James Ensor and Still Life in Belgi (1830–1930)

Rose, Rose, Rose à mes yeux

Mercatorfonds
Distributed outside the Benelux by Yale University Press

Contents

Foreword

Mu.ZEE is especially proud to kick off Ensor 2024, in general, and Ostend's festival devoted to the artist, in particular, by staging the exhibition *Rose, Rose, Rose à mes yeux: James Ensor and Still Life in Belgium (1830–1930)*. Seventy-five years after Ensor's passing, it is a true honour to organise the first exhibition to focus entirely on his still lifes, hosting it where the work of Ensor belongs: at our museum in his hometown of Ostend.

The exhibition arose from a particularly fruitful partnership between Mu.ZEE and Ensor experts: professor emeritus Dr Bart Verschaffel and Ensor committee president Sabine Taevernier, both of whom were engaged as guest curators and supported by Mu.ZEE's Dr Stefan Huygebaert. Verschaffel's decades of experience in art history led him to focus on this genre, which is essential to any understanding of Ensor's art. After all, a quarter of Ensor's painting oeuvre consists of still lifes; moreover, it was a genre he practised throughout his career. As we learn from Taevernier's contribution, for Ensor as well as for a great many other artists, the genre offered, as she notes in her essay, 'excellent terrain for experimentation' and innovation. Consequently, it was the objects surrounding him and those in his collection that he referenced for his work.

Laudably, the curators have opted to resolutely juxtapose Ensor's still lifes with works by forerunners, contemporaries and modernists: Belgian artists who, like Ensor, helped shape the still-life genre in their own way. Not quite 30 years after the exhibition *Belgische stilleven- & bloemenschilderkunst* (Belgian Still-Life and Floral Paintings)*: 1750–1914* (October 1994–January 1995), curated by Norbert Hostyn at the then Museum of Fine Arts Ostend, our museum finds itself once again the forum in which the still-life genre can be discovered. The exhibition simultaneously uncovers works that tackle still lifes in a different manner and that challenge the genre in terms of both form and content. Consequently, just as in this accompanying catalogue, the exhibition rediscovers the work of artists lost from memory. Alongside painters who had built entire careers around the decorative still life, such as Hubert Bellis and Frans Mortelmans, there are intriguing but nowadays all too often overlooked artists such as Jean-Baptiste Robie, David Émile Joseph De Noter and François Huygens.

Still life was a domestic genre that thrived in the private sphere; thus, female artists in particular devoted their talents to it in view of their exclusion from the art academies and the public sphere. They nurtured their professional careers by founding organisations such as the Cercle des Femmes Peintres (1888–93). For that reason, we are proud to confront still lifes by Ensor and his fellow artists with works by the likes of Berthe Art, Louise De Hem and Georgette Meunier. Their presence, and in some cases rediscovery, is wholly in keeping with the goals of Mu.ZEE and its focus on Belgian art from 1880 to the present day – namely, by putting more historical female artists back on the map. A masterpiece by Anna Boch is also on view once again, this coming on the heels of a recent sensational and successful monographic exhibition of her work at Mu.ZEE.

Boch, like some of the aforementioned women, exhibited paintings at art associations and salons where Ensor was also actively engaged. He inspired a great deal of the artists whose work is now on display at Mu.ZEE (such as Léon Spilliaert and Rik Wouters) alongside the work of others who in turn were points of reference for the Ostend grand master (such as Henri De Braekeleer and Alfred Verhaeren). Others, including Willy Finch and Hubert Bellis, were friends of Ensor in his youth, friends with whom he developed as an artist. It is particularly noteworthy how twentieth-century critics would take Ensor's art as a benchmark when evaluating still lifes by other artists, such as painters Walter Vaes and Albert Saverys. Reflecting the fact that Ensor continued working into the mid-twentieth century, the exhibition concludes in a similar vein by including, for example, the subtle modernism of Louis Thevenet, the Expressionism of the second Latem School, the Cubist still lifes of Marthe Donas and the Surrealism of René Magritte from the first decades of the twentieth century.

Besides the august reputations of the artists, it is the exhibition's specific selections of still lifes that lend it its strength. As the curators themselves are keen to stress, the exhibition is first and foremost an exercise in comparative viewing. It facilitates the discovery of formal strategies in an ostensibly 'dead' genre – *nature morte*: strategies that exemplify what it was that set Ensor apart and that define various aspects of modernism.

Our museum in Ensor's hometown of Ostend is presenting all of this for an international audience within impressive scenography designed by architects Guy Châtel and Kris Coremans. Their wooden structure frees the works from wall mountings, making it possible to view and simultaneously compare some 50 paintings and 20 drawings by Ensor and some one hundred works by forerunners, contemporaries and modernists.

We would like to thank not only Bart Verschaffel, Sabine Taevernier and Stefan Huygebaert for the expert analysis underpinning this catalogue and the accompanying exhibition, but also everyone on the Mu.ZEE team for their tireless commitment. The gathering together of all these works was made possible thanks solely to the valued support of our funding bodies, the sponsors and the Friends of Mu.ZEE. In addition to the many generous museums and private individuals who lent works from countries including Belgium, the Netherlands, France, Luxembourg, Germany, Austria, the United Kingdom and Switzerland, we express our particular gratitude to the Royal Museums of Fine Arts of Belgium in Brussels and the Royal Museum of Fine Arts, Antwerp, who both lent an exceptional amount of works.

We invite you to immerse yourselves in Ensor's still lifes and, together with us, appreciate their impact on the genre in Belgium. Welcome!

Dominique Savelkoul, Director, Mu.ZEE
Joost Declercq, Artistic Coordinator, Mu.ZEE

In the essays and captions, the titles of James Ensor's paintings are followed by a number starting with the letter T. These numbers correspond to those in the artist's catalogue raisonné (CR) of paintings compiled by Xavier Tricot (see Tricot 2009).

Still Lifes in Belgium, 1830–1930

Bart Verschaffel

This absolute disdain for still life!
James Ensor[1]

Noble Rose of all Roses, Rose of the hours, Rose of the winds, proud Rose of the warriors of England, diamond Rose, nostalgic Rose of fiery lands, lunar Rose, capital Rose, dreamy Rose of summer nights, Rose of poets, be always Rose, Rose, Rose in my eyes.
James Ensor[2]

Still-life painting is a composite pictorial genre that came to be defined in the seventeenth century when, following the wars of religion – particularly in the Netherlands – profane painting flourished, bringing about for the first time distinctions between and a hierarchy among types of painting. The term 'still life' reflects the fact that, instead of portraying an event or a story to which a painter must lend expression, the artist is rendering immobile, mute objects. The painter simply paints what they see. It requires little in the way of intelligence and inventiveness, and artistically speaking it is not especially prestigious. The meaning of such depictions lies solely in any associations that might derive from the image; significance can be found in allusions and in the perception of 'hidden meanings'. In the seventeenth century, the objects depicted were not yet deemed interesting in themselves – a symbolic and/or moral justification continued to be linked to their depiction.

The composition and the interpretation of still lifes were governed by a limited number of conventional iconographic formulae, such as the five senses, the seasons and, above all, the symbolism of vanitas – vanity and the transience of earthly things. The still-life genre united a variety of subgenres, but that multiplicity was held together primarily by one specific pictorial space. The floral arrangements, the fruit, vegetables and decorative objects, the 'breakfast tables', the jewellery and shells, the skulls and snuffed candles, the careworn books and the dead animals are virtually ubiquitous players within the same small theatre: a performance

1 'Ce dédain absolu pour la nature morte!' James Ensor, 'Le Salon des écrivains-peintres' (1908), in Ensor 1974, p. 21.

2 'Noble Rose entre toutes les Roses, Rose des heures, Rose des vents, Rose altière des guerriers d'Angleterre, Rose diamantée, Rose nostalgique des pays ardents, Rose lunaire, Rose capitale, Rose songeuse des nuits d'été, Rose des poètes, soyez toujours Rose, Rose, Rose à mes yeux.' James Ensor, 'Discours prononcé à Ostende au banquet Claude Bernières – Prix Verhaeren' (1923), in ibid., p. 88.

surrounded by darkness in which objects are turned towards the 'fourth wall', drawing near to the border of the scene and/or confronting the spectator, oftentimes sliding almost over the edge as if about to disappear into the dark or the void. At times they display an exuberantly triumphal opulence, but even then the reference to transience remains palpably present. This is conveyed by the pictorial space itself.[3] figs 1–3

However, the moralising meaning of the still life soon became conventional and faded away. Objects that interact with the edges as well as teeter on the verge of disappearance were employed and exaggerated still more in the eighteenth century – by Jean Baptiste Siméon Chardin, for example – but they also became exhausted as a result. The still life lost its characteristic staging and its symbolic and didactic basic meaning. It was reduced to a safe and established pictorial genre that, for that reason, became an assignment for the training of artists within traditional academia. By the early nineteenth century, still lifes consisted chiefly of floral arrangements and sumptuous still-life tableaux that could be skilfully and handsomely painted but otherwise had no further significance. Be that as it may, they were especially suitable for the decoration of bourgeois interiors and thus came to be produced *en masse*, particularly in the second half of the nineteenth century.

Regarding the output of such works in Belgium, we are able to compile a comprehensive overview of still-life painters based on the appearance of their works at the nation's salons. However, beyond mention of their names, information is generally lacking. The genre was regarded as decorative art, was ranked at the very bottom rung of the artistic ladder in terms of the academic hierarchy and was deemed suitable for the beginning of an artist's training. Still-life painting received scarcely any critical notice; museums did not collect it, and its painters and their works have been virtually forgotten by art history. The majority of extant works are in private hands. At the groundbreaking 1969 exhibition *Painting in Belgium during the Time of Henri Leys (1815–1869)* at the Royal Museum of Fine Arts, Antwerp, the first major overview of nineteenth-century art in Belgium, there was only one still life included out of 320 works: *Allegory with Skull* of 1824 by Antoine Wiertz. The 1994–5 exhibition *Belgische stilleven- & bloemenschilderkunst* (Belgian Still-Life and Floral Paintings)*: 1750–1914*, curated by Norbert Hostyn, at the former Museum of Fine Arts Ostend presented, along with some comparison works from the eighteenth century, an overview of still-life production in the nineteenth century, displaying works – almost 170 – by around 75 artists, most of whom were represented by just one painting.[4] This exhibition was the first to explore the theme and was important if only for that reason. Together with the catalogue, it provided an overview with examples, but in terms of content it barely scratched the surface.

3 Cf. Verschaffel 1997.

4 Ostend 1994–5.

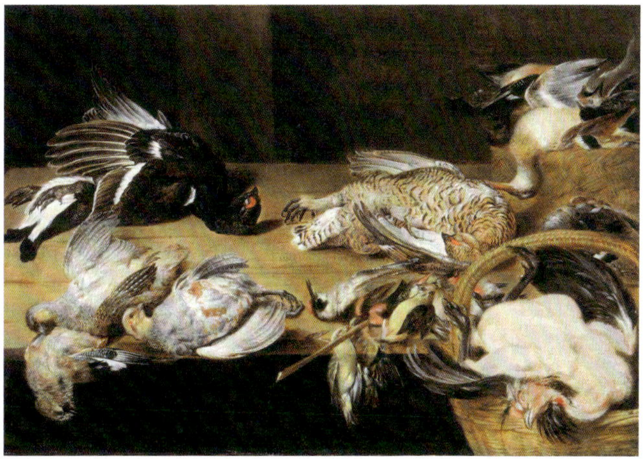

fig. 1

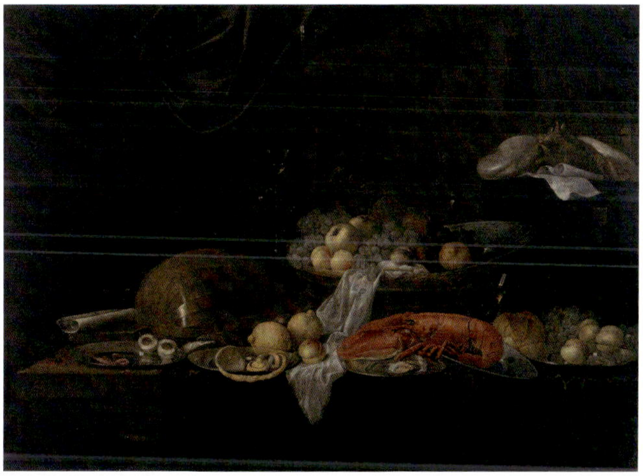

fig. 2

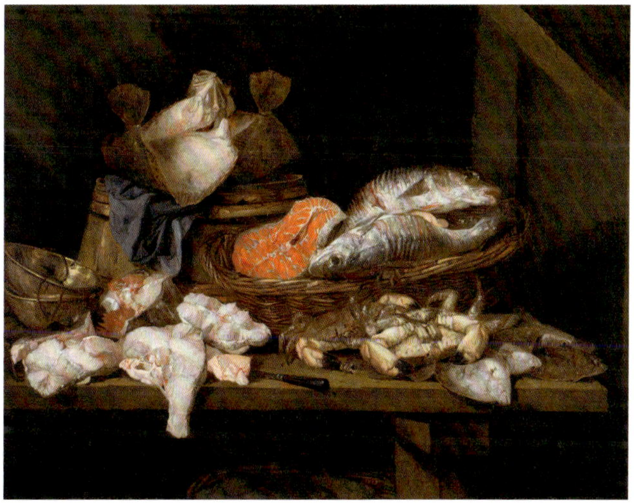

fig. 3

fig. 1 Alexander Adriaenssen, *Still Life with Dead Birds*, 1610–61, oil on panel, 70 × 100 cm. Collection City of Antwerp, Rubens House, inv. R.H.S. 213.

fig. 2 Jan van den Hecke the Elder, *Still Life with Crustacea, Fruits and a Lute*, s.d., oil on canvas, 116.7 × 162.5 cm. Museum of Fine Arts, Ghent, inv. 1902-1.

fig. 3 Abraham van Beijeren, *Still Life with Fish and Crustaceans*, 1666, oil on canvas, 97.1 × 125.9 cm. Museum of Fine Arts, Ghent, inv. 1902-A.

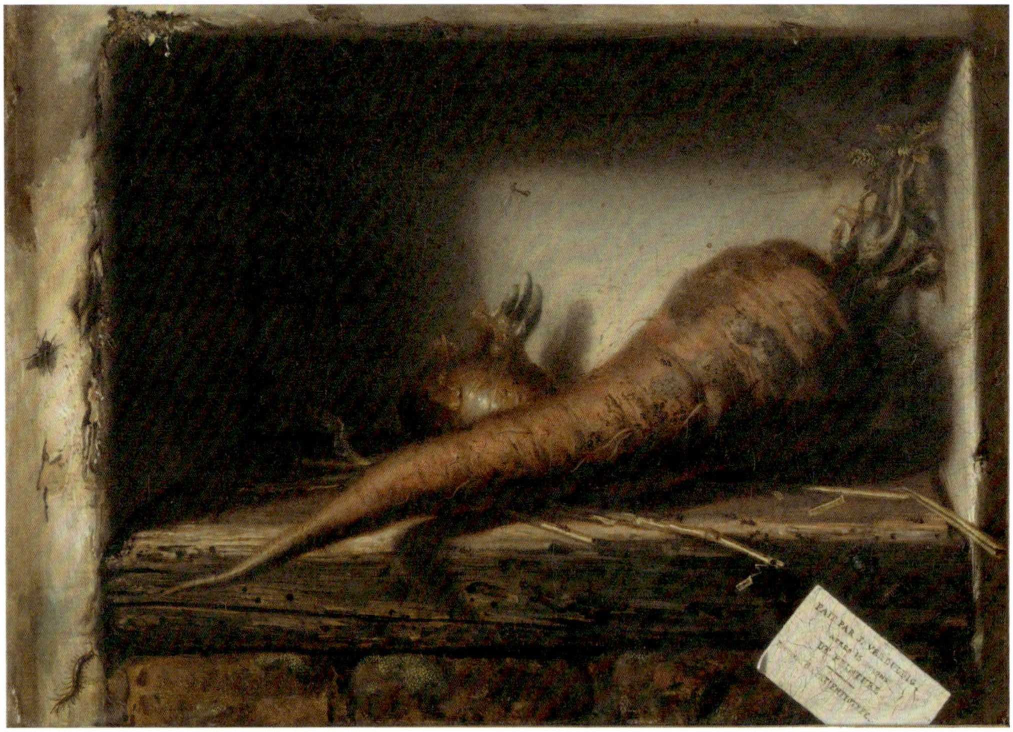

fig. 4

fig. 4 Antoine Wiertz, *A Carrot Using the Patientiotype Process*, 1840, oil on canvas, 22 × 30 cm. Royal Museums of Fine Arts of Belgium, Brussels, inv. 1936.

Nowadays it would no longer suffice simply to list artists and to catalogue paintings – the objective should be to investigate the position and significance of the pictorial genre within painting and to examine what has happened to and within the genre artistically up to the time when it tilted toward modernism in the early twentieth century.

Antoine Wiertz (1806–1865) was not a still-life painter. Apart from his *Allegory with Skull*, produced while at the academy, and a small floral arrangement, we know of only one provocative work. In 1840, ambitious to become the greatest of painters, Wiertz meticulously rendered an extremely realistic carrot. His aim in so doing was to show that he could *also* turn his hand to this kind of elementary work; above all, however, he wanted to discredit the still life and to reaffirm the superiority of history painting. The inscription for the work reads: 'FAIT PAR J. VERDULDIG. APRES 15 LEÇONS DE PEINTURE. PROCÉDÉ DU PATIENTIOTYPE' (Made by Mr Patient, after 15 lessons in painting, following the Patientiotype process). In other words: in order to paint a still life, all one needs is to have taken a few classes and, most of all, have a lot of patience! It requires no imagination, inspiration or knowledge. Afterwards, Wiertz produced romantic art depicting grandiloquent heroism overladen with meaning, at times on a monstrously large scale and with shockingly anecdotal imagery. In other words, he might be said to have relegated still lifes to the very bottom of artistic relevance. fig. 4

Ranging from Édouard Manet to Pablo Picasso, the pictorial avant-garde has painted many a still life. The conventional ingredients, the set visual formulae, the absence of narrative and meaning and the fact that the image was only to be looked at – not interpreted – made the genre particularly suitable for artistic and pictorial experimentation; the focus was wholly on the way in which the subject was presented and painted. That common denominator makes the differences visible and comparable. In that sense, along with landscapes and perhaps more so than portraits, the still life is of importance to the history of artistic modernism. In this instance, however, we shall be examining how the many variants of the traditional 'portrait of objects' survived in the nineteenth century and whether they were later infused with an artistic charge.

The Decorative Still Life: *Fleuristes et Bibelotiers*

The academies, official commissioning bodies, salons, accolades and critics invariably ranked history painting as the acme of the arts and the work of the *fleuristes et bibelotiers* (florists and trinket painters) as the nadir. Traditional patronage by the nobility and the church under the *ancien régime* had all but fallen by the wayside. This was replaced in part by commissions from the new political regime that required monumental national art; however, it was predominantly the emerging (petit) bourgeoisie and nouveaux riches who took on that mantle. They displayed their success in society through the opulence of their homes, decorating their interiors with art that was at once agreeable and amiable. Primarily this meant landscapes and animal paintings, portraits, genre paintings – historicised or otherwise – and many floral arrangements.

As a result, painters, who during their training at the academy were engaged in history painting and afterwards were permitted sporadically to create official public art (of the historicised and/or monumental type), were nonetheless mostly compelled to make a living on whatever they could sell. They worked for the art market, seeking their own niche within it; they would specialise in one genre or another, build a reputation and spend the rest of their lives producing tried and trusted images. And they created a great many in order to build a – sometimes quite ample – livelihood. For example, Louis Robbe, Eugène Verboeckhoven and Alfred Verwee painted animals; Louis Artan seascapes; Franz Courtens landscapes and seascapes; Isidore Verheyden, Théodore Baron, the brothers Xavier and César de Cock forest roads; Ferdinand De Braekeleer the Elder, Florent Willems and Constant Cap genre scenes. Among others, Jean-Baptiste Robie, David Émile Joseph De Noter, Hubert Bellis, Frans Mortelmans, Jean Capeinick, Désiré de Keghel and the majority of female painters opted for still lifes and, above all, floral arrangements. As a rule, the painters of these decorative still lifes had received adequate technical education and created astonishingly fine series of highly similar paintings. However, how was one to paint a still life that was not only well executed and beautiful from a technical perspective but also *interesting* at a time when the basic formula of the 'metaphysical' still life had been eroded and its imbued significance – its allegorical and symbolic meaning – had been lost?

The conventional theatricality of the still life's pictorial space survived into the nineteenth century, but there was a weakening of its fundamental seventeenth-century dynamics – the isolated scene, the frontality, the suction force of its edges. The still life had become a static image in a display case. This produced many decent images of artfully presented objects in which virtually nothing was 'happening'. (Among late nineteenth-century painters such as Xavier Mellery or Henri De Braekeleer, this fading away of the theatrical setting and movement and this absence of narrative and meaning resulted in a rigidity or suspense in which the objects appear to withhold their inner life – *l'âme des choses*, or the soul of things: they fall mysteriously silent or become unyielding.) Regardless, the average decorative painter did try to create artistically more ambitious images every so often.

This could be done by dividing up the pictorial space to become more interesting and visually complex, as well as by using mirrors.

Curiosities, antiquities and exotica – anything that was strange and unusual – attracted attention. Objects from the Orient, so called *souvenirs du Japon* or chinoiserie, were ubiquitous: Chinese porcelain, painted fans and fabric, Japanese prints, statuettes of Chinese sages and fantastical animals. The format of the paintings also had a role to play: a monumental work could claim artistic importance on the basis of size alone and was more suited to a museum than a standard bourgeois interior. However, to paint a monumental still life without overdoing it in some way is no easy matter. A good example of one such imposing showpiece is *Kitchen Interior* of cat. 1 1855 by Jean-Baptiste Robie (1821–1910), held in the Palais des Beaux-Arts in Lille.[5] It encapsulates all the subgenres of still life within one composition. (Baroque still-life painters such as Frans Snijders produced similar works.) Vegetables feature in the middle ground of Robie's painting and above this there is a sumptuous still life of glass and silverware and a bowl of fruit. In the foreground to the left there is an additional fish still life, while to the right there is a hunting still life with a roe and a peacock, whose tail extends to the platter bearing the fish in the foreground and serves to set off the bowl of vegetables and the opulent dishes and vases in the background.

Robie, born into a working-class family in the Marollen district of Brussels, was taught painting at the academy and eked out a living as a painter of porcelain figurines of Napoleon for British tourists in Waterloo until he made his relatively early breakthrough at the Brussels Salon of 1843. That marked the start of an especially lucrative career; in 1871, for example, the magazine *L'Art libre* reported on a work by Robie having sold for 4,700 francs, roughly four times the annual salary of a professor at the academy and eight times that of the average worker. Robie primarily painted bouquets in interiors combined with fruit and sumptuous still-life objects. Many of those works fit like jigsaw pieces in his 'synthetic work' cat. 104 from Lille, such as *Still Life with Game, Flowers and Fruits* from the cat. 105 Museum of Fine Arts, Ghent, and *Flowers, Fruits and Accessories* from the Royal Museums of Fine Arts of Belgium in Brussels. An 1894 photograph of Robie's salon-studio in Brussels shows the eclectic, exotic environment in which he lived and worked. At its fig. 5 centre is a small still-life arrangement and, surrounding it, a display of extraordinary objects and figurines he had brought back from his many trips to the Near and Far East.[6] He also painted large flower cat. 106 arrangements situated in nature, but that environment remains theatrical scenery in such cases. Works by François Huygens (1820–1905), a contemporary and fellow student, are close to those of cat. 103 Robie's. Huygens's work is usually more modest, although at times he also chances his hand at a larger format.

The best and most commonly employed strategies for artistically enhancing a still life all entail hybridisation with (elements of)

5 Schuermans 2007.

6 See 'Le Salon Indien de Jean-Baptiste Robie', in *L'Emulation: Revue mensuelle de la Société Centrale d'Architecture de Belgique*, vol. 19 (1894), pls 23–4.

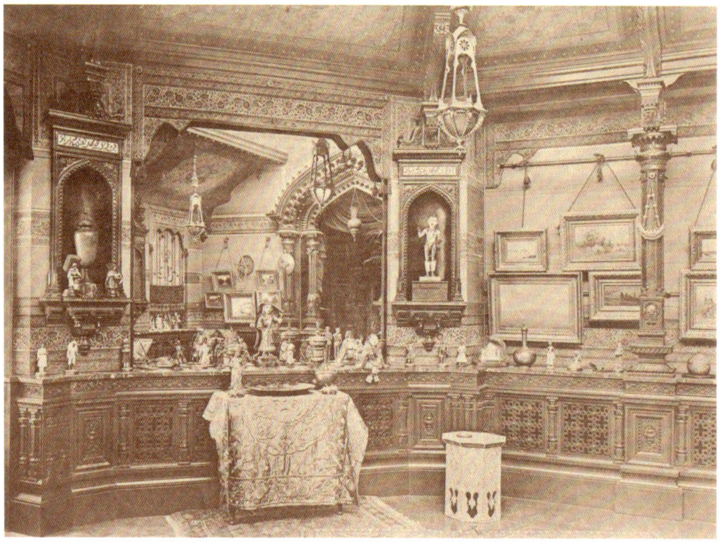

fig. 5

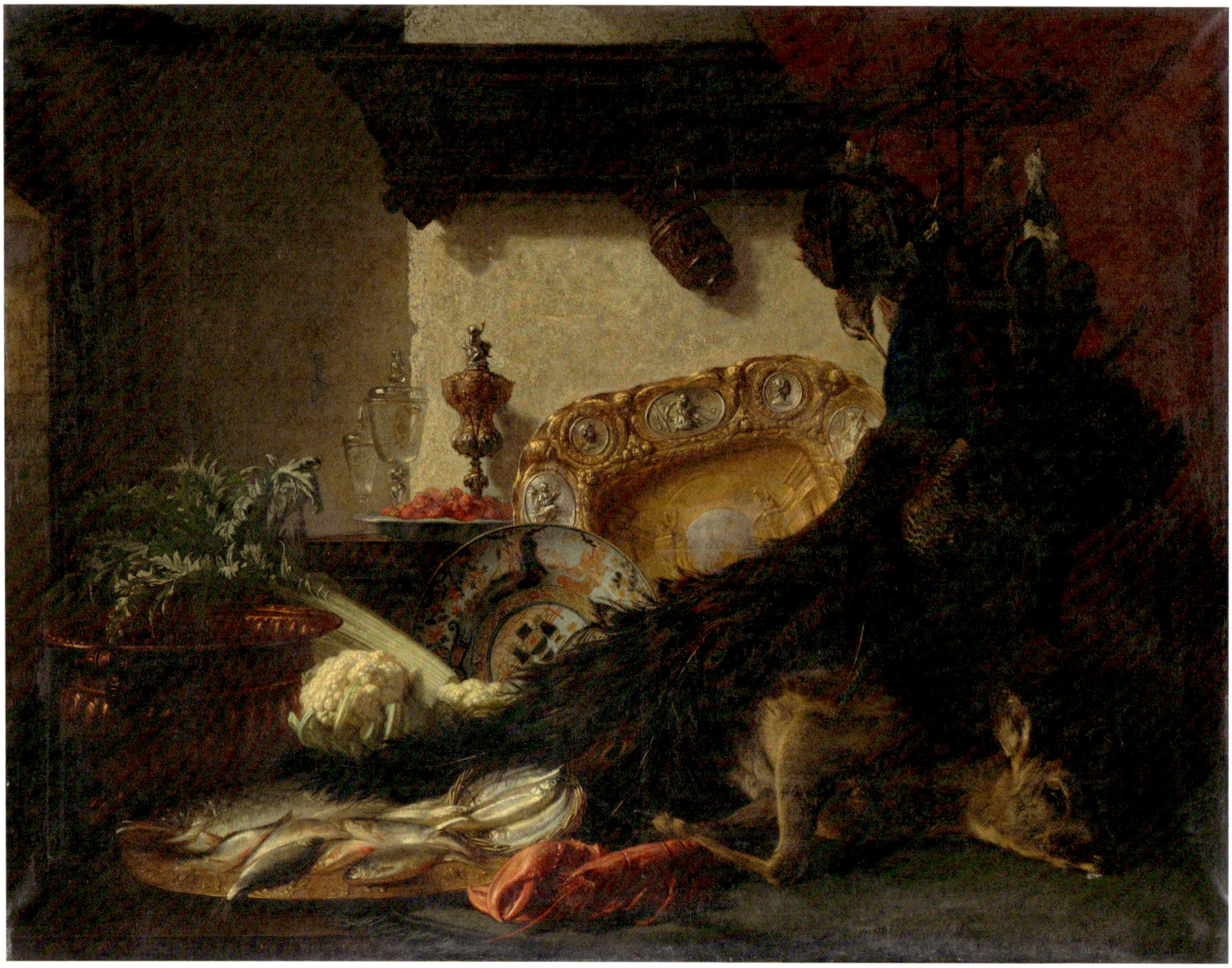

1

fig. 5 The salon-studio of Jean-Baptiste Robie, from *L'Emulation*, 1894, plate 23.
cat. 1 Jean-Baptiste Robie, *Kitchen Interior*, 1855, oil on canvas, 160 × 208 cm. Palais des Beaux-Arts de Lille, inv. P 711.

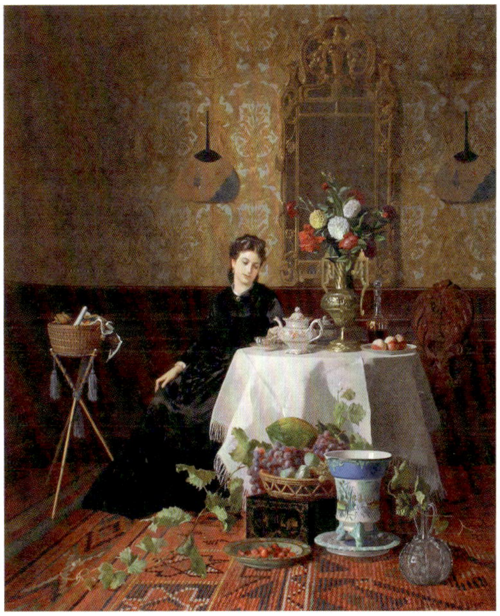

fig. 6

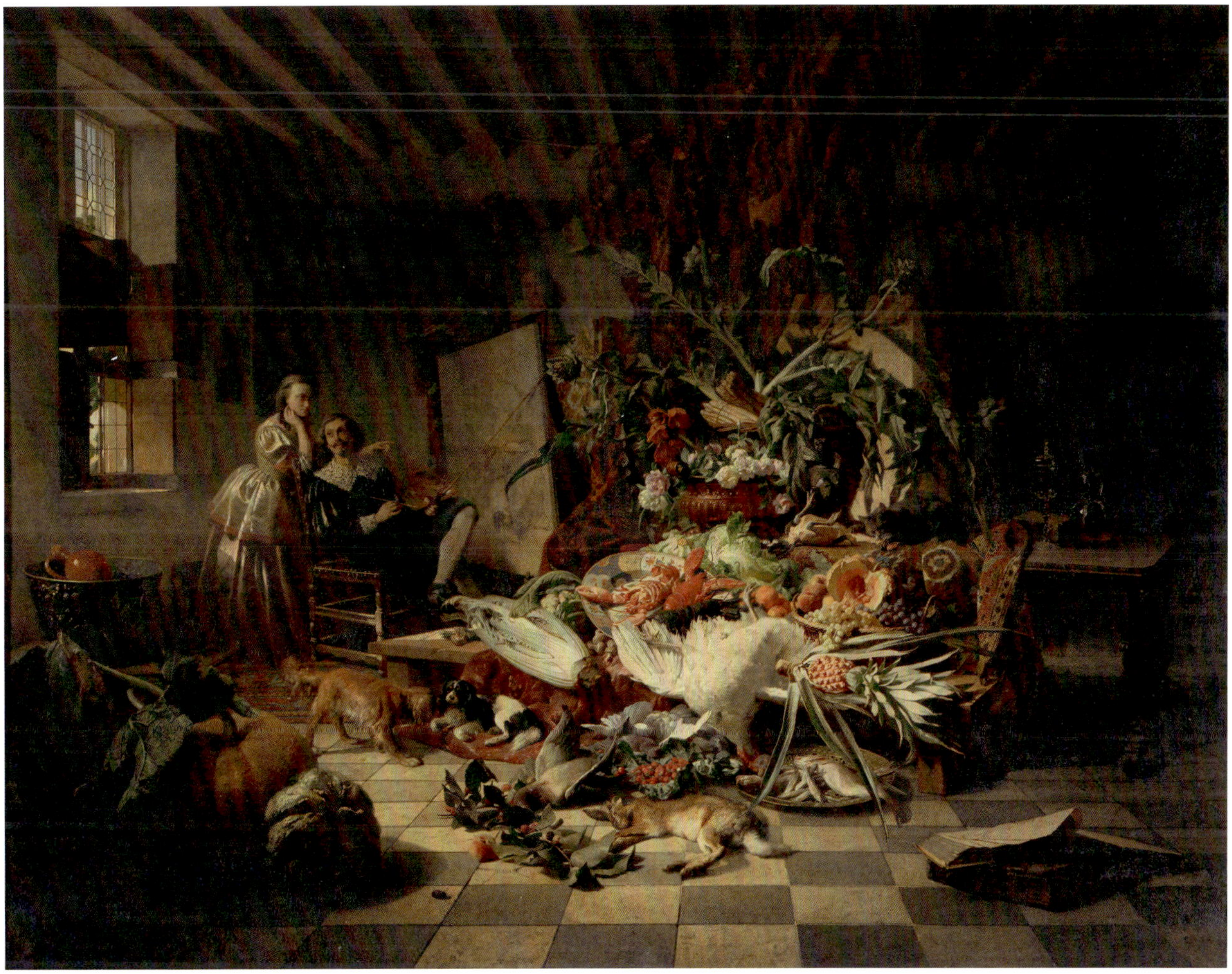

2

fig. 6 David Émile Joseph De Noter, *Tea Break*, s.d., 80.3 × 66.7 cm. Private collection, courtesy of Mark Murray Fine Paintings, New York.

cat. 2 David Émile Joseph De Noter, *Frans Snijders' Studio*, 1857, oil on canvas, 148 × 201 cm. Museum Hof van Busleyden, Mechelen, inv. S0021.

other pictorial genres. Hybrid images are intriguing. For example, still lifes come alive when adding an observer – human or animal – or a character who manipulates the objects. People have intentions, after all; they act and arouse a narrative interest of their own accord. They set a story in motion into which the dryly portrayed objects can then be inserted or, at any rate, can be related to what is happening in the scene. (Still lifes containing characters who manipulate the arrangement like 'puppet masters' date from the late sixteenth and seventeenth centuries – as in the market scenes by Pieter Aertsen and Joachim Beuckelaer, the fishmongers' stalls by Frans Snijders or the numerous still lifes with hunting motifs in which a cat, dog or bird is inspecting the spoils.) The most interesting variant in this strategy does not treat the objects as part of the furnishing of an interior, nor as the props for an action, but instead presents them as a model for a still life, as a result of which the image relates explicitly to the pictorial genre itself.

David Émile Joseph De Noter (1818–1892), belonging to the same generation as Robie and Huygens, generally employed the narrative framing strategy of a traditional still-life scene. De Noter came from Ghent and moved to Paris and then Algiers. He painted nonchalant young women full length in gently historicised interiors, a setting that appears very similar to those seen in the genre work by Ferdinand De Braekeleer the Elder, Henri Leys – who brought in De Noter to supplement his historical tableaux – or Florent Willems, as well as in Alfred Stevens's portraits of women. Besides this, however, De Noter introduced still-life ensembles displayed on the floor or laid on a table in a room that include such items as bouquets, pastries, cut fruit and vegetables, poultry and game, tableware and musical instruments.[7] The artificial configuration of all those objects, displayed frontally side-by-side and oriented towards the viewer, broke the apparent realism of the scene. As a rule, De Noter's paintings are small or modest in scale. In a monumental work, perhaps his masterpiece, from the Museum Hof van Busleyden in Mechelen, he portrayed Antwerp's Baroque still-life artist Frans Snijders at work in his studio. Snijders is painting an improbable accumulation of objects. These start off from a decorative drapery suspended from the ceiling and include a chaotic jumble of plants, fruit, dishes, crustaceans and fish, birds and game spread out over a rug draped over a table and a wooden bench, oriented towards the viewer. Moreover, throughout the studio there are all manner of additional traditional still-life objects that are missing from the central composition, including old folios, glassware and busts.

fig. 6

cat. 2

The vanitas symbolism, including the blooming and wilting of flowers, was no longer popular in the nineteenth century. Conversely, floral displays were freely associated with femininity, and women and girls arranging flowers became a popular theme. The landscape

7 Yotova 2023.

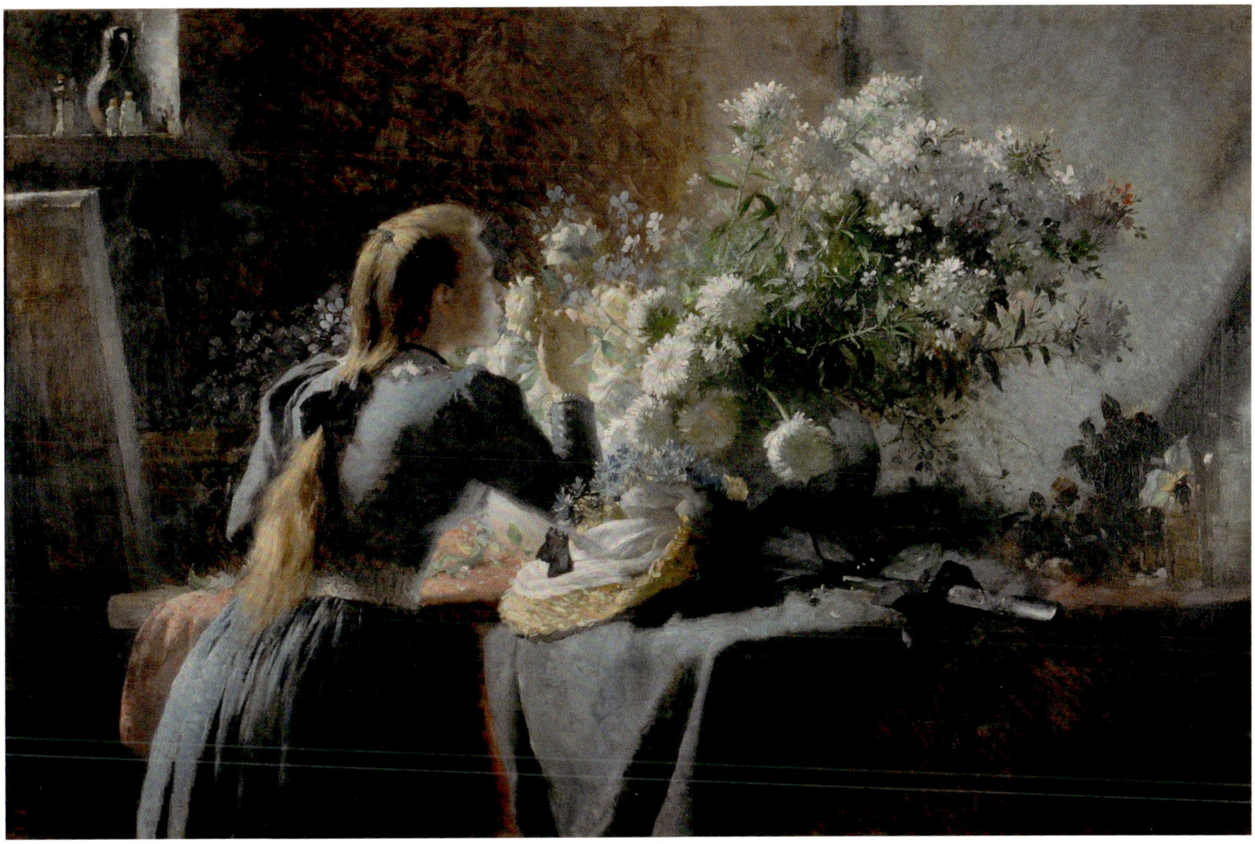

3

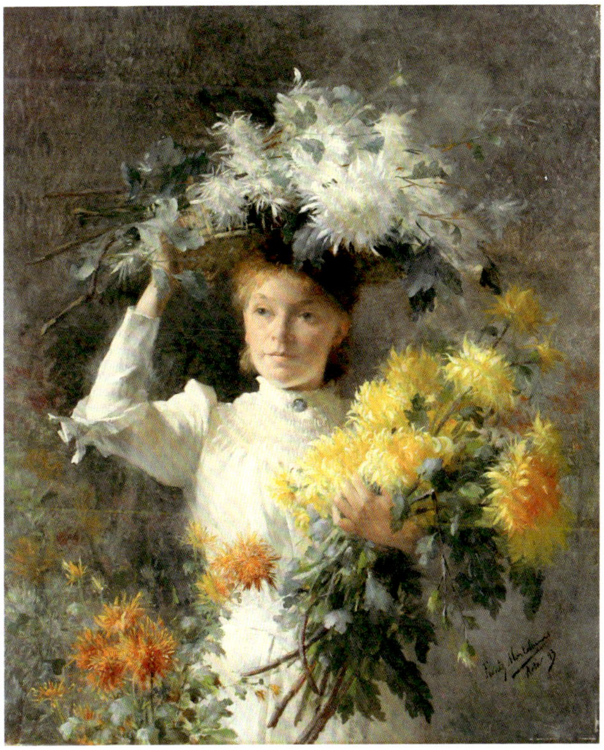

fig. 7

cat. 3 Frans Mortelmans, *Visiting the Studio*, s.d., oil on canvas, 111.5 × 171.5 cm. Collection Marthe + Félix Dony.
fig. 7 Frans Mortelmans, *Charlotte, the Painter's Youngest Sister, with Chrysanthemums in Her Arms and on Her Head*, s.d., oil on canvas, 106 × 90 cm. Private collection.

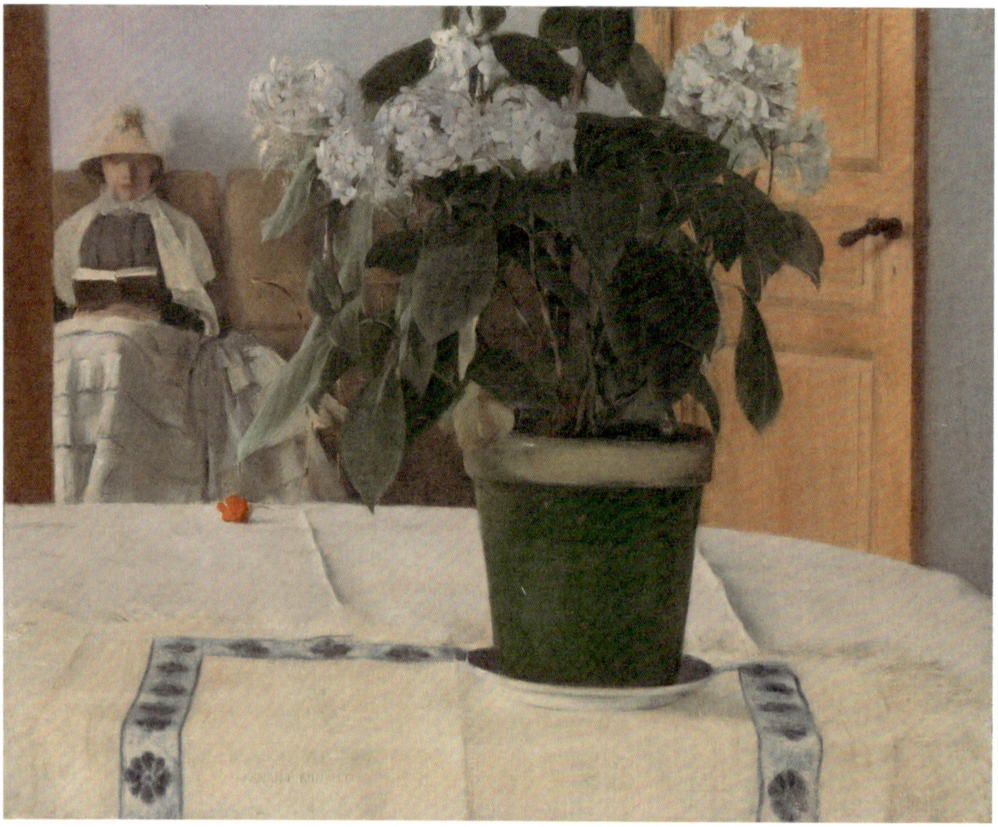

fig. 8

fig. 8 Fernand Khnopff, *Hortensia*, 1884, oil on canvas, 47.8 × 59.7 cm. The Metropolitan Museum of Art, New York, purchase, bequest of Julia W. Emmons, by exchange, and Catharine Lorillard Wolfe Collection, Wolfe Fund, and gift of Charles Hack and the Hearn Family Trust, 2015, inv. 2015.263.

painter Isidore Verheyden (1846–1905), who made still lifes only on the side, produced a fine work of a girl seated at a laid table that
cat. 122 sports a sumptuous bouquet of flowers: *The Breakfast*. Equally
cat. 3 worthy of note is *Visiting the Studio* by Frans Mortelmans (1865–1936): the girl depicted on the canvas is not admiring the flowers in the studio but, rather, taking in their scent. Mortelmans reinforced the association of young womanhood with flowers and blossoming by having the girl smell the flowers instead of arrange them, and he has her flowing hair and dress, and the blue and white of that dress, merge with the bouquet. On several occasions, Mortelmans used
fig. 7, cat. 137 characters to try out similar unusual formulae. A playful portrait of his sister wearing a flower arrangement on her head is just as quirky
cats 138, 139 as his self-portrait in the studio. The canvas *Yellow Roses in a Vase* that he is painting in that scene has been preserved. The brother of the composer Lodewijk Mortelmans, the artist was trained at the Royal Academy of Fine Arts in Antwerp – considered conservative – and participated in a few of the city's artist groups but remained on the fringes of the Belgian art (and artist) scene. He also produced landscapes, but most of his extensive oeuvre consists of masterly renditions of sumptuously painted floral still lifes, usually of roses. He continued to work as a still-life tutor at the Berchem Academy until shortly before his death in 1936.[8]

In a rare still-life painting by Fernand Khnopff (1858–1921),
fig. 8 now at the Metropolitan Museum of Art in New York, a woman is relegated to the background and the artist deliberately places a flower pot of hydrangeas in the foreground, as a result creating a particular tension by reversing the expected visual impact of figure and floral arrangement.

Instead of inserting characters, the painter can have the objects come alive and thus animate the still life, just as a landscape painter will add staffage. Comparison of two still lifes by Louis Dubois (1830–1880) demonstrates the difference between the two strategies. This Brussels painter chiefly created landscapes, animal scenes and portraits. He spent part of his training in Paris under Thomas Couture, a tutor to the likes of Édouard Manet and Henri Fantin-Latour. Together with the writer Camille Lemonnier, he was among the group of artists that founded the Société Libre des Beaux-Arts in Brussels in 1868. Dubois had intellectual interests and wrote critiques under a pseudonym, including in *L'Art libre* and *L'Art Universel*, Lemonnier's magazine. He used that medium to defend the realism of his friend Gustave Courbet and reflected on aesthetic and artistic matters such as portraiture and laughter in art. In 1872, in 'Le peintre d'histoire', he voiced criticism of 'peinture officielle' (official painting) and the traditionalism of the Royal Academy of Fine Arts in Antwerp, as well as the hierarchy of genres: 'When a work is good, the subject is of small matter. Paint a smoked herring or an emperor; it's all quite the same to me.'[9]

8 Hostyn, Schiltz and Schiltz 2009.

9 'Quand une œuvre est bonne, le sujet importe peu. Peignez un hareng-saur ou un empereur, cela m'est absolument égal.' Hout (Louis Dubois), 'Le peintre d'histoire: Étude d'après nature', in *L'Art libre*, no. 4, 1 February 1872, p. 50.

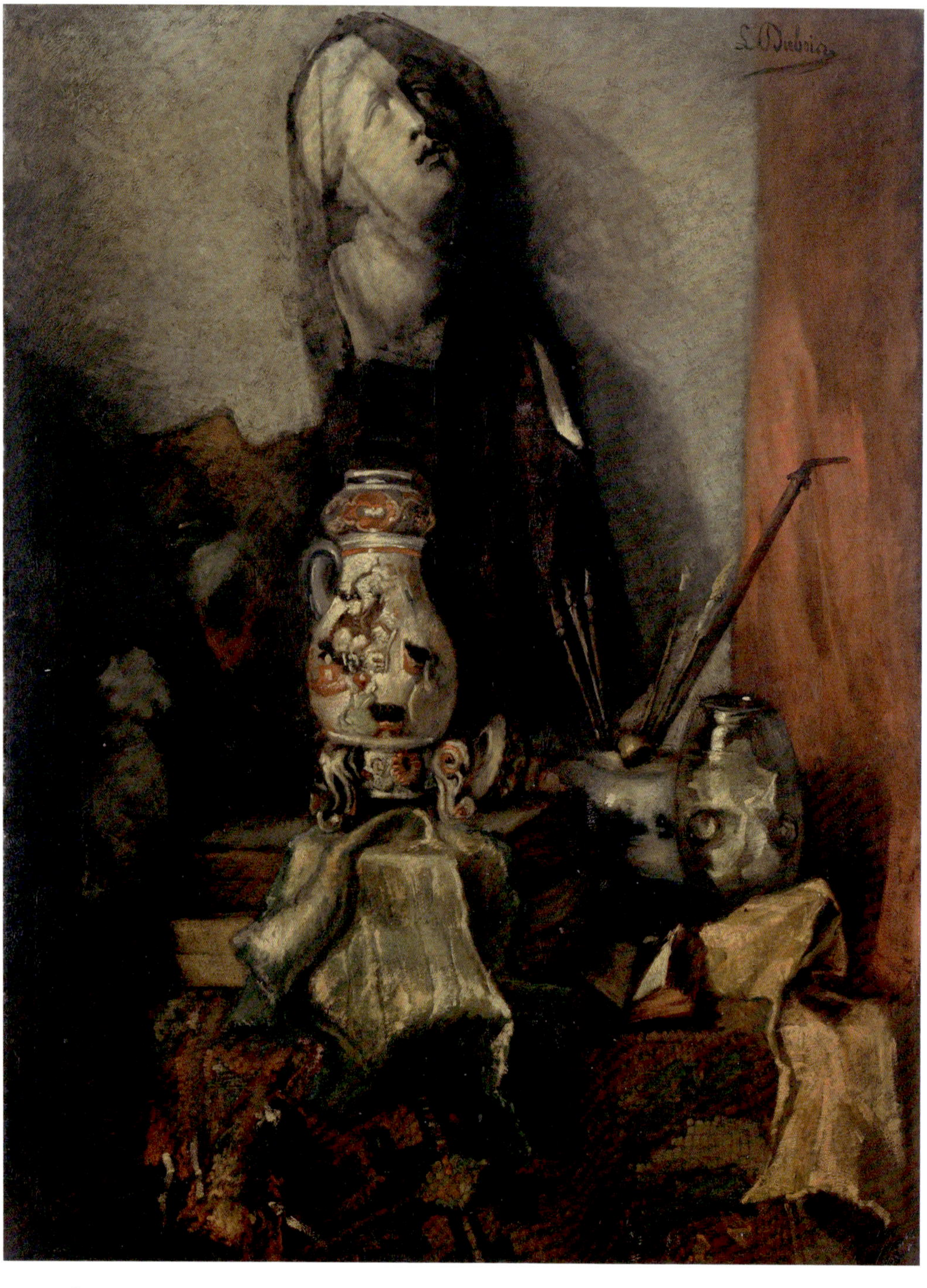

4

cat. 4 Louis Dubois, *Still Life with Studio Paraphernalia*, *c.*1855, oil on canvas, 129.7 × 98.3 cm. Museum of Fine Arts, Ghent, inv. 1924-A.

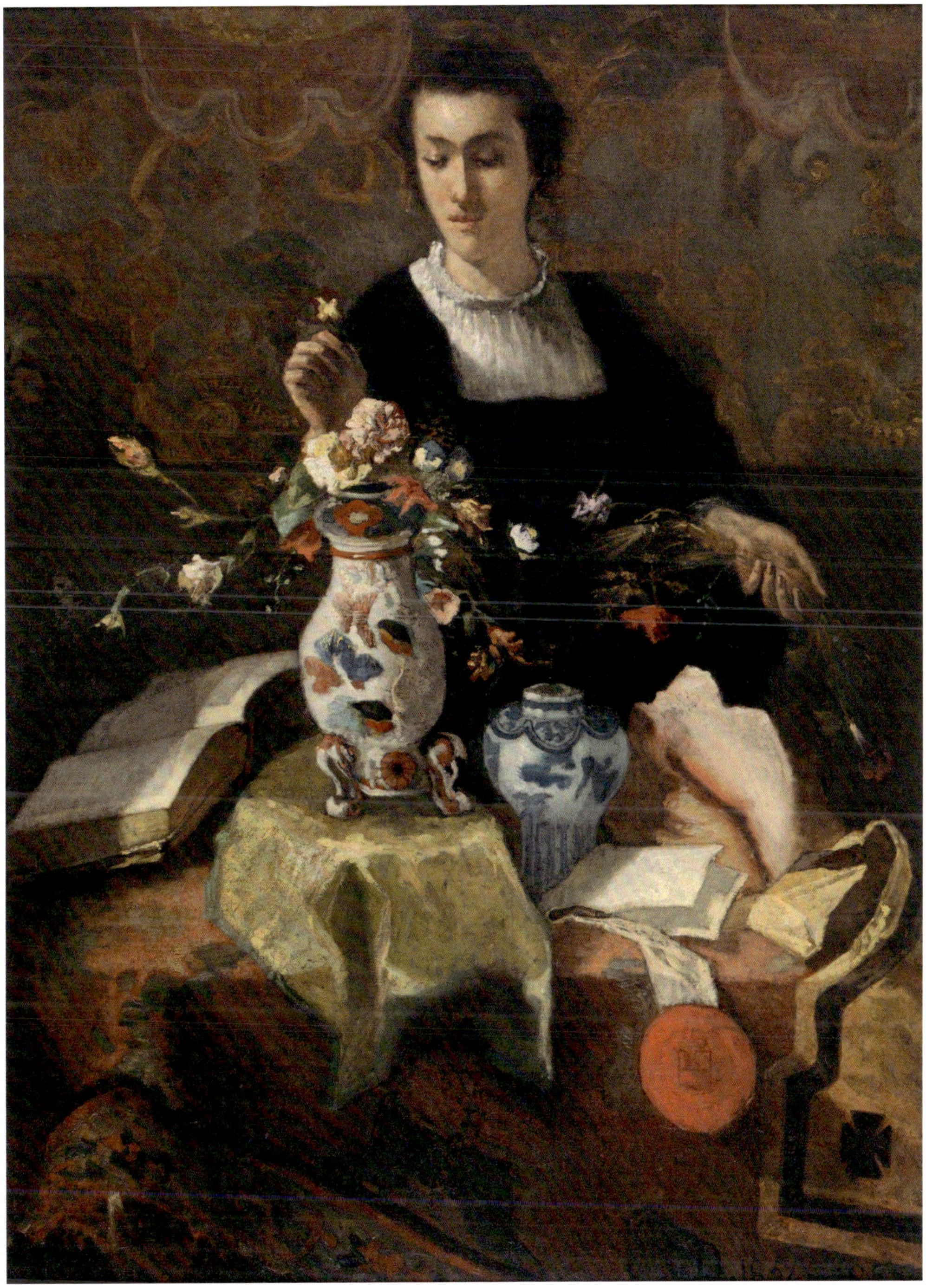

5

cat. 5 Louis Dubois, *The Woman with Bouquet*, *c.*1854–5, oil on canvas, 131 × 101 cm. Royal Museums of Fine Arts of Belgium, Brussels, inv. 4143.

In two large still lifes by Dubois, held in the Royal Museums of Fine Arts of Belgium in Brussels and the Museum of Fine Arts, Ghent, a pyramidal composition appears on the same laid table. In the middle of this there is a brightly coloured vase on a pedestal. In the Brussels version (*The Woman with Bouquet*), the scene is complemented with books, a bright red seal and a woman arranging flowers. In the Ghent version (*Still Life with Studio Paraphernalia*), he includes painter's materials, a mirroring of the vase (without flowers) and, above, where the flower arranger would have been, a plaster head of a woman bearing an emotional facial expression from beneath a widow's veil. The version containing the living woman is a bright, calm and homely image. Conversely, the version with the veiled, woebegone female face is unsettling. There is an ominous quality to *objects* that appear to live, appear to have agency and appear capable of having intentions. An object that is 'alive' turns general interest into real engagement. cat. 5 cat. 4

Human figures and faces exert a compelling attraction. An image is made more powerful by populating it with figurines, dolls, masks, sculpted or painted portraits, skulls and the like because they allow the painting to *gaze back* at the viewer. Smuggling a gaze into the scene lends the presentation of objects the presence and immediacy of a portrait. (The *tache rouge* of staffage is its equivalent in landscape painting.) The formal core of 'expressivity' or the gaze is the pupil of the eye or some variant of the *trou noir* that perforates the focal plane. René Magritte (1898–1967) demonstrated this brilliantly in a still life that he titled, most aptly, *The Portrait*: a plate with knife and fork, a glass and a bottle, and on the plate a slice of ham at the centre of which there is one open, staring eye. *The Portrait* conveys what every successful portrait manages to express; it intensifies the inadequate, artificial presence of an image by having the painting or photograph itself 'gaze' through a 'black hole'. This can be achieved with the aid of an open eye in the depicted face (preferably one eye), but it can also be done by using a black spot, a gap or a cavity, and even closed eyes can 'look'. All of this explains why still lifes with fish and dead poultry constitute a subgenre within still life and why they can sometimes be uncomfortably intense and poignant. Indeed, fish and birds cannot close their eyes; they are always looking, even when they are dead. Their staring eyes waver between life and death, and as a result they are always alien and disturbing. Their ambivalence is played out in two fish still lifes, one by Louis Dubois and another by Hubert Bellis. Dubois's work is theatrical: four fish lie next to a copper pot and an earthenware pot and some vegetables artfully displayed on a folded white tablecloth, while in the foreground, just before the edge of the canvas, we see a row of fruit. Bellis simplifies and reinforces this arrangement: one fish is laid on the table together with some lemons just in front of a wicker basket of fig. 9 cats 6, 7

crabs, closer to the viewer. Bellis's image is more horizontal than Dubois's; it pushes the gaze downwards, focusing on that solitary fish. In other, smaller still lifes, Bellis zooms in on headless salmon
cat. 8 and chopping knives, and he has the fish gaze back at the viewer with an immediacy redolent of *The Portrait*.

Hubert Bellis (1831–1902) was probably the most productive of Belgium's still-life painters of the nineteenth century. He was trained at the Brussels Academy – François-Joseph Navez was among his tutors – and in 1857, together with his younger brother Charles-Louis, opened a decorative painting business in Brussels, where, among others, the later landscape artist Guillaume Vogels would work. It was also there that the Bellis brothers set up a free open studio, L'Effort, which operated until the First World War and which would host such celebrated (still-life) painters as Louis Thevenet, Ferdinand Schirren, Jean Brusselmans and Rik Wouters. Bellis travelled a great deal for the business, taking trips abroad as well. His brother, Charles-Louis (1837–1901), also schooled as a *peintre-décorateur* at the Brussels Academy, was a landscape and seascape artist. By the end of the 1870s, the Bellis brothers were both members of the bohemian artists' association in Brussels known as La Chrysalide. It was co-founded by Louis Dubois, Théo Hannon (James Ensor's classmate and mentor) and the still-life painter Alfred Verhaeren, and it was this association that Vogels also joined, as did the young Ensor while still a student at the Brussels Academy. In October 1883, Bellis, along with Vogels and his friend Ensor – both of whom were engaged that year in the foundation of Les XX (Les Vingt) following the cessation of La Chrysalide – went on a trip to Amsterdam, where the companions are known to have visited the Frans Hals Museum. Along with Ensor, Charles-Louis Bellis – who had discovered himself a home by the sea – was one of the founders of the Cercle des Beaux-Arts d'Ostende, which organised art exhibitions between 1894 and 1896.

Hubert Bellis painted series of relatively small, convivial, not overly ambitious still lifes that include fruit, flowers, seafood and
cats 109–14 salmon. Sometimes, however, it is precisely these focused images, at times terse, that seem to possess a surprising power, albeit employing no more than shrimp or mussel shells, berries, a salmon head, a piece of meat or a few apples, with little in the way of setting and atmosphere. When objects are out of place or lack the familiarity of implements or utensils, matter can appear unexpectedly in the raw; matter not encased and protected by a bodily form, such as chunks of meat or fillets of fish, touches on the abject. Objects
cats 108, 110 then defiantly display their 'materiality'.

The still-life arrangement becomes a narrative when the painter zooms out, placing and presenting the objects as part of an interior: in the kitchen, a corner of the drawing room or a *coin d'atelier*, in front of an open window or in the garden. Situated

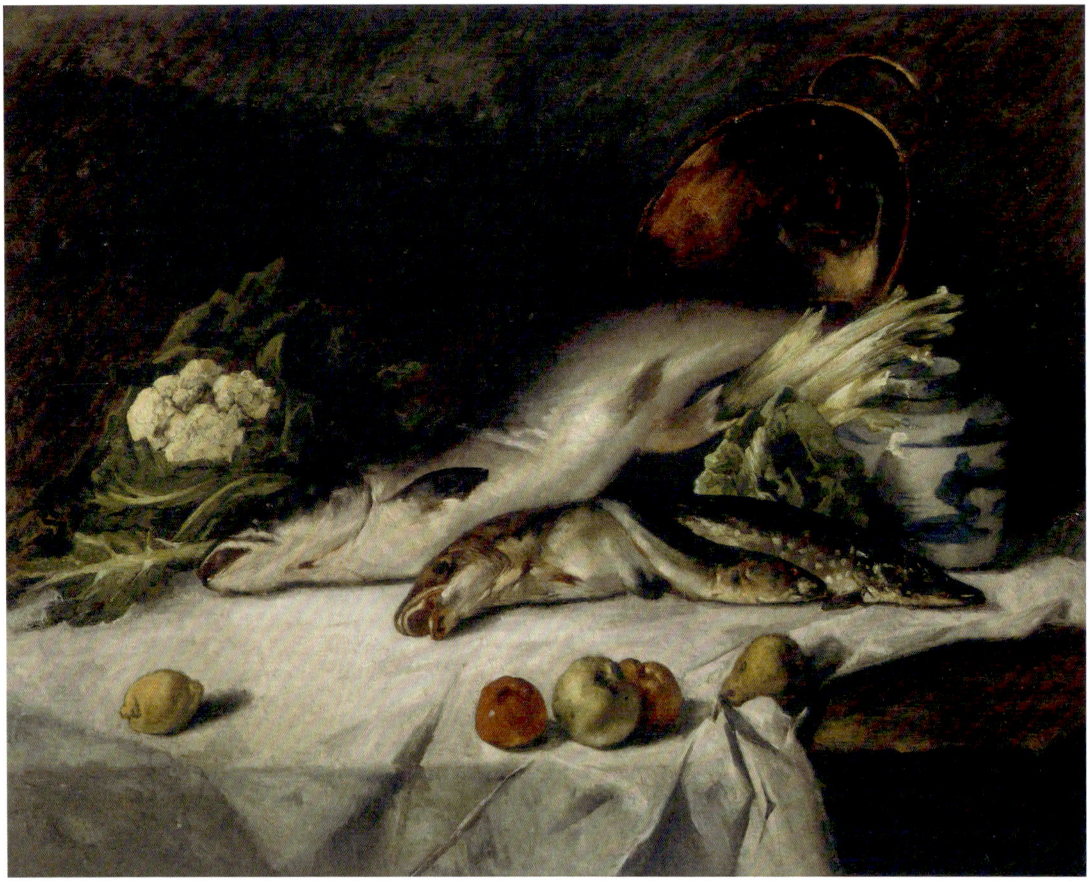

6

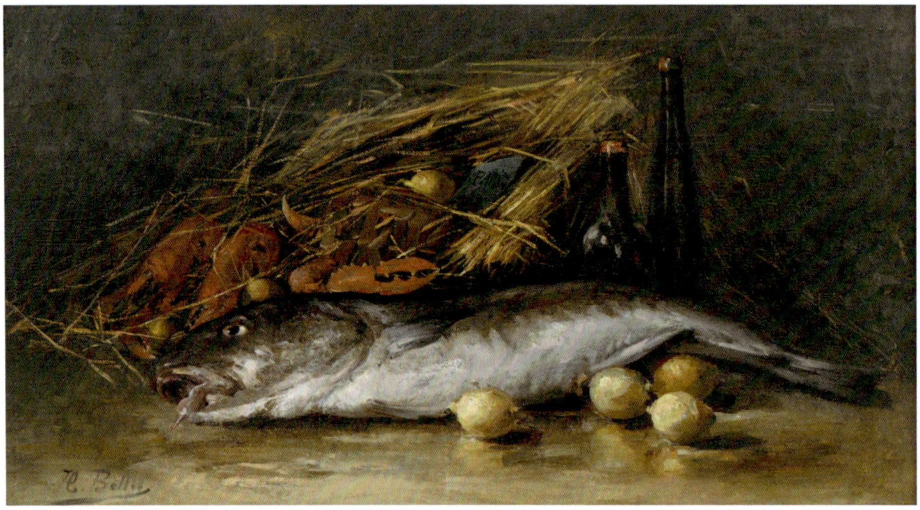

7

cat. 6 Louis Dubois, *Fish and Accessories*, 1876, oil on canvas, 109 × 141 cm. Royal Museums of Fine Arts of Belgium, Brussels, inv. 2808.

cat. 7 Hubert Bellis, *Large Fish, Red Lobsters, Lemons, Red and White Wine Bottles*, s.d., oil on canvas, 65 × 120 cm. Barat-Venker Collection, The Netherlands.

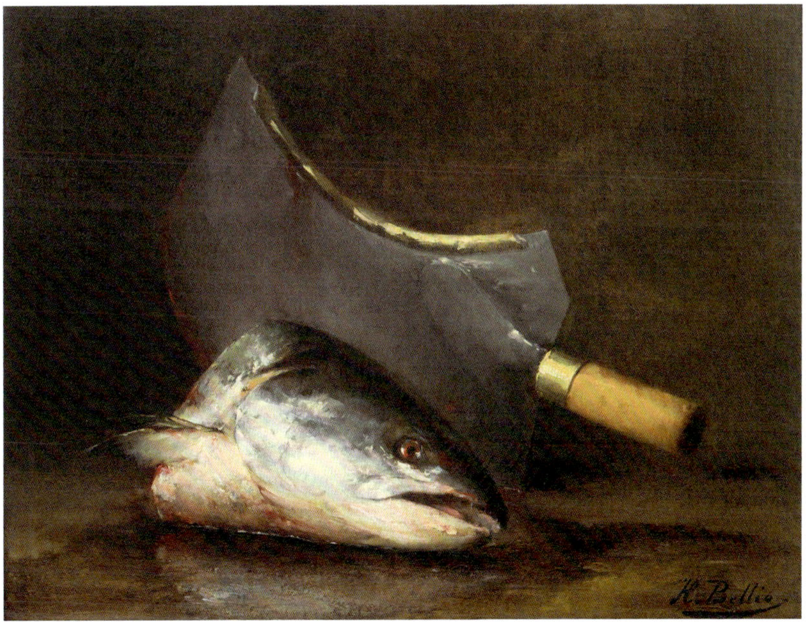

8

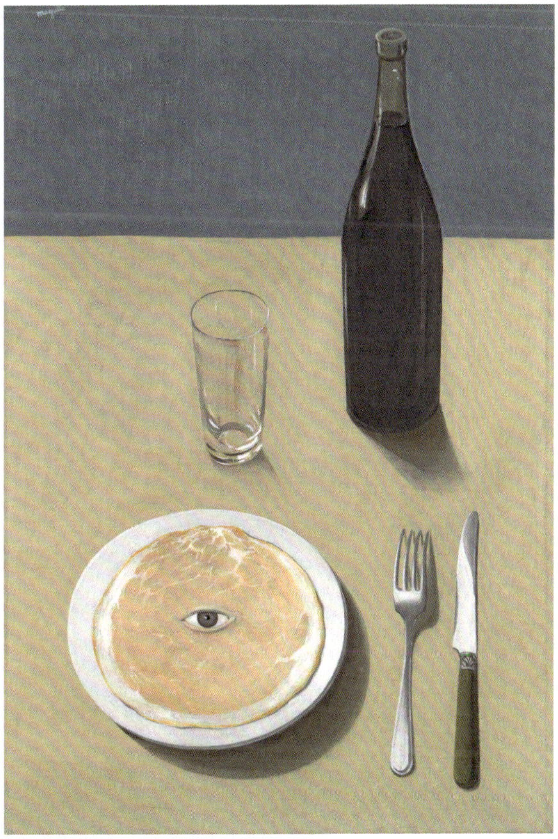

fig. 9

cat. 8 Hubert Bellis, *Still Life with a Fish Head and Cleaver*, s.d., oil on canvas, 63 × 72 cm. Collection Simonis & Buunk Kunsthandel, Ede, The Netherlands.

fig. 9 René Magritte, *The Portrait*, 1935, oil on canvas, 73.3 × 50.2 cm. The Museum of Modern Art (MoMA), New York, gift of Kay Sage Tanguy, inv. 574,1956.

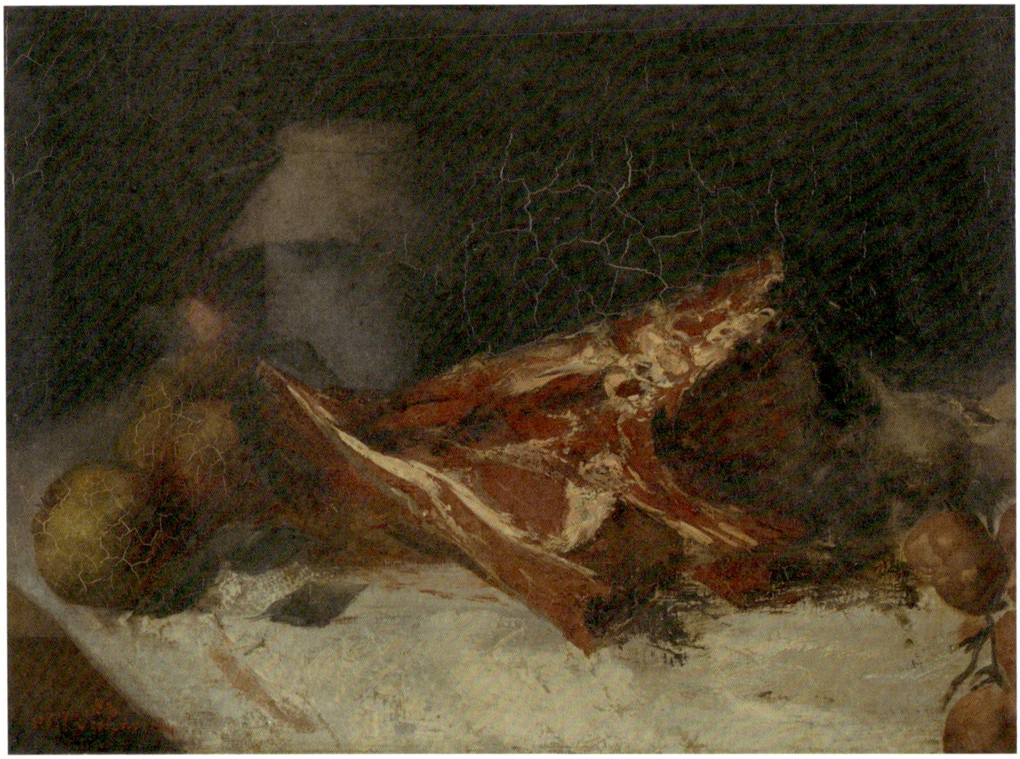

fig. 10

fig. 10 Alfred Verhaeren, *The Steak*, 1883, oil on canvas, 52.5 × 71.5 cm. The Mesdag Collection, The Hague, inv. hwm0323.

in their own miniature theatre, the objects are independent and protagonists. Conversely, a laid table in a kitchen or garden shows the objects' place in the world and the role that they play in people's lives. The history of private life and domesticity is a complex one (the home as a cocoon and a theatre, as a compendium of the world, as a prison, etc.), and nineteenth-century art uses objects to illustrate the whole spectrum of the mood of and the activity in those bourgeois, overloaded interior spaces: the forced intimacy, the sense of safety in the familiar, the faux bonhomie, the boredom, the indifferent silence, the mendacious ornaments, the twilight.

Alfred Verhaeren (1849–1924), whose (paternal) uncle was father to the poet and critic Émile Verhaeren, was also a student at the Brussels Academy, tutored by Dubois among others, and – like the Bellis brothers and Ensor – was a member of La Chrysalide. Later, in 1885, he joined the Voorwaerts group to which the *artiste-peintre* Marie de Bièvre also belonged. Verhaeren produced some well-known portraits of his famous cousin, but he also painted seascapes and still lifes of exotic figurines and dolls, as well as *coins d'atelier*: vertical, at times strikingly narrow slices of interiors, from floor to ceiling, that place the image clearly in situ. An
cat. 124 artist's studio is usually involved in the case of Verhaeren. Unlike Baroque still lifes of books, the books and folders lying around in the room and on the rug do not tumble from the canvas into the void. Domestic peace reigns here. Following a visit to Verhaeren's studio, the critic Sander Pierron wrote: 'Above the panelling there are interlaced gilded arabesques in the wrought leather hangings. On a large sheet, the lines and colours of dolls, trinkets, boxes, vehicles and wooden animals have been jumbled together. Earthenware, pewter and copper work are arranged side-by-side on an antique cabinet. A Japanese mask's grimace introduces an amusing irony to this severe environment.'[10]

Occasionally, however, he also made brash still lifes that, as in the case of works by Hubert Bellis, directly confront the viewer
fig. 10 with 'flesh'. One of those works, *The Steak*, left an impression on Ensor, as evidenced from the commemoration speech that he gave for Alfred Verhaeren in 1925 at the Royal Academy of Belgium in Brussels: '*The Steak*, the artist's principal work. All of his qualities coalesced in this instance. It allows us to surmise the love and health of his grandmothers, the butchers. A red and splendid page of blood, the powerful spectacle of the meat, trembling temptation, voluptuous cruelty, monumental insensitivity, the pink of health, the crimson sacrifice of the British ox and baron of rank, pride of the ancestral home. Oh mighty Verhaeren! The horror of the subject does not detract at all from the qualities of your painting as the work is grand and pyramidal, and its brazen beauty strikes and subjugates us.'[11]

10 'Au-dessus de la cymaise, le cuir de Cordoue entrelace des arabesques d'or. Sur une vaste toile, des jouets emmêlent les lignes et les couleurs de poupées, de polichinelles, de boîtes, de véhicules, d'animaux de bois. Des étains, des cuivres, des faïences s'alignent sur un meuble ancien. La grimace d'un masque japonais introduit dans ce cadre sévère une ironie amusante.' Pierron 1905, p. 198. See also Vanzype 1905.

11 '*L'Entrecôte*, œuvre capitale de l'artiste. Là convergent toutes ses qualités. Là, on devine l'amour et la santé de ses grand'mères les bouchères. Page rouge et superbe de sang, aspect puissant de la chair, tentation frémissante, cruauté voluptueuse, insensibilité monumentale, santé rose, immolation pourpre du bœuf britannique et baron d'envergure, orgueil de la maison ancestrale. O puissant Verhaeren! L'horreur du sujet n'a pu nuire aux qualités de ta peinture, car l'œuvre est grande et pyramidale, et son insolente beauté frappe et subjugue.' Ensor 1925, p. 113.

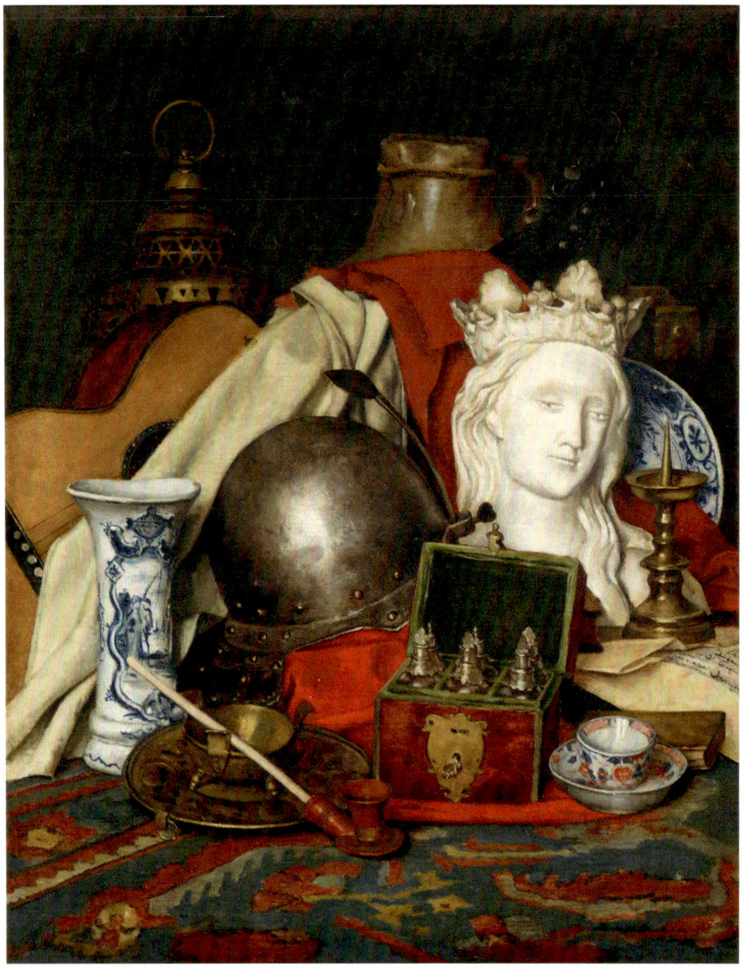

fig. 11

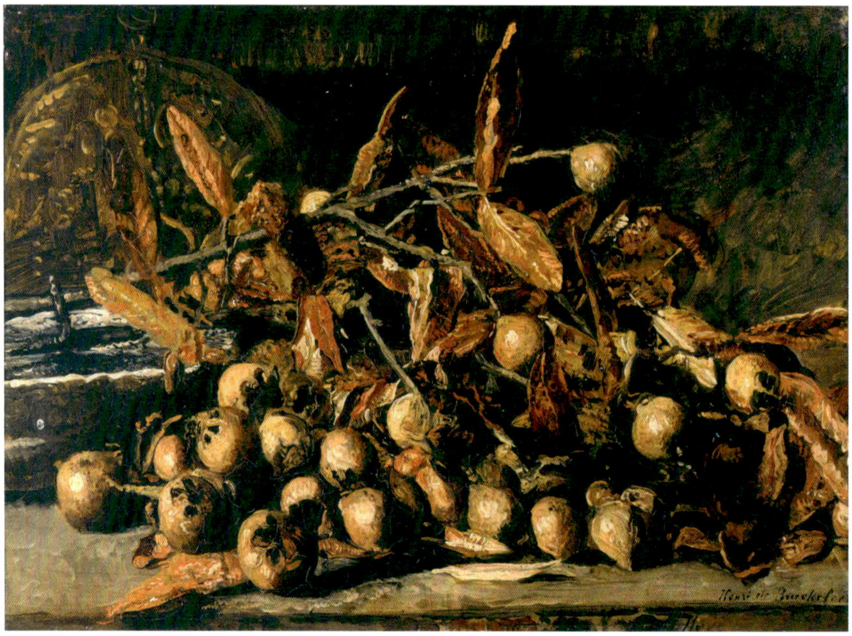

9

fig. 11 Henri De Braekeleer, *Still Life with Pipe, Helmet, Bust et al.*, *c.*1860, oil on canvas, 68 × 53 cm. Private collection, Leuven.

cat. 9 Henri De Braekeleer, *Medlars*, *c.*1886, oil on canvas, 36.5 × 51 cm. Royal Museums of Fine Arts of Belgium, Brussels, inv. 3810.

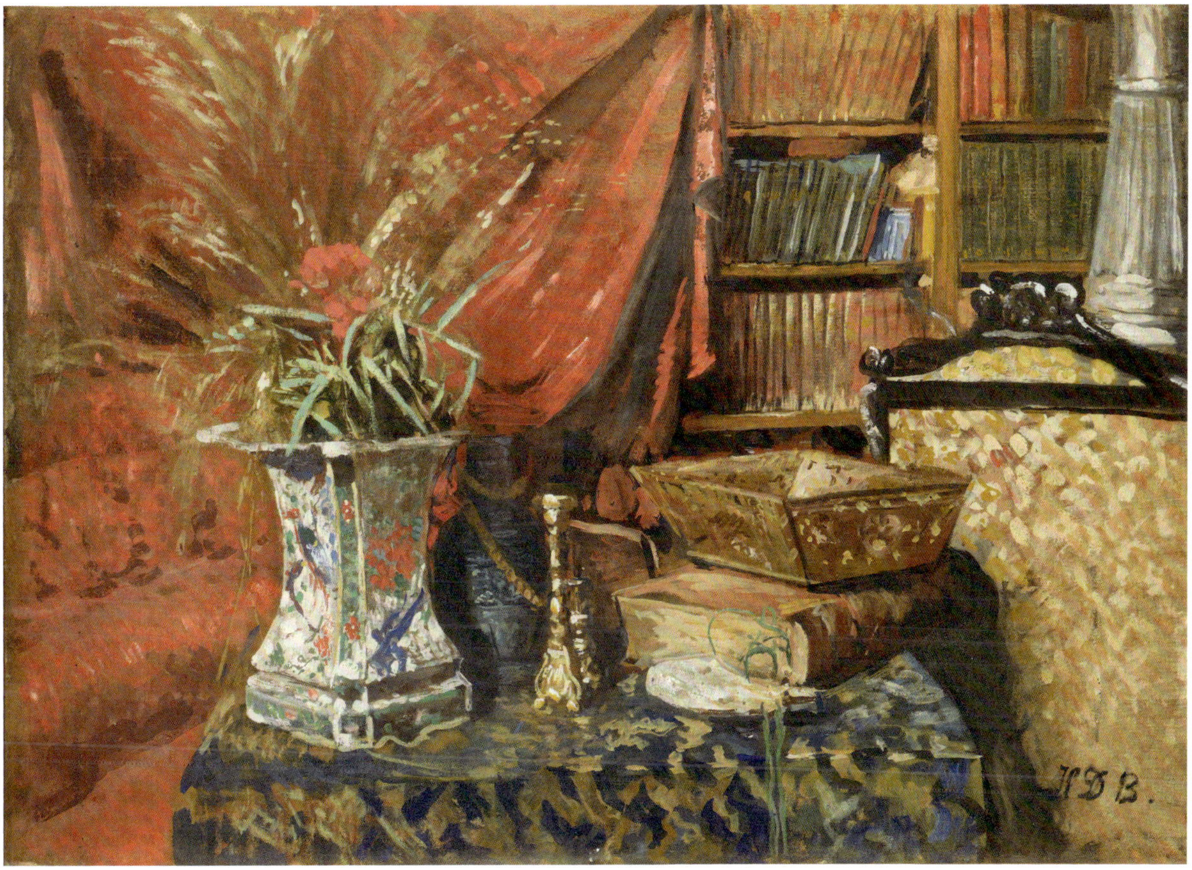

fig. 12

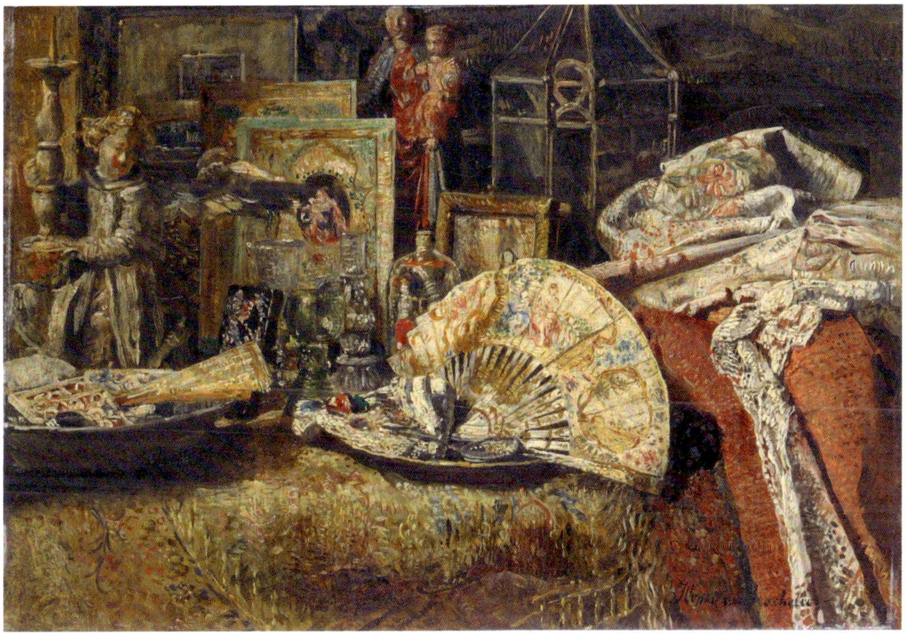

10

fig. 12 Henri De Braekeleer, *Still Life with Vase, Candlestick, Book and Basket*, 1880–85, oil on canvas, 75 × 115 cm. Private collection, Leuven.

cat. 10 Henri De Braekeleer, *Old Trinkets*, 1880–85, oil on canvas, 38 × 56 cm. Musée d'Orsay, Paris, inv. RF 1196.

Henri De Braekeleer

Henri De Braekeleer (1840–1888) was, along with Antoine Wiertz and James Ensor, a key protagonist in the story of Belgian painting from 1830 to 1900. He is a pseudo-traditional 'artist's artist' with a limited body of work little-known internationally and now faded from view in Belgium. However, at the end of his life and immediately thereafter, he was famous and praised by all the important Belgian critics and collectors; his works were purchased by museums at the highest price, and he enjoyed the respect of fellow artists, including Vincent van Gogh and Ensor: 'The admirable Henri De Braekeleer; wonderful painter, refined, meticulous to the end. …'[12]

De Braekeleer[13] was born into a prominent family of artists in Antwerp and, after his apprenticeship at the academy, trained by his father, the genre painter Ferdinand De Braekeleer the Elder, and his uncle, the then successful and internationally acclaimed history painter Henri Leys. Both were influential figures in Antwerp's art scene with good international contacts and careers in city politics. The younger artist lived in their shadow. He was a lonely and withdrawn character with an introspective life that ended sadly. Unlike other professional painters in his ambit, De Braekeleer did not seek out a specialist area in which to establish a reputation and build a career. He worked almost unnoticed on an oeuvre that did not openly refute the traditional and conventional academic art surrounding him, as Ensor and modernism would come to do later. Through the use of seemingly banal, usually slightly disturbed imagery, he eroded and undermined both pathetic and rhetorical romantic heroism, as well as the amusing anecdotal style of nineteenth-century genre art.

Between 1878 and 1882–3, De Braekeleer did little or no work, owing to an existential and artistic crisis, and/or an indeterminate illness. When he finally resumed work, a few years before his final crisis and premature demise, he painted principally still lifes. Camille Lemonnier mentions that De Braekeleer, after his bout with depression, began to paint 'small works, fruit, flowers, equipment, in order to get back on track'.[14] However, aside from this series of modest still lifes, it is De Braekeleer's oeuvre as a whole that is of importance to the still-life issue because, all things considered and as several critics have commented, it concerns the idiosyncratic existence of objects. For De Braekeleer, still life was a visual genre, but it was first and foremost a disposition of perception: he saw the world *as* a 'still life'. In his interiors, landscapes and even portraits, De Braekeleer also painted the immobile, introverted 'still life' of objects.

De Braekeleer's fascination and intimate relationship with objects gradually descended into an obsession. Lemonnier realised that De Braekeleer was losing himself in the materiality:

12 'Henri De Braekeleer, l'admirable; peintre magnifique, précieux, méticuleux jusqu'à la mort… .' Ensor 1974, p. 165.

13 My list of painting titles is drawn from the most recent (provisional) catalogue of De Braekeleer's oeuvre, compiled by Herwig Todts and André Bollen (Todts and Bollen 2019). With regard to my interpretation, I have relied on insights from my 1995 article in *De Witte Raaf* (Verschaffel 1995).

14 '[…] petits tableaux, des fruits, des fleurs, des accessoires, comme pour se mettre en train.' Lemonnier 1905, p. 41. Lemonnier was the editor-in-chief for *L'Art Universel*, in which 1,873 etchings by Henri De Braekeleer were announced. These never appeared, but it would seem from the announcement that he had by then already been in contact with De Braekeleer.

'De Braekeleer's eye is marvellous when it is a matter of establishing the tone and relief of things; but he is so much the painter that at times he ceases to be human, which is to say that his vision is more from the painter's perspective than from the human perspective of people and things. De Braekeleer is one of those types especially gifted at painting, and gifted to an extraordinary degree (like Courbet), who, by delving into surfaces, reliefs, the colourful appearance of objects, in short into matter, ends up painting living life, so varied, so manifold, so elusive, with the consistency and splendour of that matter itself.'[15]

Absorption in interior life and a focus on consistency and splendour of matter itself lead to the realm of the object. This fascination with the oppressive proximity and silent strangeness of
fig. 11 materiality is already palpable in the early work *Still Life with Pipe, Helmet, Bust et al.* from the 1860s in which the objects desperately retreat and accumulate.

His later still lifes are all small or modest in scale. These amount to a few paintings of floral arrangements and fruit still lifes using a free, impasto technique, sometimes employing a knife; a series of congested showpiece still lifes that display het-
cat. 10 erogeneous, chaotically heaped objects and materials, such as *Old*
cats 116, 118 *Trinkets* from the Musée d'Orsay; and a series of small 'breakfast pieces' that De Braekeleer painted almost in the manner of a scientist, treating the composition as an experimental installation and then using the objects as variable factors in order to gauge their effect. His arrangements with objects are palpably restless and chaotic; his florals mesmerise through the teeming vibrancy of the plants. Exceptional among the later still lifes are two freely painted large pendants from François Franck's collection. De Braekeleer
fig. 12 painted these in the free style of his small studies, but on a larger scale.

Women Painters

'It is incredible the triflingly preposterous things that people lend credit to committing to canvas. Were we in charge we would fashion separate rooms for these insignificant art creations. We wonder whether a few roses stuffed into a little pot is truly worthy of protection against wind and rain beneath the glass roof of the great hall at the Casino. If action is not taken against this, then its exhibitions will become poisoned. Those exercising this bland, meaningless genre are mostly (of course) wealthy ladies who learn this party piece as readily as they do dancing and playing the piano.'[16]

Hundreds of female painters were active in Belgium during the nineteenth century.[17] Women from the moneyed classes drew and painted as a hobby; a large contingent came from artistic families,

15 'Cet œil de de Braekeleer est merveilleux, s'il s'agit de saisir le ton et le relief des choses; mais il est tellement peintre qu'il cesse quelquefois d'être humain, c'est-à-dire qu'il voit plutôt le côté peintre que le côté humain des hommes et des choses. De Braekeleer est de ces natures spécialement douées pour la peinture, et douées à un degré extraordinaire (comme Courbet), qui, à force de s'arrêter aux surfaces, aux reliefs, à l'apparence colorée des objets, à la matière en un mot, finissent par peindre la vie vivante, si variée, si multiple, si fuyante, avec la consistance et la splendeur de la matière même.' Camille Lemonnier, 'Le Salon d'Anvers', *L'Art Universel*, no. 15, 15 September 1873, p. 127.

16 'Est-il un royaume où l'imagination et les sens affinés d'une femme puissent se plaire davantage que dans un jardin où poussent les plus belles plantes et les plus capricieuses, où les éclosions sont multiples et les odeurs enivrantes?' Karel Blondeel quotes an anonymous critic from his *Kritiek der Driejaarlijksche Kunst-Tentoonstelling in den Casino* of 1889, in Blondeel 2003, p. 56.

17 Denis Laoureux and his study group have carried out important basic research. See Caspers 2015, Namur 2016, Laoureux 2019, and Laoureux 2020, as well as Brussels 1988, Antwerp/Arnhem 1999–2000, Blondeel 2003, Creusen 2007 and Van der Stighelen 2010. See Sterckx 2012 for the work of female sculptors and Wiertz 2023 for the artistic activities of the nobility.

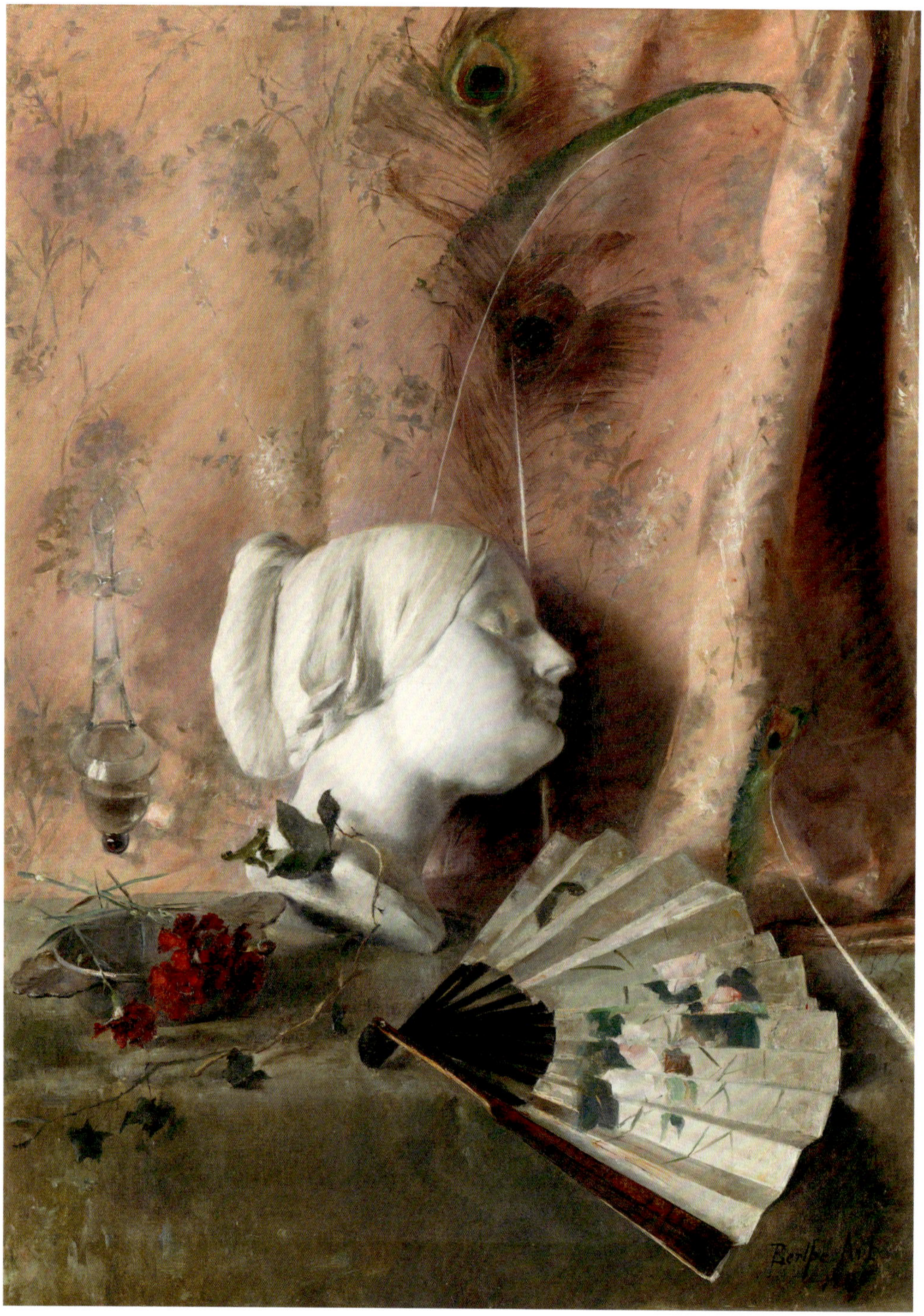

11

cat. 11 Berthe Art, *Still Life with Fan, Death Mask and Peacock Feather*, 1885, oil on canvas, 97 × 71 cm. Private collection, Kortrijk.

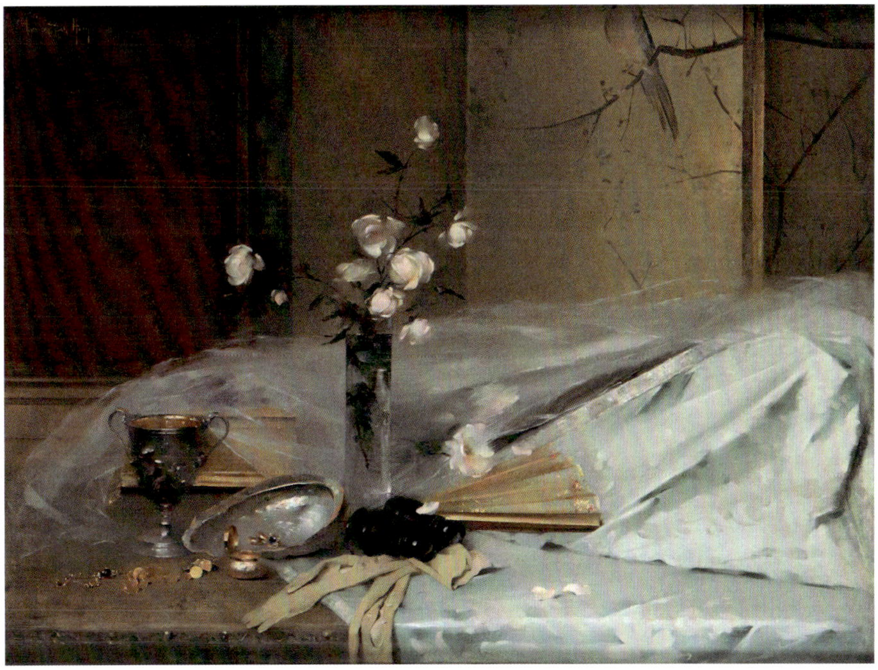

12

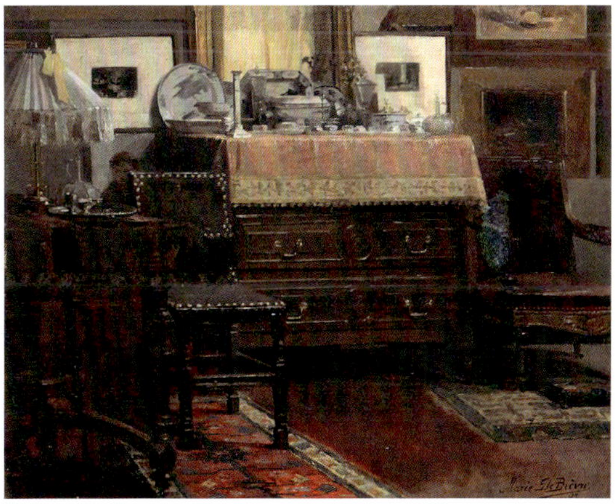

fig. 13

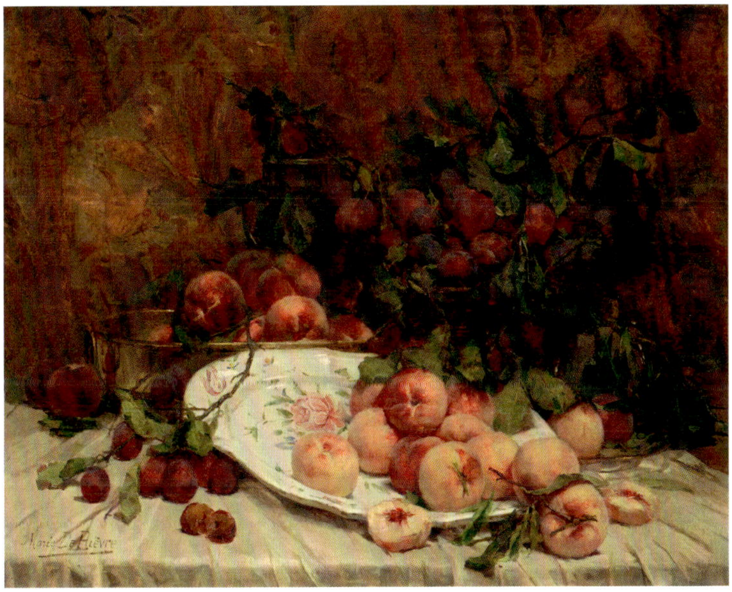

13

cat. 12 Louise De Hem, *Corner of a Lady's Boudoir*, *c.*1890, oil on canvas, 98 × 131 cm. Yper Museum, Ypres, inv. SM 000560.
fig. 13 Marie de Bièvre, *Bourgeois Interioir*, 1892, oil on canvas, 54.5 × 67 cm. Private collection.
cat. 13 Marie de Bièvre, *Peaches and Plums*, 1894 or before, oil on canvas, 74 × 94 cm. Private collection, Leuven.

while a number of them had married a painter or an artist (like the wives of De Cock, Cambier, Degouve de Nuncques, Montald and Wytsman). Nearly all of them have been forgotten by the public and neglected by art history. We know their names but, as a rule, little about their work and careers. When they participated in the salons, it almost went without saying that they did so as refined amateurs. It was generally accepted that women, particularly wives, were not meant to have a professional career, and until 1889, women were not admitted to the academies. The first courses for women at the Ghent Academy were organised in 1905. That did not prevent a number of them from having acquired thorough training as artists, typically thanks to relatives or private tutors such as Désiré de Keghel in Ghent and – in the final quarter of the nineteenth century – tuition at a few private studios such as that of Jean-François Portaels in Brussels, Alfred Stevens in Paris or Emile Claus in Ghent. But women did indeed work as 'professional artists'. This was not contested in liberal spheres or in the art scene itself. After all, they also participated in the annual salons and, above all, in the international exhibitions; they were members of the artist associations and priced their work at the same level as their average male counterparts. However, women disappeared from view in part because they practised the lesser and rather more 'decorative' artistic genres. They were excluded from academic figure studies and were certainly not deemed suited to head out alone into the open air or to paint modern life. The museums collected even less of their work than they did of their male still-life colleagues. At present, the female artists of choice that attract the attention of museums and exhibitions are those who fit to some degree within the evolution towards modernism: Anna Boch, Jenny Montigny, Juliette Wytsman, Anna De Weert and Marthe Donas, to name a few.

The situation confronting female painters was one that required them to show they were just as capable of painting as well as their male colleagues, and this fostered in them a sense that they should not be too innovative or different but, rather, that they should paint as virtuosos of convention. For that reason, they should be treated separately.

Many female artists' names crop up in the participant lists for the annual salons, but most of them disappear immediately thereafter. Like their male counterparts, female professional painters would have had a speciality and found their respective niche. They painted nature and landscapes (Euphrosine Beernaert and Marie Collart-Henrotin) and, exceptionally, history paintings (Fanny Geefs-Corr and Adèle Kindt), but the majority principally or exclusively painted still lifes and flowers. The most visible group were the members of the Cercle des Femmes Peintres. The group was active in Brussels for five years and in that time organised four exhibitions that presented the work of some 80 female artists. The group's foundation in 1888 – the year of the 'Popelin affair' concerning the admission of women to the bar association – was probably no coincidence. Founding members of the Cercle des Femmes Peintres included Berthe Art, Alice Ronner, Louise De Hem and Marie de Bièvre.

'Is there a kingdom where the imagination and refined senses of a woman might take more delight than in a garden where the loveliest and most capricious plants grow, where the blossoms are manifold and the scents intoxicating?'[18]

Berthe Art (1857–1934) worked chiefly in pastels, leaving behind a relatively large body of work numbering approximately one hundred known paintings. She came from a well-to-do and sophisticated background of art collectors with contacts in the art world. Her brother Georges worked as a literary author and translator. In the 1880s, she would visit the studio of Alfred Stevens in Paris for a few months each year. We know of her landscapes of the Côte d'Azur, but for the most part her oeuvre consists of floral
cat. 130 works and of compositions of trinkets and decorative objects. In 1904, the critic Sander Pierron wrote that 'Berthe Art is a notable exception among that intriguing group of our female painters: she combines elegance, the heightened perception that pertains to her sex, together with an expressive strength, and is an utterly male colourist'; but at the same time he characterises her work as 'feverish' (*fiévreux*) and 'restless' (*inquiet*).[19] Of special note in a private
cat. 11 collection is *Still Life with Fan, Death Mask and Peacock Feather*, showing the death mask of 'L'Inconnue de la Seine', the enigmatic portrait of a victim of drowning that inspired poets such as Rilke and Aragon. The mask suggests that Art was painting in Paris in the 1880s. She exhibited work successfully in Paris, London and elsewhere, and gained official recognition in Belgium.

Like many of her female counterparts, Alice Ronner (1857–1957) came from an important artistic family.[20] She and her sisters were schooled by their mother, Henriette Ronner-Knip, who was known for her sentimental animal portraits and for cats at play in particular. Alice shared a studio with her mother and they worked in each other's vicinity. She chiefly painted flowers and fruit, as well as some works with hunting motifs and meat. The Stadsmuseum in Lier possesses an unusually large work: a monumental interior
cat. 129 dating from 1888, *The Harp*, with the instrument behind a table on which is a cushion with a bunch of dried flowers. Her canvases were at first more realistic but after 1900 freer in style and more colourful, and she continued to paint and exhibit them well into extreme old age. A decade after the demise of the Cercle, and together with her sister Emma and Anna Boch, she was a founding member of the Galerie Lyceum, a new female painters' association in Brussels of which only a little is known about to date. She had contact with Queen Elisabeth, who visited her studio and collected her work.[21]

18 'Est-il un royaume où l'imagination et les sens affinés d'une femme puissent se plaire davantage que dans un jardin où poussent les plus belles plantes et les plus capricieuses, où les éclosions sont multiples et les odeurs enivrantes?' Pierron 1905, p. 20.

19 'Exception remarquable parmi le groupe intéressant de nos *painteresses*, Berthe Art allie à l'élégance, à la perception distingée que lui donne l'apanage de son sexe, une vigueur d'expression, de coloris absolument masculine.' Ibid., p. 19.

20 The most important contemporary source about Alice Ronner is an essay by Gustave Vanzype (Vanzype 1903). See also the master's thesis by Frédérique Van Duppen compiled in the Katlijne Van der Stighelen research group at KU Leuven (Van Duppen 2019).

21 Van Duppen 2019, pp. 67–77.

One of the most well-known female still-life painters is Louise De Hem (1866–1922)[22] from Ypres. She was tutored by her older brother-in-law Théodore Ceriez, under Alfred Stevens and in the Atelier des Dames at the Académie Julian, a private school with studios for men and women (who were also able to attend drawing classes of nude models) in Paris, where she lived for some years. In addition to still lifes, she mainly painted female portraits – at times quite monumental in scale – in the style of Stevens. She is better known owing to her sister (the heir to her estate) having donated a considerable quantity of her work to the Yper Museum, through which it was able to mount the monographic exhibition *Louise/Edith: Op handen gedragen*. Many of her compositions are influenced by seventeenth-century Baroque examples. In contrast, two works from the Yper Museum show more daring. For one large work, she sparingly arranged a few trinkets (an ornamental cup, a saucer, a fan and jewellery) around a narrow glass vase of roses. A white cloth 'flows' diagonally from the border on the right towards the foreground, carrying the trinkets with it, and slides over the edge. However, it is notable how De Hem placed another white cloth crosswise behind the first one and the vase, separating the background from the configuration in the foreground, lending the overall image depth and atmosphere as well as a quasi-landscape quality that is reinforced by the exotic folding screen with stylised birds and branches as a backdrop. In a smaller work dating from 1887, *Bust of a Young, Smiling Girl, a Carafe, a Japanese Doll and a Fan*, De Hem introduces 'expressivity' to enliven the composition and create more interest. The plaster face, the doll and the fan, forming an arc that runs from high up at the back to low down in the foreground, speak to the viewer, but at the same time each one in its own way is falling into a slumber, almost literally. De Hem painted them in the unconscious state of *objects* that are at once alive *and* inert.

cat. 12

cat. 143

Marie de Bièvre (1865–1940) is an intriguing character. She was self-taught, but a most decidedly active key figure within her generation of female painters. She took part in many exhibitions, including in France and Germany, and was involved in artist groups from a young age: a co-founder of the Cercle des Aquarellistes et des Aquafortistes Belges in 1883, of the Voorwaarts group in 1885 and of the Cercle des Femmes Peintres in 1888. She seems to have ceased painting at the time of the First World War. Her known work consists almost exclusively of still lifes. In the fruit still life *Peaches and Plums*, probably the painting of that title displayed at the Antwerp International Exposition in 1894, she pursued in masterly fashion the dynamism of the classic Baroque still life: emerging from a dark background, peaches and plums roll out of a wicker basket, a bronze dish and a porcelain plate and into the light in the foreground, all on a white tablecloth, the folds of which fan out up

cat. 13

22 Dewilde 2008.

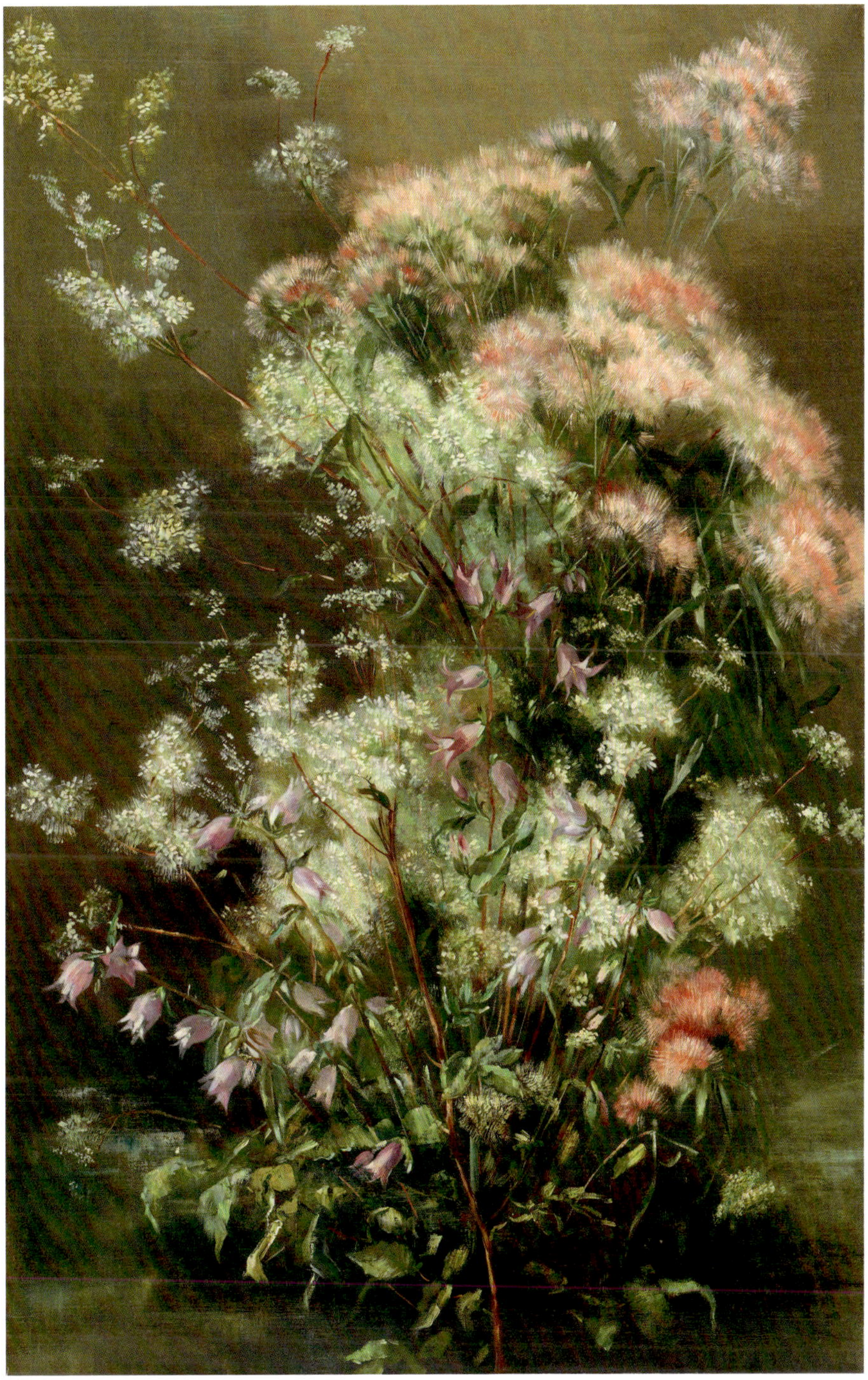

14

 cat. 14 Jeannie de Hemptinne, *Flowers*, s.d., oil on canvas, 109 × 71 cm. Private collection.

to the border of the canvas.[23] It is a bravura piece: the texture of the wicker canes, the lustre of the bronze, the sheen on the porcelain and the subtle distinctions between the fruits in the semi-darkness and in the light testify to her great artistry. A small, and probably late, work, *Physalis*, of red physalis inflorescences in a metal pot – cat. 132 the French call the *Physalis alkekengi* '*amour en cage*' – has been composed in a similarly diagonal fashion but with more contrasting colour. Once again, it demonstrates how well De Bièvre was able to render material and texture: the blue ceramic dish, the gleaming copper, the matte red of the delicate flowers, the white porcelain in the foreground. Equally intriguing are some works in which De Bièvre combines a still life of crockery with a bourgeois interior. In *Bourgeois Interior*, the almost realistic portrayal of the salon col- fig. 13 lides with an artificially arranged ensemble of cups, saucers, flowers and lamps on the dresser. This grouping is not part of the interior design, nor of everyday life, but is *posing* for the painter.

Georgette Meunier (1859–1951) also came from an artistic family. She learned to paint from her father, the engraver Jean-Baptiste Meunier whose brother was the sculptor and painter Constantin Meunier, and, as with Berthe Art, under Alfred Stevens cat. 131 in Paris. Mostly she painted still lifes of flowers and valuables.

Jeannie de Hemptinne (1865–1891) is a case apart. Descended from the family painted by François-Joseph Navez (Royal Museums of Fine Arts of Belgium), she trained at the Portaels studio in Brussels. She died young and her oeuvre is limited on that account; we know of only a dozen or so paintings by her hand, almost exclusively floral arrangements. However, an album has been pre- cats 14, 135 served that allows us to infer what these floral arrangements meant to her. A seemingly neutral genre such as the floral still life appears nonetheless to be suffused with artistic pathos, as she wrote with a romantic sigh: 'Let us love them! Let us love the wild flowers! Let them not be banished from our gardens; let them grow joyfully and freely around about us so that they bring us the wild and beneficent scent of the woods.'[24] The flower painter must choose between domesticised floral splendour in vases and bouquets and the enticing, wild beauty of 'the outdoors'.

Examples of wild-flower still lifes include a De Hemptinne work of wild flowers, a bird and a butterfly – in the family's collec- cat. 134 tion – and *The Thistles*, a lovely canvas by Pauline Jamar (1850– cat. 125 1911) from Liège and held in that city in the La Boverie collection. As regards Jamar, we know only of oil paintings and watercolours of flowers. To interpret and critically appraise the importance of these painters, and of many of their lesser colleagues, such as Clémence Jonnaert (1856–1941), Louise Coupé (1877–1945) or the sisters Valerie (1866–*c.*1948 or 1952) and Flore Geleedts (1866–1938), requires first and foremost a better understanding of their oeuvres and further documentary research.

23 Antwerp 1894.

24 'Aimons! Aimons, les fleurs sauvages! Ne les bannissons pas de nos jardins; laissons-les croitre heureuses et libres autour de nous ainsi qu'elles nous apportent la sauvage et bienfaisante odeur des bois.' *Poetry album Jeannie de Hemptinne 'J.D.H.'*, s.d. [*c.* 1880–91]. Private collection.

James Ensor

Overall, James Ensor (1860–1949) was a traditional artist whose work remained within the context of academic nineteenth-century art. He painted landscapes and seascapes, interiors and portraits, as well as many still lifes. However, he did add a genre of his own to this list. As a young painter, Ensor, at a stroke, brought innovation to the bloodless iconography of bourgeois, academic art and broke away from the conventional style of painting in which he had been taught.

James Ensor, Painter of Masks. As a student at the academy, Ensor discovered through his older fellow-student and friend, the poet, satirical playwright and painter Théo Hannon (1851–1916), in the book series *Histoire de la caricature* (1865–80) by Champfleury, the visual culture of the grotesque and the power of satire, as well as the lowbrow, the monstrous, the mask and the abject. Of that artistic tradition, so important to the human imagination and so present in the art of the Low Countries from the Gothic era to the seventeenth century, only saccharine, anecdotal genre art still persisted within the bourgeois, dignified art of the nineteenth century. The young Ensor, who had returned to Ostend after his academic studies, developed his 'mask art' based on Champfleury's compendium and illustrations, incorporating them into his own works from the mid-1880s onwards. Consequently, it was through his 'mask paintings' and some large drawings and etchings that he brought the bold tone and visual elements of this broad culture back into academic art.[25] This regeneration of iconography went hand in hand with a new style of painting.

James Ensor, Painter of Light. After 1884–5, Ensor's palette became much lighter in tone. Undoubtedly, he was highly sensitised by the atmosphere and light from the sea at Ostend. All the same, that light was not in itself his subject. He did not paint what he saw in the manner of Henri De Braekeleer, meticulously analysing the incidence of light, or in the manner of the Pointillists and Impressionists, examining and reconstructing their observations of light. His paintings are a light source in themselves; they are made of light. The painting that encapsulates his artistic change of direction, and a key work within his oeuvre, is *Masks Watching a Negro* [sic] *Tumbler* (1878/9–*c.*1890, T111). This involves a study from his student days of a Black model to which, in the early 1890s, Ensor added 'in jest' a turtle, an oil lamp and a parrot, thereafter partially overpainting it with a colourful array of masks that, uninvited, intrude into the image from the upper corner. In this way the work allows new and old art to overlap. fig. 16

At the beginning of his career, in the highly productive, magical years of 1880–82, Ensor painted a series of powerful, dark still lifes employing conventional subjects and compositions, establishing

25 Verschaffel 2018.

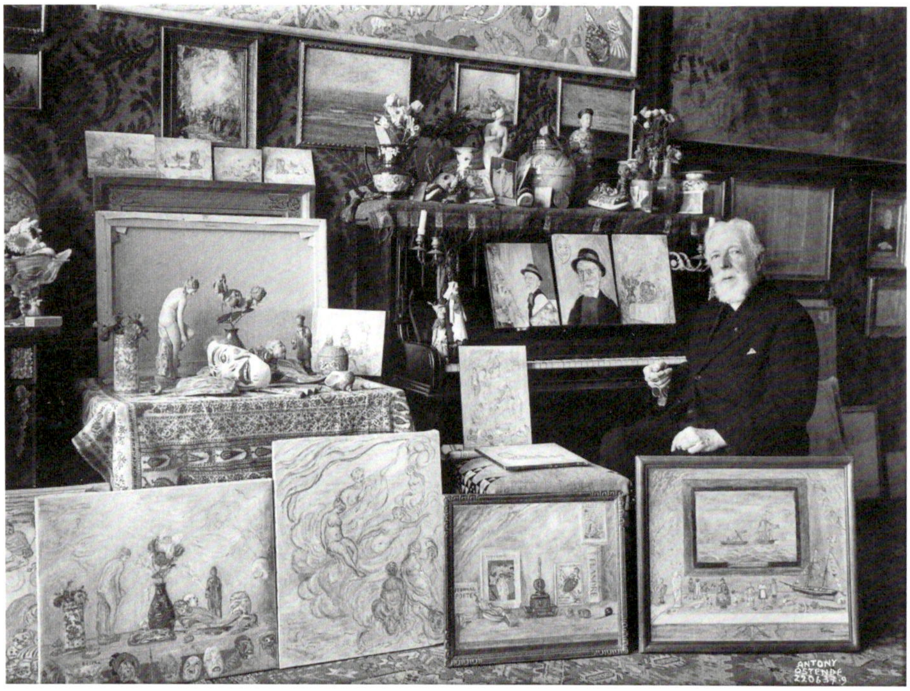

fig. 14

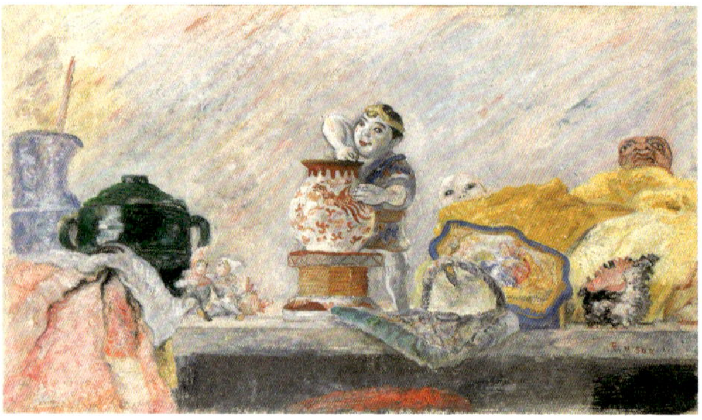

fig. 15

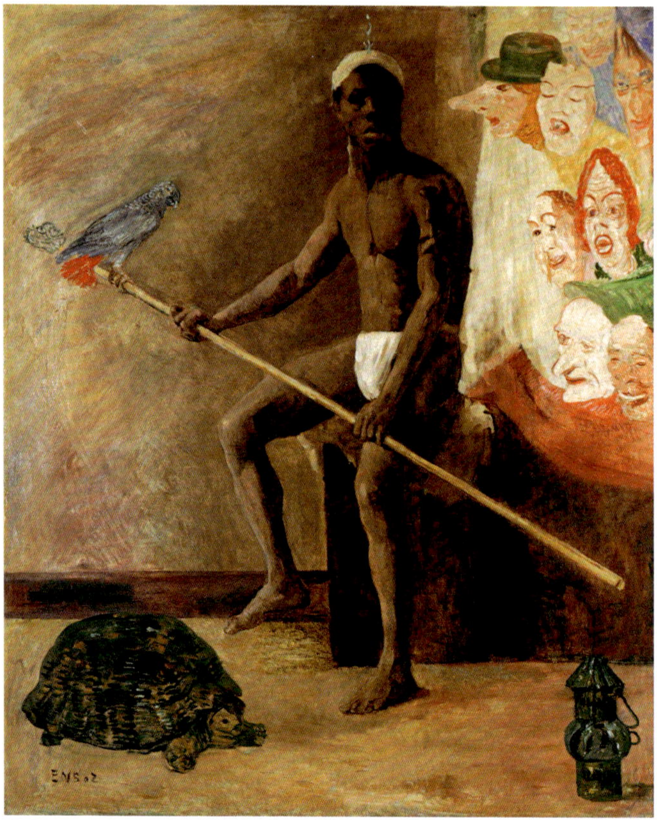

fig. 16

fig. 14 Maurice Antony, *Ensor in His Studio with a Row of Late Still Lifes and Self-portraits*, 1937. Mu.ZEE, City of Ostend Collection.
fig. 15 James Ensor, *Still Life with Chinese Porcelain Figure (Nature morte au magot)*, 1894 (?), oil on canvas, 32.5 × 56.5 cm. Private collection. CR T369.
fig. 16 James Ensor, *Masks Watching a Negro* [sic] *Tumbler (Masques regardant un nègre* [sic] *bateleur)*, 1878/9–*c.*1890, oil on canvas, 115 × 96 cm. Private collection. CR T111.

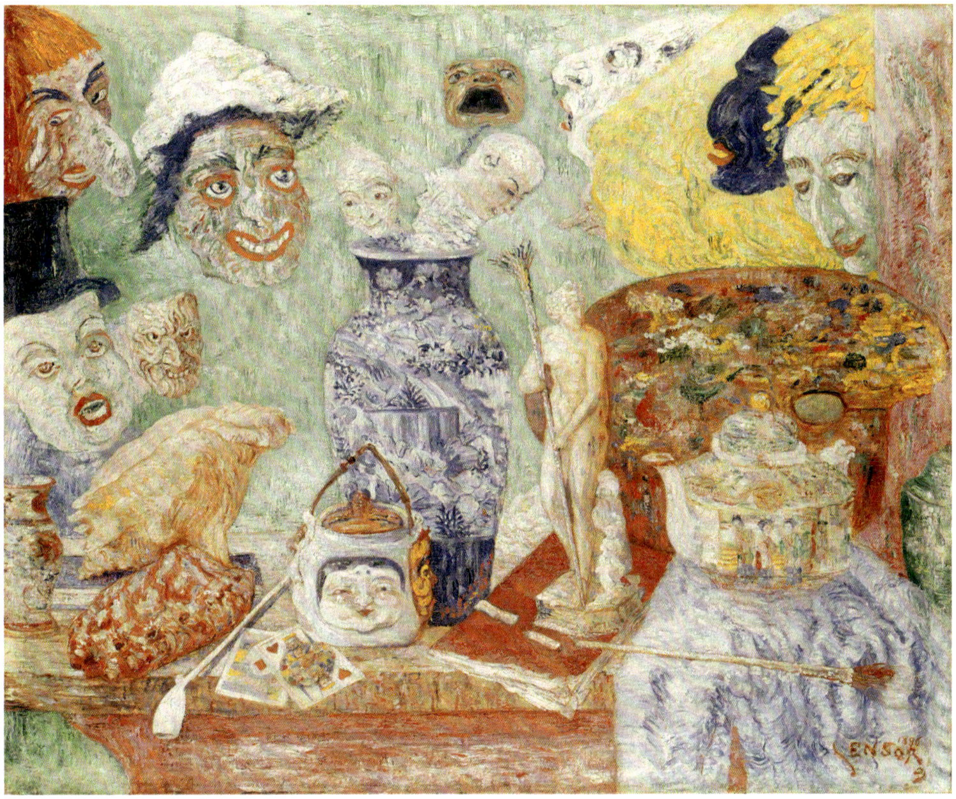

fig. 17

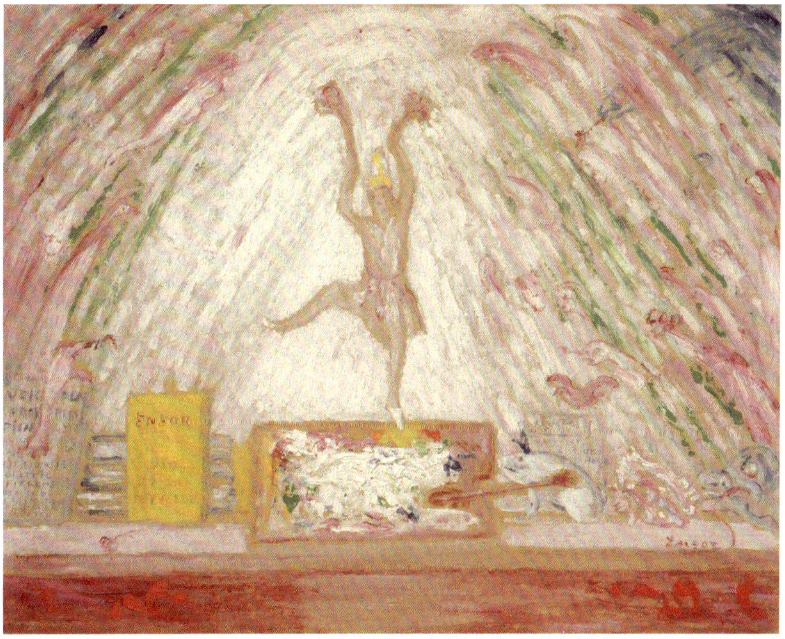

fig. 18

fig. 17 James Ensor, *Masks and Vases (Masques et potiches)*, 1896, oil on canvas, 80 × 100 cm. Hamburg, Kunsthalle, inv. 5036. CR T378.

fig. 18 James Ensor, *Offering to the Rose (L'offrande à la rose)*, 1940, oil on panel, 37.5 × 45 cm. Private collection. CR T838.

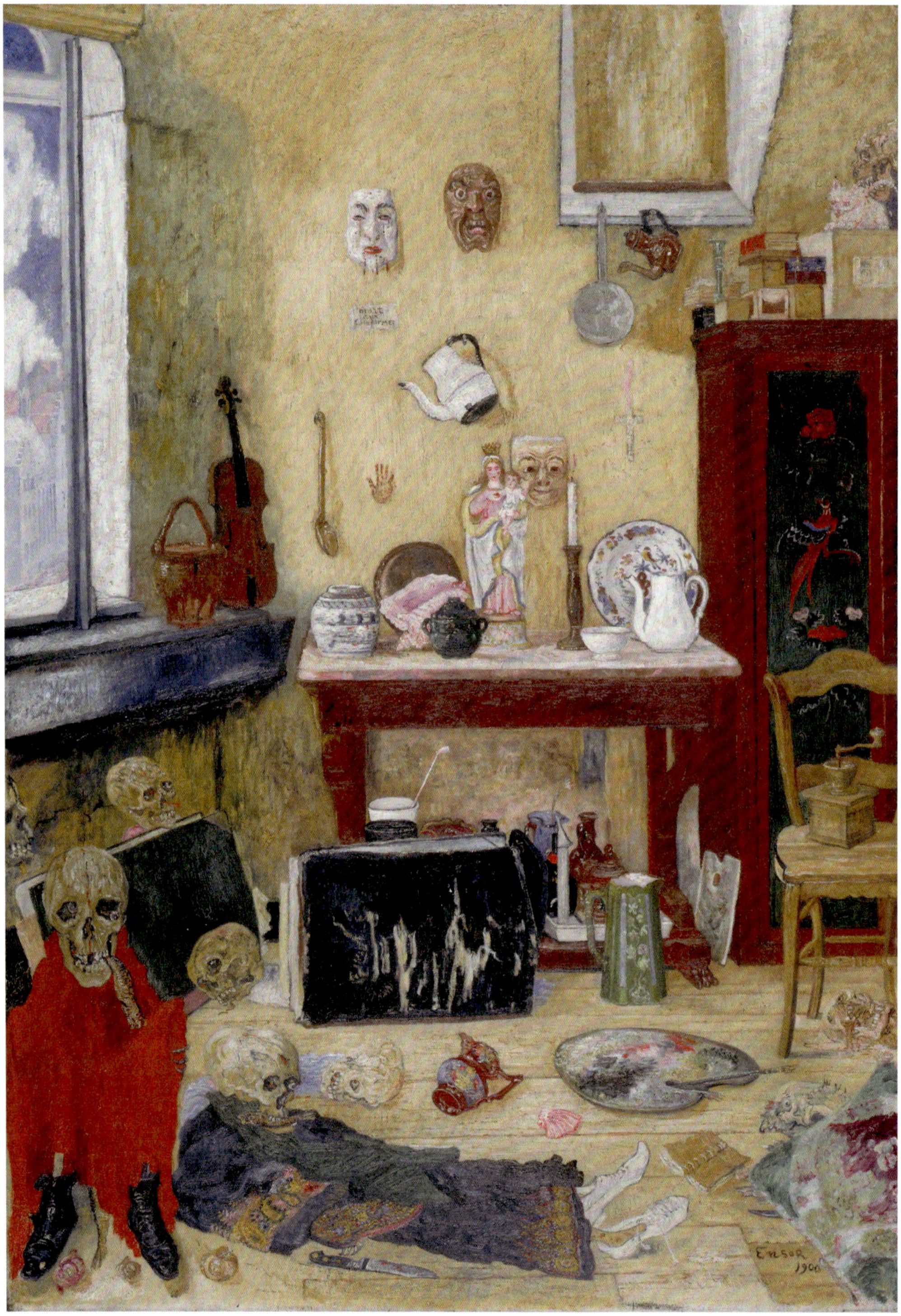

fig. 19

fig. 19 James Ensor, *Skeletons in the Studio (Squelettes à l'atelier)*, 1900, oil on canvas, 108 × 82 cm. Ottawa, National Gallery of Canada, inv. 23976. CR T394.

the basic images for that part of his oeuvre: small paintings of isolated objects such as lamps and bottles, Baroque compositions of
cat. 120 fruit and vegetables just as artists such as Willem Linnig II (1842–1890) was still painting them, floral arrangements, chinoiseries and
cats 31, 68 shells.[26] Of note amid his early still lifes are two more or less identical versions of *Blue Flask and Chicken*, a composition to which he
cat. 57 would later return, as well as the first version of *Skate and Herring*
cat. 126 (1880, T147), which Ensor painted in a joint session with his erstwhile English friend Willy Finch (1854–1930). The colours suddenly become more vivid in the mid-1880s, illuminating the images. The first masks appeared in 1887–8, and in 1889, Ensor painted *The Entry of Christ into Brussels in 1889* (1888–9, T293). In the early 1890s, this was followed once again by a series of still lifes in bright, intense colours and into which masks and grotesques came to be incorporated, contributing to the vitality of the image. Almost
fig. 38 programmatic and exemplary in nature, *Attributes of the Fine Arts* (1889, T300) is one of Ensor's most important works: a composition including an *Écorché* statuette (Flayed Man), ornamental platters, books and painter's materials, all harassed by two sets of intruding masks that – as in *Masks Watching a Negro* [sic] *Tumbler*, but this time from a background vantage point – stare impudently across the painting at the observer on the opposite side of the table. A mask lies prominently on view in the right foreground.

Assisted by his arsenal of grotesque visual elements, Ensor intensified his strategies aimed at making still lifes artistically interesting again. These semi-living beings do not blend discreetly among the objects, as do most of the display items and chinoiseries of his colleagues, but instead aggressively occupy the space. Alongside exotic figures, dolls, masks, skulls and (self-) portraits, this consists of the skate – a fish with a face that, as in humans, is turned to its belly – the queen conch and, among the vegetables and flowers, the cabbage and the rose. Ensor was keen to activate their murky symbolism and erotic associations, as in the case of the flabby skate in
cat. 41 the second version of 1892 (T350) with its flaccid tail; the many works incorporate a carnally pink 'conque indiscrète'[27] (indelicate conch) and 'folds of skin', seen in the cabbages and roses, as in *Still*
fig. 15 *Life with Chinese Porcelain Figure* (1894 (?), T369) and, in a more
fig. 17 extreme manner, *Masks and Vases* (1896, T378). A well-known
fig. 14 photograph taken by Maurice Antony in 1937 shows an elderly Ensor posing in his drawing room with a row of late still lifes and self-portraits and the protagonists in his theatre of objects.

Alongside the grotesque staffage, Ensor uses his faces and masks to observe and haunt the still-life configurations from the outside, much as his colleagues with their 'puppeteers'. One good
cat. 43 example is *Pierrot and Skeleton in Yellow Robe* (1893, T364) in the Museum of Fine Arts, Ghent, and more complex still than *Attributes of the Fine Arts*: faces loom up out of a misty background, while

26 André 1907; Antwerp 1991.
27 Ensor 1974, p. 31.

in the foreground a skeleton, Pierrot and a dwarf are engaged in dialogue, and masked faces look on from the left and right periphery, simultaneously observing both the scene and the spectators. Sometimes Ensor combined a still-life arrangement with an interior or a grotesque scene, as in *Skeletons in the Studio* (1900, T394) fig. 19
and *Interior with Three Portraits* (1938, T766). From 1894 to 1896, fig. 47
he also made a series of still lifes without grotesque additions, more traditional in intent, albeit vivid and light, in which he explored his new painting style.

Still lifes account for a quarter of Ensor's total oeuvre. It is possible to follow the significant stylistic and substantive developments in his work purely based on his still lifes. In 1905 and 1906, he frequently revisited works from his early period, now in his new, at times naive, oneiric style. An overall revision: old wine in new bottles. After 1910, he painted a remarkable number of amiable still lifes, commonly small scale, in which he revisited and alternated his stock of basic images, using the same or similar objects, in virtually identical compositions: Venus figurines or dolls from the Far East with a posy of flowers and a conch, ornamental platters and jugs, a heap of shells, apples and pears. Infrequently, one of the masked faces comes into view, but they are no longer threatening. The demons were replaced by light-footed nymphs and fairy-tale beings. Nevertheless, there is more at hand artistically than is generally thought. Particularly in this latter period, the swift and casual drawing style and the diaphanous colours transform the subject itself. Objects lose their mass and opacity, their 'materiality'; they become ethereal and start to dance and float. Take *Offering to the* fig. 18
Rose (1940, T838): a girl, the very flower of youth and beauty, rises up out of Ensor's palette, like Venus from the spume of the waves, and makes an offering to the Flower/Rose.

The Modernists

Around the turn of the century, Belgian and international art became 'modern'; artists felt compelled to use the freedom they had gained since the era of Impressionism. Within the altered conceptions of art and given the new way in which art life now organised itself outside the academies, artists could no longer choose a specialist area for themselves and build their careers upon it as the *artistes-peintres* of the nineteenth century had done. Painting was no longer a profession. The artist had to develop a personal and original body of work. Genres and subjects were secondary; it was one's own painting style, vision and expression that had priority. Above all else, a work had to be personal and unique. The artist's name became a brand. Picasso did not paint still lifes; he painted Picassos. One could still paint still lifes, of course, but true artists could no longer call themselves still-life painters. The genre conventions had become cultural heritage and were used only conditionally or ironically.

Even so, not all modernists were engaged in a radical discourse and afflicted with an unbridled thirst for experimentation. A number of 'light' modernists went along with the zeitgeist but sought their own niche in the fledgling, albeit already established, tradition of modernism. They developed a personal pictorial idiom but, erring on the side of caution, still employed the established pictorial space and vocabulary of still life and the genres; these include Louis Thevenet, Léon De Smet and others, such as Ferdinand Schirren,
cat. 163 Willem Paerels, Albert Saverys, Jos Albert and Georges Lemmen.

Louis Thevenet (1874–1930) is a minor master painter with an extensive oeuvre consisting chiefly of still lifes, interiors, village scenes and landscapes.[28] He was self-taught, had no academic training and sought his own path without much knowledge or analysis of or reference to other works. He knew about what he saw in his ambit: the work of friends such as Auguste Oleffe and of his acquaintances in the Brussels Fauvist milieu with whom he exhibited work.

Thevenet's art describes his physical environment. He painted familiar objects and places, composing new images by using the same items and furnishings. However, he is not an intimist but, rather, a realist who lived in close association with the objects and enjoyed an almost friendly, private relationship with them. He was not daydreaming, nor did he reside in memories; instead, he maintained a down-to-earth perspective on what was in front of him. He is also a realist in the way in which he painted things: it is not a matter of rendering an 'impression' but of displaying what those objects *are*. Thevenet painted them to show their own set form, colour and texture, always in full daylight – it is invariably the afternoon or summer. Thevenet's light does not dematerialise as in the case of Ensor's later works; it *articulates* and clarifies.

Thevenet called objects and their properties by their name and painted with clear didacticism; the tablecloth is radiantly white, the veneer top of the guéridon and the black lacquer of the table are gleaming and the coffee jug is reflecting light. The radiance, gleam and reflection are emphatically spelled out. His use of colour is celebratory and not subtle or nuanced. After all, colour is a permanent quality; it derives from the objects. Each colour and the strong contrasts of colours emphasise the substantiality and individuality of the objects. Apples and peaches are yellow, orange and red; the berries are green; the coffee cup is red; the bottle is blue. Thevenet keenly employs a striking degree of brilliant white and deep black, playing the one off the other, as in *The Funeral*
cats 15, 144 *March* and *Still Life*. This shows all the other colours stretched between the two unnatural extremes of the colour spectrum.

28 Lyr 1944 and 1954.

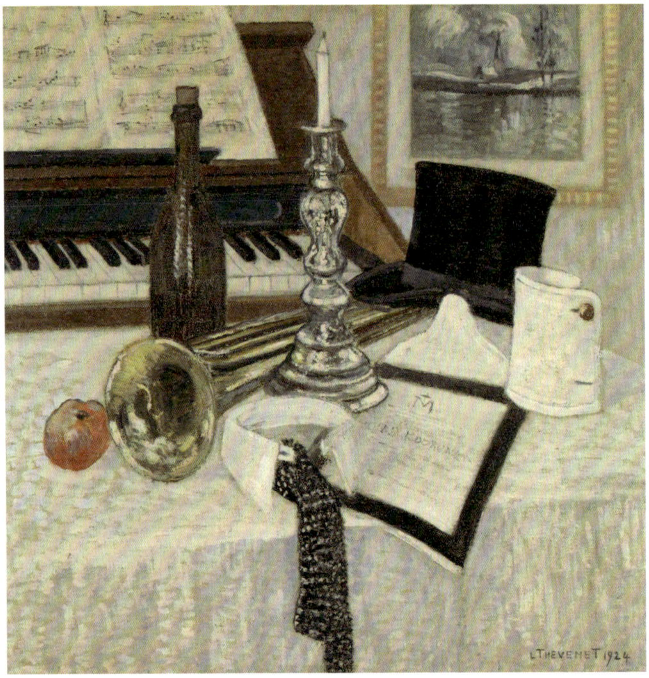

15

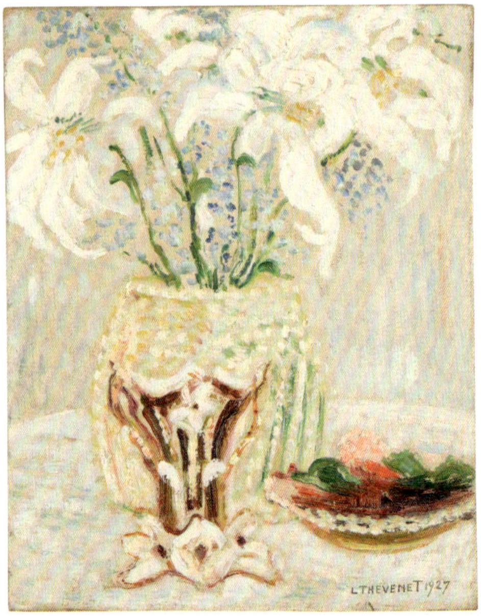

16

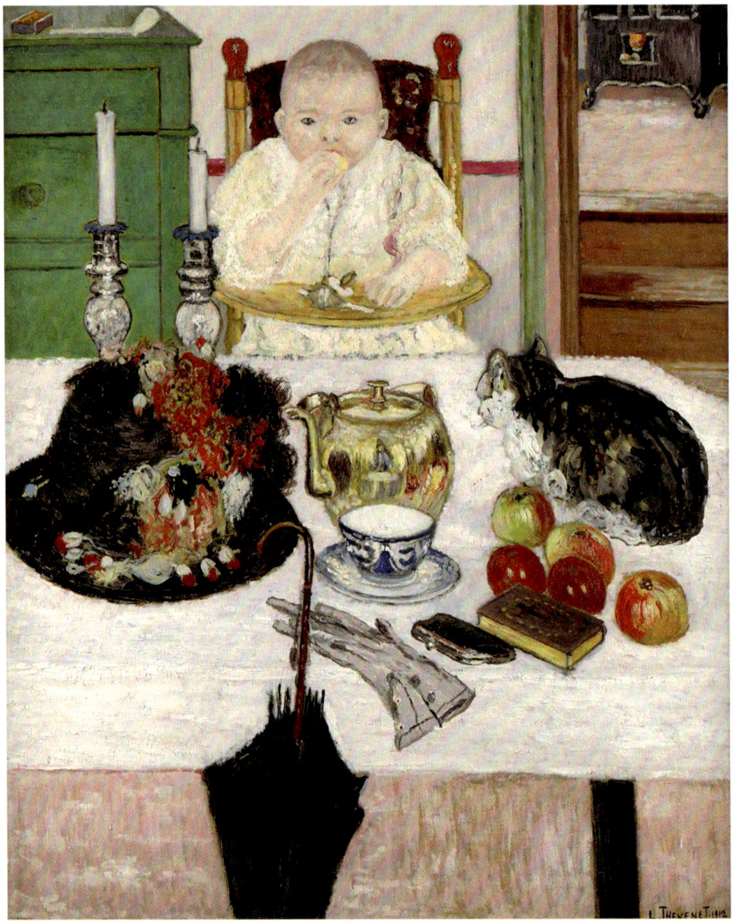

17

cat. 15 Louis Thevenet, *The Funeral March*, 1924, oil on canvas, 81 × 81 cm. Musea Brugge, inv. 0000.GRO1563.I.
cat. 16 Louis Thevenet, *Vase of Lilies*, 1927, oil on canvas, 40 × 32 cm. Private collection, Leuven.
cat. 17 Louis Thevenet, *After Mass*, 1912, oil on canvas, 109 × 88 cm. Museum of Ixelles, inv. CC 1628.

In the case of Thevenet, each still life is a close-up of an interior. He positioned the objects; we always know where we are. Everything is ordered, everything in its place. However, something is *happening* at times as well. Thevenet then *narrated* without using characters; the objects tell the story. After the funeral procession in
cat. 15 *The Funeral March*, the trumpet player's hat and starched collar are left heedlessly on the table alongside the obituary notice. In *After*
cat. 17 *Mass*, it is the umbrella, the hat, the gloves and the prayer book on the table along with the candles, the fruit and the tea that tell us that the lady of the house has returned home from church. The cat has come to sit alongside these things and is looking at a toddler who, from his vantage point, oversees everything while gnawing on a biscuit. The totality is frontal, vertical, rigidly symmetrical and composed with structural regularity. The vertical axis runs from the child in the chair to the gloves and umbrella below, and the image has been divided horizontally into three equal sections. The midsection of the scene displays a bulbous teapot reflecting the image of a teacup and above, minutely, the painter or an observer standing in front of the painting, as in a traditional still life. At the same time, the teapot is the centre of the rhombus created by the four darker visual elements: the black cat, the umbrella, the hat and the child's high chair. The upper left and right corners of the image are symmetrical, identical in form and balance each other: on the left, the chest of drawers, with the tobacco pipe and matches resting atop it; on the right, a glimpse into the room beyond and the lit stove. Likewise with the arrangement of objects on the table: the splash of colour from the flowers on the black hat to the left is in reply to the yellow and red of the apples to the right. As is customary with Thevenet, all objects are laid out alongside but separate from one another. This serves to emphasise the contrast between the dazzling white of the tablecloth and the profound black of the hat, the cat and the umbrella. The totality is made monumental and hieratic thanks to the toddler, who sits *enthroned* at the head of the table, looking the viewer straight in the eye. As with the infant Jesus in late medieval Christian art, the child has been painted in an incongruously adult fashion. The rotund, naive child's face with its intensely grave gaze from on high and his re-enactment of the Catholic ritual of consecration, together with the generally symmetrical and frontal visual composition, transform the work into archaic religious art.

Thevenet here painted in a detached and objective manner, but that does not mean that in his domestic universe everything is correct and nothing 'rubs the wrong way'. However, the rancour and resistance do not come from the objects or from the tableaux; the disquiet arises from an awkwardness or clumsiness in the actual painting. Every image fails in one way or another. For example, in
cat. 145 *The Blue Bottle*, a hat and a pair of gloves are almost shapeless. The

small vase in *Vase of Lilies* lacks sufficient curvature and volume, cat. 16
and the bowl of fruit is reduced to a painted mush. Critics, such as Georges Ramaekers, wrote about the 'gaucherie délicieuse' (refined clumsiness) of the self-taught Thevenet. Perhaps not wholly without grounds, Maurice Sulzberger even imputed to him a 'simplicité affectée' (affected simplicity).[29] Thevenet was certainly not refined in his painting. At the same time, however, it is also true that his imperfections and exaggerations do not harm his images but add flavour, and without them his oeuvre would probably have been too amiable and decorative.

Léon De Smet (1881–1966) carefully remained within the mainstream of his art genre throughout his career. He found his footing almost immediately in terms of his style of painting, atmosphere and subject matter. There is no doubt that he painted many fine impressions of landscapes and sterling floral arrangements, but his essential subject was subdued bourgeois life and the intimacy of the isolated country residence, away from the city and work, away from the world and history. Nature outdoors knows no straight lines or angles, no sharp divisions, and thus suits the gentle touch of Neo-Impressionism. Conversely, buildings and objects are consistent and have defined contours. The late Impressionist painting style of De Smet mitigates and masks the solidity and clarity of the objects and dissolves them into 'atmosphere'. He employed three principal overlapping formats: interiors, still lifes conceived as cutouts from an interior and women portrayed and positioned in their interiors. The still lifes are spacious, clearly ordered ensembles of familiar ingredients: ornamental platters, bouquets, exotic figurines, scallop shells and invariably the conch. However, De Smet's most powerful images are his nudes, which indicate that within that gentle domesticity there is nevertheless always more going on than it may seem at first glance. One extraordinary example is *Nude with*
Red Dresser. A young nude poses self-aware in front of a flam- cat. 18
ing red dresser, her almost sculpted face in profile in front of an overloaded, pyramidal still-life configuration on top of the dresser, with the ubiquitous conch, flowers in white, pink and red, a bell-jar housing the Virgin Mary and a mirror. The Egyptian face of the girl is a magnification of the face of a porcelain statuette on the dresser and becomes a part of the composition of the still life.

Is still life a genre that solely or primarily provides us with an opportunity for testing out how we *see* things and how we can *imagine* them? Is it also a locus in which to find out what those things *are*? Art that has tired of rhetorical romanticism and idealised theatrical landscapes and that, instead, desires 'reality' knows what to do and knows where it can become 'modern': outside, *en plein air* and alongside 'the everyday'. But what about the objects? In a still life, the objects are posed, made up and articulate, on-stage, in their theatre. To look closely at them, to dissect their appearance

29 René Lyr quoting Georges Ramaekers from *Samedi*, 6 October 1907, and Maurice Sulzberger from *L'Etoile Belge*, 26 February 1925, in Lyr 1944, pp. 32–3 and 91.

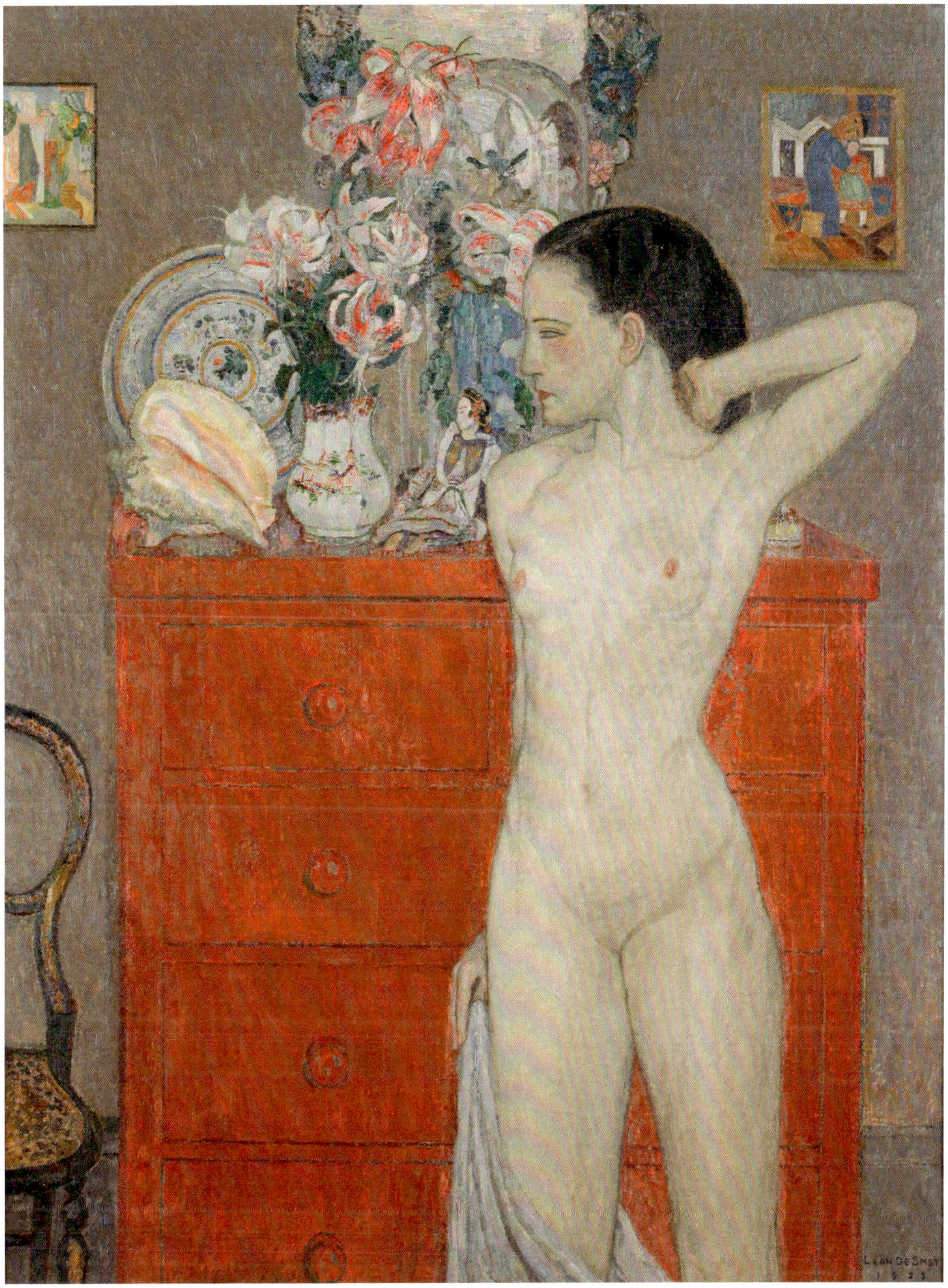

18

cat. 18 Léon De Smet, *Nude with Red Dresser*, 1921, oil on canvas, 152 × 115.5 cm. Property of the Belgian State, Collection of the Wallonia-Brussels Federation, inv. 1984.

and faithfully reconstruct it is not enough when it comes to grasping their existential nature and presence or the secret of materiality.

Within the conventional *and* modern traditions, there are still-life painters who inquire into the being of the object. The intrinsic theatrical character of the pictorial space and the expectation that the objects mean something – in other words, that they have something to do with people's lives and activities – are obstacles to this. The frontality, the prominent emptiness of the scene and the self-assurance and pathos of the pose falsify the image. One of the means of stripping away the mendacity of objects and of capturing their *reality* is the abject: the moment when the objects appear to lose their form and become *indefinable matter*. Goya's late still lifes can serve as an example of the modern still life that no longer displays the objects theatrically but finds them – cinematically – on the ground and thus emphasises their materiality and their mass. The body that has become flesh. See the small fish and meat still lifes by Hubert Bellis and the drooping necks in the various versions of Ensor's *Blue Flask and Chicken*. As a rule, Rik Wouters cats 31, 68, 73
leaves us only with the colour of the objects and is unconcerned about the objects themselves, but his *Still Life with Skinned Hare* cat. 155
and *The Skinned Rabbit B* are exceptions to this. And then there cat. 19
are the still lifes by Walter Vaes.

Born into a family of architects and artists, Walter Vaes (1882–1958) was a late bloomer within the conventional, academic tradition of the still life. He painted portraits (including of Ensor), floral arrangements and relatively small, focused still lifes, and he made etchings. Just like Thevenet, he was an artistic loner but with a traditional academic education and erudite. As a young artist in Antwerp, he joined the cultural circle De Kapel founded by François Franck, and in 1905, he co-founded Kunst van Heden. But in the midst of the emergent modernism, he was behind the times and kept painting 'traditional' still lifes in isolation instead of experimenting with form. He was judged on that account; he has not been afforded any mention in the history of modern art in Flanders. Vaes painted superb bouquets and floral arrangements, but above all it is his sober, almost minimalist still lifes that are so outstanding. Rarely did Vaes make complex compositions using many objects that interact and display variation. He favours tight close-ups of isolated objects on an indeterminate surface or dropped into a bowl or dish. These are not viewed in a theatrically frontal manner but somewhat from above, pressed downwards. Commonly, he painted different types of meat, which evoke slight disgust and which he elaborated upon at times in his etchings in fantastical and monstrous fashion. There are two distinctive and related works within his oeuvre that have as their central motif a red gurnard resting on an upturned dish. This species of fish has an unusually large head. In the work at the Royal Museum of Fine

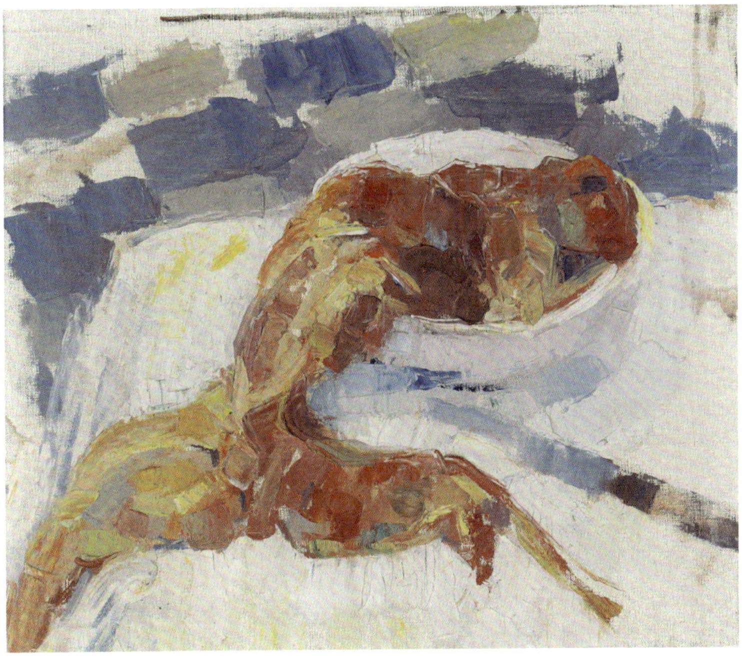

19

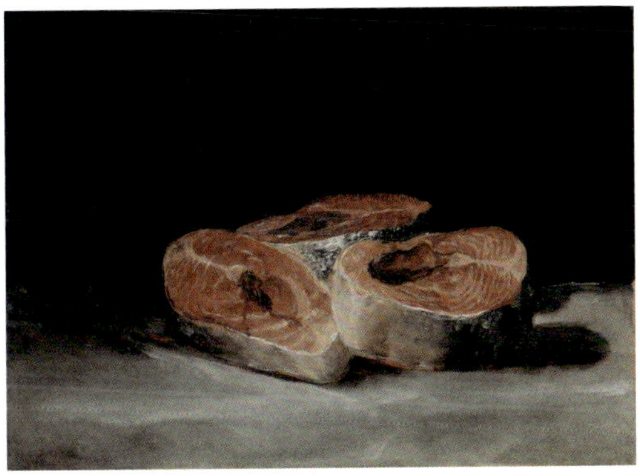

fig. 20

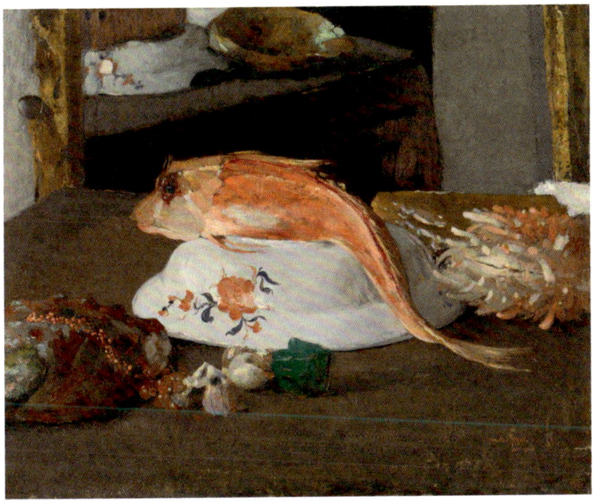

20

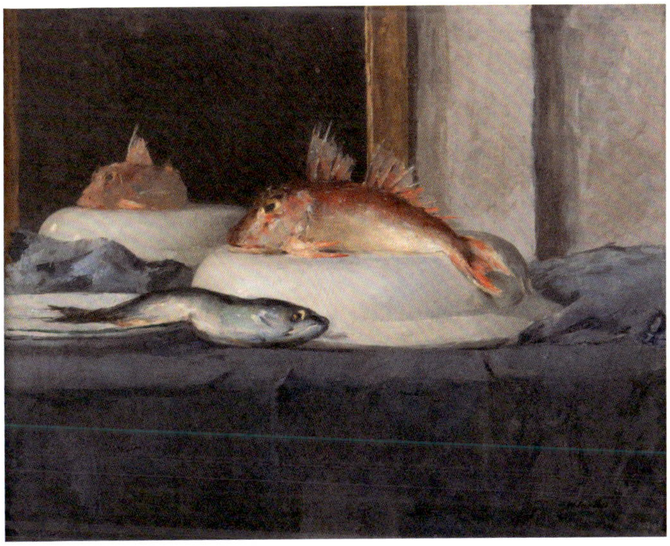

21

fig. 20 Francisco de Goya, *Still Life with Three Salmon Steaks*, 1808–12, oil on canvas, 45 × 62 cm. Collection Oskar Reinhart 'Am Römerholz', Winterthur, inv. 14.
cat. 19 Rik Wouters, *The Skinned Rabbit B*, 1908, oil on canvas, 40.2 × 47 cm. Royal Museums of Fine Arts of Belgium, Brussels, inv. 11570.
cat. 20 Walter Vaes, *Red Fish*, 1906, oil on canvas, 53.5 × 66 cm. Royal Museum of Fine Arts, Antwerp, inv. 2035.
cat. 21 Walter Vaes, *Still Life with Fish*, s.d., oil on canvas, 65.5 × 82.4 cm. Janssens Collection, Antwerp.

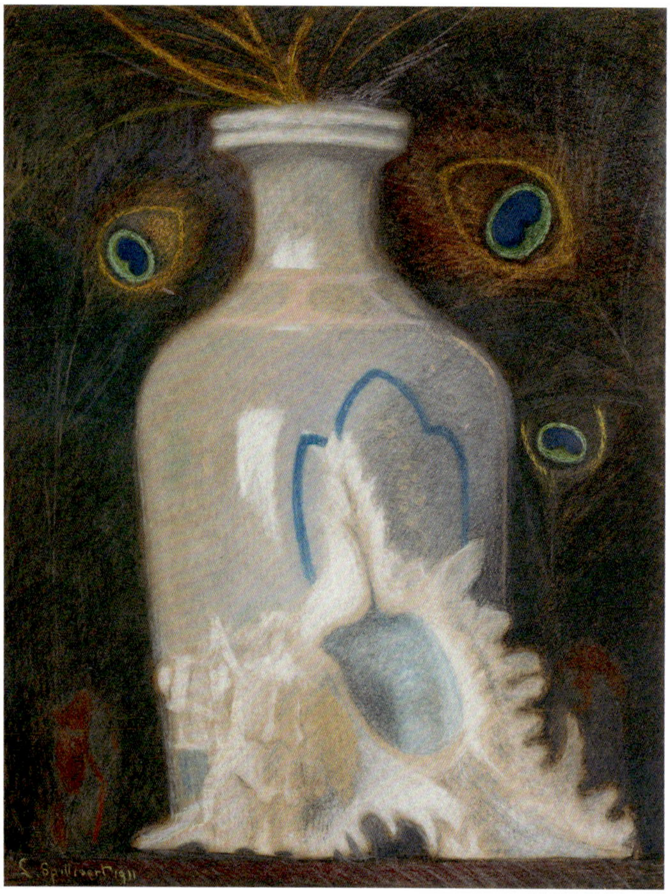

22

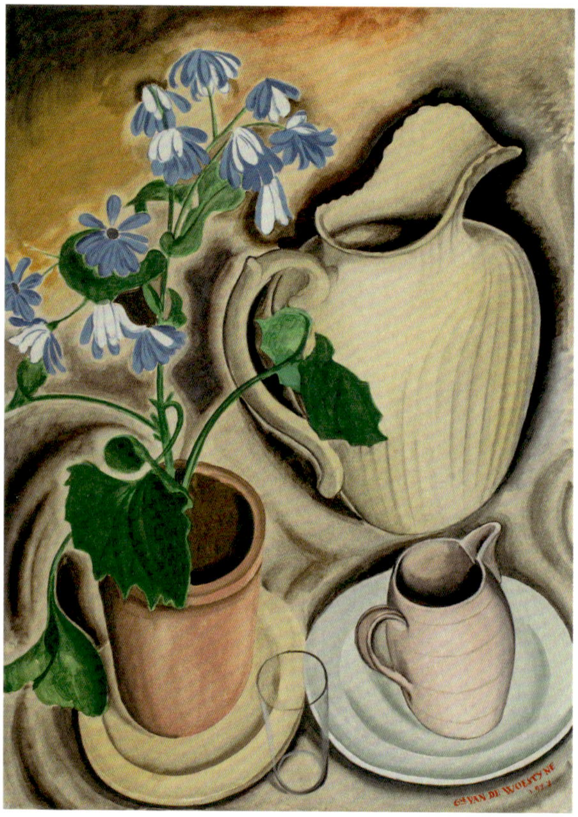

23

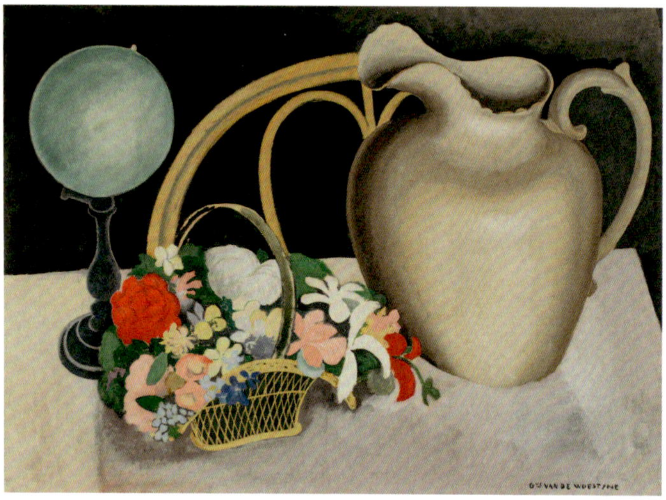

24

cat. 22 Léon Spilliaert, *Vase and Shell*, 1911, pastel on card, 89.2 × 70.2 cm. Private collection via Philip Seghers Gallery.

cat. 23 Gustave Van De Woestyne, *Still Life with Groundsel*, 1922, gouache on paper, 76.5 × 55.5 cm. Museum of Fine Arts, Ghent, inv. 2004-G.

cat. 24 Gustave Van De Woestyne, *Still Life with Globe*, *c.*1921–2, gouache and oil on Japanese paper and card, 56 × 77.5 cm. Museum of Fine Arts, Ghent, inv. 2004-H.

cat. 20 Arts, Antwerp, a mirror has been placed at an angle in the background of the painting to display both sides of the fish. In the version held in a private collection, Vaes plays on the 'staring power' of the gurnard's dead eyes and those of a coley by turning the gurnard and mirror in such a way that three fish eyes stare directly at the viewer.[30]

cat. 21

In addition to the cautious modernists, there are keen individuals who do not so much as explore or interpret the pictorial genre of the still life as appropriate and use it for their own, highly individual work. When artists such as Léon Spilliaert, Gustave Van De Woestyne or Rik Wouters created a work that looks like a still life or a portrait, they turned that iconographic and pictorial ensemble to their own ends. Naturally, their 'still lifes' are also relevant to research into the possibilities of the genre per se. Through their work, they do indeed reveal a possibility, but they exhaust it simultaneously. Their examples are inimitable; anyone who tries inevitably becomes an epigone.

Léon Spilliaert (1881–1946) did not work within, with or against the tradition or conventions of still life. It was immaterial whether he was drawing trees and plants, the beach, a dining room, a stack of boxes or decorative shells. Using his pastels – halfway between the subjective schematic of a drawing and the full likeness of a painting – he operated in a reality limbo where all things feel strange, as if bewitched, sometimes using white magic and sometimes black. In the in-between world into which Spilliaert brings the objects, they exist neither factually and corporeally, as with Thevenet, nor subjectively and internalised, as with the Impressionists and Fauvists such as Wouters. They embrace *otherworldliness* more than they do *derealisation*: the objects exist in their own right, but they are no longer what they signify to us; they are no longer that which we use them for. This means that when Spilliaert peered into that in-between world as into a mirror, he no longer recognised himself, losing himself in that 'other world'. Moreover, it means that in Spilliaert's still lifes, the objects are at once beautiful *and* incomprehensible.

Unlike images of interiors, landscapes or figures, there is something arbitrary and artificial about still lifes. The artist does not merely select and frame his subject, he creates it himself, free and able to bring all manner of elements together and to arrange improbably successful encounters between objects. One such example is
cat. 22 *Vase and Shell*. Spilliaert, like Giuseppe Arcimboldo, created a composition figure using two glaring peacock-feather eyes on either side of the neck of a large vase, some stems protruding from the top, and an unusually shaped ornamental shell mounted as 'feet' in front of the 'under-belly' of the vase.

In the 1920s and '30s, Gustave Van De Woestyne (1881–1947) painted an important series of still lifes, partly as a commission

30 Brussels 1938; Delen 1942; Corbet 1948; Lebeer 1951; Antwerp 1983; Laren/Sint-Niklaas 1987–8; Eindhoven 1999.

from the collector David van Buuren.[31] They constitute a distinct ensemble within his oeuvre. The greater part of his work revolves around the human figure and on character within those figures (i.e., on the essence of a personality). And its focus is on narrative – not on history, not on fate, fortuities and adventure, but on exemplary events and stories serving as parables. Just the essentials; no secondary matters. Pictorially, this requires simplification and austerity, visual epithets that slow down and turn actions into gestures and people into types. It can descend into caricature. After all, complexity is distracting and nuances muddy the message. What happens when this type of spiritualising art – fitting for the religiously inclined Van De Woestyne and his times – is transferred to objects? Van De Woestyne did not seek any associations or symbolism in his still lifes. Objects remain what they are. However, the *spiritualisation* in his narrative art becomes *essentialism* in his still lifes. Not religion but, rather, ontology, or the study of being: the distillation of the arbitrary existence of things into their idea. Not *an* apple, but *the* apple; not *a* basket, but *the* basket.

Van De Woestyne painted general objects, or *objets types*, using clear contours, pronounced colours and no detail. He depicted them as eternally new, without history, without traces of use, without fortuity. Two of his gouaches on paper are exemplary, produced in 1922 and held in the Museum of Fine Arts, Ghent: *Still Life with Globe* and *Still Life with Groundsel*. The principal cats 24, 23
element is twice a jug with a crenate rim. In *Still Life with Globe*, the jug is placed on a table together with a basket of flowers and a globe on an iron pedestal; in *Still Life with Groundsel*, it is accompanied by a smaller jug and flowerpot on an indeterminate surface. The location of the composition with the globe has been determined; the tabletop, the back-rest of a chair and the even black of the background tell us where we are. Conversely, in *Still Life with Groundsel*, the jug, now with a ribbed design, the striped smaller jug and the flowerpot are all floating on an undulating surface of stylised, curving and circling lines and folds, dishes and patches of shadow. The image is restless, but nothing is moving. By contrast, the jug is smooth in *Still Life with Globe* and all of the unrest and bristling is reserved for the bouquet in the basket; otherwise, nothing else is happening: the globe is a bare sphere.

Epilogue

The decline of the theatre of objects heralded the end of the traditional still life. Without their stage, the objects lacked their locus and their raisons d'être. They were lost; they could be anywhere: for example, above the nude on the sofa by Philibert Cockx (1879– cat. 25
1949).[32] Is the little dog an animal or an object? Or spread out

31 Ghent 2010.

32 Liénaux 1965; Brussels 1987.

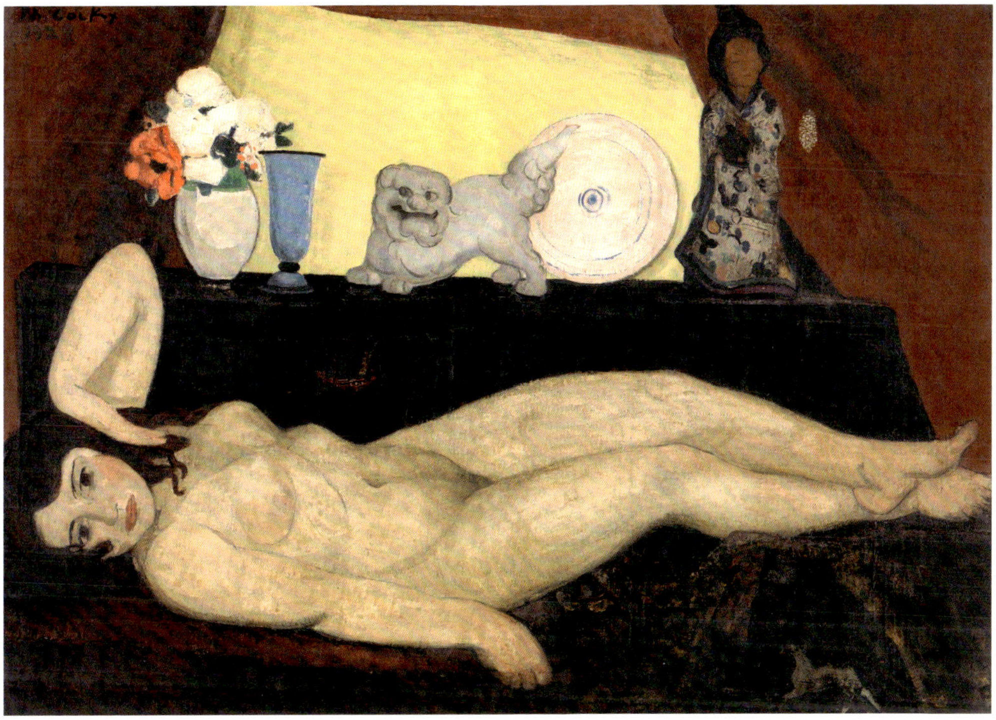

25

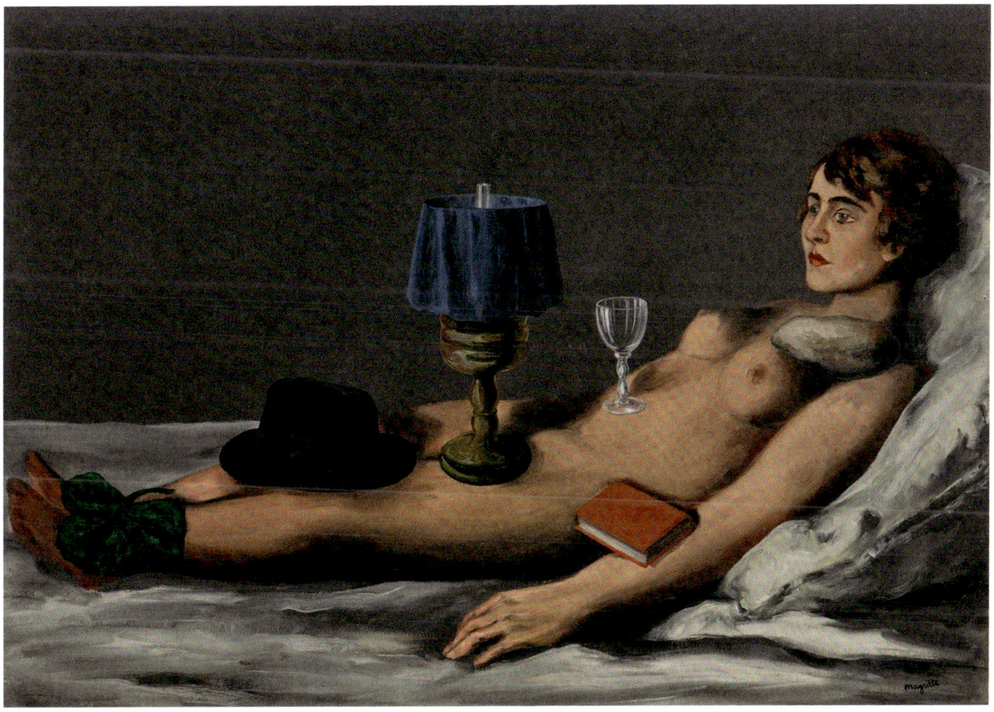

fig. 21

cat. 25 Philibert Cockx, *Lying Nude*, 1928, oil on canvas mounted on panel, 95.5 × 137.5 cm. Royal Museum of Fine Arts, Antwerp, inv. 2672.

fig. 21 René Magritte, *The Lying Nude*, 1928, oil on canvas, 81 × 116 cm. Private collection.

on the body of Georgette Magritte in *The Lying Nude*. Artistic abstraction replaces the pictorial space with a plane, proceeding to transform or reduce the objects into a visual figure and part of a planar configuration of forms and colours. Once the objects have by this means ceased to be *somewhere* and are no longer in an environment, they become surreal. fig. 21

Marthe Donas (1885–1967) was the first or at least most important Belgian modernist female painter. She created a great many still lifes between 1917 and 1927 while involved in the Parisian art scene. They show what is left of the objects after their abstraction: a colourful shadow theatre.[33] Gustave De Smet (1877–1943) illustrated the problem clearly in *Still Life*, a fascinating work from 1928 that is completely unique in his oeuvre; on the one hand, there is the 'theatre of objects', still containing some residue of the truth of 'objecthood', and, on the other hand, a planar depiction of things from which all 'reality' has evaporated. However, the critics, and perhaps also De Smet himself, saw this isolated work – wrongly – as a failed experiment. De Smet did not continue making work in this manner.[34] cat. 26 cat. 27

Jean Brusselmans (1884–1953) produced only a limited number of still lifes and floral arrangements. Up until the early 1920s, these were rather traditional, Post-Impressionistic, close-up presentations of small ensembles of objects. However, some of the paintings that prefigure his later work are striking. In these, his vantage point is from above and he is clearly cataloguing the different gathered objects. The 'leap' from the theatrical image (where the objects are together in one space, located beside and behind one another and depicted truncated and in distorted perspective) to a collage of distinctive, planar identity photographs of the objects is already apparent in two related works from 1920: *Still Life with Fan I* and *Still Life with Fan II*. They present the same ensemble of fan, jug and basket. Brusselmans takes the positioning and depth out of the picture and paints an inventory of the scene. He then proceeds to apply this composition principle to his landscapes and still lifes, sometimes tentatively, sometimes very rigorously. In so doing, he dismantles the theatrical and perspective-based pictorial space, replacing it with the image plane.[35] figs 22, 23

Still Life with Slices of Sausage is radical. The slices of sausage, the jug and the basket of apples are not placed in one space and arrangement to bring them together. Nor is there any unity of scale in which to interrelate the objects; there is no interplay. As with the upper half of the image, the lower half is plain wallpaper. The objects are depictions of themselves, pictograms, stuck to a canvas. *Still Life with Griffon* is particularly revealing. The canvas is divided horizontally into two unequal sections, with the upper section split vertically into three parts, creating a triangle in the centre. This does not merely form part of the underlying geometry into which cat. 161 fig. 26

33 Frankfurt/Ghent 2015–6.

34 Langui 1945; Boyens 1989.

35 Delevoy 1972; Ostend 2011.

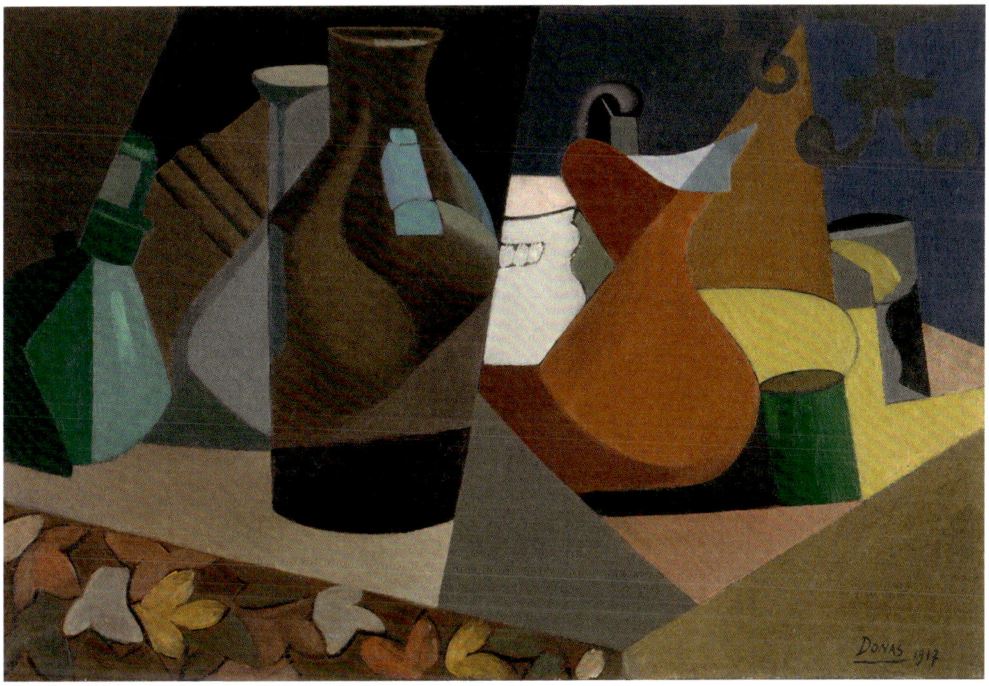

26

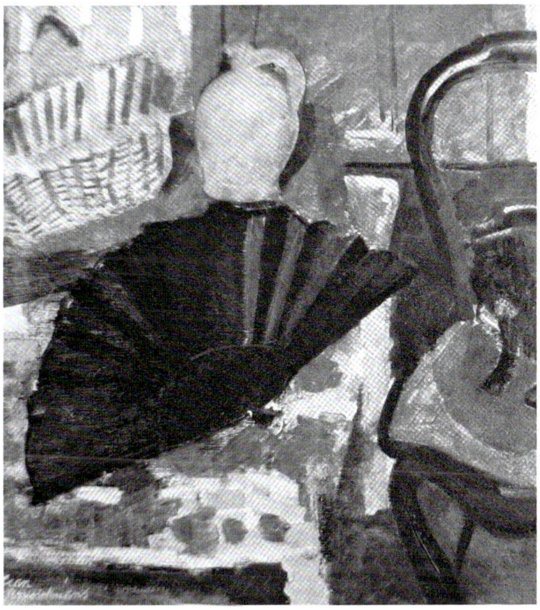

fig. 22

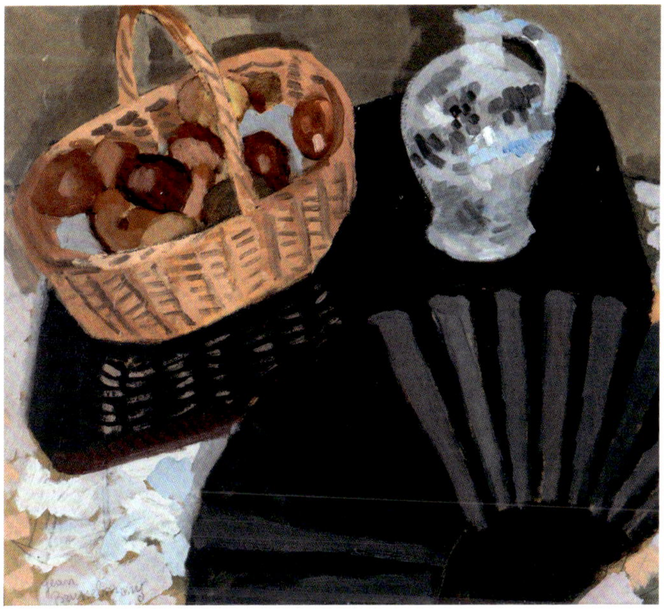

fig. 23

cat. 26 Marthe Donas, *Cubist Still Life*, 1917, oil on canvas, 34.5 × 53 cm. Royal Museum of Fine Arts, Antwerp, inv. 2948.
fig. 22 Jean Brusselmans, *Still Life with Fan I*, c.1920, oil on canvas, 67 × 64 cm. Whereabouts unknown.
fig. 23 Jean Brusselmans, *Still Life with Fan II*, c.1920, oil on wood, 47 × 54 cm. Whereabouts unknown.

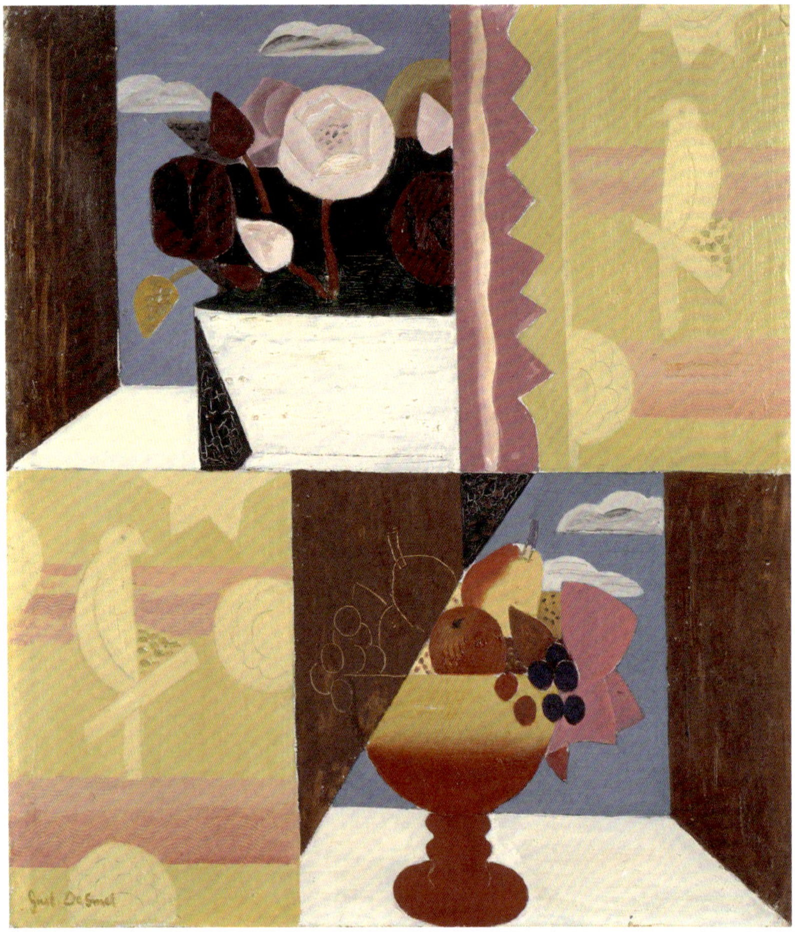

27

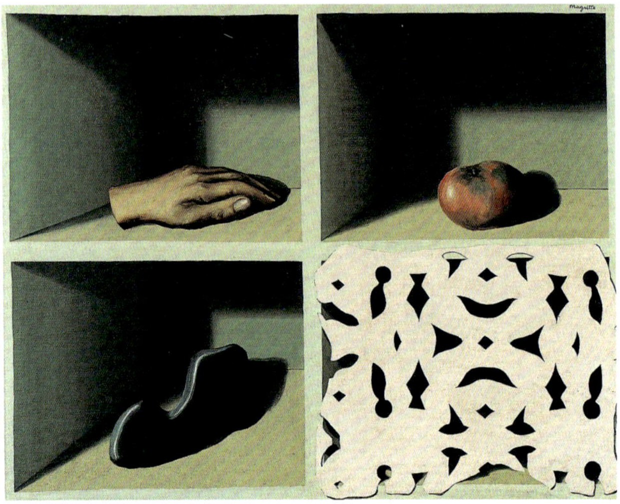

fig. 24

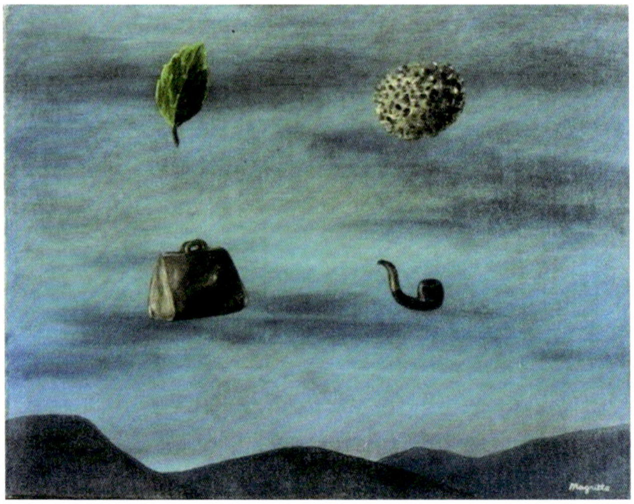

fig. 25

cat. 27 Gustave De Smet, *Still Life*, 1928, oil on canvas, 80 × 70 cm. Part of the Emanuel Hoffmann Foundation, gift from the Maja and Emanuel Hoffmann Collection 1998, permanent loan to the Öffentliche Kunstsammlung Basel, inv. H 1998.19.
fig. 24 René Magritte, *One-Night Museum*, 1927, oil on canvas, 50 × 65 cm. Private collection.
fig. 25 René Magritte, *The Future of the Voices*, 1927, oil on canvas, 50 × 65 cm. Private collection.

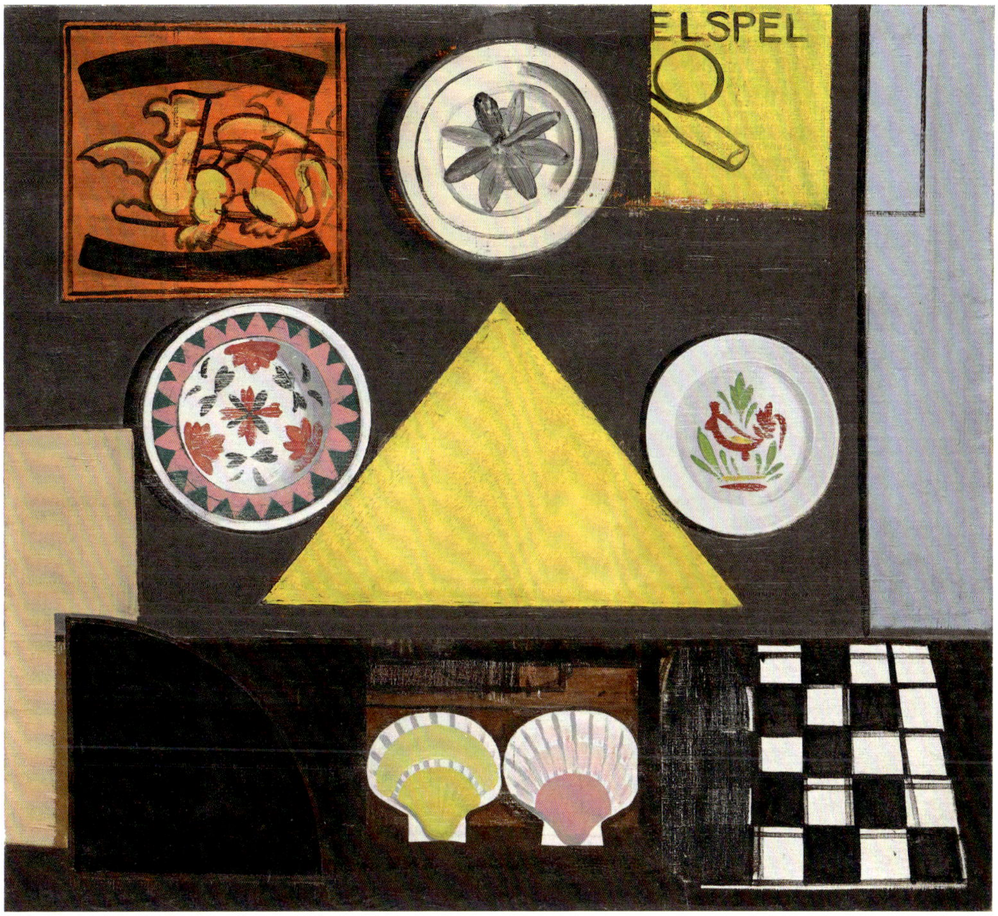

28

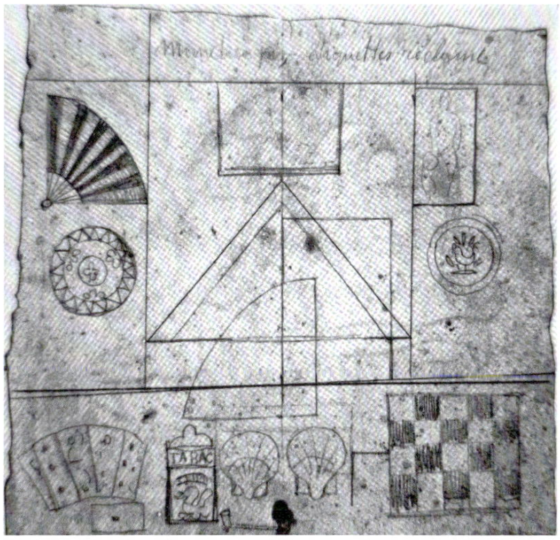

fig. 26

cat. 28 Jean Brusselmans, *Still Life with Griffon*, 1936, oil on canvas, 109.5 × 122.4 cm. Mu.ZEE, City of Ostend Collection, inv. MZ000054.

fig. 26 Jean Brusselmans, *Study for 'Still Life with Griffon'*, *c.* 1936, pencil on paper, 25.5 × 28 cm. Whereabouts unknown.

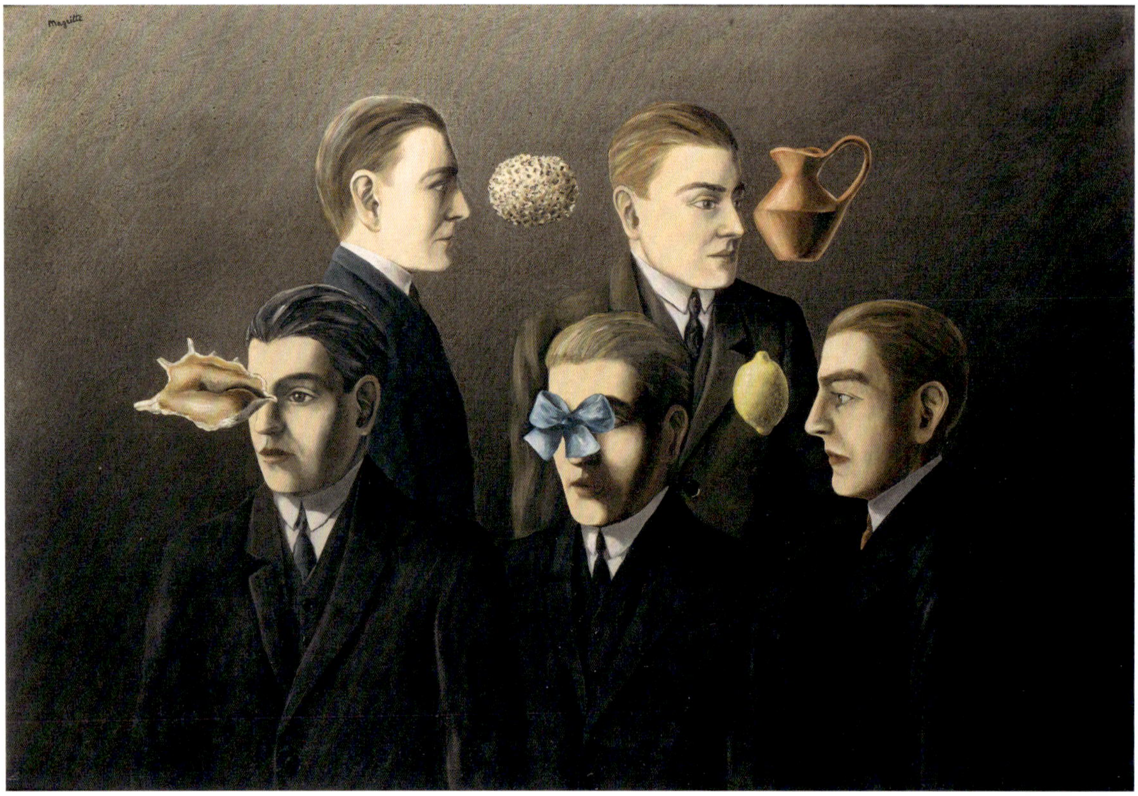

fig. 27

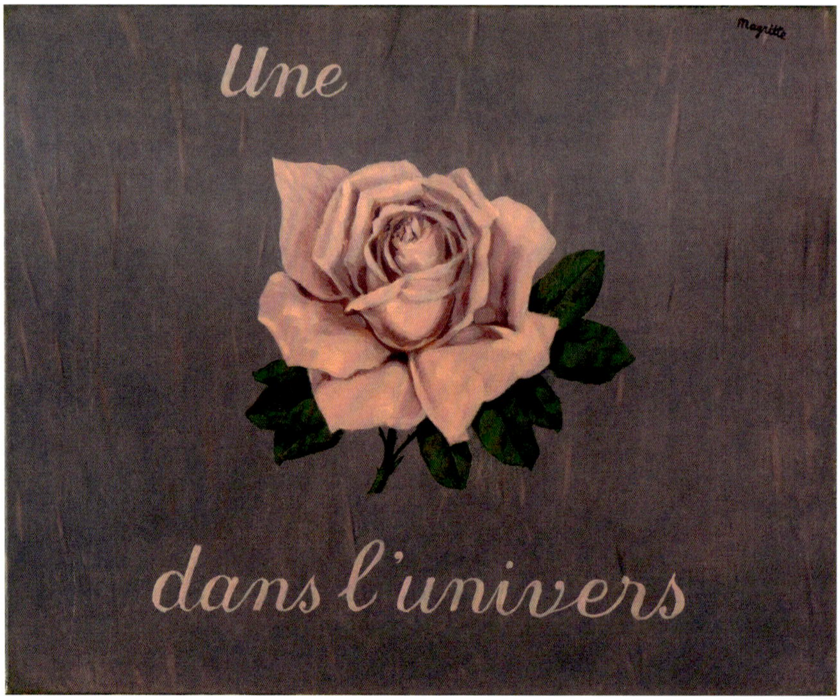

29

fig. 27 René Magritte, *Familiar Objects*, 1928, oil on canvas, 81 × 116 cm. Private collection.
cat. 29 René Magritte, *The Voice of the Absolute*, 1955, oil on canvas, 40 × 50 cm. Private collection.

the painting's visual elements are then placed. The triangle in the under-drawing is transferred to the image as an abstract coloured
cat. 28 shape and appears there as an object among the depicted objects. Rebounding from that, this serves to emphasise the essential geometric shapes of the flag, the decorative plates and the chessboard, as well as the ordered composition as a whole. The real world is very far away!

In 1948, Brusselmans produced a late work as part of a series of large Baroque versions of his planar still lifes. However, he rendered the images in such a way as to entirely cover and take over the geometric arrangement; the underlying regularity is hardly perceptible. Amid all the hustle and bustle, objects overlap, sliding against and in front of one another as if they do have some interrelationship after all and constitute a whole. They do indeed belong together: not in the world, but definitely in the history of
cat. 162 the still life. *Still Life with Fan*, of the same year, *encapsulates* the traditional still life. All of the *usual suspects* are present: the fruit and the vase of flowers, the fish, the scallop shells and the conch, the decorative platters and the fan, the artist's materials, a picture within a picture and the woman who comes to look (back).

After a few experiments with abstraction, the young René Magritte rediscovered the stage of the theatre of objects, and in 1926, he used this again for his first disturbing images. The next year, he successively painted the objects both inside and outside
figs 24, 25 their theatre: *One-Night Museum* and *The Future of the Voices*. Afterwards he made them objects of interest again, not by animating them or by having them smirk and strike fear, not by bizarrely distorting them like Ensor and not by representing them schematically like Brusselmans, but by treating them as conventional *symbols* and then combining them in improbable and startling ways. The apple and the hand or the lemon and the shell are not real things to Magritte and still less eternal essences. The foot and the shoe are wholly interchangeable. They are arbitrary symbols that
fig. 27 we keep or bear in mind (see *Familiar Objects*). The 'real' is whatever is fading out of sight behind the symbols: the universe is a mystery. The objects in the painting are not *there*, and we shall never paint them as they *are*. The painter plays with the symbols that he creates; the still life is nothing more than a parlour game,
cat. 29 as in *The Voice of the Absolute*.

James Ensor and Still Life

Sabine Taevernier

> Nature morte *is the triumph of colour and life.*
> James Ensor[1]

Of all the subjects tackled by artists, the still life is hardly the most popular. In the artistic context of the late nineteenth century, it was considered a minor genre. But let us recognise that at that point, the still life was no longer serving an audience but had become a tractable subject that the artist could manipulate at will. This lack of recognised norms afforded the artist greater creative freedom, making the genre excellent terrain for experimentation and one that James Ensor exploited to the full. Analysis of his still lifes – 'this fragment of the world that can be ordered twice, before painting and in painting'[2] – allows a better understanding of the unusual twists and turns of his art.

Ensor focused even more on still life than did Édouard Manet, for whom it was 'the touchstone of the painter'. Alongside landscapes, interiors, portraits, self-portraits and historical and biblical subjects, he painted more than two hundred still lifes, representing around a quarter of his pictorial production. As a theme it was very well suited to the enclosed world he created within the private space of his studio, much resembling the cluttered bourgeois interiors of family and friends. There, undisturbed and answerable to no one, Ensor was able to choose and arrange his objects and accessories at leisure, developing his technique and his style in complete freedom, experimenting with all kinds of compositions unthreatened by the anxieties that sometimes haunted his creative explorations. The study of his still lifes, then, allows us to follow step by step the painterly and thematic development of this gifted and unpredictable artist.

Sensitive and easily offended, Ensor tended to think of himself as misunderstood by those around him. His parents, however, had not been slow to recognise his talents and provided him with the teaching that allowed him to develop as an artist. He was tutored from age 13 by two local painters, Édouard Dubar (1803–1879) and Michel Van Cuyck (1797–1875). Both were old and at the end of their careers but were able to impart the essentials of their craft.

1 'La nature morte est le triomphe de la couleur et de la vie.' James Ensor to Edgard Picard, Ostend, 8 February 1906, in Tricot 1999, p. 537.

2 Sterling 1952, pp. 32–4.

At age 17, Ensor went not to Ghent or Antwerp, whose academies had an international reputation, but to Brussels. The attractions of the capital, whose nineteenth-century building boom had made it an international metropolis, must certainly have played a role in this choice, as might the fact that the ladies of the Ensor family liked to spend a few weeks or even a month there in the winter picking up the curios that they would sell in their shops over the summer.[3] He recalled his early work and training in a letter to the Belgian critic Jules Du Jardin:

> *From the age of 13 I was invincibly drawn to painting. My first landscapes date from that time. … In 1877 I entered the Brussels Academy, which was then headed by Jean Portaels [appointed in early 1878]. My first drawings were much admired by the teachers and I won second prize for a drawing from an ancient head. My paintings were less to their taste. My sincere landscape studies had sent me out into the open air and already I sensed the importance of light. These new experiments displeased the teachers and soon – I never really found out why – I began to be regarded as an incorrigible revolutionary. … For three years I attended the Academy's classes very regularly. I left, very much disgusted, in 1880.*[4]

The New Prophet of Light

> *The new prophet of light. … His method, his violent colourations, his scorn for form and details.*[5]

When he left the academy in 1880, without even finishing the year, Ensor was an academically trained artist with a grounding in every genre. Apart from a sketch of *The Hat-Stand* (1876, T33), still life cat. 54 had not held his attention, but his return to his own studio and his quest for subjects to paint very naturally favoured the genre. His mother's shop and its miscellany of objects and the family home with its comfortable middle-class furnishings and everyday house-

3 James Ensor to Ernest and Mariette Rousseau, Ostend, Saturday 12 October 1895, in Huys 2021, p. 417.

4 'Dès l'âge de 13 ans je fus invinciblement attiré vers la peinture. Mes premiers paysages datent de cette époque. … En 1877 j'entrai à l'académie de Bruxelles dirigée alors par Jean Portaels. Mes premiers dessins furent très admirés des professeurs et je remportais un second prix de dessin d'après tête antique. Mes peintures furent moins goûtées. Mes sincères études de paysages m'avaient fait rechercher l'air ambiant et déjà je pressentais l'importance de la lumière. Les recherches neuves déplurent aux professeurs et bientôt, je n'ai jamais bien su pourquoi, je passai pour un révolutionnaire incorrigible. … J'ai suivi pendant trois ans les cours de l'académie très régulièrement. J'ai quitté l'académie très dégoûté en 1880.' James Ensor to Jules Du Jardin, Ostend, 28 October 1899, in Tricot 1999, p. 276.

5 'Le nouveau prophète de la lumière. […] Son procédé, ses colorations violentes, son mépris de la forme et des détails.' Block 1984, p. 60.

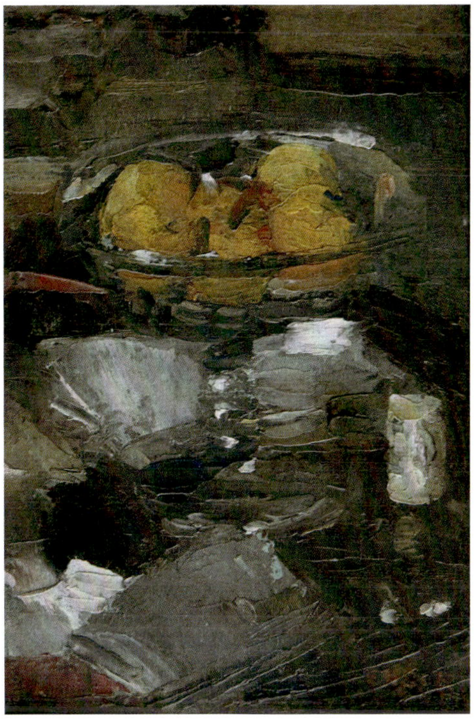

fig. 28

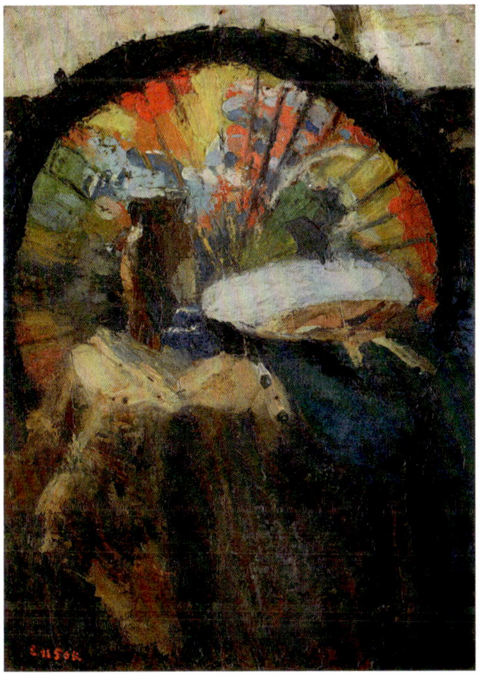

30

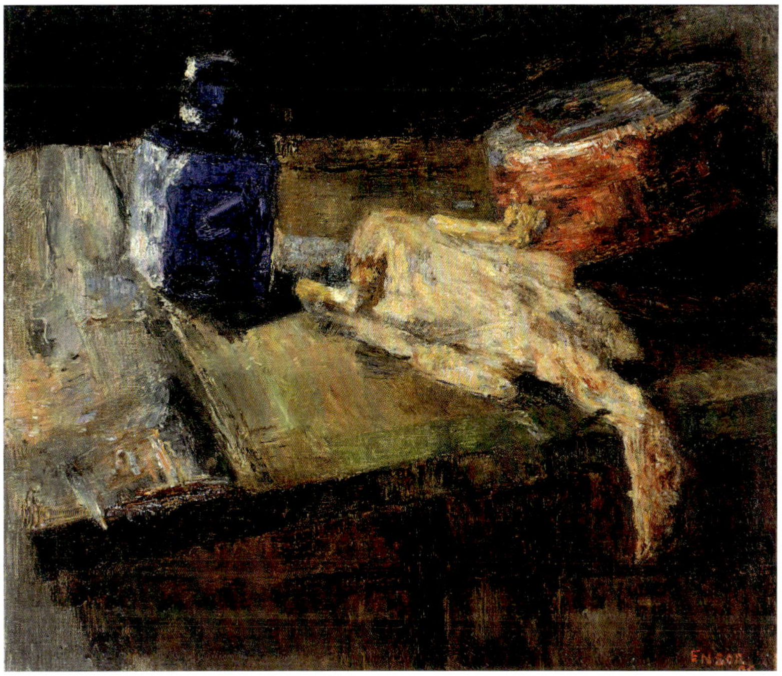

31

fig. 28 James Ensor, *Still Life with Lemons (Nature morte aux citrons)*, 1880, oil on cardboard, 26.5 × 18.5 cm. Fondation Socindec. CR T127.
cat. 30 James Ensor, *The Parasol (Le parasol)*, 1880, oil on cardboard, 31 × 22.5 cm. Vanthournout collection. CR T131.
cat. 31 James Ensor, *Blue Flask and Chicken (Flacon bleu et poulet)*, 1880, oil on canvas, 47 × 55.5 cm. Quintet Private Bank (Europe) S.A. CR T144.

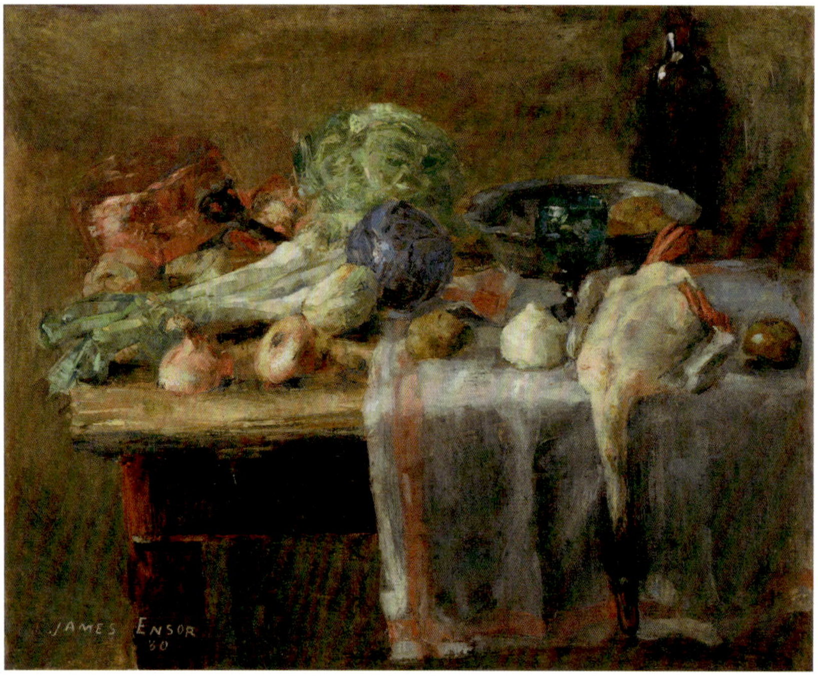

fig. 29

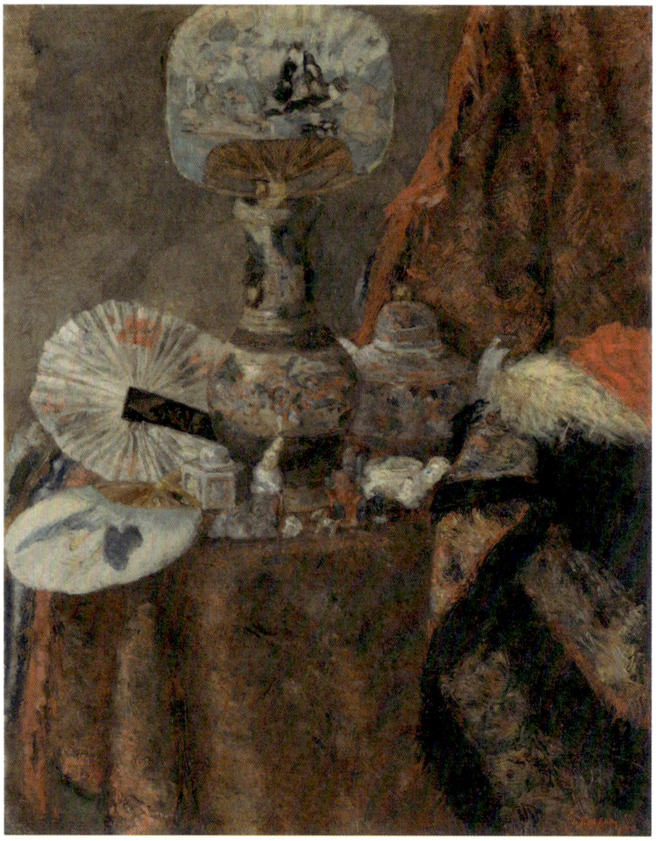

32

fig. 29 James Ensor, *Still Life with Duck (Nature morte au canard)*, 1880, oil on canvas, 80 × 100 cm. Musée des Beaux-Arts, Tournai, inv. D0936. CR T149.
cat. 32 James Ensor, *Chinoiseries, Fans and Fabrics (Chinoiseries, éventails et étoffes)*, 1880, oil on canvas, 100 × 78 cm. Royal Museum of Fine Arts, Antwerp, inv. 2076. CR T151.

hold items offered, in fact, a multitude of subjects to consider and compose. In the solitude of his attic studio with its big south-facing window[6] – high above the eastern corner of the intersection of Ostend's Rampe de Flandre and Boulevard Van Iseghem – Ensor had all the time in the world to examine his objects and study the effects of light on their forms. He thus produced a series of painted sketches of domestic objects, first on pink card and later on canvas: fabrics, small items of furniture, bottles, glass-ware, china, fruit and vegetables (T149, T131, T144).

fig. 29, cats 30, 31

The rapid, small-format sketch saw him develop a very personal manner pervaded by fault and imperfection that nonetheless reflected a direct, head-on approach to the subject more intuitive than cerebral. The light and the positioning of the object were crucial. The artist avoided the zenithal light that 'deforms and makes ugly'[7] – generally unavailable at home, in any event – choosing rather to exploit the horizontal light from windows or other lateral openings. People and objects are illuminated from front or back or obliquely, taking on different forms depending on the angle and nature of the light. Later in his career, he reflected on the importance of such an approach to a subject:

> *My friends, works of a personal vision alone will live. One must create a personal pictorial science, and be excited before beauty as before a woman one loves. Let us work with love and without fear of our faults, those inevitable and habitual companions of the great qualities. … Quality stands for uniformity in the effort to achieve certain common perfections accessible to everyone. Fault escapes conventional and banal perfections. Therefore fault is multiple, it is life, it reflects the personality of the artist and his character; it is human, it is everything, it will redeem the work.*[8]

He at the same time embarked on a series of larger compositions that testify to his academic training. Here again, he was a free spirit even as he followed the precepts of such great masters of the still life as Jan Davidsz. de Heem (1606–1684), a major figure of Baroque painting in the Low Countries. A diagonal composition, great attention to the rendering of materials and highlights and a sense of the theatrical are thus all features of Ensor's early still

6 James Ensor to André de Ridder, 2 August 1928, in Tricot 1999, p. 188.

7 Ensor 1974, p. 225.

8 'Mes amis les œuvres de vision personnelle seules resteront. Il faut se créer une science picturale personnelle et vibrer devant la beauté comme devant la femme qu'on aime. Œuvrons avec amour, ne craignant pas les défauts, compagnons habituels inévitables des grandes qualités. … Qualité signifie uniformité dans l'effort en vue d'atteindre certaines perfections communes accessibles à tous. Le défaut échappe aux perfections uniformes et banales. Le défaut est donc multiple, il est la vie et reflète la personnalité de l'artiste, son caractère, il est humain, il est tout et sauvera l'œuvre.' Ensor 1974, p. 82.

lifes in 1881–2. The table is never entirely covered, and cloth and objects are carefully arranged with colour accents so distributed as to create a balanced composition.

The subjects, all elements of a meal, are drawn from the everyday routine of the kitchen. It might be the meat and vegetables of a pot-au-feu, a ray straight from the market beside a fish basket (*Skate and Herring*, 1880, T147), a plucked chicken drooped on a cat. 57
table (*Blue Flask and Chicken*, 1880, T144), a duck with accompa- cat. 31
nying vegetables (*Still Life with Duck*, 1880, T149) or a red mullet fig. 29
set down on a blue apron accompanied by a ceramic pot and various brass items. As well as such commonplaces, Ensor liked to paint objects imported from the Far East (*Chinoiseries, Fans and* cat. 32
Fabrics, 1880, T151) or simply copied by European workshops to satisfy middle-class tastes. He liked to paint these things that delineated his own middle-class family from the working class, discovering in them an aesthetic of the chimerical, the fantastical and the exotic that would inform his painting and nourish his creative inspiration throughout his career.[9]

They would often be vases, or a tea-service with teapot, cups and caddy, accompanied by fans and opulent, colourful fabrics. While such things were household items, they also featured among the goods stocked in the shops – the one in Ostend, the other in Blankenberge – owned by his mother Marie Catherine Louise Haegheman (1835–1915) and his aunt Marie Ludovica Haegheman (1839–1916), whom he called Auntie Mimi. The ladies sold seashells, both retail and wholesale, as well as a wide range of jewellery and items in mother-of-pearl, together with chinoiseries, Chinese, Japanese and Saxony porcelain, earthenware and more. Their two shops bore the exotic name *Magasin américain* (American Store).[10] fig. 30
As Ensor recalled in a letter to Du Jardin:

> *My mother, daughter of Ostend sea-shell sellers, continued her parents' trade and I spent my childhood in the paternal [sic] shop surrounded by curiosities from the sea and the splendours of mother-of-pearl with a thousand iridescent gleams and bizarre skeletons, monsters and marine plants. The proximity of these wonders, the colours, this light-filled, gleaming opulence undoubtedly helped turn me into a painter in love with colour and sensitive to the dazzling play of light.*[11]

9 'First appearing in 1823, the term *chinoiseries* alludes to a 17th- or 18th-century European style of decorative art inspired by the arts of Asia and of China more particularly. It reflects an appetite for a Far East of the imagination, of fantasy. Its art was seen and understood as a model in its singularities and its techniques, and was admired, collected, copied and adapted', in Barthélémy Courmont, *Géopolitique des mondes asiatiques: 40 fiches illustrées pour comprendre le monde* (Paris: Editions Eyrolles), 2023, p. 31. 'It is clear, at any rate, that chinoiserie much contributed to the establishment, in the habits of life and everyday surroundings of the aristocratic classes, of an elegant and refined sociability. It answers, in fact, to a "pleasure principle" linked to one of the great underlying themes of Enlightenment thought: the quest for a lost Eden, the restoration of a world where harmony and joy prevail', in Marx 2007, p. 779.

10 Brussels 1996, pp. 52–3.

11 'Ma mère, fille de marchands de coquillages d'Ostende, continua le commerce de ses parents et j'ai passé mon enfance dans la boutique paternelle entouré de curiosités de la mer et des splendeurs des coquilles nacrées aux mille reflets irisés et des squelettes bizarres, des monstres et des plantes marines. Ce voisinage magnifique, les couleurs, cette opulence de reflets et de rayons contribuèrent certes à faire de moi, un peintre amant de la couleur et sensible aux jeux éblouissants de la lumière.' James Ensor to Jules Du Jardin, Ostend, 28 October 1899, in Tricot 1999, p. 276.

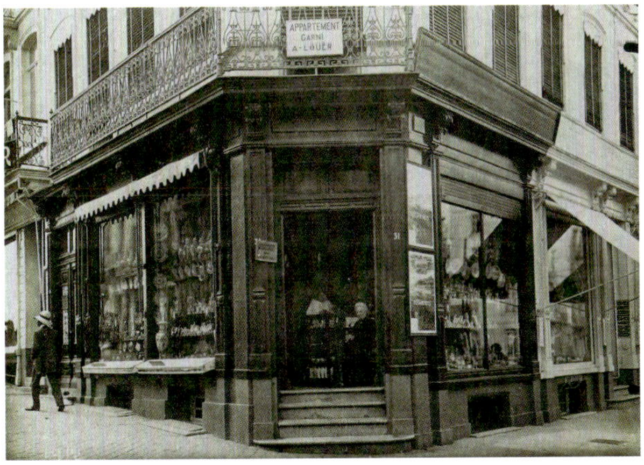

fig. 30

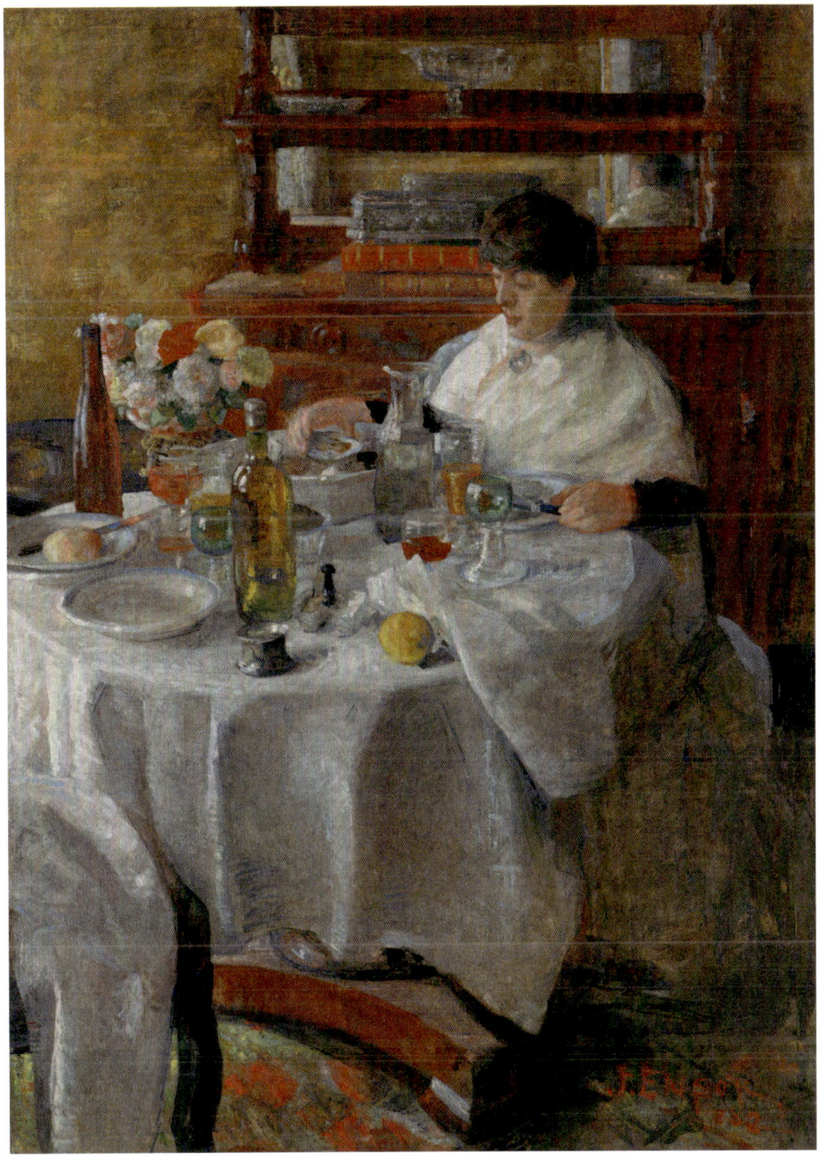

fig. 31

fig. 30 The Haegheman-Ensor family's shop at the corner of Rue de Flandre and Boulevard Van Iseghem, with Aunt Marie-Louise in the doorway, sitting next to her crutch, *c.*1905. Collection Mu.ZEE, Ostend, library.

fig. 31 James Ensor, *The Oyster-Eater (La mangeuse d'huîtres)*, 1882, oil on canvas, 207 × 150 cm. Royal Museum of Fine Arts, Antwerp, inv. 207. CR T224.

This taste for a Chinese aesthetic was directly connected with the trading activity and cultural legacy of the Ostend Company, active in the early eighteenth century.[12] With an economic boom at home, its imports from the Far East led to the growth of a luxury trade, laying the foundation for a long-lasting tradition. In the Belle Époque, Ostend still had seven shops selling seashells and decorative objects – souvenirs and seashell art but also a variety of arts and crafts.

The great freedom of the artist's style was disconcerting: the painting was blurred, governed not by the line of the object but by the light and the deformation of line it produced. The painted surface was insistently material, the way the paint was applied with brush and palette knife both structuring the subject and giving it an unfinished appearance. Ensor had devised a new way of painting intended to capture the fluidity of things as they were transformed by light, what one might call an autochthonous impressionism, an impressionism born of the softer light of the domestic interior. Many critics of the time deplored the absence of line and contour that gave the work an unfinished, embryonic air, yet at the same time they praised the facture and the radiance of the colours.[13] Ensor very soon came to be considered the leading figure of Les XX (Les Vingt), a status he would retain until 1886: 'The new prophet of light. … He alone understood it, grasped all its power, knew all its wonderful works. … His method, his violent colourations, his scorn for form and details. There are paintings by Messieurs Finch, Schlobach and Toorop that Ensor would happily sign.'[14]

Ensor grew quickly in ambition, and at the age of only 22 he painted one of his greatest works, one not itself a still life but it nonetheless makes use of still life at the heart of the composition to further develop and celebrate his innovative approach to painting. Ensor first called it *Au pays des couleurs* (In the Country of Colours), for it is they that play the most important role in the composition.[15] In *The Oyster-Eater* (1882, T224) – this being the fig. 31
title it finally received – the still life has clarity. The light hitherto exploited for its chiaroscuro effects is now omnipresent, penetrating every object and creating a play of gleam and glow that lights up Ensor's palette and envelops the human figure – here his sister Mitche – in a solitude and a melancholy typical of Symbolism. The objects are carefully disposed in relation to the window that admits the light and the mirror that reflects it in such a way as to produce a quivering luminosity. Here, the still life is exploited for its opulence. The iridescent glow of oysters and porcelain, the transparency of glasses and bottles and the chromatic range of the flowers, the foodstuffs and the drinks are all features that allow the artist to deploy his virtuosity as a painter of matter. The viewer

12 Inspired by the success of the Dutch, British and French East India companies, a number of Ostend merchants and ship-owners decided to establish a company of their own. Although commonly called the Ostend Company, it was in fact the Imperial and Royal East India Company of the Austrian Netherlands, its charter issued on 9 December 1722 by Emperor Charles VI, who encouraged his subjects to back it by himself investing 6 million florins. The company was dissolved in 1731, though its factory at Banquibazar in Bengal would remain active until 1744.

13 Brussels 1993, pp. 217–8.

14 Georges Verdavaine, 'L'exposition des XX', *Fédération artistique*, 13 February 1886, pp. 123–4, cited in Block 1984, p. 60.

15 'In the Land of Colours', section four of 'Six things you should know about Ensor's Oyster Eater', on the website of the Royal Museum of Fine Arts, Antwerp: https://kmska.be/en/oyster-eater.

is dazzled by the myriad reflections, the heightened sense of clarity, the endlessly modulating glow, caught up in a whirlpool of light.[16] While in *The Oyster-Eater* Ensor is concerned with lumi-
cat. 33 nosity, in *Seashells and Chinoiseries* (1882, T238) he engages in a variety of experiments with colour, using chiefly blues heightened with white. Red accents guide the viewer's eye in its confrontation with a jumble of objects and materials. The composition appears muddled, the objects hardly recognisable. Here the artist is treating the subject as a colourist, verging on abstraction.

Ensor's friend and patron Mariette Rousseau liked calm, untroubled paintings and regularly encouraged him to paint still lifes, occasionally sending him flowers as a prompt. In July 1884, he suggested that she should send poppies; when they arrived, he found them wonderful and wanted to paint them straight away. On 31 July, he wrote to Ernest and Mariette Rousseau: 'I'm doing the poppies and getting them successfully: I am content.'[17] *Poppies*
cat. 34 would later be retitled *Fanfare in Red* (1884, T274). The painting is worthy of its name: against a neutral background of rather muted colours is an explosion of reds; the uncertain, wobbly position of the poppies is set off by the accompanying wild flowers and foliage. This very natural, unaffected bouquet allowed Ensor the lively and unconstrained brush-work that he favoured. As for line, he delighted in being able to trace the multiplicity of deformations proper to the subject and emphasised by his own vision.

In a Chinese porcelain vase with a heron motif and in one decorated with a flower, another bouquet sent by his friends was arranged by the painter. By setting the two differently decorated vases together and filling them with peonies – the many-petalled queen of flowers, varying in colour from white and many pinks through red – Ensor prepared the subject for a painting he would
cat. 35 call simply *Peonies and Poppies* (1885, T254). After having received the flowers, he wrote to the Rousseaus:

> *Monsieur, Madame,*
> *It's fine and superb, superb!!*
> *Beautiful flowers! I'm painting them and when I see them next to the painting it saddens me. They have exquisite colours. I would like to get them into your eyes. … Who had the idea for this refined, subtle harmony of peonies and poppies? … The magnificent flowers crush the most strident of my colours. The vermilions, the black lacquers look like silk and all my old paintings appear musty*

16 Bown-Taevernier 1999, p. 33.

17 'Je fais les coquelicots et les réussis. J'en suis content.' James Ensor to Ernest and Mariette Rousseau, Ostend, 31 July 1884, in Huys 2021, p. 177.

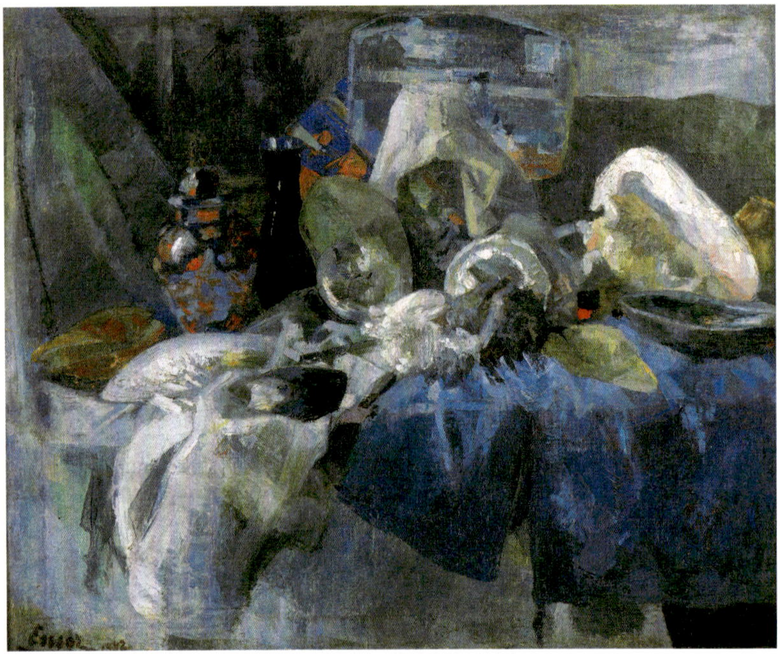

33

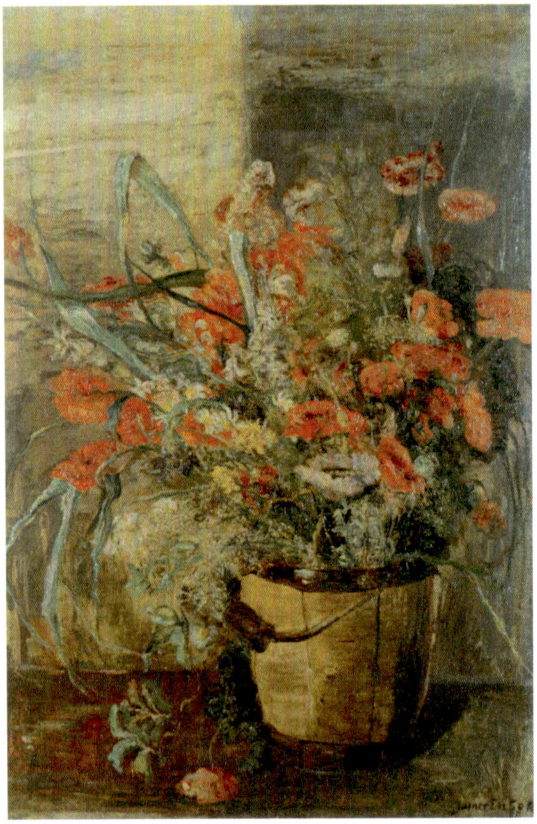

34

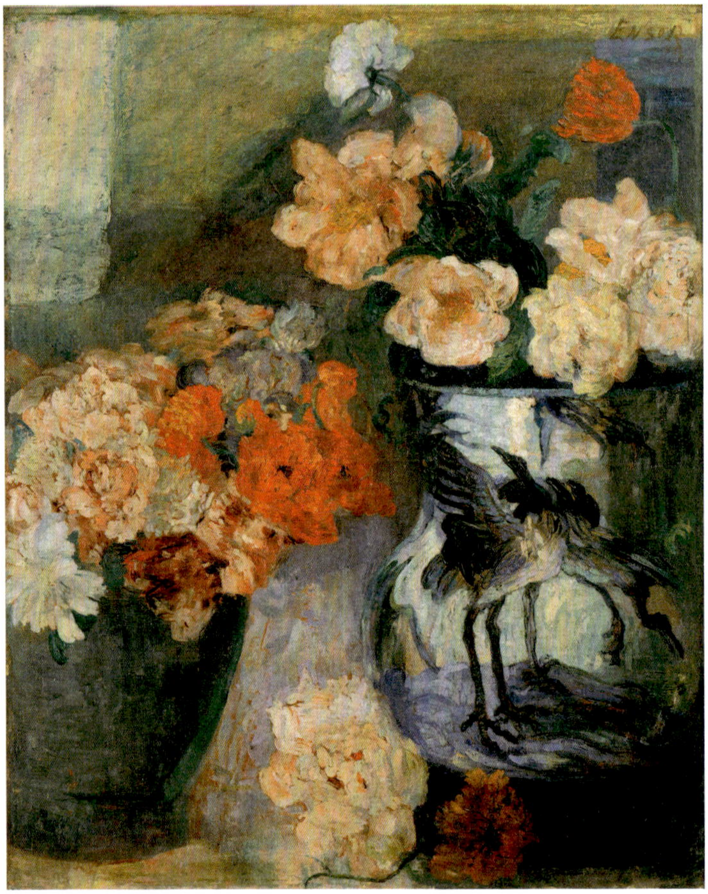

35

cat. 33 James Ensor, *Seashells and Chinoiseries (Coquillages et chinoiseries)*, 1882, oil on canvas, 80 × 100 cm. Private collection. CR T238.

cat. 34 James Ensor, *Fanfare in Red (Fanfare en rouge)*, 1884, oil on canvas, 115 × 82 cm. Private collection. CR T274.

cat. 35 James Ensor, *Peonies and Poppies (Pivoines et pavots)*, 1885, oil on canvas, 136 × 112 cm. Private collection. CR T254.

and faded. It's a firework display with bursts of scent. I'm … in a state of overexcitement and unable to do anything but paint.[18]

The light is everywhere, bringing a luminous glow to the brighter parts of the composition, but Ensor is even more so interested in colour – a 'firework display' – and line, enhanced by curves and arabesques.

Considering Ensor's still lifes, his art developed in five years from one of composition governed – indeed, held captive – by light to one dominated by colour. The year 1885 marked a high point for the painter: despite family troubles and problems with his health, he also threw himself into large compositions, enthusiastically exploring the rendering of sky and atmosphere.[19] His art had reached an apogee, heralding a change.

Visions, Fantasies and Grotesques

Why are artists enslaved to vision and disdain the light? In the deformation it imposes on line I saw an immensity to be explored, a new vision to be proclaimed.[20]

One might ask what led Ensor to depart from Impressionism and inhabit the world of masks and caricature that would rapidly become associated with him. The reasons are many, related not only to his character, his family background and his circle of friends, but also to the state of the Belgian art world in the late nineteenth century.

Thanks to the publication of the correspondence between Ensor and the Rousseaus and their son Ernest Jr, we now know more about the artist's private life, giving us a much more nuanced idea of his character and his relationships with his immediate circle. In his missives, both candid and sincere, we encounter an artist preoccupied by the self, disconcertingly inconstant, endlessly alternating between frames of reference, between real and imaginary, between different impossibilities, between unrelated styles. While this diversity made for the richness of his art, it also greatly perplexed friends and family, colleagues and critics.[21]

Between 1877 and 1898, Ensor divided his time between two cities – Ostend, the seaside resort, sleepy in the winter but frequented by fashionable society in the summer; and Brussels, the

18 'Monsieur, Madame, C'est bien et superbe, superbe!! Les belles fleurs! Je les peins et quand je les vois à côté du tableau je me désole. Elles ont des tons exquis. Je voudrais vous les faire entrer dans l'œil. … Qui est ce qui a trouvé l'accord subtil et raffiné des pivoines et des pavots? … Les magnifiques fleurs écrasent mes tons les plus violents, les vermillons. Les laques noires paraissent de la suie et toutes mes anciennes peintures prennent un air moisi et décoloré. C'est un feu d'artifice avec bombes parfumées. Je suis … en pleine surexcitation et incapable de faire autre chose que de la peinture.' James Ensor to Ernest and Mariette Rousseau, Ostend, 19 June 1885, in Huys 2021, p. 203.

19 *Large View of Ostend* (1884, T270), *Large Seascape with Sunset* (1885, T271) and *Christ Walking on the Water* (1885, T273).

20 'Pourquoi – les artistes – ne sont-ils esclaves de la vision et dédaignent-ils la lumière? Dans la déformation qu'elle fait subir à la ligne je voyais l'immensité à explorer, une nouvelle vision à imposer.' James Ensor to Pol de Mont, late 1894–early 1895, in Tricot 1999, p. 124.

21 *Lettres de James Ensor et de sa sœur Mitche aux Rousseau, ensemble composé de 400 lettres écrites entre 1883 et 1924 conservées aux Musées royaux des Beaux-Arts de Belgique*, Brussels, bequest of Marguerite Wodon-Rousseau in 1985, RMFAB, ACAB, Rousseau Fund, published in Huys 2021.

cultural and political capital of the country – and between two worlds – that of his own Ensor-Haegheman family and that of the Rousseaus, with whom he spent a great deal of time when in Brussels over the winter. He thus existed in two complementary worlds: one petty bourgeois, chiefly preoccupied with domestic matters and unconcerned for much outside; the other scholarly, curious, open to the world and humorous, witty and light-hearted. These were the poles that governed his life, each contributing to the artistic vocabulary of this unsettled and versatile figure.

In examining the history of Les XX, founded by lawyer Octave Maus on 28 October 1883, one realises how important was its annual exhibition for the development of both Ensor's art and that of his artist friends, be they Belgian, French, English, Dutch, German, Swiss, Italian, Swedish, Norwegian or American. Ensor wrote in a letter to Du Jardin:

> *In 1884, the Cercle des XX is formed.*
> *I join in the absence of anything better.*
> *The group seems odd in its make-up*
> *and to lack any precise artistic*
> *orientation.*[22]

The intention of the perceptive and enterprising Maus was to rally together a number of artistic adventurers capable of shaking up the existing canon, of producing new kinds of images, while offering the public an opportunity to gain as comprehensive an idea as possible of the modern art of the time. The group's annual exhibition was thus intended to present a judicious but unpredictable selection of truly innovative work. To expand its presence and influence, Maus also thought to feature invited artists from Belgium and elsewhere. This all helped make Brussels, between 1884 and 1893, the capital of the avant-garde, a 'crossroads where innovations met'.[23]

The first two exhibitions, in 1884 and 1885, remained in a realist vein that was overall fairly traditional, though Maus's choices did highlight the exploration of light and an inclination to Symbolism. Ensor, seen from the start as a trend-setter and admired by many artists, was already showing an interest in the carnivalesque, exhibiting *The Scandalized Masks* (T247), painted in 1883. The subject fig. 35
caused a stir but the style remained realist; the painting in fact offers a slice of life that reflects not only the artist's interest in masquerade but the problems of alcoholism within his own family.

In 1886, the presence of Claude Monet, Auguste Renoir and Odilon Redon gave the Brussels exhibition series a place on the international avant-garde scene. Renoir's *La danse l'été* and

22 'En 1884, formation du Cercle des XX. J'adhère faute de trouver mieux. Le groupe semble singulièrement composé et sans tendances précises.' James Ensor to Jules Du Jardin, Ostend, 6 October 1899, in Tricot 1999, pp. 269–70.

23 Delevoy 1981, p. 11.

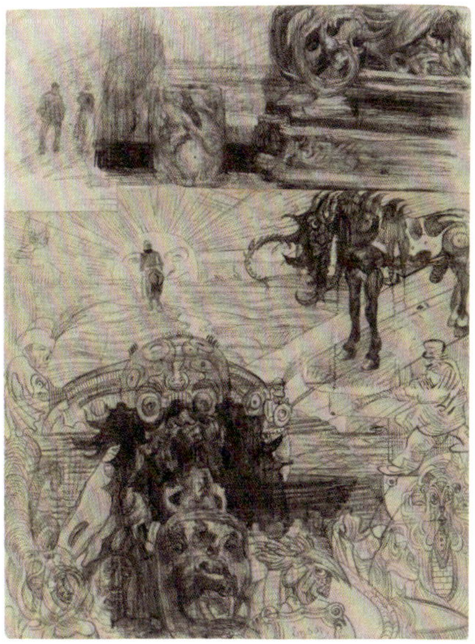

fig. 32

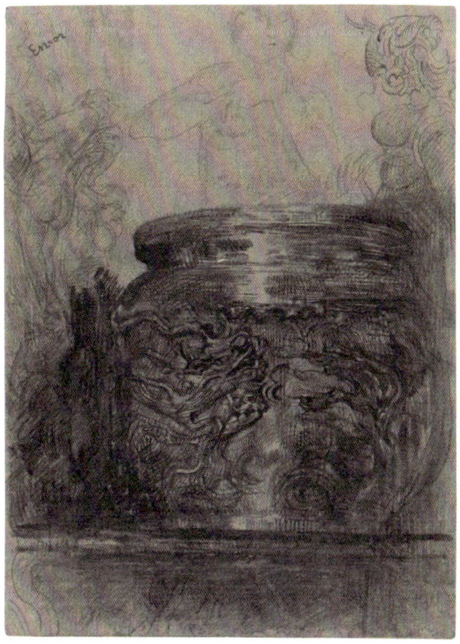

fig. 33

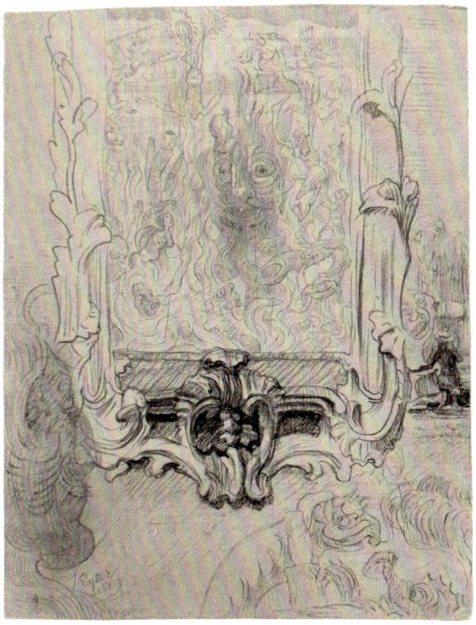

36

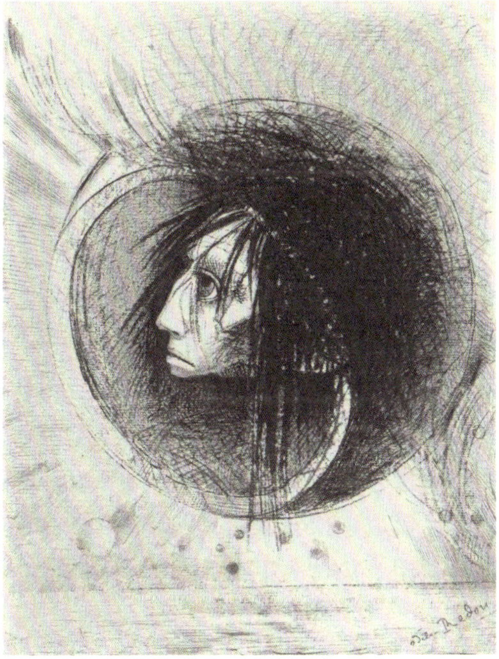

fig. 34

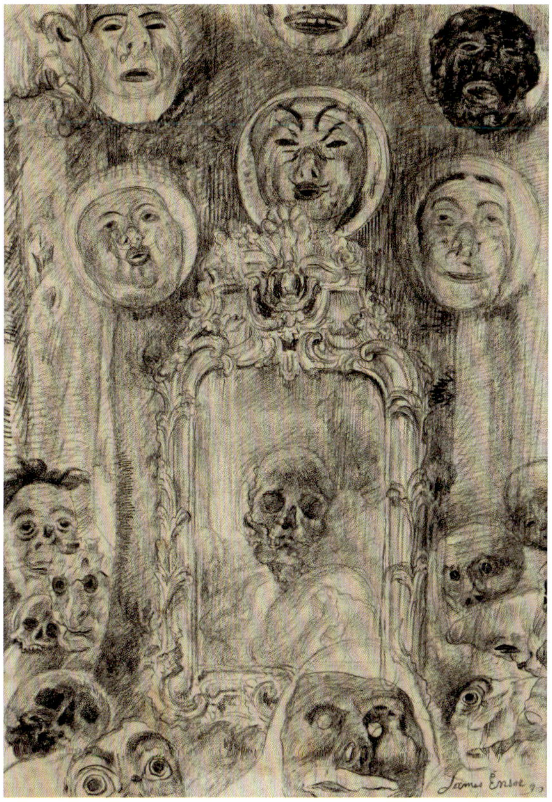

37

fig. 32 James Ensor, *Horse with Griffon's Head, Demons and Interior Fragments (Cheval avec tête de griffon, démons et fragments d'intérieur)*, 1880–83, black chalk on paper, 22.5 × 17.1 cm. Museum of Fine Arts, Ghent, inv. 1994-A.

fig. 33 James Ensor, *Bronze Pot with Apparitions (Cache-pot de bronze avec spectres)*, *c.*1880–85, *c.*1886–8, black and white chalk on paper, 25.5 × 16.5 cm. Museum of Fine Arts, Ghent, inv. 1994-B.

cat. 36 James Ensor, *The Devil's Mirror (Diable sortant de l'enfer des désirs)*, 1888, black chalk on paper, 22.5 × 17.5 cm. Private collection.

fig. 34 Odilon Redon, *Eclosion*, from the series *In the Dream (Dans le rêve: Éclosion)*, 1879, lithograph, 33.5 × 25.7 cm. Collection Kröller-Müller Museum, Otterlo, inv. KM 100.166.

cat. 37 James Ensor, *Mirror with Skeleton (Le miroir au squelette)*, 1890, black chalk on paper, 29.5 × 21.5 cm. Private collection, Brussels.

La danse l'hiver (1883)[24] and Monet's *Le Pont d'Argenteuil* (1874)[25] hung alongside Ensor's *The Oyster-Eater* (1882, T224), providing a forceful and eloquent introduction to the luminous Impressionism of the French. Ensor, however, was most particularly taken by the work of Redon, who had sent only drawings and lithographs in quest of an extraordinary world.[26]

The development of Ensor's art during 1886 clearly shows that the works Redon exhibited in Brussels in January–February fig. 34 prompted him to employ a style equally based on reality and fantasy, playing on encounter and mutual transformation. The result was the impressive series of ten drawings entitled *Aureoles of Christ or the Sensibilities of Light*,[27] shown at the 1887 exhibition and made the previous year when the artist was working with black chalk on paper and etching on copper and zinc. Drawings proliferated at this moment, and he ventured into printmaking.

Between 1886 and 1888, the drawing and etching that saw him both develop his manual dexterity and hone his imagination stood at the core of his artistic production. During this time, he returned to and transformed realist drawings of objects and interior scenes that he had produced between 1880 and 1883. The exercise stimulated his imagination, prompting the creation of beings and fantastical animals derived from the chinoiseries, the Japanese prints and the masks he had been surrounded with since a child and his studio was now full of: a horse was transformed into a hippogriff; a mirror and its moulded frame yielded a devil emerging fig. 32, cat. 36 from the hell of desire; a vase decorated with an insect and molluscs became a flea emerging from a dog's head and looking at itself in a mirror; a bronze vase of Mariette's gives us a devil sur- fig. 33 rounded by nudes; an open fire with its kitchen utensils is alive with fantastical personages and animals; from an upright piano in the corner of the room by the curtains emerges a bearded figure sud- cat. 100 denly animated by figurines born of his imagination.[28]

Like Redon, Ensor found inspiration in dreams and imagination, nurtured in his case by literature, Japanese prints and the works of Rembrandt, Bosch, Bruegel and Goya, among others. The drawings of Ernest Rousseau Sr, unfortunately little known and in good part lost, also nourished his sense of the grotesque:

> *If Monsieur Ernest is drawing do send me the sketches, I sometimes find them useful and I love their mocking acerbity.*[29]

Later, knowing that Mariette was particularly fond of these hybrid drawings, Ensor had pasted dozens together hugger-mugger on a canvas he gave her in 1893.[30] This group of 32 drawings represents

24 Two works now at the Musée d'Orsay in Paris and known as *Danse à la campagne* and *Danse à la ville*.

25 Now in the Musée d'Orsay in Paris.

26 Todts 2009, pp. 105–9.

27 Hoozee, Bown-Taevernier and Heijbroek 1987, pp. 107–17.

28 Ibid., pp. 99–105.

29 'Si Monsieur Ernest dessine envoyez-moi ces croquis, ils peuvent m'être utiles et leur accent et dérision me charment beaucoup.' James Ensor to Mariette Rousseau-Hannon, between 10 and 30 November 1888, in Huys 2021, p. 253.

30 James Ensor to Mariette Rousseau-Hannon, 2 September 1893, in ibid., p. 364.

in a way the keystone of his imaginative process. The practice of hybridisation contributed much to the development of his art and the unfolding of his artistic imagination, however indebted it might have then been to the many different sources of inspiration that had been taken up into memory, allowing him to create with great freedom, in a spirit of crazy extravagance.

Particularly prolific in drawings from 1886 to 1888, Ensor produced his largest ever works on paper, investing in them an almost euphoric energy: the series *Aureoles of Christ or the Sensibilities of Light* in 1885–6 and *The Temptation of Saint Anthony* in 1887.[31] He also created almost half his lifetime output of prints – 63 of 133 – while at the same time transforming a good number of his drawings of interiors into incongruous scenes through the insertion of very different subjects. His talents as a supremely gifted draughtsman, whose hand followed mind with disconcerting ease and simplicity, led to the development of his distinctive language, allowing him to embark on the path that would lead to masquerade becoming his trademark.

While Ensor produced only one significant painting in 1886 – *Children at Their Morning Toilet* (T282), a veritable homage to light – his need to paint returned the following year. Drawing, engraving and painting would henceforward run alongside each other, nourished by a creative imagination continuously transforming and intensifying. In 1887, he painted four museum-quality landscapes, among them *Adam and Eve Expelled from Paradise* (T287). In his letters to Mariette that year he several times mentions his artistic imagination, exuberant and fantastical even if intentionally cultivated and informed by analysis of the Old Masters:

> *I have received the mittens and the supremely interesting book. … You are very, very kind. What astounding devils! Callot [Jacques Callot, French painter, 1592–1635] was influenced. It was Hieronymus Bosch who did that. Have you seen his painting in 'l'Art ancien': a hermit tormented by devilish fish?*[32]

Responding, some years later, to Pol de Mont who had asked him whether there were artists he was especially fond of, he explained:

> *Rembrandt I really liked at first, but much later my sympathies went to Goya and Turner. I was enchanted to find two masters smitten with*

31 Hoozee, Bown-Taevernier and Heijbroek 1987, pp. 107–17, 127–8.

32 'Je reçois les mitaines et le livre suprêmement intéressant. … Quelles diableries étourdissantes! Callot a été influencé. C'est Jérôme Bosch qui a fait cela. Avez-vous vu à 'l'art Ancien' son tableau: un ermite tourmenté par des poissons diaboliques?' James Ensor to Mariette Rousseau-Hannon, 9 January 1887, in Huys 2021, p. 225.

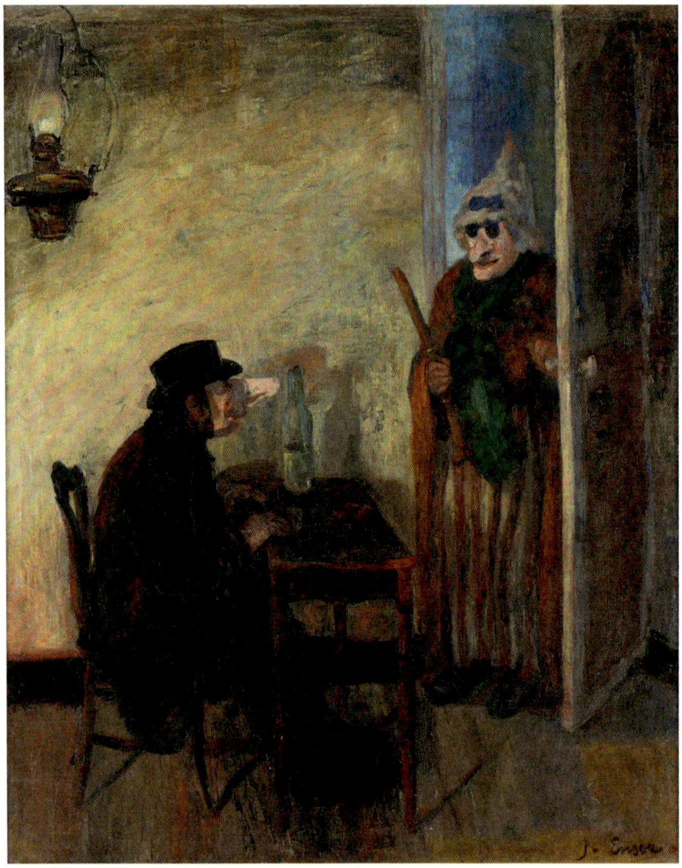

fig. 35

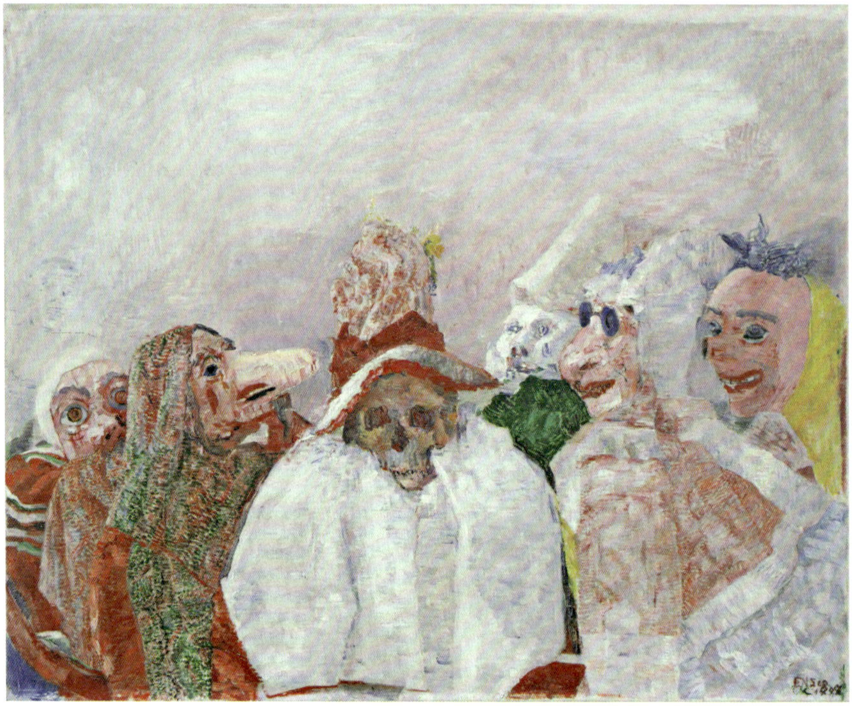

fig. 36

fig. 35 James Ensor, *The Scandalized Masks (Les masques scandalisés)*, 1883, oil on canvas, 135 × 112 cm. Royal Museums of Fine Arts of Belgium, Brussels, inv. 4190. CR T247.

fig. 36 James Ensor, *Masks Confronting Death (Masques raillant la mort)*, 1888, oil on canvas, 81.3 × 100.3 cm. The Museum of Modern Art (MoMA), New York, Mrs. Simon Guggenheim Fund, inv. 505.51. CR T289. CR T289.

light and violence. I also very much enjoyed the extraordinary inventions of Hieronymus Bosch and Pieter Brueghel. I found their works superior to those of the other Flemish masters. By a curious contradiction, there is one master of form whom I was completely unable to resist, whom I loved as I loved those geniuses: Ingres, and the oddest thing is that I never found his correctitude off-putting. He dominates, he idealises form and purifies it of all dross.[33]

In January 1887, Ensor wrote of paintings that took his breath away.[34] And in late March of that year, this highly sensitive and somewhat unbalanced artist, who did not hide the fact that he sometimes took drugs to assuage his torments, spoke to Mariette of his melancholic and susceptible imagination that enabled him to conjure up countless chimerical or fantastical characters.[35]

Painter of Masks

I enjoyed painting masks, and I have been fond of them ever since. I have in this fashion been able to contemplate the hypocritical, secret, calculating and sneaky faces of the cowards crushed by my disdainful progress. It was a fortunate choice, calling as it did for outré and violent colour.[36]

Ensor's path was laid out before him, and his masquerades when they came were no surprise. And with it all had come a change of technique, as he wrote to de Mont:

To achieve rich and varied tones, I had always mixed colours together. Unfortunately, the mixing sometimes led to discolouration and a number of paintings turned dark. I therefore changed the way I worked and began to use pure paints.[37]

33 'Rembrandt m'a plu d'abord beaucoup mais mes sympathies sont allées beaucoup plus tard à Goya et Turner. Je fus charmé de trouver deux maîtres épris de lumière et de violence. Les inventions extraordinaires de Jérôme Bosch et Pierre Brueghel me plurent extrêmement aussi. Je trouvais les œuvres supérieures à celles des autres maîtres de l'école flamande. Par une étrange contradiction, un seul maître de la forme m'a séduit despotiquement et m'a plu comme ces génies: Ingres et chose bizarre sa correction ne m'a jamais déplu. Il domine, idéalise la forme et la purifie de tout alliage.' James Ensor to Pol de Mont, late 1894–early 1895, in Tricot 1999, p. 132.

34 James Ensor to Mariette Rousseau-Hannon, between 9 and 16 January 1887, in Huys 2021, p. 227.

35 James Ensor to Mariette Rousseau-Hannon, late March 1887, in ibid., p. 230; James Ensor to Mariette Rousseau-Hannon, 16 May 1888, in ibid, p. 244.

36 'Je pris plaisir à peindre les masques. Depuis le goût du masque ne me quitte plus. J'ai pu contempler ainsi les faces hypocrites, dissimulées, intéressées et fourbes des couards écrasés par mes méprisantes évolutions. La voie était heureuse, elle appelait logiquement la couleur outrancière et violente.' James Ensor to Jules Du Jardin, 6 October 1899, in Tricot 1999, p. 271.

37 'Pour arriver à rendre les tons riches et variés, j'avais mélangé toujours les couleurs; malheureusement ces mélanges ont altéré certaines couleurs et quelques peintures ont noirci. J'ai modifié alors ma manière et appliqué les couleurs pures.' James Ensor to Pol de Mont, late 1894–early 1895, in ibid., p. 128.

Ensor's painting in 1886 and 1887 was dominated by abstract landscape as a means to explore light, but in 1888, his fascination with still life returned, and that in masterful fashion, with *Masks Confronting Death* (1888, T289), exhibited at Les XX in 1890 with the title *Scandalized Masks Mocking Death*. fig. 36

As in his earliest still lifes, the composition was essentially determined before ever setting to work on the painting, Ensor having had arranged the objects he was going to paint on a table covered with fabrics of different colours. The paints used are pure, but abundantly modulated by the addition of white, softening the severity of his unmixed colours. Against a background that recalls the marine skies of his landscapes he has arranged masks coiffed with caps and wimples around Death's head wearing a lady's hat.

It is no surprise to learn, then, that his studio was full of fabrics, masks and musical instruments, all used in staging the subjects of his works, as witnessed by journalist Maurice Des Ombiaux:

> *Ensor in his studio in Ostend, a large room under the eaves. The walls are covered in his pictures. Those for which no room can be found lie rolled up in the corners. … From beneath books, brushes, heaped stretchers and chests full of the oddest-looking masks, there peep out the beak ends of recorders. Stacked in an inaccessible corner are enough brass instruments for a carnival band.*[38]

Even if it were the fantastical visions of the previous two years that had led Ensor to Death and the masks, they are not by any means the whole reason. Sadly, cruel reality sometimes takes the upper hand. In 1887, the death of Ensor's grandmother was a hard blow to him and the rest of the family, and it was soon followed by that of his father – in the saddest of circumstances – linked to his alcoholism: 'I keep seeing my poor father. I bitterly curse the populace of Ostend. It's their doing that he is dead,' he wrote to the Rousseaus.[39]

The images he composed thus also reflect the reality of his personal life, which he represented using the story-telling capacities of the masks and the items he found around him. As in *The Scandalized Masks* of 1883 (T247), where his father wearing the long-nosed mask and his grandmother in her nightcap meet, this time they meet not in a café but in the face of Death, surrounded by other masked characters, possibly representing the people of fig. 35

38 'Ensor a son atelier à Ostende, dans une grande chambre sous les toits. Les murs sont couverts de ses toiles. Celles qui n'ont pu trouver place, gisent roulées dans les coins. … De dessous les livres, les brosses, les châssis amoncelés et des caisses pleines de masques les plus drôles, des becs de flûtes apparaissent. Dans un coin inaccessible, en tas, des instruments de cuivre pour tout un orchestre de carnaval.' Maurice Des Ombiaux, untitled article [beginning 'Avec quelques écrivains …'], *James Ensor, peintre et graveur*, special issue of *La Plume revue littéraire et artistique bimensuelle*, 15 December 1899, pp. 55–75, at pp. 74–5.

39 'Je vois toujours mon pauvre père. Je maudis âprement la populace d'Ostende. C'est par elle qu'il est mort.' James Ensor to Mariette Rousseau-Hannon, 17 or 24 April 1887, in Huys 2021, p. 233.

Ostend, this primary narrative likely being accompanied by other allusions. Within Les XX, Ensor felt a fierce hostility and hypocrisy, represented here in the grimacing mask. He was no longer the key point of reference that he had been, and he was well aware that many critics, collectors and artist friends were not ready to follow him to his 'land of derision'. This was clear to him, and he wrote to Mariette:

> *Sometimes I want not to exhibit. They will say I'm a man without conviction, a quitter, an Iscariot Impressionist. There's nothing I can do. I was seized by the need for a composition and I went along with it.*[40]

fig. 36 In *Masks Confronting Death* (1888, T289), bought by the Rousseaus at the Les XX show of 1890, Ensor abandons the reality of the inanimate objects he used in the construction of his still lifes to create a world that symbolises his own personal reality and that viewers are invited to explore. These still lifes also offer pictorial compositions that delight the eye, but beyond this the artist proposes a dialogue that those who engage in it will interpret as they wish.

Prompted by those around him, who hardly appreciated his more fantastical compositions, Ensor set aside some of his devils and again painted a series of still lifes, as he relayed to Mariette:

> *My exhibition will perhaps see me rise for a short time in your estimation, and you will see that the paintings look very good, very harmonious, soft and gentle in effect, not at all hard on the eyes, they're not intended to make any kind of bang, and what calls for attention in them is the painting and not the subject.*[41]

Ensor had thus listened to Mariette, who had begged him to paint
cat. 62 pleasant pictures as well. *Still Life with Blue Vase and Fan* (1889,
cat. 38 T297) and *Flowers and Butterflies* (1889, T299) are pure exercises in style. He took pleasure in painting a subject that afforded him a wide range of tones and shades in a work he first entitled *La note bleue* (The Blue Note). In *Flowers and Butterflies*, he seeks to awaken the senses by having Ernest's butterflies dance through space. Thanks to the painter's vision and his gift for creating dreamlike atmospheres, the still life lives again.

40 'J'ai par moment l'envie de ne pas exposer. On me traitera d'homme sans conviction, de lâcheur, d'impressionniste iscariote. Je ne puis rien y faire. Un besoin de composition m'a saisi et je me laisse aller.' James Ensor to Mariette Rousseau-Hannon, 9 January 1887, in ibid., p. 225.

41 'Mon exposition me fera peut-être monter pour quelque temps dans votre estime, et vous verrez que les peintures feront très bel effet et bonne harmonie, et que l'aspect sera très doux et ne fera pas mal aux yeux, et qu'elles ne sont pas faites pour le tapage, et que c'est surtout pour la peinture et non pour les sujets qu'elles méritent d'être regardées.' James Ensor to Mariette Rousseau-Hannon, 9 or 16 December 1889, in ibid., p. 280.

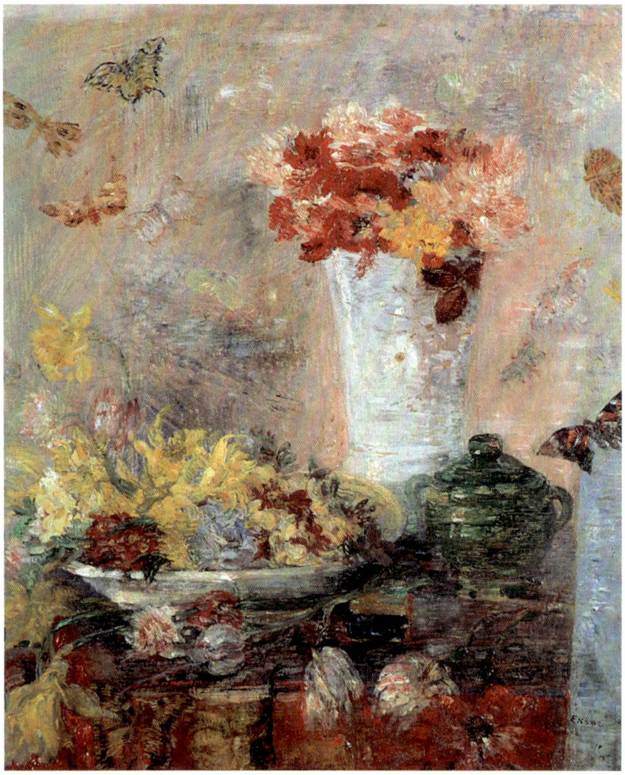

38

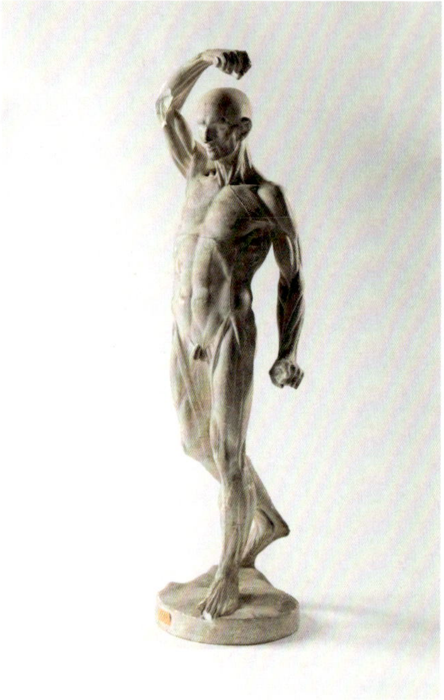

fig. 37

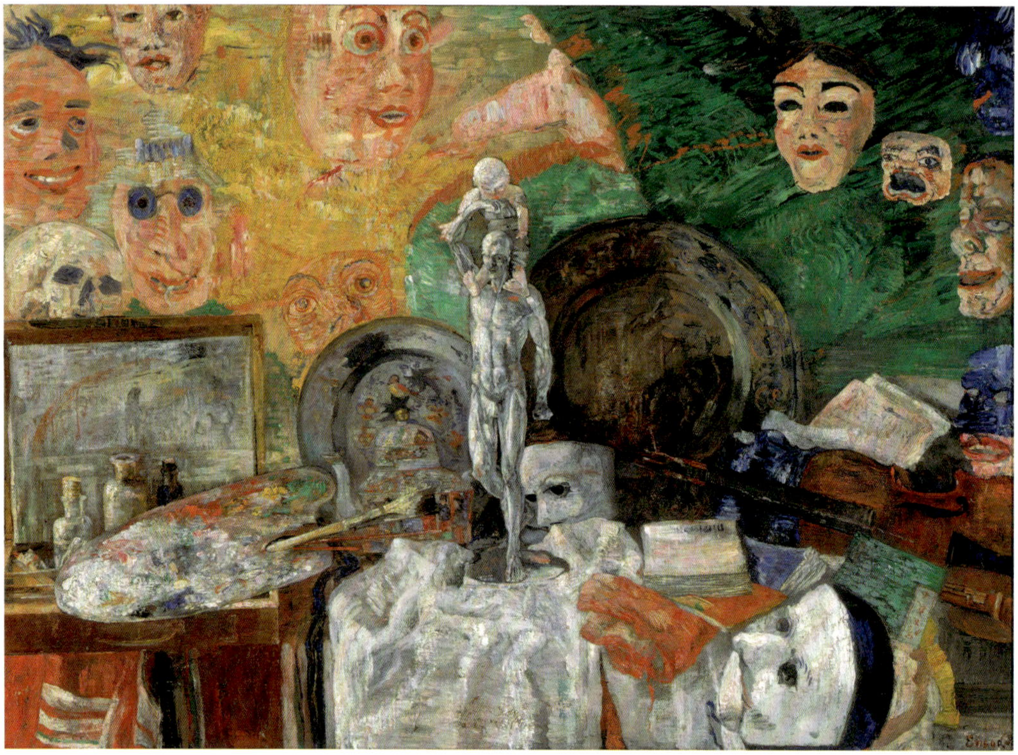

fig. 38

cat. 38 James Ensor, *Flowers and Butterflies (Fleurs et papillons)*, 1889, oil on canvas, 60 × 50 cm. Charlier Museum, Saint-Josse-ten-Noode, inv. P/161/1964. CR T299.

fig. 37 Jean-Antoine Houdon, *Écorché*, 19th century, plaster, 50 cm. Musée Carnavalet, Histoire de Paris, Paris, inv. S1787.

fig. 38 James Ensor, *Attributes of the Fine Arts (Attributs des Beaux-Arts)*, 1889, oil on canvas, 83 × 113 cm. Bavarian State Painting Collections, Neue Pinakothek, Munich, inv. 1307. CR T300.

And indeed, the Rousseaus bought *Still Life with Blue Vase and Fan* (1889, T297), and friends supported him too, Félix Buelens purchasing *Attributes of the Fine Arts* (1889, T300) and the sculptor Jacques Charlier *Flowers and Butterflies* (1889, T299).

fig. 38 In *Attributes of the Fine Arts*, today in Munich's Neue Pinakothek, Ensor gathers the artist's signature items: his brush, his palette, his paints and the canvas he's working on, but also his decorative objects, including a skull, a number of masks, his books and a violin. This is not an innocuous assemblage. In the centre he has set a studio plaster after Jean-Antoine Houdon's
fig. 37 *Écorché* (Flayed Man), which guided art students in rendering human anatomy. This exact copy, however, is transformed by the addition of a doll that floats above its shoulder, while the classical still-life composition is transmogrified by the invasive pres-
fig. 36 ence of the masks. Unlike *Masks Confronting Death*, they do not here form part of the still life but enter it from outside, reminding academic painters that the artist, perfectly capable of painting according to the rules of the academy, was himself 'flayed', and escaped to pursue the 'path of light and excess' that other artists dared not follow him on.

In its variety of forms and tones and its diversity of subject and composition, the still life in itself gave Ensor joy in painting, as well as the gratification of developing an unconventional technique and an uncommon skill. It was with a real physical pleasure that relieved him of the troubles of everyday life that he painted with such great freedom, never though departing from the characteristic density and nervosity of his line. From 1889, he would exploit in painting this manner he had developed in drawing. The shells and other gifts of the sea – fish, but also crustaceans – the fruits and the vegetables as well as the glass-ware and porcelain, all were chosen for their irregular and unexpected, even whimsical or jarring, forms.

cat. 39 In *Seashells* (1889, T298), Ensor has taken specimens from a collection as his subject. He found their variety of forms, colours and patterns fascinating, and his selection represents as wide a variety of shade and shape as possible, set against a background suggestive of a squall at sea. Pure colours model the forms but detail is done with a brush dipped in zinc white, whose lack of covering power produces an effect of transparency perfectly adapted to rendering the colour and iridescent sheen of mother-of-pearl. Here we have the native Ostender, the artist of the sea, in all his splendour. The seashell shop is an Ostend speciality, so it was not only at home but also elsewhere that Ensor was constantly confronted by seashells' variety of forms and colours:

> *Surrounded by shells and mother-of-pearl, Chinese vases and Japanese*

lacquer, many-coloured feathers and brightly patterned screens, the painter's visual imagination takes delight in composing the most uncommon and most expansive of his symphonies of colour. What notes can he strike, simultaneously soft and loud, subtle and brutal, sober and dazzling – ostensibly occasioned by some poor Oriental ornament rendered banal by fashion! And thanks to the artist's magic, his alchemy, the broad-rimmed shell with which the gloomy burgher will decorate his fireplace of painted marble will become a miracle of triumphant colour to dazzle the loveliest rooms of today's museums. Ensor is happy among this wealth of exotic bric-à-brac, amid the glowing or glassy remains of the sea.[42]

Divergent Subjects and Experimental Methods

If only I had the courage to work only from nature but I am tormented by the demon of the unknown and constantly possessed by uncertainty. As soon as I have properly grasped one thing and am certain to succeed I am compelled to give it up and begin again on a new subject, a new genre quite opposed in character. A tiring situation, a constant heartbreak.[43]

From 1889 to 1896, Ensor devoted himself to painting, either large canvases featuring carefully composed arrangements or prepared panels ranging from the very small, of around 12 by 16 centimetres, to a maximum of around 38 by 48 centimetres. The large canvases are characterised by a purely painterly approach and dominated by colour, while the works on panel explore line, primarily through arabesque, here decorative, there caricatural or driven. One might say that the former represents proper oil painting, the latter a painting drawn with the brush sometimes completed or refined by the introduction of other materials and techniques. The one is an explosion of colours that testifies to a

42 'Parmi les coquillages et les nacres, les vases de la Chine et les laques du Japon, les plumes versicolores et les écrans bariolés, l'imagination visuelle du peintre se complaît à composer ses plus rares et ses plus amples symphonies de couleurs. Les notes à la fois tendres et fortes, à la fois subtiles et brutales, à la fois sobres et éclatantes qu'il sut faire vibrer en prenant comme prétexte quelque pauvre bibelot d'Orient que la mode banalisa! Et la coquille ourlée dont le bourgeois morose ornera sa cheminée en marbre peint deviendra grâce à la magie, grâce à l'hermétisme de l'artiste, ce miracle de couleur triomphante dont s'éblouiront les salles les plus belles des musées modernes. Ensor se plaît parmi ces mille riens exotiques parmi ces dépouilles luisantes ou vitreuses de la mer.' Verhaeren 1908, p. 8.

43 'Si j'avais le courage de ne travailler que d'après nature mais je suis tourmenté par le démon de l'inconnu et constamment livré à l'incertitude. Dès que j'ai bien attrapé une chose et certain de réussir je suis forcé de lâcher et de recommencer des sujets et des genres opposés. Situation fatigante et déchirements continuels.' James Ensor to Ernest and Mariette Rousseau-Hannon, Ostend, January 1890, in Huys 2021, p. 282.

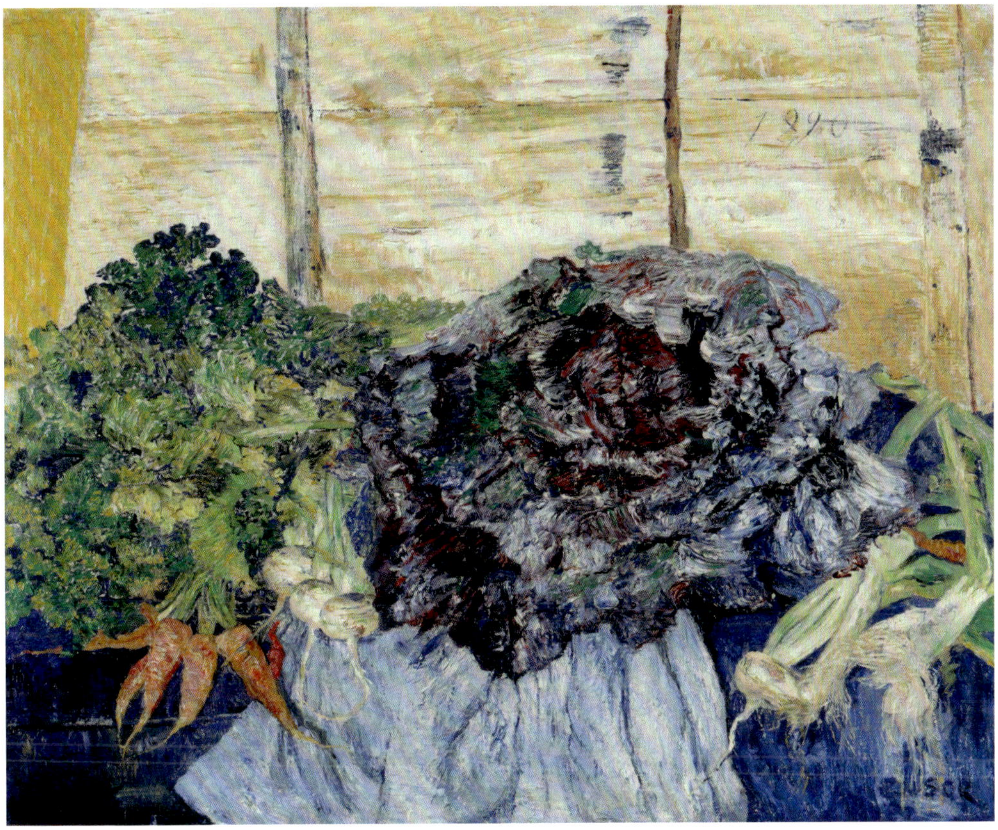

fig. 39

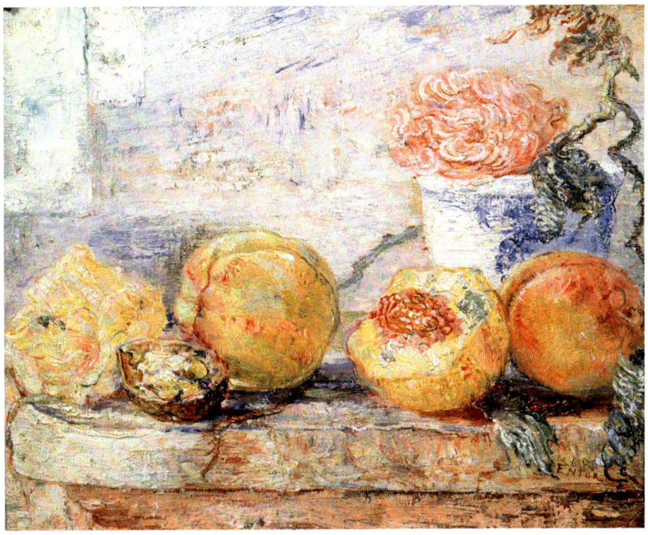

fig. 40

fig. 39 James Ensor, *Cabbages (Les choux)*, 1890, oil on canvas, 80.5 × 101 cm. Albertinum | GNM, State Art Collections, Dresden, inv. 2617. CR T314.

fig. 40 James Ensor, *The Peaches (Pêches)*, 1890, oil on panel, 19 × 23.5 cm. Private collection. CR T313.

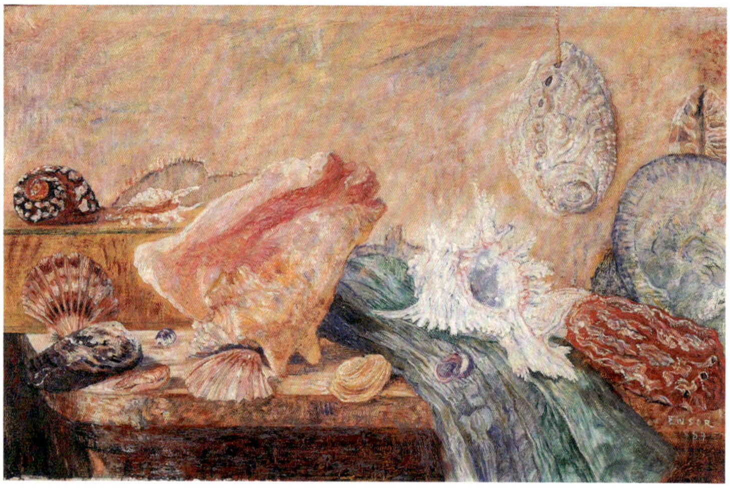

39

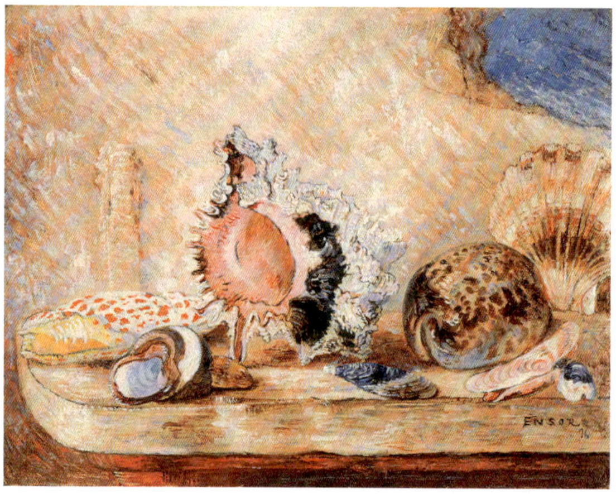

40

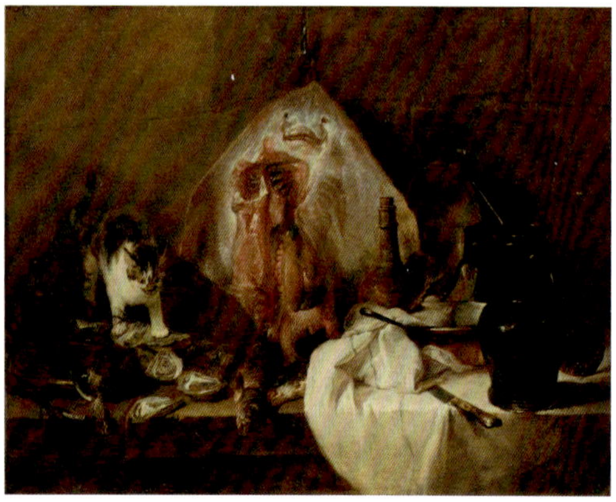

fig. 41

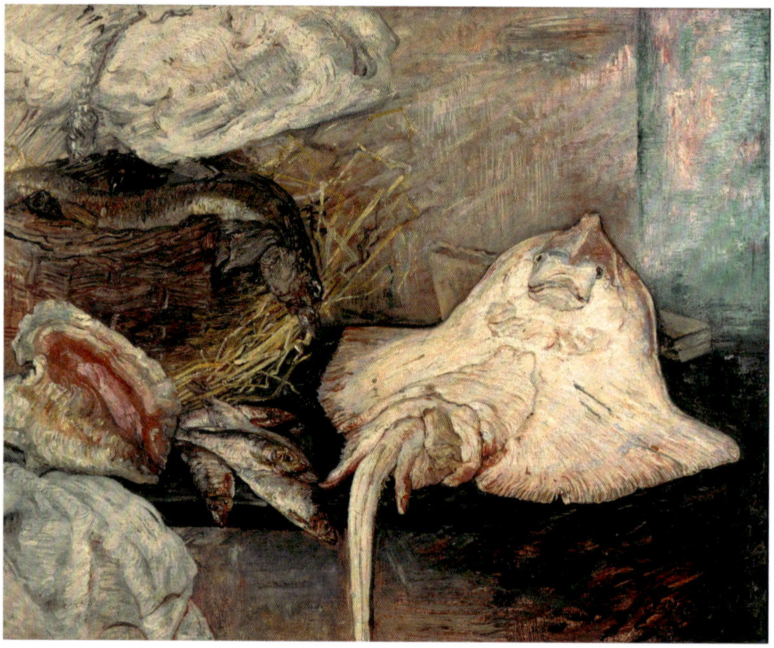

41

cat. 39 James Ensor, *Seashells (Coquillages)*, 1889, oil on canvas, 45 × 70 cm. Von der Heydt-Museum, Wuppertal, inv. G1369. CR T298.
cat. 40 James Ensor, *Seashells (Coquillages)*, 1896, oil on panel, 21 × 27 cm. Royal Museums of Fine Arts of Belgium, Brussels, inv. 11159. CR T377.
fig. 41 Jean Baptiste Siméon Chardin, *The Skate*, 1728 or earlier, oil on canvas, 114 × 146 cm, Musée du Louvre, Paris, inv. 3197.
cat. 41 James Ensor, *The Skate (La raie)*, 1892, oil on panel, 80 × 100 cm. Royal Museums of Fine Arts of Belgium, Brussels, inv. 4489. CR T350.

physical relationship with the paint, while the other is characterised by refinement and a subtlety of execution more evocative of the world of dreams.

The subjects of the large paintings are carefully composed, considered and prepared. To the artist, these were vivid, glowing subjects: 'heaps of cabbages, carrots, turnips, bloody meats and glistening, slippery fish'.[44]

Inspired by *Still Life with Vegetables* of around 1610 by Frans Snijders (1579–1657), where the cabbages seem to take over
fig. 39 the picture, Ensor embarked on *Cabbages* (1890, T314) to explore the vegetable's uneven and irregular form, the subtly shifting reds and greens of its highly variable colouration, its play with light. Helping structure the composition, the cabbages are surrounded by carrots, turnips and onions, whose accents of orange and white lend emphasis to the main subject. The light obtrusively present in the abstract yellow ground becomes completely transparent, transfiguring the whole subject while also endowing the still life with perspective. He told Mariette about his project:

> *I have painted two enormous glistening full-blown cabbages, one red, the other green. For a rest I am doing a phantasmagorical Roman Triumph. …*[45]

On panel, Ensor tackled subjects more personally significant, like friends, family and private fantasies, but did not at all neglect the fruits, flowers and shells in painting that he became dreamily content; for him they were enjoyable, rewardingly tricky subjects.[46] In these still lifes, in which he devotes himself to the stillness, charm and poetry of everyday things, even if each had been chosen for its varied and subtle colour or irregular and striking form, Ensor is close to the French painter Jean Baptiste Siméon Chardin (1699–1779). He too devoted himself to everyday objects, to the quiet and the discreet poetry of the still life, and Ensor makes many references to his paintings, discovered at the Louvre.[47]

cat. 61 In his still lifes of fruit, such as *Pear, Grapes and Nuts* (1889,
fig. 40, cat. 64 T294) and *The Peaches* (1890, T313), in *Roses* (1892, T351) and in
cat. 40 such paintings as *Seashells* (1896, T377), Ensor explores the materiality of his subjects. While the smooth, fine skin of grapes calls for the skills of highlight and transparency, nuts are there for their rugged and complex surfaces, which contrast with the velvety texture and subtly modulated tones of the peaches. Essentially decorative in intent, the rendering of the items is addressed to the eye, though evoking too the other senses, such as smell, taste and touch. This aesthetic approach reaches its apogee with *Roses*, with the titular flowers set in a clear glass and accompanied by violets. Ensor

44 '… d'amas de choux, carottes, navets, viandes saignantes, poissons gluants.' James Ensor to Mariette Rousseau-Hannon, Ostend, May 1892, in ibid., p. 326.

45 'J'ai peint deux choux énormes épanouis et rutilants, l'un rouge, l'autre vert. Pour me reposer je fais sur grand panneau un Triomphe Romain fantasmagorique. …' James Ensor to Mariette Rousseau-Hannon, Ostend, 8 December 1890, in ibid., p. 289.

46 James Ensor to Ernest and Mariette Rousseau, Ostend, 25 April 1891, in ibid., p. 300.

47 James Ensor to Mariette Rousseau-Hannon, Ostend, 27 August 1889, in ibid., p. 277. Ensor stayed in Paris in 1884 with Jan Toorop, in 1885 with Guillaume Vogels, in 1889 with Ernest and Mariette Rousseau and alone that year in June–July; ibid., p. 416, n. 2.

has opted to depict them in full bloom, maximising both the tonal range and the expressive force of the petals. One senses the pleasure taken in the careful execution of these subtle and demanding exercises, exploiting a personal technique combining oil, gouache, crayon and pastel.

Unlike the work of the same title of 1889 (T298), the *Seashells* cat. 39
of 1896 sees the artist turn to simple forms simply arranged, the objects each being subjects in themselves. Apart from their belonging to the same family, there is no real connection between the different shells. Their outlines, modelling and relief, their materiality and their colouration, these form the very subject of the composition, which though realist verges on abstraction.

Considering an artist so fond of the fanciful, a lover of grimaces and incoherences, of masks and grotesques, it is no surprise to see these find their way into his still lifes. In *Mask Looking at Crustaceans* cat. 42
(1891, T333), a powder-faced Pierrot has come to see what the artist has set on the table. A lobster, a crab, a smoked herring and a cod's head lie inanimate beside a jug, a porcelain pot and a bottle of wine with a full glass beside it. Ensor is inviting the Pierrot mask to a seafood feast. In the middle of the right-hand half of the picture and almost illegible, the letters V A E CARÊ E – *viande de Carême* (Lenten meat) – have been scratched into the paint.[48] Food permitted during the Lenten fast, the kipper and the cod's head offer a contrast with the lobster, the crab and the white wine put there to tempt Pierrot.

Elsewhere on prepared panel, Ensor lays down fine strokes of pure colour and their heightening in white in a way that lets the panel show through, reinforcing the luminosity and evanescence of the image. In *Pierrot and Skeleton in Yellow Robe* (1893, T364), a still cat. 43
life composed of familiar objects unified by various shades of a single blue is overshadowed by masks that loom out of a misty white atmosphere to invade the space and witness the encounter between Pierrot and the skeleton in its yellow robe. The figure of Pierrot is frequently encountered in the poetry and drama of the fin-de-siècle. In 1886, Théo Hannon wrote the pantomime *Pierrot macabre*, inspired by Champfleury's pieces of 40 years prior. *La Jeune Belgique*, a Belgian magazine of art and literature that Ensor followed assiduously, published Albert Giraud's *Pierrot Narcisse* the following year.[49] The *commedia dell'arte* character that became the 'snowy king of pantomime' here inhabits an evanescent world symbolised by snow, and wonders to himself: 'To live and to dream! To dream or to live? One has to choose.'[50] Constantly journeying between the world of dreams and reality, Ensor sought to render both, often mixing them together. The striking presence of the hundred or so strange-looking masks he hung in his studio

48 Antwerp 2010, p. 241, no. 225.

49 Tricot 1995, p. 53, n. 19.

50 Albert Giraud, 'Pierrot Narcisse', in *Héros et Pierrots* (Paris: Fischbacher), 1898, p. 205.

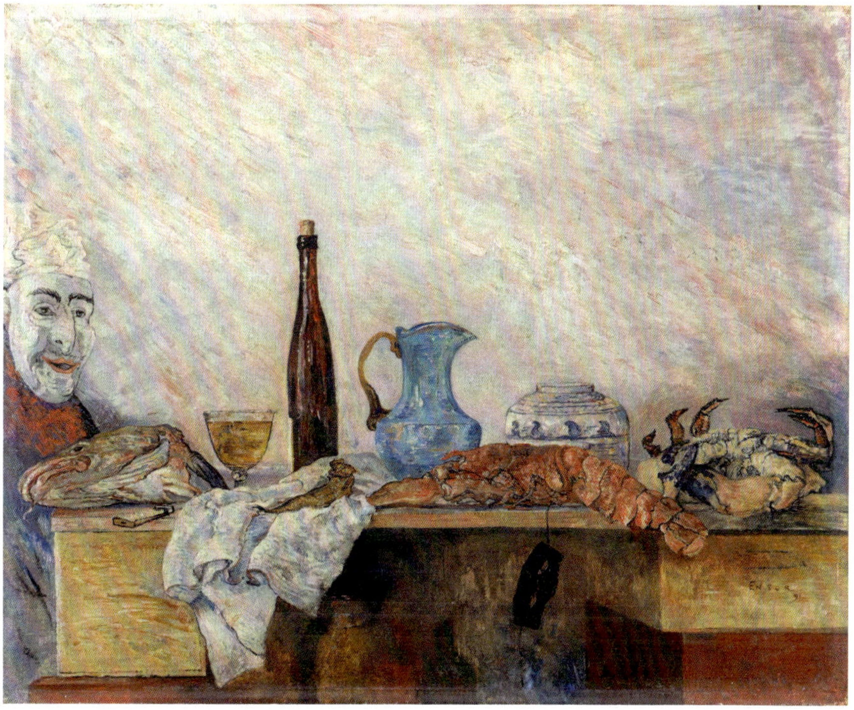

42

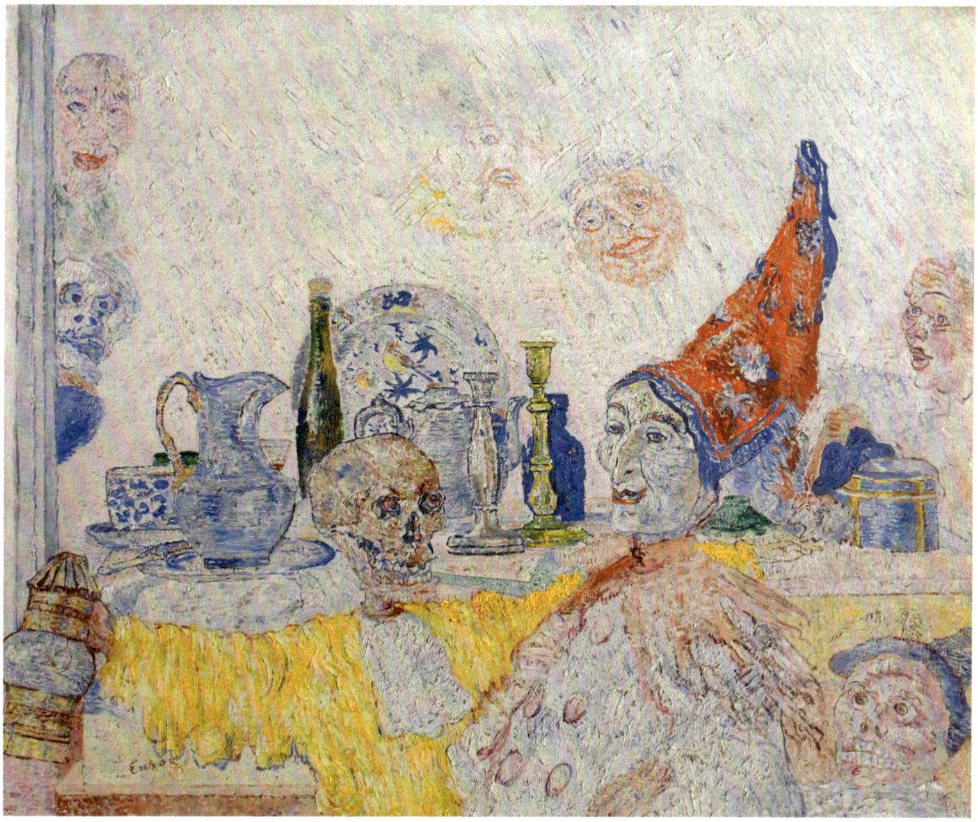

43

cat. 42 James Ensor, *Mask Looking at Crustaceans (Masque regardant des crustacés)*, 1891, oil on panel, 31 × 39 cm. Royal Museum of Fine Arts, Antwerp, inv. 1958. CR T333.
cat. 43 James Ensor, *Pierrot and Skeleton in Yellow Robe (Pierrot et squelette en jaune)*, 1893, oil on panel, 38 × 48 cm. Museum of Fine Arts, Ghent, inv. 2007-B. CR T364.

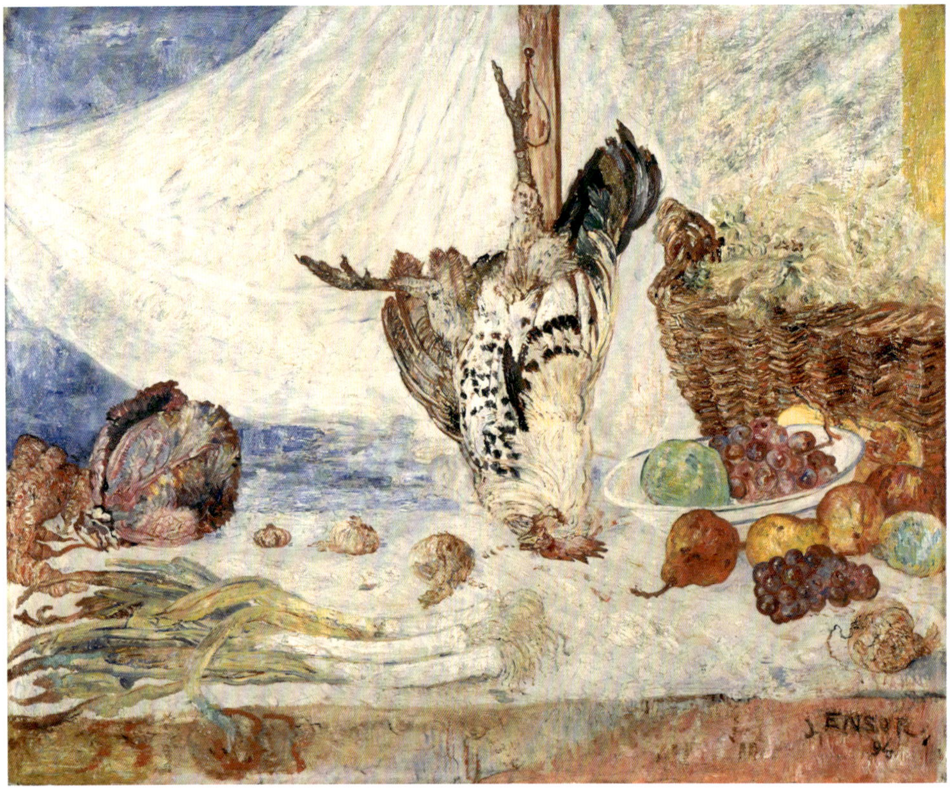

44

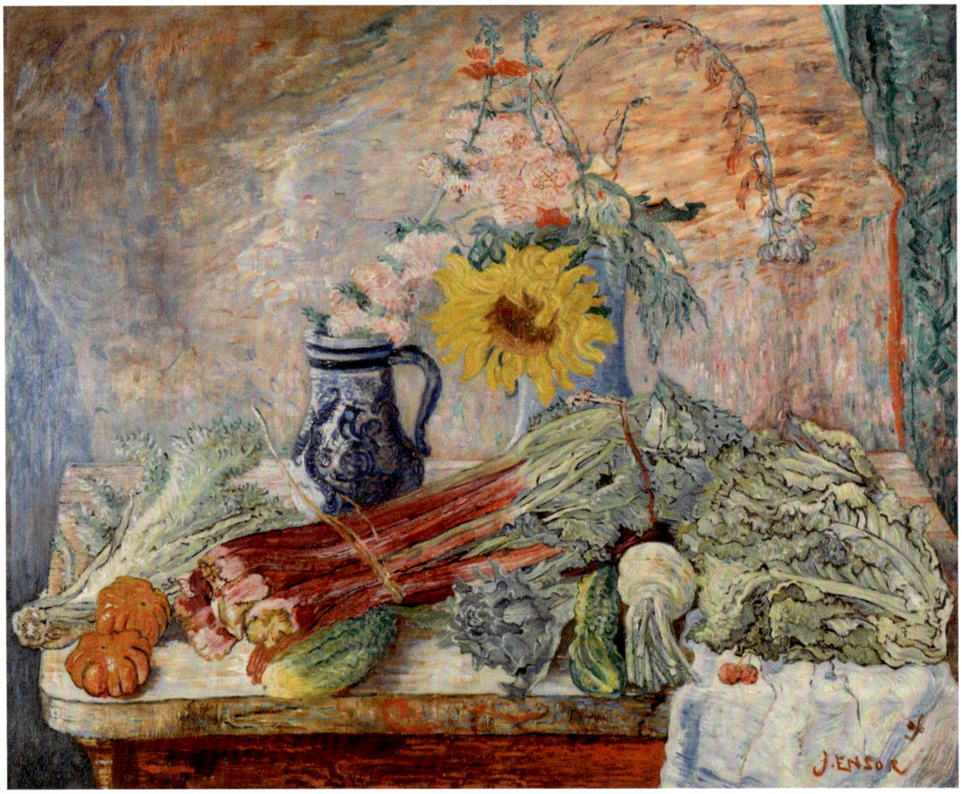

45

cat. 44 James Ensor, *The Dead Cockerel (Le coq mort)*, 1894, oil on canvas, 80 × 100 cm. Kunsthalle, Mannheim, inv. M1420. CR T367.

cat. 45 James Ensor, *Flowers and Vegetables (Fleurs et legumes)*, 1896, oil on canvas, 79 × 98 cm. Royal Museum of Fine Arts, Antwerp, inv. 1858. CR T375.

in late 1892[51] and the criminal proceedings brought against the Haegheman family and other Ostend shopkeepers[52] both help explain the robed skeleton and the masks that invade this highly theatricalised still life. However that may be, the scene itself also and above all represents a delicate and ethereal composition, one long treasured by Ensor before he sold it to Antwerp architect Joseph de Lange.

Like many other artists, Ensor liked to return to the same subjects, a fact very helpful in tracing the development of his work. Painted
cat. 57 in 1880, *Skate and Herring* (T147) is a simple, realist still life of a fish set on a table to be painted, without any ulterior motive. Twelve
fig. 41 years later, it was Chardin's *The Skate*, which had been on display at the Louvre since June 1796 and discovered by Ensor while visiting in 1889,[53] that prompted him to return to the theme. This time – as in the Chardin – the subject no longer belongs to the inanimate world proper to the still life. Lying there lifeless in the first
cat. 41 version, the skate now has its head raised, looking at the viewer (1892, T350). Already gutted, it is limp without being inert, giving the still life a theatrical dimension that recalls the artist's masquerades. Ensor was not alone in finding inspiration in the researches of Chardin, an artist concerned above all with the treatment of the subject. Paul Cézanne, Henri Matisse and later Chaïm Soutine all produced takes on Chardin's ray in the Louvre.

Ensor's encounter with Chardin continued to resonate with him for some time. Though clearly one of Ensor's carefully com-
cat. 44 posed still lifes, *The Dead Cockerel* (1894, T367) is in fact indebted to Chardin's paintings of game, while also marking the development of Ensor's painting towards a more decorative style. Hitherto close to reality, the colours begin to depart from it, while the highly theatrical composition is in no way realistic, rather suggesting a caprice deliberately staged. The different subjects are juxtaposed but lack any unifying context. They are there for their colours and materials, as elements of a symphony of forms and tones.

cat. 45 For *Flowers and Vegetables* (1896, T375), Ensor gathered all that he had found of the most baroque at the market. The tomatoes, the artichoke, the cardoons, the turnip, the salad, the rhubarb and the two cherries had not been bought to put together a meal but served rather as pretext for the artist to paint his lines and colours. The blue pot, found like the earthenware tankard in so many of Ensor's still lifes, returns again to add its own sinuous motifs to the scene. The drooping sunflower and wilted delphiniums complete this oil painting of products of nature exploited simply for their luxuriant forms and colours.

51 James Ensor to the Rousseau family, Ostend, week beginning 2 January 1893, in Huys 2021, p. 343.

52 James Ensor to Ernest Rousseau Jr, Ostend, Sunday 15 January 1893, in ibid., p. 344.

53 James Ensor to Mariette Rousseau-Hannon, Ostend, Tuesday 27 August 1889, in ibid., p. 277.

The end of Les XX's annual exhibition in 1893 and the marriage of the younger Ernest Rousseau in 1896 saw Ensor's family gradually stop spending time in Brussels in the winter, preferring the solitude of off-season Ostend. Ensor was displeased, complaining of being 'delivered up defenceless to the jeremiads and hypochondriacal grimaces of the ladies of the family'.[54]

He was approaching 40, and the extremely varied vocabulary he had developed would continue to inform his work over the following 40 years. The traditional subjects of his beginnings – the landscapes, interiors, portraits, self-portraits and still lifes – would however be transformed by colour and by the incorporation of the more fantastical elements that increasingly characterised his work. Death's head and the masks, theatre, cross-dressing, nymphs and ballet dancers would all figure in the still lifes he enjoyed treating in this way, introducing a certain vitality and humour. Ensor henceforward gave himself up to the pleasure of painting.

His *Fish and Seashells* (T373) of 1895 was painted in astonishingly traditional fashion – though Ensor was nothing if not capricious and unpredictable – before being copied around 1905 (T414). The subject is identical, down to the smallest details, including the signature and the date.[55] In the first version, the plaice, the mackerel, the little red mullet, the pink shell and the various shellfish are painted in realistic colours and retain a certain volume. In the second, the colour transforms and harmonises the whole. The red used for the background is found again in the shellfish and in the varying browns of the table, plaice and mullet. Volume has given way to lively and energetic line. More than ever, Ensor shows how he uses the subject as the means to the matter that is the real object of his investigation and the pleasure he finds in painting.

cat. 46
cat. 47

Between 1905 and 1910, Ensor went back to his well-known paintings and popular subjects to reinvent them in light, bright colours. Among the still lifes, fish, game – including *Still Life with Duck* (1880, T149 and *c.* 1905, T416) – shellfish, cabbage and miscellaneous vegetables – including *Still Life with Lantern and Vegetables* (1900 (?), T395 and 1910, T442) – were all reproduced in ways closely resembling the original versions.

fig. 29, cat. 48
cat. 67

From the beginning, chinoiserie, evoking the atmosphere of the middle-class interior, provided Ensor with one of his favourite motifs. While it is found as a subject in its own right in only 11 paintings, it features as an accessory in very many of his still lifes. His first depiction of the subject, *Chinoiseries with Fans* of 1880, is an exercise in the rendering of light and its effects on objects. By 1906 (T420), this kind of realism had been left far behind. He

fig. 42

54 '... d'être livré sans défense aux jérémiades et aux grimaces hypocondriaques des dames de chez moi.' James Ensor to Ernest and Mariette Rousseau, Ostend, Wednesday 6 January 1897, in Huys 2021, p. 440.

55 It was only later, while compiling his catalogue raisonné, that it was realised that the painting had been antedated. This was a habit of Ensor's; he liked to suggest that he had come to his innovations earlier than he really had, and he knew that his older paintings were more highly thought of.

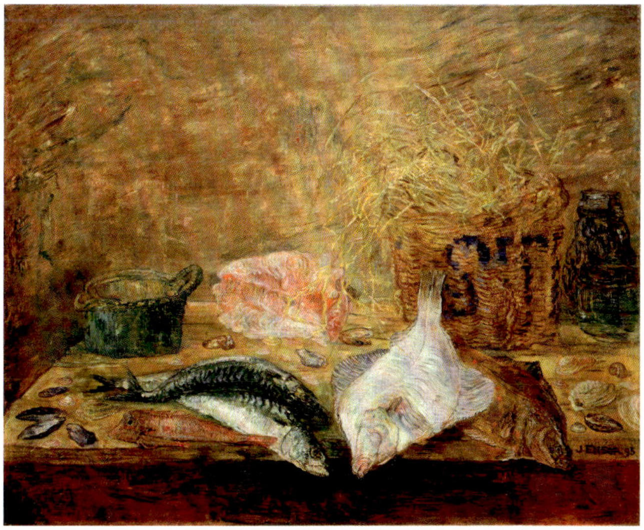

46

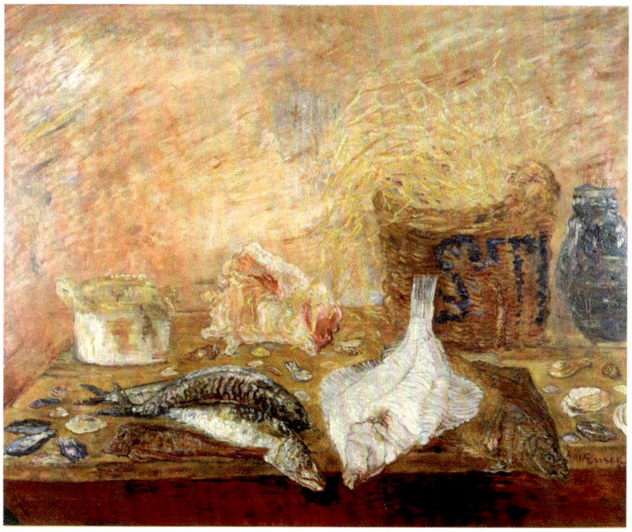

47

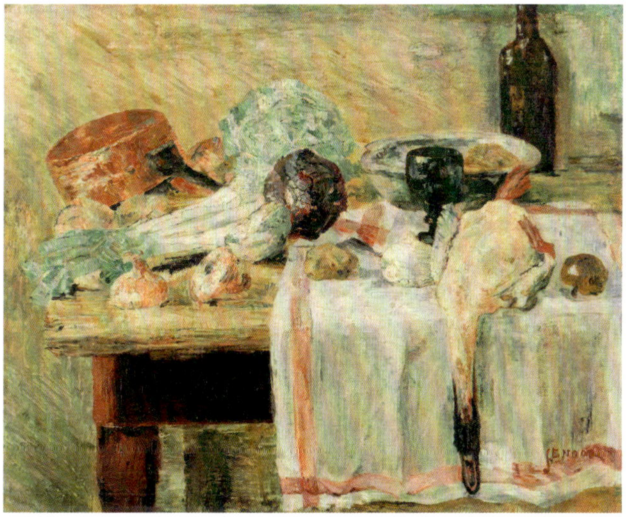

48

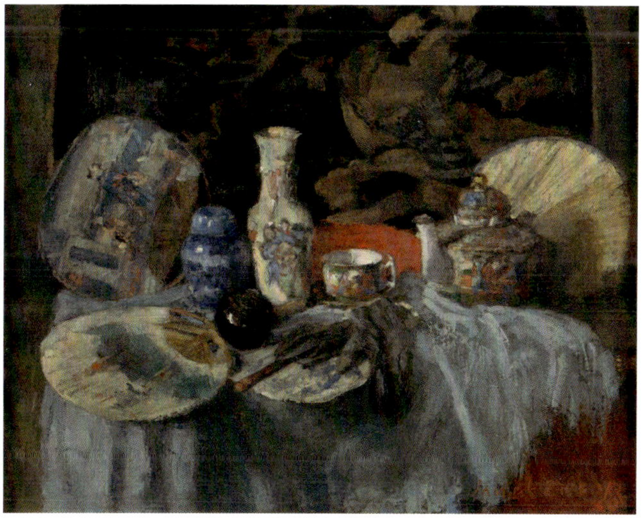

fig. 42

cat. 46 James Ensor, *Fish and Seashells (Poissons et coquillages)*, 1895, oil on canvas, 80 × 100 cm. Private collection. CR T373.

cat. 47 James Ensor, *Fish and Seashells (Poissons et coquillages)*, *c.*1905, oil on canvas, 80 × 100 cm. Private collection. CR T414.

cat. 48 James Ensor, *Still Life with Duck (Nature morte au canard)*, *c.*1905, oil on canvas, 80 × 100 cm. Collection Museum Boijmans Van Beuningen, Rotterdam. Gift of J. de Graaff and L. de Graaff-Bachiene, 1935, inv. 2047 (MK). CR T416.

fig. 42 James Ensor, *Chinoiseries with Fans (Chinoiseries aux éventails)*, 1880, oil on canvas, 80 × 100 cm. Royal Museums of Fine Arts of Belgium, Brussels, inv. 10287. CR T150.

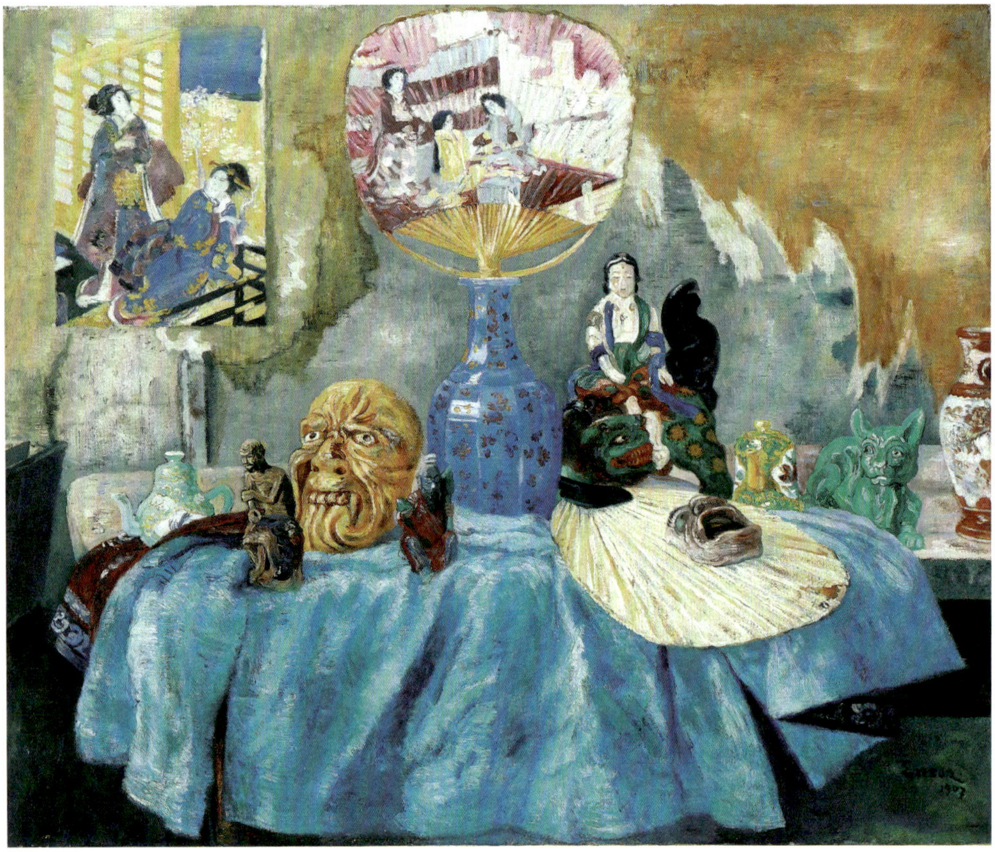

49

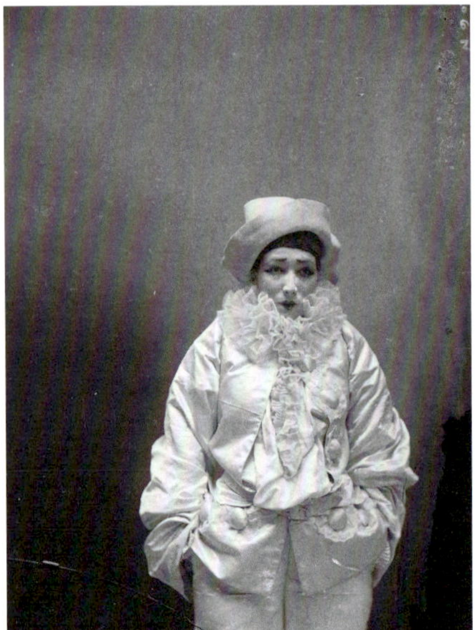

fig. 43

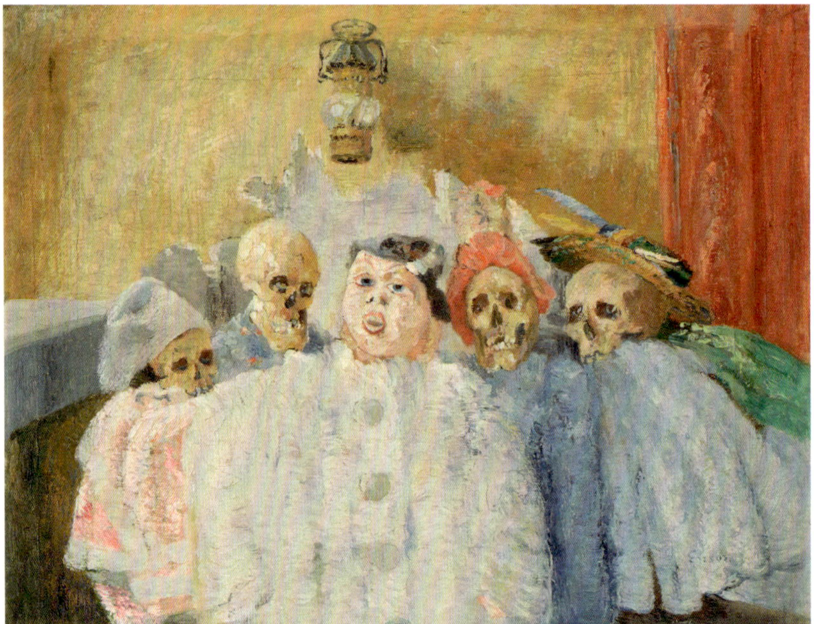

50

cat. 49 James Ensor, *Chinoiseries (Chinoiseries)*, 1907, oil on canvas, 60 × 79 cm. Museum Dhondt-Dhaenens, Deurle, inv. 000 037. CR T424.

fig. 43 Nadar, Sarah Bernhardt as Pierrot in *Pierrot assassin*, a pantomime by Jean Richepin, 1883. Médiathèque du Patrimoine et de la Photographie, Charenton-le-Pont, inv. NDR009206N.

cat. 50 James Ensor, *Pierrot and Skeletons (Pierrot et squelettes)*, *c.*1907, oil on canvas, 35.5 × 45.5 cm. Musée des Beaux-Arts, Tournai. CR T426.

frequently resorted to the combination of still life and abstract wallpaper background, carefully prepared and composed to provide him with shapes and colours. He even went so far as to depict the torn wallpaper in the dining room at home, hidden until then by sufficiently large still-life subjects.[56] In the first version from 1906, the porcelain service is translucent and the little sculptures have volume, taking their place in a theatrical but uneventful composition, while the brush-work is largely stipple. In the second version, of 1907 (T424), the artist returns to reality, applying the paint in broader strokes, which gives density to objects waiting only to be used. To enlarge the composition and create a space beyond the canvas, a vase with red and white motifs appears half-obscured at the edge of the painting. Lightness and transparency have given way to intensity of colour. Apart from a few small details, the two versions are very similar in composition, differing essentially in pictorial technique. Ensor would produce a third version in 1908 (T429).

cat. 49

As Death's head and the masks had come to be recognised as the painter's signature subjects, it is not at all surprising that this period of repetition and renewal saw him enthusiastically rework them. Popular themes like *Pierrot and Skeletons* were painted in series, with some variation.[57] The fin-de-siècle had seen Pierrot, the central figure, endowed with a particular aura: the victim of endless infidelities, the impassive dandy afflicted by a deadly melancholy, he stood for the solitary artist, the cursed poet or painter. This can be seen in many plays, first in Paul Margueritte's *Pierrot assassin de sa femme* in 1882, and then in Jean Richepin's *Pierrot assassin* a year later. Greatly interested in both theatrical cross-dressing and the morbid, the actress Sarah Bernhardt gave an unforgettable performance in the role at the Palais du Trocadéro, to be immortalised, hands in pockets, by the photographer Nadar. A recurrent figure in Ensor's art, Pierrot serves as the epitome of the issues around the relationship between the painter's personality and his art, and the place of both in society.

fig. 43

In 1905, when Ensor painted the first version of *Pierrot and Skeletons* (T411), the central figure, surrounded by dressed-up skulls, holds a bloody knife. Is this murder or suicide? Given the painter, both are possibilities. Ensor returned to the subject around 1907 (T426) in an almost identical composition, which recalls that of *Masks Confronting Death* (1888, T289), the masks here being replaced with skulls, while the central figure is no longer Death but Pierrot, an evocation of non-being, of absence. The still life is composed of inanimate objects – skulls, masks, Pierrot's costume, the varied headgear and draperies – which, as in pantomime, wait to be brought back to life by the viewer's gaze.

cat. 50
fig. 36

56 James Ensor to Mariette Rousseau-Hannon, Ostend, May 1892, in Huys 2021, p. 326.

57 These include three versions of *Pierrot and Skeletons* (T411, T425, T426) and two versions of *Skeleton Musicians* (T427, T428), as well as *From Laughter to Tears* (1908, T435) and *Skulls with Flowers* (1908–9, T436). Apart from the first version in 1905, the images of Pierrot were painted between 1907 and 1909.

Ensor was 55 when his mother Marie Catherine Louise Haegheman died, after a long illness, on 8 March 1915, aged 80. Over the three days following her death, he made the drawing on panel *My Dead* cat. 52 *Mother* and a finished version on canvas of the same title (T477), cat. 51 as well as making several drawings. The open mouth, wasted face and bony hands holding a cross show a figure consumed by old age and sickness but at last at rest in death. The image of piety she presents is echoed on the right by a statuette of the Virgin on a carved pedestal. The deceased on her deathbed is, one might say, painted at low volume, and remains in the background. The real subject of the painting is the quack preparations the artist held responsible for her death. For in the foreground, we find a still life of medicine bottles and vials, whose transparency is complemented by touches of red, blue and green that capture the attention. Here Ensor reveals himself as the anxious figure he was, worried by any sign of ill health in himself or his family. The doctors were constantly in and out of the home and he ended up reviling them as chronic failures.[58]

The following year, the artist lost his Auntie Mimi, Marie Ludovica Haegheman, his mother's sister. Apart from his own sister and her family, Ensor was now alone and without relations. In 1917, he moved to 27 Rue de Flandre, today's Maison Ensor, the building left to him by his uncle Leopold Haegheman, who had died childless in 1905. He maintained its unfrequented ground-floor shop, *La grotte aux sirènes* (Mermaid's Cave), full of porcelain, model boats and ceramic curios from China and Japan, a little museum that 'set the mood for visitors' and helped keep up the legend of the painter of masks.[59]

In the still life *Blue Chord* (1917, T496), a print of ice- fig. 44 skaters[60] is treated as a thing of value, draped in blue velvet. A work by the 57-year-old Ensor, it presides over a display of chinoiseries that recall *Chinoiseries with Fans* (1880, T150) and *Chinoiseries* fig. 42 (1906, T420), here however accompanied by a shoe of blue porcelain and flowers of an unidentifiable variety. Carefully arranged on a table, these items were chosen for their colours, Ensor contrasting the different shades of red and blue with the golden yellow of the background and of the details of many of the foreground objects. The playful notes here and there more than ever suggest an artist freed of domestic concerns and indulging in the poetry of the life of the objects.

Ensor abandoned himself to the pleasure of painting: in many of his works of this period, nothing really makes sense. Assembled to create an attractive configuration and a tonal equilibrium, objects are there for their contours and their colouring. This is true of *Still Life with Vegetables and Parrot* (1920–4, T509), whose first version dates from 1889 (T296). Inspired by Flemish Baroque painting, it recalls the work of Frans Snijders and even

58 James Ensor to Ernest and Mariette Rousseau, Ostend, Saturday 9 January 1892, in Huys 2021, pp. 320–21; James Ensor to Mariette Rousseau-Hannon, Ostend, Saturday 16 January 1892, in ibid., p. 322; James Ensor to Ernest and Mariette Rousseau, Ostend, Sunday 13 October 1893, in ibid., p. 370.

59 Legrand 1971, p. 29.

60 Taevernier 1973, no. 65.

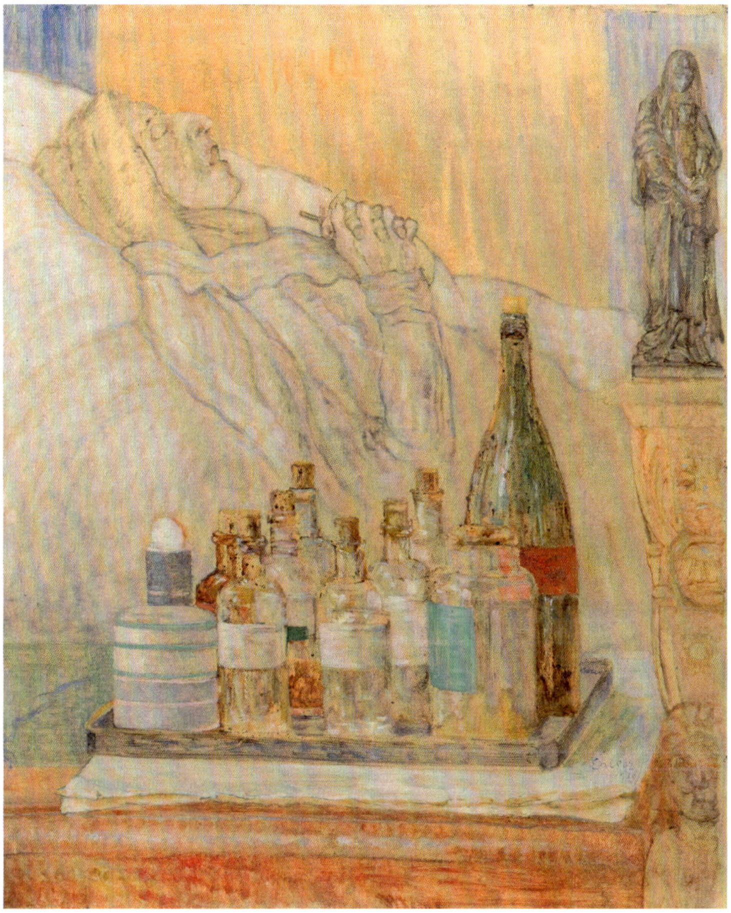

51

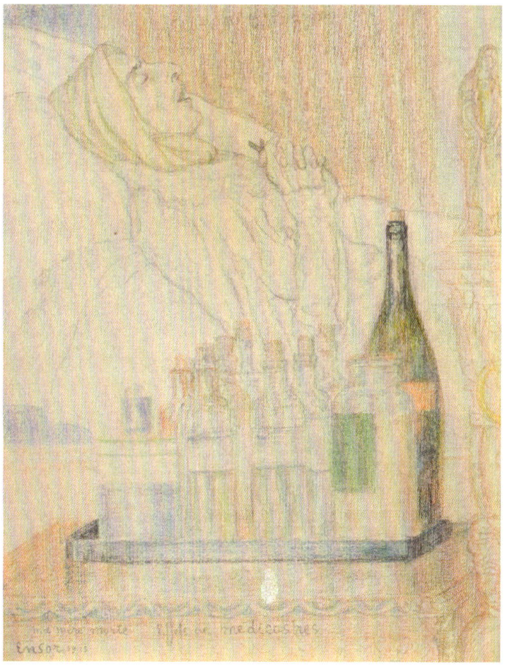

52

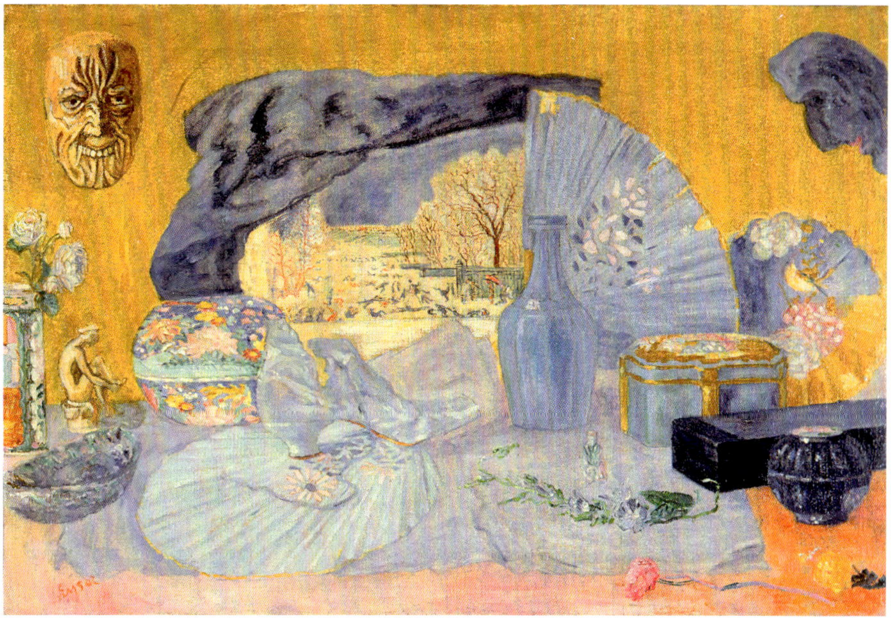

fig. 44

cat. 51 James Ensor, *My Dead Mother (Ma mère morte)*, 1915, oil on canvas, 75 × 60 cm. Mu.ZEE, City of Ostend Collection, inv. SM000713. CR T477.

cat. 52 James Ensor, *My Dead Mother: The Consequences of Quacks (Ma mère morte: Effet de médicastres)*, 1915, colour pencil on prepared panel, 23.8 × 18.3 cm. Collection Georges Hiltrop-Massenhove.

fig. 44 James Ensor, *Blue Chord (Accord bleu)*, 1917, oil on canvas, 66 × 100 cm. Private collection. CR T496.

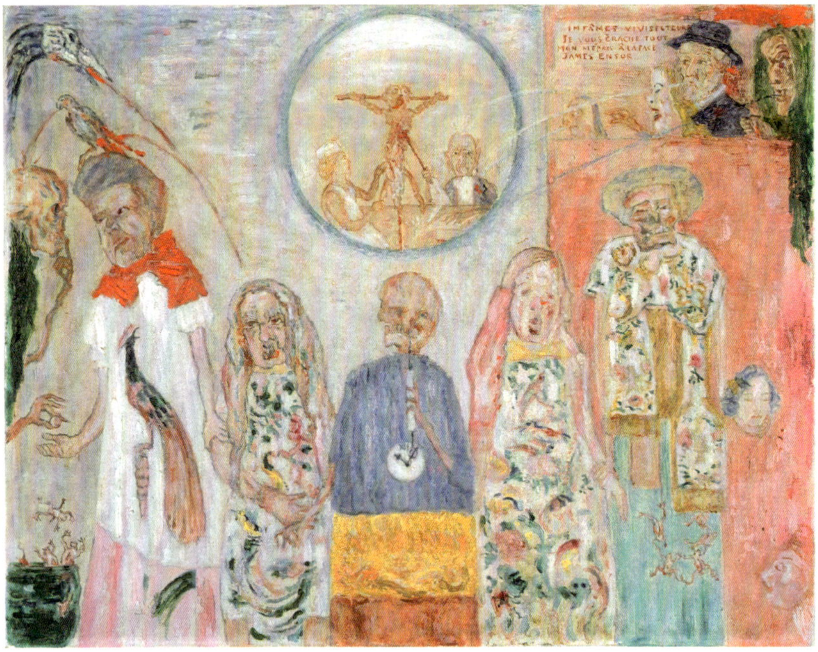

fig. 45

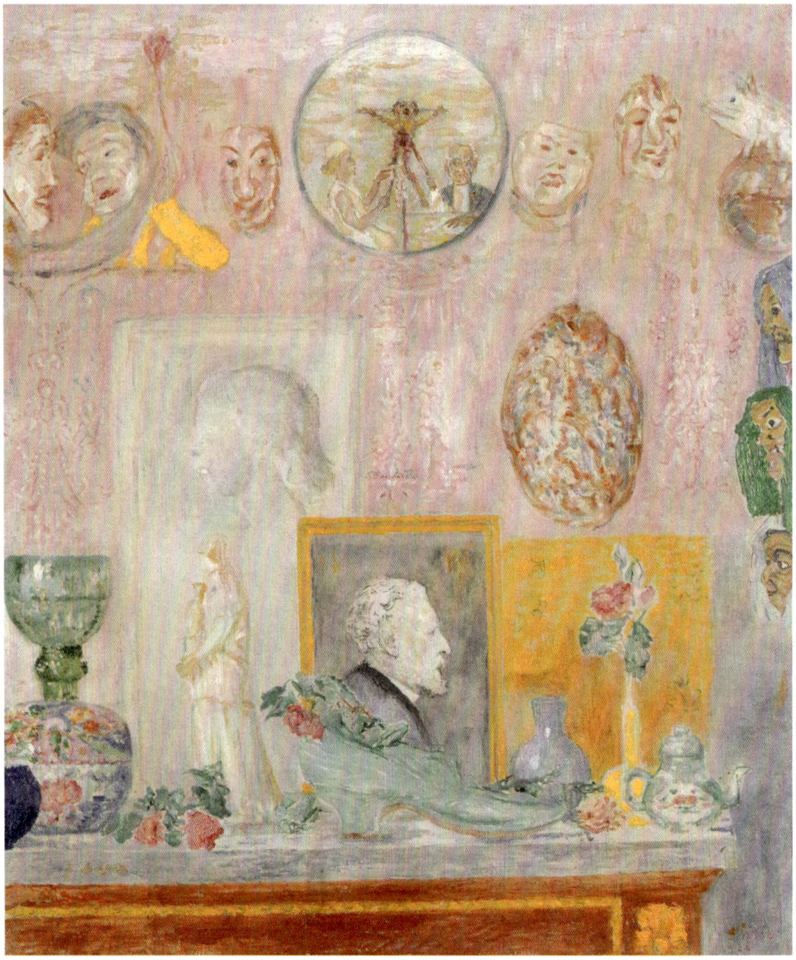

53

fig. 45 James Ensor, *The Vile Vivisectors (Les infâmes vivisecteurs)*, 1925, oil on canvas, 62 × 80 cm. Private collection. CR T529.
cat. 53 James Ensor, *Souvenirs (Souvenirs)*, 1926, oil on canvas, 70 × 60 cm. Private collection, Mortsel. CR T570.

more that of Adriaen van Utrecht (1599–1652), still-life painter par excellence, keen to show that he could paint anything at all. In this work, beneath a parrot perched on a ring sits a red cabbage, flanked on one side by a coffee-pot and on the other by a vase of flowers; on the right, a shelf above the table is laden with fruit: none of this has anything to do with a real scene – all is composition in the service of Mistress Painting.

Now and again, Ensor would venture toward a new subject, fig. 45 such as *The Vile Vivisectors* (1925, T529), but he mostly revisited familiar themes, alternating vivid and pastel colours, rearranged and enlivened by the introduction of new objects and odd little masks come to look. The still life has become a pure exercise in style, where the baroque, busy décor leads the way and animates a subject that should be lifeless in itself. Instead, the artist has transformed the objects into actors at a frivolous, playful little theatre.

Otherwise, Ensor lived among his memories and cultivated his own legend; through his work, he created his own publicity and shaped how he would be remembered by posterity. In *Souvenirs* (1926, T570), a photographic portrait of the artist is flanked by the Virgin shown beside his mother's deathbed painting of 1915. A copy of his own image of vivisection, a theme that he continued to employ, and a number of the masks and seashells he had so long surrounded himself with loom above this still life otherwise chiefly composed of china and flowers real or decorative.

While paying tribute to Jean Teugels, a magistrate and art critic of Veurne who had dedicated to the artist the book *Variations* fig. 46 *sur James Ensor* (Ostend, 1931), he reminds us in *Still Life with Book by Jean Teugels* (1938, T769) that he is now a venerated artist. fig. 47 In *Interior with Three Portraits* (1938, T766), three stages of life are represented: youth, adulthood and old age. One recognises in it his self-portrait at age 19, *Portrait of the Artist – The Little Head* cat. 53 (1879, T118); a portrait derived from his painting *Souvenirs* (1926, T570); and a contemporary portrait that presides over the whole at the centre top. Everything is there as a commemoration: the portraits, cat. 58 the paintings that mark milestones in his career – *Fans and Fabrics* (1881, T206), *Old Woman with Masks* (1889, T305), a fragment of *The Entry of Christ into Brussels in 1889* (1888–9, T293) and *The Fantastical Ballet* (1918, T502) – and the décor of masks and chinoiseries on the mantelpiece in the room with the blue wallpaper, chiming with his image as 'the painter of masks'.

Having traced this path among the still lifes and other arrangements of inanimate objects bequeathed to us by James Ensor, the very object of his painting becomes clearer. The duality of the subject – its staging and its pictorial realisation – and the diversity of themes that it supported meant that this genre was more able than

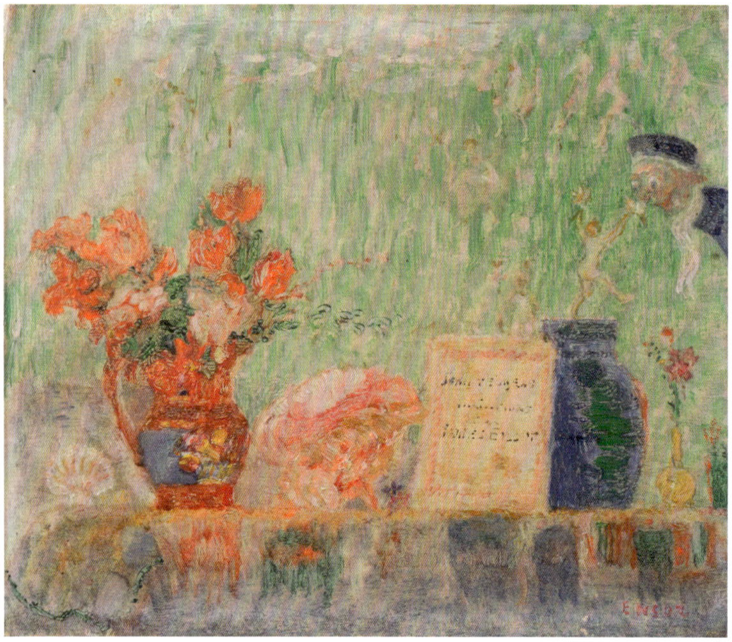

fig. 46

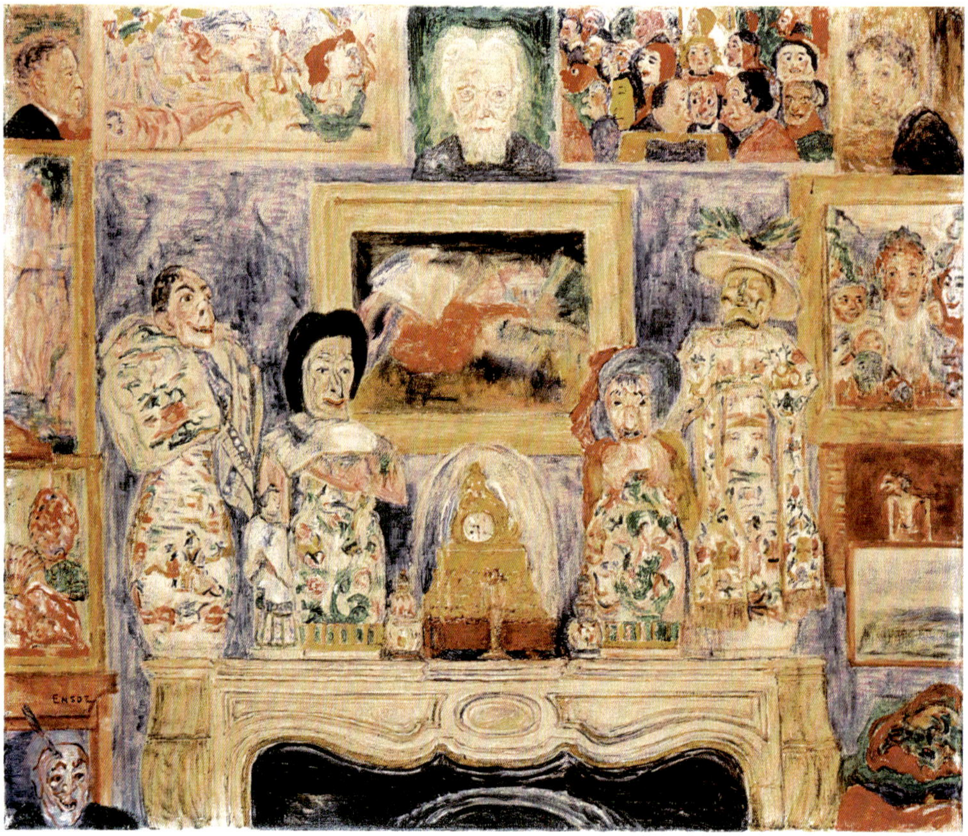

fig. 47

fig. 46 James Ensor, *Still Life with Book by Jean Teugels (Nature morte au livre de Jean Teugels)*, 1938, oil on panel, 17 × 20 cm. Private collection. CR T769.
fig. 47 James Ensor, *Interior with Three Portraits (Intérieur aux trois portraits)*, 1938, oil on canvas, 50.5 × 60.5 cm. Private collection. CR T766.

any other to reflect the artist's varied and sometimes contradictory aspirations, whether purely painterly or semiotic.

At a time when many artists embraced either Symbolism or Impressionism, Ensor had very soon decided, back in 1886, that he wanted to combine the two: Impressionism in the distortion of objects and colours by light, and Symbolism in the hermetic character of subjects rendered in puzzling and chaotic images. This alone accounts for the fact that many of his works are susceptible to a double reading. They are, on the one hand, a music of colour: '"What do these pictures represent?" Ensor was asked one day by a fascinated King Leopold. "They aren't pictures, Your Majesty", replied the painter, quite seriously, "they are symphonies!"'[61] On the other hand, many of his compositions are complex and difficult to understand. He enjoyed reading, poetry, music and studying the great masters in books and magazines and when he visited museums in Belgium, France and England. Add to this the not always easy everyday life of a personality prone to both fantasy and anxiety, and one has the amalgam from which his art arose.

His oeuvre thus offers a manifold experience; interpreting it involves a multistage process that proceeds from an initial visual approach to an in-depth analysis of the thematic content, whether social, burlesque, symbolic or personal, to arrive finally at something beyond it all that springs from his own madness. Ensor's distinctive approach allowed him to create a timeless body of work that continues to disturb through its singularity and its irregularity, but even more through its magic, when his imagination gave him no pause, and his gifted hand, obedient, was carried away by the euphoria, following without another thought.

61 Octave Maus, untitled article [beginning 'Lorsque'en 1884 …'], *James Ensor, peintre et graveur,* special issue of *La Plume revue littéraire et artistique bimensuelle*, 15 December 1899, pp. 31–5, at p. 34.

Catalogue

James Ensor

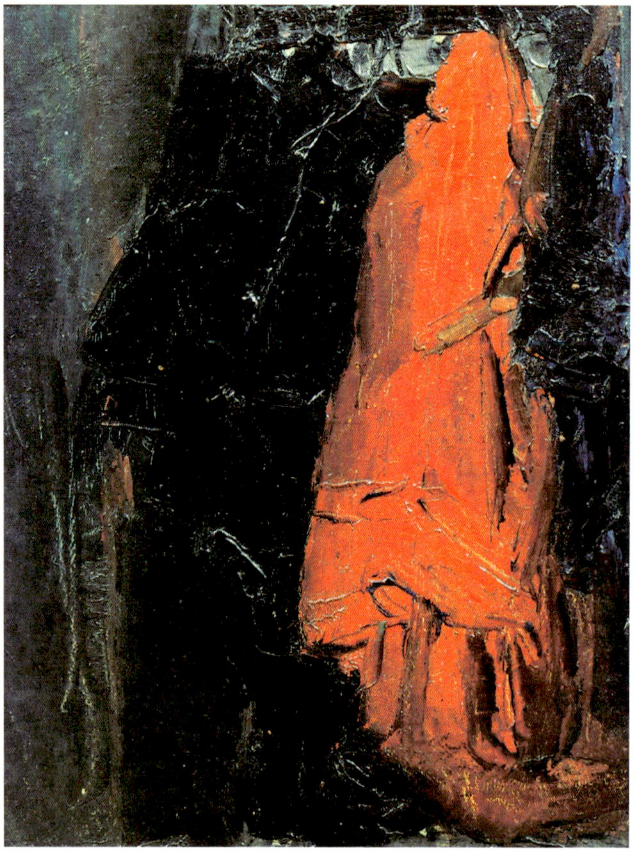

54

cat. 54 James Ensor, *The Hat-Stand (Le porte-manteau)*, 1876, oil on cardboard, 24.5 × 19 cm. Private collection. CR T33.

Biography
James Sidney Edouard Ensor (Ostend, 13 April 1860 – Ostend, 19 November 1949)

Gregory Boite

1860 James Ensor is born in Ostend to a British father, James Frederic Ensor, and a Flemish mother, Marie Catherine Louise Haegheman. For the rest of his life, he resides in Ostend, where his parents run a trinkets shop, and later his mother and aunt run a store specialising in shells and decorative objects.

1873 Ensor starts drawing and painting at an early age. He takes private lessons from local painters Michel Van Cuyck and Édouard Dubar.

1876 He creates his first works, the *cartons roses* [pink cards], painted *en plein air* in Ostend and its environs. He attends the Ostend Academy.

1877 Ensor enrols at the Royal Academy of Fine Arts in Brussels, which he attends for three years, but does not graduate.

1879 His meeting with the art critic Théo Hannon in Brussels proves to be of great importance to Ensor's development; Hannon introduces Ensor to the family of his sister Mariette Rousseau-Hannon, through which Ensor is able to build an artistic and intellectual network and, above all, gain support, acknowledgement and friendship.

1880 Ensor moves into a studio that is a room in an attic of a building at the corner of Boulevard Van Iseghem and Rue de Flandre in Ostend. Over the next few years, his paintings are notable for their free, pre-Impressionist style, with great attention to light and atmospheric effects, and the motifs often derive from his immediate surroundings. Examples of this within the still-life genre are *The Cabbage* (1880) and *The Skate* (1880).

1881 Ensor continues to be active in the Brussels art scene, owing to his membership in La Chrysalide, founded by such names as Théo Hannon and Alfred Verhaeren. The following year, he joins the artist association L'Essor together with, for example, Marie de Bievre and Georgette Meunier.

1883 Together with Willy Finch, Ensor is a co-founder of Les XX (Les Vingt), in which he plays a pioneering role. The group organises exhibitions for ten years. Ensor is supported in this by fellow Les XX member Anna Boch, who purchases his painting *Russian Music* (1881). Together with Guillaume Vogels and Hubert Bellis, he travels to the Netherlands where they visit the Rijksmuseum in Amsterdam and the Frans Hals Museum in Haarlem. The following year, he travels with Jan Toorop to Paris.

1885 From the mid-1880s, Ensor's style becomes lighter and smoother, and whereas he mixed colours in the past, he now uses undiluted colours.

1886 French artists are invited to the Salon des XX, including Claude Monet and Odilon Redon, and later Georges Seurat, who introduces Neo-Impressionism. Ensor decides from the outset to ignore the essentials of the Pointillist technique. Ensor focuses on graphic work. Influenced by Rembrandt, his etchings show particular interest in the expressive qualities of light and line.

1888 Ensor starts painting his masterpiece *The Entry of Christ into Brussels in 1889*. He also reworks previous paintings (e.g., *Self-portrait with a Flowered Hat*, 1883–8) and even adds new motifs to them, including masks, grotesque figures and fantastical beings.

1892 His first monograph is mounted by the lawyer, art critic and writer Eugène Demolder, who later organises Ensor's first solo exhibition in Brussels in 1894–5.

1894 La Libre Esthétique, founded following the disbanding of Les XX in 1893, holds its first salon. The artist also plays an active part in this association. He decides to breathe new life into Ostend's local art scene by founding the Cercle des Beaux-Arts d'Ostende, where, for example, Isidore Verheyden exhibits his *Portrait of James Ensor* of 1886.

1895 Interest in Ensor's work begins to manifest itself by degrees: museums acknowledge him in their acquisitions policy, and the Belgian State purchases *The Lamp-Lighter* (1880) for the Royal Museum of Painting and Sculpture of Belgium in Brussels, the first of Ensor's paintings to enter a museum collection.

1898 Eugène Demolder organises Ensor's first solo exhibition abroad, at the Salon des Cent in Paris. A special edition of the Parisian magazine *La Plume* is devoted to Ensor.

1899 The Kupferstichkabinett in Vienna purchases some one hundred of Ensor's engravings.

1900 After 1900, apart from a few highly inspired compositions, Ensor loses some of his ardent avant-garde style and biting satire. He looks at earlier works retrospectively and paints them in brighter, lighter tones, often referring to his own work and the world he is living in.

1901 Ensor receives support in his hometown through the museum's purchase of his entire etchings collection.

1904 Ensor meets art collector Emma Lambotte. She is a passionate supporter of his work and introduces him to the Antwerp collector, patron and decorator François Franck who, in turn, invites Ensor to exhibit work at the Antwerp artist association Kunst van Heden. It is through this association that Ensor acquires serious recognition abroad.

1906 The Lambottes give the artist a harmonium as a gift. He starts to compose music for his pantomime ballet *La gamme d'amour*, for which he writes the storyline and designs the costumes and décor.

1908 The first comprehensive monograph on Ensor is published, written by Émile Verhaeren.

1913 Rik Wouters pays tribute to Ensor with a bust of the artist. The first catalogue raisonné of his graphic work is published by Herbert von Garvens-Garvensburg, who publicises Ensor's work in Germany.

1920 In January, the public is able to view the first retrospective exhibition of Ensor's work, at Galerie Georges Giroux in Brussels.

1921 The first of Ensor's manuscripts, *Écrits de James Ensor*, is published by Sélection.

1929 Ensor is given the status of nobility by King Albert I and accordingly acquires Belgian nationality. The largest retrospective exhibition of Ensor's work to date is mounted at the Centre for Fine Arts, Brussels, where the artist debuts *The Entry of Christ into Brussels in 1889*. As a celebrated artist, Ensor plays an active role locally at the Ostend gallery Studio where Léon Spilliaert and many others also exhibit their work. Ensor regularly gives lectures there as well, including one in 1934 praising the work of painter Antoine Wiertz.

1930 In his hometown, a bust is unveiled at the Kursaal with Léon Spilliaert and others in attendance.

1949 Ensor dies on November 19 and is buried in the churchyard at the small church of Onze-Lieve-Vrouw ter Duinen in Mariakerke, Ostend.

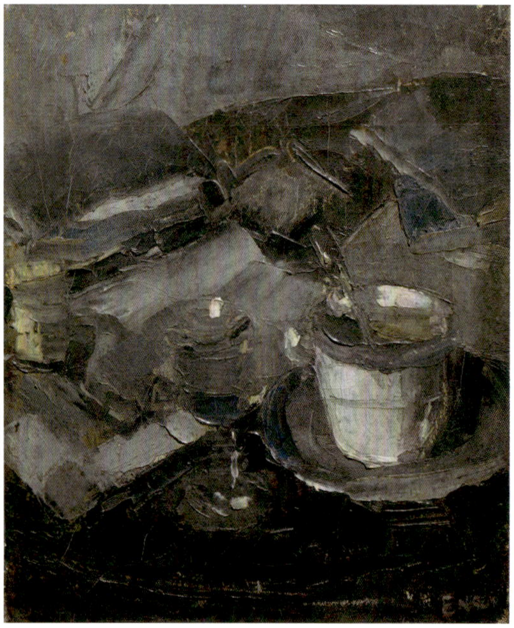

55

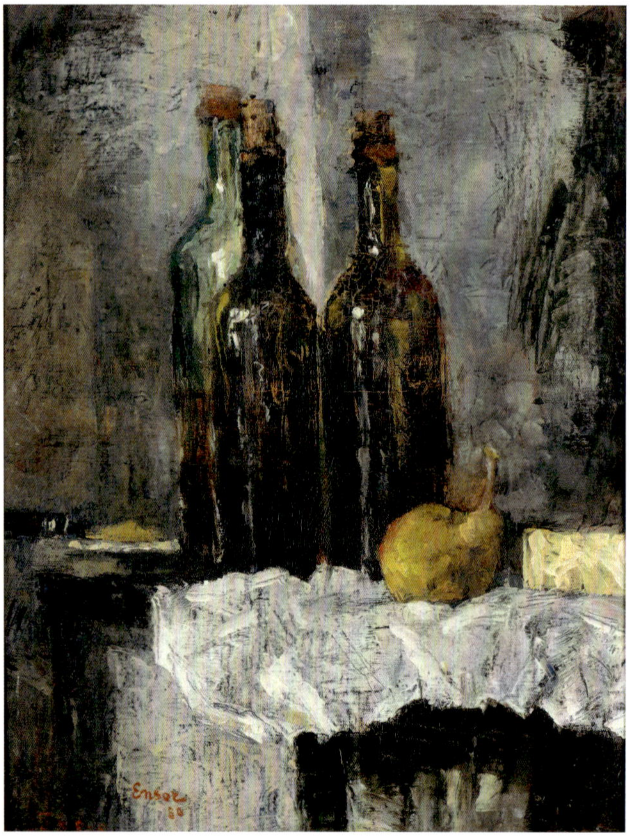

56

cat. 55 James Ensor, *The Small Coffee Cup (La petite tasse)*, *c.*1880, oil on canvas, 27.5 × 22 cm. Private collection. CR T139.

cat. 56 James Ensor, *Bottles (Les bouteilles)*, 1880, oil on canvas, 65 × 53 cm. Fondation Socindec. CR T142.

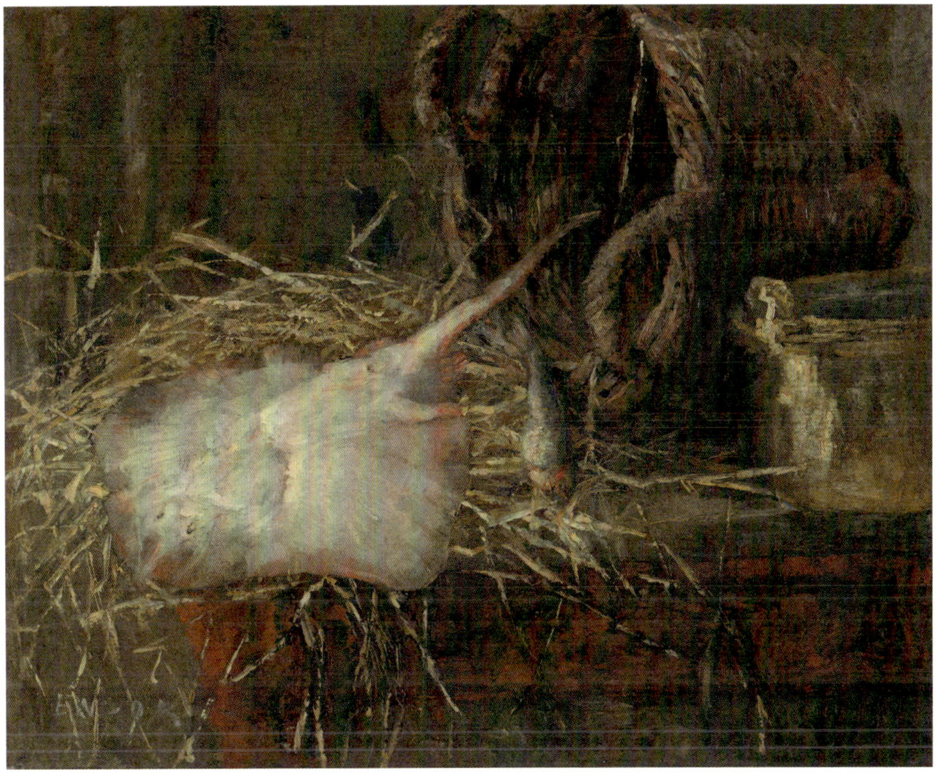

57

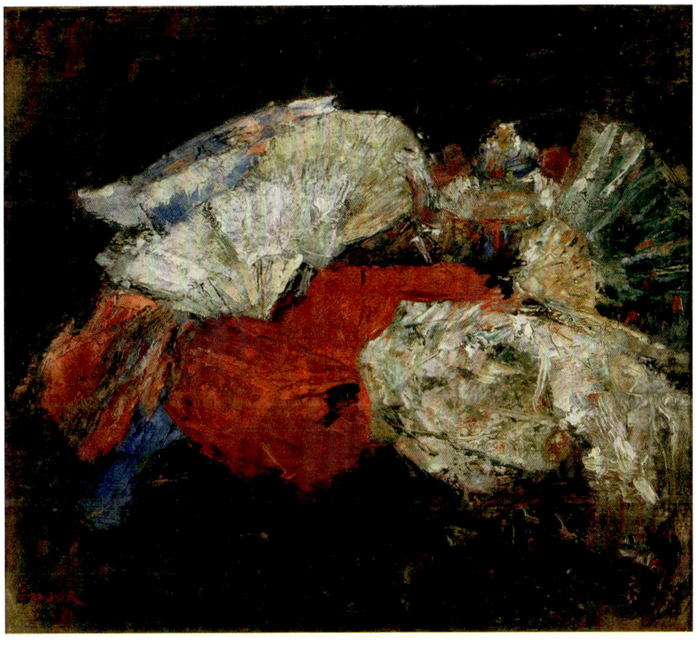

58

cat. 57 James Ensor, *Skate and Herring (Raie et hareng)*, 1880, oil on canvas, 80 × 90 cm. Royal Museum of Fine Arts, Antwerp, inv. 2188. CR T147.

cat. 58 James Ensor, *Fans and Fabrics (Éventails et étoffes)*, 1881, oil on canvas, 48 × 54 cm. Private collection, Brussels. CR T206.

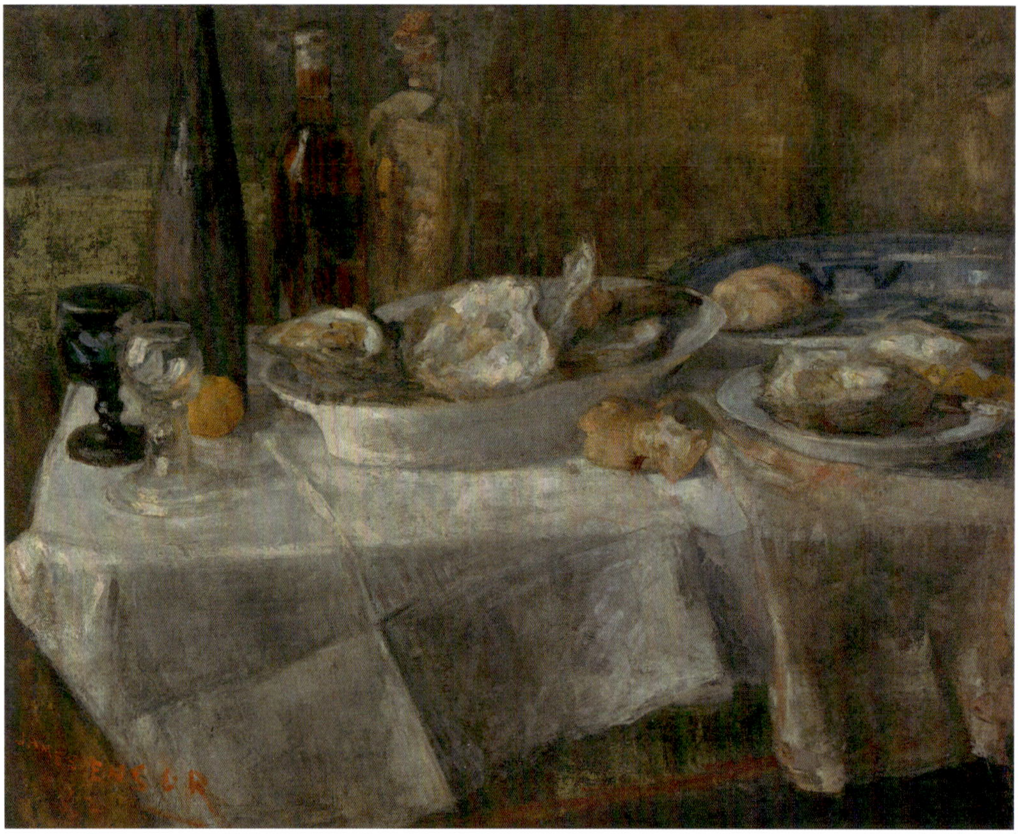

59

60

cat. 59 James Ensor, *Still Life with Oysters (Nature morte aux huîtres)*, 1882, oil on canvas, 79 × 99 cm. Royal Museum of Fine Arts, Antwerp, inv. 1412. CR T234.

cat. 60 James Ensor, *Roses, Tulips and Mimosa (Roses, tulipes et mimosa)*, 1882, oil on canvas, 48 × 58 cm. Museum Boijmans Van Beuningen, Rotterdam, acquired with the collection of D.G. van Beuningen, inv. 2602 (MK). CR T236.

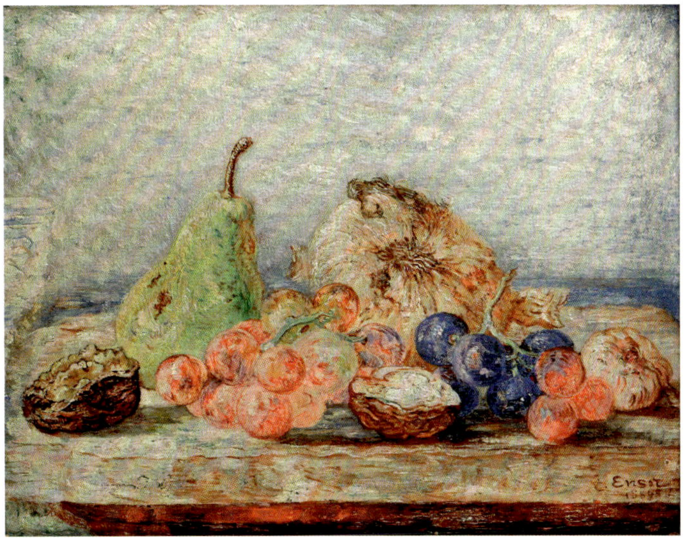

61

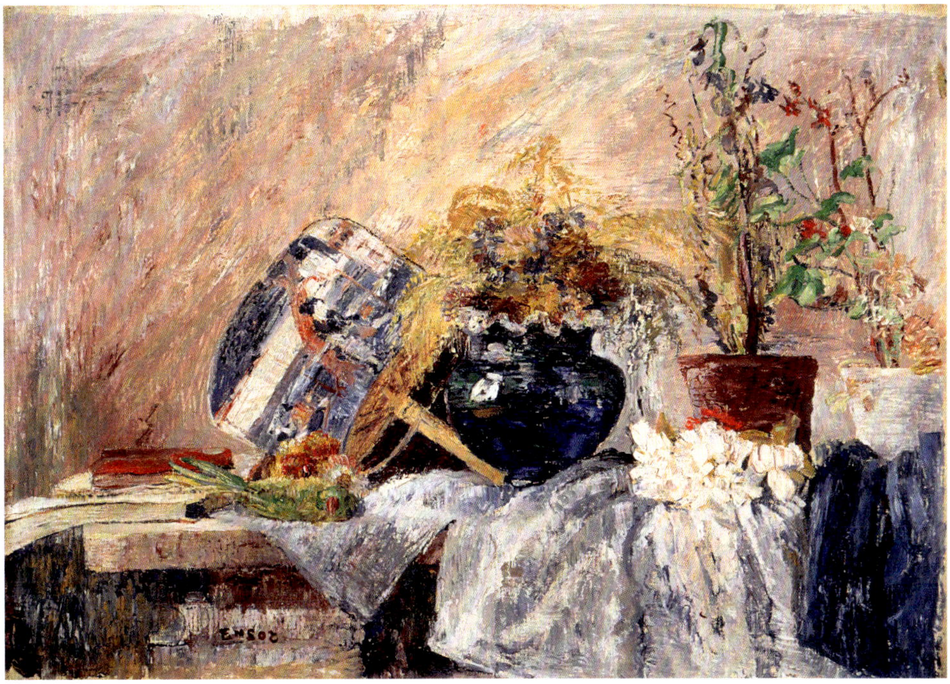

62

cat. 61 James Ensor, *Pear, Grapes and Nuts (Small Fruits) (Poire, raisins et noix (Petits fruits))*, 1889, oil on panel, 19 × 24.5 cm. Private collection. CR T294.
cat. 62 James Ensor, *Still Life with Blue Vase and Fan (Nature morte au vase et à l'éventail bleus)*, 1889, oil on canvas, 47 × 66 cm. Govaert Family. CR T297.

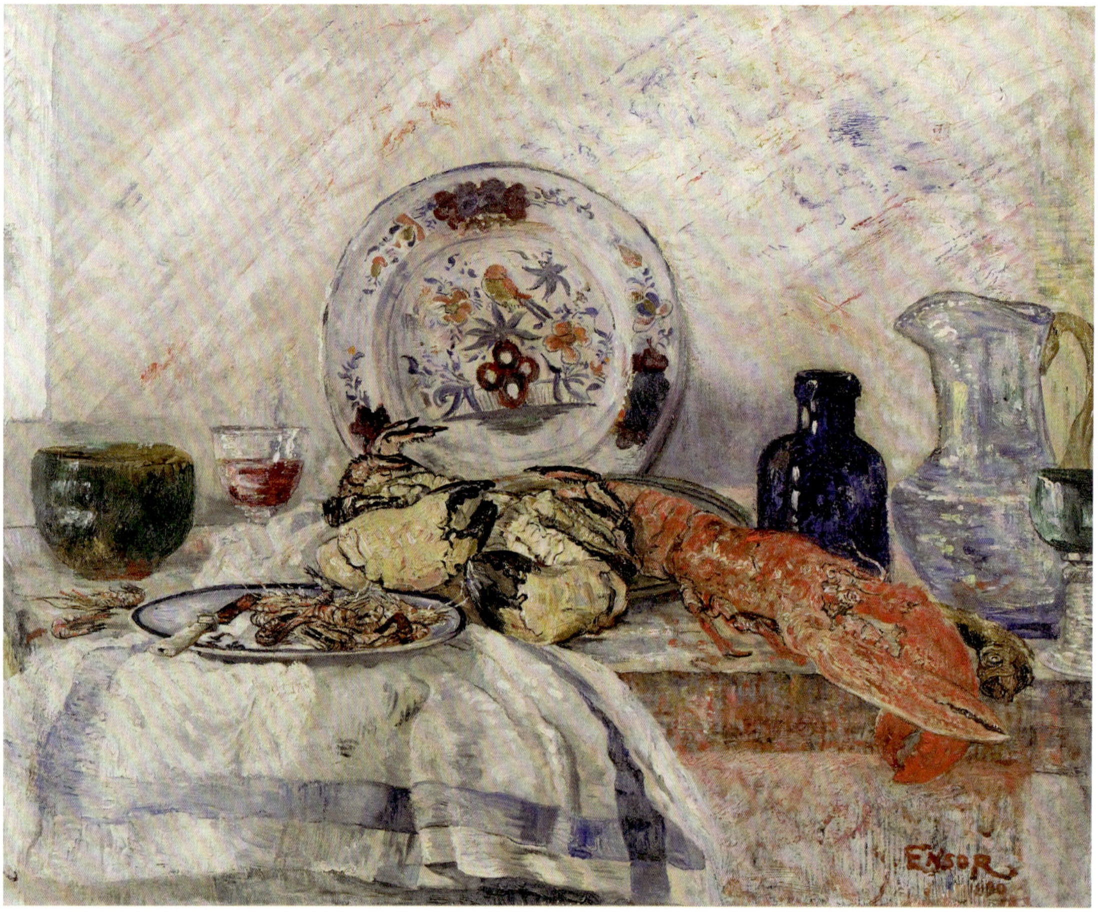

63

cat. 63 James Ensor, *Still Life with Lobster and Crab (Nature morte au homard et au crabe)*, 1890, oil on canvas, 61 × 75 cm. Private collection, Vienna. CR T315.

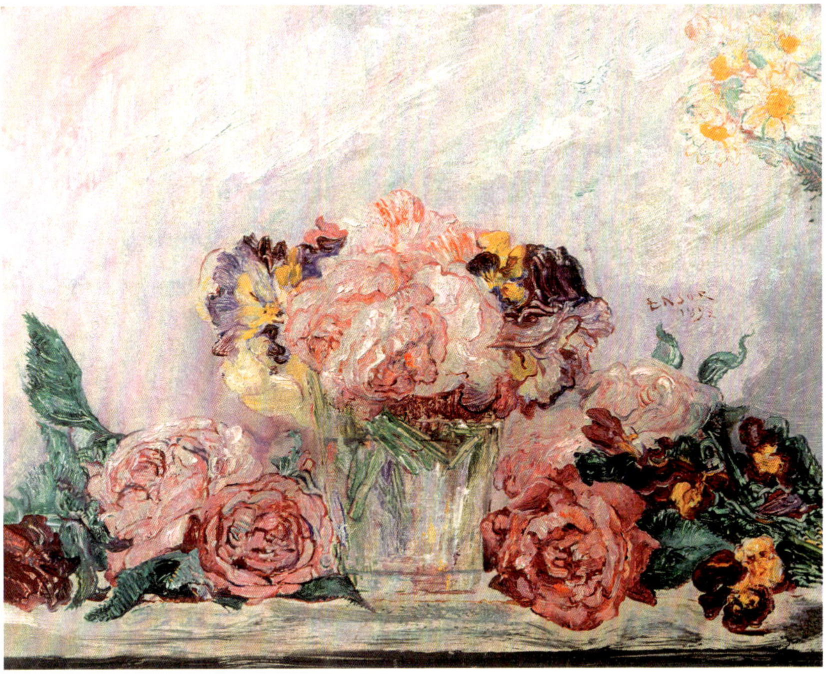

64

cat. 64 James Ensor, *Roses (Roses)*, 1892, oil on panel, 32.5 × 40 cm. Royal Museums of Fine Arts of Belgium, Brussels, inv. 11157. CR T351.

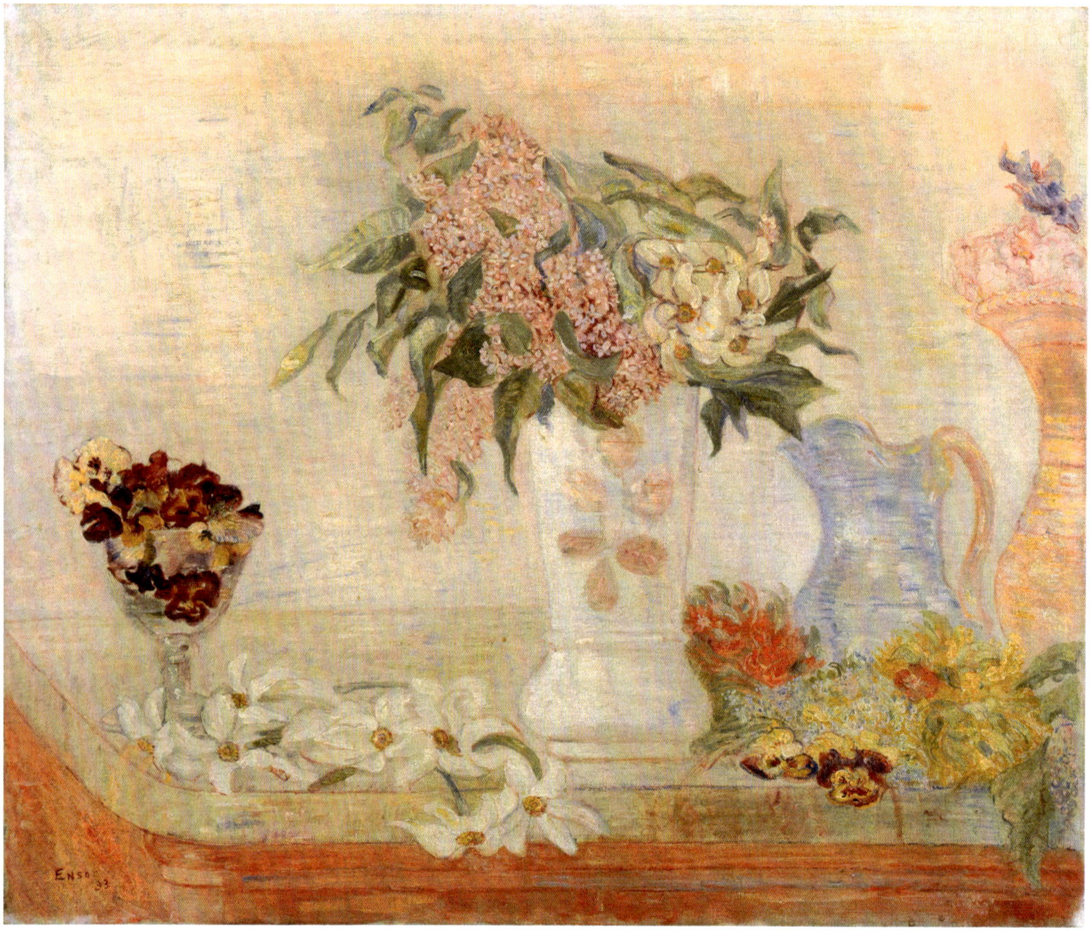

65

cat. 65 James Ensor, *Daffodils, Lilacs and Violets (Jonquilles, lilas et violettes)*, 1893, oil on canvas, 57 × 70 cm.
Private collection, courtesy Bounameaux Art Expertise. CR T366.

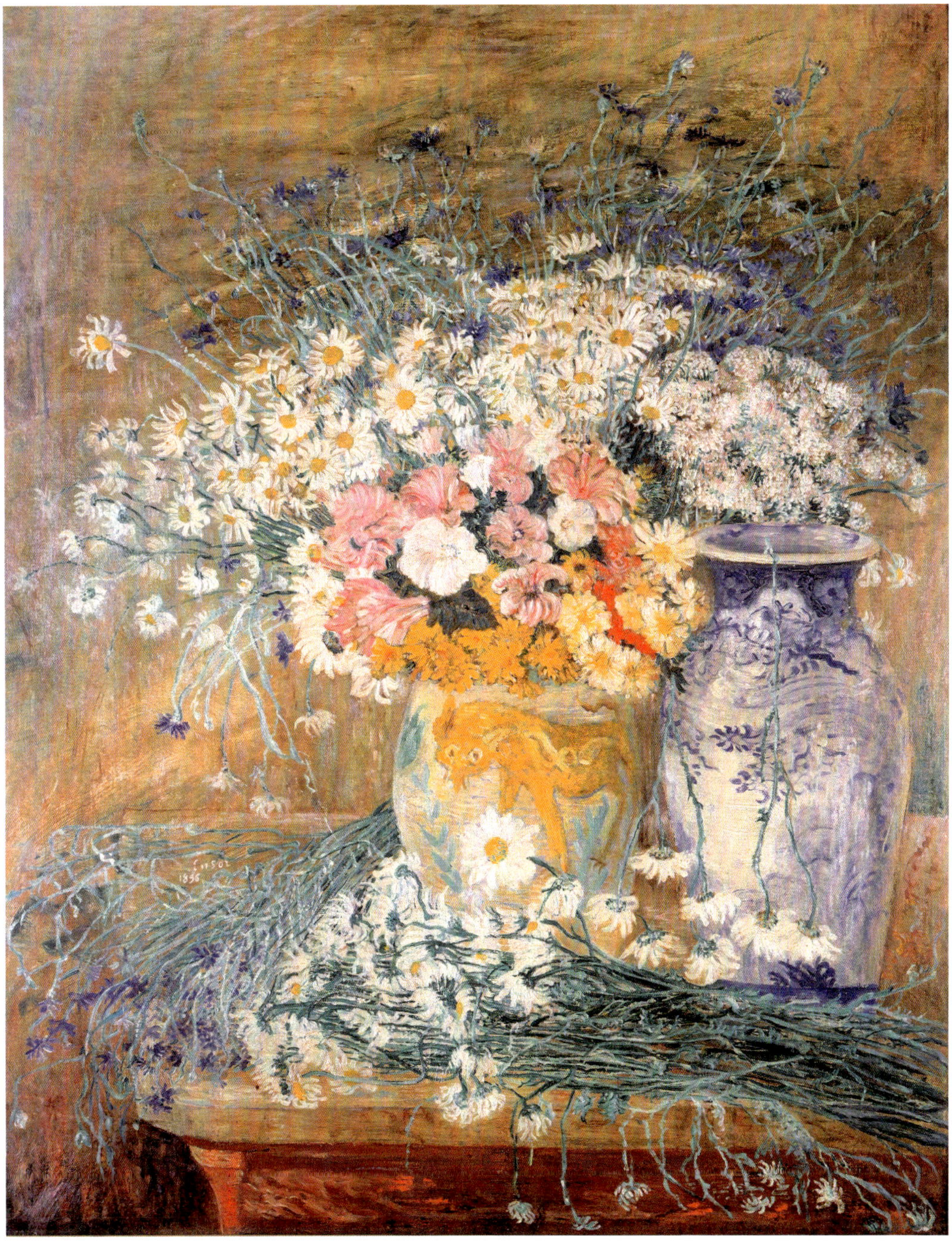

66

cat. 66 James Ensor, *Flowers and Chinese Vases (Fleurs et vases chinois)*, 1896, oil on canvas, 100 × 80 cm. Royal Museums of Fine Arts of Belgium, Brussels, inv. 6912. CR T376.

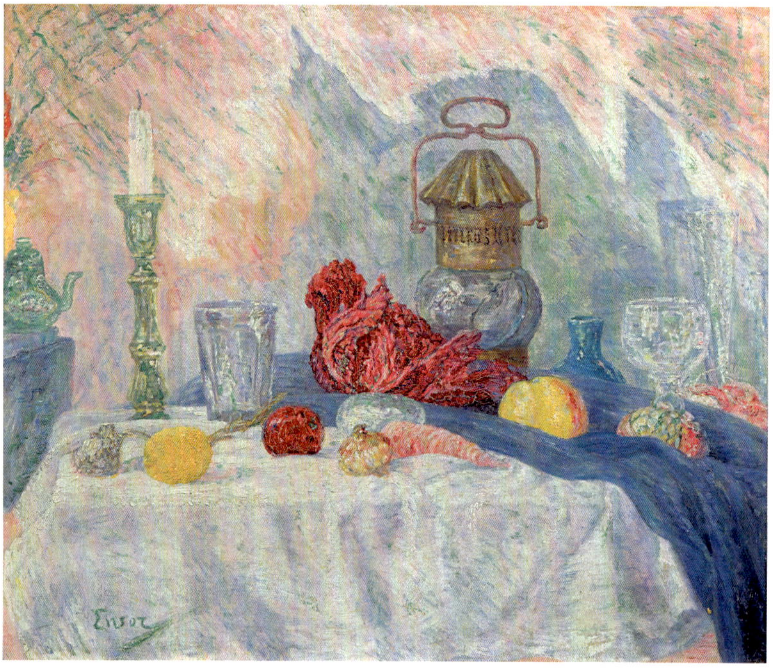

67

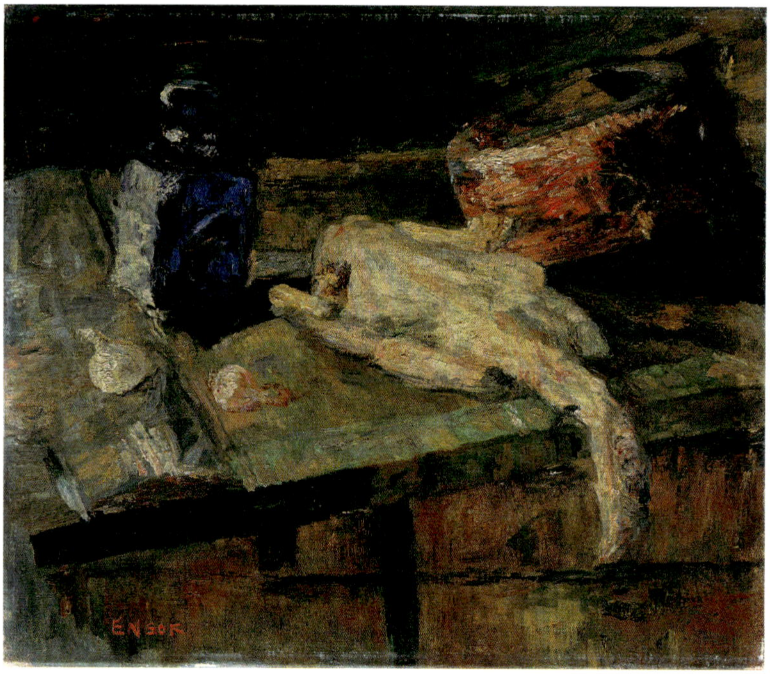

68

cat. 67 James Ensor, *Still Life with Lantern and Vegetables (Nature morte à la lanterne et aux légumes)*, 1900 (?), oil on canvas, 54.5 × 65.5 cm. The Simon Collection of Belgian Art, London. CR T395.
cat. 68 James Ensor, *Blue Flask and Chicken (Flacon bleu et poulet)*, c.1910 (?), oil on canvas, 47 × 56 cm. Belvedere, Vienna, inv. 4420. CR T453.

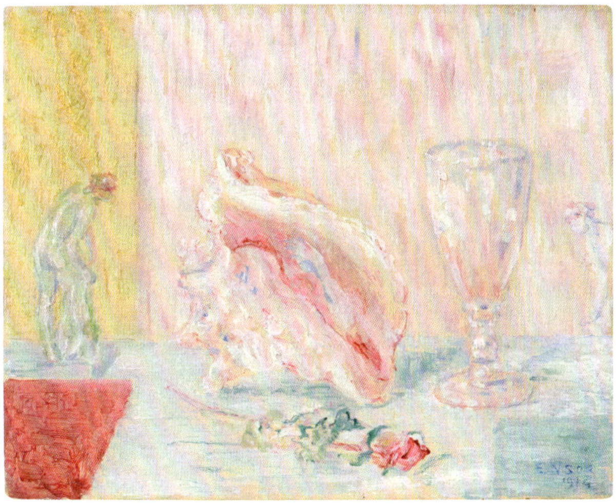

69

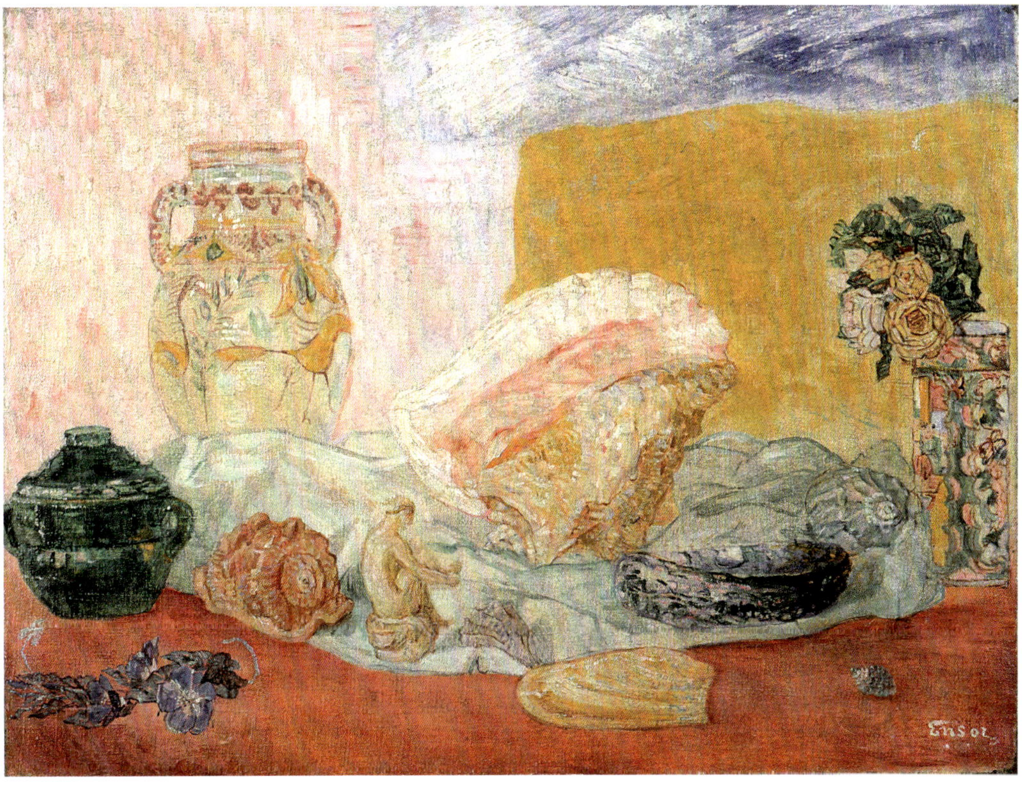

70

cat. 69 James Ensor, *The Pink Seashell (Study of Light Received between the Street and between Two Bodies of Water) (Le coquillage rose (Étude de lumière entrevue entre rue entre deux eaux))*, 1914, oil on cardboard, 19.5 × 24 cm. Private collection, Knokke. CR T471.

cat. 70 James Ensor, *Seashells, Roses and Vases (Coquillages, roses et vases)*, 1917/8, oil on canvas, 55 × 74 cm. Private collection, Bern, Switzerland. CR T497.

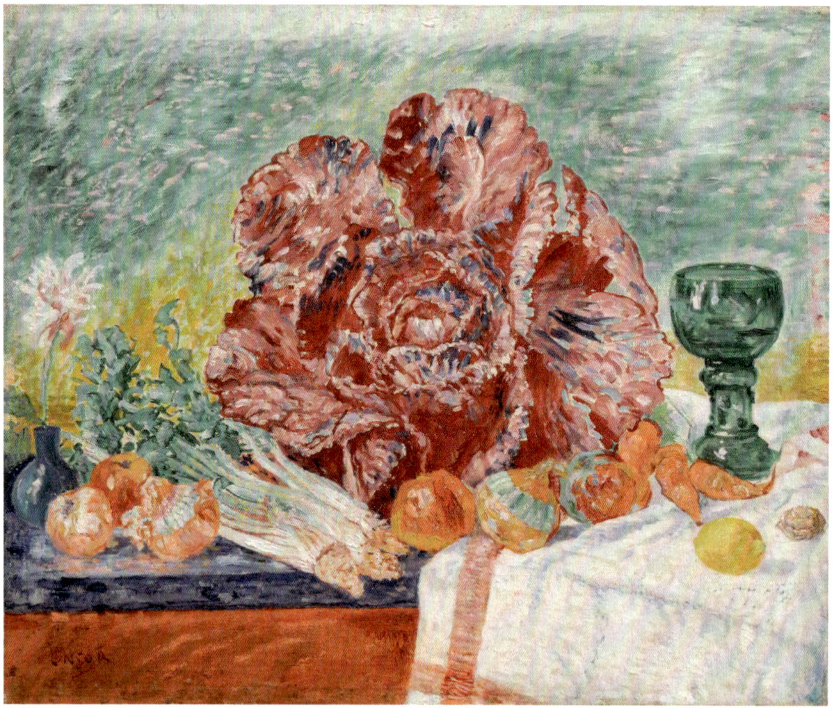

71

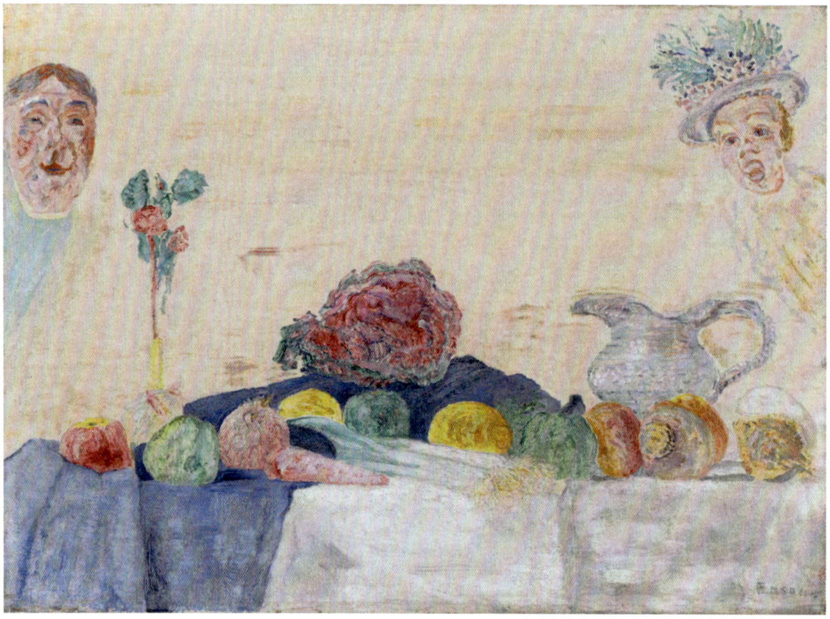

72

cat. 71 James Ensor, *Red Cabbage and Green Wine Glass (Chou rouge et verre de vin vert)*, 1925, oil on canvas, 66 × 80 cm. Private collection. CR T532.

cat. 72 James Ensor, *Red Cabbage, Fruit and Masks (Chou rouge, fruits et masques)*, *c.*1925, oil on canvas, 50.5 × 70.5 cm. Property of a Monaco Collector. CR T538.

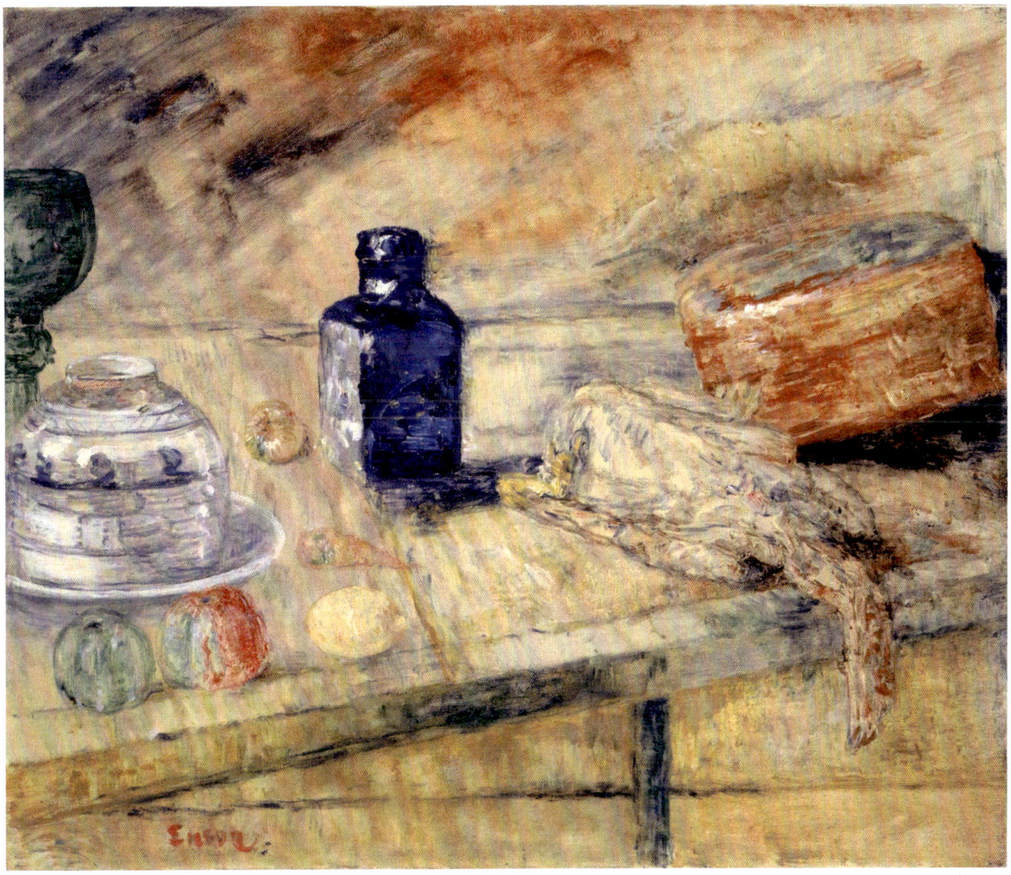

73

cat. 73 James Ensor, *Blue Flask and Chicken (Flacon bleu et poulet)*, *c.*1925, oil on canvas, 54.2 × 65.3 cm. Kunstmuseum Basel, inv. 1562, acquisition 1930. CR T540.

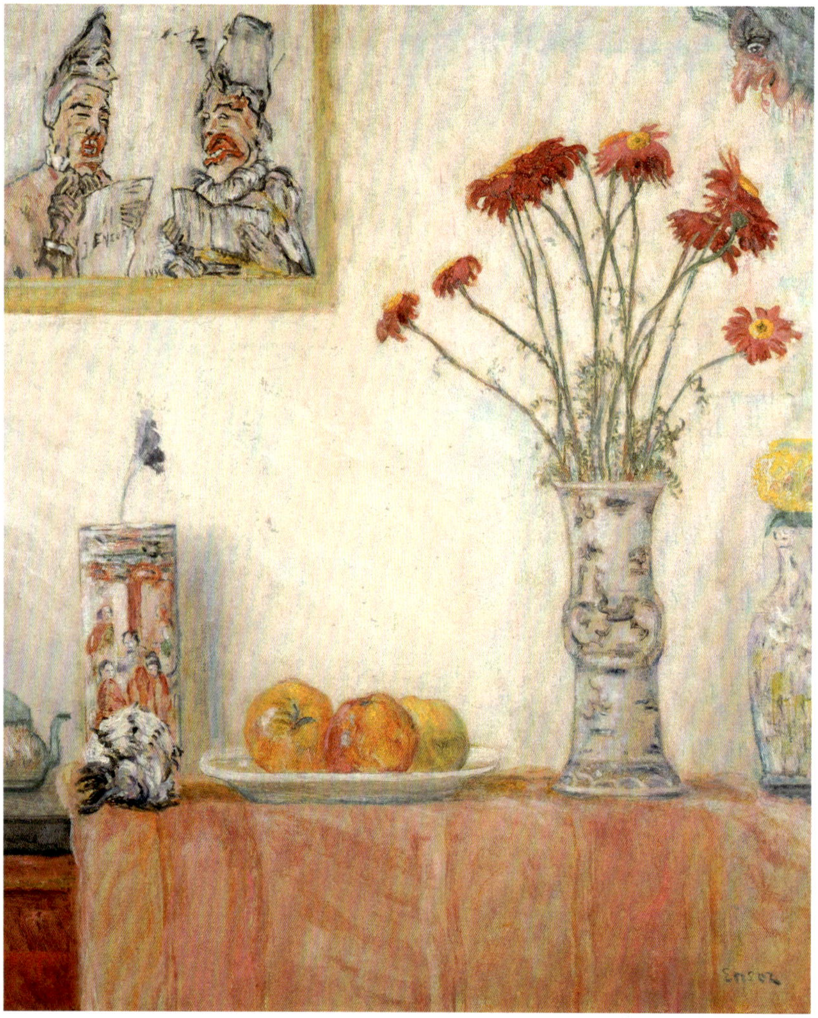

74

cat. 74 James Ensor, *Flowers, Fruit and Masks (Fleurs, fruits et masques)*, 1931, oil on canvas, 65 × 53 cm. Private collection. CR T612.

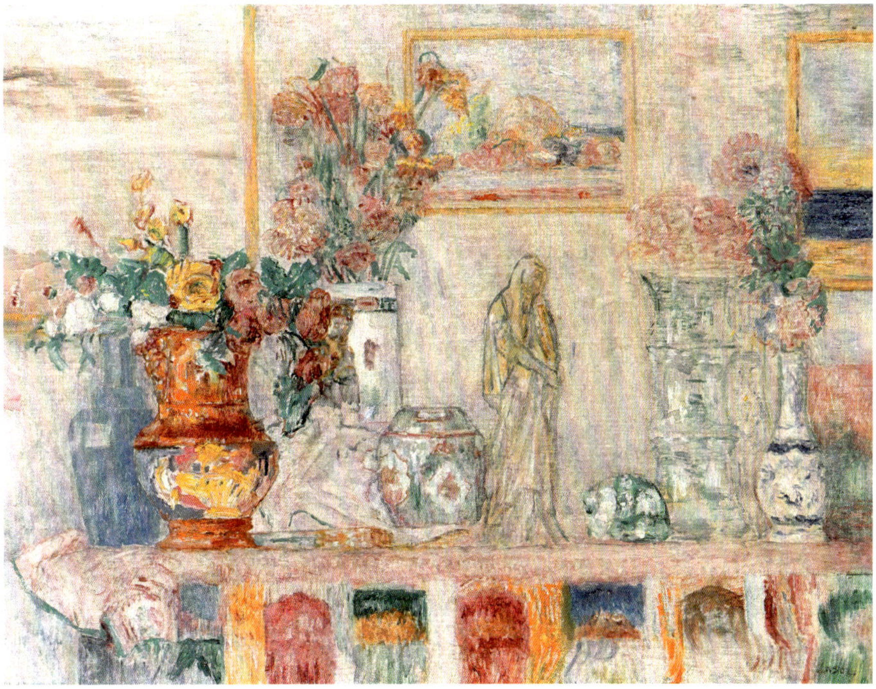

75

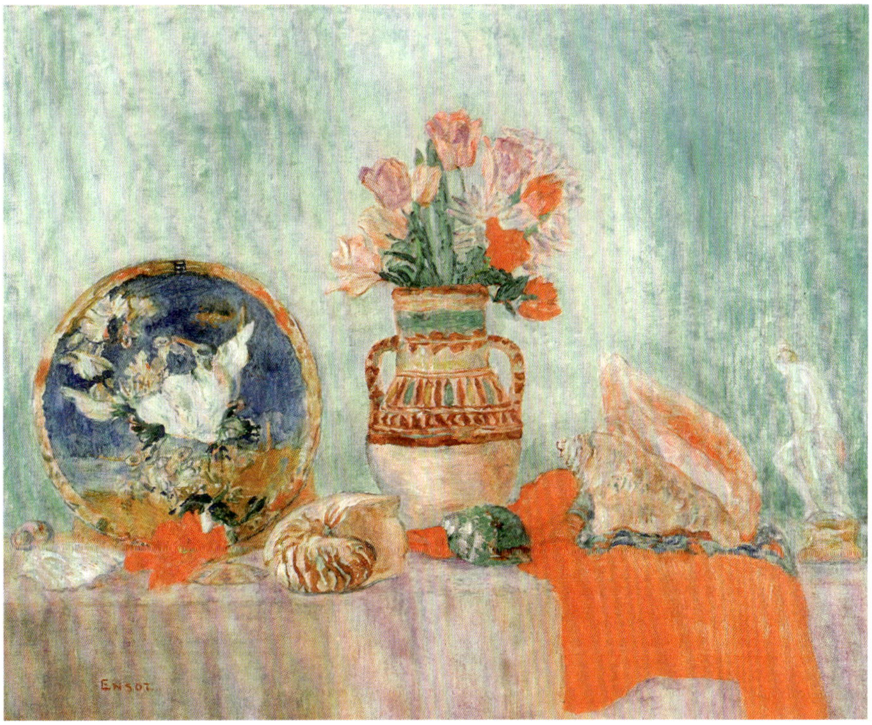

76

cat. 75 James Ensor, *Light's Caress (Caresses de lumière)*, 1934, oil on canvas, 50 × 66 cm. Private collection. CR T635.
cat. 76 James Ensor, *Light Stripped of Leaves (Lumières effeuilées)*, 1936, oil on canvas, 60.5 × 75.5 cm. Musée des Beaux-Arts / La Boverie, Liège, inv. AM 408. CR T688.

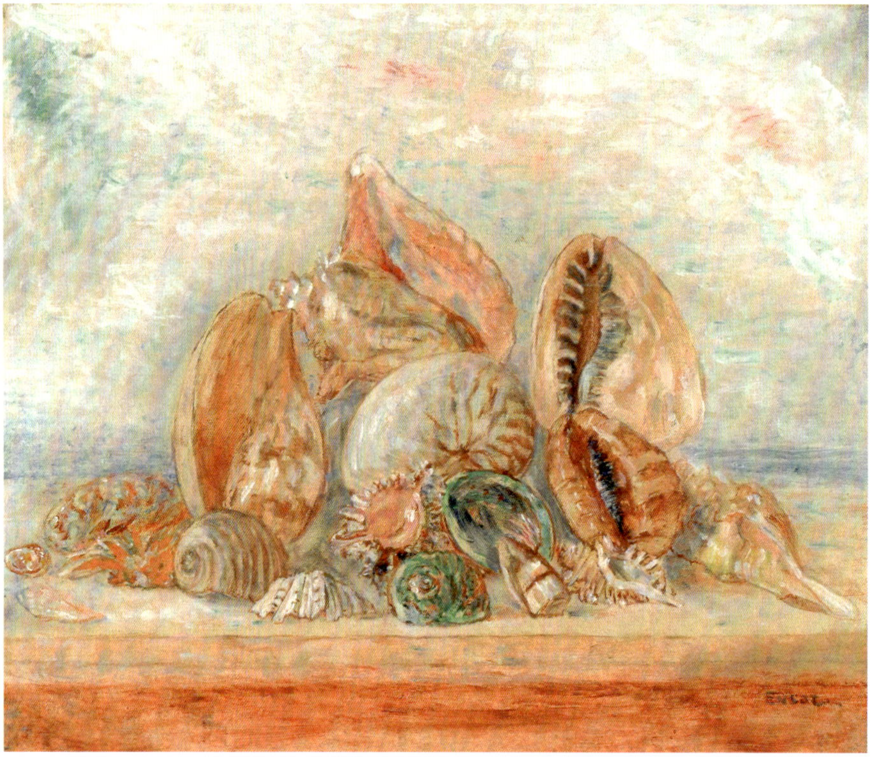

77

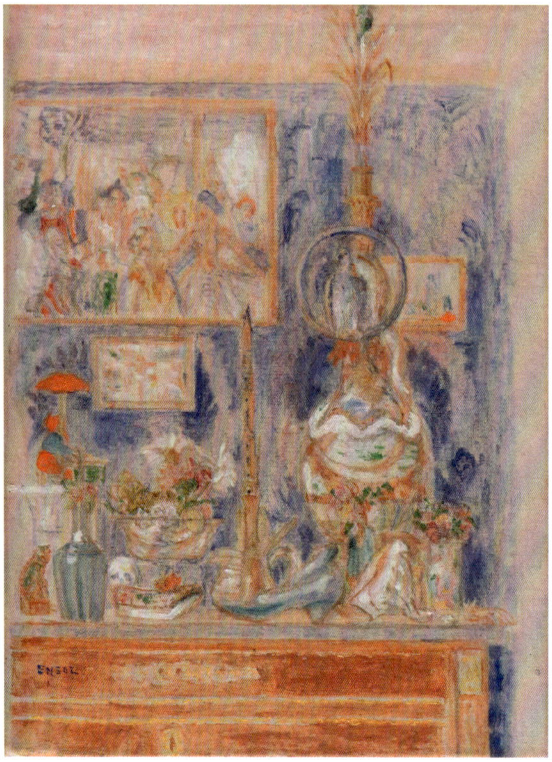

78

cat. 77 James Ensor, *Seashells (Coquillages)*, 1936, oil on canvas, 51 × 60.5 cm. Musée des Beaux-Arts / La Boverie, Liège, inv. 160. CR T701.

cat. 78 James Ensor, *A Cosy Corner at Home (Un bon coin chez moi)*, 1938, oil on canvas, 50 × 38 cm. Mu.ZEE, City of Ostend Collection, inv. SM001593. CR T781.

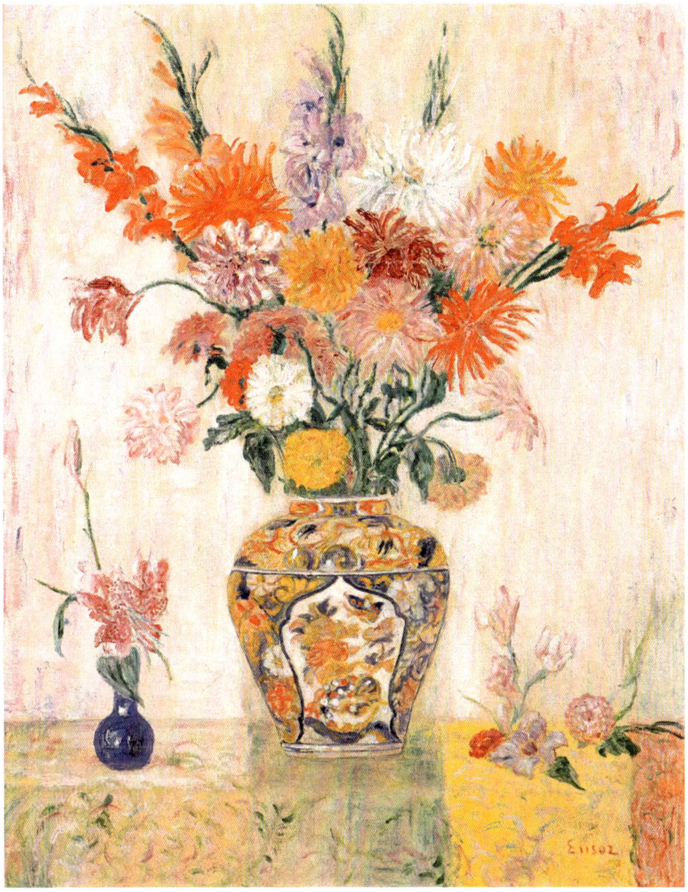

79

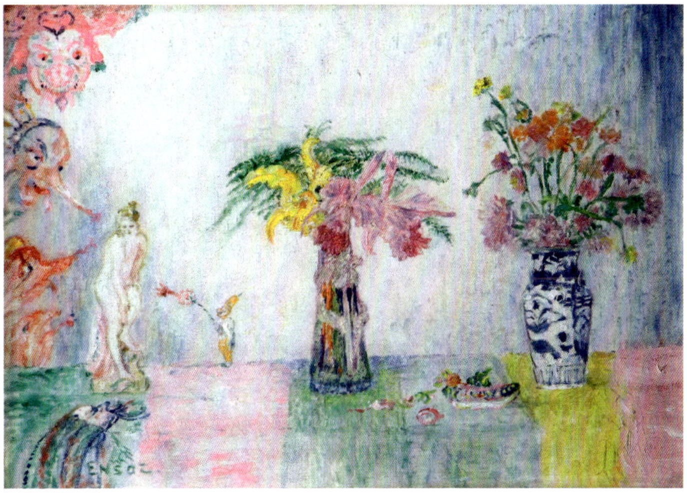

80

cat. 79 James Ensor, *Autumn Flowers (Fleurs d'automne)*, 1938, oil on canvas, 75 × 60 cm. University of Liège – Musée Wittert, Liège, inv. 24024. CR T784.

cat. 80 James Ensor, *The Language of Flowers (Le langage des fleurs)*, 1938, oil on panel, 22 × 30 cm. Musée des Beaux-Arts / La Boverie, Liège, inv. AM75. CR T785.

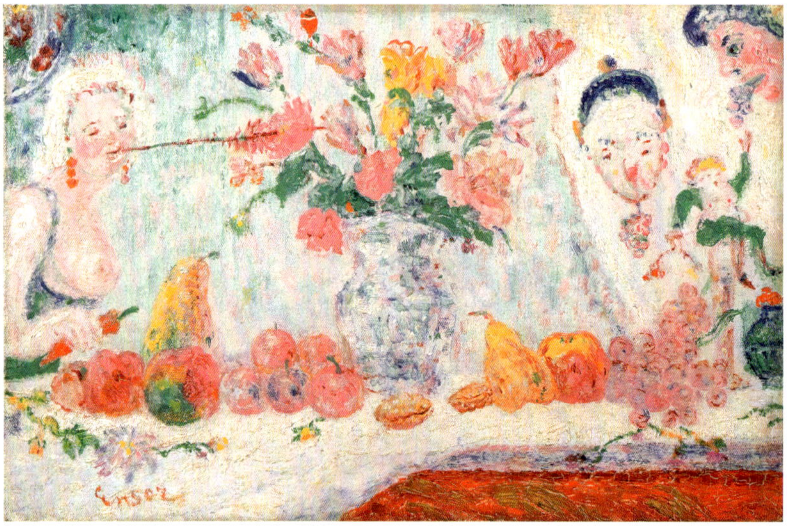

81

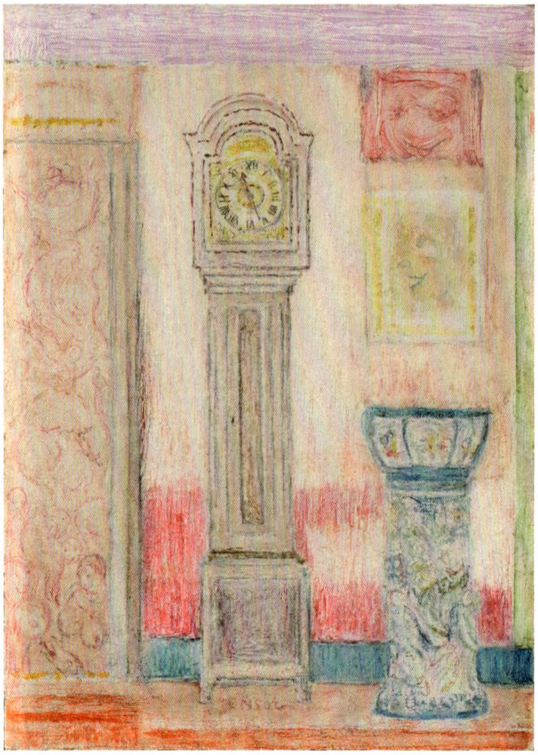

82

cat. 81 James Ensor, *Flowers and Fruit (Fleurs et fruits)*, *c.*1938, oil on panel, 16 × 24.5 cm. Frank and Eliane Demaegd-Breynaert. CR T801.

cat. 82 James Ensor, *The Old Clock (La vieille horloge)*, 1941, oil on panel, 22 × 16 cm. Private collection, courtesy Galerie Seghers, Ostend. CR T851.

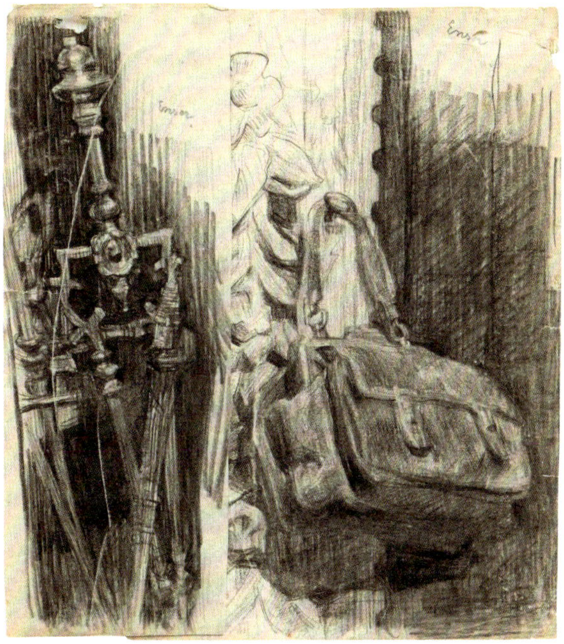

83

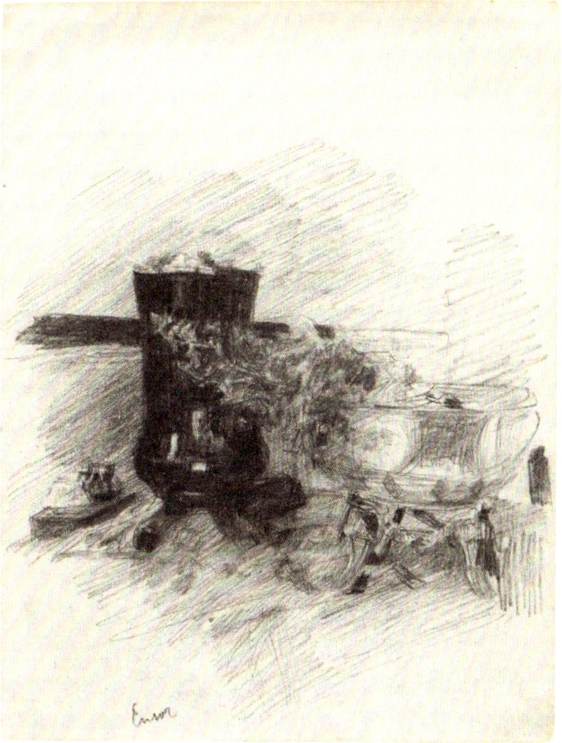

84

cat. 83 James Ensor, *Poker and Satchel (Tisonnier et gibecière)*, s.d., pencil and charcoal on paper, 22 × 17 cm. Musée des Beaux-Arts, Tournai, inv. d 0924.

cat. 84 James Ensor, *Study of Objects: Vase and Flowers (Étude d'objets: vase et fleurs)*, s.d., pencil and charcoal on paper, 22 × 17 cm. Musée des Beaux-Arts, Tournai, inv. d 0931.

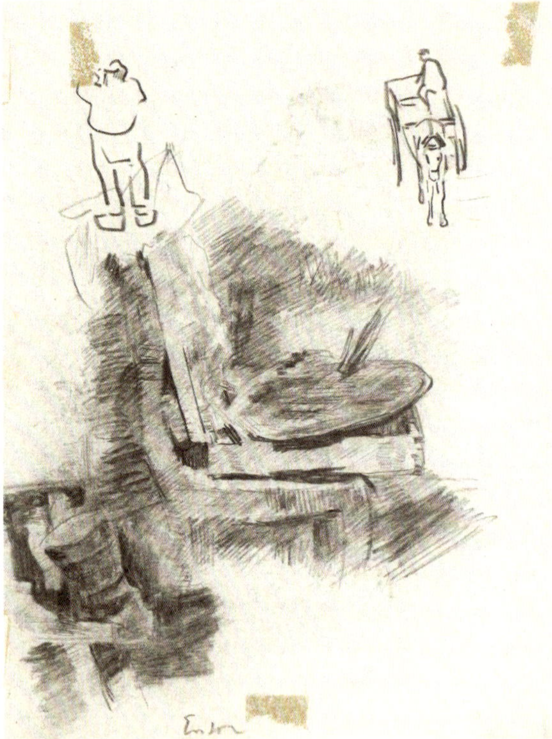

85

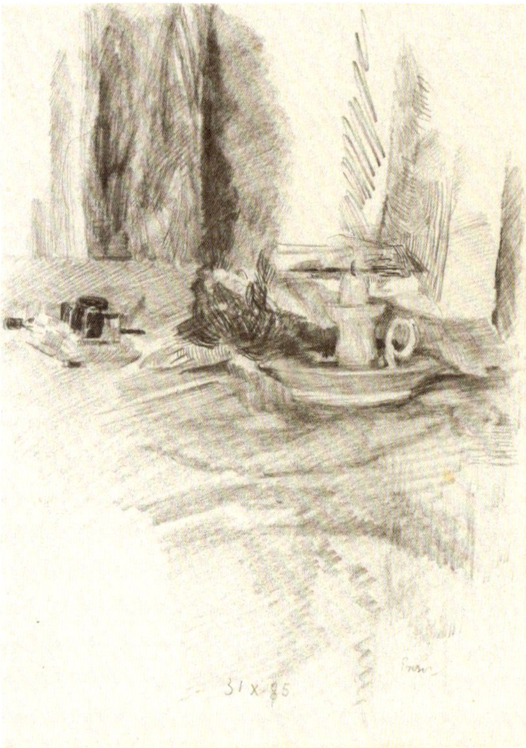

86

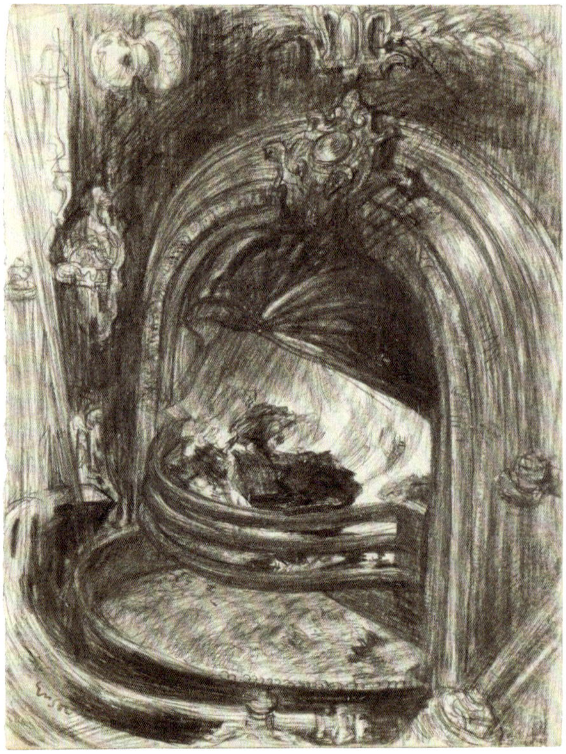

87

cat. 85 James Ensor, *Silhouettes and Palette (Silhouettes et palette de peintre)*, s.d., pencil and charcoal on paper, 22 × 17 cm. Musée des Beaux-Arts, Tournai, inv. d 0936.

cat. 86 James Ensor, *Ink Pots (Encriers)*, s.d., pencil and charcoal on paper, 22 × 17 cm. Musée des Beaux-Arts, Tournai, inv. d 0942.

cat. 87 James Ensor, *Wood Stove (Poêle à bois)*, s.d., pencil and charcoal on paper, 22 × 17 cm. Musée des Beaux-Arts, Tournai, inv. d 0951.

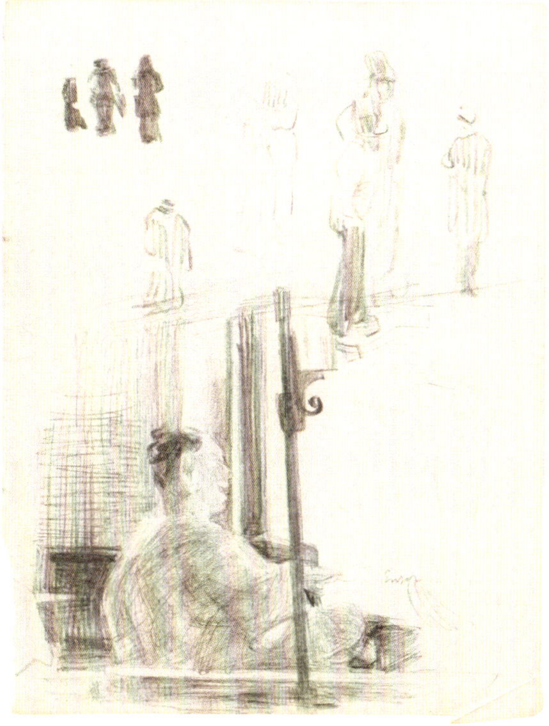

88

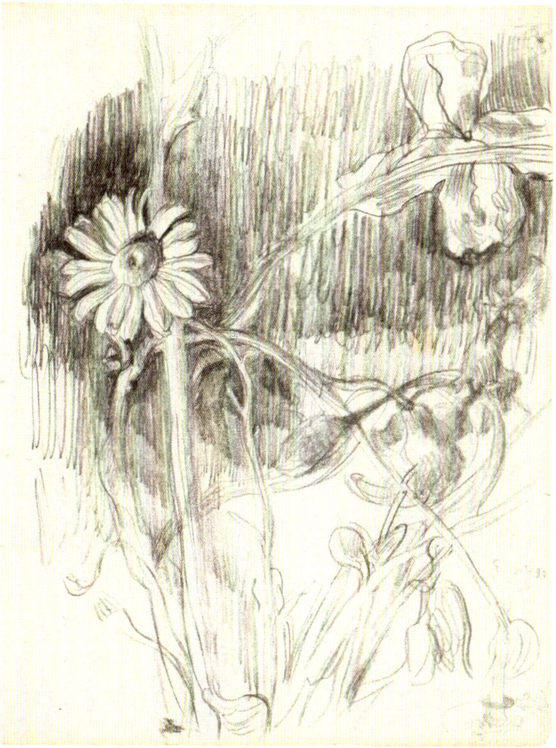

89

cat. 88 James Ensor, *Chinese Figurine (Statuette chinoise)*, s.d., pencil and charcoal on paper, 22 × 17 cm. Musée des Beaux-Arts, Tournai, inv. d 0954.

cat. 89 James Ensor, *Study of Flowers (Étude de fleurs)*, s.d., pencil and charcoal on paper, 22 × 17 cm. Musée des Beaux-Arts, Tournai, inv. d 0956.

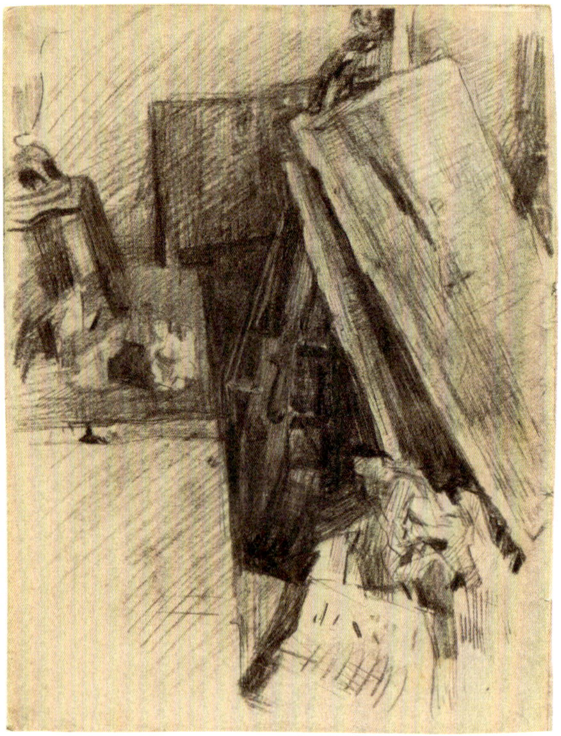

90

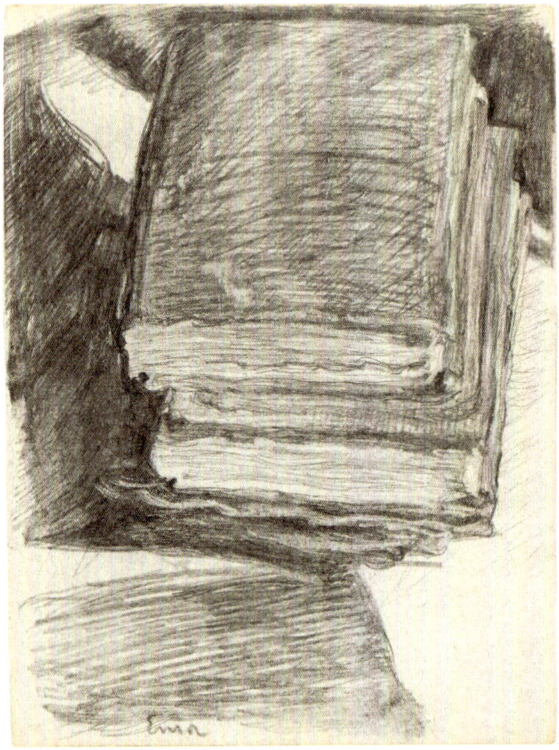

91

cat. 90 James Ensor, *Violin and Books (Violon et livres)*, s.d., pencil and charcoal on paper, 22 × 17 cm. Musée des Beaux-Arts, Tournai, inv. d 0960.

cat. 91 James Ensor, *Books (Livres)*, s.d., pencil and charcoal on paper, 22 × 17 cm. Musée des Beaux-Arts, Tournai, inv. d 0965.

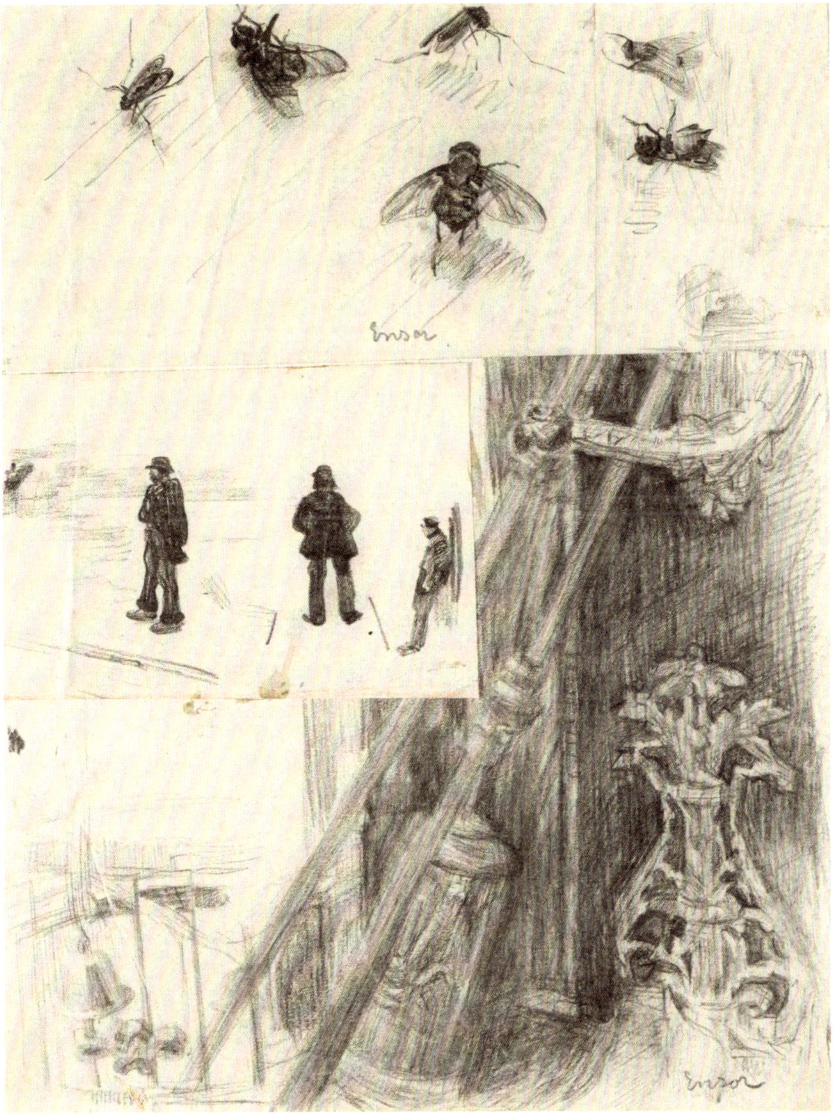

92

cat. 92 James Ensor, *Flies, Silhouettes and Assorted Objects (Mouches, silhouettes et objets divers)*, s.d., pencil and charcoal on paper, 22 × 17 cm. Musée des Beaux-Arts, Tournai, inv. d 0961.

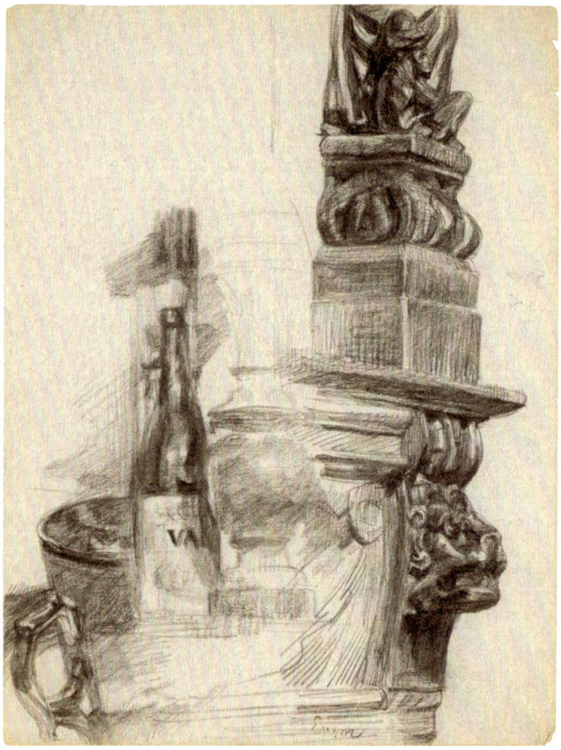

93

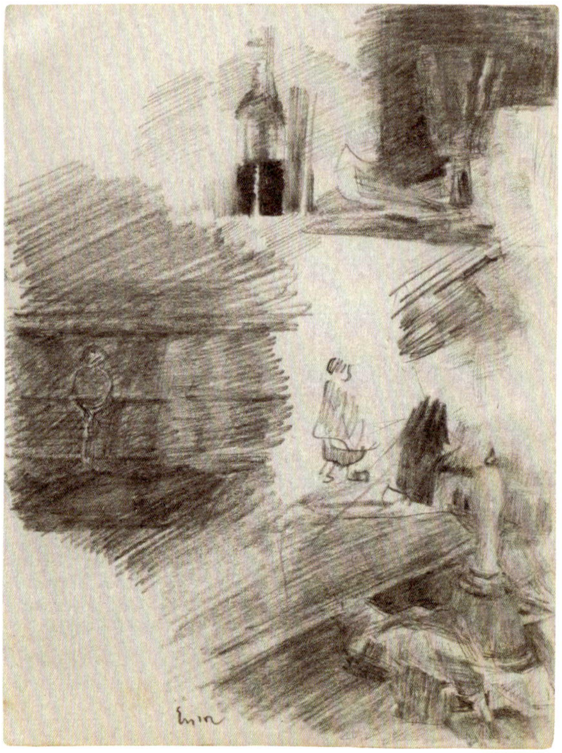

94

cat. 93 James Ensor, *Bottle and Decorative Elements (Bouteille et éléments décoratifs)*, s.d., pencil and charcoal on paper, 22 × 17 cm. Musée des Beaux-Arts, Tournai, inv. d 0967.
cat. 94 James Ensor, *Study of Objects and Silhouette (Étude d'objets et silhouette)*, s.d., pencil and charcoal on paper, 22 × 17 cm. Musée des Beaux-Arts, Tournai, inv. d 0968.

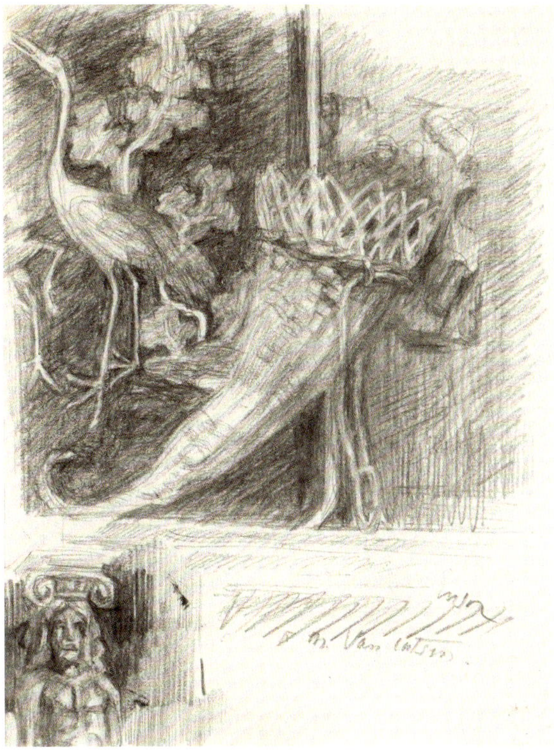

95

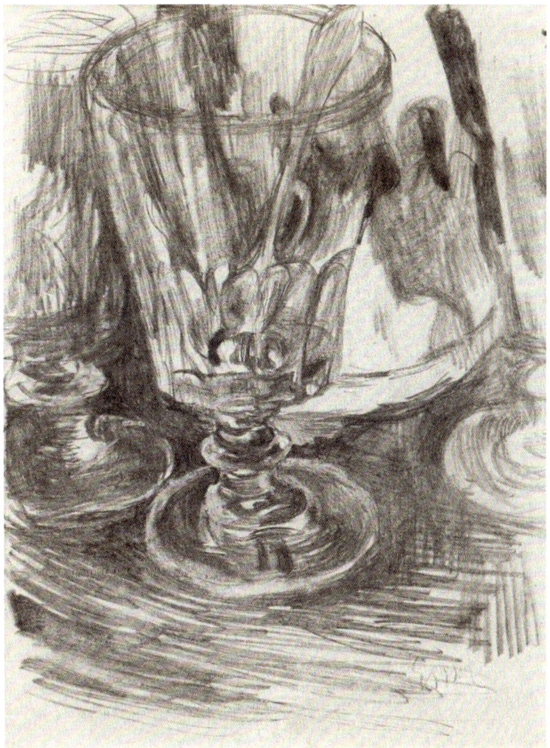

96

cat. 95 James Ensor, *Crane and Horn (Grue et corne)*, s.d., pencil and charcoal on paper, 22 × 17 cm. Musée des Beaux-Arts, Tournai, inv. d 0969.
cat. 96 James Ensor, *Wine Glass and Spoon (Verre à pied et cuillère)*, s.d., pencil and charcoal on paper, 22 × 17 cm. Musée des Beaux-Arts, Tournai, inv. d 0971.

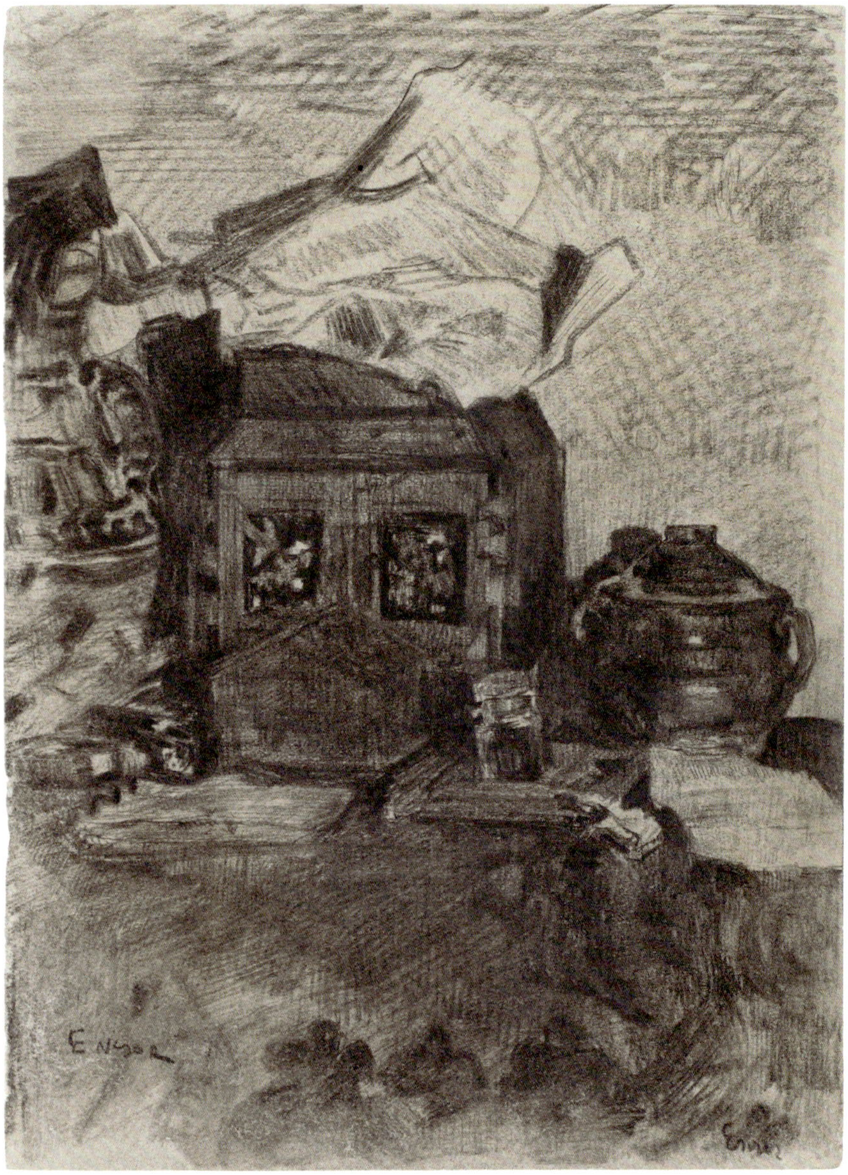

97

cat. 97 James Ensor, *The Japanese Cabinet (Le cabinet japonais)*, 1880–83, black chalk on paper, 22.5 × 16.6 cm. Dr and Mrs Rongé-Tops.

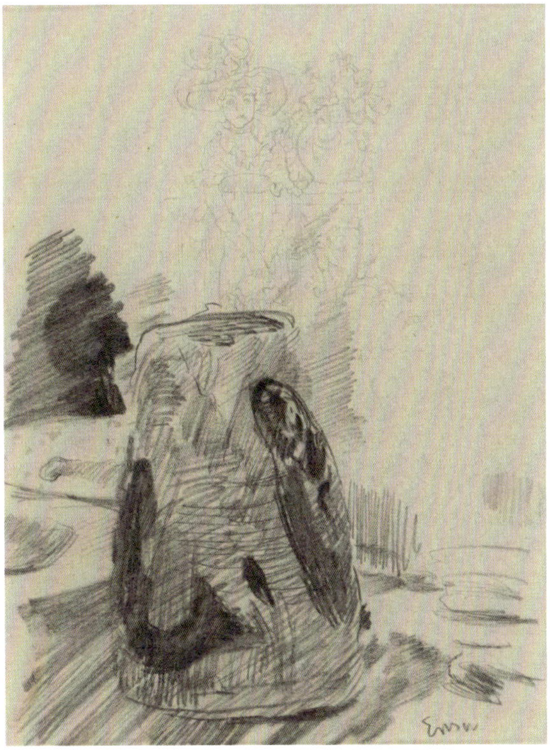

98

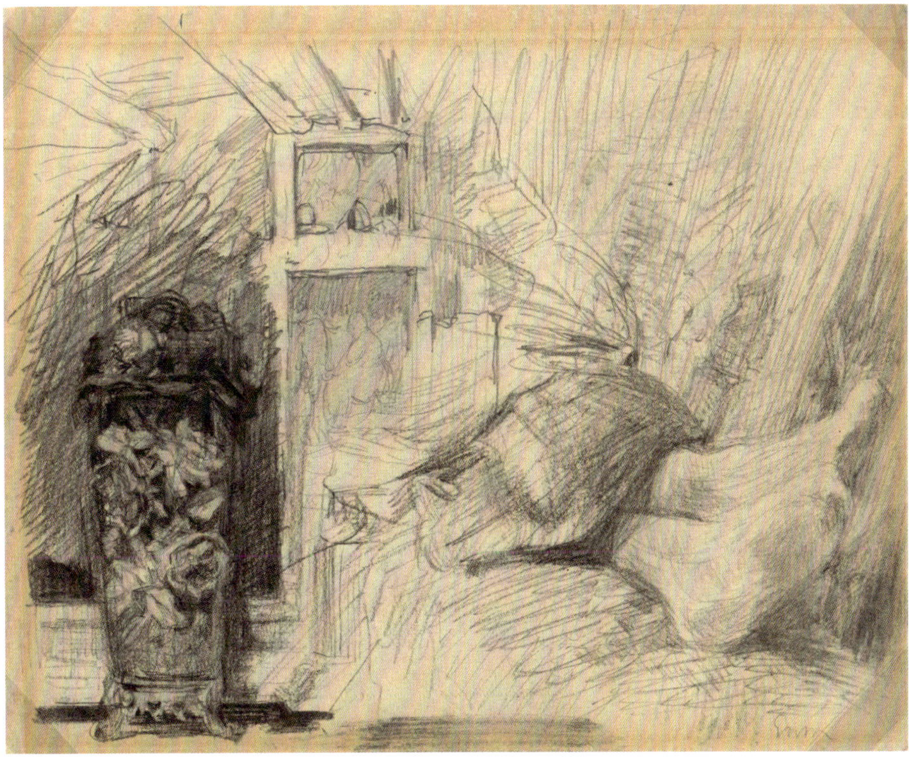

99

cat. 98 James Ensor, *Vase with Fish Motif and Woman with Vase of Flowers (Vase avec motif de pêche et femme avec vase de fleurs)*, 1880–85, pencil on paper, 21.5 × 16 cm. Mu.ZEE, City of Ostend Collection, inv. SM000329.
cat. 99 James Ensor, *Vase and Feet (Vase et pieds)*, 1880–85, pencil and charcoal on paper, 21.8 × 27.2 cm. Mu.ZEE, City of Ostend Collection, inv. SM000710a.

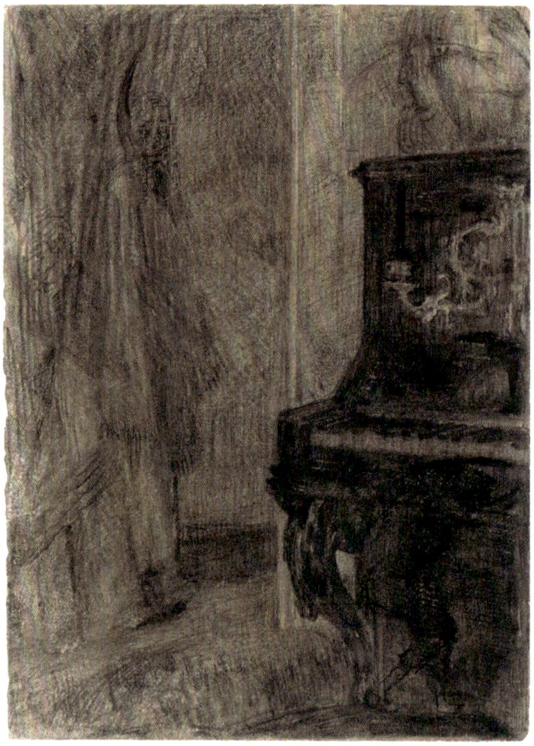

100

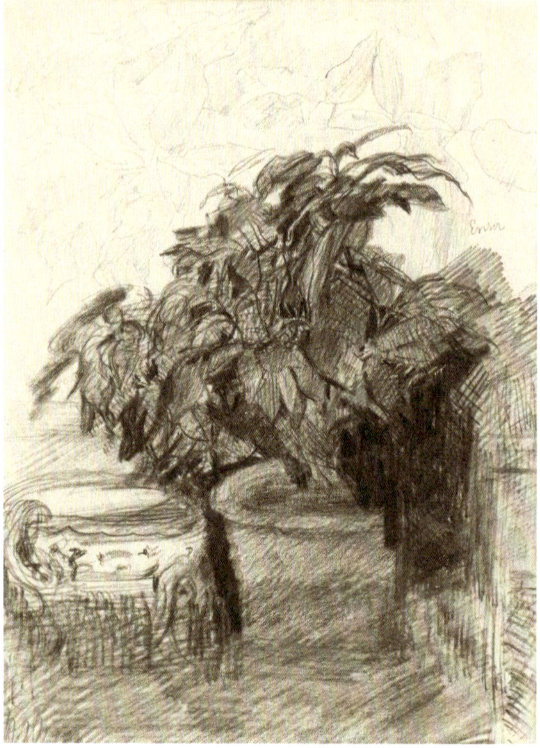

101

cat. 100 James Ensor, *The Upright Piano (Le piano droit)*, 1882, 1886–8, black chalk on paper, 22.5 × 16.5 cm. Royal Museum of Fine Arts, Antwerp, inv. 3383.

cat. 101 James Ensor, *Plant (Plante)*, 1883, pencil and charcoal on paper, 22 × 17 cm. Musée des Beaux-Arts, Tournai, inv. d 0941.

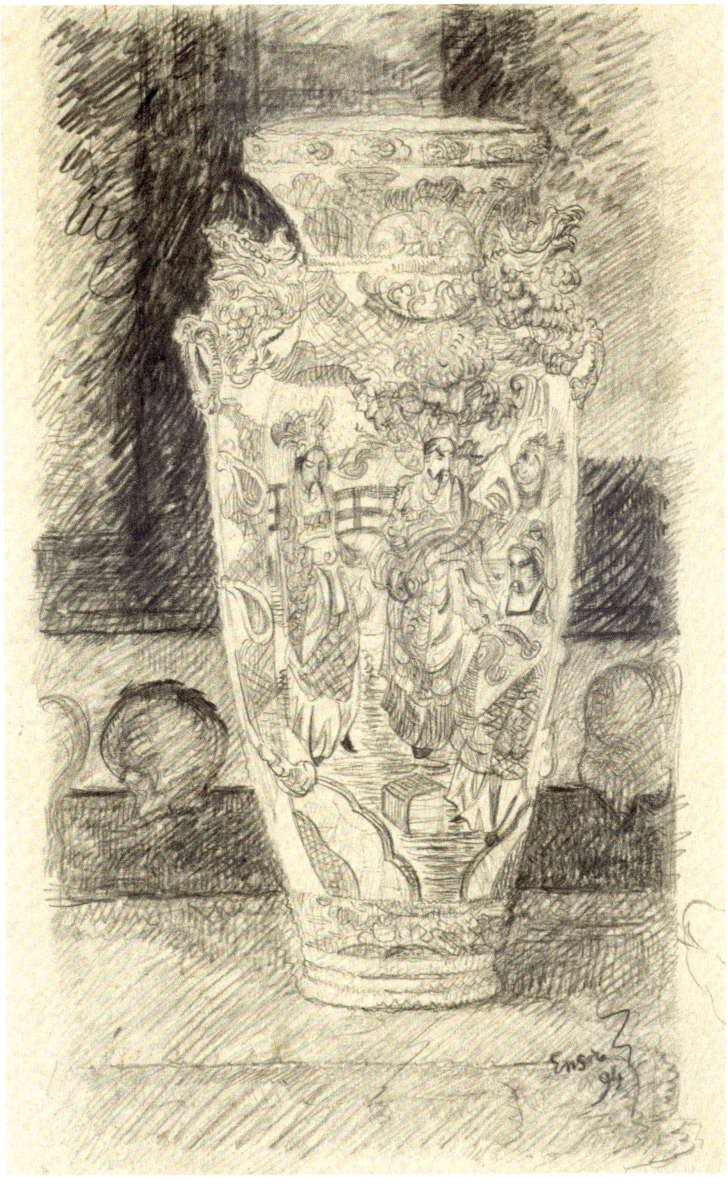

102

cat. 102 James Ensor, *Chinese Vase (Vase chinois)*, 1894, pencil and charcoal on paper, 23.5 × 15 cm. Musée des Beaux-Arts, Tournai, inv. d 0959.

Catalogue

Forerunners, Contemporaries and Modernists

Stefan Huygebaert

DAVID ÉMILE JOSEPH DE NOTER
(Ghent, 24 June 1818–Algiers, 21 January 1892)

David Émile Joseph De Noter was tutored by his father Jean Baptiste De Noter (1786–1855), a painter and copyist with an interest in archaeology. David left Ghent for Brussels and Paris, spending the final years of his life working in Algeria. Aside from the vistas that he produced there, his oeuvre consists almost entirely of interiors and still lifes. The interiors are often situated in the sixteenth or seventeenth century, following the examples of Ferdinand De Braekeleer the Elder (1792–1883) and his pupil Henri Leys (1815–1869). In certain instances, Leys and De Noter would assist each other with their works: adding figures and still lifes, respectively, which resulted in paintings with dual authorship. In his interiors, De Noter composes ensembles of a variety of objects, often with a female figure in the background, at times somewhat shrouded in the gloom and set off against an illuminating white tablecloth. Other works involve heaps of food displayed in a kitchen, sometimes in a hyperbolic pyramidal construction, and usually in chiaroscuro under direct light. When he presents a still life somewhat more in isolation, such as against a grimy wall, De Noter also focuses on depicting the supporting surface: marble tabletops, stone floors, wooden planks. Many of these elements coalesce in *Frans Snijders' Studio*. The painter Frans Snijders (1579–1657), a specialist at the type of sumptuous still life that De Noter produced, momentarily turns away from an excessively large heap of game, poultry and vegetables in chiaroscuro; the incidental light from the window also causes the dress of the woman next to the artist to become illuminated. De Noter's own unusually large painting is, if possible, even more enormous in scale than the bravura work that he is having Snijders commit to canvas.

Exhibited Work

cat. 2 David Émile Joseph De Noter, *Frans Snijders' Studio*, 1857, oil on canvas, 148 × 201 cm. Museum Hof van Busleyden, Mechelen, inv. S0021. (p. 17)

Bibliography

— Flippo 1981.
— Baetens 2020, p. 1.

FRANÇOIS HUYGENS
(Brussels, 9 April 1820–Kortenberg, 18 October 1905)

François Huygens studied at the Brussels Academy and became friends with Louis Dubois, who created a bust of him in 1870. His oeuvre is similar to that of Jean-Baptiste Robie: glossily painted still lifes of flowers, hunting motifs and shiny accessories. Revealingly, when advanced in age, Huygens was described as such in the newspaper *Le Vingtième Siècle* in response to an exhibition at the Galerie Royale: 'A "still lifer", François Huygens, a genuine and adjudicated talent; his flowers and fruit fall within traditional taste.'[1] His *Hawthorn Bouquet* of 1875 has a similar companion piece at M – Museum Leuven, one produced in the same year: in both cases, the symmetry of the bouquet is disrupted by a carelessly laid tablecloth and an ornately crafted goblet, all of which have been composed against an interior with a wall decoration.

Exhibited Work

cat. 103 François Huygens, *Hawthorn Bouquet*, 1875, oil on canvas, 131.5 × 95.5 cm. Royal Museums of Fine Arts of Belgium, Brussels, inv. 2743.

Bibliography

— S., 'Beaux-Arts', *Le Vingtième Siècle*, 29 November 1903, p. 2.
— de Mont 1921, p. 137.
— Flippo 1981.

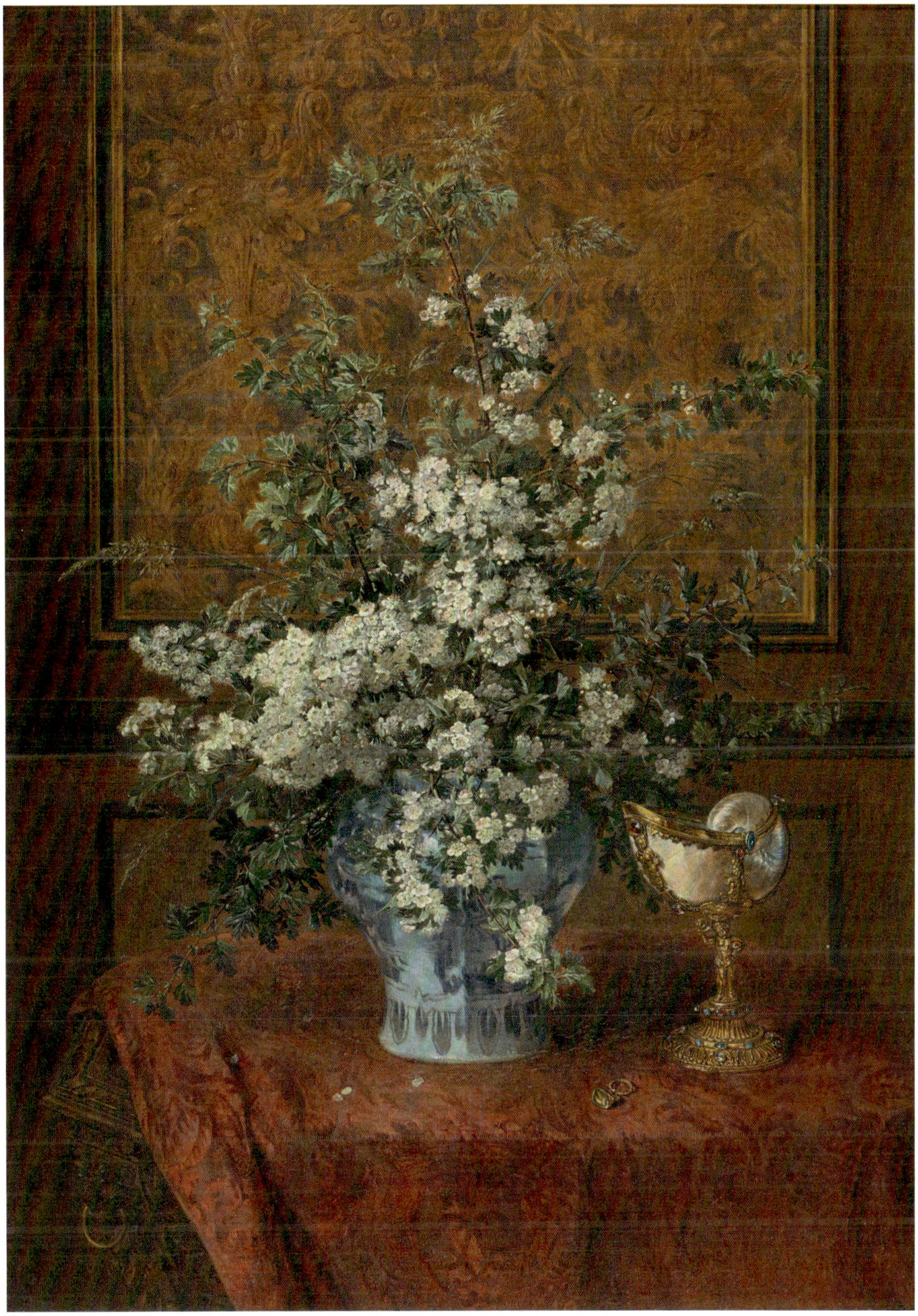

103

JEAN-BAPTISTE ROBIE
(Brussels, 19 November 1821–Brussels, 8 December 1910)

From a modest background, Jean-Baptiste Robie attended the Academy for Fine Arts in his native Brussels in 1841. There, he soon attracted notice for his floral works, after having been previously engaged in painting figurines of Napoleon for the tourist trade to earn a crust, a fact he freely imparted in his autobiography *Les débuts d'un peintre* of 1886. Robie also wrote about the many trips he embarked upon – to the Mediterranean, Great Britain and India. In his garden in Saint-Gilles, it is said he grew and tended to flowers with as much love and care as he did when committing them to canvas. Indeed, as a painter, Robie was enraptured by flowers and fruits; for that reason, he was at times associated with the French painter Simon Saint-Jean, who acquired fame with a similar oeuvre. As the critic Edmond-Louis de Taeye wrote in 1894, the qualities of Robie's works, which in terms of intellect and content have little substance, lie chiefly in the eye-catching nature of his technique, involving a delicate application and a successful composition of well-chosen and well-grouped accessories taking after the example of seventeenth-century tradition. Art movements came and went, but Robie continued to paint still lifes unaffected. According to De Taeye, the titles or listings of Robie's works were superfluous: 'It suffices to note that each of these three words, *Flowers*, *Fruit* and *Accessories*, constitutes in turn the label required to catalogue the master's paintings.'[2] Much of his oeuvre is encapsulated in the gigantic work *Kitchen Interior* of 1855, which contains simultaneously a vegetable still life, a sumptuous still life of glass-ware and silverware, a fish still life and a hunting still life.

Exhibited Works
cat. 104 Jean-Baptiste Robie, *Still Life with Game, Flowers and Fruits*, 1853, oil on canvas, 160.6 × 125.2 cm. Museum of Fine Arts, Ghent, inv. 1853-E.
cat. 1 Jean-Baptiste Robie, *Kitchen Interior*, 1855, oil on canvas, 160 × 208 cm. Palais des Beaux-Arts de Lille, inv. P 711. (p. 16)
cat. 105 Jean-Baptiste Robie, *Flowers, Fruits and Accessories*, 1875, oil on panel, 71 × 56.5 cm. Royal Museums of Fine Arts of Belgium, Brussels, inv. 2700.
cat. 106 Jean-Baptiste Robie, *Autumn Roses*, 1901, oil on panel, 104 × 125.5 cm. Royal Museums of Fine Arts of Belgium, Brussels, inv. 3604.

Bibliography

— Robie 1886.
— De Taeye 1894, pp. 171–83.
— Dujardin 1896, pp. 163–7.
— Vandevivere 1965, pp. 626–7.
— Schuermans 2007.

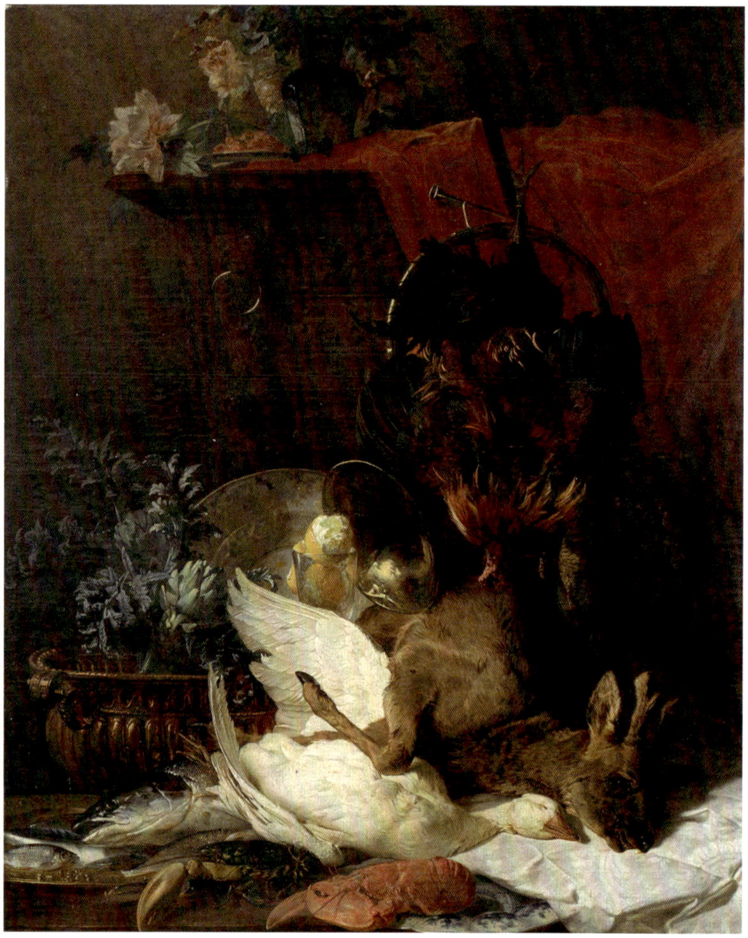

104

VIRGINIE DE SARTORIUS
(Liège, 1 August 1828–Liège, 26 April 1908)

Little is known about the floral artist Virginie de Sartorius from Liège. Born a deaf-mute to a well-to-do, high-born family, she was a pupil under Julie Van Marcke-Robert (1800–1875), a painter of flowers and fruit from Liège. This is also the genre – floral and fruit still lifes – that De Sartorius practised throughout her life and for which she won recognition. A reviewer wrote as early as 1855: 'Miss Virginie de Sartorius has painted fruit. It makes the mouth water; one might truly say that this young lady uses fruit to paint.'[3] In 1851, she rendered a composition of fruit and flowers with the bust of the then recently deceased Louise-Marie of Orléans, Queen consort of the Belgians, at its centre, with a view to the left giving on to the royal residence in Laeken. In other

105

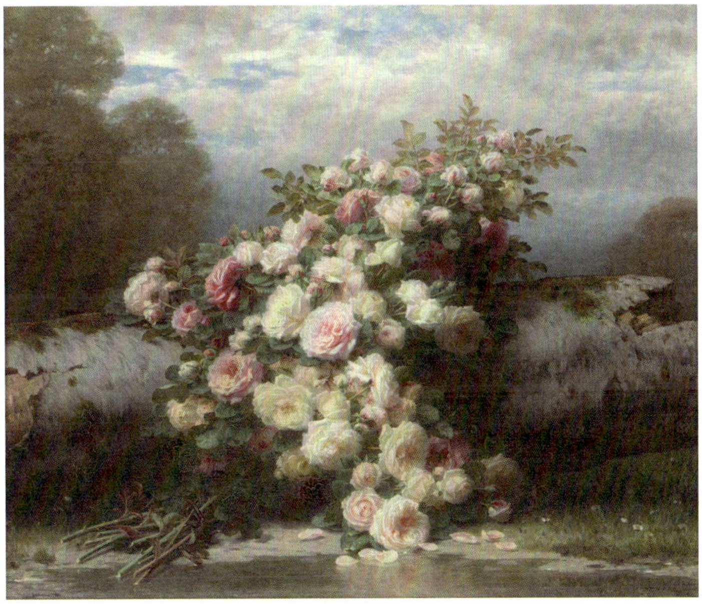

106

words, the still life would seem to be a tribute to the first Queen (consort) of the Belgians. Whether there was a direct link, we do not know for sure, but in 1853, King Leopold I purchased some of the sketches exhibited by De Sartorius in Liège. The artist remained unmarried and childless, exhibiting her work regularly at art and horticultural exhibitions both in Belgium and abroad. Just as with Augustine Vervloet and Van Marcke-Robert, the press was positive about her seventeenth-century-style still lifes. In 1861, she and Henriette Ronner-Knip (1821–1909) were awarded a second-class medal at the industrial exhibition in Metz. A year later, one of her works was purchased for the city museum of Spa, and in 1872, for the city museums of both Mons and Liège.

Exhibited Work

cat. 107 Virginie de Sartorius, *Still Life with Flowers and Bust of Louise-Marie of Orléans*, 1851, oil on canvas, 118.9 × 100.6 cm. Werner Wieland Collection.

Bibliography

— *L'Indépendance belge*, 15 September 1853, p. 2.
— Jules Lecomte, 'Exposition universelle de 1855: Beaux-Arts', *L'Indépendance belge*, 19 July 1855, pp. 1–2.
— Heuschling 1863.
— 'Décès', *La Meuse*, 27 April 1908, p. 3.
— Creusen 2007, pp. 24, 92, 107.

LOUIS DUBOIS

(Brussels, 23 December 1830–Schaerbeek, 28 April 1880)

Louis Dubois studied at the École Saint-Luc in Brussels and continued his training in Paris, where he painted under the auspices of Thomas Couture, who was also tutor to Édouard Manet, two years Dubois's junior. While in Paris, Dubois also met Gustave Courbet, whose principles in respect to realism he defended in written submissions to the Brussels magazine *L'Art libre*, the mouthpiece of the groundbreaking Société Libre des Beaux-Arts, the first avant-garde artist association in Belgium. Dubois was a founding member of the association alongside the likes of Félicien Rops (1833–1898), Isidore Verheyden and Constantin Meunier (1831–1905). In the famous group portrait kept at the Royal Museums of Fine Arts of Belgium, Dubois rests his hand on a copy of *L'Art libre*. Using his personalised palette, Dubois put into practice his written critiques of the grand historical themes employed by the preceding generation of artists, creating naturalistic and occasionally enigmatic landscapes and animal paintings. It was largely because of his palette that critics such as Camille Lemonnier linked him to the Baroque school of Jordaens. The grand scale of Dubois's paintings – including his still lifes – is also in line with that view. In one such image, a pickled herring has been wrapped in the conservative magazine *Journal des Beaux-Arts*, presided over by Adolphe Siret. Tellingly, Dubois commented, 'Paint a smoked herring or an emperor; it's all quite the same to me', as a result aligning himself with Courbet in opposition to the genre hierarchy.[4] His still lifes usually feature an impasto, creamy appearance and muted light effects. Alfred Verhaeren was among his pupils.

Exhibited Works

cat. 5 Louis Dubois, *The Woman with Bouquet*, *c.*1854–5, oil on canvas, 131 × 101 cm. Royal Museums of Fine Arts of Belgium, Brussels, inv. 4143. (p. 23)

cat. 4 Louis Dubois, *Still Life with Studio Paraphernalia*, *c.*1855, oil on canvas, 129.7 × 98.3 cm. Museum of Fine Arts, Ghent, inv. 1924-A. (p. 22)

cat. 6 Louis Dubois, *Fish and Accessories*, 1876, oil on canvas, 109 × 141 cm. Royal Museums of Fine Arts of Belgium, Brussels, inv. 2808. (p. 26)

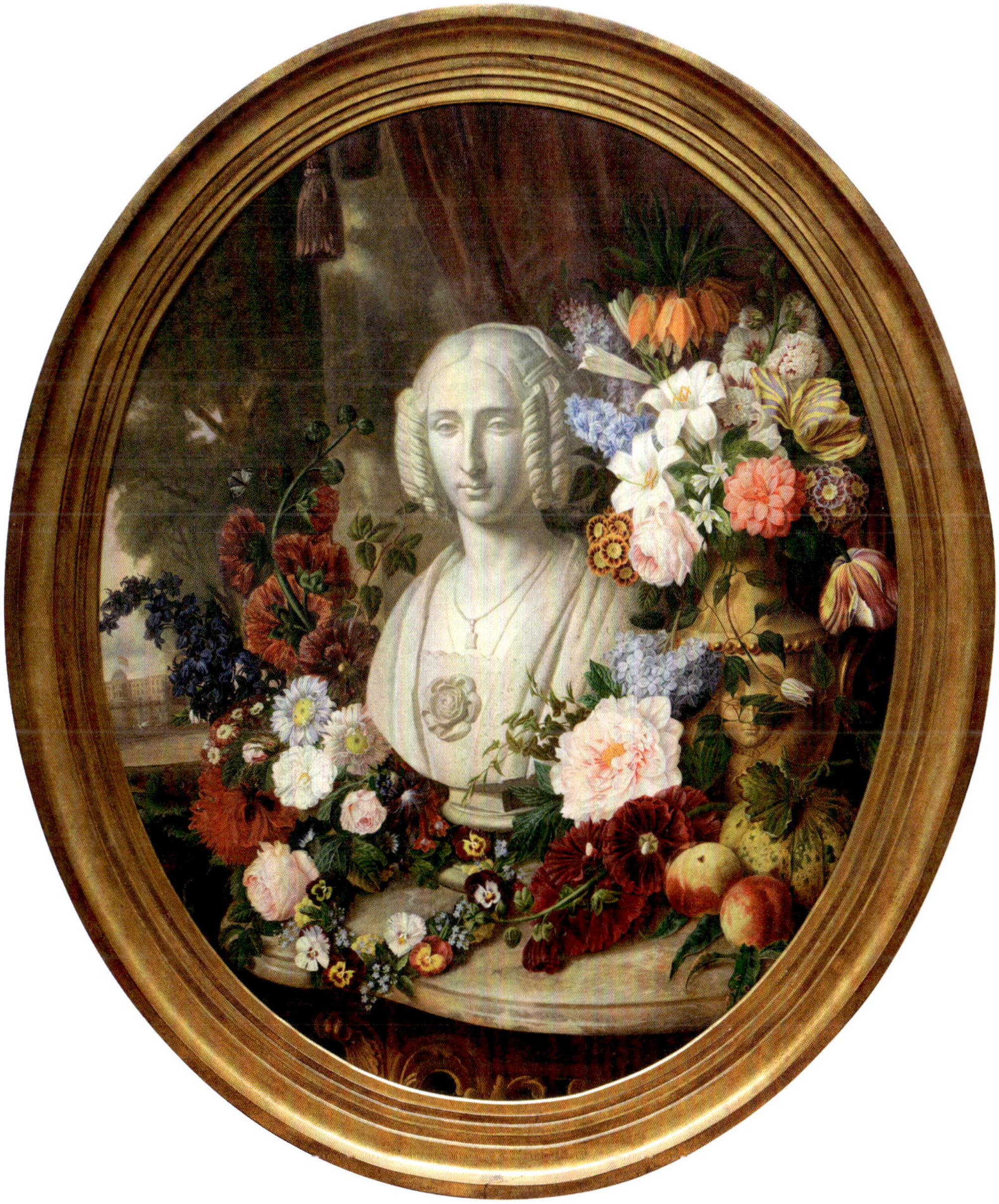

107

Bibliography
— Hout (Louis Dubois), 'Le peintre d'histoire: Étude d'après nature', *L'Art libre*, no. 4, 1 February 1872, pp. 49–51.
— Stévennart 1964, pp. 145–54.

HUBERT BELLIS
(Brussels, 6 January 1831–Schaerbeek, 16 April 1902)

Hubert Bellis studied at the academy of his native Brussels under François-Joseph Navez (1787–1869). In 1857, together with his brother Charles-Louis (1837–1901), he launched a decorative painting business, and later the painting school L'Effort, attended by such artists as Louis Thevenet, Jean Brusselmans and Rik Wouters. In October 1883, he embarked on a study trip to Amsterdam where he visited the Rijksmuseum with James Ensor and Guillaume Vogels (1836–1896) – the latter being employed at Bellis's business. Bellis was a member of the two prominent predecessors to Les XX in Brussels: L'Essor and La Chrysalide. He became known for his floral arrangements and still lifes, genres that compose his entire oeuvre. Contemporary critics referred to his still-life painting style as 'Flemish'. These works consist of picturesque, natural yet disorderly compositions painted with a swift hand and lacking in detail, resulting in a high turnover. In the obituary for this 'petit maître' (little master) of the 'petit genre' (little genre), *L'Indépendance belge* wrote tellingly: 'It is better to paint immortal oysters than to fail at heroic works of art.'[5] The newspaper was referring to the oysters so often seen in Bellis's (later) work, such as in *The Day after the Carnival*. In this suggestive, almost narrative, work, Bellis distanced himself from his own rather traditional still lifes.

Exhibited Works
cat. 108 Hubert Bellis, *Severed Fish Head and Shrimp next to a Tub*, s.d., oil on canvas, 45 × 65 cm. Barat-Venker Collection, The Netherlands.
cat. 7 Hubert Bellis, *Large Fish, Red Lobsters, Lemons, Red and White Wine Bottles*, s.d., oil on canvas, 65 × 120 cm. Barat-Venker Collection, The Netherlands. (p. 26)
cat. 109 Hubert Bellis, *Still Life with Mussels and Red Wine Glass*, s.d., oil on canvas, 21 × 36.6 cm. Barat-Venker Collection, The Netherlands.
cat. 110 Hubert Bellis, *Cutlet, Cauliflower and Endive*, s.d., oil on canvas, 38.5 × 50 cm. Barat-Venker Collection, The Netherlands.
cat. 8 Hubert Bellis, *Still Life with a Fish Head and Cleaver*, s.d., oil on canvas, 63 × 72 cm. Collection Simonis & Buunk Kunsthandel, Ede, The Netherlands. (p. 27)
cat. 111 Hubert Bellis, *Green and Yellow Pears*, s.d., oil on canvas, 36 × 45 cm. Barat-Venker Collection, The Netherlands.
cat. 112 Hubert Bellis, *Cinerarias and Azaleas in Flowerpots*, s.d., oil on canvas, 101 × 71 cm. Barat-Venker Collection, The Netherlands.
cat. 113 Hubert Bellis, *Dwarf Chrysanthemums in a Vase*, s.d., oil on canvas, 38.2 × 35 cm. Barat-Venker Collection, The Netherlands.
cat. 114 Hubert Bellis, *Rose Competition*, s.d., oil on canvas, 18 × 23.5 cm. Barat-Venker Collection, The Netherlands.
cat. 115 Hubert Bellis, *The Day after the Carnival*, s.d., oil on canvas, 100 × 150 cm. Collection M Leuven, inv. S/14/B.

Bibliography
— 'Mort du peintre Bellis', *Le Petit Bleu du Matin*, 17 April 1902, p. 1.
— 'Echos de la ville', *L'Indépendance belge*, 18 April 1902, p. 3.

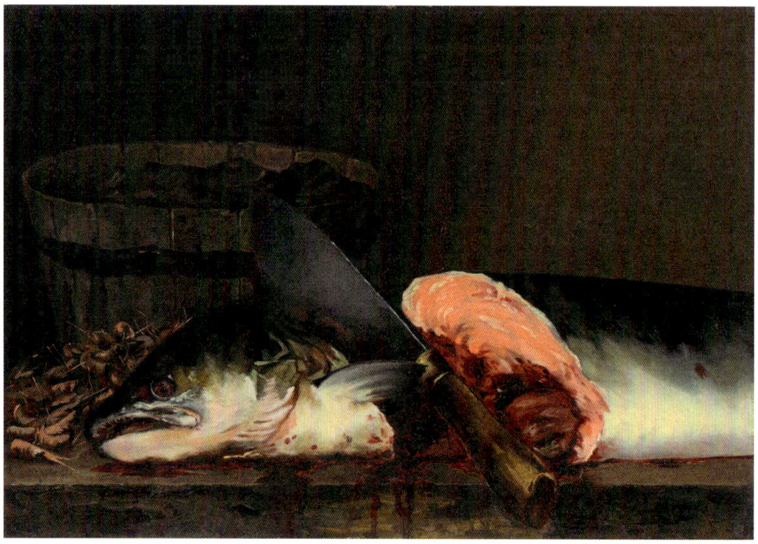

108

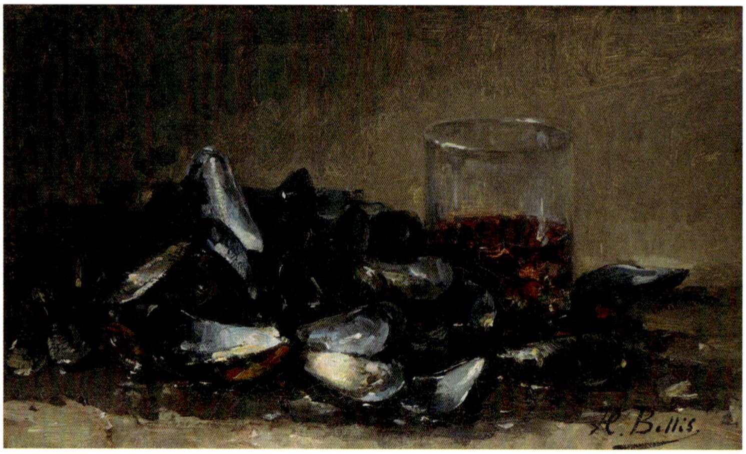

109

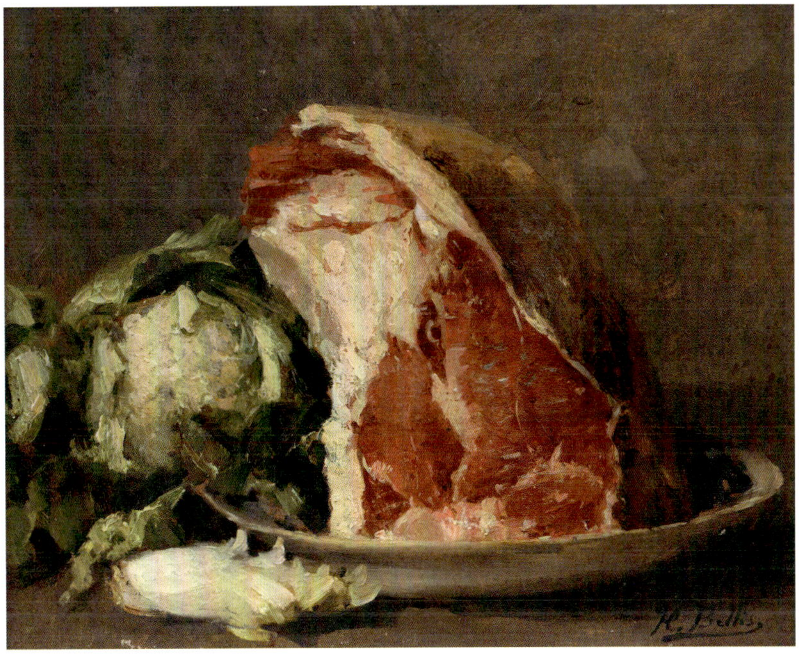

110

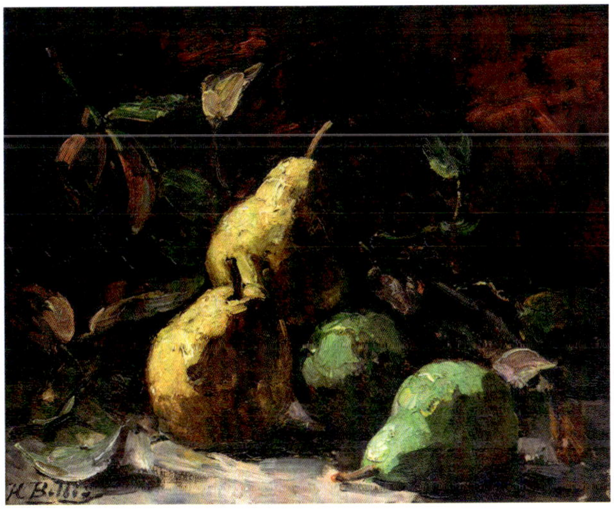

111

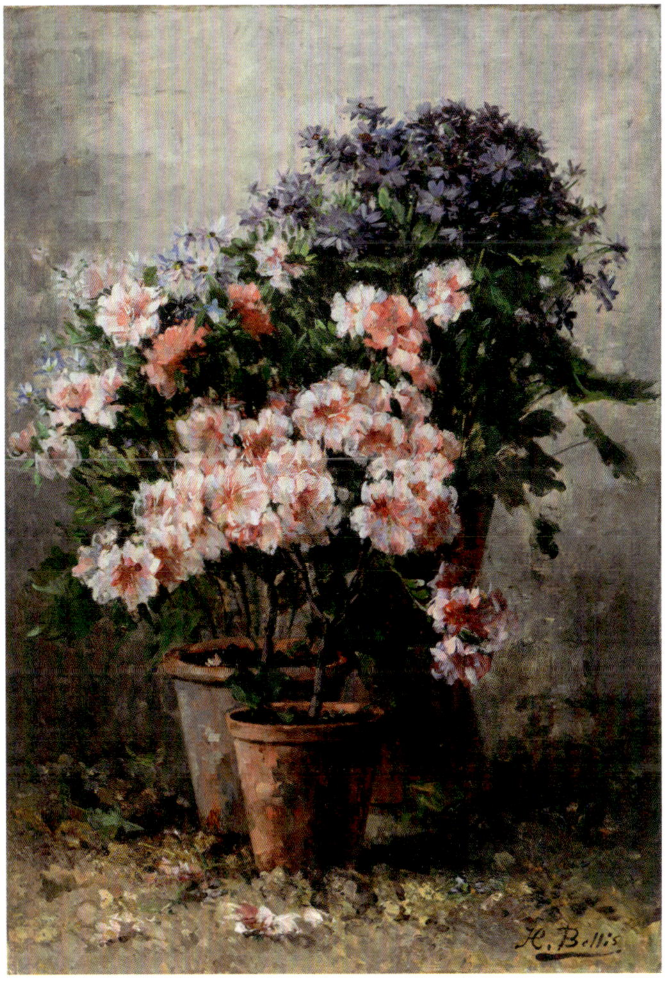

112

— Flippo 1981.
— Ostend 1994–5, pp. 37–9, 100.

HENRI DE BRAEKELEER
(Antwerp, 11 June 1840–Antwerp, 20 July 1888)

Henri De Braekeleer was the son of the romantic genre painter Ferdinand De Braekeleer the Elder (1792–1883). He painted genre works along with interiors and landscapes, but unlike his father, he did not historicise them in a faux sixteenth-century style. After taking classes from his father and at the Antwerp Academy, and thanks to his uncle Henri Leys (1815–1869), the young artist developed his own type of realism inspired by Dutch genre masters such as Pieter De Hooch (1629–1679) and Johannes Vermeer (1632–1675). He borrowed from them, among other elements, the vistas characteristic of his interiors. Owing to a contract with the Belgian art dealer Gustave Coûteaux (1815–1873) and the fact that De Braekeleer was a bachelor, he had financial security and artistic independence. Art historians would subsequently come to classify him as a pre-modernist, as with James Ensor. He ceased painting for a brief period between 1877 and 1883, probably as a result of depression. Afterwards, he embarked on a new, more productive period, exhibiting a freer, almost Impressionist style until his death in 1888. In that latter period, he chiefly produced still lifes in which the same objects would often appear, such as those from his antiquarian studio (including his own paintings). For example, the same lantern appears in *The Globe* and in *Old Trinkets*. The presence of textiles and the interplay of light and shade are characteristic of his work, particularly the golden sheen in his paintings of interiors and still lifes, which are overloaded with accessories. *Old Trinkets* is a fine example of one such chaotically crammed yet sumptuous still life.

Exhibited Works
cat. 10 Henri De Braekeleer, *Old Trinkets*, 1880–85, oil on canvas, 38 × 56 cm. Musée d'Orsay, Paris, inv. RF 1196. (p. 31)
cat. 116 Henri De Braekeleer, *Still Life*, 1881–5, oil on wood, 26.5 × 36.5 cm. Royal Museums of Fine Arts of Belgium, Brussels, inv. 4185.
cat. 117 Henri De Braekeleer, *Flowers*, 1883–7, oil on canvas, 36 × 30 cm. Royal Museums of Fine Arts of Belgium, Brussels, inv. 4077.
cat. 118 Henri De Braekeleer, *The Globe*, 1885–8, oil on canvas, 37 × 54 cm. Royal Museums of Fine Arts of Belgium, Brussels, inv. 7468.
cat. 9 Henri De Braekeleer, *Medlars*, *c.*1886, oil on canvas, 36.5 × 51 cm. Royal Museums of Fine Arts of Belgium, Brussels, inv. 3810. (p. 30)

Bibliography
— Verschaffel 1995, p. 45.
— Baetens 2010, pp. 25–41.
— Todts and Bollen 2019.

WILLEM LINNIG II
(Antwerp, 20 August 1842–Antwerp, 4 September 1890)

Willem Linnig was the son and pupil of Willem Linnig the Elder (1819–1885), an artist who worked in several genres, but who always placed his scenes in the sixteenth century, closely mimicking his tutor Henri Leys (1815–1869). Linnig the Younger studied at the Antwerp Academy. He, too, focused on interiors, genre and history scenes, townscapes and still lifes, but, unlike his father, he would sometimes place them in his own era, albeit incorporating the stylistic and compositional features of Leys's realism. Linnig pursued his career in Germany, where he taught classes at the Weimar art school between 1876 and 1882. In the period that followed, he took his

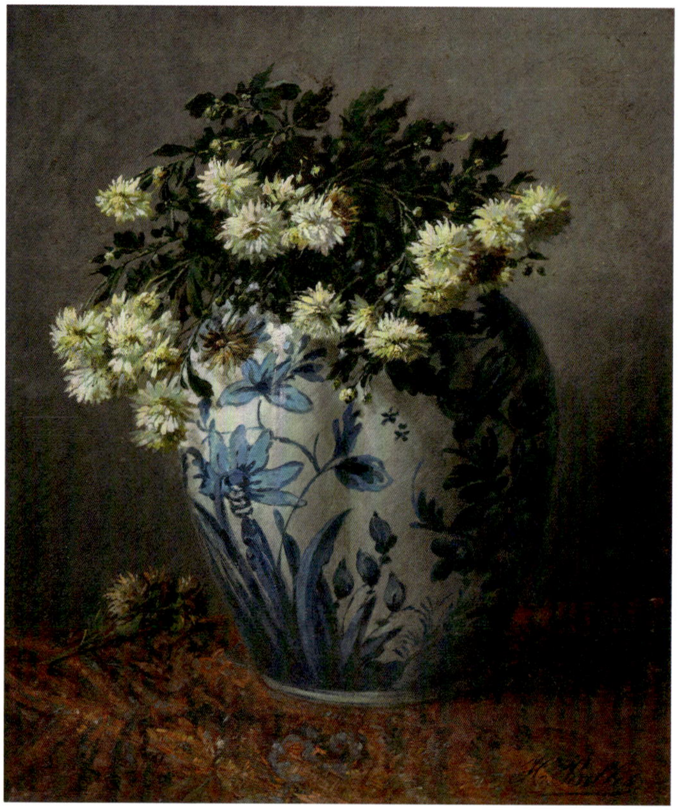

113

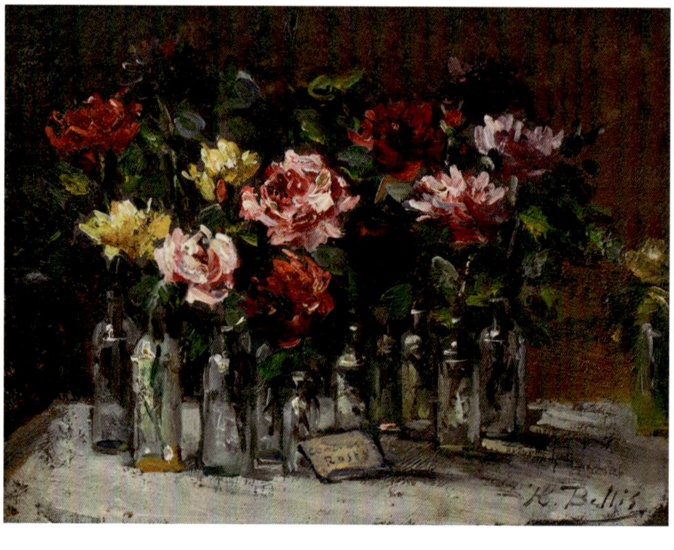

114

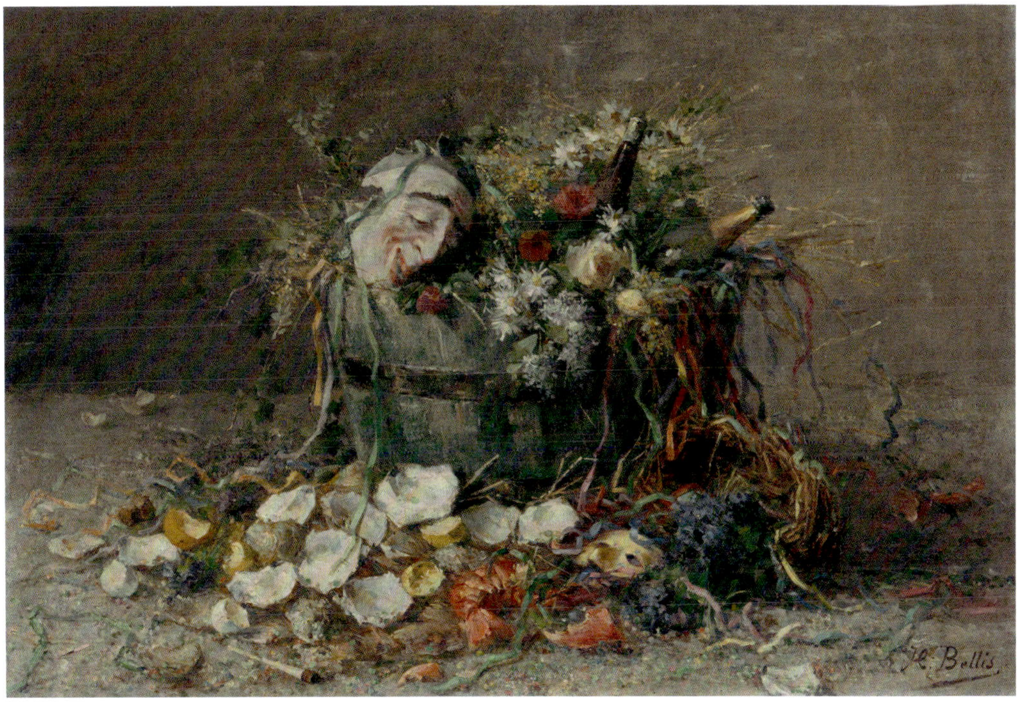

115

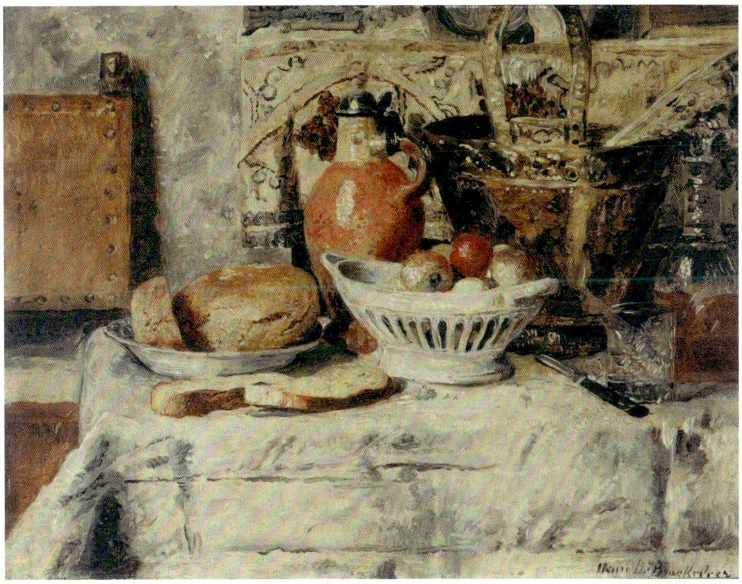

116

inspiration from the historical and literary tableaux of eighteenth-century French masters. His colourful still lifes of pastries and vegetables are characterised by their subtly sketched contour lines. *After the Wedding* is expressive in its suggestion of what preceded the wedding feast; the anecdotal details, such as the many empty bottles, discarded items of clothing and nibbling mice, are balanced by the work's lean composition using horizontal lines and brush-strokes. Those horizontals return in *Vegetables*, in which the contour lines are less evident and the various vegetables fill virtually the whole canvas with alternating areas of colour. In 1907, Belgian author and critic Paul André described Linnig's still lifes as 'celebrations of colour, outbursts of bountiful, succulent, ardent and yet fine and precise notations of everything that life and health can comprise and express, possess and reveal, and – let us simply come out with it – the poetry in seemingly inert or even vulgar objects'.[6]

Exhibited Works

cat. 119 Willem Linnig II, *After the Wedding*, 1875, oil on panel, 72 × 115 cm. Royal Museum of Fine Arts, Antwerp, inv. 2528.

cat. 120 Willem Linnig II, *Vegetables*, 1886, oil on canvas, 83 × 112 cm. Royal Museum of Fine Arts, Antwerp, inv. 2371.

Bibliography

— André 1907.
— Antwerp 1985, pp. 235–9, 252, 263.
— Antwerp 1991.

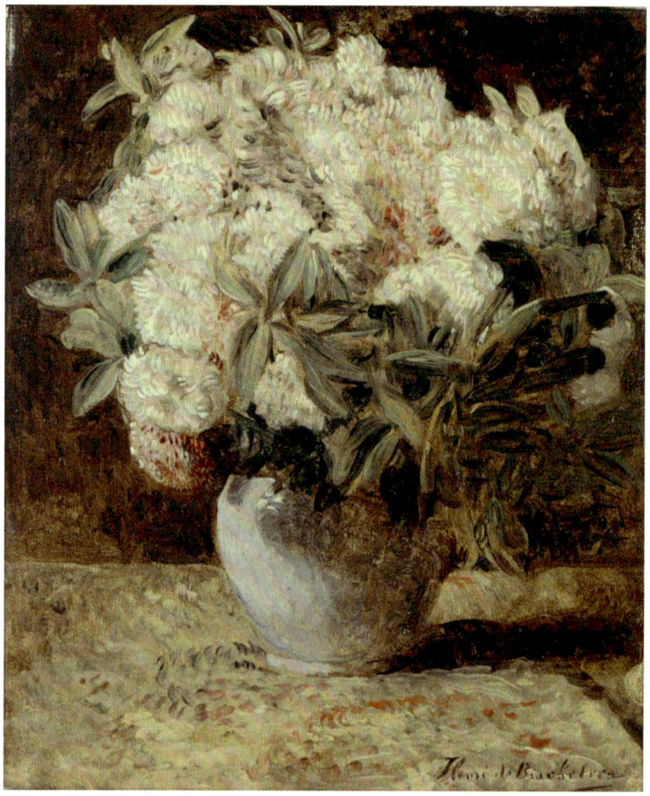

117

ISIDORE VERHEYDEN
(Antwerp, 24 January 1846–Ixelles, 1 November 1905)

Isidore Verheyden was taught by his father, Jean-François Verheyden (1806–1889), and, like Alfred Verhaeren and many others, was actively engaged at Jean-François Portaels's studio. Verheyden gained a reputation with views of the Sonian Forest, which he discovered when in Hoeilaart around 1880. His greyish landscapes painted in the open air were also appreciated by the critic Octave Maus. In the early years of the groundbreaking artist association Les XX, which Maus had founded in Brussels, Verheyden was one of its more conservative members, but he left the group in 1885 on amicable terms. He concentrated on landscapes in the Campine and Brabant regions. For some ten years, Verheyden painted with Anna Boch, who was seen as his apprentice, adopting his grey painting style in the period of 1877 to 1885. Verheyden was an accomplished portraitist, as is borne out by several handsome depictions of friends such as Constantin Meunier (1831–1905), Camille Lemonnier and Boch. Sporadically, he painted still lifes and floral arrangements, particularly in the 1870s. The traditional dark background, the muted, autumnal colour palette and the indeterminate space are reminiscent of seventeenth-century prototypes. In that same fashion, in many of his floral paintings, the transparent vases with their delicate white contours and colourful bouquets are set off against the black backdrops. *The Breakfast*, a late work, is enlivened by a young girl with a cup of tea seated at the corner of a table with lustrous objects and a floral arrangement.

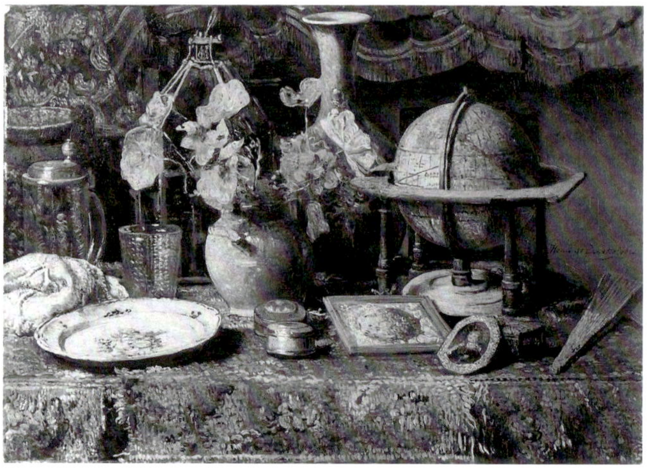

118

Exhibited Works

cat. 121 Isidore Verheyden, *Violets and Wallflowers in a Porcelain Jug*, 1873, oil on panel, 24.5 × 19 cm. Barat-Venker Collection, The Netherlands.

cat. 122 Isidore Verheyden, *The Breakfast*, *c.*1905, oil on canvas, 101.5 × 127 cm. Royal Museums of Fine Arts of Belgium, Brussels, inv. 3892.

Bibliography

— Solvay 1936–8, pp. 638–41.
— Ghent 1980, p. 175.

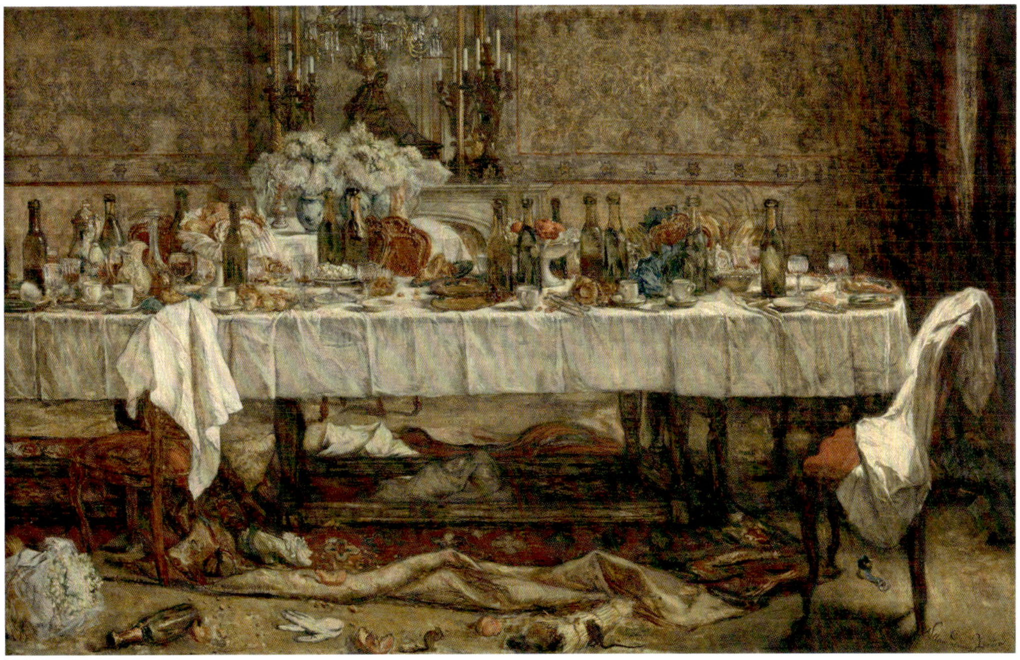

119

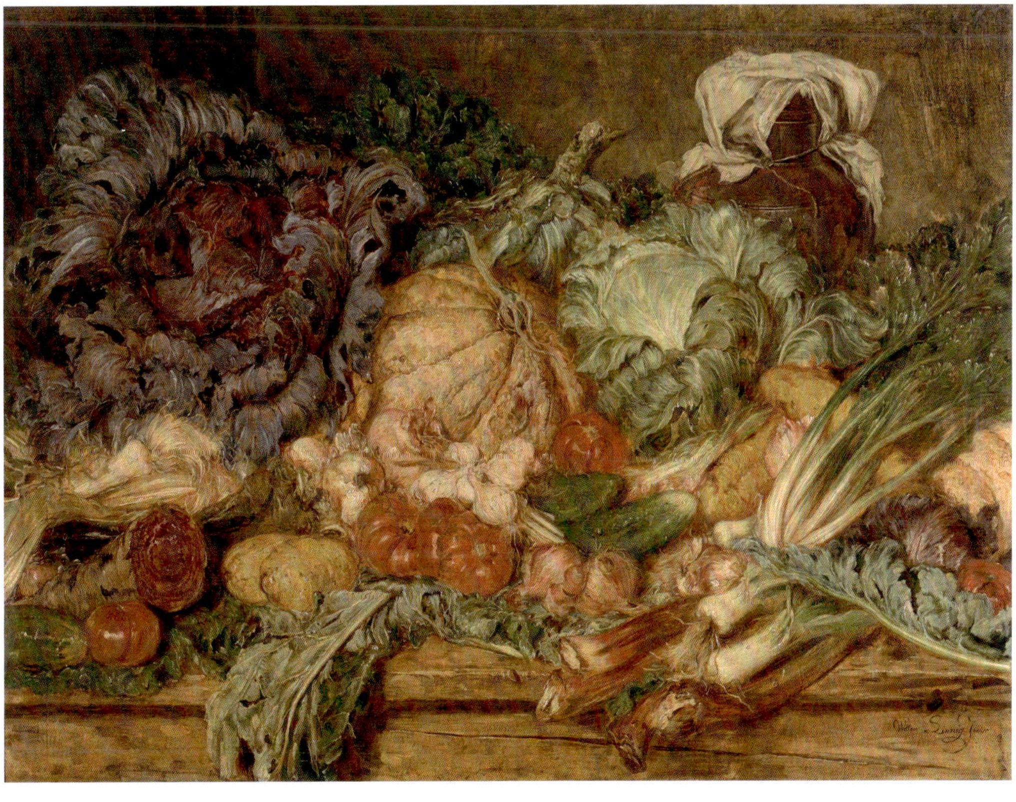

120

ANNA BOCH
(Saint-Vaast, 10 February 1848–Ixelles, 23 February 1936)

Anna Boch was the eldest daughter in a wealthy family of ceramic industrialists in Saint-Vaast near La Louvière. Following Boch's brief and fairly uninspiring tutelage under Pierre-Louis Kuhnen (1812–1877) and Euphrosine Beernaert (1831–1901), Isidore Verheyden took her in tow as a painting companion, and they worked together on the Belgian coast in the open air. The first images to arise from this partnership show Verheyden's more muted palette. In 1884, Boch became the only woman member of Les XX, where she was exposed to the artistic influences of Belgian and French Post-Impressionist avant-garde artists, such as James Ensor, Georges Seurat, Paul Signac, Vincent van Gogh and Theo Van Rysselberghe, whose works were also represented in her own celebrated art collection. Under Van Rysselberghe's influence in particular, she developed her personal version of Pointillism, employing spontaneous, comma-like brush-strokes and a bright palette. She painted landscapes, bucolic tableaux and interiors, as well as floral arrangements and still lifes exemplified by her freeness of style and a balanced composition. Equally characteristic are the works of art from her collection that surface in her still lifes and interiors. The painting *The Kitchen* was also known as *The Magpie* after the alert bird that enlivens this scene: an interior with foodstuffs. When painting this tableau, Boch employed emphatic contour lines to delineate the appealing, realistically coloured comestibles and objects. As with the inclusion of the bird, movement is incorporated through the intersecting diagonal lines of perspective as regards the table and the sideboard with the uprights of the chair. She presented the painting at the salon of the Cercle Artistique et Littéraire in Brussels in 1884. At that time, *L'Art moderne* noticed that her palette and her 'steadfast quest for reality [bore a] certain reminiscence to Louis Dubois'.[7]

Exhibited Work
cat. 123 Anna Boch, *The Kitchen*, 1883–4, oil on canvas, 86 × 137 cm. Private collection, Belgium.

Bibliography
— 'Au Cercle artistique', *L'Art moderne*, 4 May 1884, pp. 149–50.
— Thomas, Lenglez and Duroisin 2005, p. 229 (no. 149).
— Ostend 2023.

ALFRED VERHAEREN
(Brussels, 8 October 1849–Ixelles, 10 February 1924)

As a young artist, Alfred Verhaeren worked first as an illustrator of architectural plans. Following his studies at the Brussels Academy, he was tutored by Louis Dubois, whose realism left its mark on Verhaeren. He initially closely adhered to the example set by the seventeenth-century still-life masters whom he was studying, but later came under the influence of Impressionism. He excelled at still lifes and interiors. His technique is notable for smoothly painted backgrounds contrasting with an impasto application of tones and highlights. His interiors – often cluttered studio scenes– are sometimes framed and cropped in a highly idiosyncratic fashion. The same is also true of *Studio Materials*, which has an unusual height when compared with its width. In 1925, following Verhaeren's death, it was James Ensor who penned a biographical footnote on him in the *Bulletin de l'Académie royale de Belgique* of which Verhaeren had been a member since 1922. In his characteristic style, Ensor wrote about the 'foolish pucks' who failed to appreciate the beauty of withered leaves. Ensor called Verhaeren 'the most prying of our painters' and praised

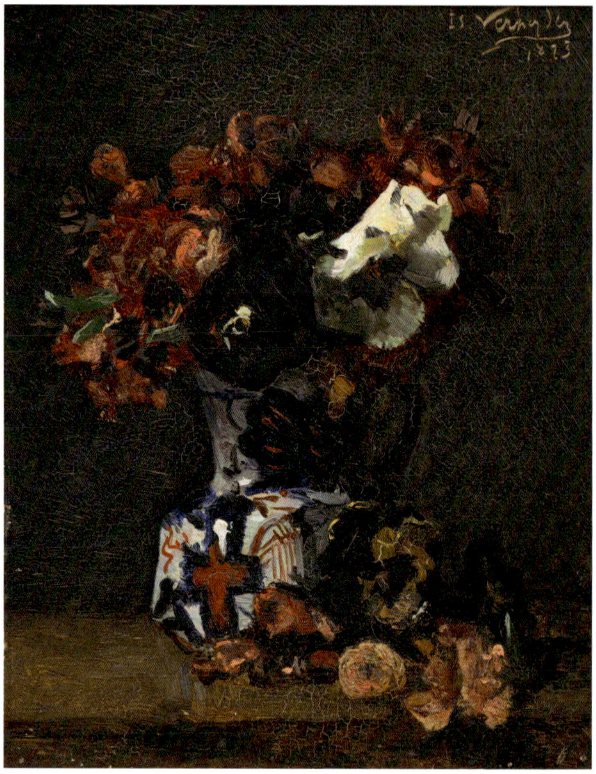
121

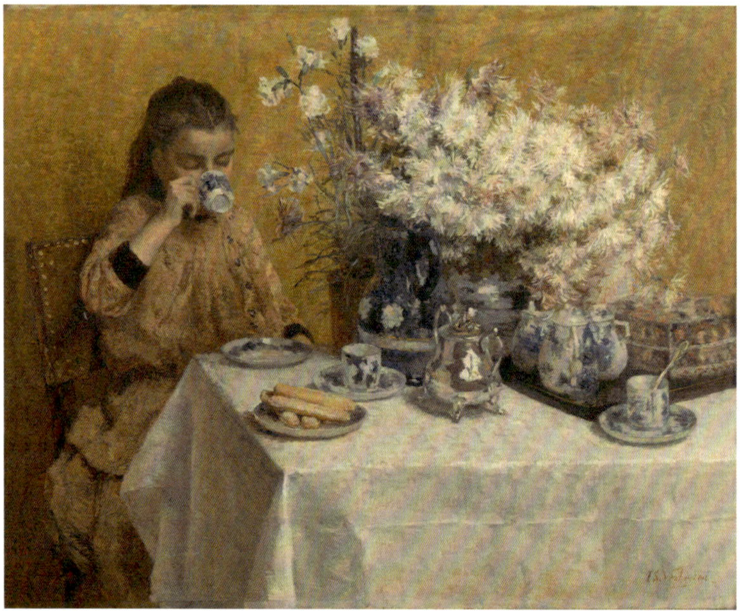
122

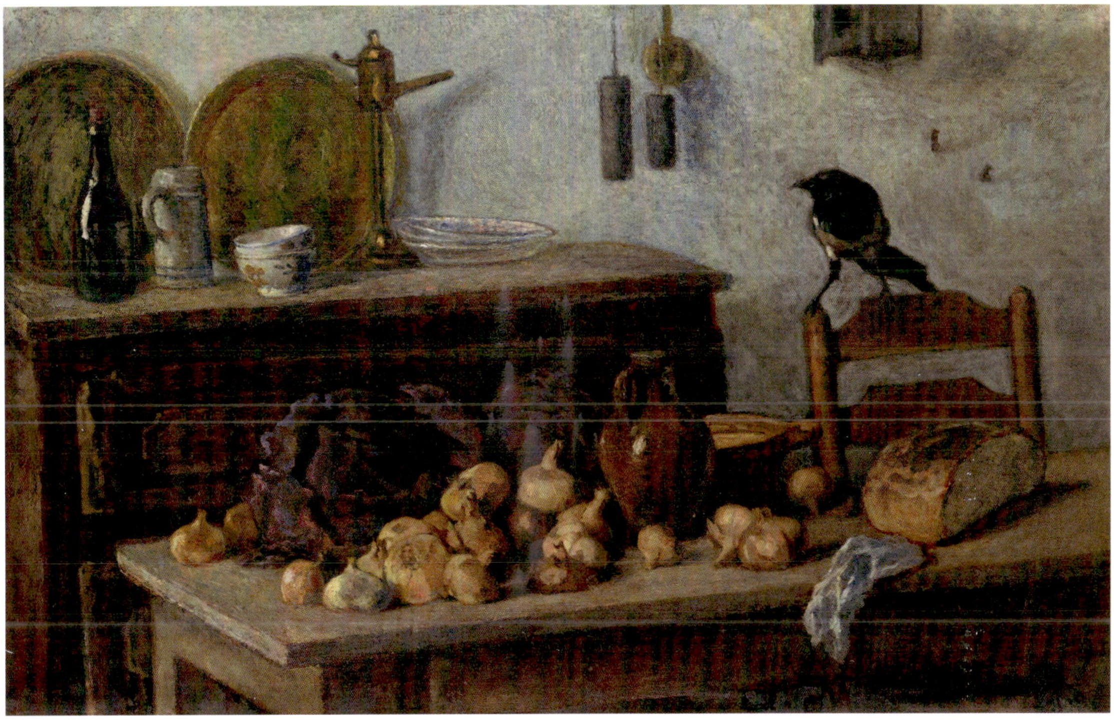

123

his traditional palette and technique, which moved him to observe: 'Our ultra-moderns have only a mediocre appreciation of the efforts made by the old painters of reality.' For Ensor, all the qualities of Verhaeren – on his mother's side the grandson of butchers – coalesced in *The Steak* (fig. 10), 'the artist's principal work'.[8] Ostend's master painter was preceded in this hymn of admiration by Alfred's younger cousin by six years Émile Verhaeren, who, as early as 1884, had sung the praises of the blood red, freshly butchered hunk of flesh, saying in conclusion: '*The Steak* is superb painting.'[9]

Exhibited Work

cat. 124 Alfred Verhaeren, *Studio Materials*, s.d., oil on canvas, 126.1 × 71.5 cm. Museum of Fine Arts, Ghent, inv. 1922-V.

Bibliography
— F. N., 'Chronique artistique', *Journal de Bruxelles*, 28 April 1889, p. 3.
— Ensor 1925, pp. 110–15.
— Sulzberger 1964.

PAULINE JAMAR
(Liège, 13 April 1850–Liège, 4 April 1911)

Pauline Jamar from Liège was sister to the architect Edmond Jamar (1853–1929). Except for a few landscapes, it was chiefly floral arrangements and still lifes that she painted throughout her career. In those still lifes, Jamar rendered a precise knowledge of nature. Among other locales, her artwork appeared at three of the four exhibitions held by the Cercle des Femmes Peintres (in 1888, 1890 and 1892) alongside works by fellow painters such as Berthe Art and Louise De Hem. Her oeuvre also comprises a considerable number of watercolours, which she exhibited within the Société Nationale des Aquarellistes et Pastellistes de Belgique. That association was founded in 1899 and around one fifth of its members were women. De Hem, Art and Jamar would also exhibit their work there jointly, as did Georgette Meunier. Jamar won awards at exhibitions in La Louvière in 1893 and in Liège in 1896. She made meticulous notes of all the exhibitions in which she participated: the triennial salons and more regional exhibitions. Denis Laoureux tallied 14 salon attendances between 1884 and 1899. She sold only three to four works a year. When, in March 1898, she exhibited her still life *The Thistles* at the Cercle des Beaux-Arts in Liège, it was remarked upon how she abandoned the trademark lightness of her watercolour still lifes in her works in oil. The image in question depicts a basket of wild flowers, as if freshly plucked, differing from her tightly arranged bouquets in vases. In 1929, *The Thistles* was donated to the Musée des Beaux-Arts in Liège by her sister Léonie Jamar.

Exhibited Work

cat. 125 Pauline Jamar, *The Thistles*, 1898 (?), oil on canvas, 63 × 91 cm. Musée des Beaux-Arts / La Boverie, Liège, inv. AW 1068.

Bibliography
— 'Beaux-Arts', *La Meuse*, 5 May 1880, p. 2.
— 'Pour le Musée des Beaux-Arts', *La Meuse*, 22 June 1929, p. 2.
— Creusen 2007, pp. 175–6.
— Laoureux 2019, p. 48.

WILLY (ALFRED WILLIAM) FINCH
(Saint-Josse-ten-Noode, 28 November 1854–Helsinki, 28 April 1930)

From age five to 20, Willy Finch lived in Ostend where his British-born parents ran the Hôtel du Phare. James Ensor became his close friend in the period 1878–88.

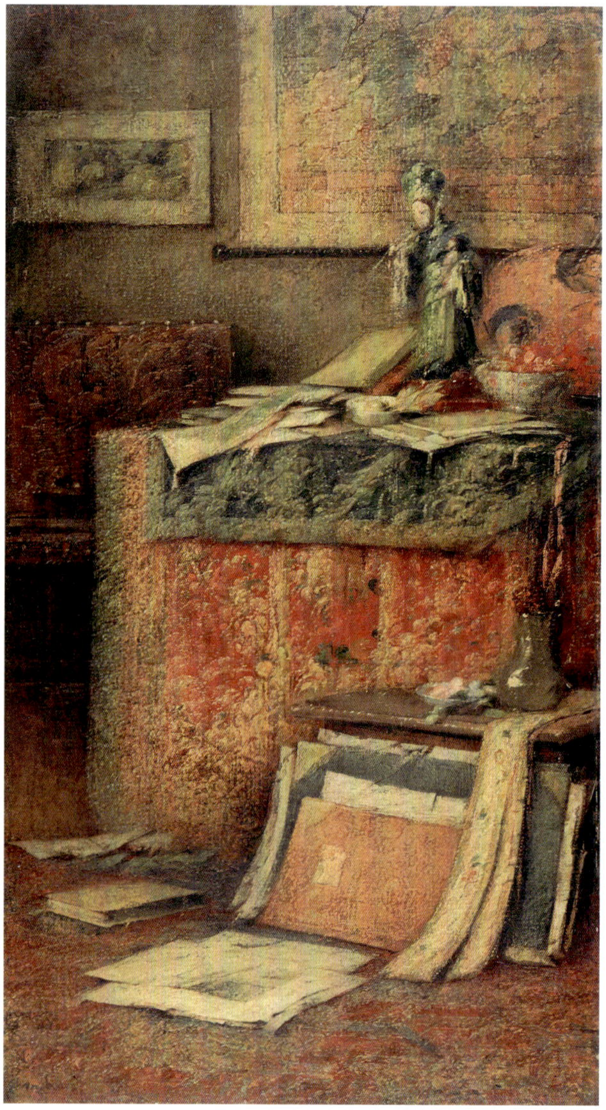

124

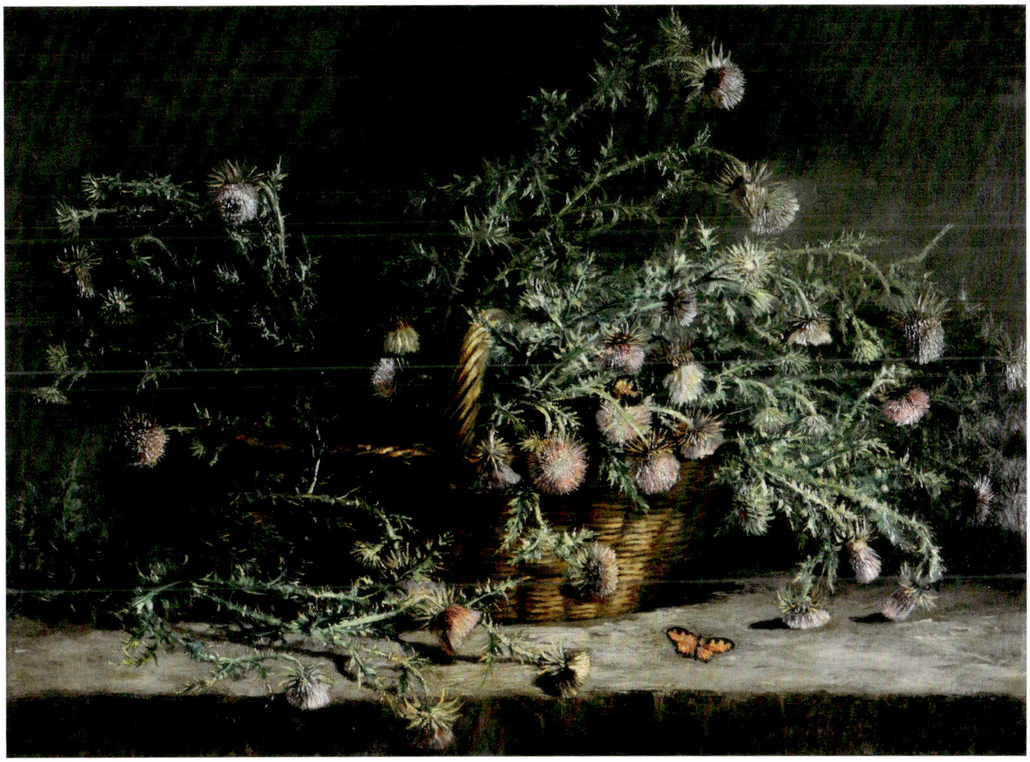

125

Sharing an artistic kinship, they were in tandem vis-à-vis choosing the dunes as a work location, certain motifs and their Brussels period. After a brief time at the Brussels Academy in 1878–9, Finch joined La Chrysalide and L'Essor. Like Ensor, he also became active as a founding member of Les XX in 1883. Just like the painting *Russian Music* (1881), in which Ensor depicts Finch and his own sister Mitche, and a number of each other's portraits, *The Skate* testifies to their friendship and collaboration. In 1880, both young artists painted the same composition from a slightly different perspective, probably sitting fraternally side by side. According to Ensor's writings, in the previous year, both of them had also painted a red gurnard on a blue table surrounded by accessories (see Ensor's *The Mullet* (1880–81)).[10] Subsequently, Finch would chiefly paint landscapes, and he became the first Belgian artist to fall under the influence of Pointillism following Georges Seurat's appearance at Les XX in 1887. Ensor was averse to Pointillism, and their friendship fizzled out. Probably with Anna Boch's encouragement, Finch also explored ceramics alongside painting, doing so variously at the company Boch Frères Keramis, at Henry van de Velde's home and in Finland, where he moved in 1902.

Exhibited Work

cat. 126 Willy Finch, *The Skate*, 1880–82, oil on canvas, 55 × 66.5 cm. Mu.ZEE, City of Ostend Collection, inv. SM001750.

Bibliography

— Derrey-Capon 1992a.
— Derrey-Capon 1992b, p. 168.
— Brussels 1992, pp. 13–17.
— Tricot 2009, pp. 257–8.

LÉON FREDERIC

(Brussels, 26 August 1856–Schaerbeek, 27 January 1940)

As the son of a goldsmith, Léon Frederic took his first lessons from the painter-decorator Charle-Albert (1821–1889). Between 1871 and 1878, he studied at the Brussels Academy and attended the popular free studio run by Jean-François Portaels, where the likes of Isidore Verheyden was also taking classes. When Frederic travelled through Italy with his friend Julien Dillens (1849–1904), a sculptor and recipient of the Prix de Rome, Frederic became inspired by the Italian and Flemish primitives. Like Dillens, he joined L'Essor and remained a member even in 1883 after the secession of Les XX. However, he was invited to exhibit his work at the latter association in 1893. Frederic is chiefly known for his monumental triptychs, an originally religious format that, as a modern primitive, he employed for works with a socio-realistic impact, although he also produced religious paintings about the lives of the saints. Working-class people of flesh and blood feature in Frederic's work in what are, nevertheless, symbolically charged everyday scenes comparable to those by the British Pre-Raphaelites. In line with the truth-to-nature principle of the latter group, Frederic's landscapes, just like his human figures, reveal close observation, such as at the Ardennes village of Nafraiture and when by the North Sea where he had a villa in Heist. This is also apparent in *The Pink Azaleas* via a window through which a rolling rural landscape appears – possibly Nafraiture. Many of Frederic's rustic interior scenes include a window of this type as a spy-hole or vista and as a device to provide illumination. In 1929, simultaneously with James Ensor, Frederic was ennobled with the hereditary title of baron.

Exhibited Work

cat. 127 Léon Frederic, *The Pink Azaleas*, s.d., oil on canvas, 69 × 52.5 cm. Courtesy Berko Collection, Knokke-Heist, Belgium.

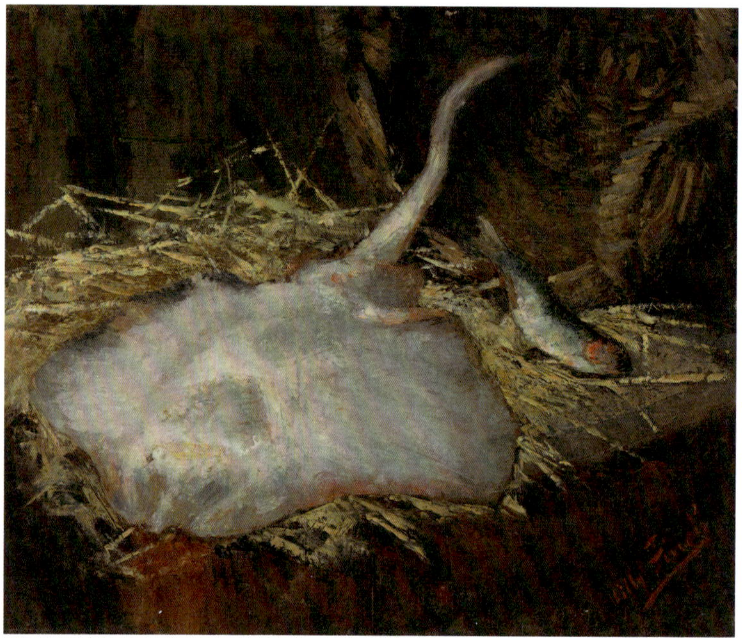

126

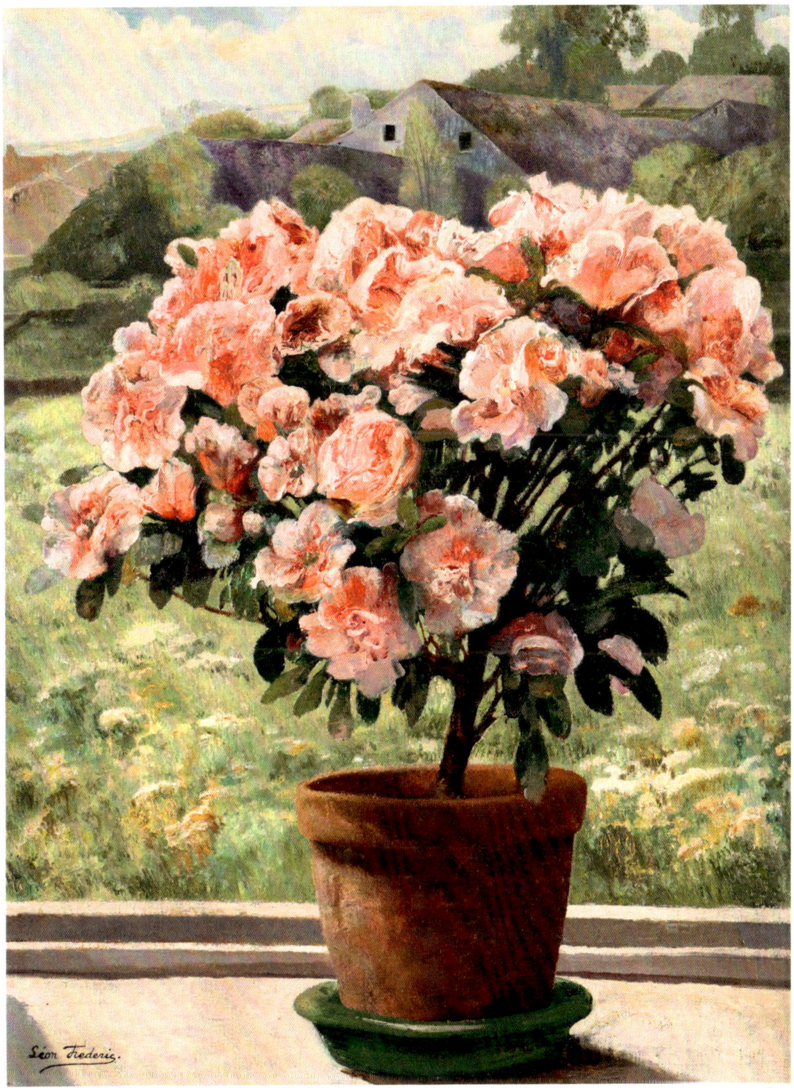

127

Bibliography
— Fernand Khnopff, 'A Belgian Painter: Leon Frederic', *The Studio* 11, no. 169, 1907, pp. 171–81.
— Ornans 2018.

ALICE RONNER
(Brussels, 9 September 1857–Ixelles, 7 July 1957)

Born into an artistic family, Alice Ronner was the daughter of Henriette Ronner-Knip (1821–1909), who achieved fame with paintings of dogs and – above all – cats at play, she herself being the daughter of the Dutch picturesque landscape painter Josephus Augustus Knip (1777–1847). Alice's brother Alfred (1852–1901) was a watercolour painter. At exhibitions around the turn of the century, Alice's work could often be seen in the company of works by Berthe Art, Georgette Meunier, Jeannie de Hemptinne and Louise De Hem, whom the critics usually mentioned in one breath or paragraph in the category assigned to floral paintings or pastels. Her particular focus was on flowers and still lifes – Fernand Khnopff (1858–1921) called her 'decidedly one of our finest painters of still-life subjects'.[11] *The Harp* takes music as its theme and displays a score for a harp, cello and violin trio (the latter instrument being only just visible on the table) by the eighteenth-century Namur harpist and composer Louis-Charles Ragué, which appears to have fallen to the floor. Just like the carelessly set-down bow and flowers, these elements bring movement into what is otherwise a lifeless composition. Employing a tried and tested formula, Ronner made the white tablecloth in the foreground shine against the dark interior. It is possible that she was using the same harp as her mother did in paintings where kittens are seen playing around it. She changed her style at the beginning of the First World War, as can be seen in *The Wicker Chair*. In 1915, the critic Paul Buschmann aptly characterised her daring new approach to painting as 'tending to extreme simplification both of harmony and technique; composed on a scale of two or three tints only, the effect is obtained by a few broad, bold touches, rendering the very structure of things before the artist's sensible eye'.[12]

Exhibited Works
cat. 129 Alice Ronner, *The Harp*, 1888, oil on canvas, 222 × 160 cm. Stadsmuseum Lier, inv. 150.
cat. 128 Alice Ronner, *The Wicker Chair*, 1915, oil on canvas, 78 × 71 cm. Musée d'Orsay, Paris, inv. RF 1979 40.

Bibliography
— Fernand Khnopff, 'Studio Talk', *The International Studio* 45, no. 179, 1912, p. 160.
— Paul Buschmann, 'Belgian Artists in England', *The International Studio* 55, no. 220, 1915, pp. 260–69.
— de Graaf 1999.

BERTHE ART
(Brussels, 26 December 1857–Saint-Gilles, 26 February 1934)

As in the cases of Georgette Meunier, Louise De Hem and many other women, Berthe Art took classes from the Belgian painter Alfred Stevens (1823–1906) in Paris. Although she did work in oils, it was her mastery of technique using pastels that was particularly impressive. Alongside a number of portraits and works including birds, her oeuvre consists chiefly of still lifes depicting flowers, trinkets, artist's studio materials and other objects. In some of her floral paintings, it is the wallcoverings in the background that attract as much attention as her flowers and vases. The gossamer fine texture of the wall textiles is reminiscent of those in Stevens's interiors, as are the chinoiserie and oriental figurines or textiles that appear in some of Art's still lifes.

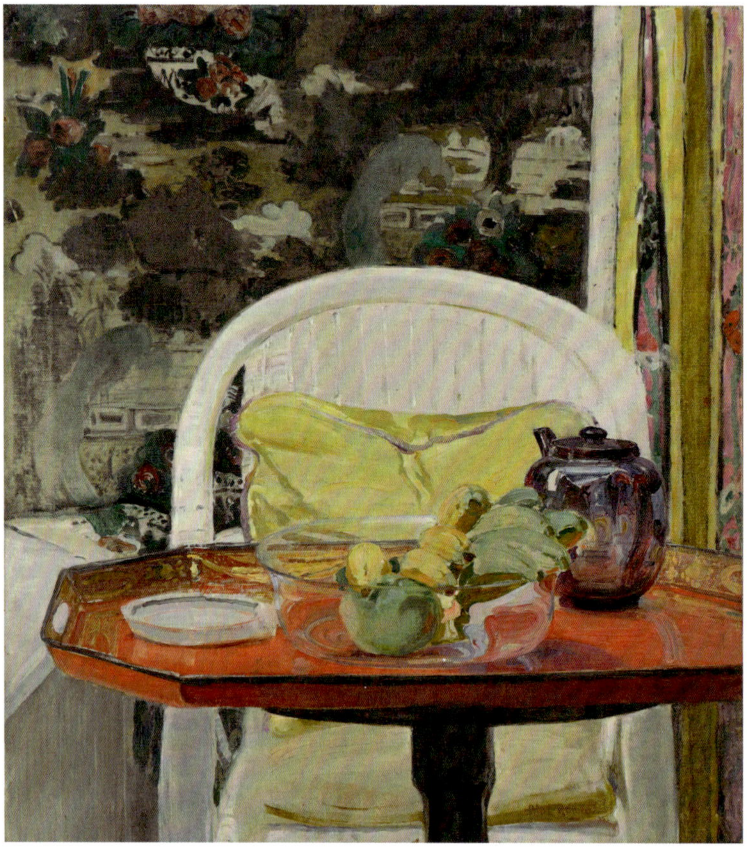

128

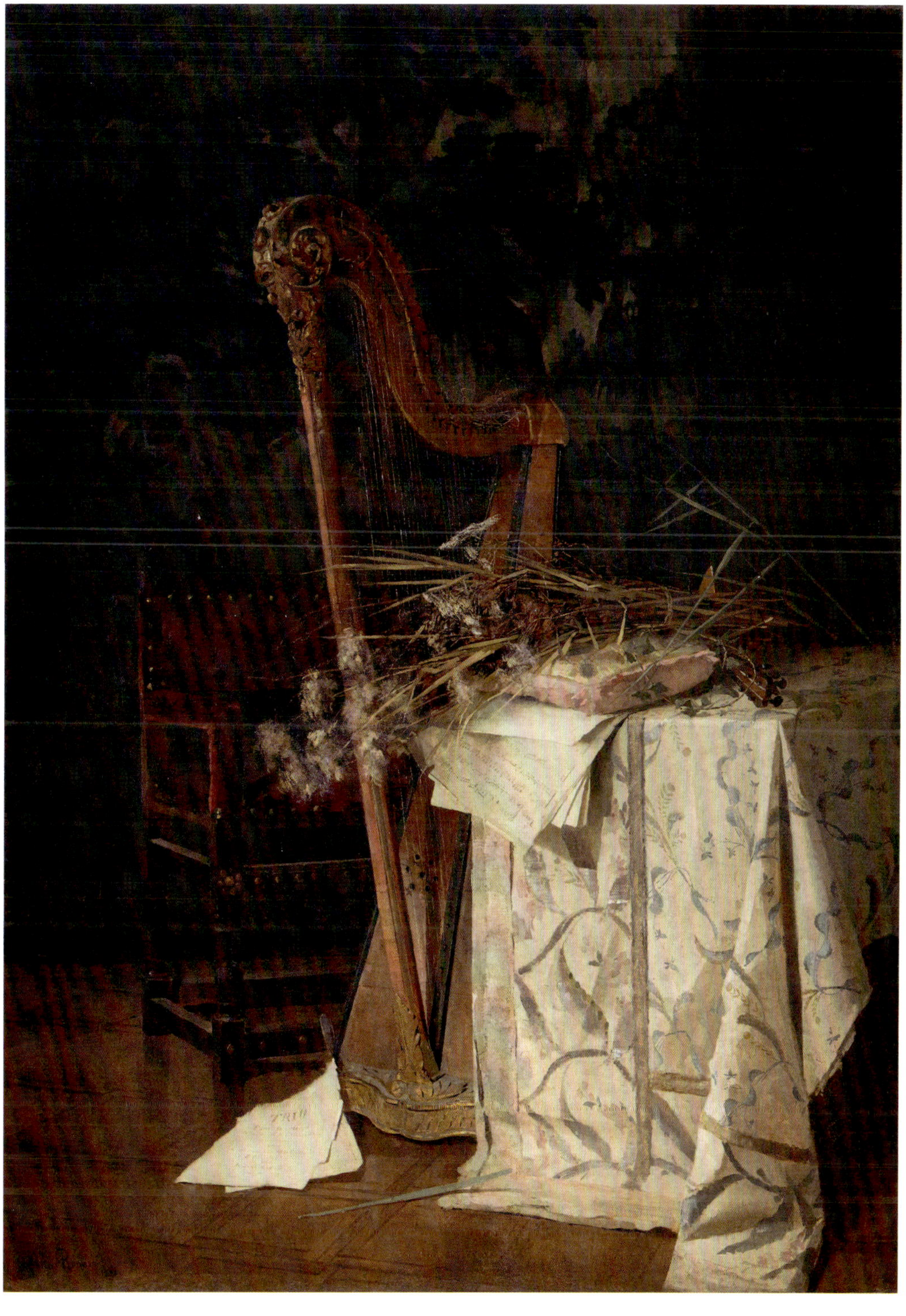

129

A case in point is the texture of the tablecloth in *Kettle and Vase with African Violets, Arum Lilies and China Asters*. In this pastel, the floral arrangement itself merges into the black and white floral motifs of the wall decoration. In *Still Life with Fan, Death Mask and Peacock Feather* of 1885, Art created a composition using light, slender objects: peacock feathers, a twig, small cut flowers, a glass flask and a half-opened oriental fan on the edge of a tabletop. All these objects seem precarious, as if they might fall from their delicate positions with only the faintest vibration or lightest of breezes. Even the central object around which all these items have been arranged – a plaster bust of a woman – is leaning against the back wall, in so doing emphasising its own fragility. The harmonious colour palette is in line with this equilibrium. According to contemporary criticism, such delicate tableaux were perceived as typically feminine and were characterised using words like 'grace' and 'charm'.

Exhibited Works

cat. 130 Berthe Art, *Kettle and Vase with African Violets, Arum Lilies and China Asters*, s.d., pastel on paper, 80 × 109 cm. Private collection, Leuven.

cat. 11 Berthe Art, *Still Life with Fan, Death Mask and Peacock Feather*, 1885, oil on canvas, 97 × 71 cm. Private collection, Kortrijk. (p. 34)

Bibliography

— Schrijvers 1999, p. 274.
— Laoureux 2019, p. 48.
— Meylaers 2023.

GEORGETTE MEUNIER
(Brussels, 7 October 1859–Brussels, 1951)

Just as in the case of her father and first tutor, the renowned print artist Jean-Baptiste Meunier (1821–1900), Georgette Meunier was an etcher, although she became celebrated chiefly as a painter of genre scenes, interiors, floral arrangements and still lifes. She studied at the Parisian studio of Alfred Stevens, a locale where at least 25 female artists from various countries underwent training, among them Berthe Art and Louise De Hem. Meunier adopted Stevens's predilection for opulent interiors with orientalist features and finely detailed depictions of textiles. Much of this is present in her pastel work *Chinoiseries*, in the centre of which Meunier places a vase surrounded by flowers and tableware; behind this is a Japanese ukiyo-e woodblock print of the sort that was popular in fin-de-siècle artistic circles. Meunier was actively involved in both La Chrysalide and L'Essor – the group from which Les XX separated – but she also exhibited work at the Société Nationale des Aquarellistes et Pastellistes de Belgique. During that association's 1902 exhibition, 12 of the 42 participants were women, including Pauline Jamar, Art and De Hem. Although author Alexia Creusen hesitates on the basis of a surname alone to state conclusively that it was *Georgette* Meunier who exhibited work at that association, it would appear from reviews that it was indeed Georgette who was there and not her uncle Constantin, a painter who, at the end of the nineteenth century, acquired a tremendous reputation as a sculptor.

Exhibited Work

cat. 131 Georgette Meunier, *Chinoiseries*, s.d., pastel on paper, 67 × 89 cm. Musée des Beaux-Arts, Tournai, inv. 450.

Bibliography

— 'Mlle Georgette Meunier', *Bruxelles féminin*, 15 April 1903, p. 8.
— Creusen 2007, pp. 70, 95, 99, 126, 228.

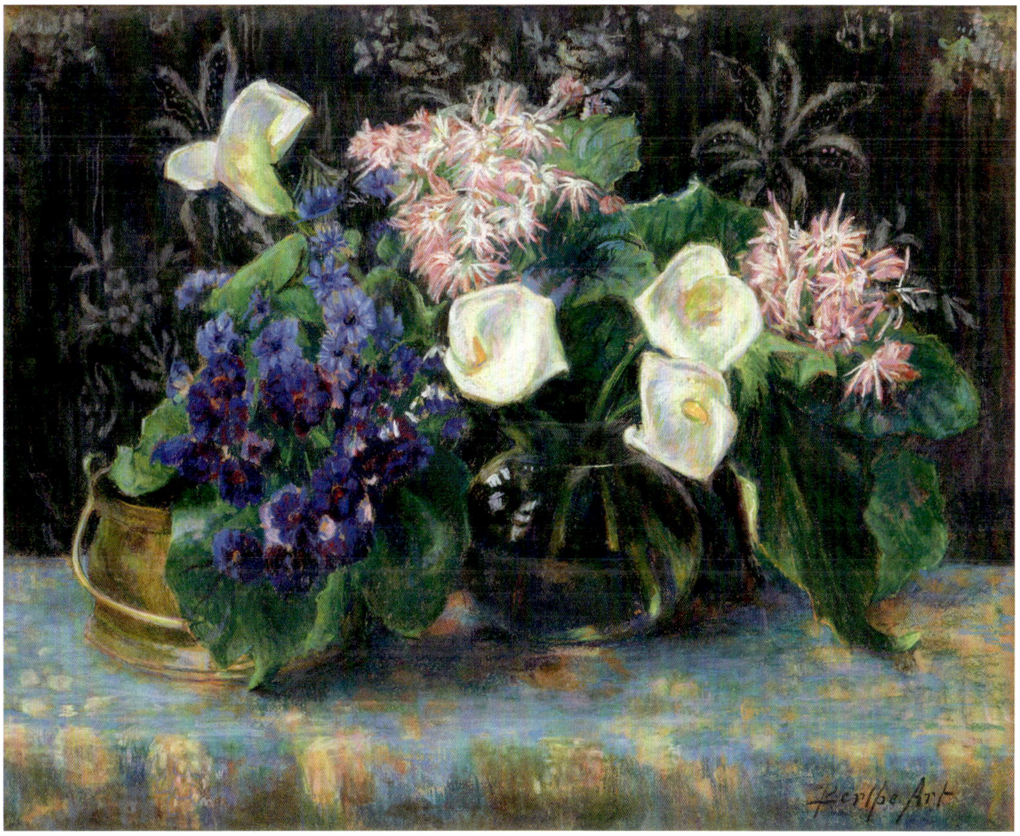

130

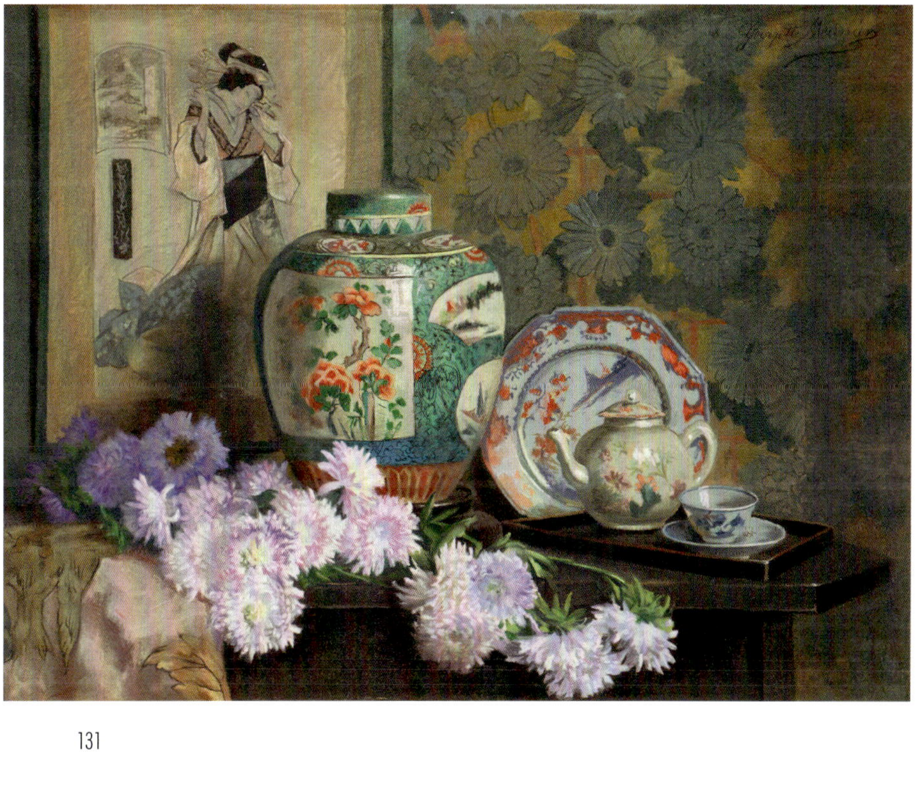

131

MARIE DE BIÈVRE

(Saint-Josse-ten-Noode, 30 January 1865–Ixelles, 7 October 1940)

Just like Jeannie de Hemptinne, the first mentions of Marie de Bièvre's attendance at a salon appear in the mid-1880s, when she exhibited floral paintings, still lifes and interiors. De Bièvre was a member of the artist association L'Essor. In response to her exhibition at the Cercle Artistique et Littéraire in Brussels in 1893, the critic writing for *L'Indépendance belge* noted how De Bièvre's artistic sense set her apart from 'so many charming women whose painting is quite as good as their virtuosity at knitting, embroidery or crochet'.[13] Four years earlier, the same newspaper had written that, logically enough, the 'chaste art' of the Belgian still life was meant for young girls: it was 'at the same time art preordained for the virginal hands and sedentary hours of latter-day Vestals'.[14] The influence of Hubert Bellis can be seen in De Bièvre's depiction of seafood.[15] Her compositions of still lifes betray an interest in setting, furnishings and wallcoverings, as well as in mirrors. In several of her works, she takes, in a sense, a step back to show what other still-life painters would have edited out, such as the dresser with tableware and porcelain figurines in *Bourgeois Interior* (fig. 13).

Exhibited Works

cat. 132 Marie de Bièvre, *Physalis*, s.d., oil on canvas, 24 × 31 cm. Private collection, Leuven.

cat. 133 Marie de Bièvre, *Azaleas and Violets*, s.d., oil on canvas, 92 × 72.5 cm. Royal Museums of Fine Arts of Belgium, Brussels, inv. 5636.

cat. 13 Marie de Bièvre, *Peaches and Plums*, 1894 or before, oil on canvas, 74 × 94 cm. Private collection, Leuven. (p. 35)

Bibliography

— 'Le Salon de Paris, 1889', *L'Indépendance belge*, 5 June 1889, p. 3.
— 'Théâtres et Beaux-Arts', *L'Indépendance belge*, 21 December 1893, p. 3.
— Flippo 1981.

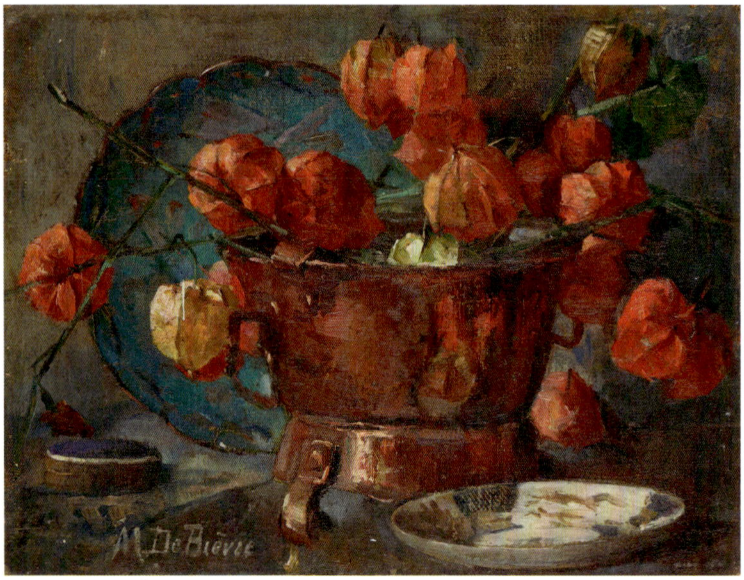

132

JEANNIE DE HEMPTINNE

(Molenbeek-Saint-Jean, 5 February 1865–Molenbeek-Saint-Jean, 14 August 1891)

Jeannie de Hemptinne was christened Jeanne-Pauline-Marguerite, the eighth of nine children born to the chemist Auguste-Ferdinand Dehemptinne (1819–1882) and Julienne Van Coillie (1822–1899). We know little about her life and any tuition she might have received. It is possible that her father taught her how to paint. She exhibited floral works at the triennial salon of 1887 in Brussels (*Poppies*) and at the salon of 1888 in Liège, where her work *Chrysanthemums* was sold. Also that year, she exhibited *Irises* and *Carnations* alongside works by Georgette Meunier, Louise De Hem, Berthe Art and Alice Ronner at the first exhibition held by the Cercle des Femmes Peintres. De Hemptinne's *Irises* was also on view at the Exposition Universelle of 1889 in Paris. In May 1891, together with the likes of Art, Meunier, Ronner and Hubert Bellis, she received an honourable mention from the *Journal de Bruxelles* in the category for floral, accessory and still-life painters at the exhibition held by the Cercle Artistique et Littéraire in Brussels. Later that year, the same newspaper published a relatively thorough obituary to mark the untimely death of the 26-year-old. This painted a picture of a woman with a talent for depicting nature as she felt it to be, but also of someone with great artistic determination, which was even linked to her premature demise. The successors to her estate possess various floral arrangements, a painted vase and

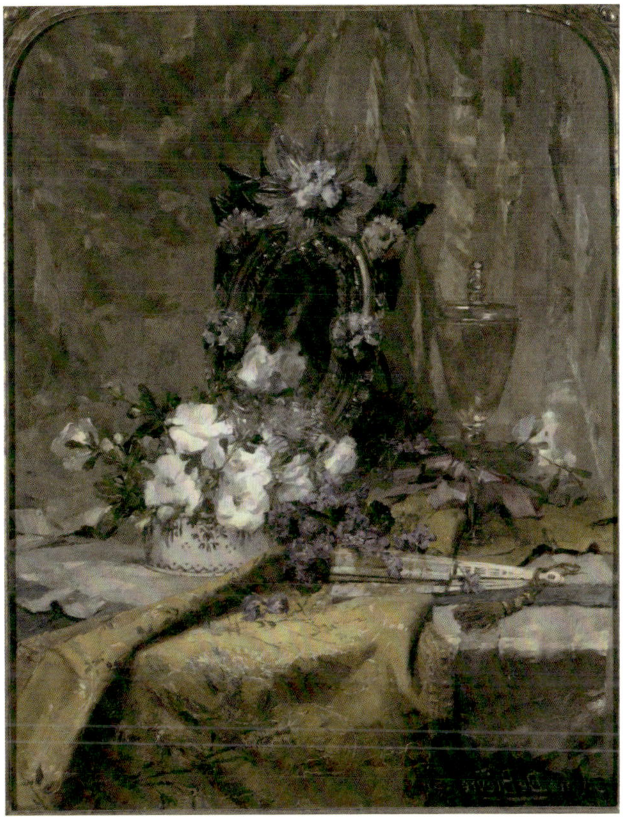

133

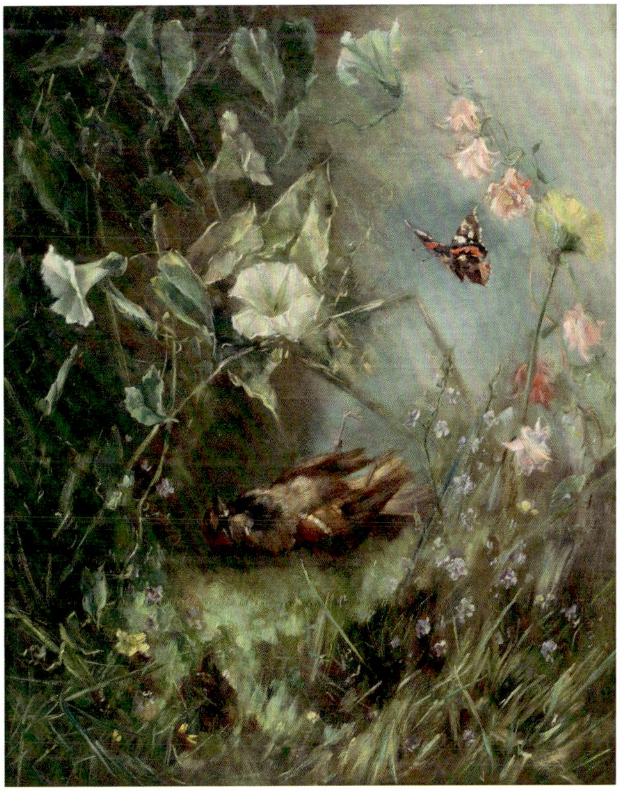

134

an album of poetry containing sketches. One of these sketches shows the same curved banisters and oriental paper lanterns visible in the small scene *Exotic Interior*. In another work, *Wild Flowers with Bird and Butterfly*, situated on a lawn, a certain sense of drama emanates from the contrast between the dead bird and the fluttering butterfly, whereas in *Flowers* the background is vague and undefined.

Exhibited Works

cat. 134 Jeannie de Hemptinne, *Wild Flowers with Bird and Butterfly*, s.d., oil on canvas, 60 × 49 cm. Private collection.
cat. 135 Jeannie de Hemptinne, *Exotic Interior*, s.d., oil on panel, 30 × 22.5 cm. Private collection.
cat. 14 Jeannie de Hemptinne, *Flowers*, s.d., oil on canvas, 109 × 71 cm. Private collection. (p. 39)

Bibliography

— *Poetry album Jeannie de Hemptinne 'J.D.H.'*, s.d. [*c.*1880–91], private collection.
— 'Chronique artistique', *Journal de Bruxelles*, 14 October 1887, p. 1.
— Tyrtée, 'Première exposition du Cercle des Femmes Peintres', *Moniteur des Arts*, 7 December 1888, p. 419.
— 'Le Salon de Paris, 1889', *L'Indépendance belge*, 5 June 1889, p. 3.
— 'Nécrologie', *Journal de Bruxelles*, 18 August 1891, p. 2.
— de Hemptinne 1984, pp. 392–400.
— Brussels 1996, p. 139.

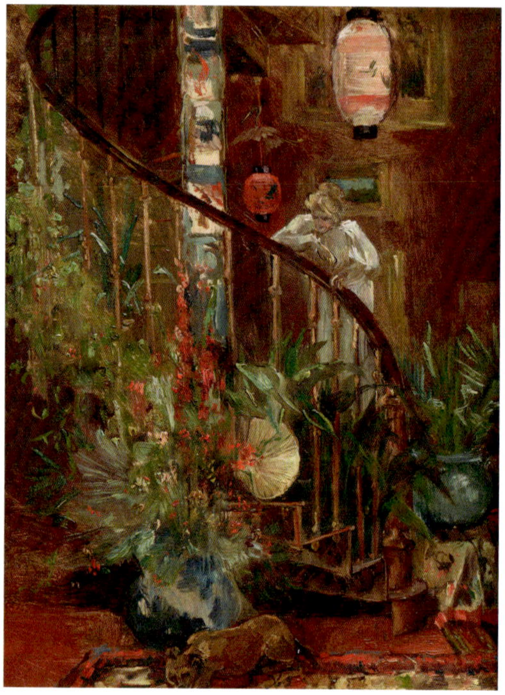

135

FRANS MORTELMANS

(Antwerp, 1 May 1865–Antwerp, 11 April 1936)

Frans Mortelmans, brother of the celebrated composer Lodewijk (1868–1952), studied at the Antwerp Academy between 1876 and 1886 and at the Higher Institute for Fine Arts from 1887 to 1891, where he subsequently became a tutor in his own right. He also taught still-life classes at the Berchem Academy after 1901 and was active in the De Scalden art association. From 1904 to 1933, he had a country estate in Kalmthout where he committed nature to canvas. However, it was on still lifes of fruit, vegetables and poultry and – above all – floral paintings that Mortelmans almost exclusively directed his focus from the late 1880s onwards. In that regard, he chiefly painted native Belgian varieties of cultivated flowers, usually as bouquets of one type, at times with colour variants, and always with a free brush-work style. Mixed bouquets and baroque, colourful explosions of different flower types failed to excite him. In the interior painting *Frans Mortelmans at His Studio in front of His Easel*, the artist illustrates the creative process for one of his actual works. Various versions were made of *Yellow Roses in a Vase*, in which one of the roses lies in front of the vase to create a certain dramatic tension. Mortelmans probably portrayed the same interior in *Visiting the Studio*, where a girl is taking in the scent of a white bouquet of flowers. The reflection in the mirror of an easel's under-frame also betrays the location of the still life in *Roses in a Vase, Bouquet of Roses on the Table*.

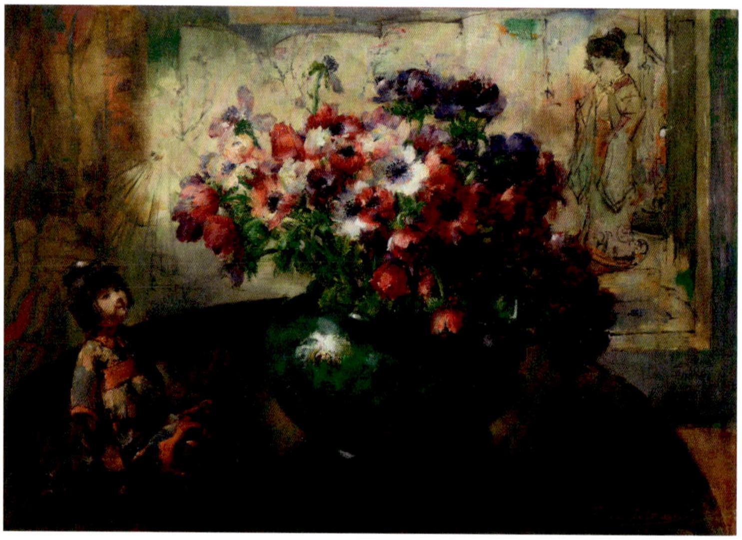

136

Exhibited Works

cat. 136 Frans Mortelmans, *Anemones in Round Vase, Japanese Doll on the Table*, s.d., oil on canvas, 58 × 83 cm. Courtesy Berko Fine Paintings, Knokke-Heist, Belgium.
cat. 137 Frans Mortelmans, *Frans Mortelmans at His Studio in front of His Easel*, s.d., oil on canvas, 60 × 48 cm. Walter Mortelmans.
cat. 138 Frans Mortelmans, *Yellow Roses in a Vase*, s.d., oil on canvas, 44 × 29 cm. Stichting Mortelmans.
cat. 139 Frans Mortelmans, *Yellow Roses in a Vase on a Pedestal Table*, s.d., oil on canvas, 79 × 48 cm. Stichting Mortelmans.

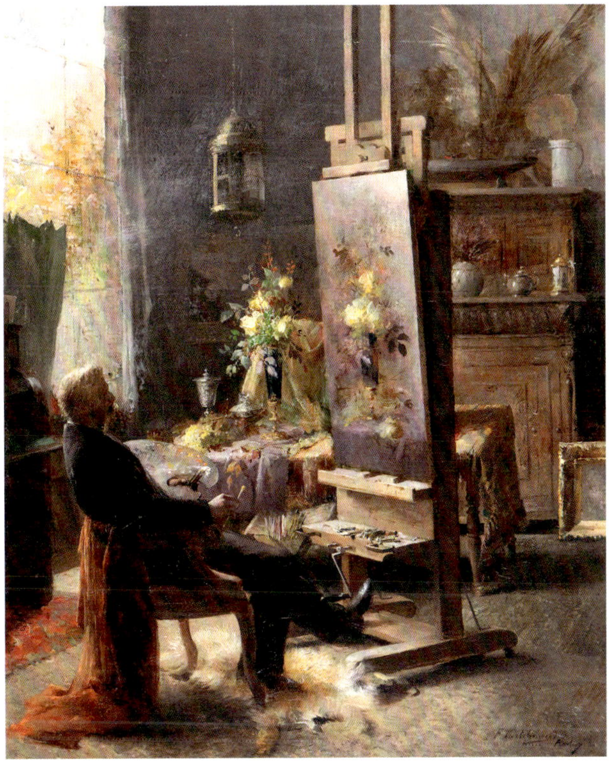

137

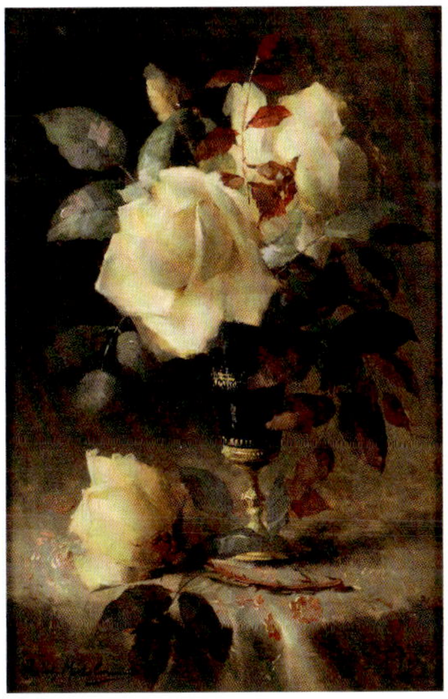

138

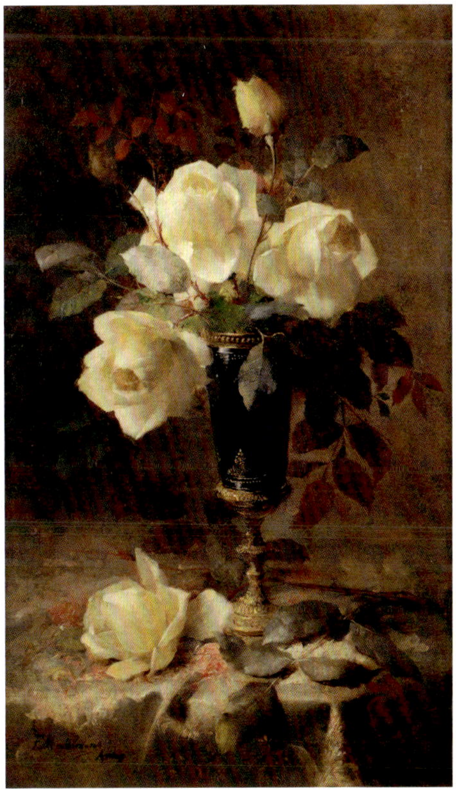

139

cat. 140 Frans Mortelmans, *Chrysanthemums in a Delftware Vase, Plate of Grapes on the Table*, s.d., oil on canvas, 58 × 70 cm. Walter Mortelmans.
cat. 141 Frans Mortelmans, *Death Mask of the Painter Wiertz*, s.d., watercolour on paper, 68 × 59 cm. Stichting Mortelmans.
cat. 142 Frans Mortelmans, *Roses in a Vase, Bouquet of Roses on the Table*, s.d., oil on canvas, 80 × 120 cm. Walter Mortelmans.
cat. 3 Frans Mortelmans, *Visiting the Studio*, s.d., oil on canvas, 111.5 × 171.5 cm. Collection Marthe + Félix Dony. (p. 19)

Bibliography
— Hostyn, Schiltz and Schiltz 2009.

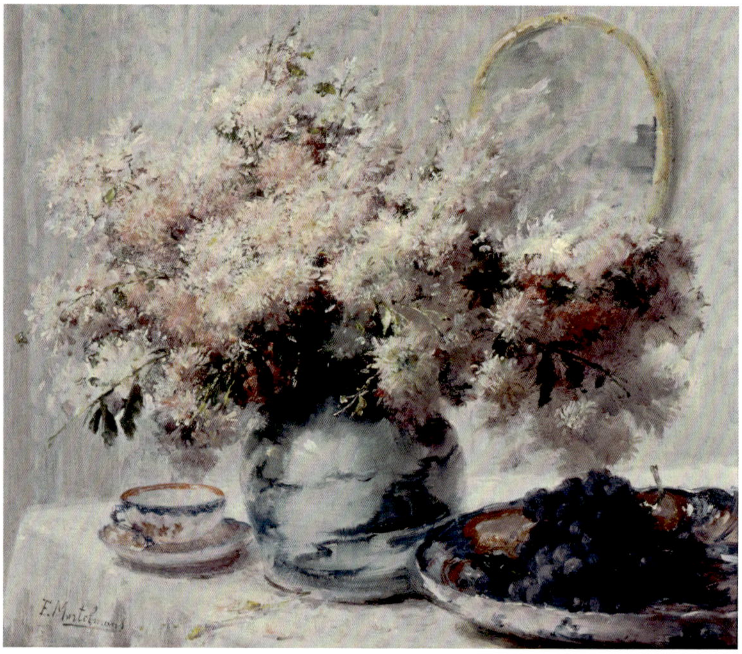

140

LOUISE DE HEM

(Ypres, 10 December 1866–Brussels, 22 November 1922)

Louise De Hem took her first art classes with Théodore Ceriez (1832–1904) who, after the death of her father, Henri Dehem, in 1872, became head of the household at the Dehem-Bartier residence. In 1876, Ceriez married Louise's sister, Hélène. Thanks to grants from her hometown and province, Louise was able to further her training as an artist variously in Brussels, chiefly in Paris under Alfred Stevens, at Fernand Cormon's free studio and at the Académie Julian: places where a great many women (and/or later members of the avant-garde) were trained. De Hem exhibited her work at a variety of salons, starting in 1885 – on her nineteenth birthday. In addition to making quite a number of portraits, which provided her with a source of income, she focused on the still-life genre in particular, employing trinkets, such as gleaming censers and carafes, but also onions or oysters. Peculiar to her style is the use of highly diluted paint applied in thin layers and, in her early works, the inclusion of darker colours mixed with bitumen. In 1905, she moved to Forest. Even more so than when working in oils, De Hem excelled in pastels, a medium in which she produced a great deal of work, particularly from her Brussels period onwards. The pastel technique affected the tonality of her oil paintings. In *Corner of a Lady's Boudoir* of around 1890, the influence of Stevens and his orientalist modishness is clear to see. The folding screen divides the background of this painting into four vertical sections. This work moved one conservative critic in *La Fédération artistique* to call back the Flemish maid from the pernicious sophistication of Stevens's Paris.[16] The latter's predilection for oriental objects is also evident in *Bust of a Young, Smiling Girl, a Carafe, a Japanese Doll and a Fan* of 1887, which is rendered in less detail.

Exhibited Works
cat. 143 Louise De Hem, *Bust of a Young, Smiling Girl, a Carafe, a Japanese Doll and a Fan*, 1887, oil on canvas, 55.5 × 38 cm. Yper Museum, Ypres, inv. SM 003261.
cat. 12 Louise De Hem, *Corner of a Lady's Boudoir*, *c.*1890, oil on canvas, 98 × 131 cm. Yper Museum, Ypres, inv. SM 000560. (p. 35)

Bibliography
— Ypres 1992.
— Dewilde 2008.

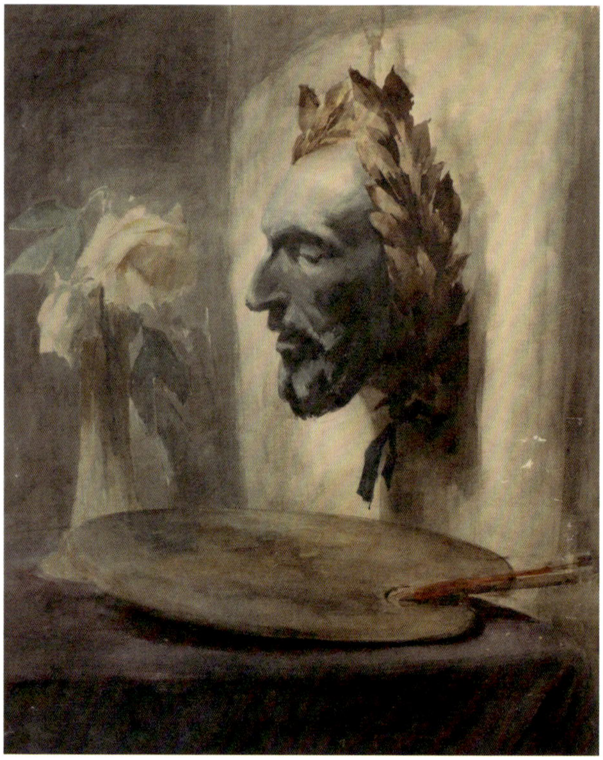

141

LOUIS THEVENET

(Bruges, 12 February 1874–Halle, 16 August 1930)

The youngest of four children, Louis Thevenet was born in 1874 into a musical family in Bruges. In that same year, the family moved to Brussels. Following the premature deaths of his parents and a few minor jobs to make ends meet, Thevenet made friendships in a

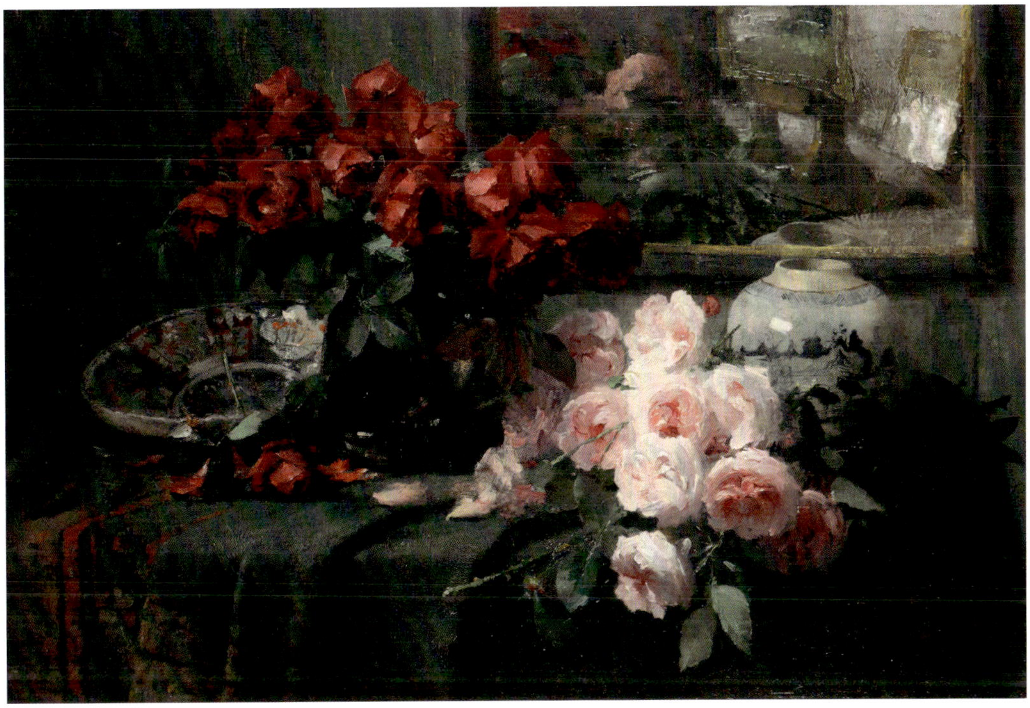

142

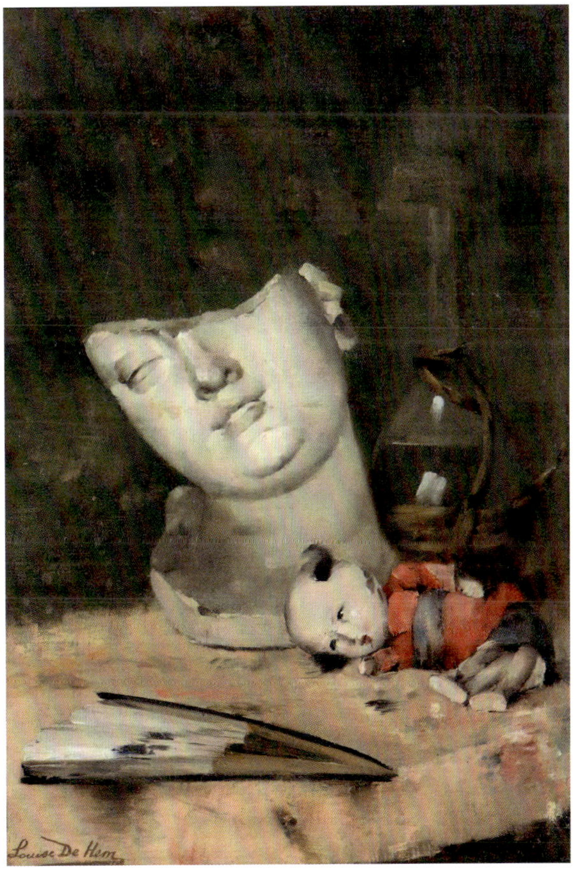

143

libertarian anarchist network, notably with the painters Pierre Scoupreman (1873–1960) and Auguste Oleffe (1867–1931), who motivated him to paint. In 1894, Thevenet began to paint in the Meuse valley and the Sonian Forest, working from nature, using an impasto technique and focusing on rustic types. Just like Jean Brusselmans, he took painting classes at the free studio L'Effort. From 1896 onwards, he concentrated on the motifs that were to make his oeuvre famous: seemingly naive and simplistic interiors and still lifes suffused in bright light and apposite hues in which the objects are largely shapes and fields of colour. The compositions are like musical harmonies or symphonies, and the human figure is generally absent or secondary, like a prop, such as the baby in *Still Life* or *After Mass,* both of 1912. After the First World War, Thevenet lived in Halle in a modest labourer's cottage filled with familiar objects that he included in his work time and again, like a statuette of the Virgin Mary in a bell-jar, a cooking pot, a harmonium and other musical instruments such as those that appear in *The Funeral March*, which recall his lifelong interest in music. In 1909, Sander Pierron wrote of Thevenet's paintings: 'Mr Thevenet does not content himself with rendering the matter, form and colour of things and the light in which they are bathed, but gives us the joy of animating the least of objects, telling us about their everyday lives, expressing to us their soul.'[17]

Exhibited Works

cat. 17 Louis Thevenet, *After Mass*, 1912, oil on canvas, 109 × 88 cm. Museum of Ixelles, inv. CC 1628. (p. 48)

cat. 144 Louis Thevenet, *Still Life*, 1912, oil on canvas, 60 × 110 cm. Artwork owned by the Province of Flemish Brabant. On loan from the provincial council, inv. 580586.

cat. 15 Louis Thevenet, *The Funeral March*, 1924, oil on canvas, 81 × 81 cm. Musea Brugge, inv. 0000.GRO1563.I. (p. 48)

cat. 16 Louis Thevenet, *Vase of Lilies*, 1927, oil on canvas, 40 × 32 cm. Private collection, Leuven. (p. 48)

cat. 145 Louis Thevenet, *The Blue Bottle*, 1927, oil on canvas, 71 × 48 cm. Private collection, Leuven.

Bibliography

— Lyr 1954.
— Halle 1990.
— Deurle 2002.
— Ekonomides 2021, pp. 35–6.

GUSTAVE DE SMET

(Ghent, 21 January 1877–Deurle, 8 October 1943)

Gustave (Gust) De Smet was the son of the decorative painter, photographer and portraitist Jules De Smet and the elder brother by four years of Léon, also an artist. Initially, Gust painted in an Impressionist style. *Still Life with Statuette* of 1911–3 dates from that time and is reminiscent of James Ensor's still lifes in terms of the application technique and use of colour.[18] The porcelain figurine of Taoist philosopher Lao Tze is still held at the Gust De Smet Municipal Museum in Sint-Martens-Latem. During his exile in the Netherlands in the First World War, De Smet, along with Frits Van den Berghe, discovered the modernist avant-garde, Fauvism, Cubism and German Expressionism. In 1906, he also became acquainted with Constant Permeke (1886–1952), and along with Paul-Gustave Van Hecke and André de Ridder, this trio would come to represent the core of Flemish Expressionism. Among his works, *Still Life* is stylistically very different from *Still Life with Statuette*. A variant of this composition was already present as a 'painting in a painting' in the double portrait *The Blue Sofa* of 1928. A preliminary draft in pencil and pastel shows how De Smet had originally wanted to depict a

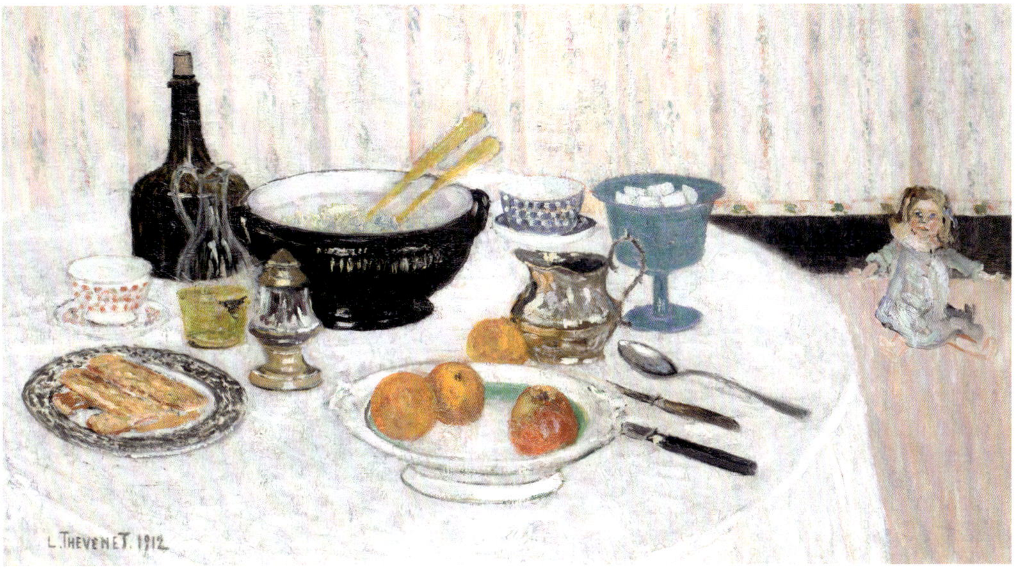

144

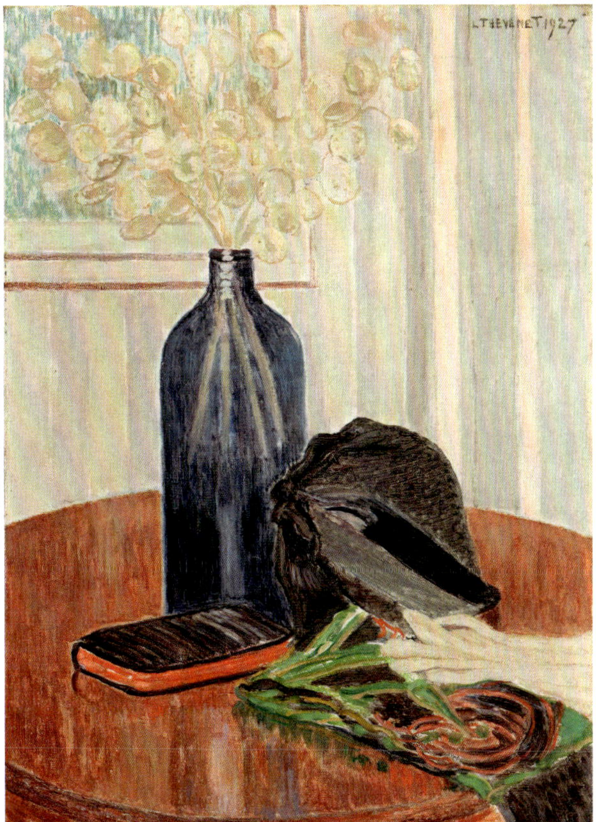

145

female nude in that part of the painting. In *Still Life*, titled *Nature morte* in 1928 in the magazine *Sélection*, the still life becomes 'simply an aesthetic game of planes and colours', where De Smet paints in his own Cubist style using paler colours and fine contours.[19] In 1945, Émile Langui, the Brussels art historian and subsequent director-general of fine arts and letters at the Department of Education, still saw it as a failed work.

Exhibited Works

cat. 146 Gustave De Smet, *Still Life with Statuette*, 1913, oil on canvas, 100 × 96.5 cm. Private collection.

cat. 27 Gustave De Smet, *Still Life*, 1928, oil on canvas, 80 × 70 cm. Part of the Emanuel Hoffmann Foundation, gift from the Maja and Emanuel Hoffmann Collection 1998, permanent loan to the Öffentliche Kunstsammlung Basel, inv. H 1998.19. (p. 60)

Bibliography

— Haesaerts, Luc, Paul Haesaerts, André de Ridder and Paul-Gustave Van Hecke, *Sélection: Chronique de la vie artistique*; *Gustave De Smet*, no. 2, 1928, p. 110.
— Langui 1945, pp. 104, 107.
— Boyens 1989.

PHILIBERT COCKX

(Ixelles, 29 April 1879 Uccle, 2 September 1949)

At age 20, Philibert Cockx was taught by a painter-decorator how to create imitation wood and marble effects. Later, he took evening classes variously at the Academy of Saint-Josse-ten-Noode, at the Brussels Academy under Isidore Verheyden and at the free studio L'Effort. Cockx rendered diverse images – nudes, portraits, genre scenes, landscapes, seascapes, still lifes and interiors – in a style halfway between Impressionism and Expressionism. Among other venues, he exhibited at La Libre Esthétique and Pour l'Art. Although author Arild Liénaux contends that Cockx never held a monographic exhibition in his lifetime, in 1937 he did exhibit 50 works in three rooms at the Cercle Artistique et Littéraire in Brussels. As in the case of Louis Thevenet, Auguste Oleffe (1867–1931) was an important pillar of artistic support as well as a friend. Cockx's paintings seem based more on dreams and visions than they are on reality. His works are characterised by harmonious colour combinations and an increasingly simplified design. The predominance of white and the facetted representation of objects in some of his still lifes from the period of the First World War are reminiscent of Rik Wouters's. During his final decades, Cockx worked in relative isolation in the hamlet of Kamerdelle in Uccle. Like Thevenet, it was the objects in his ambit that intrigued him. In *Lying Nude*, those items have been set on top of a piano above the recumbent woman, and the draped red curtains suggest a theatre scene. It is possible that Cockx had already exhibited this painting or a variant of it with a nude and a lemon-yellow background at the triennial salon of 1923 in Antwerp and at a gallery in 1924.

Exhibited Work

cat. 25 Philibert Cockx, *Lying Nude*, 1928, oil on canvas mounted on panel, 95.5 × 137.5 cm. Royal Museum of Fine Arts, Antwerp, inv. 2672. (p. 57)

Bibliography

— Joseph Conrardy, 'Au Salon triennal d'Anvers: La peinture', *Journal de Bruxelles*, 24 November 1923, p. 1.
— G. E., 'Les Expositions', *La Nation belge*, 18 November 1924, p. 3.
— C. B., 'Les Expositions: Philibert Cockx', *L'Indépendance belge*, 19 February 1937, p. 2.
— Louis Piérard, 'La mort de Philibert Cockx', *Le Peuple*, 4 September 1949, p. 2.

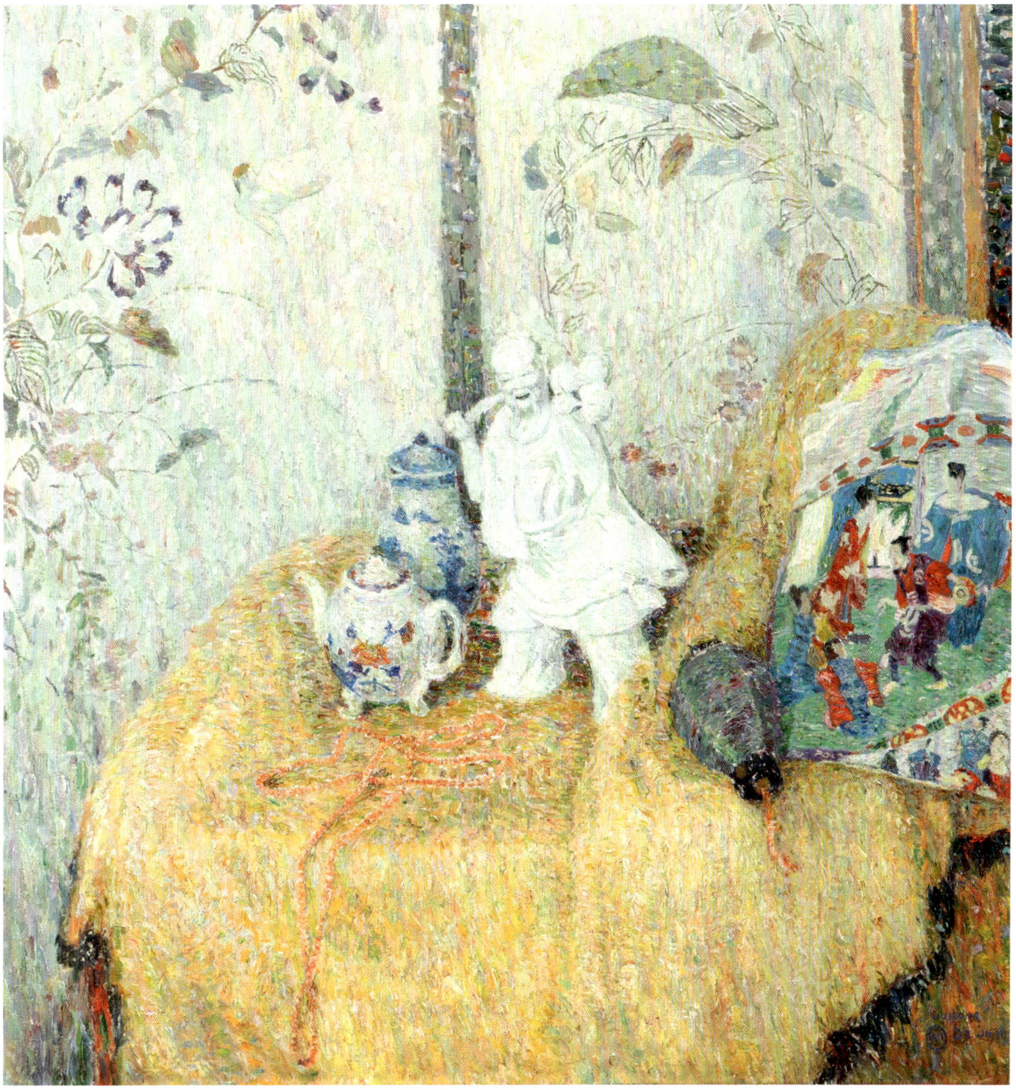

146

— Ixelles 1964.
— Liénaux 1965.

LÉON DE SMET
(Ghent, 20 July 1881–Deurle, 9 September 1966)

Léon De Smet was the son of the decorative painter, photographer and portraitist Jules De Smet and the younger brother by four years of Gustave (Gust), also an artist. He took classes at the Ghent Academy, with fellow students including Gustave Van De Woestyne. In 1901, Léon produced his first landscapes in the vicinity of Ghent at a time when he was sharing a studio with Frits Van den Berghe and others. Between 1906 and 1913, a second generation of artists coalesced in the village of Sint-Martens-Latem. Following the Symbolist-inspired mysticism of the previous generation, it was the luminism of Emile Claus (1849–1924) that served as the primary reference point for this group. At its core were the De Smet brothers, Constant Permeke (1886–1952) and Van den Berghe. De Smet fled to England during the First World War, staying in Torquay awhile, but chiefly in London, where he painted strikingly optimistic works. For a brief period, he came under the influence of his brother's Expressionist work, but in around 1930, he returned to Impressionism, and to Latem. De Smet's work shows a preference for beauty and charm: young women, porcelain and fruit, all of this often captured within interiors. Between 1905 and 1930, the human figure is almost always female; they do not seem engaged in real activity, nor do they move much, an aspect discernible in Art Nouveau and Art Deco. That passivity is present in *Nude with Red Dresser* of 1921, in which the decorative dominates in an abundantly vernacular interior – a predilection that he shared with Louis Thevenet. The bouquet of flowers is also a set element in De Smet's still lifes and interiors.

Exhibited Work

cat. 18 Léon De Smet, *Nude with Red Dresser*, 1921, oil on canvas, 152 × 115.5 cm. Property of the Belgian State, Collection of the Wallonia-Brussels Federation, inv. 1984. (p. 51)

Bibliography

— Boyens and Bosschaert 1994, pp. 230–38.

LÉON SPILLIAERT
(Ostend, 28 July 1881–Ixelles, 23 November 1946)

Ostend artist Léon Spilliaert, the son of a perfumer with a barbershop, was self-taught apart from a few months of classes at the Bruges Academy. In 1902–3, while working in Brussels for the publisher Edmond Deman, Spilliaert became acquainted with Symbolist literature and the work of Odilon Redon (1840–1916). Deman motivated Spilliaert to travel to Paris, and he arranged the artist's introduction to the Symbolist poet-critic Émile Verhaeren. Spilliaert worked almost exclusively on paper or card, using quickly applied media such as (coloured) pencil, India ink, watercolour, gouache and pastel chalk, producing in addition to this a minor graphic oeuvre. His works in the period prior to his marriage in December 1916 are largely notable for their enigmatic atmosphere: initially dark for the most part with Symbolist inspiration underlying them but, equally, with Expressionist qualities. In his idiosyncratic style, Spilliaert captured the world around him: the sea and the forsaken Ostend dike, trees in the park or locals such as fisher-women. In his particularly productive period between 1907 and 1909, he created not only his most imagination-sparking and canonised self-portraits and intriguing views of dikes, but also a vast number of interiors and still lifes – genres with which he remained engaged throughout his life. Objects from his familiar environment are keenly observed but

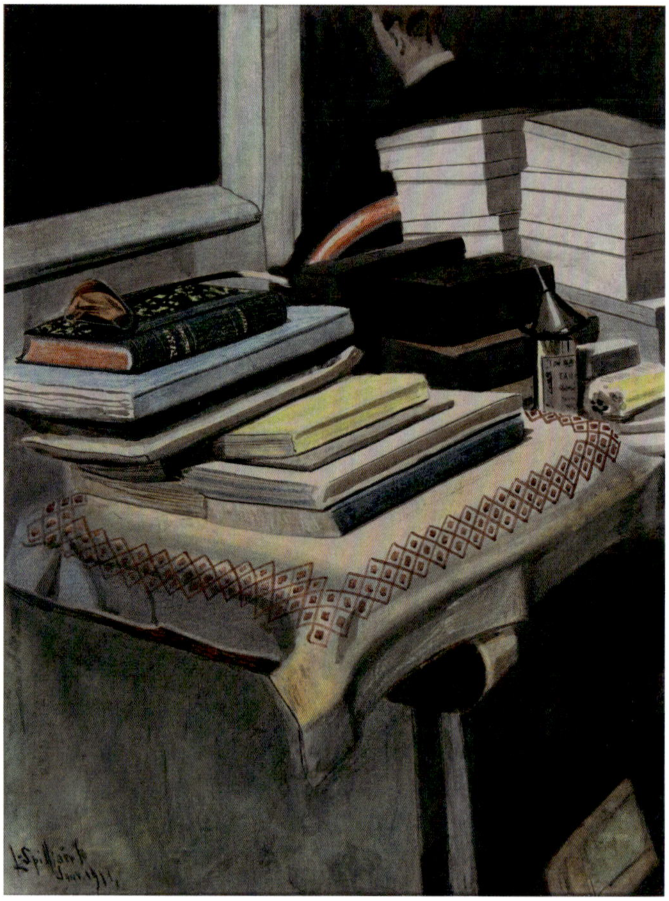

147

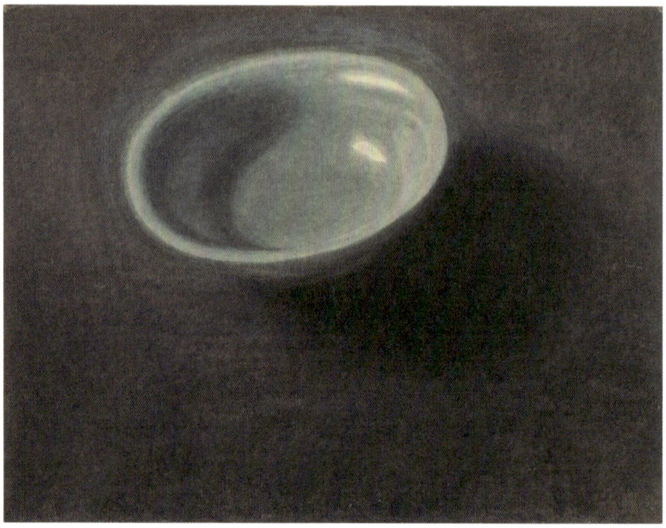

148

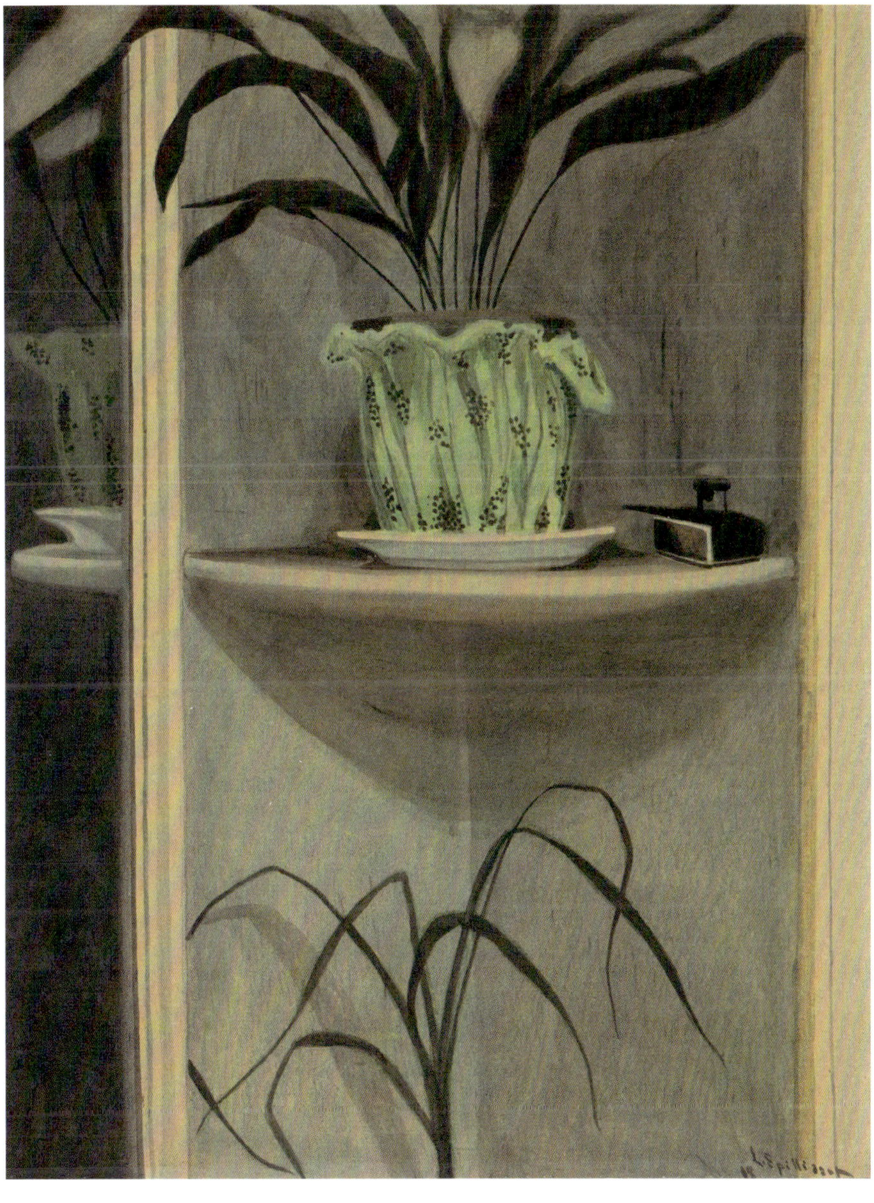

149

decontextualised, such as the eccentrically staged *The Blue Bowl* or the tightly cropped interior scene *Plants, Inkpot and Mirror* with full frontality. A figure seen from behind – probably the artist's brother – lends an uncanny feeling to *Console with Books and Boxes, Figure Seen from Behind*. The peacock tail-feathers and the gaping shell in *Vase and Shell* render the still life intense and restless.

Exhibited Works

cat. 147 Léon Spilliaert, *Console with Books and Boxes, Figure Seen from Behind*, 1907, India ink, ink wash, colour pencil, pastel, chalk, gouache and black chalk on paper, 63.4 × 48.1 cm. Private collection.

cat. 148 Léon Spilliaert, *The Blue Bowl*, 1907, India ink, gouache and pastel chalk on paper, 48 × 63 cm. Mu.ZEE, City of Ostend Collection, inv. SM000058.

cat. 149 Léon Spilliaert, *Plants, Inkpot and Mirror*, 1908, watercolour, gouache, colour pencil and India ink on paper, 64 × 49 cm. Mu.ZEE, City of Ostend Collection, inv. SM001747.

cat. 22 Léon Spilliaert, *Vase and Shell*, 1911, pastel on card, 89.2 × 70.2 cm. Private collection via Philip Seghers Gallery. (p. 54)

Bibliography

— Legrand 1981, pp. 140–43.
— Tricot 1996, pp. 7–22.
— Adriaens-Pannier 2023, pp. 70–71.
— Goldman 2023, p. 83.

GUSTAVE VAN DE WOESTYNE

(Ghent, 2 August 1881–Uccle, 21 April 1947)

In 1900, together with his brother Karel, the Ghent artist Gustave Van De Woestyne left for the village of Sint-Martens-Latem in the Leie River region. He remained there until 1909 and was the youngest member of the Symbolist-inspired first Latem School, the group that had at its core artists such as his brother, George Minne (1866–1941) and Valerius De Saedeleer (1867–1941). In 1902, Van De Woestyne became fascinated with late medieval painting and spirituality during the exhibition *Les primitifs flamands* in Bruges. The ordinary country folk of Latem turned into an important source of inspiration for his painting, which conceals a great deal of symbolism and mysticism. After the First World War, which he spent in Wales and England, Van De Woestyne came under the influence of Cubism and Expressionism. It was in galleries such as Le Centaure in Brussels where he exhibited paintings in which he had synthesised well-defined, recognisable forms and simplified colours. Some paintings display an affinity with Surrealism; André de Ridder described it as 'constructive expressionism'.[20] From 1920 to 1930, Van De Woestyne made a great many still lifes. *Still Life with Globe* and *Still Life with Groundsel*, both painted in gouache in the early 1920s, share the same formalistic fascination with an undulating water jug. Whereas the objects in the first painting have been clearly positioned with a certain degree of perspective, those in the second painting appear to be floating on some indeterminate mass. When Van De Woestyne painted *Still Life with Bananas* in 1930, his patrons were David and Alice van Buuren, for whom he produced seven still lifes between 1928 and 1931.

Exhibited Works

cat. 24 Gustave Van De Woestyne, *Still Life with Globe*, c.1921–2, gouache and oil on Japanese paper and card, 56 × 77.5 cm. Museum of Fine Arts, Ghent, inv. 2004-H. (p. 54)

cat. 23 Gustave Van De Woestyne, *Still Life with Groundsel*, 1922, gouache on paper, 76.5 × 55.5 cm. Museum of Fine Arts, Ghent, inv. 2004-G. (p. 54)

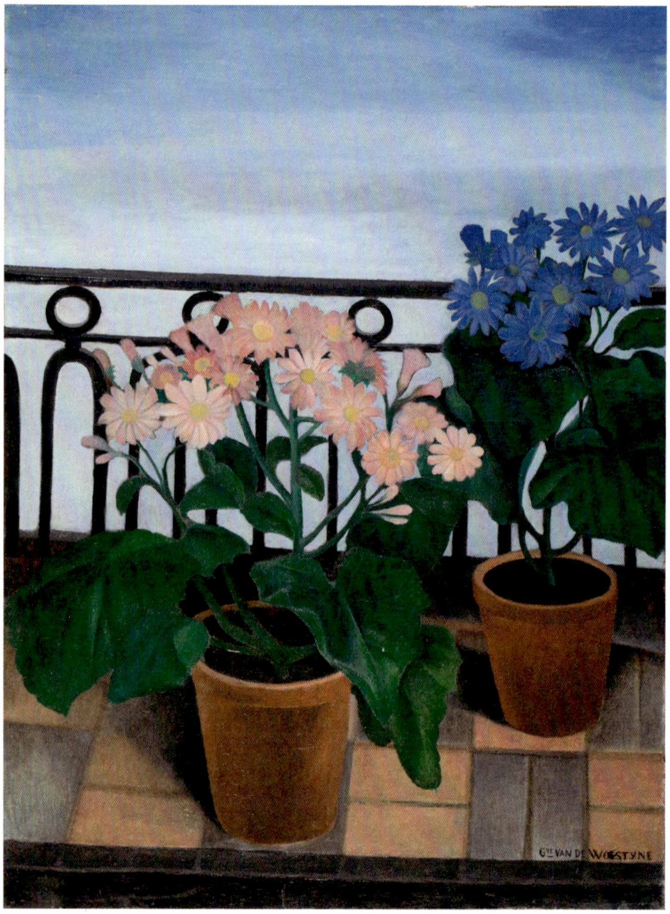

150

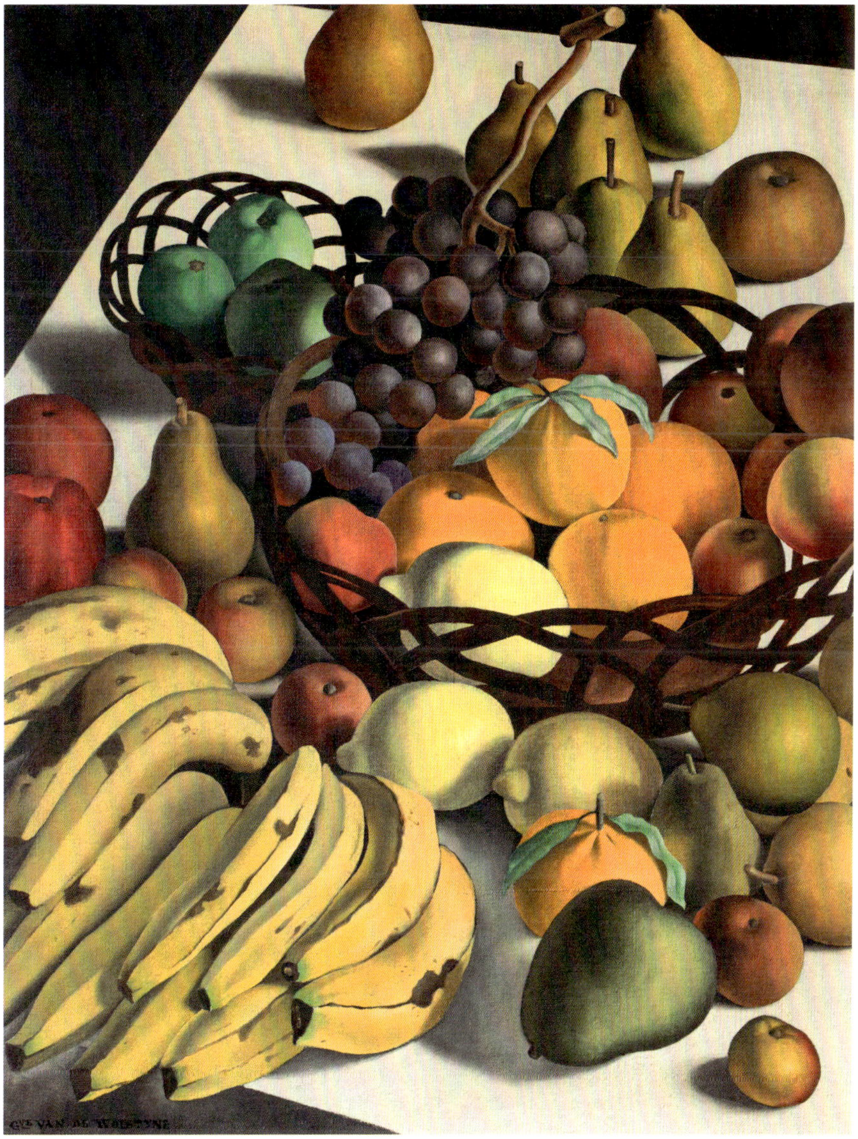

151

cat. 150 Gustave Van De Woestyne, *Balcony with Flowers (Cinerarias)*, 1929, oil on canvas, 80 × 60 cm. Museum of Fine Arts, Ghent, inv. 2015-JM.
cat. 151 Gustave Van De Woestyne, *Still Life with Bananas*, 1930, oil on canvas, 80 × 62 cm. Van Buuren Museum & Gardens, Brussels, inv. 77388.

Bibliography
— van de Woestijne 1949.
— Ghent 2010, pp. 49, 210–21.
— 's-Hertogenbosch 2022, pp. 66–103.

WALTER VAES
(Borgerhout, 12 February 1882–Antwerp, 3 April 1958)

Walter Vaes took his first art classes – initially as an engraver – from his uncle, Piet Verhaert (1852–1908), who specialised in views of old Antwerp. In 1904, following training at the Antwerp Academy, Vaes won the Prix de Rome. He practised a variety of genres and, in addition to painting landscapes, history scenes, still lifes and floral paintings, produced portraits, including one of James Ensor in 1929. In 1904, the conservative *Handelsblad* commented that 'the modernists hold him in high regard'[21] concerning his small-scale paintings in a realist-Impressionist style. A year later, Vaes was present at the inception of the Antwerp artist association Kunst van Heden, with Ensor and Léon Frederic also exhibiting work alongside him. Vaes's earliest still lifes bear Ensor's influence, incorporating motifs such as a suckling pig, a plucked cockerel or a dead duck. The use of a bird's eye view is peculiar to Vaes's style, this being how he broke away from the still life's traditional horizontal vantage point. Consequently, in one image, it is literally the belly of the titular crab that is on view. Equally idiosyncratic is the way he crops the vase in *Flowers*. First and foremost, Vaes painted physical matter – he would as soon commit a plate of fish innards to canvas as simple slices of fish – which he depicted as patches of colour arranged side by side. In 1921, the critic Pol de Mont wrote of Vaes: 'He paints fish like Linnig and meat like Verhaeren. … [H]is apples and pears [have] the startling reality of those made by Ensor.'[22]

Exhibited Works
cat. 20 Walter Vaes, *Red Fish*, 1906, oil on canvas, 53.5 × 66 cm. Royal Museum of Fine Arts, Antwerp, inv. 2035. (p. 53)
cat. 21 Walter Vaes, *Still Life with Fish*, s.d., oil on canvas, 65.5 × 82.4 cm. Janssens Collection, Antwerp. (p. 53)
cat. 152 Walter Vaes, *Flowers*, s.d., oil on canvas, 60 × 76 cm. Janssens Collection, Antwerp.
cat. 153 Walter Vaes, *Two Slices of Fish*, s.d., oil on canvas, 39 × 47 cm. Collection Museum Helmantel (former Kunsthandel Bies, Eindhoven, Netherlands).
cat. 154 Walter Vaes, *Crab*, s.d., oil on canvas, 36.6 × 44.7 cm. Royal Museum of Fine Arts, Antwerp, inv. 2876.

Bibliography
— [Albert] Plasschaert, 'Het laatste werk van Walter Vaes', *Onze kunst*, no. 30, 1916, pp. 61–71.
— de Mont 1921, pp. 138–41.
— Delen 1942, pp. 23–36.
— Sint-Niklaas 1986.

RIK WOUTERS
(Mechelen, 21 August 1882–Amsterdam, 11 July 1916)

Rik Wouters was the son of a Mechelen furniture wood-carver who taught him the wood-carving trade from an early age. He took sculpture classes at the academy, but he also began to teach himself how to

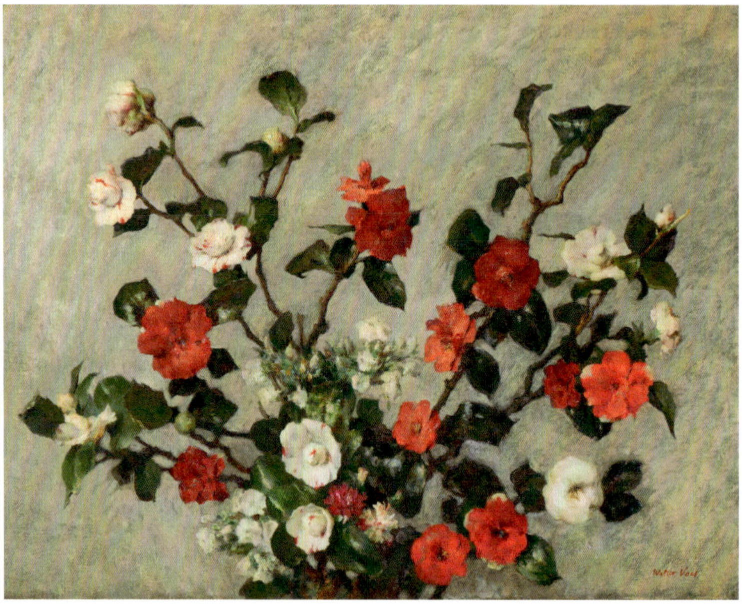

152

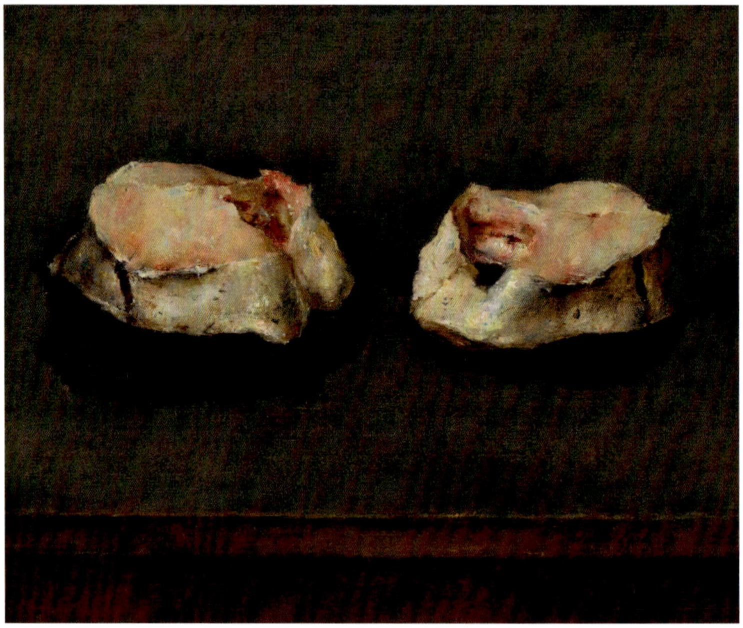

153

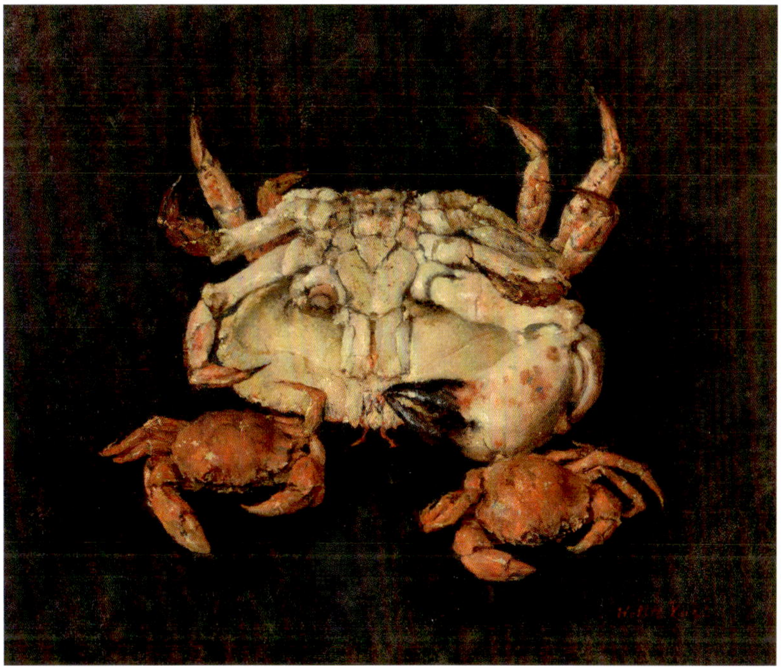

154

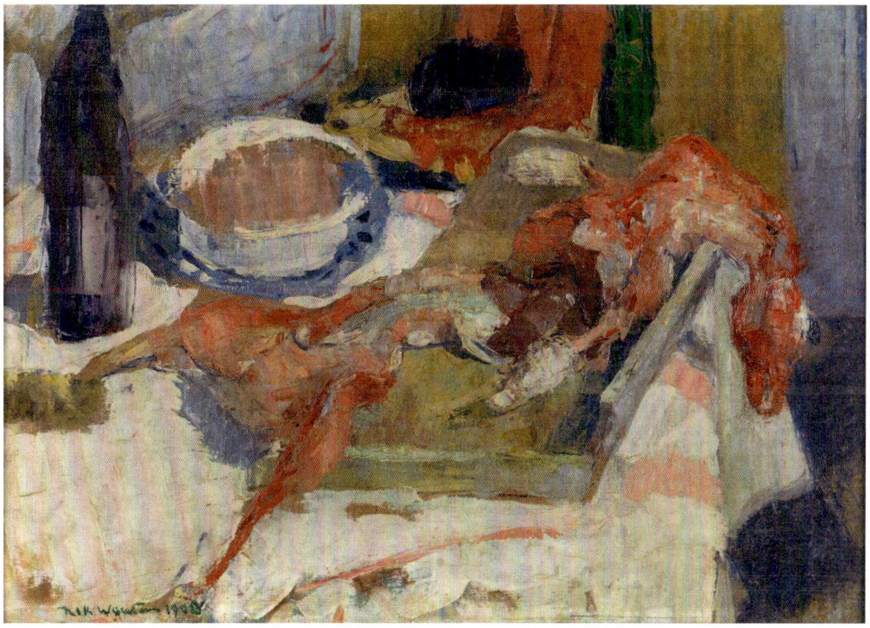

155

paint. In 1907, after he had married his lifelong muse Hélène (Nel) Duerinckx, the newly-weds moved to the Sonian Forest. Wouters's career was bolstered thanks to his friendship with gallery owner Georges Giroux in Brussels, resulting in exhibitions and a contract with monthly wages. Wouters's artistic admiration extended to James Ensor and his use of colour ('The sky is pink! God be damned, what a pink! It is unique in the history of painting', he said after having seen Ensor's works in 1913).[23] Wouters had found another hero on a previous visit to Paris in 1911: 'I have the feeling that Ensor pales in comparison to all of this', he wrote concerning the work of Paul Cézanne (1839–1906).[24] This resulted in Wouters clarifying his palette, which had already begun to comprise pure colours under Ensor's influence, colours that stand out against the grey in *Etching Table*. In his still lifes, Wouters borrowed Cézanne's sloping tabletop, such as in *Still Life with Skinned Hare*, and above all his firmness of form and abundance of colour, displayed expressly in *Apples and Artificial Flowers*, the second version of which he called *Tribute to Cézanne*. In 1913, he made an impressive bust of Ensor. As a prisoner of war in the First World War, he was treated for facial cancer in the Netherlands, losing an eye in the process. The still life *Sombre Mood* of 1915 dates from that difficult period and introduced a form of Expressionism that never fully came to fruition, owing to the painter's premature death.

Exhibited Works

cat. 19 Rik Wouters, *The Skinned Rabbit B*, 1908, oil on canvas, 40.2 × 47 cm. Royal Museums of Fine Arts of Belgium, Brussels, inv. 11570. (p. 53)

cat. 155 Rik Wouters, *Still Life with Skinned Hare*, 1908, oil on canvas, 45.2 × 66 cm. Royal Museums of Fine Arts of Belgium, Brussels, inv. 6665.

cat. 156 Rik Wouters, *Etching Table*, 1909, oil on canvas, 86 × 94 cm. Royal Museum of Fine Arts, Antwerp, inv. 2167.

cat. 157 Rik Wouters, *Green Cabbage*, 1912, oil on canvas, 111 × 100.5 cm. Royal Museums of Fine Arts of Belgium, Brussels, inv. 4864.

cat. 158 Rik Wouters, *Sombre Mood*, 1915, oil on canvas, 87 × 101 cm. Royal Museums of Fine Arts of Belgium, Brussels, inv. 4632.

cat. 159 Rik Wouters, *Apples and Artificial Flowers*, 1913, watercolour on canvas, 125.7 × 110.5 cm. KBC Bank NV, Brussels, inv. 98000441.

Bibliography

— de Mont 1921, pp. 230–32.
— Avermaete 1962.
— Min 2011.
— Brussels 2017.

FRITS VAN DEN BERGHE
(Ghent, 3 April 1883–Ghent, 29 September 1939)

Between 1904 and 1913, following four years of training at the Ghent Academy, Frits Van den Berghe spent his summers in Sint-Martens-Latem. As the son of Ghent University's librarian, he became in a sense the intellectual leader of the second artist's group at Latem. His simplified style was similar to that of his good friend Gustave De Smet. While both residing in the Netherlands during the First World War, they encountered international modernism: Cubism, Fauvism and German Expressionism. In 1922, they were living in Ostend together with Constant Permeke (1886–1952), the three of them becoming the most important artists practising what was referred to as Flemish Expressionism. Villa Malpertuis, the artist's residence of Paul-Gustave Van Hecke and Honorine (Norine) Deschrijver (1887–1977) in Afsnee by the Leie River, became a prominent meeting place, much like Galerie Sélection (1920–22) and, later, Le Centaure (1922–30), both run by Van Hecke and

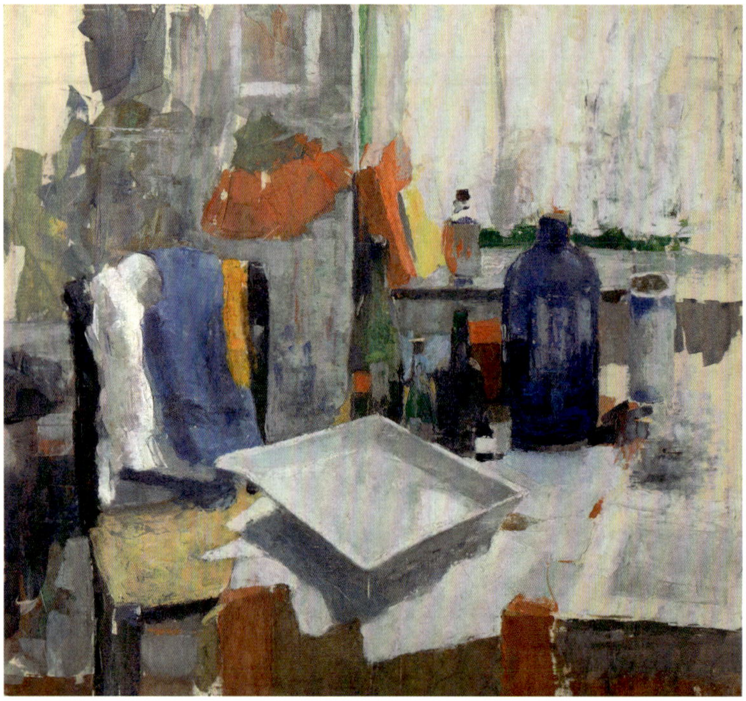

156

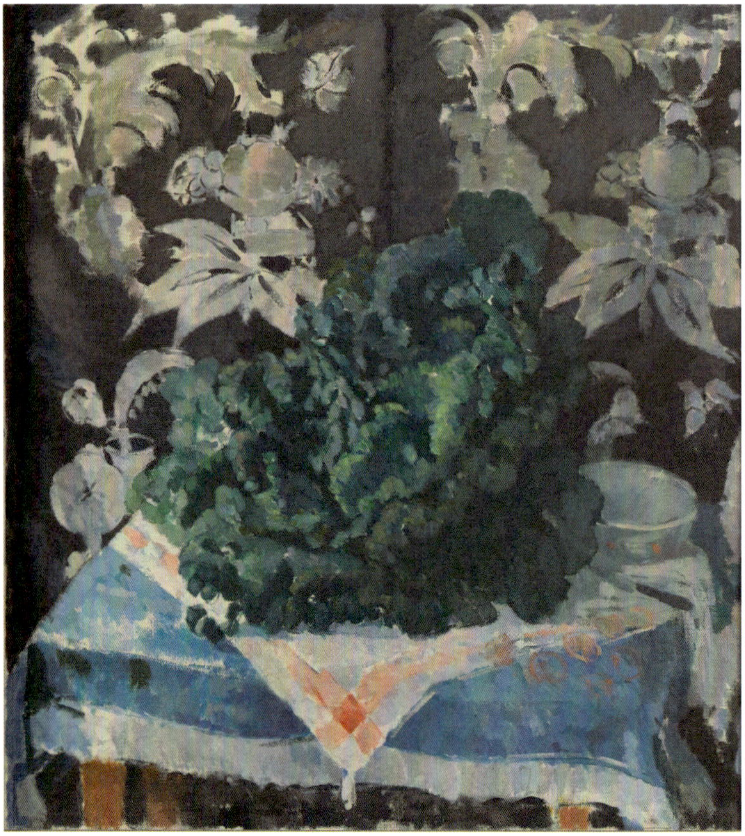

157

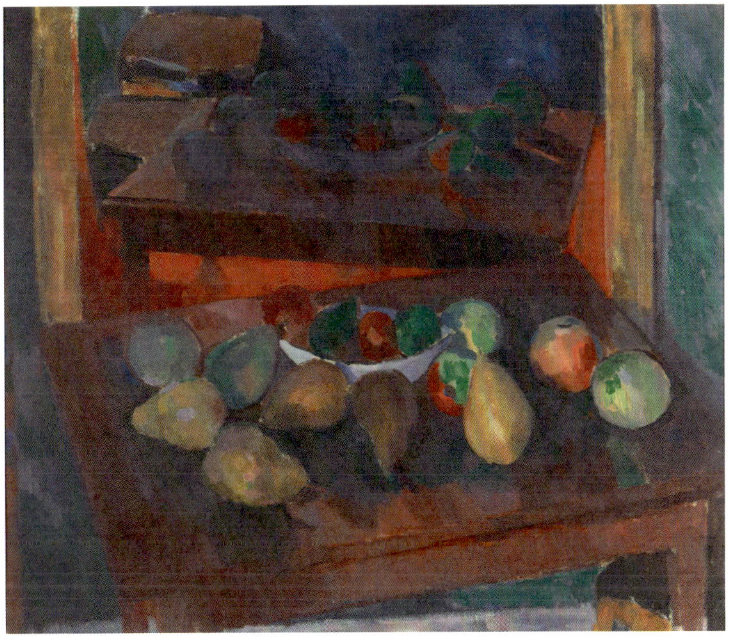

158

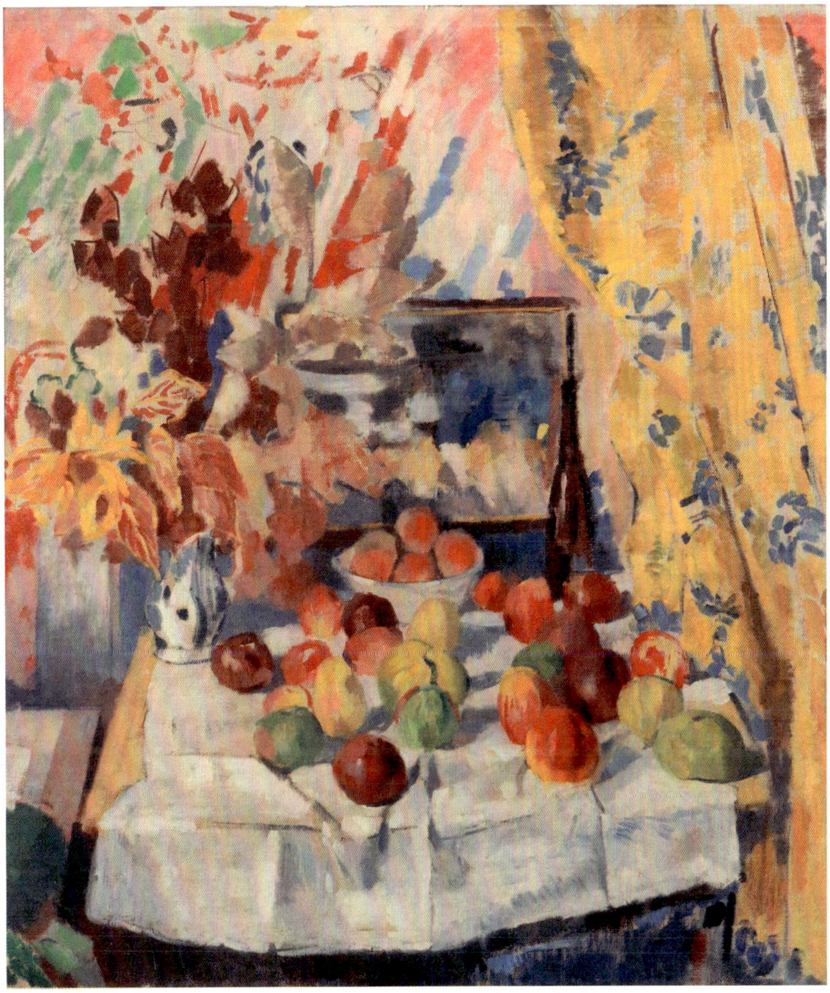

159

André de Ridder. Simplified forms and fragmentation characterise Van den Berghe's work, as do the strikingly vernacular themes and the rustic Leie River region. *Flowers over the City* of 1929, the second version of a painting made in the same year, is typical of the style between Surrealism and Expressionism sought out by Van den Berghe in his later work. After 1928, his art changed in terms of both form and content. Human destiny is at its core, employing familiar, sometimes archaic and almost archetypal motifs. The substance in this work is raw, and the city in the background – perhaps just like the society that it represents – has been eroded and lies in decay. The painting is perhaps a commentary on the typical traditional floral still life with flowers as masks and leaves as diabolical hands.

Exhibited Work

cat. 160 Frits Van den Berghe, *Flowers over the City*, 1929, oil on canvas, 126 × 97 cm. Private collection – on long-term loan at Mu.ZEE, Ostend.

Bibliography

— Langui 1968, p. 190.
— Boyens 1999, pp. 255–94, 447 (nos 654–5).
— The Hague 2023, p. 27.

JEAN BRUSSELMANS
(Brussels, 13 June 1884–Dilbeek, 9 January 1953)

Jean Brusselmans was born into a Brussels family of humble means. At age 14, he entered an apprenticeship at a lithographic printing office and took classes at the Brussels Academy, later being tutored by Isidore Verheyden. He rented a studio in 1907 in Brussels with Rik Wouters, a lifelong friend. In 1911, it was in that milieu that Brusselmans became acquainted with both James Ensor and Léon Spilliaert. Following many changes of address in the capital, in 1924 Brusselmans settled with his family in the hamlet of Koudenaerde in Dilbeek, in a house that he called Kouden Haard (Cold Hearth), a wry reference to his financial situation. Brusselmans conveyed reality on canvas in his highly idiosyncratic style, but his paintings, praised for their simplicity, did not sell well. However, he received financial support from Luc and Paul Haesaerts, who noted that, in Brusselmans's still lifes, 'everything [is] lucid, of a perplexing simplicity: the drawing has been rendered using strong lines, the forms are rough, the feeling is pure, without deviations. The paint comes straight from the tube, the composition straight from the brain, the palette straight from the heart.'[25] In the late, almost retrospective *Still Life with Fan* of 1948, Brusselmans composed a collage of objects and motifs taken from his earlier works: the fruit basket, the vase of flowers, the herrings and the scallop shells – the latter also on view in *Still Life with Griffon* of 1936. The tabletop and wall constitute one surface, and everything – including the later addition of the magazine cover featuring American actress Linda Darnell – has been reduced to simple, almost geometric forms and is indeed defined by 'strong lines'.

Exhibited Works

cat. 161 Jean Brusselmans, *Still Life with Slices of Sausage*, 1936, oil on canvas, 112 × 122 cm. Royal Museum of Fine Arts, Antwerp, inv. 3198.

cat. 28 Jean Brusselmans, *Still Life with Griffon*, 1936, oil on canvas, 109.5 × 122.4 cm. Mu.ZEE, City of Ostend Collection, inv. MZ000054. (p. 61)

cat. 162 Jean Brusselmans, *Still Life with Fan*, 1948, oil on canvas, 130 × 125 cm. Musea Brugge, inv. 1980.GRO0030.I.

Bibliography

— Delevoy 1972, pp. 73–85, 251 (no. 404), 252 (no. 406), 237 (no. 565).

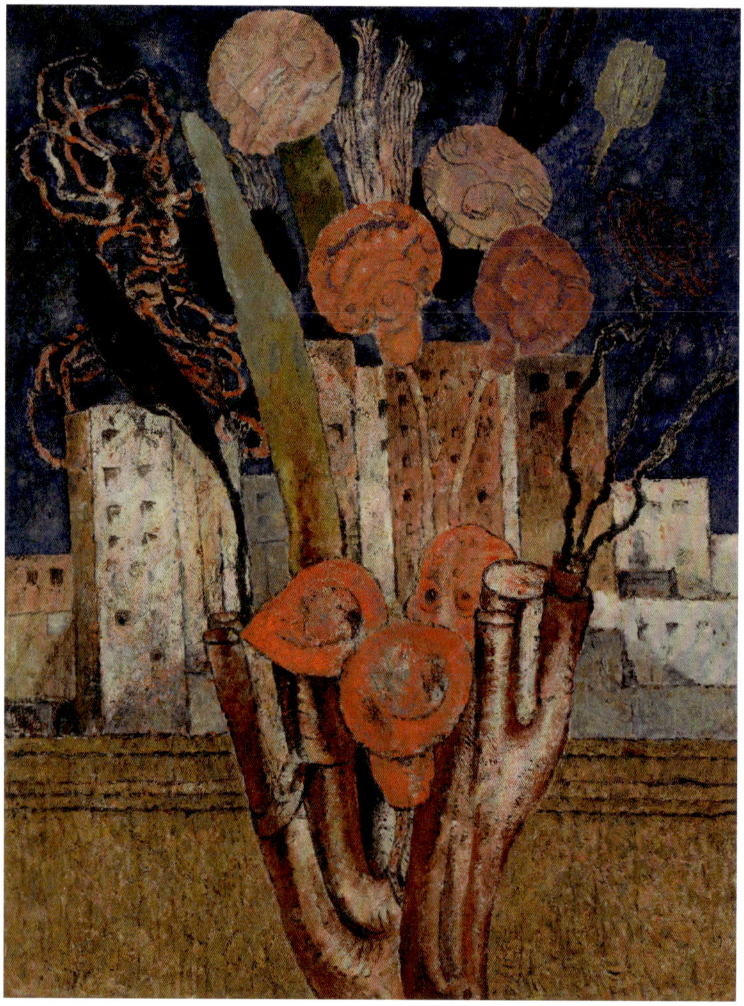

160

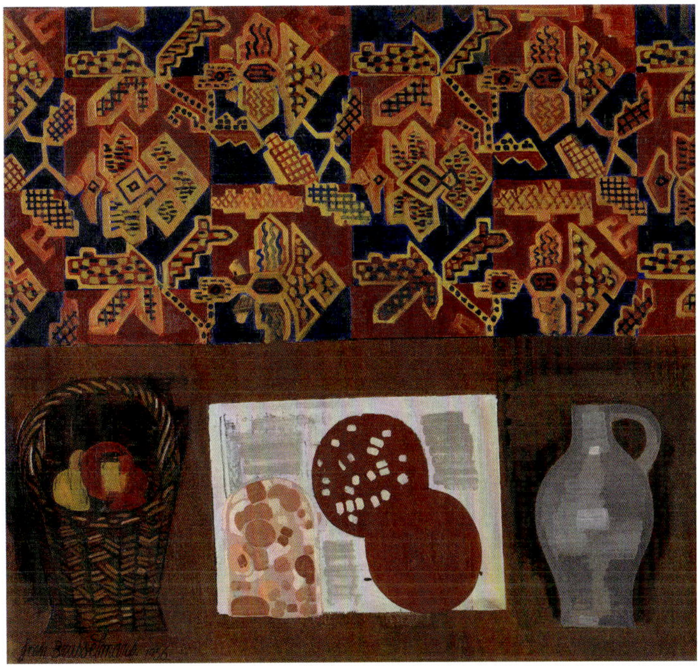

161

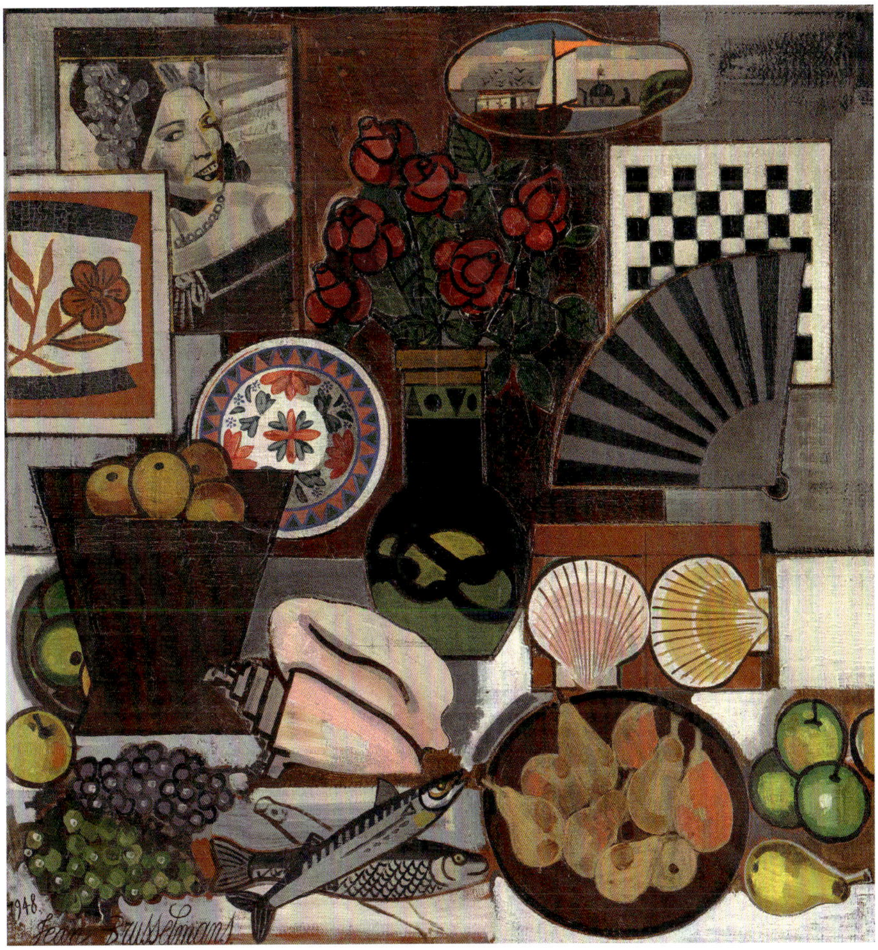

162

— Ostend 2011, pp. 63–4.
— Van Kerkhoven 2011, pp. 26–33.
— The Hague 2018.

MARTHE DONAS
(Antwerp, 26 October 1885–Audregnies, 31 January 1967)

Against the wishes of her father, who would have preferred not to see her paint floral still lifes anywhere except in their Antwerp attic, Marthe Donas joined a course for young ladies at the Antwerp Academy under such tutors as Frans van Kuyck (1852–1915). She encountered international Cubism during the First World War in Paris, following periods spent in Ireland, Great Britain and the Netherlands. The Ukrainian sculptor Alexander Archipenko (1887–1964), celebrated for his sculpture paintings, became a particularly important source of inspiration and an intimate friend. Around 1920, Donas made a name for herself in Paris under the androgynous pseudonym 'Tour' Donas in order to bypass prejudice against female artists. She also exhibited work in Berlin at Der Sturm. In 1921, she became ill, broke up with Archipenko and returned to Antwerp and went to Brabant and Brussels. She took a hiatus from painting between 1928 and the late 1940s, after which she embarked on a second career and her earlier work was rediscovered. Between 1917 and 1919, in addition to depicting female figures, Donas chiefly produced still lifes showing a concerted approach to abstraction in which objects – bottles, vases or a chair, often analogous to Archipenko's art – ultimately became unrecognisable, leaving only their colour and shape intact. Donas cited *Cubist Still Life* of 1917 as her first Cubist work in the genre. The characteristic Cubist 'broken mirror' effect is present, suggested above all by monochrome, sharply pointed planes that lend movement to the image. In 1920, the painter Otto Nebel (1892–1973) wrote about Donas's work in his role as a critic for *Der Sturm*: 'Colourful still lifes are life, which makes you smile at the title "still life" [*nature morte*, literally: "dead nature"].'[26]

Exhibited Work

cat. 26 Marthe Donas, *Cubist Still Life*, 1917, oil on canvas, 34.5 × 53 cm. Royal Museum of Fine Arts, Antwerp, inv. 2948. (p. 59)

Bibliography
— Nebel 1920.
— Frankfurt/Ghent 2015–6, pp. 13–40, 50–61.

ALBERT SAVERYS
(Deinze, 12 May 1886–Petegem, 29 April 1964)

Albert Saverys was the son of a painter-decorator. After his father's premature death in 1902, Albert was obliged to take up a position in the family business. Apart from a few drawing lessons in Deinze, he was largely self-taught in painting until his enrolment at the Ghent Academy in 1912. His early works were influenced by the luminism of Emile Claus (1849–1924) and Modest Huys (1874–1932). In Sint-Martens-Latem, before the outbreak of the First World War, Saverys became acquainted with the brothers Gust and Léon De Smet, as well as Frits Van den Berghe. However, it was mostly Japanese prints and the art of Vincent van Gogh, which he had discovered just before the war, that left an impression on the young artist, owing to their wealth of colour. Saverys continued to paint Neo-Impressionist works even after the war, employing a touch of orientalist fantasy. Although his palette became more sombre and his brush-work more Expressionist, he also created lively, almost Ensorian, fairground tableaux. In the 1920s, Saverys had Henry van de Velde build two cottage-style villas in the coastal dunes in quick succession. At that time, Saverys was popular in

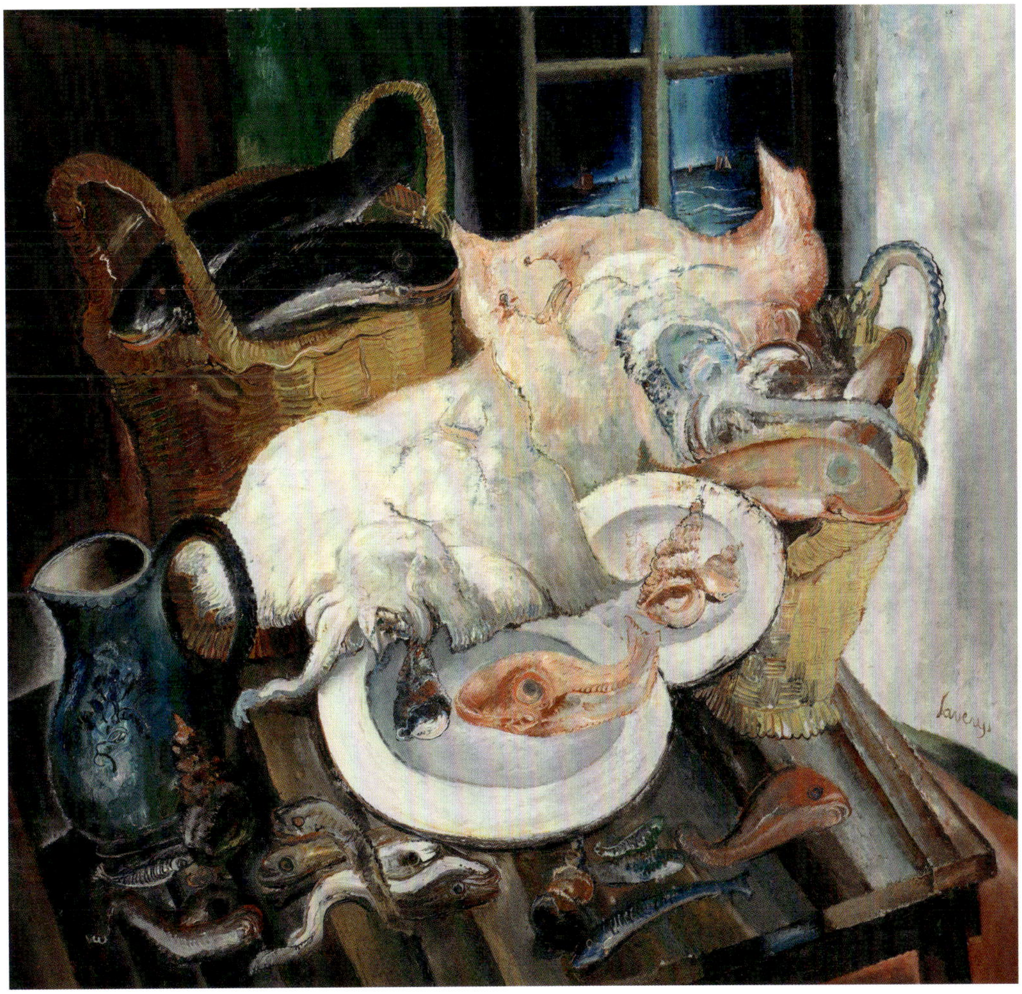

163

the Belgian art scene, and he produced a large number of fish still lifes that did well on the market. Following James Ensor's example, the skate is often the focus of attention, as in *The Two Skates* of 1926. A typical feature is the tilted table that breaks the perspective and, together with the wavy lines in the baskets and the fish, provides dynamism, while through a window we glimpse a view of the sea as the source of this natural bounty.

Exhibited Work

cat. 163 Albert Saverys, *The Two Skates*, 1926, oil on canvas, 122 × 133 cm. Museum Dhondt-Dhaenens, Deurle, inv. 000 088.

Bibliography

— Huys 1983, pp. 49–62.
— Deinze 2014, pp. 132–6.

RENÉ MAGRITTE

(Lessines, 21 November 1898–Schaerbeek, 15 August 1967)

René Magritte was the eldest child in a family from Hainaut. He attended the Brussels Academy and afterwards, to earn a living, worked briefly at a wallpaper factory. He was commissioned to make posters, illustrations and lettering by the fashion designer Honorine (Norine) Deschrijver (1887–1977), the wife of Paul-Gustave Van Hecke. In the mid-1920s, Magritte developed a style of painting in which objects were rendered to look recognisable, well defined and almost clinical, betraying the influence of Giorgio de Chirico (1888–1978). In 1927, he exhibited work at Le Centaure in Brussels, after which he spent three years in a Parisian suburb and joined the French Surrealists. After 1930, he lived the rest of his days in Brussels. Magritte's work is typified by crisp, clearly identifiable objects that become thought provoking owing to their depiction or relationship to one another. Conventions pertaining to perspective, material or scale are deliberately and blatantly broken. His fascination with objects meant that still lifes often became the focus of his work. Sometimes Magritte would petrify a still life to become a rock formation, magnify objects in an interior setting or, more frequently still, make unusual combinations and metamorphoses to engender a sense of alienation. We know a rose in a vase or garden, but not in a universe. In *The Red Model*, the first version of which (Centre Pompidou, Paris) dates from 1935, an old pair of shoes is transformed; the lifeless object (the shoe) becomes the living one (the foot) and vice versa. The painting became one of his most popular images, resulting in the creation of no fewer than six additional versions that were given different surface media and backgrounds in each instance, on canvas and on paper. In 1937, among other works, he painted a version for the British patron and poet Edward James (1907–1984), and in 1953, a version with a stone wall as the background for gallery owner Alexander Iolas (1908–1987).

Exhibited Work

cat. 164 René Magritte, *The Red Model*, 1953, oil on canvas, 38 × 46 cm. BNP Paribas Fortis Collection.

cat. 29 René Magritte, *The Voice of the Absolute*, 1955, oil on canvas, 40 × 50 cm. Private collection. (p. 62)

Bibliography

— Sylvester 1993a, pp. 205 (no. 380), 207 (no. 382), 237 (no. 428).
— Sylvester 1993b, pp. 222 (no. 795), 249–50 (no. 829).
— Sylvester 1994, pp. 96 (no. 1249), 145 (no. 1338), 154 (no. 1352).
— Draguet, Devillez and Goddeeris 2009, pp. 36, 96–8.
— Sylvester 2009, pp. 280, 384.

1 'Un "naturc-mortiste", François Huygens, talent probe et classé; ses fleurs et fruits sont dans le goût traditionnel.' S., 'Beaux-Arts', *Le Vingtième Siècle*, 29 November 1903, p. 2.

2 'Il nous suffira d'observer que ces trois mots: *Fleurs, Fruits* et *Accessoires*, fournissent tout à tour l'étiquette nécessaire pour cataloguer les tableaux du maître.' De Taeye 1894, p. 182.

3 'Mlle Virginie de Sartorius a peint des *fruits*. L'eau en vient à la bouche; on peut véritablement dire de cette demoiselle qu'elle peint avec fruit.' Jules Lecomte, 'Exposition universelle de 1855: Beaux-Arts', *L'Indépendance belge*, 19 July 1855, p. 2.

4 'Peignez un hareng-saur ou un empereur, cela m'est absolument égal.' Hout (Louis Dubois), 'Le peintre d'histoire: Étude d'après nature', *L'Art libre*, no. 4, 1 February 1872, p. 50.

5 'Mieux vaut peindre des huitres immortelles que de rater des œuvres héroïques.' 'Echos de la ville', *L'Indépendance belge*, 18 April 1902, p. 3.

6 '[...] sont des fêtes de couleur, des débauches de plantureuses, succulentes, ardentes et néanmoins fines et précises notations de tout ce que peut enclore et exprimer, posséder et révéler de vie et de santé, et – disons le mot – de Poésie, des objets apparemment inertes ou même vulgaires.' André 1907, p. 33.

7 '[...] recherche loyale de la réalité [une] certaine réminiscence de Louis Dubois'. 'Au Cercle artistique', *L'Art moderne*, 4 May 1884, p. 150.

8 '[...] les lutins follets [...] le plus flaireur de nos peintres [...] Nos ultra-modernes goûtent peu l'effort des vieux peintres du réel [...] œuvre capitale de l'artiste [...].' Ensor 1925, pp. 110–15.

9 '*L'Entrecôte* est de la peinture superbe.' Cited in Aron 1997, p. 159.

10 Brussels, RMFAB, ACAB, no. 65 568, October 1933, unpublished sheets 1933–9.

11 Fernand Khnopff, 'Studio Talk', *The International Studio* 45, no. 179, 1912, p. 160.

12 Paul Buschmann, 'Belgian Artists in England', *The International Studio* 55, no. 220, 1915, p. 266.

13 '[...] tant de charmantes femmes dont l'art de peindre vaut la virtuosité tricoteuse, brodeuse ou crocheteuse'. 'Théâtres et Beaux-Arts', *L'Indépendance belge*, 21 December 1893, p. 3.

14 '[...] en même temps l'art voué aux mains virginales et aux heures sédentaires des modernes vestales'. 'Le Salon de Paris, 1889', *L'Indépendance belge*, 5 June 1889, p. 3.

15 'Théâtres et Beaux-Arts', *L'Indépendance belge*, 21 December 1893, p. 3.

16 Cited in Dewilde 2008, p. 30.

17 'M. Thevenet ne se contente pas de rendre la matière, la forme et la couleur des choses et la lumière qui les baigne, mais nous donne la joie d'animer les moindres objets, de nous dire leur vie de tous les jours, de nous exprimer leur âme.' Sander Pierron, cited in Ekonomides 2021, pp. 35–6.

18 Boyens 1989, p. 93.

19 Ibid., p. 202.

20 Ghent 2010, p. 45.

21 'Tentoonstelling van waterverfschilderingen, pastels, etsen, enz.' *Het Handelsblad*, 17 April 1904, p. 1.

22 'Hij schildert visch als een Linnig en vleesch als een Verhaeren [...] zijn appelen en peren [hebben] de verbluffende realiteit van die, welke Ensor maakt.' de Mont 1921, p. 141.

23 'De hemel is roze! Godverdomme, wat voor een roze! Het is uniek in de geschiedenis van de schilderkunst.' Cited in Min 2011, p. 213.

24 'Ik heb het gevoel dat Ensor verbleekt bij dit alles.' Ibid., p. 145.

25 'Tout désormais y est franc, déroutant de simplicité: le dessin est tracé à gros traits, les formes sont frustes, le sentiment net, sans détour. La pâte vient tout droit du tube, la composition tout droit du cerveau, le coloris tout droit du cœur.' Haesaerts 1959, p. 205.

26 'Leben sind die Bunten Stilleben, das man lächelt über den Titel "Nature Morte".' Nebel 1920, p. 480.

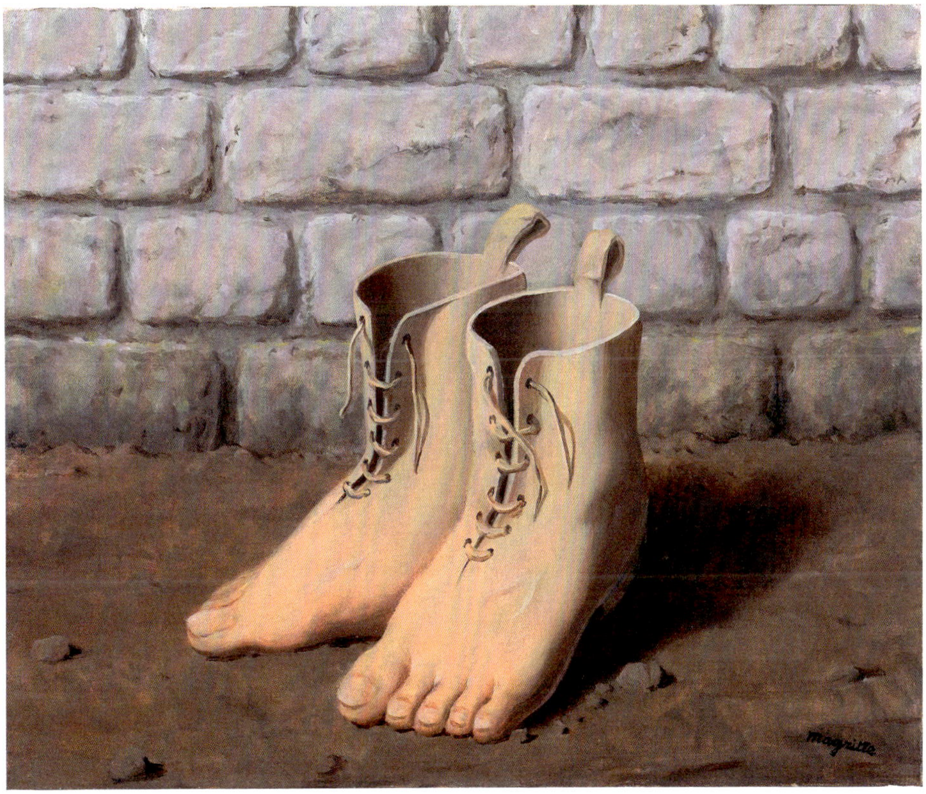

164

Bibliography

Magazine and newspaper articles published before 1950 are shown in full only in the footnotes and endnotes.

Adriaens-Pannier 2023
Adriaens-Pannier, Anne, 'Solitude féminine, intérieurs insolites', in Anne Adriaens-Pannier and Noémie Goldman (eds), *Léon Spilliaert: Avec la mer du Nord…*, exh. cat., Fondation de l'Hermitage, Lausanne, 2023 (Ghent: Snoeck), 2023, pp. 70–81

André 1907
André, Paul, *Le peintre Willem Linnig, junior: Ouvrage illustré de 32 planches en phototypie suivi du Catalogue de l'œuvre complète de l'artiste par Ben. Linnig* (Brussels: Belgique Artistique & Littéraire), 1907

Antwerp 1894
Wereldtentoonstelling der schoone kunsten, 1894: algemeene geïllustreerde catalogus, exh. cat., Koninklijke Maatschappij tot Aanmoediging der Schoone Kunsten, Antwerp, 1894 (Antwerp: Bellemans), 1894

Antwerp 1983
Schoonbaert, Lydia, and Dorine Cardyn-Oomen (eds), *Tekeningen en schilderijen van Walter Vaes*, exh. cat., Royal Museum of Fine Arts, Antwerp, 1983 (Antwerp: Royal Museum of Fine Arts), 1983

Antwerp 1985
Buyck, Jean F., Dorine Cardyn-Oomen and Herwig Todts, *Antwerpen 1900: Schilderijen en tekeningen 1880–1914*, exh. cat., Royal Museum of Fine Arts, Antwerp, 1985 (Brussels: Ministerie van de Vlaamse Gemeenschap), 1985

Antwerp 1991
Andries, Pool, et al. (ed.), *Linnig: een Antwerpse kunstenaarsdynastie in de 19de eeuw*, exh. cat., Hessenhuis, Antwerp, 1991 (Deurne: MIM), 1991

Antwerp 2010–11
Todts, Herwig, *Ensor ontmaskerd*, exh. cat., Royal Museum of Fine Arts, Antwerp, 2010–11 (Brussels: Mercatorfonds), 2010

Antwerp/Arnhem 1999–2000
Van der Stighelen, Katlijne, Mirjam Westen and Maaike Meijer (eds), *Elck zijn waerom: vrouwelijke kunstenaars in België en Nederland, 1500–1950*, exh. cat., Royal Museum of Fine Arts, Antwerp, 1999–2000 / Museum voor Moderne Kunst, Arnhem, 2000 (Ghent: Ludion), 1999

Aron 1997
Aron, Paul (ed.), *Émile Verhaeren: Écrits sur l'art (1881–1892)*, 2 vols (Brussels: Editions Labor), 1997

Avermaete 1962
Avermaete, Roger, *Rik Wouters* (Brussels: Éditions l'Arcade), 1962

Baetens 2010
Baetens, Jan Dirk, 'Vanguard Economics, Rearguard Art: Gustave Coûteaux and the Modernist Myth of the Dealer-Critic System', *Oxford Art Journal* 33, no. 1, 2010, pp. 25–41

Baetens 2020
Baetens, Jan Dirk, 'Artist-Dealer Agreements and the Nineteenth-Century Art Market: The Case of Gustave Coûteaux', *Nineteenth-Century Art Worldwide* 19, no. 1, 2020, https://doi.org/10.29411/ncaw.2020.19.1.2

Block 1984
Block, Jane, *Les XX and Belgian Avant-Gardism 1868–1894* (Ann Arbor, MI: UMI Research Press), 1984

Blondeel 2003
Blondeel, Karel, *Vrouwelijke schilders in Gent (1880–1914)*, Licentiate Thesis, Universiteit Gent, 2003

Bown-Taevernier 1999
Bown-Taevernier, Sabine, 'Het stilleven als stijlexperiment', in Gisèle Ollinger-Zinque (ed.), *Ensor*, exh. cat.,

Royal Museums of Fine Arts of Belgium, Brussels, 1999–2000 (Wommelgem: Blondé), 1999, pp. 32–7

Boyens 1989
Boyens, Piet, *Gust De Smet: Kroniek – Kunsthistorische analyse* (Antwerp: Mercatorfonds), 1989

Boyens 1999
Boyens, Piet (ed.), *Frits Van den Berghe, 1883–1939* (Antwerp: Pandora), 1999

Boyens and Bosschaert 1994
Boyens, Piet, and Hans Bosschaert, *Leon De Smet* (Tielt: Lannoo), 1994

Brussels 1938
Cornette, Arthur (ed.), *Walter Vaes*, exh. cat., Palais des Beaux-Arts, Brussels, 1938 (Brussels: Palais des Beaux-Arts), 1938

Brussels 1987
Philibert Cockx, exh. cat., City Hall, Brussels, 1987 (s.l.: s.n.), 1987

Brussels 1988
Simon, Bernadette, and Lydia De Pauw-De Veen, *9 vrouwen, 9 × kunst: vrouwelijke kunstenaars actief rond de eeuwwisseling*, exh. cat., Kredietbank, Brussels, 1988 (s.l.: Jaspaer), 1988

Brussels 1992
Roberts-Jones, Philippe, Danielle Derrey-Capon and Frederik Leen (eds), *Willy Finch 1854–1930*, exh. cat., Royal Museums of Fine Arts of Belgium, Brussels, 1992 (Brussels: Gemeentekrediet), 1992

Brussels 1993
Ollinger-Zinque, Gisèle (ed.), *Les XX: La Libre Esthétique; Cent ans après / Honderd jaar later*, exh. cat., Royal Museums of Fine Arts of Belgium, Brussels, 1993 (Brussels: Royal Museums of Fine Arts of Belgium), 1993

Brussels 1996
Beusen, Paul, and Herman Vandeveen (eds), *Bloemen in de schilderkunst van de 16de tot de 20ste eeuw*, exh. cat., Galerie van het Gemeentekrediet, Brussels, 1996 (Brussels: Gemeentekrediet), 1996

Brussels 2017
Bertrand, Olivier, et al. (ed.), *Rik Wouters: retrospectieve*, exh. cat., Royal Museums of Fine Arts of Belgium, Brussels, 2017 (Paris: Somogy Éditions d'Art), 2017

Caspers 2015
Caspers, Barbara, *Les femmes artistes et femmes d'artistes au sein des groupes artistiques des XX (1884–1893) et de la Libre Esthétique (1894–1914)*, Master's Thesis, Université Libre de Bruxelles, 2015

Corbet 1948
Corbet, August, *Walter Vaes* (Antwerp: De Sikkel), 1948

Creusen 2007
Creusen, Alexia, *Femmes artistes en Belgique: XIXe et début XXe siècle* (Paris: L'Harmattan), 2007

de Graaf 1999
de Graaf, Floor, 'Henriette Ronner-Knip', in Antwerp/Arnhem 1999–2000, p. 244

de Hemptinne 1984
de Hemptinne, Georges, 'Généalogie inédite de la branche issue de Auguste-Donat de Hemptinne', *Le Parchemin* 31, no. 234, 1984, pp. 392–400

de Mont 1921
de Mont, Pol, *De schilderkunst in België van 1830 tot 1921* (The Hague: Martinus Nijhoff), 1921

De Taeye 1894
De Taeye, Edmond-Louis, *Les artistes belges contemporains: Leur vie, leurs œuvres, leur place dans l'art* (Brussels: Alfred Castaigne), 1894

Deinze 2014
Pauwels, Peter J. H., *Albert Saverys 1886–1964*, exh. cat., Museum van Deinze en de Leiestreek, Deinze, 2014 (Ghent: Borgerhoff & Lamberigts), 2014

Delen 1942
Delen, A. J. J., *Walter Vaes* (Antwerp: Standaard Boekhandel), 1942

Delevoy 1972
Delevoy, Robert (ed.), *Jean Brusselmans* (Brussels: Laconti), 1972

Delevoy 1981
Delevoy, Robert, *Les XX, Bruxelles: Catalogue des dix expositions annuelles* (Brussels: Centre International pour l'Étude du XIXe Siècle), 1981

Derrey-Capon 1992a
Derrey-Capon, Danielle, 'Alfred William Finch van het begin tot het kunstambacht 1854–1897', in Brussels 1992, pp. 77–127

Derrey-Capon 1992b
Derrey-Capon, Danielle, 'Schilderijen', in Brussels 1992, pp. 164–75

Deurle 2002
Boyens, Piet (ed.), *Thuis, vreemd en vertrouwd: Hubert Malfait, Constant Permeke, de gebroeders Gustave en Leon de Smet, Louis Thevenet, Frits van den Berghe en Rik Wouters*, exh. cat., Museum Dhondt-Dhaenens, Deurle, 2002 (Deurle: Museum Dhondt-Dhaenens), 2002

Dewilde 2008
Dewilde, Jan, *Louise De Hem 1866–1922* (Ypres: Dienst Stedelijke Musea), 2008

Draguet, Devillez and Goddeeris 2009
Draguet, Michel, Virginie Devillez and Ingrid Goddeeris, *Magritte: Zijn oeuvre, zijn museum* (Tielt: Lannoo), 2009

Dujardin 1896
Dujardin, Jules, *L'art flamand* (Brussels: Arthur Boitte), 1896

Eindhoven 1999
Thoben, Peter (ed.), *Walter Vaes, 1882–1958: van verfijnde & gedroomde verbeelding*, exh. cat., Museum Kempenland, Eindhoven, 1999 (Eindhoven: Museum Kempenland), 1999

Ekonomides 2021
Ekonomides, Constantin, *Louis Thévenet 1874–1930: La vie est là, simple et tranquille* (Brussels: Association du Patrimoine Artistique), 2021

Ensor 1925
Ensor, James, 'Notice sur A: Verhaeren, membre de l'Académie', *Bulletin de l'Académie royale de Belgique, Classe des Beaux-Arts* 7, 1925, pp. 110–15

Ensor 1974
Ensor, James, *Mes écrits* (Liège: Éditions Nationales), 1974

Flippo 1981
Flippo, Willem M. (ed.), *Lexicon of the Belgian Romantic Painters* (Antwerp: International Art Press), 1981

Frankfurt/Ghent 2015–6
Pauwels, Peter J. H., Kristien Boon and Marcel Daloze, *Marthe Donas: A Woman Artist in the Avant-Garde*, exh. cat., Schirn Halle, Frankfurt, 2015–6 / Museum of Fine Arts, Ghent, 2016 (Ghent: Ludion; The Marthe Donas Foundation), 2015

Ghent 1980
Hoozee, Robert (ed.), *Het landschap in de Belgische kunst 1830–1914*, exh. cat., Museum of Fine Arts, Ghent, 1980 (Ghent: Museum of Fine Arts), 1980

Ghent 2010
Hoozee, Robert, and Cathérine Verleysen (eds), *Gustave Van de Woestyne*, exh. cat., Museum of Fine Arts, Ghent, 2010 (Brussels: Mercatorfonds), 2010

Goldman 2023
Goldman, Noémie, 'De l'étrange inanimé', in Anne Adriaens-Pannier and Noémie Goldman (eds), *Léon Spilliaert: Avec la mer du Nord…*, exh. cat., Fondation de l'Hermitage, Lausanne, 2023 (Ghent: Snoeck), 2023, pp. 82–95

Haesaerts 1959
Haesaerts, Paul, *Histoire de la peinture moderne en Flandre* (Brussels: Les Éditions l'Arcade), 1959

The Hague 2018
Janssen, Hans (ed.), *Jean Brusselmans 1884–1953*, exh. cat., Gemeentemuseum, The Hague, 2018 (Veurne: Hannibal), 2018

The Hague 2023
De Raedt, Thijs (ed.), *Vlaams expressionisme: Heerlijke herinneringen*, exh. cat., Kunstmuseum Den Haag, The Hague, 2023 (Veurne: Hannibal), 2023

Halle 1990
Retrospectieve Louis Thévenet, exh. cat., Oud-Jezuïetencollege, Halle, 1990 (Brussels: Gemeentekrediet), 1990

Heuschling 1863
Heuschling, Xavier, *La noblesse artiste et lettrée: Tableau historique* (Brussels: C. Muquardt; Paris: Aug. Aubry), 1863

Hoozee, Bown-Taevernier and Heijbroek 1987
Hoozee, Robert, Sabine Bown-Taevernier and Jan Frederik Heijbroek (eds), *James Ensor: Tekeningen en prenten* (Antwerp: Mercatorfonds), 1987

Hostyn, Schiltz and Schiltz 2009
Hostyn, Norbert, Ivo Schiltz and Dirk Schiltz (eds), *Frans Mortelmans 1865–1936: Virtuoos bloemenschilder* (Antwerp: Standaard Uitgeverij), 2009

Huys 1983
Huys, Paul, *Albert Saverys: Een kunstenaarsleven* (Tielt: Lannoo), 1983

Huys 2021
Huys, Jean-Philippe, *'Avec le noble crayon': Lettres de James Ensor à la famille Rousseau; Correspondance inédite dans son intégralité* (Brussels: Peter Lang), 2021

Ixelles 1964
Liénaux, Arild, *Philibert Cockx*, exh. cat., Museum of Ixelles, Ixelles, 1964 (Brussels: Meddens), 1964

Langui 1945
Langui, Émile, *Gust De Smet: De mensch en zijn werk* (Brussels: A. Manteau), 1945

Langui 1968
Langui, Émile, *Frits van den Berghe 1883–1939: De mens en zijn werk* (Antwerp: Mercatorfonds), 1968

Laoureux 2019
Laoureux, Denis, 'Le Cercle des femmes peintres de Bruxelles: un collectif, quatre expositions (1888–1893)', *Artl@s Bulletin* 8, no. 1, 2019, pp. 39–50

Laoureux 2020
Laoureux, Denis, 'Les artistes femmes dans les acquisitions d'État en Belgique (1860–1914)', in Émilie Berger and Noémie Goldman (eds), *Adjugé! Les artistes et le marché de l'art en Belgique 1850–1900*, exh. cat., Musée Félicien Rops, Namur, 2020–21 (Paris: Mare & Martin), 2020, pp. 122–33

Laren/Sint-Niklaas 1987–8
De Meester, Patty (ed.), *Walter Vaes, 1882–1958: schilderijen en aquarellen*, exh. cat., Singer Museum, Laren, 1987–8 / Stedelijk Museum, Sint-Niklaas, 1988 (Laren: Singer Museum), 1987

Lebeer 1951
Lebeer, Louis, *Walter Vaes* (Antwerp: De Scaldispers), 1951

Legrand 1971
Legrand, Francine-Claire, *Ensor, cet inconnu* (Brussels: La Renaissance du Livre), 1971

Legrand 1981
Legrand, Francine-Claire, *Léon Spilliaert in zijn tijd* (Tielt: Lannoo), 1981

Lemonnier 1905
Lemonnier, Camille, *Henri De Braekeleer: Peintre de la lumière* (Brussels: Van Oest), 1905

Liénaux 1965
Liénaux, Arild, *Philibert Cockx* (Brussels: Éditions Meddens), 1965

Lyr 1944
Lyr, René, *Mon ami Louis Thévenet* (Uccle: Éditions Nationales), 1944

Lyr 1954
Lyr, René, *Louis Thévenet* (Antwerp: De Sikkel), 1954

Marx 2007
Marx, Jacques, 'De la Chine à la chinoiserie: Échanges culturels entre la Chine, l'Europe et les Pays-Bas méridionaux (17e–18e siècles)', *Revue belge de Philologie et d'Histoire* 85, no. 3–4, 2007, pp. 735–7

Meylaers 2023
Meylaers, Francesca, *Grenzeloze expressies: De invloed van internationale exposities op het werk van Berthe Art (1857–1934) en Juliette Cambier (1879–1963)*, Master's Thesis, KU Leuven, 2023

Min 2011
Min, Eric, *Rik Wouters: een biografie* (Antwerp: De Bezige Bij), 2011

Namur 2016
Laoureux, Denis (ed.), *Femmes artistes: Les peintresses en Belgique (1880–1914)*, exh. cat., Musée Félicien Rops, Namur, 2016 (Milan: Silvana Editoriale), 2016

Nebel 1920
Nebel, Kurt, 'Die 87: Ausstellung des Sturm', *Der Cicerone: Halbmonatsschrift für die Interessen des Kunstforschers & Sammlers* 12, 1920, pp. 480–81

Ornans 2018
Thomas-Maurin, Frédérique, Lonnie Baverel and Séverine Petit, *Léon Frederic: Un autre réalisme*, exh. cat., Musée Gustave Courbet, Ornans, 2018 (Besançon: Éditions du Sekoya), 2018

Ostend 1994–5
Hostyn, Norbert (ed.), *Belgische stilleven- & bloemenschilderkunst 1750–1914: Van neo-classicisme tot post-impressionisme*, exh. cat., Museum of Fine Arts, Ostend, 1994–5 (Ostend: Stad Oostende), 1994

Ostend 1996
Florizoone, Patrick, *James Ensor: De baden in Oostende*, exh. cat., Venetiaanse Gaanderijen, Ostend, 1996 (Ghent: Snoeck-Ducaju), 1996

Ostend 2010
Van den Bossche, Phillip, Els Vermeersch and Xavier Tricot (eds), *Bij Ensor op bezoek*, exh. cat., Mu.ZEE, Ostend, 2010 (Brasschaat: Pandora), 2010

Ostend 2011
Dedobbeleer, Koenraad, and Phillip Van den Bossche (eds), *Jean Brusselmans*, exh. cat., Mu.ZEE, Ostend, 2011 (Ostend: Mu.ZEE), 2013

Ostend 2023
Devillez, Virginie, Stefan Huygebaert and Wendy Van Hoorde (eds), *Anna Boch: An Impressionist Journey*, exh. cat., Mu.ZEE, Ostend, 2023 (Veurne: Hannibal), 2023

Pierron 1905
Pierron, Sander, *Portraits d'artistes* (Brussels: Xavier Havermans Éditeur), 1905

Robie 1886
Robie, Jean-Baptiste, *Les débuts d'un peintre* (Brussels: Polleunis, Ceuterick et Lefébure), 1886

Schrijvers 1999
Schrijvers, Nanny, 'Berthe Art', in Antwerp/Arnhem 1999–2000, p. 274

Schuermans 2007
Schuermans, Brigitte, *Jean Robie 1821–1910* (Brussels: Racine), 2007

's-Hertogenbosch 2022
Boyens, Piet, *Symbolisme in Vlaanderen: De eerste generatie*, exh. cat., Het Noordbrabants Museum, 's-Hertogenbosch, 2022 (Zwolle: WBooks), 2022

Sint-Niklaas 1986
Anthurnis, Daniel, and Karel Mechiels, *Walter Vaes: tekeningen, aquarellen, pastels*, exh. cat., Stedelijk Museum, Sint-Niklaas, 1986 (Sint-Niklaas: Stedelijk Museum), 1986

Solvay 1936–8
Solvay, Lucien, 'Verheyden (Isidore)', in *Biographie nationale*, vol. 26 (Brussels: Émile Bruylant), 1936–8, cols 638–41

Sterckx 2012
Marjan Sterckx, *Sisyphus' dochters. Beeldhouwsters en hun werk in de publieke ruimte (Parijs, Londen en Brussel, ca. 1770–1953). Tekst en catalogus. 2 vols* (Brussels: Koninklijke Vlaamse Academie), 2012.

Sterling 1952
Sterling, Charles, 'En préparant l'exposition de la nature morte', *La Revue des Arts* 2, no. 1, 1952, pp. 31–6

Stévennart 1964
Stévennart, Hélène, 'Louis Dubois', in *Biographie nationale*, vol. 32 (Brussels: Émile Bruylant), 1964, cols 145–54

Sulzberger 1964
Sulzberger, Suzanne, 'Verhaeren (Alfred)', in *Biographie nationale*, vol. 32 (Brussels: Émile Bruylant), 1964, cols 705–6

Sylvester 1993a
Sylvester, David (ed.), *René Magritte: Catalogue Raisonné; Volume II, Oil Paintings and Objects 1931–1948* (Houston: Menil Foundation; Antwerp: Mercatorfonds), 1993

Sylvester 1993b
Sylvester, David (ed.), *René Magritte: Catalogue Raisonné; Volume III, Oil Paintings, Objects and Bronzes 1949–1967* (Houston: Menil Foundation; Antwerp: Mercatorfonds), 1993

Sylvester 1994
Sylvester, David (ed.), *René Magritte: Catalogue Raisonné; Volume IV, Gouaches, Temperas, Watercolours and Papiers Collés 1918–1967* (Houston: Menil Foundation; Antwerp: Mercatorfonds), 1994

Sylvester 2009
Sylvester, David, *Magritte* (Brussels: Mercatorfonds; Houston: Menil Foundation), 2009

Taevernier 1973
Taevernier, August, *James Ensor: Illustrated Catalogue of His Engravings; Their Critical Description and Inventory of the Plates* (Ghent: Erasmus), 1973

Thomas, Lenglez and Duroisin 2005
Thomas, Thérèse, Michelle Lenglez and Pierre Duroisin, *Anna Boch: Catalogue raisonné* (Brussels: Éditions Racine), 2005

Todts 2009
Todts, Herwig, 'Redon en het symbolisme', in Herwig Todts (ed.), *Goya, Redon, Ensor: Groteske schilderijen en tekeningen*, exh. cat., Royal Museum of Fine Arts, Antwerp, 2009 (Tielt: Lannoo), 2009, pp. 105–23

Todts and Bollen 2019
Todts, Herwig, and André Bollen, *Henri De Braekeleer 1840–1888: Het werk* (Brussels: Ludion; Berchem: Galerie Ronny Van de Velde), 2019

Tricot 1995
Tricot, Xavier, *Ensoriana* (Antwerp: Pandora), 1995

Tricot 1996
Tricot, Xavier, *Léon Spilliaert, de jaren 1900–1915* (Antwerp: Pandora; Ghent: Snoeck; Brussels: Gemeentekrediet van België), 1996

Tricot 1999
Tricot, Xavier, *James Ensor: Lettres* (Brussels: Labor), 1999

Tricot 2009
Tricot, Xavier, *James Ensor: Leven en werk; Oeuvrecatalogus van de schilderijen* (Brussels: Mercatorfonds), 2009

van de Woestijne 1949
van de Woestijne, Karel, 'Gustave van de Woestijne', in Karel van de Woestijne, *Verzameld werk: Deel 4; Beschouwingen over literatuur en kunst* (Bussum: Uitgeversmaatschappij C. A. J. Van Dishoeck), 1949, pp. 443–6

Van der Stighelen 2010
Van der Stighelen, Katlijne, *Vrouwenstreken: Onvergetelijke schilderessen uit de Lage landen* (Amsterdam: Amsterdam University Press; Tielt: Lannoo), 2010

Van Duppen 2019
Van Duppen, Frédèrique, *Alice Ronner (1857–1957): Een Belgische schilderes van stillevens en stillevens met bloemen*, Master's Thesis, KU Leuven, 2019

Van Kerkhoven 2011
Van Kerkhoven, Laurence, 'Jean Brusselmans', in Laurence Van Kerkhoven (ed.), *Modernisten uit het Groeningemuseum in Brugge*, exh. cat., Noordbrabants Museum, 's-Hertogenbosch, 2011 (Zwolle: Waanders), 2011, pp. 26–33

Vandevivere 1965
Vandevivere, Ignace, 'Robie (Jean)', in *Biographie nationale*, vol. 33 (Brussels: Émile Bruylant), 1965, cols 626–7

Vanzype 1903
Vanzype, Gustave, *Nos peintres*, vol. 1 (Brussels: Paul Lacomblez), 1903

Vanzype 1905
Vanzype, Gustave, *Nos peintres*, vol. 3 (Brussels: Paul Lacomblez), 1905

Verhaeren 1908
Verhaeren, Émile, *James Ensor* (Brussels: G. Van Oest & Cie.), 1908

Verschaffel 1995
Verschaffel, Bart, 'Het heimelijke van Henri De Braekeleer', *De Witte Raaf* 9, no. 54, 1995

Verschaffel 1997
Verschaffel, Bart, 'De beeldruimte van het stilleven (van Cotán tot Coorte)', *De Witte Raaf* 11, no. 67, 1997

Verschaffel 2018
Verschaffel, Bart, *Mock Humanity! Two Essays on James Ensor's Grotesques* (Ghent: A & S Books), 2018

Wiertz 2023
Wiertz, Wendy, *Adellijk en artistiek: Amateurkunstenaressen met blauw bloed in België (1815–1914)* (Leuven: Universitaire Pers Leuven), 2023

Yotova 2023
Yotova, Raya, *David De Noter: 50 Artworks (Annotated)* (North Haven, CT: self-published), 2023

Ypres 1992
Dewilde, Jan, *Louise De Hem*, exh. cat., Yper Museum, Ypres, 1992 (Ypres: Stad Ieper), 1992

Exhibited Works

Berthe Art

cat. 130 *Kettle and Vase with African Violets, Arum Lilies and China Asters*, s.d., pastel on paper, 80 × 109 cm. Private collection, Leuven.

cat. 11 *Still Life with Fan, Death Mask and Peacock Feather*, 1885, oil on canvas, 97 × 71 cm. Private collection, Kortrijk.

Hubert Bellis

cat. 108 *Severed Fish Head and Shrimp next to a Tub*, s.d., oil on canvas, 45 × 65 cm. Barat-Venker Collection, The Netherlands.

cat. 7 *Large Fish, Red Lobsters, Lemons, Red and White Wine Bottles*, s.d., oil on canvas, 65 × 120 cm. Barat-Venker Collection, The Netherlands.

cat. 109 *Still Life with Mussels and Red Wine Glass*, s.d., oil on canvas, 21 × 36.6 cm. Barat-Venker Collection, The Netherlands.

cat. 110 *Cutlet, Cauliflower and Endive*, s.d., oil on canvas, 38.5 × 50 cm. Barat-Venker Collection, The Netherlands.

cat. 8 *Still Life with a Fish Head and Cleaver*, s.d., oil on canvas, 63 × 72 cm. Collection Simonis & Buunk Kunsthandel, Ede, The Netherlands.

cat. 111 *Green and Yellow Pears*, s.d., oil on canvas, 36 × 45 cm. Barat-Venker Collection, The Netherlands.

cat. 112 *Cinerarias and Azaleas in Flowerpots*, s.d., oil on canvas, 101 × 71 cm. Barat-Venker Collection, The Netherlands.

cat. 113 *Dwarf Chrysanthemums in a Vase*, s.d., oil on canvas, 38.2 × 35 cm. Barat-Venker Collection, The Netherlands.

cat. 114 *Rose Competition*, s.d., oil on canvas, 18 × 23.5 cm. Barat-Venker Collection, The Netherlands.

cat. 115 *The Day after the Carnival*, s.d., oil on canvas, 100 × 150 cm. Collection M Leuven, inv. S/14/B.

Anna Boch

cat. 123 *The Kitchen*, 1883–4, oil on canvas, 86 × 137 cm. Private collection, Belgium.

Jean Brusselmans

cat. 161 *Still Life with Slices of Sausage*, 1936, oil on canvas, 112 × 122 cm. Royal Museum of Fine Arts, Antwerp, inv. 3198.

cat. 28 *Still Life with Griffon*, 1936, oil on canvas, 109.5 × 122.4 cm. Mu.ZEE, City of Ostend Collection, inv. MZ000054.

cat. 162 *Still Life with Fan*, 1948, oil on canvas, 130 × 125 cm. Musea Brugge, inv. 1980. GRO0030.I.

Philibert Cockx

cat. 25 *Lying Nude*, 1928, oil on canvas mounted on panel, 95.5 × 137.5 cm. Royal Museum of Fine Arts, Antwerp, inv. 2672.

Marie de Bièvre

cat. 132 *Physalis*, s.d., oil on canvas, 24 × 31 cm. Private collection, Leuven.

cat. 133 *Azaleas and Violets*, s.d., oil on canvas, 92 × 72.5 cm. Royal Museums of Fine Arts of Belgium, Brussels, inv. 5636.

cat. 13 *Peaches and Plums*, 1894 or before, oil on canvas, 74 × 94 cm. Private collection, Leuven.

Henri De Braekeleer

cat. 10 *Old Trinkets*, 1880–85, oil on canvas, 38 × 56 cm. Musée d'Orsay, Paris, inv. RF 1196.

cat. 116 *Still Life*, 1881–5, oil on wood, 26.5 × 36.5 cm. Royal Museums of Fine Arts of Belgium, Brussels, inv. 4185.

cat. 117 *Flowers*, 1883–7, oil on canvas, 36 × 30 cm. Royal Museums of Fine Arts of Belgium, Brussels, inv. 4077.

cat. 118 *The Globe*, 1885–8, oil on canvas, 37 × 54 cm. Royal Museums of Fine Arts of Belgium, Brussels, inv. 7468.

cat. 9 *Medlars*, *c.*1886, oil on canvas, 36.5 × 51 cm. Royal Museums of Fine Arts of Belgium, Brussels, inv. 3810.

Louise De Hem

cat. 143 *Bust of a Young, Smiling Girl, a Carafe, a Japanese Doll and a Fan*, 1887, oil on canvas, 55.5 × 38 cm. Yper Museum, Ypres, inv. SM 003261.

cat. 12 *Corner of a Lady's Boudoir*, *c.*1890, oil on canvas, 98 × 131 cm. Yper Museum, Ypres, inv. SM 000560.

Jeannie de Hemptinne

cat. 134 *Wild Flowers with Bird and Butterfly*, s.d., oil on canvas, 60 × 49 cm. Private collection.

cat. 135 *Exotic Interior*, s.d., oil on panel, 30 × 22.5 cm. Private collection.

cat. 14 *Flowers*, s.d., oil on canvas, 109 × 71 cm. Private collection.

David Émile Joseph De Noter

cat. 2 *Frans Snijders' Studio*, 1857, oil on canvas, 148 × 201 cm. Museum Hof van Busleyden, Mechelen, inv. S0021.

Virginie de Sartorius

cat. 107 *Still Life with Flowers and Bust of Louise-Marie of Orléans*, 1851, oil on canvas, 118.9 × 100.6 cm. Werner Wieland Collection.

Gustave De Smet

cat. 146 *Still Life with Statuette*, 1913, oil on canvas, 100 × 96.5 cm. Private collection.

cat. 27 *Still Life*, 1928, oil on canvas, 80 × 70 cm. Part of the Emanuel Hoffmann Foundation, gift from the Maja and Emanuel Hoffmann Collection 1998, permanent loan to the Öffentliche Kunstsammlung Basel, inv. H 1998.19.

Léon De Smet

cat. 18 *Nude with Red Dresser*, 1921, oil on canvas, 152 × 115.5 cm. Property of the Belgian State, Collection of the Wallonia-Brussels Federation, inv. 1984.

Marthe Donas

cat. 26 *Cubist Still Life*, 1917, oil on canvas, 34.5 × 53 cm. Royal Museum of Fine Arts, Antwerp, inv. 2948.

Louis Dubois

cat. 5 *The Woman with Bouquet*, *c.*1854–5, oil on canvas, 131 × 101 cm. Royal Museums of Fine Arts of Belgium, Brussels, inv. 4143.

cat. 4 *Still Life with Studio Paraphernalia*, *c.*1855, oil on canvas, 129.7 × 98.3 cm. Museum of Fine Arts, Ghent, inv. 1924-A.

cat. 6 *Fish and Accessories*, 1876, oil on canvas, 109 × 141 cm. Royal Museums of Fine Arts of Belgium, Brussels, inv. 2808.

James Ensor

cat. 54 *The Hat-Stand (Le porte-manteau)*, 1876, oil on cardboard, 24.5 × 19 cm. Private collection. CR T33.

cat. 30 *The Parasol (Le parasol)*, 1880, oil on cardboard, 31 × 22.5 cm. Vanthournout collection. CR T131.

cat. 55 *The Small Coffee Cup (La petite tasse)*, *c.*1880, oil on canvas, 27.5 × 22 cm. Private collection. CR T139.

cat. 56 *Bottles (Les bouteilles)*, 1880, oil on canvas, 65 × 53 cm. Fondation Socindec. CR T142.

cat. 31 *Blue Flask and Chicken (Flacon bleu et poulet)*, 1880, oil on canvas, 47 × 55.5 cm. Quintet Private Bank (Europe) S.A. CR T144.

cat. 57 *Skate and Herring (Raie et hareng)*, 1880, oil on canvas, 80 × 90 cm. Royal Museum of Fine Arts, Antwerp, inv. 2188. CR T147.

cat. 32 *Chinoiseries, Fans and Fabrics (Chinoiseries, éventails et étoffes)*, 1880, oil on canvas, 100 × 78 cm. Royal Museum of Fine Arts, Antwerp, inv. 2076. CR T151.

cat. 58 *Fans and Fabrics (Éventails et étoffes)*, 1881, oil on canvas, 48 × 54 cm. Private collection, Brussels. CR T206.

cat. 59 *Still Life with Oysters (Nature morte aux huîtres)*, 1882, oil on canvas, 79 × 99 cm. Royal Museum of Fine Arts, Antwerp, inv. 1412. CR T234.

cat. 60 *Roses, Tulips and Mimosa (Roses, tulipes et mimosa)*, 1882, oil on canvas, 48 × 58 cm. Museum Boijmans Van Beuningen, Rotterdam, acquired with the collection of D.G. van Beuningen, inv. 2602 (MK). CR T236.

cat. 33 *Seashells and Chinoiseries (Coquillages et chinoiseries)*, 1882, oil on canvas, 80 × 100 cm. Private collection. CR T238.

cat. 34 *Fanfare in Red (Fanfare en rouge)*, 1884, oil on canvas, 115 × 82 cm. Private collection. CR T274.

cat. 35 *Peonies and Poppies (Pivoines et pavots)*, 1885, oil on canvas, 136 × 112 cm. Private collection. CR T254.

cat. 61 *Pear, Grapes and Nuts (Small Fruits) (Poire, raisins et noix (Petits fruits))*, 1889, oil on panel, 19 × 24.5 cm. Private collection. CR T294.

cat. 62 *Still Life with Blue Vase and Fan (Nature morte au vase et à l'éventail bleus)*, 1889, oil on canvas, 47 × 66 cm. Govaert Family. CR T297.

cat. 39 *Seashells (Coquillages)*, 1889, oil on canvas, 45 × 70 cm. Von der Heydt-Museum, Wuppertal, inv. G1369. CR T298.

cat. 38 *Flowers and Butterflies (Fleurs et papillons)*, 1889, oil on canvas, 60 × 50 cm. Charlier Museum, Saint-Josse-ten-Noode, inv. P/161/1964. CR T299.

cat. 63 *Still Life with Lobster and Crab (Nature morte au homard et au crabe)*, 1890, oil on canvas, 61 × 75 cm. Private collection, Vienna. CR T315.

cat. 42 *Mask Looking at Crustaceans (Masque regardant des crustacés)*, 1891, oil on panel, 31 × 39 cm. Royal Museum of Fine Arts, Antwerp, inv. 1958. CR T333.

cat. 41 *The Skate (La raie)*, 1892, oil on panel, 80 × 100 cm. Royal Museums of Fine Arts of Belgium, Brussels, inv. 4489. CR T350.

cat. 64 *Roses (Roses)*, 1892, oil on panel, 32.5 × 40 cm. Royal Museums of Fine Arts of Belgium, Brussels, inv. 11157. CR T351.

cat. 43 *Pierrot and Skeleton in Yellow Robe (Pierrot et squelette en jaune)*, 1893, oil on panel, 38 × 48 cm. Museum of Fine Arts, Ghent, inv. 2007-B. CR T364.

cat. 65 *Daffodils, Lilacs and Violets (Jonquilles, lilas et violettes)*, 1893, oil on canvas, 57 × 70 cm. Private collection, courtesy Bounameaux Art Expertise. CR T366.

cat. 44 *The Dead Cockerel (Le coq mort)*, 1894, oil on canvas, 80 × 100 cm. Kunsthalle, Mannheim, inv. M1420. CR T367.

cat. 46 *Fish and Seashells (Poissons et coquillages)*, 1895, oil on canvas, 80 × 100 cm. Private collection. CR T373.

cat. 45 *Flowers and Vegetables (Fleurs et legumes)*, 1896, oil on canvas, 79 × 98 cm. Royal Museum of Fine Arts, Antwerp, inv. 1858. CR T375.

cat. 66 *Flowers and Chinese Vases (Fleurs et vases chinois)*, 1896, oil on canvas, 100 × 80 cm. Royal Museums of Fine Arts of Belgium, Brussels, inv. 6912. CR T376.

cat. 40 *Seashells (Coquillages)*, 1896, oil on panel, 21 × 27 cm. Royal Museums of Fine Arts of Belgium, Brussels, inv. 11159. CR T377.

cat. 67 *Still Life with Lantern and Vegetables (Nature morte à la lanterne et aux légumes)*, 1900 (?), oil on canvas, 54.5 × 65.5 cm. The Simon Collection of Belgian Art, London. CR T395.

cat. 47 *Fish and Seashells (Poissons et coquillages)*, *c.*1905, oil on canvas, 80 × 100 cm. Private collection. CR T414.

cat. 48 *Still Life with Duck (Nature morte au canard)*, *c.*1905, oil on canvas, 80 × 100 cm. Collection Museum Boijmans Van Beuningen, Rotterdam. Gift of J. de Graaff and L. de Graaff-Bachiene, 1935, inv. 2047 (MK). CR T416.

cat. 49 *Chinoiseries (Chinoiseries)*, 1907, oil on canvas, 60 × 79 cm. Museum Dhondt-Dhaenens, Deurle, inv. 000 037. CR T424.

cat. 50 *Pierrot and Skeletons (Pierrot et squelettes)*, *c.*1907, oil on canvas, 35.5 × 45.5 cm. Musée des Beaux-Arts, Tournai. CR T426.

cat. 68 *Blue Flask and Chicken (Flacon bleu et poulet)*, *c.*1910 (?), oil on canvas, 47 × 56 cm. Belvedere, Vienna, inv. 4420. CR T453.

cat. 69 *The Pink Seashell (Study of Light Received between the Street and between Two Bodies of Water) (Le coquillage rose (Étude de lumière entrevue entre rue entre deux eaux))*, 1914, oil on cardboard, 19.5 × 24 cm. Private collection, Knokke. CR T471.

cat. 51 *My Dead Mother (Ma mère morte)*, 1915, oil on canvas, 75 × 60 cm. Mu.ZEE, City of Ostend Collection, inv. SM000713. CR T477.

cat. 52 *My Dead Mother: The Consequences of Quacks (Ma mère morte: Effet de médicastres)*, 1915, colour pencil on prepared panel, 23.8 × 18.3 cm. Collection Georges Hiltrop-Massenhove.

cat. 70 *Seashells, Roses and Vases (Coquillages, roses et vases)*, 1917/8, oil on canvas, 55 × 74 cm. Private collection, Bern, Switzerland. CR T497.

cat. 71 *Red Cabbage and Green Wine Glass (Chou rouge et verre de vin vert)*, 1925, oil on canvas, 66 ´ 80 cm. Private collection. CR T532.

cat. 72 *Red Cabbage, Fruit and Masks (Chou rouge, fruits et masques)*, *c.*1925, oil on canvas, 50.5 × 70.5 cm. Property of a Monaco Collector. CR T538.

cat. 73 *Blue Flask and Chicken (Flacon bleu et poulet)*, *c.*1925, oil on canvas, 54.2 × 65.3 cm. Kunstmuseum Basel, inv. 1562, acquisition 1930. CR T540.

cat. 53 *Souvenirs (Souvenirs)*, 1926, oil on canvas, 70 × 60 cm. Private collection, Mortsel. CR T570.

cat. 74 *Flowers, Fruit and Masks (Fleurs, fruits et masques)*, 1931, oil on canvas, 65 × 53 cm. Private collection. CR T612.

cat. 75 *Light's Caress (Caresses de lumière)*, 1934, oil on canvas, 50 × 66 cm. Private collection. CR T635.

cat. 76 *Light Stripped of Leaves (Lumières effeuilées)*, 1936, oil on canvas, 60.5 × 75.5 cm. Musée des Beaux-Arts / La Boverie, Liège, inv. AM 408. CR T688.

cat. 77 *Seashells (Coquillages)*, 1936, oil on canvas, 51 × 60.5 cm. Musée des Beaux-Arts / La Boverie, Liège, inv. 160. CR T701.

cat. 78 *A Cosy Corner at Home (Un bon coin chez moi)*, 1938, oil on canvas, 50 × 38 cm. Mu.ZEE, City of Ostend Collection, inv. SM001593. CR T781.

cat. 79 *Autumn Flowers (Fleurs d'automne)*, 1938, oil on canvas, 75 × 60 cm. University of Liège – Musée Wittert, Liège, inv. 24024. CR T784.

cat. 80 *The Language of Flowers (Le langage des fleurs)*, 1938, oil on panel, 22 × 30 cm. Musée des Beaux-Arts / La Boverie, Liège, inv. AM75. CR T785.

cat. 81 *Flowers and Fruit (Fleurs et fruits)*, *c.*1938, oil on panel, 16 × 24.5 cm. Frank and Eliane Demaegd-Breynaert. CR T801.

cat. 82 *The Old Clock (La vieille horloge)*, 1941, oil on panel, 22 × 16 cm. Private collection, courtesy Galerie Seghers, Ostend. CR T851.

cat. 83 *Poker and Satchel (Tisonnier et gibecière)*, s.d., pencil and charcoal on paper, 22 × 17 cm. Musée des Beaux-Arts, Tournai, inv. d 0924.

cat. 84 *Study of Objects: Vase and Flowers (Étude d'objets: Vase et fleurs)*, s.d., pencil and charcoal on paper, 22 × 17 cm. Musée des Beaux-Arts, Tournai, inv. d 0931.

cat. 85 *Silhouettes and Palette (Silhouettes et palette de peintre)*, s.d., pencil and charcoal on paper, 22 × 17 cm. Musée des Beaux-Arts, Tournai, inv. d 0936.

cat. 86 *Ink Pots (Encriers)*, s.d., pencil and charcoal on paper, 22 × 17 cm. Musée des Beaux-Arts, Tournai, inv. d 0942.

cat. 87 *Wood Stove (Poêle à bois)*, s.d., pencil and charcoal on paper, 22 × 17 cm. Musée des Beaux-Arts, Tournai, inv. d 0951.

cat. 88 *Chinese Figurine (Statuette chinoise)*, s.d., pencil and charcoal on paper, 22 × 17 cm. Musée des Beaux-Arts, Tournai, inv. d 0954.

cat. 89 *Study of Flowers (Étude de fleurs)*, s.d., pencil and charcoal on paper, 22 × 17 cm. Musée des Beaux-Arts, Tournai, inv. d 0956.

cat. 90 *Violin and Books (Violon et livres)*, s.d., pencil and charcoal on paper, 22 × 17 cm. Musée des Beaux-Arts, Tournai, inv. d 0960.

cat. 92 *Flies, Silhouettes and Assorted Objects (Mouches, silhouettes et objets divers)*, s.d., pencil and charcoal on paper, 22 × 17 cm. Musée des Beaux-Arts, Tournai, inv. d 0961.

cat. 91 *Books (Livres)*, s.d., pencil and charcoal on paper, 22 × 17 cm. Musée des Beaux-Arts, Tournai, inv. d 0965.

cat. 93 *Bottle and Decorative Elements (Bouteille et éléments décoratifs)*, s.d., pencil and charcoal on paper, 22 × 17 cm. Musée des Beaux-Arts, Tournai, inv. d 0967.

cat. 94 *Study of Objects and Silhouette (Étude d'objets et silhouette)*, s.d., pencil and charcoal on paper, 22 × 17 cm. Musée des Beaux-Arts, Tournai, inv. d 0968.

cat. 95 *Crane and Horn (Grue et corne)*, s.d., pencil and charcoal on paper, 22 × 17 cm. Musée des Beaux-Arts, Tournai, inv. d 0969.

cat. 96 *Wine Glass and Spoon (Verre à pied et cuillère)*, s.d., pencil and charcoal on paper, 22 × 17 cm. Musée des Beaux-Arts, Tournai, inv. d 0971.

cat. 97 *The Japanese Cabinet (Le cabinet japonais)*, 1880–83, black chalk on paper, 22.5 × 16.6 cm. Dr and Mrs Rongé-Tops.

cat. 98 *Vase with Fish Motif and Woman with Vase of Flowers (Vase avec motif de pêche et femme avec vase de fleurs)*, 1880–85, pencil on paper, 21.5 × 16 cm. Mu.ZEE, City of Ostend Collection, inv. SM000329.

cat. 99 *Vase and Feet (Vase et pieds)*, 1880–85, pencil and charcoal on paper, 21.8 × 27.2 cm. Mu.ZEE, City of Ostend Collection, inv. SM000710a.

cat. 100 *The Upright Piano (Le piano droit)*, 1882, 1886–8, black chalk on paper, 22.5 × 16.5 cm. Royal Museum of Fine Arts, Antwerp, inv. 3383.

cat. 101 *Plant (Plante)*, 1883, pencil and charcoal on paper, 22 × 17 cm. Musée des Beaux-Arts, Tournai, inv. d 0941.

cat. 36 *The Devil's Mirror (Diable sortant de l'enfer des désirs)*, 1888, black chalk on paper, 22.5 × 17.5 cm. Private collection.

cat. 37 *Mirror with Skeleton (Le miroir au squelette)*, 1890, black chalk on paper, 29.5 × 21.5 cm. Private collection, Brussels.

cat. 102 *Chinese Vase (Vase chinois)*, 1894, pencil and charcoal on paper, 23.5 × 15 cm. Musée des Beaux-Arts, Tournai, inv. d 0959.

Willy (Alfred William) Finch

cat. 126 *The Skate*, 1880–82, oil on canvas, 55 × 66.5 cm. Mu.ZEE, City of Ostend Collection, inv. SM001750.

Léon Frederic

cat. 127 *The Pink Azaleas*, s.d., oil on canvas, 69 × 52.5 cm. Courtesy Berko Collection, Knokke-Heist, Belgium.

François Huygens

cat. 103 *Hawthorn Bouquet*, 1875, oil on canvas, 131.5 × 95.5 cm. Royal Museums of Fine Arts of Belgium, Brussels, inv. 2743.

Pauline Jamar

cat. 125 *The Thistles*, 1898 (?), oil on canvas, 63 × 91 cm. Musée des Beaux-Arts / La Boverie, Liège, inv. AW 1068.

Willem Linnig II

cat. 119 *After the Wedding*, 1875, oil on panel, 72 × 115 cm. Royal Museum of Fine Arts, Antwerp, inv. 2528.

cat. 120 *Vegetables*, 1886, oil on canvas, 83 × 112 cm. Royal Museum of Fine Arts, Antwerp, inv. 2371.

René Magritte

cat. 164 *The Red Model*, 1953, oil on canvas, 38 × 46 cm. BNP Paribas Fortis Collection.

cat. 29 *The Voice of the Absolute*, 1955, oil on canvas, 40 × 50 cm. Private collection.

Georgette Meunier

cat. 131 *Chinoiseries*, s.d., pastel on paper, 67 × 89 cm. Musée des Beaux-Arts, Tournai, inv. 450.

Frans Mortelmans

cat. 136 *Anemones in Round Vase, Japanese Doll on the Table*, s.d., oil on canvas, 58 × 83 cm. Courtesy Berko Fine Paintings, Knokke-Heist, Belgium.

cat. 137 *Frans Mortelmans at His Studio in front of His Easel*, s.d., oil on canvas, 60 × 48 cm. Walter Mortelmans.

cat. 138 *Yellow Roses in a Vase*, s.d., oil on canvas, 44 × 29 cm. Stichting Mortelmans.

cat. 139 *Yellow Roses in a Vase on a Pedestal Table*, s.d., oil on canvas, 79 × 48 cm. Stichting Mortelmans.

cat. 140 *Chrysanthemums in a Delftware Vase, Plate of Grapes on the Table*, s.d., oil on canvas, 58 × 70 cm. Walter Mortelmans.

cat. 141 *Death Mask of the Painter Wiertz*, s.d., watercolour on paper, 68 × 59 cm. Stichting Mortelmans.

cat. 142 *Roses in a Vase, Bouquet of Roses on the Table*, s.d., oil on canvas, 80 × 120 cm. Walter Mortelmans.

cat. 3 *Visiting the Studio*, s.d., oil on canvas, 111.5 × 171.5 cm. Collection Marthe + Félix Dony.

Jean-Baptiste Robie

cat. 104 *Still Life with Game, Flowers and Fruits*, 1853, oil on canvas, 160.6 × 125.2 cm. Museum of Fine Arts, Ghent, inv. 1853-E.

cat. 1 *Kitchen Interior*, 1855, oil on canvas, 160 × 208 cm. Palais des Beaux-Arts de Lille, inv. P 711.

cat. 105 *Flowers, Fruits and Accessories*, 1875, oil on panel, 71 × 56.5 cm. Royal Museums of Fine Arts of Belgium, Brussels, inv. 2700.

cat. 106 *Autumn Roses*, 1901, oil on panel, 104 × 125.5 cm. Royal Museums of Fine Arts of Belgium, Brussels, inv. 3604.

Alice Ronner

cat. 129 *The Harp*, 1888, oil on canvas, 222 × 160 cm. Stadsmuseum Lier, inv. 150.

cat. 128 *The Wicker Chair*, 1915, oil on canvas, 78 × 71 cm. Musée d'Orsay, Paris, inv. RF 1979 40.

Albert Saverys

cat. 163 *The Two Skates*, 1926, oil on canvas, 122 × 133 cm. Museum Dhondt-Dhaenens, Deurle, inv. 000 088.

Léon Spilliaert

cat. 147 *Console with Books and Boxes, Figure Seen from Behind*, 1907, India ink, ink wash, colour pencil, pastel, chalk, gouache and black chalk on paper, 63.4 × 48.1 cm. Private collection.

cat. 148 *The Blue Bowl*, 1907, India ink, gouache and pastel chalk on paper, 48 × 63 cm. Mu.ZEE, City of Ostend Collection, inv. SM000058.

cat. 149 *Plants, Inkpot and Mirror*, 1908, watercolour, gouache, colour pencil and India ink on paper, 64 × 49 cm. Mu.ZEE, City of Ostend Collection, inv. SM001747.

cat. 22 *Vase and Shell*, 1911, pastel on card, 89.2 × 70.2 cm. Private collection via Philip Seghers Gallery.

Louis Thevenet

cat. 17 *After Mass*, 1912, oil on canvas, 109 × 88 cm. Museum of Ixelles, inv. CC 1628.

cat. 144 *Still Life*, 1912, oil on canvas, 60 × 110 cm. Artwork owned by the Province of Flemish Brabant. On loan from the provincial council, inv. 580586.

cat. 15 *The Funeral March*, 1924, oil on canvas, 81 × 81 cm. Musea Brugge, inv. 0000.GRO1563.I.

cat. 16 *Vase of Lilies*, 1927, oil on canvas, 40 × 32 cm. Private collection, Leuven.

cat. 145 *The Blue Bottle*, 1927, oil on canvas, 71 × 48 cm. Private collection, Leuven.

Walter Vaes

cat. 20 *Red Fish*, 1906, oil on canvas, 53.5 × 66 cm. Royal Museum of Fine Arts, Antwerp, inv. 2035.

cat. 21 *Still Life with Fish*, s.d., oil on canvas, 65.5 × 82.4 cm. Janssens Collection, Antwerp.

cat. 153 *Two Slices of Fish*, s.d., oil on canvas, 39 × 47 cm. Collection Museum Helmantel (former Kunsthandel Bies, Eindhoven, Netherlands).

cat. 154 *Crab*, s.d., oil on canvas, 36.6 × 44.7 cm. Royal Museum of Fine Arts, Antwerp, inv. 2876.

cat. 152 *Flowers*, s.d., oil on canvas, 60 × 76 cm. Janssens Collection, Antwerp.

Gustave Van De Woestyne

cat. 24 *Still Life with Globe*, *c.*1921–2, gouache and oil on Japanese paper and card, 56 × 77.5 cm. Museum of Fine Arts, Ghent, inv. 2004-H.

cat. 23 *Still Life with Groundsel*, 1922, gouache on paper, 76.5 × 55.5 cm. Museum of Fine Arts, Ghent, inv. 2004-G.

cat. 150 *Balcony with Flowers (Cinerarias)*, 1929, oil on canvas, 80 × 60 cm. Museum of Fine Arts, Ghent, inv. 2015-JM.

cat. 151 *Still Life with Bananas*, 1930, oil on canvas, 80 × 62 cm. Van Buuren Museum & Gardens, Brussels, inv. 77388.

Frits Van den Berghe

cat. 160 *Flowers over the City*, 1929, oil on canvas, 126 × 97 cm. Private collection – on long-term loan at Mu.ZEE, Ostend.

Alfred Verhaeren

cat. 124 *Studio Materials*, s.d., oil on canvas, 126.1 × 71.5 cm. Museum of Fine Arts, Ghent, inv. 1922-V.

Isidore Verheyden

cat. 121 *Violets and Wallflowers in a Porcelain Jug*, 1873, oil on panel, 24.5 × 19 cm. Barat-Venker Collection, The Netherlands.

cat. 122 *The Breakfast*, *c.*1905, oil on canvas, 101.5 × 127 cm. Royal Museums of Fine Arts of Belgium, Brussels, inv. 3892.

Rik Wouters

cat. 19 *The Skinned Rabbit B*, 1908, oil on canvas, 40.2 × 47 cm. Royal Museums of Fine Arts of Belgium, Brussels, inv. 11570.

cat. 155 *Still Life with Skinned Hare*, 1908, oil on canvas, 45.2 × 66 cm. Royal Museums of Fine Arts of Belgium, Brussels, inv. 6665.

cat. 156 *Etching Table*, 1909, oil on canvas, 86 × 94 cm. Royal Museum of Fine Arts, Antwerp, inv. 2167.

cat. 157 *Green Cabbage*, 1912, oil on canvas, 111 × 100.5 cm. Royal Museums of Fine Arts of Belgium, Brussels, inv. 4864.

cat. 158 *Sombre Mood*, 1915, oil on canvas, 87 × 101 cm. Royal Museums of Fine Arts of Belgium, Brussels, inv. 4632.

cat. 159 *Apples and Artificial Flowers*, 1913, watercolour on canvas, 125.7 × 110.5 cm. KBC Bank NV, Brussels, inv. 98000441.

Index

Colophon

This publication accompanies the exhibition *Rose, rose, rose à mes yeux: James Ensor and Still Life in Belgium (1830–1930)* at Mu.ZEE, Ostend, from 16 December 2023 to 14 April 2024, the opening exhibition of Ensor Year 2024.

Ensor 2024

Exhibition at Mu.ZEE

Director
Dominique Savelkoul

Artistic coordinator
Joost Declercq

Business leader
Christine Van Daele

Guest curators and concept
Bart Verschaffel
Sabine Taevernier

Curator, Mu.ZEE
Stefan Huygebaert

Loan coordinators
Annelies Legein
Ilse Roosens
Gregory Boite

Conservation and collection management
Barbara de Jong
Karolien Withofs

Communication
Colette Castermans
Inge Busschaert

Public programs and education
Elise Vanhoecke
Wendy Van Hoorde

Fundraising
Inge Vekeman

Scenography
Guy Châtel
Kris Coremans

Technical realisation
Maarten Van Colen
Eddy Billiau
Ronny Malesys
Lorenzo Tjaeckx
Bram Van Hautem

Interns
Francesca Meylaers
Johanna Dams

Exhibition texts: coordination and editing
Marian Decroos

Graphic design
Chloé D'hauwe
Jef Cuypers

Mu.ZEE team
Freek Allaert, Shahida Bi Aziz, Gerda Balcaen, Bram Bekemans, Eddy Billiau, Thomas Billiau, Nancy Blieck, Gregory Boite, Hilde Brandt, Inge Busschaert, Colette Castermans, Heleen Claeys, Nina De Bruyne, Eline De Cloedt, Patricia De Jaeger, Barbara de Jong, Joost Declercq, Lizy Delheye, Herbert Deruwe, Khoshal Doust, Inne Gheeraert, Jean-Baptiste Hintjens, Stefan Huygebaert, Karine Inghelbrecht, Claudia Jaques, Christiaan Laforce, Annelies Legein, Kurt Lievens, Ronny Malesys, Tessa Mauroo, Mieke Mels, Stijn Peeters, Lars Pitteljon, Kim Plasman, Kathleen Ribbens, Ilse Roosens, Dominique Savelkoul, Inneke Schwickert, Ubah Mohamed Shil, Lorenzo Tjaeckx, Maarten Van Colen, Christine Van Daele, Wendy Van Hoorde, Johan Van Roose, Elise Vanhoecke, Inge Vekeman, Karolien Withofs

Mu.ZEE

Mu.ZEE enjoys the support of

Oostende DE STAD AAN ZEE

Flanders State of the Art

Fonds Radio Marlein managed by

King Baudouin Foundation
Working together for a better society

"The players of the National Lottery, along with the Vrienden van Mu.ZEE, are a proud partner of this unique Ensor exhibition and its immersive Wunderkammer. We applaud that James Ensor's oeuvre, of which still lifes are a substantial part, is thereby presented to the general public in an accessible way."
Frank Demeyere
Subsidy Management
National Lottery

national lottery MUCH MORE THAN JUST GAMES

VRIENDEN Mu.ZEE OOSTENDE

Mu.ZEE is grateful to the following lenders:
Barat-Venker Collection (The Netherlands)
Belvedere, Vienna
Berko Fine Paintings, Knokke-Heist, Belgium
Charlier Museum, Saint-Josse-ten-Noode
Collection BNP Paribas Fortis
Collection Marthe + Félix Dony
Collection Museum Helmantel, Westeremden, The Netherlands
Collection Simonis & Buunk Kunsthandel, Ede, The Netherlands
Collection Vanthournout
Emanuel Hoffman Foundation
Fédération Wallonie-Bruxelles
Fondation Socindec
Frank and Eliane Demaegd-Breynaert
Georges Hiltrop-Massenhove
Govaert Family
Janssens Collection, Antwerp
KBC Bank NV, Brussels
Kunsthalle Mannheim
Kunstmuseum Basel
M Leuven
Walter Mortelmans
Musea Brugge, Bruges
Musée d'Orsay, Paris
Musée des Beaux-Arts / La Boverie, Liège
Musée des Beaux-Arts de la Ville de Tournai
Musée des Beaux-Arts Lille
Museum Boijmans Van Beuningen, Rotterdam
Museum Dhondt-Dhaenens, Deurle
Museum Hof van Busleyden, Mechelen
Museum of Fine Arts, Ghent
Museum of Ixelles, Brussels
Province of Flemish Brabant
Quintet Private Bank (Europe) S.A.
Dr and Mrs Rongé-Tops
Stadsmuseum Lier
Stichting Mortelmans
The Werner Wieland Collection
University of Liège – Musée Wittert
Van Buuren Museum & Gardens, Brussels
Von der Heydt-Museum, Wuppertal
Yper Museum, Ypres

And all lenders who wish to remain anonymous

And in particular:
Royal Museum of Fine Arts, Antwerp
Royal Museums of Fine Arts of Belgium, Brussels

For their help in various forms, Mu.ZEE would like to thank:
Anne Adriaens-Pannier, Jan Dirk Baetens, Jacques Bedoret, Kunstveiling Bernaerts, Mari Bies, Kunsthandel Bies Eindhoven, Henry Bounameaux, Piet Boyens, Olivier Camus, Leen Caremans, Peter Craeymeersch, Muriel Damien, Julien De Bock, Thierry de Duve, Jelle De Rock, Oscar De Vos, Benjamin De Vuyst, Guy De Vuyst, Paul De Vylder †, Marian Decroos, Steven Decroos, Virginie Devillez, Jan Dewilde, Julia Engelmayer, Charly Herscovici, Geertrui Ivens, Max Jadot, Emmanuel Joly, Inge Ketelers, Claire Leblanc, Sylvia Liska, Mark Murray, Patricia Pálffy, Tom Raemdonck, Philippe Seghers, Bernard Steyaert, Renske Suijver, Marianne Thys, Herwig Todts, Xavier Tricot, Hildegard Van de Velde, Katlijne Van der Stighelen, Dominique Van Hove, Frederiek Van Pamel, Frederik Vandewiere, Wim Vanseveren, Mariëlle Verboven, Kathy Vincke

As well as the teams at Blackbirds, SignIt, Hiscox and Hizkia

And all who wish to remain anonymous

Catalogue

Publisher
Mercatorfonds, Brussels (Managing Director Bernard Steyaert)

Editors
Bart Verschaffel
Sabine Taevernier
Stefan Huygebaert

Texts
Gregory Boite
Stefan Huygebaert
Sabine Taevernier
Bart Verschaffel

Image editing for Mu.ZEE
Stefan Huygebaert

Translation
Dafydd Rees Roberts (French text by Sabine Taevernier)
Guy Shipton (Dutch texts by Gregory Boite, Stefan Huygebaert and Bart Verschaffel)

Copy-editing
Sheri Walter

Editorial coordination
Marianne Thys

Project coordination
Jelle De Rock (Mercatorfonds)

Graphic design and typesetting
Inge Ketelers

Printing, binding and colour separation
die Keure, Bruges

Printed on Magno Volume, 135g

www.mercatorfonds.be

ISBN 978-94-6230-363-8
D/2023/703/27
Printed in Belgium

Distributed outside the Benelux by Yale University Press, New Haven and London
www.yalebooks.com/art

ISBN 978-0-300-27319-9
LOC 2023944287

Photo credits

Every effort has been made to trace and credit all known copyright or reproduction-right holders. The publisher apologises for any errors or omissions and welcomes these being brought to their attention.

© 2008 Serge Verheylewegen, Brussels: cat. 164
© Albertinum | GNM, Staatliche Kunstsammlungen Dresden, photo Ursula-Maria Hoffmann: fig. 39
© Bayerische Staatsgemälde-sammlungen: fig. 38
© Berko Fine Paintings, Knokke-Heist, Belgium: cat. 127
© Christie's Images / Bridgeman Images: fig. 21
© Kunstbezit Provincie Vlaams-Brabant: cat. 144
© Ministère de la Culture – Médiathèque du patrimoine et de la photographie, Dist. RMN-Grand Palais / Atelier de Nadar: fig. 43
© Obrecht De Boer / IPARC, Belgium: cat. 2
© Photothèque R. Magritte / ADAGP Images, Paris, 2023: figs 24, 27; cat. 29
© Renaud Schrobiltgen, Brussels: cat. 147
© RMN-Grand Palais (Musée d'Orsay) / Franck Raux: cat. 128
© RMN-Grand Palais (Musée d'Orsay) / Hervé Lewandowski: cat. 10
© RMN-Grand Palais (Musée du Louvre) / Stéphane Maréchalle: fig. 41
© RMN-Grand Palais (PBA, Lille) / Hervé Lewandowski: cat. 1
© Royal Museums of Fine Arts of Belgium, Brussels, J. Geleyns – Art Photography: figs 4, 35, 42; cats 5, 6, 9, 19, 40, 41, 64, 66, 103, 105, 106, 116, 117, 118, 122, 133, 155, 157, 158; cover
© SABAM Belgium 2023: figs 22, 23, 26; cat. 18, 20, 21, 26, 28, 128, 129, 153, 154, 155, 161, 162, 163
© Succession René Magritte – SABAM Belgium 2023: figs 9, 21, 24, 25, 27; cats 29, 164
© Vincent Everarts: cats 18, 58, 61, 71
Adri Verburg: cats 51, 78
Antje Zeis-Loi, Medienzentrum Wuppertal: cat. 39
Belvedere, Vienna: cat. 68
Benjamin De Vuyst: fig. 23; cat. 146
bpk / Hamburger Kunsthalle: fig. 17
CC0 Paris Musées / Musée Carnavalet – Histoire de Paris: fig. 37
Cedric Verhelst: cats 98, 99, 126, 149, 160
Cedric Verhelst / Collection Museum Dhondt-Dhaenens, Deurle: cats 49, 163
Charlier Museum, Saint-Josse-ten-Noode: cat. 38
Collection Oskar Reinhart 'Am Römerholz', Winterthur: fig. 20
Collection Yper Museum: cats 12, 143
Courtesy of Mark Murray Fine Paintings, New York: fig. 6
Courtesy of Mercatorfonds: figs 15, 16, 18, 28, 40, 44, 45, 46, 47; cats 31, 33, 34, 35, 36, 46, 47, 53, 54, 56, 62, 65, 67, 74, 75, 81
Dominique Provost: fig. 33; cats 15, 115, 148
Emmanuel Joly / Musée L: cat. 21
Fabrice Schneider: cats 36, 37
Gérald Micheels: cats 76, 77, 80, 125
Ghent University Library (publication digitized on lib.ugent.be): fig. 5
H. Kessels (from: Delevoy 1972): fig. 22
Hugo Maertens: fig. 32; cats 20, 25, 26, 32, 43, 45, 55, 119, 120, 154, 156, 161, 162
KBC Bank NV, Brussels: cat. 159
Kunsthalle, Mannheim: cat. 44
Kunstmuseum Basel: cat. 73
Kunstmuseum Basel, Martin P. Bühler: cat. 27
Leopold Museum Vienna: cat. 63
NGC: fig. 19
Michel Burez: figs 2, 3; cats 4, 23, 24, 104, 124, 150
Michel Muys & Louis De Peuter: fig. 1
Mu.ZEE: fig. 30
Museum of Ixelles: cat. 17
P. Bijtebier, Brussels (from: Delevoy 1972): fig. 26
Pedro De Campos / Van Buuren Museum, 2023: cat. 151
Peter Cox (Eindhoven): cats 7, 108, 109, 110, 111, 112, 113, 114, 121, 153
Photo Antony Ostende: fig. 14
Photo Studio Tromp: cats 48, 60
Prolith AG, CH-3063 Ittigen: cat. 70
Rik Klein Gotink: figs 31, 34; cats 42, 57, 59
Simonis & Buunk Kunsthandel, Ede (The Netherlands): cat. 8
Steven Decroos: figs 11, 12, 29; cats 8, 11, 13, 14, 16, 22, 28, 30, 50, 52, 69, 82, 83, 84, 85, 86, 87, 88, 89, 90, 91, 92, 93, 94, 95, 96, 97, 101, 102, 107, 123, 129, 130, 131, 132, 134, 135, 136, 145, 152
Stichting Mortelmans: cats 3, 137, 138, 139, 140, 141, 142; fig. 7
Studio Bernaerts: fig. 13
The Metropolitan Museum of Art / Art Resource / Scala, Florence: fig. 8
The Museum of Modern Art, New York / Scala, Florence: figs 9, 36
University of Liège – Musée Wittert: cat. 79

Cover image
James Ensor, *Roses (Roses)*, 1892, oil on panel, 32.5 × 40 cm. Royal Museums of Fine Arts of Belgium, Brussels, inv. 11157. CR T351.

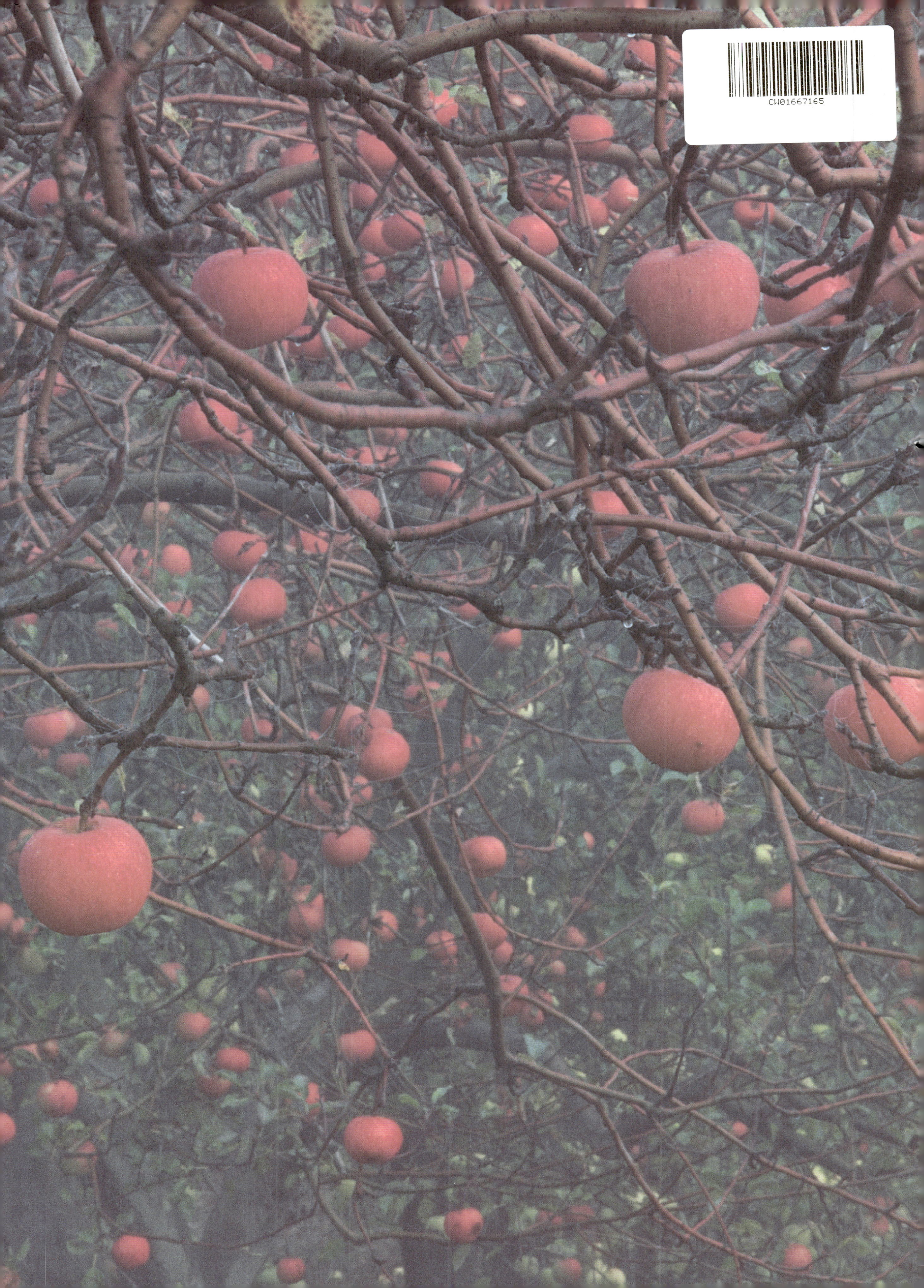

De Vier Seizoenen

EEN CULINAIRE REIS

de Lantaarn

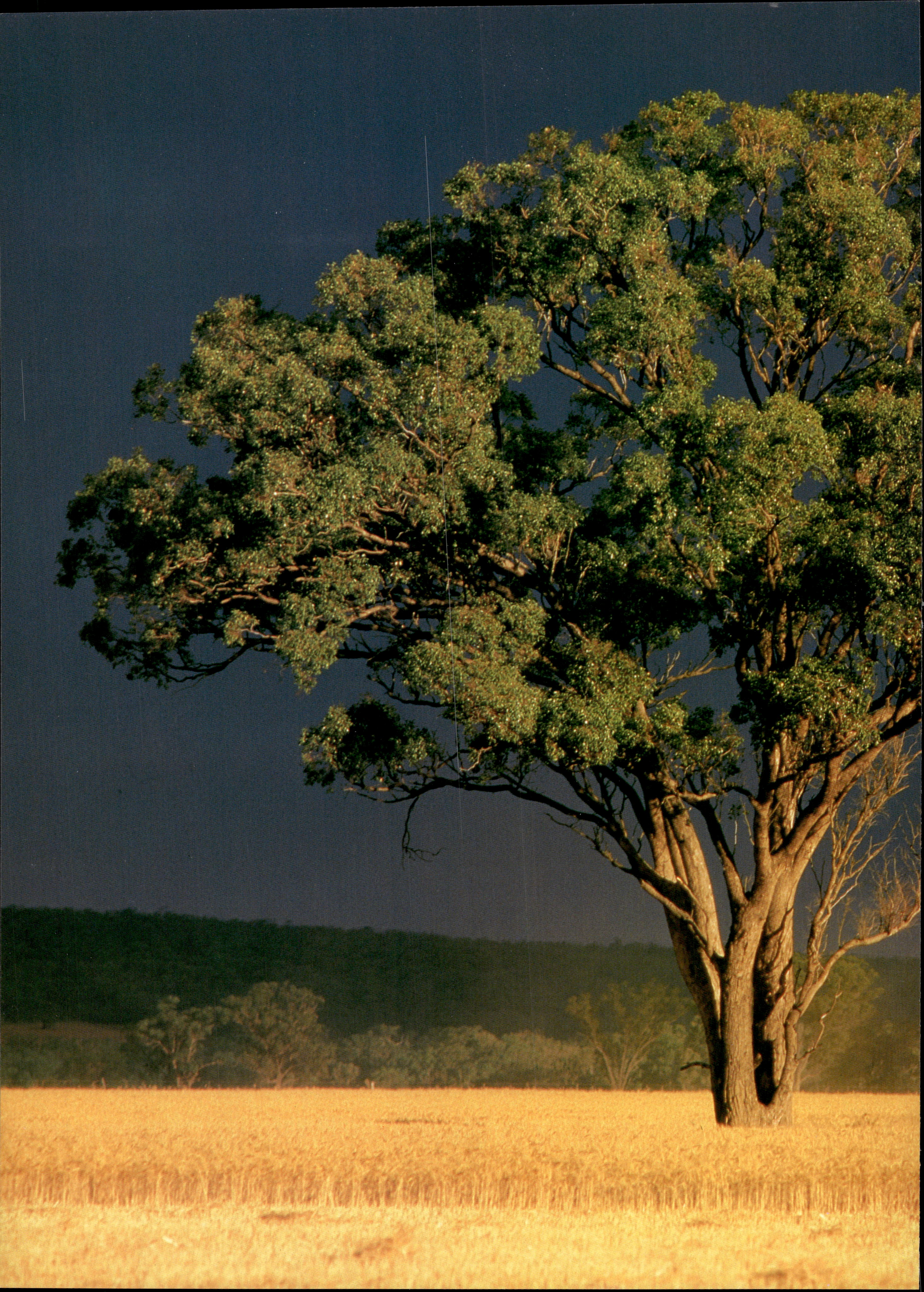

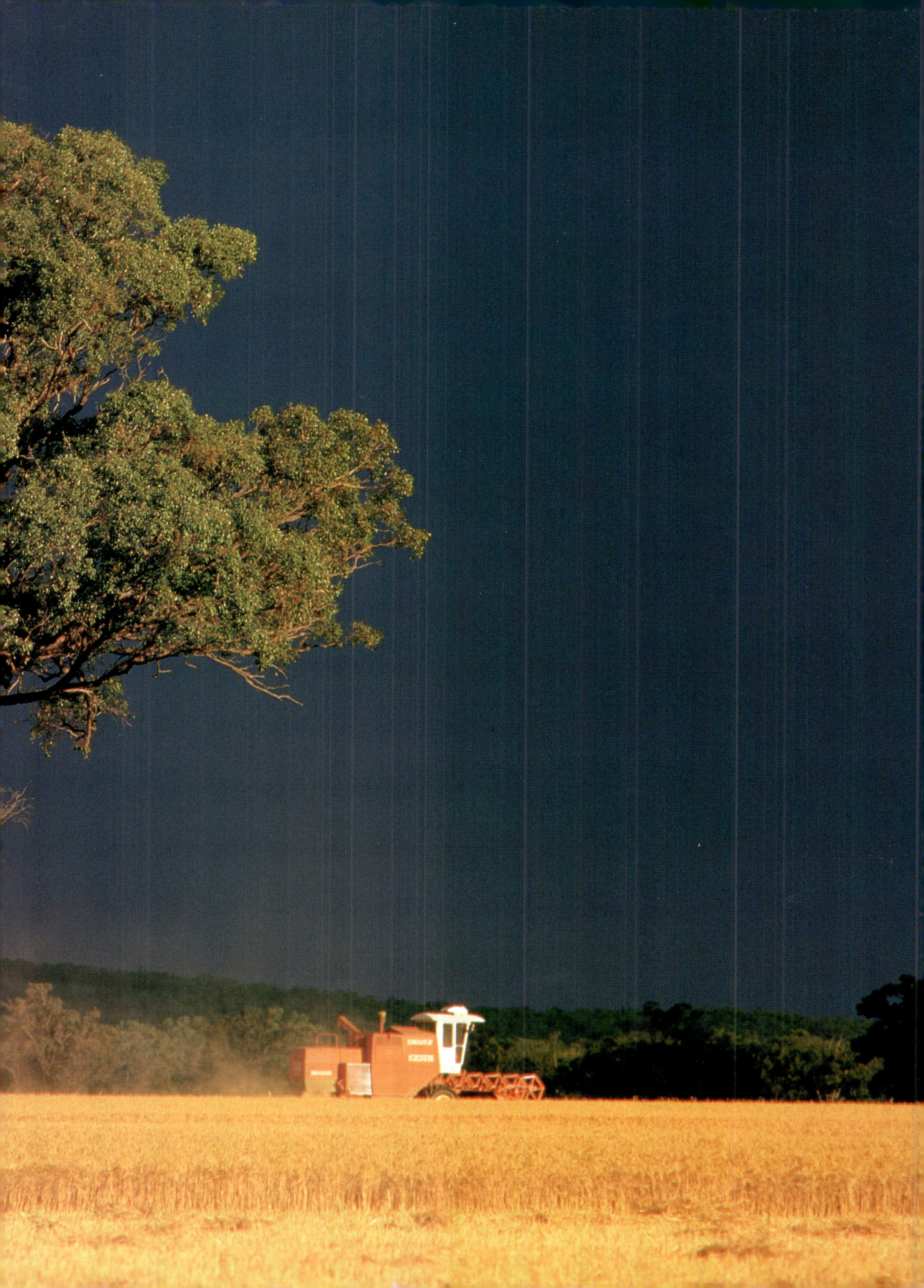

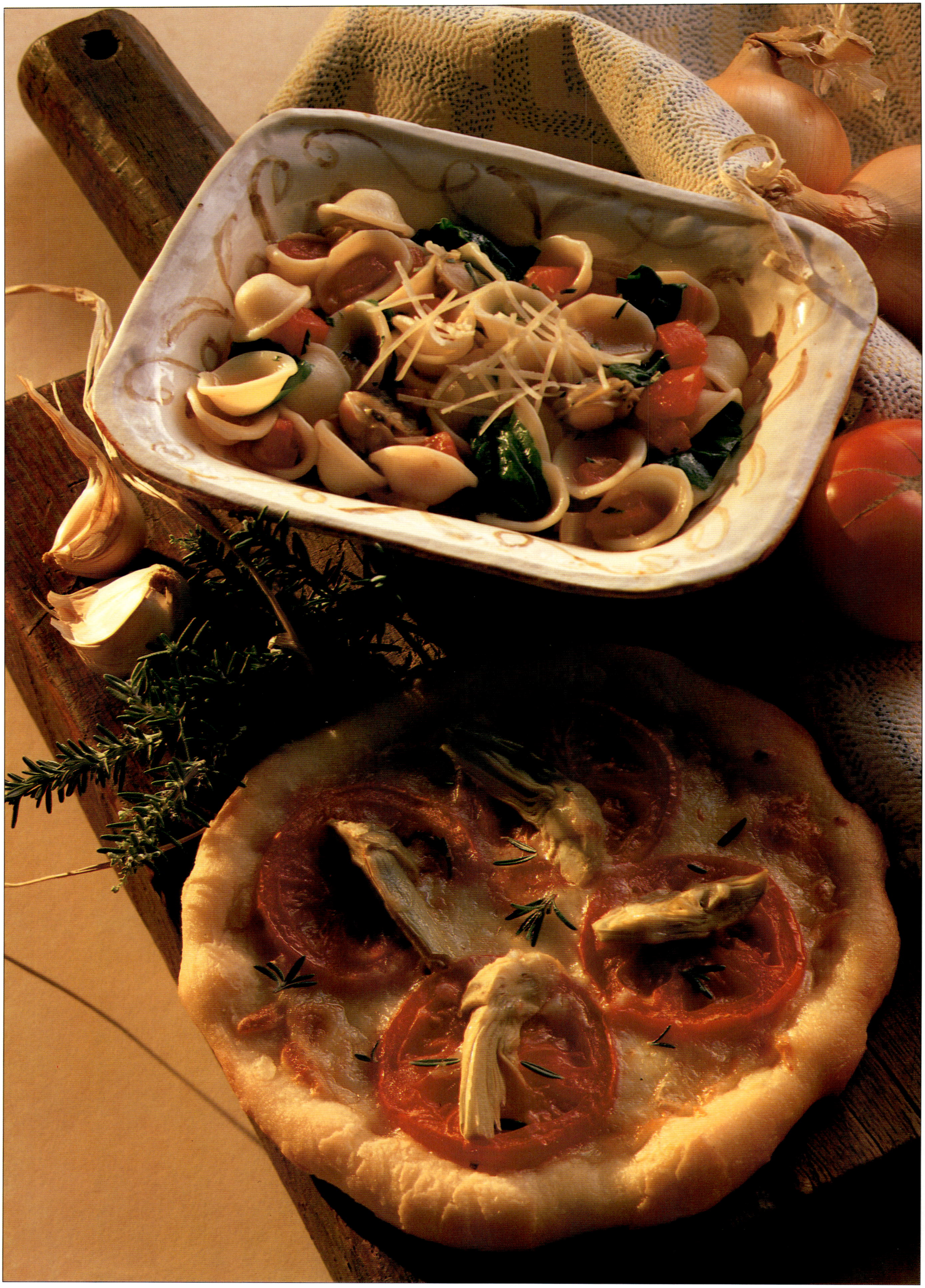

De Vier Seizoenen

EEN CULINAIRE REIS

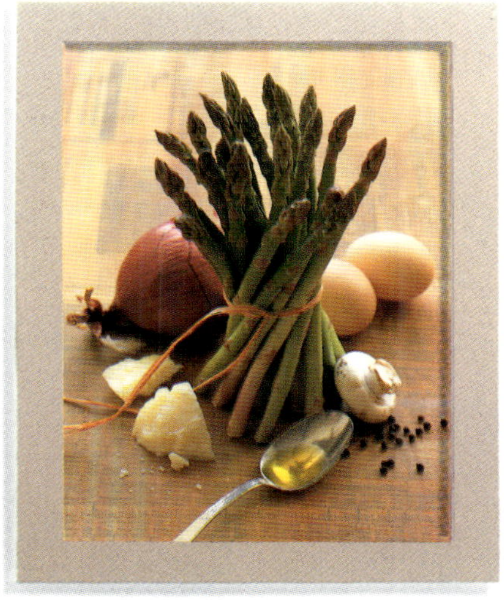

RECEPTEN

PAMELA SHELDON JOHNS

TEKST

MARY ABBOTT HESS

ASSISTENTE JANE GRANT TOUGAS

FOTO'S RECEPTEN

PHILIP SALAVERRY

STILERING

SUE WHITE

de Lantaarn

DE LANTAARN, AMSTERDAM
MCMXCV

Oorspronkelijke uitgave
Healthy Gourmet Cookbook
Geproduceerd door
Weldon Owen Inc., San Francisco

Directeur: Kevin Weldon
President: John Owen
General manager: Stuart Laurence
Directeur co-publishing: Derek Barton
Uitgeefster: Jane Fraser
Hoofdredactrice: Anne Dickerson
Redactie-assistente: Jan Hughes
Kopy-redactrice: Zipporah Collins
Bijschriften: Jane Horn
Produktie: Stephanie Sherman, Mick Bagnato
Vormgeving: Tom Morgan, Blue Design
Assistente vormgeving: Jennifer Petersen
Illustraties: Diana Reiss-Koncar
Index: Ken Dellapenta
Assistent stilering: Bruce Yim
Rekwisietenstilering: Amy Glenn
Assistent voedselfotografie: David Williams

NEDERLANDSE UITGAVE

Uitgever: Bert J. Jans
Hoofdredacteur: Jan van Gestel
Redactie-assistente: Marja Stoepman
Ontwerp omslag: Ino van Kuyk
Vertaling: Kim Maclean

De Lantaarn is een handelsmerk van
Time-Life Books B.V.

Gezet door V.O.F. Peters & Ellenbroek, Amsterdam
Produktie: Rob Peters

Vervaardigd door Mandarin Offset, Hongkong
Gedrukt in China

ISBN 90 5426 802 6
NUGI-code 421

Schutbladen: Een appelboomgaard op een nevelige herfstochtend.
Pagina 2-3: Tarwe is het meest populaire graan ter wereld. De oogst begint op een gouden akker in New South Wales in Australië.
Pagina 4, van boven naar beneden: Pasta met clams, spinazie en tomaten uit Bari, Gegrilde pizza (recepten op pagina 129).
Rechts: Een fruitverkoper op Sri Lanka staat trots voor zijn prachtig ingerichte kraam. De aantrekkingskracht van verse waar van topkwaliteit inspireert koks over de hele wereld.
Pagina 8, met de klok mee van boven: Aardbeien-champagnesorbet, Gekarameliseerde broodpudding, Ken Homs gestoofde peren (recepten op pagina 181).
Pagina 10-11: Onder het zilveren gebladerte van olijfbomen is welkome schaduw te vinden.
Pagina 62-63: Appelbomen in bloei aan de voet van Mount Hood in de V.S.
Pagina 98-99: Zonnebloemen doen een veld oplichten.
Pagina 144-145: In een boomgaard zorgt herfstgebladerte voor volop kleur.
Pagina 182-183: Een paarse gloed hangt over een akker in Oregon.

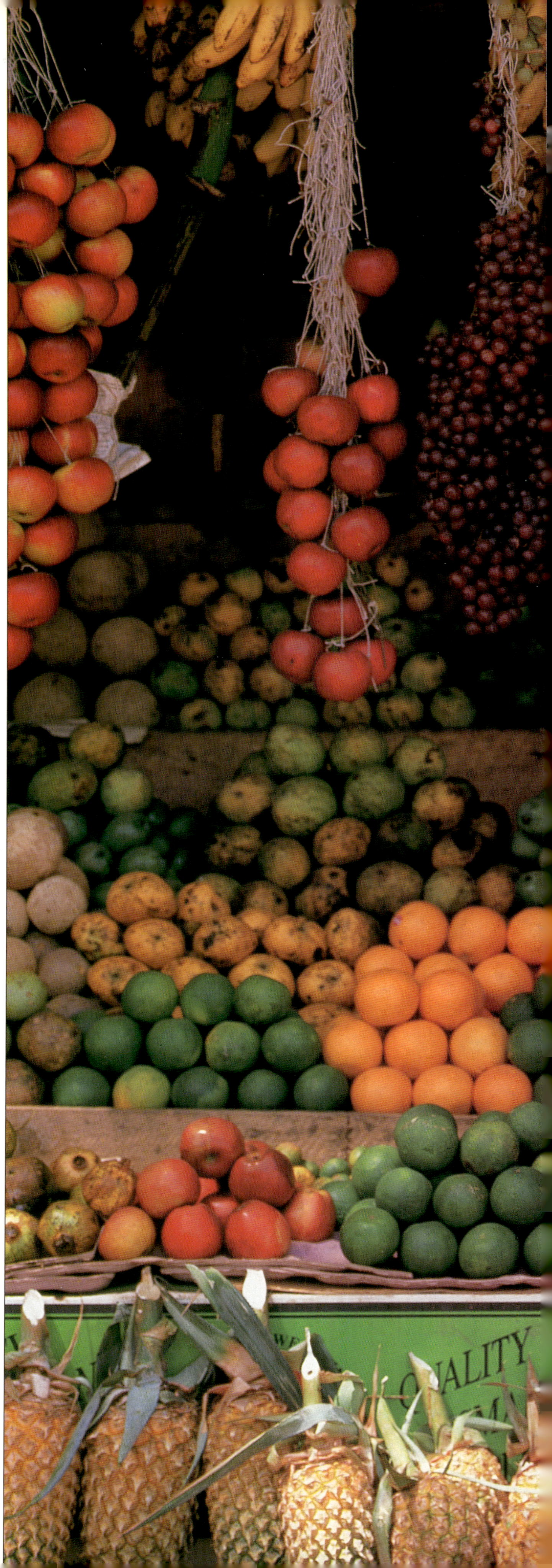

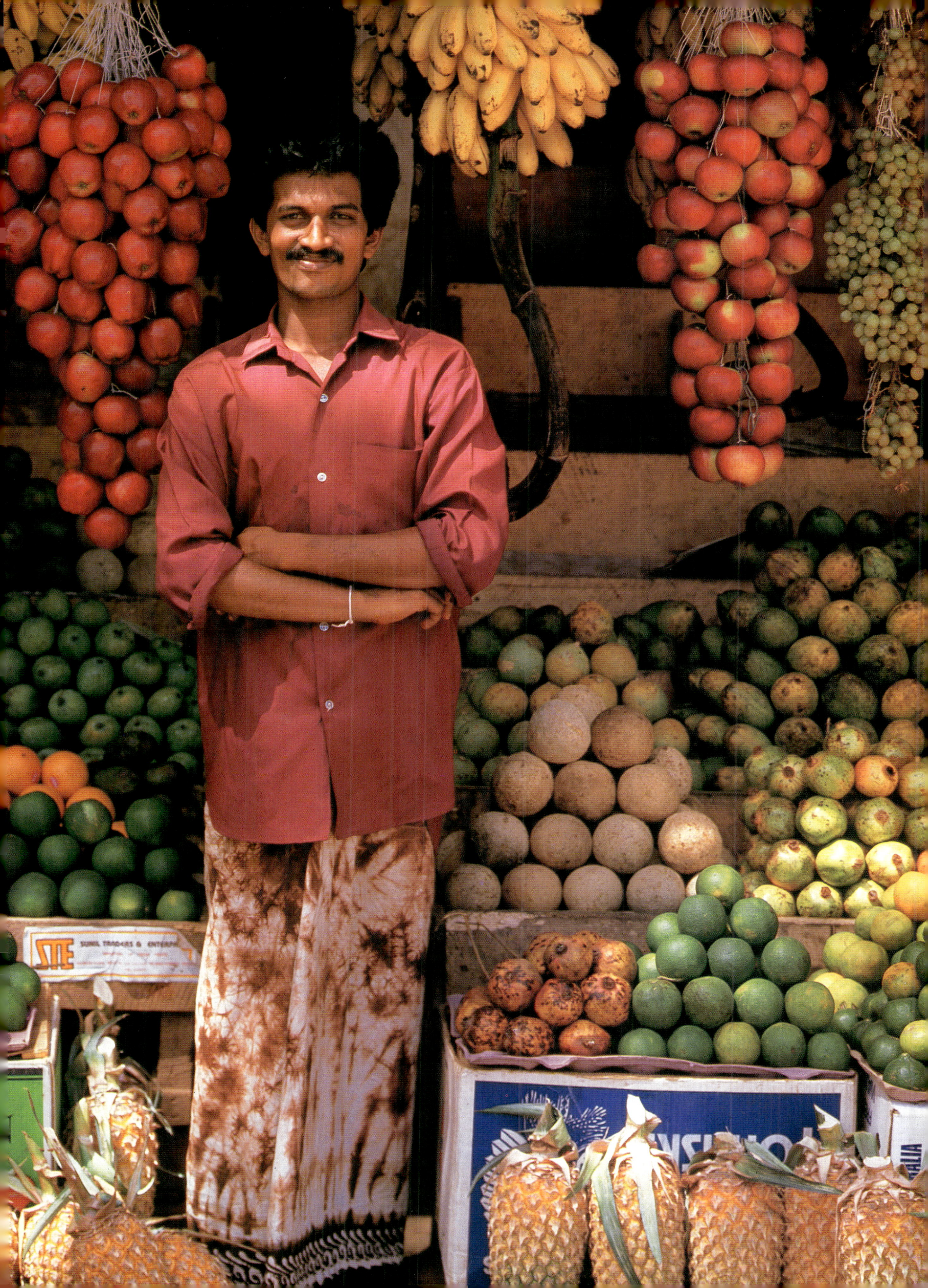
STE
SUNIL TRADERS &

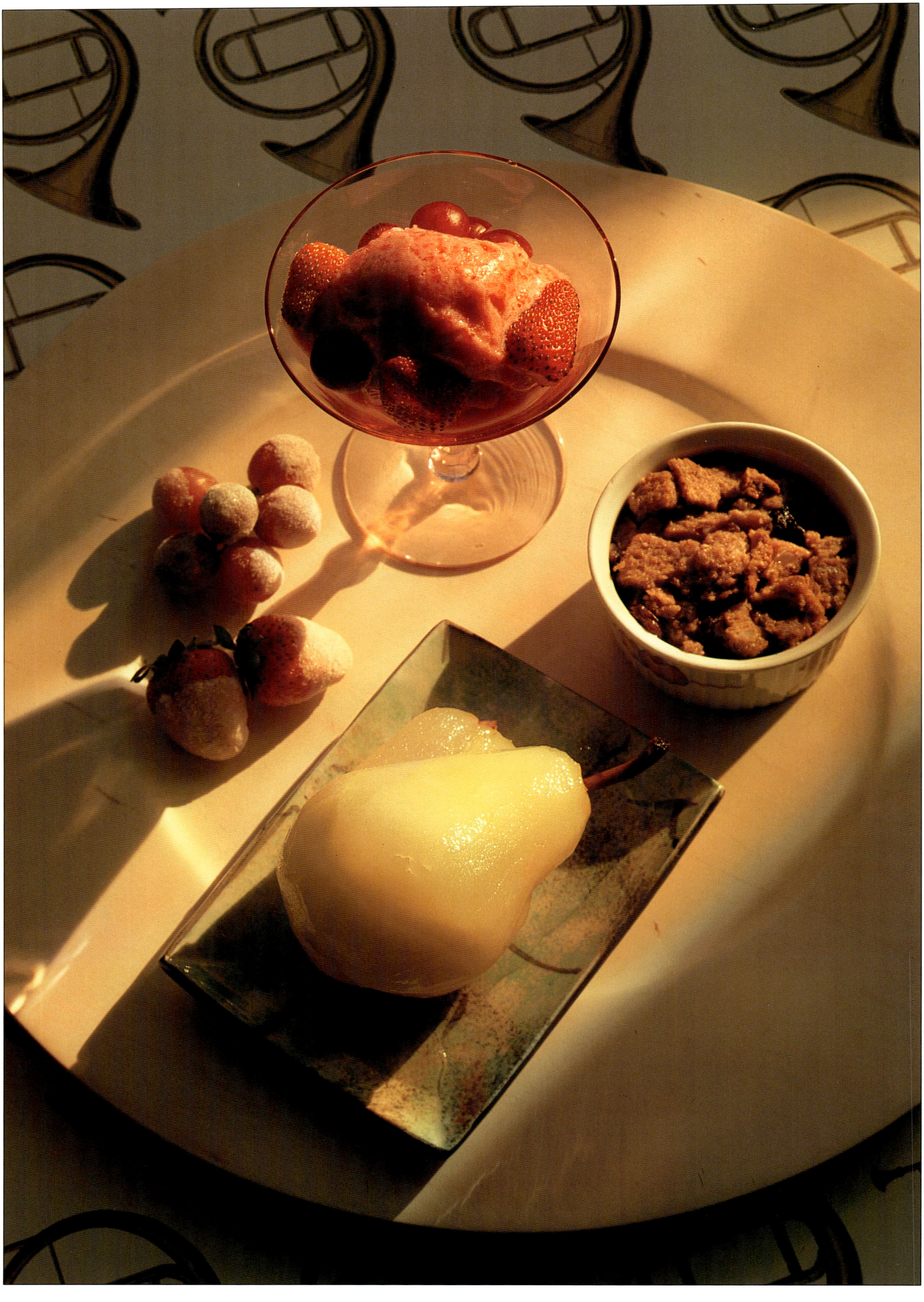

Inhoud

De Vier Seizoenen

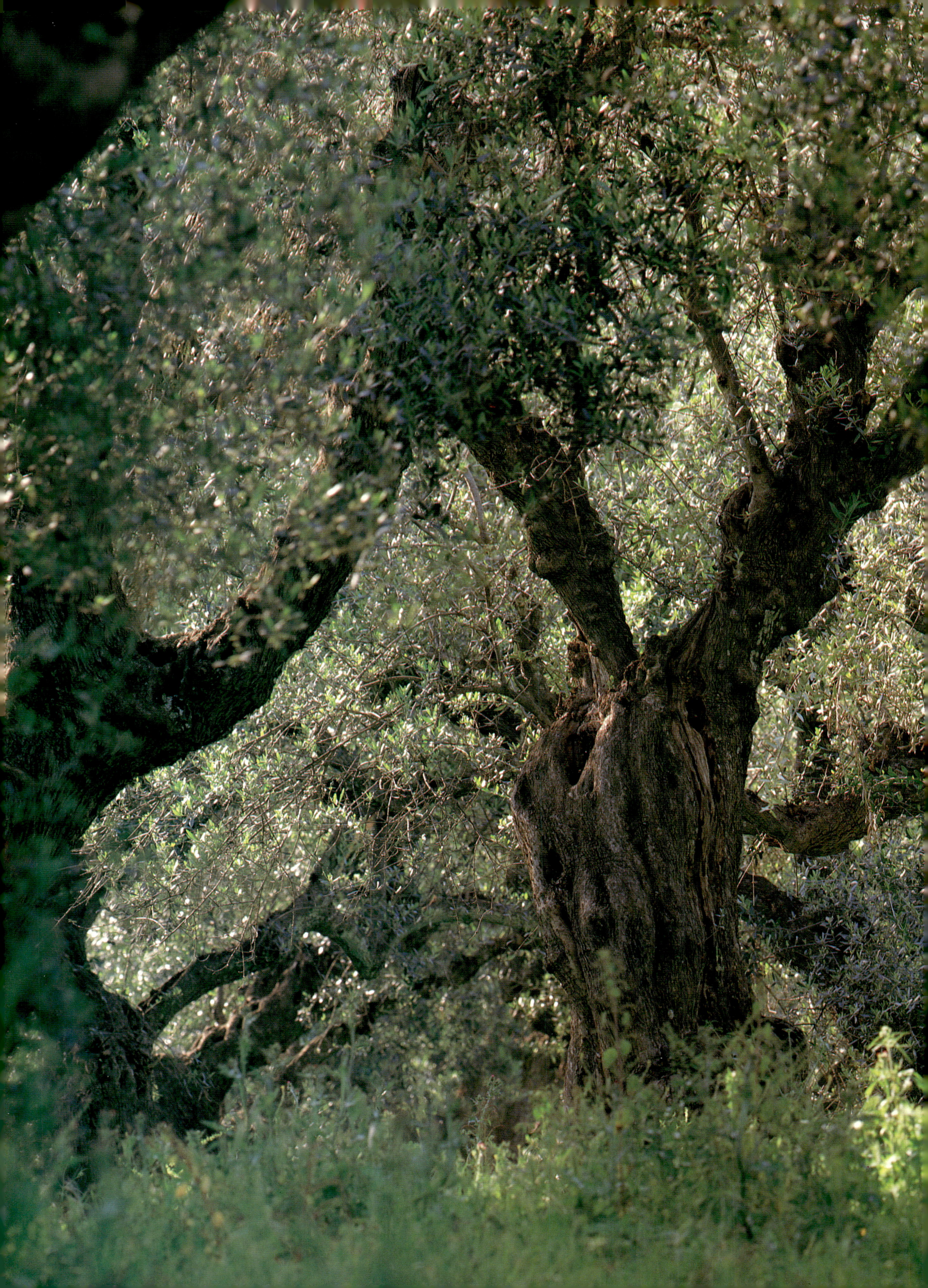

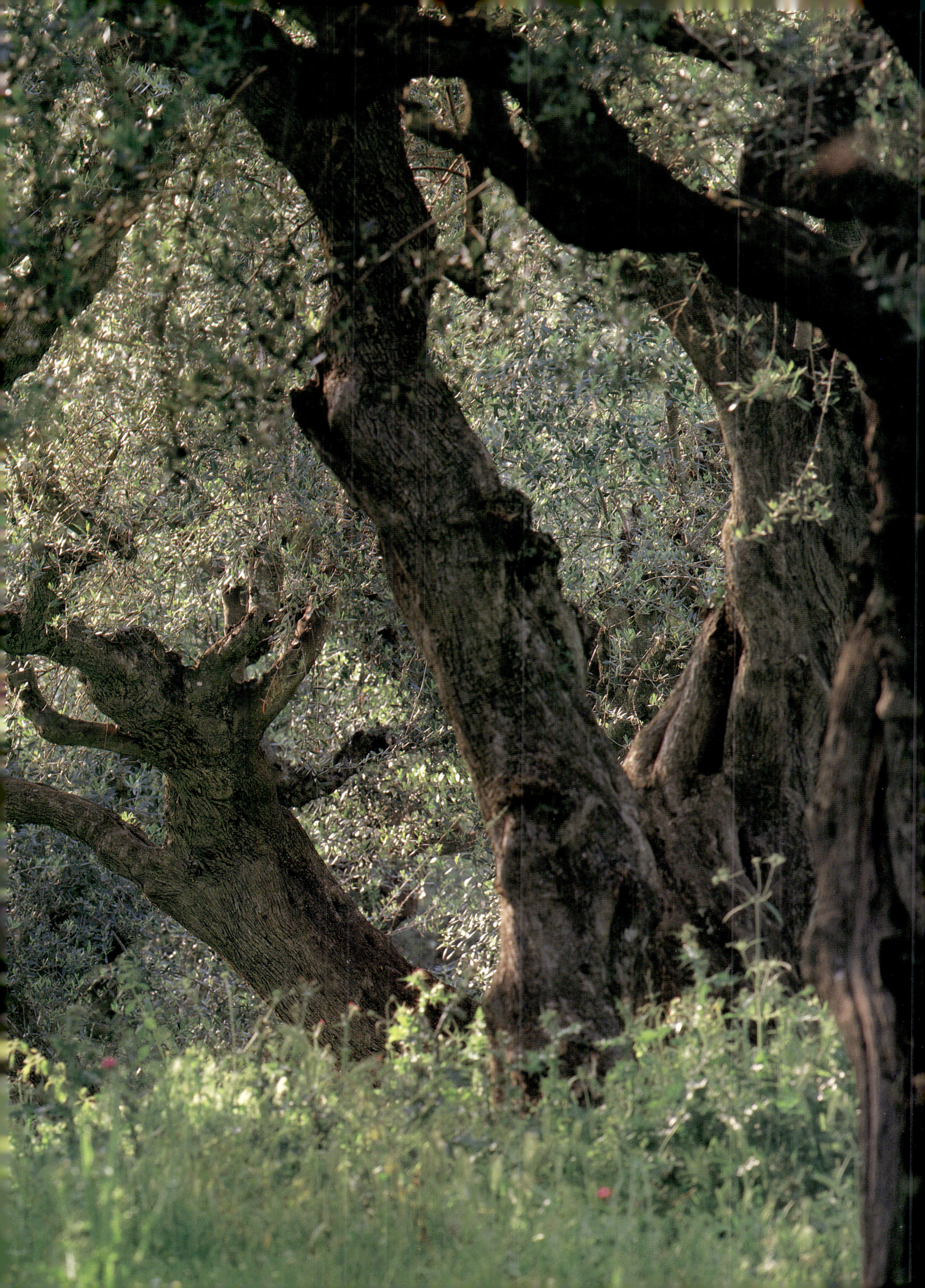

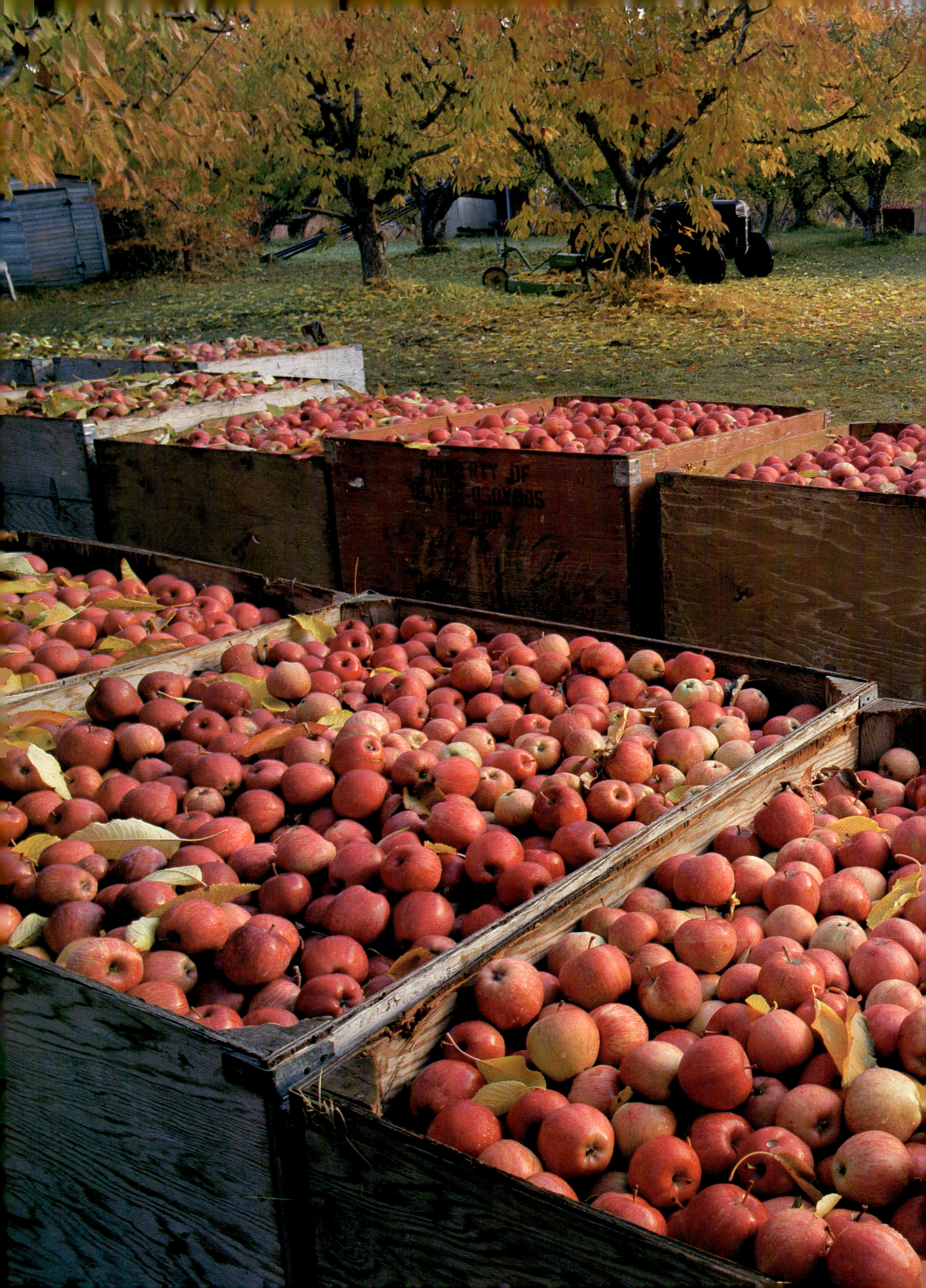
PROPERTY OF
CO-OP

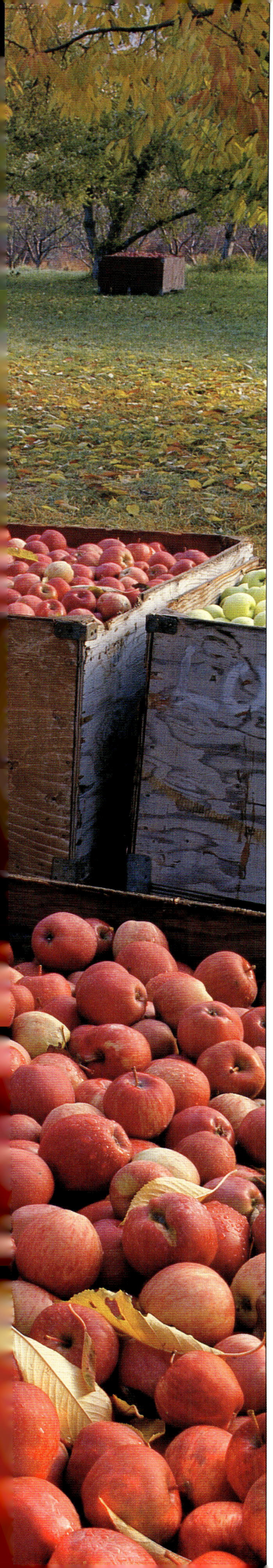

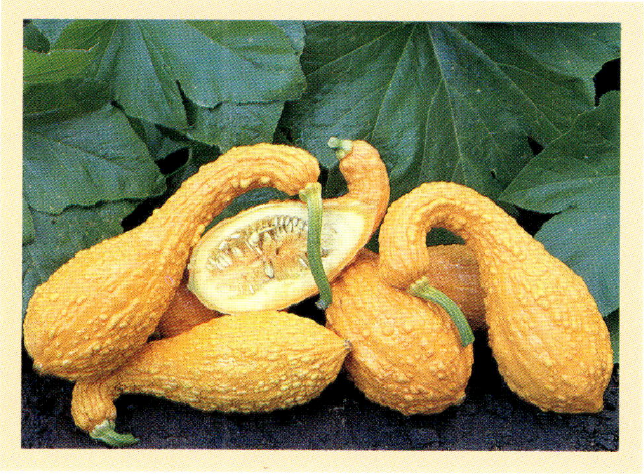

De vier seizoenen

Elk jaargetijde schenkt ons nieuwe mogelijkheden om van de rijkdom van de oogst te genieten, culturele tradities te bevestigen en smakelijk, gezond eten tot ons te nemen.

De vier seizoenen leveren ons elk aparte genoegens op eetgebied, genoegens waarmee we onze gezondheid bevorderen. Als gezondheidsoverwegingen en adviezen van voedingsdeskundigen voldoende waren om de eetgewoonten in onze samenleving te veranderen, zou dat allang geleden zijn gebeurd. Maar vaak lijkt daarbij een cruciaal element over het hoofd te zijn gezien: namelijk smaak. Als eten niet smakelijk is, eten we het niet—ongeacht hoe gezond

Boven: Een gloedvolle, gouden oogst aan pompoenen. Links: Het ene seizoen na het andere vergast de natuur ons met telkens nieuwe oogsten. Hier staan in de nazomer kisten Canadese appels op transport te wachten.

het voedsel wel mag zijn.

Jaar na jaar blijkt uit onderzoeken dat hedendaagse consumenten zich bij de keuze van voedsel in de eerste plaats laten leiden door smaak, direct gevolgd door voedingswaarde. Dit uitgangspunt moet ons doen erkennen dat smaak en voedingswaarde twee onlosmakelijk met elkaar verbonden elementen van de hele voedingsbeleving zijn.

De Vier Seizoenen is een culinaire reis die van dat uitgangspunt vertrekt. Dit boek gaat over het bereiden en genieten van heerlijk eten—optimaal van smaak, versheid, kleur, textuur *en* onontbeerlijke voedingsstoffen. De ingrediënten vormen een eerlijke oogst aan vruchten, groenten, granen en kaas; gevogelte en zeebanket, met internationale flair op smaak gebracht. U vindt een ruime etnische diversiteit in de recepten, omdat binnen de context van smaak en gezondheid "goed eten" nu eenmaal een ontdekkingsreis naar vele voedingstradities betekent.

Voor technologie en vervoer de barrières tot een wereldwijde communicatie en handel slechtten, aten mensen wat ze elk seizoen in hun omgeving vonden. In vroeger tijden was dit meestal een dieet van granen en bladgroenten dat werd aangevuld met vruchten en later met vlees. In vroege beschavingen was het verkrijgen van voedsel een belangrijke sociale activiteit, waarvoor samenwerking en het ontstaan van solidariteit vereist waren. Door het delen van maaltijden en voltrekken van rituelen raakte voedsel diep in de cultuur verankerd. Sporen van deze oude praktijken vinden we in ons dagelijks leven terug in de maaltijd voor het gezin en de viering van diverse feesten.

Door de industriële revolutie werd de afhankelijk van vers, plaatselijk verkrijgbaar voedsel iets van het verleden. Een dieet dat bestond uit samengestelde koolhydraten en vezels uit granen, vruchten en groenten werd aangevuld met geraffineerde suiker, zout, verzadigde vetten en steeds meer voorbewerkt eten. Tegenwoordig vertellen deskundigen ons dat een terugkeer naar een "primitievere" stijl van eten van wezenlijk belang voor onze gezondheid kan zijn.

In tegenstelling tot onze verre voorouders zijn seizoen en plaats geen beperking voor ons. We hebben volop keuze uit verse ingrediënten. We kunnen de smaken van ons eigen etnische erfgoed herontdekken én de culinaire tradities van anderen beleven. Het is geen verrassing dat de keukens van zovele culturen ondanks hun andere smaak zich in wezen verlaten op de granen, peulvruchten, vruchten en groenten die van elementair belang waren voor onze gezamenlijke voorouders.

De culinair schrijver Robert Barnett stelt: "Als we onze maaltijden meer baseerden op volle granen, peulvruchten, groenten en fruit…met wat vet voor de smaak en de bereiding en nu en dan zelfs behoorlijk wat vet…zouden we ontdekken dat we onze smaak wel degelijk kunnen ontwikkelen, en dat eten dat heel goed is voor onze gezondheid ook voortreffelijk kan smaken."

Al lezend in en kokend uit *De Vier Seizoenen* zult u dit standpunt met ons gaan delen. Elk jaargetijde schenkt ons nieuwe mogelijkheden om van de rijkdom van de oogst te genieten, culturele tradities te bevestigen en smakelijk, gezond eten tot ons te nemen. *De Vier Seizoenen* helpt u meedenken over het verbeteren van uw voedselkeuzes, zonder een goede smaak ten koste te laten gaan van een verantwoord voedingspatroon.

Hiernaast: Twee vrouwen handelen op een drijvende markt in Thailand. Onder: Markten zijn van oudsher ontmoetingsplaatsen. Waarschijnlijk zal deze Russische met haar verse waar ook wel wat nieuws van de dag aan haar klanten geven.

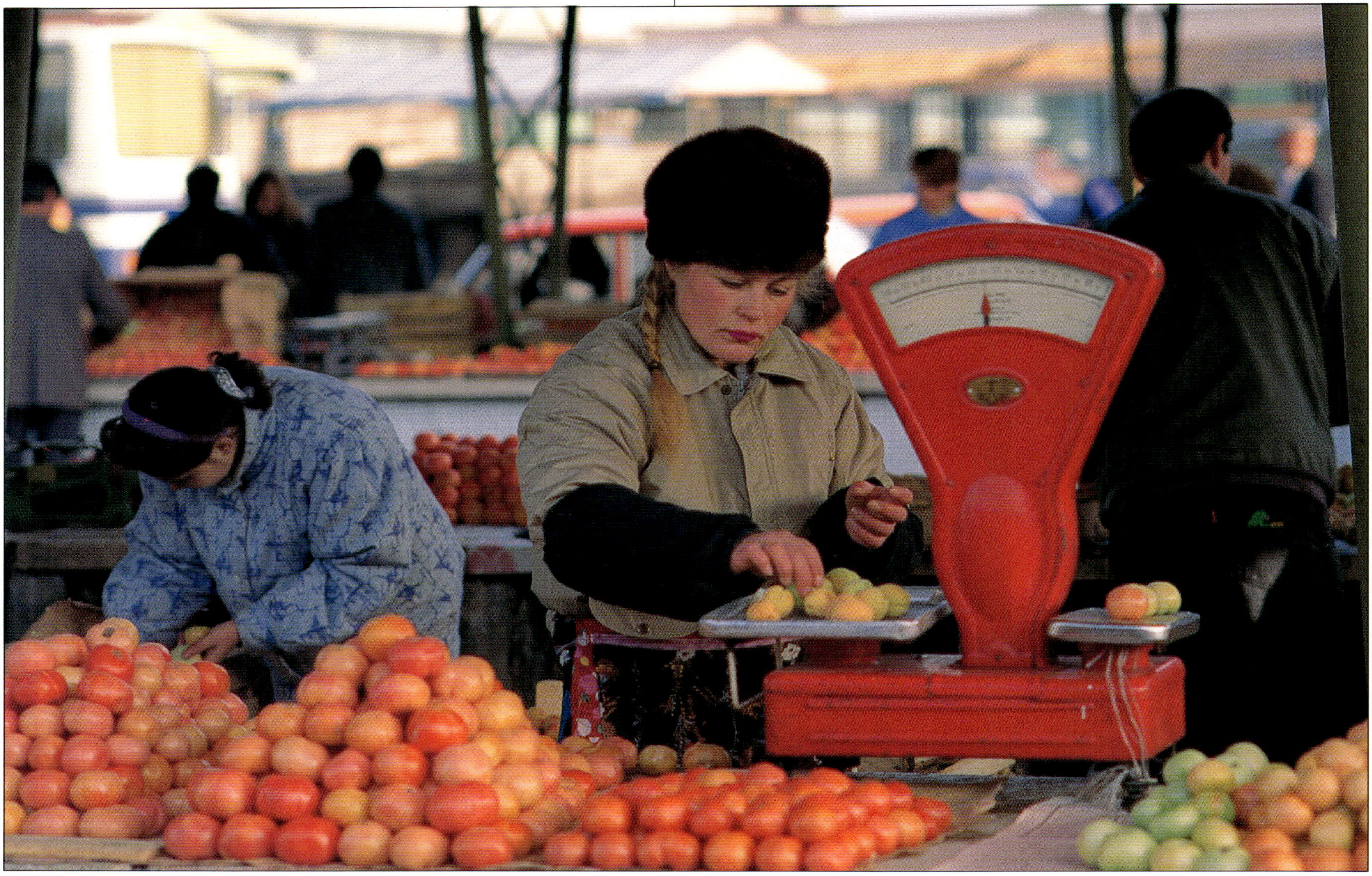

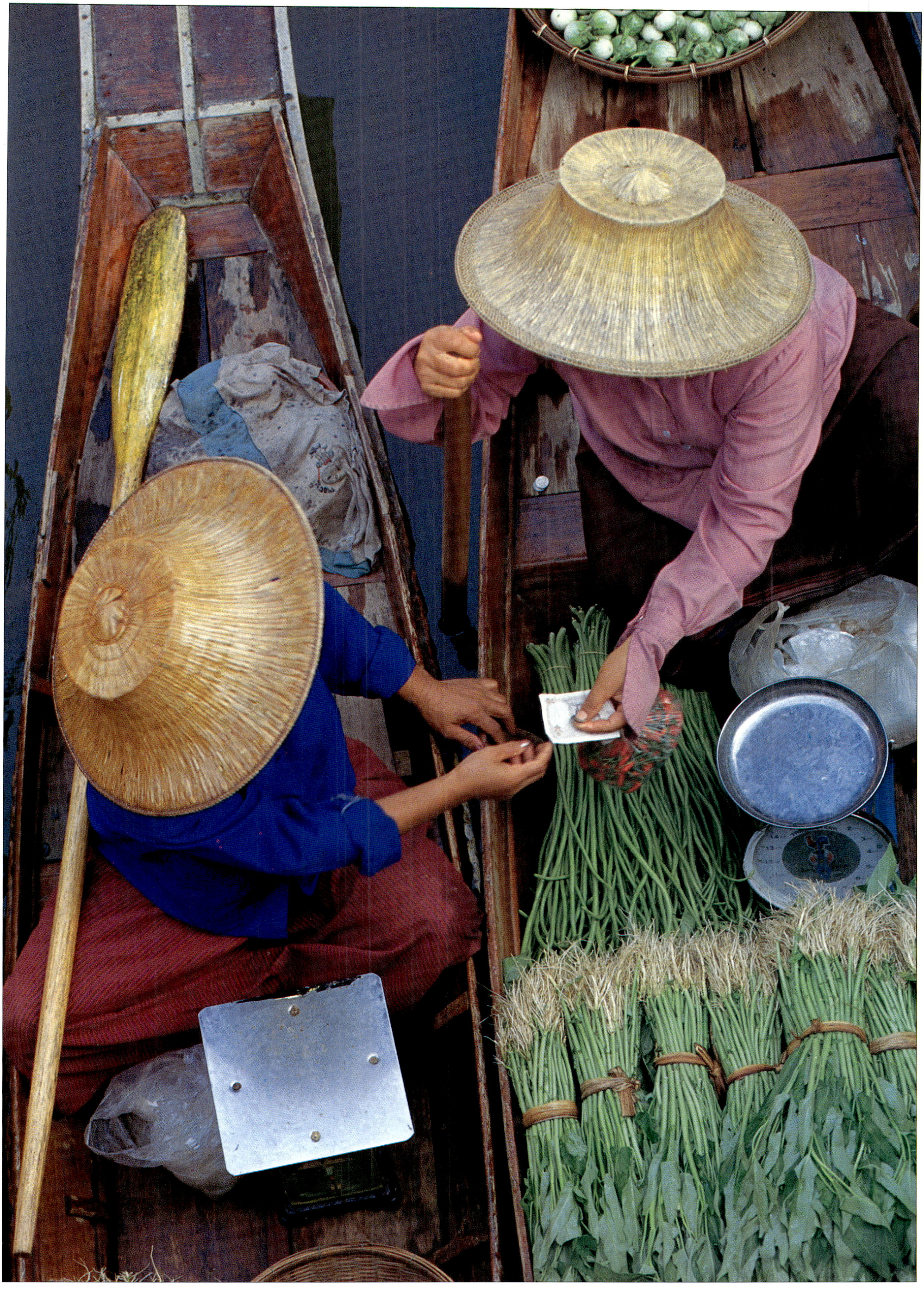

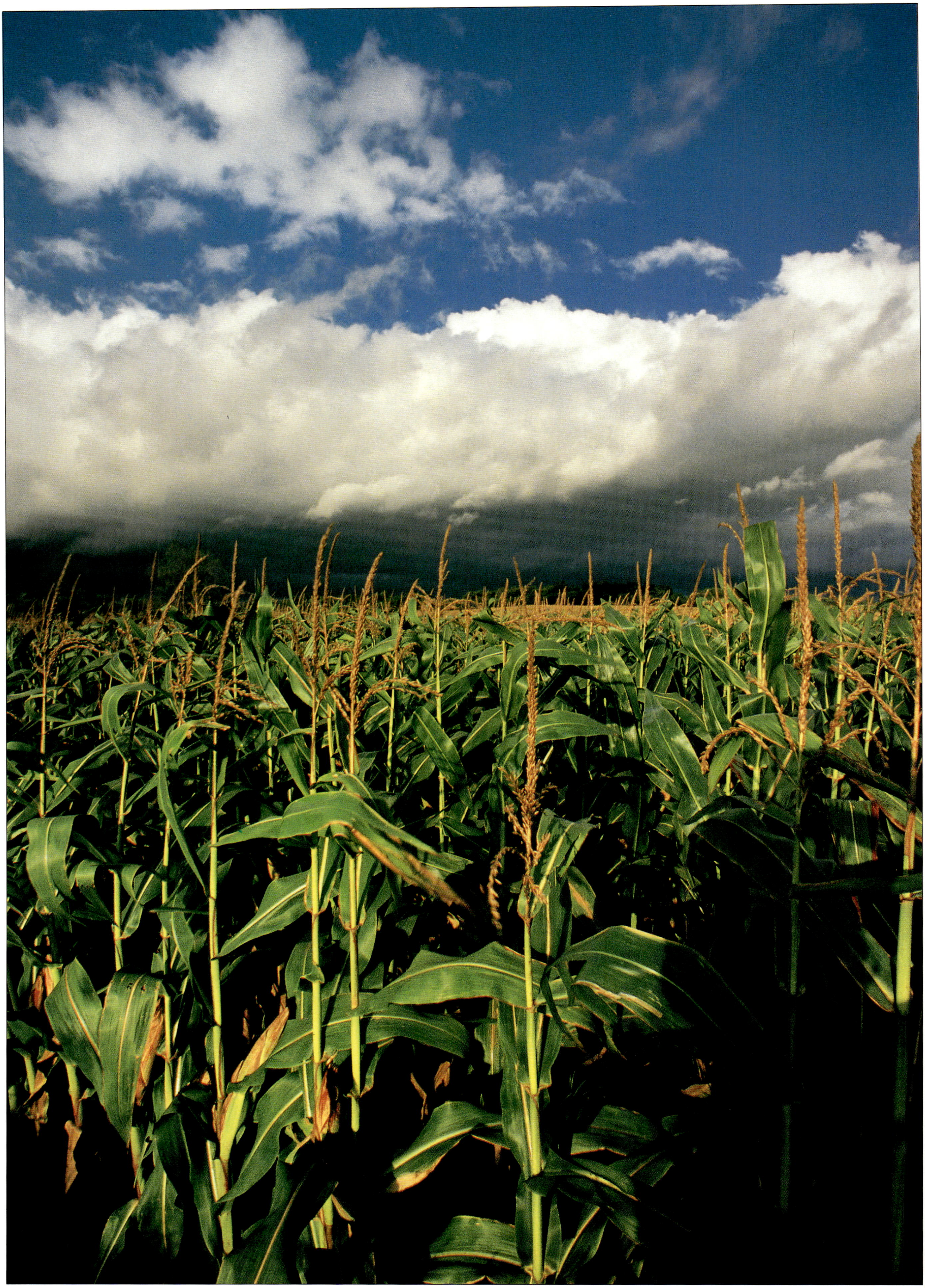

Elementaire voedingsregels

Herinnert u zich de 4 voedselcategorieën? Voor 1980 werden we aangemoedigd elke dag 2 delen uit zowel de zuivel- als de vleesgroep te eten plus 4 delen uit de vruchten- groentegroep en 4 delen uit de graangroep. Toen uit onderzoek bleek dat een juiste voedselkeuze van belang is bij de voorkoming van ziekten, kwamen diverse overheden met aanbevelingen voor de voeding, waarbij de consumptie van vet, cholesterol en natrium moest worden teruggedrongen en de opname van samengestelde koolhydraten en voedingsvezel diende te worden vergroot. Bij latere aanvullingen zijn die regels nog verder aangescherpt.

Zo werd voor een verbeterd gebruik van deze regels door de Amerikaanse overheid in 1991 de Voedselpiramide geïntroduceerd (zie pagina 25). De piramide illustreert hoe 6 voedselgroepen—granen, vruchten, groenten, vlees, zuivel en vetten/oliën/suikers—navenante bijdragen leveren aan een gezond voedingspatroon. Voor een beter begrip van de Voedselpiramide zullen we eerst de Algemene Voedingsregels bekijken.

1. EET GEVARIEERD

Mensen hebben meer dan 40 voedingsstoffen nodig, waaronder verschillende vitaminen en mineralen. Hoewel veel voedingsmiddelen verschillende voedingsstoffen bevatten, is er niet één middel dat alle stoffen bevat. Dat is één reden waarom variatie zo belangrijk is. Men kan voor de benodigde voedingsstoffen zich beter op verschillende ingrediënten verlaten dan op vitaminepillen of andere supplementaire en versterkende middelen (de toevoeging van vitaminen en mineralen aan bepaalde etenswaren). En wel hierom: voedingsstoffen die in natuurlijke combinaties voorkomen, versterken elkaar vaak. Zo levert melk bijvoorbeeld kalk, fosfor en vitamine D, die samen worden opgenomen en het beendergestel versterken. Een kalkpil bevat niet de fosfor en vitamine D die het lichaam nodig heeft voor het optimale benutten van de kalk. Bovendien ontdekken voedingsdeskundigen nog steeds meer over de rol en het belang van vele spoor-elementen in voedingswaren die niet door supplementen worden geleverd. Maar ook is het gewoon leuk om gevarieerd te eten.

Veel verschillende zaken eten, betekent niet per se veel eten. Wie een zittend bestaan leidt of wil vermageren, moet voedingswaren kiezen die caloriearm zijn, maar veel voedingsstoffen en smaak bevatten.

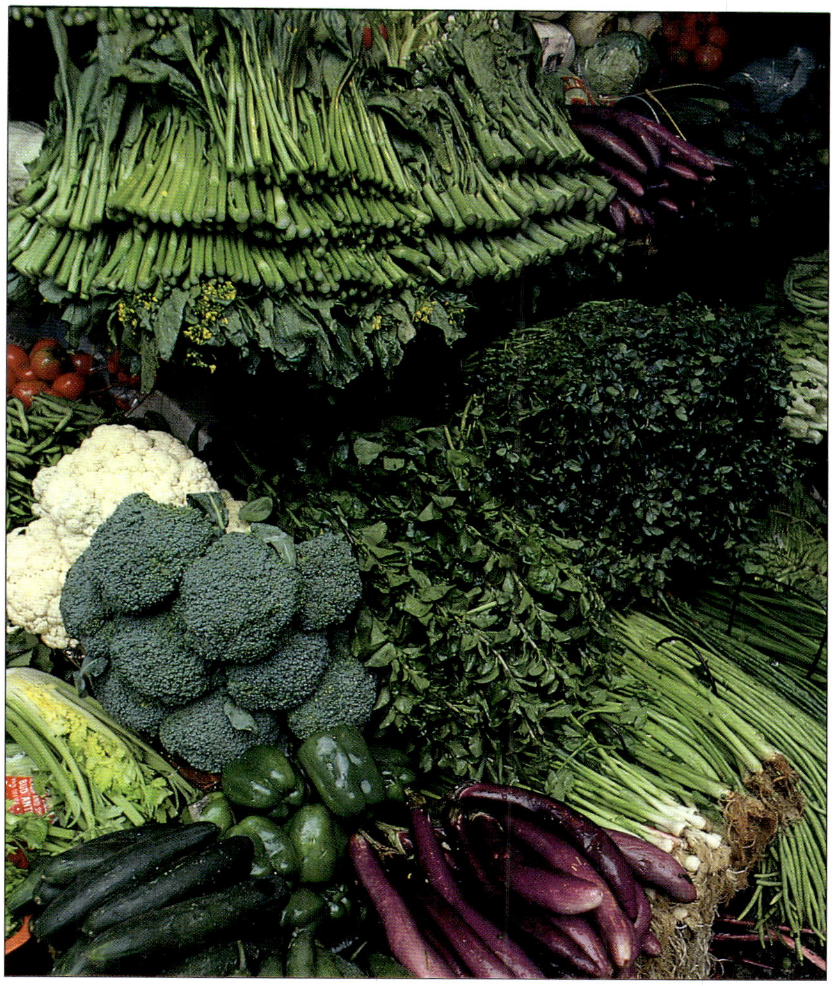

Boven: Op een openluchtmarkt in Hongkong liggen verse groenten uitgestald. Hiernaast: Onverzadigde vetten, zoals de olie die uit maïs en andere planten wordt gewonnen, blijven vloeibaar bij kamertemperatuur. Verzadigde vetten van dierlijke oorsprong blijven vast.

ALGEMENE VOEDINGSREGELS

- Eet gevarieerd.
- Blijf op een gezond gewicht.
- Kies voor een dieet met weinig vet, verzadigd vet en cholesterol.
- Kies voor een dieet met veel groenten, vruchten en graanprodukten.
- Gebruik suiker(s) met mate.
- Gebruik zout en natrium met mate.
- Gebruik alcoholhoudende drank met mate.

2. BLIJF OP EEN GEZOND GEWICHT

Het begrip "gezond gewicht' kan tot verwarring leiden, zeker in een cultuur waarin waarde wordt gehecht aan slank zijn—vaak te slank.

Een gezond gewicht hangt niet zozeer van uw verschijning af, als wel van hoeveel van uw gewicht uit vet bestaat, waar in uw lichaam het vet is opgeslagen (overgewicht in de streek rond de maag is een groter risico dan gewicht in andere gebieden) en of u door het gewicht veroorzaakte klachten hebt zoals hoge bloeddruk. Mensen worden bij het ouder worden in het algemeen meestal wat zwaarder; gewoonlijk houdt deze gewichtstoename geen risico in.

Raadpleeg een erkend diëtist of arts voor het vaststellen van uw gezonde gewicht. Wie vindt dat hij of zij voortdurend op dieet moet zijn, ook als daar geen voordelen voor de gezondheid uit voortvloeien, kan beter zijn of haar motivatie aan een onderzoek onderwerpen. Bedenk daarbij dat

VET: HET VOOR EN TEGEN

Een snelle scheikundeles. Vet bestaat uit diverse vetzuren (gewoonlijk 3). In voedsel komen gewoonlijk 24 soorten vetzuur voor. Vetzuren kunnen worden ingedeeld op basis van de lengte van de molecuulketens of de mate van verzadiging—verzadigd, enkelvoudig onverzadigd en meervoudig onverzadigd. Dit noemen we de vetsoorten.

Alle in voedsel aanwezige vet is een combinatie van verzadigde en enkelvoudig en meervoudig onverzadigde vetten. Waar één soort vet overheerst, wordt dat bepaalde voedsel zo geklassificeerd. We spreken bijvoorbeeld over het verzadigde vet in rood vlees of het enkelvoudig onverzadigde in olijfolie. (Zie de tabel onder "Vet" in de woordenlijst.) Elke soort vet beïnvloedt het menselijk lichaam op bepaalde manieren. Daarom is het raadzaam niet alleen te weten *hoeveel vet* uw dieet bevat, maar ook om *welke soorten* het gaat.

Onverzadigde vetten worden als beter voor het hart beschouwd dan verzadigde, terwijl enkelvoudig onverzadigde vetten te verkiezen zijn boven meervoudig onverzadigde. De meeste verzadigde vetten komen in dierlijke bronnen voor. Planten en vis zijn bronnen van onverzadigd vet. Tot de enkelvoudig onverzadigde vetten behoren olijf-, canola- en arachide-olie. Tot de meervoudig onverzadigde behoren maïs-, saffloer- en soja-olie. Sesamolie bevat bijna gelijke hoeveelheden meervoudig en enkelvoudig onverzadigd vet. Uitzonderingen op deze regel: kokosolie, gebruikt om voedingswaren als chips krokant te houden en veel meer verzadigd dan vet in rundvlees of boter. Omgekeerd is kippevet, hoewel van dierlijke origine, voornamelijk enkelvoudig verzadigd vet.

Van olijfolie en andere hoog enkelvoudig onverzadigde oliën wordt aangenomen dat ze het cholesterolgehalte in het bloed helpen verlagen. Dat volken in het Middellandse-Zeegebied betrekkelijk lage niveaus van cholesterol in het bloed hebben, wordt tenminste voor een deel toegeschreven aan hun gebruik van olijfolie.

Sommige voedingswaren die veel meervoudig en enkelvoudig onverzadigd vet bevatten, kunnen zodanig worden behandeld dat er vetzuren ontstaan die meervoudig of enkelvoudig onverzadigd blijven, maar als verzadigde vetten reageren, met alle gevolgen vandien voor het cholesterolniveau. Wanneer men middels hydratie vloeibare olie laat verharden tot margarine en braadvet, doen zich structurele veranderingen voor in de vetmoleculen. Daarom adviseren diëtisten veelal om zachte margarine te kiezen, omdat die minder van die nieuwe vetzuren bevat. Soms maakt boter voedsel smakelijker. Probeer boter alleen te gebruiken om de smaak van voedsel te versterken, en gebruik voor het overige vloeibare olie.

Ongeacht de voordelen die aan bepaalde vetten verbonden zijn, is het raadzaam de vetconsumptie te verminderen. Als gemiddelde wordt een totale vet-opname aanbevolen van circa 30 procent van uw calorieën over een meerdaagse periode, en het verzadigde vet tot 10 procent van de calorieën te beperken. Deze regels betekenen niet dat eten op allerlei mathematische berekeningen moet berusten, met voortdurend een calculator in de hand. Raadpleeg de Vet formule tabel hieronder voor de streefcijfers aan calorieën en grammen. Wie zich onzeker voelt, kan natuurlijk altijd bij een diëtist te rade gaan.

Gebruik de dagelijks aanbevolen hoeveelheid vet als richtlijn; zonder een streng dieet te volgen, kunt u een vetarm voedingspatroon volgen. Vrijwel alle ingrediënten kunnen in een gezond dieet passen. Het is een kwestie van kiezen—meestentijds een selectie maken uit vrij vetarme voedingsmiddelen. Op deze manier blijft er ruimte over voor een favoriete vetrijkere schotel. Als u die speciale schotels vrij vaak wilt, dient u de porties te beperken—net genoeg om er ten volle van te genieten. Bedenk dat een gezond dieet iets is dat zich over een heel leven afspeelt, en niet in geïsoleerde korte tijdsspannen.

Voor elk recept in *De Vier Seizoenen* zijn de totale hoeveelheid vet en de hoeveelheden verzadigd, enkelvoudig onverzadigd en meervoudig onverzadigd in grammen uitgerekend. Bij het voorbeeldige etiket (zie pagina 32) vindt u de hoeveelheden calorieën en vet in verpakte voedingswaren.

DE VET FORMULE

Met gebruik van de 30-procentsformule zullen uw dagelijkse streefcijfers voor calorieën uit vet, grammen vet en grammen verzadigd vet variëren naargelang de totale hoeveelheid calorieën.

Calorieën/Dag	*Calorieën uit vet (30%)*	*Grammen vet in 30% van de calorieën*	*Grammen verzadigd vet in 10% van de calorieën*
1200	360	40	13
1500	450	50	17
2000	600	67	22
2500	750	83	28
3000	900	100	33
3500	1050	117	39

voedingswaren niet van nature "goed" of "slecht" zijn. Als u zichzelf uw favoriete eten ontzegt, zult u er meer van willen en dat vaker willen. Neem gerust appeltaart, maar neem de helft van uw gebruikelijke portie. En stel u open voor nieuwe voedingsmiddelen die op smakelijke manieren worden bereid. *De Vier Seizoenen* biedt u een goed begin.

3. KIES VOOR EEN DIEET MET WEINIG VET, VERZADIGD VET EN CHOLESTEROL

In landen met een vetrijke voeding komen corpulentie en bepaalde soorten kanker meer voor dan in landen met een vetarmere voeding. Hogere gehaltes aan verzadigd vet worden in verband gebracht met hartaandoeningen. Vet bevat meer dan tweemaal zoveel calorieën als koolhydraten of eiwit. Wie een vetarm dieet eet, kan veel gemakkelijker van verschillende schotels genieten zonder teveel calorieën te consumeren.

Cholesterol is in alle lichaamsweefsel aanwezig en is van elementair belang. Van een hoge cholesterolspiegel in het bloed is echter bekend dat die riskant voor het hart is. Veel mensen verwarren cholesterolniveaus in voeding met het cholesterolniveau in hun eigen lichaam. Het grootste deel van de cholesterol in het lichaam—het serum of bloedcholesterol—wordt door het lichaam aangemaakt, dagelijks circa 1000 mg. Het bloedcholesterol zal toenemen als men voedsel eet dat veel totaalvet en met name verzadigd vet bevat. Maar enkele componenten van verzadigd vet, zoals het stearinezuur dat in rood vlees en chocola voorkomt, lijkt het bloedcholesterolniveau niet te verhogen. Bovendien helpen de in sommige vissoorten voorkomende vetzuren het risico van hartaandoeningen juist te verlagen doordat de neiging van bloed tot stollen wordt verminderd (beroertes zijn het gevolg van bloedproppen in de hersenen). Met drie keer per week vis eten, krijgt men voldoende hoeveelheden van deze beschermende vetzuren binnen.

Volgens een in november 1990 uitgevoerd onderzoek eet de gemiddelde Amerikaanse man dagelijks ongeveer 435 mg *voedings*-cholesterol, terwijl de gemiddelde Amerikaanse vrouw dagelijks 304 mg consumeert. Uit gezondheidsoverwegingen verdient het echter aanbeveling de dagelijkse hoeveelheid voedingscholesterol te beperken tot circa 300 mg. Dierlijke produkten zijn bronnen van voedingscholesterol; eierdooiers en lever bevatten bijvoorbeeld veel voedingscholesterol. Plantaardig voedsel bevat geen cholesterol, maar vetrijke voedingswaren op plantaardige basis kunnen de aanmaak van cholesterol in het lichaam stimuleren. Vol-

Kies voor een hoogwaardige voeding voor een gebalanceerd dieet dat is opgebouwd uit verschillende voedingswaren.

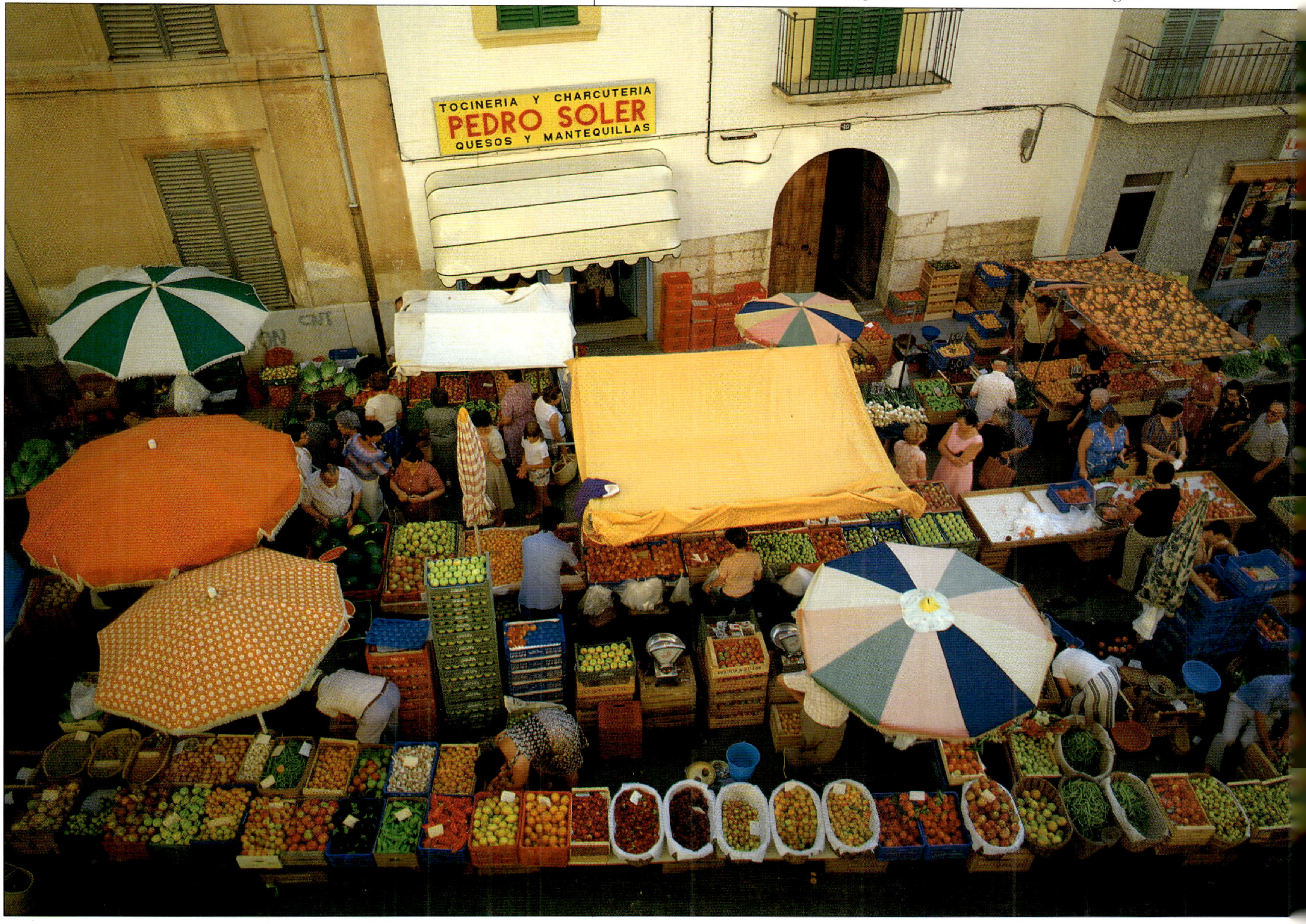

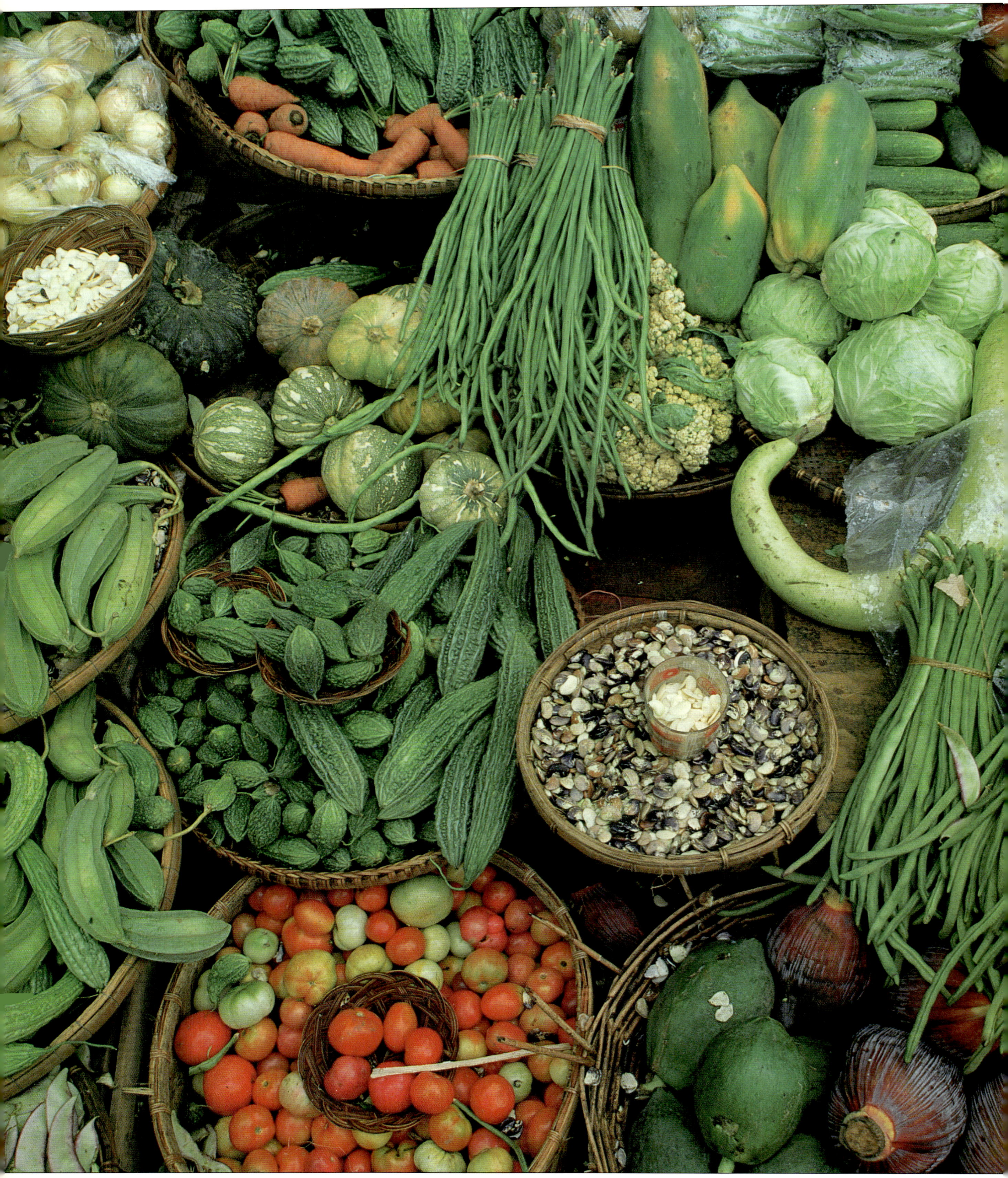

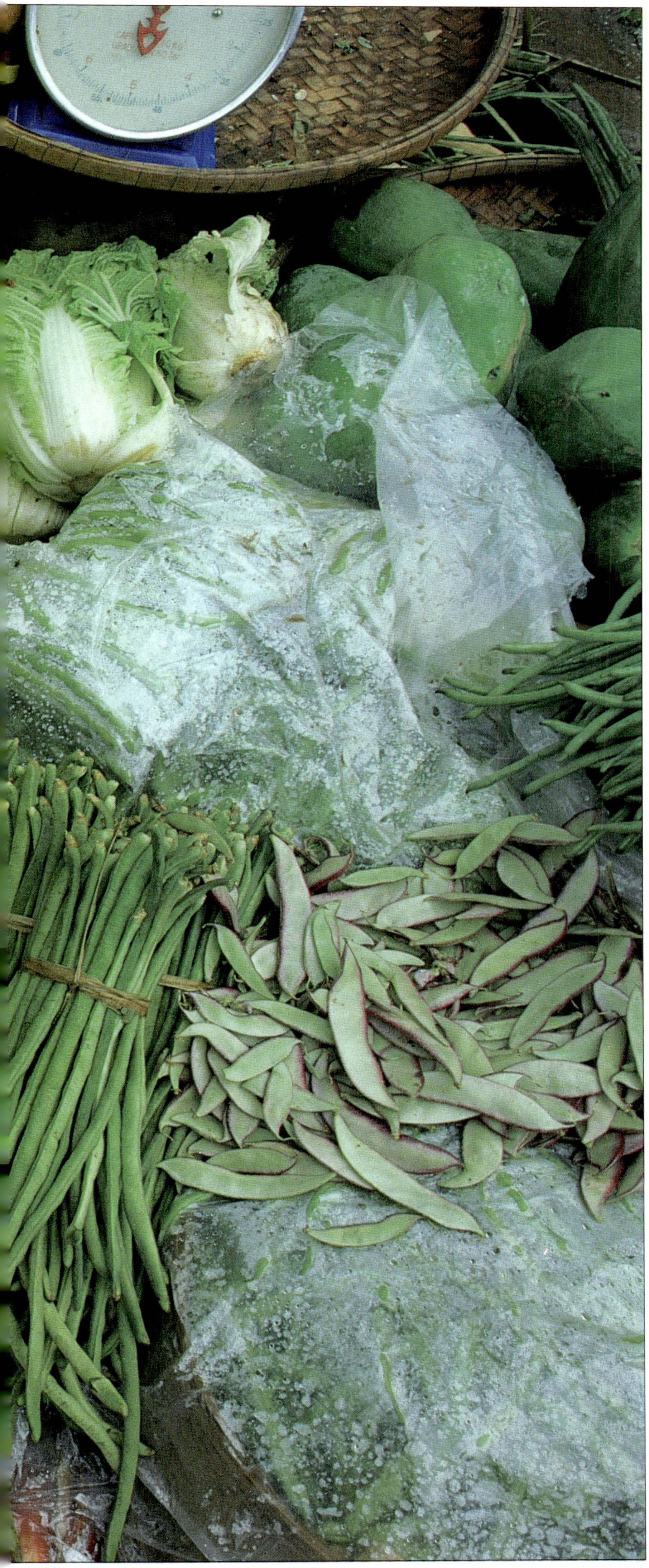

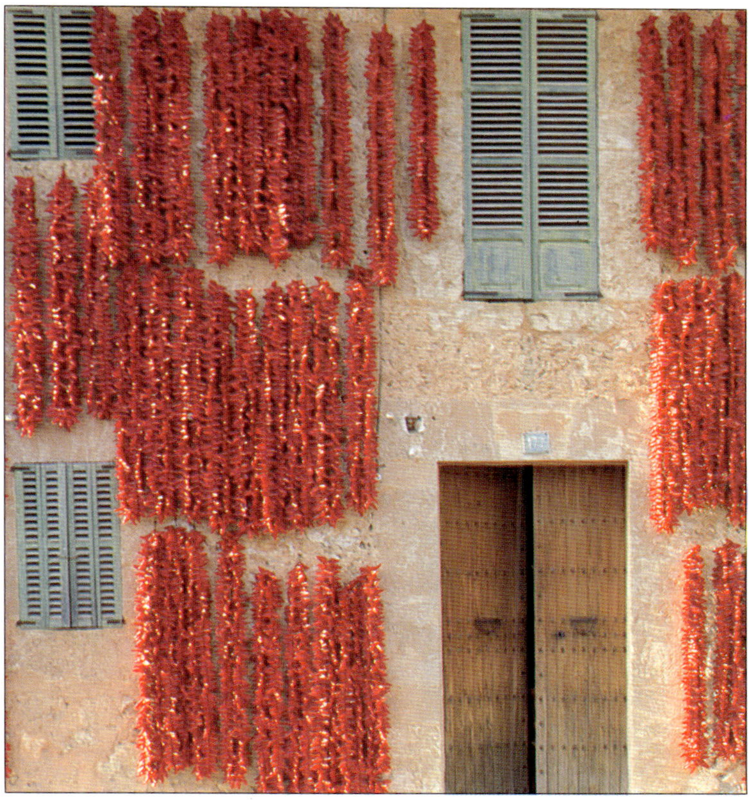

Boven: Rode chilipepers hangen te drogen in de zon op het eiland Majorca. Links: Vruchten, groenten en granen leveren niet alleen belangrijke voedingsstoffen en -vezel, maar hun textuur, smaak en kleur maken het eten ook tot een waar genoegen.

gens de huidige opvattingen is het belangrijker de hoeveelheid totaalvet en verzadigd vet terug te brengen dan de consumptie van voedingsmiddelen met cholesterol strikt te beperken. De meeste cholesterolrijke voedingsmiddelen bevatten ook veel essentiële vitaminen en mineralen. Door het beperken van voedsel van dierlijke oorsprong kunt u de benodigde opname van ijzer, kalk, zink en vitaminen te kort doen.

Voedsel dat veel oplosbare vezels bevat—gedroogde erwten en bonen, vruchten, groenten, gerst en haver—kunnen het bloedcholesterol helpen verlagen. Uit onderzoek is gebleken dat zulks met name het geval is bij meervoudig en enkelvoudig onverzadigde vetten. Maar vet blijft vet. Wie bezorgd is over zijn gewicht of het verlagen van de bloedcholesterolspiegel, moet meer groenten, vruchten en granen eten.

4. KIES EEN DIEET MET VEEL GROENTEN VRUCHTEN EN GRAANPRODUKTEN

In *De Vier Seizoenen* gaan we ervan uit dat groenten, vruchten en granen niet alleen een essentieel onderdeel van de aanbevolen gevarieerde voeding zijn, maar ook de basis vormen van de Voedselpiramide (pag. 27). Naast voedingswaarde dragen zij ook textuur, smaak en kleur bij.

Hele vruchten, groenten en granen zijn te verkiezen boven sappen en bewerkte granen omdat ze een groter scala aan voedingsstoffen en -vezel bevatten. Vezelrijke voedingsmiddelen—volle granen, peulvruchten, groenten en fruit—spelen een positieve rol in het voorkomen van hartaandoeningen en kanker. Ze helpen ook bij de bestrijding van risico's van aandoeningen aan de ingewanden. Enkele van deze eigenschappen komen uit de voedingsmiddelen zelf voort—hun unieke combinaties van voedingscomponenten en voedingsstoffen—niet alleen uit de vezels. Kies daarom vezelrijk voedsel in plaats van supplementen. Bij elk recept in *De Vier Seizoenen* staat de hoeveelheid vezel vermeld.

5. GEBRUIK SUIKER(S) MET MATE

Wie van zoet houdt (en wie doet dat niet?) hoeft niet te wanhopen. "Met mate" betekent niet "nooit". Matigen betekent kleinere porties of minder vaak. Matiging betekent ook niet circa 25 procent van de totale calorieën uit suiker consumeren. Veel voedingsmiddelen die veel toegevoegde suiker bevatten, bevatten ook veel calorieën en weinig voedingsstoffen. Niet benodigde calorieën leveren ongewenst ponden op, wat een gevaar voor de gezondheid kan inhouden.

Zoals de piek van de voedselpiramide suggereert, moeten suikerrijke voedingsmiddelen meer uitzondering dan regel zijn. Kies voor gezond zoet fruit—een voedingsmiddel met natuurlijke suikers in combinatie met vezel, vitaminen en mineralen. Het is raadzaam af te zien van snoep, frisdranken en zoete desserts. Maar krijg geen suikerfobie. Benut wat suiker voor het smaak geven aan vruchten, dranken, gebak en muesli.

Ouders zijn vaak bezorgd over de suiker in gezoete cornflakes. De toegevoegde suiker is meestal gelijk aan de suiker die veel mensen over hun cornflakes scheppen. Sommige diëtisten raden voor kinderen aan gezoete cornflakes te mengen met ongezoete, waardoor u een gezonde snack krijgt die kinderen lekker zullen vinden.

Het enige risico voor de gezondheid bij het met mate eten van suiker is het gebit. Poets uw tanden na het eten van gesuikerd voedsel of spoel de mond om met een ongezoet vocht.

Hiernaast: Hoewel de smaken kunnen verschillen, hebben de keukens van veel culturen gemeen dat ze vertrouwen op granen, peulvruchten, fruit en groenten. Op een Peruaanse markt is het een dukte van belang. Onder: Uit recent onderzoek kan worden opgemaakt dat het drinken van een of twee glazen rode wijn per dag de gezondheid kan bevorderen. Trossen Zinfandel-druiven rijpen in de Californische zon.

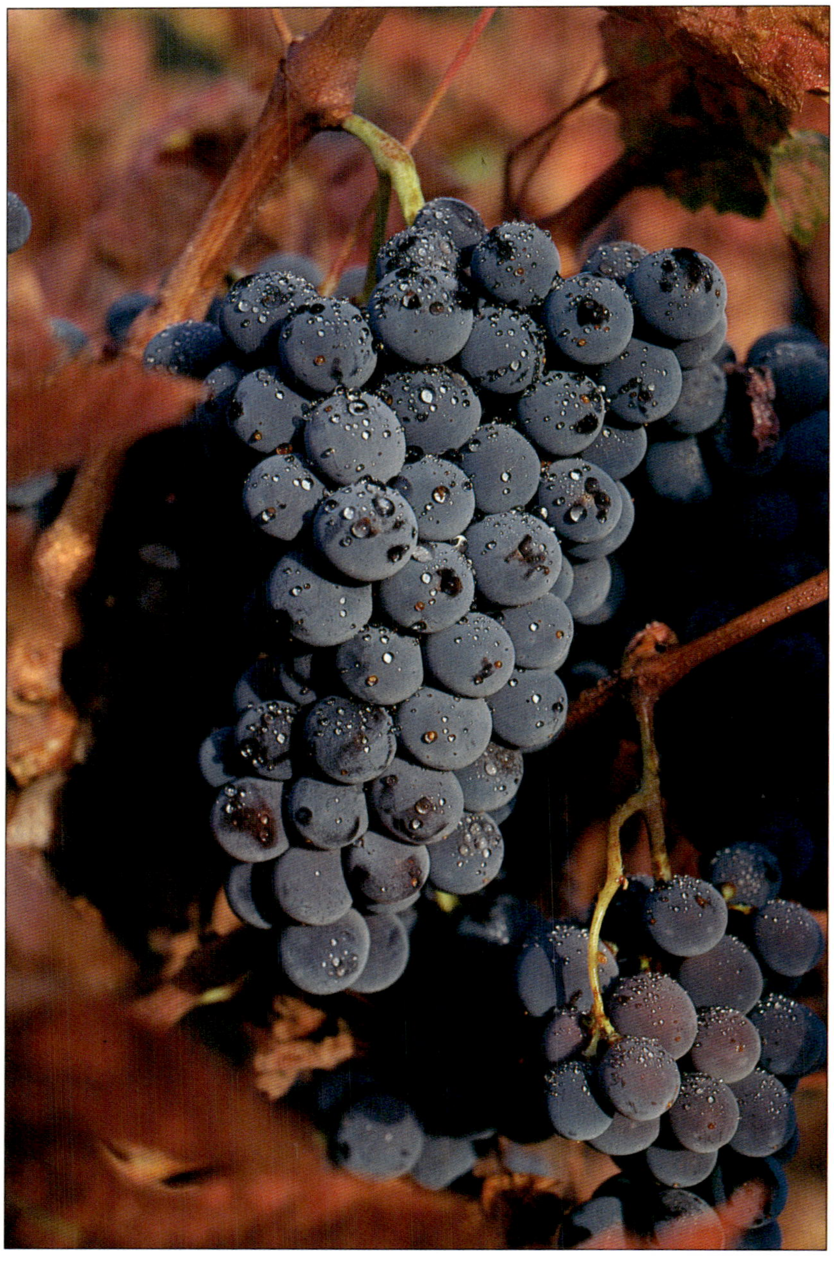

6. GEBRUIK ZOUT EN NATRIUM MET MATE

In landen met zoutarme voeding komt hoge bloeddruk minder vaak voor dan in landen als Amerika, waar mensen meestal meer zout en natrium eten dan ze nodig hebben. Een op de drie volwassen Amerikanen heeft hoge bloeddruk. Door minder zout te eten, kan deze conditie worden verlicht. Sommige mensen met hoge bloeddruk zijn niet gevoelig voor zout; het kan zijn dat zij speciale medicijnen nodig hebben.

Het valt onmogelijk te voorspellen of iemand hoge bloeddruk kan ontwikkelen en baat zou hebben bij een drastisch verminderde natriuminname. Wie over een goede nierfunctie beschikt en geen hoge bloeddruk heeft, raakt de gegeten natrium met de afvalstoffen kwijt. Dan nog bestaat de kans dat er meer natrium dan nodig wordt geconsumeerd. Het nu met de zoutgewoonte breken, is beter dan er later mee worstelen.

Voedingsdeskundigen bevelen aan dat volwassenen hun natrium-inname beperken tot 2400 mg per dag. Een theelepel zout bevat ongeveer 2300 mg. Tot natriumrijke voedingsmiddelen behoren toespijzen als soja- en Worcestershiresaus, harde kazen als Parmezaanse en Cheddar, augurken, soep in blik, gerookte vis en worst. Veel verpakte etenswaren bevatten ook veel zout. Voor elk recept in *De Vier Seizoenen* wordt de hoeveelheid natrium aangegeven.

7. GEBRUIK ALCOHOLHOUDENDE DRANK MET MATE

Alcoholische dranken leveren calorieën maar weinig of geen voedingsstoffen. Uit recent bewijs kan worden opgemaakt dat alcohol met mate, in het bijzonder rode wijn, wat voordelen voor de gezondheid kan opleveren, maar zeker is dat niet (zie pagina 48). Voor vrouwen wordt één drankje per dag als "matig" beschouwd; voor mannen twee. Een drankje is 3,75 dl gewoon bier, 1,6 dl wijn, of 0,45 dl gedistilleerd.

Wijn en andere alcoholhoudende dranken kunnen bij het koken voor de smaak worden gebruikt. Tijdens het sudderen zal de meeste alcohol verdampen, maar de smaak zal blijven. Wie gevoelig is voor alcohol kan de alcoholbevattende ingrediënten in de recepten in *De Vier Seizoenen* weglaten en vervangen door alcoholvrije wijn of vruchtesap.

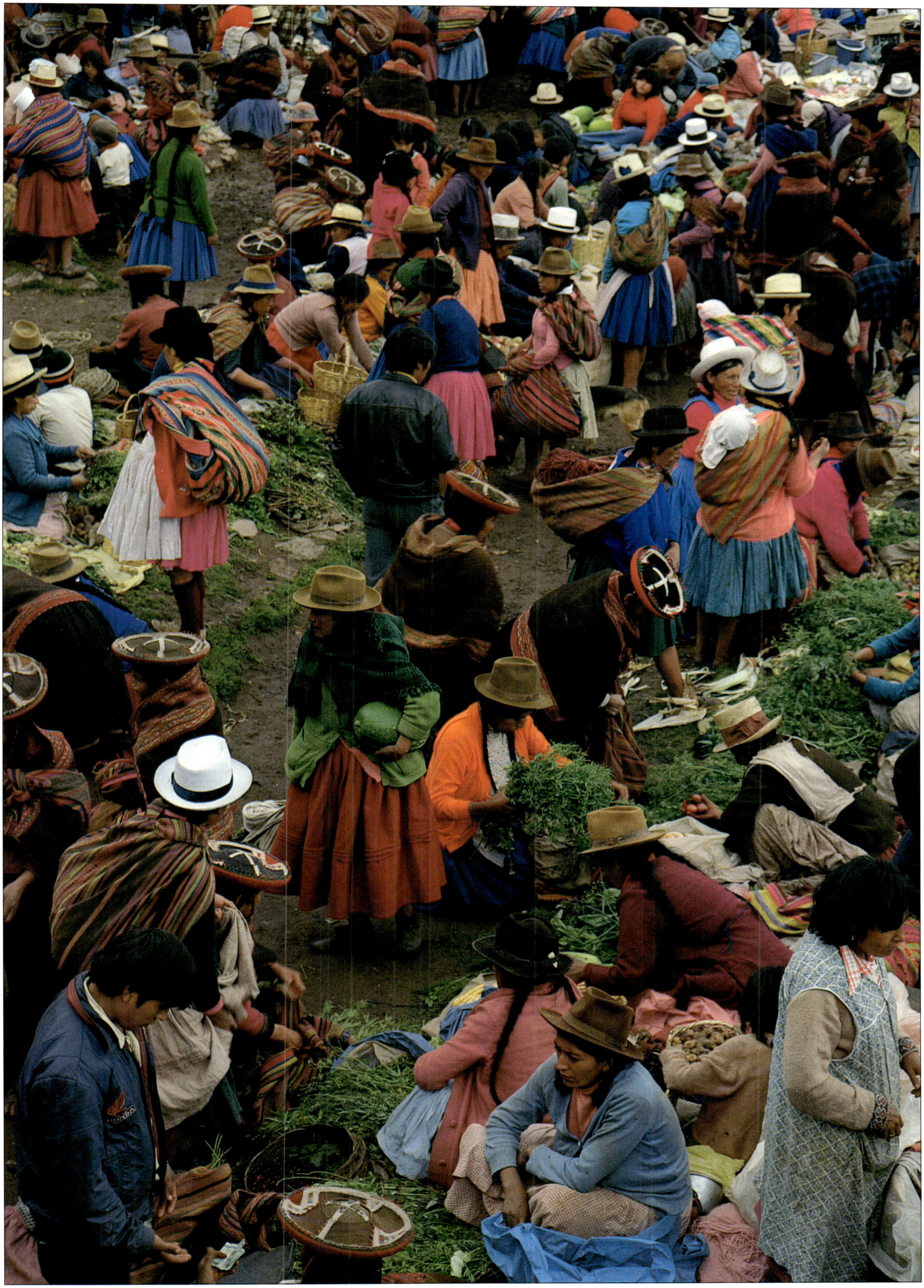

WAT IS EEN PORTIE?

Een "portie" in de Voedselpiramide is een gestandaardiseerde hoeveelheid voedsel—maar niet per se de hoeveelheid voedsel die u op uw bord schept. De meeste mensen zijn het erover eens dat 2½ dl een "glas" melk is, en dat is de portie die in de Piramide wordt gebruikt. Veel mensen eten echter meer dan 90 g bereid vlees, gevogelte of vis, of meer dan 75 g gekookte rijst of pasta als een portie. (Met de vrij kleine portie van 75 g graan is het echter makkelijker de in de Piramide aanbevolen 6-11 dagelijkse porties te bereiken.)

Helaas komen de gestandaardiseerde porties op nieuwe voedsel-etiketten niet noodzakelijkerwijs overeen met de porties in de Piramide. Op etiketten aangegeven porties komen meer overeen met de door mensen werkelijk gegeten porties. Op een etiket kunnen 2 sneden brood als een portie gelden, terwijl dat 1 snee in de Piramide is.

De zaak wordt nog gecompliceerder doordat het "voedsel-uitwisselings" systeem dat wordt gebruikt door individuen met diabetes mellitus en in diverse afslankprogramma's weer op een andere maatstaf voor porties is gebaseerd—ten minste voor sommige voedingsmiddelen. Bij gebruik van de Voedselpiramide bestaat één portie vruchtesap uit 1,8 dl. Bij het voedsel-uitwisselingssysteem varieert 1 portie vruchtesap van 1,25 dl appel- of sinaasappelsap tot 0,8 dl druiven- of pruimensap. Bij de uitwisselingssystemen wordt de portie van elk fruit aangepast, zodat elke portie een gelijke hoeveelheid koolhydraten bevat.

Bij het ontwikkelen van nieuwe regels door de Amerikaanse overheid voor de etikettering van voedingswaren drongen veel organisaties op eenvormigheid aan—ten minste tussen de etiketten en porties van de Voedselpiramide—maar helaas vergeefs. Wie de Voedselpiramide gebruikt ter regulering van de eigen voeding, hoeft de informatie over porties op etiketten alleen maar te vertalen naar porties van de Voedselpiramide.

De Voedselpiramide

Sinds het eind van de jaren '80 heeft de Amerikaanse overheid zich geconcentreerd op een groep Algemene Voedingsregels (zie pagina 17). Daarnaast zijn er internationaal ook de nodige ontwikkelingen geweest. Zo is bijvoorbeeld door hartspecialisten aangedrongen op een vet- en cholesterol-arme voeding, terwijl de kankerbestrijdingsbeweging wijst op het belang van veel groenten eten (met name de kruisbloemige soorten—zie "kruisbloemigen" in de woordenlijst) en vruchten en volle granen. Ook in andere landen zijn er soortgelijke aanbevelingen gedaan.

De huidige benadering van de Algemene Voedingsregels is gekoppeld aan een nadruk op het belang van beweging. In een subtiele maar zeer duidelijke verschuiving in perspectief, worden we nu geadviseerd te eten *wat de gezondheid bevordert*, en niet alleen wat ziekten voorkomt. En in plaats van een concentreren op elke voedingsregel of voedselgroep afzonderlijk, worden we aangemoedigd van een totaalbeeld uit te gaan. De Voedselpiramide kan daarbij behulpzaam zijn. Met behulp ervan kunnen we voedingsregels omzetten in *voedselkeuzes*.

In Amerika kwam de overheid tot het opstellen van de Voedselpiramide na uitgebreid overleg met tal van deskundigen, consumentengroepen en vertegenwoordigers van de levensmiddelenindustrie. In 1991 werd de Voedselpiramide voor het eerst gepubliceerd. Het is een grafische voorstelling—een blauwdruk—van het "totale dieet", die aanbevolen voedselgroepen en aantallen dagelijkse porties voor elke groep weergeeft. In begeleidende informatie worden de voedselsoorten in elke groep en de grootte van de porties omschreven.

De Voedselpiramide is een afbeelding van 5 groepen die rijk aan voedingswaarde zijn. (1) granen (brood, graanvlokken, rijst en pasta), (2) groenten, (3) fruit, (4) melk, yoghurt en kaas, en (5) vlees, gevogelte, vis, gedroogde bonen, eieren en noten. De aanbevolen dagelijkse hoeveelheden worden met een onder- en bovengrens aangegeven. De optimale porties zijn gebaseerd op de caloriebehoefte. Zo kunnen 6 dagelijkse porties van de granengroep ideaal zijn voor een huisvrouw of oudere volwassene die ongeveer 1600 calorieën per dag consumeert. Een atletische tienerjongen of zeer actieve volwassene die dagelijks 2800 calorieën consumeert, zal de maximale 11 aanbevolen porties brood, graanvlokken, rijst of pasta nodig hebben. Bij elk recept in *De Vier Seizoenen* wordt het aantal geleverde porties aangegeven van de specifieke voedselgroep in de Piramide waaronder het recept valt.

Een zesde voedselgroep—vetten, oliën en zoetigheid—zit in de top van de Piramide. Aanbevolen wordt om met mate van deze groep te consumeren—juist voldoende om het eten op smaak te brengen. Zo behoort een saladedressing op oliebasis tot deze groep. De bedoeling is om naar veel salade te streven met slechts een kleine hoeveelheid dressing.

Binnen elke groep zijn er *voorkeurs* keuzen. Bij brood verdienen volle granen bijvoorbeeld de voorkeur. Evenzo bevatten donkergroene en oranje groenten meer voedingswaarde dan lichter gekleurde soorten.

VAN ONDERAF WERKEN

Het concept van de Voedselpiramide berust op het begrip proportie. Hoewel de Piramide 6 groepen afbeeldt, illustreert hij tevens dat voor een optimale gezondheid sommige voedingsmiddelen in de dagelijkse voeding een grotere rol moeten spelen dan andere. Deze voedingsmiddelen bevinden zich op of bij de basis van de Piramide.

Granen: 6-11 porties. Het fundament van de Piramide wordt gevormd door voedingsmiddelen van granen die samengestelde koolhydraten, mineralen en vezel leveren: brood, graanvlokken, rijst en pasta. In tegenstelling tot wat wordt aangenomen, zijn op graan gebaseerde voedingsmiddelen niet "dikmakend". Het zijn juist de sausen op basis van boter, room en olie die de caloriewaarde omhoogjagen. Omdat iedereen behoefte heeft aan veel voedingsstoffen uit eten op graanbasis, wordt aanbevolen bij iedere maaltijd tenminste 2 porties ervan te nemen. Kies voor zaken gemaakt van meergranen of verrijkte bloem.

Eén portie staat gelijk aan 1 snee brood, 30 g kant-en-klare graanvlokken, 75 gekookte graan, rijst of pasta, 3 tot 4 kleine crackers, 1 klein plakje cake, 1 pannekoek. Vaak zullen voor een voldaan gevoel 2 porties nodig zijn. Honderdvijftig gram rijst of pasta of een heel broodje tellen voor 2 porties.

Groenten: 3-5 porties. Groenten delen de tweede laag van de Piramide met vruchten. Probeer bij elk maal behalve het ontbijt 2 porties groente te eten. Zonodig kunt u het streefcijfer bereiken met snacks als staafjes rauwe wortel. Groenten zijn van nature vetarm en leveren vitaminen als A

De voedselpiramide

Een gids bij dagelijkse voedselkeuzes

LEGENDA

● VET (VAN NATURE TOEGEVOEGD)

▼ TOEGEVOEGDE SUIKER

Symbolen voor vetten, oliën en toegevoegde suiker in eten

VETTEN, OLIËN EN ZOET
Met mate gebruiken

MELK, YOGHURT EN KAAS-GROEP
2-3 porties

GROENTEGROEP
3-5 porties

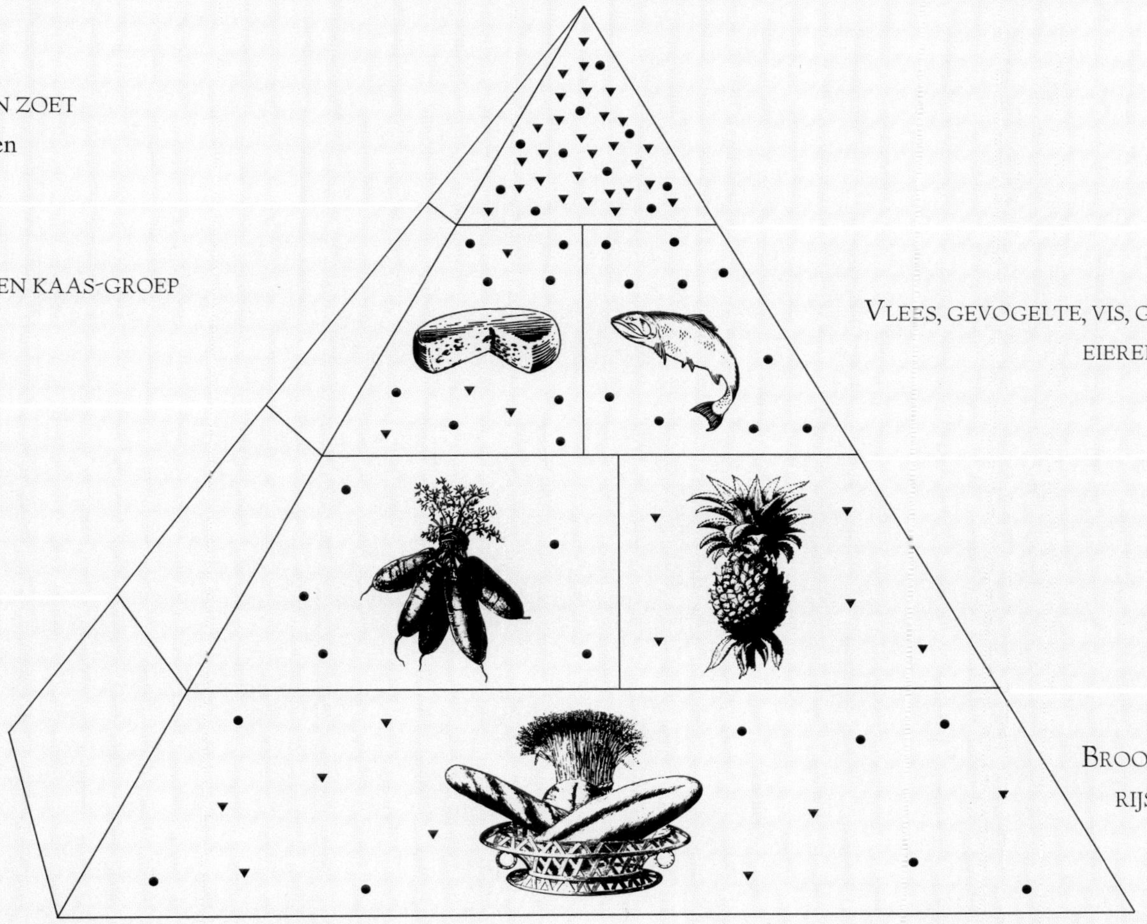

VLEES, GEVOGELTE, VIS, GEDROOGDE BONEN, EIEREN EN NOTEN GROEP
2-3 porties

FRUITGROEP
2-4 porties

BROOD, GRAANVLOKKEN, RIJST EN PASTA GROEP
6-11 porties

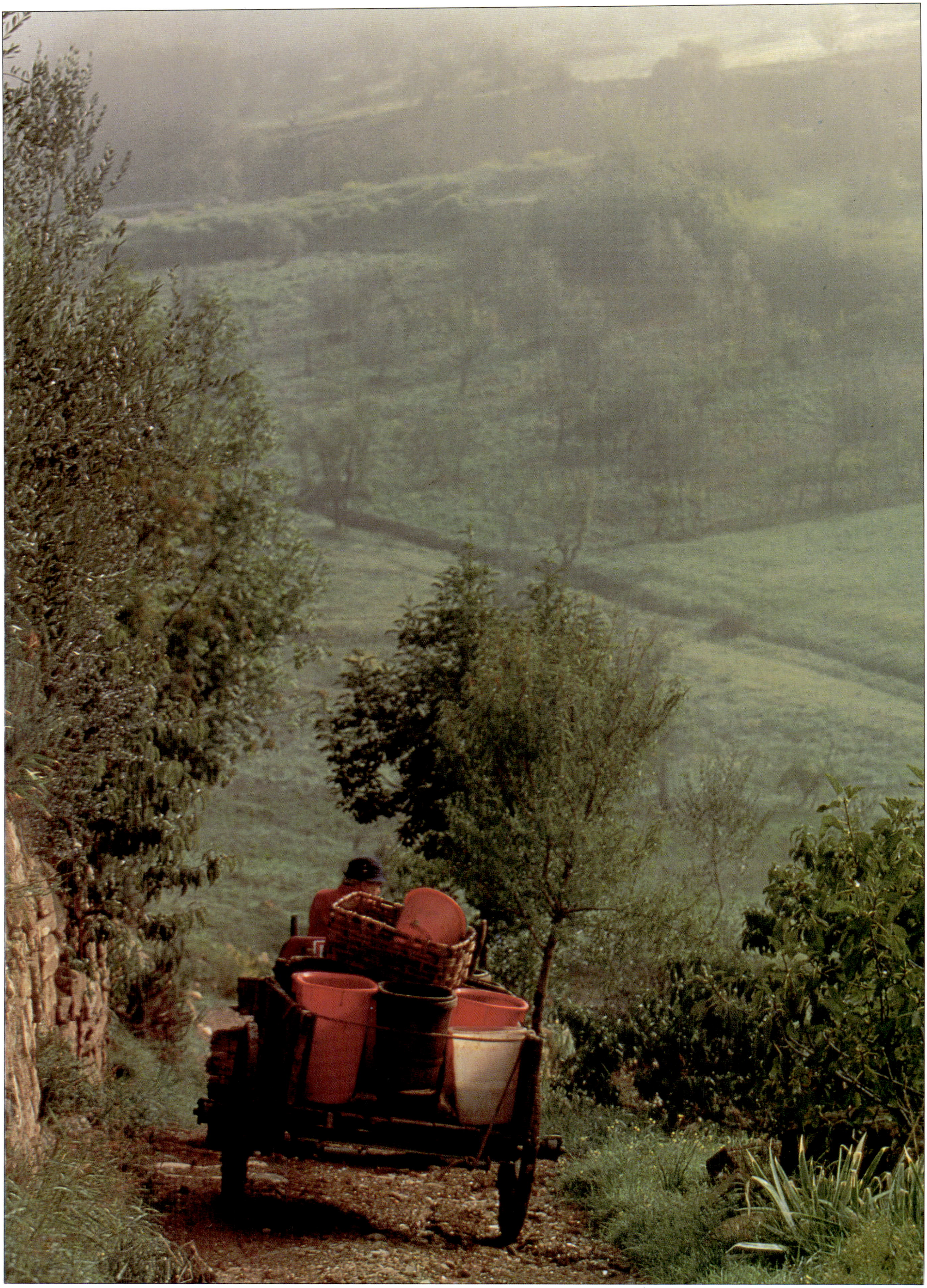

en C, foliumzuur en biotine, alsmede mineralen als ijzer. Groenten zijn ook een goede bron van vezel. De meeste mensen consumeren dagelijks slechts circa 12 g vezel terwijl men 20 tot 35 g nodig heeft!

Zorg net als bij de rest van de voeding voor variatie bij de groenten. Werp snel een blik op de groentetabel op pagina 58-60 als u vreest dat er onvoldoende keus is! Verschillende soorten groente leveren verschillende voedingsstoffen. Kook of stoom verse groenten heel kort voor het behoud van voedingsstoffen, kleur en textuur. Beperk gebakken groenten, met name natuurlijk patat frites! Wees ook voorzichtig met sausen en dressings, of, nog beter, kies waar mogelijk voor vetarme soorten.

Eén portie staat gelijk aan 100 g rauwe groenten, 50 g andere groenten (gekookt of rauw gehakt), 80 g compacte salades als aardappelsalade, en 1,8 dl groentesap. Afhankelijk van hun grootte kunnen recepten in *De Vier Seizoenen* met groenten als 2 porties tellen. (Bij sommige groenterecepten in dit boek is hier en daar wat vet gebruikt, maar juist voldoende om de smaak te versterken. Dit is in overeenstemming met de aanbevelingen van de Piramide om vetten/oliën/zoet met mate te gebruiken. Bekijk ook de inhoud en hoeveelheden van andere sausen, toespijzen en dressings met vet die u gebruikt.)

Fruit: 2-4 porties. Vruchten en 100-procents vruchtesappen leveren zowel vitamine A en C als foliumzuur en zink. Citrusvruchten, bessen en meloenen bevatten met name veel vitamine C. Hele vruchten bevatten meer vezel dan vruchtesappen. Vermijd bij gebruikt van vruchten uit blik die soorten die in siroop zitten. Waar bij fruitrecepten voor desserts suikersiroop nodig is, dient u slechts zeer weinig siroop te gebruiken. Zie de tabel op pagina 57-58 voor ideeën voor vers fruit.

Eén portie staat gelijk aan een middelgrote appel, banaan of sinaasappel, 50 g gehakte, gekookte of ingeblikte vruchten, 1,8 dl vruchtesap, of 40 g gedroogde vruchten.

Melk, yoghurt en kaas: 2-3 porties. Twee porties uit deze groep zijn voor de meeste mensen voldoende. Vrouwen in verwachting of die borstvoeding geven, tieners en jonge volwassenen onder de 25 moeten op 3 dagelijkse porties mikken. Melkprodukten leveren eiwit, vitaminen en mineralen. Melk, yoghurt en kaas zijn absoluut de beste bronnen van kalk. Veel zuivelprodukten, zoals roomijs, bevatten echter veel vet. U

Het dicht bij de natuur werken vormt een ideaal tegenwicht voor de spanningen van alledag. Op een nevelige herfstochtend gaat een Toscaanse boer op weg naar zijn wijngaard. Onder: Een Mexicaanse bakker heeft een ingenieuze manier van broodbezorgen gevonden.

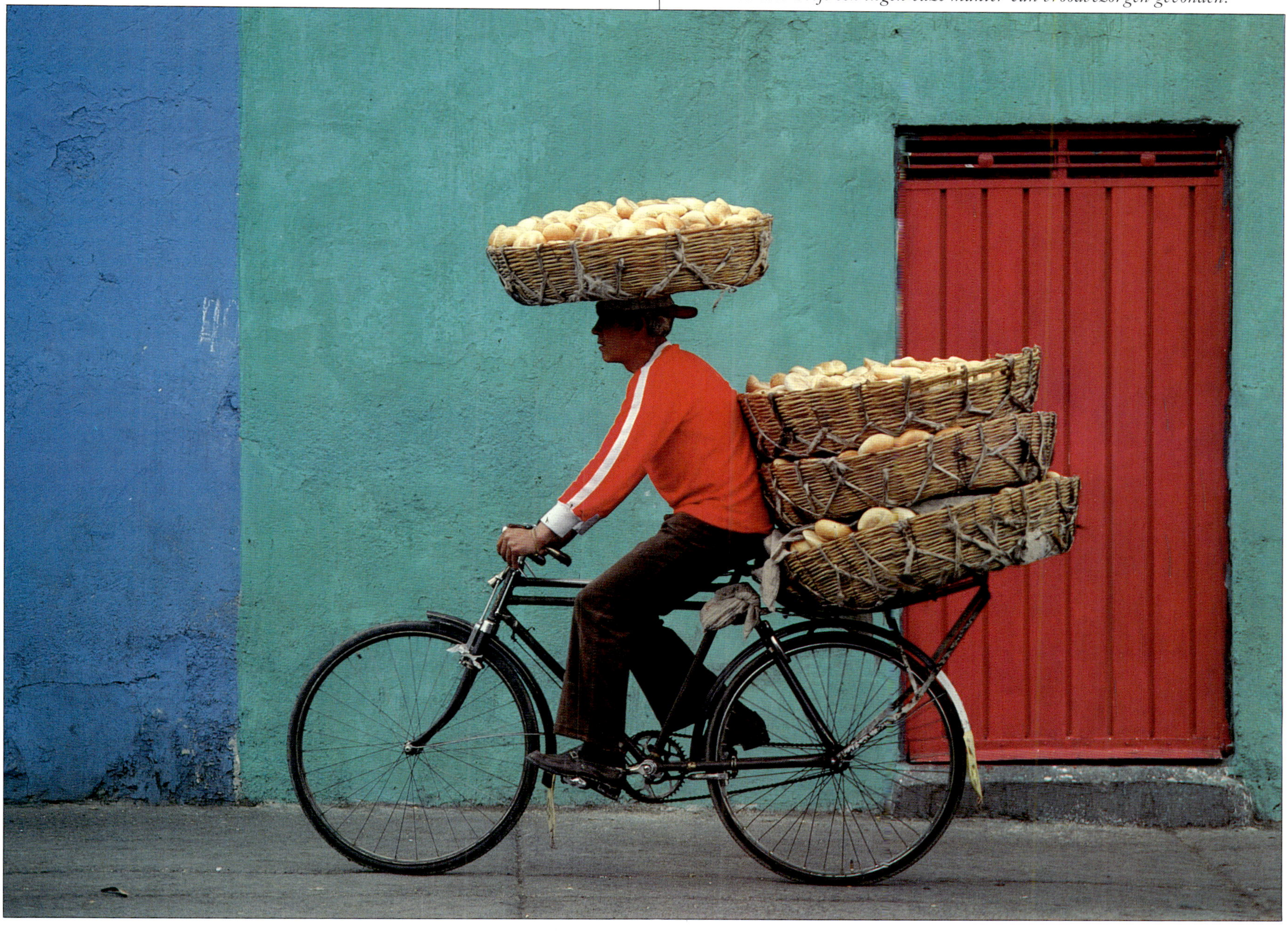

OVER VLEES

De recepten in *De Vier Seizoenen* eren de jaarlijkse oogsten aan vruchten en groenten. Maar ze gebruiken ook zeebanket, gevogelte, peulvruchten en enkele zuivelprodukten. Hoewel in dit kookboek geen receptenvoor rund-, lams-, varkens- of kalfsvlees en wild voorkomen, kan mager vlees zeker een rol spelen in een gezonde, smakelijke voeding. Mager vlees is een uitstekende bron van eiwit, ijzer, zink, fosfor, vitamine B en niacine. Een portie van 90 g mager vlees levert 20 tot 100 procent van de dagelijkse behoefte aan elk van deze voedingsstoffen in 8 procent of minder van de dagelijkse calorieën. De door vlees geleverde voedingsstoffen vindt u in de tabel voor vitaminen en mineralen na de index.

Als u vlees eet, kies dan bereid mager vlees in een portie van 90 tot 120 g. Zorg voor aanvulling door het vlees te combineren met groenten, zoals in spiezen of chili, of met granen, zoals in spaghetti met vleessaus of soep van gerst met rundvlees.

Snijd voor de bereiding alle bereikbare vet van het vlees. Als u voor de bereiding wat vet eraan laat, kunt u dit voor het opdienen verwijderen. Verwijder bij het maken van jus of saus ook het vet van braadsappen. Doe het vlees op een rooster boven deze sappen bij roosteren of braden in de oven. Gebruik voor het bakken van de stuken vlees altijd een anti-aanbak koekepan en een minimale hoeveelheid olie.

Ongeacht hoe mager het is, bevat alle vlees—dit geldt voor alle dierlijke produkten, zelfs kip en vis—20 tot 30 mg cholesterol per 30 g. Als u echter een kleine portie van 90 g eet, krijgt u maar 60 tot 90 mg cholesterol binnen minder dan een derde van het aanbevolen dagelijkse maximum van 300 mg. Daarmee houdt u ruimte over voor voedingscholesterol uit melk en andere zuivelprodukten als eieren en boter.

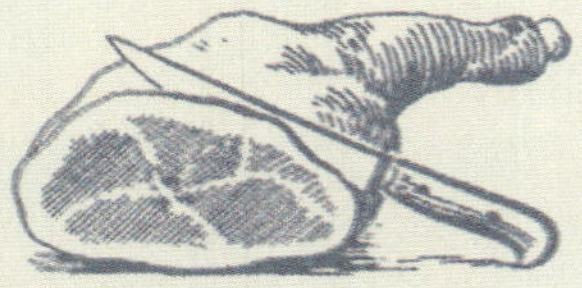

MAGERE STUKKEN

Hieronder vindt u voorbeelden van magere stukken vlees.

Per 85 g gekookte en bijgesneden portie

Soort	*Cal. (g)*	*Vet (g)*	*Vet verz. (g)*	*Chol. (mg)*
RUNDSVLEES				
Klapstuk, zonder vet	189	8,2	2,7	81
Sukadelap	183	7,1	2,6	86
Runderrollade	143	4,2	1,5	59
Vanglap	176	8,6	3,7	57
Lendebiefstuk	165	6,1	2,4	76
Haasbiefstuk	179	8,5	3,2	71
Kogelbiefstuk	176	8,0	3,1	65
Staartstuk	153	4,2	1,4	71
VARKENSVLEES				
Lenderollade	165	6,1	2,2	66
Ham, heel gebraden	187	9,4	3,2	80
Haaskarbonade, gegrild	165	6,9	2,5	70
Varkenshaas, gebraden	133	4,1	1,6	67
LAMSVLEES				
Schouderpoelet, gegrild	158	6,2	2,2	77
Lamsrollade	159	5,1	1,8	89
Lamsbout, achterstuk, geroosterd	153	5,7	2,0	74
Lamshaas, gegrild	183	8,3	3,0	80
KALFSVLEES				
Kalfsoester	171	4,5	1,3	132
Kalfspoelet, gesmoord	160	3,7	1,1	124
Kalfsschnitzel, gepaneerd, gebakken	175	5,3	1,4	96
Kalfsribstuk	151	6,3	1,8	97
VLEESWAREN				
Bacon, gegrild	156	7,2	2,4	48
Ham, mager	123	4,7	1,5	45
Rosbief, mager	150	3,3	1,4	36

kunt zonder het vet alle voedingsstoffen krijgen met halfvolle of magere melk en magere yoghurt. Magere melk levert zelfs tweemaal de hoeveelheid kalk met slechts een derde van de calorieën. Kies ook voor vetarme kazen. En als u vette kaas eet, gebruik dan kaas met een uitgesproken smaak en doe veel met weinig. Wie van roomijs houdt, moet eens ijs van magere yoghurt proberen!

Eén portie staat gelijk aan 2½ dl melk of yoghurt, 45 g natuurlijke kaas, 200 g cottage cheese, en 60 g fabriekskaas. Equivalenten voor deze groep zijn gebaseerd op de hoeveelheid kalk; in de praktijk zult u waarschijnlijk kiezen voor 100 g cottage cheese.

VLEES, GEVOGELTE, VIS, GEDROOGDE BONEN, EIEREN EN NOTEN: 2-3 PORTIES. *VLEES*, gevogelte en vis zijn uitstekende bronnen van eiwit, B-vitaminen, ijzer en zink. Gedroogde bonen, eieren en noten lijken wat geleverde voedingsstoffen betreft op vlees, maar bevatten ijzer in een vorm die niet goed door het lichaam wordt opgenomen. De beste bronnen van ijzer—een voedingsstof die met name nodig is voor vrouwen, tieners en kinderen—zijn lever; mager varkens-, rund- en lamsvlees; het

EIWIT ALTERNATIEVEN VOOR VLEES

Elk alternatief bevat 7 g eiwit, de hoeveelheid eiwit in 30 g mager vlees, vis of gevogelte (55 calorieën).

60 g gekookte broccoli of spruitjes (50 calorieën)
40 g hüttenkäse (55 calorieën)
90 g tufo of tahoe (75 calorieën)
1 groot ei (80 calorieën)
2,5 dl sojamelk (80 calorieën)
100 g gekookte peulvruchten (80 calorieën)
30 g belegen kaas (115 calorieën)
2 dl magere melk (90 calorieën)
2 dl volle melk (130 calorieën)
165 g gekookte eiernoedels (210 calorieën)
240 g havervlokken (145 calorieën)
1 klein stuk kaaspizza (170 calorieën)
30-60 g noten of zaden (150-200 calorieën)
1¾ eetlepel pindakaas (160 calorieën)
2½ eetlepel tahini (sesampasta) (220 calorieën)
2 sneden (150 g) maïsbrood (350 calorieën)

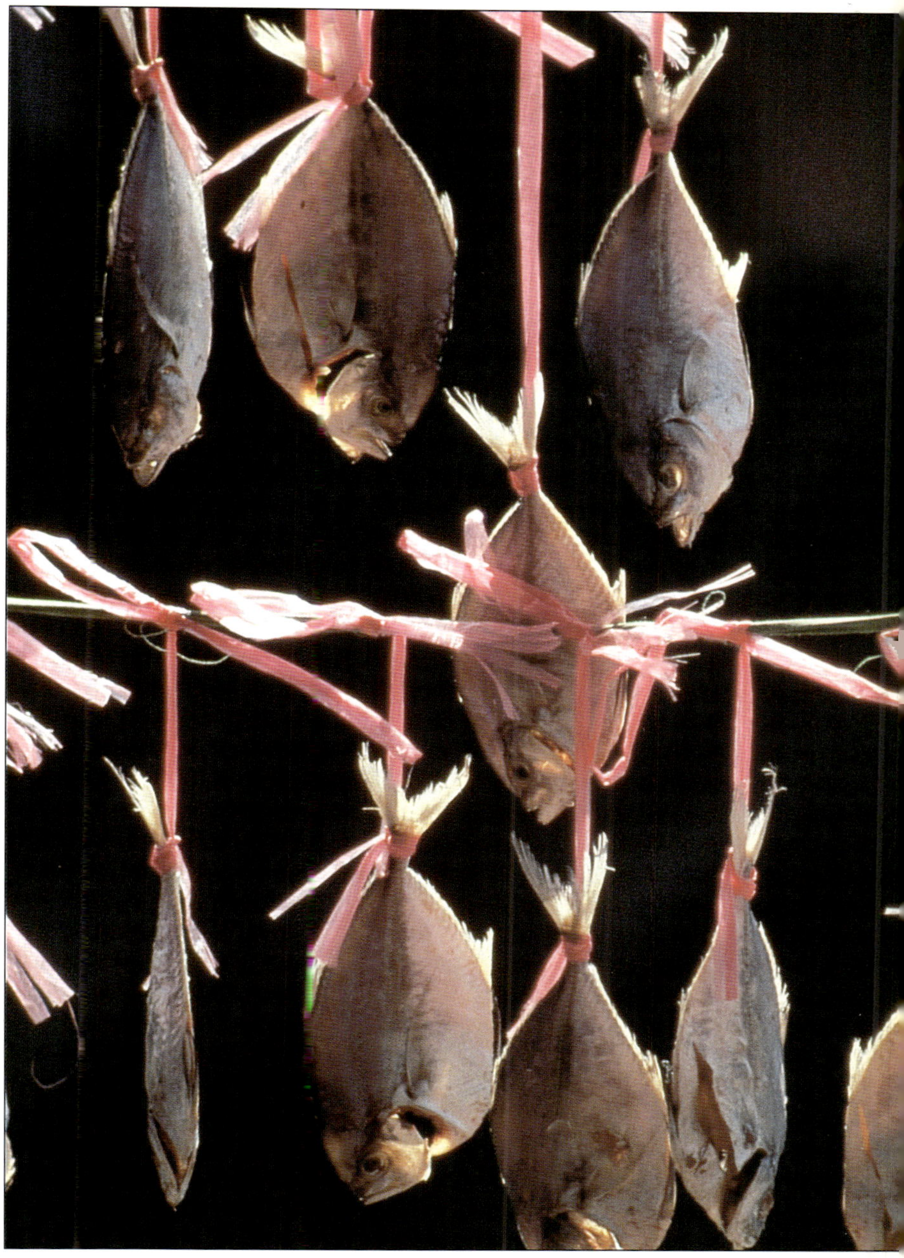

De vangst van de dag hangt te drogen in de zon in Hongkong, waar vis net als elders in Azië zeer geliefd is. Door per week drie maal vis te eten, kan men het risico van hartaandoeningen verminderen.

donkere vlees van gevogelte; vis, schaal- en schelpdieren. Buiten vlees zijn peulvruchten, volle granen, gedroogde vruchten en bladgroenten bronnen van ijzer. Uit de vleesgroep zijn mager vlees (zie pagina hiernaast), gevogelte zonder vel, schaal- en schelpdieren, vis en gedroogde bonen en peulvruchten de vetarmste keuzen. Worst en vleeswaren bevatten gewoonlijk veel vet, behalve waar anders is aangegeven. Bij de delicatessenwinkel zijn magere ham, rosbief en kalkoenborst de magerste keuzen.

Eieren bevatten heel veel voedingsstoffen, maar de dooiers bevatten veel cholesterol. Neem niet meer dan 4 hele eieren of eierdooiers per week. Wie voedingscholesterol dient te beperken, gebruikt dubbele porties eiwit. Eet ook noten met mate. Ze zijn een goede bron van eiwit, maar bevatten veel vet.

Een portie staat gelijk aan 60-90 g gekookt mager vlees, gevogelte of vis, 45 g gekookte gedroogde bonen, 1 ei, 60 g noten (of 2 eetlepels pindakaas zijn gelijk aan 30 g gekookt vlees, of ongeveer 1 portie).

VETTEN, OLIËN EN ZOET: Gebruik deze met mate. Cirkeltjes en drie-

VEGETARISCHE ALTERNATIEVEN

Verdwenen zijn de tijden waarin het woord *vegetarisch* beelden opriep van hippies en geitewollen sokken. Het vegetarisme is volledig geaccepteerd. Er is geschat dat in West-Europa 5 tot 10 procent van de mensen zichzelf als vegetariër beschouwt—van veganisten (die alle voedsel van dierlijke oorsprong vermijden) tot semi-vegetariërs (zij die zuivelprodukten en eieren eten, misschien wat vis en kip maar geen rood vlees). Zelfs mensen die rood vlees eten kunnen zichzelf echter als een soort vegetariër beschouwen. Sommigen kiezen voor "vegetarische" of vleesloze dagen.

Een van de grootste voordelen van een vegetarisch dieet is een lager dan gemiddelde consumptie van vet, verzadigd vet en cholesterol. Als gevolg daarvan hebben vegetariërs vaak een lager dan gemiddelde bloedcholesterolspiegel en een lagere bloedruk dan vleeseters. Deze factoren kunnen bij vegetariërs hartaandoeningen helpen voorkomen.

Vegetariërs hebben minder aandoeningen bij de spijsvertering en een lagere kans op suikerziekte. Het vezelrijke vegetarische dieet (of elk vezelrijk dieet) verbetert de controle op bloedsuiker, wat een voordeel is voor diabetici. Er zijn ook aanwijzingen dat vegetariërs minder risico lopen om kanker aan de dikke darm of longkanker te krijgen. Natuurlijk kunnen al deze voordelen ook iets te doen hebben met een andere levensstijl bij vegetariërs (minder roken en alcoholgebruik, meer beweging, enzovoort), die zich veelal meer om de gezondheid bekommeren dan niet-vegetariërs.

Veganisten die zorgvuldig plannen wat ze eten om er zeker van te zijn dat ze alle benodigde voedingsstoffen binnenkrijgen, lopen geen groter risico van deficiëntie dan vleeseters. En vegetariërs die enkele zuivelprodukten en wat kip of vis eten, lopen gewoonlijk minder risico van tekort aan bepaalde voedingsstoffen.

Het binnenkrijgen van voldoende vitamine B, dat alleen in dierlijke produkten voorkomt, kan een probleem zijn als iemand alle zuivelprodukten, vlees en eieren vermijdt. Echte veganisten moeten zoeken naar voedingsgistsoorten of voedsel dat is aangevuld met vitamine B_{12}.

Vooral voor vegetarische vrouwen kan het binnenkrijgen van voldoende kalk, zink en ijzer een probleem zijn. Broccoli, boerenkool, kikkererwten en peulvruchten bevatten kalk. Dat geldt ook voor met kalk aangevulde tofu. Al enkele jaren zijn er ook met kalk aangevulde sappen verkrijgbaar. Zink komt voor in erwten, linzen, tarwekiemen en tarwezemelen. Versterkte graanvlokken, peulvruchten, aardappels, gedroogde vruchten en pruimensap leveren ijzer. Het is van belang dat vegetariërs bij iedere maaltijd vruchten of groenten eten die vitamine C bevatten om zo de opname van ijzer uit plantaardig voedsel te bevorderen.

Vele granen, peulvruchten en zaden zijn goede bronnen van eiwit. In combinatie met elkaar of met groente—rode bonen met rijst, maïs met bonen, erwtensoep met roggebrood, brood met pindakaas bijvoorbeeld—is de hoeveelheid eiwit toereikend. In oude beschavingen en in gebieden waar vlees schaars of duur is, zijn deze combinaties oude vertrouwden.

Wie een of ander vegetarisch dieet volgt, moet bedenken dat variatie van het grootste belang is. Als de keuze zuiver uit gezondheidsoverwegingen is gemaakt, bedenk dan dat kleine porties mager vlees, gevogelte of vis uw streven niet zullen dwarsbomen. Bij wie de keuze is gebaseerd op godsdienstige of ecologische overwegingen dient de gezondheid prioriteit te worden gegeven door een dieet samen te stellen dat alle benodigde voedingsstoffen bevat. En ongeacht uw beweegredenen, vegetarisch of niet, kunt u op verkenning gaan in de wereld van vruchten, groenten, granen en peulvruchten die elk dieet smakelijk en gezond maken.

hoekjes in de Voedselpiramide geven de aanwezigheid aan van natuurlijk aanwezig of toegevoegd vet en suiker. Als u van de voet naar de top van de Piramide kijkt, ziet u dat vetten en suikers meer en meer voorkomen. Helemaal bovenin de Piramide komen voedingsmiddelen voor die voor veel calorieën maar voor slechts weinig vitaminen en mineralen zorgen. Vruchten, groenten en granen zijn van nature vetarm; we veranderen die hoedanigheid als we bij de bereiding olie, boter, saladedressings en vetrijke saus en jus gebruiken. Suiker maakt deel uit van het pakket voedingsstoffen dat van nature voorkomt in fruit en melk, *toegevoegde* suiker levert extra calorieën, maar slechts weinig vitaminen en mineralen.

Veel van de toegevoegde suiker in ons dieet komt uit voedsel uit de punt van de Piramide, zoals allerlei soorten snoep, frisdranken en tafelsuiker. Probeer die te vervangen door voedingsmiddelen lager in de Piramide. Kies voor snoep bijvoorbeeld verse of gedroogde vruchten. Probeer in plaats van aardappelchips zelf gepofte popcorn. Geniet in plaats van frisdranken van dranken als vruchte- en groentesappen, melk- en yoghurtdranken of mineraalwater.

Kies in plaats van snoep als zoetigheid eens fruit—een voedingsmiddel dat naast natuurlijke suikers vezel, vitaminen en mineralen bevat. Op een warme dag in Californië liggen abrikozen te drogen.

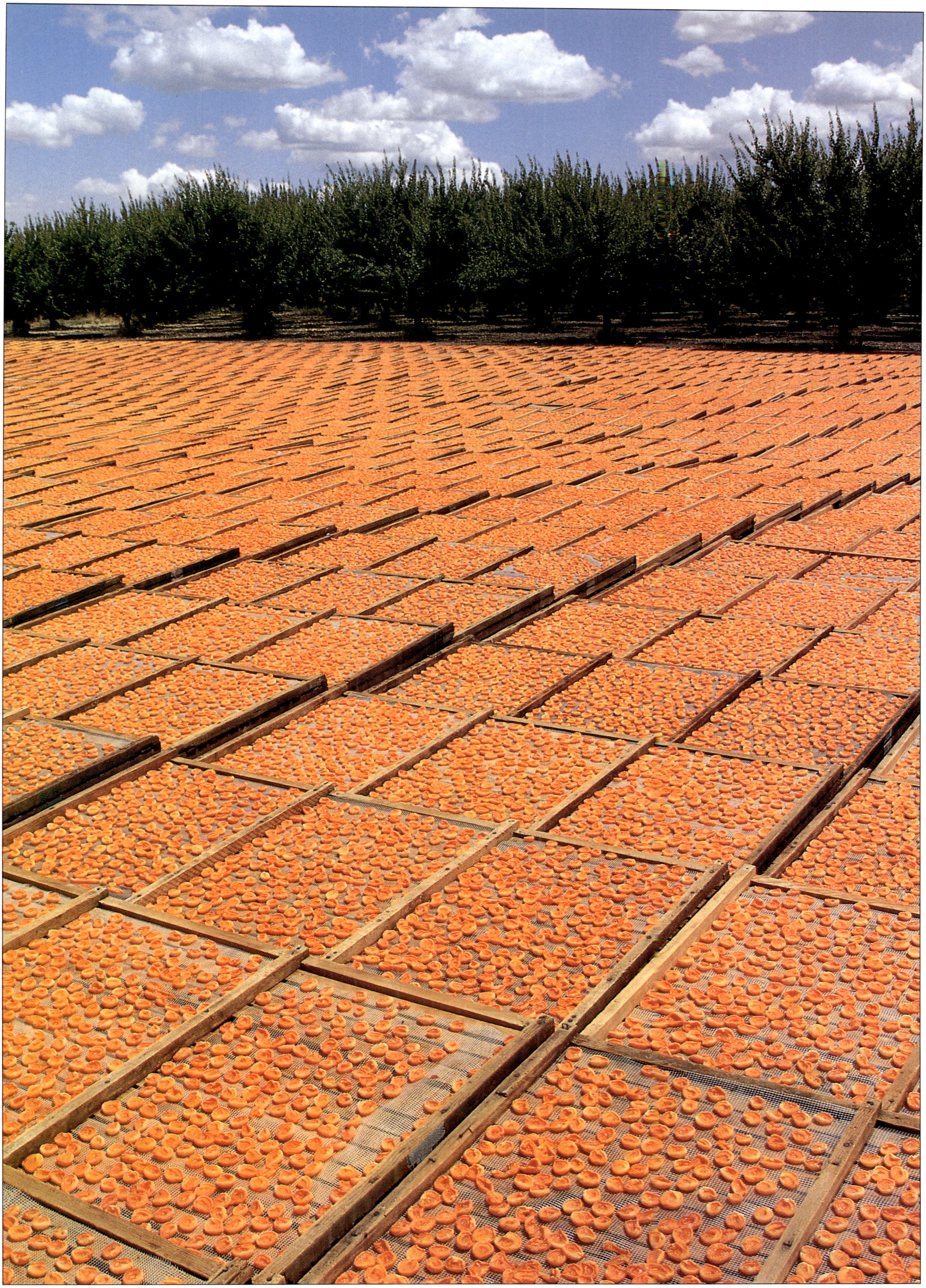

EEN VOORBEELDIG ETIKET

INFORMATIE OVER PRODUKT

Informatie over portiegrootte

Nieuwe lijst voedingsstoffen

Verdere informatie, bijv. voetnoten

Nieuwe titel voor het nieuwe etiket

Calorie-informatie

% Dagelijkse Waarden DW geven aan hoe dit voedsel in een referentiedieet van 2000 calorieën past

Dagelijkse Waarden voetnoot

Calorie-conversiewijzer

Voedingsfeiten

Portiegrootte 200 g
Porties per pak 2

Hoeveelheid per portie

Calorieën 90 Calorieën uit vet 30

	% dagelijkse waarde*
Vet totaal 3 g	**5%**
Verzadigd vet 0 g	**0%**
Cholesterol 0 mg	**0%**
Natrium 300 mg	**13%**
Totaal koolhydraten 13 g	**4%**
Voedingsvezel 3 g	**12%**
Suikers 3 g	
Eiwit 3 g	

Vitamine A 80% • Vitamine C 60%
Kalk 4% • IJzer 4%

* Procentuele Dagelijkse Waarden zijn gebaseerd op een dieet van 2000 calorieën. Afhankelijk van uw calorie-behoeften kunnen deze waarden hoger of lager zijn.

	Calorieën	2000	2500
Vet totaal	Minder dan	65 g	80 g
Verz. vet	Minder dan	20 g	25 g
Cholesterol	Minder dan	300 mg	300 mg
Natrium	Minder dan	2400 mg	2400 mg
Totaal koolhydraten		300 g	375 g
Voedingsvezel		25 g	30 g

Calorieën per gram
Vet 9 • Koolhydraten 4 • Eiwit 4

HOE U ETIKETTEN LEEST

Laatstelijk nog een goed etiket gelezen? Nog steeds bestaat er geen overeenstemming over wat etiketten over voedingsmiddelen aan informatie zouden moeten bevatten. In 1990 werd door het Amerikaanse congres besloten te komen tot het opstellen van een standaard etiket dat in de toekomst op alle voorbewerkte levensmiddelen zou moeten komen (zie boven). Dit voorstel werd inhoud gegeven door de Food and Drug Administration en het Amerikaanse Ministerie van Landbouw.

Geen onbevredigde nieuwsgierigheid meer. Geen raden naar wat er in zit. Dank zij een volledige lijst van ingrediënten, standaardporties, betrouwbare informatie betreffende de gezondheid en de inhoud van de verpakking, een klantvriendelijke opzet, wordt dit een ideaal etiket voor consumenten om een verantwoorde keus op te kunnen baseren.

ALLEEN DE FEITEN

Tot de onderwerpen die op het nieuwe etiket moeten voorkomen, behoren het totaal aantal calorieën, de calorieën uit vet, vet totaal, verzadigd vet, cholesterol, natrium, totale hoeveelheden koolhydraten, voedingsvezel, suikers, eiwit, vitamine A en C, kalk en ijzer. Uit deze 14 categorieën blijkt dat het nieuwe etiket bedoeld is controle te hebben op wat men eet en zo risico's voor de gezondheid te vermijden. Meer informatie, zoals hoeveelheden enkelvoudig onverzadigd en meervoudig onverzadigd vet, of de aanwezigheid van andere vitaminen en mineralen, is optioneel. Maar als een levensmiddel verrijkt is of wanneer een claim aangaande de gezondheid wordt gemaakt, dient dat op het etiket te worden vermeld.

Naast de informatie over voedingswaarde per portie, moet het nieuwe etiket ook Zuivelwaarden aangeven. Met uitzondering van vitaminen en mineralen worden Zuivelwaarden uitgedrukt in grammen of milligrammen en als een percentage. Elk percentage, gebaseerd op een "referentie" dieet van 2000 calorieën per dag, vertelt u hoeveel van het dagelijks "toegestane" van het betreffende ingrediënt door 1 portie van dat gerecht wordt geleverd. Als het etiket bijvoorbeeld zegt dat 1 portie voedsel 13 g vet of "20% van de Dagelijkse Waarde" bevat, weet u dat u met 1 portie 20 procent van de toegestane 65 gram vet binnen een aanbevolen dagelijks dieet van 2000 calorieën binnenkrijgt.

Als u etiketten gebruikt voor het beheersen van uw consumptie, dient u te beseffen dat de informatie is gebaseerd op een dagelijks dieet van 2000 calorieën en op de specifiek aangeven portiegrootte. Als u minder dan 2000 calorieën per dag consumeert, moet het totale percentage Dagelijkse Waarden voor vet, verzadigd vet, koolhydraten en eiwit op minder dan 100 uitkomen. Wie daarentegen meer dan 2000 calorieën per dag consumeert, zal op een percentage voor deze groepen uitkomen boven de 100 procent Dagelijkse Waarden op het etiket. De behoefte aan andere

In de loop der tijd ...

Uw behoeften aan voedingsstoffen en calorieën zijn niet hetzelfde als 10 jaar geleden. En met het verstrijken der tijd zullen ze blijven veranderen. Als algemene regel zouden volwassenen *minimaal* het lagere aantal porties van elke voedselgroep in de Voedselpiramide moeten consumeren (zie pag. 25). Met matige hoeveelheden toegevoegd vet en suiker levert deze benadering circa 1600 calorieën onvoldoende voor een huisvrouw, jongere kinderen en sommige oudere volwassenen. Afhankelijk van de lichaamsgrootte en fysieke activiteit kunnen volwassenen meer dan 1600 calorieën per dag nodig hebben. De meeste mannen en zeer actieve vrouwen kunnen bijvoorbeeld in de middelste of bovenmiddelste regionen van de Piramideporties consumeren. De lagere tot middelste cijfers zijn goed voor de meeste vrouwen. Atleten en actieve tieners, en dan met name jongens, kunnen de bovenste cijfers gebruiken.

Behoeften van vrouwen

Uit onderzoek blijkt meer en meer het verband tussen voeding en ziektepreventie bij vrouwen. Er zijn instanties die zich specifiek bezighouden met de gezondheid van vrouwen en hoe voedselkeuzes daarop van invloed kunnen zijn.

Een recente zorg is het verhogen van de kalkconsumptie in de loop van een vrouwenleven om de beendermassa op te bouwen en te onderhouden en zo osteoporose te voorkomen. Bovendien krijgen veel vrouwen niet voldoende ijzer, wat tot bloedarmoede kan leiden. (Een lage ijzer-inname kan ook tot bloedarmoede leiden bij tieners en zeer jonge kinderen.) Hartaandoeningen en borstkanker worden beide statistisch in verband gebracht met vetrijke diëten, hoewel erfelijkheid bij beide condities een belangrijke rol speelt.

Vrouwen die in verwachting kunnen raken wordt nu geadviseerd veel foliumzuur op te nemen uit groenten of supplementen, omdat over foliumzuur is ontdekt dat dat het risico van geboorte-afwijkingen kan verminderen. Algemeen wordt aangenomen dat vrouwen in verwachting of die borstvoeding geven extra kalk, ijzer en foliumzuur nodig hebben. Minstens 3 dagelijkse porties uit de zuivelgroep, plus extra granen, vruchten en groenten helpen deze grotere behoefte aan vitaminen en mineralen dekken.

Een volwassen opvatting

In 1984 bestond 11 procent van de Amerikaanse bevolking uit mensen boven de 65. Tegen 2030 zal dat cijfer stijgen tot 17 procent—50 miljoen mensen. Met deze bevolkingsgroei zal de belangstelling voor gezond, smakelijk eten toenemen. Sommige ouderen kunnen blijven eten als jongere volwassenen, maar anderen hebben minder calorieën nodig door wijzigingen in de hormoonhuishouding en stofwisseling. Bij het ouder worden raken de smaakpapillen minder gevoelig en kunnen intense smaken gewenst zijn.

Magere lichaamsmassa neemt af met het ouder worden, zodat het lichaam spierweefsel verliest en vet toevoegt. Als u minder calorieën consumeert, zorg dan dat de calorieën die u binnenkrijgt rijk aan waardevolle voedingsstoffen zijn.

Oudere mensen kunnen problemen krijgen met een minder efficiënte voedsel-opname, verminderde honger en deficiëntie aan voedingsstoffen als gevolg van medicijnen. Ze kunnen voor de versterking van hun immuniteitssysteem meer vitamine A, C en E nodig hebben, die voorkomen in vruchten, groenten en volle granen. Kalk en vitamine D zijn van belang ter vermindering van het risico van osteoporose, en ijzerrijk voedsel helpt bloedarmoede voorkomen.

Hoewel het het best is zich te verlaten op voedsel voor voedingsstoffen, kunnen mensen die door ziekte of leeftijd niet goed tot eten in staat zijn, vitaminen-mineralen-supplementen moeten nemen. Helaas kiezen veel mensen die supplementen nemen zonder advies van een deskundige de verkeerde voedingsstoffen, of nemen een onjuiste hoeveelheid, of gebruiken produkten waarvan geen aantoonbare uitwerking is bewezen. Raadpleeg daarom bij voedingsproblemen van welke aard dan ook altijd uw huisarts of diëtist.

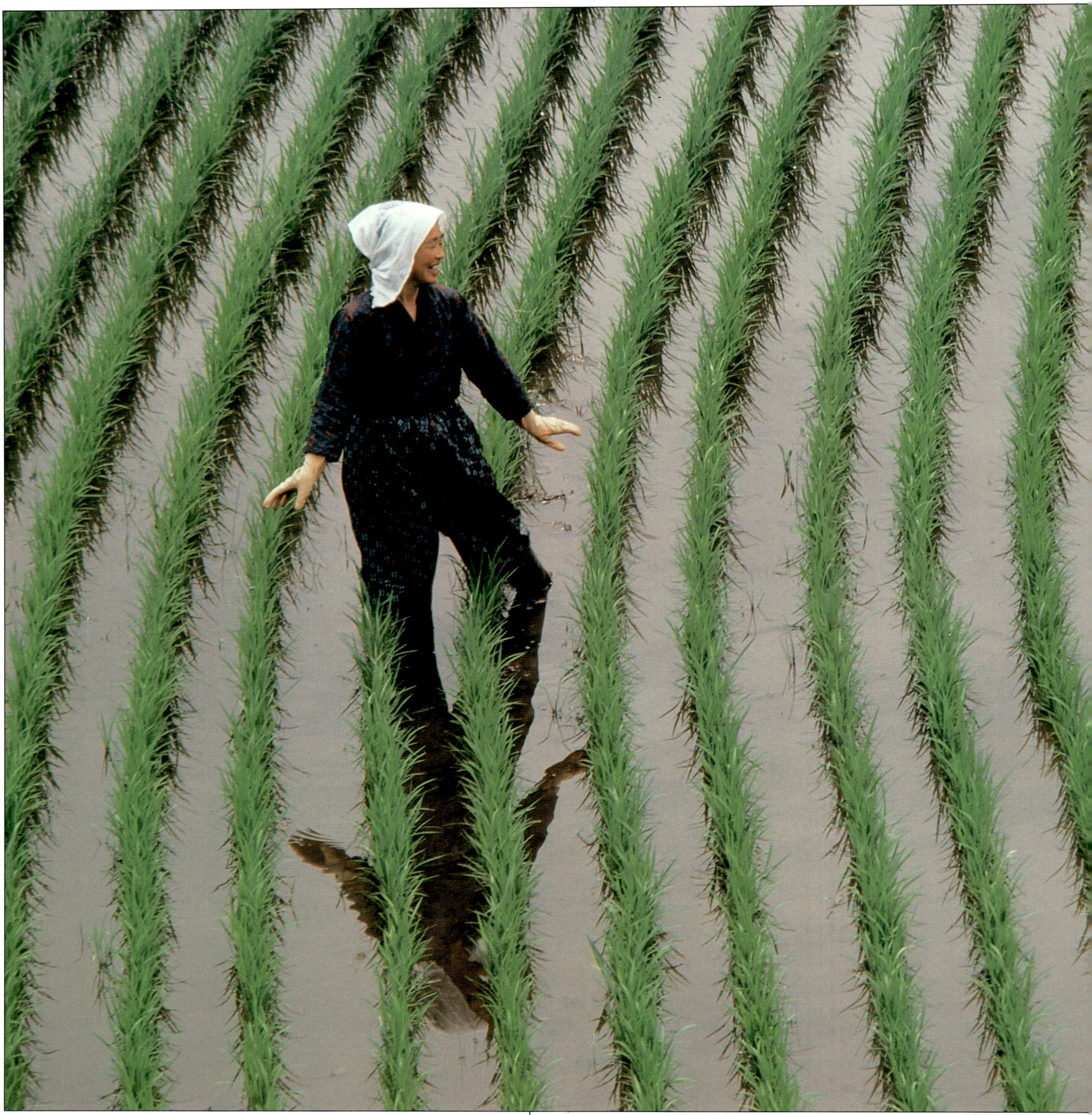

voedingsstoffen, waaronder vezel, natrium, cholesterol, vitamine A en C, ijzer en kalk, zijn niet gerelateerd aan de calorieconsumptie. Streef eenvoudig naar 100 procent van de aangegeven Dagelijkse Waarde.

Sommige etiketten bevatten ook een voetnoot voor de Dagelijkse Waarden voor 6 elementaire voedingsstoffen in zowel het 2000 als het 2500 dagelijkse calorieën dieet. Deze waarden zijn gebaseerd op algemeen aanvaarde aanbevelingen. In wezen geven de cijfers aan dat als u meer calorieën nodig hebt (of eet) u iets meer totaal vet, verzadigd vet, koolhydraten en vezel kunt eten. Ongeacht de calorie-inname adviseren voedingsdeskundigen om de cholesterolconsumptie te beperken tot een maximum van 300 mg en 2400 mg natrium per dag. Als u een goede nierfunctie hebt en u zelf of n uw familie geen last hebt van hoge bloeddruk, hoeft u natrium natuurlijk niet strikt te beperken. U zult eenvoudig afscheiden wat u ongeveer eet.

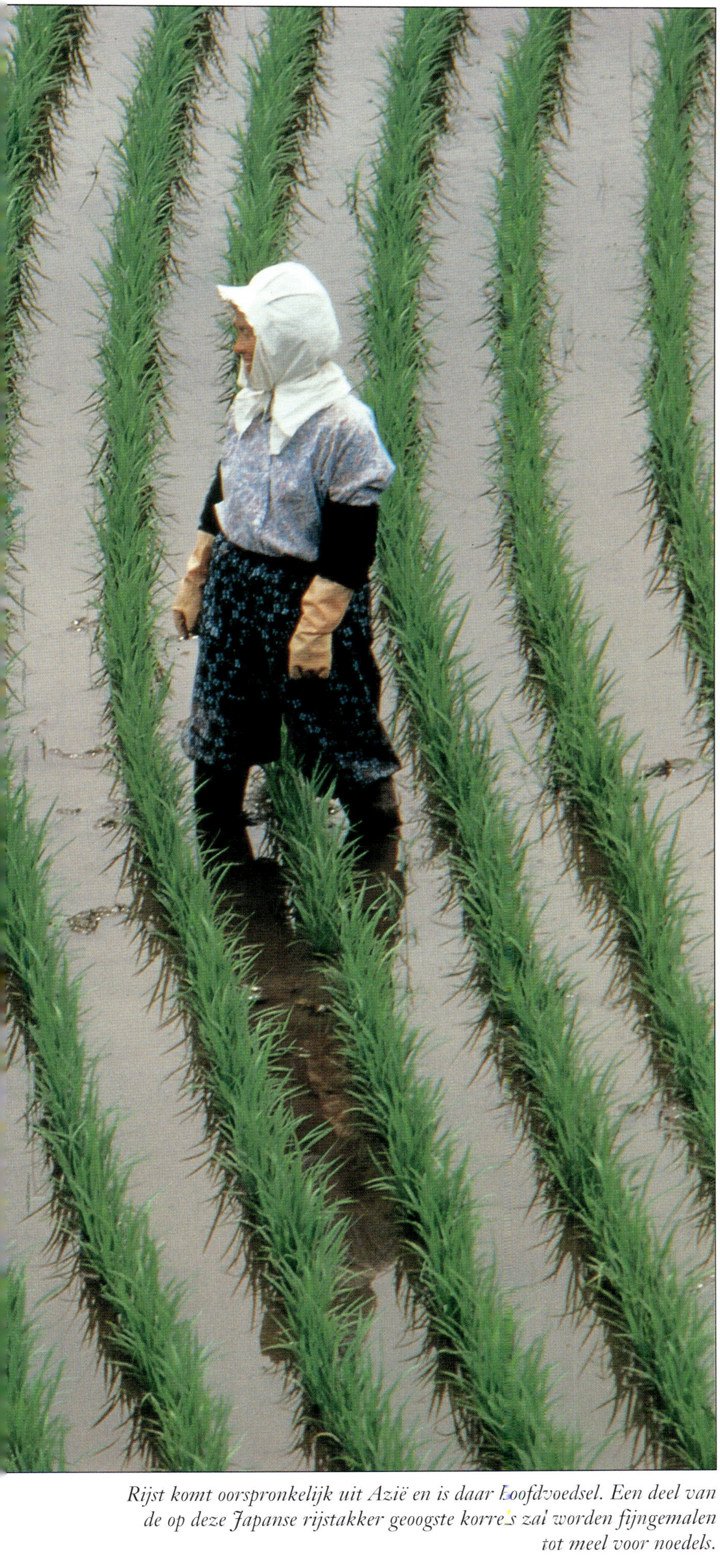

Rijst komt oorspronkelijk uit Azië en is daar hoofdvoedsel. Een deel van de op deze Japanse rijstakker geoogste korrels zal worden fijngemalen tot meel voor noedels.

HOOG EN LAAG

Beweringen over voedingswaarde hebben in het verleden tot veel verwarring geleid. Sommige onscrupuleuze fabrikanten noemden hun produkten bijvoorbeeld "cholesterolvrij" en suggereerden daarmee een uniek voordeel ten opzichte van andere produkten, terwijl het produkt van nature nooit enige cholesterol bevatte. Tegenwoordig zijn dat soort claims niet meer zo makkelijk te maken. Absolute uitspraken, zoals "natrium-arm" en "vetvrij", worden streng gecontroleerd. Alle voedsel dat "vet-arm" heet, bevat 3 gram of minder vet per portie. En produkten waarbij claims worden geïmpliceerd die op subtiele wijze suggereren dat ze op een of andere manier gezond zijn—bijvoorbeeld "hoog aan havervlokken"—moeten nu voldoen aan de vereiste criteria om de overeenkomstige absolute claim te maken—in dit geval "veel voedingsvezel".

Gezond eten

Het is op het tv-journaal en in de ochtendkrant. Het is voer voor tijdschriftartikelen, boeken, congressen en lezingen. Waar men ook kijkt, men vindt steeds meer informatie over voeding en gezondheid. Vaak zijn feiten en fictie moeilijk te scheiden. Dit is een feit: voeding kan geen chronische ziekte genezen. Maar een uitgebalanceerd dieet dat vet-arm en rijk is aan samengestelde koolhydraten, vitaminen en mineralen kan het risico van ziekten verminderen en medische behandeling ondersteunen.

KRUIDENGENEESMIDDELEN

Gewone planten, met name kruiden, worden al sinds mensenheugenis gebruikt om ziekten te weren, symptomen te helpen verlichten en, volgens sommigen, ziekten te genezen. Zo wordt van de alkaloïde olie die chilipepers heet maakt, aangenomen dat die druk op de bronchiën verlicht, bloedstolling helpt voorkomen, de stofwisseling kan versnellen en de gemoedstoestand kan verbeteren door de hersenen natuurlijke opiaten—de zogeheten endomorfinen—te laten aanmaken.

Knoflook, een lid van de familie der lelieachtigen, heeft misschien antibiotische eigenschappen. Onderzoek lijkt te suggereren dat zo'n 30 g knoflook, het equivalent van een bol, de bloedvetten vermindert, bloedstolling tegengaat en de bloeddruk wellicht verlaagt. Maar knoflook die in hoeveelheden wordt gebruikt om farmacologische resultaten te sorteren, kan tot onrust in de ingewanden leiden en een onaangename lichaamsgeur veroorzaken. Uien, die in botanisch opzicht verwant zijn aan knoflook, hebben mogelijk cholesterolverlagende en anti-carcinogene eigenschappen.

Uit onderzoek blijkt dat basilicum, komijn en geelwortel mogelijk ook anti-carcinogene eigenschappen hebben. Basilicum, koriander, dille, venkelgroen, munt, peterselie en rozemarijn zijn bronnen van bèta-caroteen. Een aantal andere kruiden en specerijen—waaronder piment, selderijzaad, kruidnagel, gember, citroengras, marjolein, peper rozemarijn en salie—hebben anti-oxidante eigenschappen. Karwij, dille, kruizemunt, marjolein en anijs kunnen als hulp bij de vertering van voedsel fungeren. Zowel kaneel als gember zijn voor het verlichten van maagklachten gebruikt.

Er zijn geen wetenschappelijk verantwoorde "aanbevelingen" voor

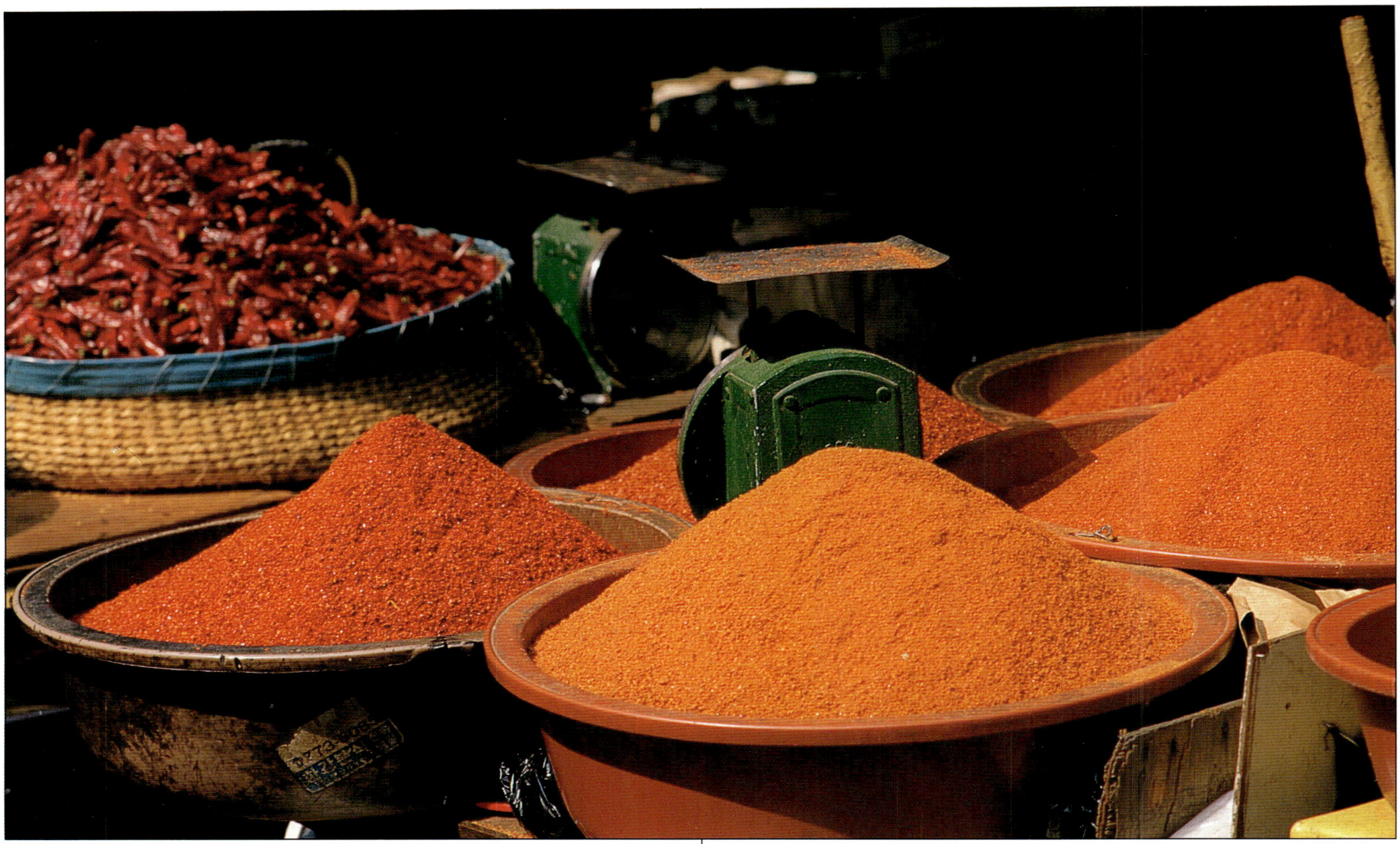

hoeveelheden kruiden en specerijen, en meer is niet per se beter. Planten en hun derivaten zitten vol verrassingen. Er is wel enig toezicht op kruidenmedicijnen en -supplementen, maar toch kunnen bijvoorbeeld in zeer geconcentreerde kruiden-oliën giftige stoffen voorkomen.

Hoewel veel medicijnen zijn gebaseerd op chemicaliën die in planten worden aangetroffen, is er meer onderzoek vereist naar de medicinale eigenschappen van planten. Gebruik vooralsnog kruiden en specerijen om de smaak en geur van eten te versterken. Als *ingrediënten* zijn ze van belang in een uitgebalanceerd, gezond en smakelijk dieet.

Hartaandoeningen zijn jaarlijks voor vele doden verantwoordelijk. Het is voor mannen en vrouwen zelfs een van de meest frequente doodsoorzaken. Volgens vele medische specialisten behoren een hoge bloed-

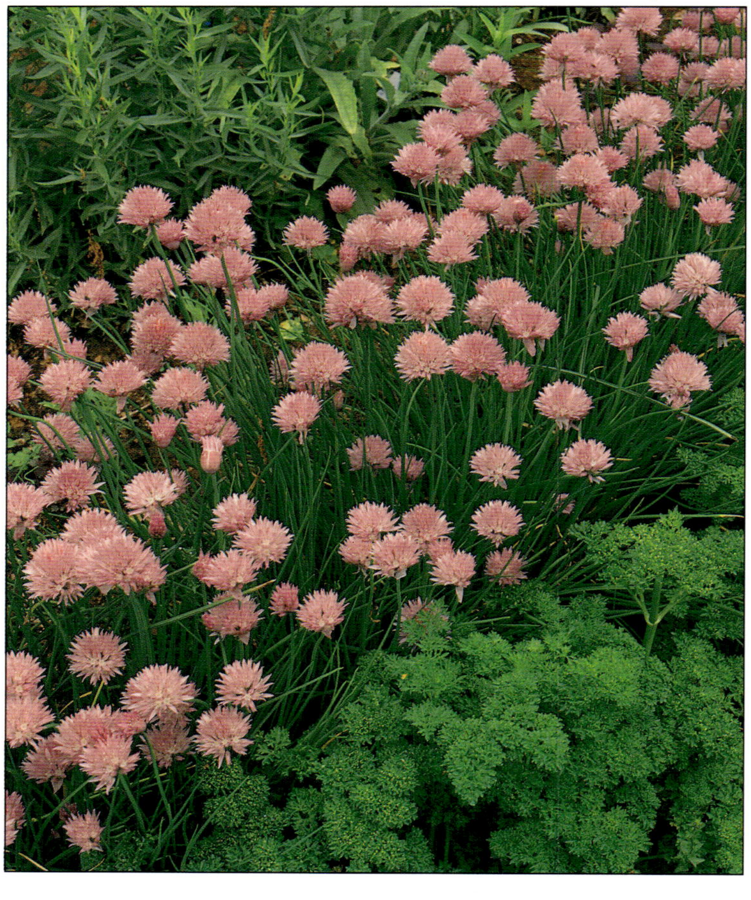

Verse kruiden zitten vol smaak, maar nemen in de tuin slechts weinig ruimte in. Gedroogde kruiden kunnen eenvoudige recepten een fantastische smaak geven. Als smaakgever zijn beide een gezond alternatief voor zout, boter en zware sausen.

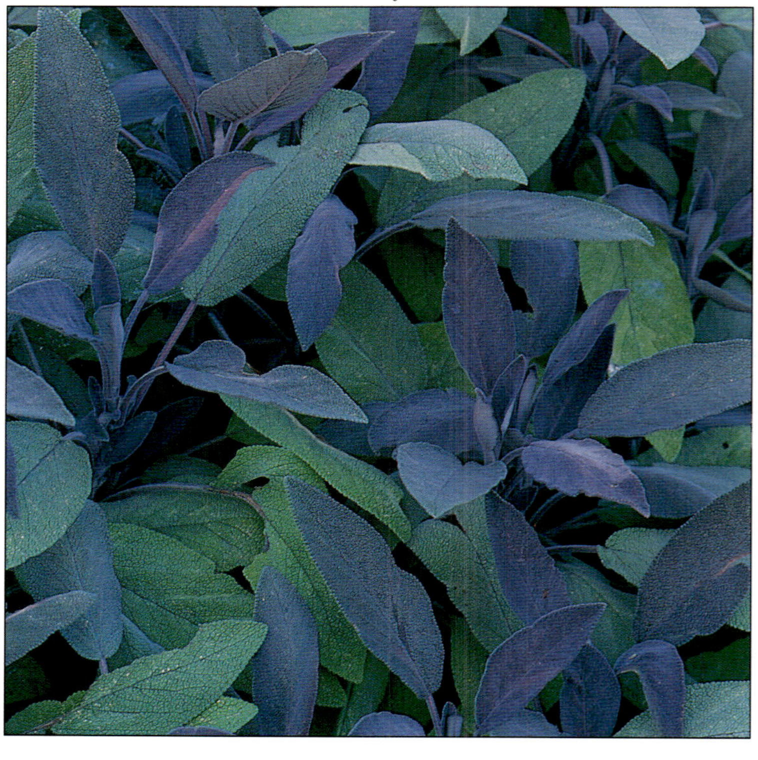

Meer smaak maar minder zout

Wrijf een kruidenmengsel in visfilets of stukken gevogelte voor het grilleren of bakken. Meng gehakte verse kruiden met broodkruim en mischien wat gemalen noten om vis of kipfilet te paneren. Doe kruiden of specerijen in groenten en granen tijdens of na het koken. Verse kruiden zijn normaal gesproken sterker van smaak, maar gedroogde kruiden zijn ook zeer geschikt wanneer verse niet verkrijgbaar zijn. Gebruik hele specerijen voor het pocheren van fruit; strooi gemalen specerijen over rauw of gekookt fruit.

Kruiden/specerijen voorbeelden van combinaties

Groenten

Aardappel	Dille, ui en peterselie
	Komijn- of karwijzaad en ui
Broccoli	Verse gember en knoflook
	Sesamzaad
Erwtjes	Munt, ui en peterselie
	Rozemarijn en marjolein
Sperziebonen	Bieslook en ingevroren geraspte citroenschil
	Marjolein, basilicum en/of rozemarijn
	Karwijzaad en mosterd
Spinazie	Nootmuskaat en ui
	Sesamzaad en verse knoflook
Tomaat	Basilicum en rozemarijn
	Kaneel en ui
Wortel	Kaneel en nootmuskaat
	Verse gember en basilicum

Fruit

Aardbeien	Kaneel
	Versgemalen zwarte peper
Appel	Kaneel, piment en nootmuskaat
	Verse gember
Banaan	Piment
	Nootmuskaat en gemberpoeder
Peer	Kardemom
	Versgemalen zwarte peper
Perzik	Nootmuskaat
	Kaneel en kruidnagel
Sinaasappel	Kaneel en kruidnagel
	Maanzaad

Granen

Pasta	Basilicum, verse knoflook en peterselie
	Verse knoflook, ui en rode peper
Rijst	Gemalen chilipeper, verse sinaasappelschil en komijn
	Kerriepoeder, gember, geelwortel en gemalen koriander
Gevogelte	Rozemarijn en tijm of marjolein
	Dragon, ui en verse knoflook
	Laurierblad, komijn en geelwortel
	Kerriepoeder, komijn, mosterd, verse knoflook en paprikapoeder
	Verse gember, kaneel, piment, anijszaad en kruidnagel
	Mosterd, verse knoflook en honing
Zeebanket	Tijm, nootmuskaat en zwarte en rode peper
	Dragon, tijm, peterselie, ui en knoflook
	Tijm, venkelzaad, zwarte en rode peper en saffraan
	Sesamzaad, gember en witte peper

Kruiden en specerijen bewaren

Koop alleen de hoeveelheid specerijen en kruiden die u voor een paar maanden denkt nodig te hebben. Bescherm deze smaakgevers door de volgende tips te volgen.

- Bewaar specerijen in luchtdichte potjes op een koele, droge plek. Te veel warmte beschadigt etherische olieën; door vochtigheid worden gemalen specerijen kleverig. Bewaar uw specerijen niet in de buurt van uw fornuis.
- Schrijf de datum op uw specerijen en kruiden wanneer u ze koopt. Gebruik oudere pakjes eerst.
- Gebruik voor het afmeten droge maatlepels om aankoeken te voorkomen.
- Sluit potjes en blikje meteen af na gebruik. Door langdurige blootstelling aan licht of lucht worden geur en smaak minder.

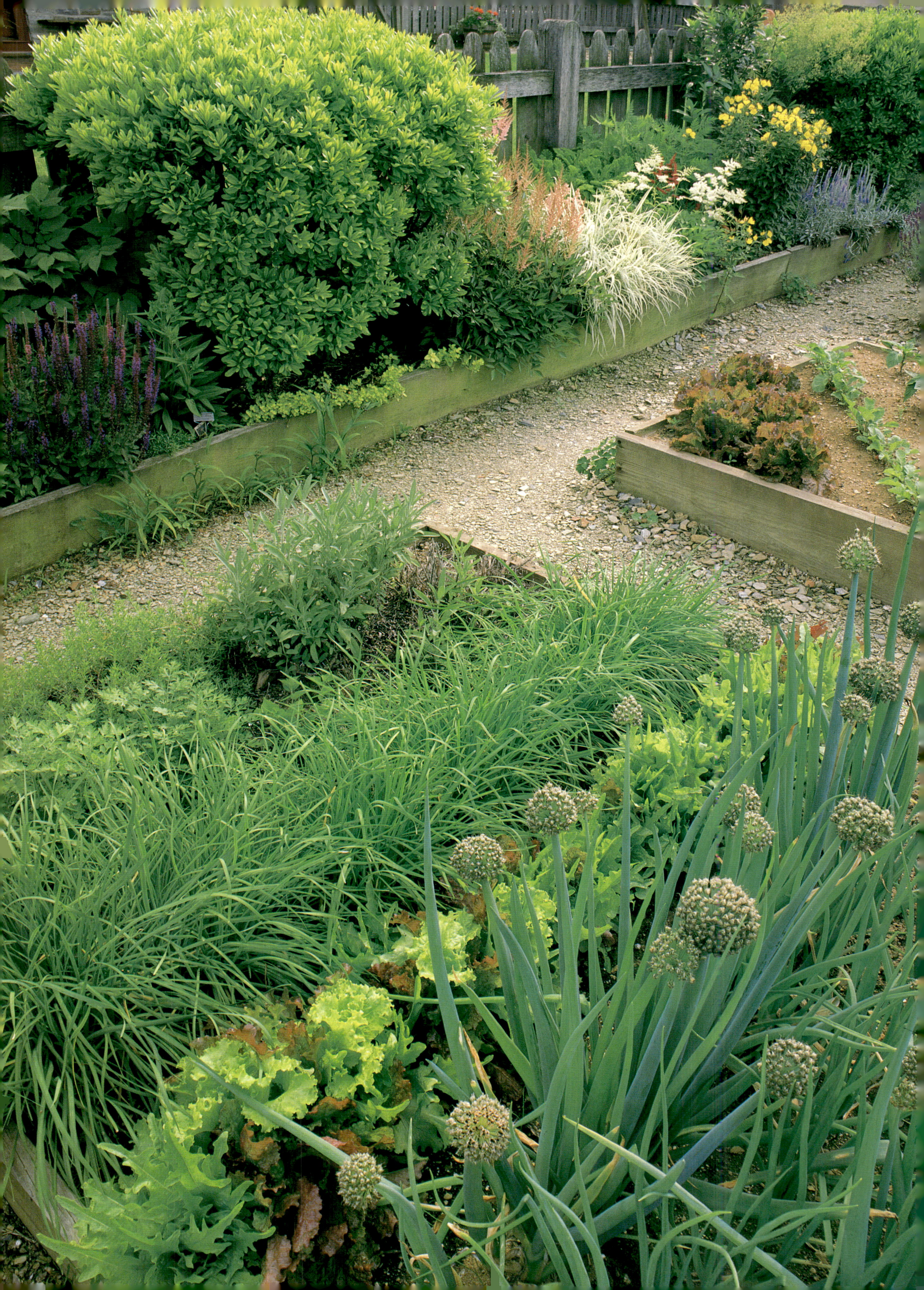

cholesterolspiegel, hoge bloeddruk en een te hoog gewicht tot de risicofactoren die hartaandoeningen veroorzaken. U kunt deze risico's controleren door middel van de Algemene Voedingsregels en de Voedselpiramide. Wees zeer voorzichtig met vet; wie teveel eet, moet het vet totaal, verzadigd vet en voedingscholesterol beperken. Vraag uw dokter uw bloedcholesterol en bloeddruk te meten. Maak keuzes op basis van uw familiehistorie, onderzoeksresultaten en persoonlijke gewoonten.

Uit onderzoek blijkt dat 40 tot 60 procent van alle kankers met voedselkeuzes samenhangen. Wetenschappers hebben ontdekt dat voedingsstoffen die worden aangetroffen in vruchten, groenten en volle granen het risico op vele soorten kanker kunnen helpen verlagen. Eet een dieet dat rijk is aan deze voedingsmiddelen en verminder uw vetconsumptie.

Bepaalde stoffen in vruchten en groenten—waaronder (maar niet uitsluitend) vezel, vitamine C en bèta-caroteen—beschermen tegen kanker. Een dieet met veel caroteen vermindert het risico van long- en huidkanker. Andere voedingsstoffen, waaronder vitamine E, selenium, vitamine B6, foliumzuur, pantotheenzuur en vitamine B_{12}, lijken ook anti-carcinogene eigenschappen te hebben. Enkele non-vitamine-, non-minerale

Als u kookt met vruchten, groenten en kruiden die van een plaatselijke boerderij of uit eigen tuin komen, levert dat weergaloos verse en smaakvolle schotels op.

Meer doen met andere smaken

Is er iets smakelijker dan een sappige, vers geplukte tomaat of maïskoorels van een kolf die zo van het land komt? Hebt u zich ooit verbaasd over de schoonheid van een verfijnde courgettebloesem of het prachtig gekrulde blad van boerenkool? We vertrouwen dezer dagen zoveel op voorbewerkt voedsel dat jongere generaties en stedelingen misschien niet eens meer weten hoe verse produkten eigenlijk smaken, aanvoelen en eruitzien.

Een reactie op de spanningvolle, gefragmenteerde levensstijl van het eind van de 20ste eeuw is een terugkeer naar de tuin geweest. Dichtbij de aarde werken, brengt ons in harmonie met de ritmes van de seizoenen. En zelf gekweekte groenten en vruchten smaken niet alleen fantastisch, maar zijn ook beduidend voordeliger. De erin gestoken arbeid is toch zeker meer ontspanning dan werk!

Als u geen stukje grond hebt dat u alleen voor een moestuin kunt bestemmen, kunt u wat groenten en bessenstruiken tussen uw eenjarige en vaste planten zetten. Sommige groenten, zoals pompoenen, hebben interessante bloemen; en sommige bloemen, zoals die van de Oostindische kers en viooltjes, leveren smakelijke ingrediënten voor een salade op. Zorg er alleen voor dat u ze zonder pesticiden of insecticiden kweekt.

Als u geen tuin hebt, kweek dan tomaten en paprika's in potten op het balkon. En vergeet vooral de kruiden niet. Die hebben maar heel weinig ruimte nodig. Met wat licht en goede zorgen kunt u die het hele jaar door op de vensterbank kweken. Met een paar snippers ervan hebt u al een hele dosis smaak om gerechten als salades of een robuuste hoofdschotel smaak te geven.

Hier zijn wat kruidentips:

- Basilicum is een eenjarige plant. Knip de steeltjes af en gebruik alleen het blad. Knip de steeltjes steeds af, zodat hij niet in bloei komt.
- Bieslook is een vaste plant. Houd de planten kort geknipt.
- Dille is een eenjarige plant. Zaai de zaadjes in fases uit, zodat u steeds een voorraad hebt. Geoogste zaadjes zijn klaar voor gebruik wanneer ze donker zijn.
- Munt is een opdringerige vaste plant. Snijd hem vaak af en geef de plant wat ruimte.
- Oregano, een vaste plant, houdt van volop zonlicht. De purperroze bloemen zijn een aanwinst voor elke tuin. Knip oude takjes af voor een optimale oogst.
- Peterselie is een tweejarige plant die als eenjarige wordt gekweekt omdat de bladvorming in het tweede jaar mager is. Peterselie gedijt het best in de volle zon. Kies voor variatie de bladpeterselie, die veel meer smaak heeft.
- Rozemarijn is een aromatische, heesterachtige vaste plant die 1 tot 1,2 meter hoog kan worden. Rozemarijn groeit het best in de volle zon. Bij koude winters moet de plant binnen worden gehouden.
- Salie is een vaste plant. Houd deze plant na de bloei kort geknipt.
- Tijm is een bossige vaste plant. Na de bloei moet de plant volledig worden teruggesnoeid om nieuwe groei te stimuleren.

Twee andere bronnen van zeer verse produkten zijn kraampjes langs de weg en lokale markten. Zo kunt u bijvoorbeeld geen ruimte hebben om in de eigen tuin spruitjes te verbouwen, maar in uw omgeving iemand vinden die dat voor u wil doen. (Het zal u verbazen hoeveel mensen—en niet alleen kinderen—nog nooit een stronk met spruitjes eraan hebben gezien.)

Door direct van boeren in uw omgeving te kopen, bent u ook verzekerd van zeer verse produkten om mee te koken. Er zijn ook boeren die gelegenheid tot "eigen pluk" geven in hun tuinen. Zo'n uitstapje is een goede manier om kinderen alles over voedsel te leren op de plek waar de produkten zelf verbouwd worden.

chemicaliën die zijn aangetroffen in vruchten en groenten activeren enzymen en vernietigen carcinogenen. Stoffen die de verspreiding van kwaadaardige tumoren tegengaan, zijn aangetroffen in sojabonen, kikkererwten en aardappels. De in yoghurt voorkomende bacteria dragen mogelijk bij aan het voorkomen van kanker aan de dikke darm. (Deze bacteria worden gebruikt voor het fermenteren van de melk en zijn "gezond"; ze helpen zelfs de spijsvertering.)

Elk jaar worden vele vrouwen getroffen door borstkanker. Hoewel de rol van de voeding bij het voorkomen van deze vorm van kanker nog niet geheel begrepen wordt, is wel bekend dat borstkanker meer voorkomt in landen waar vrouwen veel vet totaal en verzadigd vet binnenkrijgen. En er zijn aanwijzingen dat een dieet dat rijk is aan vezel en vitamine A en C het risico van borstkanker kan verminderen.

Osteoporose, het verzwakken van de botten, leidt in Amerika tot ruim 1,5 miljoen botbreuken per jaar. Van de 25 miljoen Amerikanen die aan osteoporose leiden, is het grootste deel vrouw. Hoewel er nog geen geneeswijze voor osteoporose is, kan men het helpen voorkomen, en nu is het moment om daar mee te beginnen.

Kalk is essentieel voor het terugdringen van osteoporose. De aanbevolen hoeveelheid kalk is 800 mg per dag. Adolescenten, jonge volwassenen en zwangere of borstvoeding gevende vrouwen wordt aanbevolen 1200 mg kalk per dag te consumeren. De meeste vrouwen consumeren echter slechts de helft van deze hoeveelheid. Het is verstandig bij elk maal een goede bron van kalk op te nemen. Probeer magere melk, kaas of yoghurt. Volgens sommige deskundigen dienen vrouwen na de menopauze 1500 mg kalk per dag te consumeren.

Probeer het grootste deel van de kalk uit eten te krijgen. Natuurlijk aanwezige kalk treedt in wisselwerking met andere voedingsstoffen als vitamine D voor een maximale opname. Zuivelprodukten zijn een goede bron van kalk, maar kies wel magere variëteiten. Zo'n 2,5 dl melk levert 300 mg kalk, 2,5 dl yoghurt 300-400 mg. Yoghurt, bevroren yoghurt, sardines en zalm uit blik (met graten) zijn fantastische bronnen van kalk. Donkergroene bladgroenten zijn ook een goede bron. Met kalk aangevulde vruchtesappen zijn een goed alternatief voor mensen die niet van

Hiernaast: Eten is altijd een veelzeggende uiting van cultureel erfgoed geweest. Binnen de context van smaak en gezondheid betekent "goed eten" het onderzoek en genieten van vele eettradities. Vroege beschavingen in de Nieuwe Wereld leefden van een dieet van maïs, aangevuld met andere granen en groenten. Als ze in combinatie worden gegeten, leveren deze voedingsmiddelen veel eiwit.

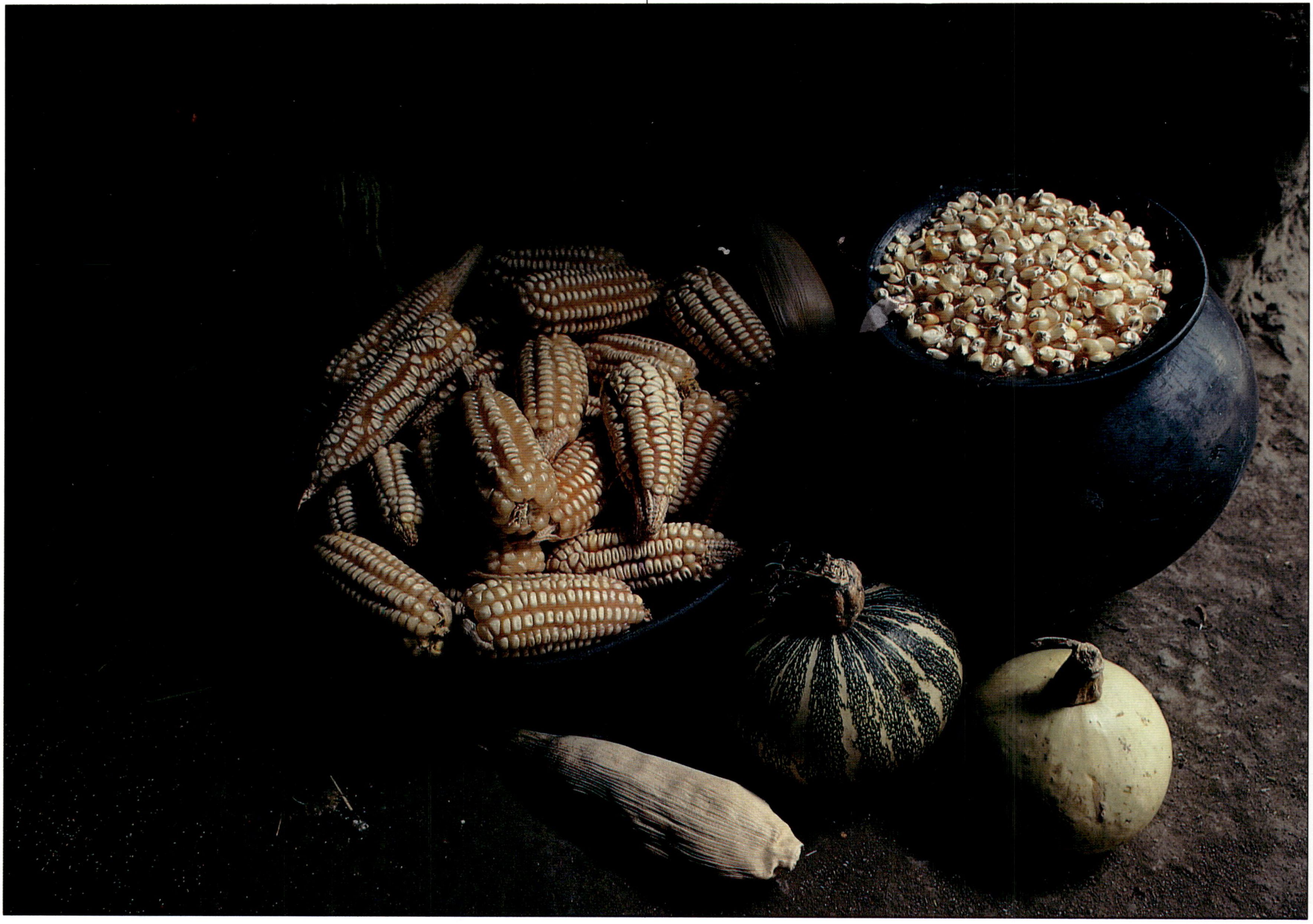

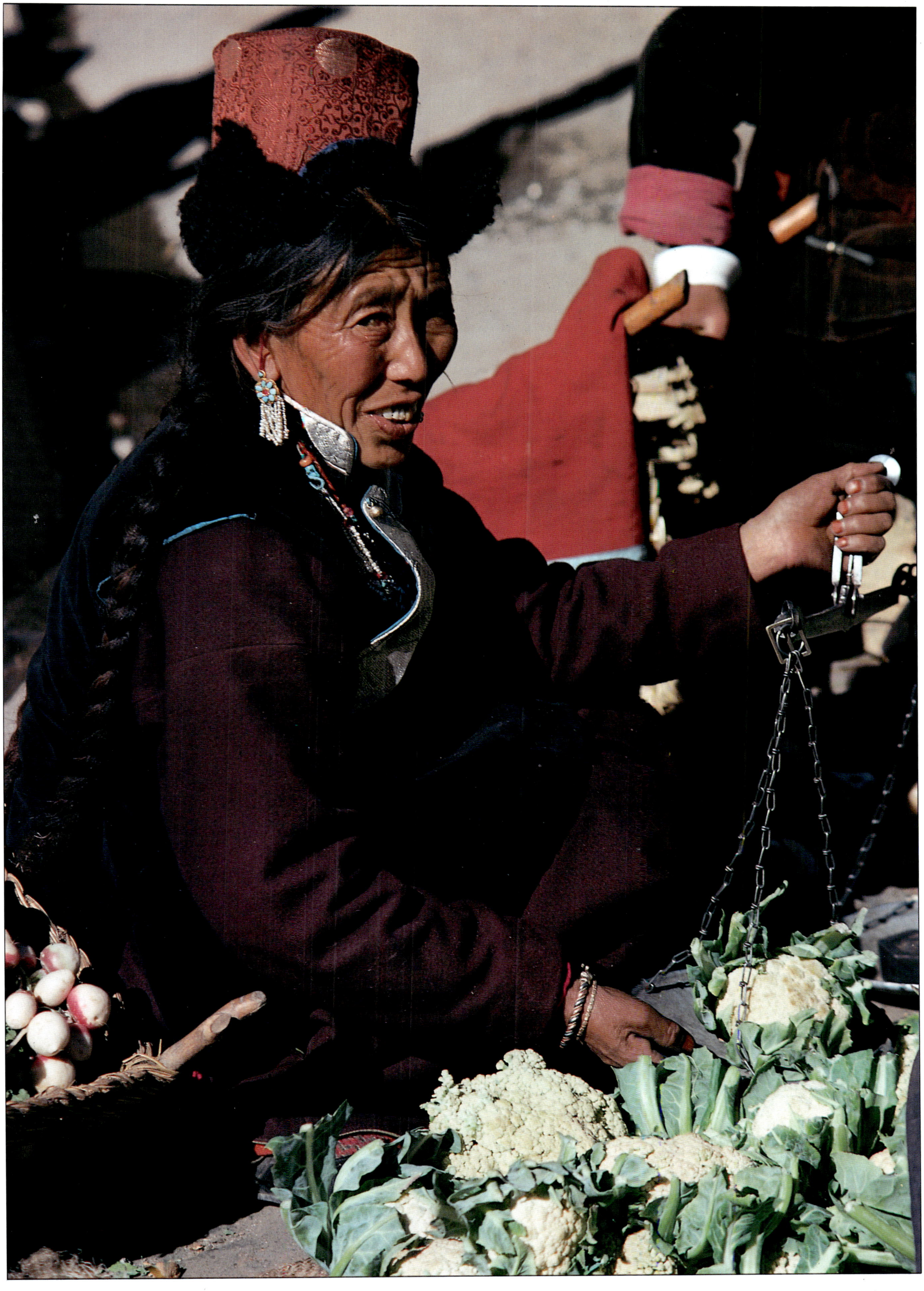

melk houden. Tegenwoordig is hier en daar met kalk verrijkt brood verkrijgbaar. Raadpleeg bij twijfel over dit punt uw dokter of diëtist omtrent wat voor u het beste is.

Een extra voordeel van een vrij kalkrijk dieet is de mogelijke verlaging van het risico van hypertensie (ook bekend als hoge bloeddruk). Hypertensie wordt echter allang in verband gebracht met natrium. Wie hoge bloeddruk heeft, of waar in de familie die aanleg voorkomt, doet er goed aan een zoutarm dieet te volgen, daar zout de meest voorkomende voedingsvorm van natrium is.

Ontwikkel een smaak voor een breed scala van kruiden, specerijen en kruiderij om uw afhankelijkheid van zout als voornaamste smaakgever te verminderen. Hierdoor zal u eetgenot toenemen, ongeacht of u aanleg voor hoge bloeddruk hebt of niet.

Behalve het onderzoek van voeding en het voorkomen van ziekten, bekijken wetenschappers ook de rol die wordt gespeeld door verschillende voedingsstoffen in de hersenchemie en immuniteit. We weten bijvoorbeeld dat tryptofaan, een bekend aminozuur dat in eiwitrijk eten voorkomt, de hersenen stimuleert tot de aanmaak van serotonine, een substantie die slaperigheid veroorzaakt en de tolerantiegrens voor pijn verhoogt. Koolhydraten leveren ook tryptofaan aan de hersenen.

Onderzoekers van het immuniteitssyteem hebben ontdekt dat zowel door voedseltekort als corpulentie dit systeem nadelig wordt beïnvloedt. Een dieet dat rijk is aan calorieën en vet, maar dat weinig essentiële voedingsstoffen bevat, kan uw bevattelijkheid voor ziekten vergroten. Antioxidanten als vitamine E en C en mineralen als zink, ijzer en selenium zijn cruciaal voor een goed functioneren van het immuniteitssysteem. Ook yoghurt versterkt dit systeem wellicht. Onderzoek bij bejaarden heeft aangetoond dat een verzwakking van het immuniteitssysteem in feite meer met een onvoldoende voeding dan met leeftijd te maken kan hebben. Op elke leeftijd wordt een goede voedingsstatus geassocieerd met een verhoogde immuniteit en weerstand tegen ziekten.

Is er op grond van deze kennis een pil die ons allen jong en gezond kan houden? Nee. Individuele voedingsstoffen werken het best in hun natuurlijke context, in een wisselwerking die nog niet geheel wordt begrepen. En een toverpil zou alle plezier van de voedselbeleving wegnemen—smaak, textuur, aroma en alle gebruiken die bepalend zijn voor de kunst, en niet de wetenschap, van koken en eten.

Doorbakken voor veiligheid

Vleessoort	*Kook tot een binnentemperatuur van*	
	Heel	*Gemalen*
Rundvlees	63°C	72°C
Varkensvlees	72°C	72°C
Lamsvlees	63°C	82°C
Kalfsvlees	72°C	72°C
Gevogelte	77°C	74°C
Gevuld gevogelte	82°C	

Voedsel goed bewaren

Iedereen streeft naar smakelijk, veilig en gezond eten. Het goed bewaren van voedsel is een uitdaging waarvoor kennis en waakzaamheid vereist zijn, zowel voor koks als overheidsinstanties. Veel mensen worden nodeloos ziek omdat ze niet op de hoogte zijn van de benodigde voorzorgsmaatregelen ter vermindering van de blootstelling aan gevaarlijke, door voedsel gedragen bacteriën, virussen, parasieten en chemische middelen. Eenvoudig gesteld, zijn de voornaamste oorzaken van voedselbesmetting een onjuiste voorbereiding, opslag en behandeling.

Er zijn drie regels waarmee u uw keuken veilig houdt:

1. Houd voedsel schoon

Was uw handen regelmatig met zeep wanneer u met voedsel omgaat, en gebruik schoon gereedschap. Was de bovenkant van blikken goed af voor u ze openmaakt; was de snijkant van uw blikopener met zeep en water. Houd alle voedsel in de koelkast goed verpakt of afgedekt.

2. Houd warm eten warm

Alle bereide voedsel moet tot minstens 60 °C worden verhit en warm worden gehouden. Laat gekookt voedsel niet langer dan 1 uur op kamertemperatuur staan.

3. Houd koud eten koud

Alle gekookte voedsel dat koud wordt opgediend of bewaard, moet u snel laten afkoelen tot 4 °C of lager in de koelkast. Vries voedsel in op -18°C. Zet resten en verse vergankelijke waar direct in de koelkast. Houd voedsel buiten de gevarenzone van 4 °-60 °C waarin bacteriën gedijen.

Hoewel een groot deel van de rijstoogst van de wereld van natte rijstvelden in laaglanden afkomstig is, wordt rijst ook op terrassen als deze op Bali verbouwd.

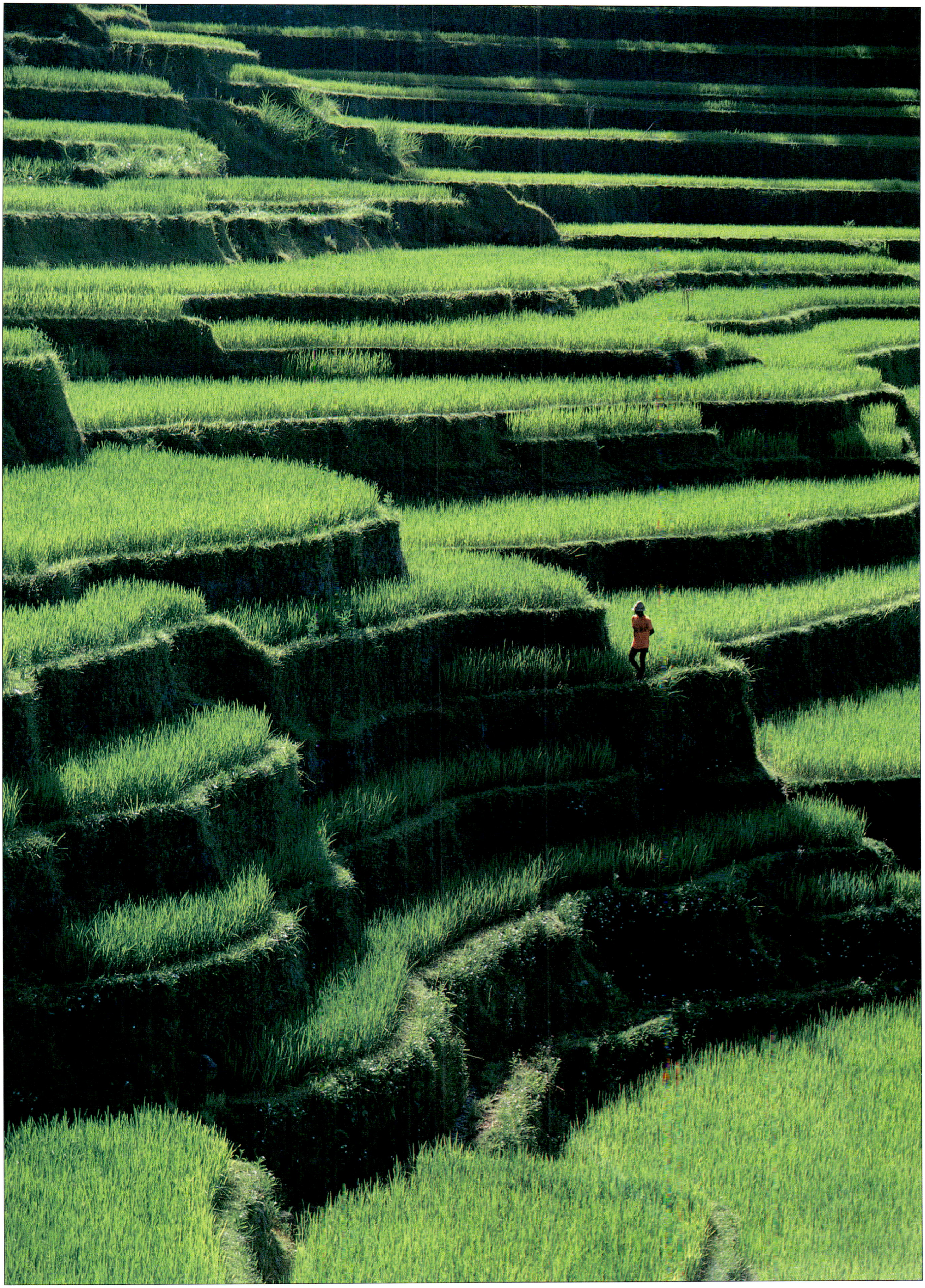

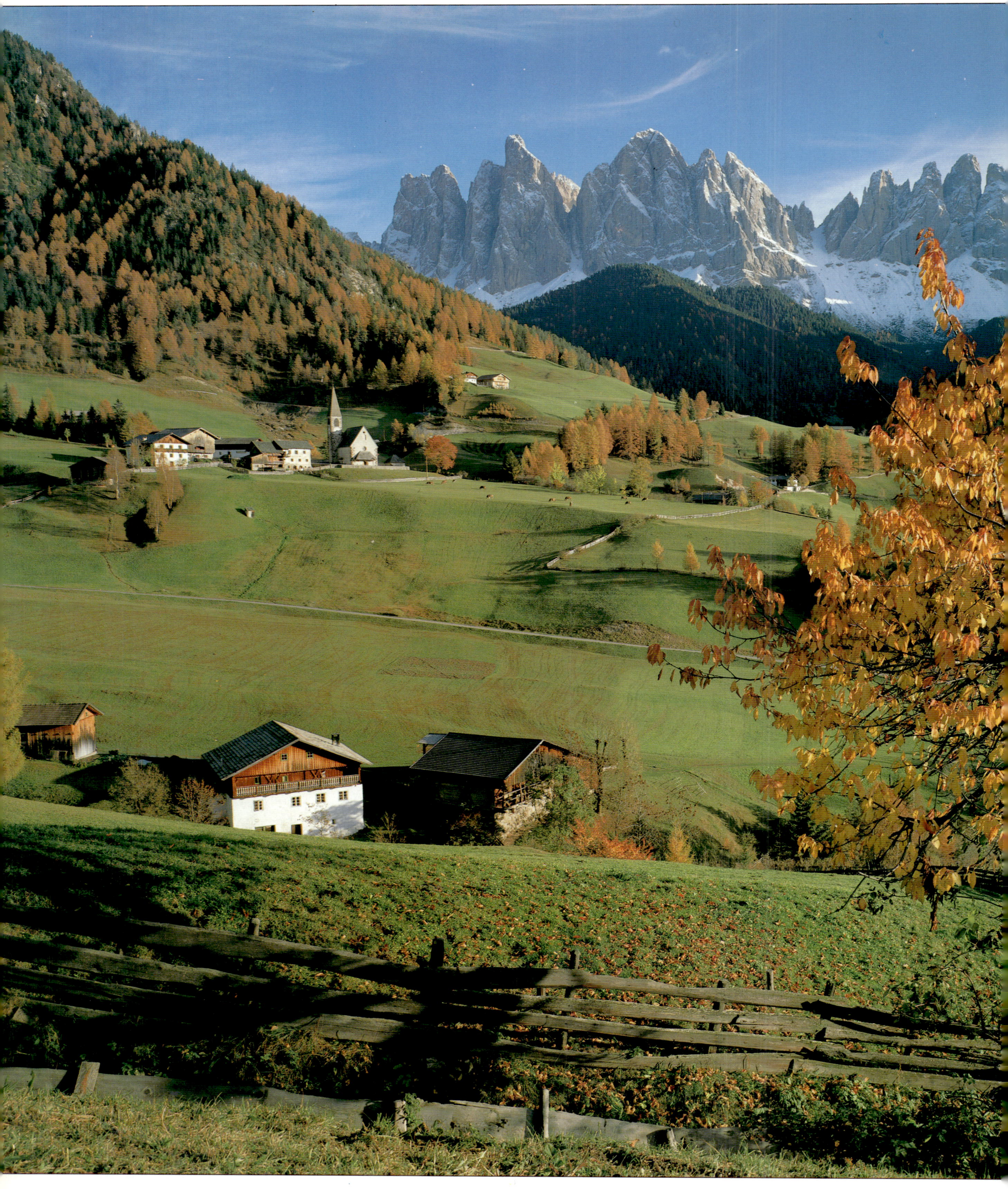

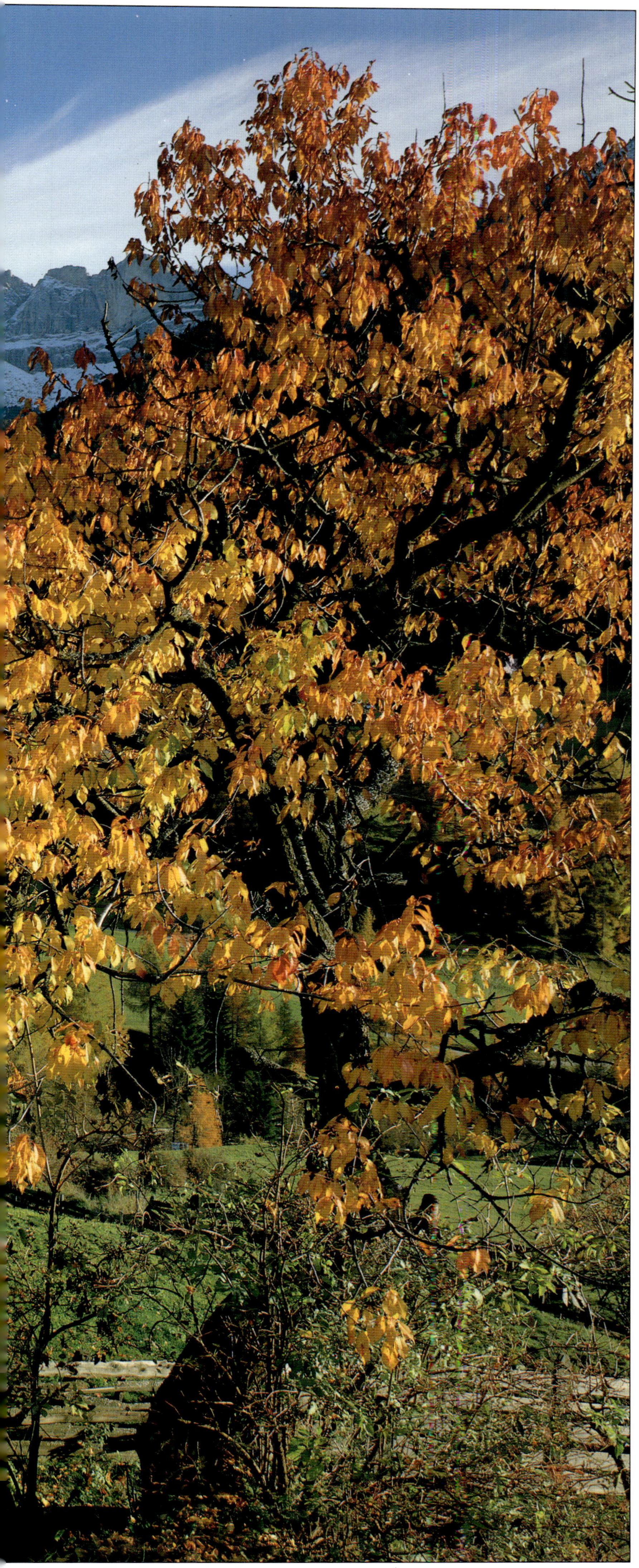

Laat bevroren voedsel ontdooien in de koelkast of onder de koude kraan. Wie voedsel in de magnetron laat ontdooien, moet het onmiddellijk bereiden. Laat voedsel nooit op kamertemperatuur ontdooien.

VEILIG MET DE MAGNETRON EN GRILL

Voor veilig werken met de magnetron en grill zijn enkele voorzorgsmaatregelen nodig. Schik voedsel zo in de magnetron dat het gelijkmatig wordt verhit. Volg bij het verwarmen van voorbewerkt eten altijd de aanwijzingen van de fabrikant op, zoals de aanwijzingen voor het keren en roeren. Zorg bij de bereiding van vlees en gevogelte in de magnetron dat altijd dezelfde binnentemperatuur wordt bereikt als bij conventioneel bereid vlees en gevogelte.

Kies voor gegrild vlees magere stukken. Er zijn aanwijzingen dat vet dat op het grill-element spat mogelijk een carcinogeen vormt die via de rook in het vlees terechtkomt. U kunt dit risico vermijden door voor het grilleren aluminiumfolie direct onder het vlees te leggen, of het vlees voor te koken in de magnetron en de grilleertijd te verkorten. Doe gegrild vlees altijd direct over op een *schoon* bord. En giet nooit een marinade met sappen van rauw vlees, gevogelte of vis over bereid eten.

KOPEN EN OPBERGEN

Zorg er bij de aanschaf van diepgevroren voedsel voor dat het solide is en dat gekoeld eten echt koud is. Koop deze ingrediënten het laatst, zeker bij warm weer. Koop geen beschadigde blikken of pakken en controleer de uiterste verkoop- en gebruiksdatum van vergankelijke waar. Berg bij thuiskomst gekoeld en ingevroren voedsel onmiddellijk op. Voorzie resten en andere levensmiddelen die u invriest onmiddellijk van een etiket met datum om "raadselpakjes" te vermijden waarvan de inhoud in kwaliteit is achteruitgegaan. Berg graanprodukten ver van warmtebronnen op. Zie de tabellen op pagina 57-60 voor tips voor het bewaren van verse vruchten en groenten. Deel uw koelkast, vriezer en kasten zo in dat u altijd makkelijk de oudste ingrediënten het eerst gebruikt.

BESTRALING EN PESTICIDEN: WAT IS WAT?

Alleen het woord roept al high-tech angstvisioenen op. Maar bestraling heeft wel een nuttige—en veilige—rol te spelen. Toch bestaan er nog wel de nodige twijfels over de voor- en nadelen van bestraling.

Bestraald eten is blootgesteld aan gammastralen die schadelijke bacteriën als salmonella vernietigen en insekten op voedsel doden. Door bestraling kan ook de bewaartijd worden verlengd doordat het rijpingsproces wordt vertraagd en door aantasting van organismen die bederf stimuleren. Bestraald eten wordt niet radioactief. Bestraling betekent wel een

In het noordoosten van Italië vormen de met sneeuw bedekte Dolomieten een fantastisch decor voor het glooiende akkerland dat de inwoners van deze streek eeuwenlang gevoed heeft.

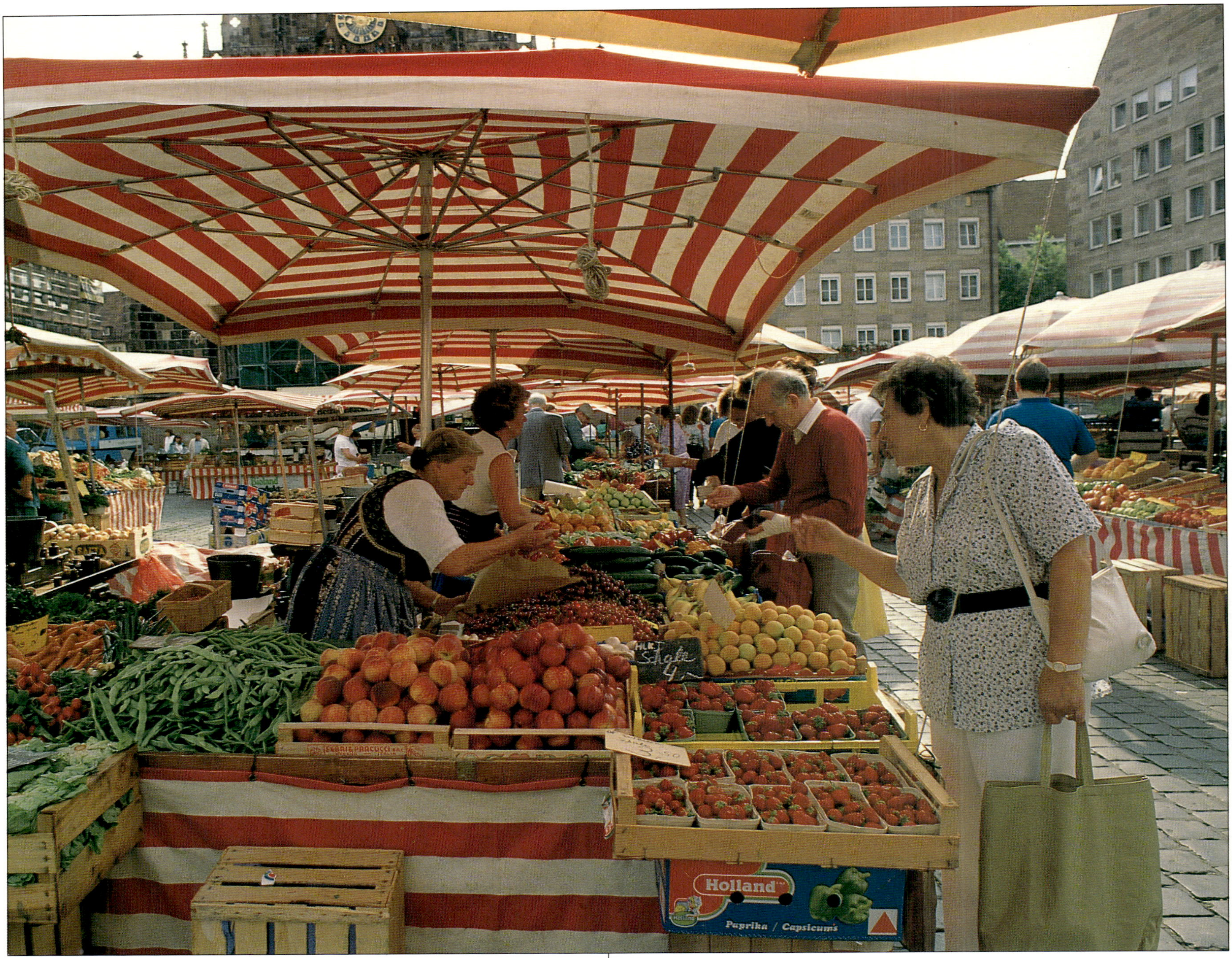

Op landelijke markten zijn altijd de mooiste seizoensprodukten te vinden. Hier keuren winkelende mensen het aanbod van de dag op een markt in het Duitse Neurenberg.

chemische verandering van het voedsel. Maar datzelfde geldt natuurlijk voor koken.

Bestralen of niet bestralen—de beslissing blijft controversieel. Bestraald gevogelte zou mogelijk een positief effect voor de volksgezondheid kunnen inhouden doordat salmonella en andere bacteriën worden vernietigd. Ook bestraling van varkensvlees is toegestaan omdat er zo minder nitriet nodig is voor het op smaak brengen en conserveren van het vlees. Het bestralen van specerijen om insekten te doden kan een beter alternatief zijn voor het gebruik van ethyleen-oxide, een chemisch middel dat mogelijke schadelijke reststoffen oplevert. Het bestralen van aardbeien met als enige oogmerk het verlengen van de bewaartijd met een week of zo, lijkt minder zinvol en meer commercieel.

In de Verenigde Staten moet alle bestraalde voedsel, behalve specerijen en enkele andere droge ingrediënten, voorzien zijn van het radura-teken. Dat ziet er zo uit.

Pesticiden worden gewoonlijk gebruikt ter beheersing van schade aan de oogst door insekten en ziekten, en om bederf te voorkomen. Evenals farmaceutische middelen worden pesticiden uitgebreid getest en gecontroleerd. Landbouwers zijn bij het gebruik aan strikte beperkingen gebonden. Dit heeft voor de consument tot gevolg dat de meeste voedingsmiddelen—of die nu vers of voorbewerkt zijn—geen waarneembare reststoffen van pesticiden bevatten.

Er zijn nu veel winkels waar organische produkten worden verkocht. Organische produkten kunnen smakelijker zijn, en mogelijk vindt u verschillende soorten organisch geteelde vruchten en groenten. Deze produkten zijn echter vrijwel altijd duurder. Organisch geteelde produkten zijn niet noodzakelijkerwijs veiliger of voedzamer dan produkten die met behulp van pesticiden zijn verbouwd. Bij onderzoek hadden deskundigen zelfs moeite om onderscheid tussen de twee produkten te maken.

Een roos is een roos is een roos? Misschien niet. Met gebruik van biotechnologie kunnen wetenschappers het reproduktieproces van een organisme manipuleren ten voordele van bepaalde genetische kenmerken. Door genetische manipulatie kunnen nu in de voedselbewerking gebruikte enzymen worden geproduceerd. Melkkoeien worden wel behandeld met een genetisch vervaardigd eiwithormoon dat de melkproduktie verhoogd.

Bij genetische manipulatie is veiligheid natuurlijk een bron van grote zorg. Is het proces te controleren? Te voorspellen? Wat zal het effect van behandelde levensmiddelen op toekomstige generaties zijn? Welke gevolgen heeft de biotechnologie voor het milieu? En wat zijn de effecten op zeer kwetsbare ecosystemen? Wat zijn de morele en sociale implicaties? Deze en andere door critici naar voren gebrachte vragen blijven een uitdaging voor de wetenschappelijke gemeenschap.

Op dit moment bestaan er geen voorschriften omtrent informatie op etiketten van genetisch gemanipuleerde levensmiddelen. Onlangs kwam als eerste genetisch gemanipuleerd produkt een tomaat op de markt die rood en rijp wordt verkocht maar een langere bewaartijd heeft. Andere genetisch gemanipuleerde produkten zullen ongetwijfeld volgen.

KWETSBARE LEVENSMIDDELEN

Door strenge voorschriften is ons voedsel in de loop der tijd veiliger geworden, maar nieuwe pathogenen vormen een uitdaging. De inmiddels beruchte *E. coli (Escherichia coli)* microbe die begin jaren '90 voor veel opschudding zorgde, werd pas in 1982 als een gevaar voor de gezondheid ontdekt. Het beste advies van de deskundigen is: neem geen risico, in het bijzonder met kwetsbare levensmiddelen waarvan bekend is dat ze incidenteel gevaarlijke organismen kunnen bevatten. Rauwe en zachtgekookte eieren, rauw en niet lang genoeg gekookt vlees en gevogelte en rauwe vis, schaal- en schelpdieren worden als risicovol voedsel beschouwd.

Eieren. Rauwe en niet lang genoeg gekookte eierdooiers kunnen een bron van de salmonellabacterie zijn. Het is aan te bevelen af te zien van zachtgekookte eieren en voorbewerkt voedsel dat als ingrediënt rauwe eieren bevat—mayonaise bijvoorbeeld. Gebruik alleen schone, onbeschadigde eieren. Verse eieren kunnen tot 3 weken in de koelkast worden bewaard, hardgekookte eieren kunt u 1 week in de koelkast bewaren.

Enkelvoudig onverzadigde olijfolie is onmisbaar in de mediterrane keuken. Dat verklaart wellicht waarom de mensen in dat gebied een relatief lage bloedcholesterolspiegel hebben.

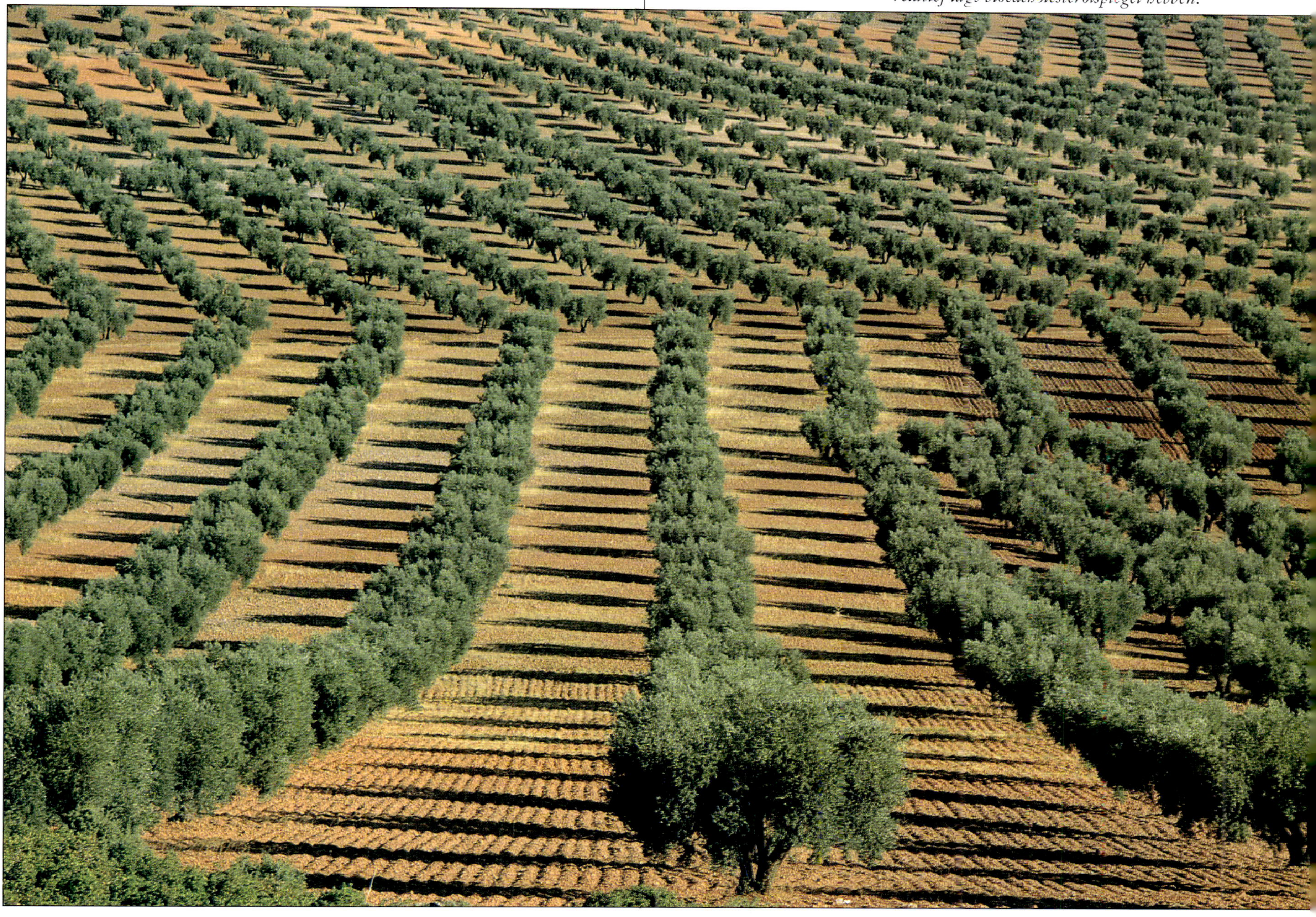

Gevogelte en vlees. Verse kip, kalkoen, eend en klein wild gevogelte kan in het koudste gedeelte van de koelkast 2 dagen worden bewaard. Uit recent onderzoek is gebleken dat veel rauw verkochte kip salmonellabacteriën bevat en daarom speciaal moet worden behandeld. Spoel rauwe kip onder de koude kraan en was *alle* oppervlakken en gerei dat in aanraking is gekomen met rauwe kip grondig af met zeep en water—inclusief het aanrecht, de snijplank, borden, bestek en uw handen. Alles dat u voor het wassen aanraakt—zelfs een kastdeur of kraan—kan besmet raken. Gelukkig worden deze bacteriën vernietigd door grondig koken.

Laat geen sappen van rauw gevogelte op andere levensmiddelen in uw koelkast druipen. Deze sappen kunnen voedsel besmetten dat u niet onmiddellijk gebruikt. Vul gevogelte vlak voor de bereiding. En onthoud dat een gevulde vogel een langere kooktijd nodig heeft. Haal vulling uit de lichaamsholte voor u resten gevogelte opbergt, en dek de vogel af met plastic folie om haar sappig te houden.

In plaats van bestraald gevogelte te kopen, is het verhitten van voedsel tot een vereiste binnentemperatuur de enige manier om te zorgen dat bacteriën worden vernietigd (zie de tabel op pagina 42). Kook vlees en gevogelte grondig en gebruik een vleesthermometer om de temperatuur te controleren. Verwarm resten tot een binnentemperatuur van minstens 72 °C; laat bij opwarmen jus en vleessausen flink aan de kook komen.

Zeebanket. Zeebanket is bijzonder voedzaam en goed voor de gezondheid, maar dient met zorg te worden behandeld. Koop uw vis altijd bij een goede visverkoper die zijn waar kent. Verse vis mag niet "vissig" of naar ammonia ruiken. Koop kleinere vis; deze soorten zijn meestal jonger en daardoor minder blootgesteld geweest aan besmette stoffen. Een verse vis moet stevig vlees hebben; heldere, bolle ogen; en een gaaf vel met een laagje erover dat als een stralend vernis oogt. Kies vismoten en filets die een doorschijnende glans en sappig, stevig vlees hebben. De schelpen van mosselen, clams en oesters moeten gesloten zijn en moeten anders bij aantikken strak dichtgaan. Bewaar schelpdieren onder een vochtige doek in het koudste deel van uw koelkast.

Koop vis die ijskoud of op ijs is bewaard. Koop geen vis die onder warme lampen ligt of lukraak ligt opgetast. Leg verse vis zo snel mogelijk in het koudste deel van uw koelkast. Spoel de vis af onder de koude kraan, dep droog met keukenpapier en doe hem in een luchtdicht afgesloten plastic zak. Gebruik verse vis binnen een dag of vries hem in.

Kook zeebanket altijd grondig. Het eten van rauwe of niet lang genoeg gekookte vis is riskant. Hij kan met bacteriën, virussen, parasietwormpjes en gevaarlijke chemische reststoffen besmet zijn. Snijd het vel af en snijd donkere stukken weg waar chemische stoffen zich kunnen ophopen. Gekookte vinvis moet ondoorschijnend zijn en het vlees moet makkelijk met een vork los te maken zijn.

Internationale waar; Gezonde tradities

In veel landen bestaat een traditionele gezonde voeding uit simpele "landelijke" kost—plaatselijk verbouwde groenten die met eenvoudige bereidingswijzen worden klaargemaakt. In het hart van verscheidene altijd populaire internationale keukens vindt u niet alleen gezondheidsbevorderende ingrediënten, maar ook duidelijk onderscheiden smaakprofielen die zich in de loop der eeuwen hebben ontwikkeld. De recepten in *De Vier Seizoenen* putten hun inspiratie—zowel voor ingrediënten als voor de smaak—vaak uit traditionele etnische keukens.

China. Het vetarme, veel koolhydraten bevattende Chinese dieet is precies wat we zouden moeten kiezen volgens vele westerse kanker-deskundigen. Rijst en tarwe zijn basisvoedingsmiddelen in China, aangevuld met meer dan 2000 groentesoorten. Voor authentieke Chinese stoofpotten en roerbakschotels is maar heel weinig olie nodig. In westerse variaties op Chinees eten ligt meer de nadruk op vlees,, gebakken ingrediënten en gesuikerde of gezouten sausen. Maak voor een meer traditionele—en meer gezonde—ervaring van rijst met gestoomde of roergebakken groenten het hoofdgerecht.

Frankrijk. In Frankrijk lijden verhoudingsgewijs minder mensen aan hartaandoeningen, ondanks het feit dat wel zo'n 37 procent van hun calorieën uit vet afkomstig is—15 procent uit verzadigd vet. Deze zogeheten Franse paradox kan worden geweten aan het feit dat de Fransen meer verse groenten en vruchten eten—beide bronnen van oxidanten die wellicht vetafzettingen op aderwanden helpen voorkomen. De Fransen gebruiken in de keuken naast boter vaak olijfolie, een enkelvoudig onverzadigd vet. Veel Franse gerechten, met name die met volle sausen, worden schitterend gepresenteerd in vrij bescheiden porties. De Fransen hebben ook een ander tempo van leven. Ze wandelen meer, eten op hun gemak en eten zelden snacks.

Hoewel de wijnconsumptie in Frankrijk vermindert, drinken de Fransen nog steeds 10 keer zoveel wijn als de Nederlanders. De rode wijn die zij bij het eten drinken kan de voedingscholesterol helpen verlagen. Uit onderzoeken kan worden opgemaakt dat een *matige* alcoholconsumptie—1 of 2 glazen per dag, niet per se beperkt tot rode wijn—enkele positieve gevolgen voor de gezondheid kan hebben. Wel hebben de Fransen meet last van leverkwalen, waaruit kan blijken dat teveel alcohol gevaarlijk voor de gezondheid is. Deze "rode-wijnconnectie" en alle andere aspecten van de Franse paradox worden diepgaand onderzocht.

Japan. Het traditionele Japanse dieet bevat weinig vet maar veel vezel, waarbij sojaprodukten, vis, groenten, noedels en rijst een rol spelen. De

Direct van de boerderij kopen betekent koken met de meest verse ingrediënten. Veel boeren verkopen hun eigen kaas en andere zuivelprodukten.

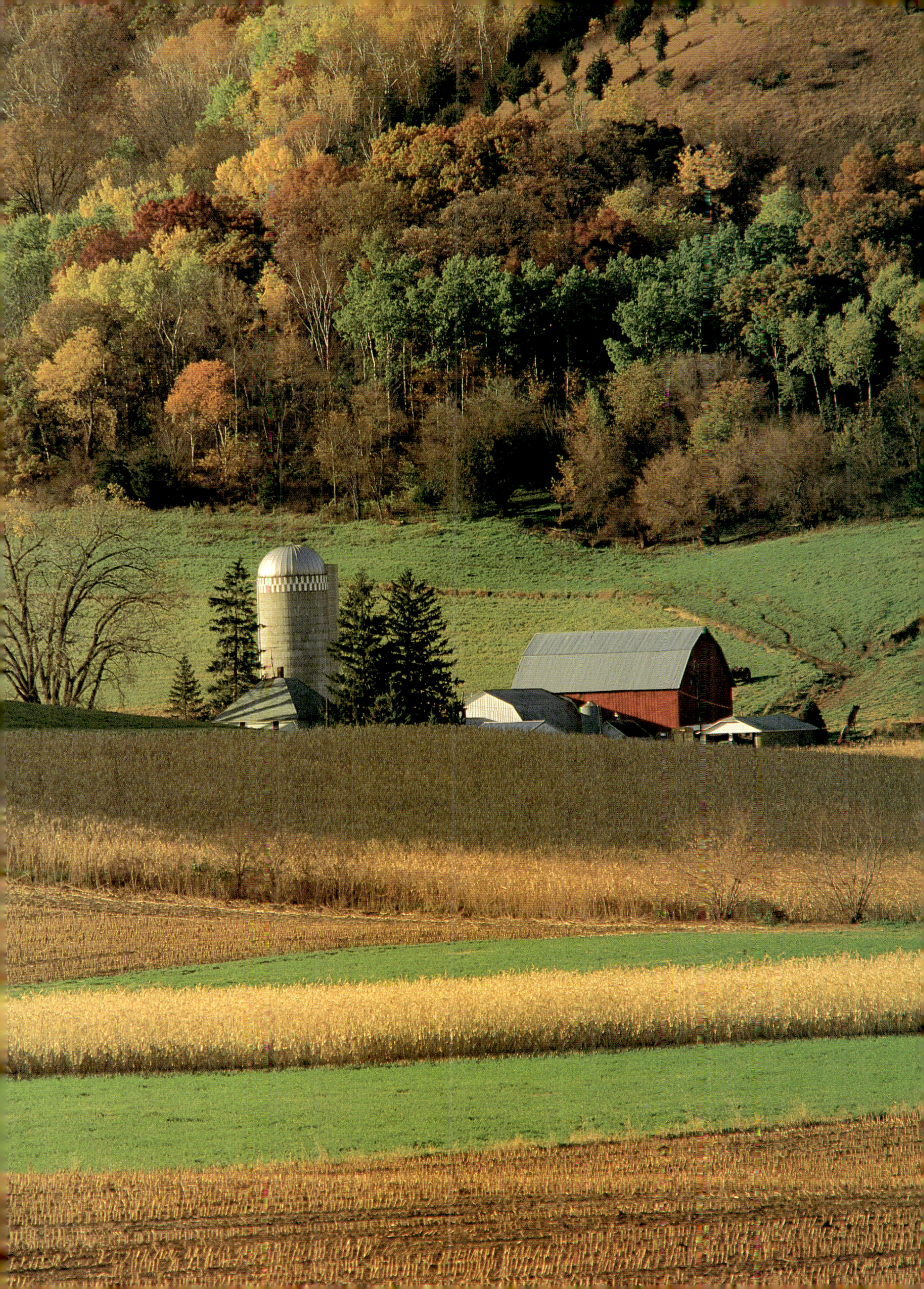

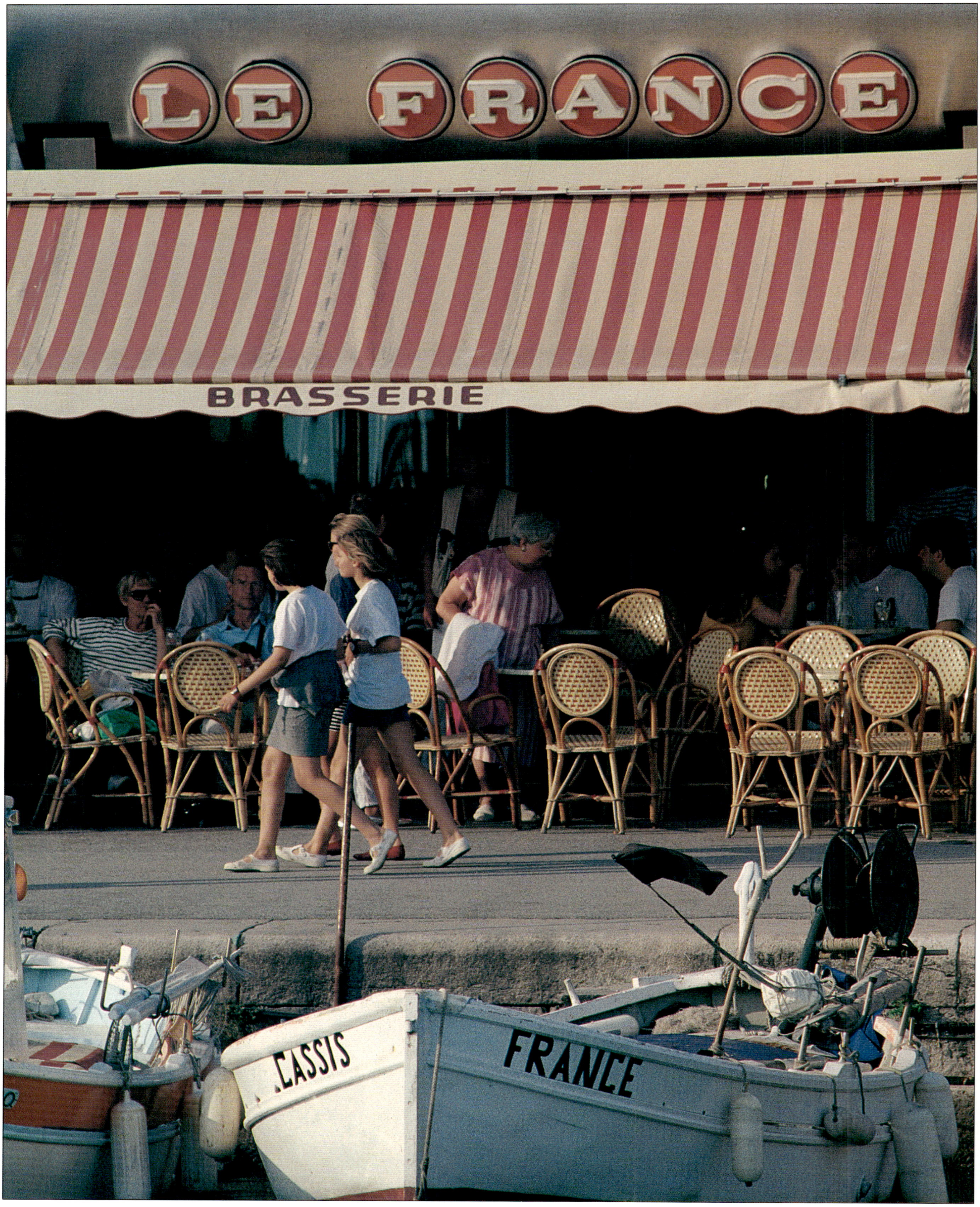
LE FRANCE
BRASSERIE
CASSIS
FRANCE

nadruk ligt op rijst of noedels—de basis van de Voedselpiramide. Vlees wordt meer als garnituur dan als hoofdgerecht gebruikt. Van dit dieet wordt gezegd dat het het aantal hartaandoeningen in Japan laag houdt. Een traditioneel Japans maal is veel meer dan eten; het is een ceremonie. Behalve een nadruk op evenwichtigheid en matiging, stellen de Japanse Algemene Voedingsregels ook dat "alle activiteiten die met voedsel en eten te maken hebben een bron van genoegen dienen te zijn".

Mediterrane gebied. Uit onderzoek van mediterrane volken is een verrassend laag cijfer van hartaandoeningen gebleken. Een typisch mediterraan dieet—zoals dat bijvoorbeeld in Zuid-Italië wordt gevonden—bestaat uit pasta, olijfolie, vruchten, groenten, brood en soms zeebanket. Over het algemeen eten mediterrane volken meer brood dan wij, en zijn peulvruchten een basisvoedsel. Zelfs het eenvoudigste mediterrane maal is een blije gebeurtenis die wordt gedeeld met familie en vrienden.

De rol van olijfolie in de mediterrane keuken is vaak belicht. Terwijl het waar is dat olijfolie, een enkelvoudig onverzadigd vet, te verkiezen is boven verzadigd en meervoudig onverzadigd vet, blijft olijfolie gewoon een vet. Wie een mediterraan dieet wil nadoen, moet geen olijfolie aan zijn voeding toevoegen, maar die gebruiken in plaats van de andere vetten die al worden gebruikt en doorgaan met de beperking van alle vet.

Mexico. Maïs, bonen, vis, kip en groenten zijn de pijlers waarop de traditionele Mexicaanse keuken rust. Het ook bij ons populair geworden Mexicaanse eten lijkt weinig op het authentieke. In de traditionele Mexicaanse keuken vormen maïs en bonen een onderdeel van elke maaltijd, waarmee complementaire eiwitten worden geleverd. De chilipepers en tomaten die zo kenmerkend voor Mexicaans eten zijn, zijn bronnen van anti-oxidante vitaminen A en C. Avocado's, het hart van guacamole, bevatten veel calorieën uit vet, maar het grootste deel van dat vet is enkelvoudig onverzadigd, en wordt daarom geacht voordelen voor de hartconditie op te leveren. Veel traditionele Mexicaanse schotels, waaronder tortilla's, worden in reuzel gebakken. Vervang reuzel door een minder zwaar vet, of bereid maïs- of bloemtortilla's met een andere methode dan bakken voor een hogere voedingswaarde.

Hiernaast: De Fransen hebben een vrij laag percentage hartaandoeningen, misschien omdat ze in een wat losser tempo van het leven genieten. Onder: In tegenstelling tot wat wel wordt beweerd, is voedsel op graanbasis als pasta niet dikmakend. In China hangen noedels te drogen aan bamboestokjes.

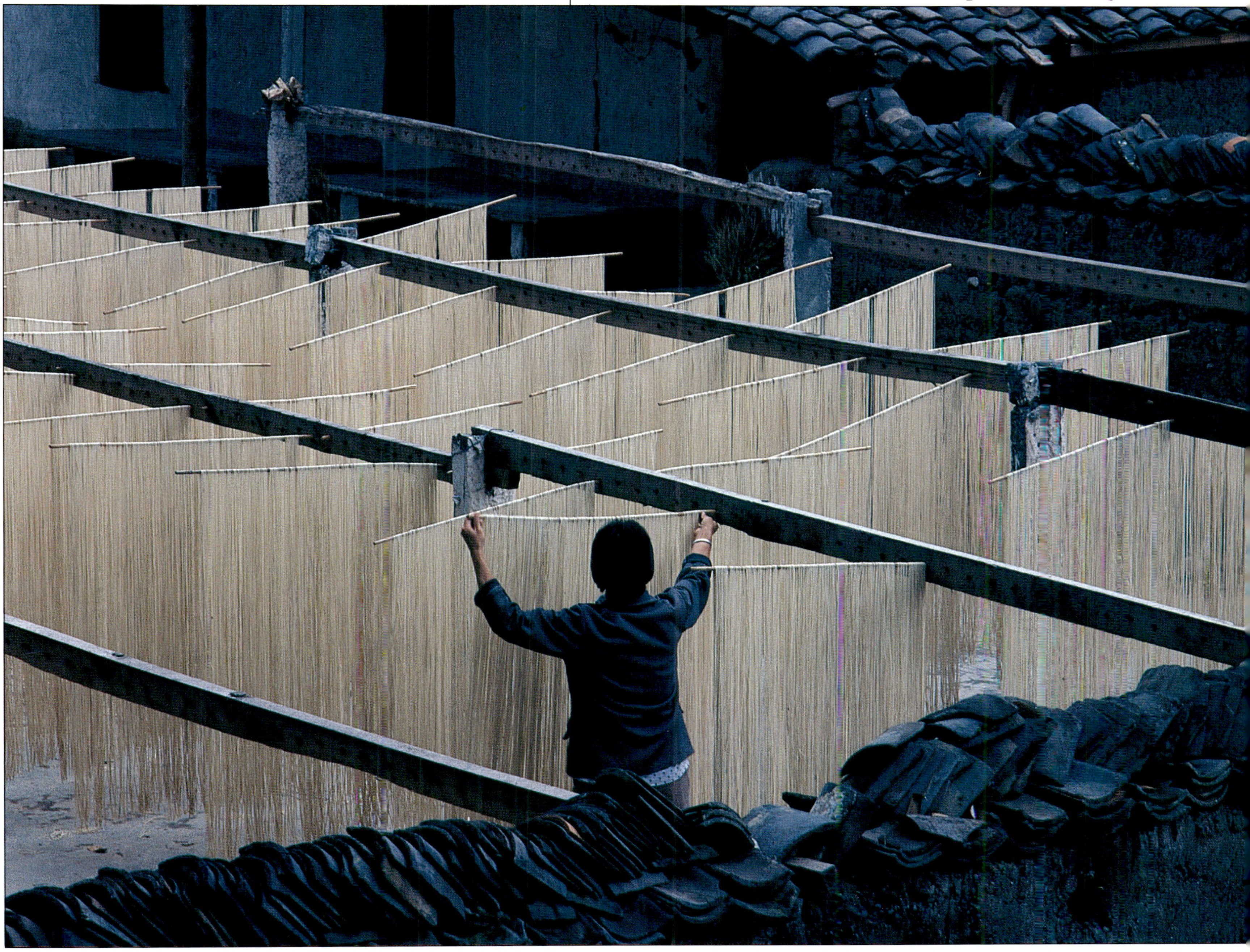

Maximale smaak

Zoals de schrijver Lionel Tiger ons voorhoudt in *The Pursuit of Pleasure*, is eten niet eenvoudig een kwestie van overleven. De Amerikaanse hoogleraar psychologie Mihaly Csikszentmihalyi heeft zelfs een onderzoek uitgevoerd naar het genoegen dat wordt beleefd aan enkele algemene, alledaagse bezigheden, waaronder koken. Csikszentmihalyi beweert dat veel koks het transformeren van rauwe ingrediënten tot maaltijden beschouwen als een soort "piek-ervaring" die orde en harmonie aan het alledaagse leven verschaft.

Hij betreurt het dat mensen die niet genoeg aandacht besteden aan wat zij eten een belangrijke bron van genoegen ontberen. Het vat krijgen op voedsel en het aankweken van smaak zijn investeringen die alle benodigde energie dubbel en dwars waard zijn. Bij het eten en koken verrijkt men de eigen belevingswereld door experimenten en avontuur.

HET TELT HOE U KOOKT

De in *De Vier Seizoenen* gebruikte bereidingswijzen spelen een belangrijke rol bij het omvormen van verse ingrediënten. Het zijn bijzonder simpele technieken, waarmee u voedsel gezond houdt en de basis legt voor een breed scala van smaken.

Stomen. Gestoomde gerechten worden zonder toegevoegd vet bereid, en stomen behoudt voedingsstoffen omdat geen deel van het voedsel direct in aanraking komt met water. Haal het eten onmiddellijk nadat het gaar is uit de stomer voor een optimale smaak. Een nadeel van gestoomd eten is soms de wat flauwe smaak. Geef niet toe aan de verleiding het te serveren met smaakvolle, vetrijke sausen. Gebruik in plaats daarvan kruiden en specerijen in het voedsel zelf en in het water.

Net gedopte erwten hoeven alleen maar heel kort te worden gestoomd om hun smaak ten volle prijs te geven.

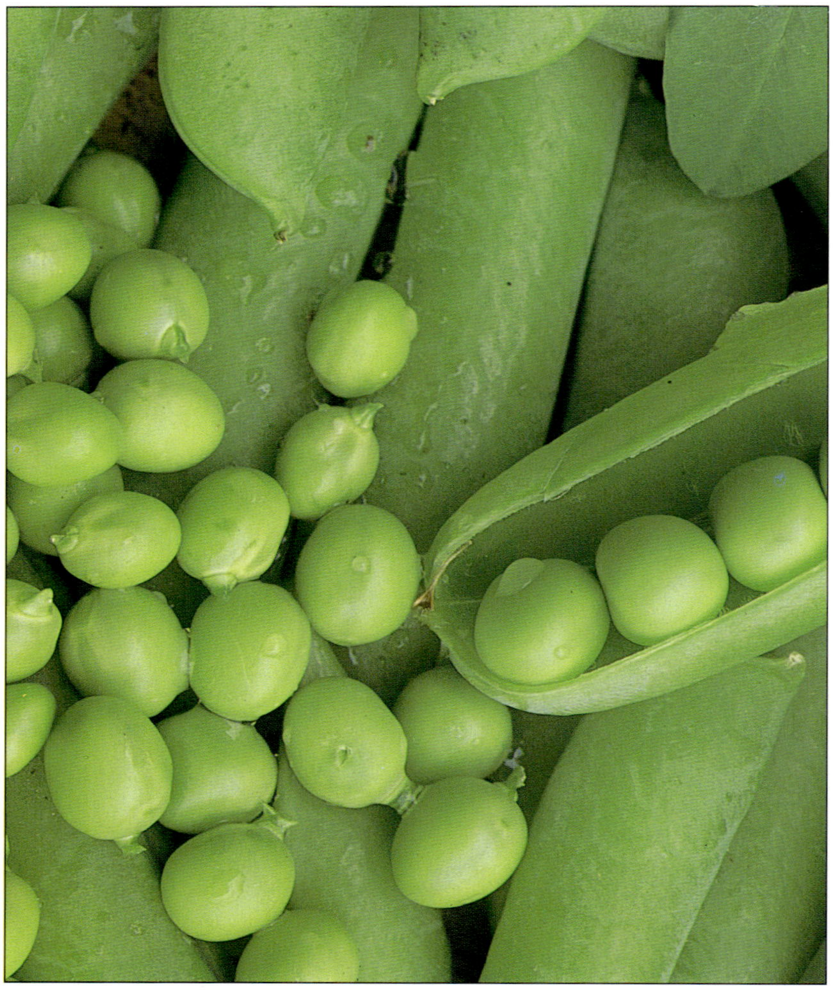

Grilleren. Zaagsel van hardhout en diverse kruiden als rozemarijn en tijm kunnen over de gloeiende kool worden gestrooid om een apart aroma aan gegrild voedsel te geven. Gedroogde kruiden moeten enkele minuten in water weken voor u ze over de houtskool strooit. Gebruik deze smaakgevers met mate; de natuurlijke smaak van het voedsel moet bewaard blijven.

Soms wordt voedsel gemarineerd voor het grilleren, zowel om het malser als om het smakelijker te maken. In *De Vier Seizoenen* worden enkele marinades op oliebasis gebruikt. Maakt u zich geen zorgen over de olie; deze wordt afgegoten en slechts een klein deel ervan wordt geconsumeerd. De voedingswaarde-analyses zijn overeenkomstig aangepast. U kunt ook olievrije marinades maken: gebruik als basis voor zulke marinades citrussap, wijn of azijn. U kunt deze marinades tijdens het grilleren over het voedsel borstelen.

Vlees, gevogelte, zeebanket, groenten en vruchten zijn zeer geschikt voor de grill. Enkele zaken moeten wellicht eerst worden voorgekookt voor ze boven de intense hitte worden afgebakken. (Zie pagina 45 voor tips betreffende marinades en grilleren.)

Braden. Bij braden wordt de ingesloten hitte van een oven voor het koken van eten gebruikt. Gebraden voedsel kan als het te gaar is droog en onappetijtelijk overkomen. Hierdoor komt men in de verleiding er zware sausen bij te geven. Als voedsel juist wordt gebraden en het vocht behouden blijft, heeft het geen vetrijke begeleiding nodig.

Hele vogels en vissen, grote stukken vlees en hele groenten noemt men meestal "gebraden", terwijl men bij visfilets, kleinere stukken vlees en gevogelte ook wel van "gebakken" spreekt—hoewel het proces in wezen identiek is. Als u gevogelte braadt met het vel ter behoud van de sappen, verwijder dan het vel voor het eten. U kunt ook wat vet aan vlees laten zitten voor vocht tijdens het braden, maar snijdt het eraf voor het opdienen. Vis- en kipfilets kunt u voor het braden door gekruid broodkruim halen. Deze deklaag helpt het vlees sappig houden.

Bakken. Van oudsher wordt gebakken voedsel bereid met olie boven een hoog vuur. Door gebruik van een anti-aanbak koekepan met een zeer kleine hoeveelheid olie kunt u het toegevoegde vet verminderen. Gehakte ui, knoflook en kruiden worden vaak gebakken voor ze aan een gerecht worden toegevoegd. Het roerbakken van fijngesneden groenten, vlees en gevogelte is eigenlijk bakken met extra omscheppen. Gebruik een anti-aanbak pan of wok en een geringe hoeveelheid kippebouillon, wijn of appelsap in plaats van vet.

Magnetron. Ideaal voor het behoud van kleur en voedingsstoffen van ingrediënten. De magnetron wordt nu in veel keukens in Nederland ge-

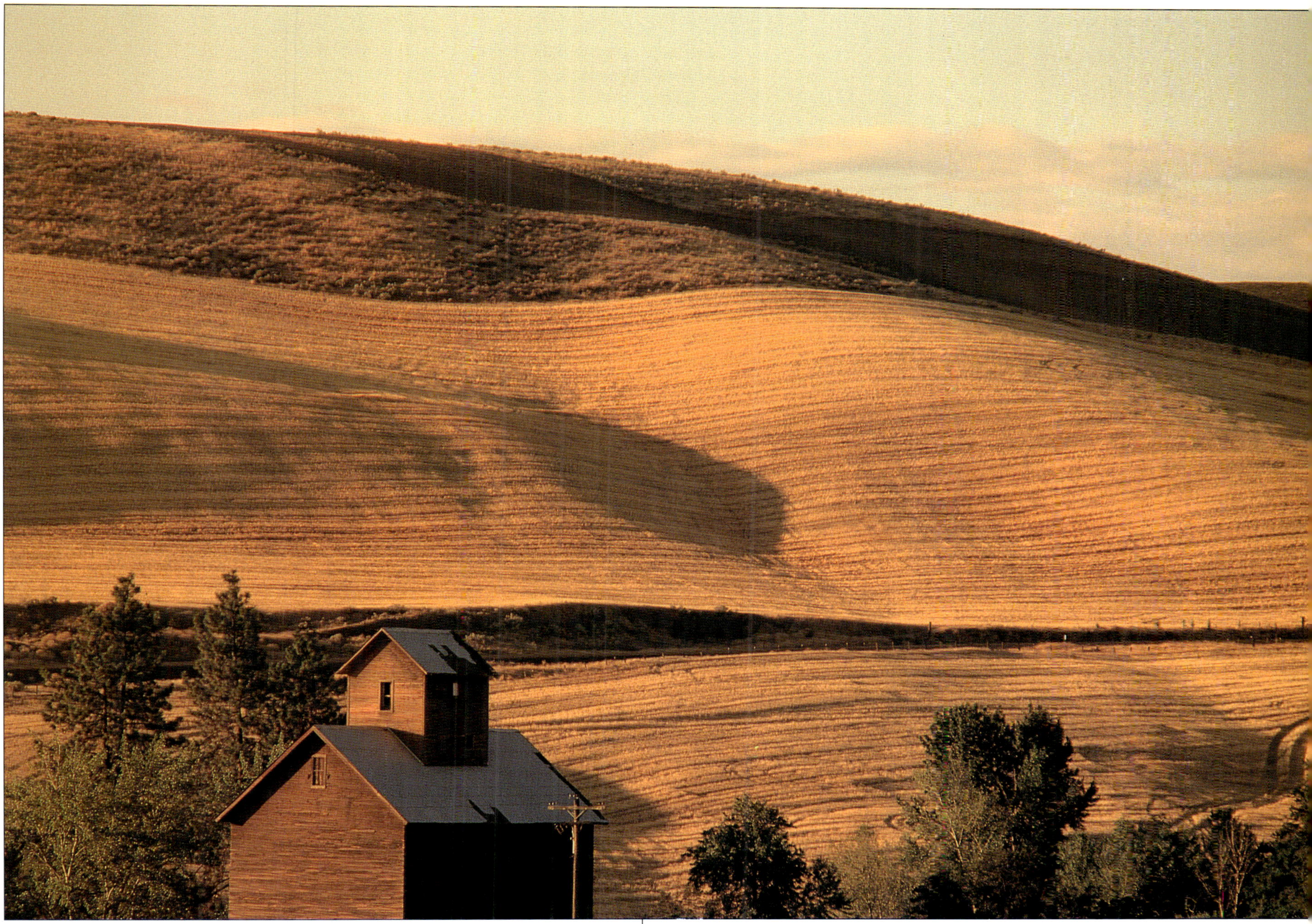

Bouwland bij Boyd in de Amerikaanse staat Oregon ademt een diepe rust.

bruikt. Bij het koken in de magnetron is geen extra vet nodig en wordt het kookproces zeer versneld.

Sommige verse groenten, zoals aardappels en pompoen, zijn uitstekende kandidaten voor de magnetron; andere, zoals sperziebonen en erwten, zijn niet zo geschikt. Van bessen maakt u in de magnetron in een wip de heerlijkste sausen.

Onthoud dat voedsel vaak ongelijkmatig kookt in de magnetron en dat u speciale schotels nodig heeft. Gebruik een magnetron-kookboek voor volledige aanwijzingen en volg nauwgezet alle instructies voor het afdekken, omroeren en draaien van schotels. (Zie pagina 45 voor meer informatie over veiligheid en de magnetron.)

EEN SMAAK VOOR ALLE SEIZOENEN

Door creatief gebruik te maken van kruiden en specerijen kunt u voor smaak zorgen bij vetarme bereidingswijzen. Hoewel de woorden *kruiden* en *specerijen* door elkaar worden gebruikt, zijn specerijen in feite afkomstig van bast, knoppen, wortels, zaden en stelen, en kruiden gewoonlijk van bladen.

Elk kruid of specerij heeft zijn karakteristieke smaak, en bepaalde combinaties zijn kenmerkend voor internationale keukens geworden. Dit betekent niet dat u op dit gebied niet meer creatief kunt zijn. Als u nieuwsgierig bent naar een onbekend vers kruid, ruik er dan aan. Kneus een blad of twee. Proef de kruiden en ruik en proef van tijdens het koken. Complementeren de smaken en aroma's elkaar? Voel u vrij om naar hartelust te experimenteren.

Gebruik bij het koken met gedroogde kruiden circa een derde van de hoeveelheid verse kruiden. Verpakte verse kruiden zijn tot aan een week in de koelkast houdbaar. Bosjes verse kruiden als peterselie kunt u in een plastic zak in de koelkast bewaren. Verpak de steeltjes eerst in vochtig papier of zet de steeltjes rechtop in wat water en dek ze van boven af met plastic folie. Was de kruiden pas kort voor gebruik.

Milde kruiden als basilicum, peterselie en dille zijn het meest smaakvol als u ze rauw of kort gekookt gebruikt en ze vlak voor het opdienen toevoegt. Sterkere kruiden als rozemarijn, laurier, salie en tijm worden voller van smaak door koken.

EEN NIEUWE KIJK OP SAUSEN

Als u denkt dat het woord *saus* een ander woord voor *vetrijk* is, hebt u het mis. De moderne sausen zijn vol van smaak op een andere manier. Inkoken, pureren, salsa's, op smaak gebrachte oliën en azijnen hebben van hollandaise en béarnaise oud nieuws gemaakt.

Bouillons en vruchtesappen kunnen langzaam worden ingekookt tot

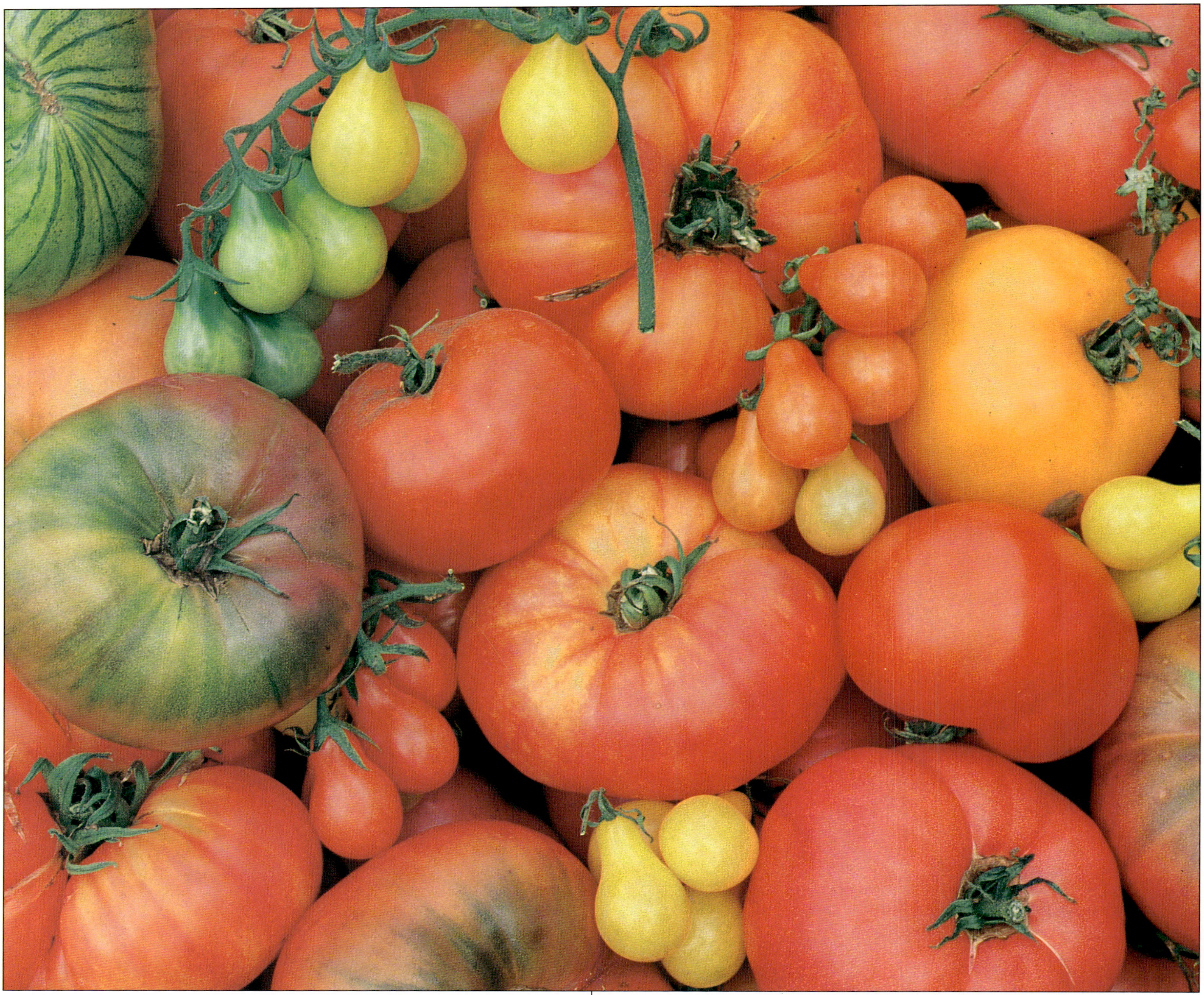

Sappige tomaten in een kleurenpalet van rood, groen, oranje en geel zingen de lof van de zomer. Met hun zoetheid zorgen ze voor een heerlijk accent in vetarme sausen en confituren.

een smaakvolle essence die robuust genoeg is om met mate toegepast fantastische resultaten te geven. In dit boek vindt u recepten voor uw eigen kippe-, vis- en groentebouillons (zie woordenlijst). Door uw eigen bouillon te maken hebt u controle over de smaak en het natriumniveau. Voeg voor een bijzondere en smakelijke saus gepureerde groenten of peulvruchten aan een ingekookte bouillon toe. Gebruik voor een "romige" saus vetvrij melkpoeder.

Kleurrijke relishes zijn een nieuwe manier om meer vruchten, groenten en peulvruchten in uw dagelijkse voeding op te nemen. Relishes hebben verschillende namen in verschillende culturen—bijvoorbeeld salsa's in Mexico, chutneys in India, sambals in Indonesië. Wat ze allemaal gemeen hebben is hun intense smaak, de gemakkelijke bereiding en hun flexibiliteit. Gebruik ze om pit te geven aan rijst en pasta, aan peulvruchten, gestoomde groenten maar bijvoorbeeld ook aan eenvoudige schotels met vlees, vis en gevogelte.

Relishes zijn al eeuwenlang een vast onderdeel van de keuken van veel culturen. Ze zijn gewoonlijk zeer gekruid, kunnen warm of koud zijn en qua textuur variëren van grof tot glad. Van oudsher hebben lokaal verkrijgbare ingrediënten een rol gespeeld in nu internationaal bekende relishes. De culinaire grenzen vervagen. Salsa's zijn niet langer uitsluitend afhankelijk van verse koriander, limoensap en chilipepers. Chutneys worden niet langer alleen bij kerrieschotels gegeven, en ook met sambals wordt geëxperimenteerd.

Aromatische oliën als sesam-, hazelnoot-, amandel- en walnootolie zijn veel intenser van smaak dan bijvoorbeeld plantaardige- of saffloerolie. Daarom kunt u met een beetje heel veel doen. Deze oliën zijn verfijnd en moeten in de koelkast worden bewaard. Een drupje balsamico azijn, *mirin* of op smaak gebrachte azijn over gestoomde groenten kan wonderen doen. Een geklopte vinaigrette over gekookte groenten en zeebanket kan in de plaats komen van een roomsaus, met beduidend minder vet maar wel meer smaak.

Snel en simpel

Tijd is een kostbaar goed. Met zoveel aanspraken op onze tijd gaan we er zuinig mee om en voelen ons schuldig als we tijd verdoen. De stuwende kracht achter de explosieve toename van kant-en-klaar eten in de afgelopen twee decennia is tijdsbesparing geweest. Hoewel enkele van deze produkten van nut kunnen zijn, hebben veel ervan alleen maar een generatie opgeleverd die niet eens weet hoe *smakelijk* zelf bereid eten van verse ingrediënten kan zijn.

Helaas hebben velen van ons niet de tijd om een alledaagse gezinsmaaltijd te bereiden, laat staan een diner, een zondagse brunch of een intiem etentje voor twee. Toch is het bereiden van een smakelijke en gezonde maaltijd van verse ingrediënten niet synoniem met een race tegen de klok om precies op tijd verscheidene tijdrovende schotels klaar te hebben. Investeer uw tijd bijvoorbeeld eens in een Toscaanse kip met rozemarijn (recept op pagina 120) of roodbaars in rode wijn (recept op pagina 189) en geef bij het hoofdgerecht een potpourri van gestoomde verse groenten met wat citroensap of een drupje azijn met wat verse vruchten. Geef wat vruchten en een stukje kaas als dessert.

Als u geen tijd voor bakken hebt, koop dan een vers meergranenbrood bij uw favoriete bakker en vergeet het besmeren met boter of margarine. Zelf gebakken brood is heerlijk als u het onversierd eet; ook voor een lunch maakt u er heerlijke sandwiches van. (Maak oudbakken brood op door er zelf melbatoost van te maken; snijd het brood in dunne sneden,

Wegwijzer voor internationale smaken

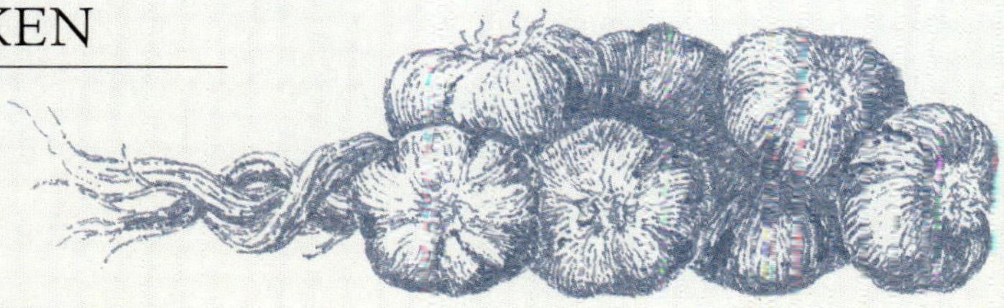

Keuken	*Smaakgevers*
Caribisch	Limoen, piment, gember, chilipeper, mosterdzaad, peper
Chinees	Verse gember, knoflook, steranijs, peper, sinaasappelschil, sojasaus, sesamzaad
Frans	Bieslook, dragon, kervel, peterselie, rozemarijn, tijm, venkel, basilicum, mosterd, zwarte peper, marjolein, munt
Grieks	Citroen, knoflook, rozemarijn, kaneel, paprika, ui, oregano
Indiaas	Chilipeper, geelwortel, komijn, fenegriek, tamarinde, mosterd, verse gember, koriander, kaneel, kruidnagel
Indonesisch	Pinda, limoen, verse gember, sesamzaad, ui, chilipeper, cayennepeper, koriander, nootmuskaat, kaneel
Italiaans	Knoflook, oregano, basilicum, rozemarijn, tijm, olijven
Japans	Verse gember, knoflook, mosterdpoeder, citroenschil, visbouillon (dashi), wasabi, sojasaus
Mexicaans	Komijn, oregano, knoflook, chilipeper, verse koriander, tamarillo (boomtomaat), ui
Marokkaans	Kardemom, foelie, piment, kruidnagel, verse gember, munt, zwarte peper, cayennepeper, koriander, komijn, ui
Noordafrikaans	Muntbladen, knoflook, sesamzaad, citroenschil, ui
Thais	Chilipeper, korianderzaad, kruidnagel, verse gember, citroengras

schik die op een bakblik en zet dat ongeveer 45 minuten in de oven op 135°C. Zo krijgt u een gezonde, brosse snack. Melbatoost met rozijnen of noten erin is net zo lekker en knapperig als een koekje.)

Wie liever tijd besteedt aan een graan- of groenteschotel dan aan een hoofdgerecht, kan een gegrilde kip erbij kopen. Geef voor extra smaak een relish of salsa bij de kip. Restjes kip kunt u in een lunchsalade of een hartige soep verwerken.

Als u een klein huishouden hebt, is de aanschaf van hele vruchten of groenten niet altijd praktisch, omdat het produkt kan bederven voor u het gebruikt. Gelukkig zijn er in supermarkten tegenwoordig verpakte gesneden groenten en vruchten verkrijgbaar die u kunt stomen, roerbakken of als snacks, desserts of relishes kunt gebruiken. In dergelijke supermarkt-afdelingen vindt u ook vers gesneden groenten als broccoli, bloemkool en wortel, en ook vruchten als meloen, ananas en sinaasappel. Deze produkten kunnen duur lijken, maar ze kosten niet meer dan weggegooide bedorven etenswaren wanneer u maar kleine hoeveelheden van diverse ingrediënten nodig hebt. En ze zijn hun geld meer dan waard als u denkt aan de smaak, variëteit, textuur, kleur en voedingsstoffen die ze aan uw maaltijden verlenen.

Voor sommige etnische schotels zijn speciale ingrediënten nodig die u in verband met tijdsbesparing in blik of diepgevroren koopt. Bevroren filodeeg is bijvoorbeeld even gemakkelijk in gebruik als veelzijdig. Kant-en-klare wontonvellen zijn in toko's verkrijgbaar. Ook ingemaakte druivebladeren zijn volop verkrijgbaar. Peulvruchten in blik zijn even rijk aan voedingsstoffen als gedroogde, geweekte bonen. Wie op de natrium-inname let, moet ze echter wel voor gebruik afspoelen. Bouillon in blik is vaak te zout; maak daarom altijd uw eigen bouillon en zoek in de woordenlijst op pagina 218 de recepten op.

Sommige vruchten en groenten in blik zijn verrassend voedzaam, maar kunnen wel veel natrium bevatten. Het etiket vertelt u hoeveel. Als u de inhoud van het blik laat uitlekken, wordt de hoeveelheid natrium drastisch verminderd.

Vergeet diepgevroren groenten niet. Door snel invriezen zijn sommige groenten "verser" dan voorraden buiten het seizoen. Kruisbloemige soorten, zoals broccoli, spruitjes en bloemkool, behouden na invriezen veel van hun smaak en textuur. Kies in het algemeen voor heel ingevroren groenten in plaats van gehakte.

Een makkelijke manier om een gezondheidsinjectie te geven aan enkele schotels die u vaak maakt, is door er wat verse vruchten of groenten aan toe te voegen. Meng voor meer kleur en knapperigheid verse druiven, blokjes appel, gehakte bleekselderij of rode paprika door uw kip- of tonijnsalade. Doe eens wat spinaziebladen op uw sandwiches en vul uw pastasausen en soepen aan met extra groenten. Als u een simpel hapje wilt, kies dan voor plakjes vers fruit. Probeer uw culinaire voorkeur eens te doorbreken door een flinke portie groenten of granen in het midden van uw bord te scheppen—de plaats die de meesten van ons gewoonlijk reserveren voor het vlees, de vis of het gevogelte.

Met vruchten en groenten kunt u een bord ook snel maar bovendien uiterst attractief garneren—tenslotte is het aanzicht een deel van het eetgenot. Groenten en fruit leveren kleur, vorm en dimensie zonder veel calorieën of vet toe te voegen.

Wat is in het seizoen?

VRUCHTEN

Hoe kunnen we ooit genoeg krijgen van rijp, sappig, zoet en heerlijk fruit met zo'n overvloedige keuze? Met zijn rijkdom aan vitaminen, mineralen en koolhydraten en als voorname bron van voedingsvezel staat fruit bovenaan wanneer het gaat om gezond en verrukkelijk eten.

De bewaartijd voor vruchten hangt af van de temperatuur, vochtigheid en rijpheid. Gebruik fruit liefst zo snel mogelijk.

Hoog scorende vruchtesoorten blijven bij ons appels, bananen, pitloze druiven en aardbeien.

GROENTEN

Een voortdurende oogst aan groenten verhoogt de smaak, textuur en schoonheid van ons dagelijks eten. Groenten zijn vetvrij, rijk aan vezel en belangrijke vitaminen en mineralen en doen dubbel dienst als gezonde en smakelijke voedselkeuzes.

De bewaartijd hangt af van de temperatuur en vochtigheid. Maar gebruik ook groenten het liefst zo snel mogelijk.

Als favoriete groentesoorten hebben wij sla, aardappels, wortels, tomaten en komkommer. Wees bij de aankoop van groenten selectief en flexibel. Kies voor de beste kwaliteit. Geniet van een variëteit aan groenten wanneer ze overvloedig verkrijgbaar zijn en optimaal van smaak en kwaliteit zijn.

FRUIT TABEL

SOORT	VERKRIJGBAAR	VERSHEID/KWALITEIT KENMERKEN	BEWAREN
Aardbeien	Vrijwel het gehele jaar (diverse produktielanden en kasteelt).	Stevige, droge egale rode vruchten met verse groene kroontjes; grote beïnvloedt smaak en kwaliteit niet; piepkleine bosaardbeitjes hebben een sterke smaak en geur.	Bewaar in de koelkast.
Abrikoos	Gehele jaar, top tussen juli en september	Gave schil, oranje kleur, sterke geur; smaak is het best wanneer de fruit rijp en zacht is	Op kamertemperatuur laten rijpen en dan in koelkast bewaren
Ananas	Gehele jaar (wisselende produktielanden).	Stevig, gaaf fruit met iets oranje kleur; wordt niet rijp na het plukken; vruchtvlees van rijpe ananassen is glanzend en nat.	Bewaar op kamertemperatuur wordt donker van kleur in koelkast; bewaar aangesneden fruit in koelkast, maar gebruik binnen 2 dagen.
Appel	Gehele jaar	Stevig, knapperig, gave, glanzende schil	In koelkast of op een koele, donkere beluchte plek
Atemoya	juni tot september	Groene schil wordt donker wanneer de fruit rijp is; rijp wanneer steeltje van de vrucht loskomt of wanneer vrucht meegeeft met zachte druk van de vingers.	Laat op kamertemperatuur rijpen en bewaar dan in de koelkast.
Avocado	Gehele jaar. Wisselende produktielanden.	Verschillende vormen, maten, kleuren en structuren; koop stevige vruchten; laat thuis rijpen; rijp wanneer vrucht meegeeft met zacht druk van de vingers.	Laat in papieren zak rijpen om donkere plekken te voorkomen en het rijpings-proces te versnellen; controleer dagelijks; bewaar nooit in de koelkast; mogelijk te pureren en dan invriezen.
Bakbananen	Gehele jaar.	Vruchten met groene schil zijn flauw en melig; vruchten met donkere schil zijn zoeter en romiger; wordt nooit rauw gegeten.	Laat op kamertemperatuur rijpen; bewaar nooit in de koelkast.
Bananen	Gehele jaar.	Heldere, gave schil, lichtgroen of lichtgeel; rijpen meestal binnen enkele dagen; verwerk overrijpe bananen met bruine vlekken in taarten en cake.	Laat op kamertemperatuur rijpen; bewaar nooit in de koelkast.
Bergbraambessen (cloudberries)	Zeldzaam. Uit Scandinavië	Stevige, droge, gele bessen.	Bewaar in de koelkast. Onmiddellijk gebruiken.
Bittersinaasappel of pomerans	November tot juli.	Dikke, zware stevige vrucht met oranje, gele of groenachtige schil.	Bewaar in de koelkast.
Blauwe bessen en bosbessen	Juli tot september.	Groot, droog sappig; mat, "bloemig" oppervlak geeft versheid aan; wilde bosbessen zijn zeer donker van kleur; gekweekte bessen wat lichter.	Bewaar in de koelkast.
Bloedsinaasappels	Januari tot maart.	Oranje of rode schil met rood vruchtvlees; stevig; zwaar in verhouding tot grootte.	Bewaar in de koelkast.
Bramen	Vrijwel het hele jaar, m.u.v. de wintermaanden.	Donkerzwart van kleur, droog en schoon; verwijder bramen die aan elkaar kleven en natte verpakking.	Bewaar in de koelkast.
Cactusvijg of woestijnvijg	Juli tot februari.	Stevig maar niet hard; rood of groenachtige fruit; diepe kleuren, niet verbleekt.	Laat op kamertemperatuur rijpen en bewaar dan in de koelkast.
Carambolas (stervrucht)	Juli tot september; december tot april (wisselende produktiegebieden)	Glazend geel wanneer rijp; randen kunnen bruin zijn; de schil is eetbaar.	Bewaar groene vruchten in een papieren zak op kamertemperatuur tot ze goudgeel en geurig zijn; bewaar dan in de koelkast.
Cherimoyas en custardappels	Gehele jaar (diverse produktielanden)	Rond, kakigroen, wat zacht.	Laat op kamertemperatuur rijpen; controleer dagelijks; bewaar rijpe vruchten in de koelkast.
Citroenen	Gehele jaar.	Dunne schil; stevig; zwaar voor de grootte.	Bewaar tot 4 weken in de koelkast.
Cranberry's	Oktober tot april.	Zeer stevige, droge, donkere glimmende bessen.	Bewaar tot 3 weken in de koelkast of vries ze in.
Dadels	Gehele jaar.	Dikke vruchten met een glimmende schil.	Tot 2 weken in de koelkast bewaren.
Druiven	Gehele jaar (diverse landen).	Stevige, dikke, droge vruchten; hele verse exemplaren hebben "bloem"; zoek gele kleur bij witte druiven en diepe kleuren in rode of blauwe rassen.	Bewaar in de koelkast.
Feijoas	Gehele jaar.	Geurige vruchten; Voelt aan als een stevige pruim wanneer hij rijp is.	Laat in een papieren zak op kamertemperatuur rijpen; bewaar dan in de koelkast.
Frambozen	Juni tot augustus.	Stevig, droog, mooie kleur; verwijder bakjes die nat zijn.	Bewaar tot 2 dagen in de koelkast.
Grapefruits	Gehele jaar.	Stevige gave schil; hoe roder de kleur van het vruchtvlees hoe zoeter.	Bewaar tot 2 weken op kamertemperatuur. Mogelijk in de koelkast te bewaren.
Guaves	Gehele jaar (diverse produktielanden).	Gele, malse vruchten met sterke geur.	Laat op kamertemperatuur rijpen tot de vrucht iets meegeeft wanneer u hem zachtjes indrukt. Controleer dagelijks en bewaar dan tot 1 dag in de koelkast.
Honingmeloenen	Augustus tot april.	Gave, geurige, roomkleurige schil, fluweelachtig maar niet zacht; sproetjes betekenen een hoog suiker-gehalte; bloesemeindpunt geeft mee als u zachtjes indrukt wanneer ze rijp zijn.	Bewaar in de koelkast.
Kantaloepmeloenen	Maart tot oktober.	Stevige, gave vruchten met een lichtgele schil.	Laat op kamertemperatuur rijpen en bewaar dan in de koelkast
Kersen	Eind mei tot eind september (diverse produktielanden).	Ronde stevige vrucht met groene steeltjes. De kleur varieert afhankelijk van het ras. Verwijder kersen die plakkerig of nat zijn.	Bewaar in de koelkast.
Kiwi's	Gehele jaar.	Dikke, stevige gave vrucht.	Laat op kamertemperatuur rijpen; bewaar dan in de koelkast.

SOORT	VERKRIJGBAAR	VERSHEID/KWALITEIT KENMERKEN	BEWAREN
Kruisbessen	Juni en juli.	Groene of rode, stevige druifachtige bessen. Wrang.	Bewaar tot 2 weken in de koelkast.
Kumquats	Gehele jaar (diverse produktielanden).	Oranje, gave schil; zware, heldere glanzende vrucht; wrang; eetbare schil.	Bewaar een aantal weken in de koelkast.
Kweeperen	Juli tot april.	Schil is geel en glad wanneer rijp; zeer geurig; nooit rauw geserveerd; altijd gekookt en gezoet.	Bewaar tot een aantal maanden op een koele, donkere plek.
Limoenen	Gehele jaar (diverse produktielanden).	Donkergroene kleur; dunne schil; zwaar voor de grootte.	Tot 4 weken houdbaar in de koelkast.
Lychees	November tot maart en juli/augustus (diverse produktielanden).	Strakke schil, met steeltjes; schil van bruin tot bruingeel.	Aantal weken houdbaar in de koelkast.
Mandarijnen	Gehele jaar; topaanvoer tussen oktober en maart.	Stevig, heldere kleur, dunne schil.	Bewaar op kamertemperatuur of in de koelkast.
Mango's	Gehele jaar (wisselende produktielanden)	Stevige, gave schil. Kleur afhankelijk van soort; moet volledig rijp zijn voor het eten.	Laat op kamertemperatuur rijpen; bewaar dan in de koelkast.
Nectarines of nectarijnen	Gehele jaar met een top tussen juli en september.	Mooie kleur, gave middelgrote tot grote vrucht.	Laat op kamertemperatuur rijpen; bewaar dan in de koelkast.
Ogenmeloenen	April tot januari.	Stevige, gave vruchten met een groengele schil.	Laat op kamertemperatuur rijpen en bewaar dan in de koelkast.
Papaja's	Gehele jaar (diverse produktielanden).	Mooie kleur; schil minstens halfgeel wanneer eetbaar.	Laat op kamertemperatuur rijpen; bewaar dan in de koelkast.
Passievruchten	Gehele jaar (diverse produktielanden).	Paars, geel of rood met stevige schil; vruchtvlees is zacht met kleine pitten.	Laat op kamertemperatuur rijpen tot de schil iets rimpelt; bewaar dan in de koelkast.
Peren	Gehele jaar (diverse produktiegebieden).	Stevige, gave vrucht; wordt zachter wanneer rijp.	Laat op kamertemperatuur rijpen en bewaar dan in de koelkast.
Persimoenen (kaki)	Gehele jaar (diverse produktielanden)	Stevige, gave vrucht; kleur, grootte en vorm verschillen per ras.	Laat op kamertemperatuur rijpen tot ze zeer zacht zijn; bewaar dan in de koelkast.
Perziken	Gehele jaar met top tussen juli en september.	Stevig, mooie kleur, gave schil. Wordt zachter wanneer rijp.	Laat op kamertemperatuur rijpen en bewaar dan in de koelkast.
Pruimen	Gehele jaar (diverse produktielanden).	Mooie kleuren met gave, glanzende schil; vele soorten, kleuren en smaken.	Laat op kamertemperatuur rijpen en bewaar dan in de koelkast.
Rabarber	Geforceerde rabarber van december tot maart, vollegrondrabarber van eind maart tot september.	Stevige stengels; mooie rood of roze; wrange smaak; altijd gekookt en gezoet; eigenlijk een groentesoort maat als een fruit gebruikt. Bladen giftig; weggooien.	Bewaar in de koelkast; ingevroren rabarber is bijzonder lekker.
Rode bessen	Juni tot augustus.	Stevige doorschijnende helderrode bessen.	Tot zes dagen in de koelkast.
Sapote of spodilla of sawo	Gehele jaar (sporadisch).	Stevige gave vrucht; zo zacht als een rijpe pruim wanneer rijp.	Laat op kamertemperatuur en bewaar dan in de koelkast maar gebruik snel; kan heel ingevroren worden.
Sinaasappels	Gehele jaar (diverse gebieden).	Dunne schil. Zwaar in verhouding van grote; stevig; kleur is afhankelijk van ras en type.	Bewaar op kamertemperatuur of in koelkast.
Tamarillos of boomtomaten	Vrijwel het gehele jaar (diverse produktielanden).	Glanzende, eivormige vruchten.	Laat op kamertemperatuur rijpen en bewaar dan in de koelkast.
Tangerine = manderijn	Februari tot juni.	Groene, tamelijke los zittend schil met een oranje kleur wanneer die rijp is; verwijder geschrompelde of bruine vruchten.	Bewaar in de koelkast.
Vijgen	April tot januari.	Lichte en donkere rassen ruiken fris. Gave huid en zachte vruchtvlees.	Bewaar in de koelkast; eet binnen 2 dagen.
Watermeloenen	Gehele jaar, echter minder in de wintermaanden.	Stevige, donkere schil; moeilijk te weten als die rijp is dus best om aangesneden watermeloen te kopen.	Bewaar aangesneden watermeloen in de koelkast; hele vruchten op kamertemperatuur.

Groente tabel

SOORT	VERKRIJGBAAR	VERSHEID/KWALITEIT KENMERKEN	BEWAREN
Aardappels: witte, rode, gele	Gehele jaar.	Stevige, droge, gave knollen zonder donkere plekken.	Bewaar nieuwe aardappel in de koelkast; bewaar oudere aardappels op een koele, donkere, droge plek.
Aardpeer	Oktober tot maart.	Stevige, lichtkleurige knollen; jonge knollen hoeven niet geschild te worden; aangesneden stukken verkleuren; houd op kleur met citroensap met water.	Bewaar in de koelkast.
Amso	Vrijwel het gehele jaar.	Jonge, groene, knapperige, ruw aanvoelende bladen.	Wikkel in folie en bewaar in de koelkast.
Andijvie	Glasandijvie van november tot juni; vollegrondsandijvie van mei tot december. Ook import uit zuidelijker landen.	Bittere donkergroene bladen. Stamppot of rauw verwerkt in saladen.	Wikkel in folie en bewaar in de koelkast.
Artisjokken	Juli tot novenber.	Stevige, strakke, verse olijfgroene bladen; grootte niet een kwaliteits factor; beste exemplaren zwaar voor de grootte.	Bewaar in de koelkast.
Asperges (wit en groen)	April tot eind juni (import het gehele jaar).	Blanke of groene stengels van gelijke lengte met een goed gesloten kop.	Wikkel in een vochtige theedoek en bewaar tot 2 dagen in de koelkast.
Aubergine	Gehele jaar.	Stevige, gave, glimmende zwarte schil met groene stengel. Middelgrote zijn vaak de lekkerste; eet alleen gekookt; Japanse ras is klein en langwerpig.	Bewaar in de koelkast.
Bieten	Gehele jaar.	Stevige, gladde, donkerrode knollen; de echt verse hebben het loof nog; kleine tot middelgrote zijn de malste.	Bewaar in de koelkast.

SOORT	VERKRIJGBAAR	VERSHEID/KWALITEIT KENMERKEN	BEWAREN
Bietenloof	Mei tot juli.	Jonge, groene, knapperige bladen.	Wikkel in folie en bewaar een paar dagen in de koelkast.
Bindsla (Romeinse sla)	Gehele jaar.	Langwerpige, smalle knapperige bladen.	Wikkel in folie en bewaar in de koelkast; was pas voor het gebruik.
Bleekselderij	Gehele jaar.	Knapperige, gave stengels.	Bewaar tot 2 weken in de koelkast.
Bloemkool	Gehele jaar.	Zware, compacte kool; geen bruine vlekken; groene bladen.	Bewaar in de koelkast.
Boerenkool	September tot maart.	Stevige, licht- of donkergroene bladen, afhankelijk van het ras.	Wikkel in folie en bewaar in de koolkast; was pas voor het gebruik.
Bos- en waspeen	Gehele jaar.	Kleine of middelgrote, mooie oranje, stevige wortel. Bospeen heeft loof. Het loof is niet eetbaar.	Verwijder het loof, wikkel in folie en bewaar in koelkast.
Broccoli	Gehele jaar.	Stevige, compacte, heldergroene bloemknoppen.	Bewaar in de koelkast.
Cassave	Gehele jaar.	Met bast bedekte wortels die fris ruiken; geen barsten of donkere plekken.	Onmiddellijk gebruiken of schillen, onder water zetten en tot 1 dag bewaren. Kan ook geschild, in stukken worden ingevroren.
Champignons (witte, kastanje, grot, Champignon de Paris)	Gehele jaar.	Droog en stevig; niet gerimpeld en zonder donkere plekken.	Wikkel losjes in papier en bewaar tot 2 dagen in de koelkast.
Chayote	Moeilijk verkrijgbaar.	Stevige, gave schil; kleine zijn malser.	Bewaar in de koelkast.
Chilipepers: Cayennepepers, Spaanse pepers, Madame Jeanette	Gehele jaar.	Dikke, knapperige, glimmende en gave vrucht.	Bewaar in een papieren zak tot 2 weken in de koelkast; mogelijk in te vriezen.
Chinese broccoli (broccolirabe, rapini)	Gehele jaar, moeilijk verkrijgbaar.	Verse groene stevige stengels met losse knoppen en kleine bladen.	Bewaar in de koelkast.
Courgette	Gehele jaar.	Groene kleur; zonder donkere plekken; stevig; kleinere exemplaren met kleine zaadjes hebben de meeste smaak; courgettebloesem is een delicatesse.	Bewaar in de koelkast; gebruik bloesem onmiddellijk.
Doperwten	Januari tot oktober.	Dikke, bolle peulen; steeltje vers en groen.	Bewaar tot 2 dagen in de koelkast.
Gemberwortel	Gehele jaar.	Niet geschrompelde, stevige wortel; kleine scheuten hebben meer smaak dan grote.	Bewaar tot 2 weken in de koelkast.
IJsbergsla	Maart tot december.	Stevige, knapperige, vaste krop.	Bewaar in de koelkast.
Jícama (yamboon)	Moeilijk verkrijgbaar.	Lichtbruine knol met gave, dunne schil.	Bewaar hele knollen tot 1 of meer weken in de koelkast; wikkel aangesneden knollen in folie.
Kardoen	September tot november.	Stevige rechte stengels; buitenste bladstelen worden meestal verwijderd.	Bewaar in de koelkast.
Knoflook	Gehele jaar.	Stevige, droge, niet uitgelopen bollen.	Bewaar op een koele, droge plek.
Knolselderij	Juli en augustus kleine, jonge knollen met veel blad, vanaf september tot mei grote knollen met of zonder een pruike blad.	Stevige, droge knollen; loof niet eetbaar.	Bewaar tot een maand in de koelkast.
Knolvenkel	Vrijwel het gehele jaar.	Middelgroot tot groot; frisse groene blaadjes en een gave witte knol.	Bewaar in de koelkast.
Komkommer	Gehele jaar.	Heldere, gladde schil, donker groen.	Bewaar in de koelkast.
Kool: rode, witte, Savooie, Chinese	Gehele jaar.	Stevige, zware, gesloten, vaste kroppen.	Bewaar tot 2 weken in de koelkast.
Koolraap	September tot mei.	Harde, hoogronde rapen.	Bewaar op een koele, droge, donkere plek. Verwijder eventuele bladen voor het bewaren.
Koolrabi	Maart tot november in afnemende hoeveelheden.	Paars of groene kleine tot middelgrote knollen.	Bewaar knollen tot 1 week in de koelkast, loof tot 3 dagen.
Kropsla	Vollegrondsla: mei tot november; glassla: oktober tot juni	Kleine kroppen met malse mooie groene of rode bladen.	Wikkel in folie en bewaar in de koelkast; was voor het gebruik, niet voor het bewaren.
Krulandijvie	Gehele jaar.	Donkergroene buitenbladen met een knapperig geel hartje.	Wikkel in folie en bewaar in de koelkast.
Lenteuitjes	Gehele jaar.	Donkergroene bladen, heldere, witte bollen.	Wikkel in folie en bewaar in de koelkast.
Limabonen	Droge bonen het gehele jaar; verse peulen zelden.	Platte, niervormige, dikke groene viltige peulen; groene boontjes hebben betere smaak dan gele of witte.	Bewaar in de koelkast.
Maïs	Vrijwel gehele jaar (diverse produktielanden).	Vers geplukte kolven, liefst met blad, sappige gladde korrels; verwijder verschrompelde, harde korrels.	Bewaar in de koelkast; eet zo gauw mogelijk na het plukken; verliest zoetigheid tijdens het bewaren.
Meiknol of meiraap	April tot november; in de winter import zonder blad.	Gladde, ronde knollen met purpere kop; stevig; zwaar in verhouding tot grootte; kleine exemplaren zijn het lekkerst.	Bewaar op een koele, donkere, droge plek.
Mierikswortel	Late herfst en winter.	Een smalle, ronde punt en een dikker knoestig eind; stevig met geenbruine of zachte plekken.	Bewaar in de koelkast.
Morieljes (verse)	Sporadisch.	Donkerbruine, kegelvormige, holle paddestoelen; vers uitziend, droog.	Bewaar in de koelkast. Gebruik binnen 1 dag.
Nopales (cactusschijven)	Verse moeilijk verkrijgbaar; verkrijgbaar in blik.	Verse: kleine, stevige schijven; verwijder de uitsteeksels met de stekels, de dikke onderkant en randen.	Wikkel in folie en bewaar 2 weken of langer in de koelkast.
Okra	Gehele jaar.	Vingerlange, vezelige doosvruchten.	Bewaar in de koelkast.

SOORT	VERKRIJGBAAR	VERSHEID/KWALITEIT KENMERKEN	BEWAREN
Paddestoelen, wilde en gekweekte; boleten, cantharellen, enoki, matsutake, oesterzwammen, shiitake, stro, trompettes des morts, wolkenoren	Gehele jaar; sporadisch.	Droog, stevig; verwijder vochtige exemplaren en exemplarenmet donkere plakken.	Wikkel losjes in papier en bewaar in de koelkast; gebruik binnen 2 dagen.
Paprika's	Gehele jaar.	Diepe heldere kleur; stevig, glad.	Wikkel in folie en bewaar in de koelkast.
Pastinaak	November tot mei.	Stevige, harde, gave, romige schil; middelgrote maat het lekkerst.	Verwijder het loof en bewaar dan in de koelkast.
Patisson	Juli tot oktober.	Wit, lichtgroen of geel van kleur, afhankelijk van het ras; kleine hebben meer smaak en zijn malser.	Bewaar in de koelkast.
Peultjes	December tot mei import, juni tot september uit eigen land en Frankrijk.	Heldere, knapperige peulen zonder donkere plekken.	Bewaar in de koelkast; gebruik binnen 2 dagen.
Pompoenen	Gehele jaar (import uit 15 landen).	Stevige, gladde of geribbelde schil, geel, groen of oranje.	Bewaar op een koele, droge plek tot 3 maanden.
Prei	Gehele jaar met een top in de herfst.	Frisse groene bladen en stevige witte schacht.	Wikkel in folie en bewaar in de koelkast.
Radijs: rode en Daikon	Radijs, maart tot augustus; daikon, het gehele jaar.	Stevig, knapperig, gaaf gewas; verse hebben nog het loof; daikons zijn grote witte pegelachtige wortels.	Verwijder het loof; bewaar dan in de koelkast.
Raketkruid (aragula, rucola, notensla)	Gehele jaar.	Frisse groene kleur.	Wikkel in folie en bewaar in koelkast
Roodlof of radicchio en rode witlof	Herfst en winter.	Frisse, rode, knapperige bladen.	Wikkel in folie en bewaar in de koelkast.
Schorseneer	Oktober tot april.	Middelgrote wortel.	Wikkel in folie en bewaar tot 2 weken in de koelkast.
Sjalotjes	Het gehele jaar.	Droge, bruinachtige schil; stevig, zonder donkere plekken en groene spruiten.	Bewaar op een koele, droge, donkere plek.
Snijbiet	Juni tot oktober.	Knapperige groene bladen.	Wikkel in folie en bewaar in de koelkast; gebruik binnen 2 dagen.
Spaghettipompoen	In beperkte mate tussen augustus en december.	Stevige, gave, kleine exemplaren zijn de lekkerste.	Bewaar op en koele, droge plek.
Sperziebonen, haricots verts, kouseband, boterbonen (gele sperziebonen)	Gehele jaar (diverse produktielanden)	Buigbaar maar knapperig, gave peulen.	Bewaar in de koelkast.
Spinazie	Gehele jaar.	Knapperige, donker groene bladen.	Wikkel in folie en bewaar in de koelkast.
Spruit- of kiemgroenten: taugé, alfalfa, enzovoort	Gehele jaar.	Frisse mooie kleur.	Bewaar in koelkast en gebruik binnen een paar dagen.
Spruitjes	Augustus tot maart.	Kleine, stevige, groene, compacte kooltjes.	Bewaar in de koelkast.
Struisveervaren	April tot juni.	Verse jonge scheuten van de struisveervaren. Moeilijk verkrijgbaar; soms ingevroren of ingemaakt in potjes.	Bewaar verse onafgespoeld in de koelkast; gebruik binnen 1 dag.
Tamarillo of boomtomaat	Sporadisch.	Stevig; droog; heldere kleur met gaaf schutblad.	Bewaar tot 1 maand in de koelkast.
Tomaten: rode, gele, pruim, vlees, tros, kers	Gehele jaar. Hoogtepunt juli tot augustus.	Gladde, heldere, gave, stevige vruchten; aan de tros gerijpte tomanten zijn het lekkerst; "geforceerde" tomaten met etheengas gerijpt; genetische gemanipuleerde tomaten hebben een verlengde houdbaarheidsperiode.	Bewaar nooit in de koelkast; bewaar op kamertemperatuur. Eet wanneer ze nog stevig zijn maar wel meegeven als u er zachtjes indrukt.
Tuinbonen	April tot juni.	Lichtgroene, grote viltige peulen; Bonen eetbaar alleen als je jong zijn; sommige mensen zijn er allergisch voor.	Bewaar in de koelkast; gebruik binnen 2 dagen.
Waterkastanjes	Sporadisch.	Zeer harde, ongerimpelde wortelstokken zonder zachte plekken.	Wikkel in folie en bewaar in de koelkast.
Waterkers	Gehele jaar.	Donkergroene, frisse bladen; stevige steeltjes.	Wikkel in folie en bewaar in de koelkast.
Witlof	Gehele jaar; laagtepunt in de zomermaanden; ruimste aanbod tussen oktober en mei.	Stevige, knapperige gave helderwitte kropjes zonder gele punten.	Wikkel in folie en bewaar in de koelkast.
Zoete aardappels	Vrijwel het gehele jaar.	Stevige, middelgrote wortels, zonder donkere plekken.	Bewaar tot 4 weken op een koele, donkere, droge plek; bewaar niet in de koelkast, anders worden ze zwart.
Zuring	April tot november.	13 cm of minder lang; heldere, knapperige, groene blaadjes.	Wikkel in folie en bewaar in de koelkast.

De voedingswaarde-analyse van *Vier Seizoenen* recepten

Bij elk recept in *De Vier Seizoenen* staat een analyse van de voedingsstoffen: calorieën, eiwit, koolhydraten, vezel, vet totaal, soorten vet (verzadigd, meervoudig onverzadigd en enkelvoudig onverzadigd), cholesterol en natrium. Deze waarden vertellen u niet alleen welke voedingsstoffen in het voedsel zitten, maar stellen u ook in staat de recepten te vergelijken met de etiketten van soortgelijke voedingswaren. Bovendien staat aangegeven welke recepten uitstekende bronnen zijn (20 procent of meer van de Dagelijkse Waarde) van ijzer, kalk, vitamine A en C. Hoeveelheden vitamine worden aangegeven in procenten van de dagelijkse behoefte eraan. De cijfers zijn afgerond. Een caloriewaarde boven 50 wordt op het dichtstbijzijnde tiental afgerond.

Soms wordt vet totaal aangegeven in minder grammen dan de *gecombineerde* som van verzadigde, meervoudig onverzadigde en enkelvoudig onverzadigde vetten. Deze afwijking ontstaat om dat we grammen vet afronden op het meest nabije volle cijfer (of de volgende 0,5 gram als het onder de 5 gram is). Bovendien zijn enkele moleculaire vetconfiguraties (aantallen koolstof-atomen in de chemische keten) *niet* opgenomen in de verzadigde-onverzadigde waarden, maar wel in het *totaal*.

Het belangrijkste is dat u op een dagelijkse basis het *totale* vet beperkt en begrijpt dat de verzadigde vetten het meeste risico voor de gezondheid inhouden. Maximaal 30 procent van de totale vetten (of 10 procent van de totale calorieën) mag uit verzadigde vetten komen. De opsplitsing van vet bij elk recept laat u de verhouding van elke soort vet zien.

De Voedselpiramide-informatie bij elk recept (weergegeven door een piramide-ikoontje onder de voedingswaarde-informatie voor elk recept) laat zien hoe dat recept bijdraagt aan het voldoen aan de dagelijks aanbevolen porties. Soms levert een recept porties uit meer dan één voedselgroep. Soms levert de gespecifieerde portie 2 porties uit één voedselgroep. Zo levert 125 gram graan 2 porties van de 6-11 aanbevolen porties per dag, omdat een standaardportie gekookt graan in de Voedselpiramide 60 gram is. Met een grotere portie zult u uw dagelijkse totalen makkelijker behalen.

In veel recepten zit een kleine hoeveelheid, maar geen volle portie, vrucht, groente, melk, olie of ander voedsel. In deze gevallen hebben we *niet* aanbevolen dat voedsel bij de dagelijkse voedselgroep-totalen te tellen. De voedingsstoffen uit deze voedselsoorten zijn natuurlijk wel opgenomen in de begeleidende informatie over de voedingswaarde. Waar recepten een ingrediënt als optioneel vermelden, is dat ingrediënt *niet* in de analyse van de voedingswaarde opgenomen.

Als recepten zeggen “zout en peper naar smaak” hebben we geen zout of peper in de berekende waarden opgenomen. Als u zout toevoegt, bevat elke theelepel gewoon zout 2300 mg natrium en bij grof zeezout 1800 mg natrium. Het toevoegen van peper is evenwel niet van invloed op de voedingswaarde.

Het aantal porties is gebaseerd op een door de receptenschrijfster gesuggereerde grootte. De voedingswaardeberekening is op die portie gebaseerd, maar u kunt natuurlijk meer of minder eten. Reken bij het plannen van maaltijden op 1½ tot 2 porties voor flinke eters.

Voor sommige recepten is kippe-, vis- of groentebouillon nodig. De recepten daarvoor vindt u in de woordenlijst.

Elk seizoen biedt nieuwe smaaksensaties; verse bosbessen zijn een mooi voorbeeld van de rijke oogst van de nazomer

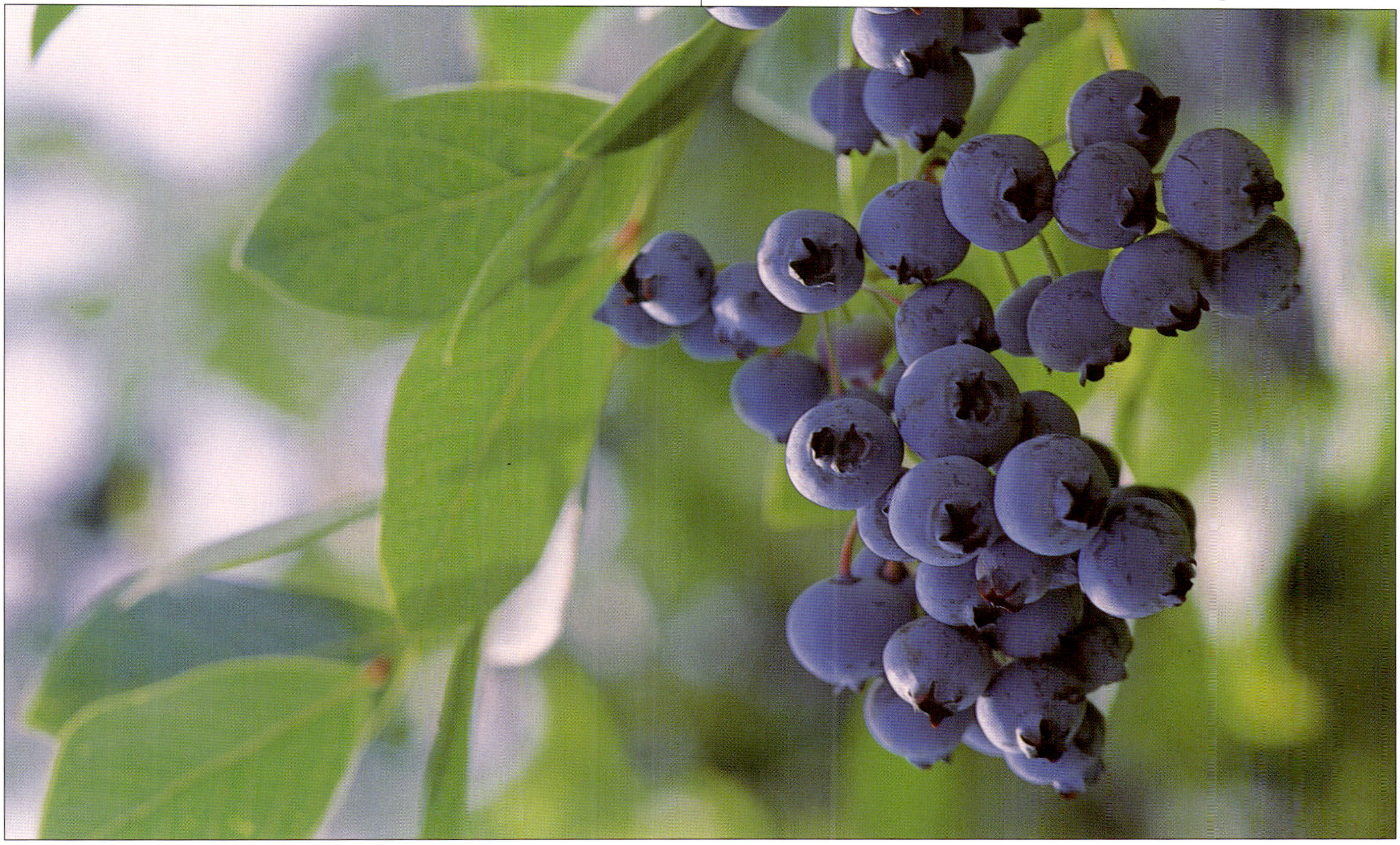

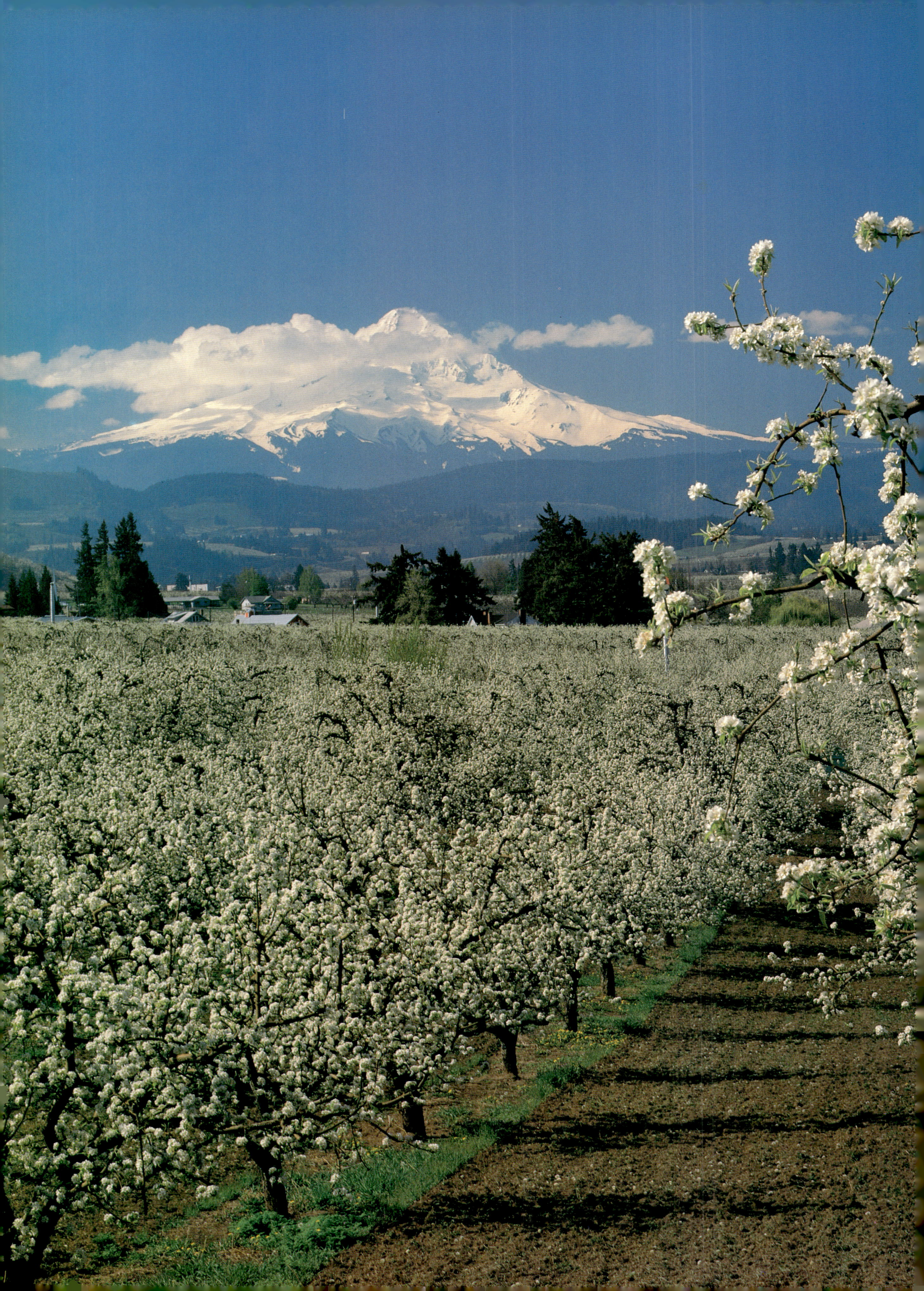

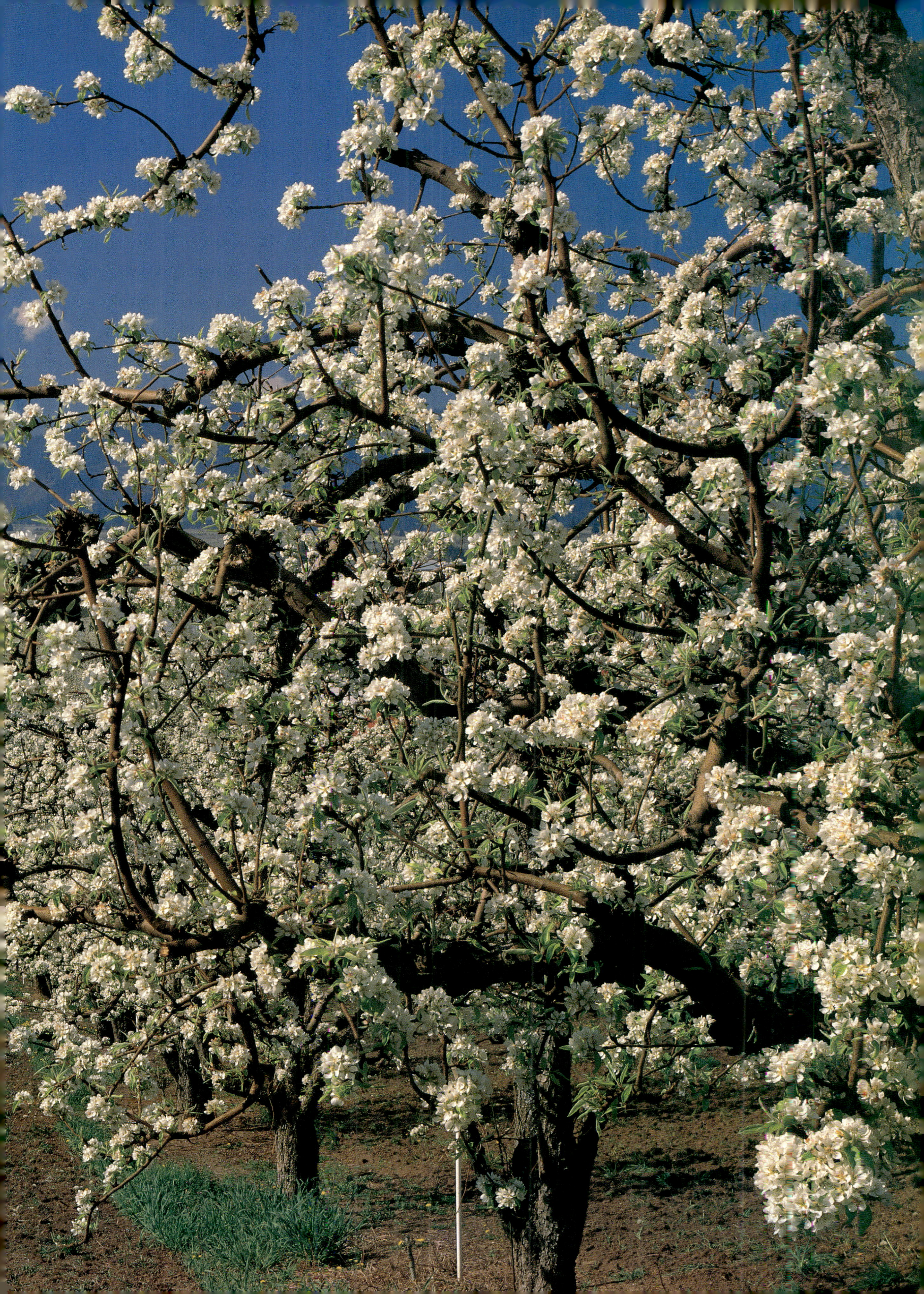

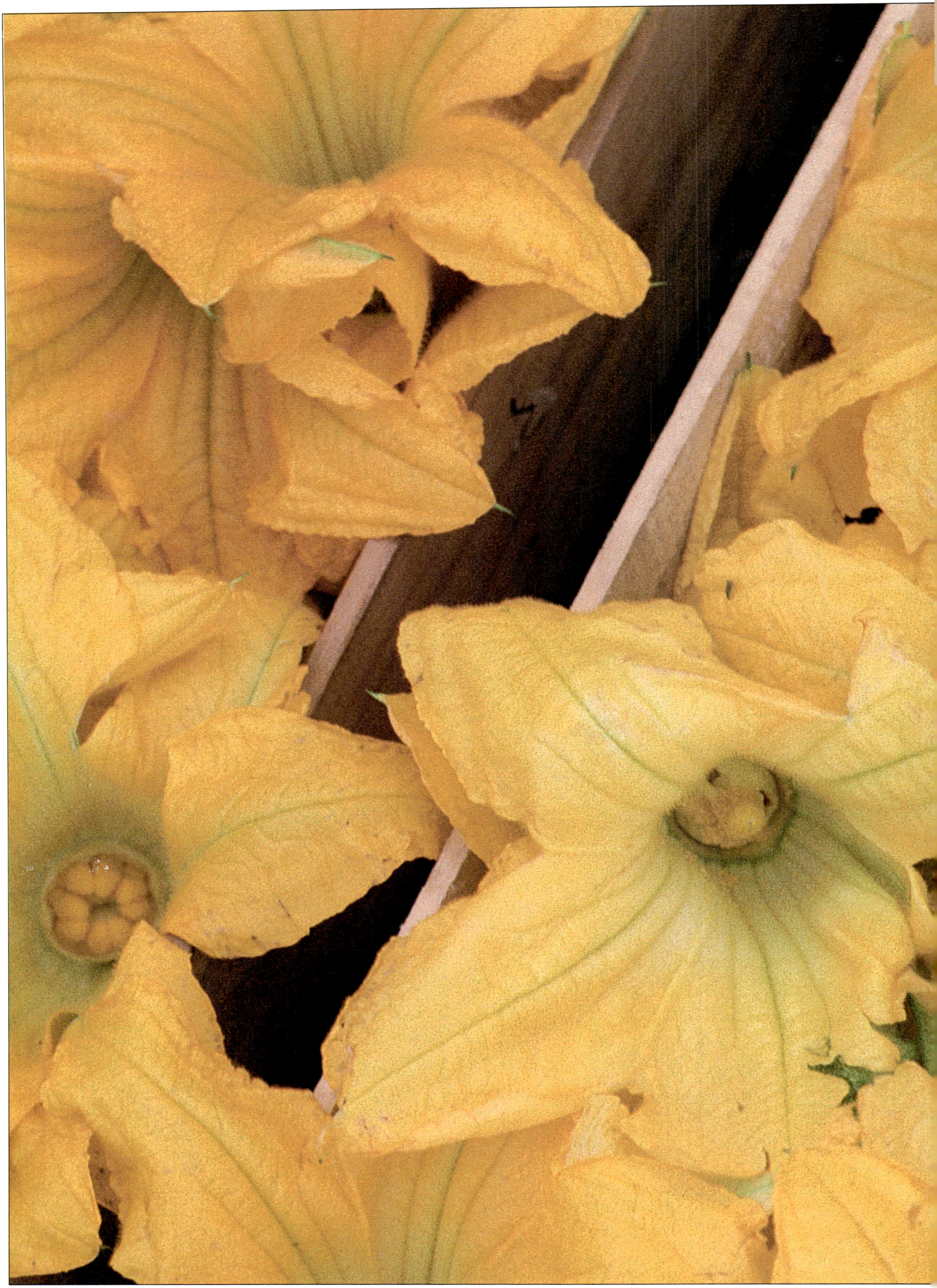

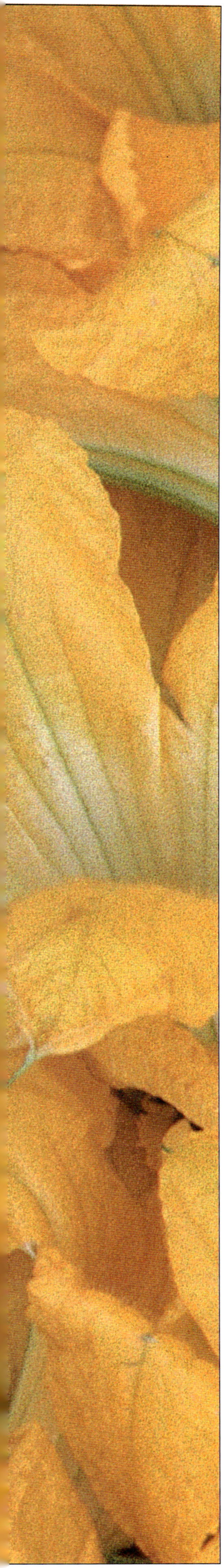

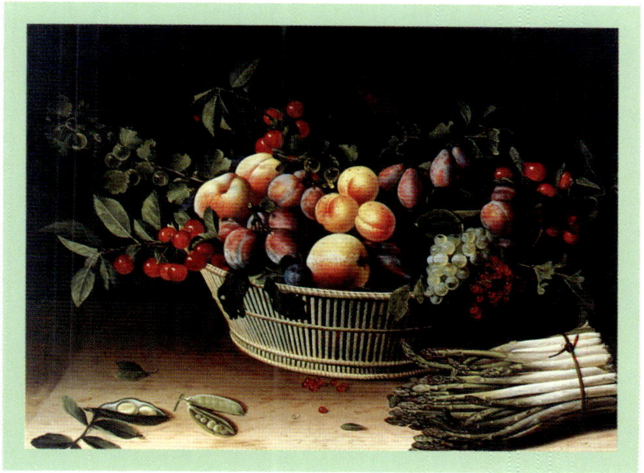

Voorjaar

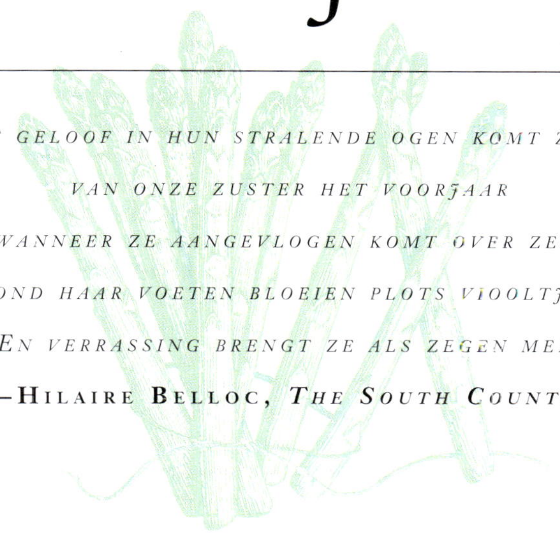

Het geloof in hun stralende ogen komt zeker
van onze zuster het voorjaar
wanneer ze aangevlogen komt over zee;
Rond haar voeten bloeien plots viooltjes,
En verrassing brengt ze als zegen mee.

—**Hilaire Belloc**, ***The South Country***

Het voorjaar is het seizoen van verse asperges, sappige aardbeien en heerlijk knapperige sla. Vier het ontwaken van de natuur met *les fleurs farcies*—courgettebloemen gevuld met ratatouille. Bij minigroenten gevuld met erwten en champignons spelen kleine aardappels, meiraapjes en pompoen een hoofdrol. Verse voorjaarserwtjes voltooien het smakelijke geheel.

Verse, jonge asperges zijn een ware lentedelicatesse. Presenteer ze gebakken in citroenboter met krabkoekjes, of verwerk ze in een heerlijke frittata met ui en champignons. Geniet van de luxe van verse frambozenazijn in een salade met zalm, linzen en malse bladgroenten.

Meergranen krenten scones met rozebladroom passen goed bij de eerste lenteframbozen of aardbeien. Fijne rozeblaadjes vormen een superieur voorjaarsgarnituur. Maak een verse aardbeiensaus bij een gemberroullade. Verse bessen en tropisch fruit zorgen voor lente-heerlijkheden. Of probeer eens een verfrissende mango lassi of een romige rabarber-sinaasappelcompote.

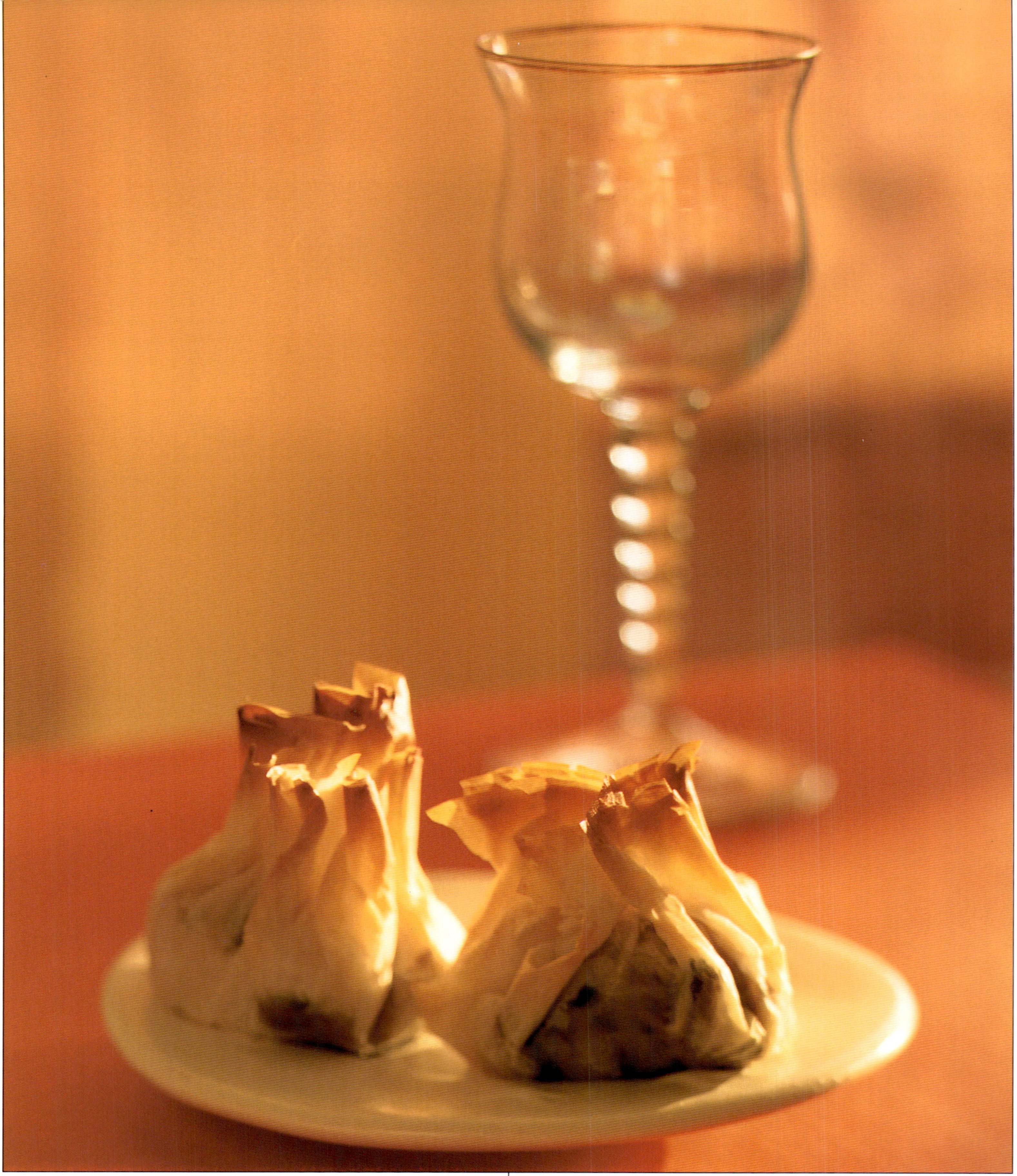

Filobuideltjes met coquilles en spinazie

HAPJES / VERENIGDE STATEN

Filobuideltjes met coquilles en spinazie

De bossige, peperachtige smaak van cantharellen wordt versterkt door wat abrikozenlikeur.

375 g verse spinazie
3 eetlepels olijfolie
2 sjalotjes, gesnipperd
2 tenen knoflook, fijngehakt
125 g verse cantharellen, julienne gesneden
2 eetlepels abrikozenlikeur
1,25 dl kippebouillon (zie woordenlijst)
500 g verse coquilles
zout en versgemalen peper naar smaak
2 eetlepels saffloerolie
500 g filodeeg

1. Verwarm de oven voor op 200°C. Bekleed een bakplaat met perkamentpapier.
2. Blancheer de spinaziebladen 15 seconden in kokend water. Laat ze onmiddellijk schrikken in ijswater om het kookproces te stoppen. Laat de spinazie goed uitlekken, knijp er zoveel mogelijk vocht uit en hak de bladen grof.

3. Verhit de olijfolie in een grote koekepan. Doe er de sjalotjes en knoflook in en laat gaar maar niet bruin fruiten. Voeg de cantharellen toe en laat 2 minuten bakken.
4. Blus de pan af met de abrikozenlikeur en laat tot een siroop inkoken. Giet er de bouillon bij en laat tot de helft inkoken.
5. Doe de spinazie en coquilles in de pan en bak ze in circa 5 minuten gaar. Breng op smaak met zout en peper. Zet weg en laat afkoelen.
6. Snijd het filodeeg in 72 rondjes van 15 cm doorsnee. Kwast 3 rondjes licht in met saffloerolie en leg ze op elkaar. Schep 2 eetlepels van de vulling op het midden van elke stapeltje, trek de randen omhoog en knijp het deeg dicht tot een pakje.
7. Schik de pakjes op de bakplaat, kwast de bovenkant in met wat saffloerolie en zet 15 minuten in de oven tot ze goudbruin zijn.
8. Doe op een voorverwarmde schaal en dien onmiddellijk op.

Voor 24 filobuideltjes

2 pakjes per portie: Calorieën 210, Eiwit 10 g, Koolhydraten 24 g, Vezel 1 g, Vet totaal 8 g (Verzadigd 1 g, Enkelvoudig onverzadigd 3,5 g, Meervoudig onverzadigd 3,5 g), Cholesterol 10 mg, Natrium 260 mg, Vitamine A 25%

▲ *1 Brood, ½ Vlees*

SOEPEN / ITALIË

Sopa di piccioncino

DUIF-SNIJBIETSOEP

Door de toevoeging van duif en snijbiet wordt dit een steviger versie van pasta e fagioli. *Geef er voor een complete maaltijd een frisse salade en knoflookcrostini (recept volgt) bij.*

100 g gedroogde witte bonen of limabonen
2 duiven, schoongemaakt en ontveld
2 eetlepels olijfolie
75 g gesnipperde ui
3 tenen knoflook, fijngehakt
1,25 dl rode wijn
1,25 dl kippebouillon (zie woordenlijst)
250 g snijbiet of bietenloof, grof gehakt
1 theelepel verse rozemarijn, fijngehakt
125 g penne (buisjespasta)
zout en versgemalen peper naar smaak
2 eetlepels versgeraspte *parmigiano reggiano* (Parmezaanse kaas) (desgewenst)

1. Zet de bonen onder koud water en laat ze een nacht weken. Giet de bonen af, zet ze weer onder water en laat ze in circa 1½ uur gaar koken. Giet de bonen af.
2. Knip de duiven in de lengte doormidden met een wildschaar of halveer ze in de lengte met een scherp mes. Spoel de druiven daarna af en dep ze droog.
3. Verhit de olijfolie in een soeppan. Doe er de ui en knoflook in en fruit ze gaar. Doe er de stukken duif in en braad ze rondom aan. Giet er de wijn en 2,5 dl van de bouillon bij; laat circa 15 minuten koken, waarbij u de stukken duif regelmatig omkeert tot ze volledig gaar zijn. Neem de duif uit de pan en laat afkoelen.
4. Giet de rest van de bouillon in de pan en breng aan de kook. Draai het vuur lager en voeg de snijbiet, rozemarijn, bonen en pasta toe. Laat 10 minuten sudderen.
5. Haal het vlees van de stukken duif en doe het vlees in de soep. Laat doorwarmen en breng op smaak met zout en peper.
6. Schep de soep in voorverwarmde soepborden, bestrooi desgewenst met de kaas en dien onmiddellijk op.

Voor 8 personen

2,5 dl per portie: Calorieën 190, Eiwit 12 g, Koolhydraten 21 g, Vezel 2 g, Vet totaal 6 g (Verzadigd 1 g, Enkelvoudig onverzadigd 3 g, Meervoudig onverzadigd 1 g), Cholesterol 25 mg, Natrium 75 mg

▲ *½ Brood, ½ Vlees*

KNOFLOOKCROSTINI

3 eetlepels olijfolie
2 tenen knoflook, fijngehakt
16 sneden stokbrood

1. Verwarm de oven voor op 190°C.
2. Verhit de olie en knoflook in een kleine pan. Kwast één kant van elke snee brood licht in met de knoflookolie en leg de sneden met de ingevette kant onder op een bakplaat.
3. Rooster het brood in de oven in 15 minuten goudbruin, waarbij u de sneden een keer omdraait. Dien onmiddellijk op.

Voor 16 sneden

per portie: Calorieën 60, Eiwit 1 g, Koolhydraten 3 g, Vezel 1 g, Vet totaal 2 g (Verzadigd 1 g, Enkelvoudig onverzadigd 0,5 g, Meervoudig onverzadigd 1 g), Cholesterol 2 mg, Natrium 2 mg

▲ *1 Brood*

Van links naar rechts: Duif-snijbietsoep, Knoflookcrostini

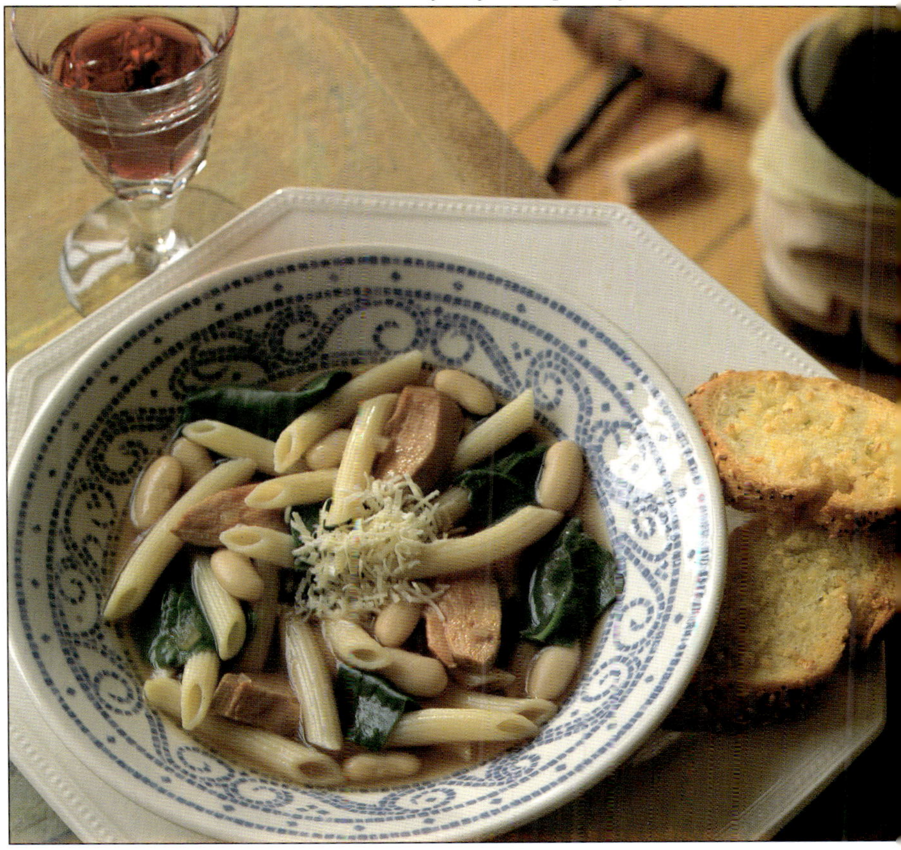

SALADES / FRANKRIJK

Salade Niçoise nouvelle

Een variant op een klassieke salade. Gebruik gegrilde verse tonijn in plaats van tonijn uit blik, die een hoog natriumgehalte heeft. Kwarteleitjes zijn zo klein dat ze veel minder cholesterol bevatten dan een henneëi.

750 g tonijnfilets
2 eetlepels vers citroensap
2 eetlepels rode wijnazijn
1 teen knoflook, fijngehakt
1½ theelepel Dijonmosterd
1,25 dl koudgeperste olijfolie
1 theelepel fijngehakte verse dragon
¼ theelepel zout
versgemalen peper naar smaak
500 g kleine nieuwe aardappels, in 10-15 minuten bijtgaar gekookt
6 baby-artisjokken, 3-4 minuten geblancheerd en in de lengte gehalveerd (zie woordenlijst)
250 g haricot verts, 30 seconden geblancheerd, of sperziebonen, 1 minuut geblancheerd (zie woordenlijst)
1 krop sla
6 hardgekookte kwarteleitjes, gepeld, in vier partjes
12 lenteuitjes, in dunne ringen gesneden
1 groene paprika, zaad en zaadlijsten verwijderd en julienne gesneden
375 g kerstomaatjes, gehalveerd
12 *Niçoise* olijven
1 eetlepel kappertjes

1. Verwarm de grill voor.
2. Snijd de tonijn in 6 porties. Grilleer de tonijn 2 minuten aan elke kant, zodat hij nog rosé van binnen is. Neem van het vuur.
3. Doe voor de dressing het citroensap, de azijn, knoflook en mosterd in een kom. Giet er al kloppend de olijfolie in een straaltje bij. Klop er de dragon en wat zout en peper door.
4. Doe de aardappels, artisjokken en haricot verts in een kom en schep om met de dressing. Laat 30 minuten marineren. Giet de groenten af en bewaar de dressing voor een ander recept.
5. Bekleed elk bord met wat sla. Schik er de groenten op. Leg een portie gegrilde tonijn op het bord en schik de rest van de ingrediënten eromheen. Zet even in de koelkast en dien op.

Voor 6 personen

1 portie: Calorieën 370, Eiwit 33 g, Koolhydraten 33 g, Vezel 5 g, Vet totaal 13 g (Verzadigd 2 g, Enkelvoudig onverzadigd 8 g, Meervoudig onverzadigd 1,5 g), Cholesterol 125 mg, Natrium 450 mg, IJzer 25%, Vitamine A 35%, Vitamine C 90%.
▲ *2 Groente, 1 Vlees*

Ingrediënten voor Frittata met ui, champignons en asperges

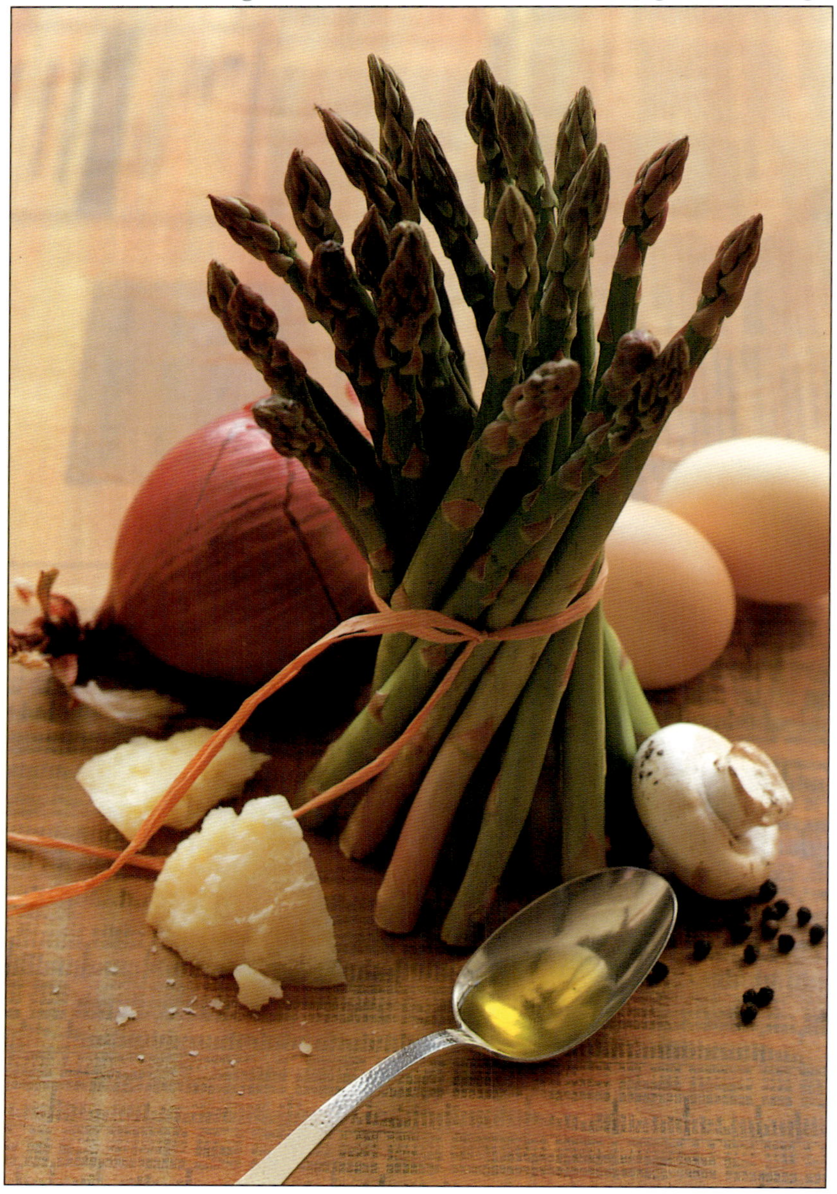

ONTBIJT / ITALIË

Frittata met ui, champignons en asperges

Deze frittata is zeer geschikt voor een brunch of als borrelhapje. U kunt een groot deel van de voorbereidingen van tevoren uitvoeren en de frittata naar wens ook van tevoren bakken en dan op kamertemperatuur serveren.

2 eetlepels olijfolie
1 rode (Spaanse) ui, in plakken van ½ cm dik gesneden
100 g champignons, in plakjes
250 g groene asperges, geblancheerd (zie woordenlijst)
8 eieren, losgeklopt
¼ theelepel zout
versgemalen peper naar smaak
30 g versgeraspte Parmezaanse kaas

1. Verwarm de oven voor op 220°C.
2. Verhit de olijfolie in een grote ovenvaste koekepan. Fruit er de ui goudgeel in. Voeg de plakjes champignon toe en bak ze tot ze gaar zijn en het vocht verdampt is. Neem de pan van het vuur.

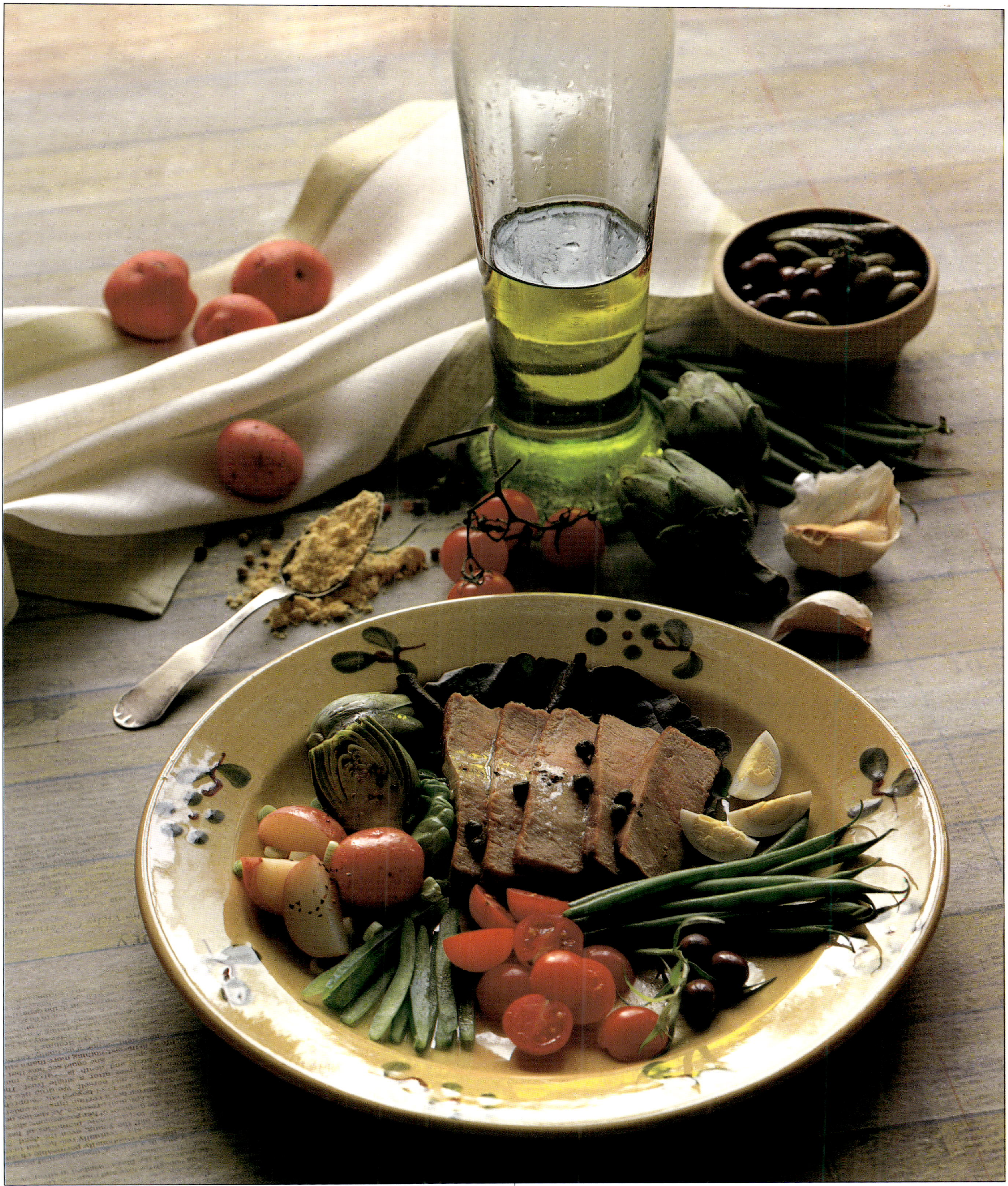

Salade Niçoise nouvelle

3. Schik de asperges op de ui en champignons. Giet de eieren over de groenten. Breng op smaak met wat zout en peper, bestrooi met de Parmezaanse kaas en zet 15-20 minuten in de oven tot een ingestoken mes er schoon uitkomt. Dien direct op of laat op kamertemperatuur komen en serveer later.

Voor 4 personen

1 portie: Calorieën 270, Eiwit 17 g, Koolhydraten 8 g, Vezel 2 g, Vet totaal 19 g (Verzadigd 5 g, Enkelvoudig onverzadigd 10 g, Meervoudig onverzadigd 2 g), Cholesterol 450 mg, Natrium 380 mg, Vitamine A 20%.

▲ *1 Groente, 1 Vlees*

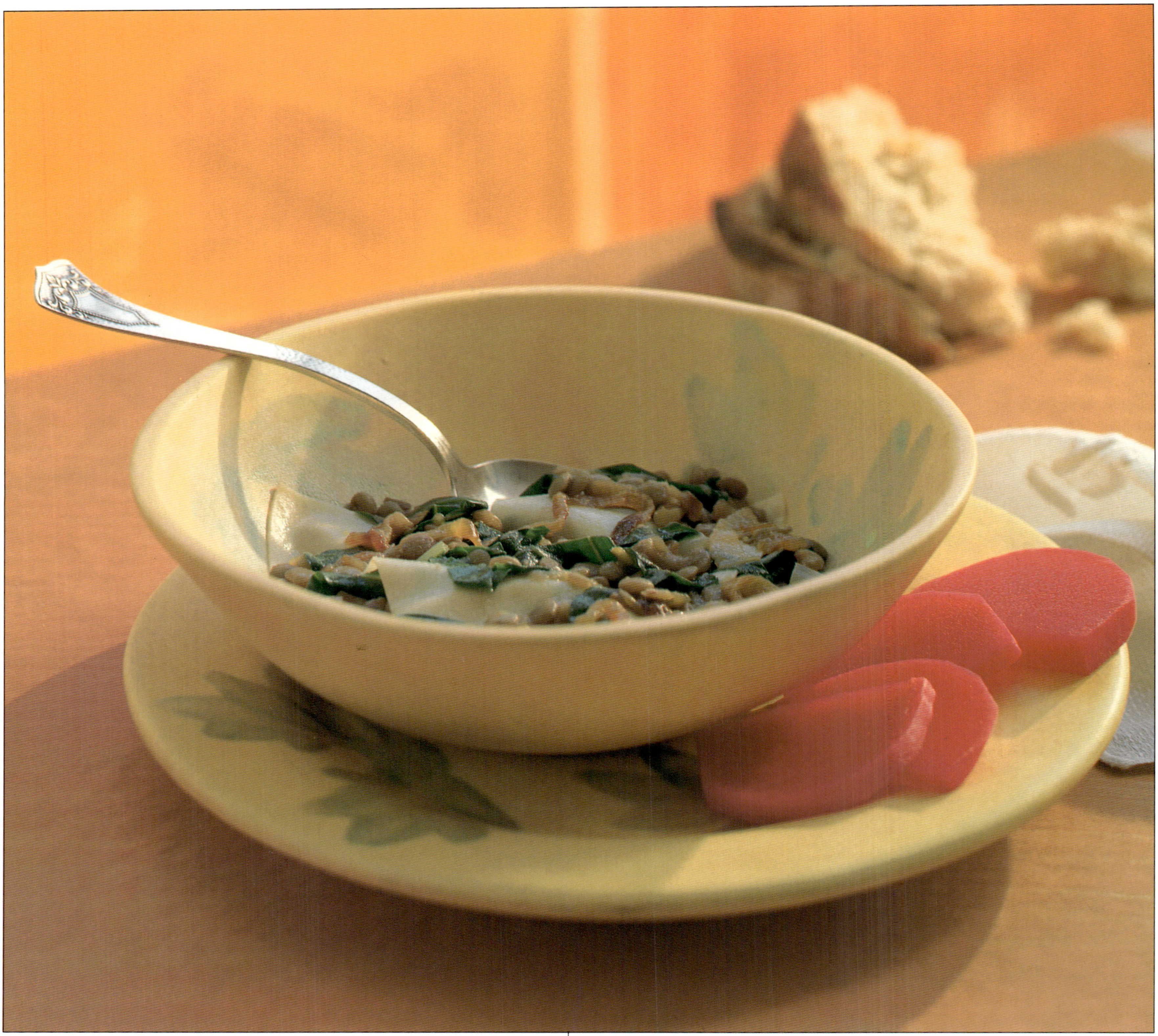

Van links naar rechts: Rushta, Ingemaakte meiraap

Rushta

Dolly Granatelli uit Santa Barbara, in Californië herinnert zich dat haar moeder dit heerlijke en voedzame Libanese gerecht maakte. De kunst is om de ui zo bruin mogelijk te bakken zonder hem te laten verbranden. Rushta *wordt per traditie met ingemaakte meiraap geserveerd (recept op de volgende pagina).*

4 grote uien, in plakken van ½ cm dik gesneden
1,2 dl olijfolie
500 g linzen, afgespoeld
1 bos (circa 400 g) snijbiet of 500 g verse spinazie, julienne gesneden
250 g verse eiernoedels, in vierkanten van 5 cm gesneden, of gedroogde noedels en 2,5 dl extra water gebruiken
zout en vers citroensap naar smaak

1. Fruit de uien onder af en toe omscheppen 10 minuten in de olijfolie in een grote pan op een middelhoog vuur. Laat de uien onder regelmatig omscheppen nog 30-40 minuten fruiten op een middelhoog vuur tot de uien zo bruin mogelijk maar niet verbrand zijn.
2. Giet er 2 liter water bij (let op voor het spetteren) en breng aan de kook. Voeg de linzen toe, draai het vuur laag en laat 20 minuten sudderen. Voeg de snijbiet toe en laat het geheel nog 10 minuten sudderen.
3. Breng de soep weer aan de kook, voeg de noedels toe en kook ze in circa 3 minuten gaar voor verse noedels en 8 minuten voor gedroogde.
4. Breng op smaak met wat zout en citroensap en dien op.

Voor 12 personen

2,5 dl per portie: Calorieën 300, Eiwit 15 g, Koolhydraten 39 g, Vezel 7 g, Vet totaal 10 g (Verzadigd 1,5 g, Enkelvoudig onverzadigd 7 g, Meervoudig onverzadigd 1 g), Cholesterol 15 mg, Natrium 40 mg, IJzer 30%, Vitamine A 50%, Vitamine C 30%.
▲ *1 Brood, 1 Groente, 1 Vlees*

GROENTEN / LIBANON

Ingemaakte meiraap

De mooie rode kleur van de meiraap is aan de biet te danken. Het zout wordt gebruikt om de meiraap het inmaakvocht beter te laten opnemen. Het meeste zout wordt afgespoeld voor de groenten in de gekruide azijn gaan. U kunt ze tot een maand in de koelkast bewaren.

1 kg meiraap, geschild en in plakken gesneden
1 rauwe biet, geschild en in plakken gesneden
2 eetlepels zeezout
3,75 dl azijn
1 theelepel suiker
3 tenen knoflook
1 chilipeper, in de lengte opengesneden (desgewenst)

1. Doe de plakken meiraap en biet in een kom. Bestrooi ze met het zout, schep om en laat 1 uur trekken.
2. Doe de azijn en suiker met 3,75 dl water in een middelgrote pan. Breng aan de kook en laat circa 3 minuten sudderen. Neem de pan van het vuur.
3. Spoel de meiraap en biet onder de kraan. Doe ze in een zuurbestendige schaal met de knoflook en chilipeper. Giet er het azijnmengsel over, dek de schaal af en zet 1 week in de koelkast voor het gebruik.

Voor 1 liter

1,25 dl per portie: Calorieën 35, Eiwit 1 g, Koolhydraten 9 g, Vezel 2 g, Vet totaal 0 g (Verzadigd 0 g, Enkelvoudig onverzadigd 0 g, Meervoudig onverzadigd 0 g), Cholesterol 0 mg, Natrium 520 mg, Vitamine C 40%.

▲ *1 Groente*

SOEPEN / MEXICO

Sopa de lima

SOEP MET LIMOEN EN COURGETTEBLOESEM

Verminder de hoeveelheid verzadigd vet door in plaats van gefrituurde chips bloemtortilla's te gebruiken die niet met reuzel zijn vervaardigd. Pas de hoeveelheid jalapeño in de soep naar eigen smaak aan.

4 bloemtortilla's
1 limoen, gehalveerd
¼ theelepel zout
1 liter kippebouillon (zie woordenlijst)
50 g gehakte rode ui
15 g verse koriander, gehakt
1 rode paprika, grof gehakt of in repen gesneden
1 courgette, overdwars in plakken van ½ cm gesneden
1 eetlepel fijngehakte verse oregano
1 theelepel fijngehakte verse tijm
600 g repen gekookte kip
2 groene chilipepers, geroosterd, ontveld en in repen gesneden (zie woordenlijst)
2 jalapeñopepers, ontzaad en overdwars in dunne reepjes gesneden
het sap van 3 limoenen
zout en versgemalen peper naar smaak
8 courgettebloesems, geblancheerd (zie woordenlijst)
2 limoenen, in partjes gesneden, ter garnering

1. Verwarm de oven voor op 180°C.
2. Wrijf de tortilla's licht in met de limoenhelften en bestrooi de tortilla's licht met zout. Snijd ze in repen van 3 cm breed en schik ze op een bakplaat. Zet 10 minuten in de oven tot ze goudbruin zijn. Zet weg.
3. Doe de kippebouillon in een grote pan en breng aan de kook. Draai het vuur lager, voeg de ui, koriander, paprika, courgette, oregano en tijm toe. Laat 10 minuten sudderen tot de groenten bijtgaar zijn. Voeg de kip, pepers en het limoensap toe en laat doorwarmen. Breng op smaak met zout en peper.
4. Doe de courgettebloesem vlak voor het serveren in de soep. Dien op met de repen tortilla en partjes limoen.

Voor 8 personen

2,5 dl per portie: Calorieën 190, Eiwit 18 g, Koolhydraten 16 g, Vezel 1 g, Vet totaal 6 g (Verzadigd 1,5 g, Enkelvoudig onverzadigd 2 g, Meervoudig onverzadigd 1,5 g), Cholesterol 45 mg, Natrium 210 mg, Vitamine C 100%.

▲ *½ Brood, 1 Vlees*

Soep met limoen en courgettebloesem

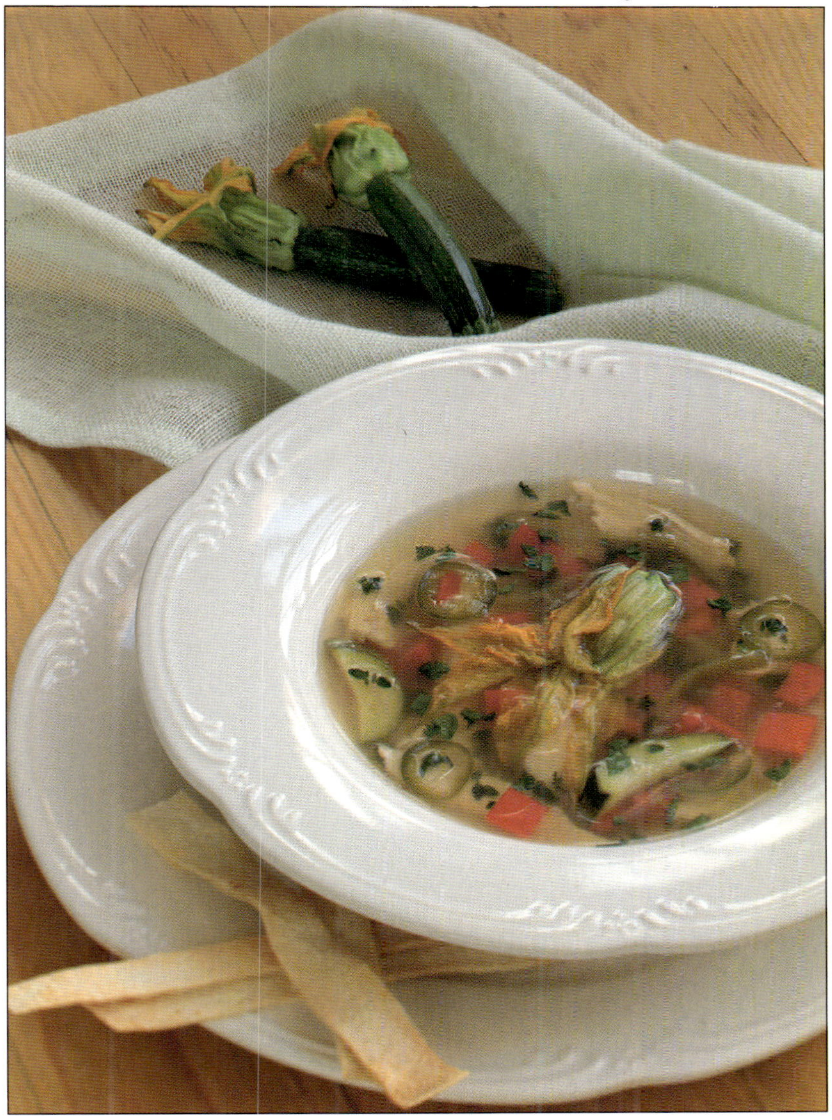

HAPJES / JAPAN

Temaki-zushi

SUSHI

Sushi is een uitstekende manier om ingrediënten te verwerken die u met mate zou moeten gebruiken. Hoewel kaviaar (tobiko) *een hoog cholesterol- en natriumgehalte heeft, is hij niet erg vet maar bevat veel vitamine* B_{12} *en omega-3 vetzuren. Avocado's zijn zeer vet, meestal enkelvoudig onverzadigd, en moeten in verband met de maximale dagelijkse portie vet met mate worden gebruikt.*

Sushi zijn makkelijk te maken en zeer geschikt voor een feest. Presenteer enkele of alle ingrediënten die hieronder staan en laat uw gasten hun eigen favorieten samenstellen. Maak eerst een paar voorbeelden op een schaal.

4 eetlepels plus 2 eetlepels rijstazijn
450 g kleefrijst
3 eetlepels suiker
½ theelepel zout
1 eetlepel zwart of wit geroosterd sesamzaad
20 vellen *nori* (gedroogd zeewier)
1 komkommer, julienne gesneden
circa 8 cm daikon of rettich, julienne gesneden
1 rode paprika, zaad en zaadlijsten verwijderd, julienne gesneden
2 wortels, geschild en julienne gesneden
250 g zeer dunne groene asperges, geblancheerd en in stukken van 5 cm gesneden (zie woordenlijst)
125 g peultjes, geblancheerd (zie woordenlijst)
½ avocado, in dunne plakken
10 groene *shiso* bladen of takjes waterkers
60 g daikonkers
100 g *enoki* paddestoelen
250 g gestoomd krabvlees
250 g rauwe garnalen, gepeld, darmkanaal verwijderd, in de lengte aan satéstokjes geregen om krullen te voorkomen en 2-3 minuten geblancheerd
60 g *tobiko* (kuit van vliegende vis)
4 eetlepels *shoyu* (natriumarme sojasaus)
1 eetlepel *wasabi*, tot een pasta gemaakt met wat water
185 g ingemaakte gember

1. Maak de *tezu* (hand-azijn) door 2 eetlepels van de rijstazijn met 2,5 dl water in een vingerkommetje te mengen. Zet weg.
2. Maak de *shari* (gekruide sushirijst). Spoel de rijst in een zeef onder de koude kraan tot het water helder blijft. Laat de rijst 1 uur uitlekken. Doe de rijst in een middelgrote pan met 5,5 dl water en leg er het deksel op. Breng aan de kook, draai het vuur laag en laat 15 minuten stomen zonder het deksel eraf te nemen. Neem de pan van het vuur, neem het deksel eraf, leg er snel een theedoek op en leg het deksel er weer op. Laat de rijst zo vervolgens 15 minuten staan.
3. Verhit de rest van de rijstazijn, de suiker en het zout in een andere pan en roer tot de suiker opgelost is. Zet weg.
4. Bevochtig de binnenkant van een grote kom met 2 theelepels van de *tezu*. Doe de rijst in de kom en roer de korrels los met een pollepel. Schep er het azijn-suikermengsel door onder voortdurend waaien om het mengsel af te koelen. Schep en waai circa 10 minuten tot alle vocht geabsorbeerd is en het mengsel volledig koel is. Zorg dat u de rijstkorrels niet beschadigt.
5. Doop uw vingers in de *tezu* en vorm de rijst tot balletjes van circa 3 cm. Knijp de balletjes zachtjes langwerpig en schik ze naast elkaar op een schaal. Bestrooi ze met het sesamzaad en dek ze af met een schone theedoek. Houd ze op kamertemperatuur tot gebruik (niet meer dan 1 uur).
6. Knip de vellen *nori* tot vierhoeken en rooster ze door ze 2 of 3 keer boven een vlam heen en weer te bewegen tot ze knapperig zijn. Stapel ze op een dienschaal.
7. Schik de komkommer, rettich, rode paprika, wortel, asperges, peultjes, avocado, *shiso* of waterkers, daikonkers, *enoki* paddestoelen, krab en garnalen op een schaal. Doe de *tobiko* in een kleine kom.
8. Doe circa 2 theelepels *shoyu* in een kleine kom voor elke gast. Geef er de *wasabi* en ingemaakte gember apart bij, zodat elke gast ze naar smaak kan toevoegen.
9. Maak de sushi door 1 vel *nori* met de glanzende kant onder in uw hand te houden. Schik er een balletje rijst en een selectie van de vullingen op, rol de *nori* op tot een hoorntje en knijp het geheel dan zachtjes aan.

Voor 6 personen (circa 48 hoorntjes)

3 hoorntjes per portie: Calorieën 190, Eiwit 11 g, Koolhydraten 30 g, Vezel 2 g, Vet totaal 2,5 g (Verzadigd 0,5 g, Enkelvoudig onverzadigd 1 g, Meervoudig onverzadigd 0,5 g), Cholesterol 50 mg, Natrium 410 mg, IJzer 30%, Vitamine A 60%, Vitamine C 30%.
▲ *½ Brood, 1 Groente, ½ Vlees*

PASTA / JAPAN

Koude sobanoedels met lenteui-sojadipsaus

Dashi, *een vis-zeewierbouillon, is een essentieel ingrediënt in de meeste Japanse recepten. U kunt* dashi *in poedervorm kopen in de meeste oosterse toko's, of u kunt het zelf maken door 1 liter water met 30 g* konbu *(gedroogd zeewier of kelp) te verhitten. Breng het mengsel tegen de kook aan, neem dan de* konbu *eruit en voeg 30 g bonitovlokjes toe. Breng het mengsel aan de kook en neem de pan dan onmiddellijk van het vuur. Zeef de bouillon voor gebruik.*

750 g gedroogde *cha-soba* (Japans boekweitnoedels bereid met groene thee)
2,5 dl dashi (zie boven)
2 eetlepels sojasaus
2 theelepels *mirin* (zoete sake) of 1 theelepel suiker
1 eetlepel suiker
3 lenteuitjes, het wit en wat van het groen in dunne plakjes gesneden
1 vel *nori* (gedroogd zeewier)
2 theelepels *wasabi*-pasta

1. Kook de *cha-soba* in 3-5 minuten gaar in kokend water. Giet ze af

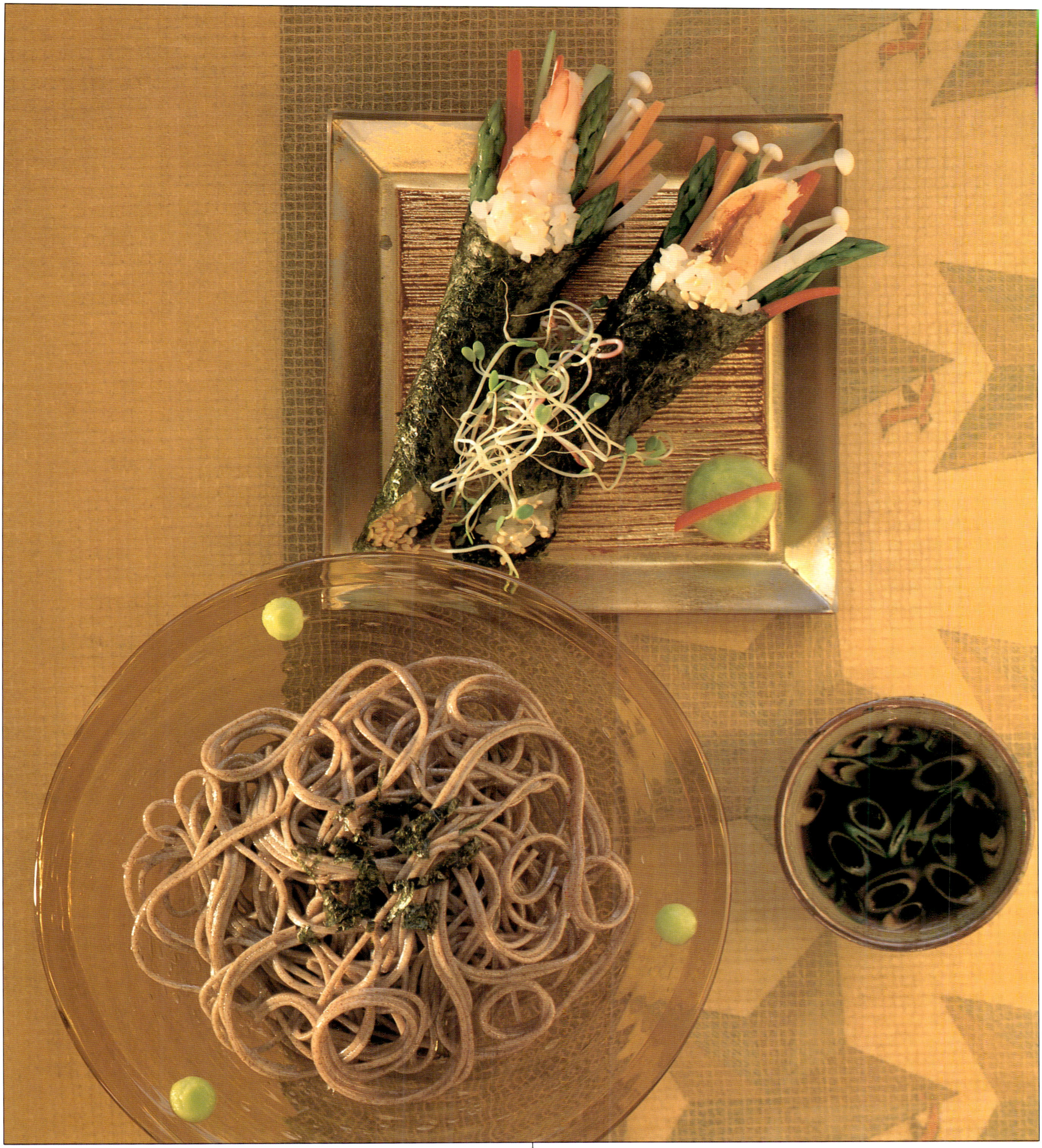

Van boven naar beneden: Temaki-zushi, Koude sobanoedels met lenteui-sojadipsaus

en spoel onder de koude kraan. Zet ze dan in de koelkast.

2. Doe voor de dipsaus de dashi, sojasaus, *mirin* en suiker in een pan en verhit het mengsel tot de suiker opgelost is. Zet in de koelkast. Schep er daarna de lenteuitjes door en verdeel de saus over 8 kommetjes.
3. Schik de *cha-soba* op 8 bamboeschaaltjes of bordjes. Rooster de *nori* door die 2 of 3 keer heen en weer over een vlam te bewegen. Snijd de *nori* in reepjes of verkruimel hem, en strooi over de noedels. Zet een kommetje dipsaus op elk schaaltje.
4. Doe wat *wasabi* op elk schaaltje en dien onmiddellijk op. Doe *wasabi* naar smaak in de dipsaus en doop er de noedels in.

Voor 8 personen

1 portie: Calorieën 310, Eiwit 13 g, Koolhydraten 67 g, Vezel 0 g, Vet totaal 1 g (Verzadigd 0 g, Enkelvoudig onverzadigd 0 g, Meervoudig onverzadigd 0 g), Cholesterol 0 mg, Natrium 1000 mg.

▲ *3 Brood*

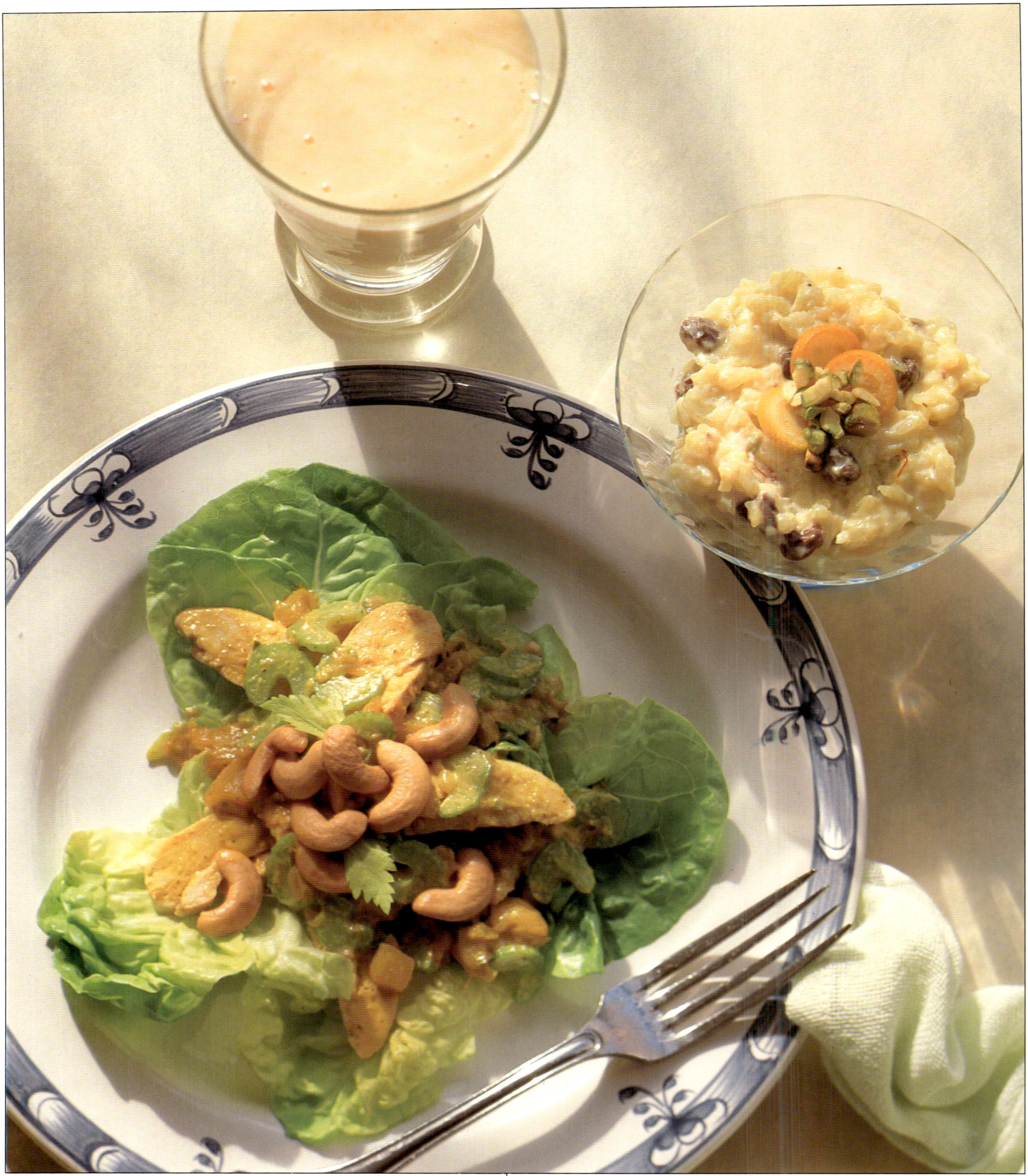

Van boven naar beneden: Mango lassi, Geurige rijstpudding, Salade van kipkerrie en mangochutney

DRANKEN / INDIA

Mango lassi

Dit romige frisse drankje bevat vrijwel geen vet en voorziet in 16% van de dagelijkse kalkbehoefte.

750 g magere yoghurt
2 rijpe mango's, geschild, ontpit en in blokjes gesneden
1 rijpe banaan
60 g suiker
20 ijsblokjes

1. Doe de yoghurt, mango, banaan en suiker in een blender en draai tot alles goed gemengd is.
2. Voeg de ijsblokjes toe en draai tot de ijsblokjes bijna helemaal verkruimeld zijn en u een schuimig mengsel hebt.
3. Schenk in gekoelde glazen en dien onmiddellijk op.

Voor 8 personen

1 glas per portie: Calorieën 130, Eiwit 5 g, Koolhydraten 24 g, Vezel 1 g, Vet totaal 2 g (Verzadigd 1 g, Enkelvoudig onverzadigd 0,5 g, Meervoudig onverzadigd 0 g), Cholesterol 5 mg, Natrium 60 mg, Vitamine A 40%, Vitamine C 25%.

▲ *½ Fruit, ½ Melk*

SALADES / GROOT-BRITTANNIË

Salade van kipkerrie en mangochutney

In de koloniale tijd in India ontdekten de Britten de specerijen en chutneys daar. Dit is geen traditioneel gerecht maar een moderne variant met traditionele ingrediënten.

4 eetlepels droge witte wijn
2 hele kipfilets, ontveld
1 teen knoflook
1 kleine verse pikante groene of rode chilipeper, ontzaad
2 eetlepels room
1 eetlepel kerriepoeder
4 eetlepels saffloerolie
versgemalen peper naar smaak
1,25 dl mangochutney (recept volgt)
6 stengels bleekselderij, overdwars in plakken gesneden
slabladen, ter garnering
35 g gehalveerde cashewnoten, ter garnering (desgewenst)

1. Verwarm de oven voor op 230°C.
2. Sprenkel de wijn over de kipfilets en zet ze onafgedekt 15 minuten in de oven. Neem de kip uit de oven en laat de filets afkoelen. Snijd de kip overdwars in plakken en doe de plakken in een grote kom. Zet weg.
3. Doe de knoflook en de chilipeper in een draaiende keukenmachine en voeg dan het kerriepoeder en de room toe. Meng goed en schraap de wand van de kom minstens één keer af. Giet er met draaiende motor geleidelijk de saffloerolie bij. Breng op smaak met versgemalen peper.
4. Schep de dressing, chutney en bleekselderij om met de kip. Bekleed een dienschaal met de slabladen, schik er de kipsalade op en garneer met de cashewnoten.

Voor 6 personen

1 portie: Calorieën 220, Eiwit 19 g, Koolhydraten 9 g, Vezel 1 g, Vet totaal 12 g (Verzadigd 2 g, Enkelvoudig onverzadigd 2 g, Meervoudig onverzadigd 7 g), Cholesterol 50 mg, Natrium 85 mg, Vitamine C 20%.

▲ *½ Fruit, 1 Vlees*

MANGOCHUTNEY

2 mango's, geschild en grof gehakt
75 g gehakte ui
100 g lichtbruine basterdsuiker
1,25 dl witte wijnazijn
4 tenen knoflook, fijngehakt
1 verse groene chilipeper, ontzaad en fijngehakt
1 eetlepel fijngehakte verse gember
¼ theelepel gemalen kruidnagel
zout en versgemalen peper naar smaak

1. Doe alle ingrediënten in een zuurbestendige pan en laat 20 minuten sudderen. Laat afkoelen en bewaar in de koelkast.

Voor 5 dl

4 eetlepels per portie: Calorieën 75, Eiwit 1 g, Koolhydraten 20 g, Vezel 1 g, Vet totaal 0 g (Verzadigd 0 g, Enkelvoudig onverzadigd 0 g, Meervoudig onverzadigd 0 g), Cholesterol 0 mg, Natrium 5 mg, Vitamine A 40%, Vitamine C 30%.

▲ *1 Fruit*

ONTBIJT / INDIA

Geurige rijstpudding

Deze romige rijstpudding is ook lekker als nagerecht. Gebruik volle melk voor een romige structuur. Serveer de pudding met een kom kumquats, vijgen en in honingwater geweekte gedroogde abrikozen (recept op pagina 216).

1,1 liter volle melk
125 g suiker
100 g *basmati*rijst, goed gespoeld
45 g rozijnen
3 eetlepels grof gehakte, geblancheerde amandelen (desgewenst; zie woordenlijst)
¼ theelepel gemalen kardemom
¼ theelepel saffraandraden
1 eetlepel grof gehakte pistachenoten (desgewenst)
100 g kumquats, in plakken (desgewenst)

1. Verhit de melk met de suiker al roerend in een grote pan tot de suiker opgelost is. Voeg de rijst toe en laat 1¼ uur sudderen onder regelmatig omscheppen. Schep desgewenst het vel dat zich zal vormen er ook door. De rijst moet volledig gaar zijn en de melk moet dik zijn geworden.
2. Voeg de rozijnen, amandelen, kardemom en saffraan toe en laat nog 10 minuten sudderen. Neem de pan van het vuur.
3. Serveer op kamertemperatuur of gekoeld. Bestrooi met de pistachenoten of plakjes kumquat.

Voor 6 personen

2 dl per portie: Calorieën 250, Eiwit 7 g, Koolhydraten 42 g, Vezel 1 g, Vet totaal 6 g (Verzadigd 4 g, Enkelvoudig onverzadigd 2 g, Meervoudig onverzadigd 0 g), Cholesterol 25 mg, Natrium 90 mg, Kalk 20%

▲ *½ Brood, 1 Melk*

ZEEBANKET / CHINA

Geurige gerookte tilapia

Een bezoeker aan China kan een indruk van het leven op de rivier krijgen door een dag aan de rivier de Li door te brengen. Met speciale boten kan men ontspannen van de rivier en een lunch genieten. Het kombuis bestaat uit een kleine verhoging achter in de boot en de lunch wordt vaak in een bamboekooi in het water gedaan en aan een lijn meegetrokken. Serveer deze gerookte vis met kouseband en champignons in zwarte-bonensaus (recept op pagina 174).

50 g rijst
50 g lichtbruine basterdsuiker
2 eetlepels sinaasappel- of mandarijneschil
4 eetlepels zwarte theeblaadjes
1 eetlepel steranijs
6 tilapia filets, 1 kg, of een andere verse vis van de baarsfamilie
2 eetlepels sojasaus
2 eetlepels rijstazijn
1 theelepel fijngehakte knoflook
¼ theelepel sesamolie
1 eetlepel reepjes sinaasappelschil

1. Maak een visroker door een wok of een grote pan met een vel aluminiumfolie te bekleden dat groot genoeg is om een soort tent te maken als u de randen dichtknijpt. Leg de rijst, suiker, sinaasappelschil, thee en steranijs op de bodem en leg er een rooster over.
2. Schik de visfilets op het rooster en knijp de folie dicht tot een tent. Rook 10 minuten op een middelhoog vuur. Neem de pan van het vuur en laat 10 minuten staan voor u de folie open doet. Doe de vis op een schaal.
3. Meng de sojasaus met de rijstazijn, knoflook en sesamolie in een kleine kom. Smeer dit mengsel over de vis, bestrooi met de sinaasappelschil en dien onmiddellijk op.

Voor 6 personen

1 filet per portie: Calorieën 200, Eiwit 32 g, Koolhydraten 8 g, Vezel 0 g, Vet totaal 4 g (Verzadigd 0,5 g, Enkelvoudig onverzadigd 1 g, Meervoudig onverzadigd 1,5 g), Cholesterol 70 mg, Natrium 360 mg
▲ *1 Vlees*

PASTA / CHINA

Chinese eiernoedels met mini-paksoi

Deze maaltijdschotel is snel klaar.

500 g verse Chinese noedels of verse smalle eiernoedels
500 g paksoi
4 eetlepels *hoisinsaus*
2 eetlepels sojasaus
2 eetlepels Chinese rijstwijn of droge sherry
2 theelepels sesamolie
2 eetlepels arachide-olie
3 tenen knoflook, in plakjes gesneden
3 lenteuitjes, in rondjes gesneden
1 eetlepel fijngehakte verse gember
4 eetlepels kippebouillon (zie woordenlijst)
1 theelepel sesamzaad

1. Kook de noedels in 3-4 minuten in kokend water bijtgaar. Giet de noedels af.
2. Snijd de taaie stronk van de paksoi. Snijd één hele krop in de lengte in vieren, blancheer 1 minuut, dompel onmiddellijk in ijswater, laat uitlekken en zet weg. Snijd de rest van de paksoi overdwars in repen en zet de stelen en de bladen apart weg.
3. Meng de *hoisinsaus* met de sojasaus, rijstwijn of sherry en sesamolie in een kleine kom.
4. Doe de arachide-olie in een wok en verhit tot de olie zeer heet is maar niet rookt. Doe er de knoflook, lenteui en gember in en roerbak 1 minuut. Voeg de in vieren en in repen gesneden paksoi toe en roerbak nog 1 minuut.
5. Voeg het *hoisinmengsel* en de kippebouillon toe en roerbak tot het vocht iets dikker is. Schep er de noedels door tot alles goed doorgewarmd is. Strooi er het sesamzaad over en dien op.

Voor 6 personen

1 portie: Calorieën 320, Eiwit 11 g, Koolhydraten 52g, Vezel 1 g, Vet totaal 8 g (Verzadigd 1,5 g, Enkelvoudig onverzadigd 0 g, Meervoudig onverzadigd 0 g), Cholesterol 55 mg, Natrium 560 mg, IJzer 20%, Vitamine A 50%, Vitamine C 70%.
▲ *2 Brood, 1 Groente*

HAPJES / CHINA

Vier seizoenenknoedels met dipsaus

Siu Mai-knoedels zijn er in vele maten en worden op straat of in theehuizen verkocht bij de dim sum. Deze knoedel wordt gezien als een symbool van de vier seizoenen.

DIPSAUS

3 eetlepels arachide-olie
20 g fijngehakte lenteuitjes
4 eetlepels sojasaus
4 theelepels suiker
1 lenteui, in dunne plakken

KNOEDELS

6 gedroogde Chinese zwarte paddestoelen
1 theelepel suiker
750 g rauwe garnalen, gepeld, darmkanaal verwijderd en grof gehakt
1 eiwit
90 g gepelde en fijngehakte verse waterkastanjes of fijngehakte waterkastanjes uit blik

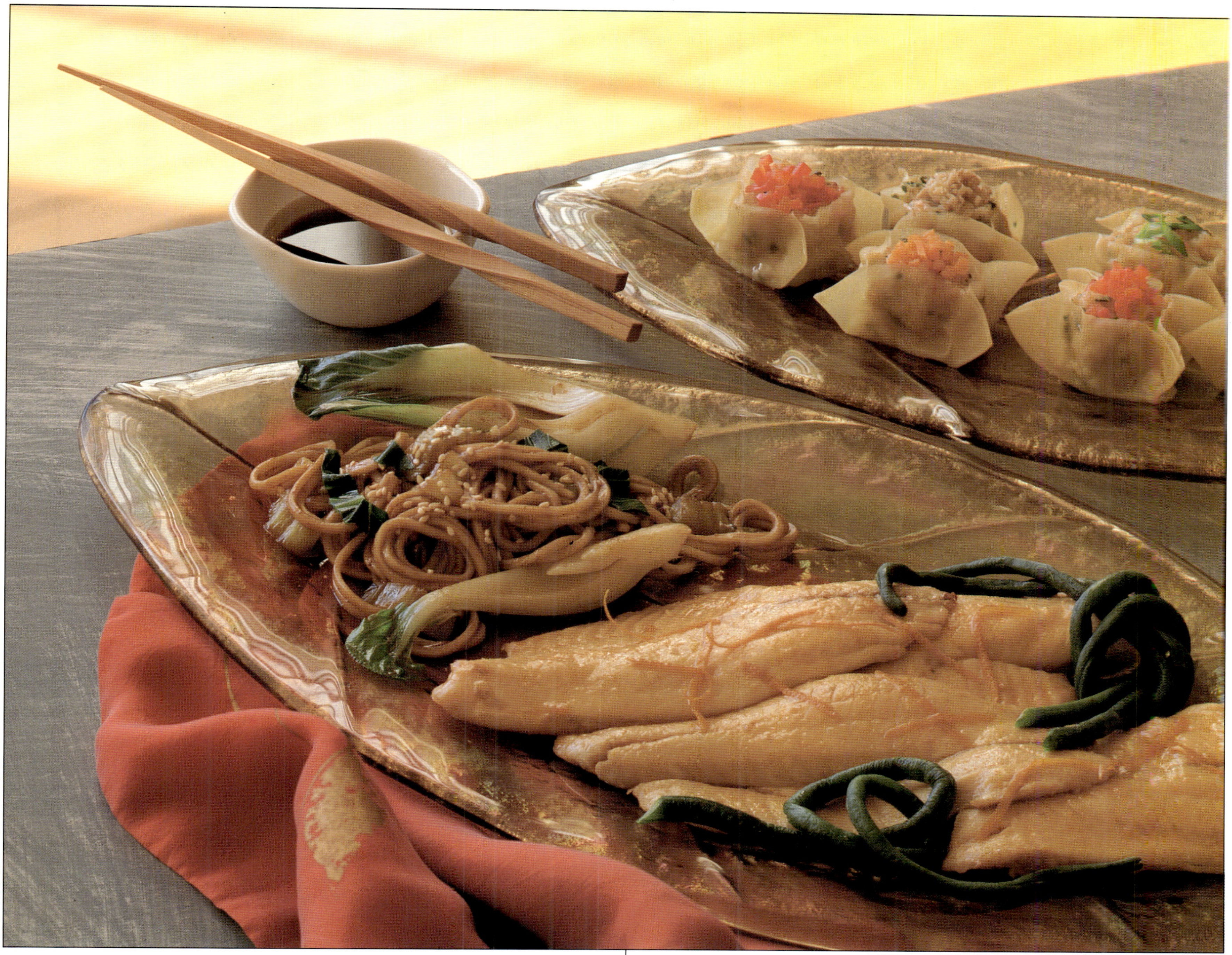

Met de klok mee van rechtsboven: Vier-seizoenenknoedels met dipsaus, Geurige gerookte tilapia, Chinese eiernoedels met mini-paksoi

1 theelepel geraspte verse gember
2 lenteuitjes, fijngehakt, plus 3 lenteuitjes, alleen het groen, zeer fijngehakt
1 theelepel fijngehakte mandarijne- of sinaasappelschil
1 eetlepel fijngehakte verse koriander
½ theelepel zout
1 theelepel maïzena
1 eetlepel Chinese rijstwijn of droge sherry
2 theelepels Chinese sesamolie
1½ theelepel arachide-olie
30 ronde wontonvellen of vierkante vellen met de hoekjes bijgesneden
1 wortel, geschild en fijngeraspt
1 rode paprika, fijngehakt
3 verse witte champignons, steeltje verwijderd, fijngehakt

1. Verhit de arachide-olie voor de dipsaus in een pan tot de olie zeer heet is en bijna rookt. Doe er de lenteuitjes in en neem de pan onmiddellijk van het vuur. Laat 10 minuten staan. Giet de olie door een zeef boven een kom, druk de uitjes aan om zoveel smaak in de olie te krijgen en gooi de uitjes weg.
2. Meng de lenteui-olie met de sojasaus en suiker in een kleine kom. Schep er de rondjes lenteui door en zet weg.
3. Zet een Chinese stoommand in een wok of grote pan en giet er zoveel water bij dat het tot aan de bodem van de mand komt. Neem de mand uit de wok en breng het water aan de kook.
4. Week de Chinese zwarte paddestoelen 20 minuten in 1,25 dl heet water en de suiker tot de paddestoelen zacht zijn. Giet ze af en verwijder de stelen. Snijd de paddestoelen in stukjes.
5. Doe de garnalen, het eiwit, de waterkastanjes, gember, 2 fijngehakte lenteuitjes, mandarijneschil, koriander en zout in een grote kom en schep alles om. Voeg de maïzena, rijstwijn, sesam- en arachide-olie toe en meng alles goed.
6. Maak de wontons door een bolle theelepel van de vulling in het midden van een wontonvel te scheppen. Breng de randen omhoog en knijp vier hoekjes in het vel tot u een open vierkantje hebt. Garneer de wontons met lenteui (lente), geraspte wortel (zomer), rode paprika (herfst) en champignon (winter).
7. Vet elke stoommand licht in met olie en schik de wontons naast elkaar in de mandjes. Stapel de mandjes op elkaar en zet ze boven het kokende water in de wok. Draai het vuur iets lager, leg het deksel op de wok en stoom 2-3 minuten. Verwissel de volgorde van de mandjes en stoom nog 2-3 minuten.

Voor 30 wontons

---

3 wontons per portie: Calorieën 230, Eiwit 17 g, Koolhydraten 21 g, Vezel 1 g, Vet totaal 7 g (Verzadigd 1,5 g, Enkelvoudig onverzadigd 3 g, Meervoudig onverzadigd 2,5 g), Cholesterol 105 mg, Natrium 700 mg, Vitamine A 50%, Vitamine C 30%.

▲ *1 Brood, 1 Vlees*

BROOD / MIDDEN-OOSTEN

Syrisch volkoren pitabrood

Vers pitabrood is geschikt voor al uw favoriete sandwichvullingen of als bijgerecht met groenten, hummus (recept op pagina 102) en baba ghanouj *(recept op pagina 103).*

1 pakje (7 g) droge gist
4 theelepels suiker
¼ theelepel zout
4 theelepels plantaardige olie
600 g bloem
300 g volkorenbloem
75 g geel maïsmeel gemengd met 75 g bloem

1. Bekleed een bakplaat met perkamentpapier en bestuif het papier met bloem.
2. Los de gist op met de suiker in 5 dl warm water (41°-46°C). Voeg het zout en de olie toe.
3. Doe het gistmengsel in een grote kom, voeg de 600 g bloem toe en meng tot een glad geheel. Schep er geleidelijk de volkorenbloem door tot het deeg te stevig is om te roeren.
4. Doe het deeg op een licht met bloem bestoven werkvlak en kneed het deeg circa 10 minuten tot het glad en elastisch is.
5. Doe het deeg in een licht met olie ingevette kom. Dek de kom af en laat het deeg circa 45 minuten rijzen tot het in volume verdubbeld is.
6. Druk de lucht uit het deeg, vorm er een bal van, dek die af en laat 30 minuten rusten.
7. Verdeel het deeg in 12 even grote ballen.
8. Bestuif een werkvlak met het maïsmeel-bloemmengsel en rol elke bal uit tot circa 15 cm doorsnee. Draai het deeg tewijl u het uitrolt, zodat het overal even dik is.
9. Schud overtollige bloem af en schik de rondjes op de bakplaat. Dek de broodjes af en laat circa 20 minuten rijzen tot ze iets uitgezet zijn.
10. Verwarm intussen de oven voor op 230°C. Keer de broodjes voorzichtig om en bak ze 5-7 minuten in de oven.

Voor 12 pitabroodjes

1 pitabroodje per portie: Calorieën 260, Eiwit 8 g, Koolhydraten 52 g, Vezel 4 g, Vet totaal 2 g (Verzadigd 0,5 g, Enkelvoudig onverzadigd 0,5 g, Meervoudig onverzadigd 1 g), Cholesterol 0 mg, Natrium 50 mg.
▲ *2 Brood*

GROENTEN / ISRAËL

Falafel

De falafels (kikkererwtenkoekjes) worden hier in een kleine hoeveelheid olie in een anti-aanbakpan gebakken in plaats van gefrituurd. Kikkererwten bevatten veel vitaminen en mineralen, zijn vezelrijk en vormen een goede vervanging voor rood vlees.

250 g kikkererwten, een nacht geweekt, of 750 g uit blik
60 g grof gehakte ui
8 tenen knoflook
3 eetlepels vers citroensap
4 eetlepels fijngehakte peterselie
2 eetlepels fijngehakte verse koriander
2 theelepels gemalen komijn
2 theelepels gemalen koriander
¼ theelepel geelwortel
¼ theelepel zout
versgemalen zwarte peper naar smaak
2 eetlepels bloem
1 theelepel bakpoeder
2 eetlepels olijfolie
3 pitabroodjes (vorig recept), gehalveerd
1 tomaat, grof gehakt
1 komkommer, geschild en in blokjes
4 eetlepels hummus (recept op pagina 102)
125 g dille-yoghurt (recept op pagina 110)

1. Giet de geweekte kikkererwten af, doe ze in een pan, giet er zoveel water bij dat ze onder staan en breng aan de kook. Draai het vuur laag en laat 1 uur sudderen. Giet ze af en laat afkoelen. (Kikkererwten in blik hoeft u alleen af te gieten.)
2. Doe de kikkererwten in een keukenmachine met de ui, knoflook, het citroensap, de peterselie en verse koriander. Draai tot een glad mengsel. Voeg de komijn, koriander en geelwortel toe en meng goed. Breng op smaak met zout en peper. Schep er de bloem en het bakpoeder door.
3. Vorm het mengsel tot 12 ronde koekjes van 5 cm doorsnee.
4. Verhit wat olijfolie in een anti-aanbak koekepan. Bak de koekjes in porties in circa 5 minuten per kant goudbruin. Houd de koekjes warm terwijl u de volgende portie bakt.
5. Serveer de falafel warm in het pitabrood met de tomaat, komkommer en hummus. Garneer met de yoghurt-dillesaus.

Voor 6 personen

1 portie: Calorieën 370, Eiwit 14 g, Koolhydraten 61 g, Vezel 6 g, Vet totaal 10 g (Verzadigd 1,5 g, Enkelvoudig onverzadigd 4,5 g, Meervoudig onverzadigd 2,5 g), Cholesterol 0 mg, Natrium 170 mg, IJzer 30%, Vitamine C 35%.
▲ *1 Vlees, 1 Brood*

VEDERWILD / MAROKKO

Tagine van piepkuikens met abrikozen en honingsaus

Tagine *is een Marokkaanse specialiteit. De naam* tagine *wijst op het gerecht zelf en op de aardewerk schotel met het kegelvormige deksel waarin het gerecht geserveerd wordt. Deze versie is van Kitty Morse, auteur van* Come with me to the kasbah: a cook's tour of Morocco. *Zij gebruikt piepkuikentjes in plaats van de traditionele duiven. U kunt vanzelfsprekend andere seizoensvruchten als vijgen gebruiken in plaats van de abrikozen. Een* tagine *is vrij machtig en de porties zijn groot, dus geef er alleen wat gestoomde rijst of couscous bij.*

3 eetlepels olijfolie
snufje Spaanse saffraan, gemalen
1 theelepel geelwortel
4 piepkuikens, elk 375-500 g
3 uien, in dunne plakken
30 g peterselie, gehakt
1,8 dl kippebouillon (zie woordenlijst)
500 g rijpe abrikozen, gehalveerd en ontpit, of 250 g gedroogde abrikozen, 20 minuten in water geweekt
1,85 dl honing
zout en versgemalen peper naar smaak
35 g hele geblancheerde amandelen, geroosterd (zie woordenlijst)

1. Doe de olie in een kleine kom met de saffraan en geelwortel. Wrijf de piepkuikens in met dit mengsel en schik ze in een passende braadpan met een deksel.
2. Doe er de helft van de ui, en peterselie en de bouillon in. Dek af en laat in circa 1 uur gaar sudderen. Doe de piepkuikens op een dienschaal en houd ze warm. Bewaar het kookvat.
3. Zet 8-10 abrikozenhelften weg ter garnering. Breng het kookvat aan de kook. Voeg de overgebleven abrikozen, ui en peterselie en de honing toe. Kook circa 10 minuten op een middelhoog vuur tot de saus tot tweederde ingekookt is. Breng op smaak met zout en peper.
4. Giet de saus over de piepkuikens, garneer met de bewaarde abrikozen en de geroosterde amandelen.

Voor 4 personen

1 kuiken per portie: Calorieën 790, Eiwit 53 g, Koolhydraten 60 g, Vezel 6 g, Vet totaal 40 g (Verzadigd 9 g, Enkelvoudig onverzadigd 20 g, Meervoudig onverzadigd 7 g), Cholesterol 155 mg, Natrium 160 mg, IJzer 25%, Vitamine A 80%, Vitamine C 45%.

▲ *2 Fruit, 2 Vlees*

Van boven naar beneden: Syrisch volkoren pitabrood, Falafel, Tagine van piepkuikens met abrikozen en honingsaus

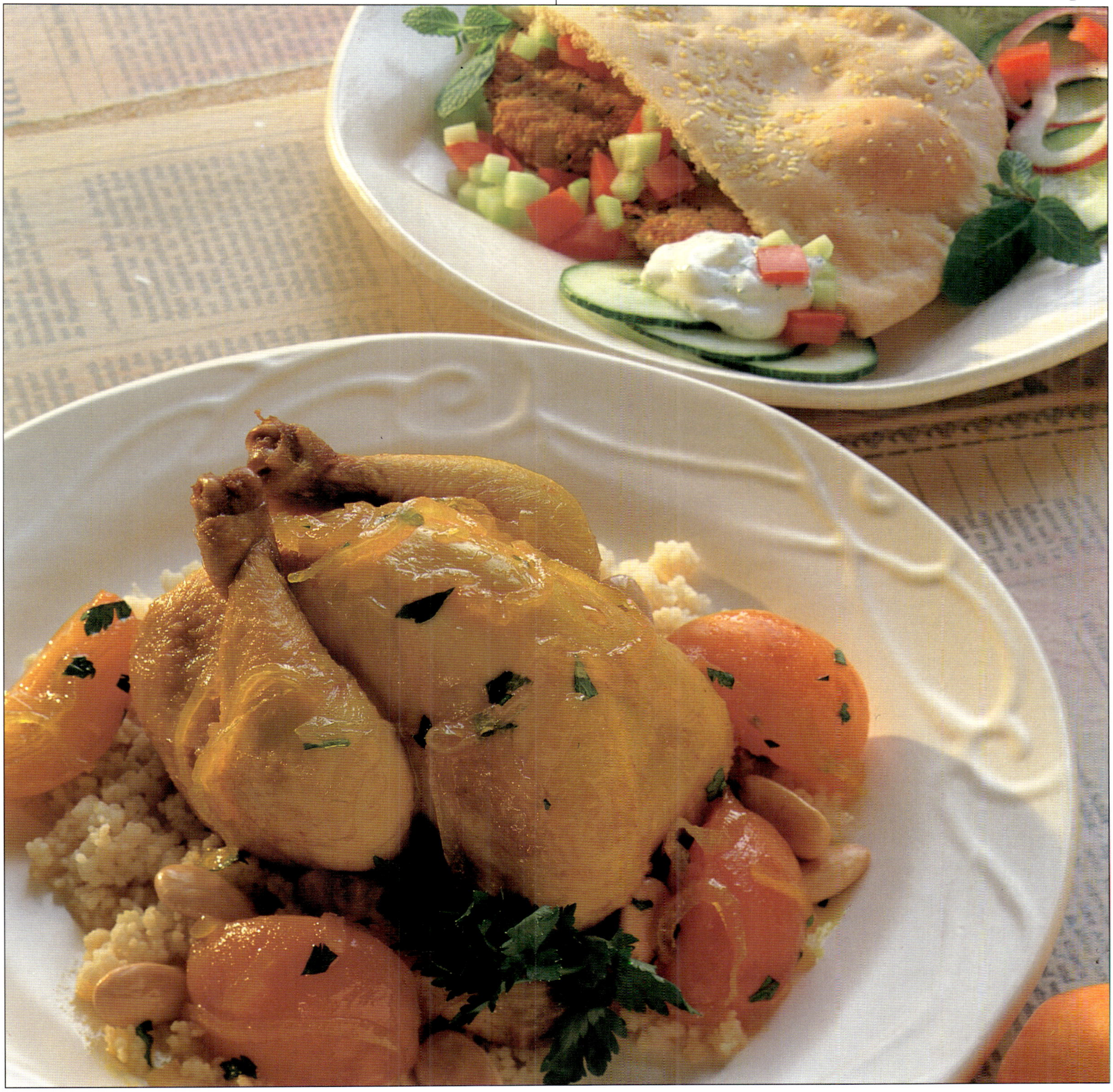

Zeebanket / Verenigde Staten

Krabkoekjes en asperges in citroenboter

Krabvlees bevat veel mineralen, waaronder zink. Zink bouwt de weerstand op. De asperges kunt u ter variatie eens vervangen door de jonge scheuten van de struisveervaren. Deze zijn ingeblikt wel in oosterse toko's verkrijgbaar.

500 g asperges of scheuten van de struisveervaren
zout naar smaak
1 eetlepel olijfolie
1 sjalotje, gesnipperd
3 eetlepels plus 1 theelepel vers citroensap
1 theelepel fijngeraspte citroenschil
4 eetlepels magere yoghurt
1 ei
½ theelepel mosterdpoeder
500 g vers krabvlees
125 g droog broodkruim
versgemalen peper naar smaak
30 g boter
2 theelepels reepjes citroenschil

1. Verwarm de oven voor op 200°C. Vet een anti-aanbak muffinvorm licht in met olie.
2. Spoel de asperges af en blancheer ze 3 minuten in kokend gezouten water. Dompel ze onmiddellijk in ijswater en giet ze dan af. Zet weg.
3. Verhit de olijfolie in een zuurbestendige pan. Doe er de sjalot in en fruit tot die gaar maar niet bruin is. Voeg 1 theelepel van het citroensap en de fijngeraspte citroenschil toe, neem de pan van het vuur en laat afkoelen.
4. Doe de yoghurt, het ei en mosterdpoeder in het afgekoelde mengsel in de pan. Schep er voorzichtig het krabvlees en broodkruim door. Breng op smaak met zout en peper.
5. Doe de muffinvorm 5 minuten in de oven. Neem de vorm eruit en schep snel volle lepels krabmengsel in elk vormpje. Bak 3-4 minuten, neem de vorm uit de oven, keer de koekjes om en doe de vorm 3-4 minuten terug in de oven, of tot de koekjes goudbruin zijn.
6. Verhit de boter in een koekepan. Doe er de asperges in en schep ze door de boter tot ze warm zijn. Voeg de rest van het citroensap en de reepjes schil toe en schep alles om. Schep de asperges uit de pan en schik ze op een dienschaal.
7. Schik de krabkoekjes op de schaal en schep er eventueel overgebleven citroenboter over. Dien onmiddellijk op.

Voor 4 personen

1 portie: Calorieën 330, Eiwit 29 g, Koolhydraten 25 g, Vezel 2 g, Vet totaal 13 g (Verzadigd 5 g, Enkelvoudig onverzadigd 5 g, Meervoudig onverzadigd 1 g), Cholesterol 120 mg, Natrium 1170 mg, Vitamine C 30%.

▲ *1 Groente, 1 Vlees*

Hapjes / Verenigde Staten

Mini-groenten gevuld met erwten en champignons

Waarmee beter de lente in te luiden dan met malse mini-groenten en erwtjes? Deze hapjes zijn perfect als onderdeel van een schaal rauwkost of als voorafje met een rode-paprikasaus (recept op pagina 90).

250 g krieltjes
250 g mini-meiraapjes
250 g mini-patissons
250 g verse doperwtjes, gedopt
2 eetlepels vers citroensap
2 theelepels fijngehakte verse peterselie
½ theelepel fijngehakte verse dragon
zout en versgemalen peper naar smaak
2 eetlepels olijfolie
2 sjalotjes, gesnipperd
1 teen knoflook, fijngehakt
500 g witte champignons, fijngehakt
½ theelepel fijngehakte verse tijm
3 eetlepels gesnipperde bieslook

1. Blancheer de krieltjes, raapjes en patissons circa 2 minuten of tot ze bijtgaar zijn. Dompel ze onmiddellijk in ijswater. Giet ze af. Snijd de bovenkant van de groenten en een dun plakje van de bodem af, zodat ze recht bli ven zitten. Schep een kuiltje uit elke groente met een bolletjesstreker. Bewaar de bolletjes voor een bouillon of soep.
2. Blancheer voor de erwtenpuree de erwtjes 1½ minuut en dompel ze onmiddellijk in ijswater. Giet ze af. Doe de erwtjes in een keukenmachine of blender en draai tot een gladde puree. Voeg het citroensap, 1 theelepel van de peterselie en de dragon toe. Breng op smaak met zout en peper. Zet weg.
3. Verhit voor de champignonvulling de olie in een middelgrote koekepan. Fruit de sjalotjes en knoflook tot ze gaar maar niet bruin zijn. Voeg de champignons toe en bak circa 5 minuten tot het vocht verdampt is. Voeg de rest van de peterselie, tijm en wat zout en peper toe. Schep het mengsel uit de pan en laat afkoelen.
4. Doe de erwtenpuree in een spuitzak en vul er de uitgeholde raapjes mee.
5. Doe het champignonmengsel in een spuitzak en vul er de uitgeholde krieltjes en patissons mee.

6 Bestrooi de groenten met de bieslook en schik ze op een dienschaal. Dien onmiddellijk op.

Voor 8 personen

1 portie: Calorieën 100, Eiwit 4 g, Koolhydraten 14 g, Vezel 3 g, Vet totaal 4 g (Verzadigd 0,5 g, Enkelvoudig onverzadigd 2,5 g, Meervoudig onverzadigd 0,5 g). Cholesterol 0 mg, Natrium 50 mg, Vitamine A 40%, Vitamine C 50%.

▲ *2 Groente*

Van boven naar beneden: Mini-groenten gevuld met erwten en champignons, Krabkoekjes en asperges in citroenboter

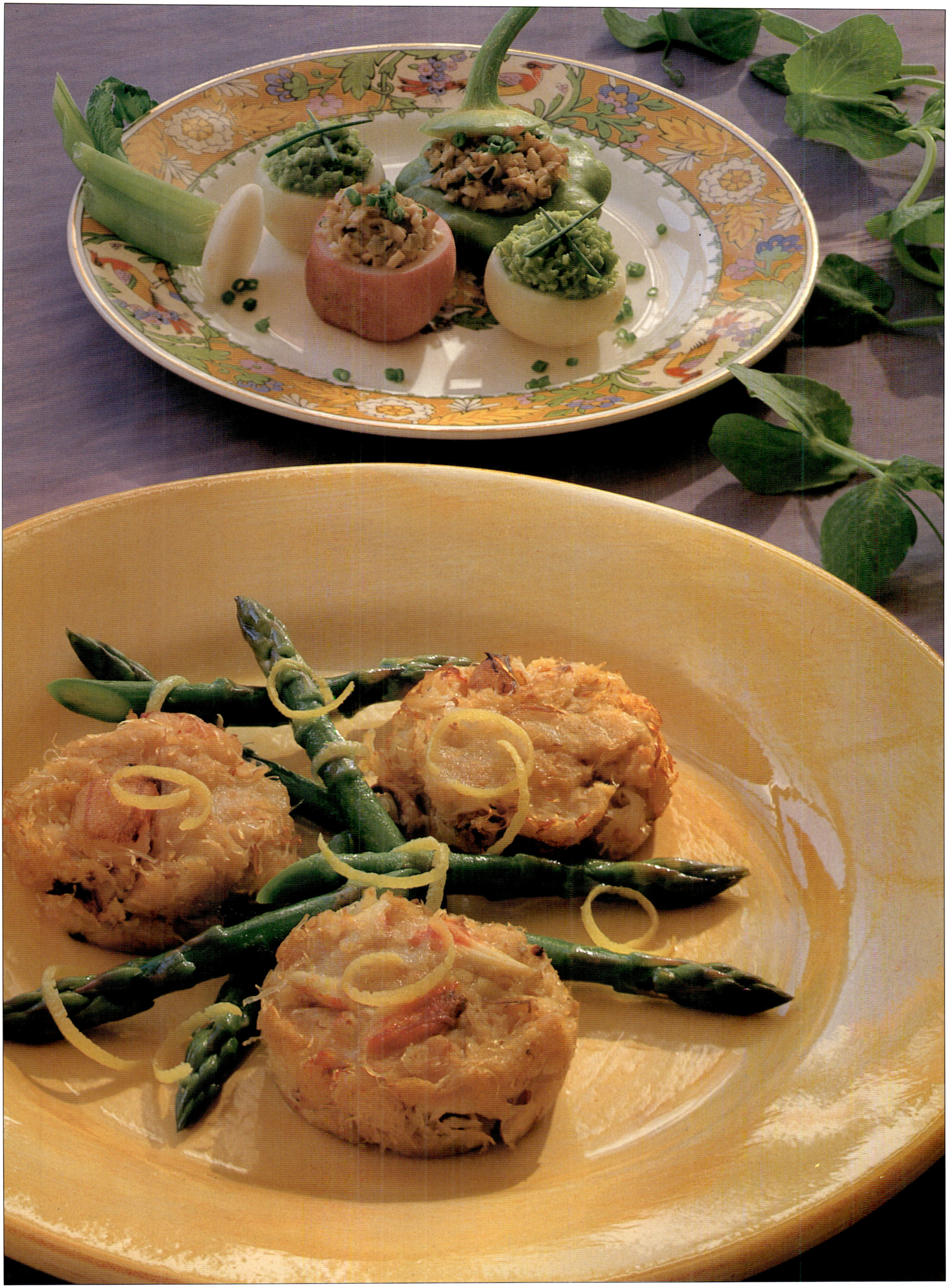

Brood / Zweden

Limpa

Zweeds roggebrood

Dit brood is altijd lekker, maar gaat vooral goed samen met zeebanket. Omdat roggebloem niet genoeg gluten heeft voor een elastisch deeg, wordt er ook een broodbloem of een glutenrijke bloem gebruikt. Het resultaat is een vrij compact en smakelijk brood.

1 pakje (7 g) droge gist
2 eetlepels lichtbruine basterdsuiker
235 g roggebloem
4 eetlepels melasse
1 theelepel venkelzaad
2 theelepels geraspte sinaasappelschil
2 eetlepels saffloerolie
1½ theelepel zout
780-800 g bloem

1. Bekleed een bakplaat met perkamentpapier.
2. Los de gist en basterdsuiker op in 5 dl warm water (41°-46°C). Voeg de roggebloem, melasse, het venkelzaad en de sinaasappelschil toe. Schep alles om tot een glad mengsel. Dek het deeg af en laat circa 1 uur staan tot het in volume verdubbeld is.
3. Schep de saffloerolie, het zout en 150 g van de bloem door het roggemengsel. Klop tot een glad mengsel. Klop telkens 75 g bloem door het deeg tot het zacht en glad is.
4. Doe het deeg op een licht met bloem bestoven werkvlak en kneed het deeg circa 10 minuten tot het glad en niet meer plakkerig is.
5. Vet een kom licht in met olie. Doe het deeg in de kom, dek af en laat circa 1 uur staan tot het deeg in volume verdubbeld is.
6. Druk de lucht uit het deeg en vorm er 2 ronde broden van. Leg ze vervolgens op de bakplaat en kerf er met een scheermes een kruis in. Dek de broden af en laat ze 1 uur staan tot ze in volume verdubbeld zijn.
7. Verwarm intussen de oven voor op 180°C.
8. Bak de broden 45-55 minuten in de oven tot ze goudbruin zijn en hol klinken wanneer u er op klopt. Laat ze afkoelen.

Voor 2 broden (24 sneden)

1 snee per portie: Calorieën 140, Eiwit 3 g, Koolhydraten 28 g, Vezel 2 g, Vet totaal 1,5 g (Verzadigd 0 g, Enkelvoudig onverzadigd 0 g, Meervoudig onverzadigd 1 g), Cholesterol 0 mg, Natrium 150 mg.
▲ *1 Brood*

Pasta / Frankrijk

Farfalle met garnalen en coquilles

75 g gesnipperde ui
3 tenen knoflook, fijngehakt
3 eetlepels olijfolie
1,25 dl droge witte wijn
3 grote tomaten, ontveld en ontzaad
2,5 dl gepureerde tomaten
1 theelepel venkelzaad
4 eetlepels half melk, half room
250 g middelgrote rauwe garnalen, gepeld en darmkanaal verwijderd
250 g coquilles
2 eetlepels Pernod
¼ theelepel zout
versgemalen peper naar smaak
500 g farfalle (vlinderpasta), bijtgaar gekookt en uitgelekt
7 g verse dragonblaadjes

1. Fruit de ui en knoflook in de olijfolie gaar maar niet bruin in een grote koekepan. Blus de pan af met de wijn en voeg dan de tomaten, gepureerde tomaten en het venkelzaad toe. Laat 30 minuten sudderen tot de saus iets dikker is.
2. Voeg de melk, room, garnalen en coquilles toe. Laat alles 5-7 minuten sudderen tot de garnalen en coquilles net gaar zijn. Breng op smaak met de Pernod, het zout en wat peper.
3. Schep de saus door de pasta, bestrooi met de dragon en dien onmiddellijk op.

Voor 6 personen

1 portie: Calorieën 480, Eiwit 26 g, Koolhydraten 69 g, Vezel 4 g, Vet totaal 11 g (Verzadigd 2 g, Enkelvoudig onverzadigd 6 g, Meervoudig onverzadigd 1,5 g), Cholesterol 75 mg, Natrium 240 mg, IJzer 30%, Vitamine A 25%, Vitamine C 60%.
▲ *2 Brood, 1 Vlees*

Salades / Frankrijk

Gebakken zalm en linzen met warme frambozenvinaigrette

Lente is de perfecte tijd voor deze gezonde salade. Kies uw favoriete slasoorten of serveer de linzen in een blaadje roodlof. Zowel linzen en zalm zijn rijk aan kalium, Vitamine B_6 en andere belangrijke voedingsstoffen.

225 g groene linzen, gespoeld en uitgelekt
1 wortel, in kleine blokjes
1 koolraap, in blokjes
75 g gesnipperde ui
4 eetlepels saffloerolie
4 zalmfilets, 1 cm dik, circa 375 g totaalgewicht
1 sjalot, gesnipperd
6 eetlepels frambozenazijn
¼ theelepel zout
versgemalen peper naar smaak
60 *mesclun* (mengsel van slasoorten: molsla, frisée, raketkruid enzovoort)
4 takjes verse kervel

1. Verwarm de oven voor op 150°C.
2. Doe de linzen en 7,5 dl water in een grote pan en breng aan de kook. Draai het vuur laag en voeg de wortel, koolraap en ui toe. Laat 20 minuten sudderen tot de linzen gaar maar niet papperig zijn. Giet af en zet weg.
3. Verhit 2 eetlepels van de olie in een grote koekepan en schroei de zalm in 2 minuten per kant dicht op een hoog vuur. Doe de filets in een ovenschaal, dek die af en houd de zalm 5 minuten warm in de oven.
4. Doe de sjalot in het bakvocht in de koekepan en fruit de sjalot gaar. Blus de pan af met 4 eetlepels van de azijn en laat iets inkoken. Breng op smaak met zout en peper. Giet de warme vinaigrette over de linzen en bewaar 4 theelepels voor de zalm. Schep de linzen goed om.
5. Schep de overgebleven azijn en olie door de *mesclun*.
6. Schik de *mesclun* op een helft van elk bord en schep de linzen op de andere helft. Schik een zalmfilet op de linzen en schep 1 theelepel van de overgebleven vinaigrette over elke filet. Garneer de zalm met de kervel en dien onmiddellijk op.

Voor 4 personen

1 portie: Calorieën 450, Eiwit 52 g, Koolhydraten 38 g, Vezel 8 g, Vet totaal 20 g (Verzadigd 2 g, Enkelvoudig onverzadigd 3,5 g, Meervoudig onverzadigd 13 g), Cholesterol 50 mg, Natrium 240 mg, IJzer 30%, Vitamine A 100%, Vitamine C 30%.

▲ *1 Groente, 1 Vlees*

Met de klok mee van rechtsboven: Zweeds roggebrood, Farfalle met garnalen en coquilles, Gebakken zalm en linzen met warme frambozenvinaigrette

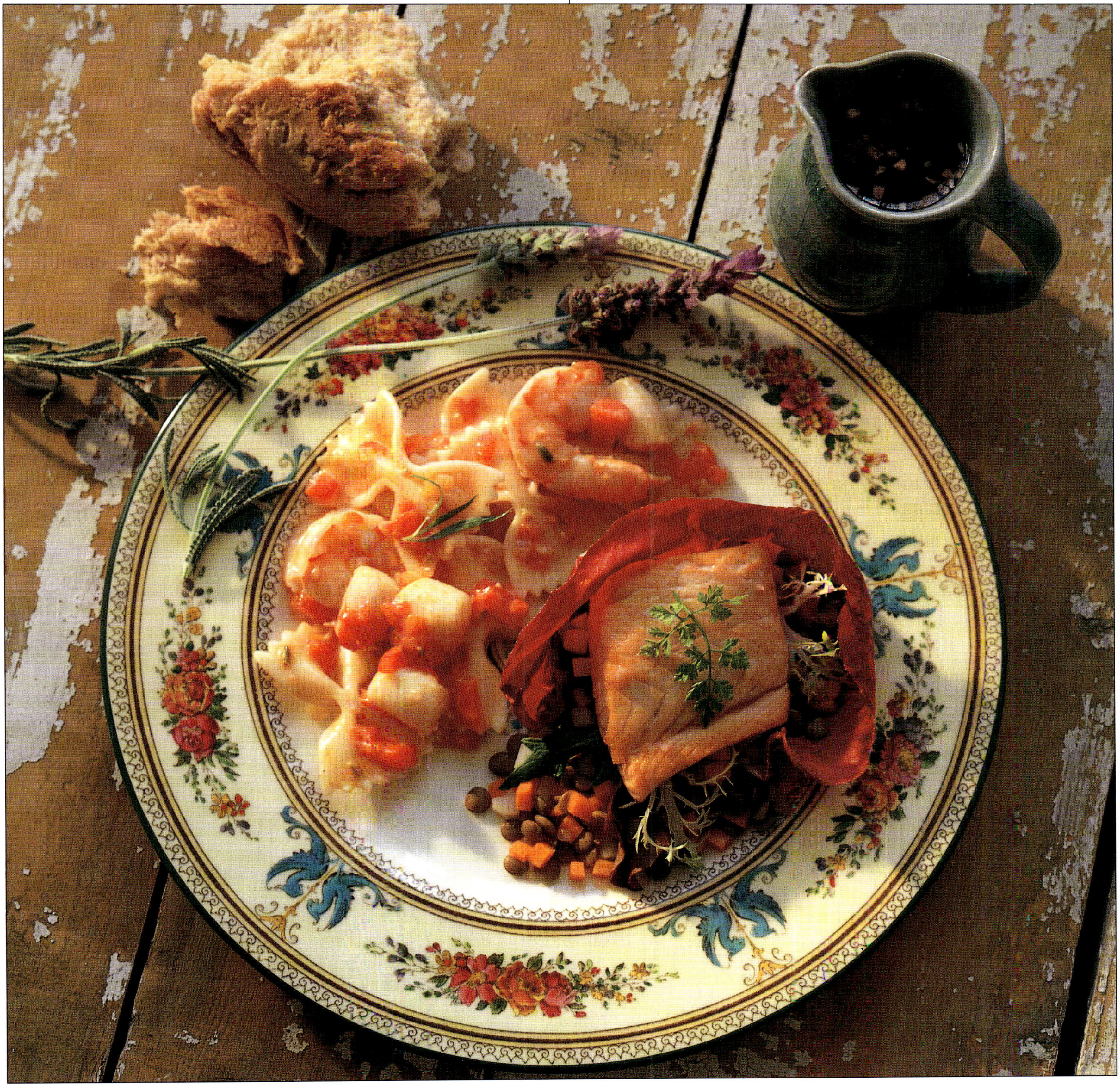

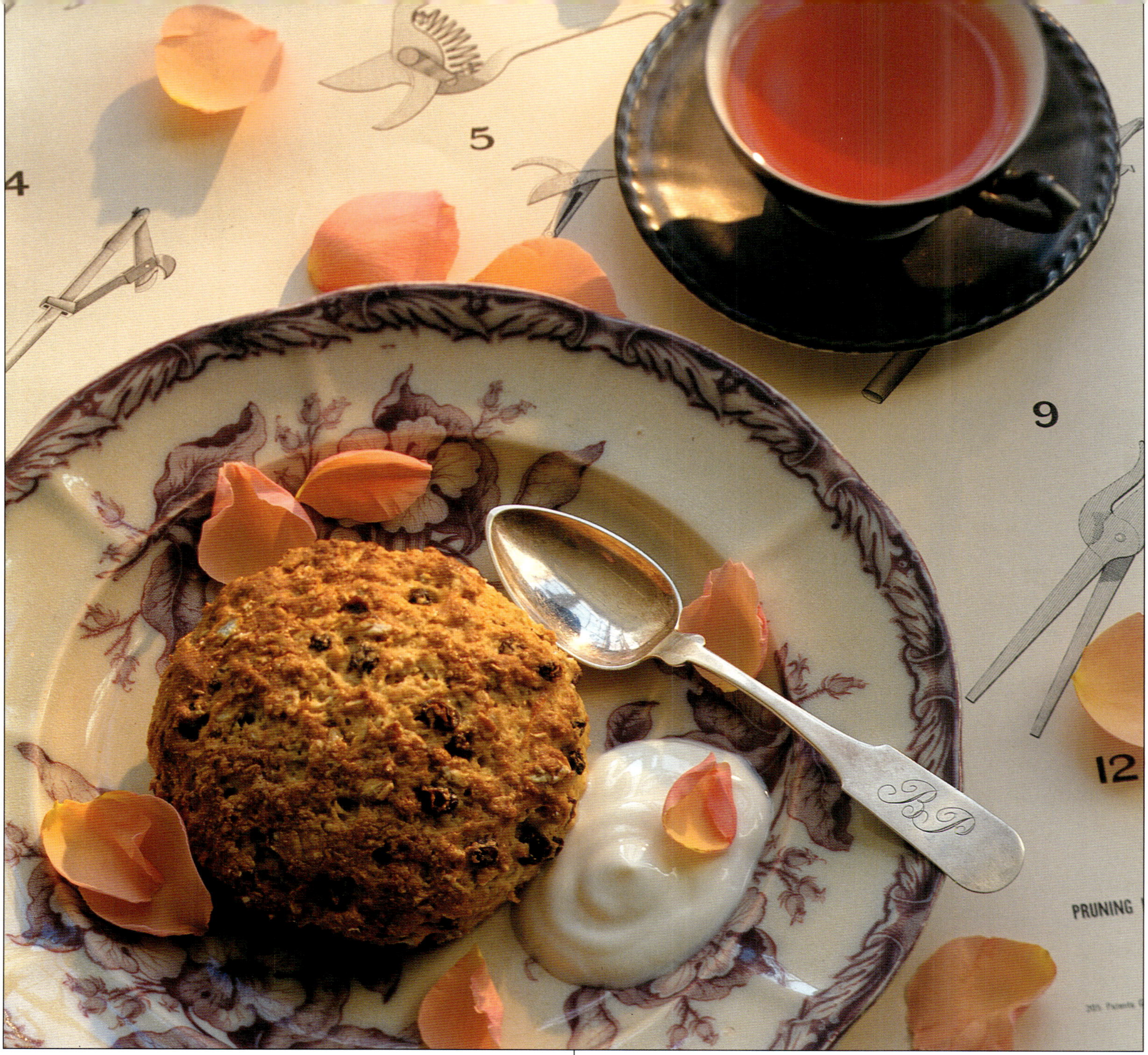

Meergranen krenten scones met rozebladroom

BROOD / GROOT-BRITTANNIË

Meergranen-krenten scones met rozebladroom

Deze hartige scones hebben een hoger eiwitgehalte dan gemiddeld door gebruik van amarantbloem. Amarantbloem heeft een hoog kalk- en ijzergehalte en is verkrijgbaar in reformwinkels. U kunt als amarantbloem niet verkrijgbaar is gewone bloem gebruiken.

250 g bloem
160 g volkorenbloem
90 g rauwe havervlokken
45 g amarantbloem
20 g tarwe- of haverzemelen
90 g suiker plus 1 eetlepel
1 eetlepel bakpoeder
1½ theelepel zuiveringszout
4,25 dl karnemelk of verse melk met 1½ eetlepel vers citroensap
2 theelepels fijngeraspte sinaasappelschil
185 g krenten
3 eetlepels magere melk
5 dl rozebladroom (recept volgt)

1. Verwarm de oven voor op 200°C. Bekleed een bakplaat met perkamentpapier.
2. Doe de bloem, volkorenbloem, havervlokken, amarantbloem en zemelen in een grote kom en schep alles om. Voeg 90 g van de suiker, het bakpoeder en zuiveringszout toe en schep om.
3. Doe de karnemelk, sinaasappelschil en krenten in een andere kom en meng goed. Voeg de droge ingrediënten toe en schep om tot ze net vochtig zijn. Meng niet te veel.
4. Doe het deeg op een licht met bloem bestoven werkvlak en rol tot 2,5 cm dik. Steek het deeg uit in rondjes van circa 7 cm met een uitsteekvorm en leg de rondjes op de bakplaat.
5. Kwast de scones in met de melk en bestrooi met de overgebleven suiker. Bak 20 minuten in de oven tot ze goudbruin zijn. Serveer de scones warm en geef er de rozebladroom bij.

Voor 12 scones

1 scone per portie: Calorieën 210, Eiwit 6 g, Koolhydraten 44 g, Vezel 4 g, Vet totaal 1,5 g (Verzadigd 0,5 g, Enkelvoudig onverzadigd 0,5 g, Meervoudig onverzadigd 0,5 g), Cholesterol 0 mg, Natrium 200 mg.
▲ *2 Brood*

ROZEBLADROOM

5 dl magere roeryoghurt, een nacht in de koelkast in een zeef laten uitlekken
3 eetlepels honing, of naar smaak
1 eetlepel rozewater
verse rozebladen

1. Doe de uitgelekte yoghurt, honing en het rozewater in een kom en schep alles om.
2. Doe in een decoratieve kom en garneer met de rozebladen.

Voor 5 dl

1 volle eetlepel per portie: Calorieën 40, Eiwit 2 g, Koolhydraten 7 g, Vezel 0 g, Vet totaal 1,5 g (Verzadigd 1 g, Enkelvoudig onverzadigd 0,5 g, Meervoudig onverzadigd 0 g), Cholesterol 0 mg Natrium 25 mg.
▲ *½ Melk*

DRANKEN / VERENIGDE STATEN

Aardbei-rabarber-sinaasappeldrank

Dit frisse fruitdrankje is heerlijk bij een middagsnack of het ontbijt en heeft door de rabarber een hoog kalkgehalte.

250 g aardbeien
1 recept rabarber-sinaasappelcompote (recept op pagina 95)
5 dl vers sinaasappelsap
10 ijsblokjes

1. Doe alle ingrediënten in een blender en draai tot een glad mengsel. Dien onmiddellijk op.

Voor 6 personen

1 glas per portie: Calorieën 160, Eiwit 2 g, Koolhydraten 40 g, Vezel 4 g, Vet totaal 1 g (Verzadigd 0 g, Enkelvoudig onverzadigd 0 g, Meervoudig onverzadigd 0 g), Cholesterol 0 mg, Natrium 5 mg, Vitamine C 180%, Kalk 10%.
▲ *2 Fruit*

ONTBIJT / VERENIGDE STATEN

Zuidwestelijk ontbijt met tomatillosalsa

U kunt dit heerlijke brunchgerecht een nacht van tevoren maken en in een decoratieve souffléschaal serveren. U kunt het ook in individuele schaaltjes maken - in dat geval bedraagt de kooktijd 35-40 minuten.

1 recept kippeworst (recept op pagina 164)
8 eiwitten
3,75 dl magere melk
5 bloemtortilla's
3,75 dl geroosterde-tomatillosalsa (recept volgt)
30 g geraspte jonge kaas (desgewenst)

1. Vet een souffléschaal licht in met olie.
2. Verkruimel de kippeworst in een kom en zet weg. Klop de eiwitten en melk in een grote maatbeker. Zet weg.
3. Schik een laag tortilla's in de souffléschaal. Strooi er wat van de kippeworst over en giet er dan wat van het eimengsel over. Ga zo door met het lagen maken en eindig met een laag tortilla. Bedek met tomatillasalsa en zet een nacht in de koelkast.
4. Verwarm de oven voor op 180°C. Strooi de geraspte kaas over de tomatillosalsa. Zet de schaal tot de helft in het water in een waterbad en zet circa 1 uur in de oven tot de bovenkant stevig aanvoelt. Dien warm op of op kamertemperatuur.

Voor 8 personen

1 portie: Calorieën 220, Eiwit 20 g, Koolhydraten 20 g, Vezel 1 g, Vet totaal 6 g (Verzadigd 1 g, Enkelvoudig onverzadigd 1,5 g, Meervoudig onverzadigd 3 g), Cholesterol 35 mg, Natrium 210 mg.
▲ *1 Brood, 1 Vlees*

TOMATILLOSALSA

Dek deze salsa af en bewaar in de koelkast tot gebruik. Salsa is ook heerlijk met rauwkost of tortillachips (zie het recept voor sopa di lima op pagina 71).

8-10 verse tomatillo's, schutblad verwijderd
1 jalapeño chilipeper of naar smaak (desgewenst)
geraspte schil van 1 citroen
3 eetlepels vers citroensap

1. Verwarm de oven voor op 180°C.
2. Schik de tomatillo's op een licht met olie ingevette bakplaat. Leg er desgewenst de jalapeño op. Rooster ze 20-25 minuten in de oven, of tot ze goudbruin en gaar zijn.
3. Doe de tomatillo's en jalapeño in een blender en draai tot een glad mengsel. Voeg de citroenschil en het sap toe en meng goed.

Voor 5 dl

4 eetlepels per portie: Calorieën 10, Eiwit 0 g, Koolhydraten 3 g, Vezel 1 g, Vet totaal 0 g (Verzadigd 0 g, Enkelvoudig onverzadigd 0 g, Meervoudig onverzadigd 0 g), Cholesterol 0 mg, Natrium 0 mg.

Van links naar rechts: Aardbei-rabarber-sinaasappeldrank, Zuidwestelijk ontbijt met tomatillosalsa

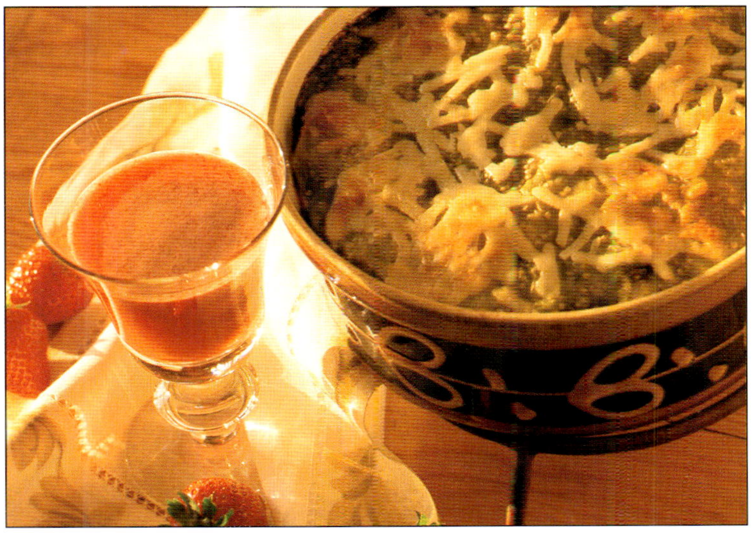

GEVOGELTE / MEXICO

Mole poplano de guajolote

KALKOEN MET CHILIPEPERSAUS

Deze stoofschotel met kalkoen is een traditioneel Mexicaans feestgerecht. Geef er warme bloemtortilla's bij. Elk mole *recept is anders. Pas de kruiden aan naar smaak en creëer uw eigen versie. Als verse* mulato *of gedroogde* poblano *chilipepers niet verkrijgbaar zijn, kunt u jalapeño pepers gebruiken om het gerecht pit te geven. U kunt de* mole *saus ook met kip of eend serveren.*

4 kg kalkoen, het vel en vet verwijderd en het vlees in blokjes gesneden
5 dl kippebouillon (zie woordenlijst), verhit tot tegen het kookpunt
1 wortel, geschild en in stukjes van 1 cm gesneden
1 ui, in stukjes van 1 cm gesneden
2 tenen knoflook, gekneusd
3 gedroogde *poblano* (milde) chilipepers
2 gedroogde *ancho* chilipepers
4 gedroogde *mulato* chilipepers
45 g rozijnen
3 cm kaneelpijp
2 hele kruidnagels
¼ theelepel heel korianderzaad
¼ theelepel anijszaad
2 eetlepels sesamzaad, geroosterd
1 maïstortilla, in stukjes gebroken
3 rijpe tomaten, ontveld
35 g *pepitas* (gepeld pompoenzaad), geroosterd
30 g Mexicaanse chocolade of extra bitter chocolade

1. Verwarm de oven voor op 180°C. Doe de stukken kalkoen in een braadslee met de kippebouillon, wortel, ui en knoflook. Dek de slee af en zet 45 minuten in de oven of tot de kalkoen gaar is. Schep de stukken kalkoen uit het kooknat. Zeef het kooknat en zet er 3,5 dl van weg en bewaar de groenten. Doe de rest van het kooknat en de stukken kalkoen in de slee en houd warm.
2. Maak de mole terwijl de kalkoen in de oven is. Week de gedroogde chilipepers en rozijnen minstens 30 minuten in warm water. Giet af. Pureer dit mengsel met 2,5 dl van het bewaarde kooknat in een blender. Doe de puree in een pan en laat 10 minuten sudderen.
3. Doe het kaneelpijpje, de kruidnagels, het koriander- en anijszaad in een middelgrote koekepan. Rooster alles op een middelhoog vuur tot de zaadjes lichtgekleurd en geurig zijn. Neem de pan van het vuur en laat alles afkoelen. Maal het zaadmengsel met 1 eetlepel van het sesamzaad fijn. Doe het mengsel in de blender met de tomaten, *pepitas*, tortilla, de bewaarde groenten en het resterende kooknat. Draai alles tot een glad mengsel en giet het dan bij de chilipeperpuree. Breek de chocolade in het mengsel en laat het geheel vervolgens 30 minuten sudderen onder af en toe omscheppen.
4. Schik de stukken kalkoen op een verwarmde schaal. Schep er de mole over, bestrooi met de rest van het sesamzaad en dien op.

Voor 10 personen

1 portie: Calorieën 330, Eiwit 45 g, Koolhydraten 12 g, Vezel 2 g, Vet totaal 11 g (Verzadigd 4 g, Enkelvoudig onverzadigd 3 g, Meervoudig onverzadigd 3,5 g), Cholesterol 110 mg, Natrium 110 mg, IJzer 25%, Vitamine C 180%.
▲ *1 Groente, 2 Vlees*

GEVOGELTE / HONGARIJE

Kip paprikás

Lecsó *is een mengsel van paprika's dat u van tevoren kunt maken, invriezen en op het laatste moment uit de vriezer halen om een snelle* paprikás *te maken. Schep de kip over noedels of rijst. Dit smakelijke eenpansgerecht bevat veel eiwit, verschillende B vitaminen, zink, ijzer en vitamine A en C.*

1 kg stukken kip, het vel en vet verwijderd
1 recept *lecsó* (recept op pagina 132)
2,5 dl kippebouillon (zie woordenlijst)
½ theelepel gedroogde marjolein
375 g eiernoedels
1,25 dl magere yoghurt
1 eetlepel bloem met 1 eetlepel water gemengd
paprikapoeder naar smaak

1. Verhit de stukken kip, *lecsó*, kippebouillon en marjolein in een grote soeppan. Leg het deksel op de pan en laat 30-35 minuten sudderen, of tot de kip gaar is.
2. Kook de noedels 10 minuten voor de kip gaar is. Giet de noedels af en schik ze op een schaal. Schep de kip en groenten met een schuimspaan uit het kooknat, schik ze over de noedels en houd alles warm.
3. Doe de yoghurt in het kooknat en verwarm. Klop er het bloempapje door en laat circa 3 minuten sudderen tot de saus iets dikker is. Breng zonodig op smaak met zout, peper en paprikapoeder. Schep de saus over de kip en dien onmiddellijk op.

Voor 6 personen

1 portie: Calorieën 465, Eiwit 34 g, Koolhydraten 58 g, Vezel 5 g, Vet totaal 11 g (Verzadigd 2,5 g, Enkelvoudig onverzadigd 5 g, Meervoudig onverzadigd 2,5 g), Cholesterol 130 mg, Natrium 310 mg, IJzer 35%, Vitamine A 55%, Vitamine C 340%.
▲ *2 Brood, 1 Groente, 1 Vlees*

Van boven naar beneden: Kip paprikás, Kalkoen met chilipepersaus, opgediend met rijst

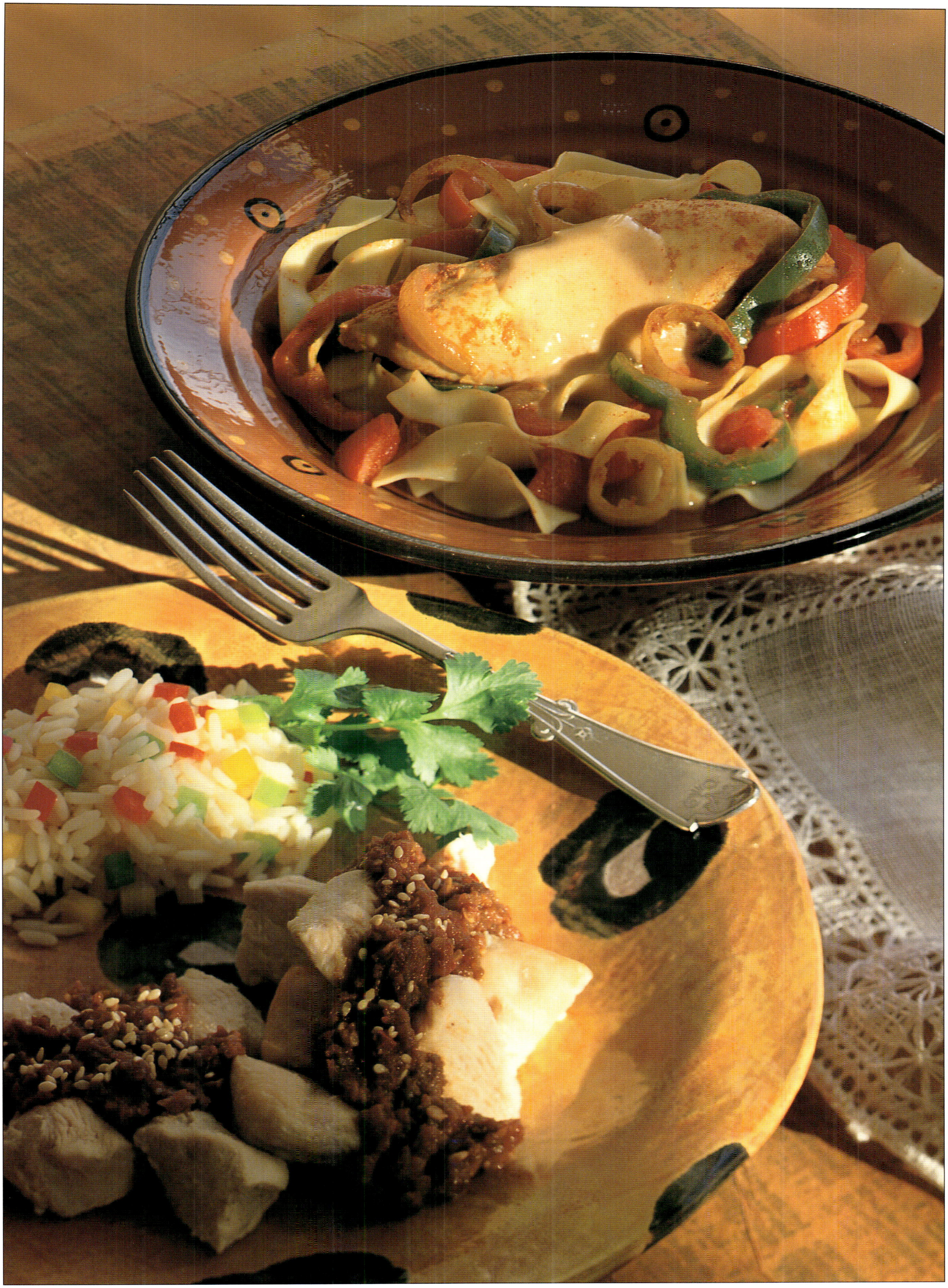

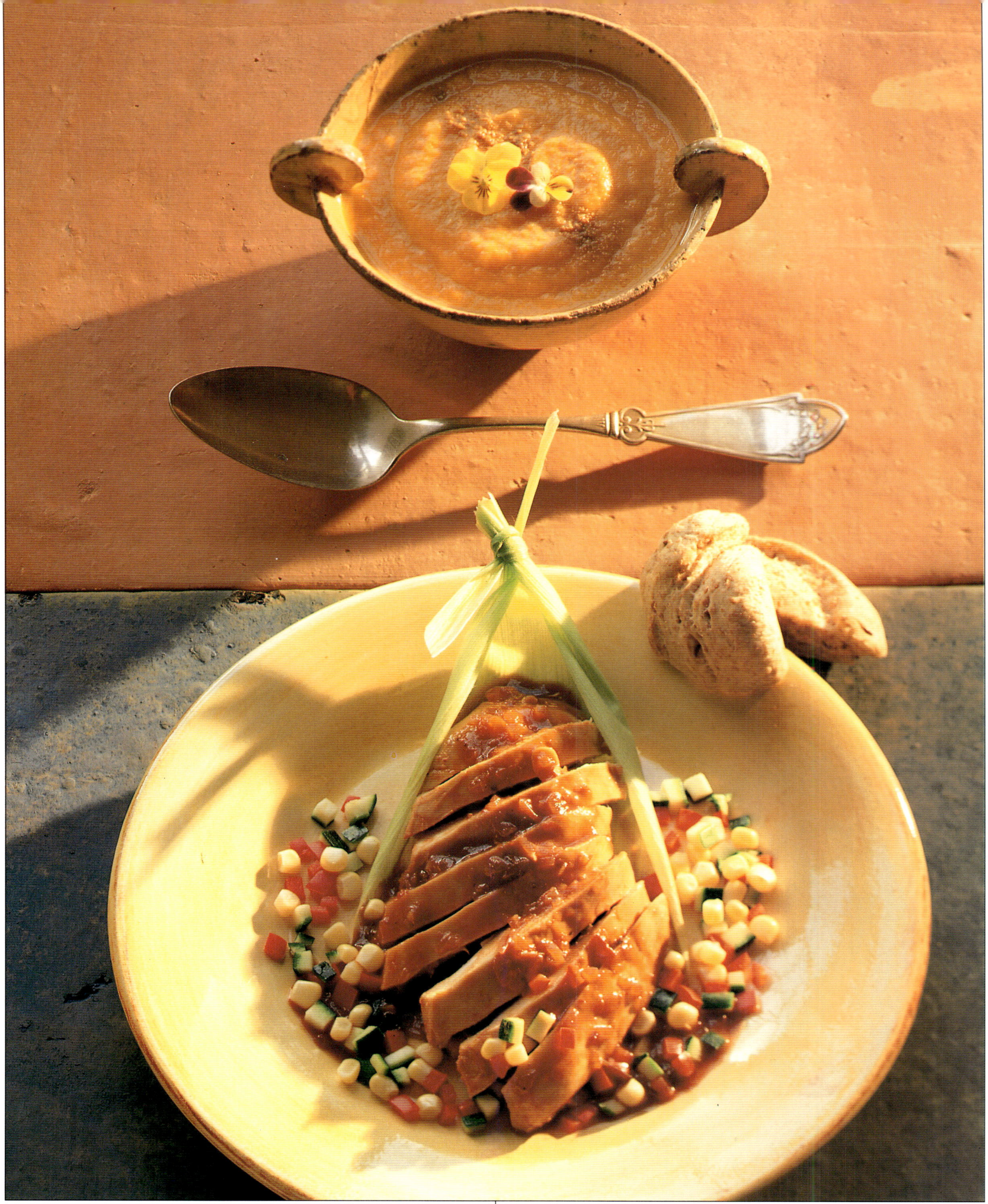

Van boven naar beneden: Romige wortel-preisoep, Volkorenbeschuit, Terracotta kipfilet met confetti

BROOD / FINLAND

Volkorenbeschuit

Dit beschuit is ideaal voor een picknick of als snack. In een luchtdichte trommel bewaard, zijn ze een week houdbaar.

1 pakje (7 g) droge gist
1½ theelepel suiker
4 eetlepels saffloerolie
1,8 dl warme magere melk
½ theelepel zout
235 g volkorenbloem
1 eetlepel karwijzaad
280 g bloem

1. Bekleed een bakplaat met perkamentpapier.
2. Los de gist en de suiker op in 4 eetlepels warm water (41°-46°C) in een grote kom.
3. Voeg de olie, melk, het zout, de volkorenbloem en het karwij-

zaad toe en schep alles om tot het deeg niet klonterig is. Schep er telkens 75 g bloem door.

4. Doe het deeg op een licht met bloem bestoven werkvlak en kneed het deeg tot het glad en niet meer plakkerig is. Verdeel het deeg in 16 gelijke stukken en vorm er ballen van. Rol de ballen tussen uw handen om ze iets langer te maken. Schik de rollen op de bakplaat, dek die af met plastic folie en laat circa 45 minuten rijzen tot ze in volume verdubbeld zijn.
5. Verwarm intussen de oven voor op 230°C. Bak de rolletjes in 10 minuten goudbruin. Neem ze uit de oven en laat op een rooster afkoelen. Zet de oven op 200°C.
6. Halveer elk rolletje in de lengte en schik ze, met de gesneden kant onder, weer op de bakplaat. Bak ze nog 10 minuten.
7. Laat het beschuit afkoelen en een nacht in de lucht drogen.

Voor 32 stuks

---

2 beschuiten per portie: Calorieën 130, Eiwit 4 g, Koolhydraten 20 g, Vezel 2 g, Vet totaal 4 g (Verzadigd 0,5 g, Enkelvoudig onverzadigd 0,5 g, Meervoudig onverzadigd 3 g), Cholesterol 0 mg, Natrium 80 mg.

▲ *1 Brood*

GEVOGELTE / MEXICO

Terracotta kipfilet met confetti

Serveer dit landelijke kipgerecht met tortilla's en ijskoude cervezas *(pils).*

2 hele kipfilets, ontveld, gehalveerd in de lengte
5 dl kippebouillon (zie woordenlijst)
3 eetlepels witte wijn
2 gedroogde milde rode chilipepers, ontzaad
2 sjalotjes, gesnipperd
3 tenen knoflook, fijngehakt
2 eetlepels plantaardige olie
1,25 dl droge witte wijn
7,5 dl vers sinaasappelsap, tot 2,5 dl ingekookt
2 eetlepels fijngehakte verse koriander
zout en versgemalen peper naar smaak
1 courgette, alleen de groene rand, in piepkleine blokjes gesneden
90 g maïskorrels
1 rode paprika, zaad en zaadlijsten verwijderd en in piepkleine blokjes gesneden

1. Verwarm de oven voor op 180°C.
2. Pocheer de kipfilets 6-7 minuten in de kippebouillon in een koekepan. Doe de filets in een ovenschaal, bewaar het kooknat en besprenkel de filets met de 3 eetlepels witte wijn. Dek de schaal af en zet 10-15 minuten in de oven terwijl u de saus maakt.
3. Week de gedroogde chilipepers 20 minuten in het bewaarde kooknat. Pureer de chilipepers en het kooknat in een blender. Zet weg.
4. Fruit de sjalotjes en knoflook in de olie tot ze gaar maar niet bruin zijn. Giet er de 1,25 dl droge wijn bij en laat inkoken tot een stroperige saus. Voeg het ingekookte sinaasappelsap en de chilipeperpuree toe. Laat de saus nog iets inkoken. Neem de pan van het vuur. Schep er de koriander en wat zout en peper door.
5. Bedek de kipfilets met de saus en garneer met de courgette, maïskorrels en paprika.

Voor 4 personen

---

1 portie: Calorieën 360, Eiwit 30 g, Koolhydraten 30 g, Vezel 2 g, Vet totaal 11 g (Verzadigd 2 g, Enkelvoudig onverzadigd 3 g, Meervoudig onverzadigd 5 g), Cholesterol 75 mg, Natrium 80 mg, Vitamine A 35%, Vitamine C 100%.

▲ *1 Groente, 1 Vlees*

SOEPEN / VERENIGDE STATEN

Romige wortel-preisoep

Om zonder slagroom toch een romige soep te krijgen, hoeft u alleen maar gekookte groenten te pureren. De wortels hebben een hoge voedingswaarde met meer dan de aanbevolen dagelijkse hoeveelheid vitamine A, veel vezel en B vitaminen. Dit veelzijdige recept is ook lekker in de herfst op basis van bloemkool of pompoen in plaats van wortels. Andere eetbare bloemen zijn onbespoten Oostindische kers, goudsbloem en viola tricolor.

1 eetlepel komijnzaad
2 eetlepels saffloerolie
3 prei, alleen het wit, in plakken van ½ cm dik
1,5 kg winterwortel, geschild en in plakken
1 liter kippebouillon (zie woordenlijst)
1,25 dl magere melk
¼ theelepel zout
versgemalen witte peper naar smaak
6 verse onbespoten bosviooltjes

1. Rooster het komijnzaad 2 minuten al schuddend in een hete droge koekepan op een middelhoog vuur. Maal het zaad in een kruidenmolen of met een deegroller tot een grof poeder. Zet even weg.
2. Verhit de olie in een middelgrote soeppan. Doe er de prei in en bak die in circa 5 minuten gaar. Voeg de gemalen komijn, op ½ theelepel na voor de garnering, toe en fruit nog 2 minuten onder af en toe omscheppen. Voeg de wortel en bouillon toe en breng aan de kook. Draai het vuur lager, leg er het deksel op en laat circa 25 minuten sudderen tot de wortels gaar zijn.
3. Pureer de soep in een blender of keukenmachine. Doe de gepureerde soep terug in de pan, giet er de melk bij en laat circa 5 minuten op een middelhoog vuur doorwarmen. Breng op smaak met zout en peper en schep dan in voorverwarmde kommen. Garneer met de gemalen komijn en bosviooltjes. Dien op.

Voor 8 personen

2,5 dl per portie: Calorieën 150, Eiwit 3 g, Koolhydraten 26 g, Vezel 6 g, Vet totaal 5 g (Verzadigd 1 g, Enkelvoudig onverzadigd 1 g, Meervoudig onverzadigd 3 g), Cholesterol 0 mg, Natrium 150 mg, Vitamine A 96%, Vitamine C 40%.

▲ *2 Groente*

Gevlochten zalm en zeebaars met twee sausen

Deze eenvoudige maar elegante presentatie van twee vissoorten wordt opgediend met twee sausen die zijn gebaseerd op de traditionele beurre blanc *(blanke botersaus). Er wordt veel minder boter gebruikt, maar de smaak wordt versterkt door de zoete paprika en de wrange zuring. In plaats van zuring kunt u bijvoorbeeld ook basilicum of verse koriander gebruiken.*

500 g zalmfilet, in de lengte in acht repen van 1 cm x 13 cm gesneden
250 g zeebaarsfilet, in de lengte in vier repen van 1 cm x 13 cm gesneden
2 dl droge witte wijn
snufje zout
versgemalen witte peper naar smaak
1 sjalotje, gesnipperd
5 dl groentebouillon ((zie woordenlijst)
1 eetlepel vers citroensap
30 g boter
1 grote rode paprika, geroosterd, ontveld en gepureerd (zie woordenlijst)
30 g verse zuring
¼ theelepel zout

1. Verwarm de oven voor op 200°C. Vet vervolgens een bakplaat licht in met olie.
2. Maak een vlecht van 2 repen zalm en 1 reep zeebaars. Snijd de punten bij. Maak in totaal 4 vlechten. Schik de vlechten op de bakplaat, sprenkel er 1 eetlepel van de wijn over en bestrooi met zout en peper.
3. Bak de visvlechten 10 minuten in de oven, of tot ze stevig aanvoelen en gaar zijn.
4. Doe intussen de sjalot en de rest van de wijn in een pan op een middelhoog vuur en kook in tot een stroperig mengsel. Giet er de bouillon bij en kook tot de helft in. Klop er met 15 g tegelijk het citroensap en de boter door tot een dikke saus.
5. Verdeel de saus in tweeën. Klop de rode paprika door één helft van de saus en pureer de zuring met de andere helft in een blender. Breng op smaak met de ¼ theelepel zout en wat peper.
6. Nappeer elk bord met de twee sausen en schik er een vlecht op.

Voor 4 personen

1 vlecht met sausen per portie: Calorieën 300, Eiwit 35 g, Koolhydraten 5 g, Vezel 1 g, Vet totaal 14 g (Verzadigd 5 g, Enkelvoudig onverzadigd 4,5 g, Meervoudig onverzadigd 3,5 g), Cholesterol 100 mg, Natrium 350 mg, Vitamine A 70%, Vitamine C 120%.
▲ *1 Vlees*

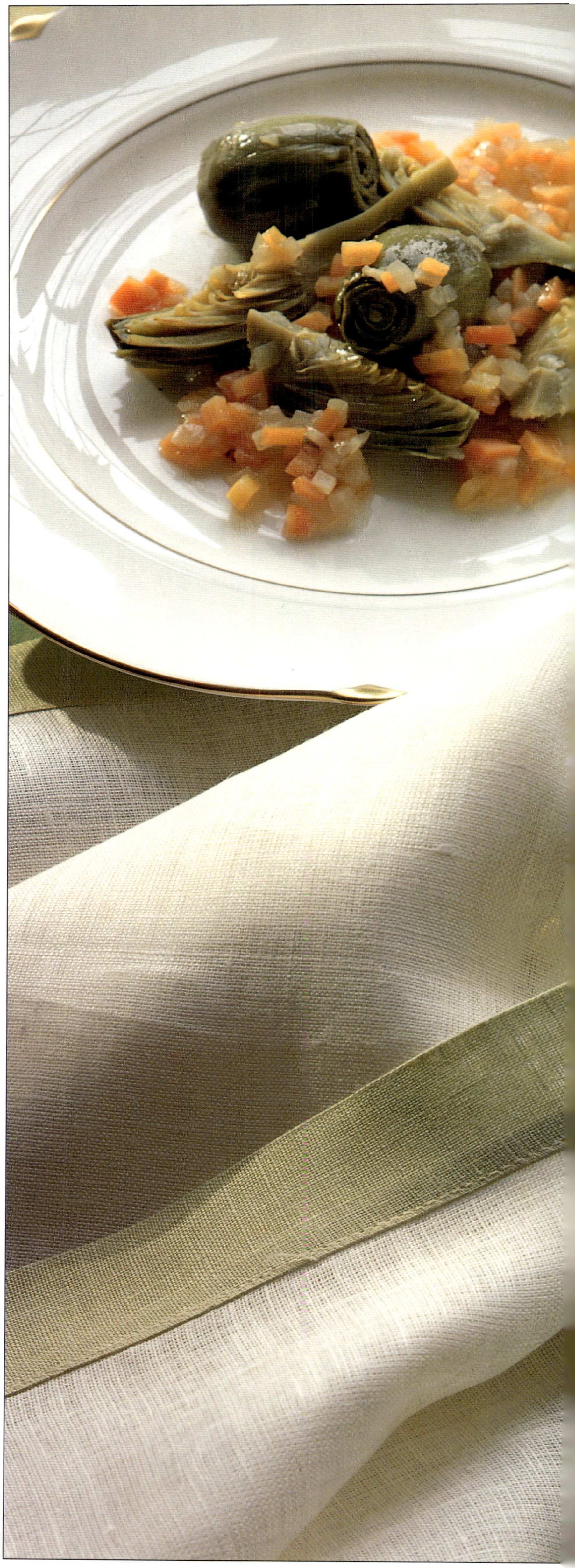

Van links naar rechts: Mini-artisjokken in witte wijn (recept pagina 92), Gevlochten zalm en zeebaars met twee sausen

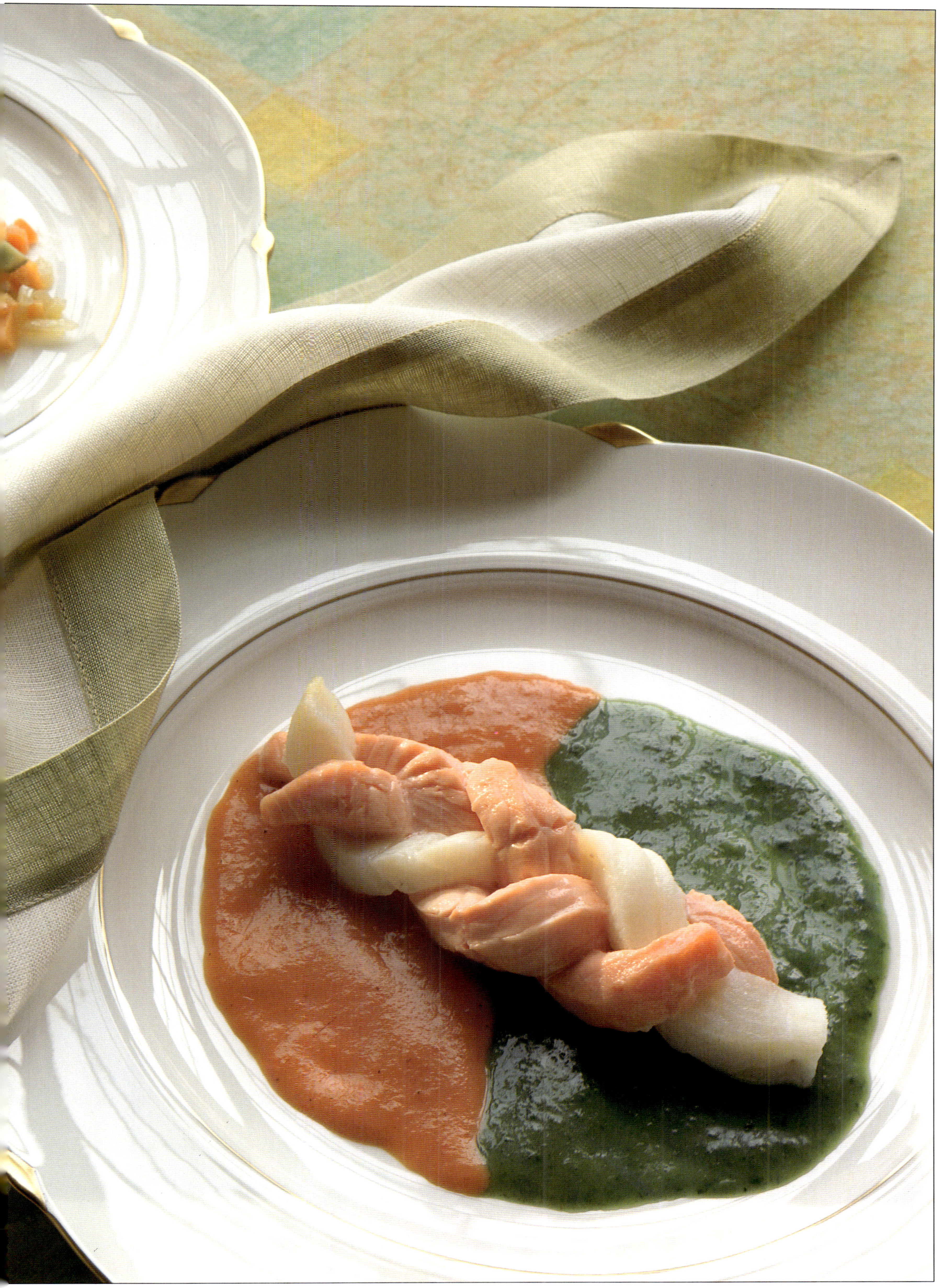

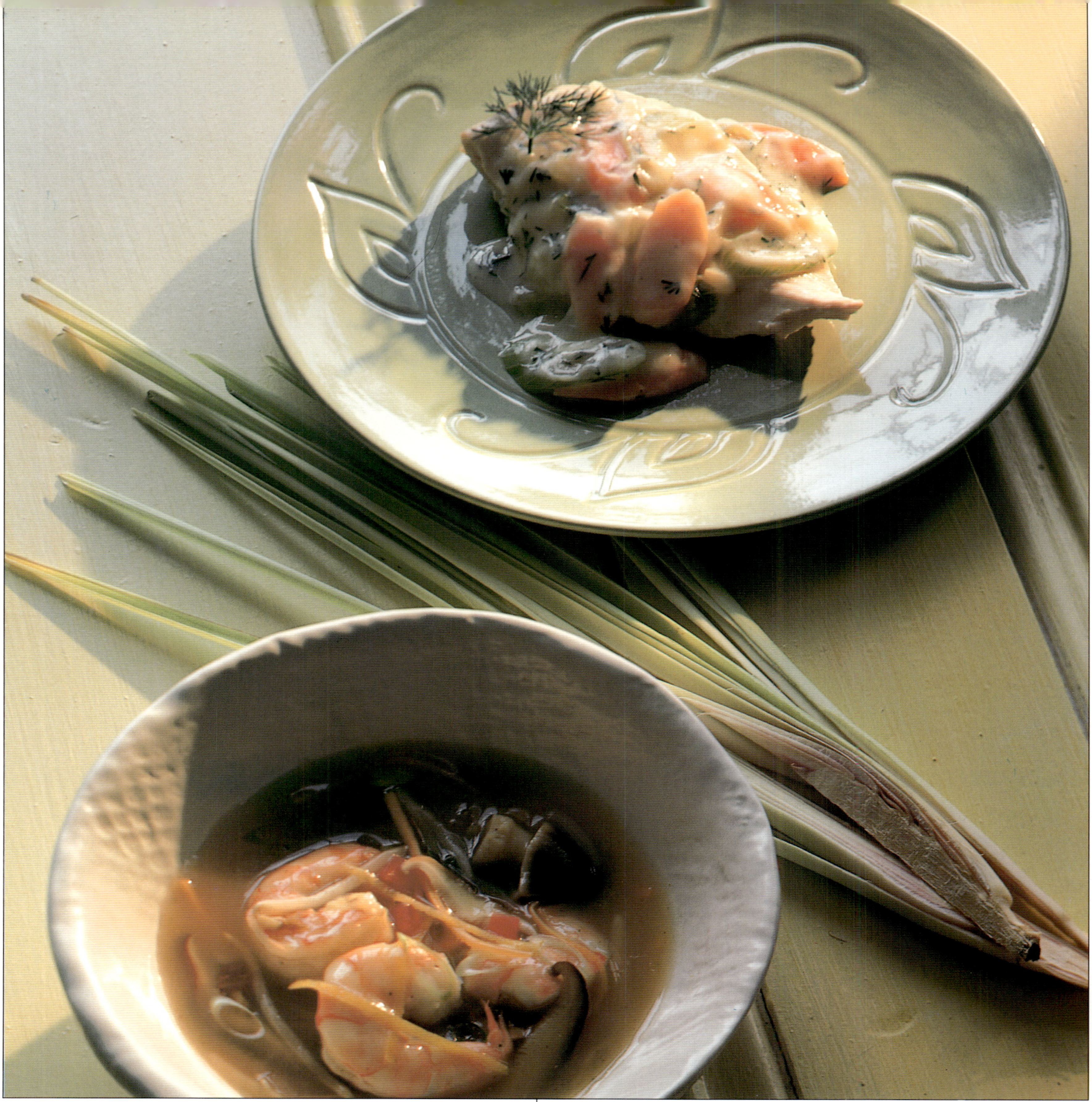

Van boven naar beneden: Kip avgolemono, Pikantzure soep

GROENTEN / FRANKRIJK

Mini-artisjokken in witte wijn

De kleine Zuidfranse paarse artisjokken zijn perfect voor dit gerecht, maar u kunt ook grote artisjokken gebruiken als u ze bijsnijdt, in de lengte in vieren snijdt, het hooi verwijdert en de kooktijd tot 20-30 minuten verlengt.

8 mini-artisjokken
1 citroen, gehalveerd
3 eetlepels olijfolie
150 g gesnipperde ui
3 tenen knoflook, fijngehakt
2 wortels, geschild en gehakt
1,8 dl droge witte wijn
1,25 dl groentebouillon (zie woordenlijst)
bouquet garni: 1 takje peterselie, 1 takje tijm, 1 laurierblad
¼ theelepel zout
versgemalen peper naar smaak

1. Snijd de punten van de artisjokken af en verwijder de taaie buintenbladen. Snijd de bodems van 4 artisjokken af zodat ze rechtop blijven staan. Halveer de andere 4 in de lengte en verwijder de fijne binnenblaadjes. Snijd de helften in de lengte doormidden. Wrijf alle aangesneden stukken in met citroen.

2. Verhit de olijfolie in een grote koekepan. Doe er de ui, knoflook en wortel in en fruit circa 3 minuten op een middelhoog vuur tot de ui gaar maar niet bruin is. Blus de pan af met de witte wijn en kook die tot tweederde in op een hoog vuur.
3. Giet er de bouillon bij en breng weer aan de kook. Draai het vuur lager en voeg het bouquet garni, zout, wat peper en de hele artisjokken (rechtop) toe. Leg het deksel op de pan en sudder 20 minuten. Voeg de gesneden artisjokken toe en laat nog 25-30 minuten sudderen onder af en toe omscheppen tot ze gaar zijn. Dien onmiddellijk op of op kamertemperatuur met wat kooknat.

Voor 4 personen *Foto op pagina 90-91*

1 portie: Calorieën 220, Eiwit 5 g, Koolhydraten 28 g, Vezel 4 g, Vet totaal 11 g (Verzadigd 1.5 g, Enkelvoudig onverzadigd 8 g, Meervoudig onverzadigd 1 g), Cholesterol 0 mg, Natrium 280 mg, Vitamine A 210%, Vitamine C 45%.

▲ *2 Groente*

SOEPEN / VIETNAM

Pikantzure soep

Peper zorgt voor het "pikante" en limoen voor het "zure" in deze soep. Gebruik deze ingrediënten naar eigen smaak.

6 middelgrote gedroogde shiitake paddestoelen, 20 minuten in heet water geweekt
1,25 dl kippebouillon (zie woordenlijst)
250 g garnalen, gepeld en darmkanalen verwijderd (bewaar de schalen)
2 stengels citroengras, witte knol in repen van 1 cm gesneden
1 wortel, julienne gesneden
4 lentuitjes, in dunne plakken gesneden
½ theelepel fijngeraspte limoenschil
100 g verse stropaddestoelen, of uit blik (straw mushrooms)
3 eetlepels maïzena opgelost in 4 eetlepels kippebouillon (zie woordenlijst)
2 eetlepels sojasaus
1 tomaat, ontveld, ontzaad en in blokjes
125 g taugé
4 eetlepels vers limoensap
1 theelepel versgemalen peper
½ theelepel sesamolie

1. Giet de shiitake af en spoel ze even onder de koude kraan. Verwijder de steeltjes. Snijd de hoedjes in dunne reepjes en zet weg.
2. Breng de kippebouillon met de bewaarde garnalenschalen aan de kook. Draai het vuur lager, sudder 10 minuten en schep de schalen met een schuimspaan uit de bouillon. Gooi de schalen weg. Voeg het citroengras, de shiitake, wortel en lenteui toe. Leg het deksel op de pan en laat 5 minuten sudderen tot de wortel gaar is.
3. Voeg de garnalen, limoenschil en stropaddestoelen toe en sudder 2-3 minuten tot de garnalen rozig en gaar zijn.
4. Meng het maïzenapapje met de sojasaus en giet het mengsel al kloppend in een straaltje in de soep. Voeg de tomaten, taugé, het limoensap en peper naar smaak toe. Neem de pan van het vuur.
5. Schep er de sesamolie door en dien onmiddellijk op.

Voor 6 personen

2,5 dl per portie: Calorieën 130, Eiwit 11 g, Koolhydraten 17 g, Vezel 2 g, Vet totaal 3 g (Verzadigd 0,5 g, Enkelvoudig onverzadigd 1 g, Meervoudig onverzadigd 1 g), Cholesterol 55 mg, Natrium 350 mg, Vitamine A 70%, Vitamine C 20%.

▲ *1 Groente, ½ Vlees*

GEVOGELTE / GRIEKENLAND

Kip avgolemono

Deze ei-citroensaus lijkt op de traditionele avgolemono-*soep en is ook heerlijk met vis. Geef er rijst of orzo bij.*

7,5 dl kippebouillon (zie woordenlijst)
125 g gehakte ui
1 wortel, geschild en in stukken van 1 cm gesneden
1 stengel bleekselderij, in stukken van 1 cm gesneden
4 tenen knoflook, gekneusd
1 laurierblad
1 takje tijm
1 kg stukken kip, vel en vet verwijderd
3 citroenen
2 eieren, gescheiden
15 g gesnipperde dille
snufje zout
versgemalen peper naar smaak
1 eetlepel maïzena opgelost in 2 eetlepels kippebouillon (desgewenst)

1. Doe de kippebouillon in een grote soeppan en breng aan de kook. Voeg de ui, wortel, bleekselderij, knoflook, het laurierblad en de tijm toe. Draai het vuur lager, voeg de kip en het sap van 1 citroen toe. Laat circa 30 minuten sudderen tot de kip gaar is. Haal er de kip uit. Zeef de bouillon en bewaar de groenten. Doe de bouillon vervolgens terug in de pan en gooi het laurierblad en de tijm weg.
2. Doe de eiwitten in een kom en klop ze schuimig. Voeg al kloppend de dooiers en dan het sap van de andere 2 citroenen toe. Giet er al kloppend geleidelijk 5 dl van de kippebouillon bij. Giet het eimengsel terug in de pan en laat de saus onder voortdurend roeren even sudderen tot hij iets dikker is. Laat de saus niet koken. Voeg de dille toe en breng op smaak met zout en peper. De saus zal dun zijn; als u een dikke saus wilt, er dan het maïzenapapje doorroeren en laten sudderen tot de saus dik is.
3. Doe de kip en de groenten terug in de saus en laat even doorwarmen. Schep alles op een schaal en dien op.

Voor 4 personen

1 portie: Calorieën 280, Eiwit 38 g, Koolhydraten 13 g, Vezel 2 g, Vet totaal 9 g (Verzadigd 3 g, Enkelvoudig onverzadigd 3 g, Meervoudig onverzadigd 2 g), Cholesterol 220 mg, Natrium 250 mg, Vitamine A 110%, Vitamine C 50%.

▲ *1 Groente, 1 Vlees*

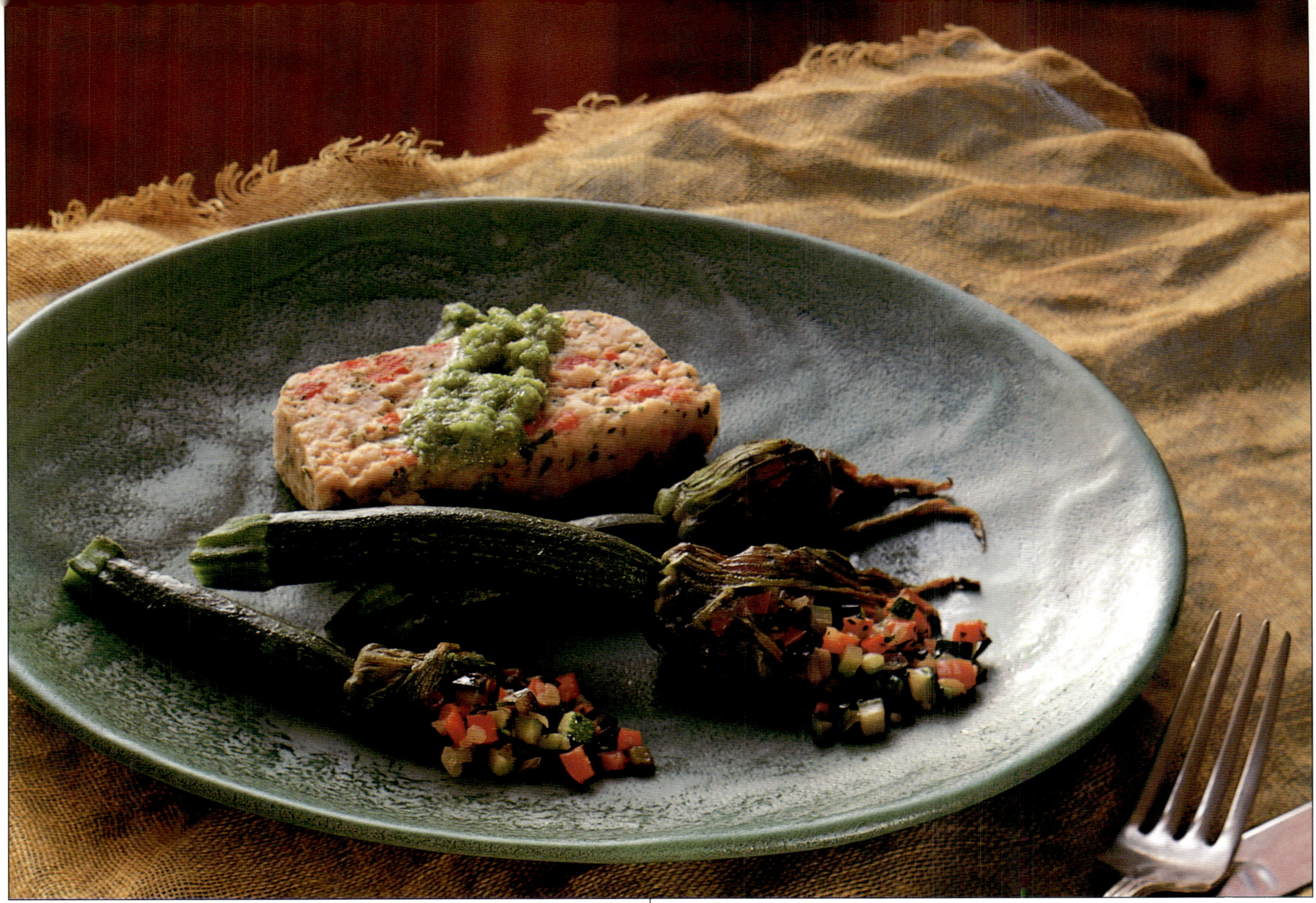

Van boven naar beneden: Zeebanketterrine met aaspergessaus, Gevulde courgettebloemen

Zeebanketterrine met aspergessaus

375 g coquilles
375 g zalmfilet
125 g rauwe garnalen, gepeld en darmkanaal verwijderd
het sap van ½ citroen
4 eetlepels droge witte wijn
4 eetlepels half melk, half room
2 eieren
¼ theelepel cayennepeper
75 g pimento (paprika uit blik), in blokjes
3 eetlepels fijngehakte verse dragon
1 eetlepel fijngehakte verse kervel
takjes verse kervel ter garnering
7,5 dl aspergessaus (recept volgt)

1. Verwarm de oven voor op 180°C. Vet een pâté- of souffléschaal van 2 liter inhoud licht in met olie.
2. Doe de coquilles, zalm en garnalen, het citroensap, de wijn, melk en room, eieren en cayennepeper in een keukenmachine en draai alles kort tot een glad mengsel. Schep er de pimento, dragon en gehakte kervel door.
3. Doe het mengsel in de ingevette schaal. Dek de schaal af met een licht met olie ingevet vel perkamentpapier. Zet de schaal in een waterbad en zet 1 uur in de oven.
4. Serveer de terrine warm of koud, garneer met de takjes kervel en geef er de aspergessaus apart bij.

Voor 12 personen

Een plak van 60 g met 4 eetlepels saus per portie: Calorieën 120, Eiwit 15 g, Koolhydraten 4 g, Vezel 0 g, Vet totaal 5 g (Verzadigd 2 g, Enkelvoudig onverzadigd 1,5 g, Meervoudig onverzadigd 1 g), Cholesterol 85 mg, Natrium 90 mg, Vitamine C 20%.
▲ *1 Vlees*

Aspergessaus

15 g boter
1 eetlepel bloem
5 dl kippebouillon (zie woordenlijst)
250 g gehakte groene asperges, geblancheerd
2 eetlepels half melk en half room

1. Verhit de boter in een pan. Roer er de bloem door en laat 2-3 minuten koken zonder bruin te laten worden. Voeg al kloppend de bouillon toe en laat onder voortdurend kloppen koken tot een dikke saus. Laat afkoelen. Doe de saus, asperges en melk en room in een blender en pureer. Zeef de saus en serveer.

Voor 7,5 dl

4 eetlepels per portie: Calorieën 20, Eiwit 1 g, Koolhydraten 2 g, Vezel 0 g, Vet totaal 2 g (Verzadigd 1 g, Enkelvoudig onverzadigd ,5 g, Meervoudig onverzadigd 0 g), Cholesterol 5 mg, Natrium 90 mg.
▲ *1 Vlees*

DESSERTS / VERENIGDE STATEN

Luchtige cakejes

Deze luchtige cakejes zijn het toppunt van een vetloos, cholesterolvrij nagerecht. Garneer met een rabarber-sinaasappelcompote (recept volgt) of andere vruchten in seizoen.

60 g cakemeel
185 g zeer fijne tafelsuiker
1 eetlepel fijngeraspte sinaasappelschil
6 grote eiwitten
½ theelepel vers citroensap
½ theelepel wijnsteenzuur
1 theelepel vanille-essence
1 eetlepel poedersuiker

1. Verwarm de oven voor op 180°C. Schik zes soufflébakjes van 2,5 dl inhoud op een bakplaat.
2. Zeef het cakemeel met 60 g van de fijne tafelsuiker. Zeef nog een keer om het zo luchtig mogelijk te maken. Schep er losjes de sinaasappelschil door en zet weg.
3. Doe de eiwitten in een zuurbestendige kom en klop ze met een handmixer schuimig. Voeg het citroensap toe en bestrooi met het wijnsteenzuur. Klop de witten weer tot er zachte pieken zijn. Voeg al kloppend met 2 eetlepels tegelijk de resterende fijne tafelsuiker toe tot de witten in volume verdubbeld zijn. Klop er de vanille door.
4. Klop het cakemeelmengsel met 2 eetlepels tegelijk met een garde door het eimengsel, maar klop niet te veel.
5. Vul de soufflébakjes voor tweederde met het beslag. Bak de cakjes 35-40 minuten in de oven tot ze goudgeel zijn en veerkrachtig aanvoelen.
6. Neem ze uit de oven, zet ze op een rooster en laat ze 10 minuten rusten. Maak de randen los met een scherp mes, haal de cakjes uit de vormpjes en laat ze verder op het rooster afkoelen. Bestuif de afgekoelde cakejes met poedersuiker en dien op.

Voor 6 personen

1 cakeje per portie: Calorieën 150, Eiwit 4 g, Koolhydraten 34 g, Vezel 0 g, Vet totaal 0 g (Verzadigd 0 g, Enkelvoudig onverzadigd 0 g, Meervoudig onverzadigd 0 g), Cholesterol 0 mg, Natrium 55 mg

▲ *1 Brood*

RABARBER-SINAASAPPELCOMPOTE

500 g verse rabarber, in stukken van 5 cm gesneden
125 g suiker
1,25 dl vers sinaasappelsap
1 theelepel geraspte sinaasappelschil
2 sinaasappels, ontpit en overdwars in plakken gesneden

1. Doe de rabarber, suiker, het sinaasappelsap en de geraspte schil in een middelgrote pan. Laat 30 minuten sudderen tot de rabarber gaar is.
2. Neem de pan van het vuur en voeg de plakken sinaasappel toe. Laat het mengsel afkoelen tot u het gaat serveren.

Voor circa 8 dl

Foto op pagina 97

1,25 dl per portie: Calorieën 110, Eiwit 1 g, Koolhydraten 27 g, Vezel 3 g, Vet totaal 0 g (Verzadigd 0 g, Enkelvoudig onverzadigd 0 g, Meervoudig onverzadigd 0 g), Cholesterol 0 mg, Natrium 3 mg, Vitamine C 70%.

▲ *1 Fruit*

HAPJES / FRANKRIJK

Les fleurs farcies

GEVULDE COURGETTEBLOEMEN

Courgettebloemen in de lente doen ons uitzien naar de komst van de zomerse courgettes. Voor dit recept wordt de buitenkant van de courgette en aubergine gebruikt. U kunt de rest van de groenten invriezen voor een andere toepassing.

24 jonge courgettes met bloemen
4 eetlepels olijfolie
3 sjalotjes, gesnipperd
2 tenen knoflook, fijngehakt
2 courgettes, buitenkant op 3 mm dik afgesneden en in piepkliene blokjes gesneden (bewaar de rest van de courgette voor een ander recept)
1 kleine, langwerpige aubergine, buitenkant op 3 mm dik afgesneden en in piepkleine blokjes gesneden
1 rode paprika, in piepkleine blokjes gesneden
5 grote basilicumbladen, in reepjes gesneden
1 theelepel fijngehakte verse peterselie
zout en versgemalen peper naar smaak

1. Verwarm de oven voor op 180°C. Vet een bakblik licht in met olie.
2. Veeg de binnenkant van de courgettebloemen schoon. Snijd de eindpunten bij en blancheer de courgettes 10 seconden in kokend gezouten water. Dompel ze onmiddellijk in ijswater om het kookproces te stoppen. Laat ze op keukenpapier uitlekken.
3. Verhit voor de ratatouille de olijfolie en fruit er de sjalotjes en knoflook in tot ze gaar maar niet bruin zijn. Voeg de blokjes courgette, aubergine en paprika toe en bak circa 2 minuten. Schep er de basilicum, peterselie en wat zout en peper door.
4. Vul elke bloem met een lepelvol ratatouille. Draai de punten van de bloemen dicht en schik de courgettes op de bakplaat. Bestrooi ze met zout en peper.
5. Dek de courgettes losjes af met aluminiumfolie en zet ze 10 minuten in de oven tot ze net gaar zijn.

Voor 8 personen

3 courgettebloemen per portie: Calorieën 80, Eiwit 1 g, Koolhydraten 3 g, Vezel 1 g, Vet totaal 7 g (Verzadigd 1 g Enkelvoudig onverzadigd 5 g, Meervoudig onverzadigd 0,5 g), Cholesterol 0 mg, Natrium 0 mg, Vitamine C 50%.

▲ *1 Groente*

DESSERTS / DUITSLAND

Kasekuchen von schwedt

KAASTAART MET COGNACKERSEN

In plaats van de kwark kunt u een mengsel hüttenkäse en ricotta gebruiken. De mueslikorst is een vetarme verrassing.

225 g muesli (recept op pagina 177), fijngemalen in een keukenmachine
60 g fijngeraspte appel
30 g boter of margarine, gesmolten
500 g kwark, of 250 g magere hüttenkäse en 250 g magere ricotta
2,5 dl magere melk
125 g suiker
2 eieren
1 theelepel vanille-essence
1 theelepel geraspte citroenschil
60 g gedroogde kersen, gehalveerd

1. Verwarm de oven voor op 180°C. Vet de bodem en randen van een springvorm van 23 cm doorsnee licht in met olie.
2. Doe de muesli, appel en boter in een middelgrote kom en schep alles om. Druk het mueslimengsel over de bodem van de springvorm en zet 13-15 minuten in de oven tot de korst goudbruin is. Laat op een rooster afkoelen.
3. Doe de kwark, melk, suiker, eieren en vanille in een keukenmachine en draai tot een glad geheel. Schep er de citroenschil en de gedroogde kersen door. Giet het beslag in de springvorm en zet 1¼ uur in de oven, of tot de taart stevig aanvoelt. Laat op een rooster afkoelen.

Voor 8 personen

1 portie: Calorieën 240, Eiwit 12 g, Koolhydraten 32 g, Vezel 2 g, Vet totaal 8 g (Verzadigd 4,5 g, Enkelvoudig onverzadigd 2,5 g, Meervoudig onverzadigd 0,5 g), Cholesterol 75 mg, Natrium 190 mg.
▲ *½ Brood, ½ Melk*

COGNACKERSEN

Deze kersen kunt u tot een maand in de koelkast bewaren. U kunt ze langer bewaren als u ze in weckpotten doet.

500 g kersen
250 g suiker
4 eetlepels witte wijnazijn
3 hele kruidnagels
1 kaneelpijpje
1,25 dl cognac

1. Verwijder de pitten en stelen van de kersen. Doe de kersen in een middelgrote kom.
2. Doe de suiker, azijn en 4 eetlepels water in een middelgrote pan. Breng al roerend aan de kook en blijf roeren tot de suiker opgelost is. Voeg de kruidnagels en het kaneelpijpje toe en laat 5 minuten sudderen.
3. Neem de pan van het vuur, giet er de cognac bij en giet het mengsel over de kersen. Laat afkoelen en zet een nacht in de koelkast.

Voor circa 1 liter

1,25 dl per portie: Calorieën 170, Eiwit 1 g, Koolhydraten 35 g, Vezel 1 g, Vet totaal 0 g (Verzadigd 0 g, Enkelvoudig onverzadigd 0 g, Meervoudig onverzadigd 0 g), Cholesterol 0 mg, Natrium 0 mg.
▲ *1 Fruit, 1 Vet/Suiker*

DESSERTS / VERENIGDE STATEN

Gemberroulade met verse aardbeiensaus

Deze vetarme taart wordt gevuld met de eerste aardbeitjes. Aardbeien zijn niet alleen heerlijk, maar een portie van 85 g bevat bijna alle voor een dag benodigde vitamine C.

750 g aardbeien, in dunne plakken
375 g suiker
2 theelepels maïzena, opgelost in 1 eetlepel water
5 grote eieren, gescheiden
¼ theelepel wijnsteenzuur
75 g gezeefd cakemeel
2 theelepels kaneel
1 theelepel gemberpoeder
2 eetlepels poedersuiker
verse aardbeiensaus (recept volgt)
12 hele aardbeien, ter garnering

1. Verwarm de oven voor op 180°C. Bekleed een bakplaat van 25 x 38 cm met perkamentpapier en laat aan één rand wat papier over hangen. Vet het perkamentpapier licht in met olie.
2. Doe voor de vulling de helft van de plakken aardbei en 125 g van de suiker in een middelgrote pan. Kook het mengel onder voortdurend roeren 10 minuten op een middelhoog vuur. Voeg het maïzenapapje toe en laat al roerend 5 minuten sudderen tot de saus wat dikker is. Laat de saus afkoelen.
3. Maak de cake door de eiwitten schuimig te kloppen in een zuurbestendige kom. Voeg het wijnsteenzuur toe en klop de witten tot zachte pieken. Voeg al kloppend met 2 eetlepels tegelijk 125 g van de overgebleven suiker toe tot er stijve maar niet droge pieken zijn.
4. Doe de dooiers en de overgebleven 125 g suiker in een grote kom en klop tot een luchtig mengsel.
5. Zeef de bloem, kaneel en gember boven een kleine kom.
6. Schep het bloemmengsel door het dooiermengsel tot alles net gemengd is. Schep er vervolgens voorzichtig het wit door. Schep het beslag direct over de bakplaat. Tik de plaat licht op het aanrecht aan om lucht te verwijderen. Bak de cake 10 minu-

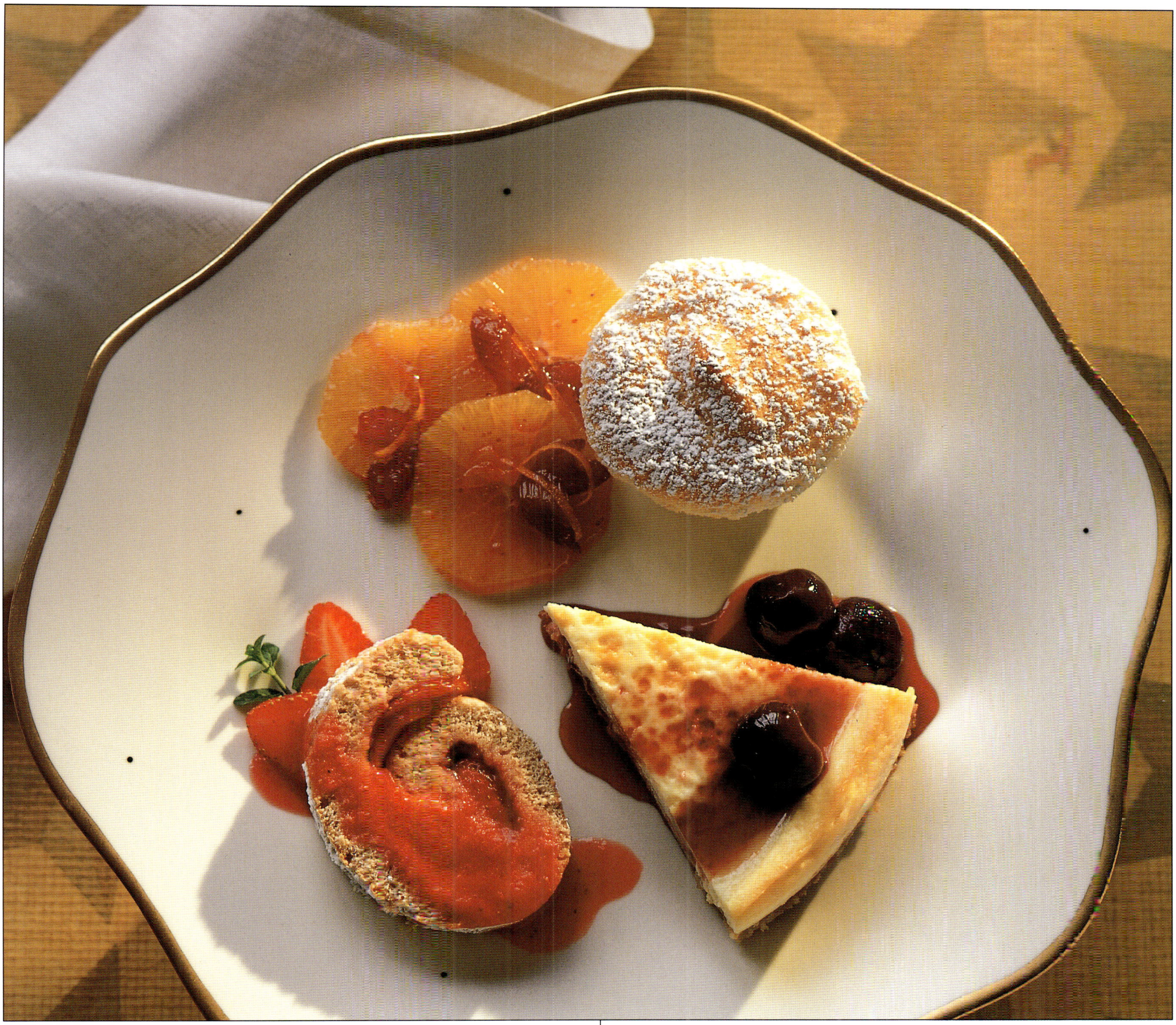

Met de klok mee van boven: Luchtige cakejes met rabarber-sinaasappelcompote (recept pagina 95), Kaastaart met cognackersen, Gemberroulade met verse aardbeiensaus

ten in de oven, of tot hij goudgeel is en stevig aanvoelt.

7. Schik een vel perkamentpapier op een werkvlak en bestuif het met wat poedersuiker. Stort de cake ondersteboven op de poedersuiker. Pel het perkament van de cakebodem.
8. Strijk de aardbeivulling uit over de cake tot 2 cm van de randen. Schik de rest van de plakken aardbei over de vulling. Rol de cake zonder beschadigen van de lange kant zo strak mogelijk op. Snijd de einden bij met een kartelmes. Leg de cake met de vouwnaad onder op een schaal en bestuif met de rest van de poedersuiker. Laat de cake 1 uur staan voor u hem aansnijdt.
9. Snijd de gemberroulade overdwars in plakken van 3 cm dik. Maak een spiegel van 2 eetlepels aardbeiensaus op elk bord en schik er een plak cake op. Garneer met een hele aardbei.

Voor 12 personen

---

1 plak met 2 eetlepels aardbeiensaus per portie: Calorieën 210, Eiwit 4 g, Koolhydraten 43 g, Vezel 3 g, Vet totaal 5 g (Verzadigd 0,5 g, Enkelvoudig onverzadigd 1 g, Meervoudig onverzadigd 0,5 g), Cholesterol 90 mg, Natrium 30 mg, Vitamine C 120%.

▲ *1 Brood, 1 Fruit*

Verse aardbeiensaus

250 g aardbeien, kroontjes verwijderd
2 eetlepels poedersuiker
het sap van 2 sinaasappels

1. Doe de aardbeien, poedersuiker en het sinaasappelsap in een blender en draai tot een puree. Druk de puree door een zeef om de pitten te verwijderen. Bewaar in de koelkast tot gebruik.

Voor 5 dl

---

6 eetlepels per portie: Calorieën 20, Eiwit 0 g, Koolhydraten 4 g, Vezel 1 g, Vet totaal 0 g (Verzadigd 0 g, Enkelvoudig onverzadigd 0 g, Meervoudig onverzadigd 0 g), Cholesterol 0 mg, Natrium 0 mg, Vitamine C 35%.

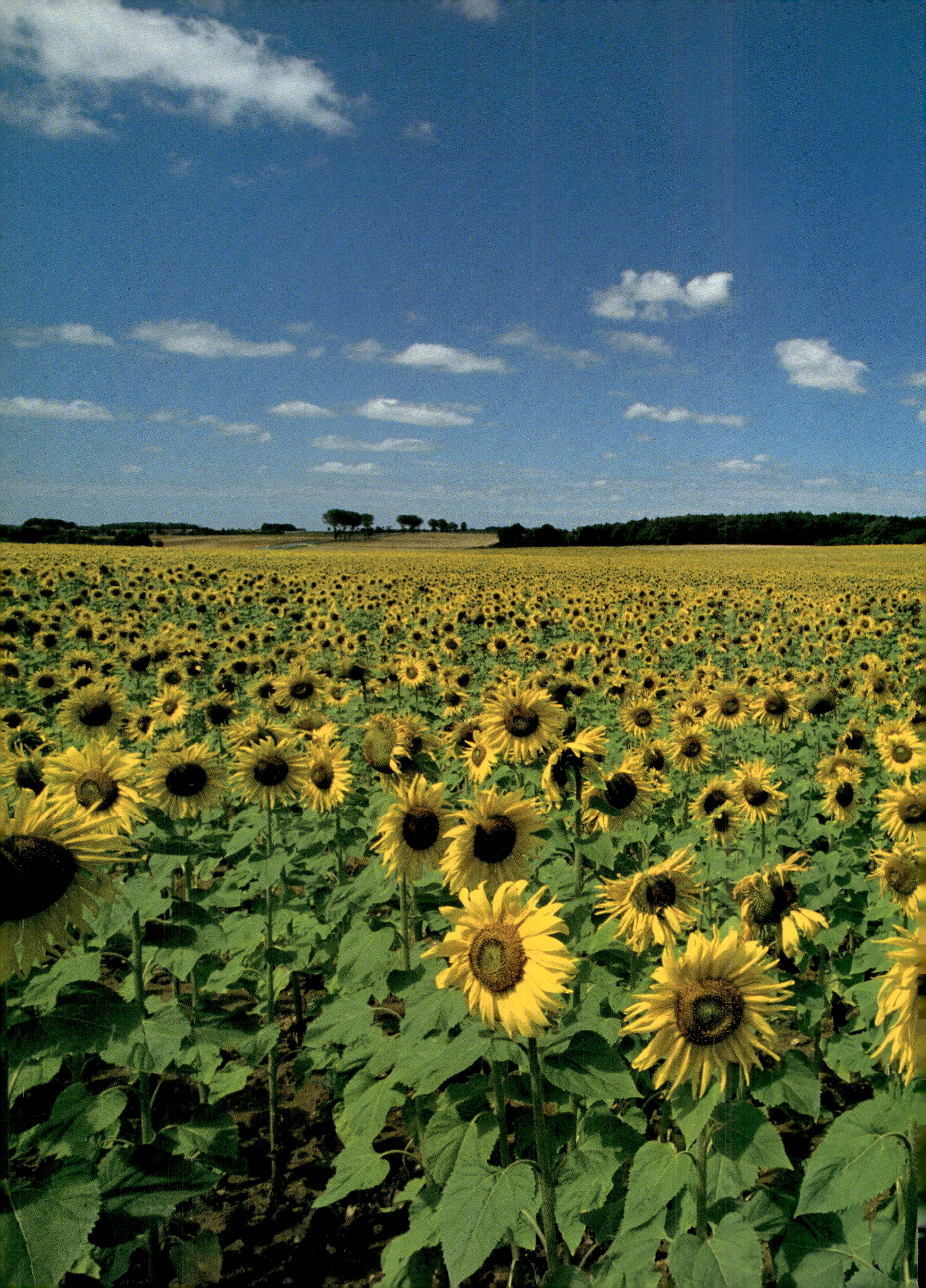

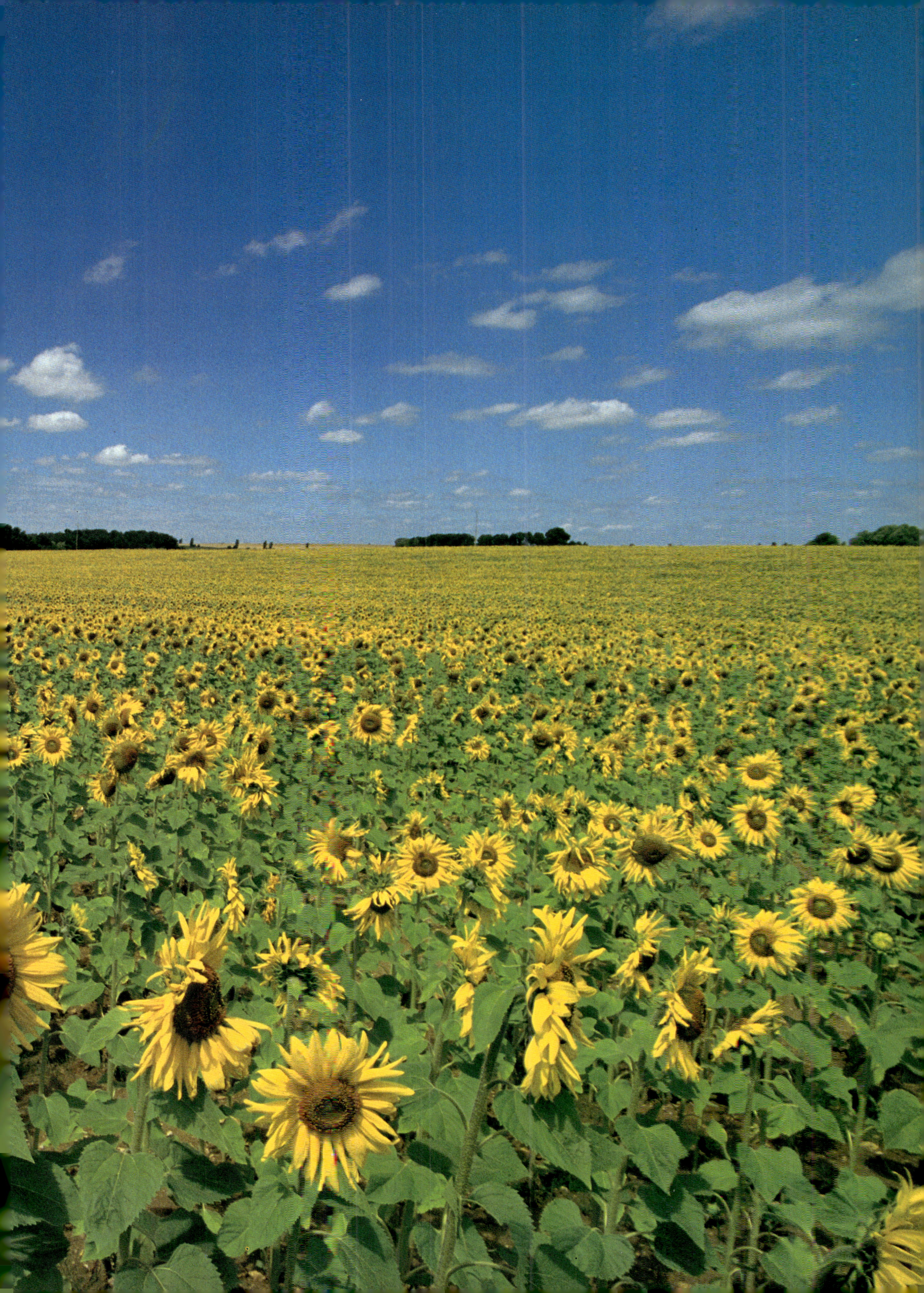

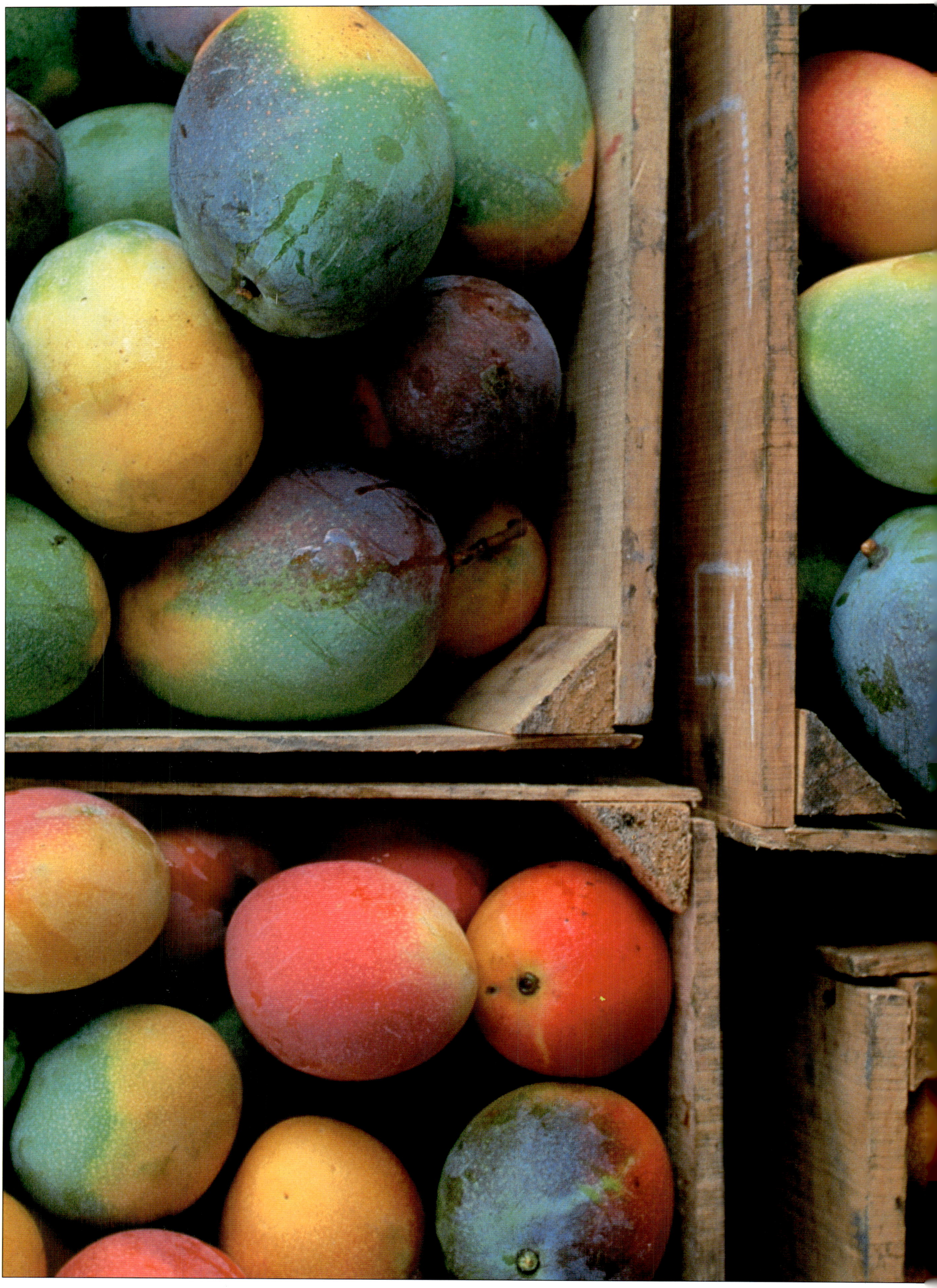

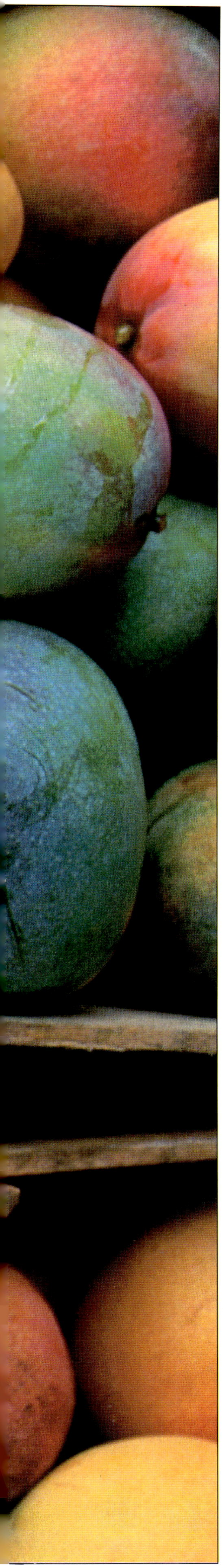

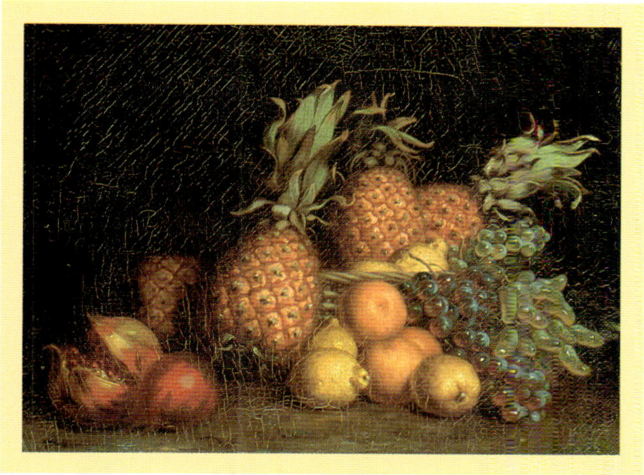

Zomer

Nu dat daar de zomer was
en overal in 't gras
bloemen vrolijk bloeiden,
zongen alle vogelen.

—Walther von der Vogelweide, *Dromenlied*

In dit seizoen van salades zijn er volop vruchten en groenten. Maak verse groenten uit de tuin aan met een vinaigrette van sappige tomaten. Geef eens een citroenvinaigrette bij een schaal crudités, een kleurrijke verzameling van rauwe en geblancheerde groenten die in hapklare stukken zijn gesneden.

Warme soepen zijn geschikt voor de wintermaanden, maar de zomer vraagt om koele variaties. Uit Denemarken is er de *yoghurtsuppe*—vetarme yoghurt gemengd met komkommer, radijs en lenteuitjes, gekruid met verse dille, dragon en munt. Of probeer een koude ananassoep: een explosie van tropische smaken en kleuren, waaronder robijnrood granaatappelzaad.

Met het lengen der dagen kan de grill worden gebruikt voor het maken van kruidige kip- of zeebanketspiezen en allerlei groenten—met name maïs aan de kolf. Completeer de maaltijd met een sangría met verse vruchten of een pittige vruchtensalsa. Maak voor ontbijten en desserts een keuze uit een vruchtencocktail, perzik clafoutis, of crêpes en sausen.

SOEPEN / DENEMARKEN

Yoghurtsoep

Een ochtendwandeling in de kruidentuin leverde deze frisse gekoelde soep op voor de lunch op een warme zomerdag. Als u gedroogde kruiden gebruikt, dient u de hoeveelheid met tweederde te verminderen.

1 komkommer, ontzaad en in blokjes
10 radijsjes, in dunne plakken
5 dl magere yoghurt
2,5 dl kippebouillon (zie woordenlijst)
1 lenteui, fijngehakt
1 eetlepel fijngehakte verse dille
1½ theelepel fijngehakte verse dragon
½ theelepel fijngehakte verse munt
zout en versgemalen peper naar smaak
4 takjes verse dille, ter garnering

1. Schep op de dille na alle ingrediënten door elkaar. Zet een paar uur voor het serveren in de koelkast. Garneer met dille.
Voor 4 personen

2,5 dl per portie: Calorieën 90, Eiwit 7 g, Koolhydraten 11 g, Vezel 1 g, Vet totaal 2 g (Verzadigd 1,5 g, Enkelvoudig onverzadigd 0,5 g, Meervoudig onverzadigd 0 g), Cholesterol 5 mg, Natrium 90 mg, Kalk 20%.

▲ *1 Melk*

GRANEN / IRAN

Perzische basmatirijst

Basmati *rijst is waarschijnlijk een van de bekendste langkorrelige rijstsoorten. Deze rijst komt oorspronkelijk uit India en wordt over de hele wereld geëxporteerd.* Basmati *bevat in verhouding weinig zetmeel en is dus niet plakkerig en wordt daarom vaak voor pilaf gebruikt.*

440 g *basmati* rijst, grondig gespoeld en een nacht in water geweekt
1 kaneelpijpje
3 hele kruidnagels
2 eetlepels saffloerolie
60 g gehakte ui
30 g pistachenoten, gedopt en grof gehakt
geraspte schil van 1 sinaasappel
90 g krenten of sultanarozijnen
15 g boter, gesmolten
1 aardappel, geschild en in de lengte in plakken van 3 mm dik gesneden

1. Verwarm de oven voor op 180°C.
2. Doe 7,5 dl water in een middelgrote pan en breng het water aan de kook. Doe er de rijst, het kaneelpijpje en de kruidnagels in en draai het vuur lager. Laat 10 minuten sudderen onder af en toe roeren. Giet overtollig water af en zet de rijst weg.
3. Verhit de olie in een grote, zware vuurvaste ovenschaal met een deksel. Fruit er de ui, pistachenoten en sinaasappelschil circa 5 minuten in tot de ui goudbruin is. Schep het mengsel uit de pan met een schuimspaan en schep het door de rijst. Schep de krenten door de rijst.
4. Kwast de wanden en bodem van de ovenschaal in met de gesmolten boter. Schik de plakken aardappel strak naast elkaar over de bodem. Schep er de rijst over en druk die stevig aan. Maak 3 diepe inkepingen met het handvat van een pollepel in de rijst zodat er stoom kan ontsnappen. Dek de rijst af met een vochtige schone theedoek om de stoom te absorberen en leg het deksel op de schaal.
5. Zet de schaal 50 minuten in de oven. Neem de schaal uit de oven en laat 10 minuten staan.
6. Neem het deksel van de ovenschaal en verwijder de theedoek. Leg een grote dienschaal op de ovenschaal en keer om. Dien op.
Voor 6 personen

2,5 dl per portie: Calorieën 380, Eiwit 7 g, Koolhydraten 67 g, Vezel 2 g, Vet totaal 9 g (Verzadigd 1,5 g, Enkelvoudig onverzadigd 2,5 g, Meervoudig onverzadigd 4 g), Cholesterol 5 mg, Natrium 5 mg, IJzer 20%.

▲ *2 Brood*

GROENTEN / MIDDEN-OOSTEN

Hummus

Tahini *is eigenlijk een sesamzaadboter die zowel veel eiwit en kalk als vet bevat. In deze versie van* hummus *worden kikkererwten gebruikt om het vetgehalte laag te houden. Meng de* hummus *met een gelijke hoeveelheid yoghurt om het vetgehalte nog lager te krijgen.* Hummus *is heerlijk als sandwichspread, als dipsaus voor groenten en natuurlijk met falafel (recept op pagina 78).*

125 g gedroogde kikkererwten, een nacht geweekt
5 dl kippebouillon (zie woordenlijst)
2 tenen knoflook
het sap van 1 citroen
1 eetlepel tahini (sesamzaadpasta)
⅛ theelepel zout
2 theelepels olijfolie
½ theelepel paprikapoeder
2 eetlepels fijngehakte verse peterselie

1. Doe de kikkererwten en kippebouillon in een middelgrote pan en laat in circa 2 uur volledig gaar sudderen. Giet ze af en bewaar de bouillon. Doe de kikkererwten in een keukenmachine met de knoflook, het citroensap, de tahini en het zout en draai tot een gladde pasta. Giet er wat van de bouillon bij tot u de gewenste structuur heeft.
2. Schep het mengsel op 4 borden en maak met de achterkant van een lepel een kuiltje in het midden. Doe ½ theelepel olijfolie in elk kuiltje. Garneer met het paprikapoeder en de peterselie.
Voor 4 personen

1,25 dl per portie: Calorieën 160, Eiwit 7 g, Koolhydraten 21 g, Vezel 2 g, Vet totaal 7 g (Verzadigd 1 g, Enkelvoudig onverzadigd 3 g, Meervoudig onverzadigd 2 g), Cholesterol 0 mg, Natrium 90 mg.

▲ *½ Vlees*

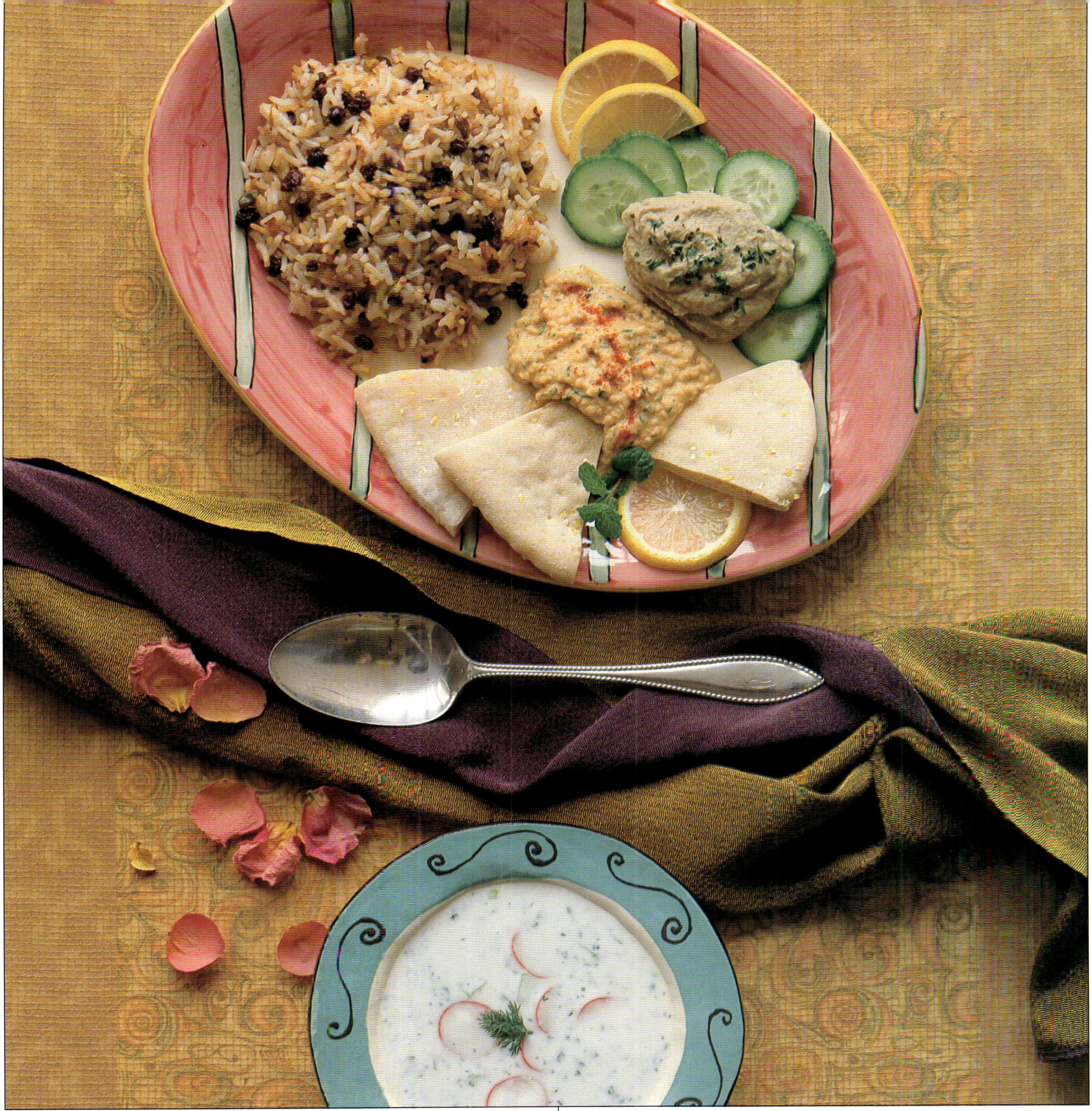

Met de klok mee van boven: Perzische basmatirijst, Baba ganouj, Hummus, Yoghurtsoep

GROENTEN / MIDDEN-OOSTEN

Baba ghanouj

Geroosterde aubergine is heerlijk als smeersel voor sandwiches of als dipsaus voor groenten.

2 grote aubergines
het sap van 2 citroenen
2 eetlepels tahini (sesamzaadpasta)
2 tenen knoflook, fijngehakt
¼ theelepel zout
versgemalen witte peper naar smaak
2 eetlepels fijngehakte verse peterselie

1. Verwarm de oven voor op 200°C. Vet een bakplaat in met olie.
2. Halveer de aubergines in de lengte en leg ze met de snijkant onder op de bakplaat. Rooster ze 40 minuten, of tot ze volledig gaar zijn. Neem ze uit de oven en laat afkoelen.
3. Schep het vruchtvlees uit de aubergines, verwijder eventuele zaden en pureer de pulp in een keukenmachine met het citroensap, de tahini en knoflook. Breng op smaak met zout en peper.
4. Doe het mengsel in een kom en bestrooi met de peterselie.

Voor 6 personen

1,25 dl per portie: Calorieën 70, Eiwit 2 g, Koolhydraten 10 g, Vezel 2 g, Vet totaal 3 g (Verzadigd 0,5 g, Enkelvoudig onverzadigd 1 g, Meervoudig onverzadigd 1 g), Cholesterol 0 mg, Natrium 110 mg

▲ *1 Groente*

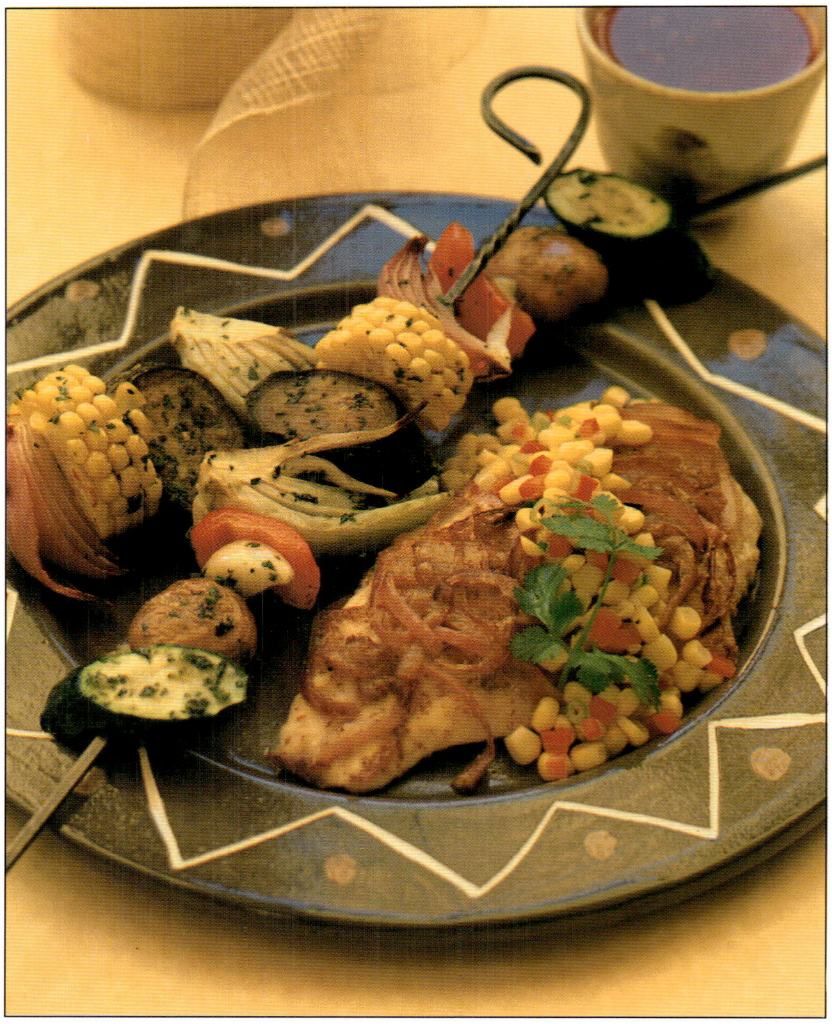

Van links naar rechts: Groentespiezen met maïs en jalapeño-olie, Meerval met mosterd-ui-korst en maïssalsa

GROENTEN / VERENIGDE STATEN

Groentespiezen met maïs en jalapeño-olie

U kunt dit Amerikaanse recept van zomerse groenten met cactusvijgsaus ook met andere groenten maken. Blancheer wintergroenten als spruitjes, wortel, aardappel, pompoen en bieten. Rijg ze aan pennen en rooster 4-5 minuten, waarbij u ze om de minuut omdraait.

4 maïskolven, bladen heel gelaten en draden verwijderd
100 g geschilde en grof gehakte cactusvijg
250 g suiker
4 eetlepels witte wijnazijn
3 tenen knoflook, fijngehakt
4 eetlepels olijfolie
1 jalapeñopeper, fijngehakt
¼ theelepel gemalen komijn
2 eetlepels fijngehakte verse koriander
1 rode paprika, in stukken van 3 cm gesneden
1 rode ui, in stukken van 3 cm gesneden
1 kleine aubergine, in plakken van 3 cm
1 courgette, in plakken van 3 cm
1 venkelknol, in 8 partjes gesneden
8 champignons, schoongeveegd en steeltjes verwijderd
16 tenen knoflook
versgemalen peper naar smaak

1. Verwarm de grill voor. Week de maïskolven in hun blad 1 uur in water.
2. Maak het cactusvijgglazuur. Doe de cactusvijg in een middelgrote pan met water en kook ze in circa 20 minuten gaar. Pureer in een blender en doe de puree terug in de pan. Voeg de suiker, azijn en fijngehakte knoflook toe en kook circa 5 minuten tot het mengsel dik is. Doe in een kom en laat afkoelen.
3. Doe voor de jalapeño-olie de olijfolie in een kleine pan. Doe er de jalapeño in en fruit 30 seconden op een laag vuur. Neem van het vuur; schep er de komijn en verse koriander door. Zet weg.
4. Rijg de paprika, ui, aubergine, courgette, venkel, champignons en tenen knoflook om en om aan 8 pennen. Schik de maïskolven (in blad) boven houtskool of onder de grill en rooster ze 10 minuten onder regelmatig omkeren. Bestrijk de groentespiezen licht met de jalapeño-olie, bestrooi ze met peper en rooster ze met de maïs 5 minuten, waarbij u ze omdraait.
5. Verwijder het blad van de maïskolven, snijd ze in stukken en bestrijk ze licht met de jalapeño-olie. Dien ze met de spiezen op met het cactusglazuur.

Voor 8 personen

1 spies per portie: Calorieën 240, Eiwit 3 g, Koolhydraten 44 g, Vezel 3 g, Vet totaal 7 g (Verzadigd 1 g, Enkelvoudig onverzadigd 5 g, Meervoudig onverzadigd 1 g), Cholesterol 0 mg, Natrium 20 mg, Vitamine C 50%.

▲ *2 Groente, 1 Vet/Suiker*

ZEEBANKET / VERENIGDE STATEN

Meerval met mosterd-ui-korst en maïssalsa

Heilbot of zalm zijn ook lekker met deze mosterd-ui-korst. U kunt de maïssalsa tot 6 uur van tevoren maken en in de koelkast bewaren. De hoeveelheid vis in dit recept levert grote porties op. Kleinere filets leveren minder calorieën en voedingsstoffen.

MAÏSSALSA

6 maïskolven
45 g rondjes lenteui
1 rode paprika, in blokjes
1 jalapeño chilipeper, fijngehakt
het sap van 1 limoen
¼ theelepel zout
versgemalen peper naar smaak

MEERVAL MET MOSTERD-UI-KORST

3 grote rode uien, julienne gesneden
2 eetlepels grove mosterd

2 eetlepels plus 1 theelepel olijfolie
4 meervalfilets, elk circa 185 g

1. Verwarm de oven voor op 180°C. Vet een bakplaat in met olie.
2. Snijd voor de salsa de maïskorrels van de kolven af. Spoel de korrels onder de koude kraan om zetmeel te verwijderen en blancheer de korrels dan 30 seconden. Laat ze goed uitlekken; schep ze om met de lenteui, paprika en jalapeño. Voeg het limoensap en wat zout en peper toe. Doe de salsa in een kom en zet weg.
3. Doe de rode ui op de bakplaat en zet die 10 minuten in de oven tot de ui goudbruin is. Neem de bakplaat uit de oven en laat de ui afkoelen.
4. Maak een pasta van de mosterd en 1 theelepel van de olijfolie. Strijk de helft van het mengsel over één kant van de visfilets. Druk de helft van de ui in de mosterdpasta op de vis.
5. Verhit de 2 eetlepels olijfolie in een vuurvaste ovenschaal. Leg de filets met de pastakant onder in de pan en bak 2 minuten op een middelhoog vuur. Smeer de pasta over de andere kant van de vis terwijl ze bakken. Keer de filets voorzichtig om en zet de schaal 8 minuten in de oven, of tot de visfilets gaar zijn en stevig aanvoelen. Dien onmiddellijk op met de salsa.

Voor 4 personen

1 filet met ¼ salsa per portie: Calorieën 470, Eiwit 37 g, Koolhydraten 45 g, Vezel 8 g, Vet totaal 17 g (Verzadigd 3 g, Enkelvoudig onverzadigd 9 g, Meervoudig onverzadigd 3,5 g) Cholesterol 100 mg, Natrium 380 mg, Vitamine A 25%, Vitamine C 100%.
▲ *1 Groente, 2 Vlees*

1 portie: Calorieën 115, Eiwit 4 g, Koolhydraten 21 g, Vezel 4 g, Vet totaal 3 g (Verzadigd 0 g, Enkelvoudig onverzadigd 0,5 g, Meervoudig onverzadigd 2 g), Cholesterol 0 mg, Natrium 25 mg, Vitamine A 190%, Vitamine C 170%.
▲ *2 Groente*

Verse citroenvinaigrette

U kunt deze dipsaus ook als een slasaus gebruiken. Door de ingekookte kippebouillon is er minder olie nodig.

1,25 dl kippebouillon (zie woordenlijst)
4 eetlepels vers citroensap
4 eetlepels witte wijnazijn
1,25 dl saffloerolie
2 theelepels fijngeraspte citroenschil
2 theelepels verse dille, stengels verwijderd
versgemalen witte peper naar smaak

1. Kook de kippebouillon tot de helft in. Laat afkoelen.
2. Doe de bouillon, het citroensap en de azijn in een kom. Giet er al kloppend geleidelijk de olie bij. Schep er de geraspte schil en de dille door en breng op smaak met de peper.

Voor 3 dl

2 eetlepels per portie: Calorieën 80, Eiwit 0 g, Koolhydraten 1 g, Vezel 0 g, Vet totaal 9 g (Verzadigd 1 g, Enkelvoudig onverzadigd 1 g, Meervoudig onverzadigd 7 g), Cholesterol 0 mg, Natrium 0 mg.
▲ *1 Vet/Suiker*

HAPJES / VERENIGDE STATEN

Rauwkost met citroenvinaigrette

125 g broccoliroosjes
125 g bloemkoolroosjes
125 g groene asperges, in stukken van 10 cm gesneden
3 wortels, geschraapt en in staafjes van 10 cm gesneden
1 kleine jícama (yam-boon), geschild en in staafjes van 10 cm gesneden
375 g kerstomaten
125 g peultjes
2 rode paprika's, in smalle repen van 10 cm lang gesneden
185 g *enoki* paddestoelen
2 stronkjes witlof, bladen losgemaakt
4 eetlepels verse citroenvinaigrette dipsaus (recept volgt)

1. Blancheer de broccoli, bloemkool, asperges en wortel 30-60 seconden in kokend water, afhankelijk van hun grootte, om de kleur te versterken en de rauwe smaak te verzwakken. Dompel ze onmiddellijk in ijswater om het kookproces te stoppen. Laat ze goed uitlekken.
2. Schik alle groenten en een kommetje op een dienschaal. Giet de dipsaus in het kommetje en dien op.

Voor 8 personen

Rauwkost met citroenvinaigrette

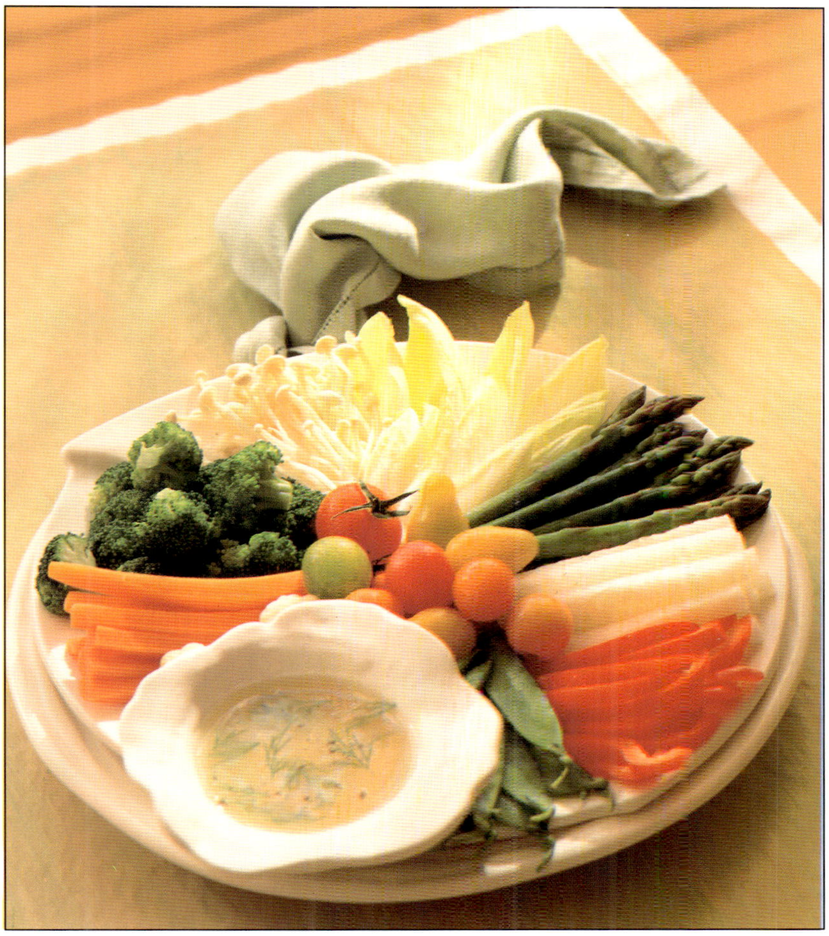

HAPJES / FRANKRIJK

Provençaalse pizza's met tomaat en basilicum

In de Provence wordt deze pizza met bladerdeeg gemaakt. Het gistdeeg in dit recept bevat minder vet.

gistdeeg (recept volgt)
1,25 dl verse gepureerde tomaten
1 eetlepel gedroogde basilicum
2 eetlepels olijfolie
2 grote verse tomaten, in plakken van ½ cm dik gesneden
1 theelepel gehakte verse tijm
1 theelepel suiker
zout en versgemalen peper naar smaak
4 grote basilicumbladen, in smalle reepjes gesneden

1. Verwarm de de oven voor op 190°C.
2. Volg de aanwijzingen 1-4 voor het gistdeeg.
3. Prik het gistdeeg in met een vork. Zet weg.
4. Zeef en bewaar het vocht van de gepureerde tomaten. Meng de gezeefde gepureerde tomaten met de gedroogde basilicum en olijfolie. Strijk het mengsel over de deegcirkels tot op 1cm van de randen.
5. Schik de plakken tomaat op het deeg, bestrooi ze met de tijm, suiker en wat zout en peper en zet ze 20 minuten in de oven. Bedruip de pizza's tijdens het bakken één of twee keer met het bewaarde tomatenvocht om te voorkomen dat ze uitdrogen. De korst moet goudbruin zijn.
6. Neem de pizza's uit de oven, bestrooi met de verse basilicum en dien onmiddellijk op.

Voor 8 personen

¼ pizza per portie: Calorieën 410, Eiwit 10 g, Koolhydraten 65 g, Vezel 3 g, Vet totaal 12 g (Verzadigd 2 g, Enkelvoudig onverzadigd 4 g, Meervoudig onverzadigd 6 g), Cholesterol 30 mg, Natrium 180 mg, IJzer 20%, Vitamine C 20%.

▲ *2 Brood, 1 Groente*

GISTDEEG

1 zakje (7 g) droge gistkorrels
60 g suiker
2,5 dl lauwe magere melk (circa 40°C)
4 eetlepels saffloerolie
1 ei
625 g ongebleekte bloem
½ theelepel zout

1. Los de gist en suiker op in een kom met de melk. Laat 5 minuten staan of tot de gist schuimt. Klop er de olie en het ei door.
2. Doe de bloem en het zout in een grote kom. Giet er al omscheppend het gistmengsel bij en meng tot u een glad deeg heeft.
3. Doe het deeg op een licht met bloem bestoven werkvlak en kneed het circa 5 minuten tot het glad en elastisch is. Doe het deeg in een schone, licht met olie ingevette kom, dek die af en laat het deeg circa 1½ uur staan tot het in volume verdubbeld is.
4. Druk de lucht uit het deeg, verdeel het in tweeën en vorm er ballen van. Rol elke bal uit op een met bloem bestoven werkvlak tot cirkels van 23 cm doorsnee en 3 mm dik. Doe de deegcirkels op 2 licht ingevette taartvormen en laat 10 minuten rusten.
5. Vul de pizza's volgens het recept.

Voor 2 pizza's

⅛ van één korst per portie: Calorieën 180, Eiwit 5 g, Koolhydraten 31 g, Vezel 1 g, Vet totaal 4 g (Verzadigd 0,5 g, Enkelvoudig onverzadigd 0,5 g, Meervoudig onverzadigd 2,5 g), Cholesterol 15 mg, Natrium 85 mg.

▲ *1 Brood*

HAPJES / FRANKRIJK

Jacques Pépins prei met tomaat en olijfolie

Dit recept verscheen voor het eerst in Today's Gourmet, *het bijbehorende kookboek voor Jacques Pépins gelijknamige televisieserie. Verse preien worden bijtgaar gekookt en lauw of op kamertemperatuur geserveerd met een pittige tomatenvinaigrette.*

4 middelgrote preien (circa 650 g), bijgesneden en gewassen
1 rijpe tomaat, ontveld, ontzaad en in blokjes van ½ cm gesneden
3 eetlepels koudgeperste olijfolie
1 eetlepel rode wijnazijn
1 eetlepel Dijonmosterd
1 theelepel Worcestershiresaus
½ theelepel zout
¼ theelepel versgemalen zwarte peper

1. Breng 5 dl water aan de kook in een roestvrijstalen pan. Doe er de prei in, breng weer aan de kook, leg het deksel op de pan en laat in circa 10 minuten zachtjes bijtgaar koken.
2. Giet de prei af en bewaar het kooknat voor een soep. Laat de prei even afkoelen en knijp er dan zoveel mogelijk vocht uit.
3. Snijd de prei in stukken van 5 cm. Schik de witte en groene stukken in een ovenschaal.
4. Meng de tomaat met de olie, azijn, mosterd, Worcestershiresaus, het zout en de peper. Schep dit mengsel over de prei en serveer lauw of op kamertemperatuur.

Voor 4 personen

1 portie: Calorieën 180, Eiwit 2 g, Koolhydraten 20 g, Vezel 2 g, Vet totaal 11 g (Verzadigd 2 g, Enkelvoudig onverzadigd 7 g, Meervoudig onverzadigd 1 g), Cholesterol 0 mg, Natrium 440 mg, Vitamine C 40%.

▲ *1 Groente, 1 Vet/Suiker*

Van boven naar beneden: Provençaalse pizza met tomaat en basilicum, Jacques Pépins prei met tomaat en olijfolie

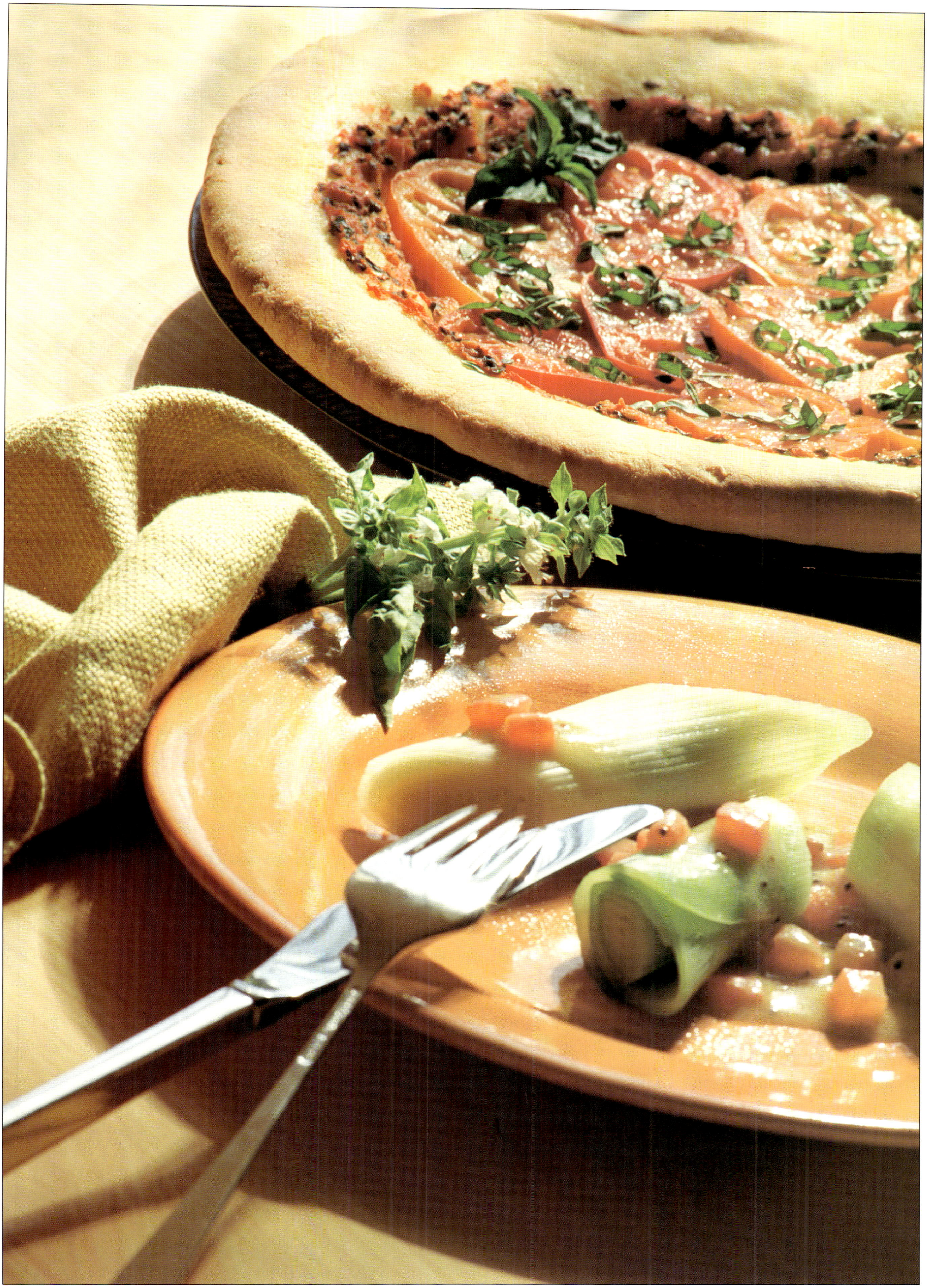

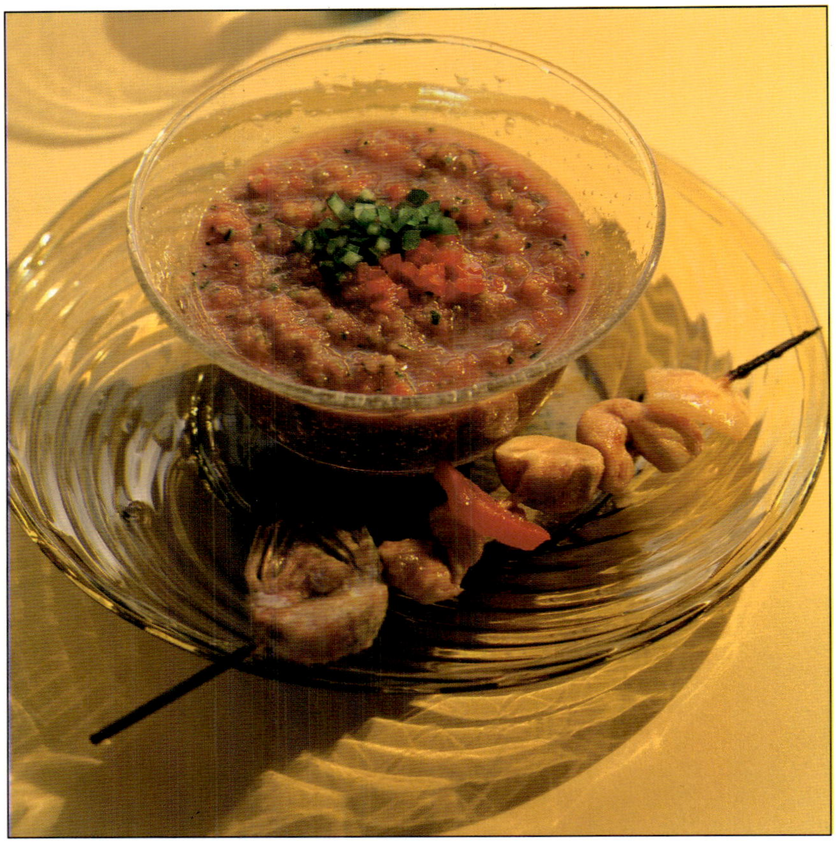

Van boven naar beneden: Andalusische gazpacho, Gegrilde kipspiesjes

SOEPEN / SPANJE

Andalusische gazpacho

Gazpacho *betekent letterlijk geweekt brood. Er zijn vele versies voor deze soep, met ingrediënten als druiven en amandelen tot zeebanket en vleesbouillon.*

1 rode paprika, ontzaad en grof gehakt
1 groene paprika, ontzaad en grof gehakt
1 komkommer, geschild en in blokjes
500 g tomaten, ontveld en grof gehakt
2 sneden oudbakken brood, korsten verwijderd, 5 minuten in water geweekt en uitgeknepen
2 tenen knoflook
2 lenteuitjes, in plakjes
2 eetlepels olijfolie
1 eetlepel sherryazijn
1 eetlepel verse peterselie, fijngehakt
½ theelepel paprikapoeder
¼ theelepel zout

1. Doe de helft van de rode paprika, groene paprika en kmkommer in een blender. Doe de rest van de ingrediënten in de blender en draai tot een glad mengsel.
2. Zet minstens 2 uur in de koelkast. Schep de soep in gekoelde kommen en garneer met de bewaarde groenten.

Voor 6 personen

2,5 dl per portie: Calorieën 90, Eiwit 2 g, Koolhydraten 11 g, Vezel 2 g, Vet totaal 5 g (Verzadigd 0,5 g, Enkelvoudig onverzadigd 3,5 g, Meervoudig onverzadigd 0,5 g), Cholesterol 0 mg, Natrium 150 mg, Vitamine A 30%, Vitamine C 100%.

▲ *2 Groente*

HAPJES / SPANJE

Gegrilde kipspiesjes

De traditie van tapas, *verschillende kleine hapjes, is nu ook bekend buiten de grenzen van Spanje. Vele restaurants en bars serveren hapjes als gemarineerde champignons, gevulde paprika's en omelet, en ook deze gegrilde kip. De beste drank hierbij is gekoelde Manzanilla, een lichtdroge sherry uit Andalusië.*

1 hele kipfilet, ontveld
2 eetlepels vers limoensap
1 eetlepel olijfolie
1 eetlepel honing
½ theelepel gemalen koriander
½ theelepel pikant paprikapoeder
2 tenen knoflook, fijngehakt
1 rode paprika, in stukken van 3 cm gesneden
1 gele paprika, in stukken van 3 cm gesneden
250 g kleine champignons
16 artisjokharten, in olijfolie gemarineerd
¼ theelepel zout
versgemalen peper naar smaak
10 g gehakte verse koriander (desgewenst)

1. Week 16 satéstokjes 30 minuten in water. Snijd de kipfilet overdwars in repen van 1 cm breed. Zet weg.
2. Meng het limoensap in een ondiepe kom met de olijfolie, honing, gemalen koriander, het paprikapoeder en de knoflook.
3. Rijg de kip, rode en gele paprika's, champignons en artisjokharten om en om aan de satéstokjes; giet er de marinade over en laat minstens 1 uur of een nacht in de koelkast marineren.
4. Bring de spiesjes op smaak met het zout en wat peper. Grilleer de spiesjes circa 2 minuten per kant boven houtskool of onder de grill, waarbij u ze één keer omdraait en met wat marinade bedruipt tot de kip gaar en goudbruin is.
5. Schik de spiesjes op een dienschaal, strooi er desgewenst de verse koriander over en dien onmiddellijk op.

Voor 16 personen

1 spies per portie: Calorieën 80, Eiwit 9 g, Koolhydraten 8 g, Vezel 1 g, Vet totaal 2 g (Verzadigd 0,5 g, Enkelvoudig onverzadigd 0,5 g, Meervoudig onverzadigd 0,5 g), Cholesterol 20 mg, Natrium 115 mg, Vitamine C 110%.

▲ *1 Groente, ½ Vlees*

SOEPEN / MEXICO

Koude ananassoep

Gekoelde soepen zijn zeer geschikt voor een lunch, maar deze is ook perfect voor een brunch.

1 grote rijpe ananas, geschild, kern verwijderd, in blokjes
1 papaja, geschild, in blokjes
de geraspte schil van 1 limoen
het sap van 2 limoenen
2 eetlepels tequila (desgewenst)
60 g suiker

1 mango, geschild en in plakken
1 stervrucht (carambola) of kiwi, de kiwi geschild, in plakken
de zaden van 1 granaatappel, circa 75 g

1. Pureer de ananas en papaja (bewaar 4 eetlepels van beide voor het garneren) in een blender of keukenmachine. Voeg de geraspte limoenschil, de helft van het limoensap, de tequila en de helft van de suiker toe en draai tot een glad mengsel. Zet 2 uur voor het serveren in de koelkast.
2. Schep de mango, stervrucht, bewaarde ananas en papaja om met het overgebleven sap en de rest van de suiker. Zet in de koelkast.
3. Giet de vruchtenpuree vlak voor het serveren in glazen. Schik er de stukjes fruit op en garneer met het granaatappelzaad.

Voor 6 personen

2,5 dl per portie: Calorieën 190, Eiwit 2 g, Koolhydraten 48 g, Vezel 5 g, Vet totaal 1 g (Verzadigd 0 g, Enkelvoudig onverzadigd 0 g, Meervoudig onverzadigd 0,5 g), Cholesterol 0 mg, Natrium 5 mg, Vitamine A 45%, Vitamine C 120%.
▲ *2 Fruit*

ONTBIJT / MEXICO

Maïspannekoeken, gepocheerde eieren en fruitsalsa

Een fruitsalsa is eenvoudig een mengsel van verse vruchten met ui en chilipeper. Verse nopales *(platte schijven van de schijf- of nopalcactus) zijn makkelijk te prepareren. Schraap er met een scherp mes of dunschiler de ogen en stekels af en spoel af. Wie geen verse* nopales *kan vinden, kan* nopales *uit blik of vers fruit als kiwi gebruiken.*

FRUITSALSA
1 papaja, geschild
125 g kleine *nopales*
1 mango, geschild en in kleine blokjes
75 g geschilde en in blokjes gesneden jícama (yamboon)
60 g gesnipperde rode ui
1 rode paprika, ontzaad en in kleine blokjes
1 jalapeño chilipeper, ontzaad en fijngehakt
1 sinaasappel, geschild en in partjes gesneden
het sap van 1 sinaasappel
zout en versgemalen peper naar smaak

MAÏSPANNEKOEKEN
280 g maïskorrels
3 eieren
7,5 dl magere melk
3 eetlepels saffloerolie
165 g bloem
140 g *masa harina*
1½ theelepel bakpoeder
¼ theelepel zout
2 eetlepels suiker

GEPOCHEERDE EIEREN
1 eetlepel vers sinaasappelsap
6 eieren

1. Maak de fruitsalsa. Haal de zaden uit de papaja en bewaar er 3 eetlepels van. Snijd de papaja in kleine blokjes en zet weg.
2. Verwijder stekels en lelijke plekken van de *nopales*. Snijd de randen bij, spoel ze af en snijd ze in blokjes. Stoom ze 2 minuten boven kokend water en dompel ze dan in ijswater. Giet af.
3. Doe de papaja, de bewaarde papajazaden, *nopales*, mango, jícama, ui, paprika, jalapeño, sinaasappelpartjes en sinaasappelsap in een grote kom. Breng op smaak met zout en peper en schep alles om. Laat 30 minuten staan.
4. Meng voor de pannekoeken de maïs met de eieren, melk en olie.
5. Doe de bloem, *masa harina*, het bakpoeder, zout en de suiker in een grote kom. Voeg het maïsmengsel toe en schep alles om.
6. Schep kleine lepels van het beslag in een anti-aanbak koekepan en bak 1 minuut per kant, waarbij u ze één keer omdraait. Houd de pannekoeken warm in een lauwe oven tot het serveren.
7. Breng voor de eieren 3 cm water in een koekepan aan de kook. Voeg het sinaasappelsap toe en draai het vuur zo laag dat het water suddert. Breek de eieren één voor één in een kleine kom en laat ze één voor één zachtjes in het water glijden. Pocheer de eieren circa 5 minuten tot het wit gestold is. Schep ze met een schuimspaan uit het water.
8. Schik een ei over 2 pannekoeken, schep er wat salsa omheen en dien onmiddellijk op.

Voor 6 personen

---

2 pannekoeken, 1 ei, 1,65 dl salsa per portie: Calorieën 520, Eiwit 21 g, Koolhydraten 72 g, Vezel 8 g, Vet totaal 18 g (Verzadigd 4 g, Enkelvoudig onverzadigd 4,5 g, Meervoudig onverzadigd 7 g), Cholesterol 335 mg, Natrium 270 mg, Vitamine A 70%, Vitamine C 70%.
▲ *2 Brood, 1 Fruit, 1 Groente, ½ Vlees, ½ Melk*

Van boven naar beneden: Koude ananassoep, Maïspannekoeken, gepocheerde eieren en fruitsalsa

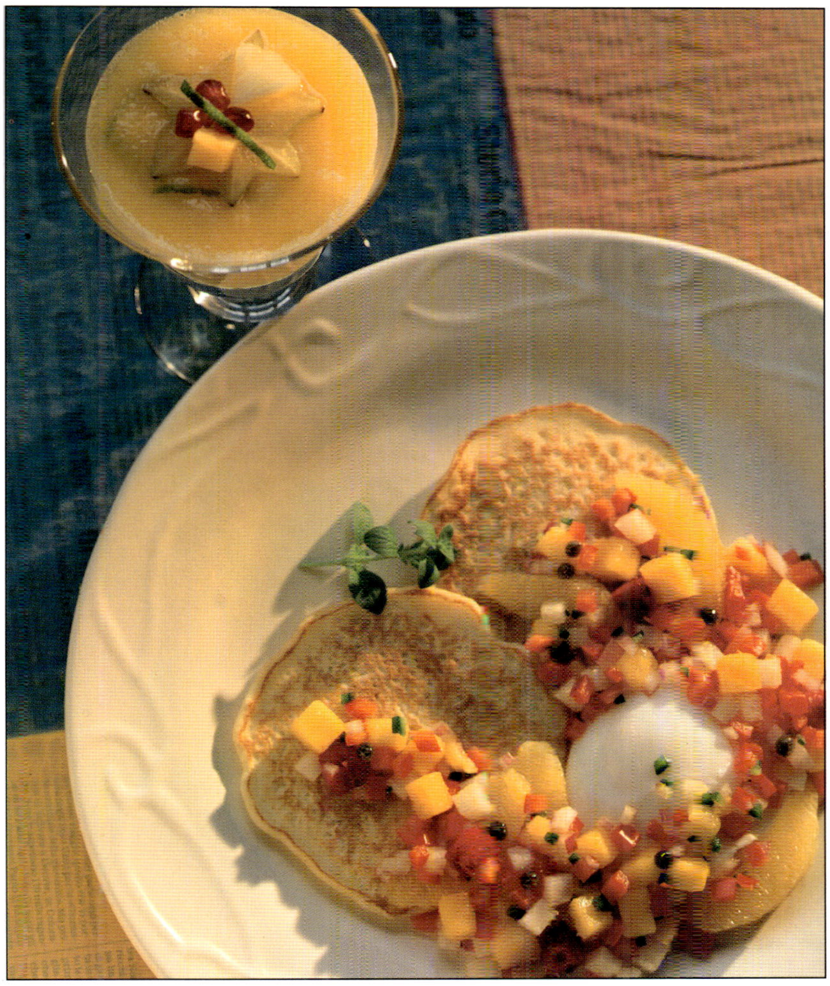

HAPJES / GRIEKENLAND

Tuinbonensalade

Serveer dit gerecht als een salade of pureer alles voor een heerlijke dipsaus met pitabrood (recept op pagina 78) en groenten. Deze salade bevat bijna de helft van de dagelijks benodigde hoeveelheid voedingsvezel en vele B-vitaminen.

500 g gedopte verse tuinbonen
2 liter kippebouillon (zie woordenlijst)
125 g gehakte ui
2 tenen knoflook, fijngehakt
1 wortel, geschild en gehakt
2 kleine courgettes, in plakken van 1 cm dik gesneden
1,25 dl vers citroensap
4 eetlepels olijfolie
½ theelepel zout
versgemalen peper naar smaak
30 g gehakte rode ui
60 g plakjes bleekselderij
1 theelepel fijngehakte verse munt
10 g fijngehakte peterselie
120 g postelein of raketkruid of een andere bladgroente naar keuze
2 tomaten, in partjes gesneden

1. Was de bonen en doe ze in een grote pan met de kippebouillon, ui, knoflook en wortel. (U kunt de bonen in een zakje van ongebleekte katoen doen, zodat u ze na het koken makkelijk uit de bouillon kunt halen.) Laat 30 minuten sudderen. Voeg de courgette toe en kook nog 10 minuten of tot de bonen gaar zijn. Giet de groenten af en zet ze weg om af te koelen. Dop de afgekoelde tuinbonen voor de tweede keer. Doe de dubbel gedopte bonen terug in het courgettemengsel.
2. Klop het citroensap door de olijfolie in een grote kom. Breng op smaak met het zout en wat peper. Voeg het afgekoelde bonenmengsel, de rode ui, bleekselderij, munt en de helft van de peterselie toe en schep alles om.
3. Schep de postelein door het bonenmengsel en schik op een dienschaal. Strooi er de rest van de peterselie over en garneer met de tomaten. Serveer op kamertemperatuur of gekoeld.

Voor 8 personen

2,5 dl per portie: Calorieën 310, Eiwit 17 g, Koolhydraten 43 g, Vezel 10 g, Vet totaal 9 g (Verzadigd 1,5 g, Enkelvoudig onverzadigd 6 g, Meervoudig onverzadigd 1,5 g), Cholesterol 0 mg, Natrium 180 mg, IJzer 25%, Vitamine A 60%, Vitamine C 40%.

▲ *1 Groente, 1 Vlees*

Van boven naar beneden: Souvlaki met yoghurt-dillesaus, Tuinbonensalade

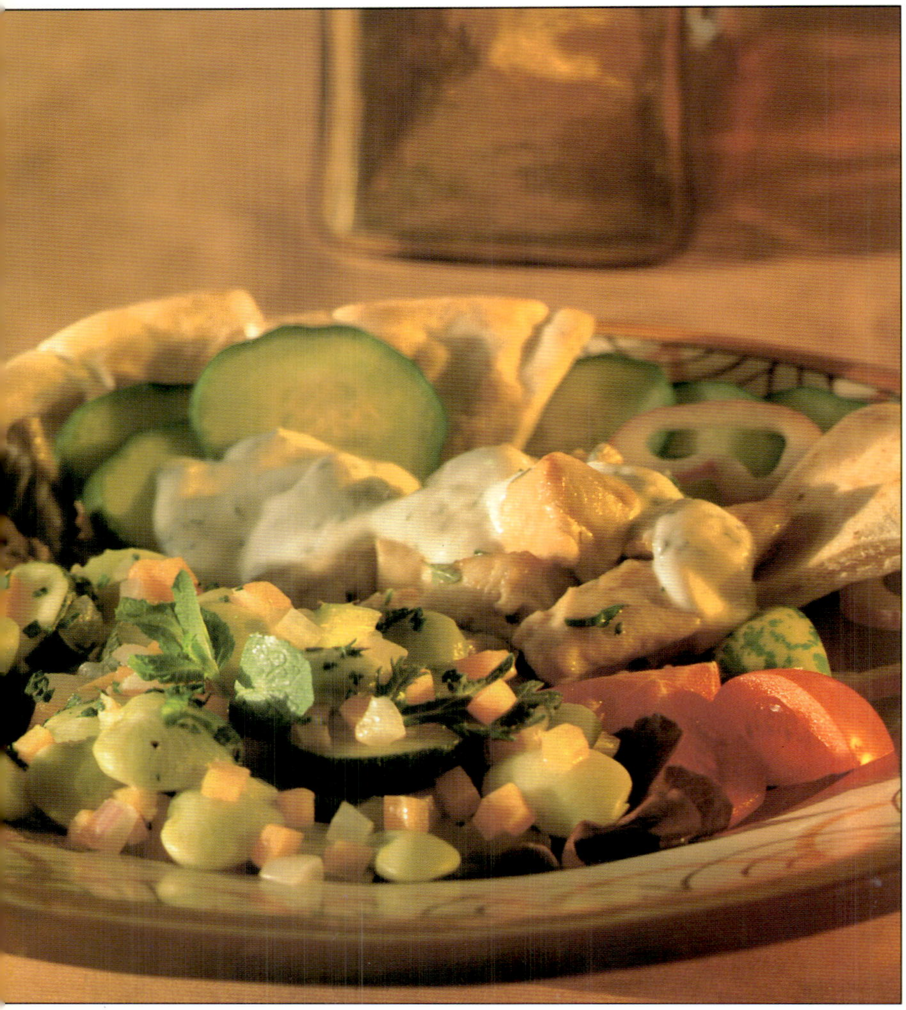

GEVOGELTE / GRIEKENLAND

Souvlaki met yoghurt-dillesaus

Souvlaki—*spiesjes van gemarineerde kip—zijn perfect voor een zomerse maaltijd. Serveer ze met plakken rijpe tomaat en rode ui, verse komkommer en een kom radijsjes. Stop alles in een verwarmd pitabrood (recept op pagina 78).*

SOUVLAKI

1,25 dl koudgeperste olijfolie
het sap van 3 citroenen
3 tenen knoflook, fijngehakt
2 theelepels fijngehakte verse oregano
1 theelepel fijngehakte verse tijm
4 laurierbladen
¼ theelepel zout
versgemalen peper
750 g kipfilet, in blokjes van 3 cm gesneden

YOGHURT-DILLESAUS

1,25 dl magere yoghurt
1½ theelepel verse dille, fijngehakt

1. Meng de olijfolie met het citroensap, de knoflook, oregano, tijm, laurierbladen, het zout en wat peper in zuurbestendige kom. Zet 3 eetlepels apart voor het bedruipen en gebruik de rest om er de kip een nacht mee in de koelkast te laten marineren.
2. Maak de yoghurt-dillesaus door de yoghurt en dille te mengen. Zet in de koelkast tot het serveren.
3. Verwarm de grill voor. Week 8 satéstokjes 20 minuten in water. Rijg de kip aan de stokjes en grilleer ze circa 6 minuten, waarbij u ze met de marinade bedruipt tot de kip goudbruin en knapperig is. Zet de kip 5 cm weg van de directe hitte en laat nog circa 6-8 minuten grilleren tot de kip volledig gaar is.

4. Bestrijk de kip licht met de bewaarde 3 eetlepels marinade, haal de stukjes van de stokjes en dien onmiddellijk op met de yoghurt-dillesaus.

Voor 4 personen

---

2 stokjes per portie plus 2 eetlepels yoghurt: Calorieën 290, Eiwit 41 g, Koolhydraten 3 g, Vezel 0 g, Vet totaal 11 g (Verzadigd 2 g, Enkelvoudig onverzadigd 7 g, Meervoudig onverzadigd 1,5 g), Cholesterol 110 mg, Natrium 150 mg.

▲ *1 Vlees*

GRANEN / FRANKRIJK

Socca

KIKKERERWTENPANNEKOEK

In Nice wordt socca, *een hartige pannekoek van kikkererwtenbloem, op de Cours Saleya-markt zo van een bakfiets verkocht. U moet er wel snel bij zijn want ze zijn zo uitverkocht.* Socca *is een heerlijk bijgerecht voor* les fleurs farcies *(recept op pagina 95) of een salade Niçoise (recept op pagina 68).*

220 g kikkererwtenbloem
½ theelepel zout
2 tenen knoflook, fijngehakt
½ theelepel gemalen komijn
2 eetlepels olijfolie

1. Klop de kikkererwtenbloem in een middelgrote kom geleidelijk door 2,5 dl koud water. Klop er het zout, de knoflook en komijn door. Dek de kom af en laat 1 uur staan.
2. Verwarm na 50 minuten de oven voor op 230°C. Vet een pizzablik van 30 cm doorsnee in met 1 eetlepel van de olijfolie.
3. Roer het beslag door en giet het in het pizzablik tot een dikte van ½ cm. Druppel er de overgebleven eetlepel olijfolie over. Zet 20 minuten in de oven tot de bovenkant goudbruin en knapperig is. Snijd in 8 punten en dien onmiddellijk op.

Voor 4 personen

---

2 punten per portie: Calorieën 220, Eiwit 8 g, Koolhydraten 26 g, Vezel 3 g, Vet totaal 9 g (Verzadigd 1 g, Enkelvoudig onverzadigd 6 g, Meervoudig onverzadigd 1,5 g), Cholesterol 0 mg, Natrium 300 mg.

▲ *2 Brood*

SOEPEN / FRANKRIJK

Franse marktsoep

De zomer is het hoogtepunt van het tomatenseizoen. Van volrijpe tomaten wordt natuurlijk de lekkerste soep gemaakt. Deze eenvouwdige tomaten-basilicumsoep krijgt zijn prachtige kleur door de toevoeging van biet. Deze lekkere en voedzame soep is een uitstekende basis voor andere verse ingrediënten als vis, aubergine, courgette, kruiden en peulvruchten, om er maar een paar op te noemen. Giet er wat extra vocht bij en u kunt rijst of pasta toevoegen.

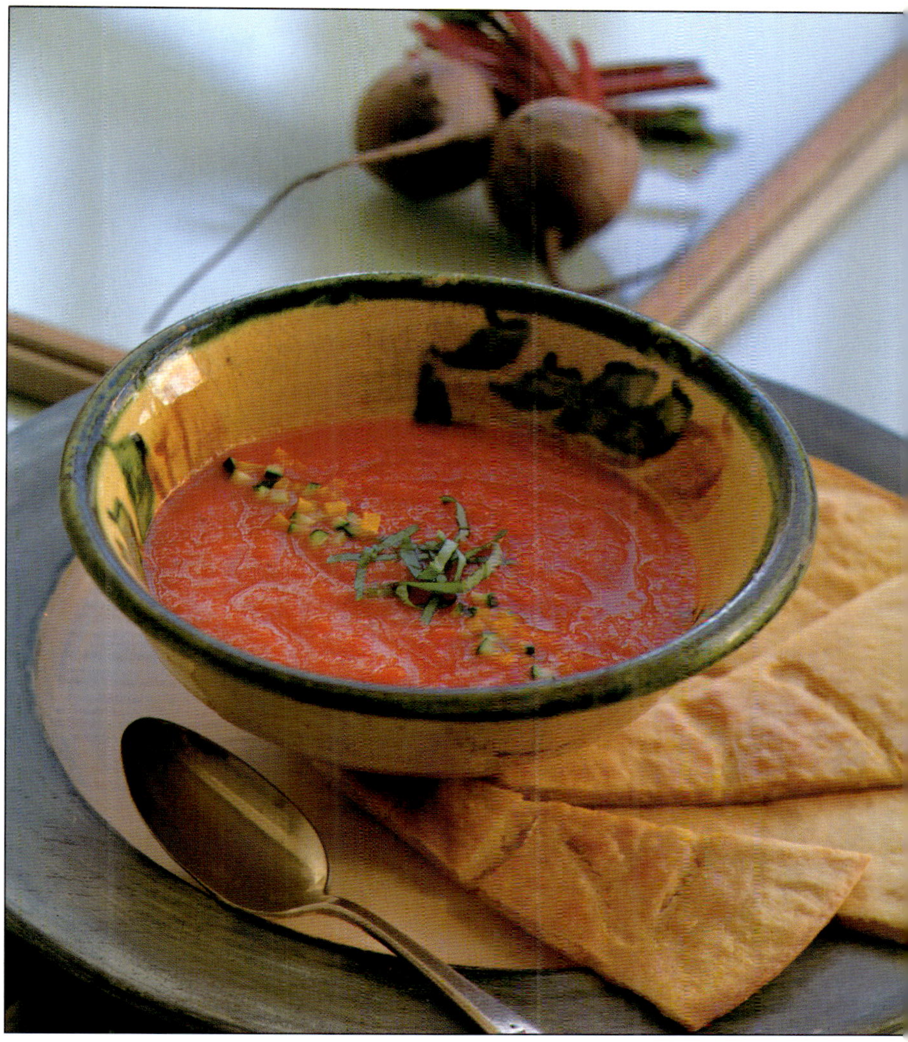

Van links naar rechts: Franse marktsoep, Kikkererwtenpannekoek

2 eetlepels olijfolie
2 uien, gehakt
2 tenen knoflook, fijngehakt
7,5 dl kippebouillon (zie woordenlijst)
1 wortel, geschild en in plakken
2 stengels bleekselderij, in dunne plakken
125 g geschilde en gehakte biet
1 kg rijpe tomaten, ontveld, ontzaad en grof gehakt
2 eetlepels tomatenpuree
zout en versgemalen peper naar smaak
3 eetlepels verse basilicumbladen, in reepjes gesneden

1. Verhit de olijfolie in een soeppan. Doe er de ui en knoflook in en fruit alles gaar. Voeg de kippebouillon, wortel, bleekselderij en biet toe en breng aan de kook. Draai het vuur lager en laat circa 10 minuten sudderen tot alle groenten gaar zijn.
2. Voeg de tomaten en puree toe en laat circa 15 minuten sudderen tot de soep dikker wordt. Pureer de soep in een blender. Doe de soep terug in de pan, breng op smaak met zout en peper en warm weer door.
3. Schep de soep in voorverwarmde kommen, garneer met de basilicum en dien op.

Voor 6 personen

2,5 dl per portie: Calorieën 120, Eiwit 3 g, Koolhydraten 16 g, Vezel 4 g, Vet totaal 6 g (Verzadigd 1 g, Enkelvoudig onverzadigd 4 g, Meervoudig onverzadigd 1 g), Cholesterol 0 mg, Natrium 40 mg, Vitamine A 90%, Vitamine C 60%.

▲ *2 Groente*

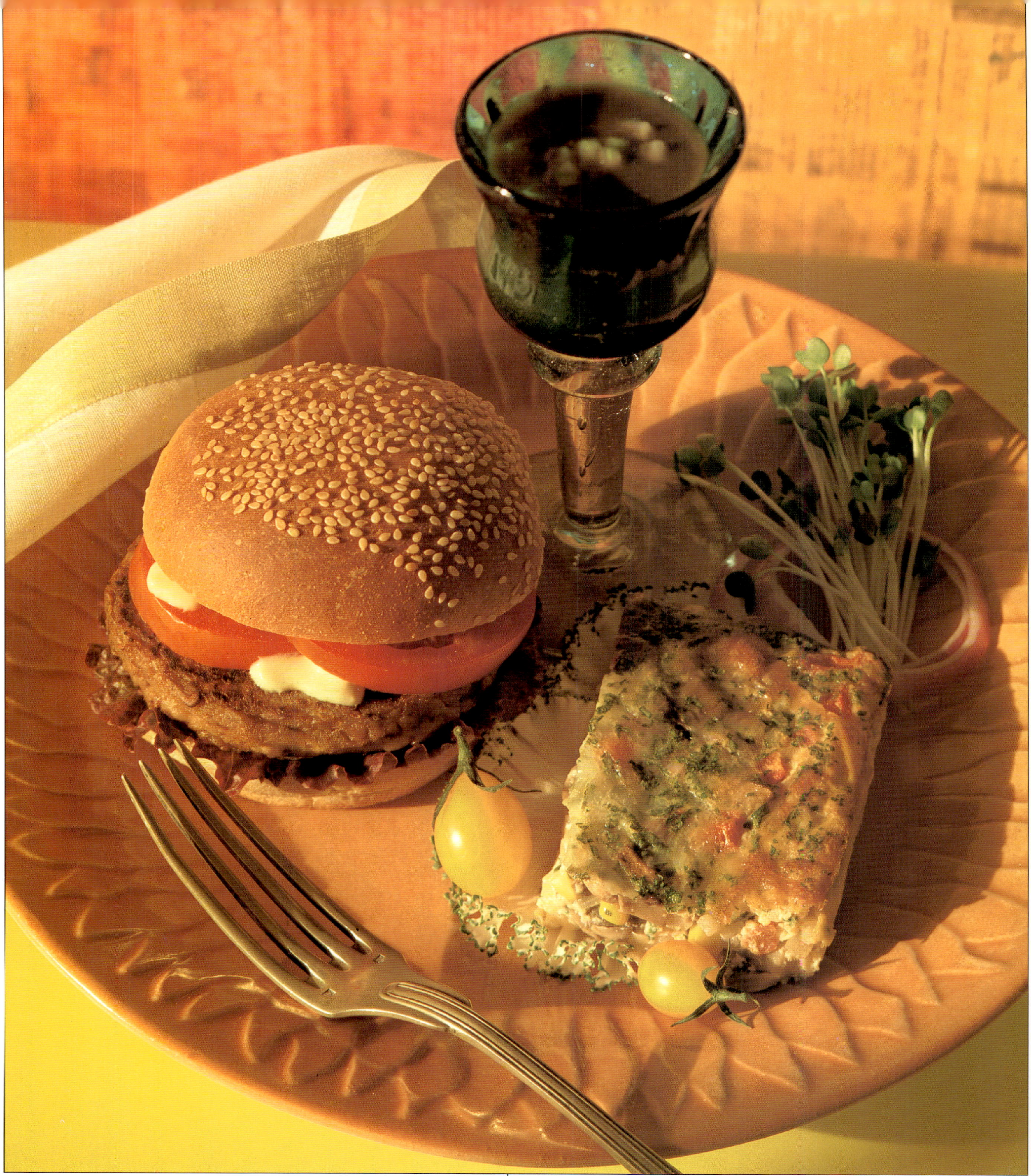

Met de klok mee van links: Burgers van adzukibonen en bruine rijst, Groentencocktail, Maïs-jícamaquiche zonder korst

DRANKEN / VERENIGDE STATEN

Groentencocktail

Een sapcentrifuge is ideaal om dit drankje te maken, maar met een blender lukt het ook. De basissmaak in dit recept is tomaat. Ze moeten rijp, zacht en sappig zijn. Als u een sapcentrifuge hebt, kunt u bleekselderij, biet en wortel toevoegen.

1 kg rijpe tomaten
4 eetlepels gemalen ijsblokjes
250 g spinaziebladen, gehakt
1 rode paprika, geroosterd, ontveld en ontzaad (zie woordenlijst)
1 komkommer, geschild
2 theelepels vers citroensap

zout en versgemalen peper naar smaak
1 theelepel Tabasco (desgewenst)

1. Hak de tomaten grof en vang zoveel mogelijk sap op; doe in een blender met de gemalen ijsblokjes en pureer. Druk dit mengsel door een fijne zeef om de zaden en pulp te verwijderen en zoveel mogelijk alle sap eruit te krijgen. Doe het sap terug in de blender. Voeg één voor één de rest van de ingrediënten toe en draai na elke toevoeging tot een glad mengsel.
2. Breng zonodig op smaak met zout en peper en serveer gekoeld.

Voor 8 personen

---

1 glas per portie: Calorieën 35, Eiwit 2 g, Koolhydraten 8 g, Vezel 3 g, Vet totaal 0 g (Verzadigd 0 g, Enkelvoudig onverzadigd 0 g, Meervoudig onverzadigd 0 g), Cholesterol 0 mg, Natrium 35 mg, Vitamine A 60%, Vitamine C 90%.

▲ *1 Groente*

GRANEN / VERENIGDE STATEN

Burgers van adzukibonen en bruine rijst

Vegetariërs zijn dol op deze graanburgers, die van buiten krokant en van binnen zacht zijn.

60 g adzuki-bonen, een nacht geweekt
60 g bruine rijst
2 eetlepels sojabonenvlokken
1 wortel, geraspt
5 dl groentebouillon (zie woordenlijst)
1 eetlepel olijfolie
60 g gehakte ui
2 tenen knoflook, fijngehakt
65 g champignons, in plakjes
1 ei, losgeklopt
2 eetlepels tarwekiemen
½ theelepel sojasaus
versgemalen peper naar smaak
70 g bloem
3 eetlepels magere yoghurt
2 eetlepels Dijonmosterd
6 volkorenbroodjes
6 bladen eikebladsla
2 tomaten, in plakken

1. Kook de bonen, bruine rijst, sojabonenvlokken en wortel 40 minuten in de groentebouillon in een middelgrote pan. Giet af.
2. Verhit de olijfolie en fruit er de ui en knoflook in circa 5 minuten goudbruin in. Voeg de champignons toe en bak tot al het vocht verdampt is. Voeg het bonenmengsel toe en laat afkoelen.
3. Doe het mengsel in een keukenmachine en draai met korte stootjes tot alles net gehakt is. Maak er geen puree van. Schep er het ei en de tarwekiemen door en breng op smaak met de sojasaus en peper. Schep er de bloem door.
4. Verhit een koekepan met een anti-aanbaklaag. Vorm 6 even grote koekjes van het bonenmengsel. Bak de koekjes circa 10 minuten op een middelhoog vuur, waarbij u ze om de 3 minuten omdraait tot ze goudbruin zijn en stevig aanvoelen.
5. Meng de yoghurt met de mosterd en smeer dit mengsel over de broodjes, leg er een koekje op en serveer met de sla en tomaten.

Voor 6 personen

---

1 burger per portie: Calorieën 330, Eiwit 12 g, Koolhydraten 53 g, Vezel 4 g, Vet totaal 8 g (Verzadigd 2 g, Enkelvoudig onverzadigd 3,5 g, Meervoudig onverzadigd 1,5 g), Cholesterol 55 mg, Natrium 510 mg, Vitamine A 80%, Vitamine C 20%.

▲ *2 Brood, 1 Groente, ½ Vlees*

ONTBIJT / VERENIGDE STATEN

Maïs-jícamaquiche zonder korst

Maak deze quiche een dag van tevoren en serveer hem de volgende dag op kamertemperatuur of opgewarmd. Een verse tomatenvinaigrette (recept op pagina 116) of salsa is er heerlijk bij.

2 eetlepels olijfolie
150 g gesnipperde ui
250 g champignons, in plakken
2 grote tomaten, ontveld, ontzaad en grof gehakt
100 g maïskorrels
75 g geschilde en gehakte jícama
3 eieren plus 2 eiwitten
3,75 dl magere melk
2 theelepels Dijonmosterd
1 eetlepel gehakte verse koriander
1 theelepel gehakte verse peterselie
½ theelepel gehakte verse oregano
¼ theelepel zout
½ theelepel paprikapoeder
30 g geraspte magere mozzarella

1. Verwarm de oven voor op 190°C. Vet een ovenschaal van 23 x 23 cm licht in met olie.
2. Verhit de olijfolie in een grote koekepan en fruit er de ui in circa 5 minuten gaar in. Voeg de champignons toe en bak tot al het vocht verdampt is. Schep er de tomaten, maïs en jícama door, doe het mengsel in de ovenschaal en zet weg.
3. Doe de eieren, eiwitten, melk, mosterd, verse koriander, peterselie, oregano, het zout en paprikapoeder in een kom en klop alles goed. Giet over de groenten en roer alles voorzichtig door.
4. Strooi er de mozzarella over en zet de quiche 35-40 minuten in de oven tot de bovenkant goudbruin is en een ingestoken mes er schoon uitkomt. Laat de quiche 10 minuten op een rooster afkoelen voor u hem aansnijdt.

Voor 6 personen

---

1 portie: Calorieën 170, Eiwit 10 g, Koolhydraten 14 g, Vezel 2 g, Vet totaal 9 g (Verzadigd 2,5 g, Enkelvoudig onverzadigd 5 g, Meervoudig onverzadigd 1 g), Cholesterol 115 mg, Natrium 260 mg, Vitamine C 30%.

▲ *1 Groente, ½ Melk*

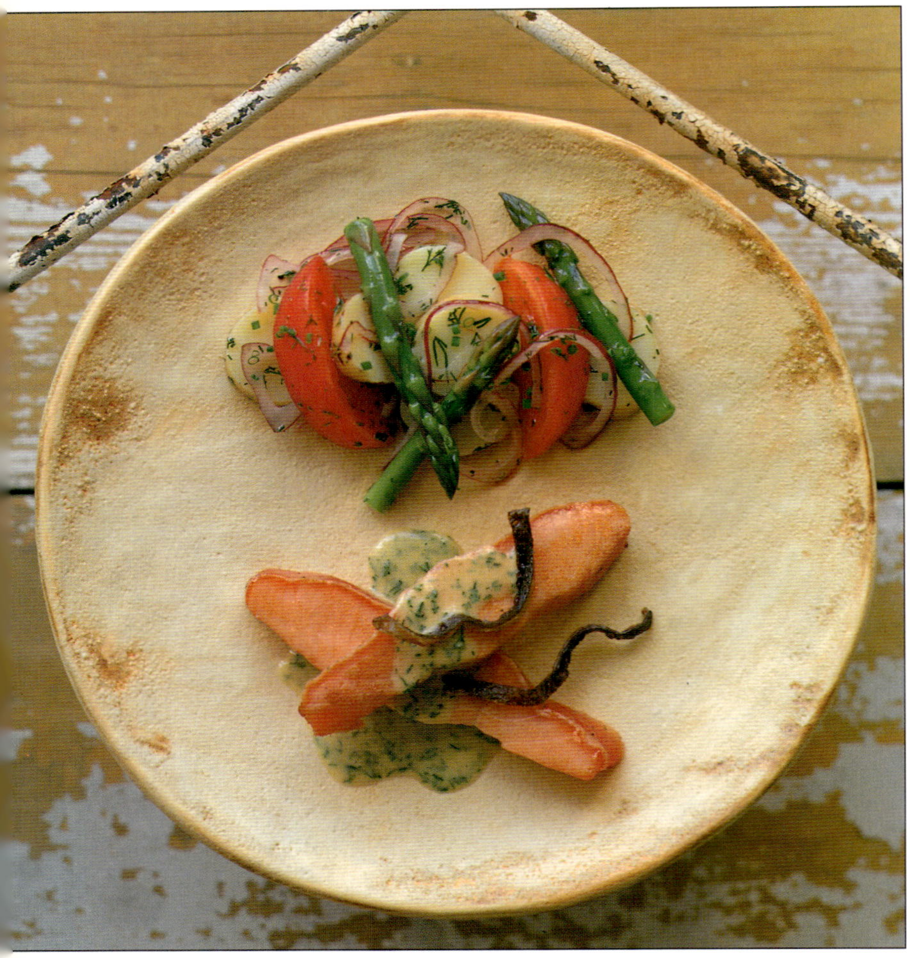

Van boven naar beneden: Zomerse aardappelsalade, Geschroeide gravlax

ZEEBANKET / ZWEDEN

Halstrad gravlax

GESCHROEIDE GRAVLAX

Chef Staffan Terje maakt een gravlax van een zalmfilet en schroeit die vervolgens dicht. Begin een dag van tevoren om de vis goed op smaak te krijgen. De zalm wordt in zout gelegd om het vocht eraan te onttrekken en het vlees steviger te maken. Daarna worden het grootste deel van het zout en de suiker verwijderd. Serveer de geschroeide gravlax met een mosterdsaus en een zomerse salade (recept hiernaast).

GRAVLAX
375 g suiker
170 g grof zeezout
20 g gesnipperde verse dille
20 g witte of zwarte peperkorrels, grof gemalen
15 g jeneverbessen, gekneusd
1 kg verse zalmfilet met vel, uit het middenstuk gesneden
MOSTERDSAUS
1,25 dl zoete en pittige mosterd
het sap van 1 citroen
2 eetlepels gesnipperde dille
5 eetlepels plantaardige olie
¼ theelepel zout
versgemalen peper naar smaak

1. Maak het inlegmengsel door de suiker, het zout, de gesnipperde dille, peperkorrels en jeneverbessen door elkaar te scheppen. Laat het mengsel 30 minuten staan.
2. Verwijder eventuele schubben en graten van de zalm.
3. Bedek de bodem van een passende zuurbestendige schaal met één kwart van het zoutmengsel. Leg er de zalm met de velkant onder op en bedek met de rest van het zoutmengsel. Dek de schaal af met plastic folie en laat 1 uur op kamertemperatuur staan. Zet dan 12 uur in de koelkast.
4. Schraap het zoutmengsel van de zalm en gooi het weg. Veeg de zalm schoon met een schone, vochtige doek.
5. Haal het vel van de zalm, snijd het vel in repen van 2 cm en zet weg. Snijd de zalm overdwars in plakken van 3 cm.
6. Klop voor de mosterdsaus de mosterd door het citroensap, de gesnipperde dille en 1 eetlepel water. Giet er al kloppend geleidelijk de olie bij. Breng op smaak met zout en peper.
7. Verhit een zware goed geoliede gietijzeren of anti-aanbak koekepan tot die heel heet is. Schroei de plakken zalm 30 seconden aan beide kanten. Schik de plakken op een dienschaal.
8. Bak de repen vel in dezelfde pan op een middelhoog vuur tot de repen knapperig zijn. Strooi ze over de zalm, schep er wat mosterdsaus over en dien onmiddellijk op.

Voor 6 personen

1 portie: Calorieën 390, Eiwit 33 g, Koolhydraten 4 g, Vezel 0 g, Vet totaal 26 g (Verzadigd 3 g, Enkelvoudig onverzadigd 14 g, Meervoudig onverzadigd 7 g), Cholesterol 95 mg, Natrium 820 mg.
▲ *1 Vlees, 1 Vet/Suiker*

SALADES / ZWEDEN

Zomerse aardappelsalade

500 g kleine nieuwe aardappels
250 g groene asperges, in stukken van 7 cm gesneden en geblancheerd (zie woordenlijst)
2 grote rijpe tomaten, ontveld en in partjes gesneden
1 rode ui, gehalveerd en in dunne plakken gesneden
3 eetlepels witte wijnazijn
2 eetlepels gesnipperde verse dille
10 g gesnipperde verse bieslook
½ theelepel suiker
snufje zout
versgemalen peper naar smaak
5 eetlepels plantaardige olie

1. Kook de ongeschilde aardappels in circa 15 minuten gaar. Giet ze af en laat afkoelen. Snijd ze in ½ cm dikke plakken en doe ze in een grote kom met de asperges, tomaten en ui.
2. Klop in een kommetje de azijn met de dille, bieslook, suiker en wat zout en peper. Giet er al kloppend geleidelijk de olie bij.
3. Schep de dressing om met de salade en dien op.

Voor 8 personen

1,85 dl per portie: Calorieën 150, Eiwit 2 g, Koolhydraten 16 g, Vezel 2 g, Vet totaal 9 g (Verzadigd 1 g, Enkelvoudig onverzadigd 5 g, Meervoudig onverzadigd 3 g), Cholesterol 0 mg, Natrium 25 mg, Vitamine C 25%.
▲ *1 Groente*

ZEEBANKET / PORTUGAL

Gemarineerde clams en mosselen

Verse clams en mosselen worden in overvloed gevangen in de Atlantische Oceaan. Kies stijf gesloten exemplaren en exemplaren die meteen dicht gaan wanneer u er op tikt. Bewaar ze onder een vochtige doek in de koelkast als u ze niet meteen wilt gebruiken, maar gebruik ze wel binnen één of twee dagen.

Schrik niet van de hoeveelheid zout: alleen een beetje wordt geabsorbeerd; de rest wordt afgegoten. U kunt 1 eetlepel geraspte citroenschil in plaats van de kappertjes gebruiken als u weinig zout gebruikt.

12 mosselen, schoongeborsteld en de baard verwijderd
12 clams, schoongeborsteld
3 eetlepels grof zeezout
2 eetlepels plus 5 eetlepels olijfolie
60 g gehakte ui
3 eetlepels gehakte verse peterselie
1 theelepel gehakte verse tijm
1,8 dl rode wijn
220 g langkorrelige rijst, gekookt volgens de aanwijzingen op de verpakking (circa 450 g gekookte rijst)
2 eetlepels rode wijnazijn
2 eetlepels kappertjes, uitgelekt
2 tomaten, ontveld, ontzaad en in blokjes
zout en versgemalen peper naar smaak

1. Doe de schone schelpdieren in koud water en voeg het zeezout toe. Laat 10 minuten trekken en giet goed af.
2. Verhit 2 eetlepels van de olijfolie in een grote koekepan. Doe er de ui in en fruit die gaar maar niet bruin. Voeg 2 eetlepels van de peterselie, de tijm, rode wijn, mosselen en clams toe. Leg het deksel op de pan en laat circa 5 minuten koken op een hoog vuur, waarbij u de pan af en toe schudt tot de schelpdieren geopend zijn. Neem de schelpdieren uit de pan en zet ze weg. Doe 75 g van de gekookte rijst in de koekepan en kook alles 10-15 minuten tot het mengsel dik is.
3. Verwarm intussen de oven voor op warm. Haal de mosselen en clams uit de schelpen en bewaar de schelpen. Doe de mosselen en clams in een zuurbestendige kom en giet er de 5 eetlepels olijfolie en de azijn over; laat 15 minuten marineren.
4. Doe de kappertjes, tomaten en de rest van de peterselie in het rijstmengsel en breng op smaak met zout en peper. Schep wat van het rijstmengsel in elke helft van de schelpen.
5. Schep de mosselen en clams met een schuimspaan uit de marinade en schik ze op de rijst in de bijpassende schelp. Houd de gevulde schelpen tot het serveren warm in de lauwe oven.
6. Schep de overgebleven rijst op een dienschaal. Schik de gevulde schelpdieren op de rijst en dien op.

Voor 4 personen

1 portie: Calorieën 310, Eiwit 10 g, Koolhydraten 44 g, Vezel 2 g, Vet totaal 10 g (Verzadigd 1,5 g, Enkelvoudig onverzadigd 7 g, Meervoudig onverzadigd 1 g), Cholesterol 15 mg, Natrium 720 mg, IJzer 40%, Vitamine C 30%.

▲ *1 Brood, 1 Vlees*

ZEEBANKET / JAPAN

Zalm-yaki

Na het marineren is deze zomerse maaltijd in minuten klaar. Geef er rondkorrelige rijst en een eenvoudige groene salade bij.

2 eetlepels vers citroensap
4 eetlepels sojasaus
4 eetlepels *mirin* (zoete keukensake)
4 eetlepels sake
500 g zalmfilet, in 4 stukken gesneden
2 eetlepels gesnipperde bieslook
1 citroen, in partjes gesneden

1. Meng het citroensap met de sojasaus, *mirin* en sake in een middelgrote kom. Laat er de zalm minstens 30 minuten in de koelkast in marineren.
2. Verwarm de grill voor.
3. Grilleer de zalm 2 minuten per kant. Bestrooi met de bieslook, garneer met de partjes citroen en dien onmiddellijk op.

Voor 4 personen

1 stuk per portie: Calorieën 200, Eiwit 24 g, Koolhydraten 1 g, Vezel 0 g, Vet totaal 10 g (Verzadigd 2 g, Enkelvoudig onverzadigd 5 g, Meervoudig onverzadigd 2 g), Cholesterol 70 mg, Natrium 260 mg.

▲ *1 Vlees*

Van links naar rechts: Gemarineerde clams en mosselen, Zalm-yaki

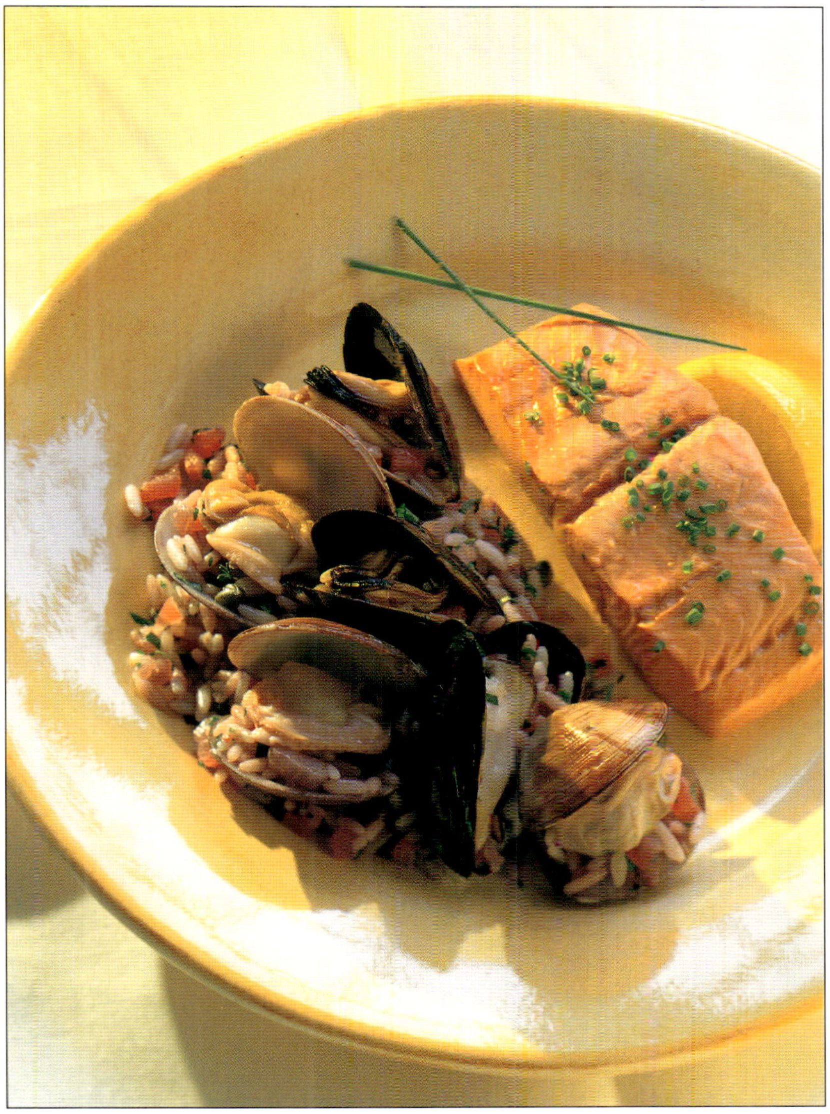

GRANEN / FRANKRIJK

Couscous

Couscous zijn piepkleine korreltjes griesmeelpasta. Gewone (in tegenstelling tot snelkokende) couscous wordt ruim een uur gestoomd in een couscoussier, *een speciale stoompan. U kunt in plaats daarvan een vergiet boven een diepe pan gebruiken. In dit recept wordt snelkokende couscous gebruikt en is een* couscoussier *niet nodig.*

1 eetlepel olijfolie
125 g gehakte ui
4 tenen knoflook, fijngehakt
1 rode paprika, fijngehakt
4,3 dl kippebouillon (zie woordenlijst)
280 g snelkokende couscous
¼ theelepel zout
versgemalen peper naar smaak
250 g Chinese broccoli of broccoli, in roosjes verdeeld

1. Verhit de olijfolie in een grote koekepan. Doe er de ui, 3 tenen knoflook en de paaprika in en fruit alles circa 3 minuten. Giet er 3,75 dl van de kippebouillon bij en breng aan de kook. Voeg de couscous toe, leg het deksel op de pan, neem de pan van het vuur en laat 5 minuten staan.
2. Verhit de rest van de kippebouillon met de overgebleven teen knoflook en het zout en wat peper in een middelgrote koekepan. Voeg de broccoli toe en laat 5 minuten sudderen.
3. Roer de couscous met een vork los en schep hem op een dienschaal. Maak een lange, smalle geul in het midden. Schik er de broccoli in en schep het kooknat over de couscous. Dien onmiddellijk op.

Voor 6 personen

2,5 dl per portie: Calorieën 230, Eiwit 8 g, Koolhydraten 42 g, Vezel 2 g, Vet totaal 3 g (Verzadigd 0,5 g, Enkelvoudig onverzadigd 2 g, Meervoudig onverzadigd 0,5 g), Cholesterol 0 mg, Natrium 115 mg, Vitamine A 25%, Vitamine C 100%.
▲ *2 Brood*

GROENTEN / FRANKRIJK

Groententian met tomatenvinaigrette

Een tian *is een Provençaalse ovale of rechthoekige aardewerk ovenschaal waarin lagen groenten en vlees worden gegratineerd en op kamertemperatuur of gekoeld worden geserveerd. Dit recept is zeer geschikt als een vegetarisch hoofdgerecht of als voorgerecht. U kunt een schaal van 1 liter inhoud gebruiken in plaats van de hieronder beschreven vier kleine schaaltjes. Dit gerecht is ook heel gezond en bevat de aanbevolen dagelijkse hoeveelheid vitamine A en C.*

2 eetlepels olijfolie
300 g gesnipperde ui
4 tenen knoflook, fijngehakt
4 tomaten, ontveld, ontzaad en grof gehakt
1 eetlepel gehakte verse basilicum
2 theelepels fijngehakte verse peterselie
1 theelepel gehakte verse tijm
1 theelepel fijngehakte verse munt
¼ theelepel zout
versgemalen peper naar smaak
2 aardappels, geschild, in zeer dunne plakken gesneden en 3 minuten geblancheerd (zie woordenlijst)
4 rode paprika's, geroosterd, ontveld en ontzaad (zie woordenlijst)
8 bladen snijbiet, kort geblancheerd, de dikke nerf uit het blad verwijderd (zie woordenlijst)
2 eetlepels vers geraspte Parmezaanse kaas
4 eetlepels verse tomatenvinaigrette (recept volgt)

1. Verwarm de oven voor op 190°C. Vet 4 *tians* of ovenschaaltjes van 2,5 dl inhoud licht in met olie.
2. Verhit de olijfolie in een grote anti-aanbak koekepan. Fruit er de ui circa 5 minuten in tot hij mooi goudbruin is. Voeg de knoflook toe en laat in circa 2 minuten gaar fruiten. Voeg de tomaten toe en bak alles nog 2 minuten. Voeg de basilicum, peterselie, tijm en munt toe; breng op smaak met het zout en wat peper. Schep alles om en neem de pan van het vuur.
3. Snijd de plakken aardappel, rode paprika en de bladen snijbiet in vierkantjes van 7 cm of zo groot als de *tians*.
4. Schep een derde van het ui-tomatenmengsel in de *tians*. Schik er om en om lagen aardappel, tomatenmengsel, snijbietbladen en rode paprika in en eindig met een schepje tomatenmengsel. Strooi er de Parmezaanse kaas over.
5. Dek de *tians* af met aluminiumfolie en zet ze 10 minuten in de oven. Verwijder de folie en zet de *tians* 15 minuten terug in de oven tot de kaas goudbruin is. Laat op een rooster afkoelen. Schep 1 eetlepel tomatenvinaigrette over elke *tian* en serveer op kamertemperatuur of gekoeld.

Voor 4 personen

1 tian *met vinaigrette per portie: Calorieën 240 , Eiwit 7 g, Koolhydraten 34 g, Vezel 6 g, Vet totaal 11 g (Verzadigd 2 g, Enkelvoudig onverzadigd 7 g, Meervoudig onverzadigd 1,5 g), Cholesterol 2 mg, Natrium 430 mg, IJzer 20%, Vitamine A 110%, Vitamine C 350%.*
▲ *2 Groente, 1 Vet/Suiker*

TOMATENVINAIGRETTE

1 eetlepel rode wijnazijn
½ theelepel grove mosterd
1 sjalotje, gesnipperd
2 eetlepels koudgeperste olijfolie
1 grote tomaat, ontveld, ontzaad en in blokjes
1 eetlepel verse basilicum, in dunne reepjes gesneden
zout en versgemalen peper naar smaak

1. Meng de azijn met de mosterd en sjalot in een kom. Druppel er al kloppend de olijfolie bij. Schep er de tomaat en basilicum door en breng op smaak met zout en peper.

Voor 1,8 dl

2 eetlepels per portie: Calorieën 50 , Eiwit 0 g, Koolhydraten 2 g, Vezel 0 g, Vet totaal 5 g (Verzadigd 0,5 g, Enkelvoudig onverzadigd 3,5 g, Meervoudig onverzadigd 0,5 g), Cholesterol 0 mg, Natrium 35 mg.
▲ *1 Vet/Suiker*

Van links naar rechts: Groententian met tomatenvinaigrette, Couscous

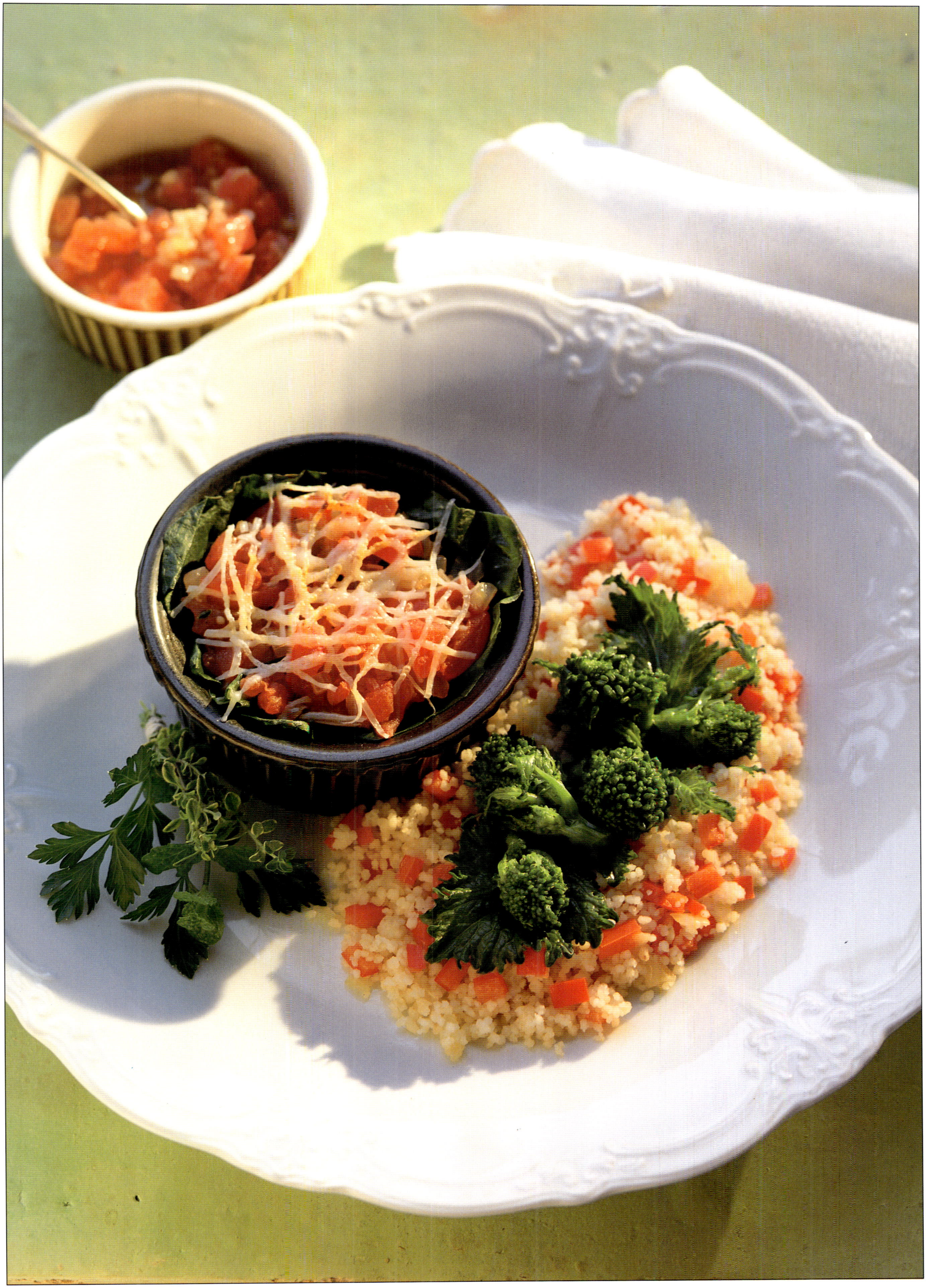

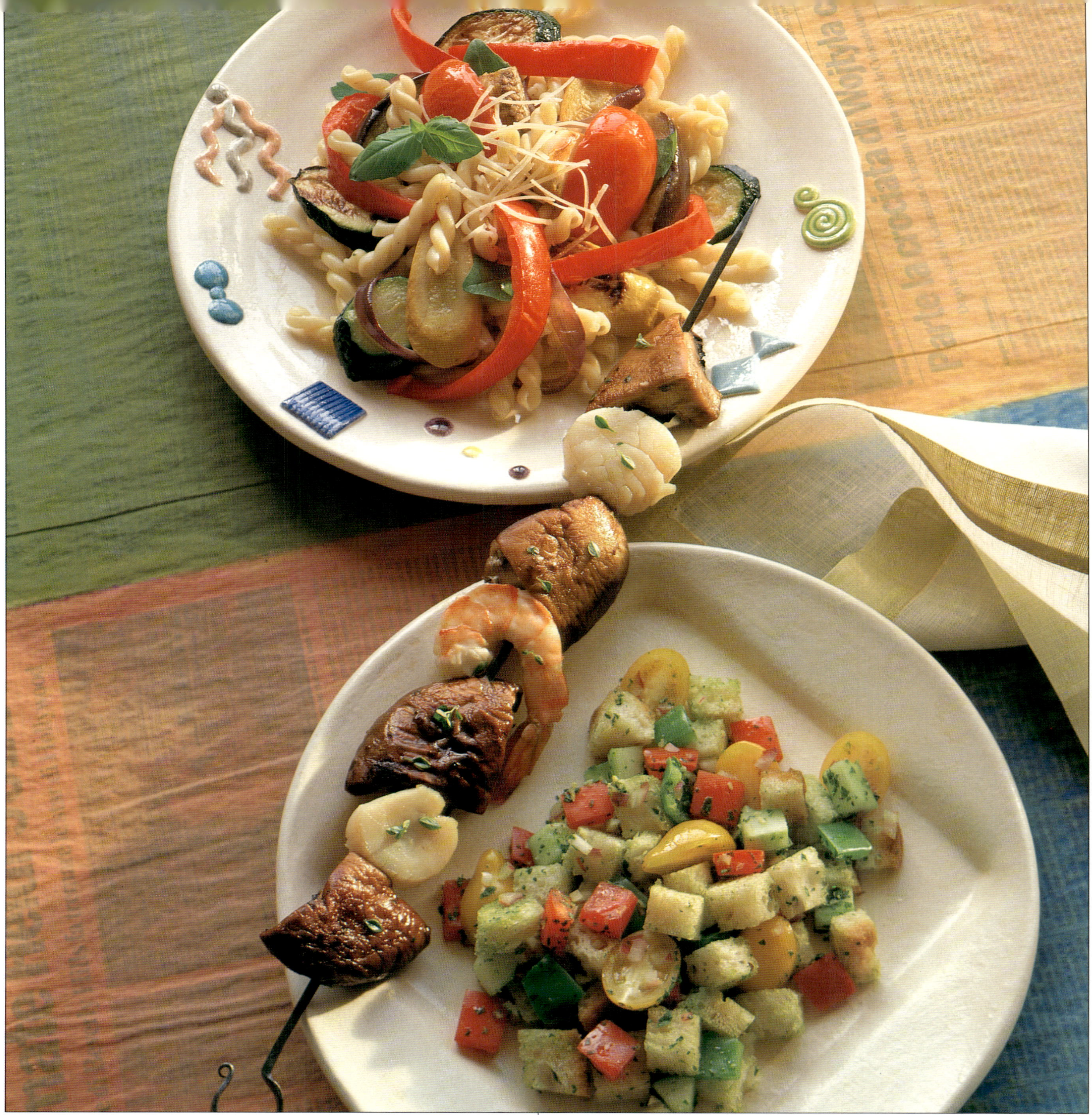

Van boven naar beneden: Marie Simmons' geroosterde groenten met gemelli, Spiesjes met zeebanket en boletes, Italiaanse broodsalade

PASTA / ITALIË

In de oven geroosterde groenten met gemelli

Marie Simmons, rubriekschrijfster en schrijfster van een aantal kookboeken, beveelt eenieder aan dit recept van haar aan te passen met groenten die in seizoen zijn. Probeer voor een lenteversie asperges, waspeen, courgette, lenteuitjes en verse dille. Het belangrijkste is om minstens 1,5 kg rauwe groenten te gebruiken omdat ze tijdens het koken de helft van hun gewicht verliezen.

1 rode paprika, gehalveerd, ontzaad en in repen van 1 cm breed gesneden
1 aubergine, bijgesneden en in repen van 1 cm dik gesneden
1 groene courgette, bijgesneden en overdwars in plakken van 1 cm dik gesneden
1 gele courgette, bijgesneden en schuin in plakken van 1 cm gesneden
1 grote rode ui, in de lengte gehalveerd en in partjes van 1 cm dik gesneden
4 tenen knoflook, gehalveerd en geplet met de platte kant van een mes
4 eetlepels koudgeperste olijfolie
4 pruimtomaten, in de lengte in vieren gesneden

¼ theelepel zout
versgemalen peper naar smaak
15 g verse basilicumblaadjes, in stukjes gescheurd
500 g *gemelli*, of een andere korte, brede pastasoort
2 eetlepels versgeraspte *parmigiano reggiano* (Parmezaanse kaas)

1. Verwarm de oven voor op 220°C.
2. Doe de paprika's, aubergine, groene en gele courgettes, rode ui en knoflook op een grote bakplaat. Druppel er de olie over en schep alles om. Rooster de groenten 30 minuten in de oven, waarbij u ze één of twee keer omschept. Doe er de tomaten bij en rooster de groenten nog circa 30 minuten tot ze aan de randen beginnen te verbranden. Neem ze uit de oven en bestrooi ze met het zout, wat peper en de basilicumblaadjes.
3. Kook intussen de pasta bijtgaar in circa 2 liter kokend water. Schep circa 1,25 dl van het pastakooknat uit de pan en zet het weg. Giet de pasta af; spoel niet af.
4. Doe de pasta in een grote, ondiepe kom of schaal. Schep er de geroosterde groenten over. Schraap met een pannelikker alle olie en kooknat van de bakplaat uit over de pasta. Druppel er de helft van het bewaarde pastakooknat over en schep alles om. Druppel er de rest van het kooknat over als de pasta te droog is. Bestrooi met de kaas en dien onmiddellijk op.

Voor 8 personen

2,5 dl per portie: Calorieën 320, Eiwit 9 g, Koolhydraten 52 g, Vezel 4 g, Vet totaal 8 g (Verzadigd 1,5 g, Enkelvoudig onverzadigd 5 g, Meervoudig onverzadigd 1 g), Cholesterol 0 mg, Natrium 110 mg, Vitamine A 30%, Vitamine C 80%.

▲ *1 Brood, 1 Groente*

SALADES / ITALIË

Panzanella

ITALIAANSE BROODSALADE

Deze salade werd verzonnen om oud brood op te maken. Als u vers brood gebruikt, moet u het eerst even roosteren voor u het in blokjes snijdt. Hoe langer deze salade staat, hoe meer dressing hij opneemt. Serveer de salade op kamertemperatuur.

170 g Italiaans brood, in blokjes van 1 cm gesneden
2 rijpe tomaten, ontzaad en in stukjes van 1 cm gesneden
185 g gele kerstomaatjes, in de lengte gehalveerd
1 komkommer, geschild, ontzaad en in stukjes van 1 cm gesneden
60 g groene paprika, ontzaad en in stukjes van 1 cm gesneden
75 g gesnipperde rode ui
3 tenen knoflook, fijngehakt
4 eetlepels rode wijnazijn
30 g verse basilicumblaadjes
4 eetlepels olijfolie
⅛ theelepel zout
versgemalen peper naar smaak
3 takjes verse basilicum, ter garnering

1. Doe de blokjes brood, rode tomaten, gele tomaten, komkommer, paprika en rode ui in een grote kom en schep alles om.
2. Pureer de knoflook met de azijn en 30 g basilicum in een blender of keukenmachine. Voeg bij draaiende motor geleidelijk de olijfolie toe. Breng op smaak met het zout en wat peper.
3. Schep de dressing door de salade, garneer met de takjes basilicum en dien onmiddellijk op.

Voor 6 personen

---

2 dl per portie: Calorieën 160, Eiwit 3 g, Koolhydraten 16 g, Vezel 2 g, Vet totaal 9 g (Verzadigd 1 g, Enkelvoudig onverzadigd 7 g, Meervoudig onverzadigd 1 g), Cholesterol 0 mg, Natrium 150 mg, Vitamine C 50%.

▲ *1 Brood, 1 Groente*

ZEEBANKET / ITALIË

Spiedini ai frutti di mare monterosso

SPIESJES MET ZEEBANKET EN BOLETEN

Aan de Italiaanse Riviera wordt veel verse vis gegeten. Geef bij dit gerecht orzo met wilde paddestoelen (recept op pagina 166).

12 grote rauwe garnalen, gepeld en darmkanaal verwijderd
24 grote coquilles
6 grote verse boleten, in vieren gesneden
4 eetlepels koudgeperste olijfolie
het sap van 1 citroen
2 theelepels gehakte verse tijm
2 tenen knoflook, fijngehakt
versgemalen peper naar smaak

1. Week 12 satéstokjes 30 minuten in water.
2. Rijg aan elk satéstokje om en om 1 garnaal, 2 coquilles en 2 stukken boleet. Leg ze op een platte, ondiepe schaal.
3. Meng in een kommetje de olijfolie met het citroensap, de tijm en knoflook. Giet dit mengsel over de spiesjes en laat minstens 1 uur of een nacht in de koelkast marineren.
4. Verwarm de grill voor.
5. Neem de spiesjes uit de marinade en bestrooi ze met wat peper. Grilleer ze 4-5 minuten, waarbij u ze regelmatig omdraait en bedruipt met de marinade tot de garnalen roze zijn en de coquilles stevig aanvoelen. Dien onmiddellijk op.

Voor 6 personen

---

2 spiesjes per portie: Calorieën 160, Eiwit 26 g, Koolhydraten 3 g, Vezel 0 g, Vet totaal 4 g (Verzadigd 0,5 g, Enkelvoudig onverzadigd 2 g, Meervoudig onverzadigd 1 g), Cholesterol 135 mg, Natrium 210 mg.

▲ *1 Vlees*

GEVOGELTE / ITALIË

Toscaanse kip met rozemarijn

In Toscane worden hele kippen opengesneden en dan opengeklapt tussen twee stukken terracotta gebakken zodat het vel knapperig wordt en het vlees sappig blijft. Dit terracotta keukengerei, een mattone, *wordt voorverwarmd en op het fornuis gebruikt. In de versie hieronder gebruiken we gereedschap dat in de meeste keukens voorhanden is.*

1 hele kip van 1,5 kg
1 citroen, gehalveerd
¼ theelepel zout
versgemalen peper naar smaak
4 theelepels olijfolie
1 eetlepel verse rozemarijnblaadjes

1. Knip of snijd de kip in de lengte doormidden langs de ruggegraat en klap de kip open door op de borst te drukken. Verwijder het vel van de borst, poten en dijen. Wrijf het vlees in met 1 citroenhelft en bestrooi met zout en peper.
2. Verhit een grote gietijzeren of anti-aanbak koekepan en doe er 2 theelepels van de olijfolie in. Leg de kip met de botkant omhoog in de pan wanneer de olie heet is. Strijk de rest van de olie over de kip en bestrooi met de rozemarijn.
3. Leg een plat bord of een andere koekepan op de kip en verzwaar dat met een groot blik of een paar bakstenen. Bak de kip 35 minuten op een middelhoog vuur, waarbij u haar om de 10 minuten omdraait.
4. Pers het sap uit de andere citroenhelft over de kip en dien onmiddellijk op.

Voor 4 personen

---

1 portie: Calorieën 270, Eiwit 35 g, Koolhydraten 1 g, Vezel 0 g, Vet totaal 14 g (Verzadigd 3 g, Enkelvoudig onverzadigd 7 g, Meervoudig onverzadigd 2,5 g), Cholesterol 110 mg, Natrium 250 mg.
▲ *1 Vlees*

GROENTEN / ITALIË

Pomodori ripieni

GEVULDE TOMATEN

Pomodori ripieni *zijn heerlijk als bijgerecht met gegrild gevogelte of zeebanket.*

8 stevige, rijpe tomaten
150 g gesnipperde ui
60 g bijgesneden en grof gehakte snijbiet
75 g blokjes gele paprika
3 tenen knoflook, fijngehakt
3 eetlepels droog broodkruim
3 eetlepels verse peterselie, fijngehakt
1 theelepel verse tijm, fijngehakt
½ theelepel verse marjolein, fijngehakt
¼ theelepel zout
versgemalen peper naar smaak
3 eetlepels versgeraspte Parmezaanse kaas

1. Verwarm de oven voor op 190°C. Vet een grote, ondiepe ovenschaal licht in met olie.
2. Halveer de tomaten overdwars. Maak de pulp los door heel voorzichtig met een scherp mes langs de randen te snijden. Zorg dat u niet door de tomaat snijdt. Schep de zaadjes en pulp vervolgens over in een grote kom. Schik de uitgeholde tomaten in een ovenschaal.
3. Schep de ui, snijbiet, paprika, knoflook, het broodkruim, de peterselie, tijm en marjolein door de zaadjes en pulp in de kom. Breng op smaak met het zout en wat peper. Schep het mengsel in de uitgeholde tomaten en bestrooi met de Parmezaanse kaas.
4. Zet de tomaten 30 minuten in de oven tot de bovenkant goudbruin is. Dien onmiddellijk op of op kamertemperatuur.

Voor 8 personen

---

1 tomaat (2 halve) per portie: Calorieën 60, Eiwit 3 g, Koolhydraten 11 g, Vezel 2 g, Vet totaal 1 g (Verzadigd 0,5 g, Enkelvoudig onverzadigd 0,5 g, Meervoudig onverzadigd 0 g), Cholesterol 2 mg, Natrium 150 mg, Vitamine A 20%, Vitamine C 80%.
▲ *1 Groente*

HAPJES / ITALIË

Bruschette con caponata alla Siciliana

SICILIAANSE TOOST MET AUBERGINERELISH

U kunt deze voedzame relish van tevoren maken en warm of op kamertemperatuur serveren. Door de aubergine te zouten onttrekt u er overtollig vocht aan. Ook krijgt de aubergine een compactere structuur en neemt daardoor minder olie op bij het bakken. Het meeste zout wordt voor het bakken afgespoeld.

1 aubergine van circa 500 g, geschild en in blokjes van 1 cm gesneden
1 theelepel zout
4 eetlepels olijfolie
4 stengels bleekselderij, in dunne plakken
1 ui, gehakt
3 tenen knoflook, fijngehakt
1 eetlepel kappertjes
2 eetlepels pijnboompitten, geroosterd
2 eetlepels rozijnen
2 theelepels suiker
4 eetlepels rode wijnazijn
185 g ontvelde en gehakte rode tomaat
zout en versgemalen peper naar smaak
16 sneden vers boerenbrood, geroosterd
40 g gehakte verse basilicum

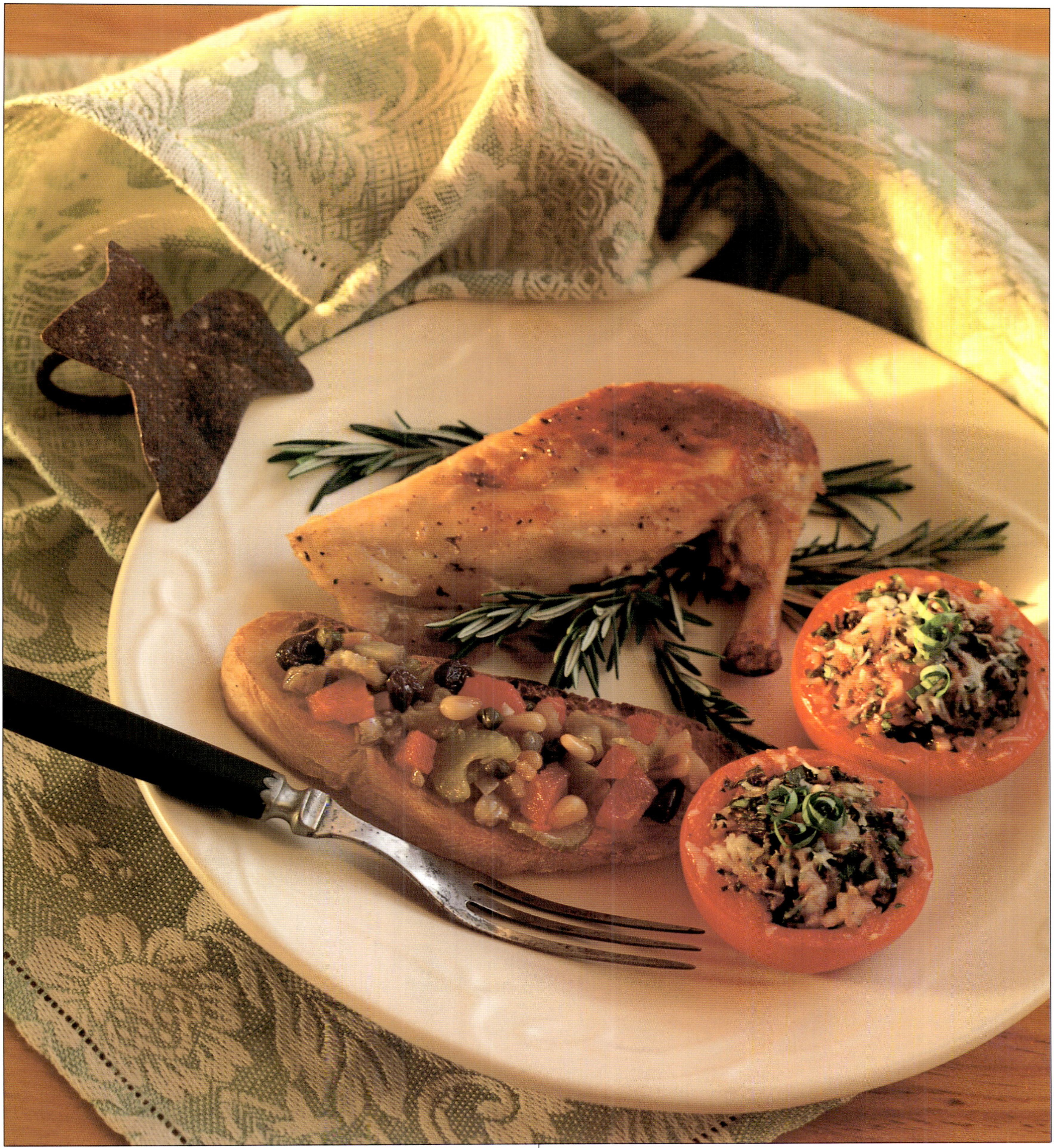

Met de klok mee van boven: Toscaanse kip met rozemarijn, Gevulde tomaten, Siciliaanse toost met auberginerelish

1. Schik 3 lagen keukenpapier op een bakplaat. Doe er de blokjes aubergine op en bestrooi met de theelepel zout. Laat 10 minuten trekken. Spoel af en dep droog met keukenpapier.
2. Verhit de olijfolie in een grote koekepan en fruit er de bleekselderij, ui en knoflook in circa 3-4 minuten goudbruin in. Schep er de aubergine door en bak in 2-3 minuten gaar.
3. Voeg de kappertjes, pijnboompitten, rozijnen, suiker en azijn toe. Kook circa 3 minuten tot de azijn verdampt is.
4. Voeg de tomaat toe en laat in circa 2 minuten doorwarmen. Breng op smaak met zout en peper.
5. Schep de relish op beboterde toostjes en garneer met de basilicum. Serveer warm of koud.

Voor 8 personen (2 sneden per persoon)

2 sneden per portie: Calorieën 280, Eiwit 8 g, Koolhydraten 44 g, Vezel 4 g, Vet totaal 8 g (Verzadigd 1 g, Enkelvoudig onverzadigd 6 g, Meervoudig onverzadigd 1 g). Cholesterol 0 mg, Natrium 600 mg.

▲ *2 Brood, 2 Groente*

Brood / Portugal

Broa

Volkoren-maïsbrood

Geef dit stevige maïsbrood bij soepen en salades.

3 dl magere melk
1 pakje (7 g) droge gist
1½ theelepel suiker
1 eetlepel olijfolie
75 g maïsgriesmeel
75 g volkorenbloem
1 theelepel zout
315-390 g bloem

1. Verhit 1,6 dl van de melk tot 40-46°C. Los er de gist en de suiker in op en laat het mengsel 5 minuten staan. Voeg de olie toe.
2. Doe het maïsgriesmeel en de volkorenbloem in een grote kom. Giet er het gistmensel bij en schep alles om tot een glad geheel. Dek de kom af met een theedoek en laat 1 uur rijzen.
3. Druk de lucht uit het deeg. Voeg de rest van de melk, het zout en 125 g van de bloem toe en schep alles om tot een glad mengsel. Doe het deeg op een met bloem bestoven werkvlak en voeg telkens 60 g tegelijk van de bloem toe en kneed tot het deeg glad en niet meer plakkerig is.
4. Vorm het deeg tot een bal, doe de deegbal in een licht met olie ingevette kom, dek die af en laat 1 uur staan tot het deeg in volume verdubbeld is.
5. Bekleed een bakplaat met perkamentpapier en bestuif dat met bloem. Druk de lucht uit het deeg, kneed het een paar keer, vorm het tot een ovaal en leg die op de bakplaat. Kerf met een scherp scheermes een X in het deeg. Dek af en laat het deeg 1 uur rijzen tot het in volume verdubbeld is.
6. Verwarm de oven voor op 190°C.
7. Bak het brood 30 minuten in de oven. Laat op een rooster afkoelen voor u het aansnijdt.

Voor 12 sneden

1 snee per portie: Calorieën 130, Eiwit 5 g, Koolhydraten 24 g, Vezel 4 g, Vet totaal 2 g (Verzadigd 0,5 g, Enkelvoudig onverzadigd 1 g, Meervoudig onverzadigd 0,5 g), Cholesterol 5 mg, Natrium 210 mg.
▲ *1 Brood*

Salades / Frankrijk

Coquilles met komkommersaus

Een verfrissende zomerse salade die caloriearm is en een hoog vitamine C-gehalte heeft.

5 dl groentebouillon (zie woordenlijst)
375 g coquilles, oranje kuit verwijderd
2 grote komkommers en 1 middelgrote komkommer
1 sjalotje, gehakt
1 eetlepel vers citroensap
2 theelepels fijngehakte verse peterselie
½ theelepel fijngehakte verse munt
⅛ theelepel zeezout
versgemalen witte peper naar smaak
125 g friséesla

1. Breng de bouillon aan de kook in een middelgrote pan. Draai het vuur lager, doe de coquilles in de bouillon en laat ze in 1-2 minuten gaar sudderen. Schep de coquilles eruit om af te koelen en bewaar 2 eetlepels van de bouillon voor de saus. Snijd de coquilles in plakken van 1 cm dik en zet ze in de koelkast.
2. Schil voor de komkommersaus de 2 grote komkommers en bewaar de schil. Halveer de komkommers in de lengte en schraap er de zaadjes uit. Snijd de komkommer in stukjes van 2 cm en doe ze in een keukenmachine. Doe er de sjalot, de bewaarde bouillon, het citroensap en de peterselie bij en draai alles tot een glad mengsel. Schep er de munt door en breng op smaak met zout en peper. Bewaar de saus tot gebruik in de koelkast.
3. Blancheer de bewaarde komkommerschil 30 seconden en dompel dan onmiddellijk in ijswater. Dep de schil droog met keukenpapier en snijd in de lengte in repen ter garnering. Zet weg.
4. Snijd de overgebleven ongeschilde komkommer overdwars in plakken van 3 mm dik. Schik de frisée in het midden van een dienschaal en schik er de plakken komkommer omheen. Schik de coquilles in het midden en garneer met wat schil. Serveer de gekoelde salade en geef er de komkommersaus apart bij.

Voor 4 personen *Foto op pagina 124*

1 portie: Calorieën 110, Eiwit 16 g, Koolhydraten 10 g, Vezel 2 g, Vet totaal 1 g (Verzadigd 0 g, Enkelvoudig onverzadigd 0 g, Meervoudig onverzadigd 0,5 g), Cholesterol 30 mg, Natrium 220 mg, Vitamine C 25%.
▲ *1 Groente, 1 Vlees*

Zeebanket / Spanje

Paella

Paella wordt per traditie in een paellapan, een diepe koekepan met twee handvatten, gemaakt, maar een grote koekepan is ook geschikt. De drie belangrijkste ingrediënten zijn rijst, olijfolie en saffraan. De rest varieert in Spanje per gebied, afhankelijk van het seizoen.

3 eetlepels olijfolie
3 tenen knoflook, fijngehakt
8 verse artisjokharten, bladen en hooi verwijderd
2 middelgrote preien, alleen het wit, julienne gesneden
1 groene paprika, julienne gesneden
1 rode paprika, julienne gesneden
3,75 dl kippebouillon (zie woordenlijst)
½ theelepel saffraandraden, in een vijzel gestampt
110 g Valencia of langkorrelige rijst
4 tomaten, ontveld en grof gehakt
250 g zeeduivel, in stukken van 5 cm gesneden
250 g rode snapper of een andere stevige witte vissoort, in stukken van 5 cm gesneden
250 g inktvis, schoongemaakt en in ½ cm dikke ringen gesneden
12 clams, schoongeborsteld
12 mosselen, schoongeborsteld

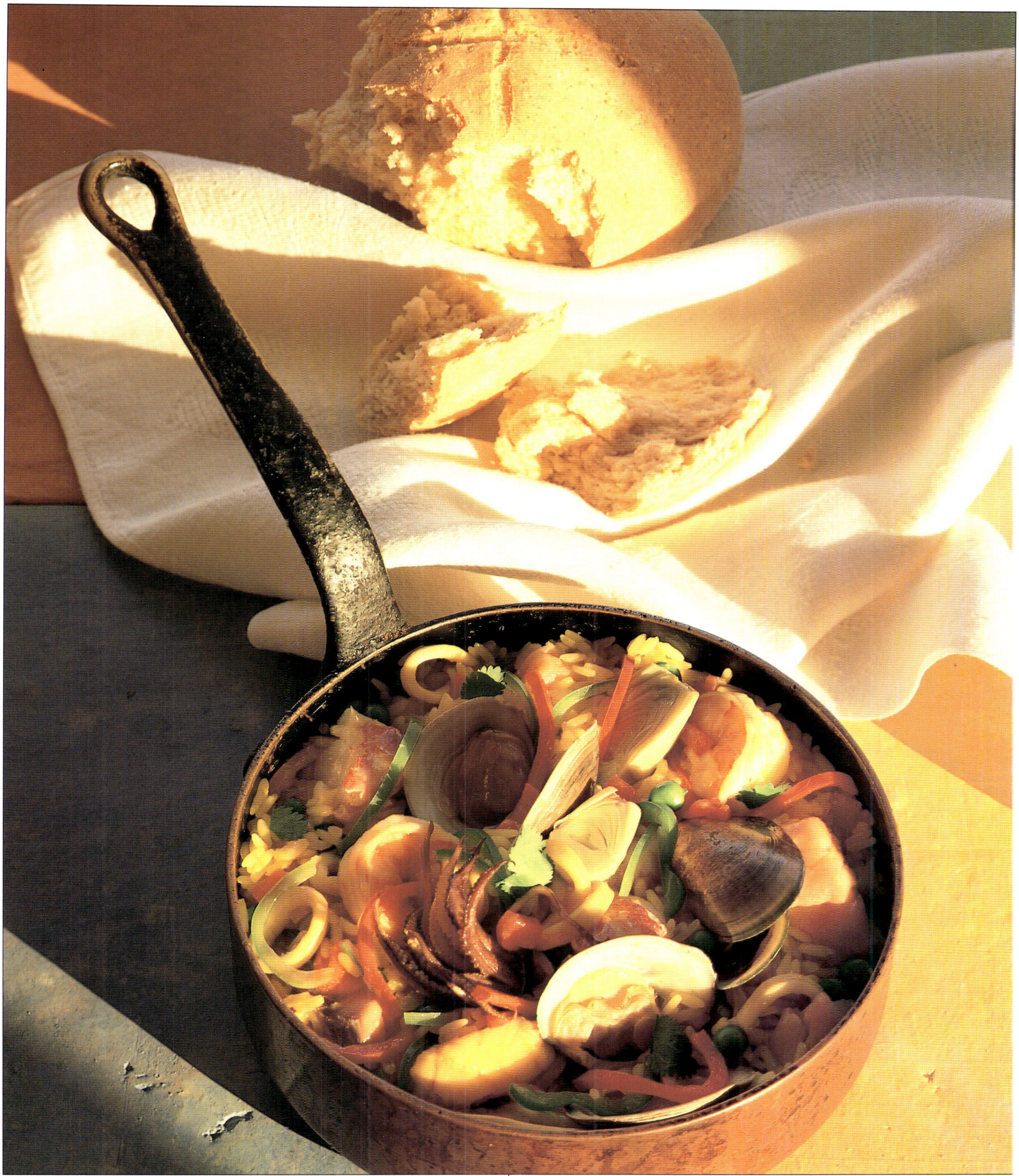

Van boven naar beneden: Volkoren-maïsbrood, Paella

8 grote rauwe garnalen, gepeld en darmkanaal verwijderd
750 g kreeft, 2 minuten voorgekookt en in de lengte gehalveerd
150 g verse doperwtjes
8 g verse korianderbladen

1. Verhit de olijfolie in een paellapan of grote koekepan. Doe er de knoflook, artisjokharten, prei en groene en rode paprika in en bak alles in circa 3 minuten gaar. Giet er de kippebouillon bij en breng aan de kook. Draai het vuur lager, voeg de saffraandraden en rijst toe en sudder 10 minuten. Voeg de tomaten, zeeduivel, snapper en inktvis toe en laat 5 minuten koken. Voeg de clams en mosselen toe en sudder 3-5 minuten tot de schelpen open zijn. Voeg de garnalen, kreeft en erwtjes toe en kook 2 minuten. Neem de pan van het vuur, leg het deksel op de pan en laat 10 minuten staan.
2. Garneer met de korianderbladen en dien op uit de paellapan

Voor 8 personen

---

1 portie: Calorieën 370, Eiwit 45 g, Koolhydraten 25 g, Vezel 2 g, Vet totaal 9 g (Verzadigd 1,5 g, Enkelvoudig onverzadigd 4,5 g, Meervoudig onverzadigd 1,5 g), Cholesterol 230 mg, Natrium 160 mg, IJzer 30%, Vitamine A 25% Vitamine 90%.

▲ *1 Groente, 1 Vlees*

Szechwan eendesalade

De bekende Chinese kipsalade wordt met geroosterde kip en komkommer gemaakt. In deze versie wordt eend gebruikt en zorgt de meloen voor een mooi contrast met de pittige saus. Restjes geroosterde eend (of kip) zijn uitstekend voor dit recept.

DRESSING

2 tenen knoflook
1 theelepel geraspte gember
1 theelepel gehakte verse koriander
1 eetlepel Chinese sesampasta of tahini als de sesampasta niet verkrijgbaar is
1 eetlepel sojasaus
2 theelepels Chinese sesamolie
1 eetlepel droge sherry
1 theelepel rijstazijn
2 theelepels suiker
½ theelepel chilipasta
¼ theelepel gemalen Szechwan peperkorrels

SALADE

280 g Chinese kool, in repen gesneden
500 g geroosterde eend of kip, zonder vel en het vlees in repen gesneden
125 g taugé, 30 seconden geblancheerd (zie woordenlijst)
1 suiker- of honingmeloen, geschild en in ½ cm dikke plakken gesneden
250 g peultjes, afgehaald, 10 seconden geblancheerd (zie woordenlijst)
1 wortel, geschild en grof geraspt

Van boven naar beneden: Coquilles met komkommersaus (recept pagina 122), Szechwan eendesalade

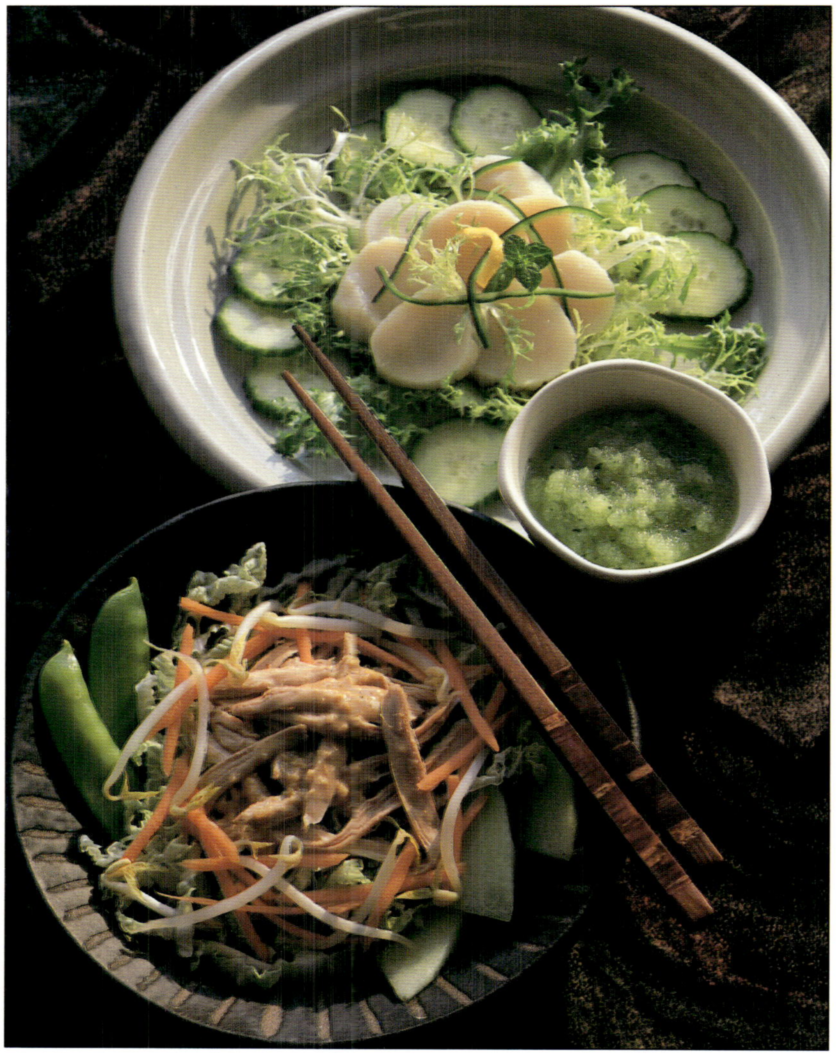

1. Pureer voor de dressing de knoflook, gember, verse koriander, sesampasta, sojasaus, sesamolie, sherry, azijn, suiker, chilipasta en peperkorrels in een blender of keukenmachine.
2. Doe de kool in een diepe kom. Schik de eend in het midden. Schik er de taugé, plakken meloen, peultjes en wortel omheen.
3. Druppel de dressing over de salade en dien op of bewaar in de koelkast.

Voor 6 personen

1 portie: Calorieën 300, Eiwit 22 g, Koolhydraten 29 g, Vezel 4 g, Vet totaal 12 g (Verzadigd 4 g, Enkelvoudig onverzadigd 4 g, Meervoudig onverzadigd 2,5 g), Cholesterol 65 mg, Natrium 230 mg, Vitamine A 80%, Vitamine C 140%.

▲ *1 Fruit, 1 Groente, 1 Vlees*

PASTA / VERENIGDE STATEN

Blauwe-maïstagliatelle met pesto van maïs en rode paprika

De blauwe-maïs en cayennepeper in de tagliatelle in dit recept verlenen dit gerecht een Tex-Mex accent. Als u weinig tijd hebt, kunt u gedroogde pasta naar keuze gebruiken.

TAGLIATELLE

300 g ongebleekte bloem
150 g blauw-maïsmeel
½ theelepel cayennepeper
1 eetlepel saffloerolie
4 eieren

PESTO

3 maïskolven met blad
2 rode paprika's, geroosterd, ontveld en ontzaad (zie woordenlijst)
10 g verse korianderbladen
3 eetlepels pijnboompitten, geroosterd
2 eetlepels saffloerolie
125 g grof gehakte ui
3 tenen knoflook, fijngehakt
3,75 dl kippebouillon (zie woordenlijst)
¼ theelepel zout
versgemalen peper naar smaak

1. Meng voor de tagliatelle de bloem met het maïsmeel en cayennepeper. Maak een kuiltje in het midden en doe er de olie en eieren in. Meng de bloem met een vork vanuit het midden naar de

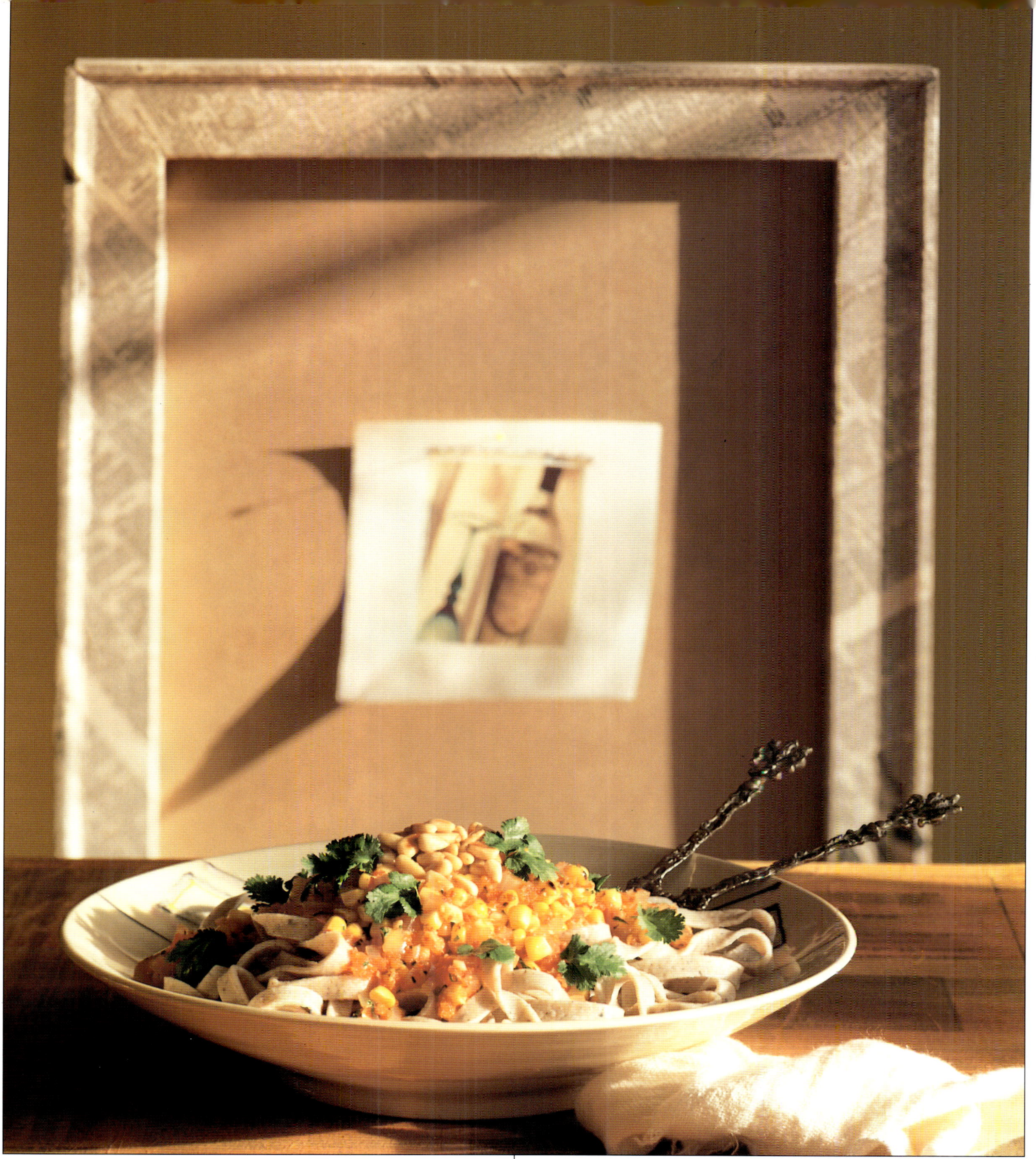

Blauwe-maïstagliatelle met pesto van maïs en rode paprika

randen en door de eieren tot alles goed gemengd is. Doe het mengsel op een met bloem bestoven werkvlak en kneed het deeg tot het glad en niet meer plakkerig is. Voeg zonodig nog wat bloem toe. Doe het deeg in een plastic zakje en laat het vervolgens 15 minuten rusten.

2. Rol het deeg uit, met een kwart tegelijk, zoals beschreven bij *Pasta* in de woordenlijst. Snijd het deeg in ½ cm brede repen en leg ze tot gebruik op een met bloem bestoven werkvlak.
3. Verwarm de grill voor wanneer u de pesto gaat maken. Verwijder de draden van de maïskolven maar houd de bladen intact. Week de kolven 15 minuten in warm water. Grilleer de maïs 5 minuten onder de grill, waarbij u de kolven regelmatig omdraait. Neem ze uit de grill en laat afkoelen. Snijd de korrels van de kolven en zet weg.
4. Pureer de rode paprika's in een keukenmachine. Voeg 3 eetlepels van de verse koriander en 1 eetlepel van de pijnboompitten toe en draai tot een gladde pasta. Zet weg.
5. Verhit de olie in een middelgrote koekepan en fruit er de ui en knoflook gaar maar niet bruin in. Voeg de kippebouillon, paprikapuree en maïskorrels toe. Laat 5-7 minuten sudderen tot het geheel iets dikker is.
6. Kook de tagliatelle in 5 minuten bijtgaar in kokend water. Giet de pasta af en doe in een kom. Breng de saus op smaak met zout en peper. Giet de saus over de pasta, bestrooi met de rest van de pijnboompitten en verse koriander en dien onmiddellijk op

Voor 6 personen

---

1 portie: Calorieën 440, Eiwit 14 g, Koolhydraten 55 g, Vezel 5 g, Vet totaal 15 g (Verzadigd 2,5 g, Enkelvoudig onverzadigd 3,5 g, Meervoudig onverzadigd 7 g), Cholesterol 145 mg, Natrium 150 mg, IJzer 25%, Vitamine A 40%, Vitamine C 90%.

▲ *2 Brood, 1 Groente*

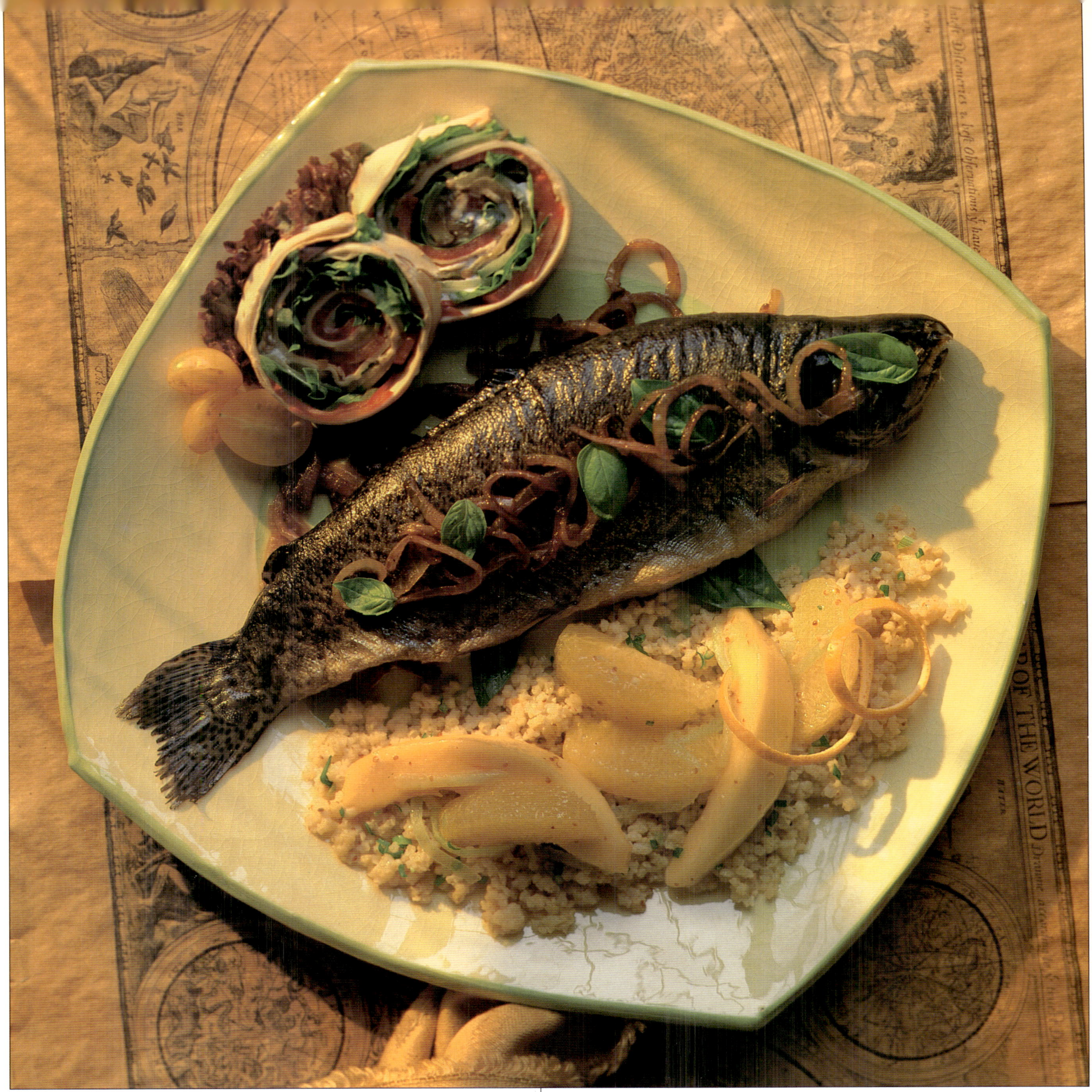

Van boven naar beneden: Mediterrane lavashrollen, Forel met basilicumvulling op gekarameliseerde uien, Gierst met papaja en sinaasappel-mosterd-vinaigrette

HAPJES / VERENIGDE STATEN

Mediterrane lavashrollen

Lavashrollen zijn heerlijk voor een buffet. U kunt ze ook als een lichte lunch serveren. De yoghurt in dit recept is een veelzijdige basis en een uitstekende vervanging voor zure room. U kunt hem als basis gebruiken voor dipsausen, smeersels en om soepen mee te binden.

4 rondjes *lavash* (recept op pagina 159)
1 aubergine, in dunne plakken
¼ theelepel zout
1,8 dl yoghurtkaas (recept volgt)
4 grote tomaten, in dunne plakken
1 krop sla
1 komkommer, in dunne plakken
7 g verse muntblaadjes, fijngehakt
zout en versgemalen peper naar smaak

1. Verwarm de grill voor.
2. Bevochtig de *lavash*, wikkel ze in een vochtige theedoek en laat 25 minuten staan.
3. Bestrooi de plakken aubergine met zout en laat 20 minuten trekken. Spoel ze af en dep ze droog. Leg de plakken op een licht met olie ingevette bakplaat en grilleer ze 1 minuut per kant.
4. Leg de zachte *lavash* op een werkvlak. Besmeer de rondjes met een derde van de yoghurtkaas. Schik er een laag tomaat, dan de

helft van de sla, dan de komkommer en ten slotte de aubergine op. Smeer er een dunne laag van de overgebleven yoghurtkaas over en bestrooi met de munt en wat zout en peper.

5. Rol het brood zo strak mogelijk op en houd de lagen op hun plaats. Wikkel de rollen strak op in plastic folie en leg ze minstens 1 uur in de koelkast.
6. Verwijder de plastic folie van de rol en zet de rol op een snijplank. Snijd de rollen in plakken van circa 2 cm dik en schik ze op een dienschaal bekleed met de overgebleven slabladen.

Voor 8 personen (4 rollen in 6-8 plakken gesneden)

3-4 plakken per portie: Calorieën 350, Eiwit 7 g, Koolhydraten 36 g, Vezel 4 g, Vet totaal 10 g (Verzadigd 1,5 g, Enkelvoudig onverzadigd 7 g, Meervoudig onverzadigd 1 g), Cholesterol 0 mg, Natrium 35 mg, Vitamine A 20%, Vitamine C 40%.

▲ *1 Brood, 1 Groente*

Yoghurtkaas

2,5 dl halfvolle roeryoghurt

1. Bekleed een vergiet met ongebleekte katoen en zet het boven een grote kom. Schep de yoghurt in het beklede vergiet en laat hem een nacht in de koelkast uitlekken.

Voor 1,8 dl

1,8 dl per portie: Calorieën 140, Eiwit 12 g, Koolhydraten 16 g, Vezel 0 g, Vet totaal 4 g (Verzadigd 2.5 g, Enkelvoudig onverzadigd 1 g, Meervoudig onverzadigd 0 g), Cholesterol 15 mg, Natrium 160 mg, Kalk 40%.

▲ *1 Melk*

Zeebanket / Verenigde Staten

Forel met basilicumvulling op gekarameliseerde uien

Wie droomt er niet van in een beek op regenboogforellen te vissen en de vangst boven een open vuur te roosteren?

4 eetlepels olijfolie
500 g uien, in zeer dunne plakken gesneden
4 eetlepels balsamico azijn
¼ theelepel zout
versgemalen peper naar smaak
4 hele forellen, elk 300-375 g, schoongemaakt
8 grote verse basilicumbladen

1. Maak een houtskoolvuur. Week houtschaafsel 30 minuten in water.
2. Verhit 3 eetlepels van de olie in een grote koekepan. Doe er de ui in en fruit ze circa 20 minuten onder regelmatig omscheppen tot ze goudbruin zijn. Voeg de azijn toe en laat in circa 2 minuten tot een siroop inkoken. Breng op smaak met zout en peper en zet weg op een dienschaal.
3. Borstel de forel van binnen en buiten in met de rest van de olijfolie. Stop 2 basilicumbladen in elke vis. Strooi het houtschaafsel over de gloeiende houtskool en grilleer de forellen in circa 4 minuten per kant goudbruin. Schik de vis op de ui en dien op.

Voor 4 personen

1 forel per portie: Calorieën 280, Eiwit 22 g, Koolhydraten 11 g, Vezel 2 g, Vet totaal 17 g (Verzadigd 2,5 g, Enkelvoudig onverzadigd 11 g, Meervoudig onverzadigd 2,5 g), Cholesterol 55 mg, Natrium 180 mg

▲ *1 Groente, 1 Vlees*

Granen / Zimbabwe

Gierst met papaja en sinaasappel-mosterd-vinaigrette

Gierst wordt in bijna heel Afrika voor couscous gebruikt. Snelkokende couscous wordt meestal van griesmeel gemaakt. Gierst bevat meer B-vitaminen en mineralen dan bruine rijst of tarwe. Dit milde en knapperige graan is ook vezelrijk.

4 lenteuitjes, fijngehakt
2 theelepels fijngehakte verse gember
1 eetlepel grove mosterd
4 eetlepels vers sinaasappelsap
4 eetlepels zonnebloemolie
⅛ theelepel zout
versgemalen peper naar smaak
1 rijpe papaja, geschild
2 sinaasappels, geschild, ontzaad en in partjes
1 groene papaja, geschild, ontzaad en grof geraspt
220 g hele of geplette gierst
7,5 dl kippebouillon (zie woordenlijst)

1. Meng in een kom de lenteui met de gember, mosterd en het sinaasappelsap voor de sinaasappel-mosterdvinaigrette. Druppel er al kloppend geleidelijk de olie bij. Breng op smaak met zout en peper en zet weg.
2. Schep de zaden uit de rijpe papaja en bewaar er 2 eetlepels van. Snijd het vruchtvlees in plakken van 1 cm dik. Schep de plakken papaja om met de sinaasappelpartjes en de geraspte groene papaja. Schep om met 4 eetlepels van de vinaigrette. Zet weg.
3. Kook de gierst 20 minuten in de sudderende kippebouillon in een afgedekte pan. Giet overtollig kooknat af en schep de overgebleven vinaigrette door de gierst. Doe de gierst op een dienschaal, schep het papajamengsel in het midden en strooi er de bewaarde papajazaden over. Dien onmiddellijk op.

Voor 8 personen

1 portie: Calorieën 210, Eiwit 4 g, Koolhydraten 30 g, Vezel 5 g, Vet totaal 9 g (Verzadigd 1 g, Enkelvoudig onverzadigd 1,5 g, Meervoudig onverzadigd 6 g), Cholesterol 0 mg, Natrium 65 mg, Vitamine A 25%, Vitamine C 100%.

▲ *1 Brood, 1 Fruit*

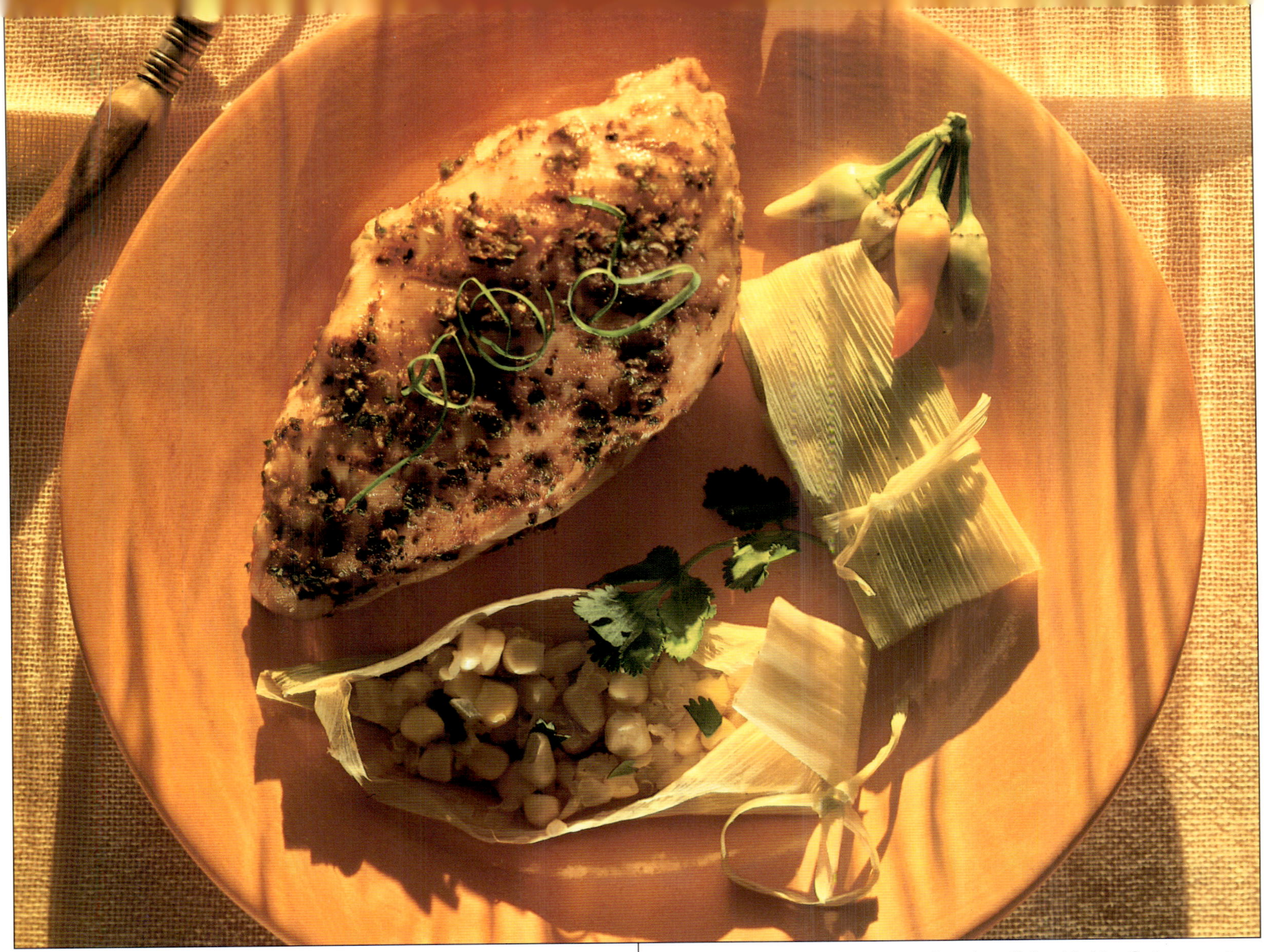

Van boven naar beneden: Gekruide kip, Quinoa, maïs en aardappel in maïsbladen gestoomd

GRANEN / BOLIVIA

Humita

QUINOA, MAÏS EN AARDAPPEL IN MAÏSBLADEN GESTOOMD

Quinoa was samen met maïs en aardappel één van de belangrijkste voedingsmiddelen van de Inca's en is waarschijnlijk al duizenden jaren oud. Quinoa heeft het hoogste eiwitgehalte van alle graansoorten. Quinoa moet voor het koken grondig gewassen worden omdat het graan een bitter laagje heeft dat als een natuurlijk insektenwerend middel werkt.

12 verse of gedroogde maïsbladen
90 g quinoa
1 middelgrote aardappel, geschild en in blokjes van ½ cm
125 g gehakte ui
370 g verse maïskorrels
10 g gehakte verse koriander
½ theelepel zout
versgemalen peper naar smaak

1. Week de maïsbladen 20 minuten in warm water.
2. Spoel de quinoa grondig af. Doe hem in een pan met 2,5 dl water, de aardappel en 60 g van de ui. Breng aan de kook, draai het vuur laag en laat 12-15 minuten sudderen tot al het water geabsorbeerd is en de graankorrels ondoorschijnend zijn. Voeg de maïs, de rest van de ui en de verse koriander toe. Breng op smaak met zout en peper.
3. Schep het mengsel in de maïsbladen, vouw de bladen dicht en schik ze in een stoommand. Stoom ze 15 minuten boven kokend water. Dien onmiddellijk op.

Voor 6 personen

2 bladen per portie: Calorieën 130, Eiwit 4 g, Koolhydraten 27 g, Vezel 4 g, Vet totaal 1 g (Verzadigd 0 g, Enkelvoudig onverzadigd 0 g, Meervoudig onverzadigd 1 g), Cholesterol 0 mg, Natrium 220 mg.

▲ *½ Brood, 1 Groente*

GEVOGELTE / JAMAICA

Gekruide kip

De kruidige marinade in dit gerecht is alom bekend in het Caribisch gebied. Hij verschilt van eiland tot eiland, maar bestaat meestal uit een mengsel van zoete specerijen en chilipepers.

½ theelepel gemalen kaneel
½ theelepel gemalen piment
¼ theelepel gemalen gember
¼ theelepel gemalen nootmuskaat
¼ theelepel gemalen kruidnagel
½ theelepel fijngehakte jalapeño chilipeper
4 lenteuitjes, grof gehakt
1 eetlepel olijfolie
zout en versgemalen peper naar smaak
4 halve kipfilets, ontveld

1. Stamp de kaneel met de piment, gember, nootmuskaat, kruidnagel, jalapeño en lenteui in een vijzel.

2. Voeg de olijfolie, het zout en wat peper toe.
3. Wrijf de pasta over de kipfilets, dek ze af en laat ze een nacht in de koelkast marineren.
4. Verwarm de grill voor en grilleer de kip 10 minuten per kant.

Voor 4 personen

½ filet per portie: Calorieën 180, Eiwit 27 g, Koolhydraten 2 g, Vezel 1 g, Vet totaal 7 g (Verzadigd 2 g, Enkelvoudig onverzadigd 4 g, Meervoudig onverzadigd 1 g), Cholesterol 75 mg, Natrium 65 mg.
▲ *1 Vlees*

PASTA / ITALIË

Orecchiette alla Barese

PASTA MET CLAMS, SPINAZIE EN TOMATEN UIT BARI

Bari is een havenstad in het zuidwesten van Apulië, een gebied met een rijk aanbod aan zeebanket uit de Adriatische Zee. Een zeer geliefde pastasoort is orecchiette, *die zo wordt genoemd omdat hij op kleine oortjes lijkt. Deze pasta is makkelijk te maken en is ook verkrijgbaar in Italiaanse delicatessenwinkels.*

150 g ongebleekte bloem
300 g volkorenbloem
36 clams, schoongeborsteld
3 eetlepels olijfolie
4 tenen knoflook, fijngehakt
60 g gehakte ui
250 g verse spinazie, grof gehakt
3 rijpe tomaten, ontveld, ontzaad en grof gehakt
1 eetlepel fijngehakte verse peterselie
¼ theelepel zout
versgemalen peper naar smaak
3 eetlepels versgeraspte *pecorino* kaas

1. Meng voor de *orecchiette* de twee bloemsoorten. Maak een kuiltje in het midden, giet er 2,5 dl water bij en schep goed om. Doe het deeg op een met bloem bestoven werkvlak en kneed het tot het glad en niet meer plakkerig is. Voeg zonodig nog wat bloem toe. Verdeel het deeg in 4 stukken, dek die af en laat 15 minuten rusten. Rol elk stuk tot een cilinder van 1 cm dik. Snijd het deeg overdwars in plakjes van 3 mm dik. Druk elke plak in het midden stevig aan met uw duim, zodat de randen omhoog komen. Laat de pasta vervolgens tot gebruik drogen op een met bloem bestoven werkvlak.
2. Doe de clams in een grote pan met een laagje water van 2 cm. Leg het deksel op de pan en kook 1 minuut op een hoog vuur. Haal alle open clams uit de pan en laat de rest nog een paar seconden koken tot ze open zijn. Laat de clams even afkoelen en haal het vlees uit de schelpen boven een kom waarin u het clamnat opvangt. Spoel het clamvlees goed af om alle zand te verwijderen en hak het vlees dan grof. Zet weg. Zeef het kooknat door ongebleekte katoen om alle zand te verwijderen en zet het kooknat daarna weg.
3. Verhit de olijfolie in een grote koekepan. Fruit er de knoflook en ui goudgeel in. Voeg de spinazie toe en bak 1 minuut. Voeg de tomaten en het bewaarde clamkooknat toe en breng aan de kook. Draai het vuur lager en voeg de *orecchiette* toe. Kook ze in 3-4 minuten bijtgaar. Voeg het bewaarde clamvlees, de peterselie en wat zout en peper toe. Bestrooi met de *pecorino* en dien op.

Voor 6 personen *Foto op pagina*

---

3 dl per portie: Calorieën 350, Eiwit 17 g, Koolhydraten 52 g, Vezel 8 g, Vet totaal 9 g (Verzadigd 2 g, Enkelvoudig onverzadigd 5 g Meervoudig onverzadigd 1 g), Cholesterol 20 mg, Natrium 200 mg, IJzer 60%, Vitamine A 60%, Vitamine C 40%.
▲ *2 Brood, 1 Groente, 1 Vlees*

HAPJES / ITALIË

Gegrilde pizza

Griesmeelbloem geeft deze korst een knapperige structuur die stevig genoeg is om te grilleren. U kunt het garnituur naar smaak aanpassen. Het grilleren boven houtskool houdt de bovenkant vers en sappig, terwijl die juist wel eens uitdroogt tijden het bakken in de oven.

1 pakje (7 g) droge gist
2 eetlepels suiker
600 g bloem
75 g griesmeelbloem
1 eetlepel zout
4 eetlepels olijfolie
125 g magere mozzarella, geraspt
2 artisjokharten, in partjes gesneden
2 pruimtomaten, in plakken gesneden
1 eetlepel rozemarijnblaadjes

1. Los de gist en de suiker op in 3,75 dl warm water (40°-46°C). Laat het mengsel 5 minuten staan tot het schuimig wordt.
2. Doe de bloem, griesmeelbloem en het zout in een grote kom. Maak een kuiltje in het midden en giet er het gistmengsel en 3 eetlepels van de olie in. Schep de natte ingrediënten door het bloemmengsel tot een stevig deeg. Doe het deeg op een licht met bloem bestoven werkvlak en kneed het tot het glad en niet meer plakkerig is. Vorm het deeg tot een bal en doe die in een licht met olie ingevette kom. Dek de kom af en laat het deeg 30 minuten rijzen.
3. Druk de lucht uit het deeg en verdeel het in 8 ballen. Dek ze af en laat ze 45 minuten rusten.
4. Maak een houtskoolvuur en kwast het rooster in met olijfolie.
5. Rol de ballen uit tot cirkels van 15 cm doorsnee en kwast ze licht in met 1 theelepel van de overgebleven olijfolie. Strooi de mozzarella over elke pizza en houd een rand van 1 cm vrij. Schik er de artisjokharten en plakken tomaat op en kwast weer licht in met de rest van de olijfolie. Bestrooi met de rozemarijnblaadjes.
6. Zet 6-8 minuten boven de houtskool tot het deeg stevig aanvoelt en goudbruin is en de kaas gesmolten is. Bak de pizza's anders 10 minuten in een op 230°C voorverwarmde oven.

Voor acht pizza's van 15 cm doorsnee *Foto op pagina*

---

1 pizza per portie: Calorieën 340, Eiwit 11 g, Koolhydraten 55 g, Vezel 3 g, Vet totaal 8 g (Verzadigd 2 g, Enkelvoudig onverzadigd 4,5 g, Meervoudig onverzadigd 1 g), Cholesterol 10 mg, Natrium 950 mg.
▲ *1 Brood, 1 Groente, ½ Melk*

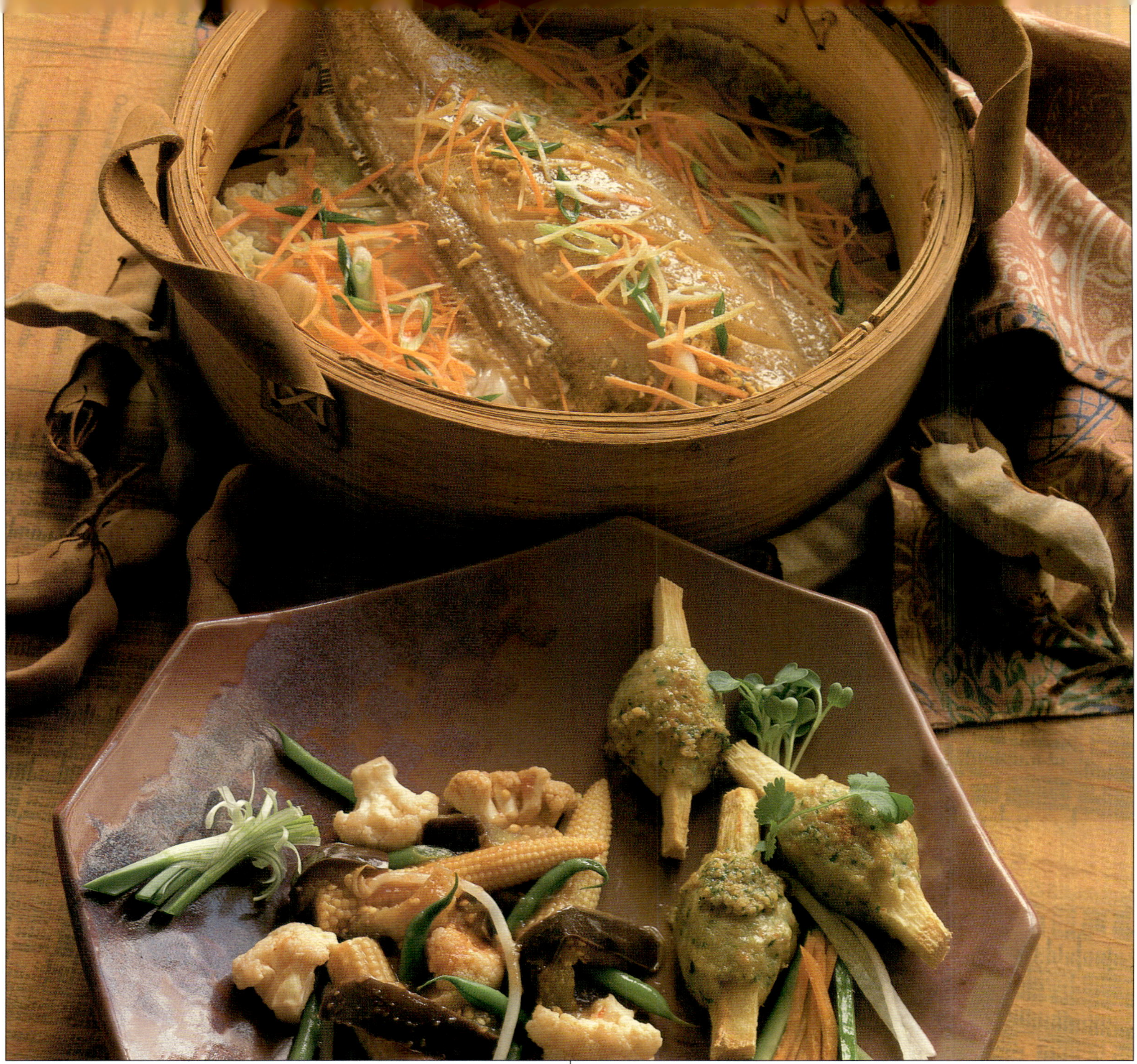

Met de klok mee van boven: Kantonese gestoomde bot, Suikerrietstaafjes met garnalenpasta en pindasaus, Pikantzure groenten

Suikerrietstaafjes met garnalenpasta en pindasaus

Dit heerlijk frisse hapje is een voorbeeld van hoezeer de Vietnamezen verse groenten waarderen. De suikerriet geeft een subtiele zoetigheid en is ook de drager van de garnalenpasta. Als er geen verse suikerriet verkrijgbaar is, kunt u suikerriet uit blik gebruiken.

Pindasaus

1 theelepel arachide-olie
2 theelepels fijngehakte knoflook
1 eetlepel fijgehakte verse koriander
2 eetlepels drooggeroosterde pinda's
2 eetlepels sojasaus
1 eetlepel suiker
¼ theelepel chilipasta, of naar smaak
4 eetlepels kippebouillon (zie woordenlijst)

Garnalen

500 g rauwe garnalen, gepeld, darmkanaal verwijderd en drooggedept
4 tenen knoflook
2 lenteuitjes, in stukken van 3 cm gesneden
1 eetlepel suiker
1 eetlepel sesamolie
1 eetlepel sojasaus
1 eiwit
1 stuk verse suikerriet of 1 uit blik, geschild en in zes stukken van 8 cm gesneden
gesorteerde verse groenten: taugé, grof geraspte wortel en rettich, julienne gesneden komkommer, gehakte verse munt en verse koriander
1 kleine krop sla
12 vellen rijstpapier

1. Verhit voor de pindasaus de arachide-olie in een kleine koekepan en fruit er de fijngehakte knoflook goudbruin in. Doe in een blender en voeg de gehakte verse koriander, pinda's, sojasaus, suiker, chilipasta en kippebouillon toe. Draai tot een glad mengsel. Giet over in een kom en zet weg.

2. Pureer de garnalen met de tenen knoflook en lenteuitjes in een keukenmachine. Voeg de suiker, sesamolie, sojasaus en het eiwit toe en draai met korte stootjes tot een pasta. Zet minstens 20 minuten in de koelkast.
3. Snijd de suikerriet in de lengte in vieren en druk de gekoelde garnalenpasta om het middelste tweederde deel van elk suikerrietstaafje. Leg de staafjes op een bakplaat en bewaar in de koelkast tot het koken.
4. Verwarm een grill voor of maak een houtskoolvuur. Vet een rooster licht in met olie. Rooster de garnalenstaafjes in circa 5-7 minuten goudbruin, waarbij u ze af en toe omdraait.
5. Schik de verse groenten op een dienschaal met de sla en het rijstpapier. Serveer de garnalenstaafjes met de groenten, het rijstpapier, kommen warm water en de pindasaus. De eters dompelen een vel rijstpapier in het warme water tot het papier zacht is en vullen het papier dan met groenten naar keuze en stukjes geroosterde garnaal die van de suikerriet zijn afgetrokken.

---

2 staafjes per portie: Calorieën 180, Eiwit 18 g, Koolhydraten 14 g, Vezel 1 g, Vet totaal 6 g (Verzadigd 1 g, Enkelvoudig onverzadigd 2 g, Meervoudig onverzadigd 0,5 g), Cholesterol 0 mg, Natrium 25 mg, Vitamine C 35%.

▲ *1 Groente, 1 Vlees*

GROENTEN / INDONESIË

Sajoer asam

PIKANTZURE GROENTEN

Tamarinde is een zoetzure vrucht met gedopte peulen die zaden bevatten. De gedroogde moes is in Indonesische speciaalzaken als asam *verkrijgbaar. Bij gebruik van de peulen moeten de dop en grove vezels worden verwijderd. Nadat de peulen 30 minuten in het water hebben geweekt, kan het vruchtvlees van de zaden worden gehaald. Meng gedroogde tamarinde met water (4 theelepels tamarinde op 1 eetlepel water). Sajoer asam is heerlijk bij geroosterde kip of als bijgerecht bij gestoomde rijst.*

125 g tamarinde
1 ui, grof gehakt
2 tenen knoflook, fijngehakt
1 liter kippebouillon (zie woordenlijst)
1 laurierblad
1 eetlepel suiker
1 aubergine, in blokjes van 5 cm gesneden
125 g sperziebonen, afgehaald en in stukjes van 3 cm gesneden
125 g bloemkool, in roosjes verdeeld
375 g verse maïs of maïs uit blik
het sap van 1 limoen
125 g taugé
½ theelepel sambal oelek, of naar smaak

1. Breek de tamarinde in stukjes en giet er 1,25 dl heet water over. Laat 10 minuten staan en wrijf dan fijn met een pollepel. Zeef en druk daarbij de tamarinde aan om zoveel mogelijk vocht eruit te krijgen. Zet het vocht weg en gooi de moes weg.
2. Pureer de knoflook en ui in een keukenmachine met 1,25 dl kippebouillon. Doe de puree in een soeppan met de rest van de kippebouillon en breng aan de kook. Voeg het laurierblad en de suiker toe en laat alles sudderen. Voeg de aubergine en sperziebonen toe en laat alles afgedekt nog 10 minuten sudderen. Voeg de bloemkool, maïs en het bewaarde tamarindevocht toe. Laat alles nog 3 tot 5 minuten koken tot de groenten bijtgaar zijn.
3. Roer het limoensap en de taugé erdoor. Voeg naar smaak sambal toe. Verwijder het laurierblad en dien onmiddellijk op.

Voor 8 personen

2,5 dl per portie: Calorieën 100, Eiwit 3 g, Koolhydraten 21 g, Vezel 3 g, Vet totaal 1 g (Verzadigd 0,5 g, Enkelvoudig onverzadigd 0,5 g Meervoudig onverzadigd 0,5 g), Cholesterol 0 mg, Natrium 25 mg, Vitamine C 35%.

▲ *2 Groente*

ZEEBANKET / CHINA

Kantonese gestoomde bot

Als u geen bamboe stoommand hebt, kunt u improviseren door een rooster in een brede pan met een deksel te zetten. Zet het rooster minstens 1 cm boven sudderend water. Stoom de visfilets 4-6 minuten, afhankelijk van de dikte.

1 kg hele bot of tong, schoongemaakt, kop en staart intact
4 eetlepels rijstwijn
1 eetlepel sojasaus
2 theelepels sesamolie
1 eetlepel fijngehakte verse gember
1 teen knoflook, fijngehakt
4 grote bladen Chinese kool
1 wortel, julienne gesneden
1 stuk verse gember van circa 5 cm, geschild en julienne gesneden
1 lenteui, schuin in dunne plakken gesneden

1. Zet de stoommand in elkaar.
2. Spoel de bot of tong af en dep dan goed droog. Maak met een 3 cm tussenruimte ondiepe, schuine inkepingen in beide kanten van de vis. Zet de vis in een ondiepe schaal.
3. Meng de rijstwijn met de sojasaus, sesamolie, fijngehakte gember en knoflook in een kleine kom. Giet dit mengsel over de vis en wrijf het in de inkepingen. Laat 30 minuten marineren.
4. Bekleed de bodem van de stoommand met de Chinese koolbladen. Leg er de vis op, bestrooi met de reepjes wortel, gember en plakken lenteui.
5. Stoom de vis 7-8 minuten of tot hij gaar is. Dien onmiddellijk op uit de stoommand.

Voor 4 personen

---

1 portie: Calorieën 180, Eiwit 33 g, Koolhydraten 3 g, Vezel 1 g, Vet totaal 3 g (Verzadigd 0,5 g, Enkelvoudig onverzadigd 0,5 g Meervoudig onverzadigd 1 g), Cholesterol 80 mg, Natrium 210 mg, Vitamine A 120%, Vitamine C 20%.

▲ *1 Vlees*

GROENTEN / HONGARIJE

Lecsó

Dit gerecht wordt in Hongarije op verschillende manieren gepresenteerd: als saus, hapje of als bijgerecht voor gevogelte of vis. U kunt het invriezen voor gebruik bij kip paprikás *(recept op pagina 86).*

2 eetlepels olijfolie
1 grote ui, in dunne plakken
250 g rode en groene paprika's, ontzaad en in plakken
250 g langwerpige (Hongaarse) lichtgele paprika's, ontzaad en in plakken
3 grote verse tomaten, ontveld, ontzaad en grof gehakt
1 eetlepel pittig Hongaars paprikapoeder, of naar smaak
2 theelepels suiker
½ theelepel zout

1. Verhit de olijfolie in een grote koekepan. Doe er de ui in en fruit die in circa 5 minuten goudgeel.
2. Voeg de paprika's toe en bak ze circa 2-3 minuten tot ze gaar maar niet bruin zijn.
3. Roer er de tomaten, het paprikapoeder, de suiker en het zout door. Laat alles doorwarmen.

Voor 4 personen

2,5 dl per portie: Calorieën 160, Eiwit 4 g, Koolhydraten 22 g, Vezel 5 g, Vet totaal 8 g (Verzadigd 1 g, Enkelvoudig onverzadigd 5 g, Meervoudig onverzadigd 1 g), Cholesterol 0 mg, Natrium 310 mg, Vitamine A 80%, Vitamine C 430%.

▲ *2 Groente*

HAPJES / CHILI

Escabeche

Escabeche *is een kruidige, koude marinade die oorspronkelijk werd gebruikt om gekookt vlees te conserveren. De term slaat ook op het marineren van rauw vlees en zeebanket in citrussap en wordt vaak "ceviche" genoemd. In dit recept wordt gepocheerde kip met verse korianderpesto gemengd en in een uitgeholde citroen geserveerd.*

4 citroenen
2 tenen knoflook
30 g verse korianderbladen
60 g pijnboompitten
3 eetlepels saffloerolie
2,5 dl kippebouillon (zie woordenlijst)
1 hele kipfilet
1 rode paprika, in blokjes
1 maïskolf, korrels afgesneden en gepocheerd (zie woordenlijst)
35 g blokjes jícama (yamboon)
zout en versgemalen peper naar smaak

1. Hol de citroenen uit; zeef de pulp en bewaar het sap. Gooi de pulp weg. Snijd een dunne plak van de bodem van elke citroenhelft zodat ze rechtop blijven staan.
2. Doe de knoflook in een draaiende keukenmachine en voeg dan de koriander, pijnboompitten, het bewaarde citroensap en de saffloerolie toe. Draai tot een gladde pasta en zet weg.
3. Breng de kippebouillon aan de kook. Doe er de kipfilet in en draai het vuur laag. Laat 20 minuten zachtjes pocheren tot de kip gaar is. Neem de kip uit de bouillon en laat afkoelen. Bewaar de bouillon voor ander gebruik.
4. Snijd de afgekoelde kip in blokjes en doe die in een kom. Schep er de paprika, maïs, jícama en korianderpesto door. Breng op smaak met zout en peper. Zet minstens 1 uur in de koelkast.
5. Schep het kipmengsel in de uitgeholde citroenen en dien onmiddellijk op.

Voor 8 personen

½ gevulde citroen per portie: Calorieën 140, Eiwit 9 g, Koolhydraten 7 g, Vezel 1 g, Vet totaal 10 g (Verzadigd 1 g, Enkelvoudig onverzadigd 2 g, Meervoudig onverzadigd 6 g), Cholesterol 20 mg, Natrium 20 mg, Vitamine C 60%.

▲ *1 Groente, ½ Vlees*

ONTBIJT / SPANJE

Piperrade

Piperrade *is een specialiteit van de Spaanse en Franse Baskische keukens en bestaat uit roerei met paprika's en tomaten. In deze versie gaan gepocheerde eieren op een bedje groenten. Geef er stokbrood en wat te drinken bij voor een complete maaltijd.*

2 eetlepels olijfolie
60 g grof gehakte ui
2 rode paprika's, ontzaad en in blokjes van 2 cm
1 groene paprika, ontzaad en in blokjes van 2 cm
1 gele paprika, ontzaad en in blokjes van 2 cm
2 grote tomaten (circa 500 g), ontveld, ontzaad en in stukjes van 2 cm
1 theelepel fijngehakte peterselie
½ theelepel fijngehakte rozemarijnblaadjes
¼ theelepel zout
versgemalen peper naar smaak
1 theelepel sherry azijn
4 eieren

1. Verhit de olijfolie in een grote koekepan en fruit er de ui in circa 5 minuten gaar in. Schep er de rode, groene en gele paprika's door en bak 5 minuten. Voeg de tomaten, peterselie en rozemarijn toe en kook nog 10 minuten. Breng op smaak met zout en peper en schep op 4 borden. Houd warm tot het serveren.
2. Breng 3 cm water aan de kook in een koekepan. Voeg de azijn toe en draai het vuur laag. Breek de eieren één voor één in een kom en laat ze zachtjes in het licht sudderende water glijden. Pocheer circa 5 minuten tot het wit gestold is. Schep ze met een schuimspaam uit het water en schik op de groenten. Dien op.

Voor 4 personen

1 portie: Calorieën 180, Eiwit 8 g, Koolhydraten 11 g, Vezel 3 g, Vet totaal 13 g (Verzadigd 2,5 g, Enkelvoudig onverzadigd 7 g, Meervoudig onverzadigd 1,5 g), Cholesterol 220 mg, Natrium 220 mg, Vitamine A 60%, Vitamine C 250%.

▲ *1 Groente, ½ Vlees*

Met de klok mee van boven: Lecsó, Piperrade, Escabeche

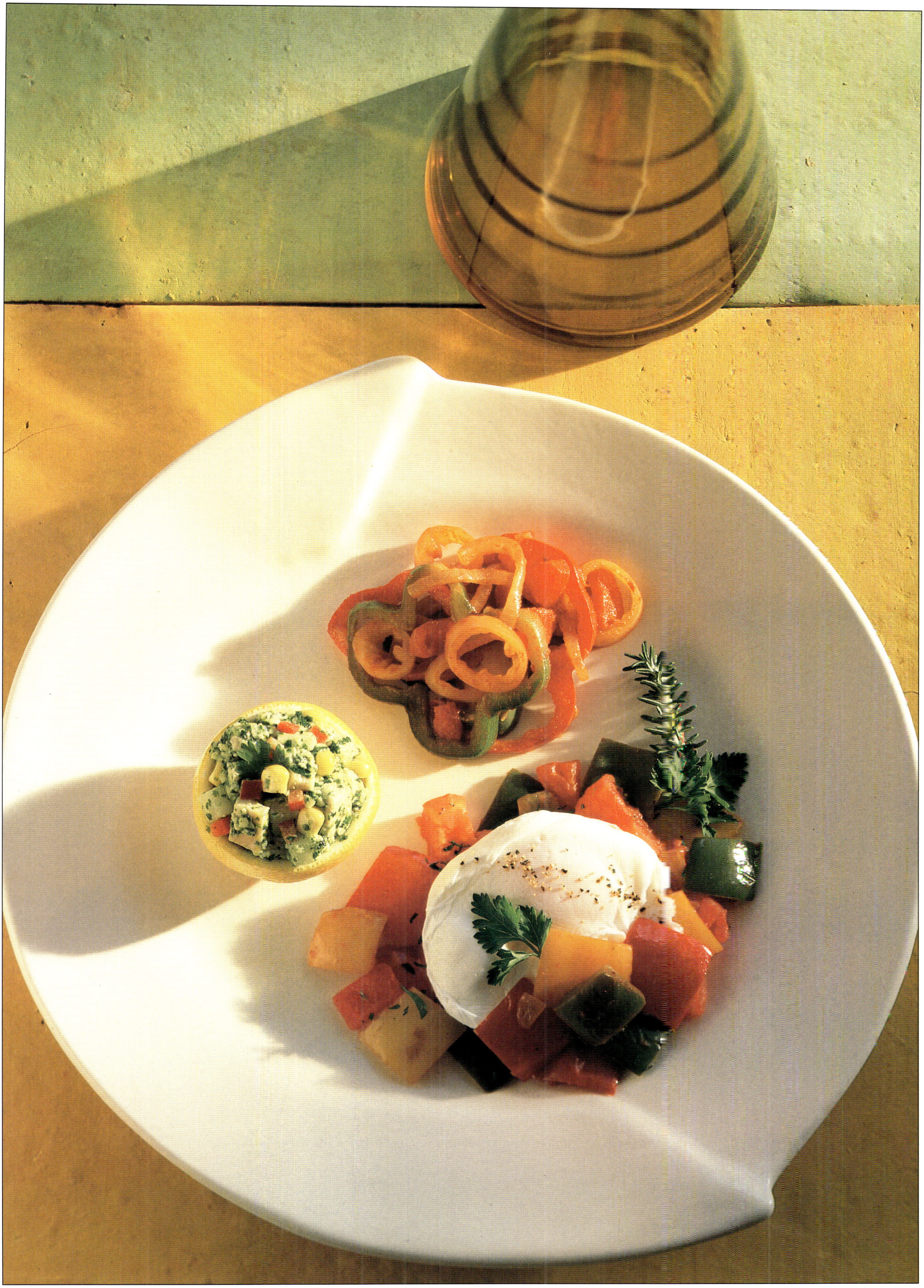

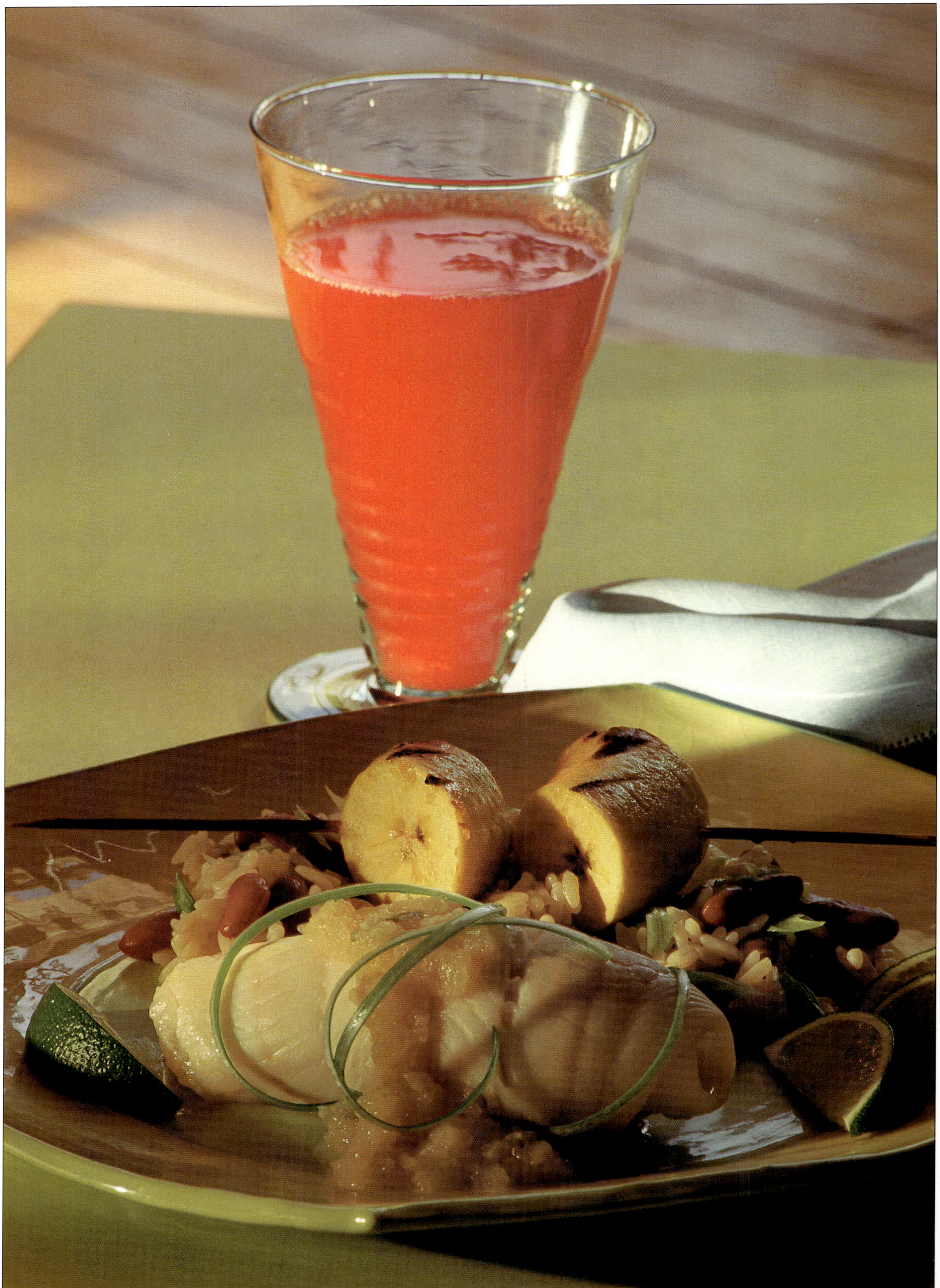

DRANKEN / CHINA

Vers watermeloensap als in Hongkong

De hitte van de zomer in Hongkong kan heel vermoeiend zijn. De leukste manier van boodschappen doen is de nachtmarkt in Kowloon, waar u ter plekke verse sappen kunt bestellen. Niets lest de dorst beter dan vers gemaakt watermeloensap.

2,5 kg watermeloen, gekoeld

1. Verwijder de schil van de meloen en snijd hem in stukken van 5 cm. Passeer de stukken door een sapcentrifuge. Verwijder anders de pitjes, pureer de meloen in een blender en zeef de puree. Dien direct op.

Voor 8 glazen

1 glas per portie: Calorieën 90, Eiwit 2 g, Koolhydraten 20 g, Vezel 2 g, Vet totaal 1 g (Verzadigd 0,5 g, Enkelvoudig onverzadigd 0 g, Meervoudig onverzadigd 0 g), Cholesterol 0 mg, Natrium 6 mg, Vitamine A 20%, Vitamine C 45%.

▲ *1 Fruit*

GROENTEN / CARIBISCH GEBIED

Gegrilde pisang met duivenbonen en rijst

Duivenbonen (gungo-erwtjes) en rijst zijn hoofdvoedsels in het Caribisch gebied. U kunt nierbonen gebruiken als duivenbonen niet verkrijgbaar zijn. Pisang is heerlijk in elk stadium van rijpheid. Hoe rijper ze zijn, hoe zoeter. Kies voor dit recept onrijpe, stevige pisangs.

150 g verse duivenbonen of 185 g gedroogde nierbonen, een nacht in water geweekt
5 dl kippebouillon (zie woordenlijst)
1,8 dl kokosmelk
2 tenen knoflook, fijngehakt
3 lenteuitjes, in dunne plakken
220 g langkorrelige rijst
zout en versgemalen peper naar smaak
3 eetlepels olijfolie
1 ui, gehakt
5 tenen knoflook, uit de knijper
1 eetlepel geraspte verse gember
5 eetlepels vers sinaasappelsap
4 grote onrijpe pisangs, gepeld

1. Doe de duivenbonen of de geweekte, uitgelekte nierbonen in een grote pan met de kippebouillon, kokosmelk en gehakte knoflook. Breng aan de kook. Draai het vuur laag en laat 20 minuten sudderen (45 minuten voor nierbonen).
2. Voeg de lentui en rijst toe, leg het deksel op de pan en laat 20 minuten koken, of tot het vocht geabsorbeerd is.
3. Breng op smaak met zout en peper en houd warm.
4. Verhit de olijfolie in een middelgrote anti-aanbak koekepan. Doe er de ui in en fruit die glazig.
5. Meng de knoflook (uit de knijper) met de gember, het sinaasappelsap en wat zout in een kleine kom. Schep dit mengsel om met de ui en laat doorwarmen. Zet weg.
6. Snijd elke pisang in 4 schuine stukken. Rijg ze aan pennen en kwast ze in met de knoflook-sinaasappelolie. Grilleer ze langzaam en keer ze regelmatig om.
7. Schep de pisang op de bonen met rijst en dien op.

Voor 8 personen

2.5 dl plus 2 stukken pisang per portie: Calorieën 390, Eiwit 6 g, Koolhydraten 71 g, Vezel 2 g, Vet totaal 12 g (Verzadigd 6 g, Enkelvoudig onverzadigd 4 g, Meervoudig onverzadigd 1 g), Cholesterol 0 mg, Natrium 15 mg, Vitamine A 30%, Vitamine C 70%.

▲ *1 Brood, 1 Fruit, ½ Vlees*

Van boven naar beneden: Vers watermeloensap als in Hongkong, Gegrilde pisang met duivenbonen en rijst, Vliegende vis met limoen, guave en ananassaus

ZEEBANKET / CARIBISCH GEBIED

Vliegende vis met limoen, guave en ananassaus

Vliegende vissen roepen beelden op van azuurblauwe Caribische wateren, maar tong of forel zijn ook zeer geschikt voor dit gerecht. Als u geen stoommand hebt, kunt u improviseren door een rooster in een ruime pan met deksel te zetten.

1 verse ananas, geschild, harde kern uitgestoken, in blokjes
1 rijpe guave, gepeld en ontzaad
2 tenen knoflook, fijngehakt
1 theelepel geraspte verse gember
¼ theelepel fijngehakte jalapeño chilipeper (desgewenst)
de geraspte schil van ½ limoen
het sap van 3 limoenen
6 vliegende vis- of tongfilets, circa 1 kg
3 lenteuitjes, in dunne plakken

1. Pureer de ananas en guave met de knoflook, gember, jalapeño, limoenschil en het limoensap in een blender.
2. Doe de puree in een pan en kook 10 minuten op een middelhoog vuur onder regelmatig roeren. Zet weg.
3. Spoel de filets af en dep ze droog. Rol de filets op en zet ze vast met cocktailprikkers. Leg de rolletjes in de stoommand en stoom ze 10 minuten boven kokend water.
4. Doe de visrolletjes op een dienschaal, schep er wat ananassaus over en garneer met de lenteuitjes.

Voor 6 personen

1 filet met saus per portie: Calorieën 240, Eiwit 30 g, Koolhydraten 27 g, Vezel 4 g, Vet totaal 3 g (Verzadigd 0,5 g, Enkelvoudig onverzadigd 0,5 g, Meervoudig onverzadigd 1 g), Cholesterol 75 mg, Natrium 125 mg, Vitamine C 100%.

▲ *1 Fruit, 1 Vlees*

Streuselkuchen

KERSEN-KRUIMELTAART

Kersen zijn in het begin van de zomer fantastisch van kwaliteit. Andere vruchten—pruimen, appels of perziken—zijn echter ook heerlijk te verwerken in deze taart.

1 pakje (7 g) droge gist
½ theelepel suiker
1,25 dl warme magere melk (40°-46°C)
3 eetlepels saffloerolie
2 eieren
125 g suiker
500 g bloem
¼ theelepel zout

Van links naar rechts: Kersen-kruimeltaart, Wortel-appel-bosbessentaart met bosbessensaus (recept pagina 139)

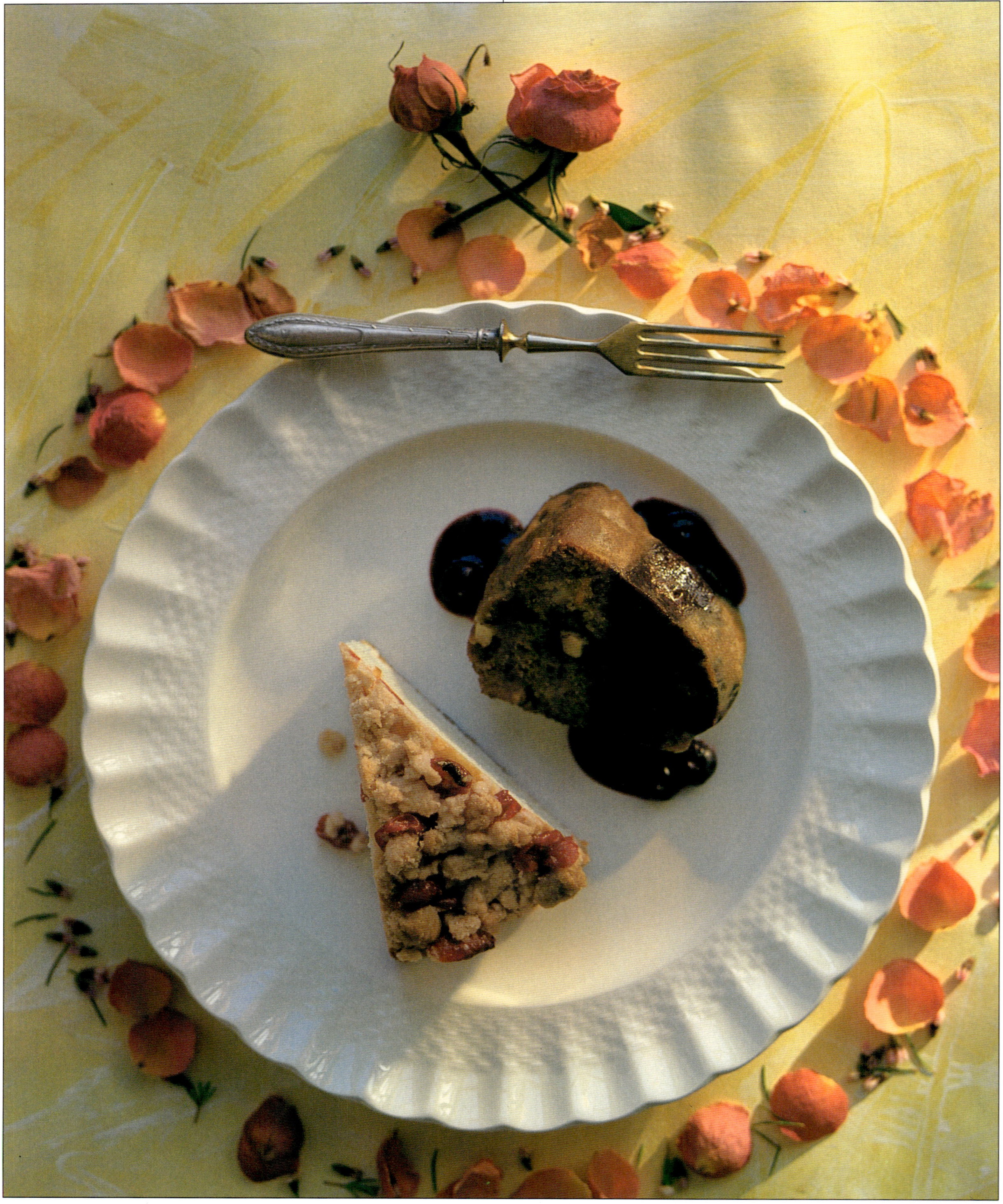

500 g verse kersen, gehalveerd en ontpit
45 g boter
de geraspte schil van ½ citroen
½ theelepel gemalen kaneel

1. Verwarm de oven voor op 190°C. Vet een springvorm van 25 cm doorsnee licht in met olie. Los de gist en de ½ theelepel suiker op in de warme melk. Laat het mengsel 5 minuten staan tot het schuimig is. Voeg de olie en eieren toe.
2. Doe 65 g van de suiker, 470 g van de bloem en het zout in de kom van een elektrische mixer met een deeghaak. Voeg het gistmengsel toe en klop tot een glad en elastisch deeg. Doe het deeg in een licht met olie ingevette kom, dek die af en laat het deeg circa 1 uur rijzen tot het in volume verdubbeld is.
3. Druk de lucht uit het deeg en kneed het circa 5 minuten. Laat het 10 minuten rusten en druk het dan in de springvorm. Dek de vorm af en laat het deeg 30 minuten rijzen.
4. Druk de kersen met de snijkant boven in het deeg.
5. Wrijf de overgebleven suiker en overgebleven bloem met de boter, geraspte schil en kaneel tot een kruimig mengsel. Strooi het mengsel over de kersen.
6. Bak de taart 30 minuten in de oven tot hij goudbruin is. Laat 10 minuten afkoelen voor u de taart aansnijdt.

Voor 12 personen

1 portie: Calorieën 240, Eiwit 6 g, Koolhydraten 41 g, Vezel 2 g, Vet totaal 8 g (Verzadigd 2,5 g, Enkelvoudig onverzadigd 2 g, Meervoudig onverzadigd 3 g), Cholesterol 45 mg, Natrium 65 mg.
▲ *1 Brood, 1 Fruit*

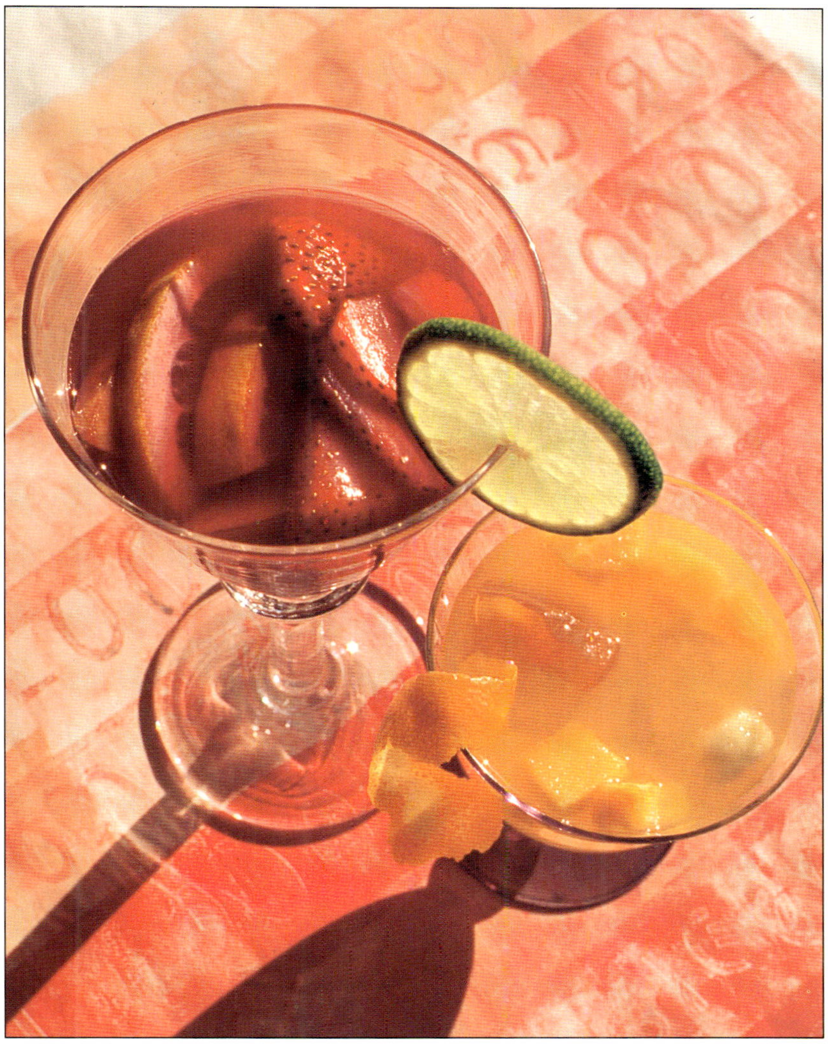

Van links naar rechts: Sangría, Tahitiaanse rumpunch

DRANKEN / SPANJE

Sangría

Serveer deze wijnpunch in een grote glazen kan om de prachtige rode kleur en de verschillende vruchten te laten zien. Voeg zonodig wat suiker toe als het sinaasappelsap te bitter is. U kunt een alchoholvrije fruitthee maken door 1 liter thee in plaats van de wijn toe te voegen.

7,5 dl droge rode wijn
3,5 dl vers sinaasappelsap
1 verse perzik, gehalveerd en in plakken
1 kleine sinaasappel, gehalveerd en in plakken
½ citroen, gehalveerd en in plakken
1 limoen, gehalveerd en in plakken
60 g aardbei, in plakjes
mineraalwater, naar smaak

1. Doe alle ingrediënten in een zuurbestendige kom en laat minstens 3 uur of een nacht in de koelkast staan.
2. Giet het mengsel in een glazen kan en geef er extra mineraalwater apart bij. Serveer in glazen die groot genoeg zijn om het fruit te bevatten.

Voor 6 glazen

1 glas per portie: Calorieën 130, Eiwit 1 g, Koolhydraten 12 g, Vezel 2 g, Vet totaal 0 g (Verzadigd 0 g, Enkelvoudig onverzadigd 0 g, Meervoudig onverzadigd 0 g), Cholesterol 0 mg, Natrium 15 mg.
▲ *1 Fruit*

DRANKEN / TAHITI

Tahitiaanse rumpunch

Tahitiaanse zomers zijn snikheet. Het beste wat men kan doen is in de schaduw zitten, vliegende vissen tellen en deze punch drinken.

1 mango, geschild, ontpit en in blokjes
1 banaan, in blokjes
1 sinaasappel, ontpit en in blokjes
1 kleine papaja, circa 250 g, geschild, ontzaad en in blokjes
1 liter ananassap
5 dl rum
2,5 dl rietsuikersiroop, of 250 g suiker in 1,25 dl kokend water opgelost en afgekoeld
het sap van 4 limoenen
2 vanillepeulen, in de lengte opengesneden
reepje sinaasappelschil, ter garnering

1. Meng alle ingrediënten behalve de schil in een kan en zet minstens 3 uur in de koelkast. Giet over ijsblokjes in glazen en dien op met een stukje schil.

Voor 8 personen

1 glas per portie: Calorieën 370, Eiwit 1 g, Koolhydraten 62 g, Vezel 2 g, Vet totaal 0 g (Verzadigd 0 g, Enkelvoudig onverzadigd 0 g, Meervoudig onverzadigd 0 g), Cholesterol 0 mg, Natrium 55 mg, Vitamine A 30%, Vitamine C 90%.
▲ *2 Fruit, 1 Vet / Suiker*

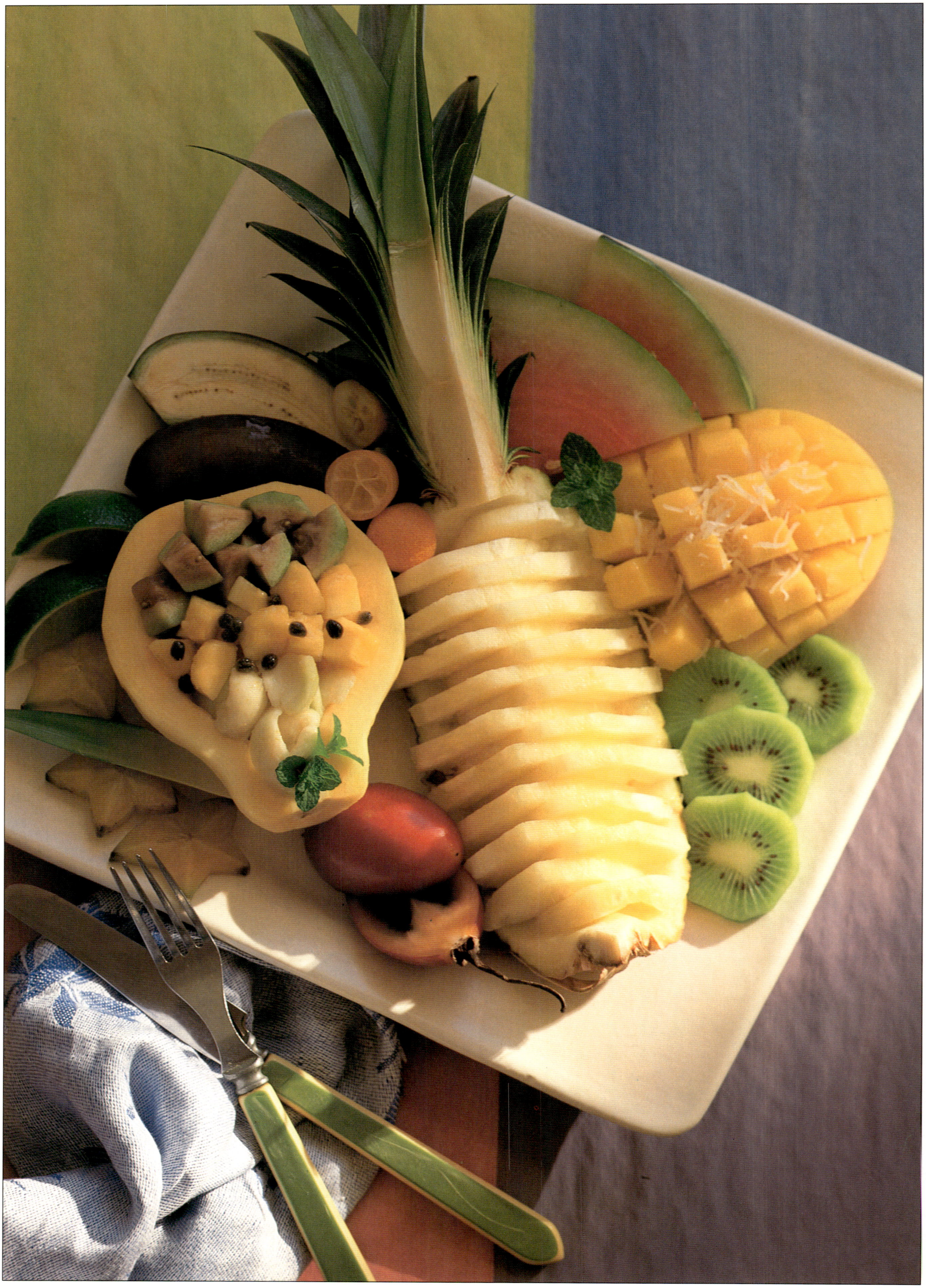

Wortel-appel-bosbessentaart met bosbessensaus

Door het gebruik van natte ingrediënten als appel en wortel in deze taart kunt u de hoeveelheid vet verminderen. U kunt de bosbessen weglaten als die niet in seizoen zijn en in plaats daarvan de taart met poedersuiker bestuiven.

235 g bloem
75 g volkorenbloem
2 theelepels bakpoeder
2 theelepels gemalen kaneel
1 theelepel zuiveringszout
¼ theelepel zout
250 g suiker
100 g lichtbruine basterdsuiker
3 eieren
1,25 dl karnemelk
1,25 dl plantaardige olie
3 wortels, grof geraspt
2 Granny Smith of Cox Orange appels, geschild en in blokjes
250 g bosbessen
7,5 dl bosbessensaus (recept volgt)

1. Verwarm de oven voor op 180°C. Vet een anti-aanbak tulbandvorm van 2½ liter inhoud licht in met olie en bestuif hem vervolgens licht met bloem.
2. Meng de bloemsoorten in een middelgrote kom. Schep er het bakpoeder, de kaneel, het zuiveringszout en zout door.
3. Klop de suiker en basterdsuiker door de eieren in een grote kom. Voeg de karnemelk, olie, wortel en appel toe. Schep er het bloemmengsel door tot alles net gemengd is. Schep er de bosbessen voorzichtig door en giet het beslag in de tulbandvorm.
4. Bak de taart 1 uur in de oven, of tot de taart van de randen loskomt. Laat de taart 15 minuten op een rooster afkoelen. Stort de taart op een dienschaal en schep er de bosbessensaus omheen.

Voor 12 personen

1 plak per portie: Calorieën 370, Eiwit 5 g, Koolhydraten 64 g, Vezel 5 g, Vet totaal 11 g (Verzadigd 1 g, Enkelvoudig onverzadigd 6 g, Meervoudig onverzadigd 3 g), Cholesterol 55 mg, Natrium 190 mg, Vitamine A 100%.

▲ *1 Brood, 2 Fruit*

Bosbessensaus

500 g bosbessen
125 g suiker
¼ theelepel gemalen kaneel
1,25 dl appelsap

1. Doe 250 g van de bosbessen, de suiker, kaneel en het appelsap in een middelgrote pan. Breng aan de kook; draai het vuur lager en laat 10 minuten sudderen. Pureer de saus in een blender en passeer dan door een zeef.
2. Schep er de overgebleven bosbessen door.

Voor 7,5 dl *Foto op pagina 136*

4 eetlepels per portie: Calorieën 70, Eiwit 0 g, Koolhydraten 16 g, Vezel 2 g, Vet totaal 0 g (Verzadigd 0 g, Enkelvoudig onverzadigd 0 g, Meervoudig onverzadigd 0 g), Cholesterol 0 mg, Natrium 0 mg.

▲ *1 Fruit*

Tropische vruchten

Tropische vruchten

Sommige tropische vruchten worden niet geëxporteerd omdat ze te teer zijn voor transport of te kort in seizoen zijn. Hieronder wordt een selectie tropische vruchten voorgesteld die tegenwoordig overal verkrijgbaar zijn. Creëer uw eigen combinatie met vruchten in seizoen als aardbeien, watermeloen, kersen, druiven en bessen. Kokos bevat circa 2 gram verzadigd vet per eetlepel, maar een beetje kokos verleent de schotel een tropische smaak en structuur.

1 rijpe papaja van circa 500 g
1 rijpe carambola (stervrucht)
1 rijpe mango
1 ananas, in de lengte in vieren gesneden, harde kern verwijderd
circa 10 appelbanaantjes
1 suiker- of honingmeloen, gehalveerd en pitjes verwijderd
4 passievruchten
4 eetlepels vers limoensap
2 eetlepels gedroogde kokos

1. Schil de papaja met een klein scherp mes en halveer hem in de lengte. Schep er de zaden uit en snijd het vruchtvlees in plakjes van 1 cm dik.
2. Verwijder eventuele draadjes langs de ribben van de carambola met een scherp mes. Snijd de stervrucht in dunne plakken.
3. Snijd de mango zo dicht mogelijk naast de pit in tweeën. Snijd het vruchtvlees van elke helft tot aan maar niet door de schil in blokjes. Draai elke helft binnenstebuiten zodat de blokjes eruit komen en snijd de schil eraf.
4. Snijd langs de rand van de schil van elk stuk ananas om het vruchtvlees los te maken, maar houd de schil intact. Snijd het vruchtvlees in plakken van 1 cm dik en schik ze weer in de schil.
5. Pel de bananen en laat ze heel of snijd ze overdwars in plakjes van 3 cm dik.
6. Schep met een bolletjessteker balletjes uit de meloen.
7. Halveer de passievruchten en schep er het vruchtvlees uit.
8. Schik de geprepareerde vruchten op een dienschaal, sprenkel er het limoensap over en garneer met de kokos. Dien op.

Voor 12 personen

1 portie: Calorieën 130, Eiwit 2 g, Koolhydraten 32 g, Vezel 4 g, Vet totaal 1 g (Verzadigd 0,5 g, Enkelvoudig onverzadigd 0 g, Meervoudig onverzadigd 0 g), Cholesterol 0 mg, Natrium 10 mg, Vitamine A 25%, Vitamine C 70%.

▲ *2 Fruit*

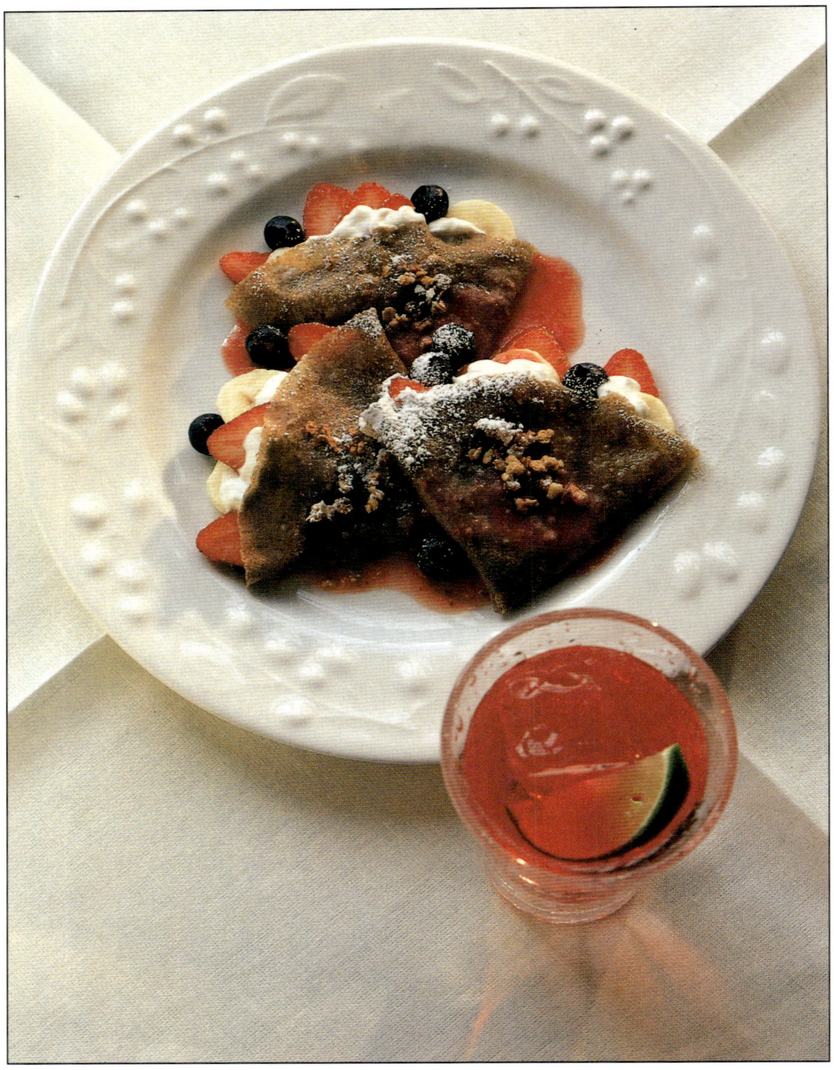

Van boven naar beneden: Boekweitcrêpes gevuld met bessen en room, Cranberry-gemberlimonade

ONTBIJT / FRANKRIJK

Boekweitcrêpes gevuld met bessen en room

De keuze is aan u—room of geen room. Probeer eens halfvolle standyoghurt. Garneer de crêpes met wat geroosterde muesli.

3 dl magere melk
2 eieren
1 eetlepel saffloerolie
½ theelepel vanille-essence
75 g bloem
75 g boekweitmeel
2 eetlepels suiker
250 g aardbeien, in plakken
250 g verse bosbessen
2 bananen, in plakken
1,25 dl slagroom, stijf geklopt met 2 eetlepels poedersuiker, of 1,25 dl halfvolle standyoghurt met vanillesmaak
1 eetlepel poedersuiker
verse aardbeiensaus (recept op pagina 97)
3 eetlepels muesli (recept op pagina 177), 7-10 minuten in een op 180°C voorverwarmde oven geroosterd

1. Meng de melk met de eieren, olie en vanille in een blender. Voeg de bloem, het meel en de suiker toe en draai het geheel tot een glad beslag.
2. Verhit een anti-aanbak koekepan. Schep er 3 eetlepels van het beslag in en laat het met een draaiende beweging van de pan over de bodem uitvloeien. Bak beide kanten 20-30 seconden tot ze goudbruin zijn. Laat de crêpes afkoelen op perkamentpapier. Stapel de gekoelde crêpes op met perkamentpapier ertussen tot gebruik.
3. Schep de aardbeien in een kom om met de bosbessen en bananen. Schep er de helft van de geklopte room of yoghurt door.
4. Schep royaal vulling in het midden van elke crêpe. Vouw één kant over de vulling en vouw dan de zijkanten om. Schik de crêpes met één kant open en de gevouwen kant onder op borden. Het is niet erg als wat van de vulling uit de crêpes loopt.
5. Bestuif de crêpes met de poedersuiker en schep wat aardbeiensaus om de crêpes heen. Garneer met een lepel van de overgebleven room of yoghurt. Bestrooi met de geroosterde muesli en dien onmiddellijk op.

Voor 8 personen

1 portie met room: Calorieën 270, Eiwit 7 g, Koolhydraten 42 g, Vezel 5 g, Vet totaal 5 g (Verzadigd 1 g, Enkelvoudig onverzadigd 1 g, Meervoudig onverzadigd 2 g), Cholesterol 55 mg, Natrium 50 mg, Vitamine C 100%.

▲ *1 Brood, 1 Fruit*

1 portie met yoghurt: Calorieën 230, Eiwit 7 g, Koolhydraten 42 g, Vezel 5 g, Vet totaal 5 g (Verzadigd 1 g, Enkelvoudig onverzadigd 1 g, Meervoudig onverzadigd 2 g), Cholesterol 55 mg, Natrium 50 mg, Vitamine C 100%.

▲ *1 Brood, 1 Fruit*

DRANKEN / VERENIGDE STATEN

Cranberry-gemberlimonade

60 g suiker
15 g fijngehakte verse gember
2 liter cranberrysap
1 limoen, in 8 partjes gesneden

1. Verhit de suiker in 1,8 dl water in een middelgrote pan en roer tot de suiker opgelost is. Voeg de gember toe en laat 5 minuten sudderen. Neem de pan van het vuur, leg er het deksel op en laat volledig afkoelen.
2. Zeef de gembersiroop, gooi de gember weg en meng het vocht met het cranberrysap. Zet de limoenade in de koelkast.
3. Giet de limonade over ijsblokjes in gekoelde glazen en garneer met een limoenpartje.

Voor 8 personen

1 glas per portie: Calorieën 180, Eiwit 0 g, Koolhydraten 45 g, Vezel 0 g, Vet totaal 0 g (Verzadigd 0 g, Enkelvoudig onverzadigd 0 g, Meervoudig onverzadigd 0 g), Cholesterol 0 mg, Natrium 10 mg, Vitamine C 180%.

▲ *1 Fruit, 1 Vet/Suiker*

Cobbler met vers geplukte zomervruchten

Een cobbler lijkt op een "crisp" of "crumble" maar in plaats van een kruimeldeeg wordt er een scone-achtig deeg gebruikt. Juli is waarschijnlijk de beste maand voor aardbeien, frambozen, bessensoorten en de eerste bramen.

750 g verse zomervruchten als frambozen, loganbessen, moerbezie, bramen, rode, witte en zwarte bessen, bosbessen, kruisbessen en/of plakjes aardbei
1,25 dl vers sinaasappelsap
125 g plus 2 theelepels suiker
1 theelepel geraspte sinaasappelschil
1 eetlepel maïzena in 1 eetlepel water opgelost
75 g bloem
snufje zout
½ theelepel gemalen kaneel
¾ theelepel bakpoeder
45 g boter
4 eetlepels magere melk
1,25 dl magere vanilleyoghurt

1. Verwarm de oven voor op 190°C. Vet een vierkante taartvorm van 23 cm doorsnee licht in met olie.
2. Maak het fruit schoon en doe alles in een grote kom.
3. Verhit het sinaasappelsap met 125 g van de suiker en de geraspte schil in een middelgrote pan en roer tot de suiker opgelost is. Draai het vuur lager, roer er het maïzenapapje door en laat 2 minuten sudderen tot het mengsel iets dikker is. Giet het mengsel over het fruit en schep alles voorzichtig om. Giet het mengsel in de taartvorm.
4. Schep de bloem door de rest van de suiker, wat zout, de kaneel en het bakpoeder in een grote kom. Snijd er de boter door met twee messen of een deegsnijder tot een kruimelig mengsel. Schep er snel de melk door. Schep wat van het mengsel langs de rand van de taartvorm en laat het fruit in het midden onbedekt.
5. Bak de cobbler 35-40 minuten in de oven tot het deeg goudbruin is. Dien onmiddellijk op met een schepje yoghurt.

Voor 8 personen

1 portie: Calorieën 190, Eiwit 3 g, Koolhydraten 35 g, Vezel 7 g, Vet totaal 5 g (Verzadigd 3 g, Enkelvoudig onverzadigd 1,5 g, Meervoudig onverzadigd 0,5 g), Cholesterol 15 mg, Natrium 60 mg, Vitamine C 50%.

▲ *1 Brood, 1 Fruit*

Cobbler met vers geplukte zomervruchten

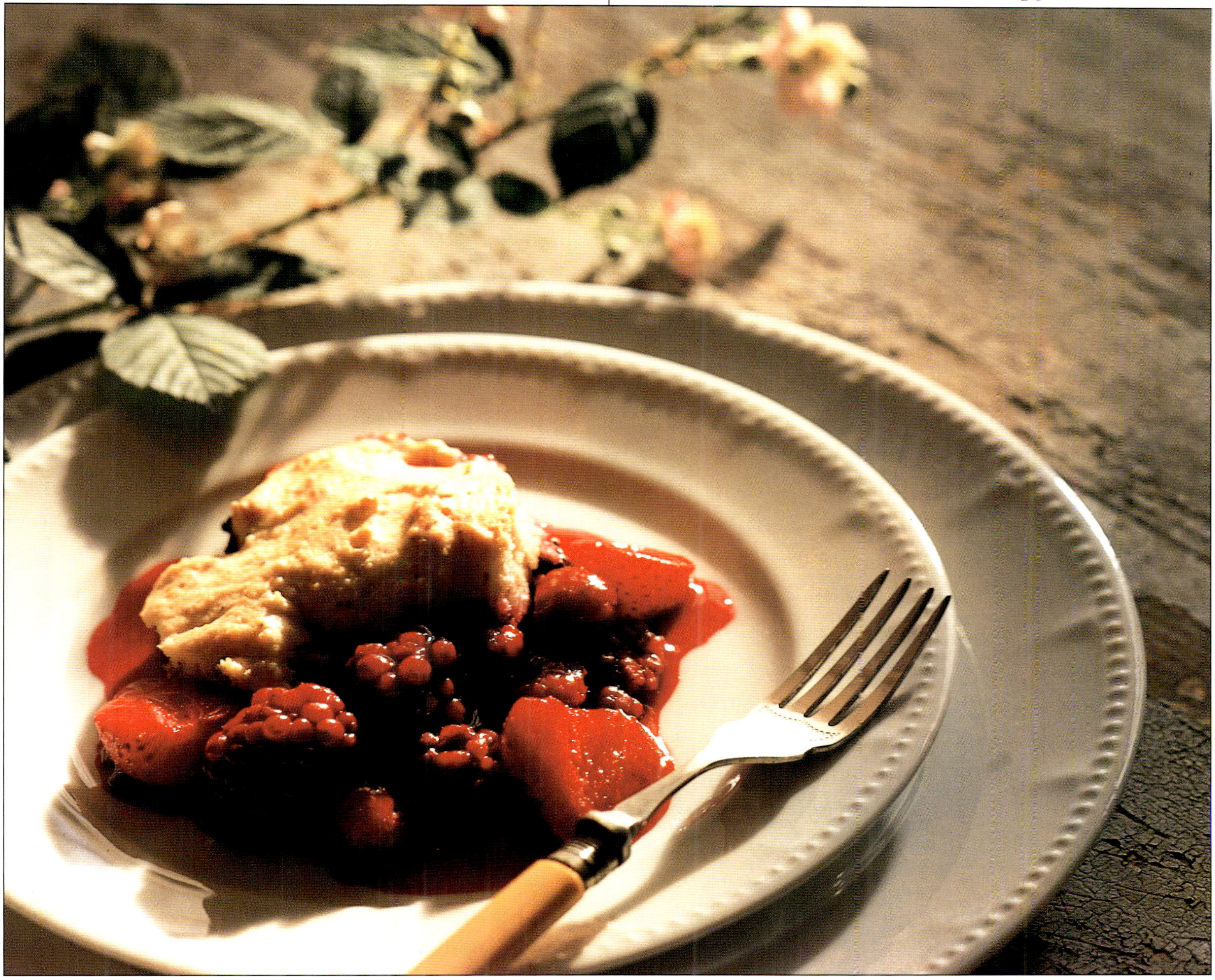

DESSERTS / FRANKRIJK

Warme abrikozensoufflé

Deze soufflé maakt indruk, maar verklap niet hoe makkelijk hij te maken is. Het fruit wordt met maïzena gebonden zodat dooiers niet nodig zijn. U kunt gedroogde abrikonen in plaats van verse gebruiken.

15 g boter, gesmolten
60 g plus 4 eetlepels suiker
6 rijpe verse abrikozen, ontpit, geschild en grof gehakt, of 185 g gedroogde abrikozen, minstens 1 uur in 1,25 dl heet water geweekt en vervolgens gepureerd
4½ theelepel maïzena, in 1 eetlepel koud water opgelost
2 eetlepels abrikozenlikeur
1 eetlepel vanille-essence
4 eiwitten
snufje wijnsteenzuur
2 eetlepels poedersuiker
poedersuiker ter garnering

1. Verwarm de oven voor op 190°C. Vet 4 soufflébakjes van 2,5 dl inhoud licht in met boter en bestuif ze met 2 eetlepels suiker.
2. Doe de rest van de suiker met 4 eetlepels water in een middelgrote pan. Breng aan de kook onder voortdurend roeren tot de suiker opgelost is. Draai het vuur lager, voeg de abrikozen of abrikozenpuree toe en laat 5 minuten sudderen tot de abrikozen gaar zijn. Voeg het maïzenapapje toe en breng al roerend aan de kook tot het mengsel dik wordt. Neem de pan van het vuur en roer er de abrikozenlikeur en vanille door. Laat afkoelen.
3. Klop de eiwitten met het wijnsteenzuur in een zuurbestendige kom tot zachte pieken. Voeg de poedersuiker toe en klop tot stijve maar niet droge pieken. Schep één derde van het geklopte eiwit voorzichtig door het abrikozenmengsel om het luchtiger te maken. Vouw er vervolgens de rest van het eiwit door.
4. Schep het eiwitmengsel in de 4 bakjes. Veeg met uw duim en wijsvinger de rand van elk bakje schoon zodat de vulling iets van de rand af is.
5. Zet de bakjes in een waterbad. Bak de soufflés 10 minuten in de oven tot ze gerezen en goudgeel zijn.
6. Bestuif de soufflés met wat poedersuiker en dien direct op.

Voor 4 personen

1 soufflé per portie: Calorieën 200, Eiwit 4 g, Koolhydraten 35 g, Vezel 1 g, Vet totaal 3 g (Verzadigd 2 g, Enkelvoudig onverzadigd 1 g, Meervoudig onverzadigd 0 g), Cholesterol 10 mg, Natrium 55 mg, Vitamine A 30%.

▲ *1 Fruit, 1 Vet/Suiker*

Perzik clafoutis

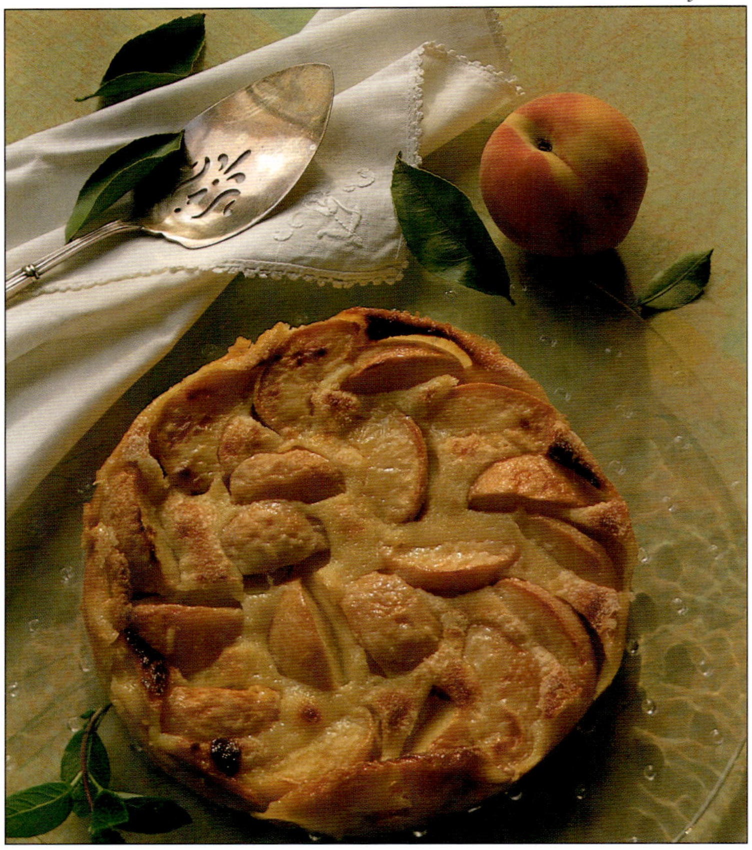

DESSERTS / ITALIË

Chocolade-sinaasappel biscotti

Sluit een maaltijd af met een paar van deze knapperige koekjes en een kopje espresso.

125 g margarine
750 g suiker
4 eierdooiers
3 eetlepels geraspte sinaasappelschil
4 eetlepels vers sinaasappelsap
470 g bloem
90 g ongezoete cacao, gezeefd
2 eetlepels bakpoeder
2 theelepels gemalen kaneel
150 g pijnboompitten, geroosterd

1. Verwarm de oven voor op 190°C. Vet een bakplaat van 25 x 38 cm licht in met olie en bestuif hem dan licht met bloem.
2. Klop de margarine met de suiker met een elektrische handmixer. Voeg de dooiers toe en klop tot een luchtig mengsel. Voeg de sinaasappelschil en het sap toe en klop alles glad.
3. Meng de bloem in een kom met de cacao, het bakpoeder, de kaneel en pijnboompitten.
4. Schep de droge ingrediënten door het beslag tot alles net gemengd is. Strijk het mengsel uit op de bakplaat en bak 15-20 minuten in de oven tot een ingestoken mes er schoon uitkomt.
5. Neem de bakplaat uit de oven en zet de temperatuur op 150°C. Snijd de cake in de lengte in 4 repen en overdwars in 12 stukken voor 48 stukjes van 3 x 6 cm. Zet elk stukje op zijn zijkant en bak ze 30-35 minuten in de oven tot ze knapperig en droog zijn. Laat ze op een rooster afkoelen.

Voor 48 koekjes

1 biscotti per portie: Calorieën 115, Eiwit 2 g, Koolhydraten 20 g, Vezel 1 g, Vet totaal 4 g (Verzadigd 1 g, Enkelvoudig onverzadigd 1,5 g, Meervoudig onverzadigd 1 g), Cholesterol 20 mg, Natrium 5 mg.

▲ *1 Brood*

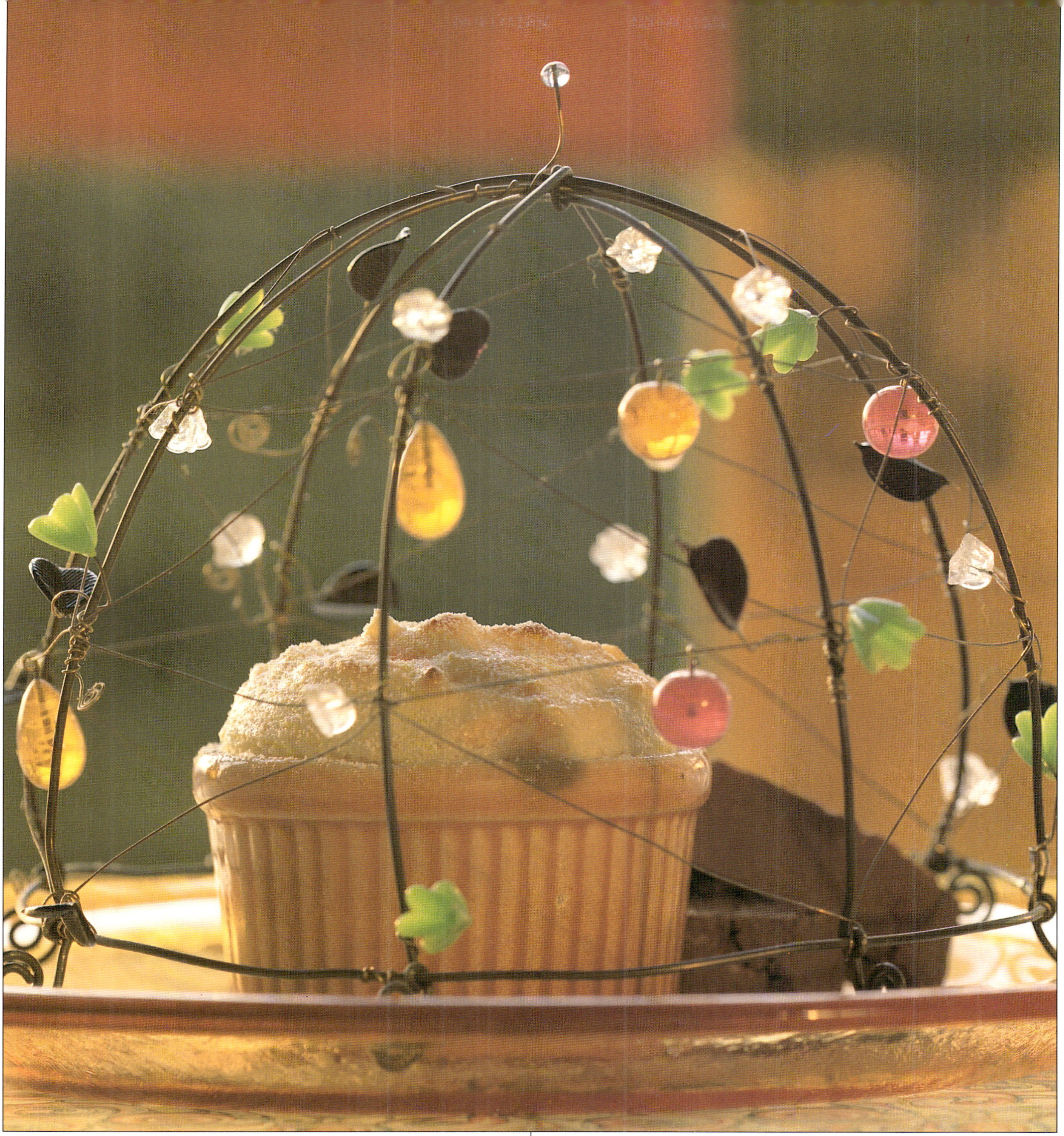

Van links naar rechts: Warme abrikozensoufflé, Chocolade-sinaasappel biscotti

Perzik clafoutis

De klassieke kersen clafoutis *komt uit de Limousin in Frankrijk.* Clafoutis *is een kruising tussen pudding en cake en kan met een soort fruit in seizoen naar keuze gemaakt worden. Deze versie wordt met perzik gemaakt; pruimen zijn ook heel geschikt.*

4 grote verse perziken (circa 750 g), geschild
125 g plus 2 eetlepels suiker
2 eieren
3 dl magere melk
1 theelepel vanille-essence
150 g bloem, gezeefd
poedersuiker, ter garnering

1. Verwarm de oven voor op 180°C. Vet een ronde taartvorm van 23 cm doorsnee licht in met olie.
2. Halveer de perziken en verwijder de pitten. Schik de helften met de snijknt onder strak naast elkaar in de vorm. Bestrooi ze met 2 eetlepels suiker en zet weg.
3. Klop 60 g van de suiker met de eieren luchtig in een grote kom; voeg de melk en vanille toe. Voeg de bloem toe en klop goed.
4. Giet het beslag over de perziken en bak 20 minuten in de oven. Bestrooi met de rest van de suiker en bak nog 15-20 minuten tot de suiker gekarameliseerd is.
5. Laat tot lauw afkoelen, bestuif met poedersuiker en dien op.

Voor 6 personen

1 portie: Calorieën 240, Eiwit 7 g, Koolhydraten 49 g, Vezel 2 g, Vet totaal 3 g (Verzadigd 1 g, Enkelvoudig onverzadigd 1 g, Meervoudig onverzadigd 0,5 g), Cholesterol 75 mg, Natrium 50 mg.

▲ *1 Brood, 1 Fruit*

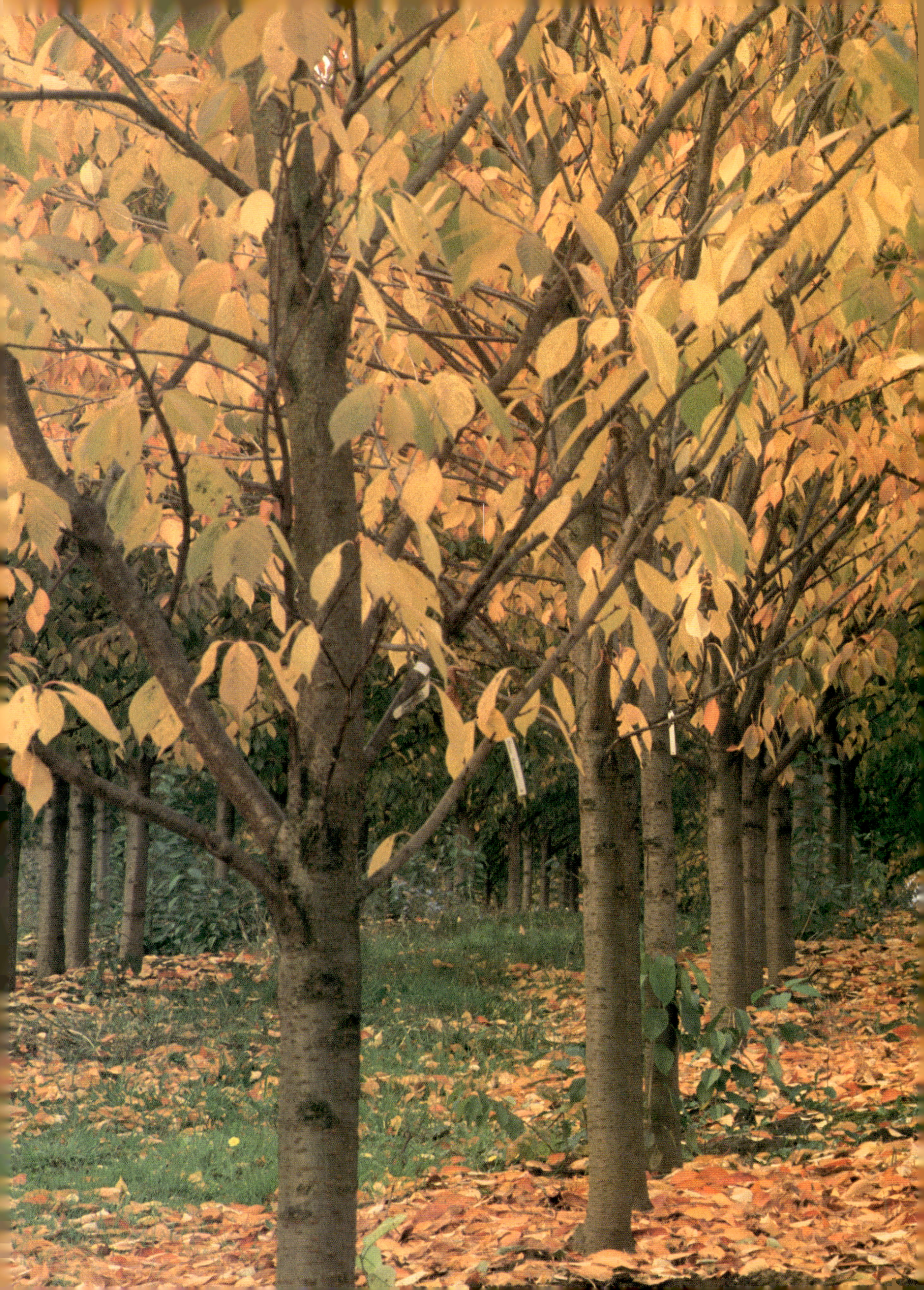

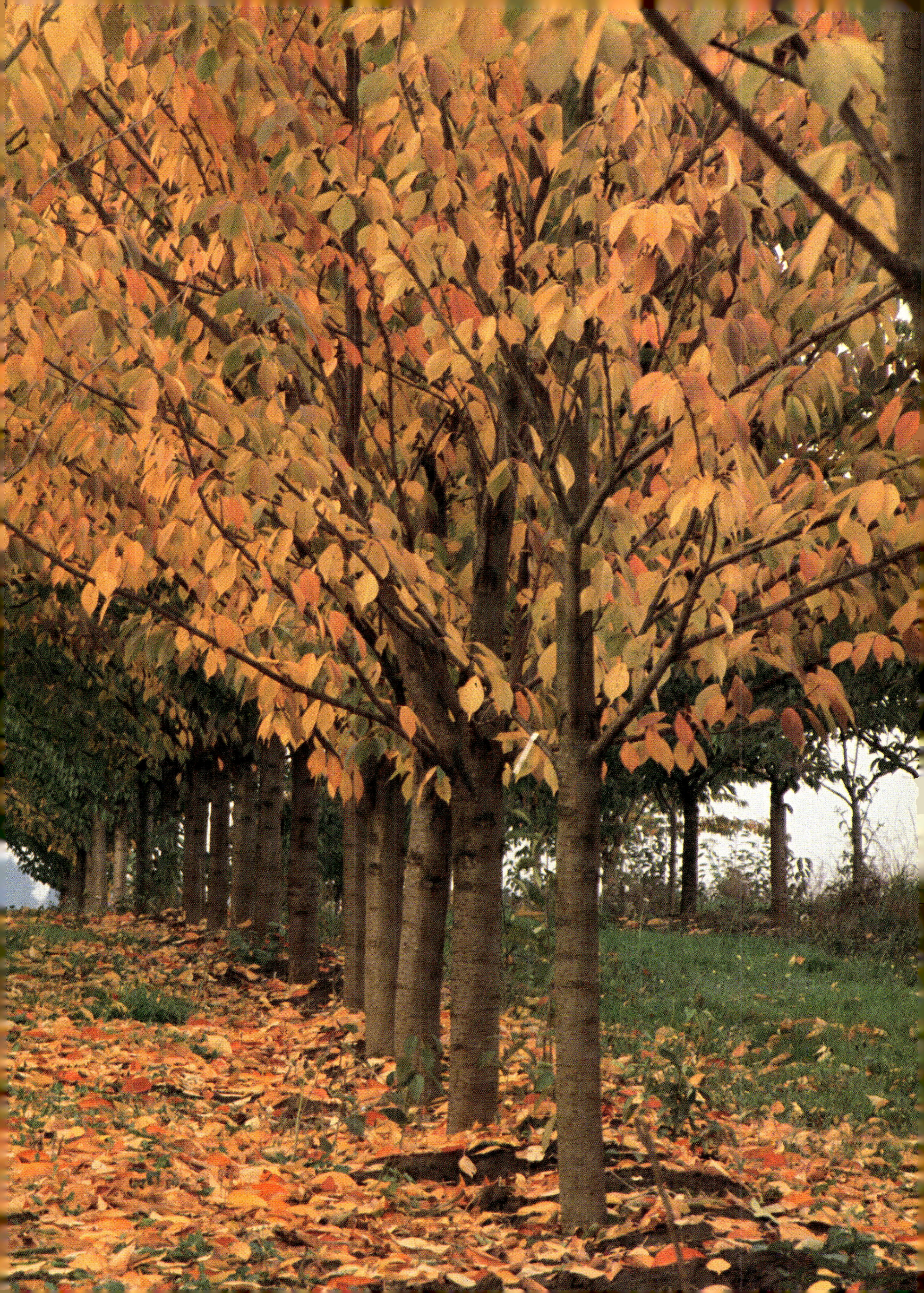

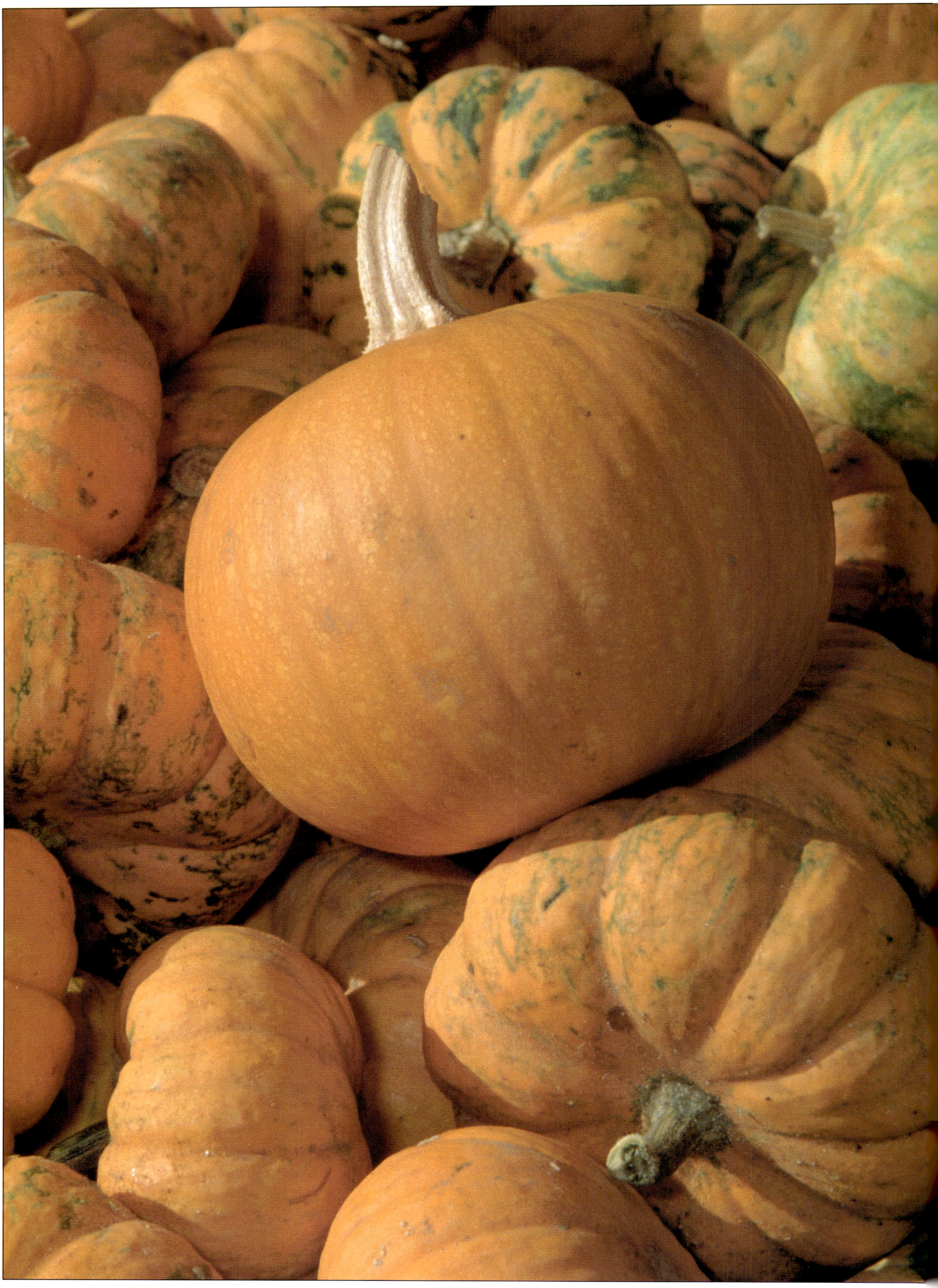

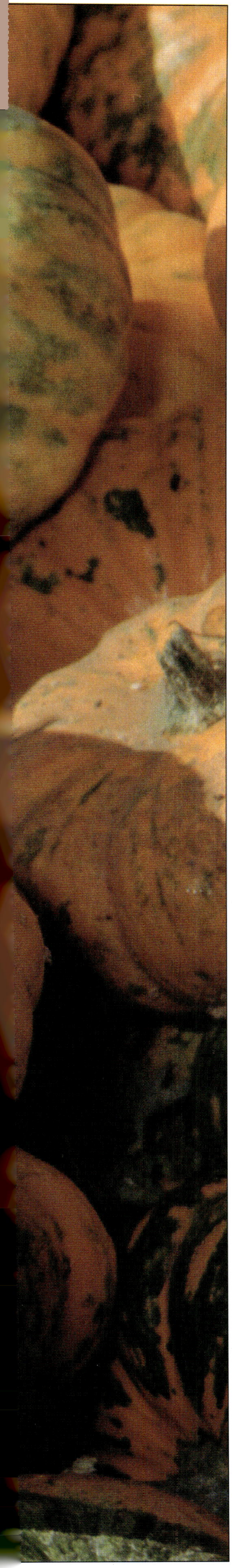

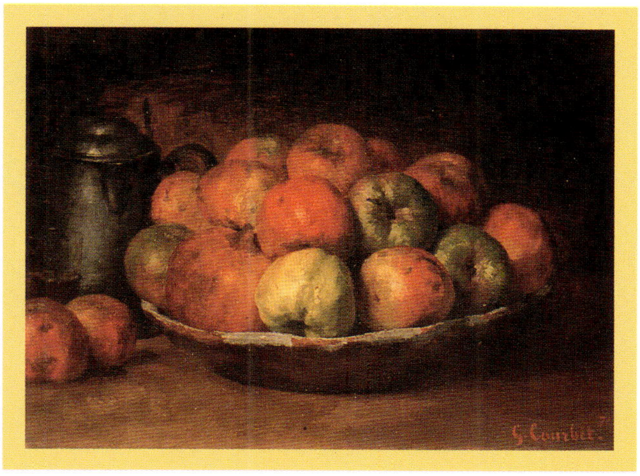

Herfst

Seizoen van mist en zoete volheid,
Boezemvriend van de rijpende zon,
Die met hem de zegening voorbereidt
Van fruit aan de wingerd bij huizen rondom.

— **John Keats, *To Autumn***

Wanneer het sprekende groen en de regenboogtinten van de zomer overgaan in pompoen-oranje, roestbruin en goud, is het tijd voor hartiger schotels.

Benut de opbrengst van de seizoensoogst aan appels. Maak met de altijd geliefde Golden Delicious een pâté met kip en appel. Kies voor latkes uit de oven met gekruide appels bijvoorbeeld Granny Smith of Cox Orange.

Denk voor koele avonden aan soepen en stoofschotels. *Pistou tomate,* een Franse verwant van de Italiaanse pesto, is een ideale manier om de rijpe tomaten van het eind van het seizoen te verwerken. De *pistou* zorgt voor smaak in een hartige groentesoep. Probeer uit Midden- en Zuid-Amerika *Pepián verde de pollo y chocla,* een stoofpot van kip en maïs. Het geheime ingrediënt *pepitas* (pompoenpitten).

Voor een feestmaal hebt u volop keuze: probeer eens kalkoenschnitzels met pruim, salie en prei. De schnitzels kunt u grilleren. Geef er met mosterd geglaceerde kastanjes, spruitjes en waspeen bij.

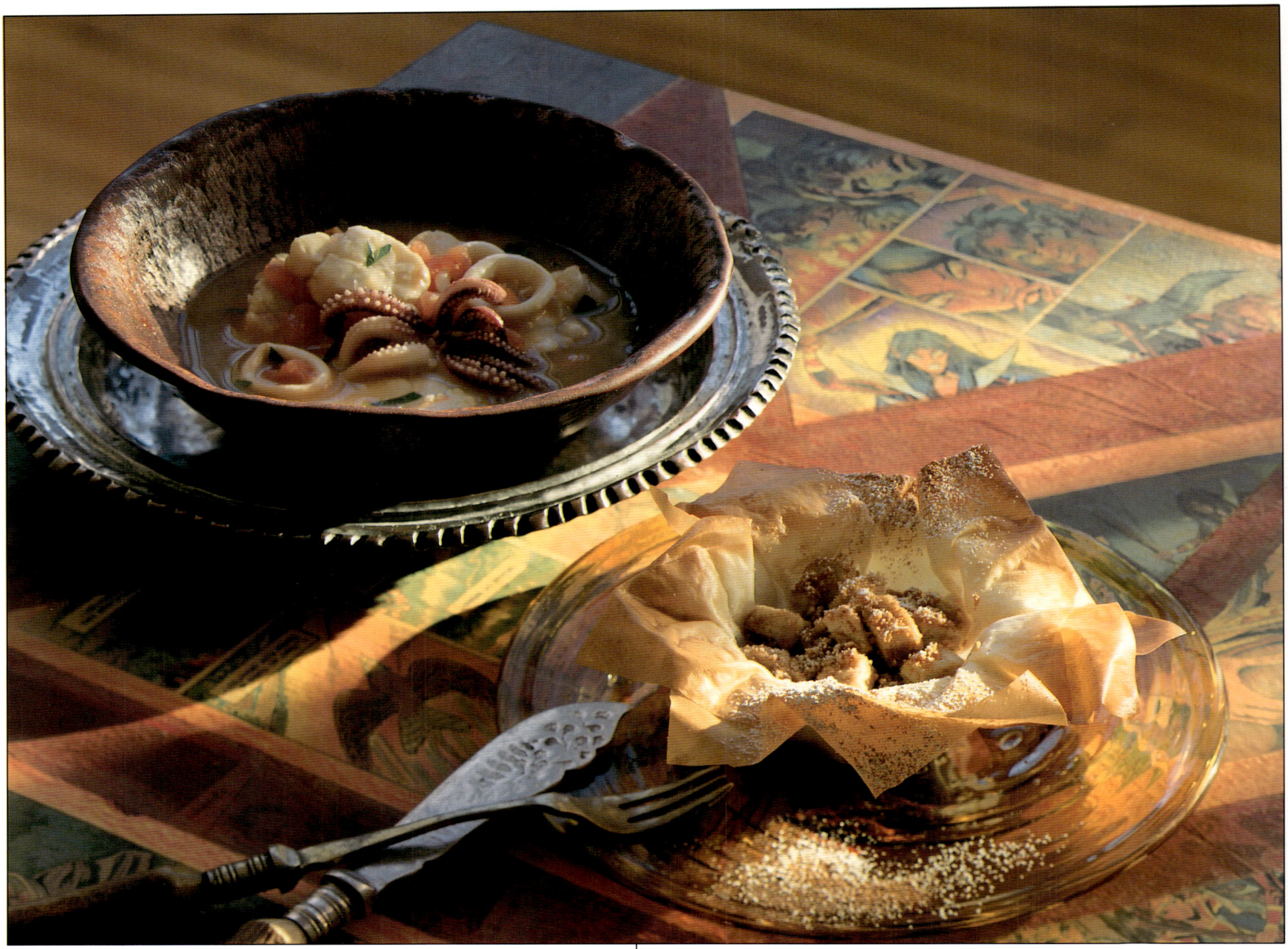

Van links naar rechts: Catalaanse vissoep, B'stilla

HAPJES / MAROKKO

B'stilla

In Marokko wordt deze zoete en hartige filo-taart boven houtskool gebakken en dan uit het vuistje gegeten, als symbool van broederschap. U kunt voor een feestje van tevoren individuele filobakjes maken en ze uit de hand eten volgens de traditie van het land van oorsprong. In dit recept wordt om het gehalte aan verzadigd vet te verminderen saffloerolie voor het inkwasten van het filodeeg gebruikt in plaats van de traditionele boter.

5 dl kippebouillon (zie woordenlijst)
500 g kipfilet
1 ui, gesnipperd
45 g grof gehakte champignons
2 eetlepels fijngehakte verse peterselie
snufje saffraandraden
3 eieren, losgeklopt
80 g amandelen, geroosterd en gemalen
1 eetlepel suiker
1 eetlepel plus ½ theelepel gemalen kaneel
¼ theelepel gemberpoeder
¼ theelepel gemalen koriander
250 g vers of bevroren filodeeg
3 eetlepels saffloerolie
30 g poedersuiker

1. Verwarm de oven voor op 200°C. Vet 2 anti-aanbak muffinblikken licht in met olie.
2. Doe de kippebouillon in een grote pan en breng aan de kook. Voeg de kipfilet, ui, champignons, peterselie en saffraan toe. Draai het vuur laag en laat de kip in circa 20 minuten gaar pocheren. Neem de kip uit het vocht en laat afkoelen. Laat de bouillon sudderen, voeg al kloppend de eieren toe (die gaan stollen) en laat circa 10 minuten sudderen tot ze romig zijn. Zeef het mengsel en bewaar het kooknat. Doe het groenten-eimengsel in een kleine kom met 1,25 dl van het kooknat en zet weg.
3. Snijd de afgekoelde kip in blokjes en zet weg.
4. Meng de amandelen in een kommetje met de suiker, ½ theelepel van de kaneel, het gemberpoeder en de koriander en zet weg.
5. Snijd het filodeeg in vierkantjes van 15 cm. Kwast 1 stuk licht in met de olie. Herhaal met nog 3 stukken en stapel ze op elkaar, waarbij u ze iedere keer een kwart slag draait. Leg elk stapeltje van 4 in een muffinvorm en druk de bodem voorzichtig aan. Maak de rest van de deegbakjes op dezelfde manier.
6. Vul elk bakje met een schepje eimengsel, een laag kipblokjes en bestrooi met wat amandelmengsel. Vouw de deeghoekjes over de vulling, kwast het deeg licht in met wat olie en bak ze in 15 minuten in de oven goudbruin.
7. Doe de taartjes op een voorverwarmde dienschaal. Meng de

poedersuiker met de rest van de kaneel, zeef dit mengsel over de *b'stilla* en dien onmiddellijk op.

Voor 24 *b'stilla*

1 b'stilla *per portie: Calorieën 110, Eiwit 7 g, Koolhydraten 9 g, Vezel 1 g, Vet totaal 5 g (Verzadigd 1 g, Enkelvoudig onverzadigd 2 g, Meervoudig onverzadigd 2 g), Cholesterol 40 mg, Natrium 65 mg.*

▲ *½ Brood, ½ Vlees*

Soep / Spanje

Catalaanse vissoep

Gebruik voor deze Spaanse vissoep uitsluitend zeer verse vis. Geschikte vissoorten zijn onder andere zonnevis, heek, tong, heilbot en verschillende schelpdieren. Vis bevat veel selenium, een spoorelement dat samen met vitamine E celbeschadiging en veroudering vertraagt.

250 g zeeduivel, in stukken van 5 cm
500 g tandbaars, in stukken van 5 cm
1 kleine inktvis (circa 100 g), schoongemaakt, overdwars in ringen gesneden, of 100 g bevroren inktvis
het sap van 1 citroen
3 eetlepels olijfolie
1 grote ui, gehakt
5 tenen knoflook, fijngehakt
1 aardappel, geschild en in blokjes
1 wortel, geschild en in blokjes
1,25 dl droge witte wijn
7,5 dl visbouillon (zie woordenlijst)
⅛ theelepel gemalen saffraan
250 g tomaten, ontveld, ontzaad en grof gehakt
3 eetlepels fijngehakte peterselie
¼ theelepel zout
versgemalen peper naar smaak

1. Doe de zeeduivel, tandbaars en inktvis in een zuurbestendige kom. Voeg het citroensap toe, schep om en zet weg.
2. Verhit de olijfolie in een grote koekepan. Fruit er de ui en knoflook in tot ze gaar maar niet bruin zijn. Voeg de aardappel en wortel toe en bak 2 minuten op een middelhoog vuur.
3. Blus de pan af met de wijn en kook tot de wijn bijna verdampt is.
4. Verhit de visbouillon in een middelgrote pan. Roer er de saffraan door tot die opgelost is. Giet de bouillon in de koekepan, voeg de tomaten en peterselie toe en breng aan de kook. Laat alles 10-15 minuten sudderen tot de groenten gaar zijn.
5. Voeg de stukken vis toe en begin met de dikste stukken. Sudder 5-7 minuten of tot de stukken vis stevig aanvoelen en gaar zijn. Breng op smaak met zout en peper. Dien onmiddellijk op uit een voorverwarmde terrine.

Voor 6 personen

2,5 dl per portie: Calorieën 230, Eiwit 24 g, Koolhydraten 13 g, Vezel 2 g, Vet totaal 9 g (Verzadigd 1 g, Enkelvoudig onverzadigd 5 g, Meervoudig onverzadigd 1 g), Cholesterol 70 mg, Natrium 160 mg, Vitamine A 70%, Vitamine C 35%.

▲ *1 Groente, 1 Vlees*

Zeebanket / Joegoslavië

Snapper in tomatensaus

Passeer rijpe, zoete tomaten door een roerzeef om de zaden en schil te verwijderen voor deze heerlijke en eenvoudige saus.

1 hele rode snapper, gefileerd, of vier filets van 185 g
1 eetlepel vers citroensap
⅛ theelepel zout
versgemalen peper naar smaak
1 eetlepel saffloerolie
30 g gehakte ui
2 tenen knoflook, fijngehakt
250 g snijbiet, stelen verwijderd en gehakt
5 eetlepels droge rode wijn
500 g rijpe tomaten, ontveld en gepureerd
2 eetlepels fijngehakte verse peterselie

1. Verwarm de oven voor op 180°C. Vet een ondiepe ovenschaal licht in met olie. Schik de filets naast elkaar in de schaal, sprenkel er het citroensap over en bestrooi met zout en peper.
2. Verhit de olie in een middelgrote koekepan. Fruit er de ui en knoflook in tot ze gaar zijn. Voeg de snijbiet toe en bak 3 minuten op een laag vuur. Giet er de wijn bij en kook 5 minuten tot de wijn iets ingekookt is. Schep er de tomaten en peterselie door en laat 5 minuten sudderen. Giet dit mengsel over de vis.
3. Bak alles 30 minuten in de oven, of tot de vis gaar is.

Voor 4 personen

1 portie: Calorieën 250, Eiwit 37 g, Koolhydraten 9 g, Vezel 2 g, Vet totaal 6 g (Verzadigd 1 g, Enkelvoudig onverzadigd 1 g, Meervoudig onverzadigd 3,5 g), Cholesterol 65 mg, Natrium 320 mg, Vitamine A 50%, Vitamine C 70%.

▲ *1 Groente, 1 Vlees*

Van boven naar beneden: Snapper in tomatensaus, Bonensoep (recept pagina 150)

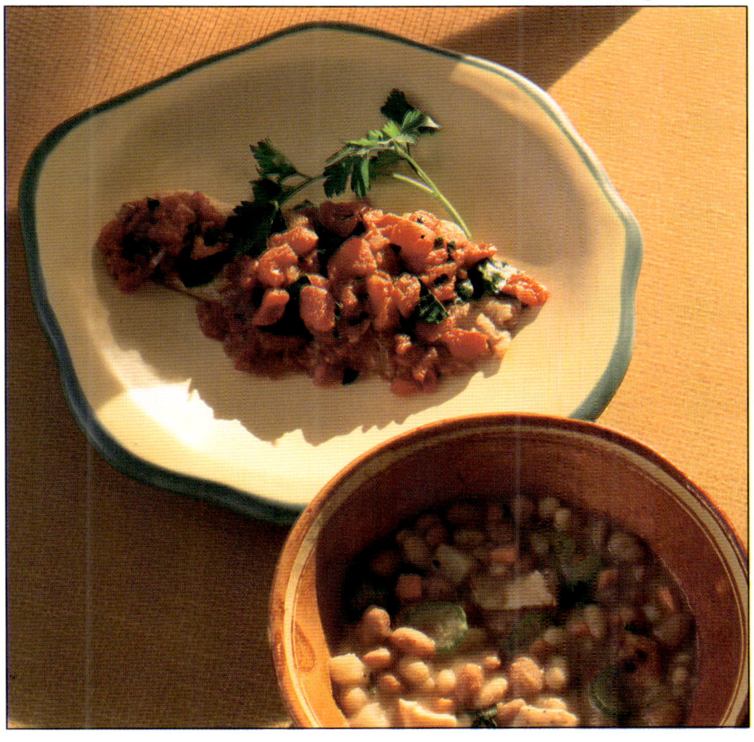

SOEP / SERVIË

Bonensoep

Gegrild vlees is een specialiteit van Servië en wordt in deze maaltijdsoep verwerkt. Door roosteren van kip aan het bot versterkt u de smaak, en door het vel te verwijderen verlaagt u het vetgehalte. Dit is een uitstekende manier om restjes gegrilde kip te verwerken. Serveer deze soep met een komkommer-tomatensalade voor een volledige en voedzame maaltijd.

250 g gedroogde kleine witte bonen
250 g gedroogde pinto-, kievits-, of nierbonen
750 g kipfilet
½ citroen
versgemalen zwarte peper naar smaak
3 eetlepels olijfolie
1 ui, gehakt
4 tenen knoflook, fijngehakt
2 liter kippebouillon (zie woordenlijst)
1 aardappel, geschild en in blokjes
2 wortels, geschild en in blokjes
2 stengels bleekselderij, in plakjes
4 eetlepels vers citroensap
¼ theelepel gedroogde tijm
¼ theelepel zout

1. Week de bonen een nacht. Giet ze af. Verwarm de grill voor.
2. Wrijf de kipfilet in met de citroenhelft. Bestrooi de kip met peper en grilleer of barbecue 12-15 minuten onder af en toe omkeren tot de kip gaar is. Neem de kip van het vuur, laat afkoelen en snijd vervolgens in stukken.
3. Verhit de olijfolie in een grote soeppan. Doe er de ui en knoflook in en fruit ze goudgeel. Voeg de bonen en kippebouillon toe, breng aan de kook en laat dan 1 uur sudderen.
4. Voeg de aardappel, wortel en bleekselderij toe en laat in circa 20 minuten gaar sudderen. Voeg de stukken kip, het citroensap, de tijm, het zout en wat peper toe. Verwarm alles en serveer in voorverwarmde soepborden.

Voor 12 personen *Foto op pagina 149*

2,5 dl per portie: Calorieën 250, Eiwit 19 g, Koolhydraten 31 g, Vezel 5 g, Vet totaal 6 g (Verzadigd 1 g, Enkelvoudig onverzadigd 3,5 g, Meervoudig onverzadigd 1 g), Cholesterol 30 mg, Natrium 95 mg, Vitamine A 70%.
▲ *1 Groente, 1 Vlees*

SOEP / CARIBISCH GEBIED

Callaloo

BLADGROENTEN-KROONSLAKSOEP

Callaloo (calalú) *is de naam van de bladen van de taroplant. Deze groente is buiten het Caribisch gebied nauwelijks verkrijgbaar, behalve misschien in blik, maar u kunt er verse spinazie of snijbiet voor in de plaats gebruiken. Madame Jeanette chilipepers zijn superheet. Draag plastic handschoenen wanneer u ze schoonmaakt en gebruik ze in deze soep naar smaak.*

3 eetlepels saffloerolie
1 grote ui, gesnipperd
½ Madame Jeanette chilipeper, ontzaad en fijngehakt
3 tenen knoflook, fijngehakt
1 liter kippebouillon (zie woordenlijst)
125 g geschilde en in blokjes van 1 cm gesneden pompoen
150 g cassave of aardappel, geschild en in blokjes van ½ cm gesneden
185 g kroonslak (conch) vlees, of een schelpdier naar keuze, in blokjes van 1 cm gesneden
185 g gaar kipvlees, in blokjes
½ theelepel gedroogde tijm
4 eetlepels vers limoensap
250 g vers *callaloo*-blad of verse spinazie, gehakt
zout en versgemalen peper naar smaak

1. Verhit de saffloerolie in een grote soeppan. Doe er de ui, Madame Jeanette en knoflook in. Fruit circa 5 minuten tot ze gaar maar niet bruin zijn. Voeg de bouillon toe en breng aan de kook.
2. Draai het vuur lager, voeg de pompoen toe en laat 15 minuten sudderen. Voeg de cassave, kroonslak, kip en tijm toe en sudder 20 minuten.
3. Schep er het limoensap en de groente door; laat 5 minuten doorwarmen en breng op smaak met zout en peper. Dien op.

Voor 6 personen

2,5 dl per portie: Calorieën 240, Eiwit 17 g, Koolhydraten 20 g, Vezel 4 g, Vet totaal 10 g (Verzadigd 1,5 g, Enkelvoudig onverzadigd 1,5 g, Meervoudig onverzadigd 6 g), Cholesterol 70 mg, Natrium 110 mg, IJzer 20%, Vitamine A 90%, Vitamine C 70%.
▲ *1 Groente, 1 Vlees*

SOEP / FINLAND

Kalakeitto

ZALM IN AARDAPPELSOEP

Scandinaviërs verwerken zalm op vele manieren. Deze eenvoudige romige soep is een favoriet en is zeer geschikt als een licht hoofdgerecht. Gele Finse aardappels zijn heel romig en binden de soep, maar u kunt rustig een andere aardappelsoort gebruiken.

1 liter visbouillon (zie woordenlijst)
500 g gele Finse aardappels, geschild en in blokjes
30 g boter of margarine
1 ui, gehakt
5 dl magere melk
375 g zalmfilet, in blokjes van 1 cm gesneden
1,25 dl droge witte wijn
15 g gesnipperde verse dille
zout en versgemalen peper naar smaak

1. Breng de visbouillon aan de kook in een grote soeppan. Voeg de aardappels toe, breng weer aan de kook en laat de aardappels

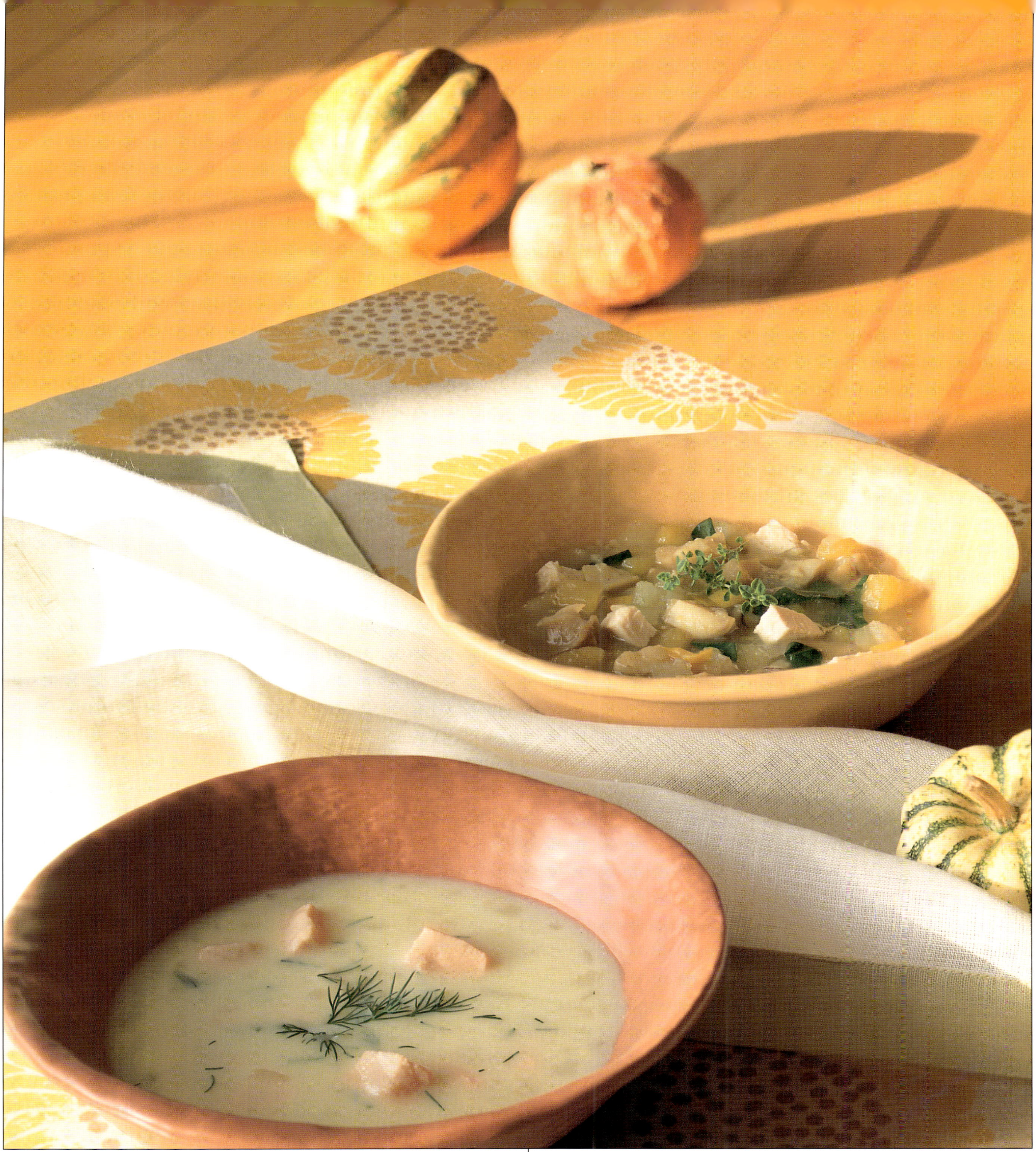

Van boven naar beneden: Bladgroenten-kroonslaksoep, Zalm in aardappelsoep

vervolgens in 15-20 minuten gaar sudderen.

2. Verhit de boter in een middelgrote pan en fruit er de ui in tot die gaar maar niet bruin is. Voeg de bloem toe en roerbak 3-4 minuten. Voeg al roerend de melk toe en laat onder voortdurend roeren circa 3 minuten sudderen tot een dik mengsel. Roer dit mengsel door de bouillon.
3. Voeg de zalm en wijn toe en kook 2 mionuten tot de zalm gaar is. Schep er de dille door en breng op smaak met zout en peper. Dien onmiddellijk op.

Voor 6 personen

2,5 dl per portie: Calorieën 270, Eiwit 17 g, Koolhydraten 26 g, Vezel 2 g, Vet totaal 10 g (Verzadigd 4 g, Enkelvoudig onverzadigd 4 g, Meervoudig onverzadigd 1,5 g), Cholesterol 50 mg, Natrium 80 mg.

▲ *1 Groente, 1 Vlees, ½ Melk*

Hapjes / Rusland

Piroshki

In Rusland en Polen worden deze pasteitjes geserveerd met soep of alleen als een licht hoofdgerecht. Kleine piroshki's zijn ook heel geschikt als hapje. Serveer ze met appelsaus of yoghurt die u hebt gemengd met wat mierikswortel.

Deeg

1 pakje (7 g) droge gist
2 theelepels suiker
1,25 dl magere melk, verwarmd tot 40°-46°C
280 g bloem
1 ei
½ theelepel zout
1 eetlepel saffloerolie

Vulling

3 eetlepels saffloerolie
75 g gesnipperde ui
1 eetlepel bloem
1,25 dl kippebouillon (zie woordenlijst)
15 g bloemkoolroosjes, geblancheerd (zie woordenlijst)
15 g broccoliroosjes, geblancheerd (zie woordenlijst)
1 kleine koolraap of meiraap, geschild, in blokjes en 2 minuten geblancheerd (zie woordenlijst)
1 kleine aardappel, geschild, in blokjes en geblancheerd (zie woordenlijst)
1 grote wortel, geschild, in blokjes en geblancheerd (zie woordenlijst)
1 eetlepel gehakte verse peterselie
zout en versgemalen peper naar smaak

1. Verwarm de oven voor op 200°C. Bekleed een bakplaat met perkamentpapier.
2. Los voor het deeg de gist en de suiker op in de melk. Laat 5 minuten staan tot een schuimig mengsel. Voeg 150 g van de bloem toe en klop tot een glad mengsel. Dek de kom af en laat 30 minuten staan.
3. Klop het ei met het zout en de ene eetlepel olie en klop door het gistmengsel. Schep er geleidelijk de rest van de bloem door. Doe het deeg op een licht met bloem bestoven werkvlak en kneed het deeg circa 5 minuten tot het glad en elastisch is. Doe het deeg in een licht met olie ingevette kom, dek die af en laat het deeg circa 1 uur staan tot het in volume verdubbeld is.
4. Verhit de 3 eetlepels olie in een pan en fruit er de ui gaar in. Roer er de ene eetlepel bloem door en roerbak in 3 minuten lichtbruin. Voeg de kippebouillon toe en roer tot het mengsel wat dikker is.
5. Schep er de bloemkool, broccoli, raap, aardappel en wortel door. Voeg de peterselie toe en breng het geheel op smaak met zout en peper.
6. Druk de lucht uit het deeg en verdeel het in 12 stukjes. Rol ze tot 3 mm dik uit op een met bloem bestoven werkvlak.
7. Schep een eetlepel van de vulling in het midden van elk rondje. Vouw de stukjes deeg in tweeën en knijp de randen dicht. Druk de randen met de tanden van een vork aan om het deeg goed dicht te maken. Schik de piroshki op de bakplaat en laat ze circa 20 minuten rijzen.
8. Bak ze 15 minuten in de oven. Zet de oven op 190°C en bak nog 10 minuten tot ze goudbruin zijn. Dien onmiddellijk op.

Voor 12 piroshki's

1 piroshki per portie: Calorieën 140, Eiwit 4 g, Koolhydraten 20 g, Vezel 2 g, Vet totaal 5 g (Verzadigd 0,5 g, Enkelvoudig onverzadigd 1 g, Meervoudig onverzadigd 3,5 g), Cholesterol 20 mg, Natrium 125 mg, Vitamine A 50%.

▲ *1 Brood*

Granen / Oekraïne

Kasha timbales

Geroosterde boekweitgrutten met prei, champignons en rodekool

Hele of geplette boekweit heeft een uitgesproken nootachtige smaak en is een smakelijk alternatief voor rijst. Boekweit bevat veel magnesium, een mineraal dat goed is voor de bloeddruk. Door de kasha voor het koken met eiwit te mengen, houdt u de korrels mooi rul. Als u een romig gerecht verkiest, kunt u die stap overslaan. Kasha is niet hetzelfde als kashi, een commercieel granenmengsel. Kashi levert wel een lekkere pilaf op en u kunt hem in dit recept in plaats van kasha gebruiken.

8 grote rodekoolbladen
170 g hele kasha (geroosterde boekweitgrutten)
1 eiwit, losgeklopt
5 dl kokende kippebouillon (zie woordenlijst)
1 wortel, geschild en in blokjes
½ theelepel gedroogde tijm
3 eetlepels saffloerolie
2 preien, alleen het wit, in dunne plakken
250 g champignons, bijgesneden en gehakt
¼ theelepel zout
versgemalen peper naar smaak
60 g krenten of sultanarozijnen
30 g grof gehakte walnoten

1. Verwarm de oven voor op 180°C. Vet 8 rechte timbaalvormpjes van 1,25 dl inhoud licht in met olie.
2. Blancheer de koolbladen circa 4 minuten in kokend water tot ze net gaar zijn. Dompel ze onmiddellijk in ijswater en dep ze droog met schone theedoeken. Zet een timbaaltje ondersteboven op elk koolblad en snijd er een passende cirkel uit. Doe de cirkel koolblad in elk timbaaltje en druk hem stevig tegen de bodem; hij zal iets boven de randen uitkomen. Zet weg. Hak de kool afsnijsels en zet ze weg.
3. Schep de kasha met het eiwit in een middelgrote kom tot de grutten er helemaal mee bedekt zijn. Verhit een grote koekepan en roerbak er de kasha in tot het eiwit droogt en de korrels rul zijn. Draai het vuur laag. Voeg de kippebouillon, wortel en tijm toe. Leg het deksel op de pan en laat alles circa 20 minuten sudderen tot het vocht geabsorbeerd is en de kasha gaar is.
4. Verhit intussen de olie in een grote koekepan; doe er de prei in en fruit die in 8-10 minuten goudbruin op een middelhoog vuur. Voeg de champignons toe en bak circa 10 minuten tot ze gaar

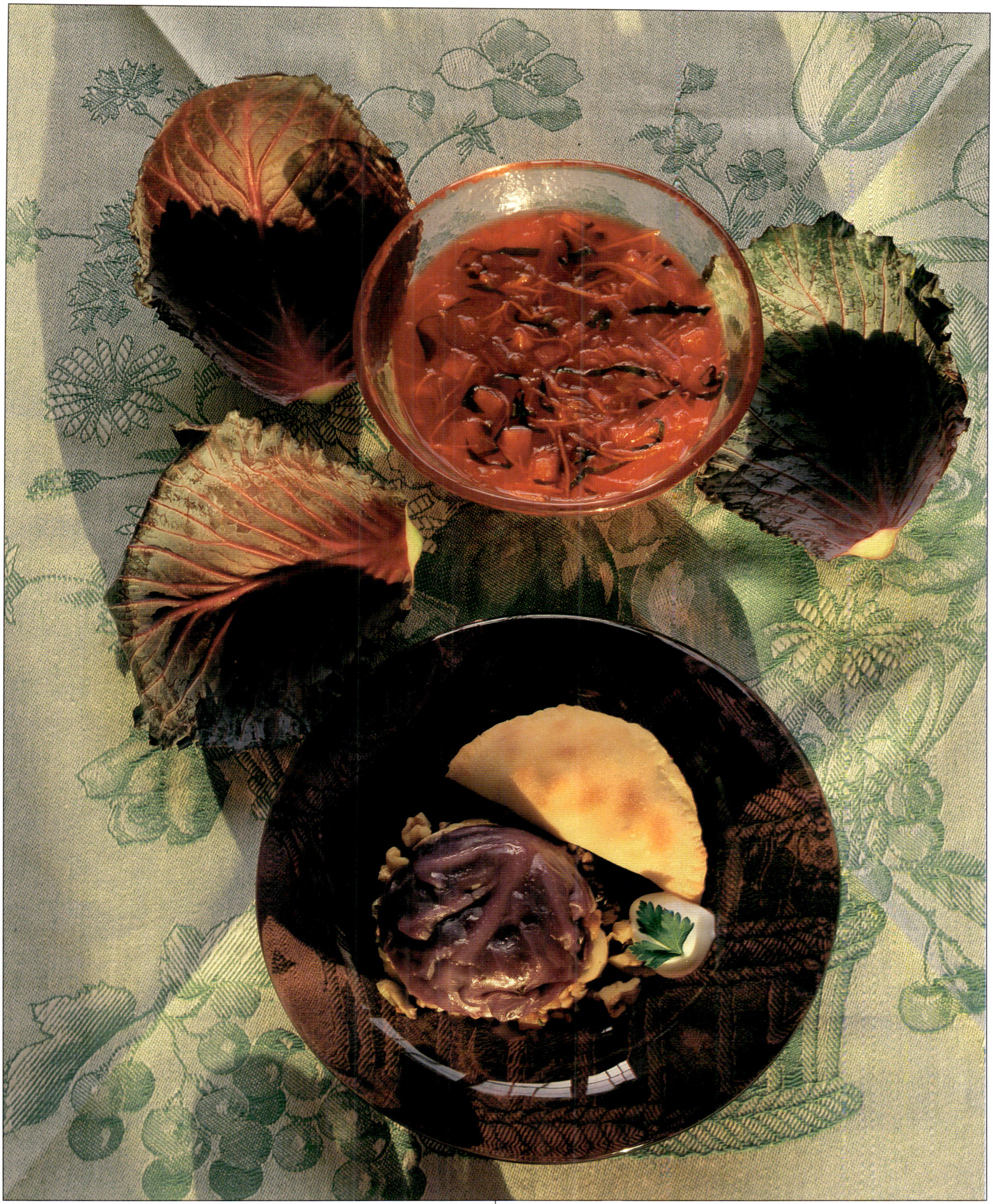

Van boven naar beneden: Borsjt (recept pagina 155), Piroshki, Geroosterde boekweitgrutten met prei, champignons en rodekool

zijn en het vocht verdampt is. Breng op smaak met zout en peper. Schep er de krenten en de bewaarde gehakte kool door. Schep het preimengsel om met de kasha.

5. Schep het kashamengsel in de timbaaltjes en druk het mengsel stevig aan. Bestrooi met de gehakte walnoten en druk die licht aan. Zet de timbaaltjes tot de helft in een waterbad en bak 20 minuten in de oven tot ze door en door warm zijn. Maak de randen los met een mes en stort ze op individuele borden.

Voor 8 personen

---

1 timbaal per portie. Calorieën 200, Eiwit 6 g, Koolhydraten 29 g, Vezel 2 g, Vet totaal 9 g (Verzadigd 1 g, Enkelvoudig onverzadigd 1,5 g, Meervoudig onverzadigd 6 g), Cholesterol 0 mg, Natrium 95 mg.

▲ *1 Brood*

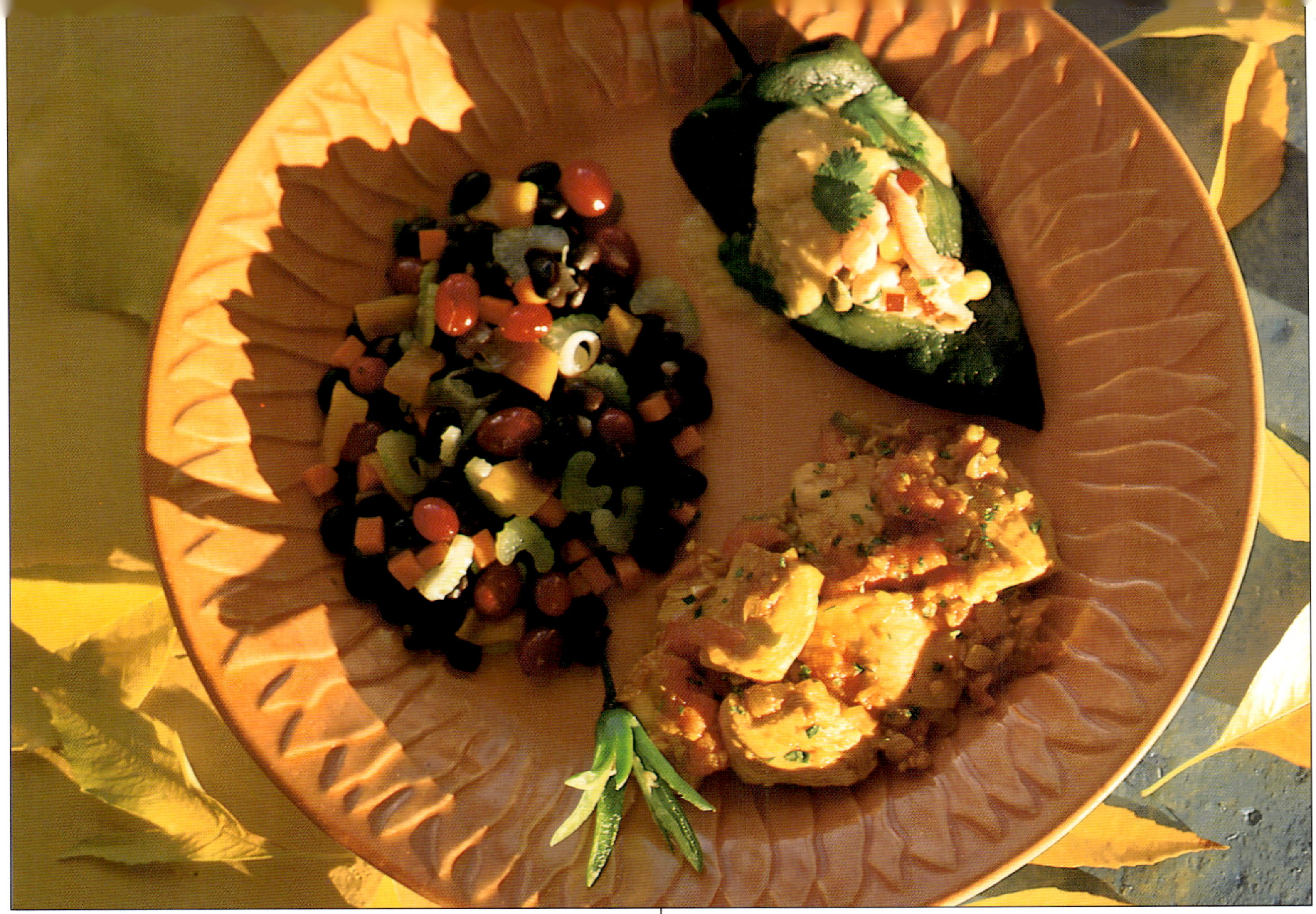

Met de klok mee van links: Zwarte-bonensalade met jalapeñodressing, Poblano-chilipepers gevuld met garnalen en krab, Tamarindekip met chilipeper

HAPJES / VERENIGDE STATEN

Poblano-chilipepers gevuld met garnalen en krab

Als verse poblanos *(milde chilipepers) niet verkrijgbaar zijn kunt u gewone paprika's of gele Turkse paprika's gebruiken.*

4 eetlepels plus 3 eetlepels olijfolie
2 sjalotjes, gesnipperd
2 gele paprika's, geroosterd, ontveld, ontzaad en in blokjes (zie woordenlijst)
3,75 dl kippebouillon (zie woordenlijst)
8 verse *poblanos* (milde chilipepers), geroosterd, ontveld en ontzaad (zie woordenlijst)
1 rode ui, gesnipperd
3 tenen knoflook, fijngehakt
125 g rauwe garnalen, gepeld, darmkanaal verwijderd en grof gehakt
2 eetlepels gehakte verse koriander
250 g vers krabvlees, gekookt en losgemaakt
maïskorrels van 1 maïskolf, geblancheerd (zie woordenlijst)
1 rode paprika, in blokjes
30 g *pepitas* (gepeld pompoenzaad), geroosterd
zout en versgemalen peper naar smaak
vers korianderblad, ter garnering

1. Verhit 3 eetlepels van de olijfolie in een middelgrote pan en fruit er de sjalotjes gaar in. Voeg de gele paprika en 2,5 dl kippebouillon toe; breng aan de kook, draai het vuur laag en laat 10 minuten sudderen. Pureer het mengsel in de blender. Doe de puree terug in de pan en houd warm tot het serveren.
2. Maak een inkeping in de zijkant van elke *poblano.* Zet weg.
3. Verhit de overgebleven olijfolie in een middelgrote koekepan en fruit er de rode ui en knoflook in 3 minuten gaar in. Blus de pan af met de rest van de bouillon en breng aan de kook. Doe er de garnalen in en kook ze in circa 3 minuten roze. Schep er de koriander, het krabvlees, de maïs, rode paprika en *pepitas* door en laat doorwarmen. Breng op smaak met zout en peper.
4. Schep de vulling in de chilipepers en schik ze op individuele borden. Schep er wat gele-paprikasaus omheen en garneer met het korianderblad. Dien onmiddellijk op.

Voor 8 personen

1 gevulde chili per portie: Calorieën 230, Eiwit 12 g, Koolhydraten 15 g, Vezel 2 g, Vet totaal 15 g (Verzadigd 2 g, Enkelvoudig onverzadigd 9,5 g, Meervoudig onverzadigd 2,5 g), Cholesterol 50 mg, Natrium 110 mg, Vitamine A 20%, Vitamine C 270%.
▲ *1 Groente, ½ Vlees, 1 Vet/Suiker*

SALADES / VERENIGDE STATEN

Zwarte-bonensalade met jalapeñodressing

Deze kleurrijke salade zorgt bij elke feestmaaltijd voor een dramatisch effect. Als cranberry's niet verkrijgbaar zijn, kunt u rode paprika gebruiken. Als verse maïs verkrijgbaar is, kunt u de maskorrels gebruiken in plaats van de gele paprika. Deze voedzame salade bevat veel vezel, B-vitaminen, ijzer en zink.

500 g gedroogde zwarte bonen, een nacht geweekt
2 tenen knoflook, fijngehakt
75 g gesnipperde ui
1 wortel, geschild en gehakt
1 stengel bleekselderij, in plakjes
1,5 dl kippebouillon (zie woordenlijst)
5 eetlepels olijfolie
125 g verse cranberry's, geblancheerd (zie woordenlijst)
75 g grof gehakte gele paprika
45 g dunne plakjes lenteui
3 eetlepels sherry azijn
1 theelepel suiker
1 verse jalapeño chilipeper, geroosterd, ontveld en gehakt (zie woordenlijst)
⅛ theelepel zout
versgemalen peper naar smaak

1. Giet en spoel de bonen af. Kook de bonen, knoflook, ui, wortel en bleekselderij 45 minuten in de kippebouillon in een grote pan tot de bonen bijtgaar zijn. Giet de bonen af en bewaar de bouillon voor een ander recept.
2. Schep 1 eetlepel olijfolie door het bonenmengsel en vervolgens de cranberry's, paprika en lenteui. Zet weg.
3. Klop de azijn in een middelgrote kom met de suiker tot de suiker opgelost is. Druppel er al kloppend de rest van de olijfolie bij. Voeg de jalapeño toe en breng op smaak met zout en peper.
4. Giet de dressing over het bonenmengsel en schep alles voorzichtig om. Serveer op kamertemperatuur of zet in de koelkast.

Voor 8 personen

2,5 dl per portie: Calorieën 310, Eiwit 13 g, Koolhydraten 43 g, Vezel 9 g, Vet totaal 10 g (Verzadigd 1,5 g, Enkelvoudig onverzadigd 7 g, Meervoudig onverzadigd 1,5 g), Cholesterol 0 mg, Natrium 50 mg, Vitamine A 50%, Vitamine C 40%, IJzer 20%, Zink 15%.

▲ *1 Groente, 1 Vlees*

GEVOGELTE / INDIA

Tamarindekip met chilipeper

Tamarindemoes of -peulen en kari *bladen zijn algemeen verkrijgbaar bij oosterse toko's.*

30 g tamarindemoes
2 theelepels suiker
3 eetlepels saffloerolie
4 gedroogde rode chilipepers
12 *kari* bladen (kerrieblad)
2 uien, gesnipperd
6 kleine groene chilipepers, in dunne ringen gesneden
6 tenen knoflook, fijngehakt
stukje verse gember van circa 3 cm, geschild en fijngehakt
2 grote tomaten, ontveld en grof gehakt
1 kg kipfilet, in stukken van 5 cm gesneden
½ theelepel geelwortel
7 g gehakt vers korianderblad

1. Breng 1,25 dl water aan de kook in een kleine pan. Doe er de tamarinemoes in en prak met een vork tot die opgelost is. Voeg de suiker toe en laat 30 minuten staan. Zeef het mengsel en druk er zoveel mogelijk van de tamarinde uit. Gooi de pulp weg en zet het sap weg.
2. Verhit de saffloerolie in een grote koekepan. Doe er de gedroogde chilipepers in en roerbak circa 1 minuut tot ze donkerbruin zijn. Voeg de *kari* bladen, ui, groene chilipepers, knoflook en gember toe en bak circa 3 minuten tot de ui gaar is. Voeg de tomaten, het tamarindesap, de kip en geelwortel toe en laat 20 minuten sudderen.
3. Doe alles op een dienschaal, bestrooi met de koriander en dien onmiddellijk op.

Voor 6 personen

1 portie: Calorieën 290, Eiwit 37 g, Koolhydraten 14 g, Vezel 2 g, Vet totaal 9 g (Verzadigd 1 g, Enkelvoudig onverzadigd 1,5 g, Meervoudig onverzadigd 5,5 g), Cholesterol 90 mg, Natrium 110 mg, Vitamine A 25%, Vitamine C 100%.

▲ *1 Groente, 1 Vlees*

SOEP / RUSLAND

Borsjt

Bieten hebben misschien het hoogste suikergehalte van alle groentesoorten, maar bevatten weinig calorieën. Bietenloof bevat volop voedingsmiddelen en smaak. U kunt deze zeer kleurrijke soep naar keuze warm of koud eten.

1,5 liter kippebouillon (zie woordenlijst)
4 eetlepels gepureerde tomaten
2 stengels bleekselderij, in dunne plakken
2 wortels, geschild en geraspt
1 ui, gehakt
1 aardappel, geschild en in blokjes
6 bieten, circa 1 kg, geschild en julienne gesneden
90 g kool, in reepjes
30 g bijgesneden en julienne gesneden bietenloof
3 eetlepels gesnipperde verse dille
2 theelepels fijngehakte verse peterselie
zout en versgemalen peper naar smaak
4 eetlepels magere yoghurt

1. Doe de kippebouillon, gepureerde tomaten, bleekselderij, wortel, ui, aardappel en bieten in een grote soeppan. Breng aan de kook en laat 20 minuten sudderen tot de groenten gaar zijn.
2. Voeg de kool en het bietenloof toe en kook nog 10 minuten.
3. Schep er de dille, peterselie en wat zout en peper door. Dien de soep warm op, gegarneerd met een schepje yoghurt.

Voor 12 personen *Foto op pagina 153*

2,5 dl per portie: Calorieën 60, Eiwit 2 g, Koolhydraten 12 g, Vezel 2 g, Vet totaal 1 g (Verzadigd 0,5 g, Enkelvoudig onverzadigd 0,5 g Meervoudig onverzadigd 0 g), Cholesterol 0 mg, Natrium 110 mg, Vitamine A 80%, Vitamine C 25%.

▲ *2 Groente*

Brood / India

Chapati

Vele Indiase broodsoorten worden gefrituurd. Dit deeg kan ook gefrituurd worden, waardoor u poories, *een andere Indiase broodsoort, krijgt. Om het vet te verminderen worden* chapati *op een droge kookplaat gebakken.*

150 g volkorenbloem
75 g bloem
snufje zout
1 eetlepel olijfolie

1. Zeef de zemelen uit de volkorenbloem. (Bewaar de zemelen voor een ander recept.) Schep de bloem en het zout door de volkorenbloem.
2. Meng de olie met 5 eetlepels warm water en roer door het bloemmengsel tot alles goed gemengd is. Doe het deeg op een licht met bloem bestoven werkvlak en kneed het deeg circa 5 minuten tot het glad en elastisch is.
3. Vorm het deeg tot een bal, doe hem in een licht met olie ingevette kom, dek die af en laat 1 uur rusten.
4. Verdeel het deeg in 4 ballen. Rol elke bal op een met bloem bestoven werkvlak uit tot een rondje van 15 cm.
5. Verhit een zware kookplaat en bak er de *chapatis* één voor één op; circa 2 minuten aan beide kanten. Draai de *chapati* om wanneer kleine bubbels verschijnen.
6. Houd de gebakken *chapati* een paar seconden aan beide kanten boven het vuur terwijl u de volgende *chapati* bakt. Wikkel de *chapati* vervolgens in aluminiumfolie of een theedoek om ze warm te houden.

Voor 4 personen

1 chapati *per portie: Calorieën 190, Eiwit 6 g, Koolhydraten 34 g, Vezel 4 g, Vet totaal 4 g (Verzadigd 0,5 g, Enkelvoudig onverzadigd 2,5 g, Meervoudig onverzadigd 0,5 g), Cholesterol 0 mg, Natrium 40 mg.*
▲ *1 Brood*

Groenten / India

Aubergine-deva

Aubergine deva *is één van de specialiteiten van het Bombay Café in Los Angeles. De eigenaars, Neela Paniz en David Chaparro, suggereren zelf een* panch puran *te maken door gelijke hoeveelheden roggezaad, Indiaas bruin mosterdzaad,* nijella *(uizaad), komijnzaad, fenegriek en venkelzaad te mengen. Er is geen vervanging voor verse* kari *bladen, behalve gedroogde* kari *bladen.*

6 kleine, smalle aubergines, in de lengte in 3 gelijke stukken gesneden (niet geschild)
3 theelepels saffloerolie
¼ theelepel zout plus zout en versgemalen peper naar smaak
1½ theelepel *panch puran* (Indiaas specerijenmengsel)
¼ theelepel venkelzaad
3 verse *kari* bladen (kerriebladen)
3 tomaten, ontveld en grof gehakt
snufje cayennepeper
2 eetlepels magere yoghurt
¼ theelepel fijngehakte knoflook
¼ theelepel fijngehakte verse gember
1 eetlepel vers korianderblad, fijngehakt

1. Verwarm de grill voor. Strijk de aubergine licht in met 1½ theelepel olie en bestrooi met zout en peper. Grilleer 2 minuten aan beide kanten. Laat afkoelen.
2. Verhit de rest van de olie in een zuurbestendige pan. Doe er de *panch puran*, het venkelzaad en de *kari* bladen in en roerbak tot het mengsel begint te spetteren.
3. Voeg de tomaten, cayennepeper en ¼ theelepel zout toe. Laat 15 minuten op een laag vuur sudderen. Zet weg.
4. Meng de yoghurt met de knoflook, gember en een snufje zout in een kleine kom.
5. Schik de gegrilde aubergine op een dienschaal. Schep het tomatenmengsel over elke plak aubergine. Garneer met een schepje yoghurtmengsel en de koriander.

Voor 6 personen

3 plakken per portie: Calorieën 65, Eiwit 2 g, Koolhydraten 10 g, Vezel 2 g, Vet totaal 3 g (Verzadigd 0,5 g, Enkelvoudig onverzadigd 0,5 g, Meervoudig onverzadigd 2 g), Cholesterol 0 mg, Natrium 135 mg, Vitamine C 20%.
▲ *1 Groente*

Groenten / India

Kroonjuwelen

Dal, *de Indiase naam voor linzen, is samen met rijst, specerijen, brood en fruit een basisvoedsel in India. Aardappels zijn ook heel belangrijk. Een gerecht met meer dan één van deze edele ingrediënten is geschikt voor mensen van adel. Probeer zo mogelijk hele specerijen te gebruiken en maal ze in een koffiemolen of stamp ze fijn in een vijzel. Fenegriekzaad heeft een unieke, licht bittere smaak en is in oosterse toko's verkrijgbaar. Serveer dit hoofdgerecht met* chapatis *(recept boven).*

100 g gedroogde groene mungbonen, één nacht geweekt
50 g gele spliterwten
50 g groene linzen
½ theelepel geelwortel
1 theelepel gemalen koriander
½ theelepel gemalen komijn
½ theelepel cayennepeper
kaneelpijpje van circa 3 cm, gemalen
½ theelepel geroosterd fenegriekzaad, gemalen
1 aardappel, geschild en in blokjes van ½ cm gesneden
3 eetlepels plantaardige olie
60 g gehakte ui
2 kleine groene chilipepers, steeltjes verwijderd, in de lengte opengesneden
3 tenen knoflook, fijngehakt
1 grote tomaat, gehakt
7 g gehakte verse koriander
5 eetlepels magere yoghurt
¼ theelepel zout
4 eetlepels vers citroensap

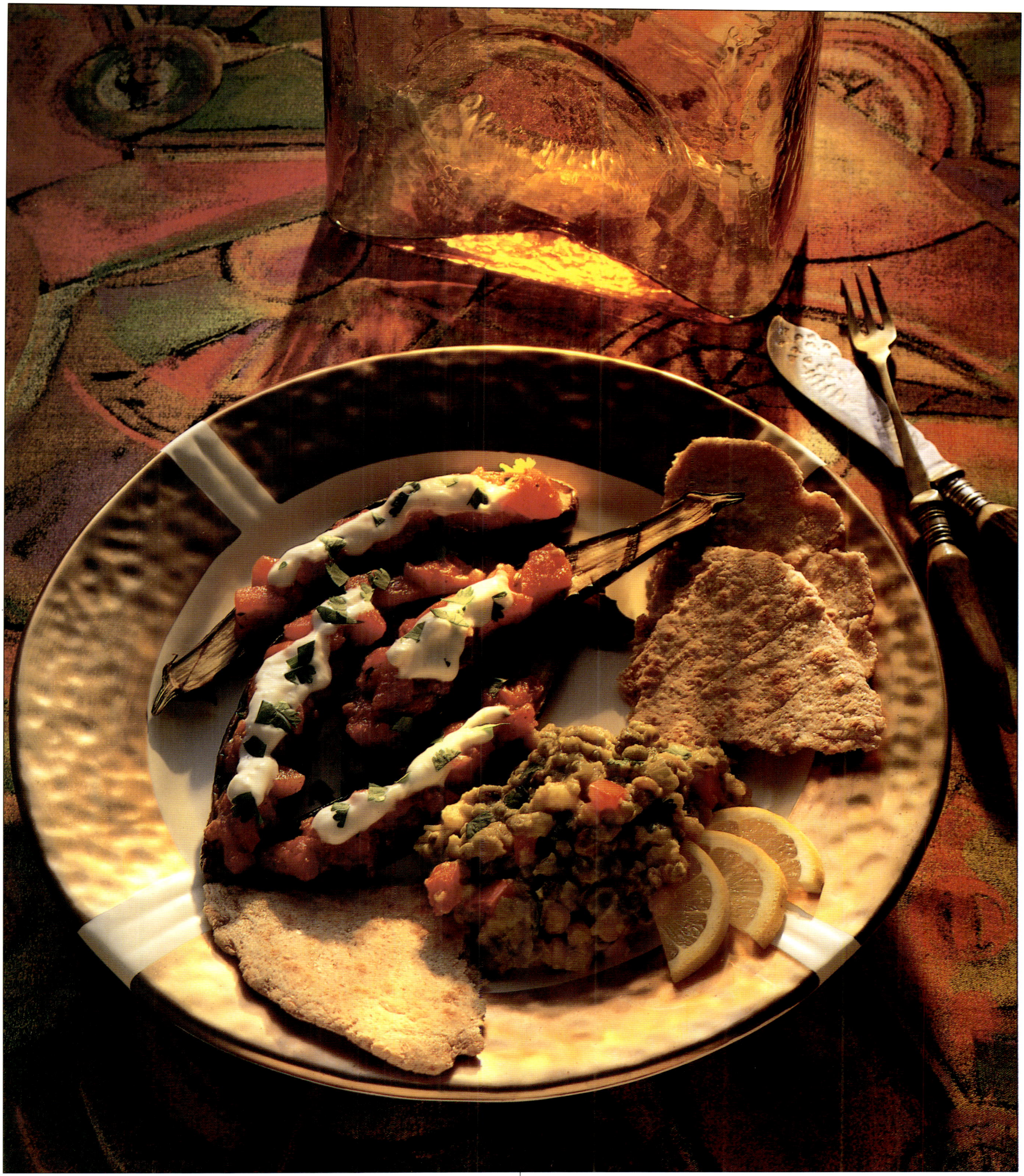

Met de klok mee van linksboven: Aubergine-deva, Chapati, Kroonjuwelen

1. Doe de mungbonen, spliterwten en linzen in een pan en zet ze onder water. Breng aan de kook en draai het vuur lager. Voeg de geelwortel, koriander, komijn, cayennepeper, kaneel en fenegriek toe en laat 40 minuten sudderen tot de peulvruchten gaar zijn. Voeg de aardappel toe en kook die in 10 minuten gaar.
2. Verhit de olie in een grote koekepan. Fruit er de ui, chilipepers en knoflook circa 5 minuten in tot ze gaar zijn. Schep er het peulvruchtenmengsel, de tomaat, verse koriander en yoghurt door. Voeg het zout en citroensap toe en dien op.

Voor 6 personen

---

1 portie: Calorieën 230, Eiwit 10 g, Koolhydraten 31 g, Vezel 4 g, Vet totaal 8 g (Verzadigd 1 g, Enkelvoudig onverzadigd 1 g, Meervoudig onverzadigd 5 g), Cholesterol 0 mg, Natrium 115 mg, Vitamine 40%.

▲ *1 Groente, ½ Vlees*

Tabbouleh

Bulghur is een soort gebroken tarwe. U kunt hem in verschillende gradaties van fijnheid kopen; kies de fijnste voor tabbouleh. U kunt deze hartige salade als hoofdgerecht serveren. Traditioneel wordt tabbouleh met een stuk bindsla opgeschept en met de hand gegeten.

185 g fijnkorrelige bulghur
1,8 dl vers citroensap
4 eetlepels olijfolie
¼ theelepel zout
versgemalen peper naar smaak
45 g gehakte verse snijpeterselie
375 g grof gehakte tomaten
45 g lentui, in dunne rondjes
4 tenen knoflook, fijngehakt
7 g muntblaadjes
8 bladen bindsla (Romeinse sla)

Van boven naar beneden: Lavash, Tabbouleh, Gevulde druivebladeren

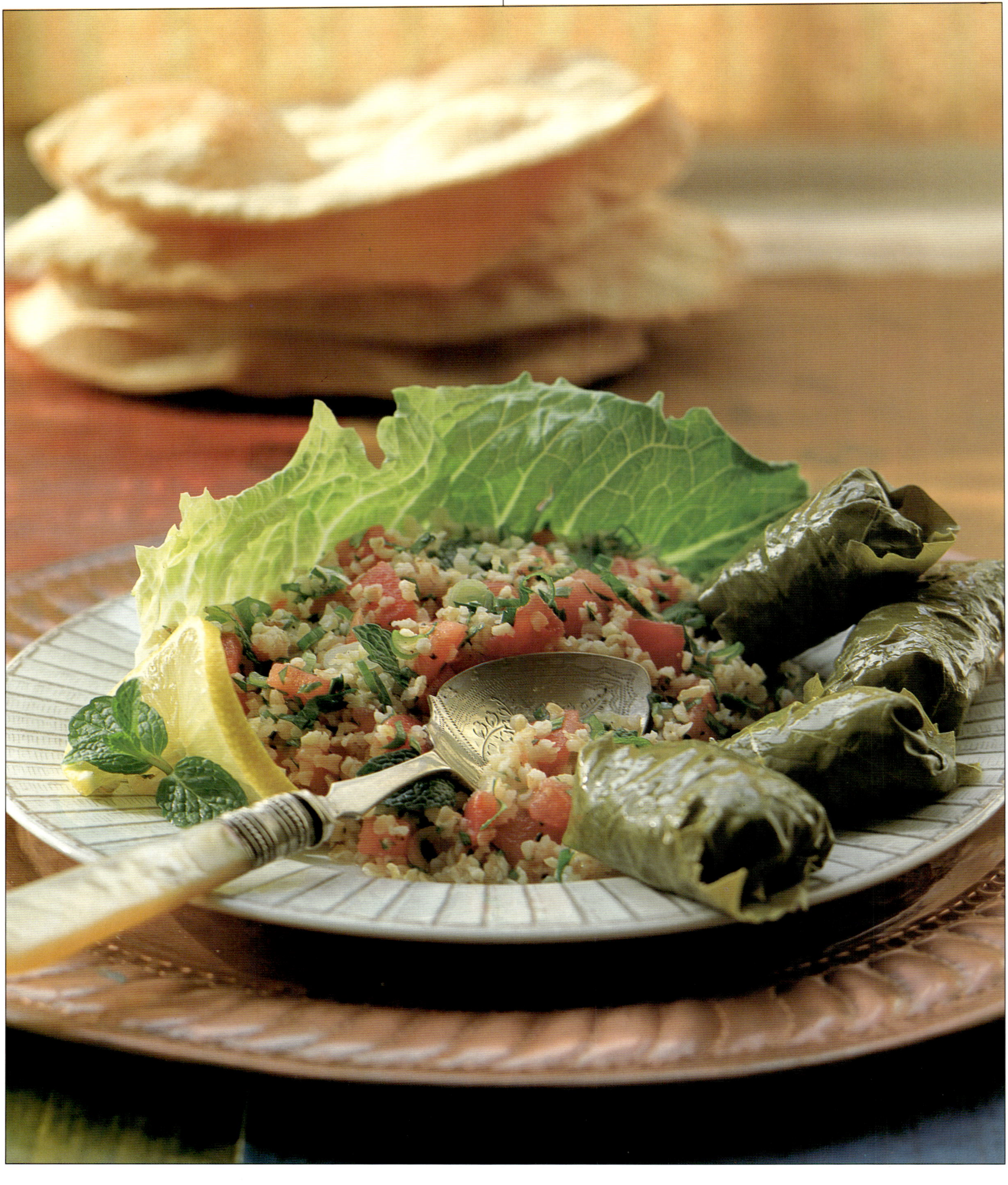

1. Week de bulghur 30 minuten in 5 dl water tot de bulghur zacht is en het vocht geabsorbeerd is.
2. Schep er het citroensap, de olijfolie en wat zout en peper door. Voeg de peterselie, tomaten, lenteui en knoflook toe. Zet minstens 2 uur in de koelkast en schep af en toe om.
3. Garneer de salade vlak voor het opdienen met de muntblaadjes. Dien de tabbouleh op en geef er de slabladen apart bij.

Voor 4 personen als hoofdgerecht, 8 als bijgerecht

2,5 dl (hoofdgerecht) per portie: Calorieën 290, Eiwit 6 g, Koolhydraten 38 g, Vezel 9 g, Vet totaal 14 g (Verzadigd 2 g, Enkelvoudig onverzadigd 10 g, Meervoudig onverzadigd 1,5 g), Cholesterol 0 mg, Natrium 170 mg, Vitamine A 35%, Vitamine C 110%.

▲ *1 Brood, 1 Groente, 1 Vet/Suiker*

HAPJES / GRIEKENLAND

Dolmas

GEVULDE DRUIVEBLADEREN

Deze heerlijke hapjes zijn perfect om zó uit de hand te eten en ze kunnen als voorgerecht geserveerd worden. Gebruik ingemaakte bladen als verse niet verkrijgbaar zijn.

40 malse druivebladeren of een potje van 375 g, steeltjes verwijderd
4 eetlepels olijfolie
75 g gesnipperde ui
45 g fijngehakte lenteui
225 g langkorrelige rijst
5 dl kippebouillon (zie woordenlijst)
het sap van 2 citroenen
1 eetlepel gesnipperde verse dille
10 g fijngehakte verse peterselie
2 theelepels gehakte verse munt
2 eetlepels pijnboompitten
45 g krenten
¼ theelepel zout
versgemalen peper naar smaak
2,5 dl dille-yoghurtsaus (recept op pagina 110)
1 citroen, in partjes gesneden

1. Blancheer verse druivebladeren 15 seconden in kokend water of spoel bladeren uit een potje af en blancheer ze dan 10 seconden. Giet ze af en dep ze droog. Leg de bladeren plat op een werkvlak met de glimmende kant onder.
2. Verhit 2 eetlepels van de olijfolie in een grote koekepan. Fruit er de ui en lenteui circa 3 minuten in tot ze gaar zijn. Voeg de rijst toe en schep om tot die met olie bedekt is. Giet de bouillon erbij en breng aan de kook. Draai het vuur lag, leg het deksel op de pan en kook 12-15 minuten tot het vocht geabsorbeerd is. Neem de pan van het vuur en schep er de helft van het citroensap, de dille, peterselie, munt, pijnboompitten en krenten door. Breng op smaak met zout en peper.
3. Schep een bolle lepel van het rijstmengsel op het steeleind van een blad. Rol het blad vanaf de onderkant één slag op, vouw de zijkanten naar binnen en rol het blad verder op tot de punt van het blad. Vul alle bladen op dezelfde manier en schik ze strak naast elkaar in een grote anti-aanbak koekepan. Sprenkel er 1 eetlepel van de olijfolie en 3 eetlepels van het citroensap over. Giet er zoveel water bij dat de dolmas net onder staan. Leg een bord op de dolmas en zet daar een gewicht op. Sudder 35 minuten en giet er zonodig wat water bij. Neem de pan dan van het vuur en laat afkoelen.
4. Giet de dolmas af en schik ze op een dienschaal. Sprenkel er de rest van de olijfolie en het citroensap over. Serveer ze op kamertemperatuur of gekoeld, met de dille-yoghurtsaus en citroen.

Voor 10 personen (40 dolmas)

---

4 dolmas per portie: Calorieën 170, Eiwit 4 g, Koolhydraten 22 g, Vezel 1 g, Vet totaal 7 g (Verzadigd 1 g, Enkelvoudig onverzadigd 4,5 g, Meervoudig onverzadigd 1 g), Cholesterol 0 mg, Natrium 260 mg.

▲ *1 Brood, 1 Groente*

BROOD / ARMENIË

Lavash

Dit knapperige, platte Armeense brood is heerlijk met dipsausen of smeersels als baba ghanouj *(recept op pagina 103) of hummus (recept op pagina 102). Bevochtig dit brood en gebruik het dan voor opgerolde sandwiches (recept op pagina 126).*

1 theelepel droge gist
1½ theelepel suiker
4 eetlepels plus 1 eetlepel olijfolie
1½ theelepel zout
320-390 g bloem
2 theelepels sesamzaad

1. Doe de gist en suiker in 2,5 dl warm water (40°-46°C) in een grote kom en laat 5 minuten staan tot het mengsel schuimt.
2. Voeg 4 eetlepels olijfolie, het zout en 150 g van de bloem toe en roer tot een glad mengsel.
3. Voeg al roerend met 75 g tegelijk de bloem toe tot u een stijf, glad deeg hebt verkregen. Doe het deeg op een licht met bloem bestoven werkvlak.
4. Kneed het deeg circa 10 minuten tot het glad en elastisch is. Doe het deeg in een licht met olie ingevette grote kom, dek die af en laat circa 1 uur staan tot het deeg in volume verdubbeld is.
5. Verwarm de oven voor op 190°C. Vet een bakplaat in met olie.
6. Druk de lucht uit het deeg en verdeel het in 4 stukken. Kneed een stuk en vorm het tot een bal. Laat die 10 minuten rusten en rol dan uit tot een cirkel van 30 cm doorsnee.
7. Rol de cirkel losjes over de deegroller en rol hem dan uit op de bakplaat. Kwast het deeg licht in met wat van de overgebleven olijfolie en bestrooi met wat sesamzaad. Bak 10-12 minuten tot een knapperig brood.
8. Rol intussen de tweede bal deeg uit. Herhaal met de rest van de ballen deeg.
9. Doe het gebakken brood direct op een rooster en laat afkoelen.

Voor 8 personen

½ rondje per portie: Calorieën 200, Eiwit 4 g, Koolhydraten 25 g, Vezel 1 g, Vet totaal 9 g (Verzadigd 1 g, Enkelvoudig onverzadigd 6 g, Meervoudig onverzadigd 1 g), Cholesterol 0 mg, Natrium 440 mg.

▲ *1 Brood*

ZEEBANKET / FRANKRIJK

Pot-au-feu de Bretagne

BRETONSE VISPOT

Langs de noordkust van Frankrijk wordt veel vis gevangen. De oester- en coquillebedden zijn rijk gevuld, en de zee bevat tal van zeeëgels, alikruiken, langoestines en vele vissoorten. Een traditionele pot-au-feu is een stoofpot van rundvlees met de bouillon als voorgerecht en het vlees en de groenten als hoofdgerecht. In deze verzie wordt er vis gebruikt.

1 kg verschillende vissoorten: zeeduivel, tarbot of tong, kabeljauw, makreel, rode snapper en zeebaars
1 kg verschillende schelp- en schaaldieren: coquilles, oesters, kreeft, krab, clams en mosselen
2 liter visbouillon (zie woordenlijst)
4 eetlepels saffloerolie
4 wortels, geschild en julienne gesneden
2 stengels bleekselderij, in dunne plakken
2 meirapen, geschild en julienne gesneden
2 uien, gehakt
1 prei, alleen het wit, gehakt
bouquet garni: 1 takje peterselie, 1 takje tijm, 1 laurierblad
¼ theelepel zout
versgemalen peper naar smaak
12 dunne sneden stokbrood, geroosterd en met knoflook ingewreven
2 theelepels fijngehakte verse peterselie

1. Ontvel en fileer de vis en snijd ze in blokken van 5 cm. Zet weg.
2. Haal de schelpdieren uit hun schelpen. Zeef er het nat uit en doe het bij de visbouillon. Borstel een aantal coquille-, clam- en mosselschelpen schoon en zet ze weg. Als u een kreeft of krab gebruikt, deze 8 minuten in kokend water koken, in tweeën splijten, de scharen openbreken en er het vlees uithalen.
3. Verhit de olie in een grote soeppan. Laat de wortel, bleekselderij, meiraap, ui en prei circa 10 minuten zweten. Voeg de visbouillon en het bouquet garni toe en breng aan de kook. Draai het vuur laag en laat alles circa 10 minuten sudderen tot de wortel en raap gaar zijn.
4. Voeg afhankelijk van de benodigde kooktijd het zeebanket toe. Dikke, compacte stukken hebben 8-10 minuten kooktijd nodig. Voeg de schelpdieren en de gekookte kreeft circa 4 minuten voor het serveren toe.
5. Zeef de stoofpot, bewaar het kooknat, doe een aantal schelpdieren terug in hun schelpen en schik alles op een dienschaal. Breng de bouillon op smaak met zout en peper.
6. Leg een snee stokbrood in elk voorverwarmd soepbord. Schep er wat bouillon over en bestrooi met de gehakte peterselie. Geef er de schaal zeebanket en groenten apart bij.

Voor 12 personen

Bretonse vispot

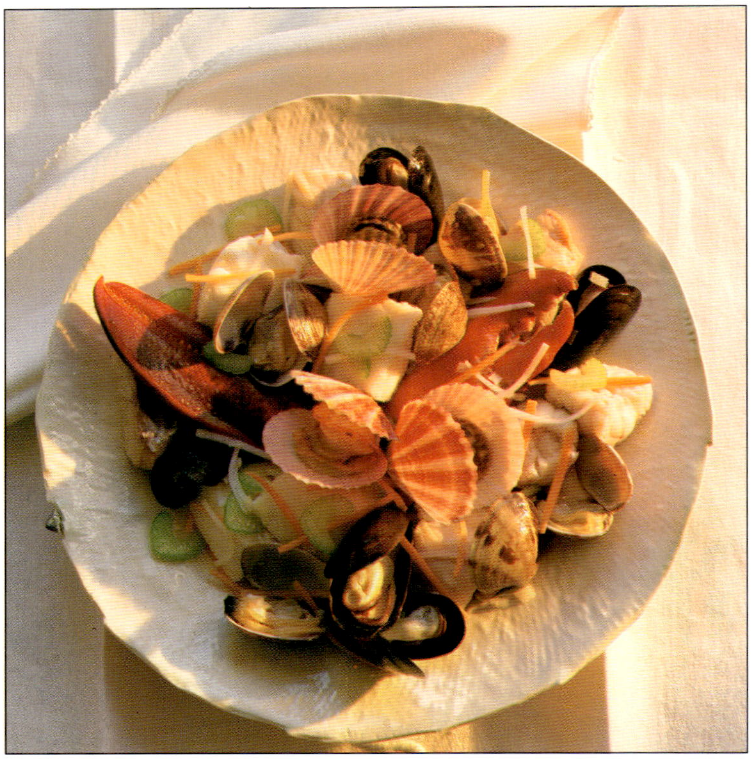

1 portie: Calorieën 260, Eiwit 25 g, Koolhydraten 20 g, Vezel 2 g, Vet totaal 7 g (Verzadigd 1 g, Enkelvoudig onverzadigd 1,5 g, Meervoudig onverzadigd 5,5 g), Cholesterol 50 mg, Natrium 330 mg, Vitamine A 140%, Vitamine C 20%.

▲ *1 Brood, 1 Groente, 1 Vlees*

HAPJES / FRANKRIJK

Pâté met kip en appel

Deze hartige pâté is heerlijk met vers stokbrood, Dijonmosterd en cornichons.

45 g boter
500 g Golden Delicious appels, geschild en in blokjes
1 grote ui, gesnipperd
1 kg kipgehakt
4 eieren
90 g droog broodkruim
60 g krenten
60 g gedroogde kersen, in 5 eetlepels rum geweekt
1,6 dl droge Marsala
3 eetlepels kappertjes
2 theelepels verkruimelde, gedroogde tijm
1 eetlepel vers citroensap
2 theelepels zout
1 theelepel geraspte citroenschil
versgemalen peper naar smaak

1. Verwarm de oven voor op 180°C. Vet een terrine van 2 liter inhoud licht in met olie.
2. Verhit de boter in een grote koekepan en fruit er de appel en ui goudbruin in. Laat afkoelen.
3. Doe het appelmengsel en de rest van de ingrediënten in een grote kom en meng met de deeghaak van een grote mixer.
4. Schep het mengsel in de terrine en strijk het mengsel glad.
5. Bak de pâté 45-50 minuten in de oven, of tot hij bruin is en van

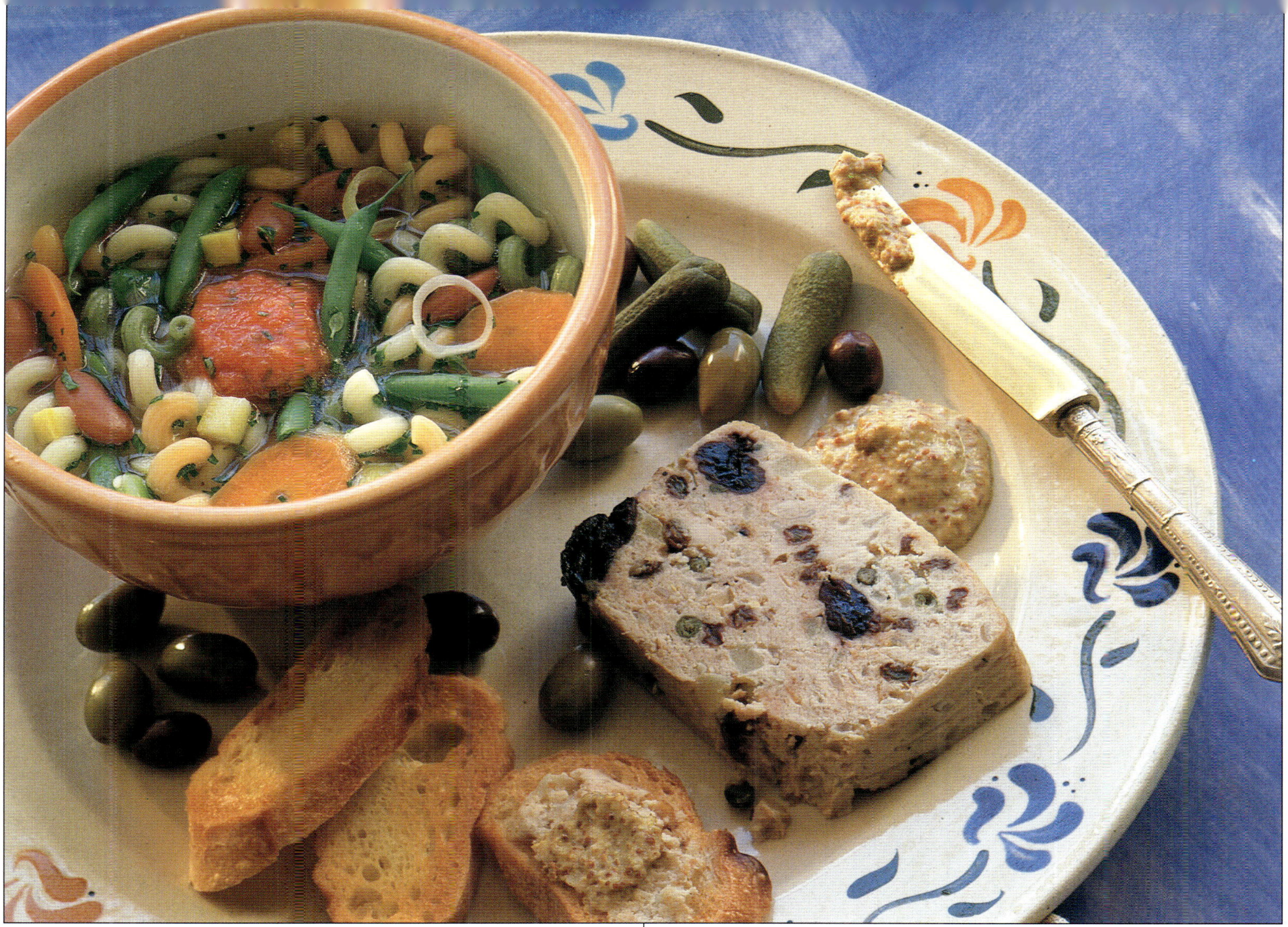

Van links naar rechts: Groentesoep met tomatenpesto, Pâté met zip en appel

de wand loskomt. Laat op een rooster afkoelen. Zet in de koelkast of serveer op kamertemperatuur.
Voor 12 personen

1 plak per portie: Calorieën 250, Eiwit 20 g, Koolhydraten 19 g, Vezel 2 g, Vet totaal 9 g (Verzadigd 3,5 g, Enkelvoudig onverzadigd 3,5 g, Meervoudig onverzadigd 1,5 g), Cholesterol 130 mg Natrium 680 mg.
▲ *1 Fruit, 1 Vlees*

SOEP / FRANKRIJK

Soupe au pistou tomate

GROENTESOEP MET TOMATENPESTO

Pistou *is een Provençaalse pasta van verse basilicum, knoflook en olijfolie en lijkt op Italiaanse pesto waarin ook Parmezaanse kaas en pijnboompitten zijn verwerkt.*

PISTOU

30 g verse basilicumblaadjes
1 rijpe tomaat, gehalveerd en ontzaad
4 tenen knoflook
2 eetlepels koudgeperste olijfolie

SOEP

2 liter kippebouillon (zie woordenlijst)
125 g verse flageolets (jonge nierbonen) of 60 g gedroogde, een nacht geweekt
125 g verse nierbonen of 60 g gedroogde, een nacht geweekt
125 g verse haricot verts of sperziebonen, afgehaald en in stukjes van 3 cm gesneden en geblancheerd (zie woordenlijst)
2 preien, overdwars in dunne plakken gesneden
125 g courgette, in blokjes
2 wortels, geschraapt en in plakjes
1 meiraap, geschild en in blokjes
½ theelepel fijngehakte verse tijm
1 eetlepel fijngehakte verse peterselie
1 laurierblad
125 g fusili (spiraalvormige pasta)
zout en versgemalen peper naar smaak

1. Maak de *pistou* door de basilicum, tomaat en knoflook fijn te malen in een keukenmachine of vijzel. Voeg de olijfolie toe en draai of stamp tot een pasta. Doe in een kom en zet weg.
2. Breng de kippebouillon aan de kook in een grote soeppan. Voeg de flageolets en nierbonen toe. Gedroogde bonen 30 minuten koken voor u verder gaat. Voeg de haricot verts, prei, courgette, wortel, meiraap, tijm, peterselie en het laurierblad toe. Laat 20 minuten sudderen, of tot de groenten gaar zijn.
3. Doe de pasta in de soep en laat nog 10 minuten koken. Breng op smaak met zout en peper.
4. Dien onmiddellijk op en geef er de *pistou* apart bij, waarna de gasten die naar smaak in de soep doen.

Voor 12 personen

2,5 dl per portie: Calorieën 130, Eiwit 5 g, Koolhydraten 21 g, Vezel 3 g, Vet totaal 4 g (Verzadigd 0,5 g, Enkelvoudig onverzadigd 2 g, Meervoudig onverzadigd 0,5 g), Cholesterol 0 mg Natrium 25 mg, Vitamine A 70%, Vitamine C 20%.
▲ *1 Groente, ½ Vlees*

GEVOGELTE / PERU

Pepián verde de pollo y choclo

STOOFPOT VAN KIP EN MAÏS

Pepián *is een Midden- en Zuidamerikaanse stoofpot met chilipepers en noten of zaden. Hij wordt vaak met rijst geserveerd.*

5 dl kippebouillon (zie woordenlijst)
1,5 kg kip in stukken, ontveld
500 g groene tomatillo's (boomtomaten), schutblad verwijderd
150 g *pepitas* (ontveld pompoenzaad), geroosterd en fijngemalen
5 jalapeño chilipepers
1 ui, gehakt
2 tenen knoflook, fijngehakt
15 g vers korianderblad
korrels van 4 maïskolven (circa 550 g)

1. Verwarm de oven voor op 200°C. Vet een ondiepe ovenschaal licht in met olie.
2. Verhit de kippebouillon in een grote soeppan. Doe er de stukken kip in en laat 30 minuten sudderen, of tot de kip gaar is.
3. Rooster intussen de tomatillo's in 10 minuten goudbruin in de oven in de ovenschaal.
4. Pureer de *pepitas*, jalapeño's, tomatillo's, ui, knoflook en korianderblad in een blender tot een glad mengsel. Doe het mengsel in een grote pan en breng aan de kook. Doe circa 2,5 dl (of meer) van het kipkooknat bij de saus tot die zo dik als room is. Voeg de maïskorrels toe en laat 5 minuten koken.
5. Schik de stukken kip op een dienschaal en schep er de saus over. Dien onmiddellijk op.

Voor 8 personen

1 portie: Calorieën 390, Eiwit 47 g, Koolhydraten 20 g, Vezel 3 g, Vet totaal 14 g (Verzadigd 3 g, Enkelvoudig onverzadigd 4,5 g, Meervoudig onverzadigd 5 g), Cholesterol 110 mg, Natrium 110 mg, Vitamine C 45%.

▲ *1 Groente, 2 Vlees*

Stoofpot van kip en maïs

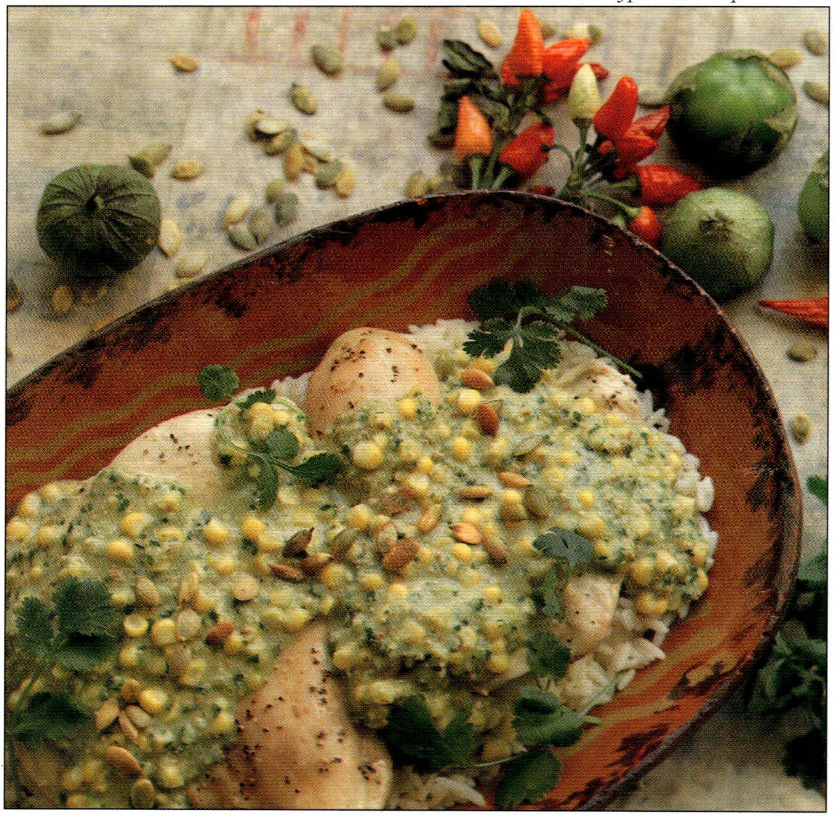

VEDERWILD / VERENIGDE STATEN

Eendeborst met perensaus

Kies rijpe, stevige peren. Het klokhuis verwijdert u eenvoudig door het met een bolletjessteker eruit te scheppen. Geef bij dit gerecht met geelwortel gekleurde aardappelpuree (recept op pagina 189) en gestoomde spinazie.

2 hele wilde-eendeborsten, in de lengte gehalveerd, gefileerd en vet verwijderd (circa 350 g)
¼ theelepel zout
versgemalen peper naar smaak
30 g boter
4 eetlepels Sauternes of droge witte wijn
2 rijpe peren, geschild, klokhuis verwijderd en in de lengte in plakken gesneden
1 sjalot, gesnipperd
250 g rijpe peren, klokhuis verwijderd en grof gehakt
5 dl kippebouillon (zie woordenlijst)
2 theelepels fijngehakte tijm
1 theelepel maïzena gemengd met 1 eetlepel kippebouillon
zout naar smaak
2 eetlepels grof gehakte geroosterde hazelnoten

1. Verwarm de oven voor op 190°C. Vet een ovenschaal licht in.
2. Bestrooi de eendeborsten met ¼ theelepel zout en wat peper. Verhit de boter tot goudbruin in een middelgrote koekepan. Schroei er de eend in 2 minuten aan beide kanten in dicht. Doe de eend in de ovenschaal en besprenkel met 2 eetlepels van de Sauternes. Dek de schaal af met aluminiumfolie en zet 10 minuten in de oven. Doe er de plakken peer bij, dek weer af en zet nog 5 minuten in de oven.
3. Fruit de sjalot en de gehakte peer 1 minuut in dezelfde koekepan. Blus de pan af met de rest van de Sauternes en de bouillon. Voeg de tijm toe en kook 5 minuten. Roer er het maïzenapapje door en laat 5 minuten zachtjes sudderen tot de saus iets dikker is en de peren gaar zijn. Breng op smaak met zout en peper.
4. Neem de eend uit de oven. Schik de peren tot waaiers op individuele borden en schik er de eendeborsten naast. Schep de saus over de eend en bestrooi met de hazelnoten. Dien op.

Voor 4 personen

1 portie: Calorieën 290, Eiwit 16 g, Koolhydraten 24 g, Vezel 4 g, Vet totaal 14 g (Verzadigd 6 g, Enkelvoudig onverzadigd 5 g, Meervoudig onverzadigd 1,5 g), Cholesterol 80 mg, Natrium 210 mg, IJzer 20%.

▲ *1 Fruit, 1 Vlees*

Eendeborst met perensaus

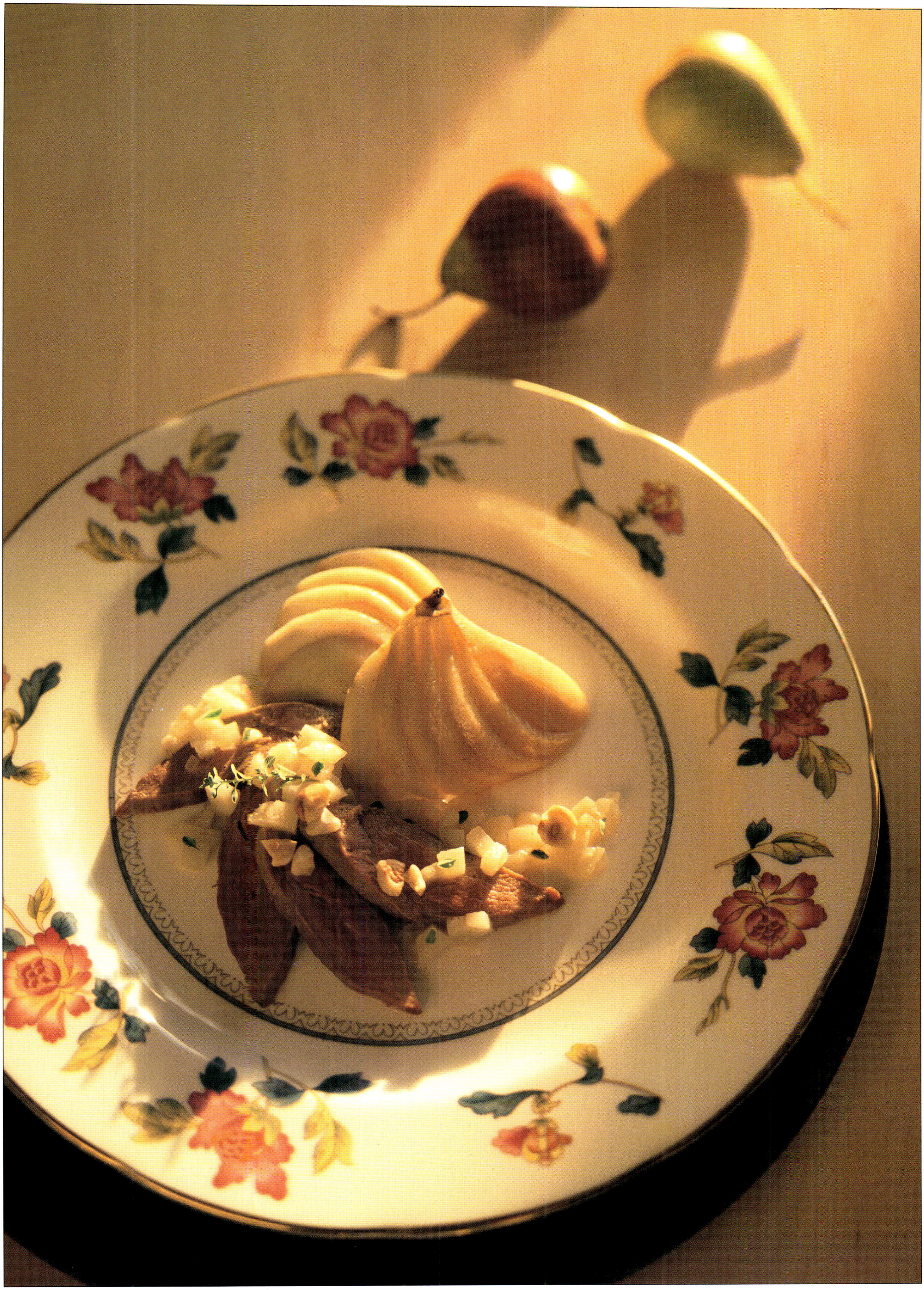

GEVOGELTE / VERENIGDE STATEN

Kippeworst in rechthoekjes

Dien deze rechthoekjes op met Himmel und Erde *(recept volgt) voor een licht diner of voorafje bij de brunch.*

500 g kipgehakt van kipfilet gemaakt
1 Cox Orange of Granny Smith appel, klokhuis verwijderd en grof geraspt
1 theelepel gemalen salie
½ theelepel verkruimelde gedroogde tijm
¼ theelepel verkruimelde gedroogde oregano
½ theelepel anijszaad
2 eetlepels saffloerolie
¾ theelepel versgemalen peper

1. Verwarm de oven voor op 180°C. Vet de bodem van een vierkante ovenschaal van 23 cm doorsnee licht in met olie.
2. Doe het kipgehakt in een middelgrote kom. Voeg de appel, salie, tijm, oregano, het anijszaad en de olie toe en schep alles vervolgens goed om.
3. Doe het mengsel in de ovenschaal en strijk het glad uit. Strooi er de peper over en zet 20 minuten in de oven.
4. Snijd in vierkantjes en dien onmiddellijk op.

Voor 4 personen

---

1 portie: Calorieën 205, Eiwit 26 g, Koolhydraten 6 g, Vezel 1 g, Vet totaal 8 g (Verzadigd 1,5 g, Enkelvoudig onverzadigd 1,5 g, Meervoudig onverzadigd 4,5 g), Cholesterol 70 mg, Natrium 60 mg.
▲ *1 Vlees*

ONTBIJT / VERENIGDE STATEN

Marion Cunninghams appelmuffins

Het recept voor deze heerlijke, voedzame muffins is afkomstig van Marion Cunningham, schrijfster van onder andere The Breakfast Book *en* The Fannie Farmer Baking Book.

500 g blokjes appel (geschild of ongeschild)
250 g suiker
2 eieren, losgeklopt
1,25 dl maïsolie
2 theelepels vanille-essence
300 g bloem
2 theelepels zuiveringszout (natriumbicarbonaat)
2 theelepels gemalen kaneel
1 theelepel zout
185 g rozijnen
45 g brokken walnoot

1. Verwarm de oven voor op 165°C. Vet een muffinblik voor 16 muffins licht in met olie.
2. Zet 3 kommen op een werkvlak. Schep de appels door de suiker in de eerste kom en zet weg. Doe de eieren, olie en vanille in de tweede kom en meng alles goed. Zeef de bloem met het zuiveringszout, de kaneel en het zout boven de derde kom en schep alles goed om.
3. Schep het eimengsel door het appelmengsel. Strooi het bloemmengsel over het appelmengsel en schep alles goed om. Strooi de rozijnen en walnoten over het beslag en schep goed om. Schep het beslag in de muffinblikken.
4. Zet de muffins 25 minuten in de oven, of tot een ingestoken satéstokje er schoon uitkomt. Dien ze warm op.

Voor 16 muffins

---

1 muffin per portie: Calorieën 240, Eiwit 3 g, Koolhydraten 37 g, Vezel 2 g, Vet totaal 9 g (Verzadigd 1,5 g, Enkelvoudig onverzadigd 2,5 g, Meervoudig onverzadigd 5 g), Cholesterol 30 mg, Natrium 320 mg.
▲ *1 Brood, 1 Fruit*

GROENTEN / DUITSLAND

Himmel und Erde

HEMEL EN AARDE

Uit de hemel komt de appel en uit de aarde komt de aardappel. Deze klassieke puree, een combinatie van zoet en hartig, wordt van oudsher bij braadworst gegeven. Himmel und Erde *is ook heerlijk bij gegrilde kip of eend.*

500 g aardappels, geschild en in blokjes
500 g meiraap, geschild en in blokjes
2 eetlepels plantaardige olie
30 g boter
1 grote ui, in plakken
1 grote zoete appel, geschild, klokhuis verwijderd en in blokjes
2 tenen knoflook, fijngehakt
1,25 dl kippebouillon (zie woordenlijst)
3 eetlepels fijngehakte peterselie
¼ theelepel zout
versgemalen witte peper naar smaak

1. Doe de aardappel en meiraap in een grote pan en zet ze onder water. Breng aan de kook, draai het vuur lager en laat ze in circa 20 minuten gaar sudderen. Giet ze af.
2. Verhit de olie en de boter in een koekepan. Doe er de ui, appel en knoflook in, dek de pan af en fruit alles circa 15 minuten tot de appel gaar is. Neem het deksel van de pan en bak alles goudbruin in circa 10 minuten op een middelhoog vuur. Giet er de kippebouillon bij.
3. Doe de helft van het ui-appelmengsel en al het aardappelmengsel in een keukenmachine en draai het geheel vervolgens met korte stootjes tot een grove puree.

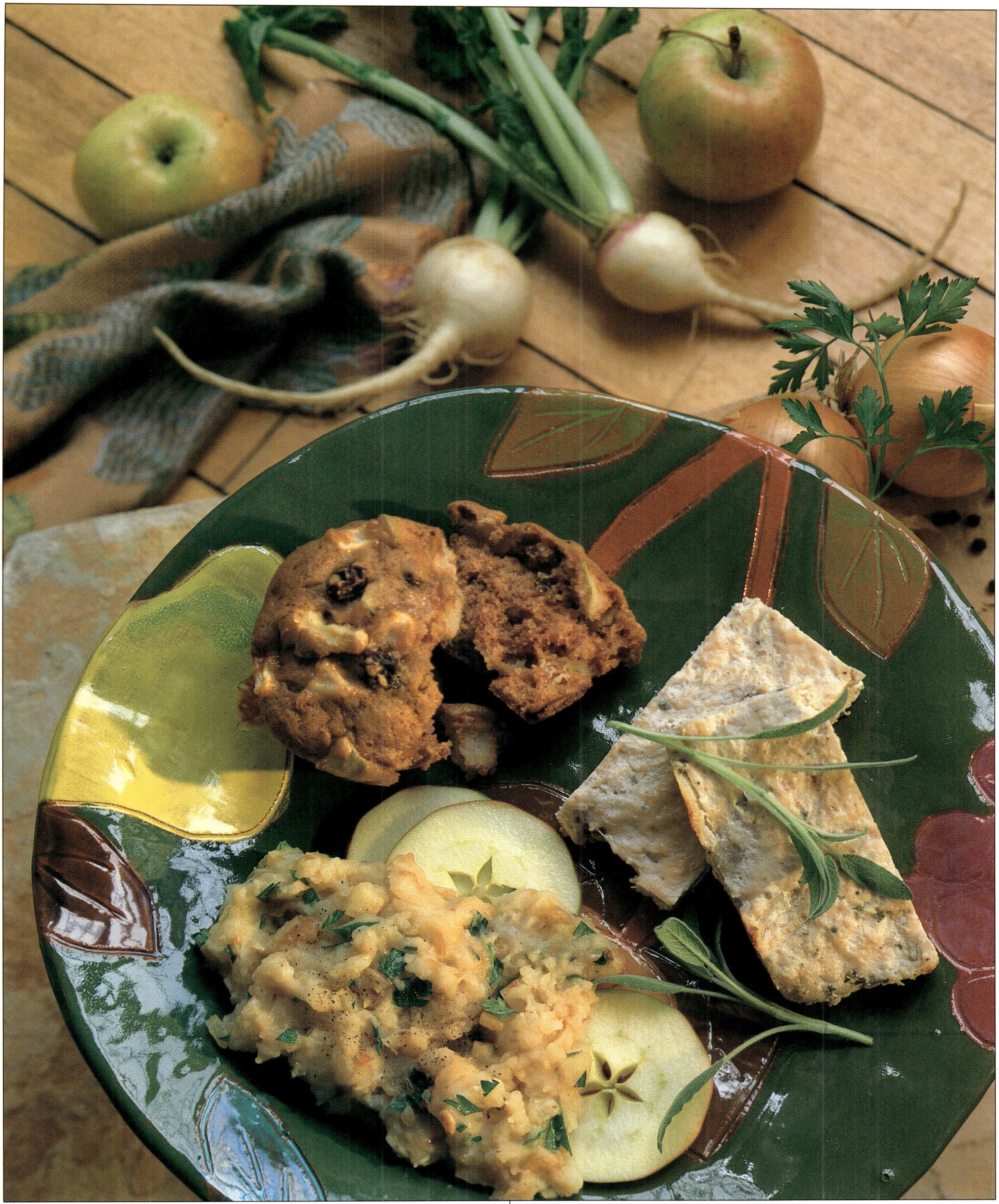

Met de klok mee van boven: Marion Cunninghams appelmuffins, Kippeworst in rechthoekjes, Hemel en aarde

4. Schep het overgebleven ui-appelmengsel door de puree. Voeg de peterselie en wat zout en peper toe. Laat alles doorwarmen en dien op.

Voor 8 personen

2,5 dl per portie: Calorieën 150, Eiwit 2 g, Koolhydraten 21 g, Vezel 3 g, Vet totaal 7 g (Verzadigd 2 g, Enkelvoudig onverzadigd 1,5 g, Meervoudig onverzadigd 3 g), Cholesterol 10 mg, Natrium 115 mg, Vitamine C 35%.

▲ *2 Groente*

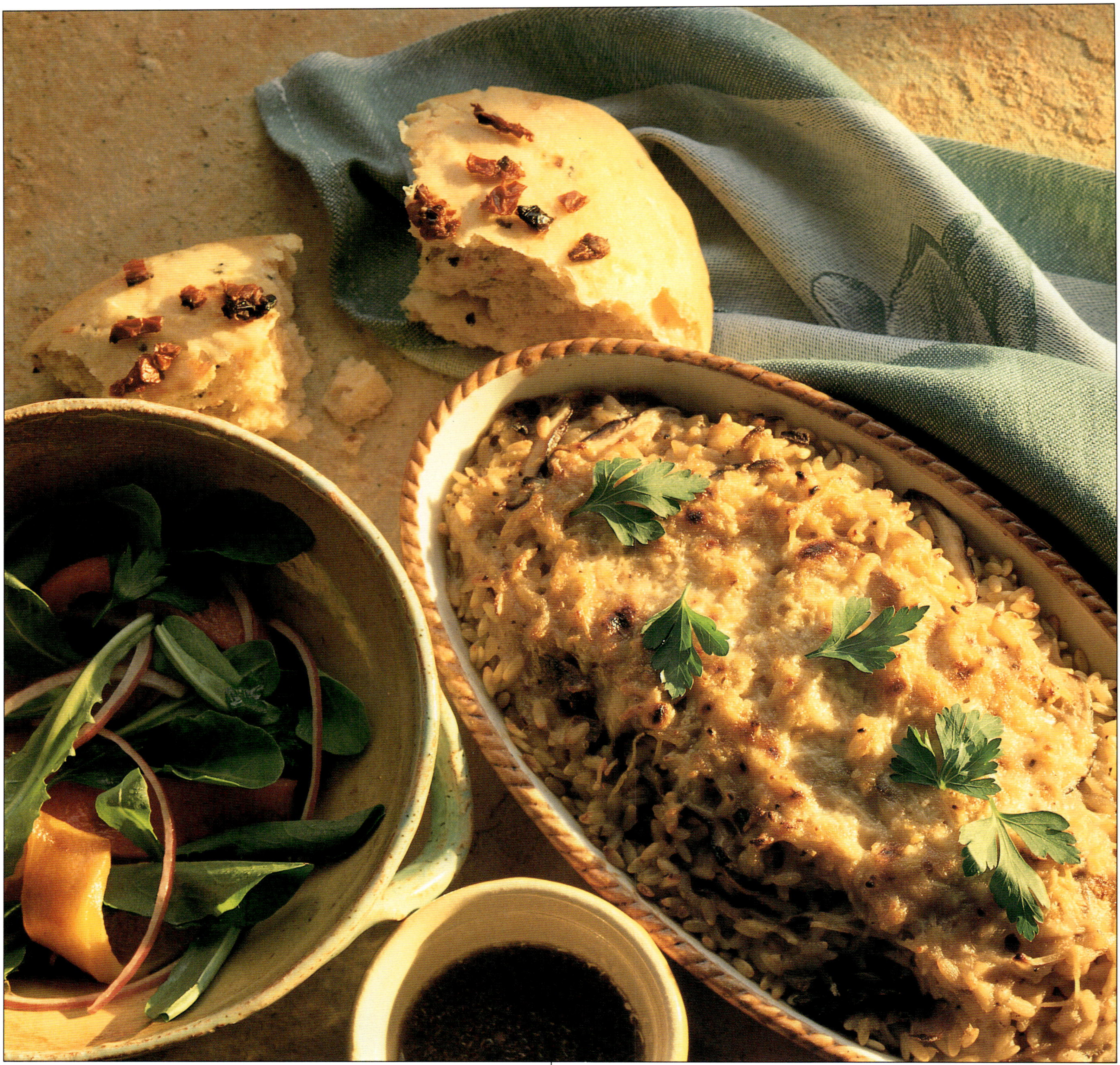

Met de klok mee van links: Geroosterde paprika en raketkruidsalade, Kruidig tomatenbrood, Orzo en paddestoelen uit de oven

PASTA / ITALIË

Orzo en paddestoelen uit de oven

Orzo is een rijstkorrelachtige pastasoort die snel gaar is. Dit gerecht lijkt een beetje op risotto zonder het langdurige roeren.

3 dl kippebouillon (zie woordenlijst)
30 g gedroogde boleten
4 eetlepels olijfolie
125 g grof gehakte rode ui
3 tenen knoflook, fijngehakt
250 g verse boleten of shiitake, bijgesneden en julienne gesneden
2 eetlepels bloem
¼ theelepel versgeraspte nootmuskaat
¼ theelepel zout
versgemalen peper naar smaak
375 g orzo, bijtgaar gekookt en uitgelekt
60 g versgeraspte Parmezaanse kaas
verse snijpeterselie, ter garnering

1. Verwarm de oven voor op 190°C. Verhit 4 eetlepels van de kippebouillon in een kleine pan en week er de gedroogde boleten 20 minuten in.
2. Verhit 2 eetlepels van de olie in een middelgrote koekepan en fruit er de ui en knoflook 2 tot 3 minuten in. Voeg de verse paddestoelen toe en bak 3 minuten. Giet er de overgebleven bouillon bij en kook circa 5 minuten tot de paddestoelen gaar zijn.

3. Schep de paddestoelen en ui met een schuimspaan uit de pan en zet ze weg. Bewaar de kippebouillon voor de saus.
4. Giet de gedroogde boleten af en bewaar het weeknat. Zet weg.
5. Verhit de overgebleven 2 eetlepels olie in een middelgrote pan en klop er de bloem door. Roerbak 2 tot 3 minuten op een middelhoog vuur om het zetmeel van de bloem te garen. Laat niet aanbranden. Giet er al kloppend de bewaarde kippebouillon en het paddestoelweeknat bij. Laat de saus op een middelhoog vuur sudderen tot de saus iets dikker is. Voeg de nootmuskaat en wat zout en peper toe.
6. Hak de geweekte boleten en doe ze bij de gare, verse paddestoelen. Schep er de orzo door.
7. Schep een dunne laag saus in een middelgrote ovenschaal. Zet 4 eetlepels van de saus weg. Schep de rest van de saus door het paddestoel-orzomengsel en schep het in de ovenschaal. Strijk er de bewaarde saus over en bestrooi met de Parmezanse kaas.
8. Zet de schaal 30 minuten in de oven. Garneer met de peterselie en dien op.

Voor 6 personen

1 portie: Calorieën 260, Eiwit 9 g, Koolhydraten 27 g, Vezel 3 g, Vet totaal 12 g (Verzadigd 3 g, Enkelvoudig onverzadigd 8 g, Meervoudig onverzadigd 1 g), Cholesterol 10 mg, Natrium 280 mg.

▲ *1 Brood, 1 Groente*

BROOD / SICILIË

Kruidig tomatenbrood

Dit boerenbrood heeft een volle tomatensmaak en gaat uitstekend samen met pasta.

4 eetlepels olijfolie
35 g gesnipperde ui
3 tenen knoflook, fijngehakt
250 g tomaten, ontveld, ontzaad en gepureerd
1 theelepel fijngehakte verse oregano
1 eetlepel fijngehakte verse tijm
2 eetlepels gehakte verse basilicum
1 pakje (7 g) droge gist
1½ eetlepel suiker
625 g bloem
75 g griesmeel (semolina)
1 eetlepel zout
16 stukken zongedroogde tomaat, 15-20 minuten in water geweekt, of 16 zongedroogde tomaten onder olie, goed uitgelekt
8 takjes verse tijm

1. Verhit 3 eetlepels van de olijfolie in een middelgrote koekepan. Doe er de ui en knoflook in en fruit circa 2 minuten tot ze gaar maar niet bruin zijn. Voeg de gepureerde tomaten, oregano, tijm en basilicum toe en neem de pan van het vuur. Zet weg.
2. Los de gist en suiker op in 1,25 dl warm water (40°-46°C). Laat 5 minuten staan tot u een schuimig mengsel hebt.
3. Doe de tomatensaus, het gistmengsel en 2,5 dl warm water in een grote kom en meng alles goed. Voeg 150 g van de bloem, het griesmeel en zout toe.
4. Voeg met 75 g tegelijk de rest van de bloem toe tot u een zacht, glad deeg hebt verkregen. Doe het deeg op een met bloem bestoven werkvlak en kneed het 7 tot 10 minuten.
5. Vorm het deeg tot een bal, dek af en laat 30 minuten rusten.
6. Verwarm de oven voor op 230°C. Vet 2 bakplaten of een ovensteen licht in met olie.
7. Druk de lucht uit het deeg en verdeel het in 4 bollen. Dek weer af en laat 45 minuten rusten.
8. Rol de bollen uit tot cirkels van 15 cm doorsnee. Kwast ze in met de overgebleven olijfolie en garneer met de zongedroogde tomaten en takjes tijm. Leg ze op de bakplaten of de steen.
9. Bak het brood 10 minuten in de oven tot de randen goudbruin zijn. Dien onmiddellijk op.

Voor 4 kleine broden (16 sneden)

1 snee per portie: Calorieën 180, Eiwit 5 g, Koolhydraten 31 g, Vezel 2 g, Vet totaal 4 g (Verzadigd 0,5 g, Enkelvoudig onverzadigd 2,5 g, Meervoudig onverzadigd 5 g), Cholesterol 0 mg, Natrium 480 mg.

▲ *1 Brood, 1 Groente*

SALADES / ITALIË

Geroosterde paprika en raketkruidsalade

De paprika's en ui worden zachter door marineren. De ui neemt de azijn op en verandert daardoor de dressing. Zet het paprika-uimengsel een nacht in de koelkast. Proef en doe er zonodig nog wat azijn bij voor u het mengsel met het raketkruid mengt.

1 grote teen knoflook
2 rode paprika's
2 gele paprika's
2 eetlepels balsamico azijn of rode wijnazijn
3 eetlepels saffloerolie
¼ theelepel zout
versgemalen peper naar smaak
60 g plakjes rode ui
60 g raketkruid
7 g snijpeterselieblad

1. Wrijf een slakom in met de knoflook. Zet weg.
2. Rooster de paprika's boven een gasvlam of onder de grill tot ze geblakerd zijn. Dompel de paprika's onmiddellijk in ijswater en ontvel ze. Verwijder het zaad en de zaadlijsten en snijd de paprika's in de lengte in repen van 2 cm breed.
3. Doe voor de dressing de azijn in een glazen of roestvrijstalen kom. Druppel er al kloppend geleidelijk de olie bij. Breng op smaak met zout en peper.
4. Schep de paprika's en ui in de slakom om met de dressing. Laat staan tot het serveren. Schep er vlak voor het serveren het raketkruid en de peterselie door. Serveer op kamertemperatuur.

Voor 6 personen

1 portie: Calorieën 80, Eiwit 1 g, Koolhydraten 5 g, Vezel 1 g, Vet totaal 7 g (Verzadigd 0,5 g, Enkelvoudig onverzadigd 1 g, Meervoudig onverzadigd 5 g), Cholesterol 0 mg, Natrium 300 mg, Vitamine A 35 %, Vitamine C 160%.

▲ *1 Groente, 1 Vet/Suiker*

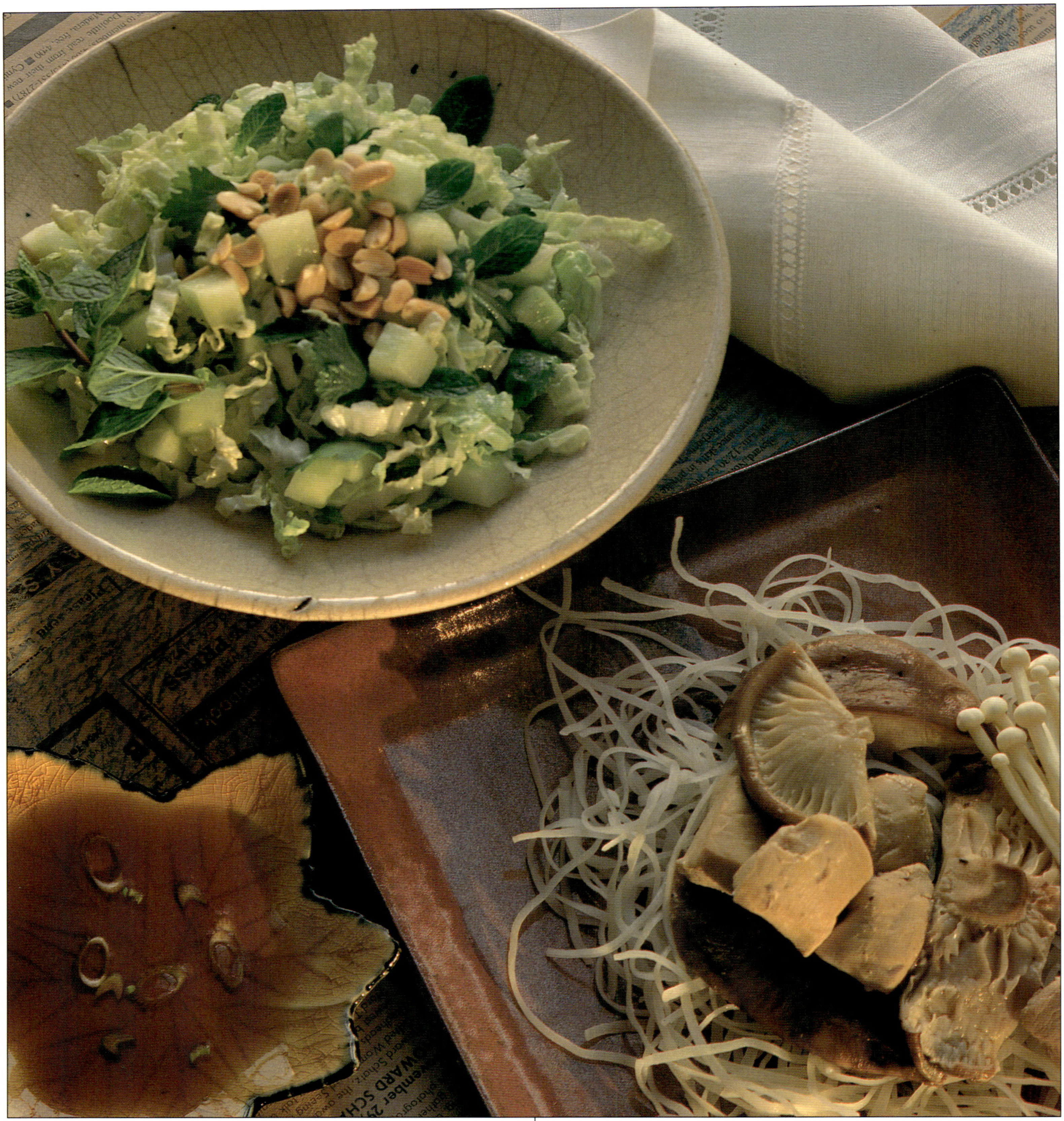

Van boven naar beneden: Thaise koolsalade, Matsutake en kip met ponzu-dipsaus

GEVOGELTE / JAPAN

Matsutake en kip met ponzu-dipsaus

Matsutake paddestoelen groeien laat in het najaar en 's winters in pijnboombossen in Japan, Korea en het noordwesten van Amerika. Ze ruiken naar deze pijnboombossen. Als matsutake *niet verkrijgbaar zijn, kunt u shiitake paddestoelen gebruiken.*

8 grote *matsutake* paddestoelen
2 hele kipfilets, in stukken van 3 cm gesneden
4 eetlepels sake
4 eetlepels natriumarme sojasaus
4 eetlepels vers citroensap
1 eetlepel gesnipperde lenteui
1 theelepel *mirin* (zoete keukensake)
125 g *harusame* (rijstnoedels), 5 minuten in warm water geweekt
60 g *enoki* paddestoelen

1. Verwarm de grill voor. Knip 4 vierkante stukken aluminiumfolie van 30 cm uit.
2. Snijd de steeltjes van de *matsutake* paddestoelen bij en snijd de hoedjes en steeltjes in dikke plakken. Schep de kip en de plakken paddestoel om met de sake en laat 20 minuten marineren.
3. Meng voor de *ponzu*-saus de sojasaus, het citroensap, lenteui en *mirin* in een kom. Doe de saus in 4 kommetjes en zet weg.

4. Giet de *harusame* af en schik op 4 borden.
5. Verdeel de paddestoelen en kip in 4 porties en schik op de folie. Vouw de randen samen zodat u luchtdichte pakjes hebt.
6. Grilleer de pakjes 4 minuten aan beide kanten. Neem het kipmengsel uit de pakjes en schik op de *harusame*. Garneer met de *enoki* paddestoelen en geef er de *ponzu*-dipsaus apart bij.

Voor 4 personen

1 portie: Calorieën 270, Eiwit 31 g, Koolhydraten 26 g, Vezel 1 g, Vet totaal 4 g (Verzadigd 1 g, Enkelvoudig onverzadigd 1 g, Meervoudig onverzadigd 1 g), Cholesterol 75 mg, Natrium 550 mg.

▲ *1 Brood, 1 Vlees*

GEVOGELTE / GROOT-BRITTANNIË

Kalkoenschnitzel met pruim, salie en prei

Met goed weer kunt u deze schnitzels barbecuen. Laat de havervlokken weg en geef er het pruim-preimengsel apart bij.

2 kalkoenfilets, elk circa 185 g, horizontaal in de lengte plakken van 5 cm dik gesneden
¼ theelepel zout
versgemalen peper naar smaak
2 eetlepels saffloerolie
3 preien, alleen het wit, julienne gesneden
2,5 dl bruine kippebouillon (zie woordenlijst)
500 g pruimen, gehalveerd en ontpit
1 eetlepel gehakte verse salie
20 g rauwe havervlokken

1. Verwarm de oven voor op 190°C. Vet een ondiepe ovenschaal licht in met olie.
2. Sla de plakken kalkoen plat met een vleeshamer of deegroller tussen 2 vellen plastic folie tot ze 2 cm dik zijn. Bestrooi ze met zout en peper.
3. Verhit de olie in een grote koekepan en bak de plakken kalkoen in circa 4 minuten aan beide kanten goudbruin. Doe ze in de schaal en zet weg.
4. Fruit de prei in 5 minuten gaar in dezelfde koekepan. Blus de pan af met de bouillon. Voeg de pruimen en salie toe en kook 5 minuten tot de bouillon iets ingekookt is.
5. Schep het pruimmengsel over de kalkoen, bestrooi met de havervlokken en zet 20 minuten in de oven.

Voor 4 personen

1 portie: Calorieën 290, Eiwit 23 g, Koolhydraten 32 g, Vezel 4 g, Vet totaal 9 g (Verzadigd 1 g, Enkelvoudig onverzadigd 1,5 g, Meervoudig onverzadigd 5,5 g), Cholesterol 55 mg, Natrium 200 mg, Vitamine C 35%.

▲ *1 Fruit, 1 Vlees*

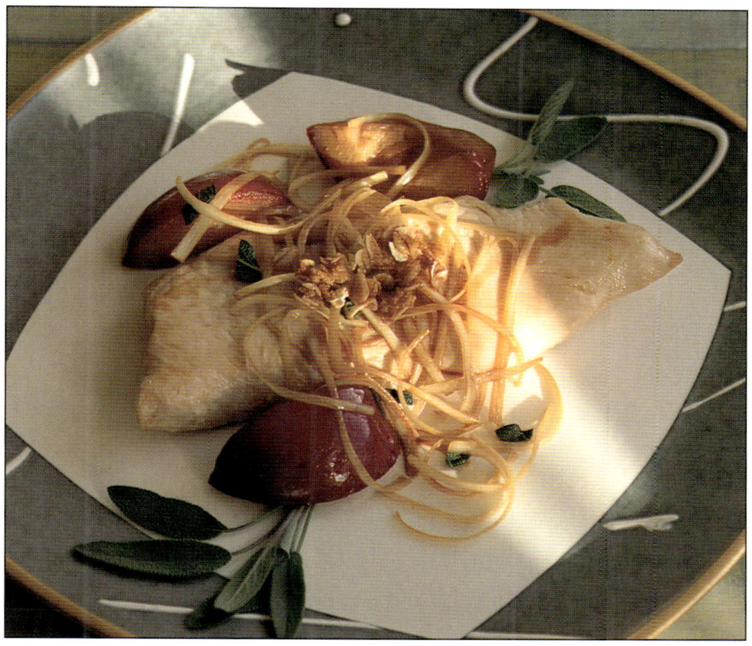

Kalkoenschnitzel met pruim, salie en prei

SALADES / THAILAND

Thaise koolsalade

Chilipepers worden veel gebruikt in de Thaise keuken. Snijd ze in plakjes en hak ze fijn voor dit recept zodat ze makkelijker te mengen zijn. Thaise groene kerriepasta is verkrijgbaar bij een goed geselecteerde oosterse toko. Als die niet verkrijgbaar is, kunt u een gelijke hoeveelheid kerriepoeder gebruiken.

2 tenen knoflook, fijngehakt
1 kleine groene chilipeper, ontzaad en overdwars in dunne plakjes (desgewenst)
3 eetlepels rijstazijn
3 eetlepels vers limoensap
2 eetlepels suiker
1 theelepel groene kerriepasta of kerriepoeder
4 eetlepels plantaardige ole
500 g Chinese kool, overdwars in dunne repen gesneden
1 komkommer, geschild, ontzaad en in blokjes
5 lenteuitjes, in dunne plakjes
7 g fijngehakte verse korianderblaadjes
7 g verse muntblaadjes
45 g grof gehakte droog geroosterde pinda's

1. Meng de knoflook met de chilipeper, rijstazijn, het limoensap, de suiker en kerriepasta in een middelgrote kom. Giet er al kloppend geleidelijk de olie bij.
2. Schep de dressing door de kool, komkommer, lenteui en verse koriander. Verdeel over 8 borden en garneer met de muntblaadjes en pinda's. Dien onmiddellijk op.

Voor 8 personen

2,5 dl per portie: Calorieën 120, Eiwit 2 g, Koolhydraten 8 g, Vezel 2 g, Vet totaal 9 g (Verzadigd 1 g, Enkelvoudig onverzadigd 2 g, Meervoudig onverzadigd 6 g), Cholesterol 0 mg, Natrium 40 mg, Vitamine A 35%, Vitamine C 50%.

▲ *2 Groente*

Vederwild / Portugal

Geroosterde kwartel met portsaus

Kies uit de vele druivensoorten één die u zelf lekker vindt. Het nadeel van pitlose druiven is dat ze soms minder smaak hebben. Het belangrijkste is dat u voor dit recept een druif met veel smaak gebruikt.

Geroosterde kwartel

8 verse kwartels
¼ theelepel zout
⅛ theelepel versgemalen zwarte peper
4 sjalotjes, gesnipperd
100 g ontpitte en grof gehakte blauwe druiven
2 eetlepels vers citroensap
6 eetlepels olijfolie

Portsaus

400 g gehalveerde en ontzade blauwe druiven
2,5 dl plus 2 theelepels port
5 dl kippebouillon (zie woordenlijst)
4 sjalotjes, gesnipperd
15 g zachte boter
2 theelepels maïzena
zout en versgemalen peper naar smaak

1. Verwarm de oven voor op 230°C.
2. Bestrooi de kwartels van binnen en buiten met ¼ theelepel zout en ⅛ theelepel peper
3. Meng de 4 sjalotjes in een kom met de grof gehakte druiven en het citroensap en schep 1 tot 2 eetlepels van het mengsel in elke vogel. Stop de punten van de vleugels onder de ruggen en bind de kwartels op.
4. Verhit de olijfolie in een grote braadslee 5 minuten in de oven. Schik de kwartels op hun zijkanten in de slee. Rooster ze 15 minuten, waarbij u ze om de 5 minuten op de andere kant keert. Leg de kwartels dan met de borstkant boven en rooster ze nog 5 minuten, of tot het sap roze is wanneer u de dij met een pen inprikt. Doe de kwartels vervolgens op een dienschaal en laat ze 5 minuten rusten.
5. Meng voor de portsaus de gehalveerde druiven, alle port op 2 theelepels na, de bouillon en sjalotjes in een middelgrote pan. Breng aan de kook, draai het vuur lager en laat het geheel 2 minuten sudderen.
6. Schep de druiven met een schuimspaan uit de saus en zet weg. Breng de saus weer aan de kook en laat tot circa 2,5 dl inkoken.
7. Prak de boter met de maïzena in een kleine kom tot een gladde pasta. Klop de pasta geleidelijk door de saus en laat 1 minuut zachtjes koken.
8. Voeg de overgebleven 2 theelepels port en de gehalveerde druiven toe en breng op smaak met zout en peper. Laat doorwarmen.
9. Schep de saus over de kwartels en dien op.

Voor 4 personen

1 kwartel met portsaus per portie: Calorieën 420, Eiwit 29 g, Koolhydraten 22 g, Vezel 1 g, Vet totaal 21 g (Verzadigd 6 g, Enkelvoudig onverzadigd 10 g, Meervoudig onverzadigd 3,5 g), Cholesterol 110 mg, Natrium 230 mg.

▲ *1 Vlees, 1 Fruit*

Pasta / Verenigde Staten

Zeebanketravioli met gekruide citrussaus

Voor zeer snel bereide verse ravioli worden in plaats van pastadeeg Chinese wontonvellen gebruikt.

Ravioli

125 g rauwe garnalen, gepeld en darmkanaal verwijderd
125 g zeebaars of een andere stevige witvissoort, gefileerd
1 theelepel fijngehakte verse dragon
1 eetlepel vers citroensap
versgemalen peper naar smaak
185 g wontonvellen of vers pastadeeg in vierkantjes van 7 cm
1 eiwit

Gekruide citrussaus

1 citroen
2 limoenen
4 sinaasappels
2 sjalotjes, gesnipperd
2 eetlepels plantaardige olie
1,25 dl droge witte wijn
4 eetlepels half melk en half room
2 theelepels fijngehakte verse dragon
1 eetlepel fijngehakte verse peterselie
versgemalen peper naar smaak

1. Hak voor de ravioli het zeebanket fijn en meng met de dragon, het citroensap en wat peper. Schep een volle lepel op een wontonvierkantje, kwast de randen in met wat eiwit en leg er een tweede wontonvel op. Druk de randen goed dicht. Maak op dezelfde manier ravioli met de rest van de ingrediënten en zet weg.
2. Snijd de schil van 1 citroen, 1 limoen en 1 sinaasappel in smalle reepjes en zet weg.
3. Fruit de sjalotjes in de olie in een middelgrote koekepan tot ze gaar maar niet bruin zijn. Blus de pan af met het sap van de citroen, limoenen en sinaasappels en de wijn. Kook in tot circa 1,25 dl. Voeg de melk en room, de reepjes schil, dragon en peterselie toe. Warm alles door en breng op smaak met peper.
4. Kook de ravioli 2 minuten in een grote pan kokend water. Giet de ravioli af en dien ze warm op met de saus.

Voor 4 personen

1 portie: Calorieën 300, Eiwit 18 g, Koolhydraten 39 g, Vezel 0 g, Vet totaal 10 g (Verzadigd 2 g, Enkelvoudig onverzadigd 1,5 g, Meervoudig onverzadigd 6 g), Cholesterol 65 mg, Natrium 320 mg, Vitamine C 100%.

▲ *1 Brood, 1 Fruit, 1 Vlees*

Soep / Verenigde Staten

Paddestoelensoep

U verkrijgt voor deze soep een gebonden effect door de paddestoelen te pureren. Zeef de soep daarna voor een gladde zijdeachtige structuur. Als u liever een boerensoep hebt, pureer dan de helft van de paddestoelen en

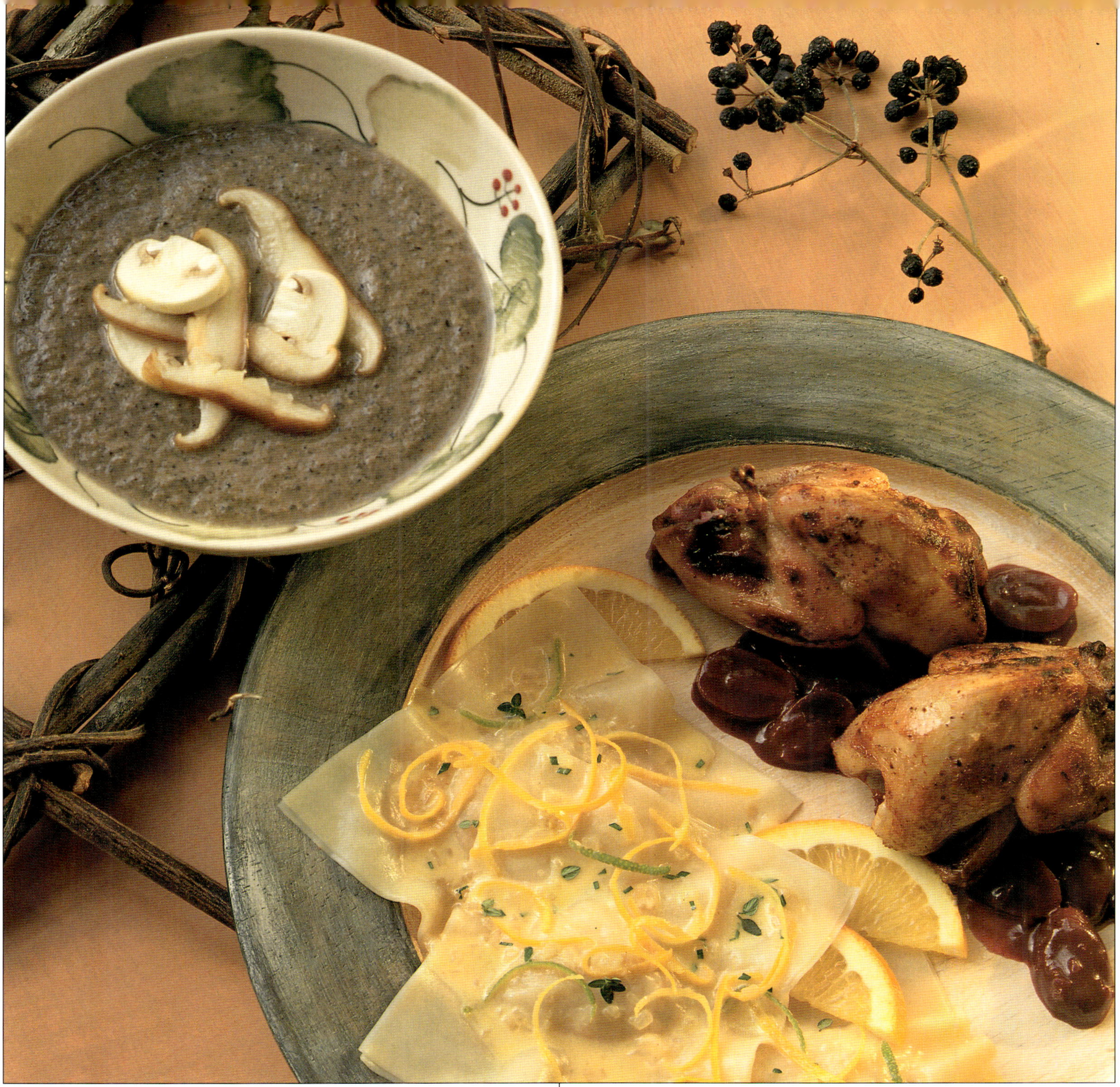

Met de klok mee van boven: Paddestoelensoep, Geroosterde kwartel met portsaus, Zeebanketravioli met gekruide citroensaus

garneer met de rest van de plakken. Fins volkorenbeschuit is heerlijk bij deze soep. Paddestoelen bevatten veel kalium, een mineraal dat belang is voor een goede spierwerking en een evenwichtige vochthuishouding.

250 g gemengde wilde paddestoelen (shiitake, morieljes, boleten, cantharellen), steeltjes bijgesneden en schoongeborsteld
500 g witte champignons, steeltjes bijgesneden en schoongeborsteld
het sap van 1 citroen
1,75 dl kippebouillon (zie woordenlijst)
60 g gedroogde boleten
2 eetlepels olijfolie
2 grote sjalotjes, gesnipperd
3 tenen knoflook, fijngehakt
1,25 dl madeira
1 theelepel gehakte verse tijm
1 eetlepel fijngehakte verse peterselie
½ theelepel zout
versgemalen peper naar smaak

1. Snijd de paddestoelen en champignons in plakken. Bewaar 16 mooie plakker ter garnering en schep ze om met het citroensap.
2. Verhit 1,25 dl van de bouillon in een kleine pan. Week er de gedroogde boleten 20 minuten in.
3. Verhit de olijfolie in een grote soeppan. Fruit er de sjalotjes en de knoflook gaar in. Voeg de plakken paddestoel en champignon toe en bak 10 minuten op een hoog vuur tot ze gaar zijn en het vocht verdampt is. Giet de gedroogde boleten af en bewaar het weeknat. Snijd de boleten en doe ze in de soeppan.
4. Blus de soeppan af met de madeira en kook in tot een een dikke puree. Giet er de overgebleven kippebouillon en het bewaarde weeknat bij en breng aan de kook.
5. Draai het vuur lager, voeg de tijm en peterselie toe en laat 30 minuten sudderen tot de soep iets dikker is. Pureer de soep in een blender, doe terug in de soeppan, breng op smaak met zout en peper en warm door. Dien onmiddellijk op en garneer elke kom met 2 van de bewaarde plakken paddestoel.

Voor 8 personen

2,5 dl per portie: Calorieën 110, Eiwit 3 g, Koolhydraten 12 g, Vezel 2 g, Vet totaal 5 g (Verzadigd 1 g, Enkelvoudig onverzadigd 3 g, Meervoudig onverzadigd 0,5 g), Cholesterol 0 mg, Natrium 160 mg.
▲ *1 Groente*

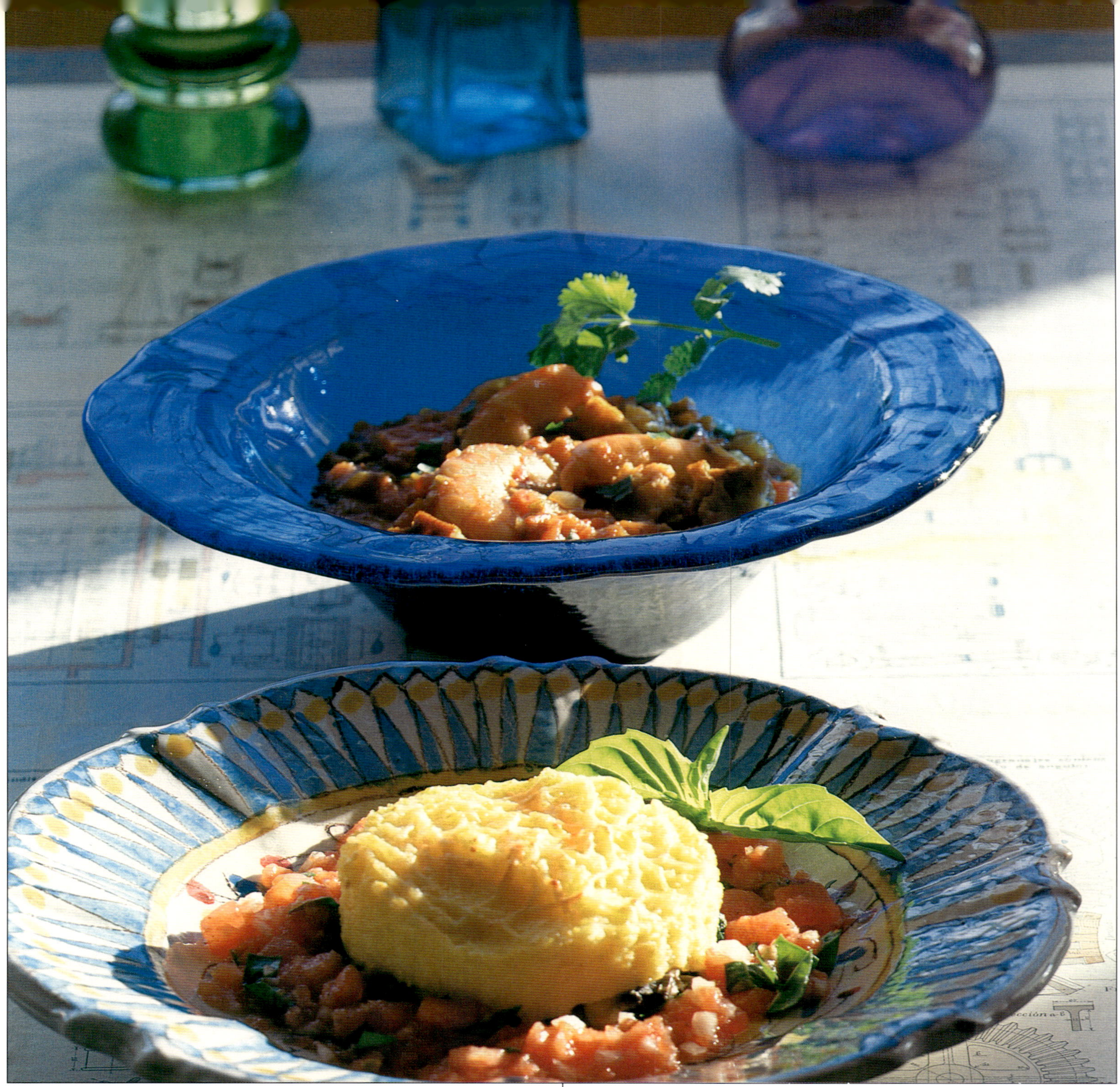

Van boven naar beneden: Garnalen-brood stoofpot, Spinazie-champignonpolenta met tomatensaus

ZEEBANKET / PORTUGAL

Migas de camarones

GARNALEN-BROOD STOOFPOT

Deze hartige stoofpot van garnalen, chilipepers, tomaten en brood is ideaal voor een koude dag.

7,5 dl kippebouillon (zie woordenlijst)
1 gedroogde milde chilipeper
2 verse milde groene chilipepers, geroosterd en ontzaad (zie woordenlijst)
3 eetlepels olijfolie
1 ui, gehakt
4 tenen knoflook, fijngehakt
1,25 dl droge witte wijn
3 eetlepels vers citroensap
500 g rauwe garnalen met schaal
4 grote tomaten, ontveld en gehakt
125 g vers brood, in stukken van 1 cm gescheurd
3 eetlepels gehakt vers korianderblad

1. Verhit 2,5 dl van de kippebouillon en week er de gedroogde chilipeper minstens 20 minuten in. Wanneer de gedroogde chilipeper zacht is hem met de verse chilipepers in een keukenmachine of blender pureren. Zet weg.
2. Verhit de olijfolie in een grote koekepan. Doe er de ui en knoflook in en fruit die in circa 3 minuten goudgeel. Giet er de wijn, het citroensap en de rest van de kippebouillon bij en breng aan de kook. Voeg de garnalen toe en laat 2 minten koken tot ze roze worden. Schep de garnalen met een schuimspaan uit de pan en laat ze afkoelen. Pel ze en verwijder de darmkanalen.
3. Breng het kooknat weer aan de kook en laat tot circa 2,5 dl inkoken. Voeg de chilipepers en tomaten toe en draai het vuur lager. Schep de gepelde garnalen en het brood door de saus. Bestrooi met de verse koriander en dien onmiddellijk op.

Voor 4 personen

1 portie: Calorieën 310, Eiwit 21 g, Koolhydraten 25 g, Vezel 4 g, Vet totaal 14 g (Verzadigd 2 g, Enkelvoudig onverzadigd 8,5 g, Meervoudig onverzadigd 2 g), Cholesterol 130 mg, Natrium 230 mg, Vitamine A 35%, Vitamine C 110%.

▲ *1 Brood, 1 Groente, 1 Vlees*

GRAAN / ITALIË

Spinazie-champignon-polenta met tomatensaus

Deze verse tomatensaus zorgt voor contrast met de gladde polenta. U kunt de polenta uit de schaal serveren of rondjes uitsteken met een uitsteekvorm van 7 cm doorsnee. Velen associëren spinazie met ijzer en kracht. Helaas wordt het ijzer in spinazie slecht opgenomen. Spinazie bevat wel veel vitaminen en mineralen.

2 eetlepels olijfolie
4 tenen knoflook, fijngehakt
250 g champignons, in plakken
500 g verse spinazie, fijngehakt
2 eetlepels fijngehakte verse peterselie
¼ theelepel zout
versgemalen peper naar smaak
1,2 liter kippebouillon (zie woordenlijst)
280 g polenta of geel griesmeel
30 g versgeraspte Parmezaanse kaas
1 liter tomatensaus (recept volgt)

1. Verwarm de oven voor op 190°C. Vet een ovenschaal van 23 x 33 cm licht in met olie.
2. Verhit de olijfolie in een middelgrote koekepan en fruit er de knoflook gaar maar niet bruin in. Voeg de champignons en spinazie toe en bak tot al het vocht verdampt is. Voeg de peterselie toe en breng op smaak met zout en peper. Zet de koekepan weg en laat afkoelen.
3. Breng de kippebouillon aan de kook in een grote pan. Voeg al kloppend geleidelijk de polenta toe. Draai het vuur middelhoog en laat onder voortdurend roeren circa 20 minuten zachtjes koken tot de polenta loslaat van de panwand.
4. Strijk het spinaziemengsel uit over de bodem van de ovenschaal. Giet er de polenta over en strijk die ook uit. Bestrooi met de Parmezaanse kaas en zet 15 minuten in de oven. Dien onmiddellijk op of laat op kamertemperatuur komen. Geef er apart een kom met tomatensaus bij.

Voor 8 personen

1 portie: Calorieën 195, Eiwit 7 g, Koolhydraten 31 g, Vezel 5 g, Vet totaal 6 g (Verzadigd 1,5 g, Enkelvoudig onverzadigd 3 g, Meervoudig onverzadigd 1 g), Cholesterol 2 mg, Natrium 200 mg, Vitamine A 80%, Vitamine C 65%.

▲ *1 Brood, 2 Groente*

TOMATENSAUS

4 tomaten, ontveld, ontzaad en in blokjes
2 tomaten, ontveld en gepureerd
het sap van 1 citroen
2 sjalotjes, gesnipperd
7 g gehakte verse basilicumblaadjes
1 eetlepel fijngehakte verse peterselie
snufje zout
versgemalen peper naar smaak

1. Meng alle ingrediënten in een decoratieve kom.

Voor 1 liter

1,25 dl per portie: Calorieën 25, Eiwit 1 g, Koolhydraten 6 g, Vezel 1 g, Vet totaal 0 g (Verzadigd 0 g, Enkelvoudig onverzadigd 0 g, Meervoudig onverzadigd 0 g), Cholesterol 0 mg, Natrium 30 mg, Vitamine C 35%.

▲ *1 Groente*

GROENTEN / BELGIË

Kastanjes en spruitjes met mosterdglazuur

Kastanje is de enige notensoort met een laag vetgehalte, en bevat bovendien wat vitamine C. Spruitjes zijn een kruisbloemige groentesoort en bevatten veel vitamine A en C.

250 g verse kastanjes of uit blik
1,25 dl kippebouillon (zie woordenlijst)
500 g spruitjes, geblancheerd (zie woordenlijst)
250 g waspeen, geschraapt en geblancheerd (zie woordenlijst)
4 eetlepels vers sinaasappelsap
15 g boter
3 eetlepels lichtbruine basterdsuiker
1 eetlepel grove mosterd
1 theelepel geraspte sinaasappelschil
zout en versgemalen peper naar smaak

1. Kerf een kruis in de kastanjes. Dompel ze 5 minuten in kokend water, giet ze af, laat afkoelen en pel ze. Zet ze weg.
2. Breng de kippebouillon aan de kook in een grote pan. Doe er de spruitjes en waspeen in en draai het vuur lager. Laat de groenten in 8 tot 10 minuten gaar sudderen. Schep ze met een schuimspaan uit de bouillon, zet ze weg en bewaar de bouillon.
3. Maak het mosterdglazuur. Verhit de bouillon in dezelfde pan en voeg het sinaasappelsap, de boter en suiker toe. Kook op een middelhoog vuur tot het mengsel tot de helft is ingekookt. Schep er de mosterd en geraspte schil door. Breng op smaak met zout en peper.
4. Schep de kastanjes, spruitjes en wortels om met het mosterdglazuur en laat alles doorwarmen. Dien onmiddellijk op.

Voor 6 personen *Foto op pagina 175*

2,5 dl per portie: Calorieën 170, Eiwit 4 g, Koolhydraten 33 g, Vezel 8 g, Vet totaal 3 g (Verzadigd 1,5 g, Enkelvoudig onverzadigd 1 g, Meervoudig onverzadigd 0,5 g), Cholesterol 5 mg, Natrium 70 mg, Vitamine A 35%, Vitamine C 150%.

▲ *2 Groente*

GROENTEN / CHINA

Kouseband en paddestoelen in zwarte-bonensaus

Als smaakgever in dit recept fungeren gefermenteerde of gezouten zwarte bonen. Deze zijn in potjes of pakjes verkrijgbaar in vele oosterse toko's. Deze ingemaakte zwarte sojabonen zijn eerst gekookt en daarna in een gekruide pekel gezet.

500 g kouseband of sperziebonen, bijgesneden
1,25 dl kippebouillon (zie woordenlijst)
30 g gedroogde zwarte Chinese paddestoelen, afgespoeld
2 eetlepels ingemaakte zwarte bonen
2 eetlepels sherry
2 tenen knoflook, fijngehakt
1 theelepel gehakte verse gember
1 theelepel maïzena gemengd met 1 eetlepel champignon-sojasaus
3 eetlepels saffloerolie
½ theelepel sesamolie
250 g shiitake paddestoelen, julienne gesneden
4 lenteuitjes, in dunne plakjes

1. Blancheer de kouseband door ze in 30 seconden in kokend water te doen (1 minuut voor sperziebonen). Dompel ze onmiddellijk in ijswater om het koken te stoppen. Giet ze af en zet weg.
2. Verhit de kippebouillon in een kleine pan. Week er de gedroogde paddestoelen minstens 30 minuten in. Schep de paddestoelen eruit en hak ze in kleine blokjes; zet weg. Zeef de bouillon door een fijne zeef en zet weg.
3. Meng de zwarte bonen met de sherry, knoflook en gember in een kleine kom. Roer om met het maïzenapapje. Zet weg.
4. Verhit de saffloerolie en sesamolie in een grote koekepan. Bak er de shiitake circa 2 minuten in. Voeg de blokjes zwarte paddestoel, kouseband, lenteui en gezeefde bouillon toe. Kook 10 minuten op een hoog vuur tot het vocht iets ingekookt is.
5. Schep er het bonenmengsel door om de saus dikker te maken en dien onmiddellijk op.

Voor 6 personen

1 portie: Calorieën 140, Eiwit 3 g, Koolhydraten 17 g, Vezel 3 g, Vet totaal 7 g (Verzadigd 1 g, Enkelvoudig onverzadigd 1 g, Meervoudig onverzadigd 5 g), Cholesterol 0 mg, Natrium 210 mg, Vitamine C 25%.

▲ *2 Groente*

Van boven naar beneden: Kouseband en in zwarte-bonensaus, Krab-en-maïssoep

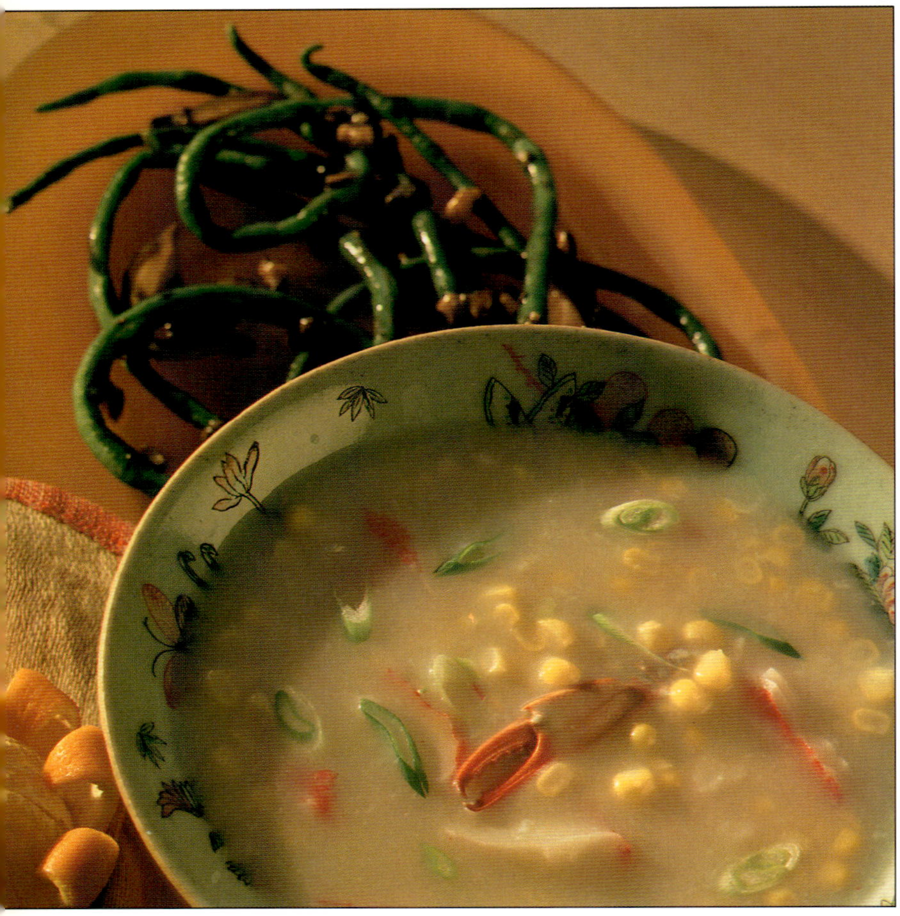

VEDERWILD / FRANKRIJK

Eendebout met pruimedanten en armagnac

Bij veel recepten wordt alleen de eendeborst gebruikt. In dit gerecht kunt u een ander heerlijk deel van de eend gebruiken. Geef er couscous of pasta bij.

185 g ontpitte pruimedanten
2,5 dl armagnac
3 eetlepels saffloerolie
3 sjalotjes, gesnipperd
4 eendebouten, vel en vet verwijderd
5 dl kippebouillon (zie woordenlijst)
2 takjes verse tijm
1 laurierblad
versgemalen peper naar smaak

1. Week de pruimedanten minstens 30 minuten in de armagnac.
2. Verhit de saffloerolie in een grote pan en fruit er de sjalotjes in circa 2 minuten gaar in. Doe er de eendebouten in en bak ze rondom lichtbruin. Blus de pan daarna af met de pruimedanten en armagnac.
3. Voeg de kippebouillon, tijm en het laurierblad toe, leg het deksel op de pan en laat 1 uur sudderen. Breng op smaak met zout en peper en dien onmiddellijk op.

Voor 4 personen

1 bout met 4 eetlepels saus per portie: Calorieën 500, Eiwit 23 g, Koolhydraten 28 g, Vezel 3 g, Vet totaal 21 g (Verzadigd 5 g, Enkelvoudig onverzadigd 4,5 g, Meervoudig onverzadigd 9 g), Cholesterol 130 mg, Natrium 135 mg, IJzer 25%, Vitamine A 20%, Vitamine C 20%.

▲ *1 Fruit, 1 Vlees*

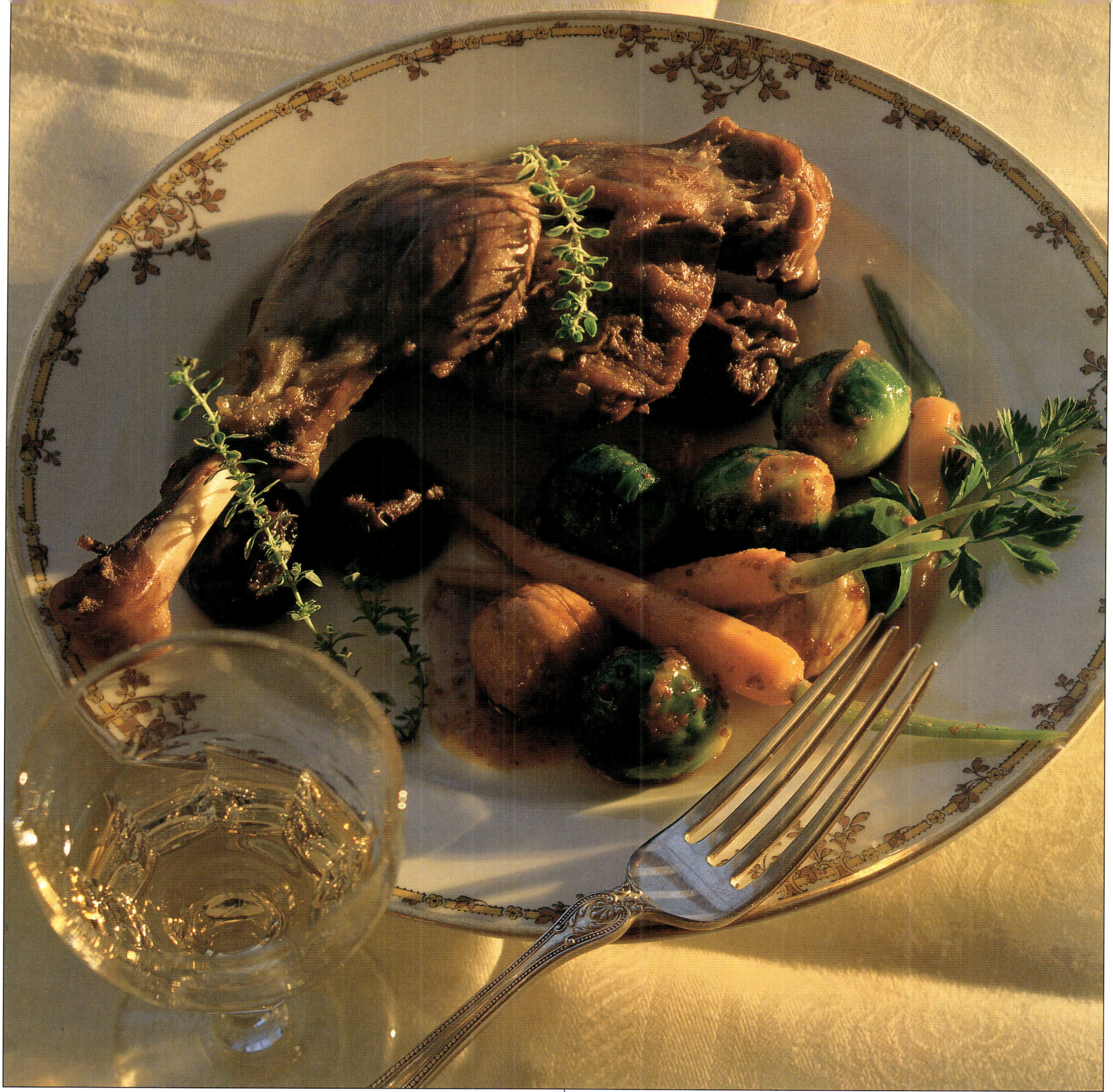

Van boven naar beneden: Eendebout met pruimedanten en armagnac, Kastanjes en spruitjes met mosterdglazuur *(recept pagina 173)*

SOEP / CHINA

Krab-en-maïssoep

Deze klassieke Chinese soep is snel klaar. Krab bevat veel zink, een belangrijk element voor het onderhoud van onze smaak en reukzin.

1 liter kippebouillon (zie woordenlijst)
½ theelepel sesamolie
250 g krabvlees
185 g verse maïskorrels
4 eetlepels magere melk
zout en versgemalen witte peper naar smaak
1 eetlepel maïzena, met 2 eetlepels kippebouillon tot een papje gemengd
2 eiwitten
2 lentuitjes, in dunne rondjes

1. Doe de kippebouillon en sesamolie in een grote soeppan en breng aan de kook. Voeg het krabvlees en de melk toe en breng weer aan de kook. Draai het vuur lager en laat nog 10 minuten sudderen. Breng op smaak met zout en peper.
2. Klop er het maïzenapapje door en laat sudderen tot de soep gebonden is.
3. Giet er al zachtjes roerend geleidelijk het eiwit bij.
4. Schep de soep in voorverwarmde soepkommen en bestrooi met de lenteui. Dien onmiddellijk op.

Voor 6 personen

2,5 dl per portie: Calorieën 100, Eiwit 10 g, Koolhydraten 8 g, Vezel 1 g, Vet totaal 2 g (Verzadigd 0,5 g, Enkelvoudig onverzadigd 1 g, Meervoudig onverzadigd 0,5 g), Cholesterol 40 mg, Natrium 140 mg, Zink 12%.

▲ *½ Vlees*

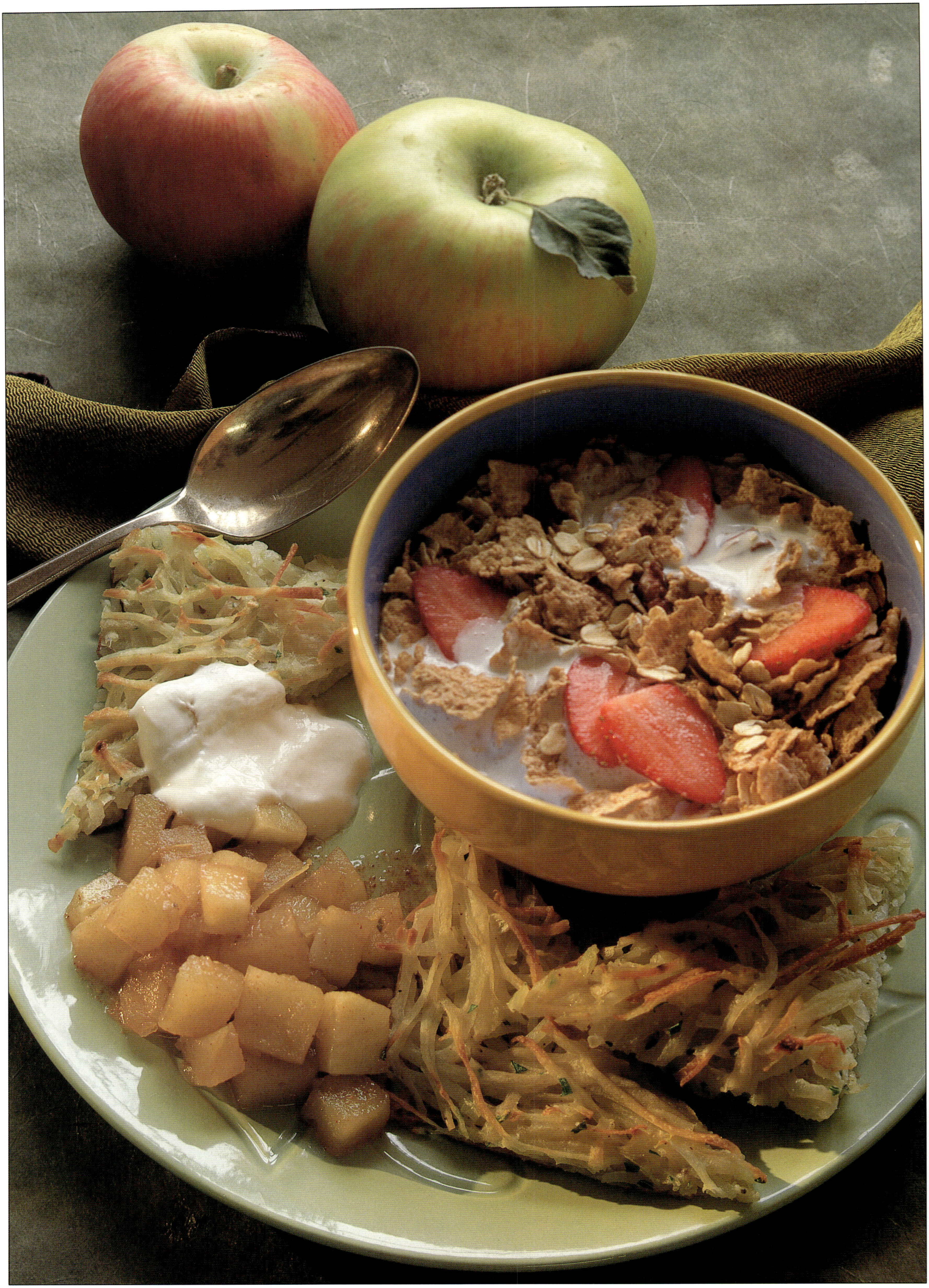

ONTBIJT / ZWITSERLAND

Muesli

Muesli werd verzonnen door een Zwiterse arts, dr. Bircher-Brenner, die naar een eiwitrijk ontbijt zocht. Het door hem gecreëerde mengel is ook vezelrijk en bevat veel vitaminen en mineralen. Muesli verschilt van cruesli doordat de granen ongekookt worden gegeten. In sommige versies worden de haver- en tarwevlokken eerst 30 minuten in water geweekt en dan na uitlekken met de andere graansoorten gemengd. Eet muesli met vers fruit als geraspte appel, plakjes banaan of aarbei, en met yoghurt of wat melk.

90 g ongekookte havervlokken
45 g tarwevlokken
20 g (4 eetlepels) tarwezemelen
2 eetlepels tarwekiemen
2 eetlepels geroosterde en grof gehakte pecannoten (desgewenst)

1. Meng alle ingrediënten in een kom.

Voor 150 g

50 g per portie: Calorieën 180, Eiwit 8 g, Koolhydraten 35 g, Vezel 6 g, Vet totaal 2,5 g (Verzadigd 0,5 g, Enkelvoudig onverzadigd 0,5 g, Meervoudig onverzadigd 1 g), Cholesterol 0 mg, Natrium 0 mg.
▲ *1 Brood*

ONTBIJT / VERENIGDE STATEN

Latkes uit de oven met gekruide appels

Latkes (aardappelpannekoeken) worden meestal in olie gebakken. Hier gaan ze in de oven om het vetgehalte te verminderen.

KRUIDIGE APPELS
3 Granny Smith of Cox Orange appels, geschild, klokhuis verwijderd en in blokjes
1,25 dl appelsap
½ theelepel fijngeraspte citroenschil
60 g suiker
1 theelepel versgemalen kaneel
½ theelepel versgeraspte nootmuskaat
¼ theelepel gemberpoeder

LATKES
6 aardappels, geschild
2 uien, gesnipperd
2 eieren
1 theelepel saffloerolie
2 eetlepels fijngehakte peterselie
75 g bloem
½ theelepel zuiveringszout (natriumbicarbonaat)
1 eetlepel vers citroensap
zout en versgemalen witte peper naar smaak
2,5 dl yoghurt

Van links naar rechts: Latkes uit de oven met gekruide appels, Muesli

1. Verwarm de oven voor op 190°C. Vet een anti-aanbak bakplaat van 32 x 43 cm licht in met olie.
2. Meng voor de kruidige appels de appels, het appelsap, de citroenschil en suiker in een middelgrote pan. Breng aan de kook. Draai het vuur lager en laat het mengsel circa 10 minuten sudderen tot de appels gaar zijn. Voeg de kaneel, nootmuskaat en gember toe. Schep over in een kom en laat afkoelen.
3. Rasp voor de latkes de aardappels en doe ze in een groot vergiet. Spoel ze onder de koude kraan, waarbij u ze zachtjes omschept tot het zetmeel weggespoeld is en het water helder blijft. Op deze manier verkleuren de aardappels voor het bakken niet. Knijp er voor het bakken zoveel mogelijk water uit.
4. Meng de aardappel met de ui, eieren, olie en peterselie in een kom. Zeef de bloem en zuiveringszout en schep door het aardappelmengsel. Voeg het citroensap en wat zout en peper toe.
5. Schep het aardappelmengsel op de bakplaat. Zet 15 minuten in de oven, of tot de latkes goudbruin zijn. Laat vervolgens 5 minuten afkoelen.
6. Snijd in vierkantjes van circa 10 cm en snijd die vervolgens in driehoekjes. Dien warm op met de gekruide appel en yoghurt.

Voor 8 personen

3 driehoekjes met appel en yoghurt per portie: Calorieën 230, Eiwit 6 g, Koolhydraten 47 g, Vezel 4 g, Vet totaal 2 g (Verzadigd 0,5 g, Enkelvoudig onverzadigd 0,5 g, Meervoudig onverzadigd 1 g), Cholesterol 55 mg, Natrium 125 mg, Vitamine C 25%.
▲ *1 Fruit, 1 Groente*

DRANKEN / VERENIGDE STATEN

Gekruide appelcider

De lekkerste cider heeft de minste behandelingen ondergaan. Dat wil zeggen dat hij niet gefilterd of gepasteuriseerd is. Dergelijke cider is in reformwinkels verkrijgbaar. Als u geen hele kruidnagel, piment of kardemom hebt, gebruik dan ¼ theelepel van elke gemalen specerij.

2 liter appelcider
4 hele kruidnagels
1 theelepel pimentbessen
1 kardemompeul, gedopt
10 kaneelpijpjes
1 sinaasappel, in dunne plakken
versgeraspte nootmuskaat naar smaak

1. Doe de appelcider in een grote, zware pan en breng aan de kook. Draai het vuur laag.
2. Wikkel de kruidnagels, pimentbessen en het kardemomzaad in een stukje ongebleekte katoen en doe in de cider. Voeg 2 van de kaneelpijpjes toe en laat 10 minuten sudderen.
3. Schep de warme cider in voorverwarmde mokken. Doe één plak sinaasappel en één van de overgebleven kaneelpijpjes in elke mok. Rasp er wat nootmuskaat over en dien onmiddellijk op.

Voor 8 personen *Foto op pagina 178*

2,5 dl per portie: Calorieën 125, Eiwit 0 g, Koolhydraten 31 g, Vezel 1 g, Vet totaal 0 g (Verzadigd 0 g, Enkelvoudig onverzadigd 0 g, Meervoudig onverzadigd 0 g), Cholesterol 0 mg, Natrium 5 mg.
▲ *1 Fruit*

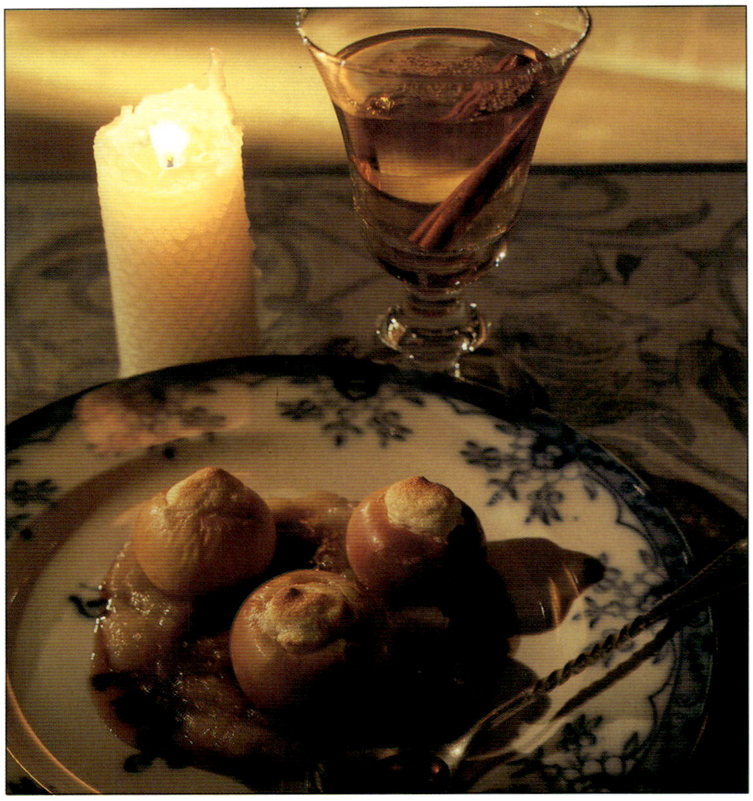

Van boven naar beneden: Gekruide appelcider (recept pagina 177), Gepofte sterappels met appelsoufflé en kaneel-rumsaus

ONTBIJT / VERENIGDE STATEN

Cruesli

Cruesli *is de uitgebreide, geroosterde versie van* muesli. Cruesli *is niet alleen een voedzaam ontbijtgerecht, maar ook een heerlijke garnering voor desserts.*

140 g ongekookte havervlokken
45 g tarwevlokken
20 g tarwezemelen
2 eetlepels gedopt pompoenzaad
2 eetlepels zonnebloempitten
1 eetlepel sesamzaad
2,5 dl appelsap
4 eetlepels honing
1 theelepel vanille-essence
1 theelepel gemalen kaneel
¼ theelepel gemalen kardemom
¼ theelepel gemberpoeder
¼ theelepel gemalen nootmuskaat
45 g gehakte dadels
45 g sultanarozijnen of krenten

1. Verwarm de oven voor op 165°C. Vet een bakplaat licht in met wat olie.
2. Schep de havervlokken door de tarwevlokken en tarwezemelen in een grote kom. Schep er het pompoenzaad, de zonnebloempitten en het sesamzaad door.
3. Doe het appelsap en de honing in een kleine pan. Verhit het mengsel al roerend op een middelhoog vuur tot de honing opgelost is. Roer er de vanille, kaneel, kardemom, gember en nootmuskaat door en neem de pan van het vuur.
4. Giet het honingmengsel over het havermengsel en schep alles goed om. Strijk het mengsel uit over de bakplaat en zet 30-35 minuten in de oven tot het bruin is, waarbij u af en toe omschept. Laat afkoelen.
5. Hak het mengsel grof en doe weer op de bakplaat. Zet nog 10-15 minuten in de oven tot het knapperig maar niet te bruin is. Laat weer afkoelen.
6. Schep er de dadels en rozijnen door en bewaar in een luchtdichte trommel.

Voor 550 g

50 g per portie: Calorieën 180, Eiwit 4 g, Koolhydraten 35 g, Vezel 4 g, Vet totaal 4 g (Verzadigd 0,5 g, Enkelvoudig onverzadigd 1 g, Meervoudig onverzadigd 2 g), Cholesterol 0 mg, Natrium 25 mg.
▲ *1 Brood*

DESSERTS / VERENIGDE STATEN

Gepofte sterappels met appelsoufflé en kaneel-rumsaus

Sterappels zijn in de herfst verkrijgbaar. Gebruik voor dit recept voor de rest van het jaar bijvoorbeeld Cox Orange of Golden Delicious; verleng in dat geval de kooktijd met 30 minuten.

GEPOFTE APPELS MET SOUFFLÉ
12 kleine sterappels of 4 grote Cox Orange of Golden Delicious
het sap van 1 citroen
1,25 dl appelsap
2 Goudrenetten of andere moesappels, geschild, klokhuis verwijderd en in blokjes
90 g suiker
½ theelepel versgemalen kaneel
¼ theelepel versgeraspte nootmuskaat
2 eiwitten

KANEEL-RUMSAUS
100 g donkerbruine basterdsuiker
1 kaneelpijpje
4 eetlepels bruine rum
2 theelepels vanille-essence

1. Verwarm de oven voor op 190°C.
2. Steek met een appelboor de klokhuizen uit de appels. Kwast de aangesneden appel licht in met wat citroensap. Doe 4 eetlepels van het appelsap in een ovenschaal die net groot genoeg is om de appels naast elkaar te bevatten. Schik de appels naast elkaar in de schaal, dek die af met aluminiumfolie en zet 15 minuten voor sterappels of 45 minuten voor Cox Orange in de oven.
3. Doe intussen de rest van het appelsap, de Goudrenetten en 60 g van de suiker in een middelgrote pan. Kook 15 minuten op een middelhoog vuur tot de appels volledig gaar zijn. Pureer het mengsel in een blender. Voeg de kaneel en nootmuskaat toe. U moet circa 5 dl appelmoes hebben. Zet weg.
4. Klop de eiwitten met 1 theelepel van het citroensap in een zuurbestendige kom tot zachte pieken. Voeg de rest van de suiker toe en klop tot stijve maar niet droge pieken. Vouw het eiwit door

2,5 dl van de appelmoes. Neem de appels uit de oven en schep het eiwitmengsel in holtes van de appels. Doe de appels dan zonder folie terug in de oven en laat 8-10 minuten bakken op 200°C, of tot de soufflé gerezen en goudbruin is. Zeef het kooknat.

5. Verhit voor de rumsaus al roerend de basterdsuiker, 4 eetlepels van het kooknat en het kaneelpijpje in een middelgrote pan tot de suiker opgelost is.
6. Laat circa 10 minuten sudderen tot de saus dik is. Roer er de rum en vanille door en giet in een voorverwarmde kom.
7. Schep de overgebleven appelmoes op 4 borden. Schik 3 sterappels of 1 Cox Orange op elk bord en geef er de saus apart bij.

Voor 4 personen

1 portie: Calorieën 330, Eiwit 2 g, Koolhydraten 74 g, Vezel 7 g, Vet totaal 1 g (Verzadigd 0 g, Enkelvoudig onverzadigd 0 g, Meervoudig onverzadigd 0 g), Cholesterol 0 mg, Natrium 35 mg, Vitamine C 30%.
▲ *2 Fruit, 1 Vet/Suiker*

ONTBIJT / VERENIGDE STATEN

Volkoren-esdoorn-siroopmuffins

Serveer deze muffins uit de oven met halfvolle yoghurt gemengd met 3 eetlepels esdoornsiroop.

300 g bloem
75 g volkorenbloem
4 eetlepels (20 g) tarwekiemen
1¼ theelepel bakpoeder
1¼ theelepel zuiveringszout (natriumbicarbonaat)
snufje zout
½ theelepel gemalen kaneel
100 g lichtbruine basterdsuiker
1,8 dl karnemelk
2 eetlepels saffloerolie
2 eieren
4 eetlepels pure esdoornsiroop
1 rijpe banaan

1. Verwarm de oven voor op 180°C. Vet een muffinvorm voor 12 muffins licht in met olie of bekleed met papieren cakevormpjes.
2. Meng de bloem in een grote kom met de volkorenbloem, 3 eetlepels van de tarwekiemen, het bakpoeder, zuiveringszout, zout, de kaneel en basterdsuiker. Zet weg.
3. Doe de karnemelk, saffloerolie, eieren, esdoornsiroop en banaan in een blender en draai tot een gladde puree.
4. Schep de natte ingrediënten snel door de droge ingrediënten tot alles net gemengd is.
5. Vul de muffinvormpjes voor tweederde met het beslag. Bestrooi met de overgebleven tarwekiemen.
6. Bak in 20 minuten in de oven goudbruin. Dien warm op.

Voor 12 muffins

1 muffin per portie: Calorieën 190, Eiwit 5 g, Koolhydraten 34 g, Vezel 2 g, Vet totaal 4 g (Verzadigd 1 g, Enkelvoudig onverzadigd 1 g, Meervoudig onverzadigd 2 g), Cholesterol 35 mg, Natrium 170 mg.
▲ *1 Brood*

Van boven naar beneden: Volkoren-esdoorsiroopmuffins, Cruesli

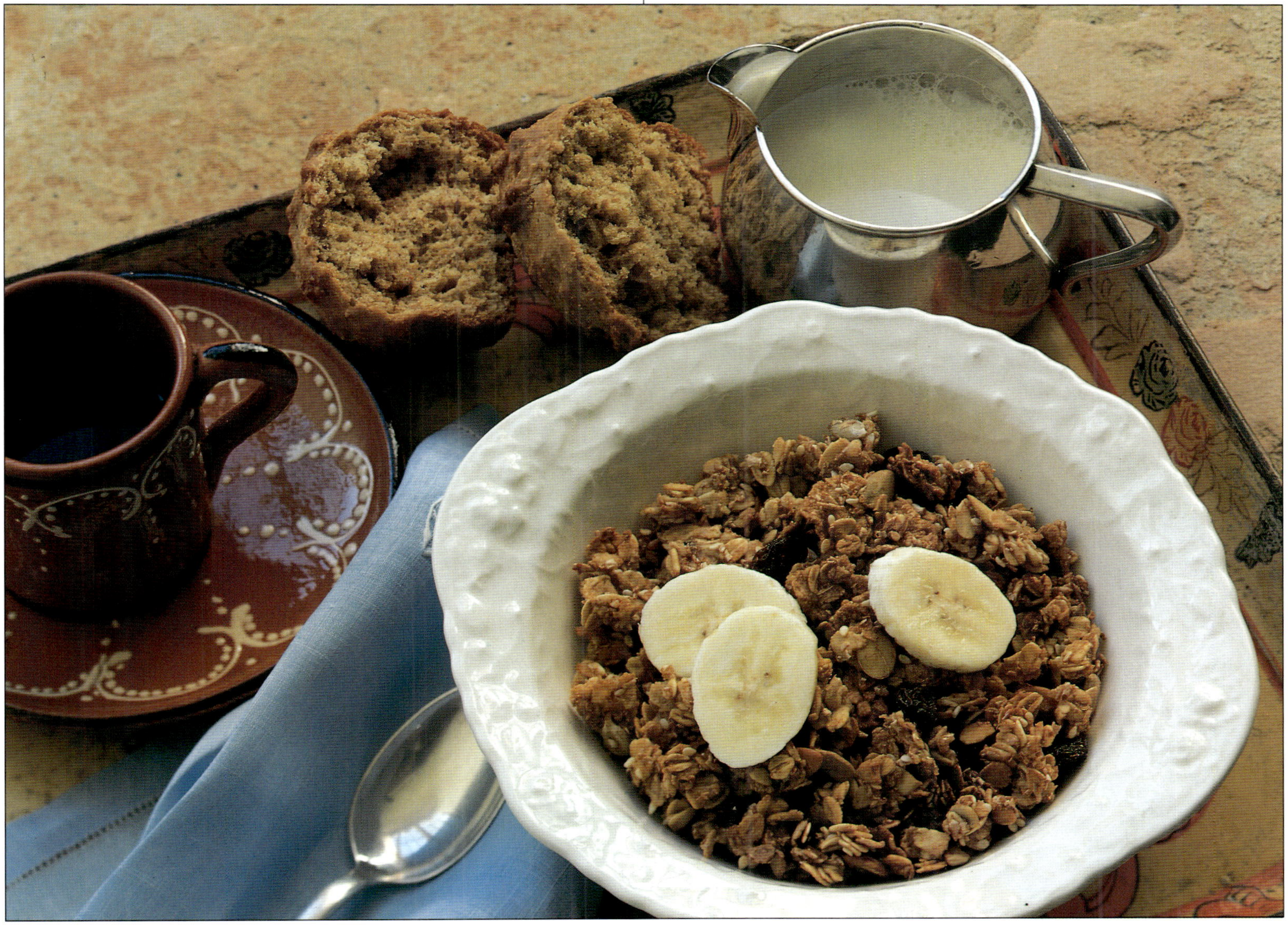

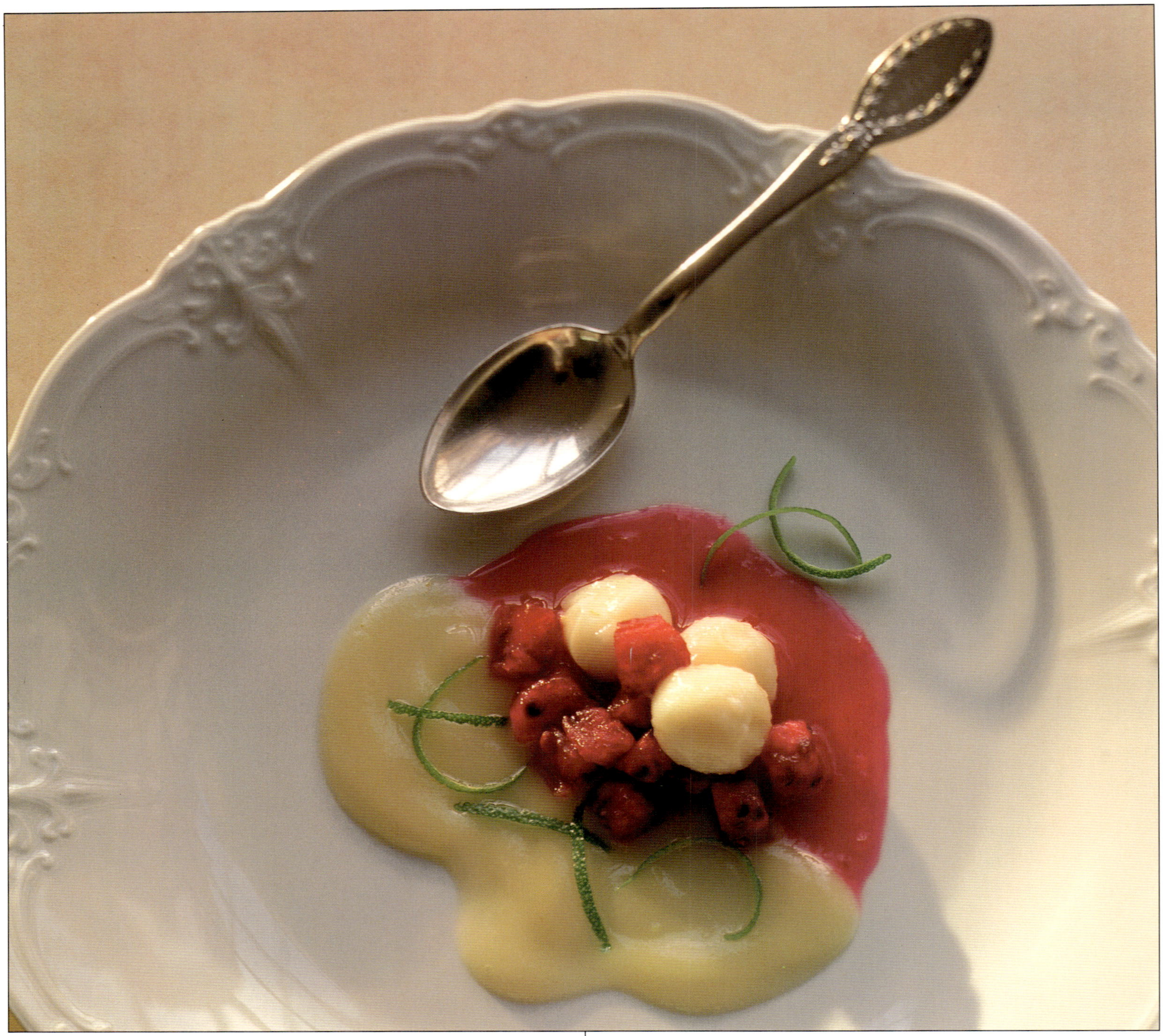

Cactusvijg en meloen met tequila en limoen

Cactusvijg en meloen met tequila en limoen

Hoewel cactusvijgen in Midden- en Noord-Amerika purperrode vruchten zijn, hebben andere variëteiten uit het Middellandse-Zeegebied en Azië romig, oranje, geel en oranje-rood vruchtvlees. Kies stevige, soepele cactusvijgen met een goede kleur. Kies stevige meloenen en laat die 3 dagen rijpen.

4 grote cactusvijgen
3 eetlepels suiker
2 eetlepels tequila
2 meloenen, elk circa 250 g, geschild en ontzaad
het sap van 1 limoen
3 eetlepels suiker
½ theelepel geraspte limoenschil

1. Schil de cactusvijgen door ze stevig met tangen vast te houden en 1 cm van elke punt te snijden. Zet de vijg op één punt en trek er vanaf één punt naar de andere een reep schil af terwijl u de vijg met de tangen vasthoudt. U kunt het geschilde stuk met uw vingers vasthouden en de rest van het schil eraf trekken.
2. Maak de cactusvijg-tequilasaus door 2 van de cactusvijgen in blokjes van 1 cm te snijden; zet weg. Pureer de overgebleven vijgen met de suiker en tequila in een blender. Zeef de puree door een fijne zeef en druk er zoveel mogelijk sap uit. Gooi de pulp weg en zet het sap tot het serveren in de koelkast.
3. Schep met een meloensteker bolletjes uit een van de meloenen en doe ze in een kom met de blokjes cactusvijg. Zet de kom daarna in de koelkast.
4. Maak de tequilasaus door de overgebleven meloen uit te scheppen en de pulp met het limoensap en suiker in een blender glad te pureren. Voeg de geraspte limoenschil toe en bewaar in de koelkast tot het serveren.
5. Schep wat cactusvijg-tequilasaus op één helft van elk bord en de meloen-limoensaus op de andere helft. Schep het gekoelde fruit in het midden.

Voor 4 personen

1 portie: Calorieën 280, Eiwit 3 g, Koolhydraten 67 g, Vezel 4 g, Vet totaal 1 g (Verzadigd 0 g, Enkelvoudig onverzadigd 0 g, Meervoudig onverzadigd 0 g), Cholesterol 0 mg, Natrium 15 mg, Vitamine C 60%.
▲ *1 Fruit*

Desserts / China

Ken Homs gestoofde peren

Desserte zijn in Chine niet het hoogtepunt van een maaltijd zoals in sommige andere landen, maar ze zijn wel meestal fris en simpel. Dit eenvoudige recept is een geschikte afsluiting voor alle maaltijden.

3 eetlepels Chinese kandijsuiker of kristalsuiker
4 rijpe, maar stevige peren, geschild, heel gelaten en uitgeboord vanaf de bodem, de steeltjes eraan
2 stukken Chinese kaneel (kassia) of kaneelpijpjes

1. Zet een stoommand klaar of leg een rooster in een wok of pan. Giet er circa 5 cm water in en breng aan de kook terwijl u de rest van de ingrediënten klaarmaakt.
2. Meng de suiker met 5 eetlepels water in een kleine pan en kook tot de suiker volledig opgelost is. Laat iets afkoelen.
3. Doe de peren, het suikerwater en de kaneel in een ondiepe kom en zet die in de stomer. Let op dat het water niet in de kom kan. Draai het vuur lager en leg het deksel op de stomer. Stoom de peren vervolgens 15 tot 25 minuten, afhankelijk van hun grootte, tot ze gaar zijn.
4. Giet het kooknat en de kaneel in een kleine pan en laat tot een siroop inkoken. Verwijder de kaneelpijpjes. Giet de siroop over de peren en dien onmiddellijk op.

Voor 4 personen *Foto op pagina 8*

1 peer met siroop per portie: Calorieën 130, Eiwit 1 g, Koolhydraten 34 g, Vezel 4 g, Vet totaal 1 g (Verzadigd 0 g, Enkelvoudig onverzadigd 0 g, Meervoudig onverzadigd 0 g), Cholesterol 0 mg, Natrium 0 mg.
▲ *1 Fruit*

Desserts / Verenigde Staten

Gekarameliseerde broodpudding

Broodpudding wordt traditioneel gemaakt met oud brood, maar voor dit recept kunt u mischien wat anders proberen als krentebrood of het hier gebruikte chocoladebrood met kersen en amandelen. Deze pudding is heerlijk met cognac-kersen (recept op pagina 96).

15 g boter
125 g plus 3 eetlepels suiker
5 dl magere melk
2 eieren
1 eetlepel vanille-essence
1 theelepel gemalen kaneel
1 heel Chocoladebrood met kersen en amandelen (recept op pagina 213), in blokjes

1. Verwarm de oven voor op 180°C.
2. Verhit de boter in een vuurvaste, rechthoekige bakvorm. Doe er de 3 eetlepels suiker in en laat al roerend op een middelhoog-vuur oplossen. Laat de suiker verder koken tot hij goudbruin is. Neem van het vuur en zet weg.
3. Klop de melk met de rest van de suiker en de eieren in een grote kom. Klop er de vanille en kaneel door. Schep er de blokjes brood door tot ze volledig met het melkmengsel bedekt zijn.
4. Giet het broodmengsel over de gekarameliseerde suiker in de vorm en druk het brood licht aan. Zet 45 minuten in de oven, of tot een ingestoken mes er schoon uitkomt.
5. Stort de pudding op een dienschaal en serveer warm.

Voor 8 personen *Foto op pagina 8*

1 portie: Calorieën 350, Eiwit 11 g, Koolhydraten 64 g, Vezel 5 g, Vet totaal 7 g (Verzadigd 2 g, Enkelvoudig onverzadigd 3 g, Meervoudig onverzadigd 1 g), Cholesterol 60 mg, Natrium 360 mg.
▲ *1 Brood*

Desserts / Groot-Brittannië

Aardbeien-champagnesorbet

Met een garnering van piepkleine champagnedruiven en bosaardbeitjes maakt u van deze eenvoudige sorbet een elegant dessert. U kunt natuurlijk gewone gehalveerde aardbeien en kleine trosjes muskaatdruiven gebruiken als de kleine niet verkrijgbaar zijn. Alcohol kan het vriesproces vertragen; begin daarom met een bevroren vruchtenbasis en voeg pas daarna de alcohol toe. Het eiwit levert een luchtiger sorbet op.

500 g rijpe aardbeien
125 g suiker
1,25 dl champagne
1 eiwit
4 kleine trosjes, circa 400 g champagnedruiven
125 g bosaardbeitjes

1. Pureer de rijpe aardbeien in een blender of keukenmachine. U moet circa 5 dl aardbeipuree hebben.
2. Meng de suiker met 4 eetlepels water in een middelgrote pan en verhit het mengsel tot de suiker opgelost is. Roer er de aardbeipuree door en zet in de koelkast tot het mengsel koud is.
3. Doe de aarbeibasis in een ijsmachine en draai tot hij deels bevroren is. Schep er de champagne door.
4. Klop het eiwit tot stijve maar niet droge pieken. Schep het eiwit dan door de aardbeibasis en doe terug in de ijsmachine. Draai tot weer deels bevroren. Zet de sorbet 1 uur voor het serveren in het vriesvak.
5. Serveer de sorbet in een ondiepe kom, garneer met de champagnedruiven en bosaardbeitjes.

Voor 4 personen *Foto op pagina 8*

1 portie: Calorieën 210, Eiwit 2 g, Koolhydraten 46 g, Vezel 5 g, Vet totaal 1 g (Verzadigd 0 g, Enkelvoudig onverzadigd 0 g, Meervoudig onverzadigd 0,5 g), Cholesterol 0 mg, Natrium 15 mg, Vitamine C 180%.
▲ *2 Fruit*

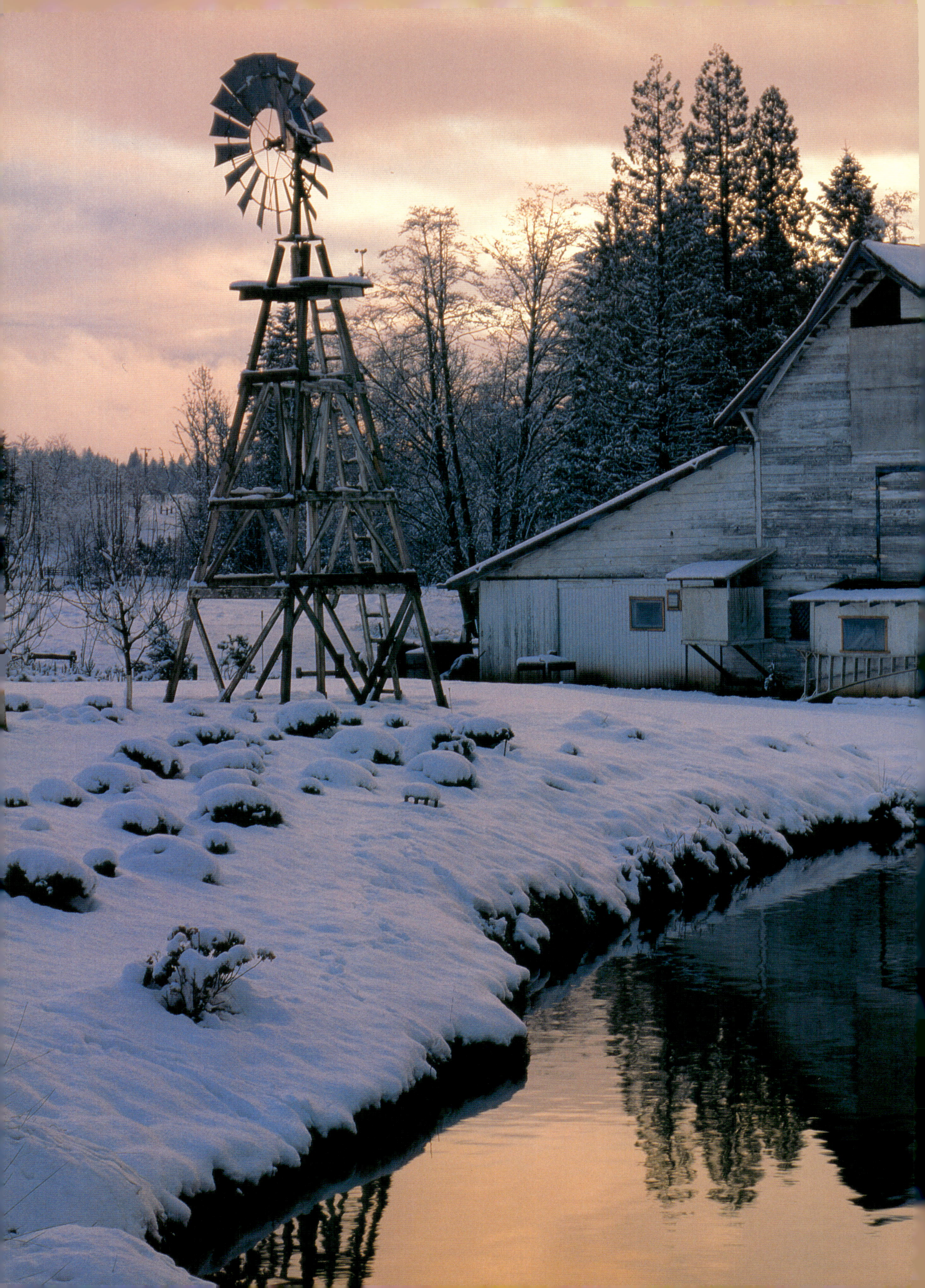

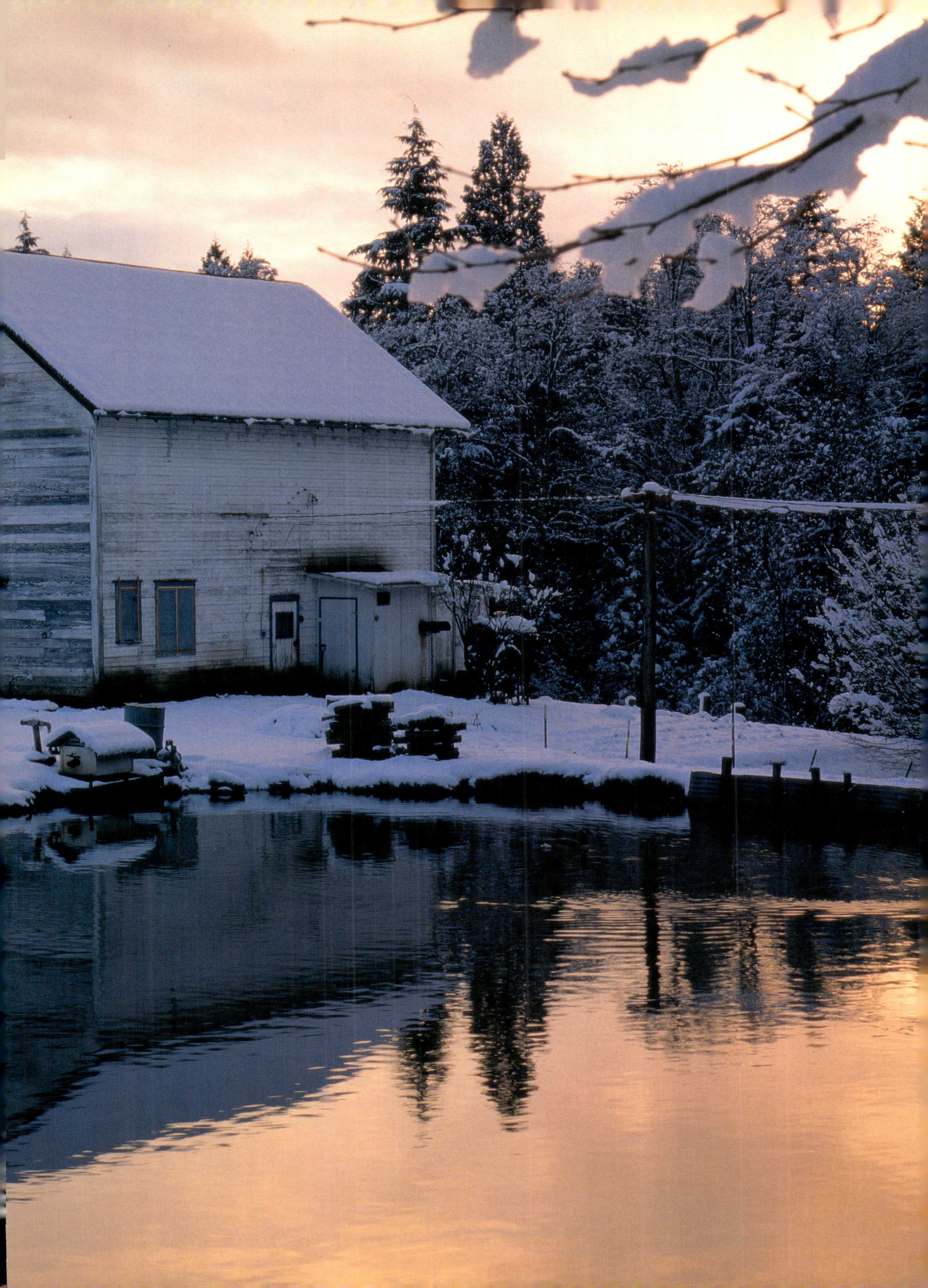

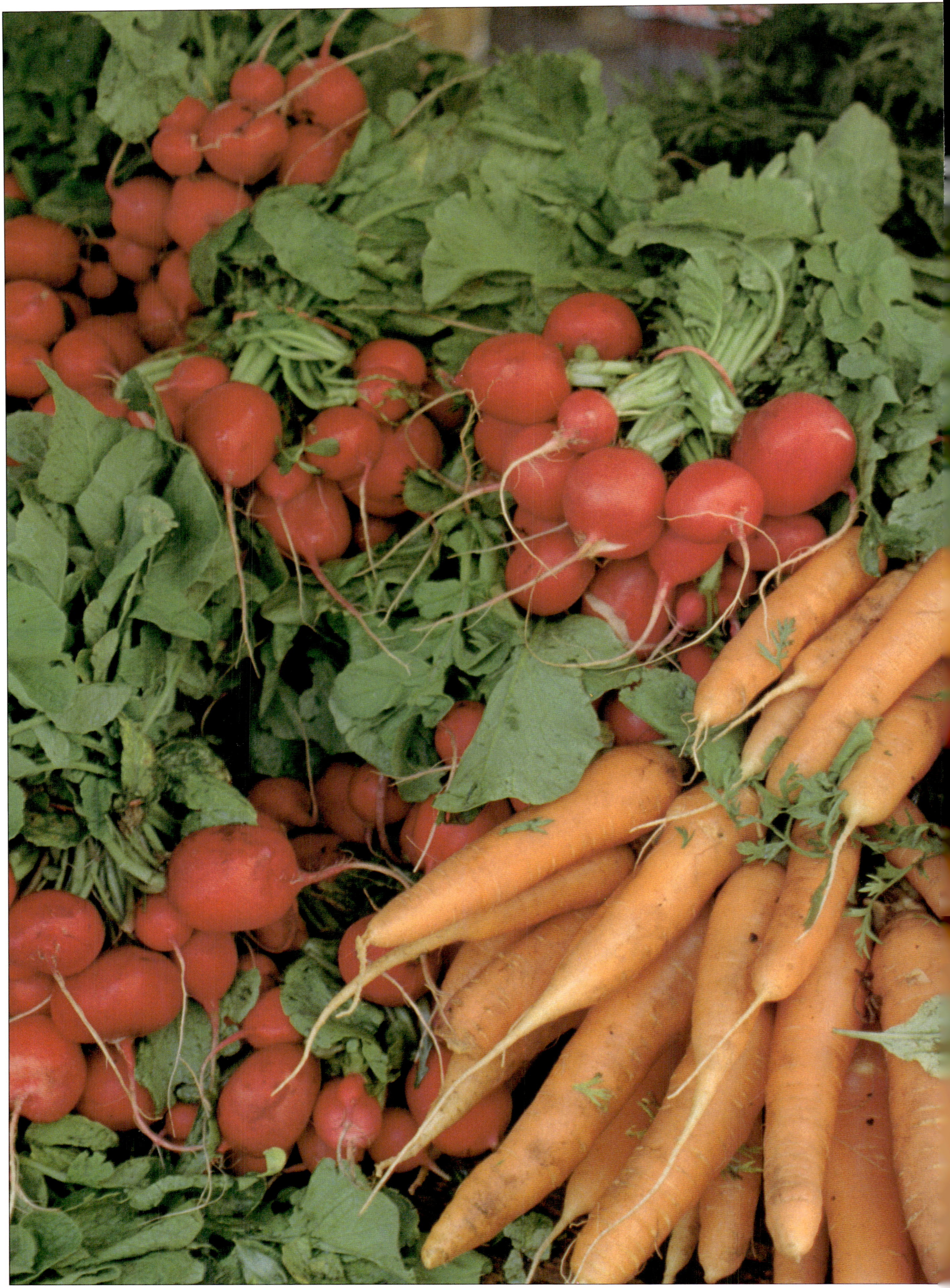

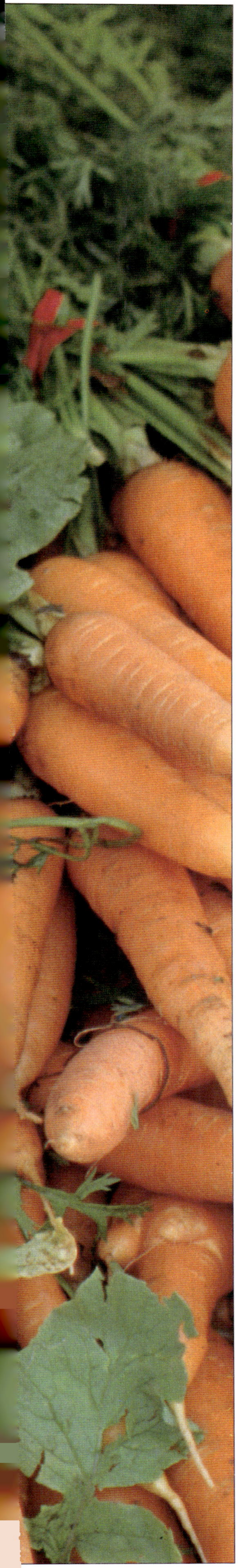

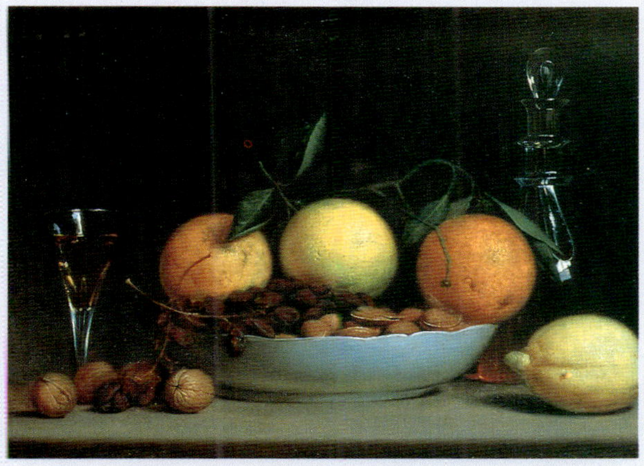

Winter

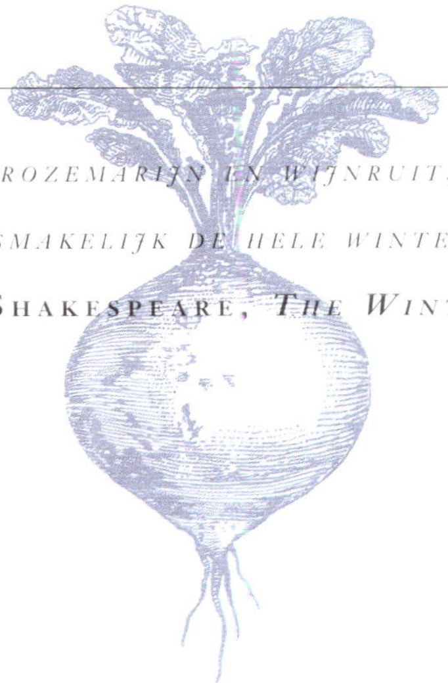

Voor u zijn er rozemarijn en wijnruit; deze blijven goed en smakelijk de hele winter door.

—William Shakespeare, *The Winter's Tale*

Het is de tijd van het jaar voor heerlijk gekruide gerechten en een overvloed aan wintergroenten. Probeer een ovenschotel van wortel- en knolgewassen—aardappels, aardperen, knolselderij, rapen en wortels. Verwarm de innerlijke mens met een aardappel-preisoep of pompoensoep met kerrie. Maak plannen voor de tuin met een Florentijnse sinaasappel-venkelsalade of een warme wintersalade van gegrilde coquilles en ui met een frisse grapefruitvinaigrette. De grapefruit zorgt voor een zomers accent in de winter.

Met de nadering der feestdagen gaan we nadenken over een feestmaal voor vrienden en familie. Begin met *Lussekatter*, de Sint Lucia-broodjes die traditioneel op kerstochtend in Zweden worden gegeten. Maak met hetzelfde deeg gevlochten brood. Vul een kalkoen of gans met wilde rijst, kastanjes en appel. Deze vulling past ook goed bij korhoender. Met een cranberry-perenchutney maakt u van restjes kalkoen iets heel bijzonders. Kies als feestdessert een warme ovenschotel van granaatappel en cranberries.

Coquillesalade met een grapefruitvinaigrette

Deze warme salade is ook geschikt als een lichte lunch.

GRAPEFRUITVINAIGRETTE

4 eetlepels vers grapefruitsap
2 eetlepels champagne-azijn of witte wijnazijn
4 eetlepels saffloerolie
30 g gesnipperde rode ui
1 theelepel geraspte grapefruitschil
¼ theelepel zout
versgemalen witte peper naar smaak

COQUILLESALADE

400 g coquilles
75 g rode ui, in stukken van 2 cm gesneden
125 g verse spinazie, in dunne reepjes gesneden
2 grapefruits, geschild, ontzaad en in partjes gesneden

1. Verwarm de grill voor. Laat 8 satéstokjes ongeveer 20 minuten in water weken.
2. Klop voor de grapefruitvinaigrette het grapefruitsap en de azijn in een middelgrote kom. Giet er al kloppend de saffloerolie in een straaltje geleidelijk bij. Voeg de gesnipperde ui en grapefruitschil toe en breng op smaak met zout en peper.
3. Rijg voor de coquillesalade de coquilles en ui aan de stokjes. Kwast ze licht in met 1 eetlepel grapefruitvinaigrette. Grilleer ze 1 minuut per kant tot de coquilles stevig aanvoelen.
4. Maak een bedje met de spinazie en schik er de spiesjes op. Strooi de partjes grapefruit om de spiesjes en druppel er de rest van de grapefruitvinaigrette over.

Voor 4 personen

1 portie: Calorieën 260, Eiwit 16 g, Koolhydraten 17 g, Vezel 3 g, Vet totaal 15 g (Verzadigd 1,5 g, Enkelvoudig onverzadigd 2 g, Meervoudig onverzadigd 11 g), Cholesterol 30 mg, Natrium 310 mg, Vitamine A 40%, Vitamine C 100%.

▲ *1 Fruit, ½ Groente, 1 Vlees*

Coquillesalade met een grapefruitvinaigrette

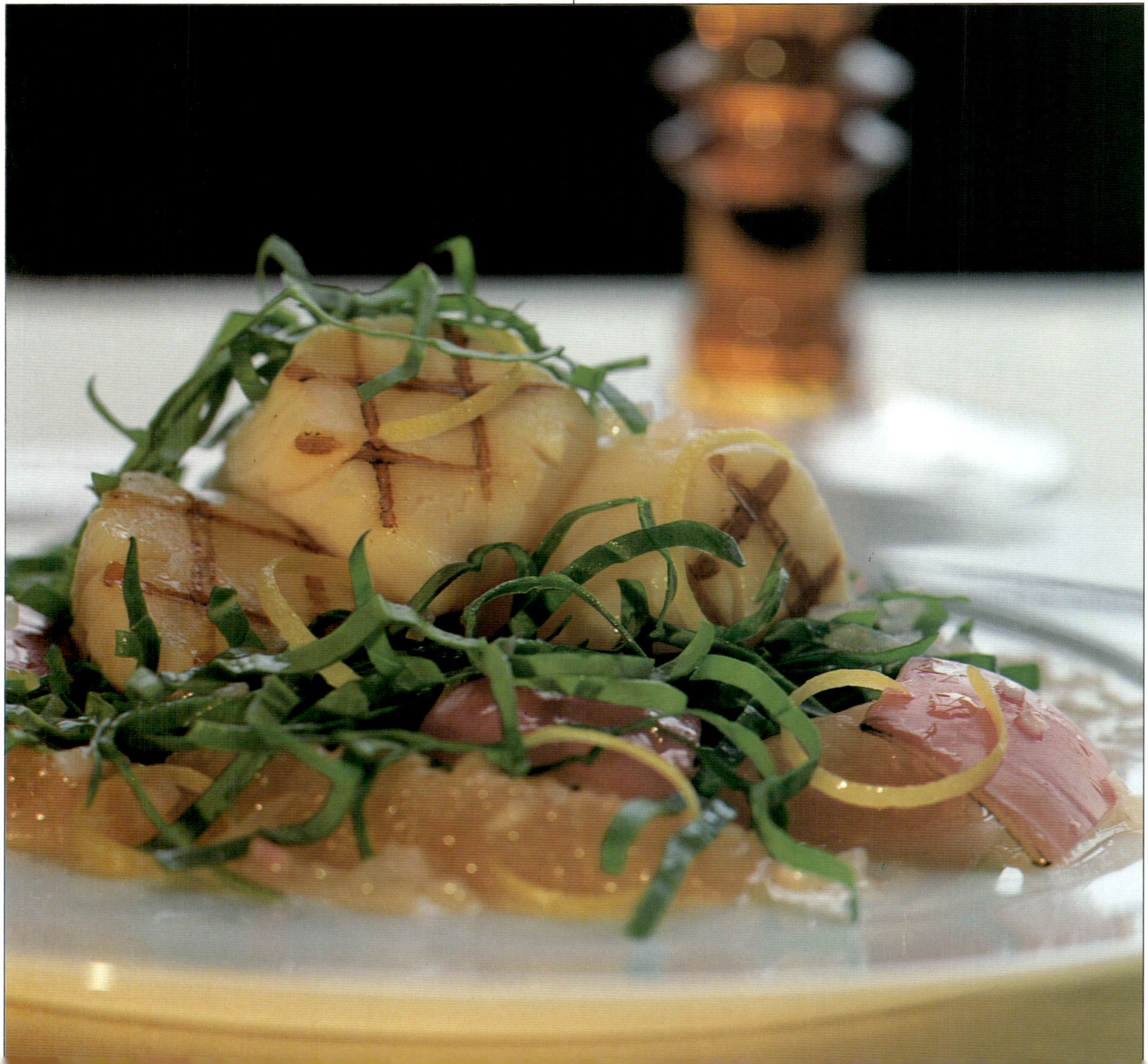

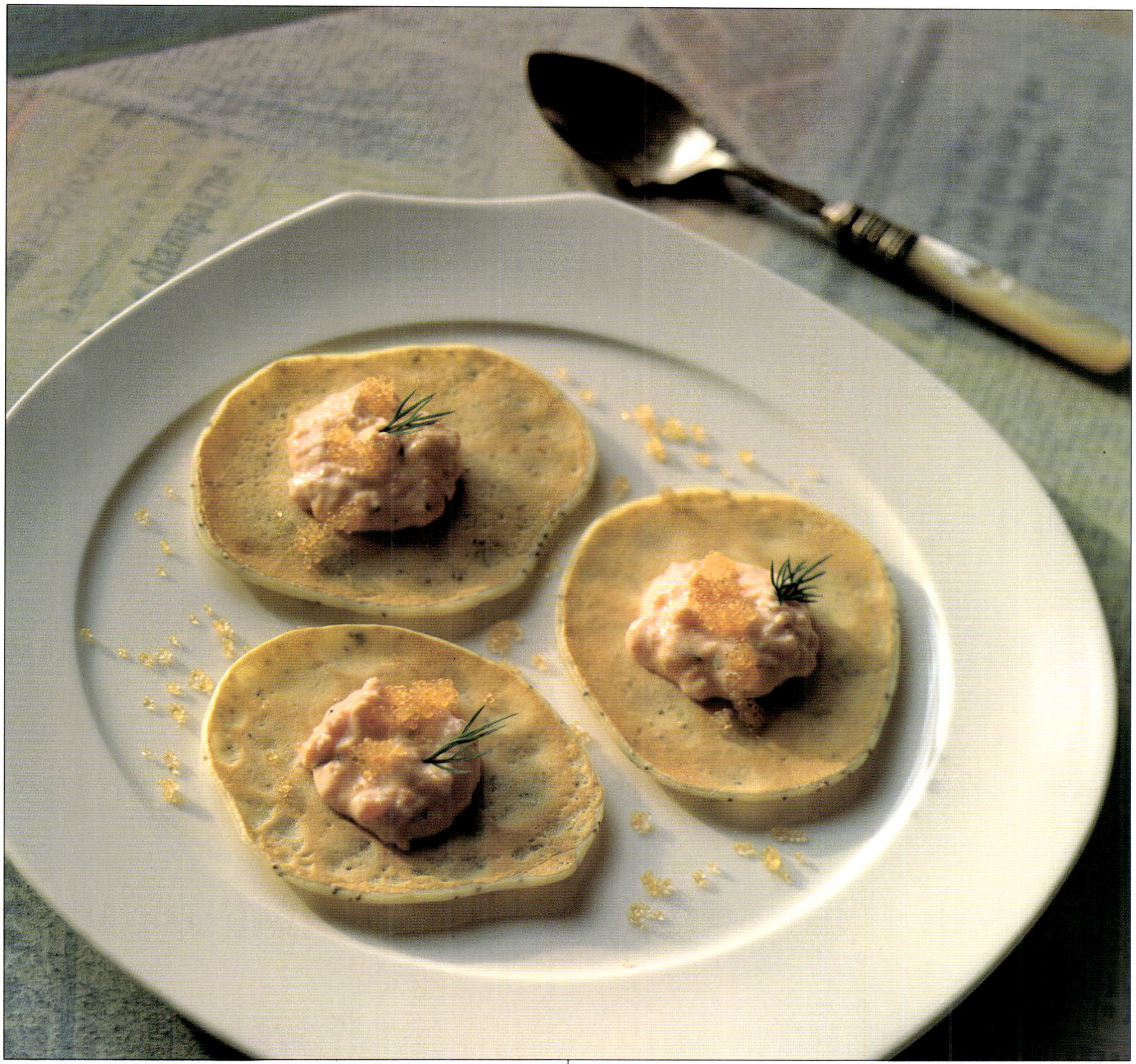

Maanzaadcrêpes met mousse van gerookte zalm

HAPJES / ZWEDEN

Maanzaadcrêpes met mousse van gerookte zalm

Deze kleine crêpes zijn iets dikker dan normaal zodat u ze makkelijk met de vingers kunt oppakken. Garneer ze met kaviaar als natrium geen probleem voor u is.

2,5 dl magere melk
1 ei
1 eetlepel saffloerolie
90 g zelfrijzend bakmeel
1 eetlepel maanzaad
1 eetlepel gesnipperde rode ui
1 eetlepel gesnipperde bieslook
2,5 dl magere yoghurt, een nacht in ongebleekte katoen uitgelekt
125 g gerookte zalm, gepureerd
2 theelepels verse dille, fijngehakt
2 eetlepels vers citroensap
2 theelepels zalmkaviaar (desgewenst)
8 takjes verse dille

1. Doe de melk, het ei en de olie in een blender en draai tot alles gemengd is. Voeg het bakmeel toe en draai tot een glad beslag. Schep er het maanzaad, de ui en bieslook door.
2. Verhit een grote anti-aanbak koekepan. Giet er acht cirkels beslag van 5 cm doorsnee in en bak ze in 45-60 seconden per kant goudbruin. Doe de crêpes op perkamentpapier en laat afkoelen.
3. Schep de uitgelekte yoghurt om met de zalm, dille en het citroensap en doe het mengsel in een spuitzak. Spuit circa 1 theelepel van de mousse op elke crêpe en garneer desgewenst met kaviaar en de dille. Dien onmiddellijk op.

Voor 8 personen

1 crêpe per portie: Calorieën 120, Eiwit 7 g, Koolhydraten 12 g, Vezel 0 g, Vet totaal 4 g (Verzadigd 1 g, Enkelvoudig onverzadigd 1 g, Meervoudig onverzadigd 2 g), Cholesterol 35 mg, Natrium 160 mg.
▲ *1 Brood, ½ Melk*

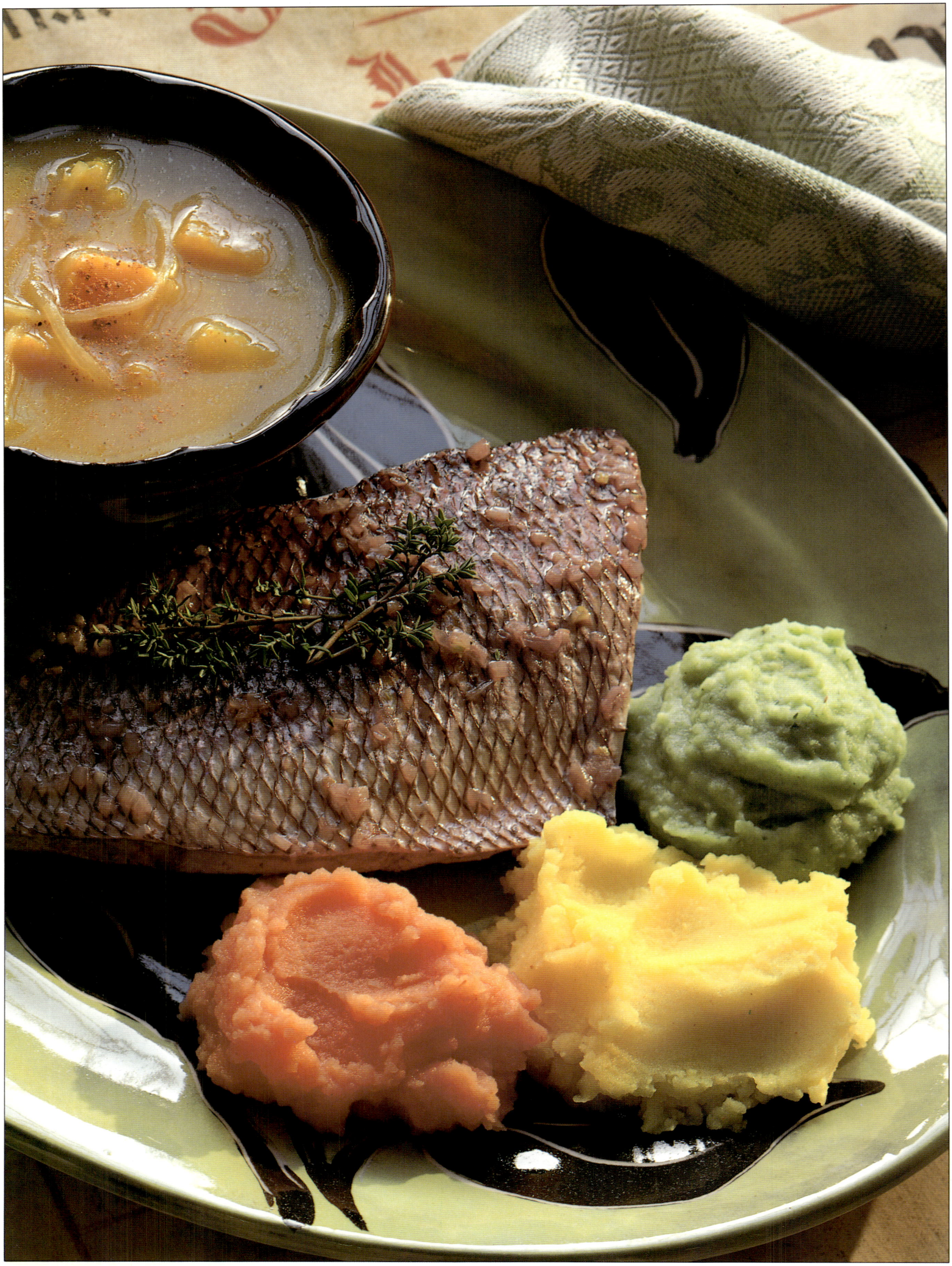

Van boven naar beneden: Pompoensoep met kerrie, Roodbaars in rode wijn,
Edna's driekleurenpurees

GROENTEN / VERENIGDE STATEN

Edna's driekleurenpurees

Deze prachtig gekleurde aardappelpurees zijn ideaal om mee te garneren. Hieronder zijn drie voorbeelden van de mogelijkheden bij het mengen van kleuren en smaken.

6 grote bloemige aardappels, geschild en in de lengte in vieren gesneden
3,75 dl karnemelk, verwarmd
2 eetlepels olijfolie
zout en versgemalen peper naar smaak
½ theelepel geelwortel
3 eetlepels *pepita* pesto (zie woordenlijst)
2 eetlepels gepureerde tomaten

1. Doe de aardappels in een grote pan en giet er zoveel koud water bij dat ze onder staan. Breng aan de kook en kook ze in circa 20 minuten gaar. Giet goed af. Pureer de aardappel met een pureeknijper of roerzeef en doe de puree terug in de pan.
2. Zet de pan op een laag vuur en schep er de karnemelk en olie door. Breng op smaak met zout en peper. Verdeel de puree over drie voorverwarmde kommen. Schep de geelwortel door de puree in de eerste kom, de pesto door de tweede en de gepureerde tomaat door de derde. Dien onmiddellijk op.

Voor 8 personen

2 dl per portie: Calorieën 180, Eiwit 4 g, Koolhydraten 24 g, Vezel 2 g, Vet totaal 8 g (Verzadigd 1,5 g, Enkelvoudig onverzadigd 5 g, Meervoudig onverzadigd 1 g), Cholesterol 5 mg, Natrium 75 mg.
▲ *1 Groente*

ZEEBANKET / NIEUW-ZEELAND

Roodbaars in rode wijn

Alle soorten brasem zijn ook geschikt om in rode wijn te pocheren. U kunt hele vis of filets pocheren; reken op circa 5 minuten per 3 cm dikte.

2 eetlepels olijfolie
3 sjalotjes, gesnipperd
7,5 dl droge rode wijn
7,5 dl visbouillon (zie woordenlijst)
bouquet garni: 1 takje peterselie, 1 takje tijm, 1 laurierblad, 5 peperkorrels
1 hele roodbaars van circa 1,5 kg
2 theelepels verse tijm, fijngehakt

1. Verhit de olie in een vispocheerpan of een andere pan die groot genoeg is voor een hele vis. Doe er de sjalotjes in en fruit ze gaar. Blus de pan af met de wijn en kook tot de helft in.
2. Voeg de visbouillon en het bouquet garni toe en breng weer aan de kook. Draai het vuur lager en leg dan de vis op het rooster. Pocheer de vis in circa 15 minuten gaar en draai af en toe om.
3. Doe de gare vis op een dienschaal, bestrooi met de tijm en dien onmiddellijk op.

Voor 4 personen

1 portie: Calorieën 160, Eiwit 33 g, Koolhydraten 0 g, Vezel 0 g, Vet totaal 2 g (Verzadigd 0 g, Enkelvoudig onverzadigd 1,5 g, Meervoudig onverzadigd 0 g), Cholesterol 45 mg, Natrium 140 mg.
▲ *1 Vlees*

SOEPEN / VERENIGDE STATEN

Pompoensoep met kerrie

Er zijn veel soorten pompoen. Sommige zijn zoet, sommige mild van smaak. De meeste hebben een hoog koolhydraatgehalte, en de oranje soorten bevatten veel vitamine A en C. U kunt voor deze kruidige soep één soort of een mengsel van verschillende soorten gebruiken. Pureer voor een romige soep alles in een blender.

500 g spaghettipompoen
500 g butterball pompoen (kleine ronde groene pompoen)
500 g Golden debut (kleine ronde oranje pompoen)
3 eetlepels saffloerolie
3 preien, alleen het wit, in plakken van ½ cm dik
3 tenen knoflook, fijngehakt
2 eetlepels kerriepoeder
1,5 dl kippebouillon (zie woordenlijst)
2 eetlepels fijngehakte peterselie
¼ theelepel zout
versgemalen peper naar smaak
¼ theelepel versgeraspte nootmuskaat

1. Halveer de spaghettipompoen in de lengte; verwijder de pitten en taaie vezels. Stoom de twee helften in circa 20 minuten gaar boven kokend water. Laat afkoelen. Schraap het afgekoelde draadachtige vruchtvlees eruit met een vork. Zet weg.
2. Schil de ander twee pompoensoorten en verwijder de pitten. Snijd ze in stukken van 3 cm en zet weg.
3. Verhit de olie in een middelgrote pan op een middelhoog vuur. Doe er de prei en knoflook in en fruit die in circa 5 minuten gaar. Roer er het kerriepoeder door en bak onder af en toe omscheppen 2 minuten. Voeg de stukken ongekookte pompoen en de bouillon toe. Breng aan de kook, draai het vuur lager en laat in circa 30 minuten gaar sudderen.
4. Pureer tweederde van het pompoenmengsel glad in een blender. Zet de andere blokken weg. Doe de puree, de blokken pompoen en de spaghettipompoen in de pan en laat circa 5 minuten op een matig vuur doorwarmen. Bestrooi met de peterselie en breng op smaak met zout, peper en nootmuskaat. Dien op.

Voor 8 personen

2,5 dl per portie: Calorieën 160, Eiwit 3 g, Koolhydraten 26 g, Vezel 3 g, Vet totaal 7 g (Verzadigd 1 g, Enkelvoudig onverzadigd 1 g, Meervoudig onverzadigd 4,5 g), Cholesterol 0 mg, Natrium 100 mg, Vitamine A 90%, Vitamine C 45%.
▲ *2 Groente*

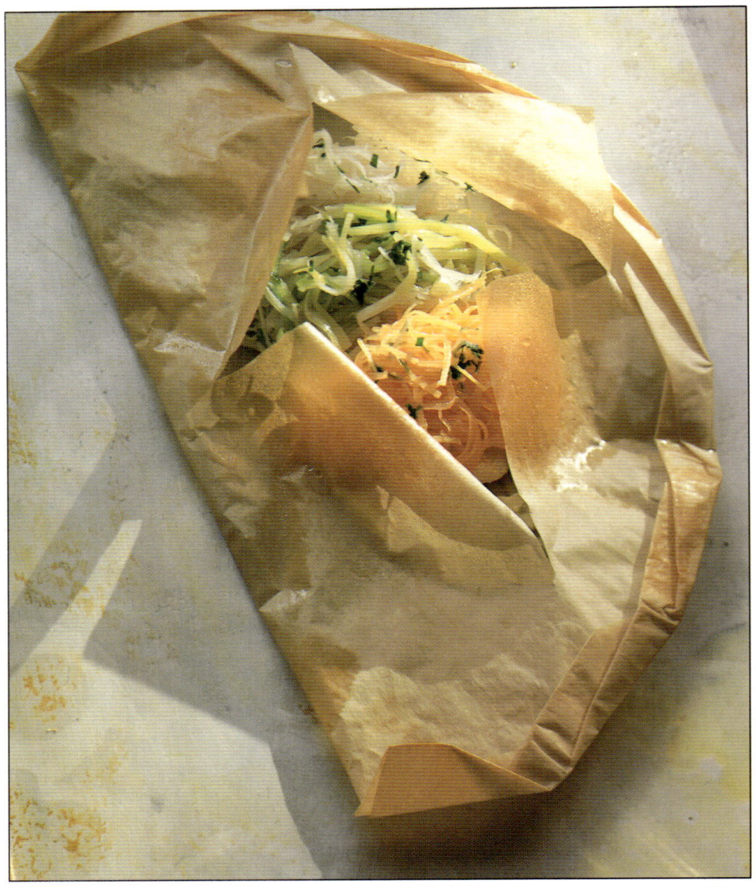

Kabeljauw en groenten en papillote

ZEEBANKET / FRANKRIJK

Kabeljauw en groenten en papillote

Door vis in perkamentpapier te koken, blijft hij sappig. Serveer het pakje ongeopend om van de geuren te genieten wanneer het papier wordt opengesneden. Vervang het citroensap door 4 eetlepels visbouillon (zie woordenlijst) als u aluminiumfolie gebruikt.

150 g geschilde en julienne gesneden wortel, 2 minuten geblacheerd (zie woordenlijst)
125 g julienne gesneden prei, 1 minuut geblacheerd (zie woordenlijst)
75 g geschilde en julienne gesneden meiraap, 2 minuten geblancheerd (zie woordenlijst)
125 g julienne gesneden knolvenkel
4 kabeljauwfilets (elk 150-180 g)
het sap van 1 citroen
¼ theelepel zout
versgemalen peper naar smaak
2 theelepels fijngehakte verse dragon
1 eetlepel fijngehakte verse peterselie
1 eetlepel saffloerolie

1. Verwarm de oven voor op 180°C. Knip 4 stukken perkamentpapier van 30 x 30 cm uit.
2. Schik de julienne gesneden groenten op de helft van elk vel perkamentpapier. Schik er een kabeljauwfilet op. Sprenkel er het citroensap over en bestrooi met het zout, wat peper, de dragon en peterselie.
3. Vouw de lege kant van het papier over de vis en groenten en knip de randen tot de vorm van een halvemaan. Knijp de randen dicht. Leg de pakjes op een bakplaat en kwast de pakjes licht in met de olie. Zet 12 minuten in de oven.
4. Dien het gerecht direct op. Laat uw gasten de pakjes aan tafel openmaken door de bovenkant te verwijderen en de bodem op het bord te laten.

Voor 4 personen

1 pakje per portie: Calorieën 190, Eiwit 27 g, Koolhydraten 11 g, Vezel 2 g, Vet totaal 5 g (Verzadigd 0,5 g, Enkelvoudig onverzadigd 0,5 g, Meervoudig onverzadigd 3 g), Cholesterol 60 mg, Natrium 260 mg, Vitamine A 200%, Vitamine C 35%.

▲ *1 Groente, 1 Vlees*

GROENTEN / VIETNAM

Wat de Zenmeester eet

Dit vegetarische hoofdgerecht van gestoomde tofu en groenten is snel klaar. Serveer met gestoomde rijst.

375 g stevige tofu (tahoe)
3 eetlepels pikante of milde bonensaus
2 eetlepels suiker
60 g cellofaannoedels
100 g gehalveerde en in plakken gesneden tomaat
20 g stropaddestoelen, vers of uit blik (straw mushooms)
30 g ui, in staafjes van 1 bij 2 cm
20 g lenteui, in stukjes van 2 cm
30 g bleekselderij, overdwars in dunne plakjes
7 g koriander of bladselderij
2 eetlepels verse gember, geschild en julienne gesneden
versgemalen peper naar smaak
5-6 verse korianderbladen
1 kleine tomaat, in partjes gesneden

1. Snijd de tofu in repen van 2 cm dik en 5 cm breed. Schik ze in de lengte met de uiteinden tegen elkaar op een dienschaal. Snijd ze om de cm overdwars in, maar niet helemaal door.
2. Meng de bonensaus in een kommetje met de suiker. Smeer 1 eetlepel van het mengsel over de tofu.
3. Week de celllofaannoedels 1 minuut in heet water; giet ze af. Schep ze om met de plakken tomaat, stropaddestoelen, ui, lenteui, bleekselderij, koriander en gember in een middelgrote kom. Voeg de rest van de bonensaus (zie 2), 4 eetlepels water en wat peper toe. Schep alles goed om.
4. Schik het groentenmengsel op de tofu.
5. Zet een bamboe stoommand in een wok of grote pan. Vul de wok of pan tot aan de bodem van de mand met water. Breng het water aan de kook en leg de schaal met tofu in de stoommand. Leg het deksel op de wok, draai het vuur iets lager en laat 5 minuten stomen.
6. Neem het bord tofu uit de stoommand. Garneer met de verse koriander en partjes tomaat en dien onmiddellijk op.

Voor 2 personen

1 portie: Calorieën 380, Eiwit 30 g, Koolhydraten 37 g, Vezel 5 g, Vet totaal 15 g (Verzadigd 2 g, Enkelvoudig onverzadigd 3,5 g, Meervoudig onverzadigd 9 g), Cholesterol 0 mg, Natrium 45 mg, IJzer 110%, Kalk 40%, Vitamine C 35%.

▲ *1 Groente, 2 Vlees*

PASTA / THAILAND

Rad na

RIJSTNOEDELS MET CHINESE BROCCOLI

Serveer dit gerecht met Thaise chilipasta, gedroogde chilipepers, ingemaakte chilipepers en wat gebakte pinda's. Alle noedelsoorten zijn geschikt voor deze hartige saus, maar rijstnoedels, verse of gedroogde, zijn bijzonder lekker. Deze verse noedels zijn al voorgekookt en moeten alleen worden opgewarmd.

4 eetlepels saffloerolie
1 teen knoflook, fijngehakt
250 g rijstnoedels, 2 cm breed
1 eetlepel sojasaus
250 g Chinese broccoli of broccoli, in stukjes gesneden
1 eetlepel Chinese bonensaus
1 eetlepel suiker
1 eetlepel *nam pla* (vissaus)
5 dl kippebouillon (zie woordenlijst)
2 eetlepels maïzena, opgelost in 3 eetlepels water

1. Verhit 2 eetlepels van de olie in een wok op een hoog vuur. Doe er de knoflook in en roerbak die snel goudbruin. Voeg de noedels en sojasaus toe en roerbak 2 tot 3 minuten tot de noedels warm zijn. Doe alles daarna op een voorverwarmde dienschaal en houd warm.
2. Doe de rest van de olie in de wok en verhit op een hoog vuur. Doe de broccoli in de hete olie en roerbak 30 seconden. Roer er snel de bonensaus, suiker, *nam pla* en kippebouillon door. Roer er het maïzenapapje door en roer 3 minuten tot de saus dik is. Schep het broccolimengsel over de noedels en dien direct op.

Voor 4 personen

1 portie: Calorieën 380, Eiwit 10 g, Koolhydraten 56 g, Vezel 2 g, Vet totaal 15 g (Verzadigd 1,5 g, Enkelvoudig onverzadigd 2 g, Meervoudig onverzadigd 11 g), Cholesterol 0 mg, Natrium 520 mg, Vitamine C 80%.

▲ *2 Brood, 1 Groente*

Van links naar rechts: Wat de Zenmeester eet, Rijstnoedels met Chinese broccoli

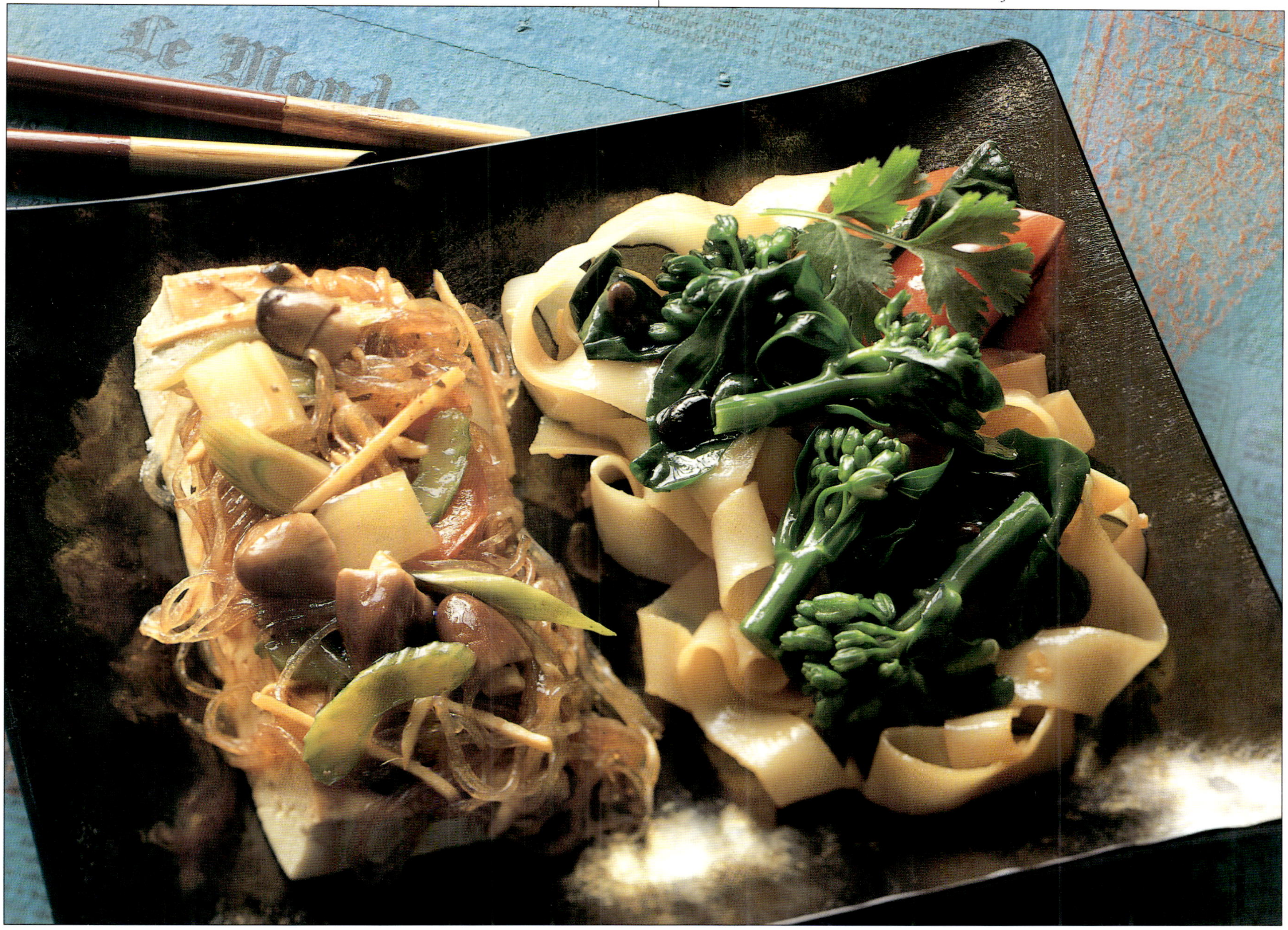

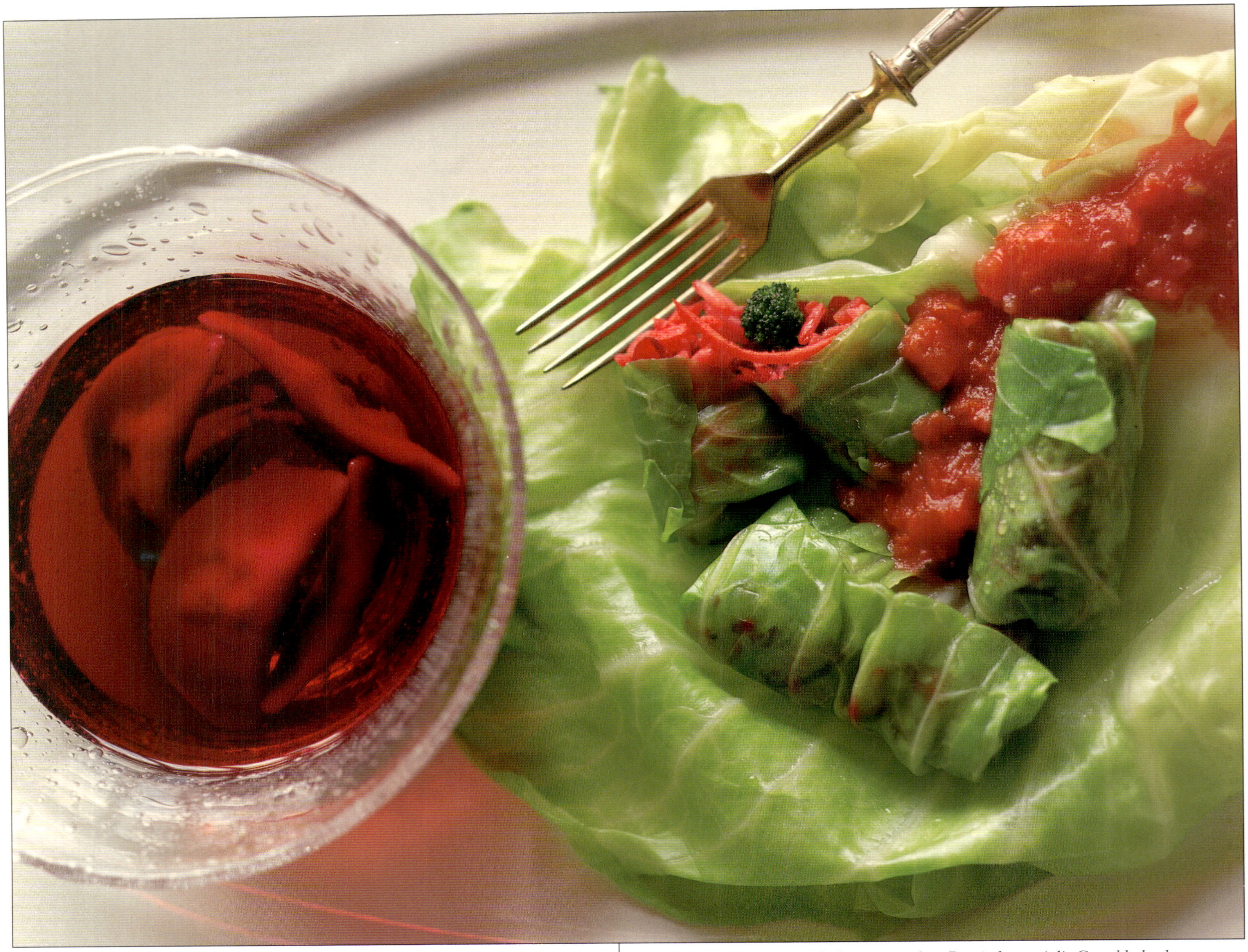

Van links naar rechts: Russische ravioli, Gevulde kool

GROENTEN / RUSLAND

Gevulde kool

Deze rolletjes zijn geschikt als bijgerecht, of als onderdeel van zakuski—*verschillende Russische hartige hapjes. Ze kunnen ook dienen als garnituur voor kippebouillon of borsjt. Kool is net als broccoli, andijvie, spruitjes en bloemkool een kruisbloemige groente en wordt geacht tegen verschillende soorten kanker te beschermen.*

1 witte kool

VULLING

4 eetlepels saffloerolie
60 g gehakte ui
2 tenen knoflook, fijngehakt
30 g broccoliroosjes
75 g geraspte biet
75 g geraspte koolraap
3,75 dl kippebouillon (zie woordenlijst)
160 g rijst
7 g peterselie, fijngehakt
45 g rozijnen
4 eetlepels gepureerde tomaten
2 eetlepels vers citroensap
¼ theelepel gemberpoeder
¼ theelepel gemalen koriander
¼ theelepel gemalen kaneel
zout en versgemalen zwarte peper naar smaak

SAUS

5 dl gepureerde tomaten
3 eetlepels lichtbruine basterdsuiker
3 eetlepels vers citroensap

1. Verwarm de oven voor op 180°C. Vet een grote, ondiepe ovenschaal licht in met olie.
2. Verwijder de taaie buitenbladen van de kool en snijd de stronk kegelvormig uit de kool.
3. Zet de hele kool onder kokend water en kook 2 tot 3 minuten of tot de bladen uit elkaar komen. Trek de bladen losjes uit elkaar en kook nog 1 tot 2 minuten, of tot de bladen volkomen soepel zijn. Giet de kool af en dompel de bladen onmiddellijk in ijswater om het kookproces te stoppen.
4. Giet de bladen af en dep ze droog met keukenpapier. Zet weg.
5. Verhit voor de vulling de olie in een grote koekepan en fruit er de ui en knoflook goudbruin in. Voeg de broccoli, biet en koolraap toe en roerbak 1 minuut. Voeg de kippebouillon en rijst toe, leg het deksel op de pan en laat 30 minuten sudderen.

6. Schep er de rest van de ingrediënten voor de vulling door.
7. Snijd het dikste deel van de hoofdnerf uit de koolbladen. Snijd met een scherp mes een rechthoek van circa 7 x 13 cm uit elk blad.
8. Schep 1 eetlepel van de vulling in het midden van elke rechthoek. Vouw een smalle kant van het blad in, vouw de zijkanten in en rol verder op. Maak de rolletjes vast met keukengaren of een cocktailprikker. Schik ze in de ovenschaal en zet weg.
9. Verhit voor de saus de gepureerde tomaten, basterdsuiker en het citroensap in een kleine pan. Laat 10 minuten sudderen.
10. Giet de saus over de rolletjes en zet 30 minuten in de oven.

Voor 16 rolletjes

---

2 rolletjes per portie: Calorieën 220, Eiwit 4 g, Koolhydraten 38 g, Vezel 4 g, Vet totaal 8 g (Verzadigd 1 g, Enkelvoudig onverzadigd 1 g, Meervoudig onverzadigd 5 g), Cholesterol 0 mg, Natrium 330 mg, Vitamine C 110%.

▲ *2 Groente*

PASTA / RUSLAND

Pelmeni

RUSSISCHE RAVIOLI

Siberische koks bewaarden deze ravioli in de sneeuw, maar uw vriesvak zal ook zeker voldoen! Per traditie worden deze ravioli in bouillon geserveerd.

1 wortel, fijngehakt
1 aardappel, fijngehakt
75 g gesnipperde ui
het sap van 1 citroen
250 g verse zalmfilet
½ theelepel mosterdpoeder
2 theelepels verse dille, gesnipperd
zout en versgemalen witte peper naar smaak
½ recept pastadeeg (zie woordenlijst), dun uitgerold
1 eiwit, losgeklopt met 1 theelepel water
2 liter borsjt (recept op pagina 155), gezeefd

1. Breng 1 liter water aan de kook in een grote pan. Doe er de wortel, aardappel, ui en op 1 eetlepel na het citroensap in. Draai het vuur lager en laat 5 minuten sudderen.
2. Voeg de zalm toe en pocheer 8 tot 10 minuten. Giet het mengsel af en laat het afkoelen.
3. Hak de zalm in kleine stukjes en schep die door de groenten.
4. Maak een papje met het mosterdpoeder en het overgebleven citroensap. Schep er de dille door en doe het papje bij het zalmmengsel. Breng op smaak met zout en peper. Zet weg.
5. Steek de pasta uit met een uitsteekvormpje van 5 cm doorsnee.
6. Schep ½ theelepel zalmmengsel in het midden van elk pastarondje. Kwast de randen in met wat eiwitmengsel en vouw in tweeën tot een halvemaanvorm. Knijp de randen dicht en let op dat de vulling niet langs de randen loopt. Leg de halvemaantjes op een licht met bloem bestoven bakplaat tot gebruik. (U kunt op dit punt aangekomen de *pelmeni* afdekken en in de koelkast zetten of ze invriezen.)
7. Verwarm de borsjt en houd hem warm.
8. Breng een ruime pan water aan de kook. Doe er de *pelmeni* in en kook ze 2 minuten. Neem ze met een schuimspaan uit de pan en laat ze uitlekken in een vergiet.
9. Doe de uitgelekte *pelmeni* in de borsjt en dien onmiddellijk op.

Voor 8 personen

---

1 portie: calorieën 250, Eiwit 11 g, Koolhydraten 36 g, Vezel 3 g, Vet totaal 6 g (Verzadigd 1,5 g, Enkelvoudig onverzadigd 2,5 g, Meervoudig onverzadigd 1 g), Cholesterol 75 mg, Natrium 150 mg, Vitamine A 130%, Vitamine C 35%.

▲ *½ Brood, 2 Groente*

GRAAN / MIDDEN-OOSTEN

Pilaf met kikkererwten, gerst en bulghur

Geplette tarwe, ook bekend al bulghur, wordt vaak in tabbouleh *(recept op pagina 158) verwerkt. Bulghur is ook lekker gemengd met andere graansoorten voor een pilaf. Dit mengsel met gierst en kikkererwten heeft een nootachtige smaak en zorgt voor volop eiwit.*

100 g gierst met vlies
1,2 liter kippebouillon (zie woordenlijst)
100 g gedroogde kikkererwten, een nacht geweekt
100 g middelfijne bulghur
2 eetlepels olijfolie
2 tenen knoflook, fijngehakt
1 ui, gehakt
60 g bleekselderij, in plakken
1 theelepel gemalen komijn
½ theelepel gemalen koriander
3 eetlepels verse peterselie, fijngehakt
¼ theelepel zout
versgemalen peper naar smaak

1. Doe de gierst en de kippebouillon in een grote soeppan en laat 30 minuten koken op een middelhoog vuur onder af en toe roeren. Voeg de uitgelekte kikkererwten toe en kook 45 minuten. Voeg de bulghur toe en laat nog 15 minuten koken. Leg het deksel op de pan, neem de pan van het vuur en zet weg.
2. Verhit de olie in een grote koekepan. Doe er de knoflook en ui in en fruit die in circa 5 minuten goudgeel. Voeg de bleekselderij toe en bak 2 minuten. Schep er het graanmengsel door.
3. Breng op smaak met de komijn, koriander, peterselie en wat zout en peper. Dien onmiddellijk op.

Voor 6 personen *Foto op pagina 195*

2,5 dl per portie: Calorieën 190, Eiwit 5 g, Koolhydraten 30 g, Vezel 6 g, Vet totaal 6 g (Verzadigd 1 g, Enkelvoudig onverzadigd 4 g, Meervoudig onverzadigd 1 g), Cholesterol 0 mg, Natrium 120 mg.

▲ *2 Brood*

Heilbot gevuld met geroosterde knoflook en zongedroogde tomaten

U kunt de heilbot door een andere stevige visfilet vervangen. Varieer dit recept door de vis te grilleren; zorg ervoor dat u de vis niet te veel vult en bind hem op met wat keukengaren.

6 bollen geroosterde knoflook (zie woordenlijst)
10 zongedroogde tomaten (droge), in warm water geweekt en julienne gesneden
1 sjalotje, gesnipperd
1 theelepel verse tijm, fijngehakt
60 g vers broodkruim, fijngemalen
1 theelepel vers citroensap
zout en versgemalen peper naar smaak
2 citroenen, in plakken van 3 mm dik gesneden
4 heilbotfilets, elk 2 cm dik en circa 185 g

1. Verwarm de oven voor op 200°C.
2. Maak eerst de vulling. Neem de tenen af van twee bollen geroosterde knoflook. Pel ze en meng ze met 8 zongedroogde tomaten, de sjalot en tijm. Schep er het broodkruim door en breng op smaak met het citroensap en wat zout en peper.
3. Vet een ovenschaal licht in met olie (gebruik wat olie van de geroosterde knoflook); bekleed de schaal met de plakken citroen.
4. Snijd de filets horizontaal bijna doormidden zodat u twee flappen hebt, als pagina's van een boek. Smeer wat vulling tussen de twee flappen en vouw ze dicht.
5. Leg de gevulde vis op de plakken citroen in de ovenschaal. Kwast de filets licht in met wat olie van de geroosterde knoflook en bestrooi ze licht met zout en peper.
6. Zet de schaal 15-18 minuten in de oven tot de vis gaar is.
7. Garneer elke portie met 1 bol van de overgebleven geroosterde knoflook en bestrooi met de rest van de zongedroogde tomaten. Dien onmiddellijk op.

Voor 4 personen

1 filet met 1 bol knoflook per portie: Calorieën 410, Eiwit 43 g, Koolhydraten 33 g, Vezel 2 g, Vet totaal 13 g (Verzadigd 2 g, Enkelvoudig onverzadigd 7 g, Meervoudig onverzadigd 2,5 g), Cholesterol 80 mg, Natrium 240 mg, Kalk 25%, Vitamine C 55%.
▲ *1 Groente, 2 Vlees*

Heilbot gevuld met geroosterde knoflook en zongedroogde tomaten

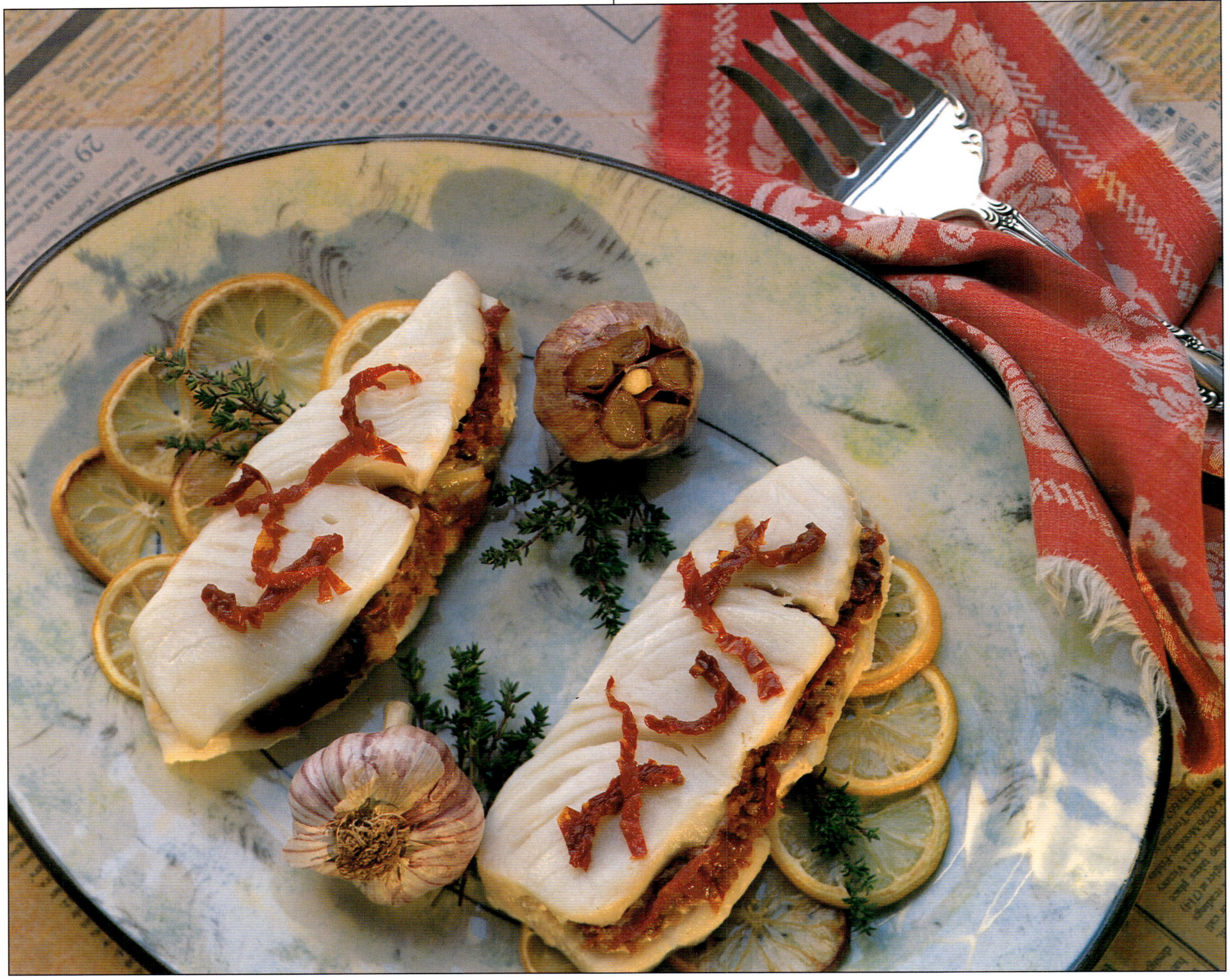

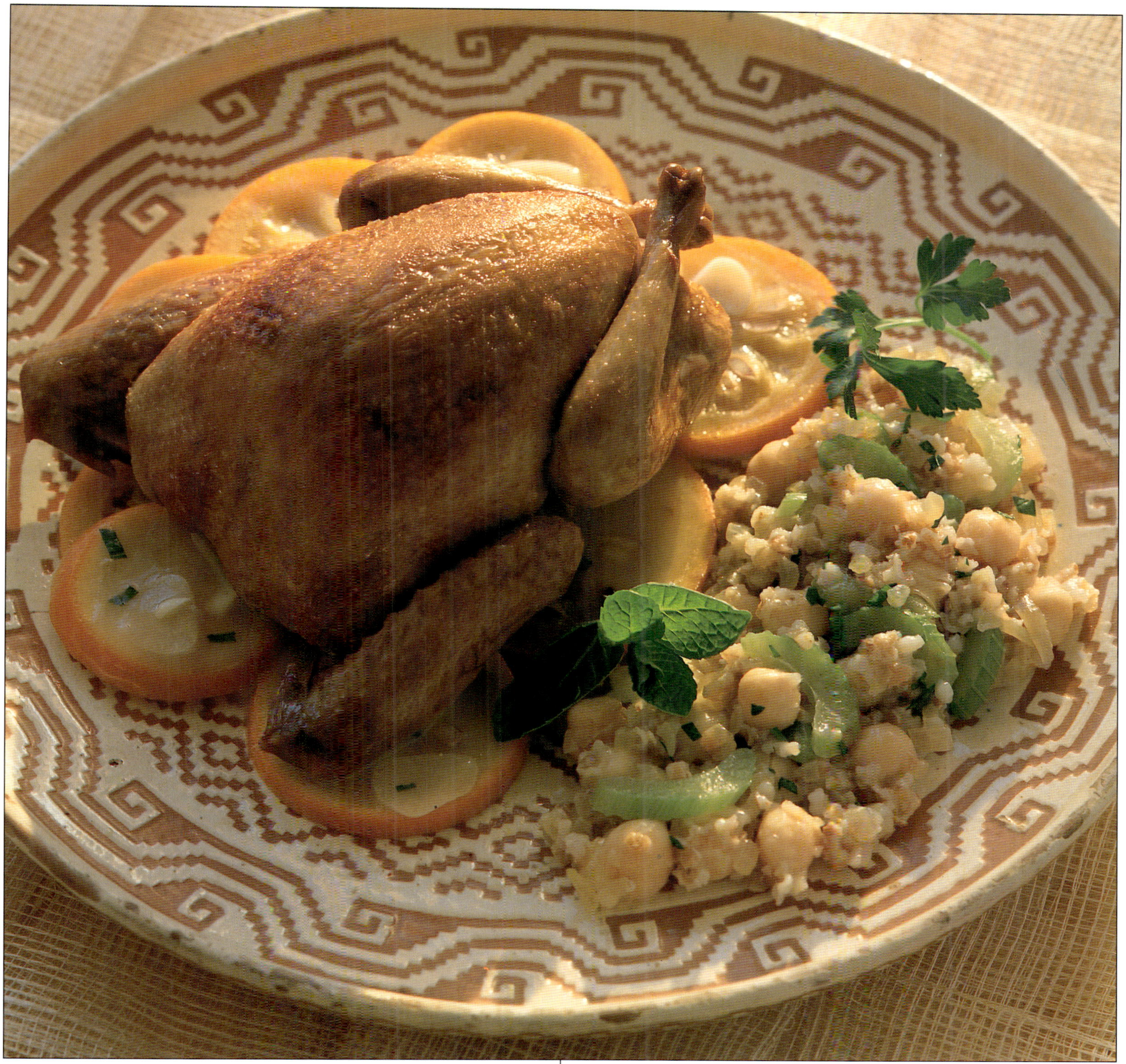

Van links naar rechts: Duiven in sinaasappelsaus, Pilaf met kikkererwten, gerst en bulghur (recept pagina 193)

GEVOGELTE / SPANJE

Duiven in sinaasappelsaus

Gebruik voor een aparte zure saus bittere (Sevilla) sinaasappels voor dit recept. Als er geen Sevilla's verkrijgbaar zijn, kunt u daarvoor in de plaats 1 zoete sinaasappel en 1 citroen gebruiken.

4 jonge duiven
3 eetlepels olijfolie
4 tenen knoflook, in plakken
4 Sevilla sinaasappels of 1 zoete sinaasappel en 1 citroen, geschild en overdwars in plakken gesneden
2,5 dl droge witte wijn
5 dl kippebouillon (zie woordenlijst)
2 eetlepels bloem gemengd met 3 eetlepels kippebouillon
1 eetlepel gehakte verse munt
¼ theelepel zout
versgemalen peper naar smaak

1. Spoel de duiven af en dep ze droog. Verhit de olijfolie in een grote braadpan en bak de duiven in circa 8-10 minuten rondom bruin op een middelhoog vuur. Draai het vuur iets lager, voeg de knoflook en sinaasappels toe en bak nog 1 minuut. Blus de pan af met de wijn en laat die 5 minuten op een middelhoog vuur inkoken. Giet er de kippebouillon bij.
2. Laat alles zonder deksel 30 minuten sudderen, waarbij u de duiven af en toe omkeert. Schep de duiven en sinaasappels over op een voorverwarmde dienschaal en houd ze warm.
3. Klop het bloempapje door het kooknat en laat 5 minuten sudderen onder af en toe kloppen, tot de saus dik is. Roer er de munt door en breng op smaak met zout en peper. Giet de saus over de duiven en dien onmiddellijk op.

Voor 4 personen

---

1 portie: Calorieën 380, Eiwit 20 g, Koolhydraten 11 g, Vezel 2 g, Vet totaal 25 g (Verzadigd 7 g, Enkelvoudig onverzadigd 14 g, Meervoudig onverzadigd 3 g), Cholesterol 100 mg, Natrium 230 mg, Vitamine C 45%.

▲ *1 Fruit, 1 Vlees*

Risotto alla Piemontese

Het gebruik van wijn met risotto is bekend, maar normaal gesproken wordt er witte wijn gebruikt. De rode wijn in dit recept geeft de risotto een prachtige kleur en een heerlijke smaak. In Piëmonte gebruikt men liefst Barolo-wijn, maar u kunt ook een Chianti of een andere volle rode wijn gebruiken.

3 eetlepels olijfolie
125 g gehakte ui
150 g kardoen, bijgesneden en in plakken van 1 cm gesneden
450 g Arborio rijst
2,5 dl droge rode wijn

Van boven naar beneden: Risotto alla Piemontese, Garnaal-venkelsalade, Gesmoorde knoflook met linguine

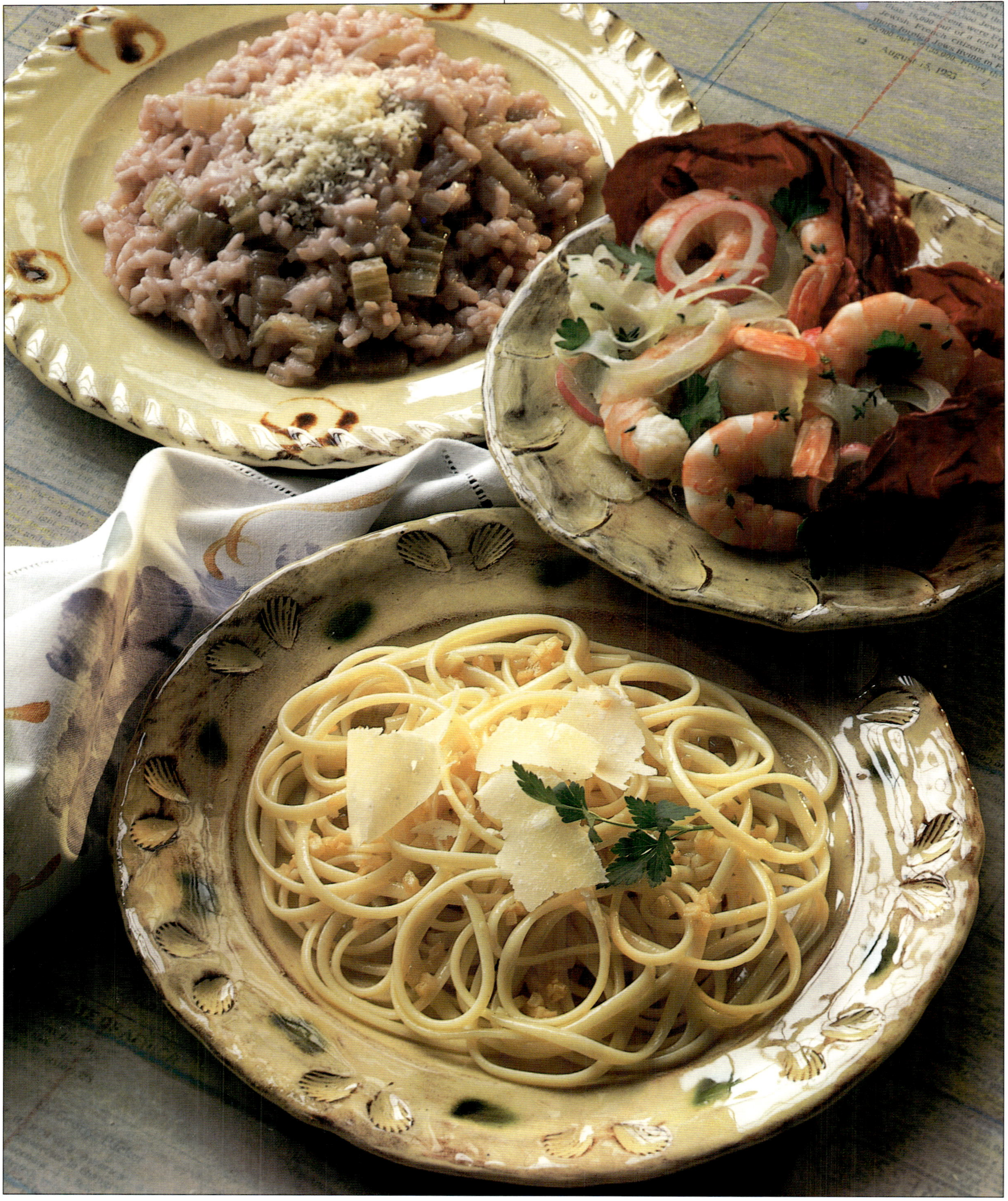

1,25-1,5 liter sudderende kippebouillon (zie woordenlijst)
¼ theelepel zout
versgemalen peper naar smaak
30 g versgeraspte Parmezaanse kaas
1 kleine witte truffel (desgewenst)

1. Verhit de olijfolie in een grote pan. Doe er de ui en kardoen in en fruit circa 8 minuten op een laag vuur tot ze gaar maar niet bruin zijn. Voeg de Arborio rijst toe en bak circa 2 minuten tot de korrels ondoorschijnend zijn.
2. Giet er de wijn bij en laat sudderen tot die geabsorbeerd is. Giet er telkens 2,5 dl van de warme bouillon bij onder voortdurend roeren tot de bouillon bijna opgenomen is voor u weer bijgiet. Breng op smaak met zout en peper.
3. Strooi er de Parmezaanse kaas over en dien onmiddellijk op. Als u witte truffel gebruikt deze in flinterdunne plakjes over elke portie schaven.

Voor 6 personen

2,5 dl per portie: Calorieën 340, Eiwit 7 g, Koolhydraten 57 g, Vezel 1 g, Vet totaal 9 g (Verzadigd 2 g, Enkelvoudig onverzadigd 6 g, Meervoudig onverzadigd 1 g), Cholesterol 3 mg, Natrium 190 mg.
▲ *2 Brood, 1 Groente*

PASTA / ITALIË

Gesmoorde knoflook met linguine

Lynne Rossetto Kaspers boek The Splendid Table: Recipes from Emilia-Romagna, The Heartland of Nothern Italian food, *is een zeer informatief boek over het eten en de culinaire invloed van dat gebied. In dit recept worden twee regionale ingrediënten verwerkt: Parmezaanse kaas en balsamico azijn. Gebruik een kwaliteits balsamico of zo mogelijk een boerenbalsamico.*

6 eetlepels koudgeperste olijfolie
8 grote tenen knoflook, grof gehakt
500 g linguine (taglialini)
zout en versgemalen zwarte peper naar smaak
125 g versgeraspte Parmezaanse kaas
8-10 theelepels balsamico azijn

1. Verhit 3 eetlepels van de olijfolie in een grote, zware koekepan op een middelhoog vuur. Doe er de knoflook in, leg het deksel op de pan en fruit de knoflook circa 5 minuten op een zeer laag vuur. Neem het deksel van de pan en laat de knoflook onder regelmatig roeren nog 8 minuten fruiten of tot hij goudgeel en volledig gaar is. Laat de knoflook niet bruin worden daar hij dan bitter wordt.
2. Breng intussen 6 liter gezouten water flink aan de kook en doe er de linguine in. Kook de pasta onder regelmatig roeren in circa 10 minuten bijtgaar. Roer circa 3 eetlepels pastakooknat door de gefruite knoflook. Giet de pasta in een vergiet.
3. Neem de pan met knoflook van het vuur en schep de knoflook door de pasta. Voeg de rest van de olijfolie toe en schep de pasta om met 2 pollepels. Breng op smaak met zout en peper. Schep er alle kaas door en doe de aangemaakte pasta in een voorverwarmde kom. Dien de pasta op en besprenkel elke portie met 1 of 2 theelepels balsamico azijn.

Voor 6 personen als hoofdgerecht, 10 als bijgerecht

---

1 portie (hoofdgerecht): Calorieën 490, Eiwit 18 g, Koolhydraten 59 g, Vezel 2 g, Vet totaal 20 g (Verzadigd 6 g, Enkelvoudig onverzadigd 12 g, Meervoudig onverzadigd 2 g), Cholesterol 15 mg, Natrium 360 mg, Kalk 30%.
▲ *2 Brood, 1 Vet/Suiker*

SALADES / ITALIË

Insalata di gamberi e finocchio

GARNAAL-VENKELSALADE

Serveer deze frisse salade als voorgerecht of lichte lunch. U kunt de salade een dag van tevoren maken en in de koelkast bewaren.

500 g rauwe garnalen, gepeld en darmkanalen verwijderd
2 venkelknollen, overdwars in zeer dunne plakken gesneden
1 kleine rode ui, in ringen gesneden
2 eetlepels rode wijnazijn
3 eetlepels koudgeperste olijfolie
¼ theelepel zout
versgemalen peper naar smaak
1 theelepel verse tijm, fijngehakt
2 eetlepels snijpeterselie
1 kropje roodlof (radicchio), bladen losgemaakt

1. Kook de garnalen circa 2 minuten in kokend water tot ze stevig aanvoelen en roze zijn. Giet ze af en laat ze afkoelen.
2. Doe de plakken venkel met de garnalen en ui in een grote slakom; zet weg.
3. Klop de azijn door de olie in een kleine kom. Breng op smaak met zout en peper. Voeg de tijm en peterselie toe en schep de dressing om met de venkel en garnalen. Zet minstens 1 uur in de koelkast voor het serveren.
4. Schep de salade op de bladen roodlof en dien op.

Voor 6 personen

---

1 portie: Calorieën 180, Eiwit 17 g, Koolhydraten 10 g, Vezel 1 g, Vet totaal 8 g (Verzadigd 1 g, Enkelvoudig onverzadigd 5 g, Meervoudig onverzadigd 1 g), Cholesterol 115 mg, Natrium 260 mg, Vitamine C 25%.
▲ *1 Groente, 1 Vlees*

HAPJES / CHINA

Gestoomde broodjes met kip en groenten

Bao, Chinese gestoomde broodjes, zijn een belangrijk onderdeel van dim sum. *Ze worden bij kraampjes verkocht met diverse vullingen. U kunt deze hapjes van tevoren klaarmaken en ze vlak voor het serveren stomen, of ze een dag van tevoren stomen en ze opwarmen. Ze zijn lekker met lenteui-dipsaus (recept op pagina 72).*

1 pakje (7 g) gedroogde gist
2 theelepels suiker
1 eetlepel plus 2 theelepels Chinese sesamolie
550-625 g bloem
3 gedroogde Chinese zwarte paddestoelen of gedroogde shiitake paddestoelen
1 eetlepel gedroogde wolkenoor paddestoelen
2 theelepels sojasaus
2 theelepels droge sherry
2 eetlepels arachide-olie
250 g kipfilet, fijngehakt
3 lenteuitjes, fijngehakt
2 tenen knoflook, fijngehakt
1 wortel, grof geraspt
2 theelepels fijngehakte verse gember
1 eetlepel maïzena, opgelost in 4 eetlepels kippebouillon (zie woordenlijst)
1 theelepel bakpoeder
45 g lenteuitjes, in dunne plakjes

1. Los de gist en de suiker op in 4 eetlepels warm water (40°-46°C). Laat 5 minuten staan tot een schuimig mengsel. Voeg dan 1 eetlepel sesamolie toe.
2. Doe 470 g van de bloem in een grote kom en voeg al kloppend geleidelijk het gistmengsel toe en klop tot een stijf deeg. Doe het deeg op een licht met bloem bestoven werkvlak en kneed er zonodig de rest van de 80-155 g bloem bij. Kneed het deeg circa 5-10 minuten tot het glad en niet meer plakkerig is. Doe het deeg in een licht met olie ingevette kom, dek die af en laat het deeg circa 1 uur rijzen tot het in volume verdubbeld is.
3. Week voor de vulling de zwarte paddestoelen en wolkenoren minstens 20 minuten in heet water. Verwijder de steeltjes; spoel de hoedjes af en hak ze fijn. Zet weg.
4. Meng de rest van de sesamolie met de sojasaus en sherry en zet het geheel weg.
5. Verhit een wok en doe er dan de arachide-olie in. Doe de kipfilet in de hete olie en roerbak circa 1 minuut. Voeg de 3 fijngehakte lenteuitjes, knoflook, wortel en gember toe en roerbak 1 minuut. Voeg de paddestoelen toe en roerbak 1 minuut. Schep er het sesam-sojamengsel door tot alle ingediënten ermee bedekt zijn. Schep er het maïzenapapje door en roerbak circa 1 minuten tot het kooknat gebonden is. Neem de wok van het vuur en laat de inhoud afkoelen.
6. Druk de lucht uit het deeg en doe het op een licht met bloem bestoven werkvlak. Strooi het bakpoeder en 45 g plakjes lenteui over het deeg en kneed het deeg daarna 5 minuten met die ingrediënten.
7. Doe een bamboe stoommand in een wok of grote pan. Vul de wok of pan met water tot aan de bodem van de mand. Neem de stoommand eruit en zet weg.
8. Knip twaalf vierkantjes van 7 cm uit vetvrij papier of ingevet perkamentpapier.
9. Verdeel het deeg in tweeën en rol elke helft uit tot een cilinder van 30 cm. Snijd elke cilinder in 6 stukjes. Druk elk stuk zachtjes aan op een licht met bloem bestoven werkvlak. Rol ze verder met een deegroller uit tot een stuk van circa 10 cm.
10. Doe 2 eetlepels vulling in het midden van elk stuk deeg. Neem de deegranden bij elkaar en maak ze verder dicht door de punten te knijpen en draaien. Doe de broodjes met de vouwnaad onder op de vierkantjes papier.
11. Schik de broodjes met hun papier 4 cm uit elkaar in stapelmanden. Dek ze af met een theedoek en laat 30 minuten rijzen.
12. Zet de manden op elkaar boven het kokende water in de wok of pot. Draai het vuur iets lager. Leg er het deksel op en stoom de broodjes 15 minuten. Verander de volgorde van de manden halverwege het stomen. Laat de strak afgedekte manden 5 minuten staan tot de stoom verdwenen is en dien dan op.

Voor 12 broodjes

1 broodje per portie: Calorieën 200, Eiwit 7 g, Koolhydraten 32 g, Vezel 2 g, Vet totaal 5 g (Verzadigd 1 g, Enkelvoudig onverzadigd 2 g, Meervoudig onverzadigd 2 g), Cholesterol 5 mg, Natrium 55 mg, Vitamine A 35%.

▲ *1 Brood, ½ Groente*

GEVOGELTE / CHINA

Kung pao kip

Dit klassieke kipgerecht is heel snel klaar. Serveer dit gerecht met gestoomde rijst als hoofdgerecht of als lichte lunch.

2 eetlepels droge sherry
1 eetlepel maïzena
1 theelepel sesamolie
versgemalen witte peper naar smaak
750 g kipfilet, in stukjes gesneden
1 eetlepel sojasaus
1 eetlepel rijstwijnazijn
4 eetlepels kippebouillon (zie woordenlijst)
3 eetlepels arachide-olie
5 kleine gedroogde chilipepers
45 g drooggeroosterde pinda's
1 theelepel fijngehakte knoflook
1 theelepel geraspte verse gember
4 lenteuitjes, in stukjes van 2 cm gesneden
150 g peultjes, bijgesneden

1. Meng 1 eetlepel sherry met de maïzena, sesamolie en peper in een grote kom. Schep er de stukjes kip door en laat ze 20 minuten marineren.
2. Meng de sojasaus met de azijn, de rest van de sherry en de kippebouillon in een kleine kom. Zet weg.

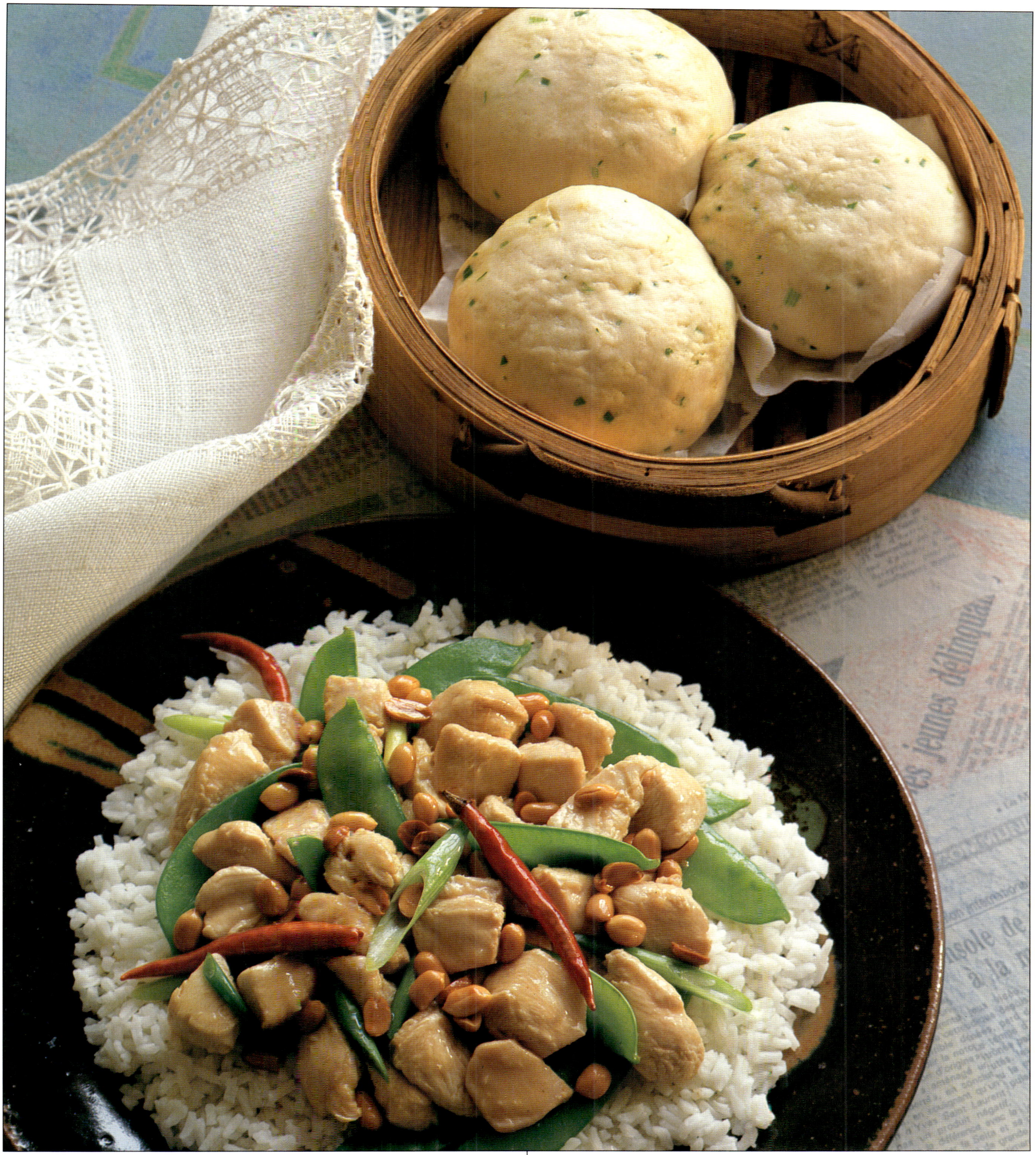

Van boven naar beneden: Gestoomde broodjes met kip en groenten, Kung pao kip

3. Verhit een wok of grote koekepan op een middelhoog vuur. Doe de arachide-olie in de hete wok en vervolgens de chilipepers en pinda's. Roerbak snel tot de chilipepers donker maar niet zwart worden. Schep met een schuimspaan de pinda's en chilipepers uit de wok en laat ze op keukenpapier uitlekken.
4. Doe de knoflook en gember in de chili-olie in de wok en roerbak snel. Voeg het kipmengsel toe en roerbak circa 3 minuten tot de kip half gaar is. Voeg de lenteuitjes en peultjes toe en roerbak 1 minuut. Schep er het sojasausmengsel door en laat circa 2 minuten koken tot het kooknat iets dikker is. Schep er de pinda's en chilipepers door en dien onmiddellijk op.

Voor 6 personen

---

1 portie: Calorieën 250, Eiwit 25 g, Koolhydraten 6 g, Vezel 2 g, Vet totaal 12 g (Verzadigd 2 g, Enkelvoudig onverzadigd 5 g, Meervoudig onverzadigd 4 g), Cholesterol 65 mg, Natrium 220 mg, Vitamine C 45%.

▲ *1 Vlees*

Faisan Normand

GEBRADEN FAZANT

In Normandië worden appels en appelcider in de herfst langs de weg verkocht. Deze ingrediënten zijn niet allen zeer geschikt voor fazant maar ook voor kip of eend.

2 fazanten, elk 1,5 kg
¼ theelepel zout
versgemalen peper naar smaak
4 sjalotjes, in plakken
2 takjes verse tijm
4 tenen knoflook, gekneusd
15 g boter
1 eetlepel olijfolie
500 g zurige stevige appels als Granny Smith of Cox Orange, geschild, klokhuizen verwijderd en in blokjes gesneden
500 g knolselderij, geschild en in staafjes gesneden
2 eetlepels calvados of cognac
4 eetlepels appelcider of ongezoet appelsap
5 dl bruine kippebouillon (zie woordenlijst)
2 theelepels verse tijm, fijngehakt

1. Verwarm de oven voor op 180°C.
2. Spoel de fazanten af, dep ze droog en bestrooi ze met zout en peper. Doe de helft van de sjalot, de takjes tijm en de knoflook in de lichaamsholte van elke fazant.
3. Verhit de boter en olijfolie in een grote koekepan. Braad de fazanten rondom aan op een hoog vuur en leg ze dan op hun zijkanten in een braadslee. Zet weg.
4. Bak de appel en knolselderij 2 minuten in dezelfde koekepan. Blus de pan af met de calvados. Voeg de cider, kippebouillon en gehakte tijm toe en laat 10 minuten sudderen. Schep de appel en knolselderij er met een schuimspaan uit en giet het kooknat over de fazanten in de braadslee.
5. Dek de braadslee af en braad de fazanten 30 minuten in de oven, waarbij u ze om de 10 minuten op de andere zijknat draait.
6. Schep de bewaarde appel en knolselderij door het kooknat in de braadslee. Leg de fazanten met de borstkant boven en laat ze onafgedekt 5 tot 7 minuten roosteren tot ze bruin zijn.
7. Doe de fazanten op een voorverwarmde dienschaal. Schep met een schuimspaan de appel en knolselderij uit de slee en schik ze om de fazanten. Schep er wat kooknat over en dien op.

Voor 8 personen

¼ fazant met saus per portie: Calorieën 410, Eiwit 49 g, Koolhydraten 18 g, Vezel 3 g, Vet totaal 16 g (Verzadigd 5 g, Enkelvoudig

Van links naar rechts: Aardappel-preisoep (recept pagina 202), Gebraden fazant, Gegratineerde groenten

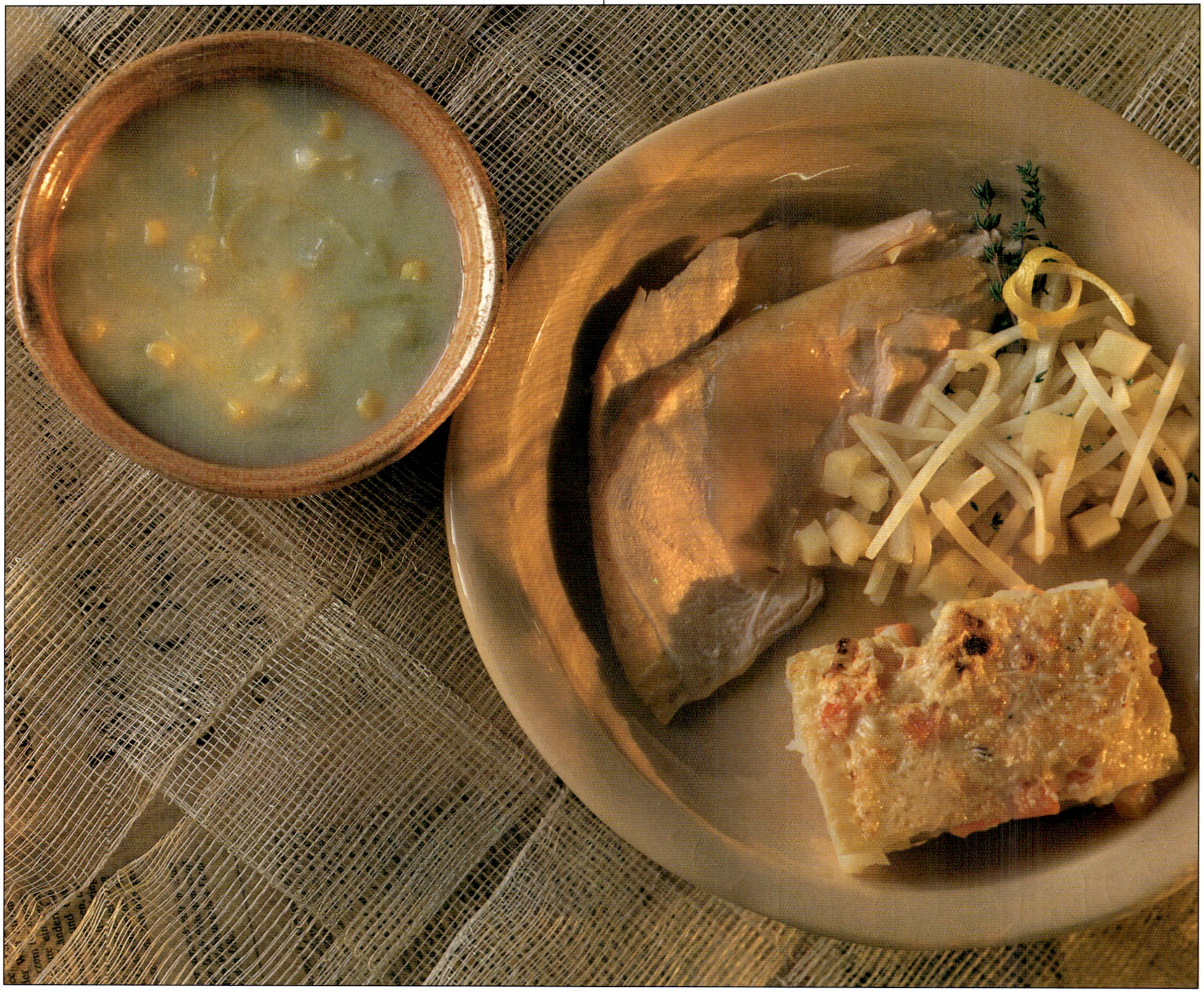

onverzadigd 8 g, Meervoudig onverzadigd 2 g), Cholesterol 100 mg, Natrium 230 mg, IJzer 20%, Vitamine C 3[illegible]%.

▲ *1 Fruit, ½ Groente, 1½ Vlees*

BROOD / BRAZILIË

Aardappelkoekjes

Dit is een mooie manier om restjes zoete aardappel op te maken. Deze koekjes krijgen hun luchtige structuur en prachtige kleur van de aardappel. Rooster de pepitas *op een droge bakplaat 10 minuten in een op 150°C voorverwarmde oven. Serveer de koekjes met uw favoriete ingemaakte fruit.*

200 g gekookte zoete aardappel
4 theelepels saffloerolie
1 eetlepel suiker
150 g bloem
1 eetlepel bakpoeder
¼ theelepel zout
4 eetlepels geroosterde *pepitas* (gepelde, gedopte pompoenpitten)

1. Verwarm de oven voor op 190°C. Bekleed een bakplaat met perkamentpapier.
2. Stamp de zoete aardappel met de saffloerolie en suiker in een grote kom fijn.
3. Meng de bloem met het bakpoeder, zout en de *pepitas* in een middelgrote kom.
4. Schep de droge ingrediënten door de aardappelpuree tot alles net gemengd is. Meng niet te veel.
5. Doe het deeg op een licht met bloem bestoven werkvlak en rol het deeg uit tot 1 cm dik. Steek er rondjes uit van 5 cm doorsnee met een uitsteekvormpje en leg de rondjes op de bakplaat.
6. Bak in 15 minuten in de oven goudbruin. Dien onmiddellijk op.

Voor 12 koekjes

---

1 koekje per portie: Calorieën 90, Eiwit 2 g, Koolhydraten 14 g, Vezel 1 g, Vet totaal 3 g (Verzadigd 0,5 g, Enkelvoudig onverzadigd 0,5 g, Meervoudig onverzadigd 2 g), Cholesterol 0 mg, Natrium 50 mg, Vitamine A 70%.

▲ *1 Brood*

GROENTEN / FRANKRIJK

Gegratineerde groenten

Bewaar wortel- en knolgewassen op een koele donkere plek. U kunt voor dit gerecht ook andere wortel- en knolgewassen gebruiken als bijvoorbeeld pastinaak, koolraap en zoete aardappel.

1 aardappel, geschild en in plakken van 3 mm dik gesneden
2 middelgrote aardperen
1 eetlepel vers citroensap
1 knolselderij, geschild en in plakken van 3 mm dik
1 meiraap, geschild en in plakken

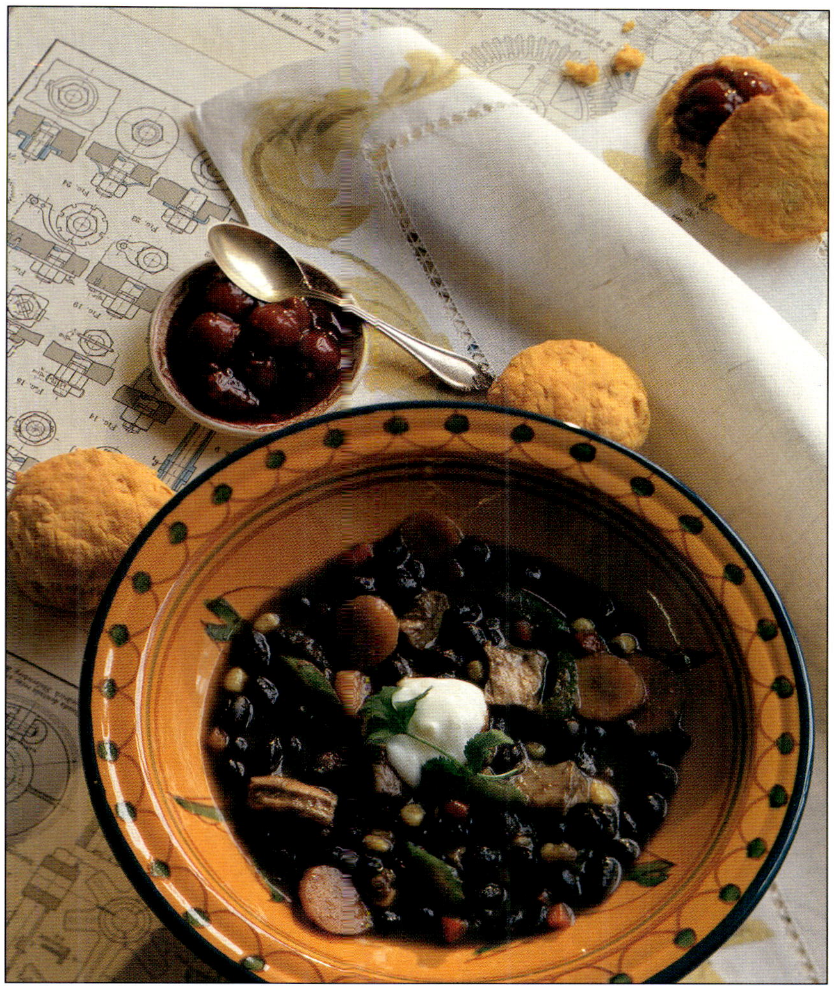

Aardappelkoekjes met vruchtenconfiture, Zwarte-bonensoep (recept pagina 206)

1 wortel, geschild en in blokjes
5 dl magere melk
¼ theelepel zout
versgemalen peper naar smaak
versgeraspte nootmuskaat naar smaak
3 eetlepels versgeraspte Parmezaanse kaas

1. Verwarm de oven voor op 190°C. Vet een ovenschaal van 2 liter inhoud licht in met olie.
2. Spoel de aardappel onder de koude kraan tot het water helder blijft. Laat uitlekken en zet weg.
3. Schil de aardperen en snijd ze in plakken van 3 mm dik. Doe ze onmiddellijk in water gemengd met het citroensap tot gebruik. Spoel ze dan onder de koude kraan tot het water helder blijft. Laat ze goed uitlekken.
4. Schik de plakken aardappel, aardpeer, knolselderij en meiraap om en om in lagen in de ovenschaal en bestrooi elke laag met wat wortel.
5. Meng de melk met wat zout, peper en nootmuskaat. Giet het mengsel over de groenten. Dek de schaal af met aluminiumfolie en zet 45 minuten in de oven tot de groenten gaar zijn. Verwijder de folie, strooi de kaas over de groenten en zet nog 10 minuten in de oven tot de bovenkant goudbruin is.

Voor 6 personen

---

1 portie: Calorieën 100, Eiwit [illegible] g, Koolhydraten 17 g, Vezel 2 g, Vet totaal 2 g (Verzadigd 1,5 g, Enkelvoudig onverzadigd 0 g, Meervoudig onverzadigd 0 g), Cholesterol 5 mg, Natrium 230 mg, Vitamine A 70%, Vitamine C 20%.

▲ *1 Groente, ½ Melk*

Soepen / Wales

Aardappel-preisoep

Wintergroenten voor een winterse soep. Verdubbel de hoeveelheden van het recept en vries de helft in voor een makkelijke maaltijd.

4 eetlepels saffloerolie
4 preien, julienne gesneden
4 tenen knoflook, fijngehakt
3 aardappels, geschild en in blokjes
7,5 dl kippebouillon (zie woordenlijst)
7,5 dl magere melk
100 g ingevroren maïskorrels
¼ theelepel zout
versgemalen peper naar smaak

1. Verhit de olie in een grote soeppan en fruit er de prei en knoflook in tot ze gaar maar niet bruin zijn.
2. Voeg de aardappel en kippebouillon toe en breng aan de kook. Draai het vuur lager en laat 15 tot 20 minuten sudderen, of tot de aardappel gaar is.
3. Pureer ongeveer de helft van de soep in een blender. Doe de puree terug in de pan en schep er de melk en maïs door. Laat de soep goed doorwarmen en breng op smaak met zout en peper.

Voor 8 personen *Foto op pagina 200*

2,5 dl per portie: Calorieën 200, Eiwit 5 g, Koolhydraten 27 g, Vezel 2 g, Vet totaal 9 g (Verzadigd 1,5 g, Enkelvoudig onverzadigd 1,5 g, Meervoudig onverzadigd 5 g), Cholesterol 5 mg, Natrium 135 mg, Vitamine C 20%.

▲ *1 Groente, ½ Melk*

Hapjes / Italië

Insalata di arànce

Sinaasappelsalade

Dit recept is van de schrijver en kook-instructeur Giuliano Bugialli in Florence. De mooie kleur van de sinaasappels en de frisse smaak van de venkel maken deze salade een prima keuze voor een voorgerecht of als onderdeel van een buffet.

4 grote sappige sinaasappels
4 struiken bleekselderij
1 venkelknol, in dunne plakken
3 eetlepels olijfolie
1 theelepel rode wijnazijn
versgemalen zwarte peper naar smaak
4 walnoten, gedopt en grof gehakt (circa 4 eetlepels)

1. Schil de sinaasappels en verwijder het wit. Snijd de sinaasappels overdwars in plakken van 1 cm dik en schik de plakken op een grote dienschaal.
2. Maak de bleekselderij schoon en haal zonodig alle draden af. Snijd ze in blokjes van 1 cm. Schik de bleekselderij en venkel over de plakken sinaasappel.
3. Meng de olie met de azijn en druppel het mengsel over de salade. Bestrooi het geheel met zout en peper en garneer met de stukjes walnoot.

Voor 8 personen

1 portie: Calorieën 130, Eiwit 2 g, Koolhydraten 16 g, Vezel 5 g, Vet totaal 7 g (Verzadigd 1 g, Enkelvoudig onverzadigd 4,5 g, Meervoudig onverzadigd 2 g), Cholesterol 0 mg, Natrium 55 mg, Vitamine C 100%.

▲ *1 Fruit, 1 Groente*

Zeebanket / Italië

Geroosterde zeeduivel en aardappels met rozemarijn

U kunt de zeeduivel door een andere vis naar keuze vervangen.

750 g rode aardappels, in stukken van 5 cm
1 ui, in plakken
2 eetlepels gehakte verse rozemarijnblaadjes
3 eetlepels olijfolie
900 g zeeduivelfilet
¼ theelepel zout
versgemalen peper naar smaak
takjes verse rozemarijn, ter garnering

1. Verwarm de oven voor op 200°C. Vet een grote braadslee licht in met olijfolie.
2. Doe de aardappel, ui, gehakte rozemarijn en 2 eetlepels olijfolie in de slee en schep alles goed om. Zet circa 25 minuten in de oven tot de aardappel gaar en goudbruin is. Schep het aardappelmengsel één keer om tijdens het roosteren.
3. Kwast de zeeduivel licht in met de rest van de olijfolie en bestrooi met zout en peper. Schep het aardappelmengsel nog een keer om en leg er de zeeduivel op. Zet 10 minuten in de oven, of tot de vis stevig aanvoelt en gaar is. Laat de vis 3 tot 4 minuten rusten; leg hem dan op een snijplank.
4. Doe het aardappelmengsel op een dienschaal. Snijd de vis in schuine plakken en schik ze op de aardappel. Garneer met de takjes rozemarijn en dien onmiddellijk op.

Voor 4 personen

1 portie: Calorieën 340, Eiwit 29 g, Koolhydraten 37 g, Vezel 4 g, Vet totaal 8 g (Verzadigd 1 g, Enkelvoudig onverzadigd 4,5 g, Meervoudig onverzadigd 1,5 g), Cholesterol 60 mg, Natrium 220 mg, Vitamine C 20%.

▲ *1 Groente, 1 Vlees*

Van beneden naar boven: Geroosterde zeeduivel en aardappels met rozemarijn, Sinaasappelsalade

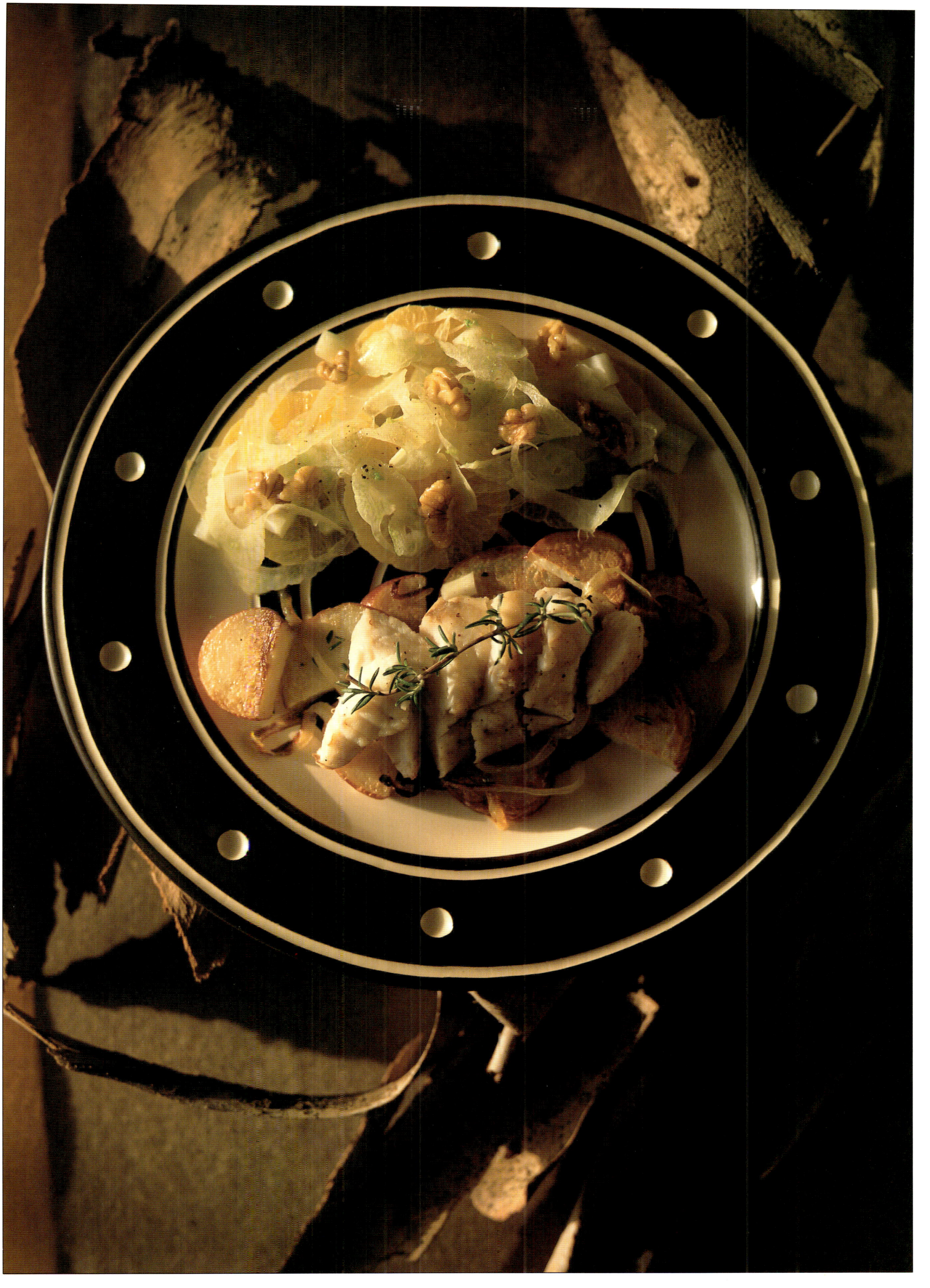

GRAAN / VERENIGDE STATEN

Wilde rijst, kastanje-appelvulling

U kunt deze heerlijke vulling gebruiken voor alle soorten gevogelte, van piepkuiken tot gans. Serveer anders als een bijgerecht met gegrild vlees of voeg 125 g cranberry's toe voor een kleurrijke versie.

185 g wilde rijst
zout naar smaak
4 preien, alleen het wit, gehakt
2 eetlepels saffloerolie
250 g verse kastanjes, geroosterd, gepeld en in plakken
2,5 dl kippebouillon (zie woordenlijst) ingekookt tot 4 eetlepels
1,25 dl calvados of droge Madeira
2 grote Granny Smith of Cox Orange appels, in blokjes
1 eetlepel verse salie, fijngehakt
2 eetlepels verse tijm, fijngehakt
7 g verse peterselie, fijngehakt
versgemalen peper naar smaak

1. Schep de wilde rijst en wat zout door 1 liter kokend water. Laat 40 tot 45 minuten onafgedekt sudderen tot het water geabsorbeerd is en de korrels gepoft zijn.
2. Fruit de prei gaar maar niet bruin in de olie op een matig vuur. Voeg de kastanjes en kippebouillon toe en kook circa 5 minuten tot het vocht verdampt is. Draai het vuur hoger, blus de pan af met de calvados of Madeira en laat tot een stroop inkoken.
3. Voeg de rest van de ingrediënten toe en schep het geheel om met de wilde rijst.

Voor 8 personen

2 dl per portie: Calorieën 230, Eiwit 5 g, Koolhydraten 45 g, Vezel 7 g, Vet totaal 5 g (Verzadigd 0,5 g, Enkelvoudig onverzadigd 1 g, Meervoudig onverzadigd 3 g), Cholesterol 0 mg, Natrium 15 mg, Vitamine C 40%.
▲ *1 Brood, ½ Fruit, ½ Groente*

VEDERWILD / VERENIGDE STATEN

Geglaceerde gans met carnberry-perenchutney

De braadtijd voor gans of kalkoen bedraagt circa 20 minuten per 500 g. Geef bij dit gerecht cranberry-perenchutney (recept volgt) en confit van ui (recept volgt) en Himmel und erde *(recept op pagina 164). Als u kalkoen in plaats van gans gebruikt, wordt het vetgehalte gehalveerd.*

GEVULDE GANS

1 gans of kalkoen van circa 5 kg
1 citroen, gehalveerd
versgemalen peper naar smaak
2 theelepels verse rozemarijn, fijngehakt
wilde rijst, kastanje- appelvulling (vorig recept)

ESDOORNSIROOPGLAZUUR

45 g margarine
3 eetlepels fijngehakte verse gember
1,25 dl pure esdoornsiroop
1,25 dl kippebouillon (zie woordenlijst)

1. Verwarm de oven voor op 220°.
2. Wrijf de buikholte van de gans of kalkoen in met de citroen en met de peper en rozemarijn. Herhaal aan de buitenkant.
3. Vul de buikholte losjes met de vulling en bind de poten samen.
4. Smelt voor het glazuur de margarine in een kleine pan. Voeg de gember toe en laat 5 minuten sudderen. Voeg de esdoornsiroop en kippebouillon toe en laat 10 minuten sudderen.
5. Leg de vogel met de borstkant boven op een rooster in een braadslee en kwast hem in met het glazuur. Dek de slee af met aluminiumfolie en rooster de vogel 15 minuten in de oven. Draai de oven op 180°C en rooster 3 uur onder regelmatig bedruipen tot u een poot makkelijk kunt bewegen of een in de dij gestoken vleesthermometer 82°C aangeeft. Verwijder de folie de laatste 15 minuten braadtijd. Als de borst al te bruin is de folie laten zitten. Controleer de gaarheid door een satéstokje in de dij te prikken: het uitlopend vocht moet helder en niet roze zijn.
6. Neem de vulling onmiddellijk uit de vogel en doe in een voorverwarmde schaal. Gooi het vet in de slee weg.
7. Laat de vogel 15 minuten op een schaal rusten voor u haar aansnijdt. Dien op met de chutney.

Voor 8 personen

120 g gans met 2 dl vulling per portie: Calorieën 610, Eiwit 33 g, Koolhydraten 50 g, Vezel 7 g, Vet totaal 31 g (Verzadigd 9 g, Enkelvoudig onverzadigd 13 g, Meervoudig onverzadigd 7 g), Cholesterol 100 mg, Natrium 100 mg, IJzer 30% Vitamine C 40 %.
▲ *2 Brood, 1 Vlees, 1 Vet/Suiker*

120 g kalkoen met 2 dl vulling per portie: Calorieën 500, Eiwit 37 g, Koolhydraten 50 g, Vezel 7 g, Vet totaal 17 g (Verzadigd 4 g, Enkelvoudig onverzadigd 5 g, Meervoudig onverzadigd 6 g), Cholesterol 95 mg, Natrium 95 mg, IJzer 25%, Vitamine C 40%.
▲ *2 Brood, 1 Vlees*

CRANBERRY-PERENCHUTNEY

Deze chutney moet een paar dagen van tevoren worden gemaakt zodat de smaken volledig tot hun recht komen. U kunt hem tot 2 weken in de koelkast bewaren.

3,75 dl witte wijnazijn
250 g suiker
100 g lichtbruine basterdsuiker
1 jalapeño peper, ontzaad en gehakt
500 g peren, geschild, klokhuizen verwijderd en in blokjes
500 g cranberry's
1 ui, gesnipperd
2 tenen knoflook, fijngehakt
100 g rozijnen
1 gele paprika, zaad en zaadlijsten verwijderd, gehakt
1 eetlepel geraspte verse gember
2 eetlepels limoensap
1 eetlepel geraspte limoenschil

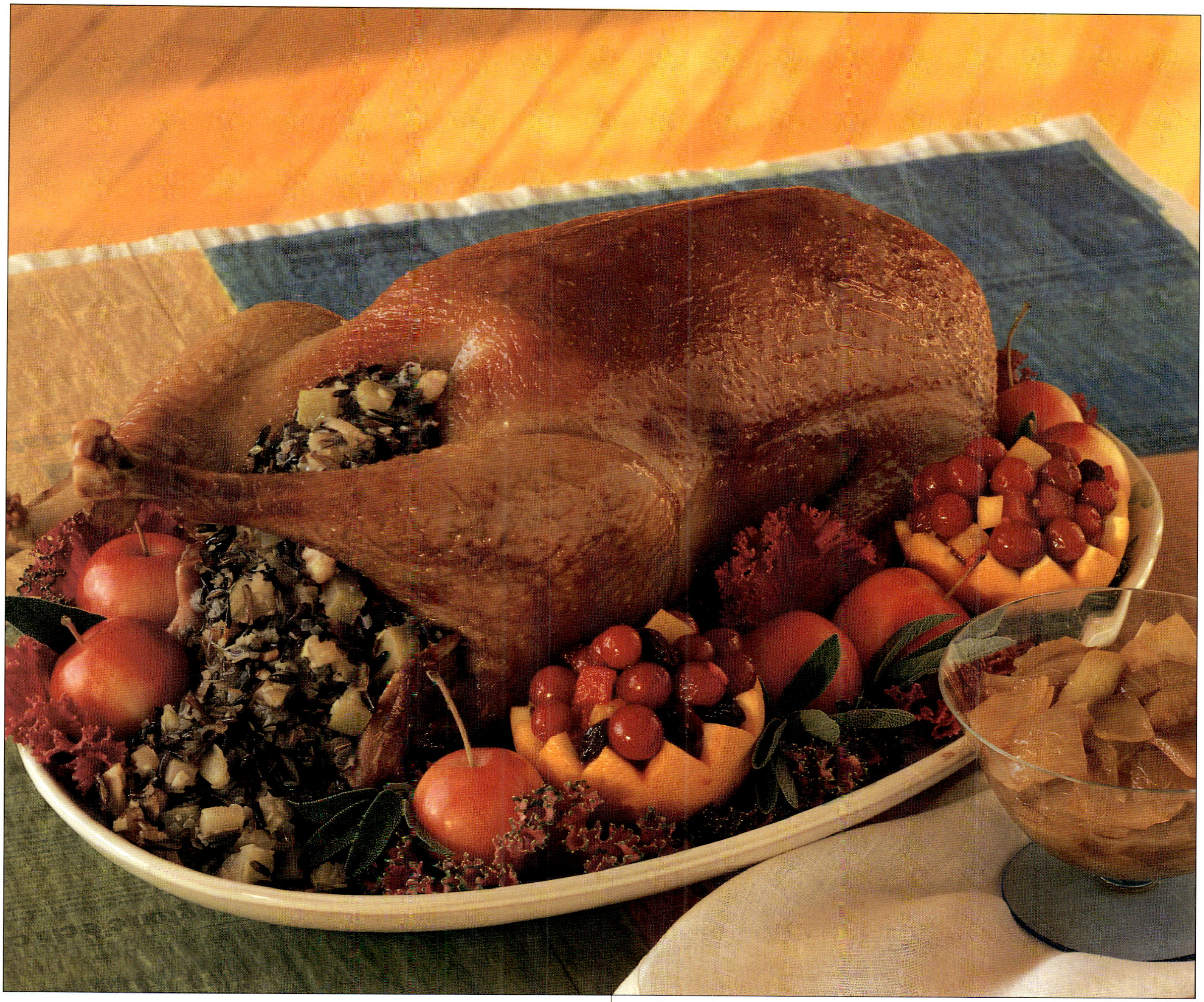

Van links naar rechts: Wilde rijst, kastanje-appelvulling, Geglaceerde gans met cranberry-perenchutney, Confit van ui

½ theelepel mosterdzaad
½ theelepel selderijzaad

1. Doe de azijn, suikersoorten en jalapeño in een zware pan. Breng aan de kook onder regelmatig roeren en schep er dan de rest van de ingrediënten door. Breng weer aan de kook, draai het vuur lager en laat 5 minuten sudderen. Neem de pan van het vuur, laat afkoelen en bewaar in de koelkast.

Voor 2 liter

4 eetlepels per portie: Calorieën 60, Eiwit 0 g, Koolhydraten 15 g, Vezel 1 g, Vet totaal 0 g (Verzadigd 0 g, Enkelvoudig onverzadigd 0 g, Meervoudig onverzadigd 0 g), Cholesterol 0 mg, Natrium 0 mg.
▲ *1 Fruit*

GROENTEN / VERENIGDE STATEN

Confit van ui

Uien bevatten relatief veel suiker, en door het koken worden ze nog zoeter. Witte uien zijn in het algemeen het zoetst of in ieder geval het minst scherp. Een confit is meestal vlees dat langzaam gebraden is in zijn eigen vet. Bij deze confit wordt dezelfde methode gebruikt.

3 eetlepels saffloerolie
2 witte uien, in stukken van 2 cm
1 prei, alleen het wit, in stukken van 2 cm
1 sjalot, fijngehakt
1,25 dl Madeira
2,5 dl kippebouillon (zie woordenlijst)

1. Verhit de olie in een grote koekepan. Doe er de ui en prei in en fruit ze circa 10 minuten op een middelhoog vuur tot ze goudbruin zijn. Voeg de sjalot toe, draai het vuur laag en laat nog 10 minuten fruiten.
2. Blus de pan af met de Madeira en laat het vocht tot een siroop inkoken. Voeg de kippebouillon toe en kook circa 15 minuten op een middelhoog vuur tot het kooknat ingekookt en dik is. Houd de confit warm tot het serveren.

Voor 7,5 dl

1,25 dl per portie: Calorieën 100, Eiwit 1 g, Koolhydraten 8 g, Vezel 1 g, Vet totaal 7 g (Verzadigd 0,5 g, Enkelvoudig onverzadigd 1 g, Meervoudig onverzadigd 5 g), Cholesterol 0 mg, Natrium 10 mg.
▲ *1 Groente*

ZEEBANKET / FRANKRIJK

Tonijn met peperkorst

Als tonijn niet verkrijgbaar is, kunt u een andere stevige vissoort als heilbot, snapper, zeebaars of zalm gebruiken.

1 theelepel saffloerolie
4 eetlepels vers citroensap
500 g moten tonijn
1 theelepel groene peperkorrels, grof gemalen
1 theelepel roze peperkorrels, grof gemalen
1 theelepel zwarte peperkorrels, grof gemalen
1 theelepel witte peperkorrels, grof gemalen
30 g boter
2 sjalotjes, gesnipperd
500 g spinazie, 5 seconden geblancheerd en uitgelekt (zie woordenlijst)
¼ theelepel zout
1 citroen, in partjes gesneden

1. Verwarm de oven voor op 200°C. Vet vervolgens een bakplaat licht in met olie.
2. Meng de olie met 1 eetlepel citroensap en kwast de tonijn in met dit mengsel.
3. Meng de peperkorrels in een kleine, ondiepe schaal. Haal de moten tonijn door de peperkorrels en druk de korrels licht aan. Leg de vis op de bakplaat. Bak de vis in circa 10 minuten gaar in de oven.
4. Smelt intussen de boter in een middelgrote koekepan. Doe er de sjalotjes in en fruit ze gaar. Voeg de spinazie toe en bak die snel aan tot hij warm is. Bestrooi het geheel met zout en de rest van het citroensap.
5. Doe de spinazie op een dienschaal en schik er de tonijn op. Dien onmiddellijk op met de partjes citroen.

Voor 4 personen

1 portie: Calorieën 260, Eiwit 30 g, Koolhydraten 8 g, Vezel 3 g, Vet totaal 13 g (Verzadigd 5 g, Enkelvoudig onverzadigd 3,5 g, Meervoudig onverzadigd 3 g), Cholesterol 60 mg, Natrium 270 mg, IJzer 30%, Vitamine A 240%, Vitamine C 30%.

▲ *1 Groente, 1 Vlees*

SOEPEN / CUBA

Zwarte-bonensoep

Traditioneel wordt zwarte-bonensoep met hamschijf gekookt, maar gerookte kip of kalkoen zijn een heerlijke vervanging. Deze soep is ook lekker zonder vlees. Bonen, samen met sommige graansoorten en ongeschilde peren, hebben het hoogste vezelgehalte. Gedroogde bonen bevatten ook ijzer, kalium, fosfor en chroom.

2 eetlepels olijfolie
6 tenen knoflook, fijngehakt
1 grote ui, gehakt
3 stengels bleekselderij, in dunne plakken
2 wortels, geschild en in dunne plakken
1 jalapeño peper, fijngehakt
8 grote tomaten, ontveld en gepureerd
250 g zwarte bonen, afgespoeld en een nacht geweekt
250 g gerookte kip of kalkoen, in blokjes
1½ theelepel geraspte sinaasappelschil
2 liter kippebouillon (zie woordenlijst)
1 eetlepel gemalen komijn
1 theelepel gemalen koriander
zout en versgemalen peper naar smaak
4 eetlepels bruine rum
1 rode paprika, in blokjes
185 g gekookte maïskorrels
4 eetlepels magere yoghurt of zure room
7 g verse koriander, fijngehakt

1. Verhit de olijfolie in een grote soeppan. Doe er de knoflook en ui in en fruit ze gaar maar niet bruin.
2. Voeg de bleekselderij, wortel, jalapeño peper, tomaten, zwarte bonen, kip, sinaasappelschil en kippebouillon toe. Breng aan de kook. Draai het vuur lager en laat onder af en toe omscheppen 2 uur onafgedekt sudderen.
3. Rooster de gemalen komijn en gemalen koriander 1 tot 2 minuten in een droge koekepan op een middelhoog vuur. Laat niet bruin worden. Schep door de gekookte soep en breng op smaak met zout en peper. Schep er de rum, paprika en maïs door en laat doorwarmen.
4. Schep de soep in voorverwarmde soepborden en garneer met wat yoghurt en verse koriander.

Voor 12 personen *Foto op pagina 201*

2,5 dl per portie: Calorieën 190, Eiwit 11 g, Koolhydraten 27 g, Vezel 6 g, Vet totaal 5 g (Verzadigd 1 g, Enkelvoudig onverzadigd 2,5 g, Meervoudig onverzadigd 1 g), Cholesterol 10 mg, Natrium 220 mg, Vitamine A 90%, Vitamine C 70%.

▲ *1 Groente, 1 Vlees*

SALADES / VERENIGDE STATEN

Sinaasappelsalade met ingemaakte ui

Deborah Madison, schrijfster van Greens *en* The Savory Way, *beveelt deze winterse salade van harte aan. Deze salade bevat bijna de helft van de dagelijks benodigde hoeveelheid vezel. Probeer een paar druppels balsamico azijn bij de sinaasappel als u wat meer pit wilt.*

INGEMAAKTE UI

1 kleine rode ui, gepeld en in dunne ringen
1 theelepel suiker
¼ theelepel zout
10 peperkorrels, grof gemalen
1,25 dl witte wijnazijn of champagne azijn

SINAASAPPELSALADE

6 navelsinaasappels
1 limoen

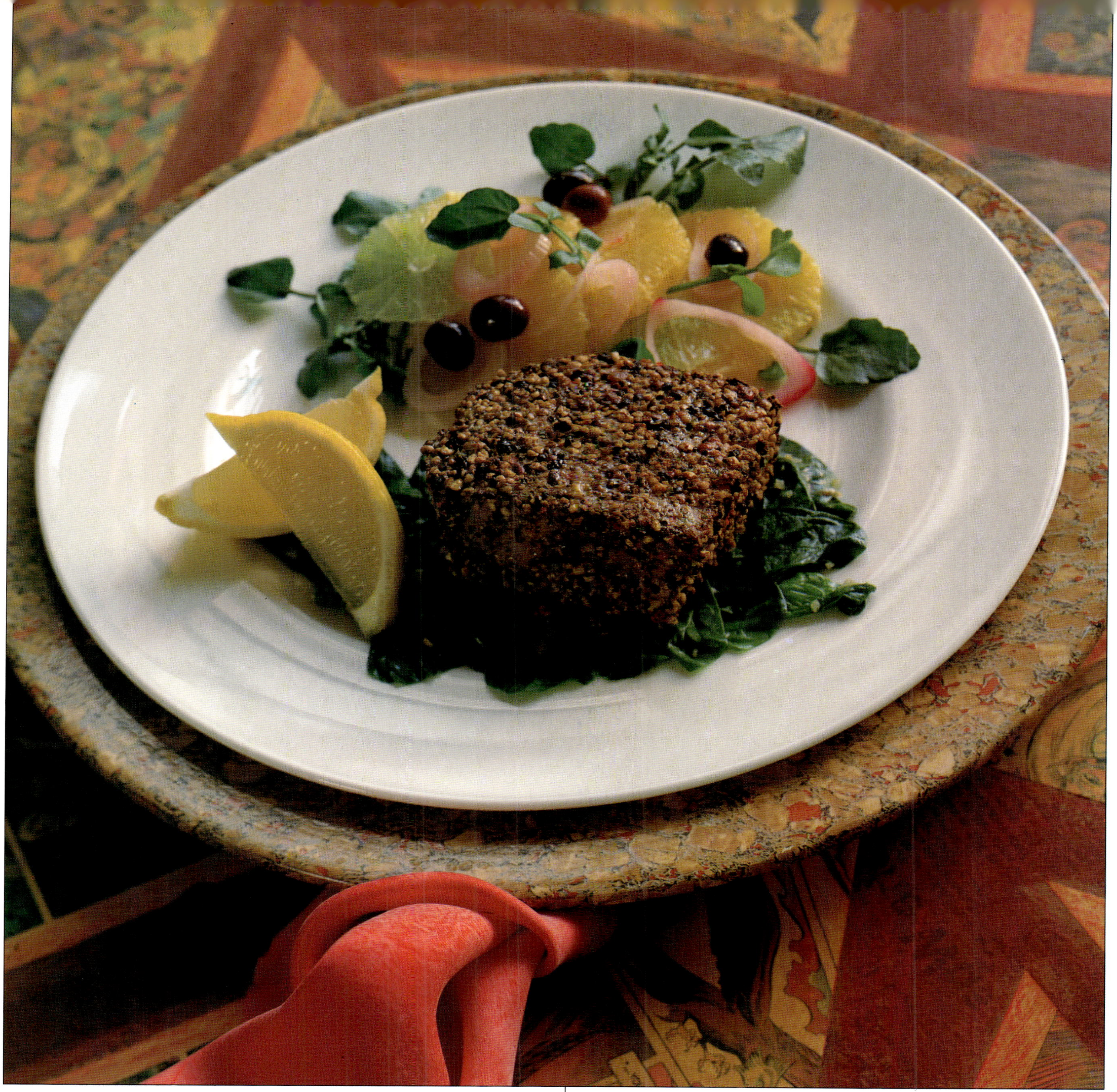

Van boven naar beneden: Sinaasappelsalade met ingemaakte ui, Tonijn met peperkorst

1 theelepel oranjebloesemwater
1 eetlepel koudgeperste olijfolie (desgewenst)
1 bosje waterkers (circa 150 g)
12 Marokkaanse of Niçoise olijven

1. Maak eerst de ingemaakte ui. Haal de uieringen uit elkaar en doe ze in een vergiet. Blancheer ze door er langzaam 1 liter kokend water over te gieten. Schud ze droog.
2. Doe de rest van de inmaak-ingrediënten in een roestvrijstalen of glazen kom met 1,25 dl koud water. Roer tot de suiker opgelost is. Voeg de geblancheerde uien toe en dompel ze onder het inmaaknat. Giet er zonodig gelijke hoeveelheden water en azijn bij. Zet minstens 20 minuten in de koelkast.
3. Schil voor de salade de sinaasappels en limoen door een kapje van de boven- en onderkant af te snijden en dan met het mes langs de randen net onder het onderhuidse wit te gaan. Snijd de sinaasappels verder overdwars in plakken van circa 1 cm dik en de limoen zo dun mogelijk. Schik de plakken sinaasappel, afgewisseld met de limoen, overlappend op een dienschaal of individuele borden. Sprenkel er het oranjebloesemwater en de olijfolie over.
4. Snijd de dikke steeltjes van de waterkers en verdeel ze in kleine takjes van circa 5 tot 7 cm lang. Schik ze om de rand van het bord. Schep de uien uit de marinade en schik ze met de olijven over de salade.

Voor 4 personen

---

1 portie: Calorieën 140, Eiwit 3 g, Koolhydraten 32 g, Vezel 11 g, Vet totaal 2 g (Verzadigd 0,5 g, Enkelvoudig onverzadigd 1,5 g, Meervoudig onverzadigd 0 g), Cholesterol 0 mg, Natrium 335 mg, Vitamine A 45%, Vitamine C 210%.

▲ *1 Fruit*

Ontbijt / Schotland

Pap van gerst, haver en tarwe

Hoewel parelgort nootachtig smaakt en sneller kookt dan gort (circa 1 uur), zijn alle zemelen er afgehaald. Gort is vezelrijk en de langere kooktijd is zeker de mooite waard. U kunt een snelkookversie van deze pap maken met gerstvlokken die circa 30 minuten moeten koken.

100 g gort
45 g grof gemalen haver
100 g geplette tarwe
½ theelepel geraspte sinaasappelschil
30 g cruesli (recept op pagina 178)
2,5 dl magere melk, verwarmd

1. Breng 1,25 liter water aan de kook. Doe er de gort in en draai het vuur lager. Leg het deksel op de pan en laat circa 1 uur sudderen onder af en toe roeren. Neem er het deksel af, voeg de haver, tarwe en sinaasappelschil toe. Laat 15 minuten sudderen tot de granen gaar zijn.
2. Schep de inhoud van de pan in voorverwarmde kommen, strooi er de cruesli over en serveer met de warme melk.

Voor 4 personen

1 portie: Calorieën 230, Eiwit 9 g, Koolhydraten 46 g, Vezel 10 g, Vet totaal 2 g (Verzadigd 0,5 g, Enkelvoudig onverzadigd 0,5 g, Meervoudig onverzadigd 0,5 g), Cholesterol 0 mg, Natrium 40 mg.
▲ *2 Brood*

Ontbijt / Verenigde Staten

Gerookte kip met aardappels uit de oven

Dit is een heerlijke manier om restjes vlees op te maken. Gerookte kip geeft dit brunchgerecht een traditionele smaak, maar u kunt ook gerookte kalkoen of gekookte kip gebruiken.

500 g nieuwe rode aadappels, ongeschild, in plakken van ½ cm dik
1,8 dl magere melk
15 g margarine, in kleine stukjes gesneden
1 grote, bloemige aardappel geschild en in blokjes
2,5 dl kippebouillon (zie woordenlijst)
2 eetlepels olijfolie
150 g gesnipperde ui
2 tenen knoflook
375 g blokjes gerookte kip
½ theelepel verse tijm, fijngehakt
1 eetlepel verse peterselie, fijngehakt
½ theelepel zout
versgemalen peper naar smaak

1. Verwarm de oven voor op 190°C. Vet een ondiepe ovenschaal licht in met olie.
2. Schik de plakken rode aardappel in de ovenschaal.
3. Breng de melk tegen de kook aan en giet over de aardappels. Verdeel er de stukjes margarine over en zet 25 tot 30 minuten in de oven, of tot de aardappels gaar zijn.
4. Doe intussen de bloemige aardappel en kippebouillon in een middelgrote pan en breng aan de kook. Draai het vuur lager en laat 15 minuten sudderen, of tot de aardappel gaar is. Giet af.
5. Verhit de olijfolie in een grote koekepan en fruit er de ui en knoflook gaar maar niet bruin in. Voeg de blokjes kip en aardappel toe en bak in 5 tot 7 minuten goudbruin. Voeg de tijm en peterselie toe en breng op smaak met zout en peper.
6. Schep het kipmengsel over de aardappel in de ovenschaal en dien onmiddellijk op.

Voor 6 personen

1 portie: Calorieën 280, Eiwit 13 g, Koolhydraten 37 g, Vezel 3 g, Vet totaal 9 g (Verzadigd 2 g, Enkelvoudig onverzadigd 5 g, Meervoudig onverzadigd 1,5 g), Cholesterol 25 mg, Natrium 830 mg, Vitamine C 30%.
▲ *1 Groente, 1 Vlees*

Brood / Ierland

Iers volkoren sodabrood

Er worden in Ierland veel verschillende versies sodabrood gemaakt en er zijn net zo veel manieren om het te maken. Deze volkoren versie is geschikt voor ontbijt of bij een pot thee in de middag. Serveer dit brood met bramenjam.

300 g volkorenmeel
150 g bloem
2 eetlepels suiker
1 eetlepel bakpoeder
½ theelepel zuiveringszout
½ theelepel zout
4 dl karnemelk of melk gemengd met 1½ eetlepel vers citroensap, op kamertemperatuur

1. Verwarm de oven voor op 180°C. Vet een ronde taartvorm licht in met olie.
2. Meng alle droge ingrediënten in een grote kom.
3. Giet er al roerend de karnemelk geleidelijk bij tot u een stijf maar niet droog deeg hebt verkregen.
4. Doe het deeg op een met bloem bestoven werkvlak en kneed het circa 3 minuten tot het glad is. Kneed niet te lang.

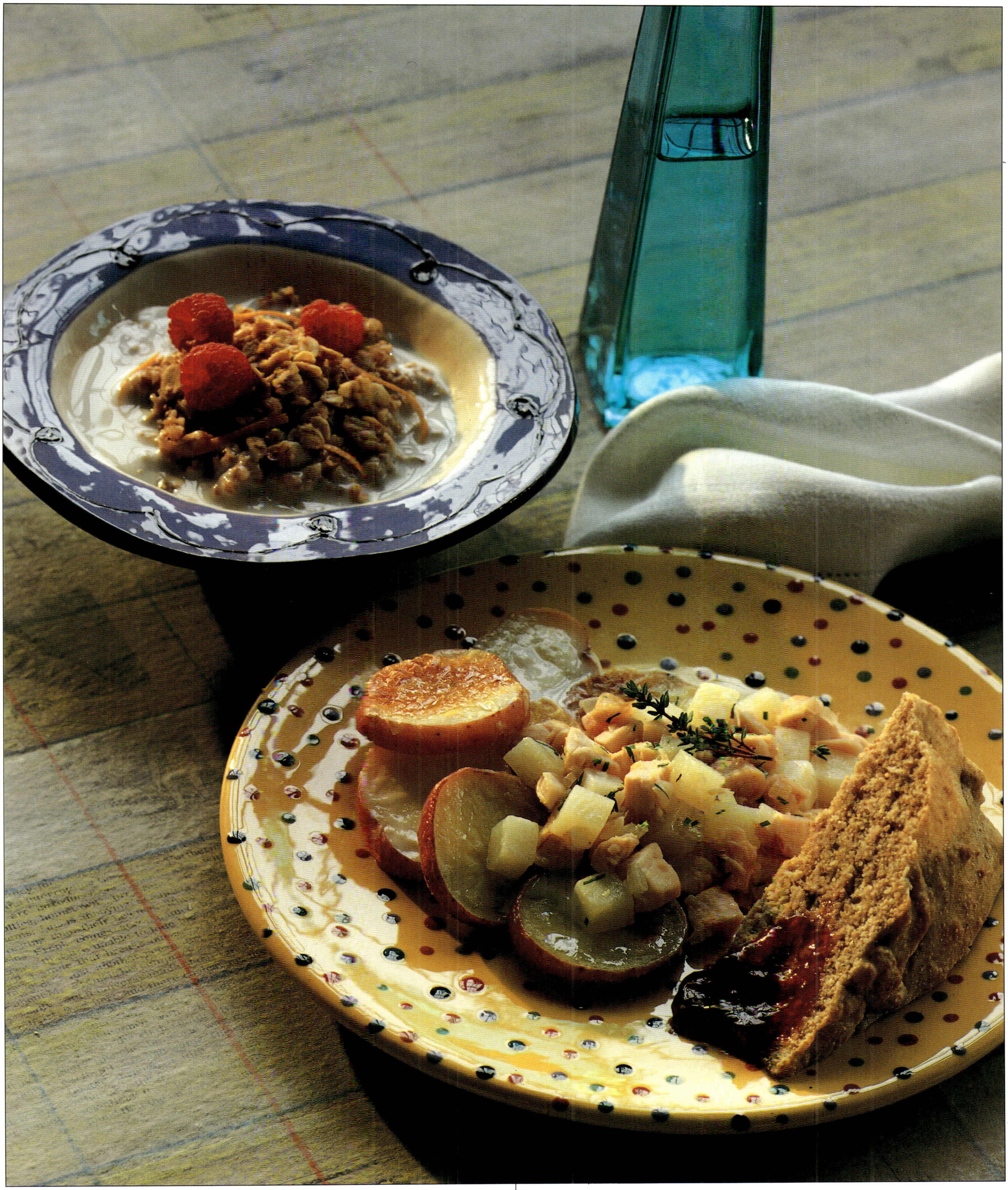

Van boven naar beneden: Pap van gerst, haver en tarwe, Gerookte kip en aardappels uit de oven, Iers volkoren sodabrood

5. Vorm een rond brood van het deeg en doe het in de taartvorm.
6. Bak het brood 35 minuten in de oven, of tot een ingestoken satéstokje er schoon uitkomt.

Voor 1 brood (8 sneden)

1 snee per portie: Calorieën 190, Eiwit 7 g, Koolhydraten 40 g, Vezel 4 g, Vet totaal 1 g (Verzadigd 0,5 g, Enkelvoudig onverzadigd 0 g, Meervoudig onverzadigd 0,5 g), Cholesterol 0 mg, Natrium 280 mg.

▲ *2 Brood*

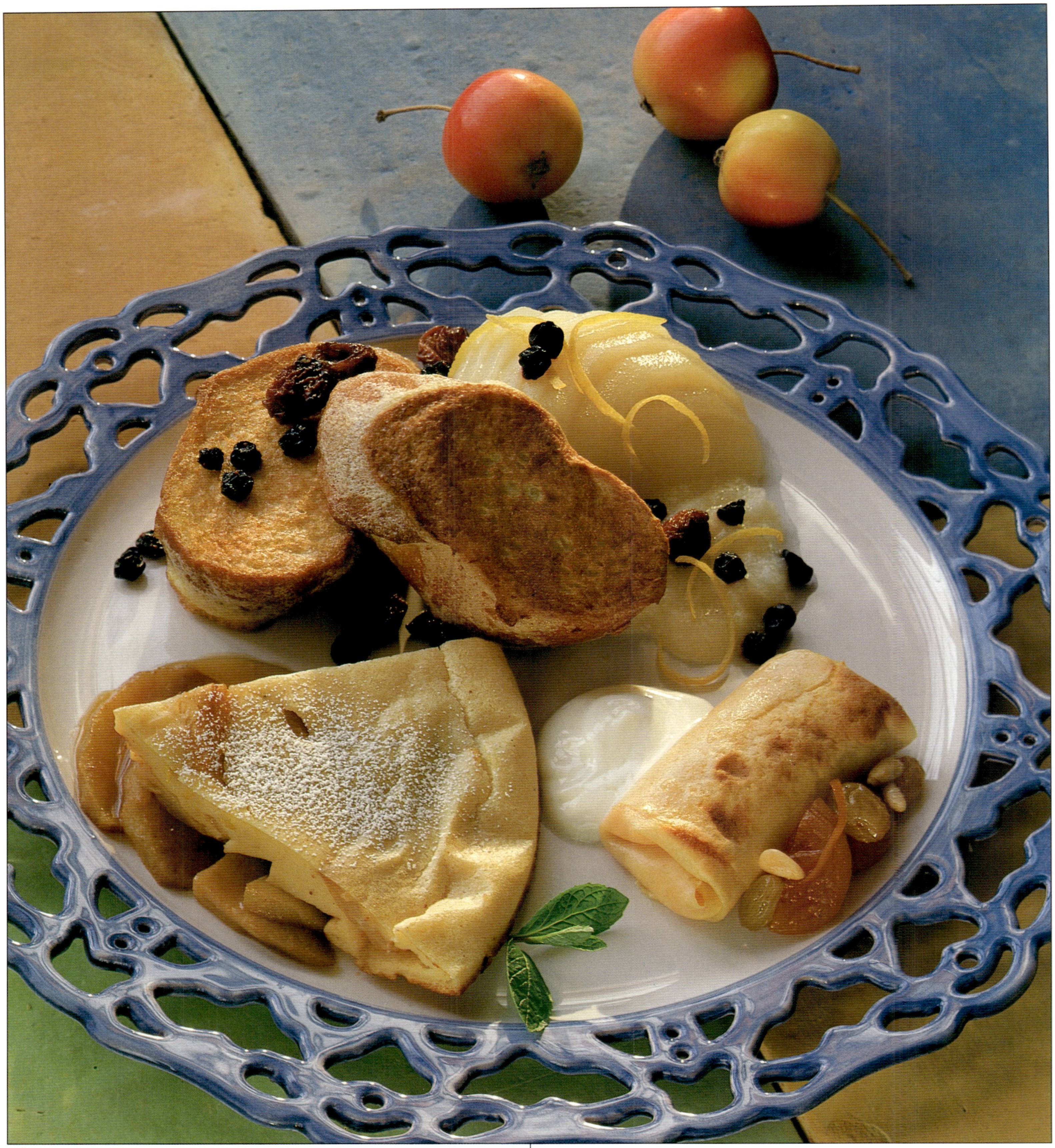

Met de klok mee van boven: Zuurdesem wentelteefjes met perensaus, Pompoenflensjes, Duitse appelpannekoek

ONTBIJT / DUITSLAND

Duitse appelpannekoek

Serveer dit gerecht 's ochtends warm met esdoornsiroop, of voor een brunch met kaneel-rumsaus (recept op pagina 178).

15 g boter
2 Golden Delicious of Granny Smith appels, geschild, klokhuizen verwijderd, in plakken van 1 cm dik gesneden
1 eetlepel suiker
½ theelepel gemalen kaneel
150 g bloem
2,5 dl magere melk
2 eieren
1 eetlepel saffloerolie
1 theelepel vanille-essence
¼ theelepel versgeraspte nootmuskaat
1 theelepel vers citroensap
½ theelepel fijngeraspte citroenschil
2 eetlepels poedersuiker

1. Verwarm de oven voor op 230°C.
2. Verhit de boter in een vuurvaste ovenschaal van 25 cm doorsnee. Doe er de appel in en fruit die gaar. Bestrooi met de suiker en kaneel. Zet de schaal in de oven en houd de appel warm.

3. Meng de bloem met de melk, eieren, olie, vanille en nootmuskaat in een blender. Schep er het citroensap en de schil door. Giet het beslag over de plakken appel en zet de schaal 15 minuten terug in de oven. Draai de temperatuur op 190°C en bak nog 10 minuten.
4. Neem de schaal uit de oven. Bestuif met poedersuiker, snijd in partjes en dien onmiddellijk op.

Voor 6 personen

1 portie: Calorieën 200, Eiwit 6 g, Koolhydraten 36 g, Vezel 2 g, Vet totaal 7 g (Verzadigd 2,5 g, Enkelvoudig onverzadigd 1,5 g, Meervoudig onverzadigd 2 g), Cholesterol 80 mg, Natrium 45 mg.

▲ *1 Brood, 1 Fruit*

ONTBIJT / VERENIGDE STATEN

Zuurdesem wentelteefjes met perensaus

Wentelteefjes en perensaus zijn voor elkaar gemaakt. Probeer de perensaus ook eens met nagerechten.

GEPOCHEERDE PERENSAUS

350 g suiker
1 theelepel geraspte citroenschil
6 rijpe, stevige peren, geschild, gehalveerd en klokhuizen verwijderd
2 theelepels vanille-essence

WENTELTEEFJES

500 g zuurdesem stokbrood
8 eiwitten
4 eieren
1 eetlepel vanille-essence
2 eetlepels suiker
1 eetlepel saffloerolie
45 g ingevroren kersen
45 g ingevroren bosbessen

1. Doe voor de saus 1 liter water met de suiker en citroenschil in een grote pan. Breng al roerend aan de kook tot de suiker opgelost is. Draai het vuur lager. Voeg de peren toe en laat ze in circa 20 minuten gaar sudderen. Schep de peren met een schuimspaan uit de siroop en laat ze afkoelen. Breng de siroop weer aan de kook en laat tot de helft inkoken.
2. Zet 6 van de afgekoelde perenhelften apart en pureer de rest in een blender. Doe de vanille en circa de helft van de ingekookte siroop bij de puree om de saus schenkbaar te maken. Zet weg.
3. Snijd voor de wentelteefjes het brood in 12 sneden en zet weg.
4. Klop de eiwitten schuimig. Klop er de hele eieren, vanille en suiker door.
5. Verhit een anti-aanbak koekepan en vet die in met de olie.
6. Haal de sneden brood door het eimengsel en bak ze in circa 2 minuten per kant goudbruin.
7. Schep wat perensaus op elk bord. Snijd de apartgehouden peerhelften in plakken. Schik 2 wentelteefjes en plakken van een peerhelft op elk bord. Garneer met de opgewarmde kersen en bosbessen en dien onmiddellijk op.

Voor 6 personen

2 sneden met saus per portie: Calorieën 520, Eiwit 17 g, Koolhydraten 99 g, Vezel 6 g, Vet totaal 8 g (Verzadigd 2 g, Enkelvoudig onverzadigd 2,5 g, Meervoudig onverzadigd 3 g), Cholesterol 150 mg, Natrium 530 mg.

▲ *2 Brood, 1 Fruit, ½ Vlees, 1 Vet/Suiker*

ONTBIJT / VERENIGDE STATEN

Pompoenflensjes

Dit zoete en hartige brunchgerecht is heerlijk met kumquats, vijgen en gedroogde abrikozen in gezoet rozewater (recept op pagina 216) en een schepje yoghurt.

1 groene pompoen (butterball) van circa 1,5 kg
¼ theelepel zout
versgeraspte nootmuskaat naar smaak
3 eieren
3 dl magere melk
2 eetlepels saffloerolie
150 g bloem
15 g boter, gesmolten

1. Verwarm de oven voor op 200°C. Vet een grote ondiepe ovenschaal licht in met olie.
2. Halveer voor de vulling de pompoen in de lengte. Schep er de pitten uit en gooi ze weg. Leg de pompoen met de aangesneden kant onder op de bakplaat en zet 35 tot 45 minuten in de oven tot hij volledig gaar is. Laat afkoelen.
3. Schil de pompoen en pureer het vruchtvlees in de blender. Breng op smaak met het zout en wat nootmuskaat en zet weg.
4. Draai voor de flensjes de eieren, melk en olie in de blender. Voeg de bloem toe en draai tot een glad mengsel.
5. Verhit een anti-aanbak crêpepan of koekepan van 15 cm doorsnee op een middelhoog vuur. Schep 2 eetlepels beslag in de pan en laat dit met een draaiende beweging van de pan over de bodem vloeien. Zet de pan weer op het vuur en bak circa 2 minuten aan één kant goudbruin. Doe het flensje op een bord en maak de rest van de flensjes op dezelfde manier. Stapel de flensjes op met telkens een vel perkamentpapier ertussen.
6. Leg een flensje met de gebakken kant onder op een werkvlak. Schep 3 eetlepels vulling vlak bij één kant van het flensje, vouw de zijkanten in en rol op.
7. Schik de flensjes naast elkaar in de ovenschaal. Kwast ze in met de gesmolten boter en zet 15 minuten in de oven tot ze goudbruin zijn.

Voor 12 personen (24 flensjes)

2 flensjes per portie: Calorieën 140, Eiwit 5 g, Koolhydraten 20 g, Vezel 2 g, Vet totaal 5 g (Verzadigd 1,5 g, Enkelvoudig onverzadigd 1 g, Meervoudig onverzadigd 2 g), Cholesterol 60 mg, Natrium 80 mg, Vitamine A 150%, Vitamine C 35%.

▲ *1 Groente, ½ Brood*

DESSERTS / ITALIË

Arànce caramelizzate di Malgieri

GEPOCHEERDE SINAASAPPELS

Dit is een recept van Nick Malgieri, chef de patisserie en auteur van Great Italian Desserts. *De geblancheerde sinaasappels met reepjes schil en sinaasappellikeur zorgen voor een dessert dat een volle smaak heeft maar wel heerlijk licht is.*

8 navelsinaasappels
375 g suiker
4 eetlepels sinaasappellikeur (Cointreau of Grand Marnier)

1. Schil met een dunschiller de schil van de navels, maar let op dat u niet het onderhuidse wit meeneemt. Snijd de schil in smalle reepjes van 3 mm. Doe ze in een kleine pan en zet ze onder water. Breng aan de kook op een laag vuur. Giet ze af, doe in een kom, zet onder koud water en zet weg.
2. Meng de suiker met 1,8 dl water in een middelgrote pan, breng aan de kook en kook circa 3 minuten tot een siroop.
3. Schil intussen de navels. Dompel de navels met 1 of 2 tegelijk in de siroop, draai het vuur laag en laat 3-4 minuten sudderen.
4. Schep de navels met een schuimspaan uit de siroop en doe ze in een dienschaal.
5. Giet de repen schil af en doe ze in de siroop. Kook het mengsel 2 minuten, of tot de schil glazig is. Neem de schill uit de siroop en garneer er de navels mee.
6. Zet de navels met schil in de koelkast. Sprenkel er vlak voor het serveren wat sinaasappellikeur over.

Voor 8 personen

1 sinaasappel per portie: Calorieën 140, Eiwit 1 g, Koolhydraten 31 g, Vezel 5 g, Vet totaal 0 g (Verzadigd 0 g, Enkelvoudig onverzadigd 0 g, Meervoudig onverzadigd 0 g), Cholesterol 0 mg, Natrium 0 mg, Vitamine C 120%.
▲ *1 Fruit*

Van boven naar beneden: Gepocheerde sinaasappels, Chocoladebrood met kersen en amandelen

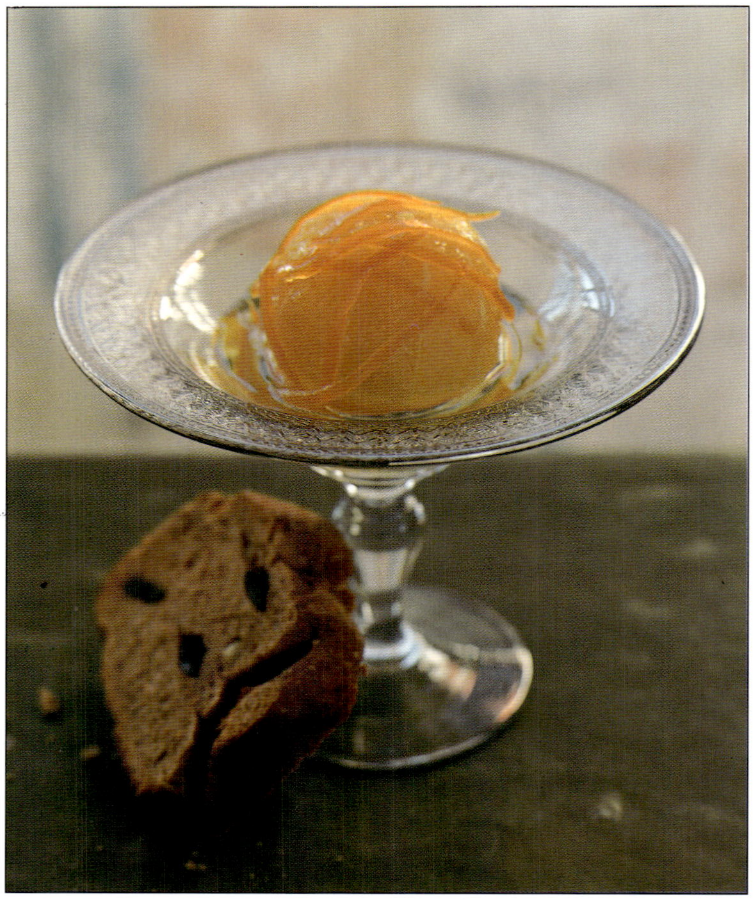

DESSERTS / VERENIGDE STATEN

Koffiesorbet

Deze sorbet is het hele jaar door de moeite waard.

90 g fijngemalen espressobonen
125 g suiker
1 eetlepel cacao
1 theelepel vanille-essence
1 eiwit

1. Doe de gemalen espressobonen in een filterzakje en zet boven een koffiepot. Giet er 6,25 dl kokend water over en laat doordruppelen. Meng de hete koffie met de suiker en cacao en roer tot de suiker opgelost is. Laat volledig afkoelen.
2. Giet het koffiemengsel in een ijsmachine en draai tot deels ingevroren.
3. Klop het eiwit tot stijve maar niet droge pieken. Schep het door het koffiemengsel en doe terug in de ijsmachine. Draai tot het mengsel weer deels ingevroren is. Zet 1 uur in het vriesvak voor het serveren.

Voor 6,25 dl

1,25 dl per portie: Calorieën 90, Eiwit 1 g, Koolhydraten 21 g, Vezel 0,5 g, Vet totaal 0 g (Verzadigd 0 g, Enkelvoudig onverzadigd 0 g, Meervoudig onverzadigd 0 g), Cholesterol 0 mg, Natrium 10 mg.
▲ *1 Vet/Suiker*

DESSERTS / VERENIGDE STATEN

Chocolade zoentjes

Met deze lichte en luchtige koekjes kunt u van chocolade genieten zonder verzadigd vet binnen te krijgen. Bewaar ze in een luchtdichte trommel.

3 eetlepels cacao
60 g poedersuiker
4 eiwitten
½ theelepel vers citroensap
125 g kristalsuiker

1. Verwarm de oven voor op 110°C. Bekleed een bakplaat met perkamentpapier.
2. Zeef de cacao met de poedersuiker boven een middelgrote kom. Zet weg.
3. Klop de eiwitten met het citroensap met een handmixer tot

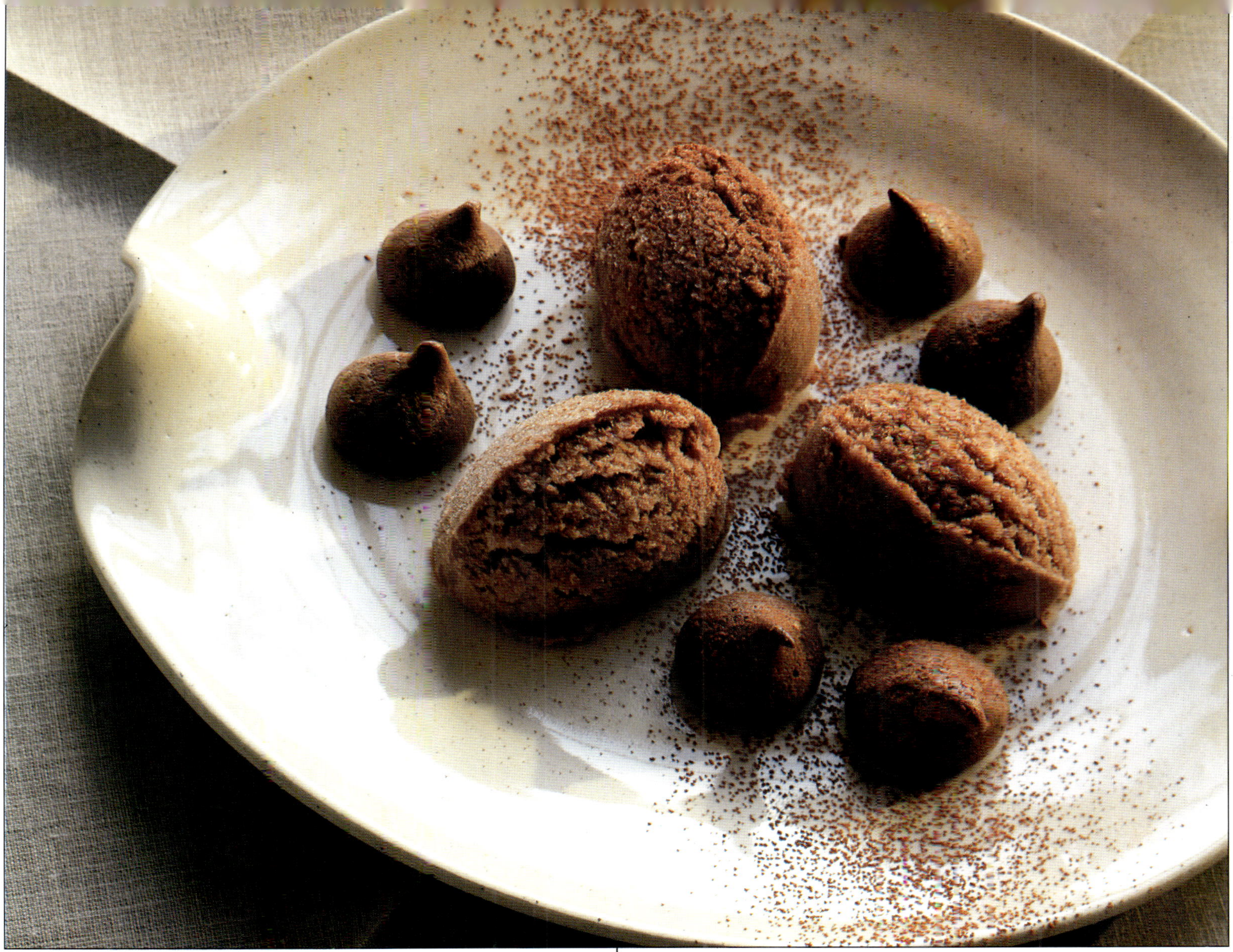

Van links naar rechts: Chocolade zoentjes, Koffiesorbet

zachte pieken. Voeg 3 eetlepels van de kristalsuiker toe en klop tot stijve pieken. Voeg de rest van de kristalsuiker toe.

4. Schep er voorzichtig het cacaomengsel door. Doe het mengsel in een spuitzak met een glad spuitmondje. Spuit "zoentjes" van 3 cm doorsnee op de bakplaat.
5. Zet de koekjes 2 uur in de oven tot ze droog en krokant zijn. Zet de oven uit en laat de koekjes 2 uur in de oven of een nacht drogen. Bewaar ze in een luchtdichte trommel.

Voor 48 koekjes

---

4 koekjes per portie: Calorieën [illegible], Eiwit 1 g, Koolhydraten 14 g, Vezel 0,5 g, Vet totaal 0 g (Verzadigd 0 g, Enkelvoudig onverzadigd 0 g, Meervoudig onverzadigd 0 g), Cholesterol 0 mg, Natrium 20 mg.

▲ *1 Vet/Suiker*

BROOD / VERENIGDE STATEN

Chocoladebrood met kersen en amandelen

3,75 dl magere melk
4 eetlepels melasse
2 theelepels zout
1 pakje (7 g) gedroogde gist
80 g tarwezemelen
150 g volkorenmeel
2 eetlepels cacao
circa 625 g bloem
140 g gedroogde kersen
65 g geroosterde, geschaafde amandelen

1. Verwarm de oven voor op 190°C. Vet twee broodvormen van 23 cm en een grote kom licht in met olie.
2. Breng de melk tegen de kook aan in een kleine pan. Neem van het vuur en roer er de melasse en het zout door. Laat op kamertemperatuur komen.
3. Doe 1,25 dl warm water (40°-46°C) in een glazen kom en roer er de gist door. Laat het mengsel vervolgens 5 minuten staan, of tot het schuimig is.
4. Doe de zemelen, het volkorenmeel, de cacao en 150 g van de bloem in een keukenmachine met een deeghaak. Giet er het lauwe melkmengsel en de opgeloste gist bij en klop goed. Voeg de kersen en amandelen toe.
5. Voeg al kloppend bijna alle overgebleven bloem toe tot het deeg goed gemengd is. Doe het deeg over op een met bloem bestoven werkvlak.
6. Kneed het deeg glad en elastisch en kneed er zonodig wat bloem bij. Doe het deeg in de ingevette kom, dek die af met plastic folie en laat circa 2 uur op een warme plek rijzen tot het deeg in volume verdubbeld is.
7. Druk de lucht uit het deeg en verdeel het in tweeën. Doe het deeg in de twee vormen, dek die af en laat het deeg circa 1½ uur rijzen tot het bijna in volume verdubbeld is.
8. Bak 40 minuten in de oven. Laat op roosters afkoelen.

Voor 2 broden (36 sneden)

---

1 snee per portie: Calorieën 100, Eiwit 3 g, Koolhydraten 20 g, Vezel 2 g, Vet totaal 1 g (Verzadigd 0 g, Enkelvoudig onverzadigd 0,5 g, Meervoudig onverzadigd 0,5 g), Cholesterol 0 mg, Natrium 140 mg.

▲ *1 Brood*

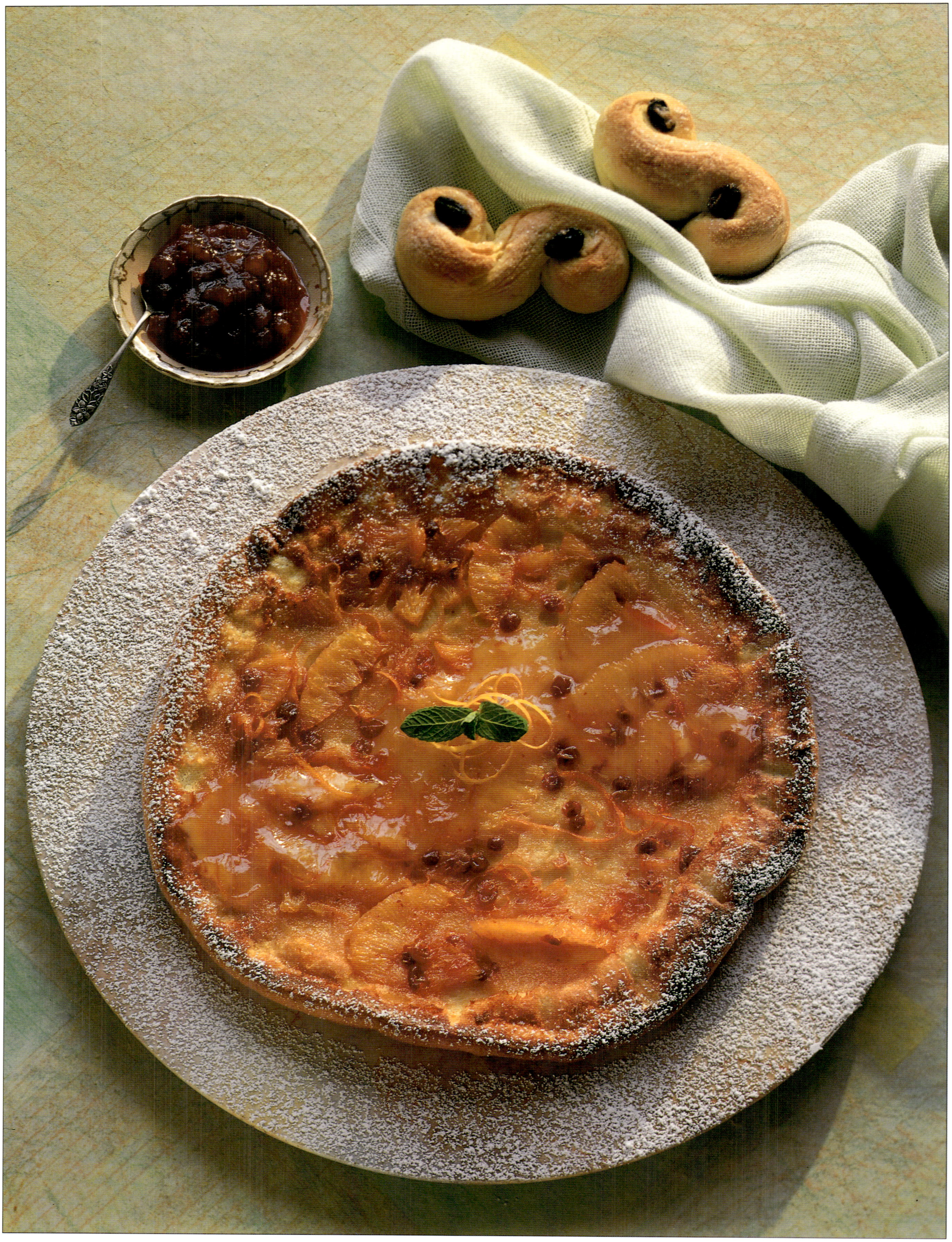

Met de klok mee van links: Bergbraambessenjam (recept pagina 216), Sint-Luciabroodjes, Omelet met sinasappel, bessen en Grand Marnier

Omelet met sinaasappel, bessen en Grand Marnier

Zorg dat alle ingrediënten klaar staan en klop de eieren op het laatste moment. Dit recept is voldoende voor één grote omelet voor vier personen.

2 sinaasappels, geschild
120 g plus 2 eetlepels suiker
15 g boter
30 g vossebessen of cranberry's
1 theelepel geraspte sinaasappelschil
4 eieren, gescheiden
¼ theelepel vers citroensap
4 eetlepels vers sinaasappelsap
2 eetlepels Grand Marnier
2 eetlepels poedersuiker, ter garnering
2,5 dl Grand Marniersaus (recept volgt)

1. Verwarm de oven voor op 200°C.
2. Snijd de sinaasappels langs de tussenschotjes uit. Schep de partjes om met de 2 eetlepels suiker.
3. Verhit de boter in een vuurvaste ovenschaal van 35 cm doorsnee. Kwast wat boter langs de randen zodat de omelet niet aanplakt. Doe er de sinaasappel, bessen en schil in en bak circa 10 minuten in de oven tot de suiker gekarameliseerd is. Zet weg.
4. Klop de eiwitten met het citroensap in een zuurbestendige kom tot zachte pieken. Voeg 60 g van de overgebleven suiker toe en klop het eiwit tot stijve maar niet droge pieken.
5. Klop de overgebleven 60 g suiker met de dooiers in een andere kom tot een licht en luchtig mengsel. Voeg al kloppend het sinaasappelsap en de Grand Marnier toe.
6. Schep het eiwit voorzichtig door het dooiermengsel.
7. Schep het omeletmengsel over het fruitmengsel in de ovenschaal en zet circa 10 minuten in de oven tot de boevenkant goudbruin is.
8. Bestuif met de suiker en geef er de Grand-Marniersaus bij.

Voor 4 personen

¼ soufflé per portie: Calorieën 290, Eiwit 7 g, Koolhydraten 48 g, Vezel 3 g, Vet totaal 8 g (Verzadigd 3,5 g, Enkelvoudig onverzadigd 3 g, Meervoudig onverzadigd 1 g), Cholesterol 230 mg, Natrium 70 mg, Vitamine C 90%.
▲ *1 Fruit, ½ Vlees*

GRAND-MARNIERSAUS

2,5 dl vers sinaasappelsap
60 g suiker
2 eetlepels sinaasappelmarmelade
1 eetlepel maïzena, gemengd met 1 eetlepel sinaasappelsap
3 eetlepels Grand Marnier

1. Verhit het sinaasappelsap met de suiker al roerend in een kleine pan tot de suiker opgelost is. Voeg de marmelade toe en roer tot die opgelost is.
2. Roer er het maïzenapapje door en laat al roerend sudderen tot de saus iets dikker is. Roer er de Grand Marnier door en dien op.

Voor 2,5 dl saus

4 eetlepels per portie: Calorieën 120, Eiwit 0 g, Koolhydraten 34 g, Vezel 0 g, Vet totaal 0 g (Verzadigd 0 g, Enkelvoudig onverzadigd 0 g, Meervoudig onverzadigd 0 g), Cholesterol 0 mg, Natrium 10 mg, Vitamine C 60%.
▲ *1 Fruit, 1 Vet/Suiker*

BROOD / ZWEDEN

Lussekatter

SINT-LUCIABROODJES

Dit recept is afkomstig van Gerd Jordano uit Santa Barbara in Californië. Zij serveerde deze broodjes vroeger iedere 13de december, Sint Luciadag, aan haar ouders. U kunt het deeg ook vlechten, tot een krans vormen en met rozijnen garneren. Het brood is heerlijk met bergbraambessenjam (recept op pagina 216).

1 pakje (7 g) gedroogde gist
5 eetlepels magere melk, gekookt en afgekoeld
75 g suiker
60 g zachte margarine
2 eieren
½ theelepel gemalen kardemom
½ theelepel zout
¼ theelepel saffraan, gemalen
400-450 g bloem
45 g rozijnen

1. Verwarm de oven voor op 180°C.
2. Los de gist op in 4 eetlepels warm water (40°-46°C). Roer er de melk, 60 g suiker, 30 g margarine, 1 van de eieren, de kardemom, het zout en de saffraan door.
3. Voeg 235 g van de bloem toe en klop tot alles goed gemengd is. Voeg al roerend geleidelijk de rest van de bloem toe tot het deeg te stijf om te roeren is.
4. Doe het deeg op een met bloem bestoven werkvlak en kneed het deeg in circa 5 minuten glad.
5. Doe het deeg in een licht met olie ingevette kom, dek af en laat het deeg circa 1 uur rijzen tot het in volume verdubbeld is.
6. Druk de lucht uit het deeg en verdeel het in 12 even grote stukken. Rol elk stuk uit tot een S-vormige cilinder; buig de eindpunten tot spiraaltjes. Schik een rozijn in elke spiraal.
7. Leg de broodjes op een licht met olie ingevette bakplaat. Smelt de rest van de margarine en strijk er de broodjes mee in.
8. Laat de broodjes circa 30 minuten rijzen tot ze in volume verdubbeld zijn. Kwast ze in met wat ei-watermengsel en bestrooi met de rest van de suiker.
9. Zet 15-20 minuten in de oven tot ze goudbruin zijn.

Voor 12 broodjes

1 broodje per portie: Calorieën 180, Eiwit 4 g, Koolhydraten 28 g, Vezel 1 g, Vet totaal 5 g (Verzadigd 1 g, Enkelvoudig onverzadigd 2 g, Meervoudig onverzadigd 1,5 g), Cholesterol 35 mg, Natrium 160 mg.
▲ *1 Brood*

DESSERTS / MIDDEN-OOSTEN

Kumquats, vijgen en gedroogde abrikozen in gezoet rozewater

Serveer deze zalige compote in gekoelde glazen of als een ontbijt bijgerecht met wafels of pannekoeken. De suiker, vezel, vitaminen en mineralen in vruchten worden versterkt tijden het drogen.

3 eetlepels honing
2 eetlepels rozewater
1 theelepel vers citroensap
250 g gedroogde vijgen
125 g gedroogde abrikozen
100 g sultanarozijnen
1 kaneelpijpje
2 steranijs
2 eetlepels pijnboompitten
125 g kumquats, gehalveerd in de lengte en ontzaad

1. Verhit 5 dl water met de honing, rozewater en het citroensap in een grote pan. Voeg de vijgen, abrikozen, rozijnen, het kaneelpijpje, de steranijs en pijnboompitten toe en laat het geheel 30 minuten sudderen.
2. Voeg de kuquats toe en laat 15 minuten sudderen. Neem de pan van het vuur en laat afkoelen. Zet minstens 3 uur of een nacht in de koelkast.

Voor 8 personen

1,65 dl per portie: Calorieën 180, Eiwit 2 g, Koolhydraten 44 g, Vezel 7 g, Vet totaal 2 g (Verzadigd 0,5 g, Enkelvoudig onverzadigd 0,5 g, Meervoudig onverzadigd 0,5 g), Cholesterol 0 mg, Natrium 5 mg, Vitamine A 20%.

▲ *2 Fruit*

DESSERTS / VERENIGDE STATEN

Gegratineerde kaki met cranberry's

Een romige kaki en cranberry pudding ligt onder een laagje plakken kaki. Fuyu en Sharon kaki's zijn de bekendste soorten van deze vrucht. Deze twee soorten zijn beide zoet en hebben niet die wrange nasmaak van tannine die andere soorten wel hebben als ze niet rijp zijn. Kaki's bevatten veel vitamine A.

3 grote, rijpe kaki's (persimoen)
2 eieren
220 g lichtbruine basterdsuiker
1,25 dl half melk, half room
125 g bloem
½ theelepel bakpoeder
½ theelepel zuiveringszout
2 theelepels gemalen kaneel
½ theelepel versgeraspte nootmuskaat
125 g verse cranberry's
15 g boter, gesmolten
1 eetlepel suiker

1. Verwarm de oven voor op 180°C. Vet 8 kleine ovenschaaltjes licht in met olie.
2. Snijd 2 kaki's in plakken van ½ cm dik. Zet weg.
3. Halveer de overgebleven kaki, schep er het vruchvlees uit en verwijder eventuele zaadjes. Pureer het vruchtvlees in een keukenmachine of blender. Doe de puree in een kom met de eieren en basterdsuiker. Meng alles goed. Schep er de melk en room door. Zet weg.
4. Meng de bloem met het bakpoeder, zuiveringszout, de kaneel en nootmuskaat. Schep door het kakimengsel tot alles net gemengd is. Schep er de cranberry's door. Meng niet te veel.
5. Giet het mengsel in de ovenschaaltjes. Schik er de plakken kaki op, kwast in met de gesmolten boter en bestrooi met de suiker. Zet 30 minuten in de oven tot een ingestoken mes er schoon uitkomt en de suiker gekarameliseerd is. Dien warm op.

Voor 8 personen

1 portie: Calorieën 230, Eiwit 4 g, Koolhydraten 45 g, Vezel 1 g, Vet totaal 5 g (Verzadigd 2,5 g, Enkelvoudig onverzadigd 1,5 g, Meervoudig onverzadigd 0,5 g), Cholesterol 65 mg, Natrium 125 mg.

▲ *½ Brood, 1 Fruit*

BROOD & ONTBIJT

Bergbraambessenjam

Bergbraambessen, lichtgele frambozen uit het noordpoolgebied, zijn hier helaas zeer moeilijk verkrijgbaar. U kunt ervoor in de plaats gewone rode frambozen gebruiken.

500 g suiker
500 g verse bergbraambessen of rode frambozen
1 theelepel vers citroensap

1. Steriliseer 3 potjes van 2,5 dl inhoud.
2. Los de suiker op in 2,5 dl water in een grote, zware pan; breng aan de kook.
3. Voeg de bessen of frambozen en het citroensap toe en breng weer aan de kook. Draai het vuur lager en laat 5 minuten sudderen. Neem de pan van het vuur.
4. Schep de jam in de gesteriliseerde potten. Sluit de potten. U kunt ook de jam eerst laten afkoelen en dan invriezen.

Voor 6,25 dl *Foto op pagina 214*

2 eetlepels per portie: Calorieën 90, Eiwit 0 g, Koolhydraten 23 g, Vezel 2 g, Vet totaal 0 g (Verzadigd 0 g, Enkelvoudig onverzadigd 0 g, Meervoudig onverzadigd 0 g), Cholesterol 0 mg, Natrium 0 mg.

▲ *1 Vet/Suiker*

Van boven naar beneden: Kumquats, vijgen en gedroogde abrikozen in gezoet rozewater, Gegratineerde kaki met cranberry's

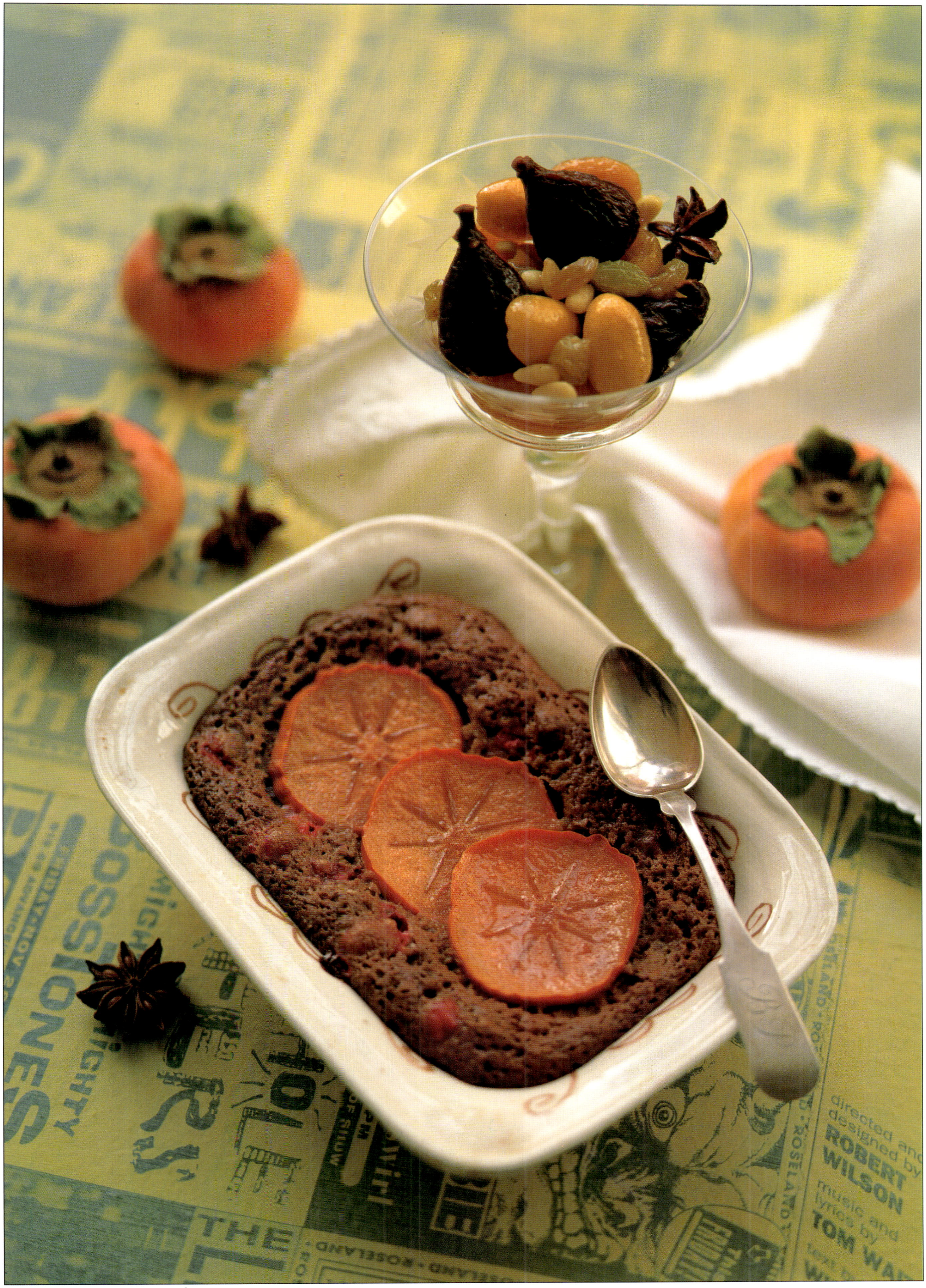
directed and
designed by
ROBERT
WILSON
music and
lyrics by

Woordenlijst

AANBEVOLEN DAGELIJKSE VOEDING: De aanbevolen dagelijkse consumptieniveaus van energie (calorieën) en vastgestelde voedingsstoffen die benodigd zijn voor een goede gezondheid.

AL DENTE: Een Italiaanse uitdrukking die letterlijk "aan de tand" betekent. Verwijst naar voedsel dat gekookt is, maar nog steeds stevig is en "bijt" heeft. Meestal gebruikt voor pasta en groenten die gekookt, maar nog stevig zijn.

AMINOZUUR: Een organisch zuur dat de basisstructuur van eiwit vormt. Er zijn 22 aminozuren in verschillende samenstellingen. Dertien ervan, de zogeheten **niet-essentiële aminozuren,** kunnen in het lichaam worden aangemaakt. De overige 9, de **essentiële aminozuren,** moeten door eiwit in de voeding worden geleverd. *Zie ook* Eiwit.

ANIJS: Een aromatische plant met zaad die wordt gebruikt in gebak, zoetigheid en gedestilleerde dranken als Pastis en Anisette. Het blad lijkt op dat van dille, maar smaakt heel anders. Anijs kan ook in salades en gekookte gerechten worden gebruikt.

ANTI-OXIDANTEN: Stoffen waarvan onderzoekers hebben ontdekt dat ze een belangrijke rol spelen in het voorkomen van ziekten doordat ze het lichaam beschermen tegen "vrije radicalen", of destructieve chemische stoffen die door oxidatie celbeschadiging veroorzaken. (Het resultaat van oxidatie is in het alledaagse leven overal om ons heen te zien: roestend metaal, ranzige olie en bros rubber zijn voorbeelden.) Oxidatie en de daarmee samenhangende veranderingen binnen menselijke cellen leiden tot ziekte en kunnen ook het verouderingsproces versnellen.

Anti-oxidanten kunnen misschien ook de oxidatie van cholesterol stoppen, en aldus het ophopen van vettige afzettingen in de aderen voorkomen, welke tot hartaanvallen en beroertes kan leiden. Uit research kan ook worden opgemaakt dat anti-oxidanten kunnen helpen staar voorkomen—een versluiering van de ooglens die minstens ten dele een gevolg is van oxidatie van eiwitten in de lens.

Vitamine E en C zijn oxidanten. Het provitamine beta-caroteen, een van de stoffen die gele en oranje vruchten en groenten hun kleur geeft, is ook een anti-oxidans. Het lichaam zet beta-caroteen om in vitamine A.

Het onderzoek naar anti-oxidanten gaat door. Wetenschappers richten zich nu op selenium, zink en andere stoffen om hun anti-oxidante eigenschappen te bepalen. Ze zijn nog niet zeker van de optimale "dosis", de beste combinatie, of de bij-effecten op lange termijn van grote doses anti-oxidanten. Momenteel bevelen de deskundigen het volgen van het Voedselpiramide-plan aan, in het bijzonder het dagelijks eten van 5-9 porties groenten en fruit, waaronder minstens 1 citrusvrucht en 1 diep-oranje vrucht of groente of donkergroene bladgroente voor vitamine C en beta-caroteen. Broccoli, asperges, avocado, perziken en boerenkool zijn bronnen van vitamine E; die komt ook voor in tarwekiemen (in volle-tarweprodukten), in maïs, zonnebloem- en soja-olie en in mayonaise. Rokers hebben meer anti-oxidanten nodig, met name vitamine C.

ARUGULA (raket): Een peperige mediterrane slagroente, bij ons ook wel notensla genoemd. Spoel en droog raket voor het gebruik goed af. Het blad kan desgewenst kort worden gebakken. Raket bevat veel vitamine A en C en ijzer.

BAIN-MARIE: Een Franse culinaire term voor de bereiding van voedsel in een heet waterbad, dat wil zeggen de schotel met het te koken voedsel plaatsen in een grote bak met heet water die in een oven wordt gezet; ook het waterbad zelf. Door deze methode kookt het voedsel gelijkmatig en blijft het vocht erin behouden.

BALSAMICO AZIJN: Een aromatische azijn die wordt geproduceerd in Emilia-Romagna in Italië door druivenmost in te koken en te laten karameliseren. Daarna fermenteert dit vocht in een serie houten vaten op lichte en droge zolders. Topkwaliteit balsamico heeft minstens 12 jaar gerijpt en wordt in druppels als toespijs gebruikt. De gewone kwaliteit balsamico die voor de recepten in dit boek benodigd is, is een mengsel van ingekookte druivenmost, wijnazijn en mogelijk wat karamel.

BERGBRAAMBESSEN: Kleine, goudkleurige wilde bessen die op kleine frambozen lijken. Ze komen in het Scandinavische noordpoolgebied voor.

BETA-CAROTEEN: Eén van een groep van carotenoïden die met vitamine A in het lichaam te maken heeft. Beta-caroteen is aanwezig in donkergroene bladgroenten en in diep-oranje en gele vruchten en groenten. Beta-caroteen is een anti-oxidans waarvan men vermoedt dat hij een rol speelt bij kankerpreventie. *Zie ook* Anti-oxidanten, Caroteen, Provitamine, Vitamine. **Vruchten en groenten die rijk zijn aan beta-caroteen:** abrikozen, asperges, broccoli, kanteloep, lenteui, mango, oosterse slasoorten, papaja, peterselie, pompoen, sla, spinazie, wortels, zoete aardappel.

BINDMIDDELEN: Zetmeelprodukten die voor het binden worden toegevoegd aan sausen, purees en soepen. Meestal gebruikt men daarvoor maïzena, arrowroot, tapioca en aardappel- of tarwebloem. Meng deze middelen met een even grote hoeveelheid water of bouillon voor u ze aan het te binden vocht toevoegt. Hiermee voorkomt u dat er klontjes ontstaan.

BLANCHEREN: Het kort onderdompelen van ingrediënten in kokend water en ze daarna meteen laten schrikken onder de koude kraan en ze laten uitlekken. Het koude water stopt het kookproces en helpt de kleur van groenten behouden. Blancheren wordt ook toegepast om het schillen van groenten en vruchten met zachte schil te vergemakkelijken. De blancheertijd hangt af van de stevigheid van het ingrediënt. **Blancheertijden:** aardappel, in plakken of blokjes: 2 minuten; asperges: 2 minuten; bloemkoolroosjes: 1 minuut; broccoliroosjes: 1 minuut; courgettes, in plakken of blokjes: 1 minuut; courgettebloemen: 10 seconden; maïskorrels: 30 seconden; meiraap, in plakken of blokjes: 2 minuten; peultjes: 15 seconden; snijbiet: 15 seconden; sperziebonen: 1 minuut; spinazie: 15 seconden; spruitjes: 2 minuten; taugé: 30 seconden; tomaten, om te ontvellen: 10 seconden; waspeen: 2-3 minuten; wortels, in plakjes: 1 minuut.

BONENSAUS: Een ingeblikt produkt van gemalen sojabonen. Verkrijgbaar in toko's.

BOUQUET GARNI: Een bosje aromatische kruiden dat wordt gebruikt om bouillons en soepen smaak te geven. Gebruik 2-3 takjes peterselie, 1 laurierblad, 1 takje tijm en 3-4 zwarte peperkorrels. De verhouding tussen kruiden en specerijen kan worden aangepast afhankelijk van het recept. Verpak het in ongebleekte katoen als het bouquet voor het serveren moet worden verwijderd.

BRADEN: Voedsel bereiden door het bloot te stellen aan directe hitte, in een oven bijvoorbeeld. Voor het braden moet vlees in de pan worden aangebraden. Bij langdurig braden kan het nodig zijn het voedsel regelmatig te bedruipen om uitdrogen te voorkomen.

BULGHUR: De volle tarwekorrel, met kiem, die voor verkoop is gekookt, gedroogd en geplet tot grove, medium of fijne korrels.

CALORIE: De eenheid van energie in koolhydraten, vet en eiwit. Een kilocalorie is de benodigde hoeveelheid warmte die nodig is om de temperatuur van 1 liter water met 1°C te verhogen.

Een gram koolhydraten of eiwit levert 4 calorieën op. Een gram vet levert 9 calorieën op. Een gram alcohol levert 7 calorieën op. Energie uit voedsel is nodig om de activiteiten van elke cel in het lichaam voort te zetten. Als we het benodigde aantal calorieën eten, blijven we op ons gewicht. Teveel calorieën eten leidt tot gewichtstoename; te weinig eten tot gewichtsverlies. Diëten die minder dan 1200 calorieën per dag leveren, kunnen niet alle voedingsstoffen bevatten die voor een goede gezondheid nodig zijn.

Soms willen mensen informatie over het **percentage calorieën uit vet** in een bepaald voedsel. Omdat elke gram vet 9 calorieën levert, bevat een portie voedsel met 2 gram vet en 50 calorieën 18 calorieën uit vet—of 36 procent. Dit percentage wordt vaak verkeerd gebruikt en begrepen. Caloriearm voedsel met slechts weinig vet lijkt vetrijk te zijn als het wordt beschouwd uit het oogpunt van het procentuele gehalte. In het voorbeeld boven vormen de 2 gram vet echter slechts 3 procent van de toegestane gemiddelde vethoeveelheid voor een dag.

Deskundigen adviseren om over een meerdaagse periode niet meer dan 30 procent van de totale calorieën uit vet op te nemen. De tabel op pagina 18 zet de verschillende calorieniveaus om in aanbevolen grammen vet. Onthoud dat 30 procent een gecombineerd totaal is, niet een hoeveelheid voor één enkele voedselsoort. In een gemiddelde dag moet u individuele voedselsoorten met meer dan 30 procent calorieën uit vet compenseren met voedsel dat weinig of geen vet bevat. In het algemeen heeft eten uit de top van de Voedselpiramide 30 procent of meer calorieën uit vet, terwijl het eten uit de onderste helft van de Piramide minder bevat. Het eten van 2 soorten uit de onderkant van de Piramide tegen 1 soort uit de bovenkant is een goede manier om uw totale calorieën uit vet op 30 procent of minder te krijgen.

CAROTEEN: Een provitamine A en oranje kleurstof die voorkomt in planten. *Zie ook* Beta-caroteen.

CHIFFONADE: Een Franse culinaire uitdrukking voor een met een scherp mes in reepjes van 3 mm tot 1 cm breed gesneden ingrediënt. Spinazie, sla en kruiden kunnen chiffonade worden gesneden.

CHILIPEPERS: Pikante pepers die veel worden gebruikt in Midden- en Zuidamerikaanse en Aziatische keukens. Voor het roosteren en verwijderen van de schil, zie *Roosteren.*

CHOLESTEROL: Een was- en vetachtige stof die wordt aangemaakt in de lever en in dierlijke produkten voorkomt. Hoewel cholesterol van essentieel belang voor het leven is, is het geen essentiële voedingsstof. Het lichaam maakt de cholesterol die het nodig heeft uit vet, eiwit en koolhydraten—met zo'n 1000 mg per dag. De uit voedsel afkomstige cholesterol is bekend als **voedingscholesterol.**

De lever maakt ook **lipoproteïnes** aan. Een van de functies daarvan is het vervoer van cholesterol door het lichaam. Zogeheten **lage-dichtheids lipoproteïnes** (LDLs) circuleren cholesterol door het systeem naar waar het nodig is voor celfuncties en de aanmaak van hormonen. Een overmaat aan LDLs draagt bij aan de vorming van afzettingen op aderwanden die kan leiden tot hartaanvallen en beroertes. **Hoge-dichtheids lipoproteïnes** (HDLs) voeren overtollige cholesterol terug naar de lever.

Een dieet met veel verzadigd vet kan het **bloedcholesterol** verhogen tot gevaarlijke niveaus, en datzelfde geldt voor voedsel dat rijk is aan voedingscholesterol, hoewel in mindere mate. Deskundigen adviseren de totale hoeveelheid bloedcholesterol onder de 200 mg per dl te houden.

CITRUSSCHIL: De helder gekleurde, dunne buitenschil van citrusvruchten, die volop smakelijke oliën bevat.

CONFIT: Vlees dat is geconserveerd door het langzaam in eigen vet te koken.

CRUDITÉS: Een assortiment rauwe en geblancheerde groenten dat als een voorgerecht wordt gegeven. Tot crudités kunnen bleekselderij, bloemkool- en broccoliroosjes, champignons, komkommer, radijsjes, paprika's, tomaten, wortels en mini-groenten behoren.

DAGELIJKSE WAARDEN: De hoeveelheden essentiële voedingsstoffen die dienen te worden geleverd door een dagelijks dieet van 2000 calorieën.

DAL: Een Indiaas woord voor gedroogde spliterwten, inzen en bonen.

DASHI: Een bouillon van vis en zeewier die een essentieel ingrediënt in veel Japanse recepten is. *Dashi* is in oosterse winkels als instant poeder verkrijgbaar. U kunt zelf *dashi* maken door 1 liter water met 30 g *kombu* (gedroogd zeewier) te verhitten. De *kombu* wordt vlak voor het vocht aan de kook komt verwijderd, waarna u 30 g *bonito* vlokken toevoegt. Breng het mengsel aan de kook en neem het dan onmiddellijk van het vuur. Zeef voor gebruik.

DEEGDEKSEL: Een bros deksel gemaakt van bloem, vet en water. Voor de meeste recepten voor deegdeksels wordt vee boter of ander vet gebruikt. Zie voor een alternatief Gistdeeg.

DEGLACEREN: Het na bakken of braden aan een pan toevoegen van wijn, bouillon of citrussap en al roerend de aangebakken deeltjes losmaken.

DIM SUM: Een assortiment kleine schotels, van noedels tot knoedels, dat in Chinese restaurants met thee als lunch of tussendoortje wordt geserveerd.

EIWIT: De structurele component van spieren, botten, kraakbeen, huid en organen. Het wordt gevormd uit 22 aminozuren, die in verschillende combinaties voorkomen. Het menselijk lichaam kan slechts 13 aminozuren aanmaken, de zogeheten **niet-essentiële**, omdat ze niet door de voeding hoeven te worden geleverd. De overige 9 aminozuren zijn **essentieel** omdat ze door de voeding moeten worden geleverd.

Als een voedingsmiddel toereikende hoeveelheden van alle 9 essentiële aminozuren bevat, wordt het een **compleet eiwit** genoemd. De meeste voedingsmiddelen uit dierlijke bronnen zijn complete eiwitten. **Incomplete eiwitten** komen meestal in plantaardige voedingsmiddelen voor en missen één of twee essentiële aminozuren. Twee of meer plantaardige voedingsmiddelen kunnen echter samen worden gegeten en zo alle essentiële aminozuren leveren. Dergelijke combinaties—bijvoorbeeld bepaalde groenten met bepaalde granen—worden **complementaire eiwitten** genoemd. Daar aminozuren enige tijd in de bloedstroom circuleren voor ze nieuw lichaams-eiwit vormen, hoeven de complementaire voedingsmiddelen niet bij één maaltijd te worden gegeten.

Het lichaam heeft elke dag een nieuwe voorraad eiwit nodig. De meeste mensen krijgen voldoende eiwitten binnen. Strikte vegetariërs moeten er echter voor zorgen dat ze voldoende groente en granen eten die bronnen van eiwit zijn om te voldoen aan hun behoefte aan essentiële aminozuren.

EMULSIE: Een mengsel van twee soorten vocht die niet goed met elkaar te mengen zijn, zoals olie en azijn. Voeg de olie heel langzaam aan de azijn toe, druppel voor druppel of in een dun straaltje, en klop voortdurend.

FILO: Een flinterdunne deegsoort die voor buideltjes of als deklaag wordt gebruikt.

FRUCTOSE: Een enkelvoudig koolhydraat en de vorm van suiker die voorkomt in de meeste vruchten en sommige groenten. *Zie ook* Koolhydraten, Suiker.

GEZONDHEIDSCLAIMS: Op etiketten kunnen specifieke gezondheidsclaims staan die voor 7 gebieden tellen.

- Voedsel dat arm is aan vet, verzadigd vet en cholesterol kan mogelijk het risico van hartaandoeningen verminderen.
- Vruchten, groenten en granen met bepaalde soorten vezel kunnen mogelijk het risico van hartaandoeningen verminderen.
- Natriumarm voedsel kan mogelijk het risico van hoge bloeddruk verminderen.
- Kalkrijk voedsel kan mogelijk het risico van osteoporose verminderen.
- Vruchten en groenten die goede bronnen zijn van vitamine C, vitamine A of vezel kunnen mogelijk het risico van sommige soorten kanker verminderen.
- Graanprodukten, vruchten of groenten die goede bronnen zijn van vezel en die weinig vet bevatten, kunnen mogelijk het risico van sommige soorten kanker verminderen.
- Vetarm voedsel kan mogelijk het risico van sommige soorten kanker verminderen.

GISTDEEG (voor quiches e.d.): Een vetarm alternatief voor korst- of bladerdeeg. Los voor een vorm van 23 cm doorsnee 7 g gedroogde gist en 60 g suiker op in 2,5 dl lauwe (circa 30°C) melk. Laat 5 minuten staan, of tot het mengsel schuimig wordt. Voeg dan 4 eetlepels saffloerolie en 1 ei toe. Klop alles goed en zet weg. Meng in een grote kom 700 g ongebleekte tarwebloem met ½ theelepel zout. Voeg het gistmengsel toe en roer of klop tot alle bloem is opgenomen en het deeg niet klonterig is. Doe het deeg over op een licht met bloem bestoven werkvlak en kneed het tot het glad en elastisch is. Doe het deeg over in een licht met olie ingevette kom, dek het af en laat het rijzen tot het in volume verdubbeld is. Druk de lucht uit het deeg, snijd het in twee even grote porties en rol elke portie tot een bal. Rol elke bal uit op een met bloem bestoven werkvlak en doe het deeg dan in licht met olie ingevette quichevormen. Laat het deeg 10 minuten rusten voor u de beklede vormen vult en ze 45 tot 50 minuten bakt in een op 190°C) voorverwarmde oven, of zolang als voor een bepaald recept nodig is.

GLUCOSE: Een suiker die de primaire brandstof is voor cellen, spieren en de hersenen. Het lichaam transformeert alle koolhydraten—enkelvoudige en samengestelde—tot glucose.

GROENTEBOUILLON: De essence van groenten, gebruikt als smaakbasis voor soepen, stoofpotten en sausen.

Verhit voor 1 liter **groentebouillon** in een ruime soeppan 3 eetlepels plantaardige olie. Voeg 8 stengels bleekselderij, 3 preien, 2 geschraapte wortels en 1 ui (alle in stukjes van zo'n 3 cm gehakt) toe. Laat zweten tot ze zacht maar niet bruin zijn. Giet er 2½ dl droge witte wijn bij en laat die tot de helft inkoken. Voeg dan 1½ liter water toe, breng het geheel aan de kook en schuim eventuele ongerechtigheden af. Draai het vuur zo laag dat de bouillon licht suddert en voeg een bouquet garni toe (3 takjes peterselie, 1 laurierblad, 2 takjes tijm en 4 zwarte peperkorrels). Laat het geheel zonder deksel 1 uur trekken, waarbij u af en toe afschuimt. Zeef de bouillon door een fijne zeef, waarbij u de groenten aandrukt om er zoveel mogelijk vocht uit te krijgen. Lat de bouillon afkoelen, zet hem dan in de koelkast en verwijder later het gestolde vet. Volg voor een **volle groentebouillon** het recept boven, maar laat de bouillon 1 uur langer trekken.

INKOKEN: Het concentreren en/of binden van een vocht door koken. Het water verdampt, waardoor het volume afneemt en de smaak sterker wordt.

JULIENNE: Een Franse culinaire term voor ingrediënten die in reepjes van circa ½ cm dik en 3 cm lang zijn gesneden. Groenten kunnen julienne worden gesneden.

KASHA: Geroosterde boekweitgrutten. Boekweit is niet verwant aan tarwe en bevat heel weinig gluten. Hele of geplette boekweit heeft een uitgesproken nootachtige smaak en is een interessant alternatief voor rijst. Door de kasha voor het koken om te scheppen met een eiwit houdt u de korrels mooi los. Voor een romiger schotel kunt u die stap weglaten.

KERRIE: Een mengsel van Indiase specerijen waartoe fenegriek, gember, kaneel, kardemom, komijnzaad, koriander, kruidnagel, kurkuma, mosterdzaad, nootmuskaat, tamarinde en gedroogde chilipeper kunnen behoren.

KIKKERERWTEN: Een peulvrucht die geliefd is in de Middenoosterse keuken.

KIPPEBOUILLON: Een essence van kip en groenten die als basis wordt gebruikt voor soepen, stoofpotten en sausen.

Doe voor **kippebouillon** in een niet-aluminium soeppan de botten van een kip van 1,5 kg, 1 geschraapte wortel, 1 stengel bleekselderij, 1 ui (alle in stukjes van 1 cm gesneden), en een bouquet garni (takje peterselie, laurierblad, takje tijm en 4-5 peperkorrels. Giet er 2 liter water bij en breng aan de kook. Draai dan de temperatuur lager en laat onder af en toe afschuimen 2 uur onafgedekt sudderen. Zeef de bouillon en zet hem koud weg tot het vet bovenop is gestold en kan worden verwijderd.

Bouillon is goed in te vriezen. Vries de bouillon bij voorkeur in in porties van ½ tot 1 liter voor later gebruik in soepen en sausen.

Voor **bruine kippebouillon** de kippebotten eerst 20 minuten roosteren in een oven op 200°C tot ze bruin zijn. Volg dan de rest van het recept boven.

Voor een **volle kippebouillon** het recept voor kippebouillon boven volgen, maar 1 uur langer laten sudderen.

KOOLHYDRATEN: Suiker, zetmeel en de meeste soorten vezel. **Enkelvoudige koolhydraten** zijn suikers—waaronder glucose, fructose uit fruit en groenten, lactose uit melk, en sucrose uit biet- of rietsuiker. **Samengestelde koolhydraten** bestaan voornamelijk uit zetmeel en vezels.

Afgezien van voedingsvezel worden koolhydraten door het lichaam afgebroken in glucose, dat voor energie wordt verbrand. Samengestelde koolhydraten worden aanbevolen boven enkelvoudige suikers (met name geraffineerde suiker) omdat ze gewoonlijk ook andere waardevolle voedingsstoffen bevatten. Bovendien komt glucose uit zetmeel langzamer in de bloedstroom terecht dan die uit suikers, waardoor de insulineproduktie en het gebruik worden beïnvloed. Dit feit is van belang voor diabetici.

Een evenwichtig dieet omvat 50-60 procent van de calorieën uit koolhydraten, met niet meer dan 15 procent van de totale calorieën afkomstig uit geraffineerde suiker.

KRUIDEN: Bladeren, bloemen en andere delen van bepaalde planten die bij het koken als smaakgevers worden gebruikt. Verse kruiden hebben een volkomen andere smaak dan hun gedroogde versies. Gebruik waar mogelijk verse. Verwijder de stelen, daar de meeste bitter zijn (een uitzondering is peterselie, die juist zeer smakelijke steeltjes heeft). Hak kruiden fijn met een vlijmscherp mes zodat u de bladen niet kneust. Als u in een recept gedroogde kruiden gebruikt, neem dan ⅓ van de opgegeven hoeveelheid verse.

KRUISBLOEMIGE GROENTEN: Een groep groenten die naar hun kruisvormige bloesem is vernoemd. Ze bevatten stoffen die enzymen lijken te activeren die carcinogenen vernietigen. De groep bestaat uit bladgroenten, bloemkool, boerenkool, broccoli, kool (alle soorten), koolraap, meiraap en spruitjes.

MAGER (als in vlees). In dit boek geldt deze uitdrukking voor vlees- en gevogelteprodukten die minder dan 10 g vet, 4 g verzadigd vet en 95 mg cholesterol per portie van 100 g bevatten.

MATTONE: Een terracotta schotel die wordt gebruikt voor het bereiden van kip op Toscaanse wijze, waarbij opengeklapte hele kippen worden verzwaard en gebakken tussen twee stukken terracotta. Dat levert een krokante buitenkant en een sappig binnenste op. De *mattone* wordt verwarmd en gaat dan boven op het fornuis.

MESCLUN: Een mengsel van jonge, bittere slagroenten en milde kruiden. Het mengsel kan bijvoorbeeld krulandijvie (of witlof), molsla, arugula, kervel en/of eikebladsla bevatten.

MINERAALSPOREN: Essentiële minerale voedingsstoffen die in het menselijk lichaam voorkomen in hoeveelheden van minder dan 5 gram, wat minder is dan 1 theelepel in uw hele lichaam. Tot deze mincromineralen behoren chromium, fluoride, mangaan, selenium en zink.

MINERALEN: Anorganische stoffen die de elementaire samenstellende delen van de aardkorst vormen. Ze worden door planten uit de aarde opgenomen en daarna gegeten door diersoorten, waaronder mensen. Van de 60 mineralen die in het menselijk lichaam worden aangetroffen, worden er 22 beschouwd als essentieel voor de menselijke voeding. De 16 belangrijkste mineralen, met hun functies en voedselbronnen, staan beschreven in de tabel die op de index volgt.

ORGANISCH GETEELD: In verwijzing naar landbouwprodukten die zijn verbouwd zonder gebruik van pesticiden of andere chemische middelen.

OXIDATIE: De combinatie van zuurstof met een ander element resulterend in de vorming van een nieuwe stof. Roest is het resultaat van de oxidatie van ijzer; ranzigheid is het resultaat van de oxidatie van vet of olie. In het menselijk lichaam is oxidatie binnen cellen een noodzakelijke chemische reactie. Antioxidanten voorkomen schade aan cellen door middel van overmatig geoxideerde deeltjes die vrije radicalen worden genoemd. *Zie ook* Anti-oxidanten, Vrije radicalen.

PADDESTOELEN: Gekweekte en wilde zwammen die bij het koken worden gebruikt. Mild smakende paddestoelen, zoals knopchampignons en *enoki*, zijn in de winkel en op markten verkrijgbaar. Veel wilde paddestoelen worden nu ook gekweekt. Bij recepten waarvoor wilde paddestoelen nodig zijn, verdient het aanbeveling ze bij een gerenommeerde winkel te kopen. Voor het zelf plukken van wilde paddestoelen is veel kennis vereist. Tot de hier verkrijgbare wilde paddestoelen behoren onder andere boleten, oesterzwammen, shiitake, morieljes, wolkenoor en cantharellen. Veel ervan zijn ook in gedroogde vorm verkrijgbaar. Laat gedroogde paddestoelen minstens 20 minuten weken in warme kippebouillon of warm water; zeef het weeknat en gebruik het voor het recept of voor een toekomstige soep of saus.

PASTA: Een deeg van bloem en vocht dat plat wordt uitgerold, in een veelheid van vormen en maten wordt gesneden en dan in kokend water of een ander vocht wordt gekookt. Pasta is een uitstekende bron van samengestelde koolhydraten en is in vele gedaanten over de hele wereld bekend. Met zijn verscheidenheid aan bloemsoorten en vormen, met of zonder eieren, is pasta een van de meest populaire gerechten ter wereld.

Maak **pastadeeg** door 500 g bloem in de kom van een keukenmachine te doen. Klop 4 eieren los met 1 eetlepel olijfolie in een kannetje met tuit. Voeg bij draaiende motor van de keukenmachine het eimengsel geleidelijk toe tot het deeg van de wand van de kom begint los te laten (de hoeveelheid toegevoegd eimengsel zal afhangen van de vochtigheid en het vochtgehalte van de bloem). Draai 30 seconden en controleer dan de structuur. Het deeg moet vochtig genoeg zijn om te kunnen worden samengeknepen, maar mag niet kleverig zijn. Neem het deeg uit de kom van de keukenmachine en kneed het met de hand tot een bal. Laat de deegbal in een plastic zak rusten.

Rol pasta uit door telkens ¼ van het deeg te nemen en de rest van het deeg in de plastic zak te houden om uitdrogen te voorkomen. Gebruik een pastamachine met slinger en begin op de breedste stand. Haal het deeg zo 8 tot 10 keer door de machine, waarbij u het deeg telkens dubbelvouwt, tot het deeg glad is. Als het deeg scheurt, is het mogelijk te vochtig; bestuif het dan met bloem en borstel daarna overtollige bloem eraf. Stel de machine een stand nauwer in en draai er de pasta *zonder vouwen* door. Herhaal deze werkwijze tweemaal bij elke volgende stand en ga daarmee door tot het deeg de gewenste dikte heeft. Laat het deeg dan iets uitdrogen en snijd het vervolgens in de gewenste vorm.

Maak voor **spinaziepasta** zo'n 400 g spinazie schoon. Stoom de spinazie kort en knijp er na even afkoelen zoveel mogelijk vocht uit. Draai de spinazie samen met de bloem in een keukenmachine voor u het eimengsel toevoegt. Volg verder het recept boven, maar gebruik slechts 3 eieren.

Maak **wortel- of bietenpasta** door 250 g wortels of bieten te schillen en ze dan te stomen of koken tot ze gaar zijn. Ga verder als bij spinaziepasta. Onthoud bij het koken van pasta dat verse pasta maar 2-3 minuten in kokend water hoeft te koken. Controleer dan of het de door u gewenste graad van gaarheid heeft. Kook pasta vooral niet te lang.

PERNOD: Een met anijszaad op smaak gebrachte likeur.

PESTO: Een smaakgevend ingrediënt dat gewoonlijk met Parmezaanse kaas, pijnboompitten, verse basilicum en olijfolie wordt gemaakt. *Pepitas*, ontvliesde pompoenpitten, die tot aan 25 procent minder vet totaal bevatten dan pijnboompitten, kunnen er voor in de plaats worden gebruikt. Aangezien dit mengsel echter in kleine hoeveelheden wordt toegepast, wordt de vetheid van de kaas en noten goed verdeeld en is niet overdadig in een portie. Probeer de basilicum ook eens te vervangen door verse koriander of zongedroogde tomaten, of gebruik in plaats van de olijfolie saffloerolie of een lichtere plantaardige olie. Een vetarme pesto zonder kaas is ook heerlijk.

Voor 60 g **pepita pesto** draait u 1 teen knoflook, 30 g vers basilicumblad, 2 eetlepels Parmezaanse kaas, 1 eetlepel geroosterde *pepitas* en 2 eetlepels olijfolie in een keukenmachine of blender. De pesto kan in de koelkast worden bewaard met een dun laagje olie erbovenop. Giet de olie af voor u de pesto gebruikt.

PEULVRUCHTEN: De groentefamilie waartoe linzen, spliterwten en verschillende soorten gedroogde bonen, alsmede pinda's (aardnoten), snijbonen, doperwten, sojabonen en alfalfa behoren. Van de 14.000 soorten peulvruchten worden er maar ongeveer 20 als voedsel gebruikt. Peulvruchten bevatten veel koolhydraten en een aantal vitaminen en mineralen. Ze bevatten ook veel oplosbare vezel en vormen een uitstekende bron van eiwit. Bijna ieders voedingspatroon kan worden verbeterd door de toevoeging van peulvruchten. Primitieve culturen waren vaak afhankelijk van peulvruchten en granen als basisvoedsel. In combinatie bieden die twee voedselsoorten een eiwitbron die gelijk is aan die van vlees, terwijl de meeste peulvruchten geen vet bevatten.

In termen van voedselgroepen worden snijbonen en doperwten als groenten beschouwd; zowel de peul als de boon van snijbonen en peultjes worden gegeten. Andere peulvruchten zitten in de voedselgroep van gedroogde bonen en noten, met vlees, gevogelte, vis en eieren. Sojabonen zijn een belangrijke bron van plantaardige olie; soja-eiwit wordt in vleesvervangingsmiddelen gebruikt. Sojasaus, tofu en miso zijn ook sojaprodukten, waarbij het vet is verwijderd. De belangrijkste toepassing van pinda's in de wereld is voor olie. Pinda's zijn vetrijke leden van de familie der peulvruchten.

Linzen en spliterwten zijn al bekend sinds 9000 v. Chr. Ze behoorden tot de eerste planten die werden verbouwd. Zowel spliterwten als linzen zijn vetarm en goede bronnen van eiwit.

Kidneybonen (nierbonen) worden in Mexico al langer dan 7000 jaar verbouwd en spelen een zeer grote rol in de Mexicaanse keuken, maar ook in de Cajun en Caribische keuken. Zwarte bonen zijn een basisvoedsel op Cuba.

Kikkererwten, die meer vet bevatten dan de meeste van hun verwanten onder de peulvruchten, zijn zeer geliefd in de Indiase en Middenoosterse keukens. Hummus wordt voornamelijk van kikkererwten gemaakt. De ijzerrijke limabonen zijn ook peulvruchten en waren eens een basisvoedsel van de Amerikaanse Indianen.

POCHEREN: Het koken van voedsel in een sudderend nat (vaak bouillon). Het nat moet heet zijn voor u er vlees, zeebanket of groenten in doet, zodat de smaak wordt ingesloten. De smaak van het vlees zal in het nat trekken als beide tegelijk worden verhit. (Daarom is kippebouillon zo smakelijk en zal het ervoor gebruikte vlees alle smaak verloren hebben.) Voeg bij het pocheren van eieren een of twee druppels azijn aan het nat toe.

PORTIE: De hoeveelheid voedsel die een persoon bij een maal zou moeten eten. De op etiketten van levensmiddelen aangegeven porties hoeven niet noodzakelijkerwijs hetzelfde te zijn als de in dit boek op basis van de Voedselpiramide aanbevolen hoeveelheden. Zie pagina 24 voor meer informatie.

PROVITAMINEN: Samengestelde eenheden die in het menselijk lichaam in actieve vitaminen kunnen worden omgezet. Zo wordt bijvoorbeeld beta-caroteen door het lichaam in vitamine A omgezet.

QUINOA: Een piepkleine graansoort die van alle granen het hoogste eiwitgehalte heeft en een compleet eiwit bevat, met de essentiële aminozuren in evenwicht. Hij moet voor gebruik goed worden afgespoeld, daar het graan een bitter deklaagje heeft dat als insektenwerend middel fungeert.

REFERENTIEDIEET: Een dagelijks dieet van 2000 calorieën dat als basis wordt gebruikt voor het etiketteren van voedingsmiddelen en de zogeheten Dagelijkse Waarden. Het is een algemene standaard voor de behoefte van een "gemiddelde" mens. *Zie ook* Dagelijkse Waarden, Etiket.

REFERENTIEVOEDSEL: Het standaard voedingsmiddel in een categorie of een gemiddelde van de 3 meest populaire merken. Deze uitdrukking wordt gebruikt voor het maken van vergelijkingen. Het is het gewone voedingsmiddel dat wordt vergeleken met een "verminderd" of "licht" middel. Zo moet een "vetarme" saladedressing met blauwe kaas minstens 25 procent minder vet bevatten dan de gewone (of referentie) dressing.

ROKEN: Het in een afgesloten ruimte blootstellen van voedsel aan rook. Oorspronkelijk was het een manier of vlees en vis te conserveren, maar deze techniek wordt nu ook gebruikt om ingrediënten een aromatische, rookachtige smaak te geven. Voorbeelden van dit soort materialen die bij het roken worden gebruikt, zijn aromatische houtsoorten, kruiden en specerijen als jeneverbes, rozemarijn, pijnboomnaalden, venkel, kaneel en sinaasappelschil.

ROOSTEREN: Voedsel bereiden door het bloot te stellen aan directe hitte, in een oven bijvoorbeeld.

Knoflook roosteren: Verwarm een oven voor op 150°C. Kerf de schil van 8 bollen knoflook in het midden in, maar snijd niet in de tenen. Verwijder de bovenste helft van de papierachtige schil zodat de tenen bloot komen. Doe de bollen knoflook in een kleine ovenschaal en giet 1,25 dl olijfolie over de knoflook. Breng op smaak met zout en versgemalen peper, strooi er 1 theelepel fijngehakte verse rozemarijn en 1 theelepel fijngehakte verse tijm over en zet de schaal 1 uur afgedekt in de oven. Verwijder het afdeksel en laat de knoflook nog 10 tot 15 minuten roosteren onder regelmatig bedruipen tot de bollen door en door gaar zijn. Laat de knoflook afkoelen voor u hem opdient. (Voor 4 tot 6 als een hapje of als bijgerecht bij een hoofdgerecht.) Bewaar de olie uit de schaal.

Roosteren wordt ook gedaan om bijvoorbeeld paprika's en chilipepers te kunnen ontvellen.

Paprika roosteren: Leg de paprika's boven een direct vuur (op een gasfornuis of onder de grill) en laat het vel blakeren. Keer de paprika's daarbij regelmatig, zodat ze gelijkmatig gaar worden. Neem de paprika's van het vuur. Doe ze in een papieren zak en sluit de zak goed af, zodat de paprika's kunnen afkoelen en uitstomen. Pel nadat de paprika's zijn afgekoeld het geblakerde vel eraf. Wat u overhoudt, is zacht en heerlijk zoet paprikavlees dat voortreffelijk is in salades, in sausen en als garnituur.

Noten roosteren: Leg de noten op een droog bakblik en zet dat 10 tot 15 minuten in een op 180°C voorverwarmde oven. Schep de noten af en toe om tot ze goudbruin zijn.

ROUX: Een klassieke Franse techniek voor het binden van vocht. Verwarm gelijke hoeveelheden boter en bloem, waarbij u minstens 5 minuten flink roert om de bloemige smaak weg te krijgen. Klop er dan het te binden vocht door en laat op een laag vuur sudderen tot de gewenste graad van gebondenheid is bereikt. Hoe langer het bloemmengsel kookt, hoe donkerder de uiteindelijke saus zal zijn.

SAFFRAAN: De gedroogde stamper van een krokussoort, gebruikt als smaakgever en om een prachtige gele kleur te geven aan een gerecht. Alleen voor de kleur kunt u kurkuma in plaats van saffraan gebruiken.

SALMONELLA: Een algemene bacterie die verantwoordelijk is voor ongeveer de helft van het aantal gevallen van voedselvergiftiging. De bacterie wordt gewoonlijk aangetroffen in rauw dierlijk voedsel als vlees, eieren en kip.

SEMOLINA (Griesmeel): Een bloemsoort die is gemaakt van grof gemalen durum (harde) tarwe.

SEROTONINE: Een chemische stof in de hersenen die door het lichaam wordt aangemaakt uit het aminozuur tryptofaan. De stof kan stemmingswijzigingen veroorzaken.

SEVICHE: Een schotel uit Midden- en Zuid-Amerika die is gebaseerd op rauw zeebanket dat men laat marineren in citrussap(pen) en mengt met chilipepers, ui, koriander en verse tomaten. De citrusmarinade "kookt" de rauwe vis, die verder niet aan hitte wordt blootgesteld.

SMOREN: Langzaam koken in een afgedekte pan met een kleine hoeveelheid vocht. Deze methode is bijzonder geschikt voor taaie ingrediënten.

STEARINEZUUR: Een verzadigd vetzuur dat wordt aangetroffen in vlees en chocolade. Uit eerder uitgevoerde onderzoeken kan worden opgemaakt dat het niet als andere verzadigde vetzuren de bloedcholesterolspiegel verhoogt.

SUCROSE: Een combinatie van fructose en glucose. Witte tafelsuiker en bruine suiker bevatten sucrose. Het komt ook op natuurlijke wijze voor in sommige groenten en vruchten.

SUIKER: Een enkelvoudig koolhydraat. In wezen zijn alle suikers wat voedingswaarde aangaat gelijk, hoewel sommige vormen—fructose bijvoorbeeld—zoeter dan andere zijn. **Glucose,** de primaire bloedsuiker is de basisbrandstof voor het lichaam. Het lichaam zet samengestelde koolhydraten (zetmeel) en de meeste fructose (vruchtensuiker) om in glucose. *Zie ook* Koolhydraten, Fructose, Glucose, Sucrose.

De volgende suikers kunnen worden tegengekomen op ingrediëntenlijsten: bruine suiker, dextrose, druivesuiker esdoornsiroop, fructose, gerstemout, glucose, honing, rietsuiker, lactose, siroop, sucrose, suiker.

SUPPLEMENTEN: Vitaminen en mineralen in pil-, poeder- of vloeibare vorm. Supplementen bevatten voedingsstoffen, maar zijn zelf geen voedsel. Mensen die aan een tekort aan vitaminen of mineralen lijden kunnen supplementen moeten nemen. Ook wordt vrouwen in verwachting of die borstvoeding geven wel aangeraden supplementen te nemen. Onderzoekers zijn bezig met research naar de mogelijkheid dat verscheidene voedingsstoffen in supplementvorm ziekten kunnen helpen voorkomen. Zij weten echter nog niet welke supplementen of hoeveel ervan veilig en effectief zullen zijn. Momenteel bevelen de meeste deskundigen nog steeds voedsel aan als de beste bron van vitaminen en mineralen.

TAJINE: Een diepe aardewerk pot met een kegelvormig deksel die in Noord-Afrika voor langdurig gekookte gerechten wordt gebruikt. Het woord *tajine* verwijst ook naar het bereide gerecht.

TAMARINDE: De vrucht in een peul van een altijdgroene boomsoort die in tropische gebieden voorkomt. Het bitterzoete vruchtvlees wordt gescheiden van de zaden en dan gedroogd of in vloeibare vorm gebracht.

TOEGEVOEGD: Bepaalde voedingsstoffen bevattend die verloren zijn gegaan bij de verwerking van een voedsel als graan, en dat bij verdere verwerking wordt vervangen. Zo verliest tarwe die wordt verwerkt tot witte bloem aanzienlijke hoeveelheden aan ongeveer 20 vitaminen en mineralen, evenals vezel. Door toevoeging worden 4 verloren gegane stoffen vervangen—thiamine, riboflavine, niacine en ijzer.

TOFU: Gestremde sojamelk die zeer eiwitrijk is en die bij marineren of koken de omringende smaken opneemt.

TRYPTOFAAN: Een aminozuur dat voorkomt in eiwit en de aanmaak stimuleert van serotonine, een chemische stof in de hersenen die stemminsveranderingen teweegbrengt.

VEGETARIËR: Een persoon die alleen of voornamelijk plantaardig voedsel eet. Strikte vegetariërs, die ook wel **veganisten** worden genoemd, eten geen voedsel van dierlijke origine. **Lactovegetariërs** hebben wel zuivelprodukten in hun voeding, maar geen vlees. **Lacto-ovovegetariërs** eten gewoonlijk kleine hoeveelheden vis of kip maar geen rood vlees. Als hun dieet zorgvuldig wordt opgesteld, lopen vegetariërs geen grotere kans op tekorten aan voedingsstoffen dan vleeseters. Veganisten dienen wel te zorgen voor voldoende eiwit, vitamine B12, kalk, ijzer en zink in hun dieet.

VERRIJKT: Een voedselsoort die toegevoegde vitaminen en mineralen bevat die er oorspronkelijk niet in aanwezig waren (of in kleinere hoeveelheden). Melk is gevitaminiseerd met vitamine A en D.

VET: Een samenstelsel van koolstof-, waterstof- en zuurstofatomen dat energie aan het lichaam levert. De meeste in voedsel voorkomende vetten zijn **triglyceriden—**drie vettige zuren en een glycerolmolecuul.

Vetzuren variëren in niveau van verzadiging, afhankelijk van het aantal meervoudige bindingen in hun chemische structuren. **Verzadigde vetzuren** hebben geen meervoudige bindingen in hun koolstofketen en komen voornamelijk in dierlijke produkten voor. Verzadigde vetten zijn gewoonlijk vast bij kamertemperatuur. **Onverzadigde vetzuren** hebben één **(enkelvoudig onverzadigd)** of meer **(meervoudig onverzadigd)** meervoudige bindingen. Onverzadigde vetten zijn afkomstig uit planten en vis en zijn vloeibaar bij kamertemperatuur. **Enkelvoudig onverzadigde vetzuren,** zoals die in olijfolie, kunnen mogelijk de bloedcholesterolspiegel helpen verlagen door de hoeveelheid lage-dichtheids lipoproteïnen (LDLs) te verminderen. Visolie bevat een meervoudig onverzadigd vetzuur dat **omega-3** wordt genoemd, en waarvan wordt vermoed dat die het risico van hartaanvallen en beroertes kan helpen verminderen. Door hydratie van meervoudig onverzadigde oliën kunnen **transvetzuren** worden ontwikkeld, die enkele eigenschappen van verzadigde vetzuren hebben.

Deskundigen adviseren om slechts 30 procent van de dagelijkse calorieën uit vet te krijgen, met maar 10 procent uit verzadigd vet. Zie ook Cholesterol, Hydratie.

SOORTEN VET IN OLIËN, BOTER EN ANDERE VETTEN

Soorten olie, enz	Verzadigd vet	Meerv. onverzadigd vet	Enkelv. onverzadigd vet	Cholesterol *(mg/eetlepel)*
Canola-olie	6%	36%	58%	0
Saffloerolie	9%	78%	13%	0
Zonnebloemolie	11%	69%	20%	0
Maïsolie	13%	62%	25%	0
Olijfolie	14%	9%	77%	0
Sesamolie	14%	42%	4%	0
Sojabonenolie	15%	61%	24%	0
Margarine	17%	32%	49%	0
Arachide-olie	18%	34%	48%	0
Kippevet	31%	21%	47%	11
Reuzel	41%	12%	47%	12
Palmolie	51%	10%	39%	0
Rundervet	52%	4%	44%	14
Botervet	66%	4%	30%	33
Kokosolie	92%	2%	6%	0

VEZEL: Het onverteerbare deel van planten. Vezel valt in twee categorieën—onoplosbaar en oplosbaar. **Onoplosbare vezel** kan aanzienlijke hoeveelheden water opnemen en bijdragen aan afvoer. Het helpt mogelijk kanker aan de dikke darm voorkomen. Bronnen van onoplosbare vezel zijn volle granen, groenten, vruchteschillen, peulvruchten, zaden en noten.

Oplosbare vezel voorkomt dat het lichaam bepaalde stoffen opneemt. Men denkt dat het de bloedcholesterolspiegel helpt verlagen en de bloedsuikerspiegel helpt reguleren. Bronnen van oplosbare vezel zijn vruchten, groenten, zaden, bruine rijst en haver.

VISBOUILLON: Een essence van vis en groenten, gebruikt als basis voor soepen, stoofpotten en sausen.

Maak **visbouillon** door 3 eetlepels plantaardige olie te verhitten in een soeppan. Voeg 1 kleine ui, 1 wortel en 1 stengel bleekselderij toe (alledrie in stukjes van ½ cm gesneden) en fruit die in circa 5 minuten zacht. Voeg 45 g in plakjes gesneden champignons en 2 kg visgraten (van witvis) toe. Kook alles circa 20 minuten op een laag vuur tot de graten uit elkaar beginnen te vallen. Voeg 5 dl droge witte wijn toe en deglaceer de pan. Voeg dan 2 liter water toe en breng alles aan de kook. Draai het vuur lager, voeg een bouquet garni toe (takje peterselie, laurierblad, takje tijm, 4-5 peperkorrels) en schuim eventuele ongerechtigheden af. Laat 30 minuten onafgedekt sudderen en schuim nu en dan af. Zeef de bouillon door kaasdoek en zet hem koud weg tot alle vet gestold is en kan worden afgeschept.

Deze bouillon is goed in te vriezen.

VITAMINEN: Organische stoffen die noodzakelijk zijn voor veel lichaamsfuncties. Vitaminen moeten worden geleverd door voedingsmiddelen (niet door supplementen); het lichaam maakt namelijk geen vitaminen aan. Hun functies en bronnen staan vermeld in de lijst na de index.

VLEESVERVANGINGSMIDDEL: Groenten-eiwit, vaak gemaakt van sojabonen, dat in recepten ter vervanging van gehakt wordt gebruikt.

VOEDINGSSTOFFEN: Stoffen die uit voedsel worden gehaald en in het lichaam worden gebruikt ter bevordering van groei, onderhoud en herstel. Tot voedingsstoffen behoren eiwitten, koolhydraten, vetten, vitaminen, mineralen en water.

VOEDINGSWAARDE CLAIMS: Uitspraken over het niveau aan voedingsstoffen in een bepaald voedingsmiddel. Zie de definities in de tabel hieronder.

DEFINITIES VAN CLAIMS OVER VOEDINGSSTOFFEN

Claim	*Hoeveelheid of Standaard*
VETVRIJ	0,5 g vet of minder per standaardportie
VERZADIGD-VETVRIJ	0,5 g verzadigd vet of minder per standaardportie
CHOLESTEROLVRIJ	Minder dan 2 mg cholesterol en 2 g of minder verzadigd vet per standaardportie
NATRIUMVRIJ	Minder dan 5 mg natrium per standaardportie
CALORIEVRIJ	Minder dan 5 calorieën per standaardportie.
SUIKERVRIJ	Minder dan 0,5 g suiker per standaardportie
VETARM	3 g vet of minder vet per standaardportie.
VERZADIGD-VETARM	3 g verzadigd vet of minder per standaardportie.
CHOLESTEROLARM	20 mg of minder cholesterol en 2 g of minder verzadigd vet per standaardportie.
NATRIUMARM	140 mg natrium of minder per standaardportie.
CALORIE-ARM	40 calorieën of minder per standaardportie.
VEZELRIJK	5 g vezel of meer per standaardportie.
GOEDE VEZEL	2,5-4,9 g vezel per standaardportie.
VERMINDERD	25% lager aan de voedingsstof dan het vergelijkbare gewone (referentie) voedingsmiddel.
GOEDE BRON	Bevat 10-19% van de Dagelijkse Waarde per portie van de voedingsstof in kwestie (bijv. goede bron van kalk)
HOOG, RIJK AAN, UITSTEKENDE BRON VAN	Bevat 20% of meer van de Dagelijkse Waarde per portie van de voedingsstof in kwestie (bijv. goede bron van kalk)
MEER, VERSTERKT, TOEGEVOEGD, VERRIJKT	Bevat minstens 10% van de Dagelijkse Waarde voor eiwit, vitaminen, mineralen en vezel per portie vergeleken met het gewone (referentie) voedingsmiddel.
LICHT	50% minder vet dan het gewone (referentie) voedingsmiddel, of 50% minder natrium dan het referentievoedingsmiddel en voedingsmiddelen die ook calorie- en vetarm zijn, of de helft minder calorieën dan het referentievoedingsmiddel, als dat laatste minder dan 50% calorieën uit vet bevat.

VOEDSELPIRAMIDE: Een grafische voorstelling die is ontwikkeld door het Amerikaanse ministerie van landbouw ter illustratie van de optimale porties van hoofd-voedselgroepen in een dieet dat de gezondheid bevordert.

VOLLE GRANEN: Graansoorten die de kiemen, endosperm, zemelen en vlies bevatten. Door het veredelingsproces worden de voedingsstofrijke kiem en de vezelrijke zemelen en vliezen verwijderd. Volle granen bevatten veel samengestelde koolhydraten en volop eiwit en vezel. Voorbeelden van volle granen zijn: boekweit, gierst, haver, havervlokken, quinoa, rogge, witte rijst, volle tarwe en zilvervliesrijst.

VRIJE RADICALEN: Uiterst reactieve atomen of moleculen met ongepaarde elektronen die andere moleculen met ongepaarde elektronen zoeken. Op celniveau komen vrije radicalen in natuurlijke vorm voor, maar ze worden ook veroorzaakt door milieufactoren als roken en bestralen. In overmaat kunnen ze genetisch materiaal in cellen vernietigen, waarna de schade tot ziekte kan leiden.

YOGHURTKAAS: Yoghurt die door het uitlekken van vocht steviger is geworden. Maak zelf yoghurtkaas door een vergiet met kaasdoek te bekleden en het vergiet op een grote kom te zetten. Schep ¼ liter gewone yoghurt in het kaasdoek, zet het geheel in de koelkast en laat het een nacht uitlekken. De yoghurt zal dan de structuur van zachte kaas hebben en kan worden uitgesmeerd op crackers of sandwiches of in sommige recepten in plaats van roomkaas worden gebruikt. Gebruik voor het beste resultaat yoghurt waaraan geen stabilisatoren zijn toegevoegd.

ZUURBESTENDIG GEREI: Keukengerei dat is gemaakt van materialen, met name roestvrij staal en glas, die niet reageren op zure ingrediënten. Vermijd aluminium, daar dat reageert met wijn, citrussap en andere zure ingrediënten, waardoor het voedsel verkleurt en van smaak verandert.

Verantwoording

Pamela Sheldon Johns wenst dank te zeggen aan haar echtgenoot en beste vriendin Courtney. Tevens dankt zij haar vrienden en medewerkers bij Jordano's, onder wie Peter; en liefs voor Janice, Keri, Robin, Laurence, Kristin, Adrienne en Kelly voor hun bijzondere steun. Ze dankt ook allen die de recepten hebben willen uitproberen. Zonder al diegenen stonden we nog steeds achter het fornuis.

Mary Abbott Hess is dankbaar voor de steun van Jane Grant Tougas, Sharon Gourley, het Amerikaanse instituut voor wijn en eten en de medewerkers van Computrition Inc., het Nationale Centrum voor Voedingsleer en Weldon Owen Inc.

De fotograaf en stilisten wensen de volgende personen en instellingen te bedanken (uit San Francisco, tenzij anders aangegeven): The Attic; Meredith Bowman; Bethanie Brandon Design; Gail Cohen, Berkeley; Cookin; Cyclamen Studios; Julie Sanders Designer, Berkeley; Ward Finer; Bea en Marty Glenn; Nancy Glenn; Rosie Glenn-Finer; Judy Goldsmith en Bernie Carrasco, J. Goldsmith Antiques; Stephanie Greenleigh; Sandra Griswold; Missy Hamilton; Glenda Jordan, Berkeley; Sue Fisher King; Mimi Koch; Luna Garcia, Venice; L'Osteria del forno; Susan Borgatti; Merna Oeberst; Paul Bauer Inc.; Susan Pascal; Bob Pool, Berkeley; Dan Schuster; Smith and Hawken Ltd., Berkeley; Tesoro, Los Angeles; Virginia Breier Gallery; WilkesHome in Wilkes Bashford; Machek Wlodarchek; The Cannery Wine Cellars.

De uitgevers wensen de volgende personen en instellingen dank te zeggen voor hun medewerking bij de totstandkoming van dit boek: Sigrid Chase, Richard VanOosterhout, Miriam Coupe, Jim Obata, Dawn Low, Janique Porcelet, Tori Ritchie, Fee-Ling Tan, Jonette Banzon, Patty Hill, Angela Williams, Laurie Wertz, Wendely Harvey, Bruce Bailey, Kim Green, Tarji Mickelson, Barbara Pool Fenzl.

Herkomst der foto's

De uitgevers wensen dank te zeggen aan de volgende fotografen en bureaus voor de toestemming tot weergave van hun foto's.

(Afkortingen: b=boven, o=onder, l=links, r=rechts)

Allstock/M. Thonig 10–11; Allstock/ Charles Krebs 12–13; Allstock/ Kristin Finnegan 100–01; Allstock/Alan Hicks 144–45; Allstock/ E.C. Stangler 184–85

Australian Picture Library/John Carnemolla 2–3; Australian Picture Library 44–45

Comstock/Jack K. Clark 31, 146-147

Ric Ergenbright 41

Michael Freeman 50, 64-65

The Granger Collection, New York, 65, 101, 147, 185

Lefever/Grushow van Grant Heilman 36 (o, l), 18

Image Bank/ Gerald Brimacrombe 49; Image Bank/Walter Bibikow 53

Impact Images/David Ryan 22, 29

Wolfgang Kaehler Photography/Wolfgang Kaehler 14, 23, 36 (b), 36 (o, r)

Dwight Kuhn Photography/Dwight Kuhn 15, 52, 54

Susan Lapides 26

Roland en Karen Muschenetz 46

Odyssey Productions, Chicago/Robert Frenck 17, 40

Brian Seed & Associates/Brian Seed 47

Stock Market/Bryan Peterson schutbladen, Stock Market/Pedro Coll 21; Stock Market/Ian Lloyd 43; Stock Market/Graic Turtle 62-63

Tony Stone Worldwide/Hugh Simon 6-7; Tony Stone Worldwide/ Laurence Monneret 15; Tony Stone Worldwide/Andy Sacks 16; Tony Stone Worldwide/Steve Vidler 19; Tony Stone Worldwide/Paul Chesley 34-35; Tony Stone Worldwide/Tony Craddock 98-99; Tony Stone Worldwide/H. Richard Johnston 182-183

Harald Sund 20–21, 27, 51

Unicorn Stock Photos/Chris Boylan 61

Index

MINERALEN

Calcium: Helpt bij de opbouw en het onderhoud van sterke botten en tanden; belangrijk voor normale zenuw- en spierfuncties en bloedstolling; voorkomt osteoporose. Voedselbronnen: Melk, kaas, yoghurt, andere zuivelprodukten, tofu, sardines en zalm uit blik als de graten worden meegegeten, bladgroenten, kikkererwten, andere peulvruchten, schelpdieren.

Chlorium: Onderhoudt de normale vochtwisseling; helpt bij het evenwicht tussen zuren en basen in het lichaam; maakt zoutzuur aan voor de spijsvertering. Voedselbronnen: Keukenzout, sojasaus, vis, schelpdieren, vlees, melk, eieren.

Chromium: Belangrijk voor glucose-omzetting. Voedselbronnen: Orgaanvlees, andere vleessoorten, kaas, volle granen, gedroogde erwten en bonen, pinda's, maïsolie, gevogelte, bladgroenten.

Fluoride: Versterkt botten en tanden; helpt misschien osteoporose voorkomen. Voedselbronnen: Gefluoriseerd water en daarin gekweekt of gekookt eten, vis, thee.

Fosfor: Helpt de groei van botten en versterking van de tanden; belangrijk voor de stofwisseling. Voedselbronnen: Melk, kaas, yoghurt, vlees, gevogelte, vis, eierdooiers, gedroogde erwten en bonen, noten, volle granen, sporen in bijna alle voedsel.

IJzer: Onmisbaar voor een goede rode-bloedcelfunctie, zuurstoftransport en cel-activiteit. Voedselbronnen: Rood vlees, lever en ander orgaanvlees, het donkere vlees van gevogelte, schelpdieren, vis, verrijkte granen, verrijkte graanprodukten, rozijnen, andere gedroogde vruchten, pruimensap, bladgroenten, peulvruchten, noten, melasse, eierdooiers; wordt het beste opgenomen uit vleesbronnen.

Jodium: Noodzakelijk voor de aanmaak van schildklierhormonen die de groei reguleren; voorkomt kropgezwellen; belangrijk voor gezonde huid, nagels en haar. Voedselbronnen: Met name keukenzout met jodium, maar ook zeebanket, zeewierprodukten, groenten uit jodiumrijke gebieden, plantaardige olie.

Kalium: Bevordert regelmatige hartslag; nodig voor zenuw- en spiercontractie; regelt de overdracht van bouwstoffen naar cellen; reguleert de vochtbalans in lichaamsweefsel en cellen; helpt de bloeddruk reguleren. Voedselbronnen: Sinaasappels, sinaasappelsap, bananen, gedroogde vruchten, tomatensap, pindakaas, spinazie, pompoen, peulvruchten, aardappels, koffie, thee, cacao, yoghurt, melasse, volle granen, vlees, gevogelte, vis.

Koper: Helpt de aanmaak van rode bloedcellen; bevordert de opname van ijzer in bloedcellen; helpt bij de aanmaak van enzymen en weefsel. Voedselbronnen: Schelpdieren, noten, lever en ander orgaanvlees, cacaopoeder, chocolade, rozijnen, maïsolie, margarine, bladgroenten, volle granen, peulvruchten, zaden, noten, gevogelte.

Magnesium: Helpt bij de groei van botten; helpt bij zenuw- en spierfuncties, waaronder het onderhoud van een normaal hartritme; nodig voor stofwisseling en celdeling. Voedselbronnen: Noten, peulvruchten, zaden, spinazie, oesters, tarwezemelen, volle granen, rauwe bladgroenten, abrikozen, vlees, cacao, chocolade.

Mangaan: Nodig voor botgroei en ontwikkeling, stofwisseling, celfunctie en normale reproduktie. Voedselbronnen: Noten, volle granen, groenten, vruchten, oploskoffie, thee, cacaopoeder, bietenloof, eierdooiers en blauwe bessen.

Molybdeen: Belangrijk voor normale celfunctie. Voedselbronnen: Erwten, bonen, graanprodukten, orgaanvlees, sommige donkergroene groenten.

Natrium: Helpt bij de regulering van het vochtgehalte in het lichaam; speelt een rol bij het onderhouden van de bloeddruk; helpt zenuwimpulsen en spiercontractie. Voedselbronnen: Keukenzout, toegevoegd zout in voorbewerkt eten, zuiveringszout, zuivelprodukten, kruiderij, sojasaus, vlees, vis, ingemaakte produkten.

Selenium: Anti-oxidans; helpt samen met vitamine E celbeschadiging bestrijden. Voedselbronnen: Vis, schelpdieren, orgaanvlees, rood vlees, eierdooiers, kip, knoflook, tonijn, tomaten, uien.

Zink: Bevordert reuk- en smaakvermogen; helpt bij normale groei en sexuele ontwikkeling; belangrijk voor embryonale groei en genezing van wonden; onderdeel van enzymen en insuline. Voedselbronnen: Oesters, krabvlees, rundvlees, lever, eieren, gevogelte, bakkersgist, volkorenbrood, peulvruchten, tarwezemelen.

VITAMINEN

Vitamine A (retinol): Belangrijk voor de ontwikkeling van gezonde ogen, huid, haar, tanden en tandvlees; verhoogt de weerstand tegen infecties; nodig voor het gezichtsvermogen; helpt bij hormoonsynthese; fungeert in caroteenvorm als anti-oxidans ter voorkoming van celbeschadiging. Voedselbronnen: Donkergroene bladgroenten (spinazie, boerenkool, spruitjes), groene asperges, geel-oranje groenten en vruchten (wortels, zoete aardappels, pompoen, abrikozen), lever, vis, gevitamineerde margarine.

Vitamine B_1 (thiamine): Nodig voor gezonde hersenen, zenuwcellen en hartfunctie; helpt bij de opname van koolhydraten, vetten en eiwitten; steunt normale eetlust. Voedselbronnen: Varkensvlees, volle granen, eierdooiers, mager vlees, orgaanvlees, gevogelte, vis, peulvruchten, noten.

Vitamine B_2 (riboflavine): Helpt bij het vrijmaken van energie uit voedsel; treedt in wisselwerking met andere B vitaminen; ondersteunt het gezichtsvermogen en een gezonde huid. Voedselbronnen: Melk en andere zuivelprodukten, mager vlees, groene bladgroenten, eieren, noten, brood.

Vitamine B_3 (niacine, nicotinezuur): Werkt samen met andere B vitaminen bij het vrijmaken van energie uit voedsel. Voedselbronnen: Vlees, gevogelte, vis, melk en andere zuivelprodukten, peulvruchten en noten.

Vitamine B_5 (pantotheenzuur): Helpt bij het vrijmaken van energie uit voedsel en in de vorming van hormonen en zenuwregulatoren. Voedselbronnen: Orgaanvlees, volle granen, peulvruchten, yoghurt.

Vitamine B_6 (pyridoxine, pyridoxal, pyridoxamine): Helpt bij de omzetting van eiwit en vetzuren; ondersteunt functies van het zenuwstelsel en de aanmaak van rode bloedcellen; helpt bij het omzetten van het aminozuur tryptofaan in niacine. Voedselbronnen: Kip, orgaanvlees, varkensvlees, groene bladgroenten, volle granen, volkorenbrood, bananen, aardappels, limabonen en andere peulvruchten, noten, avocado's, kool, bloemkool, eieren.

Foliumzuur (folinezuur): Helpt bij de aanmaak van genetische grondstoffen voor celkernstofwisseling, belangrijk bij celvervanging; werkt samen met vitamine B_{12} bij de aanmaak van rode bloedcellen. Voedselbronnen: Broccoli, groene asperges, spinazie en andere groene bladgroenten, lever en ander orgaanvlees, sinaasappels, tarwezemelen, peulvruchten, zaden.

Vitamine B_{12} (cyanocobalamine): Helpt bij de synthese van DNA in ontwikkelende cellen, de aanmaak van rode bloedcellen, de werking van het zenuwstelsel; wordt gebruikt voor de behandeling van bloedarmoede. Voedselbronnen: voornamelijk dierlijke produkten (lever, orgaanvlees, zeebanket, eierdooiers, oude kaas, melk), noten, peulvruchten.

Biotine: Nodig voor de aanmaak van vetzuren, en de opname van eiwit en koolhydraat. Voedselbronnen: Gist, eieren, lever, melk.

Vitamine C: (ascorbinezuur): Helpt in het onderhoud van gezonde botten, bindweefsel, tandvlees, capillaire buizen en tanden; verhoogt de opname van ijzer en foliumzuur; helpt bij de genezing van wonden en hormoonsynthese; als anti-oxidans voorkomt het celbeschadiging. Voedselbronnen: Citrusvruchten, (sinaasappels, grapefruit, mandarijnen, citroenen, limoenen), bessen, groene bladgroenten (broccoli, spinazie), groene en rode paprika's, tomaten, aardappels, groene asperges, papaja's, mangas.

Vitamine D (ergocalciferol en andere vormen): Nodig voor een sterk gebit en sterke botten en een goede kalkopname. Voedselbronnen: Gevitamineerde melk, vette vissoorten (haring, sardines), lever, eierdooiers, gevitamineerde margarine; ook door het lichaam aangemaakt in reactie op zonlicht.

Vitamine E: (tocoferol): Helpt bij de aanmaak van bloedcellen, spieren en gezond longweefsel; helpt het lichaam bij het gebruik van Vitamine K; als anti-oxidans voorkomt het celbeschadiging. Voedselbronnen: Tarwezemelen, maïs, sojabonen, zonnebloem- en andere plantaardige oliën; noten, zaden, olijven, groene asperges, groene bladgroenten, blauwe bessen, perziken.

Vitamine K (fyllochinon): Helpt bij bloedstolling en de regulatie van kalk in het bloed. Voedselbronnen: Broccoli, bloemkool, kool, spinazie, granen, sojabonen, lever, melk; het lichaam produceert circa de helft van de dagelijkse behoefte.

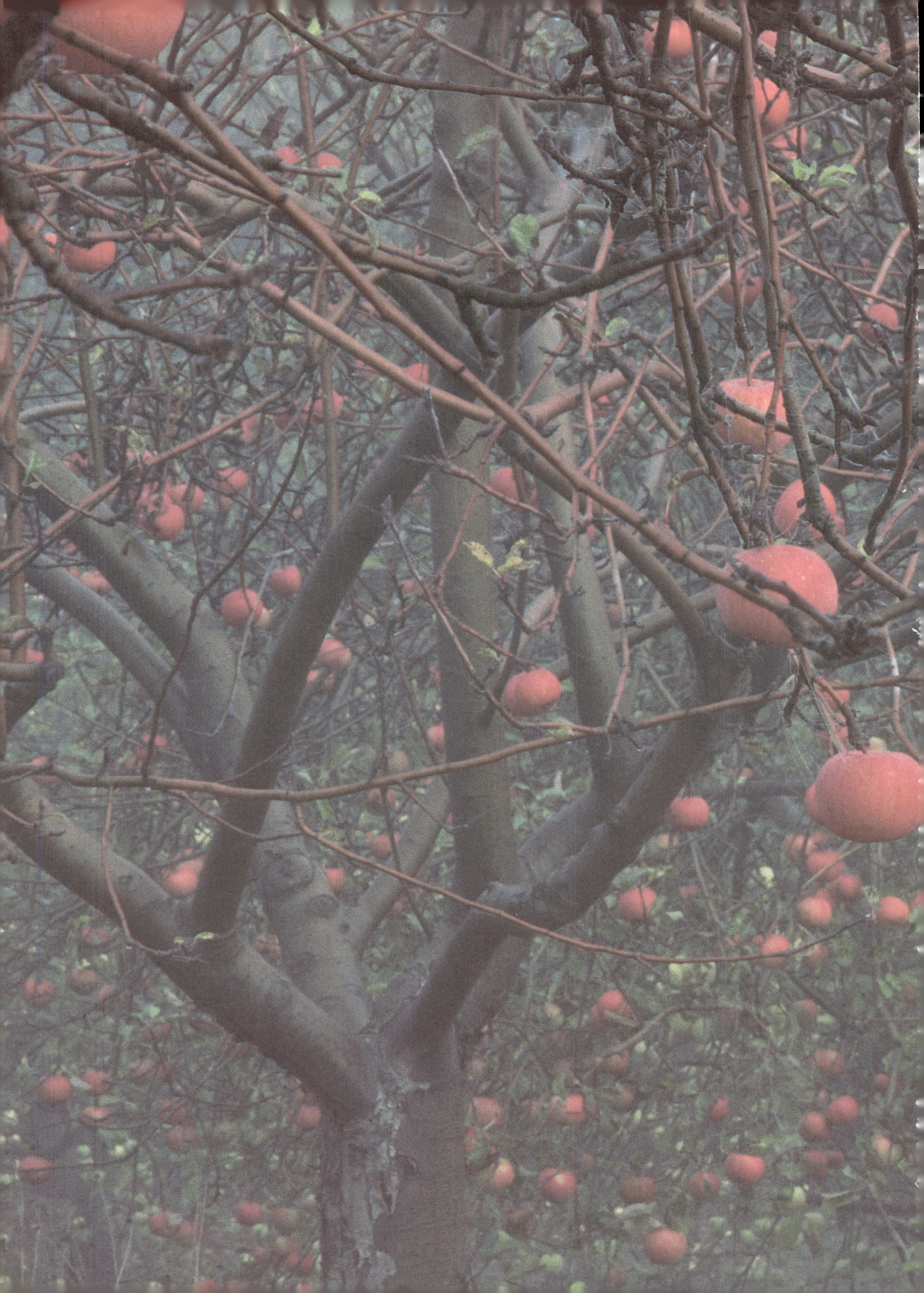